CRIMINAL LAW
CASES AND MATERIALS

Third Edition

■ ■ ■

by

Cynthia Lee
Professor of Law
The George Washington University

Angela P. Harris
Professor of Law
UC Davis School of Law

AMERICAN CASEBOOK SERIES®

Mat #41308792

444 Cedar Street, Suite 700
St. Paul, MN 55101
1-877-888-1330

Printed in the United States of America

ISBN: 978-0-314-28286-6

This book is dedicated to

Kenichi Haramoto

and

Tuck and Dorothea Lee

PREFACE

Like most Criminal Law casebooks, this book is meant to introduce students to the basic doctrines and methods of American substantive criminal law, both in jurisdictions whose penal codes continue to reflect the common law and in those jurisdictions that have adopted, in whole or in part, the Model Penal Code. Three features, however, distinguish this book from others in the field.

First, this book consistently focuses on the cultural context of substantive criminal law. Throughout the casebook, we provide readings that consider the cultural meanings of crime and the cultural meanings of punishment from the point of view of offenders, the public, and criminal justice insiders. Additionally, we provide resources for thinking about how substantive criminal law is shaped both by "legal culture"—the systematic needs of lawyers (especially prosecutors) and judges who make the criminal system run—and by the broader culture of the society in which we live. We are particularly concerned with the ways in which American culture is internally divided along lines of race, gender, class, and sexuality.

A second feature that distinguishes this book from others in the market is its treatment of substantive criminal law as a course in public law. We provide many links between criminal law and constitutional law, from the basic elements of a crime, such as the act requirement and the mens rea requirement, to particular crimes, such as conspiracy and sodomy, to constitutional doctrines that bear directly upon criminal law, such as the equal protection clause, the due process clause, and the prohibition against cruel and unusual punishment. The book also highlights some of the systemic issues raised by the use of state power against the lives and liberties of citizens, such as the fundamental "dilemma of discretion."

Finally, we have tried to make this a flexible and user-friendly book, for the law student as well as for new teachers of the subject, by providing introductory text at the beginning of each chapter (as well as at the beginning of many sections in the chapters) and by keeping the notes and questions to a minimum. We also tried to lightly edit the cases in order to give the reader fuller factual context. Because of the importance of context, we made an effort to provide additional information about the defendant or the case not provided in the judicial opinion, whenever possible.

Most of the citations and footnotes in the excerpted cases and articles have been omitted. We inserted three asterisks to indicate textual omissions from the excerpted cases and articles. Numbered footnotes indicate footnotes in the original. Footnotes in lowercase letters indicate casebook author footnotes which we have added to enhance the material.

We hope readers will find this a fresh and accessible introduction to the substantive criminal law. We also hope that students, even if they never practice criminal law, will take away a sense of its centrality in the American cultural imagination and its implications not only for the incarcerated but also for the legal system itself.

CYNTHIA LEE
ANGELA P. HARRIS

February 2014

ACKNOWLEDGMENTS

We wish to thank and acknowledge the many people who helped with the production of this casebook.

For the first edition, Angela Harris gratefully thanks her Berkeley Law students who took Criminal Law, section 4, Fall 2004, for their patience, good humor, and enthusiastic engagement with these materials as they evolved in draft. Angela Harris also thanks faculty assistant Ayn Lowry, who shepherded her through the many years of logistical nightmares that accompanied the many versions of supplemental materials that preceded the first edition of this book.

For the second edition, Angela Harris is grateful to her Criminal Law students at both Berkeley Law and the University at Buffalo, SUNY, who road-tested new materials and offered suggestions for video links and exercises. She also thanks her amazing faculty assistant at the University at Buffalo—Susan Martin, whose organization, discipline, and commitment made the copyright permissions process manageable and even (sometimes!) fun. Last but not least, the awesome Grayce Frink of Berkeley Law provided research assistance from sea to shining sea.

For the third edition, Angela Harris thanks King Hall, University of California-Davis students Laura Gallagher, Marium Lange, and Courtney Taylor. For the third edition, Angela also is grateful to all the users who joined us for the summer 2013 casebook conference generously subsidized by West, and on whose suggestions we have drawn for this substantial revision. Dean Kevin Johnson provided money for research assistance, and big ups to my King Hall colleagues Miguel Mendez and Jack Chin.

Cynthia Lee thanks the following students (in alphabetical order) from the George Washington University Law School who helped with the production of the first, second, and third editions of this casebook: Andrew Basham (third edition), Ralph Chris Berg (first edition), Dave Berman (first edition), Carrie James (third edition), Liza Meyers (first edition), Thomas Moir (first edition), Guillermo Billy Santiso (first edition), Corrina Sowden (second edition), Lauren Voss (first edition), and Masako Yoshioka (third edition). Cynthia Lee also thanks Kathryn Parente for her hard work, patience, and cheerful demeanor throughout the many drafts of the first edition of this casebook, Katharine Mason at UC Hastings College of the Law who helped prepare the manuscript for the third edition, Lesliediana Jones for assistance with copyright matters, and Jason Hawkins, Herb Somers, and Nicholas Stark for library research support. Cynthia Lee also thanks Dean Gregory Maggs, Dean Frederick Lawrence, former Dean Michael Young, and Interim Dean

Roger Trangsrud for supporting this project through research assistance and summer research stipends.

Cynthia Lee thanks her parents for the love, support, and guidance they provided during their lives. She also thanks her husband, Kenichi Haramoto, for his love, support, and guidance, without which she could not be as productive as she is today.

Finally, we both would like to thank the following colleagues for their helpful comments and suggestions for improving the third edition of this casebook: Mario Barnes, Nancy Ehrenreich, Jonathan Glader, Tamara Lawson, Melissa Murray, and Kelly Strader.

COPYRIGHT ACKNOWLEDGMENTS

We are thankful to the copyright holders who gave us permission to reprint excerpts from the following works:

Acker, James R., *The Death Penalty: An American History, 6 Contemporary Justice Review*, 169–186 (2003). Copyright © 2003 Contemporary Justice Review.

American Bar Association Journal, *Statutory Rape Laws: Does It Make Sense to Enforce Them in an Increasingly Permissive Society?*, 82 A.B.A. J. 86 (1996).

American Law Institute, Model Penal Code and Commentaries, copyright © 1962, 1980, and 1985 by The American Law Institute.

Anderson, Michelle, *Negotiating Sex*, 78 S. Cal. L. Rev. 1401 (2005).

Ashby, Charles, *The Right to Be Apathetic: Iverson Case Raises Questions About Good Samaritan Laws*, Los Angeles Daily Journal, Sept. 2, 1998, at 1.

Associated Press, *Epileptic Convicted of Assault Cleared*, Los Angeles Daily Journal, Sept. 25, 1997, at 5.

Backus, Mary Sue & Paul Marcus, *The Right to Counsel in Criminal Cases, A National Crisis*, 57 Hastings L.J. 1031 (2006). Copyright © 2006 *Hastings Law Journal*, Hastings College of the Law. Reprinted with permission.

Bair, Jeffrey, *Killer of Thief Wins Wide Support*, The San Diego Union Tribune, Dec. 27, 1994, at A–8. Copyright permission granted by the Associated Press.

Bibas, Stephanos, *Plea Bargaining Outside the Shadow of Trial*, 117 Harv. L. Rev. 2463 (2004). Copyright © 2004 Harvard Law Review Association.

Blecker, Robert, *Haven or Hell? Inside Lorton Central Prison: Experiences of Punishment Justified*, 42 Stan. L. Rev. 1149 (1990).

Brown, Kevin, *The Social Construction of a Rape Victim: Stories of African-American Males about the Rape of Desirée Washington*, in *Black Men on Race, Gender and Sexuality: A Critical Reader* (Carbado ed. 1999).

Butler, Paul D., *Race-Based Jury Nullification: Case-in-Chief*, 30 J. Marshall L. Rev. 911 (1997).

Butler, Paul, *Walking While Black: Encounters with the Police on My Street*, Legal Times, Nov. 10, 1997 at 23B. Copyright © 1997 Legal Times. Reprinted with permission.

Coker, Donna K., *Heat of Passion and Wife Killing: Men Who Batter/Men Who Kill*, 2 S. Cal. Rev. L. & Women's Stud. 71 (1992).

Cole, David, *Turning the Corner on Mass Incarceration?*, 9 Ohio St. J. Crim. L. 27 (2011). Copyright © 2011 *Ohio State Journal of Criminal Law,* Moritz College of Law—The Ohio State University. Reprinted with permission.

Coleman, Doriane Lambelet, *Individualizing Justice through Multiculturalism: The Liberals' Dilemma*, 96 Colum. L. Rev. 1093 (1996).

Cooper, Frank Rudy, *Masculinities, Post-Racialism, and the Gates Controversy: The False Equivalence Between Officer and Civilian*, 11 Nev. L.J. 1 (2010).

DeFord, William, *The Dilemma of Expressive Punishment*, 76 U. Colo. L. Rev. 843 (2005). Copyright © 2005 *University of Colorado Law Review*, University of Colorado School of Law. Reprinted with permission of the *University of Colorado Law Review* and William S. DeFord.

Delgado, Richard, *No: Selective Enforcement Targets 'Unpopular' Men*, 82 A.B.A. J. 86 (1996).

Delgado, Richard, *"Rotten Social Background": Should the Criminal Law Recognize a Defense of Severe Environmental Deprivation?*, 3 Law & Inequality J. 9 (1985).

Dressler, Joshua, *When "Heterosexual" Men Kill "Homosexual" Men: Reflections on Provocation Law, Sexual Advances, and the "Reasonable Man" Standard*, 85 J. Crim. L. & Criminology 726 (1995).

Gunning, Isabelle R., *Two Forms of Justice: Iverson Case—Nevada and California Authorities Ought to Reexamine David Cash's Actions,* L.A. Times, Sept. 21, 1998, at B5.

Harris, Paul, Black Rage Confronts the Law, pp. 4–6, 184–189 (1997). Copyright © 1997 NYU Press. Reprinted with permission.

Hart, Henry M., Jr., *The Aims of the Criminal Law*, 23 Law & Contemp. Probs. 401 (1958).

Holland, Paul, *Lawyering and Learning in Problem-Solving Courts*, 34 Wash. U. J.L. & Pol'y 185 (2010). Copyright © 2010 *Washington University Journal of Law and Policy*, Washington University Law and Paul Holland. Reprinted with permission.

Hollister, Carrie T., *The Impossible Predicament of Gina Grant*, 44 UCLA L. Rev. 913 (1997). Copyright © 1997 Carrie Walker. Reprinted with permission.

Jonsson, Patrik, *Trayvon Martin Killing in Florida Puts "Stand Your Ground" Law on Trial*, The Christian Science Monitor, March 16, 2012, pp. 10–11. Copyright © 2012 Christian Science Monitor.

Kang, Jerry, Judge Mark Bennett, Devon Carbado, Pam Casey, Nilanjana Dasgupta, David Faigman, Rachel Godsil, Anthony Greenwald, Justin Levinson, and Jennifer Mnookin, *Implicit Bias in the Courtroom*, 59 UCLA L. Rev. 1124 (2012).

Kelman, Mark, *Interpretive Construction in the Substantive Criminal Law*, 33 Stan. L. Rev. 591 (1981).

Lee, Cynthia, *Murder and the Reasonable Man: Passion and Fear in the Criminal Courtroom* (NYU Press 2003).

Leipold, Andrew D., *Race-Based Jury Nullification: A Rebuttal (Part A)*, 30 J. Marshall L. Rev. 923 (1997).

Maguigan, Holly, *Cultural Evidence and Male Violence: Are Feminists and Multiculturalist Reformers on a Collision Course in Criminal Courts?*, 70 N.Y.U. L. Rev. 36 (1995).

Mison, Robert B., *Homophobia in Manslaughter: The Homosexual Advance as Insufficient Provocation*, 80 Cal. L. Rev. 133 (1992). Copyright © 1992 California Law Review, Inc. Reprinted with permission by the California Law Review, Inc.

Morin, Richard, *Justice Isn't Blind*, Washington Post, Sept. 3, 2000, at B5.

Natapof, Alexandra, *Misdemeanors*, V85:5 Southern California Law Review (pp. 1313–1375) (2012). Copyright © 2012 *Southern California Law Review*, USC Gould School of Law. Reprinted with permission.

Oberman, Michelle, *Yes: The Risk of Psychological Harm to Girls Is Too Great*, 82 A.B.A. J. 86 (1996).

Pinard, Michael, *Collateral Consequences of Criminal Conviction: Confronting Issues of the Race and Dignity*, 85 N.Y.U.L. Rev. 457 (2010). Copyright © 2010 Michael Pinard. Reprinted with permission.

Renteln, Alison Dundes, *A Justification of the Cultural Defense as Partial Excuse*, 2 S. Cal. Rev. L. & Women's Stud. 437 (1993).

Roberts, Jenny, *Effective Plea Bargaining Counsel*, 122 Yale L.J. 2650 (2013). Copyright © 2013 *Yale Law Journal*, Yale Law School. Reprinted with permission.

Rothman, David J., *The Crime of Punishment*, The New York Review of Books, February 17, 1994, pp. 34–38. Copyright © 1994 David J. Rothman.

Taslitz, Andrew E., *Patriarchal Stories I: Cultural Rape Narratives in the Courtroom*, 5 S. Cal. Rev. L. & Women's Stud. 387 (1996).

Taylor, Laurie, *Provoked Reason in Men and Women: Heat-of-Passion Manslaughter and Imperfect Self-Defense*, 33 UCLA L. Rev. 1679 (1986).

The Christian Science Monitor for Lindsay, Leon, *Can a Person Be Free to Wander Without Worry of Arrest?*, The Christian Science Monitor, Midwestern Edition, May 12, 1982, at 3.

Theis, Sandy, *Jailed "On the Precipice" of Crime*, Newhouse News Service, August 8, 2003.

Thomas, Kendall, *Beyond the Privacy Principle*, 92 Colum. L. Rev. 1431 (1992). Copyright © 1992 Kendall Thomas. Reprinted with permission.

Umbreit, Mark S., Betty Vos, Robert B. Coates & Elizabeth Lightfoot, *Restorative Justice in the Twenty-First Century: A Social Movement Full of Opportunities and Pitfalls*, Marquette Law Review. 89(2):251–304. Copyright © 2005 *Marquette Law Review*, Marquette University Law School. Reprinted with permission.

University of Colorado Law Review for William S. DeFord, *The Dilemma of Expressive Punishment*, 76 U. Colo. L. Rev. 843 (2005).

Vidmar, Neil & Regina A. Schuller, *Juries and Expert Evidence: Social Framework Testimony*, 52 Law & Contemp. Probs. 133 (1989).

Volpp, Leti, *(Mis)identifying Culture: Asian Women and the "Cultural Defense,"* 17 Harv. Women's L.J. 57 (1994).

Volpp, Leti, *On Culture, Difference, and Domestic Violence*, 11 Am. U.J. Gender, Soc. Pol'y & Law 393 (2003).

Ward, Cynthia, *Punishing Children in the Criminal Law*, Vol. 82 Notre Dame Law Review, Pages 429–79 (2006). Copyright © 2006 *Notre Dame Law Review*, University of Notre Dame. Reprinted with permission.

SUMMARY OF CONTENTS

TABLE OF CONTENTS

TABLE OF CASES

The principal cases are in bold type.

TABLE OF AUTHORITIES

CRIMINAL LAW

CASES AND MATERIALS

Third Edition

CHAPTER 1

BASIC PRINCIPLES OF THE CRIMINAL LAW

■ ■ ■

INTRODUCTION

When law students begin their study of the criminal law, they often expect to deal with exciting search and seizure issues, illegal arrests, questionable interrogations, tainted confessions, and the like. In other words, they imagine a fun-filled course packed with the sorts of issues that occupy the episodes of TV shows like *Law & Order*. At most law schools, however, the constitutional restrictions on searches and seizures, arrests, interrogations and confessions are covered in the basic Criminal Procedure class, not Criminal Law. Criminal procedure concerns the legal limits on how people identified as possible or actual criminals may be treated by law enforcement personnel, by prosecuting attorneys, by the judiciary, and by the prison system. It is the law of criminal procedure (and to some extent the law of evidence and trial procedure) that makes for the exciting courtroom action portrayed in movies and television shows.

Substantive criminal law, however, is interesting and important in its own right. Substantive criminal law (hereafter simply *criminal law*) answers these questions: How do various jurisdictions define their criminal offenses? What are the basic elements common to every crime in the Anglo-American tradition? What does the prosecution have to prove in order for the fact-finder to find a person guilty? What are the elements of particular crimes, like murder, rape, or burglary? What distinguishes first degree from second degree murder?

Criminal law also addresses questions such as what level of punishment does the person who has committed a crime deserve? The rules of criminal law tell us what a person must do to be considered guilty of a crime, but not everyone who has technically violated a statute will be treated in the same way. Sometimes the issue is whether a person ought to be considered capable of committing a crime at all. For example, the insanity defense is based on the theory that people who commit crimes because they are insane lack the capacity to make moral choices, a prerequisite for criminal punishment. Other times, assuming the person is capable of moral choice, the issue is whether and to what extent that choice reflects values and beliefs shared by those in our society, rendering the person's actions excusable or justifiable. For example, a person who kills in the "heat of passion" is considered less blameworthy than a person who kills in cold blood. A person who kills in self-defense may not be considered blameworthy at all.

As the preceding paragraph suggests, criminal law is inextricably intertwined with issues of morality. This being the case, answers to the questions it asks may vary from person to person. Thus, criminal law in part engages one's moral intuitions, and criminal law is often taught as a branch of moral philosophy.

But people do not develop their moral intuitions in a vacuum. We grow up in a *culture*, socialized by family, friends, schools, and mass media into accepting some broad beliefs and rejecting others. Like any other culture, Anglo-American culture includes widely-held ideas about responsibility, blame, and punishment, and these ideas have shaped our criminal law. In this book, we approach criminal law as a system of cultural meaning, and Anglo-American criminal law as a reflection of Anglo-American moral culture.

This is where things get really interesting, for no culture is monolithic. First, cultural meanings change over time. Second, the same culture may contain conflicting beliefs and values. Third, cultures often contain subcultures with very different traditions and perspectives, and this is certainly true of the United States. Some of these subcultures exist because the United States is a multicultural nation, composed of immigrants (voluntary and involuntary) from many different countries. Other subcultures have emerged through the long-term effects of social inequality. Men and women, for example, are sometimes said to live in different cultures. When there is no cultural consensus on moral issues, whose view gets written into the law? Should the trier of fact—whether a judge or a jury—be educated about different cultural perspectives on a person's behavior? When does a legal rule or doctrine become so lacking in support from contemporary moral culture that it should be abolished or radically altered? What are the means by which such a rule or doctrine may be changed so as to reflect a new moral consensus? What is the proper relationship between culture and morality? These are some of the questions raised by the study of substantive criminal law.

In addition to being a system of cultural meaning, criminal law is part of a legal system, and this too raises interesting and important issues. Criminal law reflects popular morality, but law is also partly autonomous from morality. Not everything that is a moral duty is necessarily a legal duty. To what extent should criminal law reflect the minimum standards of behavior necessary to a functioning society, and to what extent should it push people to be better to one another than they might otherwise choose? What is the appropriate role for each of the different institutions that shape and enforce substantive criminal law—judges, juries, trial courts, appellate courts, and legislatures? What discretion is or should be available to each institutional actor to apply or interpret the law the way she or he sees fit? How is that discretion limited—by constitutional rules, by rules of interpretation, or by the actions of other actors within the criminal justice system?

The study of criminal law, then, is both the study of what is and what ought to be. You will learn what the rules are and also have the chance to examine critically whether those rules serve the goals of reflecting a general cultural and moral consensus. You will have the chance to ponder whether the rules strike an appropriate balance between how we would like people to act in a perfect world and what we can reasonably expect of them, and whether they facilitate the efficient and just operation of a necessarily imperfect legal system. This is not the flashy stuff of *Law & Order*, but it is just as pressing.

THE AIMS OF THE CRIMINAL LAW

Henry M. Hart, Jr.
23 Law & Contemp. Probs. 401 (1958)

* * * What do we mean by "crime" and "criminal"? Or, put more accurately, what should we understand to be "the method of the criminal law," the use of which is in question? This latter way of formulating the preliminary inquiry is more accurate, because it pictures the criminal law as a process, a way of doing something, which is what it is. * * *

What then are the characteristics of this method?

1. The method operates by means of a series of directions, or commands, formulated in general terms, telling people what they must or must not do. Mostly, the commands of the criminal law are "must-nots," or prohibitions, which can be satisfied by inaction. "Do not murder, rape, or rob." But some of them are "musts," or affirmative requirements, which can be satisfied only by taking a specifically, or relatively specifically, described kind of action. "Support your wife and children," and "File your income tax return."

2. The commands are taken as valid and binding upon all those who fall within their terms when the time comes for complying with them, whether or not they have been formulated in advance in a single authoritative set of words. They speak to members of the community, in other words, in the community's behalf, with all the power and prestige of the community behind them.

3. The commands are subject to one or more sanctions for disobedience which the community is prepared to enforce.

Thus far, it will be noticed, nothing has been said about the criminal law which is not true also of a large part of the noncriminal, or civil, law. The law of torts, the law of contracts, and almost every other branch of private law that can be mentioned operate, too, with general directions prohibiting or requiring described types of conduct, and the community's tribunals enforce these commands. What, then, is distinctive about the method of the criminal law?

Can crimes be distinguished from civil wrongs on the ground that they constitute injuries to society generally which society is interested in preventing? The difficulty is that society is interested also in the due fulfillment of contracts and the avoidance of traffic accidents and most of the other stuff of civil litigation. The civil law is framed and interpreted and enforced with a constant eye to these social interests. Does the distinction lie in the fact that proceedings to enforce the criminal law are instituted by public officials rather than private complainants? The difficulty is that public officers may also bring many kinds of "civil" enforcement actions—for an injunction, for the recovery of a "civil" penalty, or even for the detention of the defendant by public authority. Is the distinction, then, in the peculiar character of what is done to people who are adjudged to be criminals? The difficulty is that, with the possible exception of death, exactly the same kinds of unpleasant consequences, objectively considered, can be and are visited upon unsuccessful defendants in civil proceedings. * * *

4. What distinguishes a criminal from a civil sanction and all that distinguishes it, it is ventured, is the judgment of community condemnation which accompanies and justifies its imposition. As Professor Gardner wrote not long ago, in a distinct but cognate connection:

> The essence of punishment for moral delinquency lies in the criminal conviction itself. One may lose more money on the stock market than in a court-room; a prisoner of war camp may well provide a harsher environment than a state prison; death on the field of battle has the same physical characteristics as death by sentence of law. It is the expression of the community's hatred, fear, or contempt for the convict which alone characterizes physical hardship as punishment.

If this is what a "criminal" penalty is, then we can say readily enough what a "crime" is. It is not simply anything which a legislature chooses to call a "crime." It is not simply antisocial conduct which public officers are given a responsibility to suppress. It is not simply any conduct to which a legislature chooses to attach a "criminal" penalty. It is conduct which, if duly shown to have taken place, will incur a formal and solemn pronouncement of the moral condemnation of the community. * * *

At least under existing law, there is a vital difference between the situation of a patient who has been committed to a mental hospital and the situation of an inmate of a state penitentiary. The core of the difference is precisely that the patient has not incurred the moral condemnation of his community, whereas the convict has.

A. SOURCES OF CRIMINAL LAW

Law students often find criminal law frustrating because there is no nationwide criminal code. Each of the fifty states, the District of Columbia, and the federal government has its own criminal code (also known as a penal code). The United States military, in addition, has its own criminal code. Fortunately, even though criminal provisions differ from jurisdiction to jurisdiction, there are certain basic principles of criminal law which are sufficiently common to most jurisdictions to enable generalizations about the basic elements of most crimes and the basic elements of most defenses. In addition, all the criminal laws of every jurisdiction of the United States are subject to the same constraints imposed by the United States Constitution.

Because the United States began as colonies of England, all criminal codes in the United States broadly recognize the crimes and defenses developed by English judges over many centuries and then imported here. However, the definition of these crimes and defenses, and how penal codes should be read and interpreted, depends on whether one is in a jurisdiction in which the code principally follows the common law or one in which the code has incorporated reforms taken from the Model Penal Code. We can speak of these as *common law* jurisdictions and *Model Penal Code* jurisdictions.

In common law jurisdictions, judges continue to play an important role in shaping the criminal law. Courts in these jurisdictions must interpret statutes that are often very old and that may incorporate archaic language and concepts. Judges in common law jurisdictions both definitively interpret the meaning of criminal statutes and occasionally go beyond the statutes to announce new rules of their own. This book contains many excerpts from appellate court opinions in order to articulate and examine criminal law in common law jurisdictions.

Other jurisdictions have recently sought to update and reform their criminal codes. Many of these reform efforts have been influenced by the Model Penal Code (hereafter MPC). The MPC is a product of the American Law Institute (ALI), an organization composed of judges, lawyers, and law professors. When the ALI was organized, it saw itself as a body of experts that would try to influence state law by writing "restatements" of various subject matter areas, like Torts and Contracts. These restatements purported to simply set forth the common law of all the states in a clear, organized, and comprehensive way, but in fact they often incorporated significant reforms. The ALI hoped that the states would change their own laws to conform with the restatements, and many of these restatements have been highly influential with state legislatures.

When it came to the criminal law, the ALI concluded that the statutory and case law of the various states was such a hopelessly confusing and obsolete mishmash that "restatement" would be the wrong word. Instead, the ALI drafted its own model criminal code from scratch. Drafting of the MPC began in 1952, and in 1962, after thirteen tentative drafts with accompanying explanatory Commentaries, the ALI approved and published its Proposed Official Draft of the MPC. Although no state has adopted the MPC in its entirety, between 1962 and 1984 thirty-four states enacted completely new criminal codes, influenced to some extent by the MPC. In these jurisdictions, the language of the statute is more important than prior decisions of judges in figuring out "what the law is." You will find excerpts from the MPC in the Appendix to this casebook.

In common law jurisdictions, then, one primarily relies on the decisions of judges to find out what the criminal law is; in MPC jurisdictions, one primarily relies on the statutory language itself. In both kinds of jurisdictions, however, criminal law is influenced by federal law.[a] The most important source of federal law is the United States Constitution. The Constitution does not specifically set forth any crimes or defenses. However, some provisions of the Constitution set limitations on the way states can criminally punish behavior. We will examine some of these limitations in Chapter 2.

B. JUSTIFICATIONS FOR PUNISHMENT

The arguments traditionally used to justify criminal punishment come from moral philosophy. These moral justifications for punishment are not only discussed by theorists, but are frequently used by policymakers in public debate and by attorneys and judges in legal proceedings to evaluate the efficiency and fairness of the criminal justice system. Legislators and judges use concepts taken from moral philosophy when writing or revising criminal statutes, when sentencing convicted criminals, and when making "policy" arguments about the fairness of a law. We therefore need to briefly examine these philosophical principles in order to understand the traditional justifications for punishment.

Traditional moral reasoning is usually divided into two types: *consequentialist* and *nonconsequentialist.* The consequentialist believes that actions are morally right if, and only if, they result in desirable consequences. The primary consequentialist theory of punishment is called *utilitarianism.* Utilitarians tend to look forward at the predictable effects of punishment on the offender and/or society. The nonconsequentialist, in contrast, believes that actions are morally right or wrong in themselves, regardless of the consequences. The primary

[a] Congress has no general constitutional authority to make criminal law, so the principal authority for enacting criminal statutes lies with the states, rather than the federal government. However, Congress does enact many criminal statutes (including, for example, drug laws) by virtue of its power over interstate commerce. Congress also has the authority to make criminal law for the District of Columbia, for the military, and for territories under its jurisdiction, such as Indian reservations.

nonconsequentialist theory of punishment is called *retributivism*. Retributivists typically look backwards at the harm caused by the crime and attempt to calibrate the punishment to the crime. Debates over criminal law and policy usually involve a mixture of utilitarian and retributivist arguments.

The first excerpt in this section, a famous English case, provides fodder for a rich discussion regarding the basic theories of punishment. The second excerpt represents a contemporary American use of the traditional justifications for punishment in a sentencing decision. The third excerpt looks at the traditional justifications for punishment as they play out in a contemporary American prison.

REGINA V. DUDLEY AND STEPHENS

Queen's Bench Division
14 Q.B.D. 273 (1884)

* * * The two prisoners, Thomas Dudley and Edwin Stephens, were indicted for the wilful murder of Richard Parker on July 25, 1884, on the high seas, within the jurisdiction of the Admiralty of England. They were tried at the winter assizes at Exeter on Nov. 6, 1884, before Huddleston, B., when at the suggestion of the learned judge, the jury returned a special verdict, setting out the facts, and referred the matter to the Divisional Court for its decision.

The special verdict was as follows:

The jurors, upon their oath, say and find that, on July 5, 1884, the prisoners, with one Brooks, all able-bodied English seamen, and the deceased, also an English boy, between seventeen and eighteen years of age, the crew of an English yacht, were cast away in a storm on the high seas, 1,600 miles from the Cape of Good Hope, and were compelled to put into an open boat. That in this boat they had no supply of water and no supply of food, except two 1 lb. tins of turnips, and for three days they had nothing else to subsist upon. That on the fourth day they caught a small turtle, upon which they subsisted for a few days, and this was the only food they had up to the twentieth day, when the act now in question was committed. That on the twelfth day the remains of the turtle were entirely consumed, and for the next eight days they had nothing to eat. That they had no fresh water, except such rain as they from time to time caught in their oilskin capes. That the boat was drifting on the ocean, and it was probably more than a thousand miles away from land. That on the eighteenth day, when they had been seven days without food and five without water, the prisoners spoke to Brooks as to what should be done if no succour came, and suggested that someone should be sacrificed to save the rest, but Brooks dissented, and the boy to whom they were understood to refer was not consulted. That on July 24, the day before the act now in question, the prisoner Dudley proposed to Stephens and to Brooks that lots should be cast who should be put to death to save the rest, but Brooks refused to consent, and it was not put to the boy, and in point of fact there was no drawing of lots. That on that day the prisoners spoke of their having families, and suggested that it would be better to kill the boy that their lives should be saved, and the prisoner Dudley proposed that if there was no vessel in sight by the morrow morning the boy should be killed. That next day, July 25, no vessel appearing, Dudley told Brooks that he had better go and have a sleep, and made signs to Stephens and Brooks that the boy had better be killed. The prisoner Stephens agreed to the act, but Brooks dissented from it. That the boy was then lying at the bottom of the boat quite helpless, and extremely weakened by famine and by drinking sea water, and unable to make any resistance, nor did he ever assent to his being killed. The prisoner, Captain Dudley, offered a prayer, asking forgiveness for them all if either of them should be tempted to commit a rash act, and that their souls might be saved. That the prisoner Dudley, with the assent of the prisoner Stephens, went to the boy, and telling him that his time was come, put a knife into his throat and killed him then and there. That the three men fed upon the body and blood of the boy for four days. That on the fourth day after the act had been committed, the boat was picked up by a passing vessel, and the prisoners were rescued still alive, but in the lowest state of prostration. That they were carried to the port of Falmouth, and committed for trial at Exeter. That, if the men had not fed upon the body of the boy, they would probably not have survived to be so picked up and rescued, but would within the four days have died of famine. That the boy, being in a much weaker condition, was likely to have died before them. That at the time of the act in question there was no sail in sight, nor any reasonable prospect of relief. That under the circumstances there appeared to the prisoners every probability that, unless they then fed, or very soon fed, upon the boy or one of themselves, they would die of starvation. That there was no appreciable chance of saving life except by killing someone for the others to eat. That assuming any necessity to kill anybody, there was no greater necessity for killing the boy than any of the three men.

But whether [the killing of Parker by Dudley and Stephens] be felony and murder or not the said jurors so as aforesaid chosen, tried, and sworn, are ignorant, and pray the advice of the court thereupon.

Dec. 9, 1884.

The following judgment of the court was delivered by LORD COLERIDGE, C.J.—

The two prisoners, Thomas Dudley and Edwin Stephens, were indicted for the murder of Richard Parker on the high seas on July 25 in the present year. They were tried before Huddleston, B., at Exeter on Nov. 6, and, under the direction of my learned brother, the jury returned a special verdict, the legal effect of which has been argued before us, and on which we are now to pronounce judgment. From the facts, stated with the cold precision of a special verdict, it appears sufficiently that the prisoners were subject to terrible temptation and to sufferings which might break down the bodily power of the strongest man, and try the conscience of the best. Other details yet more harrowing, facts still more loathsome and appalling, were presented to the jury, and are to be found recorded in my learned brother's notes. But nevertheless this is clear, that the prisoners put to death a weak and unoffending boy upon the chance of preserving their own lives by feeding upon his flesh and blood after he was killed, and with a certainty of depriving him of any possible chance of survival. The verdict finds in terms that: "if the men had not fed upon the body of the boy, they would probably not have survived . . . " and that "the boy, being in a much weaker condition, was likely to have died before them." They might possibly have been picked up next day by a passing ship; they might possibly not have been picked up at all; in either case it is obvious that the killing of the boy would have been an unnecessary and profitless act. It is found by the verdict that the boy was incapable of resistance, and, in fact, made none; and it is not even suggested that his death was due to any violence on his part attempted against, or even so much as feared by, them who killed him. Under these circumstances the jury say they are ignorant whether those who killed him were guilty of murder, and have referred it to this court to say what [are] the legal consequences which follow from the facts which they have found.

[HIS LORDSHIP dealt with objections taken by counsel for the prisoners which do not call for report, and continued:] There remains to be considered the real question in the case—whether killing, under the circumstances set forth in the verdict, be or be not murder. * * *

First, it is said that it follows, from various definitions of murder in books of authority—which definitions imply, if they do not state, the doctrine—that, in order to save your own life you may lawfully take away the life of another, when that other is neither attempting nor threatening yours, nor is guilty of any illegal act whatever towards you or anyone else. But, if these definitions be looked at, they will not be found to sustain the contention. * * * [I]t is clear that Bracton is speaking of necessity in the ordinary sense, the repelling by violence—violence justified so far as it was necessary for the object—any illegal violence used towards oneself. * * * Lord Hale regarded the private necessity which justified, and alone justified, the taking the life of another for the safeguard of one own's to be what is commonly called self-defence. . . . Lord Hale himself has made it clear, for, in the chapter in which he deals with the exemption created by compulsion or necessity, he thus expresses himself (1 Hale, P.C. 51):

> If a man be desperately assaulted, and in peril of death, and cannot otherwise escape, unless to satisfy his assailant's fury he

> will kill an innocent person then present, the fear and actual force will not acquit him of the crime and punishment of murder if he commit the act, for he ought rather to die himself than to kill an innocent; but if he cannot otherwise save his own life, the law permits him in his own defence to kill the assailant, for, by the violence of the assault and the offence committed upon him by the assailant himself, the law of nature and necessity hath made him his own protector. * * *

Is there, then, any authority for the proposition which has been presented to us? Decided cases there are none. * * *

Except for the purpose of testing how far the conservation of a man's own life is in all cases and under all circumstances an absolute, unqualified, and paramount duty, we exclude from our consideration all the incidents of war. We are dealing with a case of private homicide, not one imposed upon men in the service of their Sovereign or in the defence of their country. It is admitted that deliberate killing of this unoffending and unresisting boy was clearly murder, unless the killing can be justified by some well-recognised excuse admitted by the law. It is further admitted that there was in this case no such excuse, unless the killing was justified by what has been called necessity. But the temptation to the act which existed here was not what the law has ever called necessity. Nor is this to be regretted. Though law and morality are not the same, and though many things may be immoral which are not necessarily illegal, yet the absolute divorce of law from morality would be of fatal consequence, and such divorce would follow if the temptation to murder in this case were to be held by law an absolute defence of it. It is not so.

To preserve one's life is generally speaking, a duty, but it may be the plainest and the highest duty to sacrifice it. War is full of instances in which it is a man's duty not to live, but to die. The duty, in case of shipwreck, of a captain to his crew, of the crew to the passengers, of soldiers to women and children * * *—these duties impose on men the moral necessity, not of the preservation, but of the sacrifice, of their lives for others, from which in no country—least of all it is to be hoped in England—will men ever shrink, as indeed they have not shrunk. It is not correct, therefore, to say that there is any absolute and unqualified necessity to preserve one's life. * * *

It would be a very easy and cheap display of commonplace learning to quote from Greek and Latin authors, from Horace, from Juvenal, from Cicero, from Euripides, passage after passage, in which the duty of dying for others has been laid down in glowing and emphatic language as resulting from the principles of heathen ethics; it is enough in a Christian country to remind ourselves of the Great Example whom we profess to follow. It is not needful to point out the awful danger of admitting the principle which has been contended for. Who is to be the judge of this sort of necessity? By what measure is the comparative value of lives to be measured? Is it to be strength, or intellect, or what? It is plain that the principle leaves to him who is to profit by it to determine the necessity which will justify him in deliberately taking another's life to save his own. In this case the weakest, the youngest, the most unresisting was chosen. Was it more necessary to kill him than one of the grown men? The answer must be, No. * * *

There is no path safe for judges to tread but to ascertain the law to the best of their ability, and to declare it according to their judgment, and if in any case the law appears to be too severe on individuals, to leave it to the Sovereign to exercise that prerogative of mercy which the Constitution has entrusted to the hands fittest to dispense it. It must not be supposed that, in refusing to admit temptation to be an excuse for crime, it is forgotten how terrible the temptation was, how awful the suffering, how hard in such trials to keep the judgment straight and the conduct pure. We are often compelled to set up standards we cannot reach ourselves, and to lay down rules which we could not ourselves satisfy. But a man has no right to declare temptation to be an excuse, though he might himself have yielded to it, nor allow compassion for the criminal to change or weaken in any manner the legal definition of the crime. It is, therefore, our duty to declare that the prisoners' act in this case was wilful murder; that the facts as stated in the verdict are no legal justification of the homicide; and to say that, in our unanimous opinion, they are, upon this special verdict, guilty of murder.

The Lord Chief Justice thereupon passed sentence of death in the usual form.[a]

Judgment for the Crown.

NOTE

Do you think the sentence of death was an appropriate punishment? Consider four different theories of punishment: (1) deterrence, which can either be general (punishment to deter others from committing the same or similar offenses) or specific (punishment to deter the individual defendant from committing the same crime in the future), (2) rehabilitation (reforming the defendant through vocational training, counseling, drug rehabilitation, etc.), (3) incapacitation (incarceration to keep the defendant away from other members of society), and (4) retribution (giving the defendant what he deserves).

---

[a] Apparently, a pardon had been arranged in advance, so even though Dudley and Stephens were sentenced to death, they served only six months in prison. Leo Katz, BAD ACTS AND GUILTY MINDS: CONUNDRUMS OF THE CRIMINAL LAW 25 (1987). Haunted by memories of what happened on the dinghy, Stephens lost his mental faculties. *Id.* Dudley moved to Australia, became an opium addict, and then died of the bubonic plague. *Id.*

PEOPLE V. SUITTE

New York State Supreme Court, Appellate Division
455 N.Y.S.2d 675, 90 A.D.2d 80 (N.Y. App. Div. 1982)

LAZER, JUSTICE PRESIDING.

The defendant has pleaded guilty to criminal possession of a weapon in the fourth degree, a class A misdemeanor. The sentence we review consists of 30 days of imprisonment and three years of probation, the jail time to be a condition of and to run concurrently with the period of probation. Execution of the sentence has been stayed pending this appeal. * * *

When arrested in January, 1981, for unauthorized use of a motor vehicle, based on what seems to have been a misunderstanding, James Suitte was found to possess a loaded Sterling .25 calibre automatic pistol. Although Mr. Suitte had registered the gun in North Carolina when he acquired it there in 1973, he carried it unlicensed in this State for the seven and one-half-year period preceding his arrest. College educated for three years, Mr. Suitte is 46 years old, has been married for 25 years, and has two children, aged 14 and 21 years. He has never before been convicted of a crime. Although he admits he was aware of New York's gun licensing requirement, he claims that the gun was necessary for protection because the tailor shop he operates is located in a high crime area of the Bronx.

The plea of guilty was a bargained one. Originally charged with the class D felony of criminal possession of a weapon in the third degree, Mr. Suitte was permitted to plead to the misdemeanor of possession in the fourth degree. In imposing sentence under the new gun statute and its mandatory one year imprisonment provision—publicized in the State as the "toughest gun law in the country"—the sentencing Judge found the mandatory one year jail provision too severe. He noted, however, "the Legislature, the community and indeed this Court [are] concerned with the proliferation of guns and the possession of guns by individuals in the community, regardless of the reasons, and we have such a possession in this case." He then exercised his discretion under the statute and imposed a jail sentence of 30 days plus three years' probation. The jail portion of the sentence is the focus of the appeal.

The new gun statute has substantially increased the penal sanctions for possession and sale of illegal weapons. The major change from previous law is the mandatory imposition of a prison sentence of at least one year upon conviction of possession of a loaded weapon outside the home or place of business. The legislation contains additional procedures, however, which, inter alia, permit imposition of a lesser sentence upon conviction of possession in the fourth degree if "the court having regard to the nature and circumstances of the crime and to the history and character of the defendant, is of the opinion that such sentence would be unduly harsh." This mitigation inquiry relative to possession in the fourth degree is limited to individuals who have not been convicted of either a felony or a class A misdemeanor within the preceding five years. Other provisions of the new law prohibit preindictment plea bargaining, restrict post-indictment plea bargaining and expedite the processing of licensing requests.

The statute is an obvious expression of the State's reaction to the current avalanche of gun-related crimes. In approving the law, Governor Carey proclaimed:

> We must bring an end to the proliferation of illegal handguns in New York and the intolerable assaults on law enforcement officers and law-abiding citizens. We must let it be known that New York has the toughest gun law in the country and that it will be strictly enforced. We are determined to rid our streets of those who would do violence to its citizens.

The Governor viewed the amended gun law as even more stringent than that of Massachusetts, which had been considered the strictest in the country. Mayor Koch termed the legislation "a significant first step in the fight to remove illegal handguns from the streets of our city."

Early returns on the law—later ones are not available—indicate that applications for gun licenses have increased, fewer gun possession cases have been reduced to misdemeanors, and sentences of incarceration have been imposed in more instances than before the law. Slightly more than half of the adults convicted of gun possession received at least the mandatory one-year minimum.

Whatever its ultimate success in a nation bedeviled by handguns, there can be no doubt that the State's 1980 legislation represents a vivid manifestation of public policy intended to make illegal possession of guns a serious criminal offense accompanied by the strong prospect of punishment by penal servitude. While we note our colleague's negative view of the wisdom of the statute, it is not for the court to pass on the wisdom of the Legislature, for that body "has latitude in determining which ills of society require criminal sanctions, and in imposing, as it reasonably views them, punishments, even mandatory ones, appropriate to each." We turn, then, to the role of the judiciary in enforcing this public mandate that the crime of illegal possession of a gun be impressed upon all as a serious offense against society.

It is scarcely worth repetition to observe that a sentencing determination is a matter committed to the exercise of the sentencing court's discretion, for it is that court's primary responsibility. Sentencing involves consideration of the crimes charged, the particular circumstances of the offender, and the purposes of a penal sanction.

As has been oft-stated, the four principal objectives of punishment are deterrence, rehabilitation, retribution and isolation. While deterrence includes individual deterrence directed at preventing the specific offender from repeating the same or other criminal acts, it also includes general deterrence which aims to discourage the general public from recourse to crime. Rehabilitation is directed, of course, at reform of the individual, while retribution includes "the reaffirmation of societal norms for the purpose of maintaining respect for the norms themselves," community condemnation, and the community's emotional desire to punish the offender. Isolation serves simply to segregate the offender from society so as to prevent criminal conduct during the period of incarceration. It is clear that the principal aim of the 1980 gun legislation is general deterrence.

The most difficult problem confronting the sentencing judge is determination of the priority and relationship between the objectives of punishment, a matter of considerable and continuing debate. Inevitably, there are bound to be differences of opinion in the relative values assigned these factors in particular cases. The theories frequently are in unavoidable and constant conflict and those that prevail in the sentencer's mind obviously decide the degree of punishment. Much of the controversy and criticism swirling about the contemporary sentencing scene relates to inequitable disparities between sentences for the same or similar crimes. The disparities derive primarily from differing philosophies and attitudes of judges and a lack of consensus concerning the goals of criminal justice.

Appellate review of sentences obviously is a useful means of diminishing sentencing disparity and ensuring the imposition of fair sentences. Nevertheless, the limited nature of appellate review of sentences is a recognition that "the sentencing decision is a matter committed to the exercise of the [sentencing] court's discretion." A reviewing court lacks some of the first-hand knowledge of the case that the sentencing judge is in a position to obtain, and therefore the sentencer's decision should be afforded high respect. As a consequence, abuse of discretion is the test most frequently cited as the one to be applied. The abuse of discretion standard is especially befitted to an era in which most convictions derive from plea bargains where the bargaining leverages of the respective parties to the agreement are ofttimes more important in fixing the degree of the crime pleaded to and the other limits of the sentence to be imposed than matters of guilt, fault, character, mitigative circumstances or other factors which might otherwise seem more relevant. Nevertheless, since the Legislature has empowered us to modify sentences "as a matter of discretion in the interest of justice" and our general review powers include the right to do whatever the trial court could have done even in matters entrusted to the discretion of that court, we can substitute our own discretion for that of a trial court which has not abused its discretion in the imposition of a sentence. The power to substitute discretion helps us to meet recommended sentence review standards by making any disposition the sentencing court could have made, except an increased sentence. Without the substitution power, our ability to rectify sentencing disparities, reach extraordinary situations, and effectively set sentencing policy through the development of sentencing criteria, would be sorely handicapped.

Appellate review determines whether the sentence is excessive to the extent that there was a failure to observe the principles of sentencing. In such review, the court takes a "second look" at the sentences in light of the societal aims which such sanctions should achieve. But in reducing any sentence, the appellate body must be sensitive to the fact that its actions become guidelines for the trial court to follow in the imposition of future sentences under circumstances similar to the case reviewed.

In the current case, there has been no abuse of discretion and we perceive neither a failure to observe sentencing principles nor a need to impose a different view of discretion than that of the sentencing judge. True, the defendant does not appear to be a danger to society or in apparent need of rehabilitation. It is plain, however, that the sentencing court viewed general deterrence as the overriding principle, and we cannot say that the emphasis was erroneous or that the interests of justice call for a reduction. Deterrence is the primary and essential postulate of almost all criminal law systems. In this era of conflict between the adherents of the rehabilitation model and those who advocate determinative sentencing, it is hardly debatable that prisons do deter even if the degree of deterrence and the types of persons deterred remain in dispute. Even when imposing an "individualized" sentence, the judge may look beyond the offender to the presumed effect of the sentence on others. Indeed, the primary purpose behind mandatory sentence laws is to impose swift and certain punishment on the offender. A short definite period of confinement under the circumstances has been seen as the most effective method of deterrence. As Marvin Frankel has written, general deterrence may be satisfied through "relatively short but substantially inexorable sentences to prison." Some commentators have concluded that lesser punishment for firearm crimes, e.g., fines, probation or suspended sentences, is not significant enough to have any real deterrent effect.

In emphasizing the mandatory minimum sentence and the purpose of deterrence, the new gun legislation intended to convey to the public a "get tough" message on crime. In this regard, the advertisements heralding the new law are significant; thus: "If you get caught carrying an illegal handgun, you'll go to jail for one year. No plea bargaining. No judges feeling sorry for you. Just one year in jail."

With such a background, we cannot view the new gun law as containing a blanket exception of first offenders from the scope of its penal provisions. The statute's provisions for mitigation are not carte blanche for the commission of one offense free of the threat of a sentence of custodial detention. The sense of the new law is to deter all unlicensed handgun possessions, whether the offense is the first or a repeat. The special mitigation inquiry is not intended to provide automatic probation for those without prior criminal records. The penalty to be imposed is a matter for the trial court's broad discretion within the limits imposed by the Legislature. In balancing the public and private interests represented in the criminal justice process, the sentencing court's decision in this case was neither inconsistent with sound sentencing principles, nor inappropriate. We see nothing obscene about a 30-day jail sentence (which is subject to a 10-day reduction for good behavior) for possession of a gun, particularly when the defendant has a history of carrying the weapon for over seven years with knowledge of the law's requirements.

Reduction of the current sentence by this court would proclaim to those listening that the new gun law presents no threat of jail to first criminal offenders. Such a reduction would also declare to the trial bench that a judge who imposes a 30-day jail sentence on such a first offender has either abused his discretion or that this court disagrees with the sentencer's evaluation of the relevant sentencing factors. Finally, reduction would be this court's expression that violation of the gun law is nothing serious.

Accordingly, the sentence is affirmed.

O'CONNOR, JUSTICE (dissenting).

In his usual scholarly and impelling style, my esteemed confrere of the majority, Justice LAZER, reviews the principles and discusses the rationale attendant upon sentencing and its appellate review. And so we go pell mell on our merry, merry way! More crimes are committed, more police make more arrests, more D.A.'s process more cases, more judges commit more people to jail, and here, the majority would affirm a jail sentence despite the presence of what, by any standard, was an abuse of sentencing discretion that warrants, nay demands, a reduction to probation. I cannot agree.

Recently released Justice Department figures for 1981 indicate that there were 369,000 adults in Federal and State prisons at the end of that year, plus nearly 157,000 in local jails. The National Council on Crime and Delinquency reports that the United States trails only the Soviet Union and South Africa (what a combination!) in its per capita rate of incarceration and, contrary to popular belief, in the severity of the punishments it inflicts! And in spite of it all, the crime rate continues to soar. * * *

It seems to me that it's about time we begin to find, in matters such as this where no violence or even threat of violence is present, alternatives to jail. I further believe that rather than joining those who bend before the incessant cry of a rightly outraged public for vengeance we, as appellate judges, should seek to put some sanity into the sentences we approve under these circumstances.

I agree with the principle, articulated in the majority opinion, that an appellate court ought not disturb a sentence in the absence of an abuse of discretion by the sentencing court or unless the interest of justice so requires. I further agree that a workable test for applying this principle is whether the alleged excessiveness of the challenged sentence in fact demonstrates a failure by the sentencing court to observe the purposes of sentencing: individual and general deterrence, rehabilitation, retribution and isolation. I can even agree to the soundness of visiting upon one individual a punishment greater than would have been his had the sentencing court not decided to make an example of him in order to curb sharply a sudden manifestation in the general public of pernicious conduct previously endemic to certain subclasses, e.g., drug abuse, or to overcome widespread public intransigence to legislated curbs on historically unregulated conduct such as gun possession. But I disagree with the majority's statement that the sentencing judge, rather than this court, may on an ad hoc basis, subject only to personal predilections, establish the coefficients to the four variables of deterrence, rehabilitation, retribution and isolation in this sentencing formula. This court should not abdicate its responsibility for the assignment of appropriate, if somewhat inexact, weights to these factors in the discharge of its obligation to control sentencing discretion within the overarching limits fixed by the Penal Law.

Is it just or proper that we permit one sentencing judge to count general deterrence as the overriding factor in this gun possession case under the new anti-gun law, with the implication that another sentencing judge in a factually identical case may switch the emphasis in the formula to another factor, e.g., rehabilitation? Bear in mind that the difference resulting from our toleration of such ad hoc legislating by sentencing judges is incarceration, and I most vehemently reject any argument that incarceration is but a gentle escalation of sanctions to the point at which a real deterrent effect can finally be ascertained operating on the populace. After all, 30 days in the county jail will surely cripple the spirit of any otherwise law-abiding citizen who honestly believed that the cost of unlawfully possessing a gun (discounted tremendously by the infinitesimally small probability of being caught) outweighed the benefit of protecting his life while conducting his livelihood in an urban war zone. I submit that it is we, as the Appellate Division, that should assign the approximate values to the parameters of the sentencing formula (to the extent possible), and that we should restrict sentencing judges to their proper role in applying this legal formula, as so weighted, to the facts as they find them in individual cases.

I pose the questions:

(1) Is it a proper exercise of discretion to sentence to jail a first offender who poses no serious threat to the community?

(2) Does the nature of the crime here committed make it a serious threat to the community?

With these thoughts in mind, let us look at the case at bar.

On the morning of January 20, 1981, while driving through Nassau County on his way to his place of business in New York City, the defendant was stopped and arrested on a bench warrant charging him with the unauthorized use of a motor vehicle.

The validity of that warrant, or the merits of the complaint upon which it was issued, are not before the court at this time, but it should be noted that it is defendant's contention that the charge is totally without substance, arising, he alleges, out of a misunderstanding involving the return by him of a rented automobile.

Be that as it may, upon his arrest he was found in possession of a loaded Sterling .25 caliber automatic pistol. He was promptly charged with the crime of criminal possession of a weapon in the third degree, a class D felony, was convicted on his plea of guilty to possession in the fourth degree, a class A misdemeanor, and was sentenced to three years' probation with the special condition that he serve a determinate sentence of 30 days in the Nassau County Correctional Center. Execution of that sentence has been stayed pending appeal.

Upon appeal to this court as excessive, that sentence has been affirmed by my confreres of the majority. I respectfully disagree and strongly suggest that under the facts and circumstances here extant, it is totally inappropriate and completely counterproductive to impose a jail sentence for however short a period of time.

An objective review of the record establishes that this defendant, a successful businessman, with three years of college education, is married and the father of two children, a daughter, aged 21, and a son, 14 years of age.

Since 1973 the defendant has owned and operated a custom tailer [sic] shop which is located in a high-crime area of the Bronx. A prior owner of the shop had been stabbed during one of several robberies that took place before defendant became the proprietor. The defendant lawfully purchased the gun in question in North Carolina and properly registered it in that State.

According to the arresting officers, the defendant was "very cooperative" when arrested, and readily admitted that he knew that it was illegal to carry an unregistered pistol in New York City and stated that although he had inquired about obtaining a gun permit, he had never completed the process. The defendant told the police that he thought he needed the gun for self-protection.

The Probation Report contains this significant appraisal:

> The present offense is the defendant's only criminal conviction and his first criminal charge in 21 years. He appears to be a devoted father and husband, as well as a productive member of society. There is no evidence of criminal intent in his possession of this weapon and his desire for protection in his business neighborhood is justified.

No one can sustain this defendant, or any person, in the illegal possession of a loaded firearm. It is a clear violation of law and calls for an appropriate sanction and penalty. But under the clear and compelling circumstances here present, is it appropriate or fair or just to send this first offender off to jail for 30 days, 10 days or even one day? To me, such a sentence based upon these facts is cruel and harsh and borders on the obscene.

It is beyond cavil that violent crime is ever on the increase and that it is, in all its terrifying aspects, continuously creating conditions of unspeakable horror on the streets of our cities. Out of these jungle conditions in crescendo fashion, the cry of an aroused and frightened public is heard demanding, with good reason, swift and effective measures to contain and to curtail the monstrous abominations which are daily visited upon them. The fire is fueled by those who should and do know better but who, seizing upon a popular theme, pick up the cry and, by some total distortion of reason, imply that the fault lies with the judiciary and suggest that tougher and longer prison sentences are the solution. The Legislature responds by passing more and more mandatory sentencing laws and the press and other news media not infrequently give at least tacit approval to such measures. And all the time, judges, sitting in the eye of the storm, know that the catastrophic rise in crime bespeaks a failure not alone of society, but of the family, the church, the schools, the home and of the economic and political structure of the State itself. We know, too, that there are as many reasons for crime as there are people who commit it and we have long since learned that there is no simple solution or ready answer to the problem. I have previously expressed my disapproval of mandatory sentences because of a firmly held opinion that mandatory sentences give to a worried and frightened public the illusion of protection, that they do not deter the criminal and, worst of all, that they incapacitate a major section of the system of criminal justice in denying discretion to the courts. Are we really ready to give up on the theory that the punishment fit the crime?

To the issue before us—to tack on an additional jail sentence for the possession and/or use of the gun, loaded or unloaded, in or about the commission of a crime, makes much sense and may even be effective. However, to send an otherwise law-abiding citizen to jail on his first offense under the facts of this case makes no sense, accomplishes no good and creates nothing but untoward hardship and bitterness. I respectfully dissent and would modify the sentence by striking the 30-day period of incarceration.

HAVEN OR HELL? INSIDE LORTON CENTRAL PRISON: EXPERIENCES OF PUNISHMENT JUSTIFIED

Robert Blecker[a]
42 Stan. L. Rev. 1149 (1990)

I. INTRODUCTION

* * *

A. *The Problem: Justifying Punishment*

Why and how should we punish these criminals? A fearful and furious citizen may demand: "First, get them off the streets; keep them away from us. Make them suffer: They deserve it. Teach them a lesson they will not forget. And let their pain and suffering be an example to others. Maybe then, having been punished, someday, somehow, these criminals will feel remorse, change their attitudes, and productively reintegrate into society." Drawing upon sentiments and concepts implicit in the Bible and the works of Plato, Hobbes, Beccaria, Kant, Bentham, and a host of contemporary commentators, the citizen urges that punishment serve as incapacitation, retribution, general deterrence, specific deterrence, and rehabilitation.

The precise definition of each concept differs with each advocate, antagonist, or analyst. Essentially, however, *incapacitation* is rendering harmless to society a person otherwise inclined to crime. *Retribution* is the intentional infliction of pain and suffering on a criminal to the extent he deserves it because he has willingly committed a crime. *General deterrence* is the pressure that the example of one criminal's pain and suffering exerts on potential criminals to forgo their contemplated crimes. *Specific deterrence* is the pressure that unpleasant memories of incarceration exert on a released convict, which cause him to obey the law. *Rehabilitation* is the acquisition of skills or values which convert a criminal into a law-abiding citizen. * * *

---

[a] Robert Blecker, a criminal law professor at New York Law School, interviewed street criminals in Lorton prison and on the streets of Washington, D.C. from 1986 to 1999.

Those who do [prioritize] among the various justifications or purposes of punishment, almost without exception address the problem conceptually, as a matter of logic or philosophy. Without discussion, they assume that an appropriate blend of retribution, deterrence, incapacitation, and rehabilitation ultimately translates into a number, or number range, such as "10 years in prison" or "5-to-15 years in prison." A legislature or court need merely increase or decrease the length of the "sentence" to increase or decrease retribution, rehabilitation, deterrence, or incapacitation. Often this abstraction is obscured: the number *becomes* the punishment rather than a symbol of its duration which is only one dimension of a prisoner's actual pain and suffering.

Punishment, however, is not merely the quantity of time in prison. *The reality of each criminal's punishment consists in the experience of that punishment.* What actually happens to prisoners—their daily pain and suffering inside prison—is the only true measure of whether the traditional concepts have meaning, the traditional goals are fulfilled, the traditional definitions apply. Only through the prisoners' experience can we test the categories, clarify these concepts, and set priorities. * * * This study, then, attempts to bridge the gap between traditional penal philosophy and the actual experience of punishment. * * *

II. INSIDE LORTON CENTRAL

Retribution, deterrence (general and specific), rehabilitation, and incapacitation represent overlapping and antithetical perspectives on why, when, and to what degree criminals should undergo pain and suffering through punishment. In order to evaluate these various definitions, justifications, and goals of punishment, therefore, we need to know whether and how prisoners do in fact suffer inside Lorton Central.

Of course everyone's "bit"—time spent in prison—is different. One individual feels a loss of freedom more or less than another. A forced separation from home, and the streets, and entrance into a new prison environment can be more or less painful. Losing family ties may cause a criminal to suffer differently at different stages of life. And in the course of each day, moment to moment, a prisoner's experience of prison changes. * * *

C. Haven or Hell?

* * * What is the real experience of Lorton? Obviously it depends. Some guys breeze through it; others live in agony. Even Douglas Wright who called Lorton a "playground" qualified it: "[A] playground to all those youngsters who don't know what's happening."

Almost uniformly the older inmates condemn Lorton Central as a "deathtrap." "You can get killed because you have no protection," said Danny Bethel, one of many prisoners who has been stabbed. "You can't go to a dark room; you can't take a bucket and wash your clothes without realizing it's possible you might not come out. It's no such place as that you're guaranteed to see tomorrow. You go to bed with a nightmare, and the only peace that you ever get is not waking up at all." * * *

III. THE EXPERIENCE OF LORTON CENTRAL JUSTIFIED

A. Retribution

> He who kills a man shall be put to death. . . . When a man causes a disfigurement in his neighbor, as he has done it shall be done to him, fracture for fracture, eye for eye, tooth for tooth; as he has disfigured a man, he shall be disfigured. *Leviticus 24:17–20*

Retribution is perhaps the oldest measure of punishment: like for like—pain and suffering for pain and suffering. The Bible commands: "[A]s he has done, it shall be done to him." Scorned by a shrinking majority of scholars, retribution continues to be embraced by a large majority of citizens. Retributivists have recognized that strict repayment is not always possible: If a criminal takes out the only eye of a one-eyed man, surely to take out only one of his two good eyes is not full retribution, whereas to take them both out is not exact recompense. Retribution has advanced beyond exact retaliation to become what it is today—*proportional punishment.* Punishment should be proportional to the gravity of the crime.

Retributivists differ as to the appropriate length and intensity of punishment attaching to particular crimes. Some may see violent crime as incomparably more deserving of punishment than non-violent crime; others may feel that crimes which affect the public generally, such as illegally dumping toxic wastes, or cheating the elderly out of their life savings, or a public official's bribe-receiving deserve the greater punishment. * * * Since Aristotle, *malum in se,* a thing bad in itself, has been distinguished from *malum prohibitum,* a thing bad only because defined as illegal, or as inmate Alvin Hines called it, "a man-made crime." Murder, rape, robbery: These are serious crimes, bad in themselves. But is selling drugs? In 1990, a small but respectable chorus including judges and legislators calls for the legalization of narcotics. Yet, during this era of prohibition, many prisoners are serving very long and painful sentences for engaging in truly consensual transactions that perhaps should not be illegal, while others for whom killing is a business decision, who maintain deadly workplaces or poison our water are sentenced to community service or not punished at all. Is this proportional? * * *

In theory, prison life should be tougher for serious felons, and by privileges and courtesies extended, it should be relatively more comfortable for less serious offenders. But inside Lorton Central, theory and reality do not match.

Inside Central a man's crime is virtually ignored. Officers routinely deny that they treat a prisoner with an eye to his record, to his crime, to his "evil" choice that brought him to prison. Captain Frank Townshend, a long-time, well-respected, tough-but-fair officer, insisted that he never looks at a man's record when he deals with him lest he be "prejudiced. Everyone is entitled to the same treatment here, regardless of what they did to get here. What a man is in here for is not our concern." * * *

All officers interviewed agreed: They never consult a man's record, and sometimes for good reasons. "If you know a man is a murderer, you may fear him, and he will sense that. They pick up those things," said one officer, "so I don't want to know. I make it a point not to know." One female officer offered a similar rationale. She does not check the records, for if she discovers a man is a rapist, she will feel apprehensive about disciplining him. Even when officers do know the criminals' records, they do not treat the more serious offenders more harshly. Rather, they concentrate on behavior which may cause problems in prison. "Inside, a thief is more dangerous than a murderer," observed Sergeant Shipley. "The thief will continue to steal whenever he can, and get himself or someone else stabbed or killed. So he's the one, day to day, that you have to come down hard on." * * *

Overwhelmingly then, by their actions and attitudes consistent with official D.C. Department of Corrections policy, officers and inmates reject retribution as a goal of punishment on the inside for past conduct on the outside. To them, the judge metes out punishment by setting the number of years during which all inmates will be equally deprived of liberty. The officers see no point in trying to make prison more painful for prisoners because they "deserve" it, unless they deserve it for their conduct inside prison. By consciously ignoring prisoners' criminal records, however, officers unwittingly help sever the essential retributive connection between the past crime committed and the present punishment experienced. As Captain Townshend said, "It's none of my business. What a man is like in here is what I concerned with, not what he did out there."

The prisoners further help cut all connection between crime on the street and punishment inside the joint. With the exception of rape which they scorn, and child molestation or crimes against the elderly for which a prisoner may be ostracized or physically attacked, whatever a person did on the outside is his own business. Each man is a hustler, trying to survive. * * *

B. General Deterrence

Deterrence lies at the very source of Western culture. Although the Old Testament is retributive in its measure of punishment—an eye for an eye—it is fundamentally deterrent in its justification and purpose. Over and over, the Bible calls for harsh punishment, not only because an individual deserves it on account of his past transgression, but also for the future benefit it will bring to others: "[T]hen you shall do to him as he had meant to do to his brother. . . . And the rest shall hear, and fear, and shall never again commit any such evil among you." * * *

According to the psychology expounded by Beccaria and Bentham, a rational pleasure seeker defers immediate illegal gratification because a threat of future punishment weighs decisively in his pleasure/pain, cost/benefit calculus. Convicts as well as commentators dismiss this psychology of the rational prudent calculating maximizer as fantastic—an ideal inapplicable to the streets: General deterrence is unreal and unworkable; people do not consciously weigh costs and benefits before they engage in crime.

A litmus question to the inmates at Lorton Central—"Before you pulled the trigger [or robbed] did you ever think about what would happen if you were caught?"—revealed minds unconcerned with future punishment in moments immediately surrounding the criminal act:

"Nah, never thought about it," said inmate David Basnight, "until one time, and that's probably why I got caught. I just stood there, looking at the camera, thinking."

"Did you ever think about getting caught?" inmate Harry Rowe was asked.

"No."

"Never occurred to you?"

"No."

"Never thought about going to jail?"

"Well, *I'd been told,* but you know, I ain't never really thought about it. . . . "

"And the day you did it, it never passed through your mind that 'Hey, I might get caught, this might be the last day'?"

"No, I ain't think . . . that weren't on my mind. Just getting the money and getting away."

The pressing problem of the moment—getting away—includes not getting shot, and not getting caught, which may subconsciously include a future trial and eventually a prison term. But conscious calculation is not so much of punishment as of pulling it off and escaping. * * *

"Seeing another hustler fall, you say 'he did something foolish,' something you're not going to do," mused Itchy Brooks. "Sometimes a guy try to find out what he did so he won't do the same. That's the only deterrent effect that has."

When the possibility of being caught only causes a more disciplined hustler to take greater precautions or to switch to safer crimes, has deterrence succeeded?

Some criminals may be undeterrable because they do not calculate, but others are undeterrable because they do. "I had a job," said inmate Wade Briggs, "but I saw that the same amount of money it took me four weeks to work for, I could make in one day." * * *

"If I worked, there wasn't much chance of my getting more than a few thousand dollars a year and here's a chance of my getting two hundred fifty thousand dollars in a day or so. It was worth it to take the risk. Plus the federal statistics show that only a little over half of all bank robbers are caught. And eighty percent of those just ran in and grabbed the stuff. People in the banks are instructed not to create the kind of situation where somebody's going to get hurt. Because the money's insured. And really the professional is not going there to hurt nobody. He's going there to get the money. Since he knows they're instructed not to offer resistance, that's the way it's done." * * *

"The average black kid in the ghetto after that first knockdown knows that the old bootstrap trick is not really there," observed Sergeant Edmonds. "And he just takes a look around at his aunts and uncles, his parents and cousins, and he assesses how far they reached up this ladder of success. How much have they gained? And he is saying to himself 'Gee they don't got very much, old raggedy clothes, living in a run-down dump.' Then he looks right across the street. Here Joe Slick pulls up: He's got this great big shiny car, the best looking clothes on, he got his jewelry on, he's got a fine looking woman with him. The guy says 'Now that's what I want,' because this guy's got it. He is not equating that with the whole picture, but he is looking at the for-now." * * *

Family visits at Lorton could provide a most compelling occasion for images and pain to combine and produce maximum deterrence. But they don't.

Sergeant Edmonds reminisced about his first year at the prison: "It was Christmas of '80. We had a tree down in the visiting hall and in the cell blocks. And as the kids came in, the fathers came out of their cells carrying gifts. It was a mixed emotion day for me, to look at the picture we projected to the younger kids when they came here to visit. Just to watch the expression on their faces, how they would light up when they came through the control area out front. * * * They were all aglow, watching this door, waiting for their father to come through that door into that visiting hall. And they just ran to him and flung themselves on him. It made you conscious of your younger existence. And how you felt about your father. My father was in the military, so we had that kind of 'father's home, boat's in!' He's going to be here in a few minutes and everybody is all excited about it. And everybody is rushing to him. It gave me the same kind of feeling watching them.

"But by the same token, it made the children feel that this was a good place, because all the good things that occurred to them in a family sense were occurring right here inside an institution where their father was locked away at. And being punished at. So it did not build a sense of 'this is a bad place;' it built the sense of 'this is a good place'—the experience for a lot of them, of seeing for the first time both parents together, hugging and embracing and enjoying each other's company. And the kids running around the visiting hall or out in the field, having a good time with other kids from their neighborhoods within the city. * * *

"When the kids visit, you give them your best smile," Itchy agreed. "We're relaxed; nothing jumps off at the visiting hall. But they don't see our face change as we leave the hall." * * *

C. Incapacitation

Originally prison's sole purpose was to hold prisoners until trial or punishment. Today, incarceration—taking criminals from the streets and confining them—remains prison's front line, and perhaps bottom line, justification. The experience inside may not be retributive, it may not rehabilitate the inmate, nor deter him or others, but at least that criminal is removed from society and to the prison, where he is disabled from committing further crimes. * * *

Even though sentences have gotten much longer and inmates believe escape is not that difficult today, very few prisoners plan or attempt it. * * * What keeps them inside? Less a fear of being shot while scaling the fence, than the punishment which follows an unsuccessful escape attempt: Transfer. Lorton, Virginia is easily accessible to Washington, D.C. As Reggie Brooks said, "They got three or four of their little buddies serving life sentences with them here, and they're in heaven." A transfer to Wala Wala [*sic*], Leavenworth or another remote prison cuts off an inmate from his family, friends, his familiar environment. Punishing escape with transfer deters; it is also ironically retributive.

An inmate who does not escape, however, is not necessarily incapacitated. Incapacitation requires more than confinement. While incarcerated, an inmate must commit no crimes against society. Prisoners inside Central rarely assault visitors, teachers, counselors, or officers, mostly because they fear transfer. But prisoners often kill prisoners. Inside Lorton Central serious stabbings and murder attempts are an everyday event. Every inmate who wants a weapon has one. * * *

Prisoners disagree over which is more dangerous, the joint or the streets. Inside Lorton Central there are very few guns, whereas the streets of Washington, D.C. have become a battlefield. On the other hand, in the closed environment inside Central, there is nowhere to run, nowhere to hide. On the street when a guy cuts in line or "rips you off," you can ignore it. You will probably never see him again. But inside Lorton Central, with everyone watching on the side-lines, you must counter such disrespect, or others will take advantage of you. "In the street when you're doing something wrong you're seldom doing it in your neighborhood," said Johnny. "Lorton is the neighborhood. Each time you take a pair of tennis shoes, a radio, a sweatsuit, you risk your life." * * *

Thus, from the outside, the prisoners of Lorton Central seem to be incapacitated. Rarely do they cross the perimeter or even test it. Inside the prison, however, crime—the sale and possession of narcotics, theft, assault, and murder—is rampant. In the words of inmate Pete Arnold, "It's a fucking zoo."

D. Specific Deterrence

In theory, then, having committed no crimes while he is incarcerated, the prisoner, once released, carries with him painful memories of his prison experience, which continue to haunt him, pressuring him to avoid criminality and live the straight life. In theory.

If, as Hobbes defined it, memory is "decaying sense," then painful prison memories have a very short half-life: "In twenty-five days you've forgotten the experience of twenty-five years," said Itchy Brooks. "All the lessons you learned." Pressed in the streets, memories of Lorton quickly fade. The immediate dangers, the uncertainty, and the insecurity can seem worse than life in Central with its "three hots and a cot."

"I know what the penitentiary is about. I've dealt with it," said Leo Simms. "Inside, I guess I know I can deal with it. If you check my records it seems I am able to deal with the institution better than I do with the street. You can institutionalize a person. I know what to expect here. I can be inside any institution for a week, and I can close my eyes and know the routine from hour to hour. It doesn't offer me any challenges. It's a lesser threat than I would have in the street. The decisions you have to make in the free world you don't have to make here. I know it's sad to say, a guy my age, but you can get in the habit of having people make decisions for you. You have many guys in this institution that cry every day about wanting to get out, but their actions dictate different, because in their heart they can't really want to go, because they don't know how to make it out there. * * *

Dr. Reynolds, Chief [Psychologist] at Maximum, summed it up bleakly: "Before the first time, they don't think about it; after the first time they get used to it." "When I was on the street," said Robert Moffitt, "I used to say to myself 'I wish I could go to jail for about six months or a year maybe, just to get myself together.' Jail is about the only place a man can get himself cleaned up." Specific deterrence fails miserably when prison becomes a refuge.

For some inmates, Central is not so much a refuge, but an acceptable, if unpleasant, necessity. "I operate on the premise of my being a hustler and this [is] part of it, part of the game that comes with it. It's a deterrent as far as educational things," said Rodney Hunt. "I won't make the same mistakes in the future. I'll do it another way." * * *

"You come here for stealing a car, you leave here knowing how to crack a safe," Itchy said. "This is a crime factory."

Prison experience, then, fails as a specific deterrent for the ex-convict on the streets who remembers it as a refuge, or accepts it as an inevitable part of hustling life. And the experience fails to specifically deter those it makes more cautious or those ex-convicts it opens up to new criminal opportunities. Most perversely, out on the street, specific deterrence fails when a convict's obvious indifference to repeating a long bit may make him an even more effective hustler. His threats are credible—"I've done hard time; I can do it again."

He may come out more vicious than he went in. "Prison is not a healthy place to be," said Itchy. "The people in the community say, 'Well, it's not intended to be. We don't want it to be.' Fine, so when a guy come to the gate to blow your fucking head off, then that's what you apparently wanted. You should have expected it. Because that's exactly what the fuck you're doing. When you put a man in prison and you say 'life,' then make that life. Or you're asking for it."

"What do you do with a Doberman Pinscher when you want him to be mean? You make him hungry and keep him chained up, restrained from everything. When you let him loose he goes wild. It's no different with us," Itchy said. "You in such a state of deprivation when you leave here, you want *everything* and you want it *now*. You don't want to wait. You've been waiting too long. You've been waiting on too many lines. You done took shit from too many people. You ain't taking any more shit.

"So when you go on the street with that attitude you're dangerous. And that's that. This is a monster. But where did that monster come from? You were a small monster when you came but you're a giant one when you go out of here." * * *

Why, then, doesn't every ex-prisoner return to prison? Why is any Lorton Central ex-con ever deterred? Two factors, often noted in the literature, were reflected inside the prison. "I would never come back to this place," insisted Danny Bethel. "I've overstayed my welcome. I'm too old for it and I can't take it no more. There comes a time in all of us where it's time to quit. There's no force, there's no power that can make me commit a crime. My time's over; I'm just not coming back." For many, like Bethel, Johnny, and Leo, the aging process itself makes specific deterrence work. * * *

Family is the great motivator. "It would be a lot different for me if I had a second chance," mused Earl Grier. "What it boils down to on this charge and me doing this time, is that it really wasn't worth it compared to what I have lost. * * *

E. Rehabilitation: "An Eye Patch For An Eye"

* * * Rehabilitation—or reformation—essentially consists of the acquisition of attitudes, values, habits and skills by which an "enlightened" criminal comes to value himself as a member of a society in which he can function productively and lawfully. This glossy definition is appealing, but reveals little of the rehabilitative process with its pitfalls and problems. * * *

1. Back out, back in.

"This place is not working," observed Sergeant Edmonds, stating the obvious. "But you cannot change it inside and not change the outside. Even if a guy has good intentions, and says, 'I am going to get out and go straight, be a good father, be a good provider.' He goes back out into the system we are in. He is a convicted criminal. That's one strike against him. He's black or Hispanic, so he's got two strikes against him. When he gets back out there, who's going to hire him? The average business really does not want a convict employee. What did he do? Can he be trusted? How will other employees feel with him around? So if he gets a job, it's going to be a low-level, low-paying job. But his aspirations are as high as anybody else's out there. He wants the American dream too. A lot of them get into crime because they want the American dream. The reasons that brought him here never changed. The have-nots want to have." * * *

Itchy described the psychological corrosion of a prisoner, released after a long bit, initially determined to stay out: "You're going in the street," said Itchy, "with the fifty dollars they give you and you have a whole new situation where you haven't been making no decisions for four or five years and now you have to make them all. You haven't had to do nothing but make ugly faces and look tough in here to get by. Now looking tough don't get you nothing. So you're out there and all your good intentions, all that shit don't amount to a hill of beans, because it's back to real life, it's back to the survival struggle. . . . You're out there and everything is falling apart; everybody's got a family except you—yours fell apart a long time ago while you were in here.

"And your buddies come by and say 'let's take a drink.' 'Man, no, I got some things I'm trying to do' and that lasts for awhile. Because you see yourself accomplishing something, you see yourself trying to do something. But then after a few months go by and you're still in the same situation you was, you see yourself making no progress, your prospects are the same as the day you came out. Nobody's seriously offering you anything. You got some people telling you 'well if you go down and sit outside the union somebody will come by and offer you a day's work.' What is a day's work going to do toward paying the rent? You don't got enough money to more than get you a drink, or buy you some dope and put yourself out of your misery. The next thing you know, you find that all this stuff about Lorton is fuzzy in your mind. 'Damn, I sure did rough in Lorton. But at least somebody had their foot on my neck and kept me from doing better. Now, here, nobody got their foot on my neck and I still can't do better.' Then you start backsliding. You start going around with your buddies and doing things you hadn't planned on doing."

"When you leave here," said Johnny, "You don't have no money. The people you know in the street are hustling. A guy may offer you some drugs, or somebody going to say 'Here's five or six hundred dollars. Go downtown and get yourself a couple of outfits.' And then the same guy, a couple of days later, going to say 'Hey, what you doing?' And you say 'I ain't doing nothing yet. I'm still looking around.' In the course of a few weeks you're getting back into the swing of things. And then this guy come back again in the Mercedes Benz or the BMW and that six is gone. And he say 'Hey, you ready to go to work now?' And you say, 'Of course.' "
* * *

Some prisoners, however, nearing the end of their term can look forward to returning to society with a home, a family, a job. Sergeant Edmonds portrayed the pressure on them: * * * "The same people that came to visit him, the same lady, children came to visit him, now have to alter their life to fit him in. Before, they didn't have to do that. They just had Tuesdays, Thursdays, Saturdays and Sundays to visit in two hour blocks and back to whatever they were doing. Now he is there full-time. They have to integrate him into their being. Slap! 'I am back.' He wants to carry the same authoritative manner that he had when they came for those couple of hours visit. In charge. But they have lived independent of him, with the exception of the visits. Resentment builds. He is now a liability instead of an asset. Because he's not making the kind of money that is going to help motivate and lift them. What little that they now have, have to be shared with someone else. The food bill goes up. The use of the automobile is shared. All of the things that they had, now have to be shared with this guy. Even though they love him, this is a sharing thing now.

"He notices that the irritation factor is setting in, arguments ensue, words are exchanged. Now, it is crystal clear to him that something is wrong here. By now, the woman is saying 'Jesus, man, you're a drain on the family, you got to bring some money in here, we ain't going to live like this.'

"And it gets back to 'What do I know how to do?' Back on the Avenue. You are talking to your friends. You have resisted them. Maybe for six or seven months. You have resisted the temptation to put the package in your hand, or do a deal to make some money. A lot of the guys who have gotten out, the guys they see on the streets, those same role models are still out there living the high life, wads of money.

"One day you are coming up out of McDonald's, dirty and greasy, going home into the shit, arguments, and all that because you are not providing. You're choking, you are stifling them to death. And he says 'Give me the package; fuck McDonald's.' He knows from that point he's on his way home. This is his home, Lorton. The rhetoric is the rhetoric. This is home." * * *

F. The Unjustified Experience at Lorton: A Summary

Traditionally, the principal definitions, justifications, and purposes of punishment—retribution, general deterrence, specific deterrence, incapacitation, and rehabilitation—have been singly advocated in the literature. Inside Lorton Central they have been singularly violated. * * * Lorton Central may be unique among prisons in the United States, but in its failure to achieve the traditional goals of punishment, it suffers their common fate. The problem may lie in the categories themselves, used for centuries by legislatures, courts, philosophers, and law professors, with a most casual relationship to reality.

THE DILEMMA OF EXPRESSIVE PUNISHMENT

William S. DeFord

76 U. Colo. L. Rev. 843 (2005)[a]

Introduction: The Dilemma

In January 1990, Utah State Senator Paul T. Fordham presented a bill designed to address Utah's problem with criminal street gangs. Speaking to the legislators, he said, "I think we need to send a message to these organized people that there isn't a place for them in Utah." The medium that Senator Fordham chose for this message was a sentence enhancement that increased the minimum sentence for crimes committed "in concert with two or more persons." It is common for legislators to say that the intent of a sentence enhancement or other punishment scheme is to "send a message." * * *

I. Why Punishment Must Be Expressive

* * *

A. Expressive Theories of Punishment

In 1929, A.C. Ewing wrote that rehabilitating criminals requires that we inflict suffering on them because the criminal [:]

> must realize the badness of what he has been doing, and since his previous actions make it very doubtful whether he will do so of his own accord, this badness must be "brought home to him" and the consciousness of it stamped on his mind by suffering. The infliction of pain is society's way of impressing on him that he has done wrong.

[a] William S. DeFord, *The Dilemma of Expressive Punishment*, 76 U. Colo. L. Rev. 843 (2005). Reprinted with permission of the *University of Colorado Law Review*.

Punishments, then, should educate criminals and express the proper moral standing of criminal acts. It is significant that expressive theories use the word express and not communicate; the latter suggests a meeting of the minds, a communion between speaker and hearer. The word express, however, suggests a kind of force, descending from the Latin ex premere, meaning to press out, like pressing oil from an olive. Look again at the Ewing passage above. In describing punishment, he uses the words "stamped" and "impressing," both of which connote the same kind of downward force that expression in its original meaning possessed. If punishment is a kind of language, it is a language that depends on a vocabulary of force.

Even before A.C. Ewing wrote the article quoted above about how punishment should express moral condemnation, a handful of philosophers and legal theorists had suggested that punishments were or should be expressive. J.F. Stephen * * * argued that the criminal law should affirmatively seek to express the public's moral indignation aroused by crime. This moral indignation should not be discouraged but instead is perfectly legitimate and indeed should be ratified by the punishments we inflict. "[T]he whole criminal law is based on the principle that it is morally right to hate criminals." When the law inflicts a punishment, according to Stephen, it allows expression of hatred for and vindictiveness toward the criminal that would be inappropriate in other fora. The criminal law channels the public's revenge so that "the criminal law stands to the passion of revenge in much the same relation as marriage to the sexual appetite." Similar to Stephen's version of expressive punishment, Henry M. Hart—quoting George K. Gardner—wrote that while physical hardships can come from many sources like wars and market downturns, "[i]t is the expression of the community's hatred, fear, or contempt for the convict which alone characterizes physical hardship as punishment." Without some expressive element, then, punishment would be identical to any other physical hardship. * * *

In recent years, expressive theories of law have abounded, championed by Cass Sunstein, Richard McAdams, Robert Nozick, and Lawrence Lessig, to name a few. Each theorist describes a subtly different way that the law influences behavior by what it says. This Part examines one theory of expressive law, formulated by Dan M. Kahan. I have chosen Kahan's treatment of expressive law because it is a particularly cogent argument about punishment * * * instead of the expressive function of law generally.

B. Kahan and the Language of Punishment

Kahan's article, *What Do Alternative Sanctions Mean?*, explains why "[i]mprisonment is the punishment of choice in American jurisdictions," although "theorists of widely divergent orientations—from economics-minded conservatives to reform-minded civil libertarians—are united in their support for alternative sanctions." This disconnect between theory and practice, Kahan argues, exists because alternative sanctions, like community service or fines, lack the power to express condemnation in the same way that imprisonment can. Alternative sanctions too often express the wrong things. Fines, for example, express that "you may do what you have done, but you must pay for the privilege." Community service is ambiguous in what it expresses because it involves activities worthy of praise and admiration. Alternative sanctions are politically unacceptable because they represent a "mismatch between the suffering that a sanction imposes and the meaning that [the sanction] has for society."

* * * Kahan's solution? The rediscovery of shame. Shaming punishments have the benefits of other alternative sanctions—especially that they are less costly than imprisonment—but also, argues Kahan, shaming punishments "express appropriate moral condemnation," and thus are more politically acceptable than other alternative sanctions. The article does not say specifically how shaming punishments express condemnation, only that they do. To be fair to Kahan, however, the ability of shaming to express condemnation may be self-evident. Take the case of the woman who was ordered to wear a sign that read, "I am a convicted child molester." If this punishment was able to make the criminal feel ashamed, that shame resulted from some expression of condemnation implicit in the punishment. The criminal felt shame because she stood condemned by the community, in front of the community. * * *

Even if criminals are not ashamed by shaming punishments, the message is nevertheless out there, and the public's anger is assuaged. Kahan writes,

> [t]he public's realization that not all offenders view such punishments as disgraceful, however, does not diminish the resonance of either shaming penalties or imprisonment as symbols of the community's moral disapproval. If anything, the perception that the offender is not shamed by what is commonly understood to be shameful would reinforce onlookers' conclusion that he is depraved and worthy of condemnation. * * *

II. Why Punishment Is Not Expressive

The messages that criminal punishments send are complex to the point of incoherence in three ways. First, the audiences of these messages are undefined and confused. Second, the speakers of the messages are complex, institutional speakers, obscuring the intents of the messages. And when the intent behind a message is confused, the message itself is confused. Third, the messages themselves are ambiguous, inconsistent, and sometimes contradictory. * * *

A. The Problem of Audience: To Whom Does Punishment Speak?

* * *

When Senator Fordham said, "I think we need to send a message to these organized people that there isn't a place for them in Utah," he seems to announce who the intended audience is for the message they are sending. "These organized people," he said. The punishment is intended to send a message to gang members. This presents several possibilities. First, the message could be intended for the recipients of the punishment, that is, the gang members who have been convicted of gang-related crimes and who will therefore serve the additional prison time required by the new law. Second, "these organized people" could be anyone who commits gang-related crimes, whether they have been caught and convicted or not. Third, the audience for the message could be all gang members. The message, then, would be designed to keep them from committing crimes. After all, Senator Fordham directs his message to "these organized people," which could mean any gang member. Fourth, the message could be directed to the public in general, to express the notion that their fears and their hostilities regarding gang activity are being vindicated. Further, the message could be to the public, telling them not to join gangs. But notice the structure of the legal formulation: the statute provides that crimes committed in concert with two or more persons merit a greater penalty than if the crime was committed alone. The law itself does not tell anyone not to join a gang or commit crimes in concert with others. It merely describes conditions under which the judge is constrained to hand down an enhanced punishment. The addressee of the statute is not any of those listed above, but instead the statute is addressed to judges and prosecutors. They are the ones who are expected to read the punishment legislation and act on it. As Drury Stevenson argues,

> most of the sanctions in our codebooks are to be meted out to citizen violators; but being the recipient of the punishment is not the same as being the addressee of the injunction to mete out the punishment. If a military officer commands his men to shoot at the enemy, his men are the addressees, not the enemy, even though it is the enemy who is shot.

Although not the addressees, gang members may "overhear" a message sent from legislatures to judges and prosecutors, either by seeing a report of the new law in the newspaper or on television, by experiencing the punishment that the statute prescribes, or by observing a friend receive the punishment. But the legislature has no control over the message by the time the gang member receives it, or should receive it. The legislature is no longer sending any message, and the recipients of the message (judges and prosecutors), or those who "overhear" the message (the press, for example), now may not deliver the message to others in the way that the legislature intends. For example, the newspaper may criticize the new legislation for unfairly targeting low-income minors, undercutting the moral condemnation that members of the legislature seemed to intend. Or the judge could hand down the enhanced sentence with no accompanying explanation that the punishment was enhanced because the crime was gang-related. Again, no message of moral condemnation of gang activity is expressed to anyone but the judge and prosecutor. * * *

The audiences of punishment's messages are as complex as the messages, and as the complexity mounts, so does the message's ambiguity. Utterances are clearest when they are focused on a single addressee or class of addressees. The more they try to say different things to different people, the more the messages are confused. * * *

C. The Problems of Ambiguity and Inconsistency: What Does Punishment Say?

* * * The ambiguities of the messages of punishment come from two sources: first, the structural limitations of punishment as a kind of language, and second, the inconsistencies in the way that punishment is applied. * * * Unlike spoken or written languages which derive their meaning from shared understandings about what words and grammatical structures mean, there is no operative and shared understanding of what a prison sentence means. There is no dictionary to define it for us, no grammar to chart the relations between terms. * * * We are left, then, with many alternative reactions according to personal interpretations of what the punishment means.

The second source of ambiguity—inconsistencies in the way that punishment is applied—is the subject of the next two subsections. * * *

1. Inconsistency between the Punishment and the Message

Punishment and the messages it seeks to send are often inconsistent because the means of punishment (force, violence, imprisonment, exacting fines, etc.) are similar to the actions the message seeks to condemn. * * * Punishments as mirror images of the crimes may have tremendous retributive value, but they lose the power to condemn those actions when the state undertakes them in response. Think of the confused message that a child receives when she is spanked for hitting her brother. Whether or not the spanking is legitimate, the message is confusing because the moral status of hitting another person is problematized when the authority figure (here, the parent) simultaneously hits and condemns hitting. Whatever the moral differences between inflicting suffering as legal punishment and inflicting suffering as crime, to the convict, crime and punishment may look similar enough to send the opposite message than society intends to send. The similarities between crime and punishment send this message: that we as a society believe that it is appropriate, even necessary, to take people's lives, property, and autonomy by force, to make others suffer, to deprive them of their families, their privacy, and their human agency. These are cast as justified human actions. These are some of the messages of imprisonment, and they confuse, even contradict, any message that hopes to reinforce social norms against doing violence or infringing on the autonomy of others.

2. Inconsistencies between Punishments

* * *

In 1984, Congress passed the Sentencing Guidelines and Policy Statements of the Sentencing Reform Act ("SRA"). The SRA was designed to "eliminate sentencing disparities and state[s] explicitly that race, gender, ethnicity, and income should not affect the sentence length." * * * Since the promulgation of sentencing guidelines, there has been increased scholarly scrutiny of racial, gender, and social class disparities in criminal sentencing. In a study promulgated by the U.S. Sentencing Commission, it was found that mandatory minimums actually worked against the most important goal of determinate sentencing. The Commission found that sentence enhancements actually promoted sentence disparity instead of alleviating it. This is because sentence enhancements do not eliminate discretion in sentencing; they merely shift the discretion from the judge to the prosecutor. If the prosecutor decides to pursue an enhancing factor and proves her case, the mandatory nature of the sentencing scheme means that the judge is bound to apply the enhancement. But the prosecutor often will not pursue the enhancement, or will only use it as a bargaining chip in plea bargaining. More damning, the study also found that sentence disparity under mandatory enhancement schemes was correlated with the race of the defendant. Sentences of white defendants were more likely to fall below mandatory minimums than those of black or Hispanic defendants. * * *

* * * Shawn D. Bushway and Anne Morrison Piehl, in a study of punishments under Maryland's sentencing guidelines, found that African Americans had twenty percent longer sentences than whites. "We find more judicial discretion and greater racial disparity than is generally found in the literature." Similarly, David B. Mustard found that "blacks, males, and offenders with low levels of education and income receive substantially longer sentences" than whites, females, and educated offenders.

If the studies are correct and if these punishments are meant to send a message, it is, among other things, a troubling message of racial, gender, and economic inequality. If punishment expresses condemnation, it says that African Americans and Latinos are more worthy of condemnation than whites even when their behavior is the same. If punishment offers an education in morals, as Jean Hampton argues, it teaches a morality of racial, social, economic, and gender hierarchies. Of course, some punishments send the opposite message, as when Martha Stewart was convicted and one of the jurors said that the verdict "sends a message to bigwigs in corporations. . . . They have to abide by the law. No one is above the law." My point here is not that punishments are always unequal and unjust. It is simply that because of the complexity of the messages that punishments send, in the aggregate, punishments send messages that most of us would not endorse. The complexity of punishment's social messages means that the messages are less predictable and coherent than we would like.

NOTE

In 2006, Professor Dan Kahan, who had previously supported the idea of shaming punishments, wrote, "The time has come for me to recant." Dan M. Kahan, *What's Really Wrong with Shaming Sanctions*, 84 TEX. L. REV. 2075, 2075 (2006). Kahan explained that he had realized that shaming punishments send a message that social conformity is good and individuality bad, a message that is deeply at odds with the values of many Americans:

> [T]he aesthetics of shame seem inescapably to conjure up the specter of hierarchy and coerced conformity. This is especially true for the more ritualized forms of shaming. When a court orders a man convicted of harassing his ex-wife to permit her to spit in his face, as happened in one well-publicized case, the law announces, and invites members of the consuming public to infer, that the offender is contemptibly low in status. When a court orders an offender to engage in an abject form of public apology, it asserts, at least symbolically, the right of the community not just to impose disabilities on those who break the law, but also to force them to renounce their deviant values. For some, even milder publicity sanctions—the posting of the pictures of men convicted of soliciting prostitutes on billboards or internet sites—project a frightening image of the state self-consciously wielding the cudgel of public denunciation to cow reluctant individuals into obedience with communal norms.

Kahan, 84 TEX. L. REV. at 2088. Kahan now believes that imprisonment is a better punishment because it permits people with many different value systems to embrace it for different reasons:

> An immensely rich and ambiguous institution, imprisonment not only condemns, but condemns in a multiplicity of registers that make it simultaneously agreeable to persons of diverse cultural outlooks: hierarchists can see it as supplying a delicious form of debasement for those who resist their proper place in the social order; communitarians, a fitting gesture of banishment for those who wrongfully renounce social obligation; individualists, a

> reciprocal deprivation of liberty for those who fail to respect the liberty of others; and egalitarians, a uniquely democratic metric of punishment for persons who enjoy value by virtue of their capacity for autonomy. Neither the ascendancy of imprisonment nor its stubborn persistence can be understood without an appreciation of the political advantages it has enjoyed over rival forms of punishment by virtue of its expressive overdetermination.

Id. at 2089–90.

Although Kahan has recanted, other advocates support a different theory of criminal justice that involves shame: "restorative justice," which involves the idea of "reintegrative shaming."

C. THE PRESUMPTION OF INNOCENCE AND PROOF BEYOND A REASONABLE DOUBT

In American litigation, criminal trials begin with the prosecution's attempt to establish the defendant's guilt. The reason why the prosecution goes first in a trial is the presumption of innocence, which has been described by the Supreme Court as "that bedrock 'axiomatic and elementary' principle whose 'enforcement lies at the foundation of the administration of our criminal law.'" *In re Winship*, 397 U.S. 358, 90 S.Ct. 1068, 25 L.Ed.2d 368 (1970). The formal way of saying that the prosecution has the responsibility for establishing the defendant's guilt—rather than the defendant having the responsibility for establishing his or her innocence—is that in a criminal case, the prosecution bears the *burden of proof*.[a]

The *standard of proof* in litigation describes the level of certainty the fact-finder must reach before ruling for the party with the burden of proof. In an American criminal trial, the prosecution's standard of proof is "beyond a reasonable doubt." This is the most difficult standard of proof to meet in American law; in civil cases, in contrast, the standard is usually "a preponderance of the evidence," meaning "more likely than not."

Why is the burden of proof in a criminal trial so onerous? In *Winship*, the Supreme Court set forth some reasons for placing such a heavy burden on the government:

> The reasonable-doubt standard . . . is a prime instrument for reducing the risk of convictions resting on factual error. * * * "[A]

---

[a] There are two types of burdens of proof: the *burden of production* and the *burden of persuasion*. The burden of production is the initial responsibility to produce evidence in support of a claim. The burden of persuasion is the ultimate responsibility of proving that a given offense was committed or that the elements of an asserted defense are either present (the defendant's position) or absent (the prosecutor's position). In a criminal case, the burden of persuasion as to charged offenses always rests with the prosecution. The burden of persuasion as to a defense may rest with the prosecution or the defendant, depending on the type of defense asserted. For simplicity's sake, however, it is common to speak of the "burden of proof."

> person accused of a crime . . . would be at a severe disadvantage, a disadvantage amounting to a lack of fundamental fairness, if he could be adjudged guilty and imprisoned for years on the strength of the same evidence as would suffice in a civil case."
>
> The requirement of proof beyond a reasonable doubt has this vital role in our criminal procedure for cogent reasons. The accused during a criminal prosecution has at stake interests of immense importance, both because of the possibility that he may lose his liberty upon conviction and because of the certainty that he would be stigmatized by the conviction. Accordingly, a society that values the good name and freedom of every individual should not condemn a man for commission of a crime when there is reasonable doubt about his guilt. * * *
>
> Moreover, use of the reasonable-doubt standard is indispensable to command the respect and confidence of the community in applications of the criminal law. It is critical that the moral force of the criminal law not be diluted by a standard of proof that leaves people in doubt whether innocent men are being condemned. * * *

The reasonable doubt standard is not just a good idea; it is the law. In *Winship*, the Court held that the Due Process Clause of the Fifth and Fourteenth Amendments of the U.S. Constitution "protects the accused against conviction except upon proof beyond a reasonable doubt of every fact necessary to constitute the crime with which he is charged." 397 U.S. at 364.

Because the prosecution always retains the burden of proof beyond a reasonable doubt in order to secure a conviction, one possible defense strategy is simply to create a reasonable doubt about some element of the crime. This kind of strategy is sometimes described as a *case-in-chief* defense, or a *prima facie* case defense. Suppose, for example, that the defendant has been charged with theft, and one element of that crime is the intentional taking of the property of another. By simply creating a reasonable doubt about whether the taking was intentional or merely accidental, the defense can win and the defendant can be acquitted. This kind of defense may not require the introduction of any evidence; it requires only that the defendant "poke holes" in the prosecution's story.

However, a second strategy is also available to the defense: admitting the basic crime, but arguing for acquittal based on extenuating circumstances. For instance, the defendant can admit that she took the victim's property, but argue that the taking was justified: she stole the victim's fire extinguisher in order to put out a fire that would have otherwise killed an entire family of innocent people. Or, the defendant can admit she stole the property, but argue that she should nevertheless be excused from criminal punishment because she believed the fire extinguisher was actually a transmission device for messages from Saturn, and she needed to receive and translate these messages in order to save the Earth. This kind of defense—in which the defendant admits guilt as to the charged offense, but claims she nevertheless should be acquitted of that offense either because she was justified in acting the way she did or because she should be excused—is called an *affirmative defense.* In contrast to the burden of persuasion for the case in chief, which always remains on the prosecution as a matter of constitutional law, the legislature may place the burden of persuasion regarding an affirmative defense on the defendant. In such a case, the defendant has the responsibility to prove the elements of any justification or excuse defense[b] he or she asserts at trial. In situations in which the legislature has allocated the burden of persuasion to the defendant, the defendant is usually required to prove the affirmative defense by a preponderance of the evidence, the same standard used in civil trials.

What does "reasonable doubt" mean? Consider the following model jury instructions.

CRIMINAL JURY INSTRUCTIONS FOR THE DISTRICT OF COLUMBIA

Instruction 2.108—REASONABLE DOUBT

Young Lawyers Section of the Bar Association of the District of Columbia (5th ed., 2013)

The government has the burden of proving [name of the defendant] guilty beyond a reasonable doubt. In civil cases, it is only necessary to prove that a fact is more likely true than not, or, in some cases, that its truth is highly probable. In criminal cases such as this one, the government's proof must be more powerful than that. It must be beyond a reasonable doubt. Reasonable doubt, as the name implies, is a doubt based on reason—a doubt for which you have a reason based upon the evidence or lack of evidence in the case. If, after careful, honest, and impartial consideration of all the evidence, you cannot say that you are firmly convinced of the defendant's guilt, then you have a reasonable doubt.

Reasonable doubt is the kind of doubt that would cause a reasonable person, after careful and thoughtful reflection, to hesitate to act in the graver or more important matters in life. However, it is not an imaginary doubt, nor a doubt based on speculation or guesswork; it is a doubt based on reason. The government is not required to prove guilt beyond all doubt, or to a mathematical or scientific certainty. Its burden is to prove guilt beyond a reasonable doubt.

---

[b] The distinction between justifications and excuses is discussed in Chapter 10.

CALIFORNIA JURY INSTRUCTIONS—CRIMINAL

2.90. Presumption of Innocence–Reasonable Doubt–Burden of Proof
7th ed., West, 2003

A defendant in a criminal action is presumed to be innocent until the contrary is proved, and in case of a reasonable doubt whether [his] [her] guilt is satisfactorily shown, [he] [she] is entitled to a verdict of not guilty. This presumption places upon the People the burden of proving [him] [her] guilty beyond a reasonable doubt.

Reasonable doubt is defined as follows: It is not a mere possible doubt; because everything relating to human affairs is open to some possible or imaginary doubt. It is that state of the case which, after the entire comparison and consideration of all the evidence, leaves the minds of the jurors in that condition that they cannot say they feel an abiding conviction of the truth of the charge.

D. STANDARDS OF REVIEW

Before a criminal trial has ended, at the close of the prosecution's case in chief, a defendant may move for a "directed verdict" of acquittal, in which the judge directs the jury to acquit for lack of evidence. After the trial is completed, if the defendant is convicted, he or she may appeal the conviction to a higher court for review of the sufficiency of the evidence. What standard of proof should the trial judge apply to a motion for directed verdict? What standard of proof should an appellate court apply when reviewing the evidence supporting a conviction?

It may be surprising, at first glance, to learn that in these situations the trial judge and the appellate judge or judges do not apply the reasonable doubt standard. Instead, the standard of review is a more complex one. On a motion for a directed verdict, the trial judge asks herself or himself, not whether the prosecution has proved its case beyond a reasonable doubt, but whether the prosecution has introduced sufficient evidence such that a rational jury *could* decide that the prosecution has proved its case beyond a reasonable doubt. On an appeal based on the sufficiency of the evidence, the question for the appellate court is, again, not whether the prosecution has proved its case beyond a reasonable doubt, but rather whether a rational jury *could have*, on the evidence presented, found the defendant guilty beyond a reasonable doubt. These standards suggest that when the trial court is deciding whether to free the defendant without the jury's input or in spite of the jury's belief that the defendant should be convicted, the appellate court will give the prosecution, not the defendant, the benefit of the doubt. The following case helps illuminate this counter-intuitive standard of review.

CURLEY V. UNITED STATES

United States Court of Appeals, District of Columbia
160 F.2d 229 (D.C. Cir. 1947)

PRETTYMAN, ASSOCIATE JUSTICE.

Appellants were indicted for violation of the mail fraud statute and for conspiracy to violate that statute. Trial was had before a jury. At the conclusion of the case for the prosecution, the defendants moved for directed verdicts of acquittal. The court denied the motions. Defendants Curley and Fuller stood on the motions and offered no evidence. Defendant Smith presented eight character witnesses and proffered certain documentary evidence. These three defendants were convicted on the conspiracy count. * * * The appeals were consolidated for argument.

[Curley and the other defendants were members of "the Group," a business organization involved in government procurement for housing and defense-related contracts.]

* * * In the negotiation of the contracts, representations were made in the name of the Group as to business controlled by it, its staff, its assets, and the existing status of various government projects. The money was received by the Group under agreements that it be held as deposits and returned if contemplated business projects did not materialize. The representations were false, and the agreements were not kept, except that three refunds were made from funds paid in by other people. The Group was represented as having within its control the designation of contractors on certain government housing projects and war work. It had none. It represented [itself] as having large amounts of cash in bank and extensive security holdings. It had no such amounts or holdings. Certain housing projects were represented as having been approved by the Federal Housing Administration. They had not been. Commitments on financing were represented as having been made by financial institutions on certain projects. No such commitments had been made. These various representations were inducements for the contracts made by the Group with its customers or clients. They were made verbally, in letters, in contract agreements, and in a brochure widely distributed. The money received as deposits was not held but was spent as received. * * *

[Curley's claim at trial was that, although he served as President of the Group, there was no proof that he was involved in any significant way in the fraudulent activities of the Group.]

The functions of the jury include the determination of the credibility of witnesses, the weighing of the evidence, and the drawing of justifiable inferences of fact from proven facts. It is the function of the judge to deny the jury any opportunity to operate beyond its province. The jury may not be permitted to conjecture merely, or to conclude upon pure speculation or from passion, prejudice or sympathy. The critical point in this boundary is the existence or non-existence of a reasonable doubt as to guilt. If the evidence is such that reasonable jurymen must necessarily have such a doubt, the judge must require acquittal, because no other result is permissible within the fixed bounds of jury consideration. But if a reasonable mind might fairly have a reasonable doubt or might fairly not have one, the case is for the jury, and the decision is for the jurors to make. The law recognizes that the scope of a reasonable mind is broad. Its conclusion is not always a point certain, but, upon given evidence, may be one of a number of conclusions. Both innocence and guilt beyond reasonable doubt may lie fairly within the limits of reasonable conclusion from given facts. The judge's function is exhausted when he determines that the evidence does or does not permit the conclusion of guilt beyond reasonable doubt within the fair operation of a reasonable mind.

The true rule, therefore, is that a trial judge, in passing upon a motion for directed verdict of acquittal, must determine whether upon the evidence, giving full play to the right of the jury to determine credibility, weigh the evidence, and draw justifiable inferences of fact, a reasonable mind might fairly conclude guilt beyond a reasonable doubt. If he concludes that upon the evidence there must be such a doubt in a reasonable mind, he must grant the motion; or, to state it another way, if there is no evidence upon which a reasonable mind might fairly conclude guilt beyond reasonable doubt, the motion must be granted. If he concludes that either of the two results, a reasonable doubt or no reasonable doubt, is fairly possible, he must let the jury decide the matter. In a given case, particularly one of circumstantial evidence, that determination may depend upon the difference between pure speculation and legitimate inference from proven facts. The task of the judge in such case is not easy, for the rule of reason is frequently difficult to apply, but we know of no way to avoid that difficulty. * * *

The crucial question at this point seems to us to be whether [Curley] knew of the wrongful acts being committed in the name of the Group. Because, if he knew, reasonable minds might fairly conclude that he must necessarily have been a participant in the scheme, i.e., a conspirator; that no other hypothesis is consistent with that knowledge and his acts. Was such knowledge on his part a legitimate inference from the proven facts? It seems to us that it was. He was president of the corporation. He was frequently in its offices. He introduced customers. He personally attempted to arrange with a bank for a "loan" which was to be left on deposit, a sham depiction of financial substance. The misrepresentations made by the Group were total, not incidental or occasional. They were made not to occasional customers or clients but to all of them. The misrepresentations were not as to whether a group, in control of certain contracts, was also in control of others; this Group had control of no contracts whatever. The misrepresentations were not as to incidents of the staff and organization of the Group; it had no staff worthy of the name. The Group did not have funds which it might legitimately use for operating expenses and, by inadvertence or misconduct of an individual, dip into other funds which it was obligated to hold on deposit; it had no funds whatever, other than the deposits. Occasional, incidental or partial misrepresentation or misappropriation by one officer of a corporation may be unimpressive as a basis for imputing knowledge to another officer; but total misrepresentation of the corporate affairs and total diversion of funds is substantial ground for an inference of knowledge on the part of an active and experienced president. The jury might fairly and legitimately infer as a fact from the proven facts that Curley knew of the wrongs being committed. As we have said, if he knew, his proven activities with and on behalf of the Group might fairly lead, if not compel, reasonable men to conclude that he must necessarily have been a participant in the plans of the Group. It cannot be said that upon all this evidence reasonable minds must necessarily doubt that Curley was a participant in the activities of the Group. * * *

The decision in the case rests squarely upon the rule of law governing the action of the trial judge upon the motion for directed verdict of acquittal and the action of an appellate court upon a verdict of conviction. We agree, as Curley contends, that upon the evidence reasonable minds might have had a reasonable doubt. As much might be said in many, if not in most, criminal cases. The jury, within the realm of reason, might have concluded that it was possible that Curley was merely a figurehead, that he had complete faith in Fuller, that he never asked any questions, that he was never informed as to the contents of contracts with customers or the financial statements or the use of the money; in short, that it was possible that he was as much put upon as were the customers. If the jury had concluded that such was a reasonable possibility, it might have had a reasonable doubt as to guilt. But, as we have stated, that possibility is not the criterion which determines the action of the trial judge upon the motion for directed verdict and is not the basis upon which this court must test the validity of the verdict and the judgment. If the evidence reasonably permits a verdict of acquittal or a verdict of guilt, the decision is for the jury to make. In such case, an appellate court cannot disturb the judgment of the jury. If we ourselves doubted Curley's guilt, that doubt would be legally immaterial, in view of the evidence and the rule of law applicable. However, we think it proper to add, under the circumstances of the case, that to us, as to the jury, there is no doubt. * * *

Affirmed.

WILBUR K. MILLER, ASSOCIATE JUSTICE (dissenting).

It is my view that the jury should have been instructed to find the appellant, James M. Curley, not guilty. The wrongs were done by Fuller. Curley made no representations to anybody. He did not participate in negotiations with customers. He signed no letters, executed no contracts.

He did not know of the brochure or the financial statement. He received no money or other thing of value. All this is admitted, even recited, in the court's opinion.

Whether Curley was guilty depended therefore, on whether he knew of the wrongful acts being committed in the name of the Group. That, the court correctly says, is the crucial question with respect to him. There was no criminal intent if he did not know. If he knew, then it would follow that he had become a conspirator with Fuller. But the evidence of knowledge must be clear, not equivocal.

It is true, of course, that whether Curley had knowledge of Fuller's wrongdoing could not be proved directly, but could only be inferred from what Curley did. Nevertheless, the presumption of innocence insists that there be no equivocation in that proof. As always, it must convince beyond a reasonable doubt. If it be not of that quality, if it be not clear but equivocal, then the jury must not be permitted to speculate that the defendant is guilty. * * *

To prove guilt beyond a reasonable doubt does not mean merely to prove certain facts which are as consistent with innocence as guilt. To me the expression means to submit evidence which produces in the minds of the jurors an abiding and conscientious conviction, to a moral certainty, that the accused is guilty. I am aware of the fact that his classic paraphrase of proof beyond a reasonable doubt by Chief Justice Shaw of Massachusetts has been criticized of late, but I do not agree with the critics. Reasonable doubt is not eliminated by evidence from which the jury may draw either of two irreconcilable inferences. * * *

E. THE ROLE OF COUNSEL

AMERICAN BAR ASSOCIATION

Ethical Standards for Defense and Prosecution Function

Ethical Standards for the Defense Function

Standard 4–1.2 The Function of Defense Counsel

(a) Counsel for the accused is an essential component of the administration of criminal justice. A court properly constituted to hear a criminal case must be viewed as a tripartite entity consisting of the judge (and jury, where appropriate), counsel for the prosecution, and counsel for the accused.

(b) The basic duty defense counsel owes to the administration of justice and as an officer of the court is to serve as the accused's counselor and advocate with courage and devotion and to render effective, quality representation.

(c) Since the death penalty differs from other criminal penalties in its finality, defense counsel in a capital case should respond to this difference by making extraordinary efforts on behalf of the accused. * * *

(d) Defense counsel should seek to reform and improve the administration of criminal justice. When inadequacies or injustices in the substantive or procedural law come to defense counsel's attention, he or she should stimulate efforts for remedial action.

(e) Defense counsel, in common with all members of the bar, is subject to standards of conduct stated in statutes, rules, decisions of courts, and codes, canons, or other standards of professional conduct. Defense counsel has no duty to execute any directive of the accused which does not comport with law or such standards. Defense counsel is the professional representative of the accused, not the accused's alter ego.

(f) Defense counsel should not intentionally misrepresent matters of fact or law to the court.

Standard 4–1.6 Trial Lawyer's Duty to Administration of Justice

(a) The bar should encourage through every available means the widest possible participation in the defense of criminal cases by lawyers. Lawyers should be encouraged to qualify themselves for participation in criminal cases both by formal training and through experience as associate counsel.

(b) All such qualified lawyers should stand ready to undertake the defense of an accused regardless of public hostility toward the accused or personal distaste for the offense charged or the person of the defendant.

Standard 4–7.7 Argument to the Jury * * *

(a) Defense counsel should not make arguments calculated to appeal to the prejudices of the jury.

(b) Defense counsel should refrain from argument which would divert the jury from its duty to decide the case on the evidence.

Ethical Standards for the Prosecution Function

Standard 3–1.2 The Function of the Prosecutor

(a) The office of the prosecutor is charged with responsibility for prosecutions in its jurisdiction.

(b) The prosecutor is an administrator of justice, and advocate, and an officer of the court; the prosecutor must exercise sound discretion in the performance of his or her functions.

(c) The duty of the prosecutor is to seek justice, not merely to convict.

(d) It is an important function of the prosecutor to seek to reform and improve the administration of criminal justice. When inadequacies or injustices in the substantive or procedural law come to the prosecutor's attention, he or she should stimulate efforts for remedial action.

Standard 3–3.4 Decision to Charge

(a) The decision to institute criminal charges should be initially and primarily the responsibility of the prosecutor. * * *

(c) The prosecutor should establish standards and procedures for evaluating complaints to determine whether criminal prosecutions should be instituted. * * *

Standard 3–3.8 Discretion as to Noncriminal Disposition

(a) The prosecutor should consider in appropriate cases the availability of noncriminal disposition, formal or informal, in deciding whether to press criminal charges which would otherwise be supported by probable cause; especially in the case of a first offender, the nature of the offense may warrant noncriminal disposition.

(b) Prosecutors should be familiar with the resources of social service agencies which can assist in the evaluation of cases for diversion from the criminal process.

Standard 3–3.9 Discretion in the Charging Decision

(a) A prosecutor should not institute, or cause to be instituted, or permit the continued pendency of criminal charges when the prosecutor knows that the charges are not supported by probable cause. * * *

(b) The prosecutor is not obliged to present all charges which the evidence might support. The prosecutor may in some circumstances and for good cause consistent with the public interest decline to prosecute, notwithstanding that sufficient evidence may exist which would support a conviction. Illustrative of the factors which the prosecutor may properly consider in exercising his or her discretion are:

(i) The prosecutor's reasonable doubt that the accused is in fact guilty;

(ii) The extent of the harm caused by the offense;

(iii) The disproportion of the authorized punishment in relation to the particular offense or the offender;

(iv) Possible improper motives of the complainant;

(v) Reluctance of the victim to testify;

(vi) Cooperation of the accused in the apprehension or conviction of others; and

(vii) Availability and likelihood of prosecution by another jurisdiction.

(c) A prosecutor should not be compelled by his or her supervisor to prosecute a case in which he or she has a reasonable doubt about the guilt of the accused.

(d) In making the decision to prosecute, the prosecutor should give no weight to the personal or political advantages or disadvantages which might be involved or to a desire to enhance his or her record of convictions.

* * *

Standard 3–6.1 Role in Sentencing

(a) The prosecutor should not make the severity of sentences the index of his or her effectiveness. To the extent that the prosecutor becomes involved in the sentencing process, he or she should seek to assure that a fair and informed judgment is made on the sentence and to avoid unfair sentence disparities.

F. THE ROLE OF THE JURY

The jury plays an influential role in the criminal justice system.[a] The Sixth Amendment to the U.S. Constitution guarantees that "in all criminal prosecutions, the accused shall enjoy the right to a speedy and public trial by an impartial jury." This means that unless the defendant waives his or her right to a jury trial and elects to be tried by a judge, his guilt or innocence will be determined by a jury of twelve individuals.

Although the judge gives jurors detailed instructions on the law they are supposed to apply to the case, the jury is not strictly obligated to follow the law. If the jury acquits the defendant even in the face of overwhelming evidence of guilt, the judge is not permitted to punish the jury nor can the judge overturn the jury's not guilty verdict. The act of returning a verdict contrary to law is called *jury nullification*.

[a] In the federal courts and in most state courts, the defendant is tried before a jury of 12 persons and the jury's verdict must be unanimous. If the jury cannot come to a unanimous verdict, the judge will declare a mistrial due to a hung jury and the prosecutor may either re-file charges or drop the case. Some states permit non-unanimous verdicts. Some states permit juries to be comprised of less than twelve persons. The Supreme Court has upheld the use of non-unanimous jury verdicts and juries of less than twelve persons. *See, e.g.*, Apodaca v. Oregon, 406 U.S. 404, 92 S.Ct. 1628, 32 L.Ed.2d 184 (1972), Johnson v. Louisiana, 406 U.S. 356, 92 S.Ct. 1620, 32 L.Ed.2d 152 (1972). If, however, a six-person jury is used, its verdict must be unanimous. Burch v. Louisiana, 441 U.S. 130, 99 S.Ct. 1623, 60 L.Ed.2d 96 (1979).

A longstanding debate exists over whether jurors should be informed of their power to nullify. On the one hand are individuals who, like the members of the Fully Informed Jury Association (FIJA), believe that jurors should be informed of their power to ignore the law so that justice can be done in all cases, not simply in the cases in which a member of the jury happens to know of the nullification power and tells his fellow jurors. FIJA members have shown up on the steps of courthouses, passing out leaflets informing potential jurors of their power to bring in a verdict of conscience when they find that a law is objectionable, unjust or unfair.

On the other hand are individuals who believe that jury nullification threatens the rule of law and invites chaos. According to these individuals, if jurors feel they are free to reach any verdict they choose regardless of the law, jury verdicts are likely to produce widely disparate treatment for similarly situated defendants.

In 1995, law professor Paul Butler ignited a new debate in the nullification arena when he suggested in the Yale Law Journal that African American jurors should engage in racially based jury nullification in cases involving African American defendants charged with non-violent crimes. An excerpt from one of Professor Butler's subsequent writings as well as a powerful response by Andrew Leipold follow *People v. Williams*, a case in which the California Supreme Court had to decide whether a trial judge acted properly when he discharged a juror who admitted that he was uncomfortable convicting an 18-year-old male defendant of statutory rape for having what the defendant claimed was consensual sex with his 16-year-old girlfriend. If the jury has the power to acquit even in the face of overwhelming evidence of guilt, is it fair for a judge to discharge a juror who seems inclined to exercise this power?

PEOPLE V. WILLIAMS

Supreme Court of California
25 Cal.4th 441, 21 P.3d 1209, 106 Cal.Rptr.2d 295 (2001)

GEORGE, C.J.

* * * [T]he charges in this case arose from three incidents involving defendant and his former girlfriend. Only the first incident is relevant to the issue upon which we granted review.

At the time of the December 31, 1994, incident, defendant was 18 years of age and his girlfriend, Jennifer B., was 16 years of age. Both defendant and Jennifer B. testified that they engaged in sexual intercourse on that date; however, defendant testified it was consensual, and Jennifer B. testified defendant forced her to engage in intercourse by threatening her with knives.

At trial, prior to the attorneys' closing arguments, the court indicated that it would instruct the jury that it could convict defendant of unlawful sexual intercourse with a minor as a lesser offense included within the charged offense of rape. Defendant's objection was overruled.

During argument, defense counsel made the following statement: "Something else has happened in this case. * * * They have added misdemeanors to all the charges you heard. They added statutory rape suddenly without notice or preparation. Now, what is the role of a juror on the statutory misdemeanor rape? Your role as a juror is to fairly apply the law. That's why we don't want computers. We need the input of fair people, [defendant]'s peers, if you will. Law as you know is not uniformly applied. I can see five cars speeding and the highway patrol is not likely to arrest any of the five. Mores, custom[s] change. Times change. And the law must be applied fairly. So if the law is not being applied fairly, that's why you need fair jurors. Now there is a case called *Duncan versus Alaska*. It's the Supreme Court of the United States. And I would like to read to you just two lines: 'The guarantee of jury trial in the federal and state Constitutions reflect a profound judgment about the way in which law should be enforced and justice administered. A right to jury trial is granted to criminal defendants in order to prevent oppression by the government.' And further on in the case at the end are the lovely words, 'A jury may, at times, afford a higher justice by refusing to enforce harsh laws.' Please understand."[2]

During the first day of deliberations, the trial court received a message from the jury foreperson indicating that Juror No. 10 "refuses to adhere to Judge's instruction to uphold the law in regard to rape and statutory rape, Section 261.5(b) of the Penal Code. He believes the law is wrong and, therefore, will not hear any discussions." In response, the trial court questioned Juror No. 10 outside the presence of the other jurors:

THE COURT: [I]t's been reported to me that you refuse to follow my instructions on the law in regard to rape and unlawful sexual intercourse, that you believe the law to be wrong and, therefore, you will not hear any discussion on that subject. Is that correct?

[JUROR]: Pretty much, yes.

THE COURT: All right. Are you governed by what was said during argument by counsel?

[JUROR]: Yes.

---

[2] The language quoted by defense counsel actually is from the decision in *Duncan v. Louisiana*. The "lovely words" quoted by defense counsel appear in Justice Harlan's dissenting opinion. Defense counsel did not quote the parenthetical phrase following those words, which raises concerns about the concept of juror nullification: "A jury may, at times, afford a higher justice by refusing to enforce harsh laws (although it necessarily does so haphazardly, raising the questions whether arbitrary enforcement of harsh laws is better than total enforcement, and whether the jury system is to be defended on the ground that jurors sometimes disobey their oaths)."

THE COURT: You understand that there was an improper suggestion and that it's a violation of the Rules of Professional Conduct?

[JUROR]: No, I don't know that.

THE COURT: All right. Well, I'm telling you that's what it was. And I would remind you too that you took an oath at the outset of the case in the following language: 'Do you and each of you understand and agree that you will well and truly try the cause now pending before this Court and a true verdict render according only to the evidence presented to you and to the instructions of the Court.' You understand that if you would not follow the instructions that have been given to you by the court that you would be violating that oath? Do you understand that?

[JUROR]: I understand that.

THE COURT: Are you willing to abide by the requirements of your oath?

[JUROR]: I simply cannot see staining a man, a young man, for the rest of his life for what I believe to be a wrong reason.

THE COURT: Well, you understand that statutory rape or unlawful sexual intercourse has been described to you as a misdemeanor? Did you follow that in the instructions?

[JUROR]: I've been told it is a misdemeanor. I still don't see—if it were a $10 fine, I just don't see convicting a man and staining his record for the rest of his life. I think that is wrong. I'm sorry, Judge.

THE COURT: What you're saying is not the law either concerning that particular aspect.

[JUROR]: I'm trying as best I can, Judge. And I'm willing to follow all the rules and regulations on the entire rest of the charges, but on that particular charge, I just feel duty-bound to object.

THE COURT: So you're not willing then to follow your oath?

[JUROR]: That is correct.

The trial court, over defendant's objection, excused Juror No. 10, replaced him with an alternate juror, and instructed the jury to begin its deliberations anew. The next day, the jury convicted defendant of the above described charges, including unlawful sexual intercourse with a minor.

III

A trial court's authority to discharge a juror is granted by Penal Code section 1089, which provides in pertinent part: "If at any time, whether before or after the final submission of the case to the jury, a juror dies or becomes ill, or upon other good cause shown to the court is found to be unable to perform his duty, or if a juror requests a discharge and good cause appears therefor [sic], the court may order him to be discharged and draw the name of an alternate, who shall then take his place in the jury box, and be subject to the same rules and regulations as though he had been selected as one of the original jurors." "We review for abuse of discretion the trial court's determination to discharge a juror and order an alternate to serve. If there is any substantial evidence supporting the trial court's ruling, we will uphold it." * * *

A juror who refuses to follow the court's instructions is "unable to perform his duty" within the meaning of Penal Code section 1089. As soon as a jury is selected, each juror must agree to render a true verdict " 'according only to the evidence presented . . . and *to the instructions of the court.*' " * * *

Defendant contends, however, that the trial court's order denied him his right to trial by jury, because Juror No. 10 properly was exercising his alleged right to engage in juror nullification by refusing to follow the law regarding unlawful sexual intercourse with a minor. But defendant has cited no case, and we are aware of none, that holds that a trial court violates the defendant's right to a jury trial by excusing a juror who refuses to follow the law. The circumstance that, as a practical matter, the jury in a criminal case may have the ability to disregard the court's instructions in the defendant's favor without recourse by the prosecution does not diminish the trial court's authority to discharge a juror who, the court learns, is unable or unwilling to follow the court's instructions.

It long has been recognized that, in some instances, a jury has the ability to disregard, or nullify, the law. A jury has the ability to acquit a criminal defendant against the weight of the evidence. A jury in a criminal case may return inconsistent verdicts. A court may not direct a jury to enter a guilty verdict "no matter how conclusive the evidence." * * *

The jury's power to nullify the law is the consequence of a number of specific procedural protections granted criminal defendants. Chief Justice Bird, quoting Judge Learned Hand's description of jury nullification as the jury's " 'assumption of a power which they had no right to exercise, but to which they were disposed through lenity,' " observed: "This power is attributable to two unique features of criminal trials. First, a criminal jury has the right to return a general verdict which does not specify how it applied the law to the facts, or for that matter, what law was applied or what facts were found. * * * Second, the constitutional double jeopardy bar prevents an appellate court from disregarding the jury's verdict in favor of the defendant and ordering a new trial on the same charge." The United States Supreme Court has referred to the ability of a jury in a criminal case to nullify the law in the defendant's favor as "the unreviewable power of a jury to return a verdict of not guilty for impermissible reasons."[6]

But the circumstance that the prosecution may be powerless to challenge a jury verdict or finding that is prompted by the jury's refusal to apply a particular law does not lessen the obligation of each juror to obey the court's instructions. More than a century ago, the United States Supreme Court recognized that jurors are required to follow the trial court's instructions. * * *

This view has deep roots. In 1835, in *United States v. Battiste,* Justice Story, sitting as a circuit justice, instructed the jury in a criminal case that they were the judges of the facts, but not of the law, stating: "[T]hey have the physical power to disregard the law, as laid down to them by the court. But I deny, that, in any case, civil or criminal, they have the moral right to decide the law according to their own notions, or pleasure. On the contrary, I hold it the most sacred constitutional right of every party accused of a crime, that the jury should respond as to the facts, and the court as to the law. It is the duty of the court to instruct the jury as to the law; and it is the duty of the jury to follow the law, as it is laid down by the court. This is the right of every citizen; and it is his only protection. If the jury were at liberty to settle the law for themselves, the effect would be, not only that the law itself would be most uncertain, from the different views, which different juries might take of it; but in case of error, there would be no remedy or redress by the injured party; for the court would not have any right to review the law as it had been settled by the jury. Indeed, it would be almost impracticable to ascertain, what the law, as settled by the jury, actually was. * * * Every person accused as a criminal has a right to be tried according to the law of the land, the fixed law of the land; and not by the law as a jury may understand it, or choose, from wantonness, or ignorance, or accidental mistake, to interpret it."

In *United States v. Powell,* the high court reaffirmed the rule that verdicts in a criminal prosecution need not be consistent but, at the same time, the court recognized that jurors are obligated to follow the law. * * * The court explained the rule permitting inconsistent verdicts in criminal cases "as a recognition of the jury's historic function, in criminal trials, as a check against arbitrary or oppressive exercises of power by the Executive Branch." (*Ibid.*; see also *Williams v. Florida* ["The purpose of the jury trial . . . is to prevent oppression by the Government. . . . Given

---

[6] A jury is able to nullify the law only under certain limited circumstances. In a civil case, the jury's ability to nullify a law is sharply curtailed. The court may direct the jury in a civil case to enter a particular verdict, and a verdict that is not supported by substantial evidence or is contrary to the law may be vacated on a motion for new trial or the resulting judgment may be reversed on appeal. Even in a criminal prosecution, the jury's ability to nullify the law is limited when it acts to the defendant's detriment. If the evidence is "insufficient to sustain a conviction," the court "shall order the entry of a judgment of acquittal." A verdict convicting a defendant that is not supported by substantial evidence, or is contrary to law, may be vacated on a motion for new trial, or the resulting judgment may be reversed on appeal.

this purpose, the essential feature of a jury obviously lies in the interposition between the accused and his accuser of the commonsense judgment of a group of laymen, and in the community participation and shared responsibility that results from that group's determination of guilt or innocence"].) * * *

[I]t is important not to encourage or glorify the jury's power to disregard the law. While that power has, on some occasions, achieved just results, it also has led to verdicts based upon bigotry and racism.[9] A jury that disregards the law and, instead, reaches a verdict based upon the personal views and beliefs of the jurors violates one of our nation's most basic precepts: that we are "a government of laws and not men."

The only case cited by the parties or that we have found that has addressed the specific issue raised in the present case—i.e., whether a trial court may remove a juror who discloses, during jury deliberations, that he or she will not apply the law as instructed by the court—is *U.S. v. Thomas,* involving a prosecution for violation of federal narcotics laws. In *Thomas,* pursuant to the provisions of rule 23(b) of the Federal Rules of Criminal Procedure permitting the court to dismiss a juror for "just cause" and have a verdict returned by the remaining 11 jurors, a juror was dismissed during deliberations. The court of appeals held "that—as an obvious violation of a juror's oath and duty—a refusal to apply the law as set forth by the court constitutes grounds for dismissal under Rule 23(b)." Restating "some basic principles regarding the character of our jury system," the Court of Appeals concluded: "Nullification is, by definition, a violation of a juror's oath to apply the law as instructed by the court. . . . We categorically reject the idea that, in a society committed to the rule of law, jury nullification is desirable or that courts may permit it to occur when it is within their authority to prevent."

The court in *Thomas* added: " 'A jury has no more "*right*" to find a "guilty" defendant "not guilty" than it has to find a "not guilty" defendant "guilty," and the fact that the former cannot be corrected by a court, while the latter can be, does not create a right out of the power to misapply the law. Such verdicts are lawless, a denial of due process and constitute an exercise of erroneously seized power.' "

---

[9] Jury nullification includes "acquittals by all-white, southern juries of white defendants who killed, assaulted, or harassed civil rights activists or African Americans generally." As one federal circuit court has observed:

> [A]lthough the early history of our country includes the occasional *Zenger* trial or acquittals in fugitive slave cases, more recent history presents numerous and notorious examples of jurors nullifying—cases that reveal the destructive potential of a practice Professor Randall Kennedy of the Harvard Law School has rightly termed a "sabotage of justice." Consider, for example, the two hung juries in the 1964 trials of Byron De La Beckwith in Mississippi for the murder of NAACP field secretary Medgar Evers, or the 1955 acquittal of J.W. Millam and Roy Bryant for the murder of fourteen-year-old Emmett Till—shameful examples of how nullification has been used to sanction murder and lynching.

Although the court in *Thomas* ultimately concluded that the trial court in that case had erred in dismissing the juror in question, because the record suggested that the juror's views may well have been motivated by doubts about the defendant's guilt rather than by an intent to nullify the law, the *Thomas* opinion left no doubt that when the record does establish that a deliberating juror is unwilling to apply the law as instructed by the court, "a juror's purposeful disregard of the law as set forth in the court's instruction may constitute just cause for that juror's removal under Rule 23(b)." * * *

In the present case there is ample evidence in the record to support the trial court's finding that Juror No. 10 was unable to perform his duties as a juror. The juror stated that he objected to the law concerning unlawful sexual intercourse and expressly confirmed that he was unwilling to abide by his oath to follow the court's instructions. The juror's inability to perform his duties thus appears in the record "as a demonstrable reality." The trial court acted properly in excusing Juror No. 10 on this basis.

IV

Jury nullification raises issues that go to the heart of our constitutional form of government. These issues sometimes arise when defendants, as a matter of conscience, choose to violate laws as a means of protest, or to violate laws they view as unjust. Such cases cause us to examine the meaning of the cherished right to trial by jury.

It is striking that the debate over juror nullification remains vigorous after more than a hundred years. But it is equally significant that, during this time, no published authority has restricted a trial court's authority to discharge a juror when the record demonstrates that the juror is unable or unwilling to follow the court's instructions.

"Championing a jury's refusal to apply the law as instructed is inconsistent with the very notion of the rule of law. As the young Abraham Lincoln said in a related context, 'let me not be understood as saying there are no bad laws, or that grievances may not arise for the redress of which no legal provisions have been made. I mean to say no such thing. But I do mean to say that although bad laws, if they exist, should be repealed as soon as possible, still, while they continue in force, for the sake of example, they should be religiously observed.' "

Encouraging a jury to nullify a law it finds unjust or to act as the "conscience of the community" by disregarding the court's instructions may sound lofty, but such unchecked and unreviewable power can lead to verdicts based upon bigotry and racism. Jurors who do not feel bound to follow the law can act capriciously, to the detriment of the accused. In addition to refusing to follow laws they view as unjust, such jurors could choose to disregard instructions mandated by the Legislature not to read media accounts of the trial, not to discuss the case with others, or not to conduct their own investigation by visiting the crime scene. The jury might feel free to ignore the presumption of innocence or find the defendant guilty even though some jurors harbor a reasonable doubt. A jury might disregard an instruction not to draw an inference from the exercise of a privilege and assume the defendant must be guilty if he or she chooses not to testify. In a capital case, a juror could vote to impose the death penalty without considering mitigating evidence. Some jurors might decide not to view a defendant's confession with caution or not require corroboration of the testimony of an accomplice. A jury even might determine that deliberations are too difficult and decide the defendant's guilt by the flip of a coin.

These are just a few of the many instructions required by the Legislature that a juror might choose to ignore if encouraged to nullify the law.

Jury nullification is contrary to our ideal of equal justice for all and permits both the prosecution's case and the defendant's fate to depend upon the whims of a particular jury, rather than upon the equal application of settled rules of law. As one commentator has noted: "When jurors enter a verdict in contravention of what the law authorizes and requires, they subvert the rule of law and subject citizens—defendants, witnesses, victims, and everyone affected by criminal justice administration—to power based on the subjective predilections of twelve individuals. They affect the rule of men, not law." A nullifying jury is essentially a lawless jury.

We reaffirm, therefore, the basic rule that jurors are required to determine the facts and render a verdict in accordance with the court's instructions on the law. A juror who is "unable or unwilling to do so is unable to perform his [or her] duty" as a juror and may be discharged.

V

The judgment of the Court of Appeal is affirmed.

NOTE

Judges disagree over whether jury nullification is a good or bad thing and whether it is proper for a trial court to discharge a juror who expresses reservations about convicting the defendant. In 2011, the Ninth Circuit Court of Appeals reversed a California defendant's murder conviction on the ground that her Sixth Amendment right to a jury trial was violated by the trial judge's dismissal of a known holdout juror who had expressed reservations to fellow jurors about convicting the defendant of murder. Williams v. Cavasoz, 646 F.3d 626 (9th Cir 2011).

Although many judges refuse to permit defense counsel to inform the jury of its power to nullify, on June 29, 2012, the governor of New Hampshire signed into law a bill that provides, "In all criminal proceedings the court shall permit the defense to inform the jury of its right to judge the facts and the application of the law in relation to the facts in controversy." This law went into effect on January 1, 2013, and is codified at N.H. Rev. Stat. § 519:23–a (2013).

The constitutions of Indiana, Maryland, and Georgia contain provisions which empower the jury to determine both law and fact, but courts have limited the application of these provisions. The Indiana Constitution provides that "[i]n all criminal cases whatever, the jury shall have the right to determine the law and the facts[,]" but it has been held that "that right is not without limitation[ ] . . . [and the jury] may not arbitrarily reject the instructions of the court." Fuquay v. Indiana, 583 N.E.2d 154, 156 (Ind. Ct. App. 1991). Maryland's constitution states that "[i]n the trial of all criminal cases, the Jury shall be the Judges of Law, as well as of fact," but the Fourth Circuit Court of Appeals of Maryland has indicated that juries in criminal cases are not given unrestricted powers in applying the law, and in fact, "[t]he powers of the jury are hedged in a number of ways." Wyley v. Warden, Maryland Penitentiary, 372 F.2d 742, 743–44 (4th Cir. 1967). The Georgia Constitution provides that "[i]n criminal cases . . . the jury shall be the judges of the law and the facts." Yet, "it has long been settled that this language . . . means that jurors are 'made absolutely and exclusively judges of the facts in the case [and] they are, in this sense only, judges of the law.' " Hall v. State, 201 Ga.App. 133, 410 S.E.2d 448, 451 (Ct. App. 1991) (quoting Harris v. State, 190 Ga. 258, 9 S.E.2d 183 (1940)).

RACE-BASED JURY NULLIFICATION: CASE-IN-CHIEF

Paul D. Butler
30 J. Marshall L. Rev. 911 (1997)

* * *

I was a Special Assistant United States Attorney in the District of Columbia. I represented the United States of America and used that power to put African-American people in prison. Like a lot of prosecutors, that pretty much was my job description. While at the U.S. Attorney's Office, I saw and did things that profoundly changed the way that I viewed my work as a prosecutor and my responsibilities as an African-American man.

* * * The reality is this: as we speak, one-third of African-American young men are under criminal justice supervision. The reality is that, as we speak, over half of the women in state prison are African-American and over half of the men in federal and state prisons are African-American.

My journey took me to the academy. I teach criminal law. My students learned that prison is for people who are the most dangerous and the most immoral in our society. Is there anyone here who really believes that over half of the most immoral and dangerous people in the United States are African-American when they constitute only 12 percent of the population? When I look at those statistics, I think that punishment, prison, and criminal law have become the way that we treat the problems of the poor, especially poor African-American people. I think that is immoral. I am confident that one day we, as a society, will understand that, but African-American people cannot afford to wait that long. If the present rate of incarceration of African-Americans continues, by the year 2010 the majority of African-American men between the ages of 18 and 40 will be in prison, the majority.

Now, to prevent that kind of "just us" justice, I advocate a program of black self-help outside and inside the courtroom. Outside the courtroom self-help includes the kind of community-building efforts that many of us are already engaged in: mentoring, tutoring, after-school programs, providing legal and medical care to the poor, working with inmates, and taking better care of our families. * * * Inside the courtroom self-help includes the responsible use of prosecutorial discretion, especially by black prosecutors. It also includes selective jury nullification for victimless crimes. I am going to spend the balance of my time talking about selective jury nullification because it is part of my solution to the unfairness in the criminal justice system.

* * * According to the Department of Justice, for virtually every crime African-Americans are disproportionately arrested, prosecuted, convicted and imprisoned.

That is true of murder, manslaughter, rape, drug possession, drug distribution, theft and gambling. Why is that? Why do African-Americans commit so many crimes, or do they really? Maybe it is just discrimination that accounts for this apparent disproportionate black criminality. To give you a sense of the justice of selective nullification, I am going to describe quickly two racial critiques of American criminal justice: a liberal critique, and one that I call radical, although the radical critique is made by a lot of people who do not think of themselves as radical.

First, I will discuss the liberal racial critique of American justice. According to the critique, American criminal justice is racist because it is controlled primarily by white people who are unable to escape the culture's dominant message of white supremacy. Therefore, white people are inevitably, even if unintentionally, prejudiced. These white actors include legislatures, police, prosecutors, judges and jurors. These white actors exercise their discretion to make and enforce the criminal law in a discriminatory fashion.

Sometimes this discrimination is overt, as in the case of people like Mark Fuhrman or the police officers who beat up Rodney King. Sometimes it is unintentional, such as a white juror who invariably credits the testimony of a white witness over a black witness. I think that the most persuasive case for the liberal critique is with drug cases. According to the Department of Justice, black people do not commit any more drug offenses than whites. They are about 12 percent of drug offenders, which is exactly proportionate to their share of the population. Now, I know this does not surprise all of you who have been on college campuses, and if you think about it, it is probably consistent with our knowledge of the real world, too. * * *

The Department of Justice agrees, and the conclusion is borne out by statistics. But get this: of people who are incarcerated for drug use, African-Americans are more than 70 percent. African-Americans are 12 percent of the offenders, but 74 percent of the people locked up for the offense. That sounds like discrimination, and when I talk to my police and prosecutor friends, they agree that it is a kind of discrimination. However, many make the argument that it is discrimination that is good for the black community: it is more law enforcement, which is a good thing. When I talk about my proposal for nullification, we will come back to that idea. For now, understand that I think that drug offenses are the best argument for the liberal critique on American criminal justice.

However, I mentioned another critique, one that I called radical. What is this critique? What is the radical critique of why there are so many more blacks in prison than whites and other minorities? The radical critique does not discount the role of discrimination in accounting for this racial disparity, but it also does not say that most or all of the blame is due to discrimination. It offers a more structural fundamental explanation for black crime. * * *

* * * The answer to why there is so much black crime is rooted more in sociology than in either psychology or biology. Prominent American criminologist Norval Morris says that "an adverse social and subcultural background is statistically more criminogenic than psychosis." How about that? So, unsurprisingly then, virtually all of the sociological theories predict high levels of African-American criminal behavior. A short quote, if you will indulge me, from Michael Tonry:

> Crime by young disadvantaged black men [does not] result primarily from their individual moral failures but from their misfortune of being born in places and times and under circumstances that make crime, drug use and gang membership look like reasonable choices, choices from a narrow range of not very attractive options.

* * * One interesting thing is what the liberal and the radical critiques do not say. They do not say that prison is a bad place for every African-American criminal. Rather, liberal critics tend to say that law enforcement in the white community should be leveled up to law enforcement in the black community. For example, white communities should have the same kind of police presence. * * * Alternatively, these

critics might say that law enforcement should be leveled down in black communities. For example, the government should not prosecute black drug users and sellers any more than it prosecutes white or Asian-American or Latino drug users and sellers.

Our radical critics, on the other hand, might encourage incarceration of African-Americans when it has some proven social benefit, some utilitarian benefit, usually like rehabilitation or incapacitation or sentencing with a proven deterrent effect. This is an important point because one almost never hears any racial critic saying that black murderers or rapists or child abusers should not be punished. That includes African-American jurors who engage in jury nullification. In fact, in my experience, black jurors are happy to send violent black criminals to prison, because these jurors, like most jurors, have good sense. It is almost always in the interests of the community to isolate dangerous people, even if the reason those people are dangerous might be due to circumstances beyond their control.

What are the costs to the black community of so much law enforcement? What are the costs of having one out of three of our young men under criminal justice supervision? Racial critics identify many costs: economic and social costs, including the lack of a black male presence particularly in the African-American community; the lack of male role models and male income; the perceived dearth or the lack of marriage-eligible African-American men, among others. So when we start talking about specific cases in which nullification would occur, I will mention drug cases as one great example. You might say, "Well, that's not a victimless crime." I ask you to keep in mind that law enforcement is also not victimless. Law enforcement also has opportunity costs.

* * * Nullification is a partial cure that I come to reluctantly and for moral reasons. To me it is not enough to say that there is a power to nullify; there also has to be some moral basis for this power. In the article I make several moral claims as to the power. * * * I am going to quickly tell you about two.

One is this phenomenon of democratic domination. It is a critical race concept. The reason why I believe that African-American jurors have a moral claim to selective nullification is based on this idea that they do not effectively have a say; they do not have the say that they should in the making of the law. They are the victims of the tyranny of the majority. * * * Let me tell you how it works in the context of the criminal justice system. With every crime bill, the Black Political Caucus—the national one or the one in the state—will make the argument, "Hey, guys, instead of spending all this money building prisons, let's spend some money on rehabilitation, on job training, on education. Those are the root causes of crime." In the Black Political Caucus' belief, the white majority will just say no. It will be legislated away, as we saw happen in the two most recent crime bills. That is always the case. * * * We know that there are better ways to stop crime than prison building, including, for example, financial incentives for kids to stay in school. Rand Corporation released a report that said you prevent more crime per dollar spent by giving kids money to stay in school than you do by building prisons.

The second most powerful way to stop crime is parental training, teaching some of these kids who are having babies how to be good parents. Studies show that such training prevents more crime than the deterrent effect of prison. Now, that does not shock a lot of you. It does not shock a lot of legislators either, but, unfortunately, the majority seems to prefer the punishment regime. We have certainly seen that with powder cocaine versus crack cocaine today. You all know the disparity: you get the same punishment for one gram of crack that you get for 100 grams of powder.[a] A lot of African-Americans and other people thought that that was unfair. The political majority's response to the African-American community was, "Well, if you don't like racially biased disparity, don't acquit crack dealers; what you ought to do is change the law." The way you change the federal sentencing law is to lobby the U.S. Sentencing Commission. At least that is the way you always did it before this proposal for jury nullification.

The Sentencing Commission was lobbied by civil rights groups, and they agreed that that disparity was unfair. They recommended to the U.S. Congress and to the President that the crack-versus-powder disparity be changed. However, for some reason the U.S. Congress and the President, Bill Clinton, just said no. They preferred the punishment regime. Again, this is typical when it comes to the way lawmakers deal with the criminal justice system as it applies to African-Americans. "Democratic domination" is Derrick Bell's name for it, and for me it is a moral reason as to why nullification is appropriate.

The third moral claim African-Americans have to the power of jury nullification is what I call the symbolic role of black jurors. If you look at Supreme Court cases, they often have the occasion to discuss black jurors. They do so because of our country's sad history of excluding black people from juries. The Court said that is a bad thing because black jurors serve this symbolic function. Essentially they symbolize the fairness and the impartiality of the law. The Court says that excluding black jurors undermines public confidence in the criminal justice system. The Court has also found that black jurors are especially important in race-related cases.

---

[a] Butler refers to the extreme federal punishment differential between possession of powder cocaine and possession of crack cocaine that existed prior to 2008. *See, e.g.*, U.S. SENTENCING COMM'N, FEDERAL SENTENCING GUIDELINES MANUAL § 2D1.1(c) (1994). For a discussion of a similar punishment regime in the state of Minnesota, *see State v. Russell* in Chapter 2.

* * * What about an African-American juror who endorses racial critiques of the American criminal justice system? She does not hold any confidence in the integrity of the system. So if she is aware of the implicit message that the Supreme Court says her presence sends, maybe she does not want to be the vehicle for that message.

Again, that brings us to selective nullification. For violent crimes, for crimes with victims, there should be no nullification. If the juror is convinced beyond a reasonable doubt in such cases, then she should convict and be happy to do so. In my experience prosecuting cases for violent crimes, Washington, D.C. jurors are happy to put those people in prison. It is in everybody's interests to get those people off the streets, and certainly these jurors are acting in their self interests. In Chicago, for example, jurors know that nullified, violent African-American criminals are not going to move to the largely white communities of Bridgeport or Cicero; they are going to move to the predominantly black South Shore, they are going to move to the primarily African-American West Side. Thus, these jurors have no interest in emancipating violent African-American criminals. The problem is that separating violent criminals from their communities is not the main use of prisons. Most people are in prison for nonviolent conduct.

[As] for drug offenses, . . . I think that jurors in those cases should consider nullification. For possession cases, I encourage nullification. For distribution cases I do not encourage it, but I think it is an option that jurors should consider. Jurors should weigh factors that judges weigh now in the sentencing determination. For example, I would never encourage nullification for anyone who sells drugs to children. I might well suggest it for a nonviolent distributor of marijuana. There are two purposes of this selective nullification: black self-help, and, less importantly, political protest. The black self-help prevents people from being punished when there are better alternatives, as I discussed earlier.

The political protest part is to encourage an end to this madness of locking up African-Americans when white people do not get locked up for the identical crimes. Again, this is borne out by those drug statistics. According to the Justice Department, black people do not use drugs any more than whites—it is just that African-Americans get locked up more for drug charges. People ask what the black community would look like if drug offenders were not incarcerated. We know the answer to that: it would look like the white community. Again, the white community does not resort to the punishment regime for dealing with drug problems. I agree with that. I think punishment is not a smart way to deal with substance abuse. I think that when it comes to law enforcement, what is good enough for white people is good enough for African-Americans.

I hope that nullification would encourage rehabilitation for non-criminal means of dealing with the problem. I do not like drugs. I wish people would not use them. I have seen them ruin people's lives. I might also add that I have seen alcohol ruin people's lives, but I also do not support locking up alcohol users and distributors. So I hope that nullification will spark the return of rehabilitation and crime prevention.

* * *

"Is American criminal justice just?" To me the answer is obviously not. There are too many African-Americans in prison who do not belong there. Do you really think that 50 percent of the most dangerous and immoral people in the United States are black? That is what our justice system tells us about black people. If you do not agree with that, if you do not believe that, then you must agree that we need fundamental change.

The second question is, "If not jury nullification, then what?" I do not want to hear that African-Americans should write to Congress. We tried that. It did not work. The house that African-Americans live in is on fire, and when your house is on fire, you do not write to Congress. You do not ask the people who set the fire to put it out; you leave the building. That is what my proposal for selective jury nullification encourages.

RACE-BASED JURY NULLIFICATION: REBUTTAL (PART A)

Andrew D. Leipold
30 J. Marshall L. Rev. 923 (1997)

* * * [D]o I think that the criminal justice system is perfect the way it is? Of course not. Do I think there are severe problems involving race and justice? Of course I do. Do I think the answer is selective jury nullification? Not even remotely.

Professor Butler says he does not want to hear us suggest that the answer is to write to Congress. That answer fails, he says, because right now the house is on fire, suggesting that more dramatic and more immediate action is needed. But even if the house is on fire, I do not think we should embrace a solution that involves fanning the flames and making the fire worse. This is what I fear selective race-based jury nullification will do.

Let me briefly outline a few of my concerns about Professor Butler's plan. The first two are technical, lawyer-type arguments. The last two address philosophical concerns I have about his proposal.

The first technical point involves the impact of Professor Butler's proposal on the makeup of juries. I agree with Paul entirely about the importance of African-Americans serving on juries. * * * It is critically important to have juries that are reflective of community sentiments and community norms. Given this, we should ask ourselves what juries will look like if large numbers of African-American potential jurors were to embrace the Butler plan. I think the answer, without a doubt, is that there would be fewer African-Americans seated on juries than there are today. * * *

If potential African-American jurors were to embrace the Butler plan, and if they were honest during voir dire, their belief in jury nullification would at least give prosecutors a race-neutral explanation for removing these jurors with their peremptory strikes. In addition, if the jurors were candid in admitting that they came to the jury box with a very strong presumption of acquitting a defendant regardless of what the facts show, such jurors could almost certainly be removed for cause. Since there are no limits on the number of challenges for cause, every African-American juror who believed in race-based nullification might be excused in certain cases. The result would inevitably be juries that are less diverse; this surely cannot be part of the solution that Professor Butler seeks.

My second technical argument is that juries are incapable of making reasoned nullification decisions, because at trial they will not be given the information they need. At the heart of Professor Butler's plan is the notion that juries should engage in a cost-benefit analysis when deciding whether to convict. Jurors are supposed to look at the defendant and ask, "Even if this defendant committed the crime charged, what are the rewards of keeping this person out of jail, and what are the risks to the community of letting this person stay free?" The problem is that juries will never hear the evidence that would help them answer this question.

Consider the problem in the context of a simple drug possession case. If we were sitting on a jury, what would we like to know about the defendant before we decided whether to nullify his conviction? We would probably want to know whether the defendant is contrite. We would want to know whether he had a criminal record, and if so, how serious were his prior crimes. We might want to know whether there was anyone else involved in the crime who is more blameworthy. We might wonder how the prosecution enforces this crime against others: are African-Americans disproportionately targeted or arrested for this type of crime? We might also want to know about the potential sentences the defendant would face if convicted; under our cost-benefit analysis, we might be more willing to nullify if the defendant faced a stiff, mandatory sentence.

The problem is that almost none of this information is admissible at trial. Defendants cannot be forced to testify, so the jurors will often be unable to evaluate the defendant's contrition. Evidence of prior crimes is usually inadmissible, as is information on possible sentences or the prosecution's enforcement scheme. In short, through no fault of their own, jurors just will not be able to engage in a meaningful cost-benefit analysis. The best they would be able to do is speculate, based on what they think might be going on, rather than on what is actually going on in the case at hand. * * *

There are undoubtedly other groups that will feel that they, too, do not get a fair shake from the criminal justice system and they, too, should come to the jury box with an eye toward nullifying the convictions of members of their groups. "What's so bad about that," you ask? "Maybe that's the way all juries should decide cases." The problem with nullification is that once we tell a jury, directly or indirectly, that it is okay to engage in an uninformed cost-benefit analysis, we have no moral basis for complaining about any decision that a jury makes.

Assume that a jury nullifies in the case of a young African-American defendant who has been charged with simple possession. Maybe this is a good result: maybe in that specific case, society is better off keeping another African-American kid out of jail, away from a very harsh sentence. But now assume that the next jury comes back and says, "Yes, we think this defendant battered his wife, but you know, she decided to stay in the marriage rather than get a divorce, it looks like she provoked him by spending too much time at her job, she was nagging him, et cetera, and we are not going to send this guy to jail." When a jury recently acquitted a defendant who had raped a woman at knife point because the woman was "asking for it" by dressing in a provocative manner, this also sounded like a cost-benefit analysis. We might be repelled by this reasoning, but we do not have any standing to complain about the process by which the outcome was reached. Those juries also engaged in a cost-benefit analysis, the same process approved of by the Butler plan. * * *

The final concern I have is at the broadest philosophical level. It is a comment that makes me very sad to have to raise at all: whether you go to jail or get set free should not depend on the color of your skin. Using race as the reason for acquitting or convicting is a bad idea, and no matter how strategic the reasoning and no matter how good our intentions, it is still wrong. It is wrong because it encourages the kind of stereotyping that had led to problems in the first place. It is wrong because we are telling people that they will never get equal justice in the courts and so you should take whatever you can get, however you can get it, and be satisfied with that. In short, the plan raises the flag of surrender in the fight for equal justice under the law.

G. STATUTORY INTERPRETATION

As we have seen, the primary source of criminal law in the United States is statutory law. No statute, however, is self-interpreting, and judges play an important role in deciding what a particular statute means and how it should apply to particular cases. Whether the jurisdiction is one whose penal code is based on the common law of England or one whose penal code has incorporated the Model Penal Code in whole or in part, judges must develop ways to interpret statutes to serve a number of goals. These goals include respecting the "plain language" of the statutory text; discerning and effectuating the intent of the legislature or, in the case of an initiative, the voters; and making sure that the interpretation of a particular statute in one case does not contradict its interpretation in another case.

Judges in England and the United States have developed a body of informal rules over time to help them interpret statutes. Some of these rules address what values a judge should prioritize when reading a statute: for example, the rule that the interpreter should always begin with the text of the statute itself. Other rules concern efficiency in the administration of justice: for example, the rule that statutes should be interpreted in such a way as to avoid constitutional problems. Still other rules address grammar and syntax issues that frequently arise in textual interpretation. Two of these—*noscitur a sociis* and *ejusdem generis*—are described in the case that follows. Finally, some rules of statutory interpretation, such as the "rule of lenity" also discussed in the following case, reflect basic principles of fairness: under the rule of lenity, all doubts when reading a criminal statute should be resolved in favor of the defendant, in recognition of the important liberty interests at stake and the presumption of innocence. Collectively, these various sorts of interpretive rules are referred to as "canons of statutory construction."

This alternative term for statutory interpretation—"statutory construction"—reminds us that the process of interpretation is as much an art as a science. Although judges are supposed to apply the law and not make it, when statutory language is broad, ambiguous, or outdated, the line between applying and making can become exceedingly fine. Indeed, as students of literary interpretation know, to read a text is always in some sense to "construct" its meaning. In Chapter 2, we will explore some of the constitutional implications of the fuzzy boundary between discovering and making meaning.

UNITED STATES V. DAURAY

United States Court of Appeals for the Second Circuit
215 F.3d 257 (2d Cir. 2000)

JACOBS, CIRCUIT JUDGE:

Defendant-appellant Charles Dauray was arrested in possession of pictures (or photocopies of pictures) cut from one or more magazines. He was convicted following a jury trial in the United States District Court for the District of Connecticut of violating 18 U.S.C. § 2252(a)(4)(B), which punishes the possession of (inter alia) "matter," three or more in number, "which contain any visual depiction" of minors engaging in sexually explicit conduct. On appeal from the judgment of conviction, Dauray argues that the wording of § 2252(a)(4)(B)—which has since been amended—is ambiguous as applied to possession of three or more pictures, and that the rule of lenity should therefore apply to resolve this ambiguity in his favor. We agree, reverse the conviction, and direct that the indictment be dismissed.

BACKGROUND

On May 13, 1994, an officer of the Connecticut Department of Environmental Protection approached Dauray's car in a state park and found Dauray in possession of thirteen unbound pictures of minors. The pictures were pieces of magazine pages and photocopies of those pages. On November 18, 1998, a federal grand jury returned a one-count indictment, charging Dauray with possessing child pornography in violation of 18 U.S.C. § 2252(a)(4)(B). The version of the statute then in force punished the possession of "3 or more books, magazines, periodicals, films, video tapes, or other matter" that have passed in interstate or foreign commerce and "which contain any visual depiction" showing (or produced by using) a minor engaged in sexually explicit conduct. 18 U.S.C. § 2252(a)(4)(B) (1994) (amended 1998). The statute defined "sexually explicit conduct" in part as "actual or simulated—lascivious exhibition of the genitals or pubic area of any person."

Dauray and the government stipulated at trial to the facts that bear upon this appeal. One stipulation provided that "[i] on or about May 13, 1994, Charles Dauray possessed the visual depictions which have been introduced into evidence; and [ii] Charles Dauray was aware of the contents of these visual depictions and thus he knew that genitalia of minors appear in each of them." A second stipulation was that the visual depictions were transported in interstate commerce. The jury therefore had only to decide whether the visual depictions showed "minor[s] engaging in sexually explicit conduct," i.e., whether they depicted the "lascivious exhibition of the genitals or pubic area." The jury found Dauray guilty, and by special interrogatory specified the four of the thirteen pieces of evidence that met the statutory definition.

The district court then considered Dauray's pretrial motion, on which the court had earlier reserved decision, to dismiss the indictment for failure to charge an offense. Dauray argued that each of the four pictures specified by the jury was in itself a "visual depiction" and therefore could not be "other matter which contain any visual depiction." Therefore, he reasoned, the indictment failed to charge an offense. The district court concluded that the pictures Dauray possessed were "other matter" within the plain meaning of § 2252(a)(4)(B), and for the same reason denied Dauray's request to apply the rule of lenity.

Dauray was sentenced on April 30, 1999 to 36 months of imprisonment, followed by three years of supervised release, and a $50 special assessment.

DISCUSSION

The statute under which Dauray was convicted has since been amended. At the time, the statute provided in pertinent part:

> (a) Any person who—
>
> (4) . . .
>
> (B) knowingly possesses *3 or more* books, magazines, periodicals, films, video tapes, or *other matter which contain any visual depiction* that has been mailed, or has been shipped or transported in interstate or foreign commerce, or which was produced using materials which have been mailed or so shipped or transported, by any means including by computer, if—
>
> (i) the producing of such visual depiction involves the use of a minor engaging in sexually explicit conduct; and
>
> (ii) such visual depiction is of such conduct;
>
> shall be punished as provided in subsection (b) of this section.

18 U.S.C. § 2252(a)(4)(B) (1994) (emphasis added).

The question presented on appeal is whether individual pictures are "other matter which contain any visual depiction" within the meaning of § 2252(a)(4)(B). This question of first impression is one of law, which we review de novo.

Notwithstanding diligent efforts to construe § 2252(a)(4)(B), we conclude that it can be read either to support or to defeat this indictment. We therefore apply the rule of lenity to resolve the ambiguity in Dauray's favor.

I.

A. Plain Meaning.

Our starting point in statutory interpretation is the statute's plain meaning, if it has one. Congress provided no definition of the terms "other matter" or "contain." We therefore consider the ordinary, common-sense meaning of the words.

Among the several dictionary definitions of the verb "to contain," Dauray presses one, and the government emphasizes another. (i) "To contain" means "to have within: hold." Webster's Third New International Dictionary 491 (unabridged ed.1981). Dauray argues that a picture is not a thing that contains itself. Thus in the natural meaning of the word, a pictorial magazine "contains" pictures, but it is at best redundant to say that a picture "contains" a picture. (ii) "To contain" also means "to consist of wholly or in part: comprise; include," *id.*, and the government argues that each underlying piece of paper is "matter" (as opposed perhaps to anti-matter) that contains the picture printed on it. It is also possible, applying this latter meaning, to say that each picture, composed of paper and ink, is matter that contains its imagery.

The district court assumed that Congress meant to employ both meanings. The district court thus recognized that one critical word of the statute lends itself to (at least) two meanings, only one of which can sustain the conviction, but then assumed, without resort to tools of construction, that the statutory language was drafted to support every meaning that would impose punishment. Resort to tools of construction is necessary in this case, however, to decide whether the language used gave adequate notice that this defendant's conduct was forbidden by this statute.

The plain meaning of another critical term—"other matter"—is also elusive. The dictionary defines "matter" as "the substance of which a physical object is composed." Webster's Third New International Dictionary 1394. Everything is more or less organized matter (as Napoleon observed). But Congress employed "matter" in a specific context, as the final, general term at the end of a list. We must "consider not only the bare meaning of the word but also its placement and purpose in the statutory scheme. '[T]he meaning of statutory language, plain or not, depends on context.'" Other courts have construed "other matter" in § 2252(a)(4)(B) as "simply something which, at a minimum, must be capable of containing a visual depiction." These definitions are unhelpful for our purposes.

There is no doubt that a pictorial magazine is "matter" that "contains" visual images. But no court that has construed § 2252(a)(4)(B) has considered whether a loose photograph clipped from such a magazine is itself "matter" that "contains" a visual image. The First Circuit recently held that a single negative film strip containing three images constituted only one piece of "matter" under § 2252(a)(4)(B). The court noted that "[h]ad Congress meant for the number of images to be the relevant criterion, it would have likely stated as much." The case concerned the character of singular "matter" containing multiple images, not whether each image—if loosed from the container—could itself constitute prohibited "matter."

Every other case that construes the term "other matter" has involved whether an individual computer graphics file is a "matter." These cases consider whether a computer file has the capacity to "contain a visual depiction," whether the general term "other matter" extends the statute's prohibition to a medium that is unenumerated in the list (and unlikely to have been thought of when the statute was drafted), and whether the proper analog to a graphics file is a page in a book or a book in a library. These cases have no evident bearing on whether a single magazine (which it was no crime to possess at the time of Dauray's arrest, no matter how many pages and pictures it contained) can become prohibited material simply by detaching the staples that bind the pages. * * *

B. Canons of Construction.

Because the government and Dauray each rely on a reasonable meaning of § 2252(a)(4)(B), we resort to the canons of statutory interpretation to help resolve the ambiguity.

1. Lists and Other Associated Terms. Two related canons inform our analysis of the meaning of "other matter." First, the meaning of doubtful terms or phrases may be determined by reference to their relationship with other associated words or phrases (*noscitur a sociis*). Second, "where general words follow a specific enumeration of persons or things, the general words should be limited to persons or things similar to those specifically enumerated" (*ejusdem generis*). In this case, "other matter" should be construed to complete the class of items or things in the list preceding it, namely "books, magazines, periodicals, films, [or] video tapes."

Dauray argues that the listed items form a category of picture containers that can enclose within them multiple visual depictions. Because a picture taken from a magazine is not itself a picture container, like books or magazines, but is rather a thing abstracted from its container, Dauray contends that a picture in itself cannot be considered "other matter" within the meaning of the statute, and that possession of three of them is not prohibited.

But these canons equally support the government's argument. The list—at a sufficient level of generality, and completed by the catch-all "other matter"—can be read to include any physical medium or method capable of presenting visual depictions. A picture cut from a magazine, considered as paper and ink employed to exhibit images, can be said to contain an image or as many images as can be perceived in a picture or photograph, which depends on how one looks at it.

2. Statutory Structure. "[A] statute is to be considered in all its parts when construing any one of them." The Protection of Children Against Sexual Exploitation Act contains four substantive subsections (of which § 2252(a)(4) is one): § 2252(a)(1) prohibits the interstate transportation of child pornography; § 2252(a)(2) prohibits the receipt or distribution of it; and § 2252(a)(3) prohibits its sale or possession with intent to sell. Only § 2252(a)(4) specifies that the conduct forbidden involves "books, magazines, periodicals, films, video tapes or other matter which contain" the pornography. The others more simply forbid "any visual depiction" of child pornography, period. Dauray and the government both find support in this statutory structure.

According to Dauray, the different drafting demonstrates that Congress knew how to prohibit the possession of individual pictures if it wanted to do so. The plain language of the other sections—each of which targets "any visual depiction"—is such that if Dauray had transported, distributed or sold the pictures he merely possessed, he would have violated the law unambiguously.

But the government could argue: that the transport, distribution and sale of child pornography are most harmful to children, and were therefore prohibited regardless of the medium or number of visual depictions; that Congress did not want to cast so fine a net in the context of mere possession in order to assure that the accidental possessor of one piece of pornography avoids liability while the collector does not; and that Congress implemented the distinction by punishing only persons who possess a threshold number (three) of anything that contains pornographic images, i.e., "books, magazines, periodicals, films, video tapes or other matter." If the statute simply read "3 or more visual depictions," then the accidental possession of one pictorial magazine could violate the statute. The difference between the language in § 2252(a)(4) and the other subsections is therefore (according to this view) fully consistent with a congressional intent to punish the possession of three or more individual pictures, postcards, posters, still frames, or even fragments of magazine pages.

3. Statutory Amendment. A statute should be construed to be consistent with subsequent statutory amendments. In 1998, Congress amended the statute by replacing "3 or more" with "1 or more" of the same list of "books, magazines, periodicals, films, video tapes or other matter." At the same time, Congress established an affirmative defense for a defendant who could show that he possessed "less than three matters containing" child pornography and "promptly and in good faith . . . took reasonable steps to destroy" the pornography or report it to law enforcement officials without disseminating it to others. According to the government, the list, with its catch-all of "other matter," is designed to reach even an individual photograph. That could have been accomplished without the list, however, by an amendment that simply prohibits possession of "1 or more visual depictions." Dauray argues with some force that the list is superfluous post-amendment unless it serves to distinguish a "container" such as a magazine, from its contents, such as individual pictures cut from the magazine's pages. The government on this appeal makes no response to this argument, which is not to say that no response can be made.

4. Avoiding Absurdity. A statute should be interpreted in a way that avoids absurd results. Whichever interpretation one accepts, the statute tends to produce absurd results. Dauray's reading would prohibit the possession of three books, each of which contains one image, but allow the possession of stacks of unbound photographs. Equally absurd, the government's reading would prohibit the possession of three individual

photographs (unless they were mounted in a single album), but allow the possession of two thick illustrated tomes.

C. Legislative History.

When the plain language and canons of statutory interpretation fail to resolve statutory ambiguity, we will resort to legislative history. Unfortunately, "[e]xamination of [§ 2252's] legislative history . . . reveals no insight as to what Congress intended the precise scope of 'other matter' to be." * * *

II.

Due process requires that a criminal statute "give fair warning of the conduct that it makes a crime." "[B]efore a man can be punished as a criminal under the Federal law his case must be 'plainly and unmistakably' within the provisions of some statute." The rule of lenity springs from this fair warning requirement. "In criminal prosecutions the rule of lenity requires that ambiguities in the statute be resolved in the defendant's favor." This expedient "ensures fair warning by so resolving ambiguity in a criminal statute as to apply it only to conduct clearly covered."

But "[b]ecause the meaning of language is inherently contextual," the Supreme Court has "declined to deem a statute 'ambiguous' for purposes of lenity merely because it was possible to articulate a construction more narrow than that urged by the Government." "Instead, [the Court has] always reserved lenity for those situations in which a reasonable doubt persists about a statute's intended scope even after resort to 'the language and structure, legislative history, and motivating policies' of the statute." It is a "doctrine of last resort."

Here, we have done what we can. We have read the plain language of § 2252(a)(4)(B), considered the traditional canons of statutory construction, looked for legislative history, and canvassed potentially relevant case law. And we are left with no more than a guess as to the proper meaning of the ambiguous language here.

While it is true that "our role as a court is to apply the provision as written, not as we would write it," the statute's ambiguity makes it impossible for us to apply the provision in this case without simply guessing about congressional intent. Indeed, the government conceded at oral argument that Dauray would not have violated the statute had his pictures been found in a photo album rather than in an unbound stack.

The government did not show that the pictures at issue were taken from more than a single magazine. At the time of Dauray's arrest, the statute did not forbid possession of such a magazine. Nor did the statute give Dauray notice that removing several pictures from the magazine, and keeping them, would subject him to criminal penalties. This result is unconstitutionally surprising. Under these circumstances, we must apply the rule of lenity and resolve the ambiguity in Dauray's favor.

CONCLUSION

For the foregoing reasons, the judgment is hereby reversed.

KATZMANN, CIRCUIT JUDGE, dissenting.

I respectfully dissent from the majority's well-argued opinion. I would not apply the rule of lenity in this case. In *Muscarello v. U.S.*, the Supreme Court stated that the "simple existence of some statutory ambiguity . . . is not sufficient to warrant application of that rule, for most statutes are ambiguous to some degree." The Court continued: "To invoke the rule, we must conclude that there is a grievous ambiguity or uncertainty in the statute." I do not think that there is such a "grievous ambiguity or uncertainty" in the statute before us, or that we can make "no more than a guess as to what Congress intended." The statute requires that the visual depiction be contained within books, magazines, periodicals, films, video tapes, or other matter. The word "contain" in the statute, consistent with its purposes, could mean both "comprise" and "hold" and still, in my view, not lead to "grievous ambiguity or uncertainty." Nothing in the statute itself or in the legislative record suggests that Congress did not intend to use both ordinary meanings of the word "contain." It makes sense, given the statute's purposes, that a photograph could be understood—quite naturally—to "contain" a visual depiction.

I fully agree with the majority that the statute could result in some incongruous interpretations. But in the end, I conclude that we must "apply the provision as written, not as we would write it."

CHAPTER 2

CONSTITUTIONAL LIMITATIONS ON THE POWER TO PUNISH

■ ■ ■

INTRODUCTION

Although legislatures have primary authority for making criminal laws, all United States law, whether criminal or civil, is subject to the requirements of the United States Constitution. In addition, each state has its own constitution, which is binding upon the law of that state. Although constitutional opinions are scattered throughout this book, this chapter focuses on three federal constitutional limitations that are particularly fundamental to understanding criminal law. These limitations are: (1) the "void for vagueness" doctrine applied to state and federal governments through the Due Process Clause of the Fifth and Fourteenth Amendments, (2) the Cruel and Unusual Punishment Clause of the Eighth Amendment, and (3) the Equal Protection Clause of the Fourteenth Amendment.

In addition to introducing the reader to these substantive restrictions on legislative power to create and punish crimes, this chapter introduces the reader to some of the tensions that emerge from the system of separation of powers and the federal system in the United States. Under the system of separation of powers, the legislature is the body primarily charged with passing laws that reflect the will of the general public at any given time. The judiciary's task is to protect non-majority interests and enforce the long-term, fundamental interests of the people as a whole by enforcing constitutional guarantees. The courts, then, often find themselves caught between the desire to carry out the will of the majority and the desire to restrain the majority in the name of fundamental principles.

Our federal system of government also produces dilemmas for judges interpreting the U.S. Constitution. For example, in theory, individual states should have the latitude to pursue different paths, and pass laws that reflect the will of their own voters. This suggests that criminal law will look very different in different states. The fact that the Constitution has nationwide application, however, creates a pressure toward uniformity. As we will see, the tensions emerging both from the system of separation of powers and from the system of federalism often emerge in subtle (and sometimes not-so-subtle) battles between courts, between courts and legislatures, and sometimes within courts.

Finally, a common theme of this chapter and Chapter One is the theme of discretion. Although one of the aims of the criminal law, as we will see in *Papachristou v. Jacksonville*, is to subject all citizens equally to "the rule of law," in fact, discretion in the system cannot be eliminated, only exposed and subjected to scrutiny. We have already seen this to be true in the case of jury nullification: the structure of the American system gives juries unreviewable discretion to free people being tried for a crime. In this chapter, we will see how judges have made an effort to control or challenge the discretion of police and prosecutors, how legislatures have attempted to control the discretion of judges, and how judges attempt to control the discretion of legislatures. The majority in *McCleskey v. Kemp* concedes that some level of discretion in the criminal justice system is inevitable, but suggests that this discretion is both good and bad. Is it possible to limit the "bad" exercise of discretion and maintain the "good?"

A. FOURTEENTH AMENDMENT DUE PROCESS: VOID FOR VAGUENESS DOCTRINE

The Due Process Clause of the Fifth and Fourteenth Amendments ("nor shall any person . . . be deprived of life, liberty, or property, without due process of law") has been interpreted to impose upon legislatures the duty to draft statutes that are clearly understandable. This requirement serves two purposes: providing fair notice to citizens of what conduct is prohibited, and, perhaps more importantly, limiting police discretion to arrest and jury discretion to imprison people they don't like. *Papachristou v. Jacksonville, Kolender v. Lawson,* and *Chicago v. Morales* illustrate how this "void for vagueness" doctrine works.

PAPACHRISTOU V. CITY OF JACKSONVILLE

Supreme Court of the United States
405 U.S. 156, 92 S.Ct. 839, 31 L.Ed.2d 110 (1972)

MR. JUSTICE DOUGLAS delivered the opinion of the Court.

This case involves eight defendants who were convicted in a Florida municipal court of violating a Jacksonville, Florida, vagrancy ordinance.[1]

---

[1] Jacksonville Ordinance Code § 26–57 provided at the time of these arrests and convictions as follows:

> Rogues and vagabonds, or dissolute persons who go about begging, common gamblers, persons who use juggling or unlawful games or plays, common drunkards, common night walkers, thieves, pilferers or pickpockets, traders in stolen property, lewd, wanton and lascivious persons, keepers of gambling places, common railers and brawlers, persons wandering or strolling around from place to place without any lawful purpose or object, habitual loafers, disorderly persons, persons neglecting all lawful business and habitually spending their time by frequenting houses of ill fame, gaming houses, or places where alcoholic beverages are sold or served, persons able to work but habitually

Their convictions, entailing fines and jail sentences (some of which were suspended), were affirmed by the Florida Circuit Court in a consolidated appeal. * * * The case is here on a petition for certiorari, which we granted. For reasons which will appear, we reverse.

At issue are five consolidated cases. Margaret Papachristou, Betty Calloway, Eugene Eddie Melton, and Leonard Johnson were all arrested early on a Sunday morning, and charged with vagrancy—"prowling by auto."

Jimmy Lee Smith and Milton Henry were charged with vagrancy—"vagabonds."

Henry Edward Heath and a codefendant were arrested for vagrancy—"loitering" and "common thief."

Thomas Owen Campbell was charged with vagrancy—"common thief."

Hugh Brown was charged with vagrancy—"disorderly loitering on street" and "disorderly conduct—resisting arrest with violence."

The facts are stipulated. Papachristou and Calloway are white females. Melton and Johnson are black males. Papachristou was enrolled in a job-training program sponsored by the State Employment Service at Florida Junior College in Jacksonville. Calloway was a typing and shorthand teacher at a state mental institution located near Jacksonville. She was the owner of the automobile in which the four defendants were arrested. Melton was a Vietnam war veteran who had been released from the Navy after nine months in a veterans' hospital. On the date of his arrest he was a part-time computer helper while attending college as a full-time student in Jacksonville. Johnson was a tow-motor operator in a grocery chain warehouse and was a lifelong resident of Jacksonville.

At the time of their arrest the four of them were riding in Calloway's car on the main thoroughfare in Jacksonville. They had left a restaurant owned by Johnson's uncle where they had eaten and were on their way to a nightclub. The arresting officers denied that the racial mixture in the car played any part in the decision to make the arrest. The arrest, they said, was made because the defendants had stopped near a used-car lot which had been broken into several times. There was, however, no evidence of any breaking and entering on the night in question.

---

living upon the earnings of their wives or minor children shall be deemed vagrants and, upon conviction in the Municipal Court shall be punished as provided for Class D offenses.

Class D offenses at the time of these arrests and convictions were punishable by 90 days' imprisonment, $500 fine, or both. Jacksonville Ordinance Code § 1–8 (1965). The maximum punishment has since been reduced to 75 days or $450. § 304.101 (1971).

We are advised that at present the Jacksonville vagrancy ordinance is § 330.107 and identical with the earlier one except that 'juggling' has been eliminated.

Of these four charged with "prowling by auto" none had been previously arrested except Papachristou who had once been convicted of a municipal offense.

Jimmy Lee Smith and Milton Henry (who is not a petitioner) were arrested between 9 and 10 a.m. on a weekday in downtown Jacksonville, while waiting for a friend who was to lend them a car so they could apply for a job at a produce company. Smith was a part-time produce worker and part-time organizer for a Negro political group. He had a common-law wife and three children supported by him and his wife. He had been arrested several times but convicted only once. Smith's companion, Henry, was an 18-year-old high school student with no previous record of arrest.

This morning it was cold, and Smith had no jacket, so they went briefly into a dry cleaning shop to wait, but left when requested to do so. They thereafter walked back and forth two or three times over a two-block stretch looking for their friend. The store owners, who apparently were wary of Smith and his companion, summoned two police officers who searched the men and found neither had a weapon. But they were arrested because the officers said they had no identification and because the officers did not believe their story.

Heath and a codefendant were arrested for "loitering" and for "common thief." Both were residents of Jacksonville, Heath having lived there all his life and being employed at an automobile body shop. Heath had previously been arrested but his codefendant had no arrest record. Heath and his companion were arrested when they drove up to a residence shared by Heath's girlfriend and some other girls. Some police officers were already there in the process of arresting another man. When Heath and his companion started backing out of the driveway, the officers signaled to them to stop and asked them to get out of the car, which they did. Thereupon they and the automobile were searched. Although no contraband or incriminating evidence was found, they were both arrested, Heath being charged with being a "common thief" because he was reputed to be a thief. The codefendant was charged with "loitering" because he was standing in the driveway, an act which the officers admitted was done only at their command.

[The facts describing the arrests of Campbell and Brown have been omitted.]

This ordinance is void for vagueness, both in the sense that it "fails to give a person of ordinary intelligence fair notice that his contemplated conduct is forbidden by the statute," and because it encourages arbitrary and erratic arrests and convictions. * * *

Living under a rule of law entails various suppositions, one of which is that "(all persons) are entitled to be informed as to what the State commands or forbids." * * *

The poor among us, the minorities, the average householder are not in business and not alerted to the regulatory schemes of vagrancy laws; and we assume they would have no understanding of their meaning and impact if they read them. Nor are they protected from being caught in the vagrancy net by the necessity of having a specific intent to commit an unlawful act.

The Jacksonville ordinance makes criminal activities which by modern standards are normally innocent. "Nightwalking" is one. Florida construes the ordinance not to make criminal one night's wandering, only the "habitual" wanderer or, as the ordinance describes it, "common night walkers." We know, however, from experience that sleepless people often walk at night, perhaps hopeful that sleep-inducing relaxation will result.

Luis Munoz-Marin, former Governor of Puerto Rico, commented once that "loafing" was a national virtue in his Commonwealth and that it should be encouraged. It is, however, a crime in Jacksonville.

"(P)ersons able to work but habitually living upon the earnings of their wives or minor children"—like habitually living "without visible means of support"—might implicate unemployed pillars of the community who have married rich wives.

"(P)ersons able to work but habitually living upon the earnings of their wives or minor children" may also embrace unemployed people out of the labor market, by reason of a recession or disemployed by reason of technological or so-called structural displacements.

Persons "wandering or strolling" from place to place have been extolled by Walt Whitman and Vachel Lindsay. The qualification "without any lawful purpose or object" may be a trap for innocent acts. Persons "neglecting all lawful business and habitually spending their time by frequenting . . . places where alcoholic beverages are sold or served" would literally embrace many members of golf clubs and city clubs. * * *

The difficulty is that these activities are historically part of the amenities of life as we have known them. They are not mentioned in the Constitution or in the Bill of Rights. These unwritten amenities have been in part responsible for giving our people the feeling of independence and self-confidence, the feeling of creativity. These amenities have dignified the right of dissent and have honored the right to be nonconformists and the right to defy submissiveness. They have encouraged lives of high spirits rather than hushed, suffocating silence. * * *

This aspect of the vagrancy ordinance before us is suggested by what this Court said in 1876 about a broad criminal statute enacted by Congress: "It would certainly be dangerous if the legislature could set a net large enough to catch all possible offenders, and leave it to the courts to step inside and say who could be rightfully detained, and who should be set at large."

While that was a federal case, the due process implications are equally applicable to the States and to this vagrancy ordinance. Here the net cast is large, not to give the courts the power to pick and choose but to increase the arsenal of the police. * * *

Another aspect of the ordinance's vagueness appears when we focus, not on the lack of notice given a potential offender, but on the effect of the unfettered discretion it places in the hands of the Jacksonville police. Caleb Foote, an early student of this subject, has called the vagrancy-type law as offering "punishment by analogy." Such crimes, though long common in Russia, are not compatible with our constitutional system. We allow our police to make arrests only on "probable cause," a Fourth and Fourteenth Amendment standard applicable to the States as well as to the Federal Government. Arresting a person on suspicion, like arresting a person for investigation, is foreign to our system, even when the arrest is for past criminality. Future criminality, however, is the common justification for the presence of vagrancy statutes. * * *

Those generally implicated by the imprecise terms of the ordinance—poor people, nonconformists, dissenters, idlers—may be required to comport themselves according to the life style deemed appropriate by the Jacksonville police and the courts. Where, as here, there are no standards governing the exercise of the discretion granted by the ordinance, the scheme permits and encourages an arbitrary and discriminatory enforcement of the law. It furnishes a convenient tool for "harsh and discriminatory enforcement by local prosecuting officials, against particular groups deemed to merit their displeasure." It results in a regime in which the poor and the unpopular are permitted to "stand on a public sidewalk . . . only at the whim of any police officer." * * *

A presumption that people who might walk or loaf or loiter or stroll or frequent houses where liquor is sold, or who are supported by their wives or who look suspicious to the police are to become future criminals is too precarious for a rule of law. The implicit presumption in these generalized vagrancy standards—that crime is being nipped in the bud—is too extravagant to deserve extended treatment. Of course, vagrancy statutes are useful to the police. Of course, they are nets making easy the roundup of so-called undesirables. But the rule of law implies equality and justice in its application. Vagrancy laws of the Jacksonville type teach that the scales of justice are so tipped that even-handed administration of the law is not possible. The rule of law, evenly applied to minorities as well as majorities, to the poor as well as the rich, is the great mucilage that holds society together.

The Jacksonville ordinance cannot be squared with our constitutional standards and is plainly unconstitutional.

Reversed.

KOLENDER V. LAWSON

Supreme Court of the United States
461 U.S. 352, 103 S.Ct. 1855, 75 L.Ed.2d 903 (1983)

JUSTICE O'CONNOR delivered the opinion of the Court.

This appeal presents a * * * challenge to a criminal statute that requires persons who loiter or wander on the streets to provide a "credible and reliable" identification and to account for their presence when requested by a peace officer under circumstances that would justify a stop under the standards of *Terry v. Ohio*.[a] We conclude that the statute as it has been construed is unconstitutionally vague within the meaning of the Due Process Clause of the Fourteenth Amendment by failing to clarify what is contemplated by the requirement that a suspect provide a "credible and reliable" identification. Accordingly, we affirm the judgment of the court below.

I

Appellee Edward Lawson was detained or arrested on approximately 15 occasions between March 1975 and January 1977 pursuant to Cal. Penal Code Ann. § 647(e).[2] Lawson was prosecuted only twice, and was convicted once. The second charge was dismissed.

Lawson then brought a civil action in the District Court for the Southern District of California seeking a declaratory judgment that § 647(e)[c] is unconstitutional, a mandatory injunction to restrain

---

[a] *Terry v. Ohio*, 392 U.S. 1 (1968), held that the police have the power to stop and question any person upon "reasonable suspicion" of criminal activity, and the further power to frisk that person upon reasonable suspicion that the suspect is armed and dangerous. This kind of stop is called a *Terry* detention or *Terry* stop.

[2] The District Court failed to find facts concerning the particular occasions on which Lawson was detained or arrested under § 647(e). However, the trial transcript contains numerous descriptions of the stops given both by Lawson and by the police officers who detained him. For example, one police officer testified that he stopped Lawson while walking on an otherwise vacant street because it was late at night, the area was isolated, and the area was located close to a high crime area. Another officer testified that he detained Lawson, who was walking at a late hour in a business area where some businesses were still open, and asked for identification because burglaries had been committed by unknown persons in the general area. The appellee states that he has never been stopped by police for any reason apart from his detentions under § 647(e).

[c] California Penal Code Ann. § 647(e) (West 1970) provides:

> Every person who commits any of the following acts is guilty of disorderly conduct, a misdemeanor: . . . (e) Who loiters or wanders upon the streets or from place to place without apparent reason or business and who refuses to identify himself and to account for his presence when requested by any peace officer so to do, if the

enforcement of the statute, and compensatory and punitive damages against the various officers who detained him. The District Court found that § 647(e) was overbroad because "a person who is stopped on less than probable cause cannot be punished for failing to identify himself." The District Court enjoined enforcement of the statute, but held that Lawson could not recover damages because the officers involved acted in the good-faith belief that each detention or arrest was lawful. * * *

The Court of Appeals affirmed the District Court determination as to the unconstitutionality of § 647(e). * * *

The officers appealed to this Court from that portion of the judgment of the Court of Appeals which declared § 647(e) unconstitutional and which enjoined its enforcement. We noted probable jurisdiction pursuant to 28 U.S.C. § 1254(2).

II

In the courts below, Lawson mounted an attack on the facial validity of § 647(e). "In evaluating a facial challenge to a state law, a federal court must, of course, consider any limiting construction that a state court or enforcement agency has proffered." As construed by the California Court of Appeal, § 647(e) requires that an individual provide "credible and reliable" identification when requested by a police officer who has reasonable suspicion of criminal activity sufficient to justify a *Terry* detention. "Credible and reliable" identification is defined by the State Court of Appeal as identification "carrying reasonable assurance that the identification is authentic and providing means for later getting in touch with the person who has identified himself." In addition, a suspect may be required to "*account for his presence* . . . to the extent that it assists in producing credible and reliable identification. . . . " Under the terms of the statute, failure of the individual to provide "credible and reliable" identification permits the arrest.

III

Our Constitution is designed to maximize individual freedoms within a framework of ordered liberty. Statutory limitations on those freedoms are examined for substantive authority and content as well as for definiteness or certainty of expression.

As generally stated, the void-for-vagueness doctrine requires that a penal statute define the criminal offense with sufficient definiteness that ordinary people can understand what conduct is prohibited and in a manner that does not encourage arbitrary and discriminatory enforcement. Although the doctrine focuses both on actual notice to citizens and arbitrary enforcement, we have recognized recently that the

---

surrounding circumstances are such as to indicate to a reasonable man that the public safety demands such identification.

more important aspect of the vagueness doctrine "is not actual notice, but the other principal element of the doctrine—the requirement that a legislature establish minimal guidelines to govern law enforcement." Where the legislature fails to provide such minimal guidelines, a criminal statute may permit "a standardless sweep [that] allows policemen, prosecutors, and juries to pursue their personal predilections."

Section 647(e), as presently drafted and as construed by the state courts, contains no standard for determining what a suspect has to do in order to satisfy the requirement to provide a "credible and reliable" identification. As such, the statute vests virtually complete discretion in the hands of the police to determine whether the suspect has satisfied the statute and must be permitted to go on his way in the absence of probable cause to arrest. An individual, whom police may think is suspicious but do not have probable cause to believe has committed a crime, is entitled to continue to walk the public streets "only at the whim of any police officer" who happens to stop that individual under § 647(e). Our concern here is based upon the "potential for arbitrarily suppressing First Amendment liberties. . . . " In addition, § 647(e) implicates consideration of the constitutional right to freedom of movement. * * *

At oral argument, the appellants confirmed that a suspect violates § 647(e) unless "the officer [is] satisfied that the identification is reliable." In giving examples of how suspects would satisfy the requirement, appellants explained that a jogger, who was not carrying identification, could, depending on the particular officer, be required to answer a series of questions concerning the route that he followed to arrive at the place where the officers detained him, or could satisfy the identification requirement simply by reciting his name and address.

It is clear that the full discretion accorded to the police to determine whether the suspect has provided a "credible and reliable" identification necessarily "[entrusts] lawmaking 'to the moment-to-moment judgment of the policeman on his beat.' " Section 647(e) "furnishes a convenient tool for 'harsh and discriminatory enforcement by local prosecuting officials, against particular groups deemed to merit their displeasure,' " and "confers on police a virtually unrestrained power to arrest and charge persons with a violation." In providing that a detention under § 647(e) may occur only where there is the level of suspicion sufficient to justify a *Terry* stop, the State ensures the existence of "neutral limitations on the conduct of individual officers." Although the initial detention is justified, the State fails to establish standards by which the officers may determine whether the suspect has complied with the subsequent identification requirement.

Appellants stress the need for strengthened law enforcement tools to combat the epidemic of crime that plagues our Nation. The concern of our citizens with curbing criminal activity is certainly a matter requiring the attention of all branches of government. As weighty as this concern is, however, it cannot justify legislation that would otherwise fail to meet constitutional standards for definiteness and clarity. Section 647(e), as presently construed, requires that "suspicious" persons satisfy some undefined identification requirement, or face criminal punishment. Although due process does not require "impossible standards" of clarity, this is not a case where further precision in the statutory language is either impossible or impractical.

IV

We conclude § 647(e) is unconstitutionally vague on its face because it encourages arbitrary enforcement by failing to describe with sufficient particularity what a suspect must do in order to satisfy the statute. Accordingly, the judgment of the Court of Appeals is affirmed, and the case is remanded for further proceedings consistent with this opinion.

It is so ordered.

[JUSTICE BRENNAN'S concurring opinion and JUSTICE WHITE'S dissenting opinion have been omitted.]

NOTE

Ten years after the Supreme Court decided *Kolender v. Lawson*, Lawson was detained once again by police responding "to a call that a black man was driving 'too slowly' past an elementary school in a predominantly white neighborhood."[a] Lawson explained that the reason he was driving slowly was because he was near a school.[b]

CAN A PERSON BE FREE TO WANDER WITHOUT WORRY OF ARREST?

Leon Lindsay

The Christian Science Monitor, Midwestern Edition, May 12, 1982, at 3[a]

Edward C. Lawson is not a lawyer, but one day next fall he plans to stand before the US Supreme Court and argue his case—a right of any citizen, though few have taken advantage of it. When Mr. Lawson appears before the high court bench, the justices may hear an impressive plea based on what he calls "the most important part of the Bill of Rights"—the Fourth Amendment, which guarantees "The right of the people to be secure in their persons . . . against unreasonable searches and seizures. . . . "

[a] I. Bennett Capers, *Policing, Race, and Place*, 44 HARV. C.R.–C.L. L. REV. 43, 60 (2009), *citing* Patricia Ward Biederman, *Charges Against Activist Dropped*, L.A. TIMES, May 9, 1993, at J4.

[b] *Id.*

[a] This article first appeared in *The Christian Science Monitor* on May 12, 1982 and is reproduced with permission.

They also will see—unless court protocol requires that he cut his hair and wear a business suit—what might have prompted San Diego police to detain or arrest him more than 15 times between March 1975 and January 1977. They will at least see what Lawson believes is the chief reason for these incidents: He is black.

Prosecuted twice for violating Section 647(e) of the California Penal Code, an anti-vagrancy law, Lawson was convicted once. That began a five-year process of appeals that will culminate in the Supreme Court. Lawson is a bachelor in his mid-30s who heads his own San Francisco-based consulting and entrepreneurial firm. A vegetarian who says he does not smoke, drink, or "do dope," he also is a firm advocate of physical and mental fitness. To help maintain both, Lawson says, he walks everywhere he can. Distances of 10 or 12 miles do not faze him, nor is he concerned about the time consumed.

What did San Diego policemen, patrolling residential or business streets in their cruisers, see that prompted them to stop him? They saw a tall, slender black man striding along the sidewalk or roadside, most likely wearing a plain T-shirt and white trousers. The most outstanding feature is his hair; braided in the style of the Rastafarian religious sect (of which he is not a member), it is just below shoulder length. On his feet are sneakers or basketball shoes. And, if it is late at night and perhaps a little chilly, Lawson might wear a loose-fitting white jacket much like those worn by hospital workers.

Apparently because police saw Lawson walking at certain times and in certain areas in which his presence seemed unusual, they stopped him and demanded identification. He says that the first few times it happened he presented the identification he always carries and explained his presence. After a while, however, he began to feel that this was wrong, and he would ask the police why they wanted him to account for himself. Thus the 15 documented occasions, one of which led to his conviction. * * *

Appeals in the case labeled *Lawson v. Kolender* (San Diego Police Chief William Kolender) led through state courts to the US District Court, where the judge overruled the conviction and the statute. * * *

The case then went to the federal Court of Appeals (Ninth Circuit), which on Oct. 15, 1981, upheld the district court's decision holding 647(e) unconstitutional and also ruled that a jury trial must be held to determine whether the policemen had acted in good faith and whether Lawson could collect the $150,000 in damages he seeks. The court of appeals held that the California law * * * "violates the due process clause because it encourages arbitrary and discriminatory enforcement." The court also said that the law "contains a vague enforcement standard which is susceptible to arbitrary enforcement; or . . . fails to give fair and adequate notice of the type of conduct prohibited."

Lawyers for the state attorney general's office and the City of San Diego, who appealed that decision to the Supreme Court, hold that the law is needed by police to help prevent crimes such as robbery, burglary, and rape. They hold that there has been sufficient experience with this and similar laws across the United States to establish safe guidelines for its enforcement. * * *

Although Lawson attended college only sporadically and puts little value on formal education, the New York City native is articulate and well-informed. He has no record other than the one conviction in San Diego. He makes clear that he does not believe it was his hair or the way he dressed that caused police to stop him. Laws like 647(e), he asserts, are directed "against the prevailing minority" in many US cities. "In certain places that means blacks. In other places it means Hispanics. Hippies in the 1960s would routinely and consistently find themselves describing to someone (in law enforcement) where they were going or what they were doing. * * * "The law becomes a form of instantaneous punishment, to discourage certain kinds of people from being in certain areas," says Lawson. "There is nothing unique about what happened to me. . . . What they were doing was that they were stopping a black who was in an area or (out at) a time that they deemed he should not be." * * *

WALKING WHILE BLACK: ENCOUNTERS WITH THE POLICE ON MY STREET

Paul Butler[a]
Legal Times, Nov. 10, 1997, at 23[b]

Sometimes being a scholar of criminal procedure and a black man seems redundant.

I am walking in the most beautiful neighborhood in the District of Columbia. Though I'm coming home from work, I feel as though I'm on a nature walk: I spy deer and raccoons and hear ridiculously noisy birds. And even more unusual in Washington: black and white people. Living next door to each other. It's more like Disney World than the stereotypical image of Washington, D.C.

It is the neighborhood where I am fortunate enough to reside, and I am ashamed that the walk is unfamiliar; it is occasioned by my broken car. The time is about 9 p.m., and the streets are mostly deserted. When I'm about three blocks from home, a Metropolitan Police car, passing by, slows down. I keep walking, and the car makes a right turn, circles the

---

[a] Paul Butler is a Professor of Law at Georgetown University Law Center in Washington, D.C.

[b] This article is reprinted with permission from *Legal Times*, a publication of American Lawyer Media. (1-800-933-4317 * subscriptions@legaltimes.com * www.legaltimes.biz).

block, and meets me. There are three officers inside. Their greeting is, "Do you live around here?"

I have been in this place before. I know that answering the question will be the beginning, not the end, of an unpleasant conversation—"Where do you live?" "It's kind of cold to be walking, isn't it?" "Can I see some I.D.?"—that I don't feel like having.

So I ask a question instead: "Why do you want to know?" The three officers exchange a glance—the "we got a smartass on our hands" glance. I get it a lot.

"Is it against the law to walk on the sidewalk if I don't live around here?" When no response is immediately forthcoming, I say, "Have a nice evening, officers," and head toward home.

The police now use an investigative technique that probably has a name other than cat-and-mouse, but that is the most accurate description. They park their car on the side of the road, turn off their lights, and watch me walk. When I pass out of their range of vision, they zip the car up to where they can see me.

In this fashion we arrive on the block where I live. I have a question, and so I stop and wait. For once, I have the power to summon the police immediately, quicker even than the president, who lives about seven miles away. Sure enough, as soon as I pause, the car does too. The police and I have a conversation, consisting mostly of questions.

"Why are you following me?"

"Why won't you tell us where you live?"

"What made you stop me?"

"We don't see a lot of people walking in this neighborhood."

"Are you following me because I'm black?"

"No, we're black too."

This answer is true, but it is not responsive. I ask the officers if they have ever been followed around a store by a security guard. They all say yes. The senior officer—a sergeant—says that it doesn't bother her because she knows she's not a thief.

I ask if that's how the kid in the Eddie Bauer case should have felt. A Prince George's County police officer, moonlighting as a security guard, made an African-American teen-ager take off the shirt he was wearing and go home to get a receipt in order to prove that he had not stolen the shirt from the store. Testifying about how that made him feel, the black man-child cried. The case had been in the news the previous week because a jury awarded the boy $850,000. Nonetheless, the sergeant says she isn't aware of it.

The officers tell me that they're suspicious because this is not a neighborhood where they usually see people walking. Furthermore, they know everybody who lives in the neighborhood and they don't know me. I ask if they know who lives there, pointing down the road to the house where I have lived for 14 months. Yes, they answer, yes, they do.

And so I walk. I walk up my stairs. I sit on my porch. I wait. I wait because I am a professor of criminal procedure. I wait because I remember the last time, with different officers, in a different place, when I "cooperated." Which meant that I let them search my car. Or rather, I let one search while the other watched me. With his hand resting near his gun. On 16th Street. Cars whizzed by. I pretended that I was invisible.

Now the officers park their car and position its spotlight on my face. All three of them join me on my porch.

"Do you live here?"

"Yes, I do."

"Can we see some identification?"

"No, you may not."

During the antebellum period of our nation's history, blacks were required to carry proof of their status, slave or free, at all times. Any black unsupervised by a white was suspect. In North Carolina, to make it easier for law enforcement, nonslave blacks had to wear shoulder patches with the word "free."

The District of Columbia, through its three agents standing on my porch, tells me: "If you live here, go inside. It's too cold to be out."

I am content where I am. So, the police announce, are they. They will not leave me until I produce some I.D. or enter the house.

I have arrived home late because I worked late, writing about a book for the Harvard Law Review. The book, which I'm carrying in my knapsack, is Race, Crime and the Law, by Randall Kennedy. Since apparently none of us has anything better to do, I take the book out of my sack and show the officers Chapter 4, "Race, Law, and Suspicion: Using Color as a Proxy for Dangerousness." The chapter contains several stories just like this one. It quotes Harvard Professor Henry Louis Gates Jr. * * * "There's a moving violation that many African-Americans know as D.W.B.: Driving While Black."

But this, I announce, is the first time I've ever heard of "walking while black." I point to the big window of my beautiful house. I tell the police that I have seen people, mostly white, walking down the street at all times of the day and night, and I have never heard them questioned about their right to be there. That is why I will not show them my identification. This is not apartheid South Africa, and I don't need a pass card.

The officers are not interested. In fact, they announce, they're getting angry. There have been burglaries in this neighborhood and car vandalism. The police are just doing their job, and I—I am wasting the taxpayers' money. One officer theorizes that I'm homeless. Another believes that I'm on drugs. The one thing of which they are certain is that I don't live here in the house on whose porch I sit. And when they find out who I "really" am, I will be guilty of unlawful entry, a misdemeanor. * * *

The sergeant tells me that since I'm being "evasive," she will interview my neighbors. The two officers who remain radio for backup. They give the dispatcher the wrong address, and I correct them. Soon a second patrol car, with two more officers, arrives. I am cold but stubborn.

Finally, my neighbor comes outside and identifies me. I'm free now—free to be left alone. Free to walk on a public street. Free to sit on my porch, even if it is cold.

But first, we—the five law enforcement officers and I—look to my neighbor for vindication, a moral to justify the last hour of our lives. My neighbor is black like us. He says that he is always happy to see police patrolling the neighborhood. But, he adds, many white people walk late at night, and they are not questioned about their right to be there. My neighbor tells the officers that they are always welcome to stop by his house for coffee. And he goes home. The sergeant invites me to a crime prevention meeting at the police station in a few weeks. Then the five officers get into their two cars and drive away.

As for me, I'm still searching for a moral. My neighborhood does not seem so beautiful anymore. I got my car repaired right away: I had enjoyed the walk, but I dreaded the next set of officers. Sometimes I prefer to leave criminal procedure at the office. Sometimes I like a walk to be simply a walk.

But sometimes I am willing for my walk to serve as a hypothetical, for the police, and for you, reader, about the Fourth Amendment and its protection against unreasonable government intrusion. If I had a television show, I would say, "Kids, don't try this at home." It is unfortunate, but other uppity Negroes have gotten themselves shot for less than what I did. The officers I encountered were professional, even if the male officers were not especially polite. They never led me to believe that they would physically harm me or even falsely arrest me. It is sad that I should feel grateful for that, but I do.

One reason that I felt safer with the officers was because they were African-American. They might stop me because I'm black, but I didn't think they would be as quick on the draw as nonblack officers, who are more susceptible to the hype. The black officer's construct of me—a black man walking in a neighborhood where people don't often walk at night—was burglary suspect, or homeless person, or drug addict. The white officer's construct—even during a traffic stop—is violent black man. At least that is what is communicated by the approach with the hand on the gun, the order to exit the car, and the patdown search. Not every time, but often enough.

Because the officers were black, I was especially angry. They should've known better.

What is reasonable law enforcement? There are neighborhoods in this city that covet police officers as concerned about crime prevention as these officers seemed to be. Like my neighbor, I had been pleased to see police patrols—at least until the police patrolled me. Still, I could excuse the intrusion as the price of life in the big city if everybody had to pay the price. But everybody does not. Ultimately, my protest is less about privacy and more about discrimination.

Most courts say that police may consider race in assessing suspicion. It is probably true that there are more black than white burglars and car thieves in the District. In *United States v. Weaver*, the U.S. Court of Appeals for the 8th Circuit said of racial profiles: [F]acts are not to be ignored simply because they may be unpleasant. . . . Race, when coupled with other factors is a lawful factor in the decision to approach and ultimately detain a suspect. We wish it were otherwise, but we take the facts as they are presented to us, not as we would like them to be.

But the fact is also that most of the black people who walk in my neighborhood are, like me, law-abiding. And the fact is that some white people are not law-abiding. Race is so imprecise a proxy for criminality that it is, in the end, useless.

The police officers made me an offer before they left. If I wanted to know when they stopped white people who walked in my neighborhood, they would tell me. They would ring my doorbell any time, day or night, to let me know. Ironically, considering the officers' lack of interest in Professor Kennedy's book, their offer is also his suggestion. Kennedy believes in colorblindness, including in assessments of suspicion. He writes:

> [I]nstead of placing a racial tax on minorities, government should, if necessary, increase taxes across the board. . . . It should be forced to inconvenience everyone . . . by subjecting all . . . to questioning. The reform I support, in other words, does not entail lessened policing. It only insists that the costs of policing be allocated on a nonracial basis.

I turned down the offer, thinking that the police might begin to question every walker in my neighborhood just to make a point. That would not make me feel any safer, and it would inconvenience the neighbors.

In retrospect, I made the wrong decision. I hadn't wanted to draw the enmity of my neighbors by causing them to be treated like criminal suspects. Or like black men. Sometimes the law gets me confused about the difference. Kennedy is correct: It is a confusion everyone should share.

NOTE

In the summer of 2009, numerous newspaper, magazine, and television outlets covered the story of Professor Henry Louis Gates, Jr., a Harvard professor arrested by a local police officer on suspicion of having committed a break-in at his own home. The controversy culminated in an awkward "beer summit" held by President Barack Obama with both the professor and the officer. Professor Frank Rudy Cooper argues in the following excerpt that masculinity norms, combined with an arguably vague statute that gave police wide discretionary authority, led to the incident and the public brouhaha over it.

MASCULINITIES, POST-RACIALISM, AND THE GATES CONTROVERSY: THE FALSE EQUIVALENCE BETWEEN OFFICER AND CIVILIAN

Frank Rudy Cooper
11 NEV. L.J. 1 (2010)

Part of the reason the Gates affair so thoroughly captured the public's imagination for more than two weeks in the summer of 2009 is that it involved three very interesting characters. One was a working-class Irish kid who had made good and moved from the city to the suburbs but still policed his hometown. The other was a world-famous black male professor at one of the world's most well-known universities. And then there was the President of the United States, Barack Obama, also a black male, who managed to become the leader of this country despite being a racial minority.

The incident also highlighted significant social issues that have divided the country. The obvious one was race, which has literally rent this nation asunder and simmers beneath many political issues. Here, it was represented by the issue of racial profiling, which drew the nation's attention prior to September 11, 2001, but seems to have faded into a non-controversy. There were also class issues represented by the dichotomy between the "townie" cop and the privileged professor. Lastly, but quite significantly, was the issue of machismo, which made a rare appearance in our public thought thanks to the "pissing contest" between these parties. * * *

A. Crowley's Report

[Arresting officer James] Crowley begins the substantive part of his Incident Report by noting that he was uniformed and on the 7:00 a.m. to 3:30 p.m. shift when the relevant events occurred. At approximately 12:44 p.m., he was driving on Harvard Street, near Ware Street in the Harvard Square area. He overheard a * * * broadcast of a possible break-in in progress on Ware Street. Lucia Whalen made the 911 call. * * *

Crowley's Incident Report states he responded to the dispatcher's call because he was nearby. * * * As he climbed the porch and reached the front door of Gates' home Whalen called out to him. The report continues, "She went on to tell me that she observed what appeared to be two black males with backpacks on the porch." Later, Whalen denied she ever specified that the suspects were black. Crowley further claims "[Whalen] told me that her suspicions were aroused when she observed one of the men wedging his shoulder into the door as if he was trying to force entry." This might also contradict Whalen's account, as the recording describes her as calling on behalf of an older woman who was the one who saw the events in full. * * *

At this point, Crowley says he saw an older black man in the foyer * * * through the glass of the front door. * * * With the door still shut, Crowley asked if Gates would step onto the porch and speak with him, to which Gates replied, "[N]o, I will not," and asked Crowley to identify himself.

According to the report, while Crowley was explaining he was investigating a potential break-in, Gates opened the door and asked, "[W]hy, because I'm a black man in America?" Crowley says he asked Gates if anyone else was in the house and "[w]hile yelling, [Gates] told me it was none of my business and accused me of being a racist police officer." * * * Gates then allegedly told Crowley he "had no idea who [he] was 'messing' with and that [he] had not heard the last of it."

Crowley asked Gates to provide photo identification. Gates initially refused and demanded that Crowley show him identification, but Gates later supplied a Harvard University identification card. * * *

Next, Crowley reports that as he exited the front door he heard Gates yelling another request for his name. Crowley again told Gates he would speak with him outside. According to Crowley, "My reason for wanting to leave the residence was that Gates was yelling very loud and the acoustics of the kitchen and foyer were making it difficult for me to transmit pertinent information to * * * other responding units." * * *

Crowley's language then mirrors the case law on arrests for disorderly conduct, which requires tumultuous behavior in front of onlookers:

> Due to the tumultuous manner Gates had exhibited in his residence as well as his continued tumultuous behavior outside the residence, in view of the public, I warned Gates that he was becoming disorderly. Gates ignored my warning and continued to yell, which drew the attention of both the police officers and citizens, who appeared surprised and alarmed by Gates's outburst. For a second time I warned Gates to calm down. . . . Gates again ignored my warning and continued to yell at me. It was at this time that I informed Gates that he was under arrest.

* * *

B. Gates's View

For Gates, the event begins quite differently and has a very different tenor. He had just returned from China. With the help of his driver, he had forced open the door of his house, which had been jammed. He says he was already on the phone with the Harvard Real Estate Office about this problem when Crowley came onto his porch. Gates further says that when he opened the door to see why a police officer was on his porch, Crowley immediately asked him to step outside. Gates says that he instead remained in his home and asked Crowley why he was there. When Crowley told Gates he was investigating a 911 call about a breaking and entering, Gates said he lived there and was on Harvard's faculty. According to Gates, Crowley demanded proof of those facts. When Gates turned to walk into his kitchen where he had left his wallet, Crowley followed him into the house. Gates says he then handed Crowley both his state and Harvard identification cards.

According to Gates, he made at least three requests for Crowley's name and badge number. Crowley did not respond to these requests. Gates says he then told Crowley, "You're not responding because I'm a black man, and you're a white officer." According to Gates, Crowley's only response was to turn and walk out of Gates's house. When Gates followed Crowley to his front door, he was surprised to see additional police officers on his front porch. Gates then asked one of Crowley's fellow officers for Crowley's name and badge number. When Gates stepped onto his front porch, Crowley handcuffed him.

Gates specifically refutes Crowley's story in two ways. First, he claims he never explicitly called Crowley racist. As evidence that he does not "walk around calling white people racist," Gates points out that he is half-white, was married to a white woman, and has children who are part-white. Second, he says he could not have been particularly loud because he was recovering from a bronchial infection.

C. Obama's Comment and the "Beer Summit"

As Crowley's arrest of Gates was becoming a national controversy, President Obama held a rare news conference during primetime in order to promote national healthcare. During the press conference, a reporter asked Obama what he thought of the arrest. Obama responded as follows:

> Now, I don't know, not having been there and not seeing all the facts, what role race played. But I think it's fair to say, number one, any of us would be pretty angry, number two, that the Cambridge police acted stupidly in arresting somebody when there was already proof that they were in their own home, and, number three, what I think we know separate and apart from this incident is that there's a long history in this country of African-Americans and Latinos being stopped by law enforcement disproportionately. . . . That's just a fact.

The media instantly boiled the three-part answer down to headlines about Obama's choice of the words the "Cambridge police acted stupidly." Cambridge Police Commissioner Robert Haas took offense, saying, "It deeply hurts the pride of this agency." Nationally, police unions were critical of Obama and demanded an apology. Republicans pounced on the issue as a means of criticizing both Obama and Massachusetts elected officials.

In the wake of this criticism, * * * [Obama's] spokesman, Robert Gibbs, said Obama wanted to clarify that he was not calling Crowley stupid. Obama himself said he thought "it was a pretty straightforward commentary that you probably don't need to handcuff a guy, a middle-aged man who uses a cane, who is in his own home." Obama went on to say he had "extraordinary respect" for police work and he understood that Crowley was an "outstanding" officer.

Meanwhile, Obama suffered a significant drop in his poll numbers. The relationship between Obama's "stupidly" comment and white flight from supporting him seems obvious from news reports:

> The president's approval ratings fell, especially among working-class whites, as the focus of the Gates story shifted from details about the incident to Obama's remarks, the poll said. Among whites in general, more disapprove than approve of his comments by a two-to-one margin.

Whites, especially working-class whites, sided with Crowley and against Gates and Obama, and Obama paid a heavy price for his comments in the polls.

The controversy appeared unresolvable until Obama invited the parties to the White House to discuss the event. The event was quickly dubbed the "beer summit" based on the idea that the three men would talk over a beer. * * * In the end, the summit had the desired effect of putting the controversy to rest with a dénouement wherein the media concentrated on what beers the men would choose.

D. The Discretion Inherent in the Massachusetts Disorderly Conduct Law

One potential objection to the argument that Crowley's arrest of Gates was brought about by the way in which identities came together in this context is that this was simply a matter of a man being disorderly. That is, one could argue Crowley's actions were dictated by the law. This seems unlikely because the disorderly conduct law in question is so vague that it could be applied much more frequently than it actually is applied. If the disorderly conduct law were applied in all cases where there was probable cause of a violation, one could assume many more people would be arrested for disorderly conduct. That not being the case, we have to assume that police exercise their discretion to avoid making arrests under the disorderly conduct law.

The Massachusetts disorderly conduct law provides as follows:

> (a) Common night walkers, common street walkers, both male and female, persons who with offensive and disorderly acts or language accost or annoy persons of the opposite sex, lewd, wanton and lascivious persons in speech or behavior, keepers of noisy and disorderly houses, and persons guilty of indecent exposure shall be punished by imprisonment in a jail or house of correction for not more than 6 months, or by a fine of not more than $200, or by both such fine and imprisonment.
>
> (b) Disorderly persons and disturbers of the peace, for the first offense, shall be punished by a fine of not more than $150. On a second or subsequent offense, such person shall be punished by imprisonment in a jail or house of correction for not more than 6 months, or by a fine of not more than $200, or by both such fine and imprisonment.

This language is obviously very broad. It should come as no surprise Crowley could believe he had probable cause to make an arrest on this basis.

Perhaps because of the expansive scope of the statute's coverage, the Massachusetts Supreme Judicial Court has narrowed the scope of its application. For a variety of public disturbance codes, the Court defines "disorderly" as requiring some degree of purposeful or reckless mens rea. In light of that construction, standard jury instructions divide the offense into three elements. First, the Commonwealth must prove the defendant committed at least one of the following actions: he either engaged in fighting or threatening; engaged in violent or tumultuous behavior; or created a hazardous or physically offensive condition by an act that served no legitimate purpose. Second, the Commonwealth must prove the defendant's actions were reasonably likely to affect the public. Third, the Commonwealth must prove the defendant either intended to cause public inconvenience, annoyance, or alarm, or recklessly created a risk of public inconvenience, annoyance, or alarm.

It now becomes clear why Crowley used the word tumultuous to describe Gates's conduct. Gates did not engage in fighting, threatening, or violent behavior. Nor did he create a hazardous or physically offensive condition. Therefore, in order to charge Gates with disorderly conduct, Crowley had to describe Gates's actions as "tumultuous."

It is possible that the definition of disorderly conduct also drove Crowley to lure Gates onto the porch. The definition mandates that the defendant act with purpose to cause a public inconvenience, annoyance, or alarm, or recklessly create risk thereof. By its very definition, an individual's home is not a public place. By remaining inside his home, it would have been difficult for Crowley to contend that Gates purposely or recklessly acted to cause a public inconvenience, annoyance, or alarm. Thus, Crowley might have brought Gates to his porch so that he could charge him with disorderly conduct within the meaning of the statute.

But this legal analysis fails to explain why Crowley chose to arrest Gates. The statute, even as narrowed, grants officers broad discretion to make arrests. Many police interactions will allow such an arrest. But there has been no public outcry over the statute that would suggest such arrests are made nearly as often as they could be. It seems that officers often exercise their discretion not to use this tool. Gates's behavior alone cannot explain Crowley's decision to use this law to make an arrest. * * *

III. The Arrest as a Masculinity Contest

Some might suggest that Crowley arrested Gates solely because of his attitude. * * * But to say Gates was arrested for his attitude begs important questions regarding what, precisely, about Gates's attitude prompted his arrest: Would a similarly situated white man have been arrested? Would a similarly situated black woman have been arrested?

Sociologist and legal scholar Bernard Harcourt provides a succinct answer to the first of those questions. * * * Specifically,

> [I]t is hard to imagine that Sergeant Crowley would have arrested a white Harvard professor of equal stature or status. . . .
> * * *

* * * Crowley need not be explicitly racist to have believed the pervasive stereotype of black men being dangerous. One needs only a cursory look at the extensive literature on implicit bias to see that even a well-meaning police officer is likely to have an anti-black bias that will influence his behavior.

So, would this incident have played out differently if Gates had been white? Of course. As Harcourt notes, race implicitly influences every juncture of the interaction between a white police officer and a black suspect. * * * As Harcourt writes, "It is clear that Professor Gates believed that he was being profiled. It is also clear that Sergeant Crowley understood that he was being accused of racial profiling."

A preliminary answer to the question of whether Crowley would have arrested a similarly situated woman is "no." The fact that Crowley and Gates are both men created a greater likelihood the parties would not back down from their positions. * * *

Pioneering masculinites theorist Michael Kimmel says that men are engaged in "homosocial" competition. * * * Men collect evidence of success—money, power, women—to show other men they are manly. * * *

* * * Manhood is * * * a never-ending test of whether one's behaviors measure up to the ideal form of manhood. But the rules of the hegemonic form of U.S. masculinity—(1) denigrate contrast figures, such as women, (2) accrue tokens of success, (3) hold one's emotions in check, and (4) be aggressive—are unrealizable. It is difficult, if not impossible, for any man to embody these characteristics of the ideal man at every given moment and over the course of his lifetime. Men are always subject to being "unmask[ed]" as less than manly. The need to prove masculinity is thus a constant source of anxiety. * * *

A core aspect of the hegemonic pattern of police officer identity * * * is the officer's sense he must enact a command presence. One has command presence when one takes charge of a situation. * * * Command presence is also associated with the physical control of suspects. It is justified by the need to control dangerous suspects. When misused, it can amount to police brutality. * * *

A corollary of the fact that police officers' senses of self are tied up with their ability to enact command presence is an unwritten rule that civilians must show deference to the badge. * * *

When someone issues a challenge to a fight, he creates a masculinity contest because he has challenged the masculinity of the other * * *. If the other fights, the initiator will now have his masculinity judged based on his performance. * * *

[Crowley and Gates] were in a masculinity contest at the time of the arrest in at least three ways. First, there was the issue of whether or not Gates would follow Crowley's request and leave his house. * * * Gates's refusal of this request challenged Crowley's police authority, and thus his masculinity. Simultaneously, Crowley's insistence that Gates leave the house challenged Gates's masculinity. Would Gates stand his ground or back down? * * *

[Another] way in which the Gates arrest became a masculinity contest was Gates's later request for, and Crowley's refusal to give, an apology. Crowley accused Gates of bad behavior with his arrest for disorderly conduct. Gates counter-claimed bad behavior by calling Crowley a racist. The request for an apology was a continuation of the masculinity contest. Now the question was whether or not Crowley would apologize to Gates. Would he stand his ground or back down? Of course, he stood his ground, and this masculinity contest became a national event.

Ultimately, we should understand Crowley's decision to arrest Gates as more than racial profiling. It should also be understood as a product of machismo. Although it is hard to imagine that a famous white Harvard professor (e.g., Alan Dershowitz) would have been arrested after the officer identified him and determined he did not commit a crime, it is also hard to imagine that a famous black female Harvard professor (e.g., Lani Guinier) would have been arrested under these circumstances. In order to fully understand the arrest, it is necessary to see it as a multidimensional product of Crowley and Gates's races, Gates's claim of racism, Crowley's sensitivity to that charge, the relative class positions of the parties, and the fact that they are both men.

NOTE

In *Arrest Efficiency and the Fourth Amendment*, Professor L. Song Richardson explains why even a well-meaning police officer might perceive the behavior of a Black person as suspicious while thinking the same behavior engaged in by someone who appears White is not suspicious at all:

> * * * The science of implicit social cognition demonstrates that individuals of all races have implicit biases in the form of stereotypes and prejudices that can negatively and nonconsciously affect behavior towards blacks. The implicit stereotype consists of the cultural stereotype of blacks, especially young men, as violent, hostile, aggressive, and dangerous. In the policing context, implicit stereotypes can cause an officer who harbors no conscious racial animosity and who rejects using race as a proxy for criminality to unintentionally treat individuals differently based solely upon their physical appearance.
>
> As a result of implicit biases, an officer might evaluate behaviors engaged in by individuals who appear black as suspicious even as identical behavior by those who appear white would go unnoticed. In other words, even when officers are not intentionally engaged in conscious racial profiling, implicit biases can lead to a lower threshold for finding identical behavior suspicious when engaged in by blacks than by whites.

L. Song Richardson, *Arrest Efficiency and the Fourth Amendment*, 95 MINN. L. REV. 2035, 2039 (2011).

IMPLICIT BIAS IN THE COURTROOM

Jerry Kang, Judge Mark Bennett, Devon Carbado, Pam Casey, Nilanjana Dasgupta, David Faigman, Rachel Godsil, Anthony Greenwald, Justin Levinson, and Jennifer Mnookin
59 UCLA L. Rev. 1124 (2012)

Over the past thirty years, cognitive and social psychologists have demonstrated that human beings think and act in ways that are often not rational. We suffer from a long litany of biases, most of them having nothing to do with gender, ethnicity, or race. For example, we have an oddly stubborn tendency to "anchor" to numbers, judgments, or assessments that we have been exposed to and use them as starting points for future judgments—even if those anchors are objectively wrong. We exhibit an "endowment effect," with irrational attachments to arbitrary initial distributions of property, rights, and grants of other entitlements. We suffer from "hindsight bias" and believe that what turns out to be the case today should have been easily foreseen yesterday. * * *

One type of bias is driven by attitudes and stereotypes that we have about social categories, such as genders and races. An attitude is an association between some concept (in this case a social group) and an evaluative valence, either positive or negative. A stereotype is an association between a concept (again, in this case a social group) and a trait. Although interconnected, attitudes and stereotypes should be distinguished because a positive attitude does not foreclose negative stereotypes and vice versa. For instance, one might have a positive overall attitude toward African Americans and yet still associate them with weapons. Or, one might have a positive stereotype of Asian Americans as mathematically able but still have a negative attitude towards them.

The conventional wisdom has been that these social cognitions—attitudes and stereotypes about social groups—are explicit, in the sense that they are both consciously accessible through introspection and endorsed by the person as appropriate. Indeed, this understanding has shaped much of current antidiscrimination law. The conventional wisdom is also that the social cognitions that individuals hold are relatively stable in the sense that they operate in the same way over time and across different situations.

However, recent findings in the mind sciences, especially implicit social cognition (ISC), have undermined these conventional beliefs. As detailed below, attitudes and stereotypes may also be implicit, in the sense that they are not conventionally accessible through introspection. Accordingly, their impact on a person's decisionmaking and behaviors does not depend on that person's awareness of possessing these attitudes or stereotypes. In this way, they can function automatically, including in ways that the person would not endorse as appropriate if he or she did have conscious awareness.* * *

Consider * * * some of the crucial milestones in a criminal case flowing to trial. First, on the basis of a crime report, the police investigate particular neighborhoods and persons of interest and ultimately arrest a suspect. Second, the prosecutor decides to charge the suspect with a particular crime. Third, the judge makes decisions about bail and pre-trial detention. Fourth, the defendant decides whether to accept a plea bargain, after consulting his defense attorney, often a public defender or court-appointed private counsel. Fifth, if the case goes to trial, the judge manages the proceedings while the jury decides whether the defendant is guilty. Finally, if convicted, the defendant must be sentenced. At each of these stages, implicit biases can have an important impact. * * *

1. Police Encounter

Blackness and criminality. If we implicitly associate certain groups, such as African Americans, with certain attributes, such as criminality, then it should not be surprising that police may behave in a manner consistent with those implicit stereotypes. In other words, biases could shape whether an officer decides to stop an individual for questioning in the first place, elects to interrogate briefly or at length, decides to frisk the individual, and concludes the encounter with an arrest versus a warning. These biases could contribute to the substantial racial disparities that have been widely documented in policing.

2. Charge and Plea Bargain

Journalistic investigations have uncovered some statistical evidence that racial minorities are treated worse than Whites in the charging decisions of prosecutors. * * *

For example, in a 1985 study of charging decisions by prosecutors in Los Angeles, researchers found prosecutors more likely to press charges against Black than White defendants, and determined that these charging disparities could not be accounted for by race neutral factors such as prior record, seriousness of charge, or use of a weapon. * * * At the federal level, a U.S. Sentencing Commission report found that prosecutors were more apt to offer White defendants generous plea bargains with sentences below the prescribed guidelines than Black or Latino defendants. * * *

[T]he conditions under which implicit biases translate most readily into discriminatory behavior are when people have wide discretion, exercised quickly, with little accountability. Prosecutors function in just such environments. * * *

3. Trial

a. Jury

If the case goes to the jury, what do we know about how implicit biases might influence the factfinder's decisionmaking? There is a long line of research on racial discrimination by jurors, mostly in the criminal context. Notwithstanding some mixed findings, the general research consensus is that jurors of one race tend to show bias against defendants who belong to another race ("racial outgroups"). For example, White jurors will treat Black defendants worse than they treat comparable White defendants. * * *

One might assume that juror bias against racial outgroups would be greater when the case is somehow racially charged or inflamed, as opposed to those instances when race does not explicitly figure in the crime. Interestingly, many experiments have demonstrated just the opposite. Sam Sommers and Phoebe Ellsworth explain the counterintuitive phenomenon in this way: When the case is "racially charged," jurors—who want to be fair—respond by being more careful and thoughtful about race and their own assumptions and thus do not show bias in their deliberations and outcomes. By contrast, when the case is not racially charged, even though there is a Black defendant and a White victim, jurors are not especially vigilant about the possibility of racial bias influencing their decisionmaking. These findings are more consistent with an implicit bias story than a concealed explicit bias story. * * *

b. Judge

* * * [D]ata show that when the race of the defendant is explicitly identified to judges in the context of a psychology study * * *, judges are strongly motivated to be fair, which prompts a different response from White judges (who may think to themselves, "whatever else, make sure not to treat the Black defendants worse") than Black judges (who may think "give the benefit of the doubt to Black defendants"). However, when race is not explicitly identified but implicitly primed * * *, perhaps the judges' motivation to be accurate and fair is not on full alert.

4. Sentencing

There is evidence that African Americans are treated worse than similarly situated Whites in sentencing. For example, federal Black defendants were sentenced to 12 percent longer sentences under the Sentencing Reform Act of 1984, and Black defendants are subject disproportionately to the death penalty. * * *

JUSTICE ISN'T BLIND

Richard Morin[a]

Washington Post, September 3, 2000, at B5

A black man is run over and killed by a drunken driver. A typical sentence: two years in prison. A white man is run over and killed by a drunken driver. A typical sentence: four years in prison. A white woman is run over and killed by a drunken driver. A typical sentence: seven years in prison.

Three similar crimes. Three equally blameless victims. Three different punishments—a pattern that is entirely common, assert two economists who have studied the influence of victims' sex and race on sentencing in homicide cases.

Edward Glaeser of Harvard University and Bruce Sacerdote of Dartmouth College found that people convicted of vehicular homicide, for example, received sentences that were 56 percent longer if they killed a woman than if the victim had been a man. But a driver who killed a black person got a sentence that was 53 percent shorter than he would have received if the victim had been white, if all other key factors about the crime, the killer and the victim held constant. * * *

Glaeser and Sacerdote based their conclusions on a random sampling of 2,800 homicide cases drawn from prosecutors' files in 33 urban counties by the Bureau of Justice Statistics. The data set included the characteristics of the offenders, the victims and the outcomes of the trials. That allowed the researchers to control for the effects of factors such as the killers' and victims' prior criminal histories, the type of offense and details of the crime—in addition to personal characteristics such as age, gender, race and income. They confirmed some key findings with data from Alabama, a state with similarly complete records and a relatively large number of vehicular homicides.

The sentencing pattern for the crime of vehicular homicide is particularly noteworthy, they say, because its victims are "essentially random." Unlike other types of homicides, victims of vehicular homicide typically are people who happened by chance to be in the wrong place at the wrong time—the perfect natural experiment to test the impact of the victim's race, gender and other characteristics on sentencing.

They also found these effects were large in other types of homicides. Overall, "murderers who kill black victims receive 26.8 percent shorter sentences" than they would have received if the victims had been white, they wrote. "Murderers who kill male victims receive 40.6 percent shorter sentences [than murderers who kill female victims]," other key factors being equal.

---

[a] Richard Morin is a former staff writer and columnist for The Washington Post.

They also found that the race of the victims had far more to do with sentence length than the race of the killers, after controlling for various factors including the defendants' prior criminal records.

What explains the apparent tendency of judges and juries to go lighter on killers whose victims are black but throw the book at killers whose victims are women? One troubling possibility suggested by Glaeser and Sacerdote: "vengeance." That's a factor that some social scientists argue is important, though rarely acknowledged, in sentencing decisions. In the case of female victims, they argue that vengeance may take the form of outrage over the death of an "innocent" woman to produce a disproportionately long sentence. But in the case of black victims, they speculate that this "taste for vengeance" may take a different form—overt or, more likely, unconscious racism that significantly devalues the life of a black victim by going lighter on the convicted killer. "The racial effects may be despicable," they concluded—but apparently they are all too real.

CITY OF CHICAGO V. MORALES

Supreme Court of the United States
527 U.S. 41, 119 S.Ct. 1849, 144 L.Ed.2d 67 (1999)

JUSTICE STEVENS announced the judgment of the Court and delivered the opinion of the Court with respect to Parts I, II, and V, and an opinion with respect to Parts III, IV, and VI, in which JUSTICE SOUTER and JUSTICE GINSBURG join.

In 1992, the Chicago City Council enacted the Gang Congregation Ordinance, which prohibits "criminal street gang members" from "loitering" with one another or with other persons in any public place. The question presented is whether the Supreme Court of Illinois correctly held that the ordinance violates the Due Process Clause of the Fourteenth Amendment to the Federal Constitution.

I

Before the ordinance was adopted, the city council's Committee on Police and Fire conducted hearings to explore the problems created by the city's street gangs, and more particularly, the consequences of public loitering by gang members. Witnesses included residents of the neighborhoods where gang members are most active, as well as some of the aldermen who represent those areas. * * *

The council found that a continuing increase in criminal street gang activity was largely responsible for the city's rising murder rate, as well as an escalation of violent and drug related crimes. It noted that in many neighborhoods throughout the city, "the burgeoning presence of street gang members in public places has intimidated many law abiding citizens." Furthermore, the council stated that gang members "establish control over identifiable areas . . . by loitering in those areas and intimidating others from entering those areas; and . . . members of criminal street gangs avoid arrest by committing no offense punishable under existing laws when they know the police are present. . . ." It further found that "loitering in public places by criminal street gang members creates a justifiable fear for the safety of persons and property in the area" and that "aggressive action is necessary to preserve the city's streets and other public places so that the public may use such places without fear." Moreover, the council concluded that the city "has an interest in discouraging all persons from loitering in public places with criminal gang members."

The ordinance creates a criminal offense punishable by a fine of up to $500, imprisonment for not more than six months, and a requirement to perform up to 120 hours of community service. Commission of the offense involves four predicates. First, the police officer must reasonably believe that at least one of the two or more persons present in a "public place" is a "criminal street gang member." Second, the persons must be "loitering," which the ordinance defines as "remaining in any one place with no apparent purpose." Third, the officer must then order "all" of the persons to disperse and remove themselves "from the area." Fourth, a person must disobey the officer's order. If any person, whether a gang member or not, disobeys the officer's order, that person is guilty of violating the ordinance.

Two months after the ordinance was adopted, the Chicago Police Department promulgated General Order 92–4 to provide guidelines to govern its enforcement. That order purported to establish limitations on the enforcement discretion of police officers "to ensure that the anti-gang loitering ordinance is not enforced in an arbitrary or discriminatory way." The limitations confine the authority to arrest gang members who violate the ordinance to sworn "members of the Gang Crime Section" and certain other designated officers, and establish detailed criteria for defining street gangs and membership in such gangs. In addition, the order directs district commanders to "designate areas in which the presence of gang members has a demonstrable effect on the activities of law abiding persons in the surrounding community," and provides that the ordinance "will be enforced only within the designated areas." The city, however, does not release the locations of these "designated areas" to the public.

II

During the three years of its enforcement, the police issued over 89,000 dispersal orders and arrested over 42,000 people for violating the ordinance. * * *

We granted certiorari, and now affirm. Like the Illinois Supreme Court, we conclude that the ordinance enacted by the city of Chicago is unconstitutionally vague.

III

The basic factual predicate for the city's ordinance is not in dispute. As the city argues in its brief, "the very presence of a large collection of obviously brazen, insistent, and lawless gang members and hangers-on on the public ways intimidates residents, who become afraid even to leave their homes and go about their business. That, in turn, imperils community residents' sense of safety and security, detracts from property values, and can ultimately destabilize entire neighborhoods." The findings in the ordinance explain that it was motivated by these concerns. We have no doubt that a law that directly prohibited such intimidating conduct would be constitutional, but this ordinance broadly covers a significant amount of additional activity. Uncertainty about the scope of that additional coverage provides the basis for respondents' claim that the ordinance is too vague. * * *

[A]s the United States recognizes, the freedom to loiter for innocent purposes is part of the "liberty" protected by the Due Process Clause of the Fourteenth Amendment. We have expressly identified this "right to remove from one place to another according to inclination" as "an attribute of personal liberty" protected by the Constitution. Indeed, it is apparent that an individual's decision to remain in a public place of his choice is as much a part of his liberty as the freedom of movement inside frontiers that is "a part of our heritage" or the right to move "to whatsoever place one's own inclination may direct" identified in Blackstone's Commentaries. * * *

Vagueness may invalidate a criminal law for either of two independent reasons. First, it may fail to provide the kind of notice that will enable ordinary people to understand what conduct it prohibits; second, it may authorize and even encourage arbitrary and discriminatory enforcement. Accordingly, we first consider whether the ordinance provides fair notice to the citizen and then discuss its potential for arbitrary enforcement.

IV

"It is established that a law fails to meet the requirements of the Due Process Clause if it is so vague and standardless that it leaves the public uncertain as to the conduct it prohibits. . . . " The Illinois Supreme Court recognized that the term "loiter" may have a common and accepted meaning, but the definition of that term in this ordinance—"to remain in any one place with no apparent purpose"—does not. It is difficult to imagine how any citizen of the city of Chicago standing in a public place with a group of people would know if he or she had an "apparent purpose." If she were talking to another person, would she have an apparent purpose? If she were frequently checking her watch and looking expectantly down the street, would she have an apparent purpose?

Since the city cannot conceivably have meant to criminalize each instance a citizen stands in public with a gang member, the vagueness that dooms this ordinance is not the product of uncertainty about the normal meaning of "loitering," but rather about what loitering is covered by the ordinance and what is not. The Illinois Supreme Court emphasized the law's failure to distinguish between innocent conduct and conduct threatening harm.[24] * * *

The city's principal response to this concern about adequate notice is that loiterers are not subject to sanction until after they have failed to comply with an officer's order to disperse. * * * We find this response unpersuasive for at least two reasons.

First, the purpose of the fair notice requirement is to enable the ordinary citizen to conform his or her conduct to the law. "No one may be required at peril of life, liberty or property to speculate as to the meaning of penal statutes." Although it is true that a loiterer is not subject to criminal sanctions unless he or she disobeys a dispersal order, the loitering is the conduct that the ordinance is designed to prohibit. If the loitering is in fact harmless and innocent, the dispersal order itself is an unjustified impairment of liberty. If the police are able to decide arbitrarily which members of the public they will order to disperse, then the Chicago ordinance becomes indistinguishable from the law we held invalid in *Shuttlesworth v. Birmingham.* Because an officer may issue an order only after prohibited conduct has already occurred, it cannot provide the kind of advance notice that will protect the putative loiterer from being ordered to disperse. Such an order cannot retroactively give adequate warning of the boundary between the permissible and the impermissible applications of the law. * * *

V

The broad sweep of the ordinance also violates " 'the requirement that a legislature establish minimal guidelines to govern law enforcement.' " There are no such guidelines in the ordinance. In any public place in the city of Chicago, persons who stand or sit in the company of a gang member may be ordered to disperse unless their purpose is apparent. * * * It matters not whether the reason that a gang member and his father, for example, might loiter near Wrigley Field is to rob an unsuspecting fan or just to get a glimpse of Sammy Sosa leaving the ballpark; in either event, if their purpose is not apparent to a nearby police officer, she may—indeed, she "shall"—order them to disperse. * * *

---

[24] One of the trial courts that invalidated the ordinance gave the following illustration: "Suppose a group of gang members were playing basketball in the park, while waiting for a drug delivery. Their apparent purpose is that they are in the park to play ball. The actual purpose is that they are waiting for drugs. Under this definition of loitering, a group of people innocently sitting in a park discussing their futures would be arrested, while the 'basketball players' awaiting a drug delivery would be left alone."

VI

* * * We recognize the serious and difficult problems testified to by the citizens of Chicago that led to the enactment of this ordinance. "We are mindful that the preservation of liberty depends in part on the maintenance of social order." However, in this instance the city has enacted an ordinance that affords too much discretion to the police and too little notice to citizens who wish to use the public streets.

Accordingly, the judgment of the Supreme Court of Illinois is

Affirmed.

JUSTICE SCALIA, dissenting.

The citizens of Chicago were once free to drive about the city at whatever speed they wished. At some point Chicagoans (or perhaps Illinoisans) decided this would not do, and imposed prophylactic speed limits designed to assure safe operation by the average (or perhaps even subaverage) driver with the average (or perhaps even subaverage) vehicle. This infringed upon the "freedom" of all citizens, but was not unconstitutional.

Similarly, the citizens of Chicago were once free to stand around and gawk at the scene of an accident. At some point Chicagoans discovered that this obstructed traffic and caused more accidents. They did not make the practice unlawful, but they did authorize police officers to order the crowd to disperse, and imposed penalties for refusal to obey such an order. Again, this prophylactic measure infringed upon the "freedom" of all citizens, but was not unconstitutional.

Until the ordinance that is before us today was adopted, the citizens of Chicago were free to stand about in public places with no apparent purpose—to engage, that is, in conduct that appeared to be loitering. In recent years, however, the city has been afflicted with criminal street gangs. As reflected in the record before us, these gangs congregated in public places to deal in drugs, and to terrorize the neighborhoods by demonstrating control over their "turf." Many residents of the inner city felt that they were prisoners in their own homes. Once again, Chicagoans decided that to eliminate the problem it was worth restricting some of the freedom that they once enjoyed. The means they took was similar to the second, and more mild, example given above rather than the first: Loitering was not made unlawful, but when a group of people occupied a public place without an apparent purpose and in the company of a known gang member, police officers were authorized to order them to disperse, and the failure to obey such an order was made unlawful. The minor limitation upon the free state of nature that this prophylactic arrangement imposed upon all Chicagoans seemed to them (and it seems to me) a small price to pay for liberation of their streets. * * *

JUSTICE THOMAS, with whom THE CHIEF JUSTICE and JUSTICE SCALIA join, dissenting.

The duly elected members of the Chicago City Council enacted the ordinance at issue as part of a larger effort to prevent gangs from establishing dominion over the public streets. By invalidating Chicago's ordinance, I fear that the Court has unnecessarily sentenced law-abiding citizens to lives of terror and misery. The ordinance is not vague. "Any fool would know that a particular category of conduct would be within [its] reach." Nor does it violate the Due Process Clause. The asserted "freedom to loiter for innocent purposes," is in no way " 'deeply rooted in this Nation's history and tradition.' " I dissent.

I

The human costs exacted by criminal street gangs are inestimable. In many of our Nation's cities, gangs have "virtually overtaken certain neighborhoods, contributing to the economic and social decline of these areas and causing fear and lifestyle changes among law-abiding residents." Gangs fill the daily lives of many of our poorest and most vulnerable citizens with a terror that the Court does not give sufficient consideration, often relegating them to the status of prisoners in their own homes.

The city of Chicago has suffered the devastation wrought by this national tragedy. Last year, in an effort to curb plummeting attendance, the Chicago Public Schools hired dozens of adults to escort children to school. The youngsters had become too terrified of gang violence to leave their homes alone. The children's fears were not unfounded. In 1996, the Chicago Police Department estimated that there were 132 criminal street gangs in the city. Between 1987 and 1994, these gangs were involved in 63,141 criminal incidents, including 21,689 nonlethal violent crimes and 894 homicides. Many of these criminal incidents and homicides result from gang "turf battles," which take place on the public streets and place innocent residents in grave danger.

Before enacting its ordinance, the Chicago City Council held extensive hearings on the problems of gang loitering. Concerned citizens appeared to testify poignantly as to how gangs disrupt their daily lives. Ordinary citizens like Ms. D'Ivory Gordon explained that she struggled just to walk to work:

> When I walk out my door, these guys are out there. . . . They watch you. . . . They know where you live. They know what time you leave, what time you come home. I am afraid of them. I have even come to the point now that I carry a meat cleaver to work with me. . . . I don't want to hurt anyone, and I don't want to be hurt. We need to clean these corners up. Clean these communities up and take it back from them.

Eighty-eight-year-old Susan Mary Jackson echoed her sentiments, testifying, "We used to have a nice neighborhood. We don't have it anymore. . . . I am scared to go out in the daytime. . . . you can't pass because they are standing. I am afraid to go to the store. I don't go to the store because I am afraid. At my age if they look at me real hard, I be ready to holler." Another long-time resident testified:

> I have never had the terror that I feel everyday when I walk down the streets of Chicago. . . . I have had my windows broken out. I have had guns pulled on me. I have been threatened. I get intimidated on a daily basis, and it's come to the point where I say, well, do I go out today. Do I put my ax in my briefcase. Do I walk around dressed like a bum so I am not looking rich or got any money or anything like that.

Following these hearings, the council found that "criminal street gangs establish control over identifiable areas . . . by loitering in those areas and intimidating others from entering those areas." It further found that the mere presence of gang members "intimidates many law abiding citizens" and "creates a justifiable fear for the safety of persons and property in the area." It is the product of this democratic process—the council's attempt to address these social ills—that we are asked to pass judgment upon today.

II

As part of its ongoing effort to curb the deleterious effects of criminal street gangs, the citizens of Chicago sensibly decided to return to basics. The ordinance does nothing more than confirm the well-established principle that the police have the duty and the power to maintain the public peace, and, when necessary, to disperse groups of individuals who threaten it. * * *

Today, the Court focuses extensively on the "rights" of gang members and their companions. It can safely do so—the people who will have to live with the consequences of today's opinion do not live in our neighborhoods. Rather, the people who will suffer from our lofty pronouncements are people like Ms. Susan Mary Jackson; people who have seen their neighborhoods literally destroyed by gangs and violence and drugs. They are good, decent people who must struggle to overcome their desperate situation, against all odds, in order to raise their families, earn a living, and remain good citizens. As one resident described, "There is only about maybe one or two percent of the people in the city causing these problems maybe, but it's keeping 98 percent of us in our houses and off the streets and afraid to shop." By focusing exclusively on the imagined "rights" of the two percent, the Court today has denied our most vulnerable citizens the very thing that JUSTICE STEVENS elevates above all else—the "freedom of movement." And that is a shame. I respectfully dissent.

[The concurring opinions of JUSTICE O'CONNOR and JUSTICE KENNEDY have been omitted.]

NOTE

Tracey Meares and Dan Kahan explain why the anti-gang loitering ordinance passed by the Chicago City Council in the summer of 1992 was favored by residents of the mostly poor, minority, inner-city neighborhoods where the ordinance would likely be enforced:

> In fact, it may be precisely because they care so deeply about [the youths likely to be affected by the anti-gang loitering ordinance] that residents of the inner-city prefer relatively mild gang loitering and curfew laws over draconian penalty enhancements for gang crimes, severe mandatory minimum prison sentences for drug distribution, and similarly punitive measures. Inner-city residents may believe these harsher penalties visit an intolerably destructive toll on the whole community. The pervasive sense of linked fate between the majority of inner city residents and the youths affected by curfews and gang loitering ordinances again furnishes a compelling reason not to second guess the community's determination that such measures enhance rather than detract from liberty.

Tracey L. Meares and Dan M. Kahan, *The Wages of Antiquated Procedural Thinking: A Critique of Chicago v. Morales*, 1998 U. CHI. LEGAL F. 197, at 210.

B. THE EIGHTH AMENDMENT: CRUEL AND UNUSUAL PUNISHMENT AND THE PRINCIPLE OF PROPORTIONALITY

The Eighth Amendment states, "Excessive bail shall not be required, nor excessive fines imposed, nor cruel and unusual punishments inflicted." Although the Supreme Court has been internally divided on this issue, a majority of Justices have maintained that punishments that are out of proportion to the crime violate the cruel and unusual punishment clause. *Kennedy v. Louisiana* examines whether the death penalty is cruel and unusual punishment for the rape of a child. *Graham v. Florida* represents a recent effort by the Court to reconcile its decisions involving the death penalty with its decisions involving penalties other than death in the Eighth Amendment context. In *Ewing v. California,* the Supreme Court upholds California's three strikes law against an Eighth Amendment challenge.

KENNEDY V. LOUISIANA

Supreme Court of the United States
554 U.S. 407, 128 S.Ct. 2641, 171 L.Ed.2d 525 (2008)

JUSTICE KENNEDY delivered the opinion of the Court.

* * * Patrick Kennedy, the petitioner here, seeks to set aside his death sentence under the Eighth Amendment. He was charged by the respondent, the State of Louisiana, with the aggravated rape of his then—8-year-old stepdaughter. After a jury trial petitioner was convicted and sentenced to death under a state statute authorizing capital punishment for the rape of a child under 12 years of age. This case presents the question whether the Constitution bars respondent from imposing the death penalty for the rape of a child where the crime did not result, and was not intended to result, in death of the victim. * * *

I

Petitioner's crime was one that cannot be recounted in these pages in a way sufficient to capture in full the hurt and horror inflicted on his victim or to convey the revulsion society, and the jury that represents it, sought to express by sentencing petitioner to death. At 9:18 a.m. on March 2, 1998, petitioner called 911 to report that his stepdaughter, referred to here as L. H., had been raped. He told the 911 operator that L.H. had been in the garage while he readied his son for school. Upon hearing loud screaming, petitioner said, he ran outside and found L.H. in the side yard. Two neighborhood boys, petitioner told the operator, had dragged L.H. from the garage to the yard, pushed her down, and raped her. Petitioner claimed he saw one of the boys riding away on a blue 10-speed bicycle. * * *

L.H. was transported to the Children's Hospital. An expert in pediatric forensic medicine testified that L. H.'s injuries were the most severe he had seen from a sexual assault in his four years of practice. * * * *

Eight days after the crime, and despite L. H.'s insistence that petitioner was not the offender, petitioner was arrested for the rape. The State's investigation had drawn the accuracy of petitioner and L. H.'s story into question. * * *

* * * On June 22, 1998, L.H. was returned home and told her mother for the first time that petitioner had raped her. And on December 16, 1999, about 21 months after the rape, L.H. recorded her accusation in a videotaped interview with the Child Advocacy Center.

The State charged petitioner with aggravated rape of a child under La. Stat. Ann. § 14:42 and sought the death penalty. At all times relevant to petitioner's case, the statute provided:

"A. Aggravated rape is a rape committed . . . where the anal or vaginal sexual intercourse is deemed to be without lawful consent of the victim because it is committed under any one or more of the following circumstances: . . .

(4) When the victim is under the age of twelve years. Lack of knowledge of the victim's age shall not be a defense.

D. Whoever commits the crime of aggravated rape shall be punished by life imprisonment at hard labor without benefit of parole, probation, or suspension of sentence.

(1) However, if the victim was under the age of twelve years, as provided by Paragraph A(4) of this Section:

(a) And if the district attorney seeks a capital verdict, the offender shall be punished by death or life imprisonment at hard labor without benefit of parole, probation, or suspension of sentence, in accordance with the determination of the jury." * * *

The trial began in August 2003. L.H. was then 13 years old. She testified that she " 'woke up one morning and Patrick was on top of [her].' " She remembered petitioner bringing her "[a] cup of orange juice and pills chopped up in it" after the rape and overhearing him on the telephone saying she had become a "young lady." She acknowledged that she had accused two neighborhood boys but testified petitioner told her to say this and that it was untrue.

The jury having found petitioner guilty of aggravated rape, the penalty phase ensued. The State presented the testimony of S.L., who is the cousin and goddaughter of petitioner's ex-wife. S.L. testified that petitioner sexually abused her three times when she was eight years old and that the last time involved sexual intercourse. She did not tell anyone until two years later and did not pursue legal action.

The jury unanimously determined that petitioner should be sentenced to death. The Supreme Court of Louisiana affirmed. * * *

The court acknowledged that petitioner would be the first person executed for committing child rape since La. Stat. Ann. § 14:42 was amended in 1995 and that Louisiana is in the minority of jurisdictions that authorize the death penalty for the crime of child rape. * * *

[T]he Supreme Court of Louisiana rejected petitioner's argument that the death penalty for the rape of a child under 12 years is disproportionate and upheld the constitutionality of the statute. * * *

We granted certiorari.

II

The Eighth Amendment, applicable to the States through the Fourteenth Amendment, provides that "[e]xcessive bail shall not be required, nor excessive fines imposed, nor cruel and unusual punishments inflicted." The Amendment proscribes "all excessive punishments, as well as cruel and unusual punishments that may or may not be excessive." * * * [T]he Eighth Amendment's protection against excessive or cruel and unusual punishments flows from the basic "precept of justice that punishment for [a] crime should be graduated and proportioned to [the] offense." Whether this requirement has been fulfilled is determined not by the standards that prevailed when the Eighth Amendment was adopted in 1791 but by the norms that "currently prevail." The Amendment "draw[s] its meaning from the evolving standards of decency that mark the progress of a maturing society." This is because "[t]he standard of extreme cruelty is not merely descriptive, but necessarily embodies a moral judgment. The standard itself remains the same, but its applicability must change as the basic mores of society change."

Evolving standards of decency must embrace and express respect for the dignity of the person, and the punishment of criminals must conform to that rule. As we shall discuss, punishment is justified under one or more of three principal rationales: rehabilitation, deterrence, and retribution. It is the last of these, retribution, that most often can contradict the law's own ends. This is of particular concern when the Court interprets the meaning of the Eighth Amendment in capital cases. When the law punishes by death, it risks its own sudden descent into brutality, transgressing the constitutional commitment to decency and restraint.

For these reasons we have explained that capital punishment must "be limited to those offenders who commit 'a narrow category of the most serious crimes' and whose extreme culpability makes them 'the most deserving of execution.'" Though the death penalty is not invariably unconstitutional, the Court insists upon confining the instances in which the punishment can be imposed.

Applying this principle, we held in *Roper* and *Atkins* that the execution of juveniles and mentally retarded persons are punishments violative of the Eighth Amendment because the offender had a diminished personal responsibility for the crime. The Court further has held that the death penalty can be disproportionate to the crime itself where the crime did not result, or was not intended to result, in death of the victim. In *Coker v. Georgia*, for instance, the Court held it would be unconstitutional to execute an offender who had raped an adult woman. And in *Enmund v. Florida*, the Court overturned the capital sentence of a defendant who aided and abetted a robbery during which a murder was committed but did not himself kill, attempt to kill, or intend that a killing would take place. On the other hand, in *Tison v. Arizona*, the Court allowed the defendants' death sentences to stand where they did not themselves kill the victims but their involvement in the events leading up to the murders was active, recklessly indifferent, and substantial.

In these cases the Court has been guided by "objective indicia of society's standards, as expressed in legislative enactments and state practice with respect to executions." The inquiry does not end there, however. * * * Whether the death penalty is disproportionate to the crime committed depends as well upon the standards elaborated by controlling precedents and by the Court's own understanding and interpretation of the Eighth Amendment's text, history, meaning, and purpose. * * *

III

A

The existence of objective indicia of consensus against making a crime punishable by death was a relevant concern in *Roper*, *Atkins*, *Coker*, and *Enmund*, and we follow the approach of those cases here. The history of the death penalty for the crime of rape is an instructive beginning point.

In 1925, 18 States, the District of Columbia, and the Federal Government had statutes that authorized the death penalty for the rape of a child or an adult. Between 1930 and 1964, 455 people were executed for those crimes. To our knowledge the last individual executed for the rape of a child was Ronald Wolfe in 1964.

In 1972, *Furman* invalidated most of the state statutes authorizing the death penalty for the crime of rape; and in *Furman*'s aftermath only six States reenacted their capital rape provisions. Three—States Georgia, North Carolina, and Louisiana—did so with respect to all rape offenses. Three States—Florida, Mississippi, and Tennessee—did so with respect only to child rape. All six statutes were later invalidated under state or federal law.

Louisiana reintroduced the death penalty for rape of a child in 1995. * * * Five States have since followed Louisiana's lead: Georgia; Montana; Oklahoma; South Carolina; and Texas. * * *

By contrast, 44 States have not made child rape a capital offense. As for federal law, Congress in the Federal Death Penalty Act of 1994 expanded the number of federal crimes for which the death penalty is a permissible sentence, including certain nonhomicide offenses; but it did not do the same for child rape or abuse.* * *

* * * Both in *Atkins* and in *Roper*, we noted that the practice of executing mentally retarded and juvenile offenders was infrequent. Only five States had executed an offender known to have an IQ below 70 between 1989 and 2002; and only three States had executed a juvenile offender between 1995 and 2005. * * *

The evidence of a national consensus with respect to the death penalty for child rapists, as with respect to juveniles, mentally retarded offenders, and vicarious felony murderers, shows divided opinion but, on balance, an opinion against it. Thirty-seven jurisdictions—36 States plus the Federal Government—have the death penalty. As mentioned above, only six of those jurisdictions authorize the death penalty for rape of a child. Though our review of national consensus is not confined to tallying the number of States with applicable death penalty legislation, it is of significance that, in 45 jurisdictions, petitioner could not be executed for child rape of any kind. That number surpasses the 30 States in *Atkins* and *Roper* and the 42 States in *Enmund* that prohibited the death penalty under the circumstances those cases considered. * * *

D

There are measures of consensus other than legislation. Statistics about the number of executions may inform the consideration whether capital punishment for the crime of child rape is regarded as unacceptable in our society. These statistics confirm our determination from our review of state statutes that there is a social consensus against the death penalty for the crime of child rape.

Nine States—Florida, Georgia, Louisiana, Mississippi, Montana, Oklahoma, South Carolina, Tennessee, and Texas—have permitted capital punishment for adult or child rape for some length of time between the Court's 1972 decision in *Furman* and today. Yet no individual has been executed for the rape of an adult or child since 1964, and no execution for any other nonhomicide offense has been conducted since 1963.

Louisiana is the only State since 1964 that has sentenced an individual to death for the crime of child rape; and petitioner and Richard Davis, who was convicted and sentenced to death for the aggravated rape of a 5-year-old child by a Louisiana jury in December 2007, are the only two individuals now on death row in the United States for a nonhomicide offense. * * *

IV

A

As we have said in other Eighth Amendment cases, objective evidence of contemporary values as it relates to punishment for child rape is entitled to great weight, but it does not end our inquiry. "[T]he Constitution contemplates that in the end our own judgment will be brought to bear on the question of the acceptability of the death penalty under the Eighth Amendment." We turn, then, to the resolution of the question before us, which is informed by our precedents and our own understanding of the Constitution and the rights it secures.

It must be acknowledged that there are moral grounds to question a rule barring capital punishment for a crime against an individual that did not result in death. These facts illustrate the point. Here the victim's fright, the sense of betrayal, and the nature of her injuries caused more prolonged physical and mental suffering than, say, a sudden killing by an unseen assassin. The attack was not just on her but on her childhood. * * * Rape has a permanent psychological, emotional, and sometimes physical impact on the child. We cannot dismiss the years of long anguish that must be endured by the victim of child rape.

It does not follow, though, that capital punishment is a proportionate penalty for the crime. The constitutional prohibition against excessive or cruel and unusual punishments mandates that the State's power to punish "be exercised within the limits of civilized standards." Evolving standards of decency that mark the progress of a maturing society counsel us to be most hesitant before interpreting the Eighth Amendment to allow the extension of the death penalty, a hesitation that has special force where no life was taken in the commission of the crime. It is an established principle that decency, in its essence, presumes respect for the individual and thus moderation or restraint in the application of capital punishment. * * *

* * * We said in *Coker* of adult rape:

> We do not discount the seriousness of rape as a crime. It is highly reprehensible, both in a moral sense and in its almost total contempt for the personal integrity and autonomy of the female victim. . . . Short of homicide, it is the "ultimate violation of self. . . . " [But] [t]he murderer kills; the rapist, if no more than that, does not. . . . We have the abiding conviction that the death penalty, which "is unique in its severity and irrevocability," is an excessive penalty for the rapist who, as such, does not take human life. * * *

Consistent with evolving standards of decency and the teachings of our precedents we conclude that, in determining whether the death penalty is excessive, there is a distinction between intentional first-degree murder on the one hand and nonhomicide crimes against individual persons, even including child rape, on the other. The latter crimes may be devastating in their harm, as here, but "in terms of moral depravity and of the injury to the person and to the public," they cannot be compared to murder in their "severity and irrevocability." * * *

V

* * * The Court, it will be argued, by the act of addressing the constitutionality of the death penalty, intrudes upon the consensus-making process. By imposing a negative restraint, the argument runs, the Court makes it more difficult for consensus to change or emerge. The

Court, according to the criticism, itself becomes enmeshed in the process, part judge and part the maker of that which it judges.

These concerns overlook the meaning and full substance of the established proposition that the Eighth Amendment is defined by "the evolving standards of decency that mark the progress of a maturing society." Confirmed by repeated, consistent rulings of this Court, this principle requires that use of the death penalty be restrained. The rule of evolving standards of decency with specific marks on the way to full progress and mature judgment means that resort to the penalty must be reserved for the worst of crimes and limited in its instances of application. In most cases justice is not better served by terminating the life of the perpetrator rather than confining him and preserving the possibility that he and the system will find ways to allow him to understand the enormity of his offense. Difficulties in administering the penalty to ensure against its arbitrary and capricious application require adherence to a rule reserving its use, at this stage of evolving standards and in cases of crimes against individuals, for crimes that take the life of the victim.

The judgment of the Supreme Court of Louisiana upholding the capital sentence is reversed. This case is remanded for further proceedings not inconsistent with this opinion.

It is so ordered.

[The dissenting opinion of JUSTICE ALITO, with whom THE CHIEF JUSTICE, JUSTICE SCALIA, and JUSTICE THOMAS join, has been omitted.]

GRAHAM V. FLORIDA

United States Supreme Court
560 U.S. 48, 130 S.Ct. 2011 (2010)

JUSTICE KENNEDY delivered the opinion of the Court.

The issue before the Court is whether the Constitution permits a juvenile offender to be sentenced to life in prison without parole for a nonhomicide crime. * * * Petitioner challenges the sentence under the Eighth Amendment's Cruel and Unusual Punishments Clause, made applicable to the States by the Due Process Clause of the Fourteenth Amendment.

I

Petitioner is Terrance Jamar Graham. He was born on January 6, 1987. Graham's parents were addicted to crack cocaine, and their drug use persisted in his early years. Graham was diagnosed with attention deficit hyperactivity disorder in elementary school. He began drinking alcohol and using tobacco at age 9 and smoked marijuana at age 13.

In July 2003, when Graham was age 16, he and three other school-age youths attempted to rob a barbeque restaurant in Jacksonville,

Florida. One youth, who worked at the restaurant, left the back door unlocked just before closing time. Graham and another youth, wearing masks, entered through the unlocked door. Graham's masked accomplice twice struck the restaurant manager in the back of the head with a metal bar. When the manager started yelling at the assailant and Graham, the two youths ran out and escaped in a car driven by the third accomplice. The restaurant manager required stitches for his head injury. No money was taken.

Graham was arrested for the robbery attempt. Under Florida law, it is within a prosecutor's discretion whether to charge 16- and 17-year-olds as adults or juveniles for most felony crimes. Graham's prosecutor elected to charge Graham as an adult. The charges against Graham were armed burglary with assault or battery, a first-degree felony carrying a maximum penalty of life imprisonment without the possibility of parole, and attempted armed-robbery, a second-degree felony carrying a maximum penalty of 15 years' imprisonment.

On December 18, 2003, Graham pleaded guilty to both charges under a plea agreement. Graham wrote a letter to the trial court. After reciting "this is my first and last time getting in trouble," he continued, "I've decided to turn my life around." Graham said "I made a promise to God and myself that if I get a second chance, I'm going to do whatever it takes to get to the [National Football League]."

The trial court accepted the plea agreement. The court withheld adjudication of guilt as to both charges and sentenced Graham to concurrent 3-year terms of probation. Graham was required to spend the first 12 months of his probation in the county jail, but he received credit for the time he had served awaiting trial, and was released on June 25, 2004.

Less than 6 months later, on the night of December 2, 2004, Graham again was arrested. The State's case was as follows: Earlier that evening, Graham participated in a home invasion robbery. His two accomplices were Meigo Bailey and Kirkland Lawrence, both 20-year-old men. According to the State, at 7 p.m. that night, Graham, Bailey, and Lawrence knocked on the door of the home where Carlos Rodriguez lived. Graham, followed by Bailey and Lawrence, forcibly entered the home and held a pistol to Rodriguez's chest. For the next 30 minutes, the three held Rodriguez and another man, a friend of Rodriguez, at gunpoint while they ransacked the home searching for money. Before leaving, Graham and his accomplices barricaded Rodriguez and his friend inside a closet.

The State further alleged that Graham, Bailey, and Lawrence, later the same evening, attempted a second robbery, during which Bailey was shot. Graham, who had borrowed his father's car, drove Bailey and Lawrence to the hospital and left them there. As Graham drove away, a police sergeant signaled him to stop. Graham continued at a high speed but crashed into a telephone pole. He tried to flee on foot but was apprehended. Three handguns were found in his car.

When detectives interviewed Graham, he denied involvement in the crimes. He said he encountered Bailey and Lawrence only after Bailey had been shot. One of the detectives told Graham that the victims of the home invasion had identified him. He asked Graham, "Aside from the two robberies tonight how many more were you involved in?" Graham responded, "Two to three before tonight." The night that Graham allegedly committed the robbery, he was 34 days short of his 18th birthday.

On December 13, 2004, Graham's probation officer filed with the trial court an affidavit asserting that Graham had violated the conditions of his probation by possessing a firearm, committing crimes, and associating with persons engaged in criminal activity. The trial court held hearings on Graham's violations about a year later. * * *

Graham * * * admitted violating probation conditions by fleeing. The State presented evidence related to the home invasion, including testimony from the victims. The trial court * * * found that Graham had violated his probation by committing a home invasion robbery, by possessing a firearm, and by associating with persons engaged in criminal activity.

The trial court held a sentencing hearing. Under Florida law the minimum sentence Graham could receive absent a downward departure by the judge was 5 years' imprisonment. The maximum was life imprisonment. * * *

After hearing Graham's testimony, the trial court explained the sentence it was about to pronounce:

> Mr. Graham, as I look back on your case, yours is really candidly a sad situation. You had, as far as I can tell, you have quite a family structure. You had a lot of people who wanted to try and help you get your life turned around including the court system, and you had a judge who took the step to try and give you direction through his probation order to give you a chance to get back onto track. And at the time you seemed through your letters that that is exactly what you wanted to do. And I don't know why it is that you threw your life away. I don't know why.
>
> But you did, and that is what is so sad about this today is that you have actually been given a chance to get through this, the original charge, which were very serious charges to begin with. . . . The attempted robbery with a weapon was a very serious charge.
>
> . . . . .

> [I]n a very short period of time you were back before the Court on a violation of this probation, and then here you are two years later standing before me, literally the—facing a life sentence as to—up to life as to count 1 and up to 15 years as to count 2.
>
> And I don't understand why you would be given such a great opportunity to do something with your life and why you would throw it away. The only thing that I can rationalize is that you decided that this is how you were going to lead your life and that there is nothing that we can do for you. And as the state pointed out, that this is an escalating pattern of criminal conduct on your part and that we can't help you any further. We can't do anything to deter you. This is the way you are going to lead your life, and I don't know why you are going to. You've made that decision. I have no idea. But, evidently, that is what you decided to do.
>
> So then it becomes a focus, if I can't do anything to help you, if I can't do anything to get you back on the right path, then I have to start focusing on the community and trying to protect the community from your actions. And, unfortunately, that is where we are today is I don't see where I can do anything to help you any further. You've evidently decided this is the direction you're going to take in life, and it's unfortunate that you made that choice.
>
> I have reviewed the statute. I don't see where any further juvenile sanctions would be appropriate. I don't see where any youthful offender sanctions would be appropriate. Given your escalating pattern of criminal conduct, it is apparent to the Court that you have decided that this is the way you are going to live your life and that the only thing I can do now is to try and protect the community from your actions.

The trial court * * * sentenced [Graham] to the maximum sentence authorized by law on each charge: life imprisonment for the armed burglary and 15 years for the attempted armed robbery. Because Florida has abolished its parole system, a life sentence gives a defendant no possibility of release unless he is granted executive clemency.

Graham filed a motion in the trial court challenging his sentence under the Eighth Amendment. * * * The First District Court of Appeal of Florida affirmed, concluding that Graham's sentence was not grossly disproportionate to his crimes. * * * The court concluded further that Graham was incapable of rehabilitation. Although Graham "was given an unheard of probationary sentence for a life felony, . . . wrote a letter expressing his remorse and promising to refrain from the commission of further crime, and . . . had a strong family structure to support him, the court noted, he "rejected his second chance and chose to continue committing crimes at an escalating pace." The Florida Supreme Court denied review.

We granted certiorari.

II

The Eighth Amendment states: "Excessive bail shall not be required, nor excessive fines imposed, nor cruel and unusual punishments inflicted." To determine whether a punishment is cruel and unusual, courts must look beyond historical conceptions to " 'the evolving standards of decency that mark the progress of a maturing society.' " "This is because '[t]he standard of extreme cruelty is not merely descriptive, but necessarily embodies a moral judgment. The standard itself remains the same, but its applicability must change as the basic mores of society change.' "

The Cruel and Unusual Punishments Clause prohibits the imposition of inherently barbaric punishments under all circumstances. "[P]unishments of torture," for example, "are forbidden." These cases underscore the essential principle that, under the Eighth Amendment, the State must respect the human attributes even of those who have committed serious crimes.

For the most part, however, the Court's precedents consider punishments challenged not as inherently barbaric but as disproportionate to the crime. The concept of proportionality is central to the Eighth Amendment. Embodied in the Constitution's ban on cruel and unusual punishments is the "precept of justice that punishment for crime should be graduated and proportioned to [the] offense."

The Court's cases addressing the proportionality of sentences fall within two general classifications. The first involves challenges to the length of term-of-years sentences given all the circumstances in a particular case. The second comprises cases in which the Court implements the proportionality standard by certain categorical restrictions on the death penalty.

In the first classification the Court considers all of the circumstances of the case to determine whether the sentence is unconstitutionally excessive. Under this approach, the Court has held unconstitutional a life without parole sentence for the defendant's seventh nonviolent felony, the crime of passing a worthless check. In other cases, however, it has been difficult for the challenger to establish a lack of proportionality. A leading case is *Harmelin v. Michigan,* in which the offender was sentenced under state law to life without parole for possessing a large quantity of cocaine. * * *

The controlling opinion in *Harmelin* explained its approach for determining whether a sentence for a term of years is grossly disproportionate for a particular defendant's crime. A court must begin by comparing the gravity of the offense and the severity of the sentence. "[I]n the rare case in which [this] threshold comparison . . . leads to an inference of gross disproportionality" the court should then compare the defendant's sentence with the sentences received by other offenders in the same jurisdiction and with the sentences imposed for the same crime in other jurisdictions. If this comparative analysis "validate[s] an initial judgment that [the] sentence is grossly disproportionate," the sentence is cruel and unusual.

The second classification of cases has used categorical rules to define Eighth Amendment standards. The previous cases in this classification involved the death penalty. The classification in turn consists of two subsets, one considering the nature of the offense, the other considering the characteristics of the offender. With respect to the nature of the offense, the Court has concluded that capital punishment is impermissible for nonhomicide crimes against individuals. In cases turning on the characteristics of the offender, the Court has adopted categorical rules prohibiting the death penalty for defendants who committed their crimes before the age of 18, or whose intellectual functioning is in a low range.

In the cases adopting categorical rules the Court has taken the following approach. The Court first considers "objective indicia of society's standards, as expressed in legislative enactments and state practice" to determine whether there is a national consensus against the sentencing practice at issue. Next, guided by "the standards elaborated by controlling precedents and by the Court's own understanding and interpretation of the Eighth Amendment's text, history, meaning, and purpose," the Court must determine in the exercise of its own independent judgment whether the punishment in question violates the Constitution.

The present case involves an issue the Court has not considered previously: a categorical challenge to a term-of-years sentence. The approach in cases such as *Harmelin* * * * is suited for considering a gross proportionality challenge to a particular defendant's sentence, but here a sentencing practice itself is in question. This case implicates a particular type of sentence as it applies to an entire class of offenders who have committed a range of crimes. As a result, a threshold comparison between the severity of the penalty and the gravity of the crime does not advance the analysis. Here, in addressing the question presented, the appropriate analysis is the one used in cases that involved the categorical approach * * *.

III

A

The analysis begins with objective indicia of national consensus. "[T]he 'clearest and most reliable objective evidence of contemporary values is the legislation enacted by the country's legislatures.'" Six jurisdictions do not allow life without parole sentences for any juvenile offenders. Seven jurisdictions permit life without parole for juvenile offenders, but only for homicide crimes. Thirty-seven States as well as the District of Columbia permit sentences of life without parole for a juvenile nonhomicide offender in some circumstances. Federal law also allows for the possibility of life without parole for offenders as young as 13. Relying on this metric, the State and its *amici* argue that there is no national consensus against the sentencing practice at issue.

This argument is incomplete and unavailing. "There are measures of consensus other than legislation." Actual sentencing practices are an important part of the Court's inquiry into consensus. Here, an examination of actual sentencing practices in jurisdictions where the sentence in question is permitted by statute discloses a consensus against its use. Although these statutory schemes contain no explicit prohibition on sentences of life without parole for juvenile nonhomicide offenders, those sentences are most infrequent. According to a recent study, nationwide there are only 109 juvenile offenders serving sentences of life without parole for nonhomicide offenses. * * *

B

Community consensus, while "entitled to great weight," is not itself determinative of whether a punishment is cruel and unusual. In accordance with the constitutional design, "the task of interpreting the Eighth Amendment remains our responsibility." The judicial exercise of independent judgment requires consideration of the culpability of the offenders at issue in light of their crimes and characteristics, along with the severity of the punishment in question. In this inquiry the Court also considers whether the challenged sentencing practice serves legitimate penological goals.

Roper established that because juveniles have lessened culpability they are less deserving of the most severe punishments. As compared to adults, juveniles have a "lack of maturity and an underdeveloped sense of responsibility'"; they "are more vulnerable or susceptible to negative influences and outside pressures, including peer pressure"; and their characters are "not as well formed." These salient characteristics mean that "[i]t is difficult even for expert psychologists to differentiate between the juvenile offender whose crime reflects unfortunate yet transient immaturity, and the rare juvenile offender whose crime reflects irreparable corruption." Accordingly, "juvenile offenders cannot with reliability be classified among the worst offenders." A juvenile is not absolved of responsibility for his actions, but his transgression "is not as morally reprehensible as that of an adult."

No recent data provide reason to reconsider the Court's observations in *Roper* about the nature of juveniles. As petitioner's *amici* point out, developments in psychology and brain science continue to show fundamental differences between juvenile and adult minds. For example, parts of the brain involved in behavior control continue to mature through late adolescence. Juveniles are more capable of change than are adults, and their actions are less likely to be evidence of "irretrievably depraved character" than are the actions of adults. It remains true that "[f]rom a moral standpoint it would be misguided to equate the failings of a minor with those of an adult, for a greater possibility exists that a minor's character deficiencies will be reformed." These matters relate to the status of the offenders in question; and it is relevant to consider next the nature of the offenses to which this harsh penalty might apply.

The Court has recognized that defendants who do not kill, intend to kill, or foresee that life will be taken are categorically less deserving of the most serious forms of punishment than are murderers. There is a line "between homicide and other serious violent offenses against the individual." Serious nonhomicide crimes "may be devastating in their harm . . . but 'in terms of moral depravity and of the injury to the person and to the public,' . . . they cannot be compared to murder in their 'severity and irrevocability.' " This is because "[l]ife is over for the victim of the murderer," but for the victim of even a very serious nonhomicide crime, "life . . . is not over and normally is not beyond repair." Although an offense like robbery or rape is "a serious crime deserving serious punishment," those crimes differ from homicide crimes in a moral sense.

It follows that, when compared to an adult murderer, a juvenile offender who did not kill or intend to kill has a twice diminished moral culpability. The age of the offender and the nature of the crime each bear on the analysis.

As for the punishment, life without parole is "the second most severe penalty permitted by law." It is true that a death sentence is "unique in its severity and irrevocability," yet life without parole sentences share some characteristics with death sentences that are shared by no other sentences. The State does not execute the offender sentenced to life without parole, but the sentence alters the offender's life by a forfeiture that is irrevocable. It deprives the convict of the most basic liberties without giving hope of restoration, except perhaps by executive clemency—the remote possibility of which does not mitigate the harshness of the sentence. As one court observed in overturning a life without parole sentence for a juvenile defendant, this sentence "means denial of hope; it means that good behavior and character improvement are immaterial; it means that whatever the future might hold in store for the mind and spirit of [the convict], he will remain in prison for the rest of his days." * * *

Life without parole is an especially harsh punishment for a juvenile. Under this sentence a juvenile offender will on average serve more years and a greater percentage of his life in prison than an adult offender. A 16-year-old and a 75-year-old each sentenced to life without parole receive the same punishment in name only. This reality cannot be ignored.

The penological justifications for the sentencing practice are also relevant to the analysis. * * * A sentence lacking any legitimate penological justification is by its nature disproportionate to the offense. With respect to life without parole for juvenile nonhomicide offenders, none of the goals of penal sanctions that have been recognized as legitimate—retribution, deterrence, incapacitation, and rehabilitation—provides an adequate justification.

Retribution is a legitimate reason to punish, but it cannot support the sentence at issue here. Society is entitled to impose severe sanctions on a juvenile nonhomicide offender to express its condemnation of the crime and to seek restoration of the moral imbalance caused by the offense. But "[t]he heart of the retribution rationale is that a criminal sentence must be directly related to the personal culpability of the criminal offender." And as *Roper* observed, "[w]hether viewed as an attempt to express the community's moral outrage or as an attempt to right the balance for the wrong to the victim, the case for retribution is not as strong with a minor as with an adult." The case becomes even weaker with respect to a juvenile who did not commit homicide. * * * [R]etribution does not justify imposing the second most severe penalty on the less culpable juvenile nonhomicide offender.

Deterrence does not suffice to justify the sentence either. *Roper* noted that "the same characteristics that render juveniles less culpable than adults suggest . . . that juveniles will be less susceptible to deterrence." Because juveniles' "lack of maturity and underdeveloped sense of responsibility . . . often result in impetuous and ill-considered actions and decisions," they are less likely to take a possible punishment into consideration when making decisions. * * * Here, in light of juvenile nonhomicide offenders' diminished moral responsibility, any limited deterrent effect provided by life without parole is not enough to justify the sentence.

Incapacitation, a third legitimate reason for imprisonment, does not justify the life without parole sentence in question here. Recidivism is a serious risk to public safety, and so incapacitation is an important goal. But while incapacitation may be a legitimate penological goal sufficient to justify life without parole in other contexts, it is inadequate to justify that punishment for juveniles who did not commit homicide. To justify life without parole on the assumption that the juvenile offender forever will be a danger to society requires the sentencer to make a judgment that the juvenile is incorrigible. The characteristics of juveniles make that judgment questionable. * * *

Here one cannot dispute that this defendant posed an immediate risk, for he had committed, we can assume, serious crimes early in his term of supervised release and despite his own assurances of reform. Graham deserved to be separated from society for some time in order to prevent what the trial court described as an "escalating pattern of criminal conduct," but it does not follow that he would be a risk to society for the rest of his life. Even if the State's judgment that Graham was incorrigible were later corroborated by prison misbehavior or failure to mature, the sentence was still disproportionate because that judgment was made at the outset. A life without parole sentence improperly denies the juvenile offender a chance to demonstrate growth and maturity. * * *

Finally there is rehabilitation, a penological goal that forms the basis of parole systems. * * *

A sentence of life imprisonment without parole, however, cannot be justified by the goal of rehabilitation. The penalty forswears altogether the rehabilitative ideal. By denying the defendant the right to reenter the community, the State makes an irrevocable judgment about that person's value and place in society. This judgment is not appropriate in light of a juvenile nonhomicide offender's capacity for change and limited moral culpability. * * * As one *amicus* notes, defendants serving life without parole sentences are often denied access to vocational training and other rehabilitative services that are available to other inmates. For juvenile offenders, who are most in need of and receptive to rehabilitation, the absence of rehabilitative opportunities or treatment makes the disproportionality of the sentence all the more evident.

In sum, penological theory is not adequate to justify life without parole for juvenile nonhomicide offenders. This determination; the limited culpability of juvenile nonhomicide offenders; and the severity of life without parole sentences all lead to the conclusion that the sentencing practice under consideration is cruel and unusual. This Court now holds that for a juvenile offender who did not commit homicide the Eighth Amendment forbids the sentence of life without parole. * * * Because "[t]he age of 18 is the point where society draws the line for many purposes between childhood and adulthood," those who were below that age when the offense was committed may not be sentenced to life without parole for a nonhomicide crime.

A State is not required to guarantee eventual freedom to a juvenile offender convicted of a nonhomicide crime. What the State must do, however, is give defendants like Graham some meaningful opportunity to obtain release based on demonstrated maturity and rehabilitation. * * * It bears emphasis, however, that while the Eighth Amendment forbids a State from imposing a life without parole sentence on a juvenile nonhomicide offender, it does not require the State to release that offender during his natural life. Those who commit truly horrifying crimes as juveniles may turn out to be irredeemable, and thus deserving of incarceration for the duration of their lives. The Eighth Amendment does not foreclose the possibility that persons convicted of nonhomicide crimes committed before adulthood will remain behind bars for life. It does forbid States from making the judgment at the outset that those offenders never will be fit to reenter society. * * *

D

There is support for our conclusion in the fact that, in continuing to impose life without parole sentences on juveniles who did not commit homicide, the United States adheres to a sentencing practice rejected the world over. This observation does not control our decision. The judgments of other nations and the international community are not dispositive as to the meaning of the Eighth Amendment. But " '[t]he climate of international opinion concerning the acceptability of a particular punishment' " is also " 'not irrelevant.' " The Court has looked beyond our Nation's borders for support for its independent conclusion that a particular punishment is cruel and unusual.

Today we continue that longstanding practice in noting the global consensus against the sentencing practice in question. A recent study concluded that only 11 nations authorize life without parole for juvenile offenders under any circumstances; and only 2 of them, the United States and Israel, ever impose the punishment in practice. * * *

Thus, as petitioner contends and respondent does not contest, the United States is the only Nation that imposes life without parole sentences on juvenile nonhomicide offenders. We also note, as petitioner and his *amici* emphasize, that Article 37(a) of the United Nations Convention on the Rights of the Child, ratified by every nation except the United States and Somalia, prohibits the imposition of "life imprisonment without possibility of release . . . for offences committed by persons below eighteen years of age." As we concluded in *Roper* with respect to the juvenile death penalty, "the United States now stands alone in a world that has turned its face against" life without parole for juvenile nonhomicide offenders.

The State's *amici* stress that no international legal agreement that is binding on the United States prohibits life without parole for juvenile offenders and thus urge us to ignore the international consensus. These arguments miss the mark. The question before us is not whether international law prohibits the United States from imposing the sentence at issue in this case. The question is whether that punishment is cruel and unusual. In that inquiry, "the overwhelming weight of international opinion against" life without parole for nonhomicide offenses committed by juveniles "provide[s] respected and significant confirmation for our own conclusions." * * *

The Constitution prohibits the imposition of a life without parole sentence on a juvenile offender who did not commit homicide. A State need not guarantee the offender eventual release, but if it imposes a sentence of life it must provide him or her with some realistic opportunity to obtain release before the end of that term. The judgment of the First District Court of Appeal of Florida is reversed, and the case is remanded for further proceedings not inconsistent with this opinion.

It is so ordered.

[The concurring opinion of JUSTICE STEVENS, with whom JUSTICE GINSBURG and JUSTICE SOTOMAYOR join, has been omitted.]

[The concurring opinion of CHIEF JUSTICE ROBERTS has also been omitted.]

JUSTICE THOMAS, dissenting, with whom JUSTICE SCALIA joins, and with whom JUSTICE ALITO joins as to Parts I and III. * * *

[T]he Court concludes that juveniles are less culpable than adults because, as compared to adults, they "have a ' "lack of maturity and an underdeveloped sense of responsibility," ' " and "their characters are 'not as well formed.' " As a general matter, this statement is entirely consistent with the evidence * * * that judges and juries impose the sentence at issue quite infrequently, despite legislative authorization to do so in many more cases. Our society tends to treat the average juvenile as less culpable than the average adult. But the question here does not involve the average juvenile. The question, instead, is whether the Constitution prohibits judges and juries from *ever* concluding that an offender under the age of 18 has demonstrated sufficient depravity and incorrigibility to warrant his permanent incarceration.

In holding that the Constitution imposes such a ban, the Court cites "developments in psychology and brain science" indicating that juvenile minds "continue to mature through late adolescence," and that juveniles are "more likely [than adults] to engage in risky behaviors." But even if such generalizations from social science were relevant to constitutional rulemaking, the Court misstates the data on which it relies.

The Court equates the propensity of a fairly substantial number of youths to engage in "risky" or antisocial behaviors with the propensity of a much smaller group to commit violent crimes. But research relied upon by the *amici* cited in the Court's opinion differentiates between adolescents for whom antisocial behavior is a fleeting symptom and those for whom it is a lifelong pattern. See Moffitt, Adolescence-Limited and Life-Course-Persistent Antisocial Behavior: A Developmental Taxonomy,

100 Psychological Rev. 674, 678 (1993) (cited in APA Brief 8, 17, 20) (distinguishing between adolescents who are "antisocial only during adolescence" and a smaller group who engage in antisocial behavior "at every life stage" despite "drift[ing] through successive systems aimed at curbing their deviance"). That research further suggests that the pattern of behavior in the latter group often sets in before 18. See Moffitt, *supra,* at 684 ("The well-documented resistance of antisocial personality disorder to treatments of all kinds seems to suggest that the life-course-persistent style is fixed sometime before age 18"). And, notably, it suggests that violence itself is evidence that an adolescent offender's antisocial behavior is *not* transient. See Moffitt, A Review of Research on the Taxonomy of Life-Course Persistent Versus Adolescence-Limited Antisocial Behavior, in Taking Stock: the Status of Criminological Theory 277, 292–293 (F. Cullen, J. Wright, & K. Blevins eds.2006) (observing that "life-course persistent" males "tended to specialize in serious offenses (carrying a hidden weapon, assault, robbery, violating court orders), whereas adolescence-limited" ones "specialized in non-serious offenses (theft less than $5, public drunkenness, giving false information on application forms, pirating computer software, etc.)").

In sum, even if it were relevant, none of this psychological or sociological data is sufficient to support the Court's " 'moral' " conclusion that youth defeats culpability in *every* case.

The Court responds that a categorical rule is nonetheless necessary to prevent the " 'unacceptable likelihood' " that a judge or jury, unduly swayed by " 'the brutality or cold-blooded nature' " of a juvenile's nonhomicide crime, will sentence him to a life-without-parole sentence for which he possesses " 'insufficient culpability.' " I find that justification entirely insufficient. The integrity of our criminal justice system depends on the ability of citizens to stand between the defendant and an outraged public and dispassionately determine his guilt and the proper amount of punishment based on the evidence presented. That process necessarily admits of human error. But so does the process of judging in which we engage. As between the two, I find far more "unacceptable" that this Court, swayed by studies reflecting the general tendencies of youth, decree that the people of this country are not fit to decide for themselves when the rare case requires different treatment.

[JUSTICE ALITO's dissenting opinion has been omitted.]

EWING V. CALIFORNIA

Supreme Court of the United States
538 U.S. 11, 123 S.Ct. 1179, 155 L.Ed.2d 108 (2003)

JUSTICE O'CONNOR announced the judgment of the Court and delivered an opinion in which THE CHIEF JUSTICE and JUSTICE KENNEDY join.

In this case, we decide whether the Eighth Amendment prohibits the State of California from sentencing a repeat felon to a prison term of 25 years to life under the State's "Three Strikes and You're Out" law.

I

A

California's three strikes law reflects a shift in the State's sentencing policies toward incapacitating and deterring repeat offenders who threaten the public safety. The law was designed "to ensure longer prison sentences and greater punishment for those who commit a felony and have been previously convicted of serious and/or violent felony offenses." * * *

B

California's current three strikes law consists of two virtually identical statutory schemes "designed to increase the prison terms of repeat felons." When a defendant is convicted of a felony, and he has previously been convicted of one or more prior felonies defined as "serious" or "violent" in Cal. Penal Code Ann. §§ 667.5 and 1192.7, sentencing is conducted pursuant to the three strikes law. Prior convictions must be alleged in the charging document, and the defendant has a right to a jury determination that the prosecution has proved the prior convictions beyond a reasonable doubt.

If the defendant has one prior "serious" or "violent" felony conviction, he must be sentenced to "twice the term otherwise provided as punishment for the current felony conviction." If the defendant has two or more prior "serious" or "violent" felony convictions, he must receive "an indeterminate term of life imprisonment [with the possibility of parole]." * * *

C

On parole from a 9-year prison term, petitioner Gary Ewing walked into the pro shop of the El Segundo Golf Course in Los Angeles County on March 12, 2000. He walked out with three golf clubs, priced at $399 apiece, concealed in his pants leg. A shop employee, whose suspicions were aroused when he observed Ewing limp out of the pro shop, telephoned the police. The police apprehended Ewing in the parking lot.

Ewing is no stranger to the criminal justice system. In 1984, at the age of 22, he pleaded guilty to theft. The court sentenced him to six months in jail (suspended), three years' probation, and a $300 fine. In 1988, he was convicted of felony grand theft auto and sentenced to one year in jail and three years' probation. After Ewing completed probation, however, the sentencing court reduced the crime to a misdemeanor, permitted Ewing to withdraw his guilty plea, and dismissed the case. In 1990, he was convicted of petty theft with a prior and sentenced to 60 days in the county jail and three years' probation. In 1992, Ewing was convicted of battery and sentenced to 30 days in the county jail and two years' summary probation. One month later, he was convicted of theft and sentenced to 10 days in the county jail and 12 months' probation. In January 1993, Ewing was convicted of burglary and sentenced to 60 days in the county jail and one year's summary probation. In February 1993, he was convicted of possessing drug paraphernalia and sentenced to six months in the county jail and three years' probation. In July 1993, he was convicted of appropriating lost property and sentenced to 10 days in the county jail and two years' summary probation. In September 1993, he was convicted of unlawfully possessing a firearm and trespassing and sentenced to 30 days in the county jail and one year's probation.

In October and November 1993, Ewing committed three burglaries and one robbery at a Long Beach, California, apartment complex over a 5-week period. He awakened one of his victims, asleep on her living room sofa, as he tried to disconnect her video cassette recorder from the television in that room. When she screamed, Ewing ran out the front door. On another occasion, Ewing accosted a victim in the mailroom of the apartment complex. Ewing claimed to have a gun and ordered the victim to hand over his wallet. When the victim resisted, Ewing produced a knife and forced the victim back to the apartment itself. While Ewing rifled through the bedroom, the victim fled the apartment screaming for help. Ewing absconded with the victim's money and credit cards.

On December 9, 1993, Ewing was arrested on the premises of the apartment complex for trespassing and lying to a police officer. The knife used in the robbery and a glass cocaine pipe were later found in the back seat of the patrol car used to transport Ewing to the police station. A jury convicted Ewing of first-degree robbery and three counts of residential burglary. Sentenced to nine years and eight months in prison, Ewing was paroled in 1999.

Only 10 months later, Ewing stole the golf clubs at issue in this case. He was charged with, and ultimately convicted of, one count of felony grand theft of personal property in excess of $400. As required by the three strikes law, the prosecutor formally alleged, and the trial court later found, that Ewing had been convicted previously of four serious or violent felonies for the three burglaries and the robbery in the Long Beach apartment complex.

At the sentencing hearing, Ewing asked the court to reduce the conviction for grand theft, a "wobbler" under California law, to a misdemeanor so as to avoid a three strikes sentence.[c] Ewing also asked the trial court to exercise its discretion to dismiss the allegations of some

[c] Under California law, certain offenses may be charged as either a felony or a misdemeanor. These offenses are known as "wobblers." The trial court can reduce a "wobbler" charged as a felony to a misdemeanor to avoid implementing a 3 strikes sentence.

or all of his prior serious or violent felony convictions, again for purposes of avoiding a three strikes sentence. * * *

In the end, the trial judge determined that the grand theft should remain a felony. The court also ruled that the four prior strikes for the three burglaries and the robbery in Long Beach should stand. As a newly convicted felon with two or more "serious" or "violent" felony convictions in his past, Ewing was sentenced under the three strikes law to 25 years to life.

The California Court of Appeal affirmed in an unpublished opinion. * * * The Supreme Court of California denied Ewing's petition for review, and we granted certiorari. We now affirm.

II

* * *

[I]n *Solem v. Helm,* 463 U.S. 277 (1983), we held that the Eighth Amendment prohibited "a life sentence without possibility of parole for a seventh nonviolent felony." The triggering offense in *Solem* was "uttering a 'no account' check for $100." We specifically stated that the Eighth Amendment's ban on cruel and unusual punishments "prohibits . . . sentences that are disproportionate to the crime committed," and that the "constitutional principle of proportionality has been recognized explicitly in this Court for almost a century." The *Solem* Court then explained that three factors may be relevant to a determination of whether a sentence is so disproportionate that it violates the Eighth Amendment: "(i) the gravity of the offense and the harshness of the penalty; (ii) the sentences imposed on other criminals in the same jurisdiction; and (iii) the sentences imposed for commission of the same crime in other jurisdictions." Applying these factors in *Solem,* we struck down the defendant's sentence of life without parole. * * *

Eight years after *Solem,* we grappled with the proportionality issue again in *Harmelin v. Michigan. Harmelin* was not a recidivism case, but rather involved a first-time offender convicted of possessing 672 grams of cocaine. He was sentenced to life in prison without possibility of parole. A majority of the Court rejected Harmelin's claim that his sentence was so grossly disproportionate that it violated the Eighth Amendment. The Court, however, could not agree on why his proportionality argument failed. Justice Scalia, joined by The Chief Justice, wrote that the proportionality principle was "an aspect of our death penalty jurisprudence, rather than a generalizable aspect of Eighth Amendment law." He would thus have declined to apply gross disproportionality principles except in reviewing capital sentences.

Justice Kennedy, joined by two other Members of the Court, concurred in part and concurred in the judgment. Justice Kennedy specifically recognized that "the Eighth Amendment proportionality principle also applies to noncapital sentences." He then identified four principles of proportionality review—"the primacy of the legislature, the variety of legitimate penological schemes, the nature of our federal system, and the requirement that proportionality review be guided by objective factors"—that "inform the final one: The Eighth Amendment does not require strict proportionality between crime and sentence. Rather, it forbids only extreme sentences that are 'grossly disproportionate' to the crime." Justice Kennedy's concurrence also stated that *Solem* "did not mandate" comparative analysis "within and between jurisdictions."

The proportionality principles in our cases distilled in Justice Kennedy concurrence guide our application of the Eighth Amendment in the new context that we are called upon to consider.

B

For many years, most States have had laws providing for enhanced sentencing of repeat offenders. Yet between 1993 and 1995, three strikes laws effected a sea change in criminal sentencing throughout the Nation. These laws responded to widespread public concerns about crime by targeting the class of offenders who pose the greatest threat to public safety: career criminals. As one of the chief architects of California's three strikes law has explained: "Three Strikes was intended to go beyond simply making sentences tougher. It was intended to be a focused effort to create a sentencing policy that would use the judicial system to reduce serious and violent crime."

Throughout the States, legislatures enacting three strikes laws made a deliberate policy choice that individuals who have repeatedly engaged in serious or violent criminal behavior, and whose conduct has not been deterred by more conventional approaches to punishment, must be isolated from society in order to protect the public safety. Though three strikes laws may be relatively new, our tradition of deferring to state legislatures in making and implementing such important policy decisions is longstanding.

Our traditional deference to legislative policy choices finds a corollary in the principle that the Constitution "does not mandate adoption of any one penological theory." A sentence can have a variety of justifications, such as incapacitation, deterrence, retribution, or rehabilitation. Some or all of these justifications may play a role in a State's sentencing scheme. Selecting the sentencing rationales is generally a policy choice to be made by state legislatures, not federal courts.

When the California Legislature enacted the three strikes law, it made a judgment that protecting the public safety requires incapacitating criminals who have already been convicted of at least one serious or violent crime. Nothing in the Eighth Amendment prohibits California from making that choice. To the contrary, our cases establish that "States have a valid interest in deterring and segregating habitual criminals." Recidivism has long been recognized as a legitimate basis for increased punishment.

California's justification is no pretext. Recidivism is a serious public safety concern in California and throughout the Nation. According to a recent report, approximately 67 percent of former inmates released from state prisons were charged with at least one "serious" new crime within three years of their release. In particular, released property offenders like Ewing had higher recidivism rates than those released after committing violent, drug, or public-order offenses. * * *

The State's interest in deterring crime also lends some support to the three strikes law. We have long viewed both incapacitation and deterrence as rationales for recidivism statutes: "[A] recidivist statute['s] . . . primary goals are to deter repeat offenders and, at some point in the life of one who repeatedly commits criminal offenses serious enough to be punished as felonies, to segregate that person from the rest of society for an extended period of time." Four years after the passage of California's three strikes law, the recidivism rate of parolees returned to prison for the commission of a new crime dropped by nearly 25 percent. Even more dramatically:

> [A]n unintended but positive consequence of 'Three Strikes' has been the impact on parolees leaving the state. More California parolees are now leaving the state than parolees from other jurisdictions entering California. This striking turnaround started in 1994. It was the first time more parolees left the state than entered since 1976. This trend has continued and in 1997 more than 1,000 net parolees left California.

To be sure, California's three strikes law has sparked controversy. Critics have doubted the law's wisdom, cost-efficiency, and effectiveness in reaching its goals. This criticism is appropriately directed at the legislature, which has primary responsibility for making the difficult policy choices that underlie any criminal sentencing scheme. We do not sit as a "superlegislature" to second-guess these policy choices. It is enough that the State of California has a reasonable basis for believing that dramatically enhanced sentences for habitual felons "advances the goals of [its] criminal justice system in any substantial way."

III

Against this backdrop, we consider Ewing's claim that his three strikes sentence of 25 years to life is unconstitutionally disproportionate to his offense of "shoplifting three golf clubs." We first address the gravity of the offense compared to the harshness of the penalty.[a] At the threshold, we note that Ewing incorrectly frames the issue. The gravity of his offense was not merely "shoplifting three golf clubs." Rather, Ewing was convicted of felony grand theft for stealing nearly $1,200 worth of merchandise after previously having been convicted of at least two "violent" or "serious" felonies. Even standing alone, Ewing's theft should not be taken lightly. His crime was certainly not "one of the most passive felonies a person could commit." To the contrary, the Supreme Court of California has noted the "seriousness" of grand theft in the context of proportionality review. Theft of $1,200 in property is a felony under federal law and in the vast majority of States.

That grand theft is a "wobbler" under California law is of no moment. Though California courts have discretion to reduce a felony grand theft charge to a misdemeanor, it remains a felony for all purposes "unless and until the trial court imposes a misdemeanor sentence." * * * In Ewing's case, however, the trial judge justifiably exercised her discretion not to extend such lenient treatment given Ewing's long criminal history.

In weighing the gravity of Ewing's offense, we must place on the scales not only his current felony, but also his long history of felony recidivism. Any other approach would fail to accord proper deference to the policy judgments that find expression in the legislature's choice of sanctions. In imposing a three strikes sentence, the State's interest is not merely punishing the offense of conviction, or the "triggering" offense: "It is in addition the interest . . . in dealing in a harsher manner with those who by repeated criminal acts have shown that they are simply incapable of conforming to the norms of society as established by its criminal law." To give full effect to the State's choice of this legitimate penological goal, our proportionality review of Ewing's sentence must take that goal into account.

Ewing's sentence is justified by the State's public-safety interest in incapacitating and deterring recidivist felons, and amply supported by his own long, serious criminal record. Ewing has been convicted of numerous misdemeanor and felony offenses, served nine separate terms of incarceration, and committed most of his crimes while on probation or parole. His prior "strikes" were serious felonies including robbery and three residential burglaries. To be sure, Ewing's sentence is a long one. But it reflects a rational legislative judgment, entitled to deference, that offenders who have committed serious or violent felonies and who continue to commit felonies must be incapacitated. The State of California

---

[a] Justice O'Connor's opinion addresses only one of the three factors outlined in *Solem v. Helm*, the gravity of the offense and the harshness of the penalty. O'Connor does not go on to compare Ewing's sentence to sentences imposed on other criminals in California, nor does she compare Ewing's sentence to sentences imposed for commission of the same crime in other jurisdictions. Justice Kennedy, concurring in *Harmelin v. Michigan*, expressed the view that such comparative analysis is not mandatory.

"was entitled to place upon [Ewing] the onus of one who is simply unable to bring his conduct within the social norms prescribed by the criminal law of the State."

We hold that Ewing's sentence of 25 years to life in prison, imposed for the offense of felony grand theft under the three strikes law, is not grossly disproportionate and therefore does not violate the Eighth Amendment's prohibition on cruel and unusual punishments. The judgment of the California Court of Appeal is affirmed.

It is so ordered.

JUSTICE SCALIA, concurring.

In my opinion in *Harmelin v. Michigan* [501 U.S. 957, 984, 985, 111 S.Ct. 2680, 115 L.Ed.2d 836 (1991)], I concluded that the Eighth Amendment's prohibition of "cruel and unusual punishments" was aimed at excluding only certain modes of punishment, and was not a "guarantee against disproportionate sentences." Out of respect for the principle of stare decisis, I might nonetheless accept the contrary holding of *Solem v. Helm*—that the Eighth Amendment contains a narrow proportionality principle—if I felt I could intelligently apply it. This case demonstrates why I cannot.

Proportionality—the notion that the punishment should fit the crime—is inherently a concept tied to the penological goal of retribution. "[I]t becomes difficult even to speak intelligently of 'proportionality,' once deterrence and rehabilitation are given significant weight,"—not to mention giving weight to the purpose of California's three strikes law: incapacitation. In the present case, the game is up once the plurality has acknowledged that "the Constitution does not mandate adoption of any one penological theory," and that a "sentence can have a variety of justifications, such as incapacitation, deterrence, retribution, or rehabilitation." That acknowledgment having been made, it no longer suffices merely to assess "the gravity of the offense compared to the harshness of the penalty;" that classic description of the proportionality principle (alone and in itself quite resistant to policy-free, legal analysis) now becomes merely the "first" step of the inquiry. Having completed that step (by a discussion which, in all fairness, does not convincingly establish that 25-years-to-life is a "proportionate" punishment for stealing three golf clubs), the plurality must then add an analysis to show that "Ewing's sentence is justified by the State's public-safety interest in incapacitating and deterring recidivist felons."

Which indeed it is—though why that has anything to do with the principle of proportionality is a mystery. Perhaps the plurality should revise its terminology, so that what it reads into the Eighth Amendment is not the unstated proposition that all punishment should be reasonably proportionate to the gravity of the offense, but rather the unstated proposition that all punishment should reasonably pursue the multiple purposes of the criminal law. That formulation would make it clearer than ever, of course, that the plurality is not applying law but evaluating policy.

Because I agree that petitioner's sentence does not violate the Eighth Amendment's prohibition against cruel and unusual punishments, I concur in the judgment.

[The concurring opinion of JUSTICE THOMAS and the dissents of JUSTICES STEVENS and BREYER, joined by JUSTICES SOUTER and GINSBURG, have been omitted.]

NOTE

The harshness of California's Three Strikes Law became the focus of attention in 2012. In November of that year, California voters passed Proposition 36, revising California's Three Strikes Law to impose life sentences only when the third felony conviction is "serious" or "violent." Cheryl Hurd, Samantha Tata, and Jason Kandel, *Prop. 36 Passes; Will Modify California Three Strikes Law*, NBC Bay Area, Nov. 8, 2012, *available at* http://www.nbcbayarea.com/news/local/177871121.html (last visited Mar. 4, 2014). *See also* Bob Egelko, *Prop. 36's '3 Strikes' Change Working, Lawyers Say*, SFGate, Sept. 9, 2013, *available at* http://www.sfgate.com/crime/article/Prop–36–s–3–strikes-change-working-lawyers-say–4800057.php (last visited Nov. 29, 2013).

C. EQUAL PROTECTION

The Equal Protection Clause of the Fourteenth Amendment (understood by the courts to apply to the federal government through the Fifth Amendment Due Process Clause) prohibits each state government from denying to "any person within its jurisdiction the equal protection of the laws." This clause has been interpreted by the courts to prohibit governments from treating people differently based on their race unless such treatment serves a "compelling state interest" and is "narrowly tailored" to serve that interest. This standard is commonly referred to as "strict scrutiny," because very few government actions can satisfy this stringent test.[a]

Over the last few decades, however, the Supreme Court has applied this so-called "strict scrutiny" only to racial discrimination that is "intentional." Unintentional conduct that results in people being treated differently on the basis of their race is subjected to a much lower level of scrutiny: In such cases, the court only asks if the state action has a "rational basis." *McCleskey v. Kemp* illustrates the Supreme Court's

[a] Discrimination based on gender is subjected to intermediate scrutiny, a slightly more generous standard.

approach to the "discriminatory intent" requirement in the context of criminal law.

MCCLESKEY V. KEMP

Supreme Court of the United States
481 U.S. 279, 107 S.Ct. 1756, 95 L.Ed.2d 262 (1987)

JUSTICE POWELL delivered the opinion of the Court.

* * *

I

McCleskey, a black man, was convicted of two counts of armed robbery and one count of murder in the Superior Court of Fulton County, Georgia, on October 12, 1978. McCleskey's convictions arose out of the robbery of a furniture store and the killing of a white police officer during the course of the robbery. The evidence at trial indicated that McCleskey and three accomplices planned and carried out the robbery. All four were armed. McCleskey entered the front of the store while the other three entered the rear. McCleskey secured the front of the store by rounding up the customers and forcing them to lie face down on the floor. The other three rounded up the employees in the rear and tied them up with tape. The manager was forced at gunpoint to turn over the store receipts, his watch, and $6. During the course of the robbery, a police officer, answering a silent alarm, entered the store through the front door. As he was walking down the center aisle of the store, two shots were fired. Both struck the officer. One hit him in the face and killed him.

Several weeks later, McCleskey was arrested in connection with an unrelated offense. He confessed that he had participated in the furniture store robbery, but denied that he had shot the police officer. At trial, the State introduced evidence that at least one of the bullets that struck the officer was fired from a .38 caliber Rossi revolver. This description matched the description of the gun that McCleskey had carried during the robbery. The State also introduced the testimony of two witnesses who had heard McCleskey admit to the shooting.

The jury convicted McCleskey of murder. At the penalty hearing, the jury heard arguments as to the appropriate sentence. Under Georgia law, the jury could not consider imposing the death penalty unless it found beyond a reasonable doubt that the murder was accompanied by one of the statutory aggravating circumstances. The jury in this case found two aggravating circumstances to exist beyond a reasonable doubt: the murder was committed during the course of an armed robbery; and the murder was committed upon a peace officer engaged in the performance of his duties. In making its decision whether to impose the death sentence, the jury considered the mitigating and aggravating circumstances of McCleskey's conduct. McCleskey offered no mitigating evidence. The jury recommended that he be sentenced to death on the murder charge and to consecutive life sentences on the armed robbery charges. The court followed the jury's recommendation and sentenced McCleskey to death. * * *

[After unsuccessfully appealing his convictions,] McCleskey next filed a petition for a writ of habeas corpus in the Federal District Court for the Northern District of Georgia. His petition raised 18 claims, one of which was that the Georgia capital sentencing process is administered in a racially discriminatory manner in violation of the Eighth and Fourteenth Amendments to the United States Constitution. In support of his claim, McCleskey proffered a statistical study performed by Professors David C. Baldus, Charles Pulaski, and George Woodworth (the Baldus study) that purports to show a disparity in the imposition of the death sentence in Georgia based on the race of the murder victim and, to a lesser extent, the race of the defendant. The Baldus study is actually two sophisticated statistical studies that examine over 2,000 murder cases that occurred in Georgia during the 1970's. The raw numbers collected by Professor Baldus indicate that defendants charged with killing white persons received the death penalty in 11% of the cases, but defendants charged with killing blacks received the death penalty in only 1% of the cases. The raw numbers also indicate a reverse racial disparity according to the race of the defendant: 4% of the black defendants received the death penalty, as opposed to 7% of the white defendants.

Baldus also divided the cases according to the combination of the race of the defendant and the race of the victim. He found that the death penalty was assessed in 22% of the cases involving black defendants and white victims; 8% of the cases involving white defendants and white victims; 1% of the cases involving black defendants and black victims; and 3% of the cases involving white defendants and black victims. Similarly, Baldus found that prosecutors sought the death penalty in 70% of the cases involving black defendants and white victims; 32% of the cases involving white defendants and white victims; 15% of the cases involving black defendants and black victims; and 19% of the cases involving white defendants and black victims.

Baldus subjected his data to an extensive analysis, taking account of 230 variables that could have explained the disparities on nonracial grounds. One of his models concludes that, even after taking account of 39 nonracial variables, defendants charged with killing white victims were 4.3 times as likely to receive a death sentence as defendants charged with killing blacks. According to this model, black defendants were 1.1 times as likely to receive a death sentence as other defendants. Thus, the Baldus study indicates that black defendants, such as McCleskey, who kill white victims have the greatest likelihood of receiving the death penalty. * * *

II

McCleskey's first claim is that the Georgia capital punishment statute violates the Equal Protection Clause of the Fourteenth Amendment.[7] He argues that race has infected the administration of Georgia's statute in two ways: persons who murder whites are more likely to be sentenced to death than persons who murder blacks, and black murderers are more likely to be sentenced to death than white murderers. As a black defendant who killed a white victim, McCleskey claims that the Baldus study demonstrates that he was discriminated against because of his race and because of the race of his victim. In its broadest form, McCleskey's claim of discrimination extends to every actor in the Georgia capital sentencing process, from the prosecutor who sought the death penalty and the jury that imposed the sentence, to the State itself that enacted the capital punishment statute and allows it to remain in effect despite its allegedly discriminatory application. We agree with the Court of Appeals, and every other court that has considered such a challenge, that this claim must fail.

A

Our analysis begins with the basic principle that a defendant who alleges an equal protection violation has the burden of proving "the existence of purposeful discrimination." A corollary to this principle is that a criminal defendant must prove that the purposeful discrimination "had a discriminatory effect" on him. Thus, to prevail under the Equal Protection Clause, McCleskey must prove that the decisionmakers in *his* case acted with discriminatory purpose. He offers no evidence specific to his own case that would support an inference that racial considerations played a part in his sentence. Instead, he relies solely on the Baldus study. McCleskey argues that the Baldus study compels an inference that his sentence rests on purposeful discrimination. McCleskey's claim that these statistics are sufficient proof of discrimination, without regard to the facts of a particular case, would extend to all capital cases in Georgia, at least where the victim was white and the defendant is black.

The Court has accepted statistics as proof of intent to discriminate in certain limited contexts. First, this Court has accepted statistical disparities as proof of an equal protection violation in the selection of the jury venire in a particular district. Although statistical proof normally must present a "stark" pattern to be accepted as the sole proof of

[7] Although the District Court rejected the findings of the Baldus study as flawed, the Court of Appeals assumed that the study is valid and reached the constitutional issues. Accordingly, those issues are before us. As did the Court of Appeals, we assume the study is valid statistically without reviewing the factual findings of the District Court. Our assumption that the Baldus study is statistically valid does not include the assumption that the study shows that racial considerations actually enter into any sentencing decisions in Georgia. Even a sophisticated multiple-regression analysis such as the Baldus study can only demonstrate a *risk* that the factor of race entered into some capital sentencing decisions and a necessarily lesser risk that race entered into any particular sentencing decision.

discriminatory intent under the Constitution, "because of the nature of the jury-selection task, . . . we have permitted a finding of constitutional violation even when the statistical pattern does not approach [such] extremes." Second, this Court has accepted statistics in the form of multiple-regression analysis to prove statutory violations under Title VII of the Civil Rights Act of 1964.[a]

But the nature of the capital sentencing decision, and the relationship of the statistics to that decision, are fundamentally different from the corresponding elements in the venire-selection or Title VII cases. Most importantly, each particular decision to impose the death penalty is made by a petit jury selected from a properly constituted venire. Each jury is unique in its composition, and the Constitution requires that its decision rest on consideration of innumerable factors that vary according to the characteristics of the individual defendant and the facts of the particular capital offense. Thus, the application of an inference drawn from the general statistics to a specific decision in a trial and sentencing simply is not comparable to the application of an inference drawn from general statistics to a specific venire-selection or Title VII case. In those cases, the statistics relate to fewer entities, and fewer variables are relevant to the challenged decisions.

Another important difference between the cases in which we have accepted statistics as proof of discriminatory intent and this case is that, in the venire-selection and Title VII contexts, the decisionmaker has an opportunity to explain the statistical disparity. Here, the State has no practical opportunity to rebut the Baldus study. "Controlling considerations of . . . public policy" dictate that jurors "cannot be called . . . to testify to the motives and influences that led to their verdict." Similarly, the policy considerations behind a prosecutor's traditionally "wide discretion" suggest the impropriety of our requiring prosecutors to defend their decisions to seek death penalties, "often years after they were made." Moreover, absent far stronger proof, it is unnecessary to seek such a rebuttal, because a legitimate and unchallenged explanation for the decision is apparent from the record: McCleskey committed an act for which the United States Constitution and Georgia laws permit imposition of the death penalty.

Finally, McCleskey's statistical proffer must be viewed in the context of his challenge. McCleskey challenges decisions at the heart of the State's criminal justice system. "One of society's most basic tasks is that of protecting the lives of its citizens and one of the most basic ways in which it achieves the task is through criminal laws against murder." Implementation of these laws necessarily requires discretionary judgments. Because discretion is essential to the criminal justice process,

[a] Title VII of the Civil Rights Act of 1964 forbids employers from discriminating in their employment practices on the basis of race, color, religion, sex, or national origin.

This completely misses the point. π didn't argue that his crime didn't "deserve" the death penalty. Its that if you as a state apply the Death Penalty, you need to do so in a racially nuetral manner.

we would demand exceptionally clear proof before we would infer that the discretion has been abused. The unique nature of the decisions at issue in this case also counsels against adopting such an inference from the disparities indicated by the Baldus study. Accordingly, we hold that the Baldus study is clearly insufficient to support an inference that any of the decisionmakers in McCleskey's case acted with discriminatory purpose.

B

McCleskey also suggests that the Baldus study proves that the State as a whole has acted with a discriminatory purpose. He appears to argue that the State has violated the Equal Protection Clause by adopting the capital punishment statute and allowing it to remain in force despite its allegedly discriminatory application. But " 'discriminatory purpose' . . . implies more than intent as volition or intent as awareness of consequences. It implies that the decisionmaker, in this case a state legislature, selected or reaffirmed a particular course of action at least in part 'because of,' not merely 'in spite of,' its adverse effects upon an identifiable group." For this claim to prevail, McCleskey would have to prove that the Georgia Legislature enacted or maintained the death penalty statute *because of* an anticipated racially discriminatory effect. In *Gregg v. Georgia* this Court found that the Georgia capital sentencing system could operate in a fair and neutral manner. There was no evidence then, and there is none now, that the Georgia Legislature enacted the capital punishment statute to further a racially discriminatory purpose. * * *

* * * Accordingly, we reject McCleskey's equal protection claims. * * *

III

McCleskey also argues that the Baldus study demonstrates that the Georgia capital sentencing system violates the Eighth Amendment. * * * To evaluate McCleskey's challenge, we must examine exactly what the Baldus study may show. Even Professor Baldus does not contend that his statistics *prove* that race enters into any capital sentencing decisions or that race was a factor in McCleskey's particular case. Statistics at most may show only a likelihood that a particular factor entered into some decisions. There is, of course, some risk of racial prejudice influencing a jury's decision in a criminal case. There are similar risks that other kinds of prejudice will influence other criminal trials. The question "is at what point that risk becomes constitutionally unacceptable," McCleskey asks us to accept the likelihood allegedly shown by the Baldus study as the constitutional measure of an unacceptable risk of racial prejudice influencing capital sentencing decisions. This we decline to do. * * *

McCleskey's argument that the Constitution condemns the discretion allowed decisionmakers in the Georgia capital sentencing system is antithetical to the fundamental role of discretion in our criminal justice system. Discretion in the criminal justice system offers substantial benefits to the criminal defendant. Not only can a jury decline to impose the death sentence, it can decline to convict or choose to convict of a lesser offense. Whereas decisions against a defendant's interest may be reversed by the trial judge or on appeal, these discretionary exercises of leniency are final and unreviewable. Similarly, the capacity of prosecutorial discretion to provide individualized justice is "firmly entrenched in American law." As we have noted, a prosecutor can decline to charge, offer a plea bargain, or decline to seek a death sentence in any particular case. Of course, "the power to be lenient [also] is the power to discriminate," but a capital punishment system that did not allow for discretionary acts of leniency "would be totally alien to our notions of criminal justice."

C

At most, the Baldus study indicates a discrepancy that appears to correlate with race. Apparent disparities in sentencing are an inevitable part of our criminal justice system. * * * As this Court has recognized, any mode for determining guilt or punishment "has its weaknesses and the potential for misuse." * * * Where the discretion that is fundamental to our criminal process is involved, we decline to assume that what is unexplained is invidious. In light of the safeguards designed to minimize racial bias in the process, the fundamental value of jury trial in our criminal justice system, and the benefits that discretion provides to criminal defendants, we hold that the Baldus study does not demonstrate a constitutionally significant risk of racial bias affecting the Georgia capital sentencing process.

We have held that discretion in a capital punishment system is necessary to satisfy the Constitution. Yet, the dissent now claims that the "discretion afforded such prosecutors and jurors in the Georgia capital sentencing system" violates the Constitution by creating "opportunities for racial considerations to influence criminal proceedings." The dissent contends that in Georgia "no guidelines govern prosecutorial decisions . . . and [that] Georgia provides juries with no list of aggravating and mitigating factors, nor any standard for balancing them against one another." Prosecutorial decisions necessarily involve both judgmental and factual decisions that vary from case to case. Thus, it is difficult to imagine guidelines that would produce the predictability sought by the dissent without sacrificing the discretion essential to a humane and fair system of criminal justice. Indeed, the dissent suggests no such guidelines for prosecutorial discretion.

Two additional concerns inform our decision in this case. First, McCleskey's claim, taken to its logical conclusion, throws into serious question the principles that underlie our entire criminal justice system. The Eighth Amendment is not limited in application to capital punishment, but applies to all penalties. Thus, if we accepted McCleskey's claim that racial bias has impermissibly tainted the capital sentencing decision, we could soon be faced with similar claims as to other types of penalty. Moreover, the claim that his sentence rests on the irrelevant factor of race easily could be extended to apply to claims based on unexplained discrepancies that correlate to membership in other minority groups, and even to gender. Similarly, since McCleskey's claim relates to the race of his victim, other claims could apply with equally logical force to statistical disparities that correlate with the race or sex of other actors in the criminal justice system, such as defense attorneys or judges. Also, there is no logical reason that such a claim need be limited to racial or sexual bias. If arbitrary and capricious punishment is the touchstone under the Eighth Amendment, such a claim could—at least in theory—be based upon any arbitrary variable, such as the defendant's facial characteristics, or the physical attractiveness of the defendant or the victim, that some statistical study indicates may be influential in jury decisionmaking. As these examples illustrate, there is no limiting principle to the type of challenge brought by McCleskey.* * *

Second, McCleskey's arguments are best presented to the legislative bodies. It is not the responsibility—or indeed even the right—of this Court to determine the appropriate punishment for particular crimes. It is the legislatures, the elected representatives of the people, that are "constituted to respond to the will and consequently the moral values of the people." Legislatures also are better qualified to weigh and "evaluate the results of statistical studies in terms of their own local conditions and with a flexibility of approach that is not available to the courts." * * *

Accordingly, we affirm the judgment of the Court of Appeals for the Eleventh Circuit.

It is so ordered.

JUSTICE BRENNAN, with whom JUSTICE MARSHALL joins, and with whom JUSTICE BLACKMUN and JUSTICE STEVENS join in all but Part I, dissenting.

I

Adhering to my view that the death penalty is in all circumstances cruel and unusual punishment forbidden by the Eighth and Fourteenth Amendments, I would vacate the decision below insofar as it left undisturbed the death sentence imposed in this case. This Court observes that "the *Gregg*-type statute imposes unprecedented safeguards in the special context of capital punishment," which "ensure a degree of care in the imposition of the death penalty that can be described only as unique." Notwithstanding these efforts, murder defendants in Georgia with white victims are more than four times as likely to receive the death sentence as are defendants with black victims. Nothing could convey more powerfully the intractable reality of the death penalty: "that the effort to eliminate arbitrariness in the infliction of that ultimate sanction is so plainly doomed to failure that it—and the death penalty—must be abandoned altogether."

Even if I did not hold this position, however, I would reverse the Court of Appeals, for petitioner McCleskey has clearly demonstrated that his death sentence was imposed in violation of the Eighth and Fourteenth Amendments. * * *

II

At some point in this case, Warren McCleskey doubtless asked his lawyer whether a jury was likely to sentence him to die. A candid reply to this question would have been disturbing. First, counsel would have to tell McCleskey that few of the details of the crime or of McCleskey's past criminal conduct were more important than the fact that his victim was white. Furthermore, counsel would feel bound to tell McCleskey that defendants charged with killing white victims in Georgia are 4.3 times as likely to be sentenced to death as defendants charged with killing blacks. In addition, frankness would compel the disclosure that it was more likely than not that the race of McCleskey's victim would determine whether he received a death sentence: 6 of every 11 defendants convicted of killing a white person would not have received the death penalty if their victims had been black, while, among defendants with aggravating and mitigating factors comparable to McCleskey's, 20 of every 34 would not have been sentenced to die if their victims had been black. Finally, the assessment would not be complete without the information that cases involving black defendants and white victims are more likely to result in a death sentence than cases featuring any other racial combination of defendant and victim. The story could be told in a variety of ways, but McCleskey could not fail to grasp its essential narrative line: there was a significant chance that race would play a prominent role in determining if he lived or died. * * *

IV

The Court cites four reasons for shrinking from the implications of McCleskey's evidence: the desirability of discretion for actors in the criminal justice system, the existence of statutory safeguards against abuse of that discretion, the potential consequences for broader challenges to criminal sentencing, and an understanding of the contours of the judicial role. While these concerns underscore the need for sober deliberation, they do not justify rejecting evidence as convincing as McCleskey has presented.

The Court maintains that petitioner's claim "is antithetical to the fundamental role of discretion in our criminal justice system." It states that "where the discretion that is fundamental to our criminal process is involved, we decline to assume that what is unexplained is invidious."

Reliance on race in imposing capital punishment, however, is antithetical to the very rationale for granting sentencing discretion. Discretion is a means, not an end. It is bestowed in order to permit the sentencer to "trea[t] each defendant in a capital case with that degree of respect due the uniqueness of the individual." The decision to impose the punishment of death must be based on a "particularized consideration of relevant aspects of the character and record of each convicted defendant." Failure to conduct such an individualized moral inquiry "treats all persons convicted of a designated offense not as unique individual human beings, but as members of a faceless, undifferentiated mass to be subjected to the blind infliction of the penalty of death."

Considering the race of a defendant or victim in deciding if the death penalty should be imposed is completely at odds with this concern that an individual be evaluated as a unique human being. Decisions influenced by race rest in part on a categorical assessment of the worth of human beings according to color, insensitive to whatever qualities the individuals in question may possess. Enhanced willingness to impose the death sentence on black defendants, or diminished willingness to render such a sentence when blacks are victims, reflects a devaluation of the lives of black persons. When confronted with evidence that race more likely than not plays such a role in a capital sentencing system, it is plainly insufficient to say that the importance of discretion demands that the risk be higher before we will act—for in such a case the very end that discretion is designed to serve is being undermined. * * *

The Court next states that its unwillingness to regard petitioner's evidence as sufficient is based in part on the fear that recognition of McCleskey's claim would open the door to widespread challenges to all aspects of criminal sentencing. Taken on its face, such a statement seems to suggest a fear of too much justice. Yet surely the majority would acknowledge that if striking evidence indicated that other minority groups, or women, or even persons with blond hair, were disproportionately sentenced to death, such a state of affairs would be repugnant to deeply rooted conceptions of fairness. The prospect that there may be more widespread abuse than McCleskey documents may be dismaying, but it does not justify complete abdication of our judicial role. The Constitution was framed fundamentally as a bulwark against governmental power, and preventing the arbitrary administration of punishment is a basic ideal of any society that purports to be governed by the rule of law.

In fairness, the Court's fear that McCleskey's claim is an invitation to descend a slippery slope also rests on the realization that any humanly imposed system of penalties will exhibit some imperfection. Yet to reject

McCleskey's powerful evidence on this basis is to ignore both the qualitatively different character of the death penalty and the particular repugnance of racial discrimination, considerations which may properly be taken into account in determining whether various punishments are "cruel and unusual." Furthermore, it fails to take account of the unprecedented refinement and strength of the Baldus study.

It hardly needs reiteration that this Court has consistently acknowledged the uniqueness of the punishment of death. "Death, in its finality, differs more from life imprisonment than a 100-year prison term differs from one of only a year or two. Because of that qualitative difference, there is a corresponding difference in the need for reliability in the determination that death is the appropriate punishment." Furthermore, the relative interests of the state and the defendant differ dramatically in the death penalty context. The marginal benefits accruing to the state from obtaining the death penalty rather than life imprisonment are considerably less than the marginal difference to the defendant between death and life in prison. Such a disparity is an additional reason for tolerating scant arbitrariness in capital sentencing. * * *

The Court also maintains that accepting McCleskey's claim would pose a threat to all sentencing because of the prospect that a correlation might be demonstrated between sentencing outcomes and other personal characteristics. Again, such a view is indifferent to the considerations that enter into a determination whether punishment is "cruel and unusual." Race is a consideration whose influence is expressly constitutionally proscribed. We have expressed a moral commitment, as embodied in our fundamental law, that this specific characteristic should not be the basis for allotting burdens and benefits. Three constitutional amendments, and numerous statutes, have been prompted specifically by the desire to address the effects of racism. "Over the years, this Court has consistently repudiated 'distinctions between citizens solely because of their ancestry' as being 'odious to a free people whose institutions are founded upon the doctrine of equality.' " Furthermore, we have explicitly acknowledged the illegitimacy of race as a consideration in capital sentencing. That a decision to impose the death penalty could be influenced by *race* is thus a particularly repugnant prospect, and evidence that race may play even a modest role in levying a death sentence should be enough to characterize that sentence as "cruel and unusual." * * *

It is tempting to pretend that minorities on death row share a fate in no way connected to our own, that our treatment of them sounds no echoes beyond the chambers in which they die. Such an illusion is ultimately corrosive, for the reverberations of injustice are not so easily confined. "The destinies of the two races in this country are indissolubly linked together," and the way in which we choose those who will die reveals the depth of moral commitment among the living. * * *

[JUSTICE BLACKMUN's dissenting opinion has been omitted.]

NOTE

In light of recent research on implicit bias, *see* Kang et al., *supra*, does it make sense to require explicit proof of discriminatory intent? In 2009, North Carolina Governor Beverly Perdue signed the Racial Justice Act into law. 'The Racial Justice Act's opening provision declared that "[n]o person shall be subject to or given a sentence of death or shall be executed pursuant to any judgment that was sought or obtained on the basis of race." N.C. GEN. STAT. § 15A–2010. Importantly, it provided that "[i]f the court finds that race was a significant factor in decisions to seek or impose the sentence of death . . . the death sentence imposed by the judgment shall be vacated." *Id.* In contrast to *McCleskey v. Kemp*, North Carolina's Racial Justice Act allowed courts to consider statistical evidence identifying bias in and across cases as proof of racial discrimination. Barbara O'Brien & Catherine M. Grosso, *Beyond Batson's Scrutiny: A Preliminary Look at Racial Disparities in Prosecutorial Peremptory Strikes Following the Passage of the North Carolina Racial Justice Act*, 46 U.C. DAVIS L. REV. 1623, 1626 (2013).

In April 2010, two days before the 25th anniversary of *McCleskey v. Kemp*, a judge issued the first decision under the Racial Justice Act, commuting the death sentence of Marcus Reymond Robinson to life without parole. Campbell Robinson, "*Bias Law Used to Move a Man Off Death Row*," N.Y. TIMES, Apr. 20, 2012, *available at* http://www.nytimes.com/2012/04/21/us/north-carolina-law-used-to-set-aside-a-death-sentence.html. Robinson had been sentenced to death for kidnapping a 17-year-old boy, shooting him to death, and stealing his car and $27 from his wallet. Based on a statistical study of racial disparities during jury selection, Judge Gregory A. Weeks of Cumberland County Superior Court found that "race was a materially, practically and statistically significant factor" in the jury selection process—not only in Mr. Robinson's trial, but in trials across the county and the state. His 167-page ruling concluded, in fact, that there was intentional discrimination "at every level."

On June 19, 2013, Republican governor Pat McCrory signed legislation repealing the act. "Nearly every person on death row, regardless of race, has appealed their death sentence under the Racial Justice Act," McCrory told the press. "The state's district attorneys are nearly unanimous in their bipartisan conclusion that the Racial Justice Act created a judicial loophole to avoid the death penalty and not a path to justice." Matt Smith, "*Racial Justice Act Repealed in North Carolina*," CNN, June 20, 2013, *available at* http://www.cnn.com/2013/06/20/justice/north-carolina-death-penalty (last visited December 1, 2013). At the time the CNN report was published, even though African-Americans made up approximately 22 percent of the state's population, they constituted "53% of the 153 convicts awaiting execution in North Carolina." *Id.*

CHAPTER 3

THE ACTUS REUS REQUIREMENT

■ ■ ■

INTRODUCTION

Most crimes in the United States consist of four basic elements: (1) a voluntary act (or omission when there is a legal duty to act) that results in some kind of social harm (in legalese, an "actus reus"); (2) a prohibited mental state (in legalese, a "mens rea," or guilty mind); (3) a chain of causation that links the defendant's actions with the social harm; and (4) concurrence between the mens rea and the actus reus. This chapter examines the actus reus requirement.

The actus reus requirement can be thought of as an umbrella term that ties together several loosely related doctrines or concepts. First, there is the notion that in the United States, a person should not be convicted solely on the basis of her thoughts, but also must have done something that caused some sort of social harm. Second, the defendant's act must have been voluntary. Third is the general rule that there can be no criminal liability for an omission unless the person who failed to act had a legal duty to act. Finally, there is the notion that "status crimes" are unconstitutional: people should only be criminally punished for their conduct, not simply for being a certain kind of person.

A. THE PROSCRIPTION AGAINST THOUGHT CRIMES

One of the basic principles of criminal law is that the state cannot punish a person merely because he has bad thoughts. The criminal law generally requires an act in addition to a culpable mind-set before an individual can be held criminally liable.

The next two excerpts explore the limits of this principle. Can or should an individual be punished for writing about evil deeds in his private journal? Can or should one be punished more severely if he commits a violent crime against an individual because of his race, religion, national origin, gender, or sexual orientation? Is there a principled reason for drawing a distinction between these two types of cases?

JAILED "ON THE PRECIPICE" OF CRIME

Sandy Theis
Newhouse News Service, August 8, 2003[a]

Instead of acting on his fantasies, Brian Dalton confronted his demons by writing a journal filled with fictional tales of child molestation and torture.

For this thought crime, Dalton became the first person in America imprisoned for fictitious writings. His case is being watched closely by constitutional scholars who argue that personal diaries are protected by the First Amendment, and by anti-pornography crusaders who counter that Dalton is a threat to society.

There is little dispute that Dalton is a troubled man. His writings were so graphic that grand jurors asked police to stop reading them after just two pages, and a psychologist hired by the prosecution said they were among the most disturbing things he'd encountered in his 21-year practice. Dalton's stories center on three children, ages 10 and 11, who are caged in a basement, molested and sexually tortured. Yet court records show no evidence that he acted on these dark fantasies.

Still, Dalton pleaded guilty in July 2001 to pandering obscenity involving a minor,[b] a crime that falls under Ohio's broadly written pornography law.

"I remember testifying against the language when I was the ACLU director," said Benson Wolman, one of Dalton's lawyers and a former director of the American Civil Liberties Union of Ohio. "It says no person shall 'create, reproduce or publish' these materials, and I remember giving testimony to the effect of: 'wait a minute. This means that if somebody writes something down in a diary they can be prosecuted for it.' And I was assured that 'no, no our prosecutors wouldn't do anything like that.' "

Not only did Franklin County (Columbus) prosecutors go after Dalton, but his initial lawyer, Isabella Dixon-Thomas (now a candidate for Columbus city attorney) never raised the obvious First Amendment or privacy issues posed by the case. She later asked to withdraw Dalton's guilty plea so she could raise them, but the trial judge refused her request.

Dalton is serving a seven-year prison sentence.

---

[a] Reprinted courtesy of Newhouse News Service.

[b] The Ohio statute criminalizing "pandering obscenity involving a minor" defines the crime as creating, reproducing, publishing, advertising, selling, delivering, displaying, buying, procuring, possessing, etc. any obscene material that has a minor as one of its participants or portrayed observers. Ohio Rev. Code Ann. § 2907.321 (West 2009).

The ACLU eventually intervened. On July 17, an appeals court dismissed the guilty plea, said Dalton was denied his constitutional right to an effective lawyer, and sent the case back for a new trial.[c]

Franklin County Prosecutor Ron O'Brien said he would ask the Ohio Supreme Court to hear the case.

The case is noteworthy for the issues it raises, as well as the players involved.

Along with top-tier ACLU lawyers from the left, Dalton's legal team includes Jeff Sutton, President George W. Bush's newest appointee to the 6th U.S. Circuit Court of Appeals and a lawyer the left has loved to hate. According to Wolman, "Sutton called up and volunteered; he was astounded by what happened in the trial court."

The appeals court appeared to share his astonishment.

The scholarly but blunt opinion details mistakes made by the trial judge and by Dixon-Thomas, saying she erroneously concluded that some of Dalton's writings were based on the molestation of his cousin rather than a fictional character. This misunderstanding was significant, the appeals court said, because it affected her legal advice to Dalton. As the appeals court noted, "The private possession of obscene material is constitutionally protected. . . . However, the private possession of child pornography may be constitutionally prohibited."

Prosecutors are trying to keep Dalton locked up, arguing his wicked writings are part of a pattern that proves he is a threat to society. They contend that he had "admitted to prior sex offenses," although he was never charged, and say some of this writings show that he "is on the precipice of offending against another real child."

Prosecutors also note what is perhaps the case's greatest irony: Dalton's past psychological treatment required him "to keep a 'deviant sexual fantasy' journal." The writings helped to monitor his fantasies and teach Dalton how to avoid "triggers" that would spark his deviant behavior.

In other words, Dalton's writings were therapeutic not pornographic.

NOTE

The idea that "thought crimes" are prohibited under American law suggests that the defendant must have committed some kind of action in addition to having thoughts in order to be prosecuted. Drawing a bright line between thought and action, however, is not easy. Reality looks more like a

[c] In March 2004, Franklin County Common Pleas Judge David Cain dismissed the child pornography charge against Dalton, ruling that the statute under which he was charged only applies to acts involving real children and noting that it was clear that Dalton stories were never intended to be distributed. *See Porn Charge Tossed in Journal Case*, CHI. TRIB., March 5, 2004, at 20.

continuum of intertwined thought and action from the first fleeting idea related to a criminal act to the completed crime. At what point along that continuum is it appropriate for the police to step in? The criminal law tries to answer this question through its treatment of the so-called "inchoate" crimes which endeavor to criminalize conduct leading up to the completed social harm, so that the police may apprehend a person before the social harm occurs.[a]

The next case, *Wisconsin v. Mitchell*, examines the controversial subject of hate crimes law. In response to crimes of violence with racist or bigoted overtones, legislatures at both the state and federal levels have passed a variety of penal laws specifically addressing hate crimes. *See* FREDERICK M. LAWRENCE, PUNISHING HATE: BIAS CRIMES UNDER AMERICAN LAW (Harv. Univ. Press 1999) (Appendix A). Critics of hate crimes laws have argued that increasing the penalty for a crime because the defendant was motivated by racial or other bias amounts to criminalizing bad thoughts in violation of the First Amendment. Zachary Wolfe describes the difference between laws punishing hate crimes and laws punishing hate speech:

> Generally, prosecution under a hate crime statute requires that the individual committed some predicate offense set out in the statute with the animus specified in a hate crime statute, with the statute operating to enhance the punishment imposed for the predicate offense. Those statutes that do not depend on the commission of a predicate offense, and simply punish the utterance of racist or bigoted speech, or the commission of bigoted acts that are substantially equivalent to speech, are hate speech laws. * * *

ZACHARY J. WOLFE, HATE CRIMES LAW § 11:1 (West 2012).

WISCONSIN V. MITCHELL

Supreme Court of the United States
508 U.S. 476, 113 S.Ct. 2194, 124 L.Ed.2d 436 (1993)

REHNQUIST, CHIEF JUSTICE.

Respondent Todd Mitchell's sentence for aggravated battery was enhanced because he intentionally selected his victim on account of the victim's race. The question presented in this case is whether this penalty enhancement is prohibited by the First and Fourteenth Amendments. We hold that it is not.

On the evening of October 7, 1989, a group of young black men and boys, including Mitchell, gathered at an apartment complex in Kenosha, Wisconsin. Several members of the group discussed a scene from the motion picture "Mississippi Burning," in which a white man beat a young black boy who was praying. The group moved outside and Mitchell asked them: " 'Do you all feel hyped up to move on some white people?' " Shortly

---

[a] The inchoate crimes are discussed in Chapters 11 and 13.

thereafter, a young white boy approached the group on the opposite side of the street where they were standing. As the boy walked by, Mitchell said: " 'You all want to fuck somebody up? There goes a white boy; go get him.' " Mitchell counted to three and pointed in the boy's direction. The group ran toward the boy, beat him severely, and stole his tennis shoes. The boy was rendered unconscious and remained in a coma for four days.

After a jury trial in the Circuit Court for Kenosha County, Mitchell was convicted of aggravated battery. That offense ordinarily carries a maximum sentence of two years' imprisonment. But because the jury found that Mitchell had intentionally selected his victim because of the boy's race, the maximum sentence for Mitchell's offense was increased to seven years under § 939.645. That provision enhances the maximum penalty for an offense whenever the defendant "[i]ntentionally selects the person against whom the crime . . . is committed . . . because of the race, religion, color, disability, sexual orientation, national origin or ancestry of that person . . . ." The Circuit Court sentenced Mitchell to four years' imprisonment for the aggravated battery.

Mitchell unsuccessfully sought postconviction relief in the Circuit Court. Then he appealed his conviction and sentence, challenging the constitutionality of Wisconsin's penalty-enhancement provision on First Amendment grounds. The Wisconsin Court of Appeals rejected Mitchell's challenge, but the Wisconsin Supreme Court reversed. The Supreme Court held that the statute "violates the First Amendment directly by punishing what the legislature has deemed to be offensive thought." It rejected the State's contention "that the statute punishes only the 'conduct' of intentional selection of a victim." According to the court, "[t]he statute punishes the 'because of' aspect of the defendant's selection, the *reason* the defendant selected the victim, the *motive* behind the selection." And under *R.A.V. v. St. Paul*, "the Wisconsin legislature cannot criminalize bigoted thought with which it disagrees."

We granted certiorari because of the importance of the question presented and the existence of a conflict of authority among state high courts on the constitutionality of statutes similar to Wisconsin's penalty-enhancement provision. We reverse. * * *

The State argues that the statute does not punish bigoted thought, as the Supreme Court of Wisconsin said, but instead punishes only conduct. While this argument is literally correct, it does not dispose of Mitchell's First Amendment challenge. To be sure, our cases reject the "view that an apparently limitless variety of conduct can be labeled 'speech' whenever the person engaging in the conduct intends thereby to express an idea." Thus, a physical assault is not by any stretch of the imagination expressive conduct protected by the First Amendment.

But the fact remains that under the Wisconsin statute the same criminal conduct may be more heavily punished if the victim is selected because of his race or other protected status than if no such motive obtained. Thus, although the statute punishes criminal conduct, it enhances the maximum penalty for conduct motivated by a discriminatory point of view more severely than the same conduct engaged in for some other reason or for no reason at all. Because the only reason for the enhancement is the defendant's discriminatory motive for selecting his victim, Mitchell argues (and the Wisconsin Supreme Court held) that the statute violates the First Amendment by punishing offenders' bigoted beliefs.

Traditionally, sentencing judges have considered a wide variety of factors in addition to evidence bearing on guilt in determining what sentence to impose on a convicted defendant. The defendant's motive for committing the offense is one important factor. Thus, in many States the commission of a murder, or other capital offense, for pecuniary gain is a separate aggravating circumstance under the capital sentencing statute.

But it is equally true that a defendant's abstract beliefs, however obnoxious to most people, may not be taken into consideration by a sentencing judge. In *Dawson*, the State introduced evidence at a capital sentencing hearing that the defendant was a member of a white supremacist prison gang. Because "the evidence proved nothing more than [the defendant's] abstract beliefs," we held that its admission violated the defendant's First Amendment rights. In so holding, however, we emphasized that "the Constitution does not erect a *per se* barrier to the admission of evidence concerning one's beliefs and associations at sentencing simply because those beliefs and associations are protected by the First Amendment." Thus, in *Barclay v. Florida*, we allowed the sentencing judge to take into account the defendant's racial animus towards his victim. The evidence in that case showed that the defendant's membership in the Black Liberation Army and desire to provoke a "race war" were related to the murder of a white man for which he was convicted. Because "the elements of racial hatred in [the] murder" were relevant to several aggravating factors, we held that the trial judge permissibly took this evidence into account in sentencing the defendant to death.

Mitchell suggests that *Dawson* and *Barclay* are inapposite because they did not involve application of a penalty-enhancement provision. But in *Barclay* we held that it was permissible for the sentencing court to consider the defendant's racial animus in determining whether he should be sentenced to death, surely the most severe "enhancement" of all. And the fact that the Wisconsin Legislature has decided, as a general matter, that bias-motivated offenses warrant greater maximum penalties across the board does not alter the result here. For the primary responsibility for fixing criminal penalties lies with the legislature. * * *

Moreover, the Wisconsin statute singles out for enhancement bias-inspired conduct because this conduct is thought to inflict greater individual and societal harm. For example, according to the State and its *amici,* bias-motivated crimes are more likely to provoke retaliatory crimes, inflict distinct emotional harms on their victims, and incite community unrest. The State's desire to redress these perceived harms provides an adequate explanation for its penalty-enhancement provision over and above mere disagreement with offenders' beliefs or biases. * * *

For the foregoing reasons, we hold that Mitchell's First Amendment rights were not violated by the application of the Wisconsin penalty-enhancement provision in sentencing him. The judgment of the Supreme Court of Wisconsin is therefore reversed, and the case is remanded for further proceedings not inconsistent with this opinion.

It is so ordered.

B. THE VOLUNTARY ACT REQUIREMENT

In general, a person cannot be convicted of a crime unless he or she commits a voluntary (i.e. volitional) act that causes social harm. A volitional act is a movement of the body willed by the actor. Professor Joshua Dressler explains the difference between volitional and non-volitional acts:

> [Consider] the difference in meaning of the following two sentences: (1) "I raised my arm;" and (2) "My arm came up." Both statements suggest that a bodily movement has occurred. Yet, the difference in language expresses our understanding of the difference between a voluntary act (as described in the first sentence) and an involuntary one (the second sentence). In both cases, the arm movement was the result of impulses from the actor's brain. But, in the first sentence, the implication is that the act was the result of something more than mere physiological brain activity. That extra "something" was the more sophisticated thought process that goes into the "decision" to raise one's arm. . . . With a voluntary act, a human being—a person—and not simply an organ of a human being, causes the bodily action.
>
> Thus, when *D*'s arm strikes V as the result of an epileptic seizure, we sense that *D's* body, but not *D* the person, has caused the impact. The movement of *D*'s arm is similar to a tree branch bending in the wind and striking *V*. When *D* "wills" her arm to move, however, we feel that *D*, and not simply her body, is responsible for *V*'s injury. Her "acting self" is implicated. A

personal, human agency is involved in causing the bodily contact.[a]

Habitual acts are generally considered volitional even if "the actor is unaware of what she is doing as she is doing it." Dressler explains:

> One should be careful not to assume that an act is involuntary simply because the actor is unaware of what she is doing as she is doing it. For example, people act habitually: a chain-smoker may light up a cigarette "without thinking" a driver coming home from work may change lanes on the freeway at precisely the same place each day, without even noticing that she is doing this. Although, at our best, we are aware of both our external and internal (mental) surroundings, sometimes we "don't notice that [we] notice . . . [We are] aware of everything except [ourselves]." In this sense, consciousness is a matter of degree, and the law treats habitual acts as falling on the voluntary side of the continuum.[b]

Martin v. State involves a man who was forcibly removed from his home by police and then charged with being drunk in public. *State v. Decina*, involves the actions of a man who suffered an epileptic seizure at the wheel of his car with fatal consequences. The Court of Appeals of New York appears to deviate from the general rule that one cannot be held criminally liable for non-volitional acts, focusing most of its opinion on the recklessness of Mr. Decina's conduct which is really a question of mens rea. Thinking about this case from an actus reus perspective, are you persuaded that Mr. Decina's voluntary acts caused the social harm at issue in the case?

MARTIN V. STATE

Alabama Court of Appeals
31 Ala.App. 334, 17 So.2d 427 (1944)

SIMPSON, JUDGE.

Appellant was convicted of being drunk on a public highway, and appeals. Officers of the law arrested him at his home and took him onto the highway, where he allegedly committed the proscribed acts, viz., manifested a drunken condition by using loud and profane language.

The pertinent provisions of our statute are: "Any person who, while intoxicated or drunk, appears in any public place where one or more persons are present, * * * and manifests a drunken condition by boisterous or indecent conduct, or loud and profane discourse, shall, on conviction, be fined," etc.

---

[a] Joshua Dressler, UNDERSTANDING CRIMINAL LAW § 9.02[C][2] (6th ed. 2012).

[b] *Id.*

Under the plain terms of this statute, a voluntary appearance is presupposed. The rule has been declared, and we think it sound, that an accusation of drunkenness in a designated public place cannot be established by proof that the accused, while in an intoxicated condition, was involuntarily and forcibly carried to that place by the arresting officer.

Conviction of appellant was contrary to this announced principle and, in our view, erroneous. * * *

Reversed and rendered.

STATE V. DECINA

Court of Appeals of New York
2 N.Y.2d 133, 138 N.E.2d 799, 157 N.Y.S.2d 558 (1956)

FROESSEL, JUDGE.

At about 3:30 p.m. on March 14, 1955, a bright, sunny day, defendant was driving, alone in his car, in a northerly direction on Delaware Avenue in the city of Buffalo. The portion of Delaware Avenue here involved is 60 feet wide. At a point south of an overhead viaduct of the Erie Railroad, defendant's car swerved to the left, across the center line in the street, so that it was completely in the south lane, traveling 35 to 40 miles per hour.

It then veered sharply to the right, crossing Delaware Avenue and mounting the easterly curb at a point beneath the viaduct and continued thereafter at a speed estimated to have been about 50 or 60 miles per hour or more. During this latter swerve, a pedestrian testified that he saw defendant's hand above his head; another witness said he saw defendant's left arm bent over the wheel, and his right hand extended towards the right door.

A group of six schoolgirls were walking north on the easterly sidewalk of Delaware Avenue, two in front and four slightly in the rear, when defendant's car struck them from behind. One of the girls escaped injury by jumping against the wall of the viaduct. The bodies of the children struck were propelled northward onto the street and the lawn in front of a coal company, located to the north of the Erie viaduct on Delaware Avenue. Three of the children, 6 to 12 years old, were found dead on arrival by the medical examiner, and a fourth child, 7 years old, died in a hospital two days later as a result of injuries sustained in the accident.

After striking the children, defendant's car continued on the easterly sidewalk, and then swerved back onto Delaware Avenue once more. It continued in a northerly direction, passing under a second viaduct before it again veered to the right and remounted the easterly curb, striking and breaking a metal lamppost. With its horn blowing steadily—apparently because defendant was "stooped over" the steering wheel—the car proceeded on the sidewalk until it finally crashed through a 7 ¼-inch brick wall of a grocery store, injuring at least one customer and causing considerable property damage.

When the car came to a halt in the store, with its horn still blowing, several fires had been ignited. Defendant was stooped over in the car and was "bobbing a little." To one witness he appeared dazed, to another unconscious, lying back with his hands off the wheel. Various people present shouted to defendant to turn off the ignition of his car, and "within a matter of seconds the horn stopped blowing and the car did shut off."

Defendant was pulled out of the car by a number of bystanders and laid down on the sidewalk. To a policeman who came on the scene shortly he appeared "injured, dazed" another witness said that "he looked as though he was knocked out, and his arm seemed to be bleeding." An injured customer in the store, after receiving first aid, pressed defendant for an explanation of the accident and he told her: "I blacked out from the bridge."

When the police arrived, defendant attempted to rise, staggered and appeared dazed and unsteady. When informed that he was under arrest, and would have to accompany the police to the station house, he resisted and, when he tried to get away, was handcuffed. The foregoing evidence was adduced by the People, and is virtually undisputed—defendant did not take the stand nor did he produce any witnesses.

From the police station defendant was taken to the E. J. Meyer Memorial Hospital, a county institution, arriving at 5:30 p.m. * * *

On the evening of that day, after an interne [sic] had visited and treated defendant and given orders for therapy, Dr. Wechter, a resident physician in the hospital and a member of its staff, came to his room. * * *

He asked defendant how he felt and what had happened. Defendant, who still felt a little dizzy or blurry, said that as he was driving he noticed a jerking of his right hand, which warned him that he might develop a convulsion, and that as he tried to steer the car over to the curb he felt himself becoming unconscious, and he thought he had a convulsion. He was aware that children were in front of his car, but did not know whether he had struck them.

Defendant then proceeded to relate to Dr. Wechter his past medical history, namely, that at the age of 7 he was struck by an auto and suffered a marked loss of hearing. In 1946 he was treated in this same hospital for an illness during which he had some convulsions. Several burr holes were made in his skull and a brain abscess was drained. Following this operation defendant had no convulsions from 1946 through 1950. In 1950 he had four convulsions, caused by scar tissue on the brain.

From 1950 to 1954 he experienced about 10 or 20 seizures a year, in which his right hand would jump although he remained fully conscious. In 1954, he had 4 or 5 generalized seizures with loss of consciousness, the last being in September, 1954, a few months before the accident. Thereafter he had more hospitalization, a spinal tap, consultation with a neurologist, and took medication daily to help prevent seizures.

On the basis of this medical history, Dr. Wechter made a diagnosis of Jacksonian epilepsy, and was of the opinion that defendant had a seizure at the time of the accident. Other members of the hospital staff performed blood tests and took an electroencephalogram during defendant's three-day stay there. The testimony of Dr. Wechter is the only testimony before the trial court showing that defendant had epilepsy, suffered an attack at the time of the accident, and had knowledge of his susceptibility to such attacks.

Defendant was indicted and charged with violating section 1053–a of the Penal Law. Following his conviction, after a demurrer[a] to the indictment was overruled, the Appellate Division, while holding that the demurrer was properly overruled, reversed on the law, the facts having been "examined" and found "sufficient." * * *

We turn first to the subject of defendant's cross appeal, namely, that his demurrer should have been sustained, since the *indictment* here does not charge a crime. The indictment states essentially that defendant, *knowing* "that he was subject to epileptic attacks or other disorder rendering him likely to lose consciousness for a considerable period of time," was culpably negligent "in that he *consciously* undertook to and *did operate* his Buick sedan on a public highway" (emphasis supplied) and "while so doing" suffered such an attack which caused said automobile "to travel at a fast and reckless rate of speed, jumping the curb and driving over the sidewalk" causing the death of 4 persons. In our opinion, this clearly states a violation of section 1053–a of the Penal Law.[b] The statute does not require that a defendant must deliberately intend to kill a human being, for that would be murder. Nor does the statute require that he knowingly and consciously follow the precise path that leads to death and destruction. It is sufficient, we have said, when his conduct manifests a "disregard of the consequences which may ensue from the act, and indifference to the rights of others. No clearer definition, applicable to the hundreds of varying circumstances that may arise, can be given. Under a

[a] A demurrer is a pleading filed by the defendant, which admits the matters of fact alleged in the complaint, but alleges that they are insufficient as a matter of law to state a cause of action.

[b] Section 1053–a, Criminal negligence in operation of vehicle resulting in death, provided that "A person who operates or drives any vehicle of any kind in a reckless or culpably negligent manner, whereby a human being is killed, is guilty of criminal negligence in the operation of a vehicle resulting in death." New York courts had previously held that the terms "criminal negligence" and "culpably negligent" represented a state of mind closer to recklessness than ordinary negligence.

given state of facts, whether negligence is culpable is a question of judgment."

Assuming the truth of the indictment, as we must on a demurrer, this defendant knew he was subject to epileptic attacks and seizures that might strike at any time. He also knew that a moving motor vehicle uncontrolled on a public highway is a highly dangerous instrumentality capable of unrestrained destruction. With this *knowledge*, and without anyone accompanying him, he deliberately took a chance by making a conscious choice of a course of action, in disregard of the consequences which he knew might follow from his conscious act, and which in this case did ensue. How can we say as a matter of law that this did not amount to culpable negligence within the meaning of section 1053–a?

To hold otherwise would be to say that a man may freely indulge himself in liquor in the same hope that it will not affect his driving, and if it later develops that ensuing intoxication causes dangerous and reckless driving resulting in death, his unconsciousness or involuntariness at that time would relieve him from prosecution under the statute. His awareness of a condition which he knows may produce such consequences as here, and his disregard of the consequences, renders him liable for culpable negligence, as the courts below have properly held. To have a sudden sleeping spell, an unexpected heart or other disabling attack, without any prior knowledge or warning thereof, is an altogether different situation, and there is simply no basis for comparing such cases with the flagrant disregard manifested here. * * *

Accordingly, the Appellate Division properly sustained the lower court's order overruling the demurrer.

JUDGE DESMOND, concurring in part and dissenting in part.

I agree that the judgment of conviction cannot stand[c] but I think the indictment should be dismissed because it alleges no crime. Defendant's demurrer should have been sustained.

The indictment charges that defendant knowing that "he was subject to epileptic attacks or other disorder rendering him likely to lose consciousness" suffered "an attack and loss of consciousness which caused the said automobile operated by the said defendant to travel at a fast and reckless rate of speed" and to jump a curb and run onto the sidewalk "thereby striking and causing the death" of 4 children. Horrible as this occurrence was and whatever necessity it may show for new licensing and driving laws, nevertheless this indictment charges no crime known to the New York statutes. Our duty is to dismiss it.

---

[c] In a part of the opinion not reproduced here, the court found that the defendant's communications with the doctor should not have been admitted into evidence and that the judgment of conviction was properly reversed.

Section 1053–a of the Penal Law describes the crime of "criminal negligence in the operation of a vehicle resulting in death." Declared to be guilty of that crime is "A person who operates or drives any vehicle of any kind in a reckless or culpably negligent manner, whereby a human being is killed." The essentials of the crime are, therefore, first, vehicle operation in a culpably negligent *manner*, and, second, the resulting death of a person. This indictment asserts that defendant violated section 1053–a, but it then proceeds in the language quoted in the next-above paragraph of this opinion to describe the way in which defendant is supposed to have offended against that statute. That descriptive matter shows that defendant did *not* violate section 1053–a. No *operation* of an automobile in a reckless manner is charged against defendant. The excessive speed of the car and its jumping the curb were "caused," says the indictment itself, by defendant's prior "attack and loss of consciousness." Therefore, what defendant is accused of is *not* reckless or culpably negligent driving, which necessarily connotes and involves consciousness and volition. The fatal assault by this car was after and because of defendant's failure of consciousness. To say that one drove a car in a reckless manner in that his unconscious condition caused the car to travel recklessly is to make two mutually contradictory assertions. One cannot be "reckless" while unconscious. One cannot while unconscious "operate" a car in a culpably negligent manner or in any other "manner." The statute makes criminal a particular kind of knowing, voluntary, immediate operation. It does not touch at all the involuntary presence of an unconscious person at the wheel of an uncontrolled vehicle. To negative the possibility of applying section 1053–a to these alleged facts we do not even have to resort to the rule that all criminal statutes are closely and strictly construed in favor of the citizen and that no act or omission is criminal unless specifically and in terms so labeled by a clearly worded statute. * * *

Numerous are the diseases and other conditions of a human being which make it possible or even likely that the afflicted person will lose control of his automobile. Epilepsy, coronary involvements, circulatory diseases, nephritis, uremic poisoning, diabetes, Meniere's syndrome, a tendency to fits of sneezing, locking of the knee, muscular contractions—any of these common conditions may cause loss of control of a vehicle for a period long enough to cause a fatal accident. An automobile traveling at only 30 miles an hour goes 44 feet in a second. Just what is the court holding here? No less than this: that a driver whose brief blackout lets his car run amuck and kill another has killed that other by reckless driving. But any such "recklessness" consists necessarily not of the erratic behavior of the automobile while its driver is unconscious, but of his driving at all when he knew he was subject to such attacks. Thus, it must be that such a blackout-prone driver is guilty of reckless driving whenever and as soon as he steps into the driver's seat of a vehicle. Every time he drives, accident or no accident, he is subject to criminal prosecution for reckless driving or to revocation of his operator's license. * * *

When section 1053–a was new it was assailed as unconstitutional on the ground that the language "operates or drives any vehicle of any kind in a reckless or culpably negligent manner" was too indefinite since a driver could only guess as to what acts or omissions were meant. * * * [G]iving section 1053–a the new meaning assigned to it permits punishment of one who did not drive in any forbidden manner but should not have driven at all, according to the present theory. No motorist suffering from any serious malady or infirmity can with impunity drive any automobile at any time or place, since no one can know what physical conditions make it "reckless" or "culpably negligent" to drive an automobile. Such a construction of a criminal statute offends against due process and against justice and fairness. * * *

A whole new approach may be necessary to the problem of issuing or refusing drivers' licenses to epileptics and persons similarly afflicted. But the absence of adequate licensing controls cannot in law or in justice be supplied by criminal prosecutions of drivers who have violated neither the language nor the intendment of any criminal law.

Entirely without pertinence here is any consideration of driving while intoxicated or while sleepy, since those are conditions presently known to the driver, not mere future possibilities or probabilities.

The demurrer should be sustained and the indictment dismissed.

INTERPRETIVE CONSTRUCTION IN THE SUBSTANTIVE CRIMINAL LAW

Mark Kelman
33 Stan. L. Rev. 591 (1981)

Legal argument can be made only *after* a fact pattern is characterized by interpretive constructs. Once these constructs operate, a single legal result seems inevitable, a result seemingly deduced on general principle. These constructs appear both in conscious and unconscious forms in standard legal discourse. * * *

* * *

The voluntary act requirement. Unconscious shifting between broad and narrow time frames * * * arises in applying the criminal law's voluntary act requirement. In *Martin v. State*, police officers arrested the defendant at his home and took him onto a public highway, where the defendant used loud and profane language. He was convicted under a statute prohibiting public exhibition of a drunken condition. The appellate court reversed, holding that the defendant was involuntarily and forcibly carried to the public place by the arresting officers. The court concluded, uncontroversially, that an involuntary act cannot give rise to liability. But in *People v. Decina*, the court sustained the defendant's conviction for negligent homicide, though at the time his car struck the victims, he was unconscious as a result of an epileptic fit, not voluntarily operating the vehicle. The court held that the defendant was culpable because he had made a conscious decision to drive, knowing that an epileptic attack was possible.

The hidden interpretive time-framing construct becomes visible when one tries to square *Martin* with *Decina*. In *Decina*, the court opened up the time frame, declaring that if the defendant commits a voluntary act at time one which poses a risk of causing an involuntary harm later—drives the car knowing he is a blackout-prone epileptic—then the second act—crashing while unconscious—will be deemed voluntary. But the defendant in *Martin*, as well, may have done *something* voluntarily (before the police came) that posed a risk that he would get arrested and carried into public in his drunken state. While it is plausible that Martin was arrested on an old warrant and could not foresee that he would wind up in public on this occasion, it is quite possible that the defendant was arrested for activity he was engaging in at home: for instance, beating his wife. Why did the court not consider saying that the voluntary act at time one (wife beating) both posed a risk of and caused a harmful involuntary act at time two (public drunkenness) and assessing the voluntariness of the alleged criminal act with reference to the wider time-framed scenario? It cannot be that the involuntary, harmful act at time two was unforeseeable. The probability of an epileptic blackout is almost certainly far lower than the probability of ending up in public after engaging in behavior likely to draw police attention. * * *

EPILEPTIC CONVICTED OF ASSAULT CLEARED

Associated Press[a]
Los Angeles Daily Journal, Sept. 25, 1997, at 5[b]

ARLINGTON, Va.—A man with epilepsy who was convicted of assault for grabbing a woman's arm during a seizure has been cleared after convincing a judge that he wasn't in control of himself. Scott D. Vining was found guilty in July after he grabbed the woman on a commuter train in the Washington suburbs and refused to let go. A third passenger intervened. On Tuesday, when he had been scheduled to be sentenced, Arlington County Judge Griffin T. Garnett Jr. dismissed the verdict after seeing videotapes of Vining having seizures, including some in which he lunged at people. The tapes were shot over six days at George

[a] Reprinted with permission of The Associated Press.

[b] Copyright 2003 Daily Journal Corp. Reprinted with permission. The Daily Journal's definition of reprint and posting permission does not include the copying by third parties.

Washington University Hospital. Vining voluntarily stopped taking his medication to prove that his epilepsy could cause the behavior he exhibited on May 19. The prosecutor who had obtained Vining's conviction joined the defense in seeking the dismissal.

In finding Vining guilty, Garnett had discounted a letter from the man's doctor and testimony about his previous seizures. Vining, 35, had faced up to a year in jail and a $2,500 fine.

The woman Vining grabbed on the train, Lavita Haugabrook, was not in court Tuesday, but her mother and stepfather were and were distressed by the judge's decision. "I don't believe this," said Diane Johnson, shaking her head. "He hasn't said one time, 'I'm sorry.' " Outside the courtroom, however, Vining did just that. "I am deeply, deeply sorry about what your daughter experienced," he told Ms. Johnson. "I had no knowledge . . . If I had, I would have done everything humanly possible to explain what happened."

Alexandra K. Finucane, vice president of the Epilepsy Foundation of America, said the case "demonstrates the crying need for educating not only the general public about epilepsy but also the police, prosecutors and even the judiciary."

C. LIABILITY FOR OMISSIONS

Despite the general rule that a voluntary act that causes the social harm is necessary to satisfy the actus reus requirement, criminal liability can be based upon an omission if the defendant had a legal duty to act and was physically capable of acting. The omission which replaces the voluntary act must also cause the social harm, and the defendant must act with the requisite mens rea in order to be convicted of the offense.

The courts have recognized five situations in which individuals have a legal duty to act:

(1) when there is a *special relationship* between the defendant and the victim, such as the relationship between husbands and wives, parents and children, and masters and servants;

(2) when the defendant enters into a *contract* which requires him either explicitly or implicitly to act in a particular way (e.g., a contractual duty to provide care to an elderly individual);

(3) when there is a *statutory duty* to act (such as the duty to pay federal taxes found in the Internal Revenue Code);

(4) when the defendant *creates the risk* of harm to the victim; and

(5) when the defendant, who otherwise would not have a duty to act, *voluntarily assumes care* of a person in need of help.

In order to be held criminally liable for an omission, the defendant must have been physically capable of acting. For example, if the defendant is a mother whose child falls into a swimming pool, the mother ordinarily would have a duty to rescue her child (or at least attempt such a rescue) because of the special relationship recognized by courts between parents and their children. If the mother just stands there and watches her child drown, not jumping into the swimming pool to attempt a rescue, she could be charged with negligent homicide as long as she had the requisite mental state required for commission of that crime. Given the "physically capable of acting" requirement, however, if the mother did not know how to swim or could not swim because of some physical limitation, then she could not be held criminally liable for her failure to jump into the pool. She might, however, be held criminally liable for failing to throw her child a life preserver if a life preserver was available and she was physically capable of throwing it to her child.

Additionally, the defendant must have known of the facts giving rise to the need for action. For example, if a mother is swimming in a lake and does not know that her daughter is drowning five feet away from her, the mother cannot be held liable for her failure to rescue her daughter.

The first three cases in this section discuss some of the ways a person can be held criminally liable for a failure to act. The remaining materials examine the general American rule that there is no legal duty to rescue a total stranger. In particular, these materials explore the question whether it is wise to adopt Good Samaritan statutes that attempt to reverse the general American rule by imposing a statutory duty to rescue or at least call for help when one knows that another individual is in need of assistance.

1. ESTABLISHING THE LEGAL DUTY TO ACT

PEOPLE V. BEARDSLEY

Supreme Court of Michigan
150 Mich. 206, 113 N.W. 1128 (1907)

MCALVAY, J.C.

Respondent was convicted of manslaughter before the circuit court for Oakland county, and was sentenced to the State prison at Jackson for a minimum term of one year and a maximum term not to exceed five years. He was a married man living at Pontiac, and at the time the facts herein narrated occurred, he was working as a bartender and clerk at the Columbia Hotel. He lived with his wife in Pontiac, occupying two rooms on the ground floor of a house. Other rooms were rented to tenants, as was also one living room in the basement. His wife being temporarily absent from the city, respondent arranged with a woman named Blanche Burns, who at the time was working at another hotel, to go to his apartments with him. He had been acquainted with her for some time. They knew each other's habits and character. They had drunk liquor together, and had on two occasions been in Detroit and spent the night together in houses of assignation. On the evening of Saturday, March 18, 1905, he met her at the place where she worked, and they went together to his place of residence. They at once began to drink and continued to drink steadily, and remained together, day and night, from that time until the afternoon of the Monday following, except when respondent went to his work on Sunday afternoon. There was liquor at these rooms, and when it was all used they were served with bottles of whiskey and beer by a young man who worked at the Columbia Hotel, and who also attended respondent's fires at the house. He was the only person who saw them in the house during the time they were there together. Respondent gave orders for liquor by telephone. On Monday afternoon, about one o'clock, the young man went to the house to see if anything was wanted. At this time he heard respondent say they must fix up the rooms, and the woman must not be found there by his wife, who was likely to return at any time. During this visit to the house the woman sent the young man to a drug store to purchase, with money she gave him, camphor and morphine tablets. He procured both articles. There were six grains of morphine in quarter-grain tablets. She concealed the morphine from respondent's notice, and was discovered putting something into her mouth by him and the young man as they were returning from the other room after taking a drink of beer. She in fact was taking morphine. Respondent struck the box from her hand. Some of the tablets fell on the floor, and of these, respondent crushed several with his foot. She picked up and swallowed two of them, and the young man put two of them in the spittoon. Altogether it is probable she took from three to four grains of morphine. The young man went away soon after this. Respondent called him by telephone about an hour later, and after he came to the house requested him to take the woman into the room in the basement which was occupied by a Mr. Skoba. She was in a stupor and did not rouse when spoken to. Respondent was too intoxicated to be of any assistance and the young man proceeded to take her downstairs. While doing this Skoba arrived, and together they put her in his room on the bed. Respondent requested Skoba to look after her, and let her out the back way when she waked up. Between nine and ten o'clock in the evening Skoba became alarmed at her condition. He at once called the city marshal and a doctor. An examination by them disclosed that she was dead.

Many errors are assigned by respondent, who asks to have his conviction set aside. The principal assignments of error are based upon the charge of the court, and refusal to give certain requests to charge, and are upon the theory that under the undisputed evidence in the case, as claimed by the people and detailed by the people's witnesses, the respondent should have been acquitted and discharged. In the brief of the prosecutor his position is stated as follows:

> It is the theory of the prosecution that the facts and circumstances attending the death of Blanche Burns in the house of respondent were such as to lay upon him a duty to care for her, and the duty to take steps for her protection, the failure to take which, was sufficient to constitute such an omission as would render him legally responsible for her death. * * * There is no claim on the part of the people that the respondent was in any way an active agent in bringing about the death of Blanche Burns, but simply that he owed her a duty which he failed to perform, and that in consequence of such failure on his part she came to her death.

Upon this theory a conviction was asked and secured.

The law recognizes that under some circumstances the omission of a duty owed by one individual to another, where such omission results in the death of the one to whom the duty is owing, will make the other chargeable with manslaughter. This rule of law is always based upon the proposition that the duty neglected must be a legal duty, and not a mere moral obligation. It must be a duty imposed by law or by contract, and the omission to perform the duty must be the immediate and direct cause of death.

Although the literature upon the subject is quite meagre and the cases few, nevertheless, the authorities are in harmony as to the relationship which must exist between the parties to create the duty, the omission of which establishes legal responsibility. One authority has briefly and correctly stated the rule, which the prosecution claims should be applied to the case at bar, as follows:

> If a person who sustains to another the legal relation of protector, as husband to wife, parent to child, master to seaman, etc., knowing such person to be in peril of life, willfully or negligently fails to make such reasonable and proper efforts to rescue him as he might have done without jeopardizing his own life or the lives of others, he is guilty of manslaughter at least, if by reason of his omission of duty the dependent person dies.
>
> So one who from domestic relationship, public duty, voluntary choice, or otherwise, has the custody and care of a human being, helpless either from imprisonment, infancy, sickness, age, imbecility, or other incapacity of mind or body, is bound to execute the charge with proper diligence and will be held guilty of manslaughter, if by culpable negligence he lets the helpless creature die.

The following brief digest of cases gives the result of our examination of American and English authorities, where the doctrine of criminal liability was involved when death resulted from an omission to perform a claimed duty. We discuss no cases where statutory provisions are involved. In *Territory v. Manton,* a husband was convicted of manslaughter for leaving his intoxicated wife one winter's night lying in the snow, from which exposure she died. The conviction was sustained on the ground that a legal duty rested upon him to care for and protect his wife, and that his neglect to perform that duty, resulting in her death, he was properly convicted.

State v. Smith is a similar case. A husband neglected to provide clothing and shelter for his insane wife. He left her in a bare room without fire during severe winter weather. Her death resulted. The charge in the indictment is predicated upon a known legal duty of the husband to furnish his wife with suitable protection.

In *State v. Behm,* the conviction of a mother of manslaughter for exposing her infant child without protection, was affirmed upon the same ground.

State v. Noakes was a prosecution and conviction of a husband and wife for manslaughter. A child of a maid servant was born under their roof. They were charged with neglecting to furnish it with proper care. In addition to announcing the principle in support of which the case is already cited, the court said:

> To create a criminal liability for neglect by nonfeasance, the neglect must also be of a personal, legal duty, the natural and ordinary consequences of neglecting which would be dangerous to life.

In reversing the case for error in the charge—not necessary to here set forth—the court expressly stated that it did not concede that respondents were under a legal duty to care for this child because it was permitted to be born under their roof, and declined to pass upon that question. * * *

The case of *Regina v. Nicholls,* was a prosecution of a penniless old woman, a grandmother, for neglecting to supply an infant grandchild left in her charge with sufficient food and proper care. The case was tried at assizes in Stafford before Brett, J., who said to the jury:

> If a grown up person chooses to undertake the charge of a human creature, helpless either from infancy, simplicity, lunacy, or other infirmity, he is bound to execute that charge without (at all events) wicked negligence, and if a person who has chosen to take charge of a helpless creature lets it die by wicked negligence, that person is guilty of manslaughter.

* * * The charge of this nisi prius judge recognizes the principle that a person may voluntarily assume the care of a helpless human being, and having assumed it, will be held to be under an implied legal duty to care

for and protect such person. The duty assumed being that of caretaker and protector to the exclusion of all others.

Another English case decided in the appellate court, Lord Coleridge, C.J., delivering the opinion, is *Regina v. Instan*. An unmarried woman without means lived with and was maintained by her aged aunt. The aunt suddenly became very sick, and for ten days before her death was unable to attend to herself, to move about, or to do anything to procure assistance. Before her death no one but the prisoner had any knowledge of her condition. The prisoner continued to live in the house at the cost of the deceased and took in the food supplied by the tradespeople. The prisoner did not give food to the deceased, or give or procure any medical or nursing attendance for her; nor did she give notice to any neighbor of her condition or wants, although she had abundant opportunity and occasion to do so. In the opinion, Lord Coleridge, speaking for the court, said:

> It is not correct to say that every moral obligation is a legal duty; but every legal duty is founded upon a moral obligation. In this case, as in most cases, the legal duty can be nothing else than taking upon one's self the performance of the moral obligation. There is no question whatever that it was this woman's clear duty to impart to the deceased so much of that food, which was taken into the house for both and paid for by the deceased, as was necessary to sustain her life. The deceased could not get it for herself. She could only get it through the prisoner. It was the prisoner's clear duty at common law to supply it to the deceased, and that duty she did not perform. Nor is there any question that the prisoner's failure to discharge her legal duty, if it did not directly cause, at any rate accelerated, the death of the deceased. There is no case directly on the point; but it would be a slur and a stigma upon our law if there could be any doubt as to the law to be derived from the principle of decided cases, if cases were necessary. There was a clear moral obligation, and a legal duty founded upon it; a duty willfully disregarded and the death was at least accelerated, if not caused, by the nonperformance of the legal duty.

* * *

Seeking for a proper determination of the case at bar by the application of the legal principles involved, we must eliminate from the case all consideration of mere moral obligation, and discover whether respondent was under a legal duty towards Blanche Burns at the time of her death, knowing her to be in peril of her life, which required him to make all reasonable and proper effort to save her; the omission to perform which duty would make him responsible for her death. This is the important and determining question in this case. If we hold that such legal duty rested upon respondent it must arise by implication from the facts and circumstances already recited. The record in this case discloses that the deceased was a woman past 30 years of age. She had been twice married. She was accustomed to visiting saloons and to the use of intoxicants. She previously had made assignations with this man in Detroit at least twice. There is no evidence or claim from this record that any duress, fraud, or deceit had been practiced upon her. On the contrary it appears that she went upon this carouse with respondent voluntarily and so continued to remain with him. Her entire conduct indicates that she had ample experience in such affairs.

It is urged by the prosecutor that the respondent "stood towards this woman for the time being in the place of her natural guardian and protector, and as such owed her a clear legal duty which he completely failed to perform." The cases cited and digested establish that no such legal duty is created based upon a mere moral obligation. The fact that this woman was in his house created no such legal duty as exists in law and is due from a husband towards his wife, as seems to be intimated by the prosecutor's brief. Such an inference would be very repugnant to our moral sense. Respondent had assumed either in fact or by implication no care or control over his companion. Had this been a case where two men under like circumstances had voluntarily gone on a debauch together and one had attempted suicide, no one would claim that this doctrine of legal duty could be invoked to hold the other criminally responsible for omitting to make effort to rescue his companion. How can the fact that in this case one of the parties was a woman, change the principle of law applicable to it? Deriving and applying the law in this case from the principle of decided cases, we do not find that such legal duty as is contended for existed in fact or by implication on the part of respondent towards the deceased, the omission of which involved criminal liability. We find no more apt words to apply to this case than those used by Mr. Justice Field in *United States v. Knowles*:

> In the absence of such obligations, it is undoubtedly the moral duty of every person to extend to others assistance when in danger; * * * and if such efforts should be omitted by any one when they could be made without imperiling his own life, he would, by his conduct, draw upon himself the just censure and reproach of good men; but this is the only punishment to which he would be subjected by society.

Other questions discussed in the briefs need not be considered. The conviction is set aside, and respondent is ordered discharged.

COMMONWEALTH V. HOWARD

Superior Court of Pennsylvania
265 Pa.Super. 535, 402 A.2d 674 (1979)

HOFFMAN, JUDGE:

Appellant contends that the Commonwealth failed to prove her guilty of involuntary manslaughter beyond a reasonable doubt because the evidence was insufficient to prove that her actions were reckless or directly caused the death of her five year old daughter. We conclude that the evidence was sufficient to prove all the essential elements of the crime, and therefore, we affirm.

Appellant resided with her daughter and a boyfriend, Edward Watts. For a period of several weeks before the child's death, Watts regularly beat the child and subjected her to various forms of sadistic abuse. Appellant also struck the child on occasion, sometimes with a belt or strap. On the evening of March 5, 1977, during the course of a beating by Watts, the child fell and hit her head on a piece of furniture. When appellant could not awaken her child the next morning, Watts called the police and fabricated a story to explain the child's injuries, which included a bloodied nose and bruised forehead. The child was pronounced dead on arrival at a local hospital. The stated cause of death was multiple injuries to the head and trunk.[1]

Under Section 2504 of our Crimes Code, 18 Pa.C.S.A. § 2504, "A person is guilty of involuntary manslaughter when as a direct result of the doing of an unlawful act in a reckless or grossly negligent manner, or the doing of a lawful act in a reckless or grossly negligent manner, he causes the death of another person." Although there was evidence in the record that appellant struck her child on occasion, the lower court in this waiver trial premised appellant's culpability on her failure to protect her child from the more regular and severe beatings inflicted upon her by Watts. We affirm because we conclude that the evidence was sufficient to prove that appellant's failure to protect the child was a direct cause of her death, and that such failure was reckless or grossly negligent under the circumstances.

Preliminarily we note that an omission to act may create criminal culpability under our Crimes Code even though the law defining the offense, as here, requires an "act," where "a duty to perform the omitted

[1] A post-mortem examination of the child revealed 43 major categories of external wounds. Of these, some were recent, some were several days old, and others were more remote. The medical examiner also described numerous internal injuries to the child, including extensive contusions of the scalp, a bilateral subdural hemorrhage, internal bleeding and swelling in the brain, laceration of the lung tissues, and a remote fracture of the right sixth rib (since healed), which indicated the injury was at least several weeks old and probably older. The examiner stated that the internal injuries were the result of the same multiple blunt impacts on the child body which caused the various external injuries. Some of the child injuries also revealed various types of sadistic torture practiced upon her, which we will not detail here.

act is otherwise imposed by law." 18 Pa.C.S.A. § 301(b)(2). Here, appellant and the victim stood in the relation of parent and child. A parent has the legal duty to protect her child, and the discharge of this duty requires affirmative performance.

Next we must examine whether the child's death was "a direct result of" appellant's failure to protect her child from Watts' beatings and abuse. While the immediate cause of the child's death was multiple injuries to the head and trunk, inflicted on the child by Watts over a period of several weeks, appellant may still be held culpable for her continuing failure to protect the child during all that time. * * * [W]e hold that appellant's failure to protect her child from Watts' savagery was a direct cause of death sufficient to impose criminal culpability.

Lastly, we must consider whether appellant's failure to protect her child was, under these circumstances, reckless or grossly negligent. Section 302(b)(3) of the Crimes Code, 18 Pa.C.S.A. § 302(b)(3) states:

> A person acts recklessly with respect to a material element of an offense when he consciously disregards a substantial and unjustifiable risk that the material element exists or will result from his conduct. The risk must be of such a nature and degree that, considering the nature and intent of the actor's conduct and the circumstances known to him, its disregard involves a gross deviation from the standard of conduct that a reasonable person would observe in the actor's situation.

* * *

Here appellant witnessed and had full knowledge of a continuing pattern of severe beatings, abuse, and sadistic torture inflicted on her child by Watts over a period of at least several weeks. However, appellant did nothing to protect her child. She never evicted or even discouraged Watts. She never reported anything to the public authorities. Taken together with the evidence of different ages and severity of the child's injuries this is sufficient to show that appellant consciously disregarded a manifestly apparent risk to the health and safety of her young child and that this neglect was a gross deviation from the standard of conduct the reasonable parent would observe under the circumstances. It is this long period of knowing yet apathetic acquiescence in her child's undoubted agony which satisfies the culpability requirements of the involuntary manslaughter statute.

Judgment of sentence affirmed.

COMMONWEALTH V. PESTINIKAS

Superior Court of Pennsylvania
421 Pa.Super. 371, 617 A.2d 1339 (1992)

WIEAND, J.

The principal issue in this appeal is whether a person can be prosecuted criminally for murder when his or her failure to perform a contract to provide food and medical care for another has caused the death of such other person. The trial court answered this question in the affirmative and instructed the jury accordingly. The jury thereafter found Walter and Helen Pestinikas guilty of murder of the third degree in connection with the starvation and dehydration death of ninety-two (92) year old Joseph Kly. On direct appeal from the judgment of sentence, the defendants contend that the trial court misapplied the law and gave the jury incorrect instructions. They argue, therefore, that they are entitled to an arrest of judgment because of the insufficiency of the evidence against them or at least a new trial because of the trial court's erroneous instructions to the jury. * * *

Joseph Kly met Walter and Helen Pestinikas in the latter part of 1981 when Kly consulted them about prearranging his funeral. In March, 1982, Kly, who had been living with a stepson, was hospitalized and diagnosed as suffering from Zenker's diverticulum, a weakness in the walls of the esophagus, which caused him to have trouble swallowing food. In the hospital, Kly was given food which he was able to swallow and, as a result, regained some of the weight which he had lost. When he was about to be discharged, he expressed a desire not to return to his stepson's home and sent word to appellants that he wanted to speak with them. As a consequence, arrangements were made for appellants to care for Kly in their home on Main Street in Scranton, Lackawanna County.

Kly was discharged from the hospital on April 12, 1982. When appellants came for him on that day they were instructed by medical personnel regarding the care which was required for Kly and were given a prescription to have filled for him. Arrangements were also made for a visiting nurse to come to appellants' home to administer vitamin B-12 supplements to Kly. Appellants agreed orally to follow the medical instructions and to supply Kly with food, shelter, care and the medicine which he required.

According to the evidence, the prescription was never filled, and the visiting nurse was told by appellants that Kly did not want the vitamin supplement shots and that her services, therefore, were not required. Instead of giving Kly a room in their home, appellants removed him to a rural part of Lackawanna County, where they placed him in the enclosed porch of a building, which they owned, known as the Stage Coach Inn. This porch was approximately nine feet by thirty feet, with no insulation, no refrigeration, no bathroom, no sink and no telephone. The walls contained cracks which exposed the room to outside weather conditions. Kly's predicament was compounded by appellants' affirmative efforts to conceal his whereabouts. Thus, they gave misleading information in response to inquiries, telling members of Kly's family that they did not know where he had gone and others that he was living in their home.

After Kly was discharged from the hospital, appellants took Kly to the bank and had their names added to his savings account. Later, Kly's money was transferred into an account in the names of Kly or Helen Pestinikas, pursuant to which moneys could be withdrawn without Kly's signature. Bank records reveal that from May, 1982, to July, 1983, appellants withdrew amounts roughly consistent with the three hundred ($300) dollars per month which Kly had agreed to pay for his care. Beginning in August, 1983 and continuing until Kly's death in November, 1984, however, appellants withdrew much larger sums so that when Kly died, a balance of only fifty-five ($55) dollars remained. In the interim, appellants had withdrawn in excess of thirty thousand ($30,000) dollars.

On the afternoon of November 15, 1984, when police and an ambulance crew arrived in response to a call by appellants, Kly's dead body appeared emaciated, with his ribs and sternum greatly pronounced. Mrs. Pestinikas told police that she and her husband had taken care of Kly for three hundred ($300) dollars per month and that she had given him cookies and orange juice at 11:30 a.m. on the morning of his death. A subsequent autopsy, however, revealed that Kly had been dead at that time and may have been dead for as many as thirty-nine (39) hours before his body was found. The cause of death was determined to be starvation and dehydration. Expert testimony opined that Kly would have experienced pain and suffering over a long period of time before he died.

At trial, the Commonwealth contended that after contracting orally to provide food, shelter, care and necessary medicine for Kly, appellants engaged in a course of conduct calculated to deprive Kly of those things necessary to maintain life and thereby cause his death. The trial court instructed the jury that appellants could not be found guilty of a malicious killing for failing to provide food, shelter and necessary medicines to Kly unless a duty to do so had been imposed upon them by contract. The court instructed the jury, inter alia, as follows:

> In order for you to convict the defendants on any of the homicide charges or the criminal conspiracy or recklessly endangering charges, you must first find beyond a reasonable doubt that the defendants had a legal duty of care to Joseph Kly.
>
> There are but two situations in which Pennsylvania law imposes criminal liability for the failure to perform an act. One of these is where the express language of the law defining the offense provides for criminal [liability] based upon such a failure. The other is where the law otherwise imposes a duty to act.

> Unless you find beyond a reasonable doubt that an oral contract imposed a duty to act upon Walter and Helen Pestinikas, you must acquit the defendants.

Appellants contend that this was error.

The applicable law appears at 18 Pa.C.S. § 301(a) and (b) as follows:

> (a) General rule.—A person is not guilty of an offense unless his liability is based on conduct which includes a voluntary act or the omission to perform an act of which he is physically capable.
>
> (b) Omission as basis of liability.—Liability for the commission of an offense may not be based on an omission unaccompanied by action unless:
>
> (1) the omission is expressly made sufficient by the law defining the offense; or
>
> (2) a duty to perform the omitted act is otherwise imposed by law.

With respect to subsection (b), Toll, in his invaluable work on the Pennsylvania Crimes Code, has commented

> . . . [Subsection (b)] states the conventional position with respect to omissions unaccompanied by action as a basis of liability. Unless the omission is expressly made sufficient by the law defining the offense, a duty to perform the omitted act must have been otherwise imposed by law for the omission to have the same standing as a voluntary act for purposes of liability. It should, of course, suffice, as the courts now hold, that the duty arises under some branch of the civil law. If it does, this minimal requirement is satisfied, though whether the omission constitutes an offense depends as well on many other factors. * * *

In *Jones v. United States* the court stated:

> There are at least four situations in which the failure to act may constitute breach of a legal duty. One can be held criminally liable: first, where a statute imposes a duty to care for another; second, where one stands in a certain status relationship to another; third, where one has assumed a contractual duty to care for another; and fourth, where one has voluntarily assumed the care of another and so secluded the helpless person as to prevent others from rendering aid.

[T]he duty must be one which the party is bound to perform by law or by contract, and not one the performance of which depends simply upon his humanity, or his sense of justice or propriety. It has been said that a legal duty to assist another does not arise out of a mere moral duty. * * *

Consistently with this legal thinking we hold that when, in 18 Pa.C.S. § 301(b)(2), the statute provides that an omission to do an act can be the basis for criminal liability if a duty to perform the omitted act has been imposed by law, the legislature intended to distinguish between a legal duty to act and merely a moral duty to act. A duty to act imposed by contract is legally enforceable and, therefore, creates a legal duty. It follows that a failure to perform a duty imposed by contract may be the basis for a charge of criminal homicide if such failure causes the death of another person and all other elements of the offense are present. Because there was evidence in the instant case that Kly's death had been caused by appellants' failure to provide the food and medical care which they had agreed by oral contract to provide for him, their omission to act was sufficient to support a conviction for criminal homicide, and the trial court was correct when it instructed the jury accordingly.

Our holding is not that every breach of contract can become the basis for a finding of homicide resulting from an omission to act. A criminal act involves both a physical and mental aspect. An omission to act can satisfy the physical aspect of criminal conduct only if there is a duty to act imposed by law. A failure to provide food and medicine, in this case, could not have been made the basis for prosecuting a stranger who learned of Kly's condition and failed to act. Even where there is a duty imposed by contract, moreover, the omission to act will not support a prosecution for homicide in the absence of the necessary mens rea. For murder, there must be malice. Without a malicious intent, an omission to perform duties having their foundation in contract cannot support a conviction for murder. In the instant case, therefore, the jury was required to find that appellants, by virtue of contract, had undertaken responsibility for providing necessary care for Kly to the exclusion of the members of Kly's family. This would impose upon them a legal duty to act to preserve Kly's life. If they maliciously set upon a course of withholding food and medicine and thereby caused Kly's death, appellants could be found guilty of murder. * * *

Having found no valid reason for disturbing the jury's verdicts, we conclude that the judgments of sentence must be, as they are,

AFFIRMED.

[The dissenting opinion by J. DEL SOLE has been omitted.]

2. THE "NO DUTY TO RESCUE" RULE

THE RIGHT TO BE APATHETIC: IVERSON CASE RAISES QUESTIONS ABOUT GOOD SAMARITAN LAWS

Charles Ashby
Los Angeles Daily Journal, Sept. 2, 1998, at 1[a]

LAS VEGAS—Ignore thy neighbor. That is every American's right. That may seem morally reprehensible, but long-established legal precedent in the United States releases Americans from any duty to help one another. Unless the situation involves withholding evidence of a crime or helping to cover one up, it is not illegal, in most states, to witness a crime or accident and then fail to step in to prevent it or fail to report it to authorities.

Which is why charges will not be filed against 20-year-old David Cash, the Los Angeles man who seemingly could have stopped the brutal sexual assault and strangulation of a 7-year-old girl in a Nevada casino last year, a Clark County, Nev[ada], prosecutor said. Despite the growing outcry for charges against Cash, Ben Graham, chief deputy district attorney for the Clark County district attorney's office, said he will not be prosecuted. "Clark County has come under a lot of intense pressure because of this," Graham said. "But he really didn't violate any crime." There is not enough evidence to charge Cash with any crime, he said, whether it is obstruction of justice or accessory after the fact, since he neither gained anything from the crime nor actively tried to cover it up. To be guilty as an accessory, Graham explained, a person has to aid, abet or encourage someone to commit a crime.

Common-Law Line of Authority

"What you have is a long, long common-law line of authority that unless you're in a special class or in a special relationship, you really have no duty to act," Graham said. "Historically, mere presence, being there when a crime is committed, is not chargeable. Our laws are basically laws of 'do not.' We seldom require anyone to go do anything." He sees the moral question, on the other hand, as a simple one: Anyone should have done whatever he could to stop the murder of Sherrice Iverson, he said.

Iverson was killed during the wee hours of May 25, 1997, as she played in a casino in Primm, Nevada. As her father gambled, two Long Beach buddies, Cash and Jeremy Strohmeyer, 19, struck up a game of tag with the child. When she dashed into the women's bathroom, Strohmeyer followed her, then Cash. In the restroom—as he peered over the stall—Cash reportedly watched as Strohmeyer began to sexually assault the girl. He then left the restroom, telling no one what he saw, according to an interview in the Los Angeles Times.

While Cash expressed sympathy for Strohmeyer, he displayed a notable absence of feeling for the child—and no regret for not reporting the crime. "I'm not going to get upset over someone else's life," Cash reportedly said. "I just worry about myself first. I'm not going to lose sleep over somebody else's problems."

Strohmeyer has been charged with murder in the sexual assault and strangulation of the girl. If convicted at the trial, which began Monday, Strohmeyer could face a death sentence.[b] He is being represented by Los Angeles criminal defense attorney Leslie Abramson.

Clark County defense lawyer Tom Pitaro * * * sees a defense if Cash were to be charged with a crime. * * * "If you were defending him, you would say he didn't have a duty to do anything; therefore, he didn't cause any harm. He just didn't prevent any—and there's no [law] against that."

Whether there should be is a subject of mounting national interest. In recent years, the idea of requiring intervention gained ground in several states and with respect to certain types of people, for instance children. Teachers gained new legal responsibilities in recent years, requiring them to report suspected child-abuse cases, Pitaro said. Failure to do so can result in civil and, in some states, criminal penalties.

Nevada Assemblyman Richard Perkins, D-Clark County, has requested that a [G]ood Samaritan bill be drafted to make silence such as Cash's illegal. Currently only Minnesota, Wisconsin, Vermont, Rhode Island and Massachusetts have duty-to-rescue laws that apply to the general public. Other states have considered the idea, chiefly since Princess Diana's death in Paris last year, when paparazzi following the car were said to be taking pictures of the accident rather than helping those inside. France long has had a [Good] Samaritan law that requires people who witness accidents to assist in some way. * * *

Those states that make it criminal not to offer aid also safeguard the person offering the aid through general liability protections. And a person is not expected to render aid that would endanger oneself or cause a person to neglect a duty to others. Pitaro says any good defense lawyer would see those "protections" as loopholes in the law that would allow an easy acquittal.

The oldest "general duty to rescue" law in the United States is Wisconsin's, approved in 1983. As a result, there is little case law interpreting it. Wisconsin's law carries a misdemeanor punishment for failing to follow it. It was upheld by the Wisconsin Court of Appeals in 1994 in *State v. LaPlante*, 521 N.W.2d 448. In that case, the court said to gain a conviction, the prosecution must prove that the accused believed a

[b] After this article was published, Strohmeyer pled guilty to murder in exchange for an agreement by prosecutors not to seek the death penalty. He was sentenced to life without the possibility of parole.

crime was being committed and that a victim was exposed to bodily harm, said Gary Watchke, legislative analyst for the Wisconsin Legislative Reference Bureau.

[Good] Samaritan laws that govern professionals, such as a doctor, firefighter or police officer, are different, Watchke said. Such professionals accept responsibility to people they do not personally know because of the nature of their jobs. Good Samaritan laws are needed to protect them from liability, encouraging them to help when they are needed, he said.

TWO FORMS OF JUSTICE: IVERSON CASE—NEVADA AND CALIFORNIA AUTHORITIES OUGHT TO REEXAMINE DAVID CASH'S ACTIONS

Isabelle R. Gunning
L.A. Times, Sept. 21, 1998, at B5

One year and four months ago, Jeremy Strohmeyer followed little 7-year-old Sherrice Iverson into a casino ladies' room. His friend, David Cash, followed after them. There, Strohmeyer kidnapped, sexually assaulted and strangled Sherrice to death while Cash, according to his own testimony, watched the assault begin and then left without notifying authorities. Strohmeyer pleaded guilty to all the crimes, facing a lifetime in prison, and Cash remains at UC Berkeley. The disparate legal treatment of two young men who both appear so morally culpable has raised a lot of passions, causing even a noted criminal defense attorney, Strohmeyer's own Leslie Abramson, to call angrily for some retribution against Cash.

So why hasn't Cash been charged? Many in the African American community believe that the whole case is about race. South-Central activists were highly critical of the Nevada district attorney's willingness to accept a plea offer from Strohmeyer, wondering if the prosecution wouldn't have been more eager to seek the death penalty through a trial if the victim were white and wealthy. Maybe. As a former public defender, it seems to me that the deal was typical when a defendant faces a real possibility of the death penalty. Moreover, as an opponent of the death penalty, I agree with Sherrice's father when he said, "Killing that boy won't bring my baby back."

But when it comes to Cash, I wonder. This is not Mississippi in 1963. There is no great racist plot. Indeed, the public unease and outrage against Cash is a multiracial affair with blacks and browns, whites and reds, yellows and "mixeds" all horrified by his actions and indifference. But is there a subtle, perhaps unconscious combination of racial and class privilege causing the authorities to balk at charging a young middle-class white man with a bright future at an elite public university? Would they be so hesitant if he were darker hued, had no high school degree and had the uncertain economic future that too many young, poor black and brown men face?

It is said that neither Nevada nor California can charge Cash because neither state has a "Good Samaritan" law—and they should. I disagree with the pundits who oppose such laws with concerns that range from the infrequency with which Vermont uses its law to the suggestion that these laws turn "us into informants on each other." It doesn't matter if the new law is rarely used. Ideally, we hope that all criminal laws will rarely need to be used. What matters is that we believe that the moral obligation to help under certain circumstances is important. If so, then we should have a law for whenever it is needed. And these laws have less to do with us becoming informants on each other and everything to do with what we should already be doing for each other: helping each other out in times of need, regardless of our differences, because we are all part of a community. * * *

3. SAMPLE GOOD SAMARITAN STATUTES

HAWAII'S GOOD SAMARITAN STATUTE

Haw. Rev. Stat. Ann. § 663–1.6. (1995)

[§ 663–1.6]. Duty to assist.

(a) Any person at the scene of a crime who knows that a victim of the crime is suffering from serious physical harm shall obtain or attempt to obtain aid from law enforcement or medical personnel if the person can do so without danger or peril to any person. Any person who violates this subsection is guilty of a petty misdemeanor.

(b) Any person who provides reasonable assistance in compliance with subsection (a) shall not be liable in civil damages unless the person's acts constitute gross negligence or wanton acts or omissions, or unless the person receives or expects to receive remuneration. Nothing contained in this subsection shall alter existing law with respect to tort liability of a physician licensed to practice under the laws of this State committed in the ordinary course of the physician's practice.

(c) Any person who fails to provide reasonable assistance in compliance with subsection (a) shall not be liable for any civil damages.

VERMONT'S GOOD SAMARITAN STATUTE

Vt. Stat. Ann. tit. 12, § 519 (2002)

§ 519 Emergency medical care

(a) A person who knows that another is exposed to grave physical harm shall, to the extent that the same can be rendered without danger or peril to himself or without interference with important duties owed to others, give reasonable assistance to the exposed person unless that assistance or care is being provided by others.

(b) A person who provides reasonable assistance in compliance with subsection (a) of this section shall not be liable in civil damages unless his acts constitute gross negligence or unless he will receive or expects to receive remuneration. Nothing contained in this subsection shall alter existing law with respect to tort liability of a practitioner of the healing arts for acts committed in the ordinary course of his practice.

(c) A person who willfully violates subsection (a) of this section shall be fined not more than $100.00.

D. THE PROHIBITION AGAINST "STATUS CRIMES"

One aspect of the act requirement has been constitutionalized: the idea that people should be punished only for their conduct and not being a certain kind of person. In *Robinson v. California*, the first case in this section, the United States Supreme Court addressed the question whether the state of California could punish a person for being a narcotics addict. In *Powell v. Texas*, the Court had to decide whether the state of Texas could punish a chronic alcoholic for being drunk in public. Both defendants argued that because of their addictions, their conduct was not entirely voluntary. As you read these cases, think about whether you are persuaded by the Court's explanation for treating the two cases differently.

ROBINSON V. CALIFORNIA

Supreme Court of the United States
370 U.S. 660, 82 S.Ct. 1417, 8 L.Ed.2d 758 (1962)

STEWART, JUSTICE.

A California statute makes it a criminal offense for a person to "be addicted to the use of narcotics." This appeal draws into question the constitutionality of that provision of the state law, as construed by the California courts in the present case.

The appellant was convicted after a jury trial in the Municipal Court of Los Angeles. The evidence against him was given by two Los Angeles police officers. Officer Brown testified that he had had occasion to examine the appellant's arms one evening on a street in Los Angeles some four months before the trial. The officer testified that at that time he had observed "scar tissue and discoloration on the inside" of the appellant's right arm, and "what appeared to be numerous needle marks and a scab which was approximately three inches below the crook of the elbow" on the appellant's left arm. The officer also testified that the appellant under questioning had admitted to the occasional use of narcotics. * * *

The appellant testified in his own behalf, denying the alleged conversations with the police officers and denying that he had ever used narcotics or been addicted to their use. He explained the marks on his arms as resulting from an allergic condition contracted during his military service. His testimony was corroborated by two witnesses.

The trial judge instructed the jury that the statute made it a misdemeanor for a person "either to use narcotics, or to be addicted to the use of narcotics. . . . That portion of the statute referring to the 'use' of narcotics is based upon the 'act' of using. That portion of the statute referring to 'addicted to the use' of narcotics is based upon a condition or status. They are not identical. . . . To be addicted to the use of narcotics is said to be a status or condition and not an act. It is a continuing offense and differs from most other offenses in the fact that [it] is chronic rather than acute; that it continues after it is complete and subjects the offender to arrest at any time before he reforms. The existence of such a chronic condition may be ascertained from a single examination, if the characteristic reactions of that condition be found present."

The judge further instructed the jury that the appellant could be convicted under a general verdict if the jury agreed *either* that he was of the "status" *or* had committed the "act" denounced by the statute. "All that the People must show is either that the defendant did use a narcotic in Los Angeles County, or that while in the City of Los Angeles he was addicted to the use of narcotics. . . ."

Under these instructions the jury returned a verdict finding the appellant "guilty of the offense charged." * * * We noted probable jurisdiction of this appeal because it squarely presents the issue whether the statute as construed by the California courts in this case is repugnant to the Fourteenth Amendment of the Constitution. * * *

It would be possible to construe the statute under which the appellant was convicted as one which is operative only upon proof of the actual use of narcotics within the State's jurisdiction. But the California courts have not so construed this law. * * *

This statute, therefore, is not one which punishes a person for the use of narcotics, for their purchase, sale or possession, or for antisocial or disorderly behavior resulting from their administration. It is not a law which even purports to provide or require medical treatment. Rather, we deal with a statute which makes the "status" of narcotic addiction a criminal offense, for which the offender may be prosecuted "at any time before he reforms." California has said that a person can be continuously guilty of this offense, whether or not he has ever used or possessed any narcotics within the State, and whether or not he has been guilty of any antisocial behavior there.

It is unlikely that any State at this moment in history would attempt to make it a criminal offense for a person to be mentally ill, or a leper, or to be afflicted with a venereal disease. A State might determine that the general health and welfare require that the victims of these and other human afflictions be dealt with by compulsory treatment, involving quarantine, confinement, or sequestration. But, in the light of contemporary human knowledge, a law which made a criminal offense of such a disease would doubtless be universally thought to be an infliction of cruel and unusual punishment in violation of the Eighth and Fourteenth Amendments.

We cannot but consider the statute before us as of the same category. In this Court counsel for the State recognized that narcotic addiction is an illness. Indeed, it is apparently an illness which may be contracted innocently or involuntarily. We hold that a state law which imprisons a person thus afflicted as a criminal, even though he has never touched any narcotic drug within the State or been guilty of any irregular behaviour there, inflicts a cruel and unusual punishment in violation of the Fourteenth Amendment. To be sure, imprisonment for ninety days is not, in the abstract, a punishment which is either cruel or unusual. But the question cannot be considered in the abstract. Even one day in prison would be a cruel and unusual punishment for the "crime" of having a common cold.

We are not unmindful that the vicious evils of the narcotics traffic have occasioned the grave concern of government. There are, as we have said, countless fronts on which those evils may be legitimately attacked. We deal in this case only with an individual provision of a particularized local law as it has so far been interpreted by the California courts.

Reversed.

JUSTICE CLARK, dissenting.

The Court finds § 11721 of California's Health and Safety Code, making it an offense to "be addicted to the use of narcotics," violative of due process as "a cruel and unusual punishment." I cannot agree. * * *

Apart from prohibiting specific acts such as the purchase, possession and sale of narcotics, California has taken certain legislative steps in regard to the status of being a narcotic addict—a condition commonly recognized as a threat to the State and to the individual. The Code deals with this problem in realistic stages. At its incipiency narcotic addiction is handled under § 11721 of the Health and Safety Code which is at issue here. It provides that a person found to be addicted to the use of narcotics shall serve a term in the county jail of not less than 90 days nor more than one year, with the minimum 90-day confinement applying in all cases without exception. Provision is made for parole with periodic tests to detect readdiction. * * *

Where narcotic addiction has progressed beyond the incipient, volitional stage, California provides for commitment of three months to two years in a state hospital. * * * This proceeding is clearly civil in nature with a purpose of rehabilitation and cure. * * * Thus, the "criminal" provision applies to the incipient narcotic addict who retains self-control, requiring confinement of three months to one year and parole with frequent tests to detect renewed use of drugs. Its overriding purpose is to cure the less seriously addicted person by preventing further use. On the other hand, the "civil" commitment provision deals with addicts who have lost the power of self-control, requiring hospitalization of up to two years. Each deals with a different type of addict but with a common purpose. * * *

In the instant case the proceedings against the petitioner were brought under the volitional-addict section. There was testimony that he had been using drugs only four months with three to four relatively mild doses a week. At arrest and trial he appeared normal. His testimony was clear and concise, being simply that he had never used drugs. The scabs and pocks on his arms and body were caused, he said, by "overseas shots" administered during army service preparatory to foreign assignment. He was very articulate in his testimony but the jury did not believe him, apparently because he had told the clinical expert while being examined after arrest that he had been using drugs, as I have stated above. The officer who arrested him also testified to like statements and to scabs—some 10 or 15 days old—showing narcotic injections. There was no evidence in the record of withdrawal symptoms. Obviously he could not have been committed under § 5355 as one who had completely "lost the power of self-control." The jury was instructed that narcotic "addiction" as used in § 11721 meant strongly disposed to a taste or practice or habit of its use, indicated by the use of narcotics often or daily. A general verdict was returned against petitioner, and he was ordered confined for 90 days to be followed by a two-year parole during which he was required to take periodic Nalline tests. * * *

The majority acknowledges, as it must, that a State can punish persons who purchase, possess or use narcotics. Although none of these acts are harmful to society in themselves, the State constitutionally may attempt to deter and prevent them through punishment because of the grave threat of future harmful conduct which they pose. Narcotics addiction—including the incipient, volitional addiction to which this provision speaks—is no different. California courts have taken judicial notice that "the inordinate use of a narcotic drug tends to create an irresistible craving and forms a habit for its continued use until one becomes an addict, and he respects no convention or obligation and will lie, steal, or use any other base means to gratify his passion for the drug, being lost to all considerations of duty or social position." Can this Court deny the legislative and judicial judgment of California that incipient, volitional narcotic addiction poses a threat of serious crime similar to the threat inherent in the purchase or possession of narcotics? And if such a threat is inherent in addiction, can this Court say that California is powerless to deter it by punishment?

It is no answer to suggest that we are dealing with an involuntary status and thus penal sanctions will be ineffective and unfair. The section at issue applies only to persons who use narcotics often or even daily but not to the point of losing self-control. When dealing with involuntary addicts California moves only through § 5355 of its Welfare Institutions Code which clearly is not penal. Even if it could be argued that § 11721 may not be limited to volitional addicts, the petitioner in the instant case undeniably retained the power of self-control and thus to him the statute would be constitutional. Moreover, "status" offenses have long been known and recognized in the criminal law. A ready example is drunkenness, which plainly is as involuntary after addiction to alcohol as is the taking of drugs. * * *

I would affirm the judgment.

[JUSTICE DOUGLAS' and JUSTICE HARLAN'S concurring opinions and JUSTICE WHITE'S dissenting opinion have been omitted.]

POWELL V. TEXAS

Supreme Court of the United States
392 U.S. 514, 88 S.Ct. 2145, 20 L.Ed.2d 1254 (1968)

MR. JUSTICE MARSHALL announced the judgment of the Court and delivered an opinion in which THE CHIEF JUSTICE, MR. JUSTICE BLACK, and MR. JUSTICE HARLAN join.

In late December 1966, appellant was arrested and charged with being found in a state of intoxication in a public place, in violation of Texas Penal Code, Art. 477 (1952), which reads as follows:

> Whoever shall get drunk or be found in a state of intoxication in any public place, or at any private house except his own, shall be fined not exceeding one hundred dollars.

Appellant was tried in the Corporation Court of Austin, Texas, found guilty, and fined $20. He appealed to the County Court at Law No. 1 of Travis County, Texas, where a trial *de novo* was held. His counsel urged that appellant was "afflicted with the disease of chronic alcoholism," that "his appearance in public [while drunk was] . . . not of his own volition," and therefore that to punish him criminally for that conduct would be cruel and unusual, in violation of the Eighth and Fourteenth Amendments to the United States Constitution.

The trial judge in the county court, sitting without a jury, made certain findings of fact but ruled as a matter of law that chronic alcoholism was not a defense to the charge. He found appellant guilty, and fined him $50. There being no further right to appeal within the Texas judicial system, appellant appealed to this Court; we noted probable jurisdiction.

I.

The principal testimony was that of Dr. David Wade, a Fellow of the American Medical Association, duly certificated in psychiatry. His testimony consumed a total of 17 pages in the trial transcript. Five of those pages were taken up with a recitation of Dr. Wade's qualifications. In the next 12 pages Dr. Wade was examined by appellant's counsel, cross-examined by the State, and re-examined by the defense, and those 12 pages contain virtually all the material developed at trial which is relevant to the constitutional issue we face here. Dr. Wade sketched the outlines of the "disease" concept of alcoholism; noted that there is no generally accepted definition of "alcoholism" alluded to the ongoing debate within the medical profession over whether alcohol is actually physically "addicting" or merely psychologically "habituating" and concluded that in either case a "chronic alcoholic" is an "involuntary drinker," who is "powerless not to drink," and who "loses his self-control over his drinking." He testified that he had examined appellant, and that appellant is a "chronic alcoholic," who "by the time he has reached [the state of intoxication] . . . is not able to control his behavior, and [who] . . . has reached this point because he has an uncontrollable compulsion to drink." Dr. Wade also responded in the negative to the question whether appellant has "the willpower to resist the constant excessive consumption of alcohol." He added that in his opinion jailing appellant without medical attention would operate neither to rehabilitate him nor to lessen his desire for alcohol.

On cross-examination, Dr. Wade admitted that when appellant was sober he knew the difference between right and wrong, and he responded affirmatively to the question whether appellant's act of taking the first drink in any given instance when he was sober was a "voluntary exercise of his will." Qualifying his answer, Dr. Wade stated that "these individuals have a compulsion, and this compulsion, while not completely overpowering, is a very strong influence, an exceedingly strong influence, and this compulsion coupled with the firm belief in their mind that they are going to be able to handle it from now on causes their judgment to be somewhat clouded."

Appellant testified concerning the history of his drinking problem. He reviewed his many arrests for drunkenness; testified that he was unable to stop drinking; stated that when he was intoxicated he had no control over his actions and could not remember them later, but that he did not become violent; and admitted that he did not remember his arrest on the occasion for which he was being tried. On cross-examination, appellant admitted that he had had one drink on the morning of the trial and had been able to discontinue drinking. In relevant part, the cross-examination went as follows:

> "Q. You took that one at eight o'clock because you wanted to drink?
>
> "A. Yes, sir.
>
> "Q. And you knew that if you drank it, you could keep on drinking and get drunk?
>
> "A. Well, I was supposed to be here on trial, and I didn't take but that one drink.
>
> "Q. You knew you had to be here this afternoon, but this morning you took one drink and then you knew that you couldn't afford to drink any more and come to court; is that right?
>
> "A. Yes, sir, that's right.
>
> "Q. So you exercised your will power and kept from drinking anything today except that one drink?
>
> "A. Yes, sir, that's right.

* * *

> On redirect examination, appellant lawyer elicited the following:
>
> "Q. Leroy, isn't the real reason why you just had one drink today because you just had enough money to buy one drink?
>
> "A. Well, that was just give [sic] to me.
>
> "Q. In other words, you didn't have any money with which you could buy any drinks yourself?
>
> "A. No, sir, that was give [sic] to me.

"Q. And that's really what controlled the amount you drank this morning, isn't it?

"A. Yes, sir.

"Q. Leroy, when you start drinking, do you have any control over how many drinks you can take?

"A. No, sir."

Evidence in the case then closed. The State made no effort to obtain expert psychiatric testimony of its own, or even to explore with appellant's witness the question of appellant's power to control the frequency, timing, and location of his drinking bouts, or the substantial disagreement within the medical profession concerning the nature of the disease, the efficacy of treatment and the prerequisites for effective treatment. It did nothing to examine or illuminate what Dr. Wade might have meant by his reference to a "compulsion" which was "not completely overpowering," but which was "an exceedingly strong influence," or to inquire into the question of the proper role of such a "compulsion" in constitutional adjudication. Instead, the State contented itself with a brief argument that appellant had no defense to the charge because he "is legally sane and knows the difference between right and wrong." * * *

III.

Appellant claims that his conviction on the facts of this case would violate the Cruel and Unusual Punishment Clause of the Eighth Amendment as applied to the States through the Fourteenth Amendment. The primary purpose of that clause has always been considered, and properly so, to be directed at the method or kind of punishment imposed for the violation of criminal statutes; the nature of the conduct made criminal is ordinarily relevant only to the fitness of the punishment imposed.

Appellant, however, seeks to come within the application of the Cruel and Unusual Punishment Clause announced in *Robinson v. California,* 370 U.S. 660 (1962), which involved a state statute making it a crime to "be addicted to the use of narcotics." This Court held there that "a state law which imprisons a person thus afflicted [with narcotic addiction] as a criminal, even though he has never touched any narcotic drug within the State or been guilty of any irregular behavior there, inflicts a cruel and unusual punishment . . . . "

On its face the present case does not fall within that holding, since appellant was convicted, not for being a chronic alcoholic, but for being in public while drunk on a particular occasion. The State of Texas thus has not sought to punish a mere status, as California did in *Robinson;* nor has it attempted to regulate appellant's behavior in the privacy of his own home. Rather, it has imposed upon appellant a criminal sanction for public behavior which may create substantial health and safety hazards, both for appellant and for members of the general public, and which offends the moral and esthetic sensibilities of a large segment of the community. This seems a far cry from convicting one for being an addict, being a chronic alcoholic, being "mentally ill, or a leper . . . . " * * *

It is suggested in dissent that *Robinson* stands for the "simple" but "subtle" principle that "[criminal] penalties may not be inflicted upon a person for being in a condition he is powerless to change." In that view, appellant's "condition" of public intoxication was "occasioned by a compulsion symptomatic of the disease" of chronic alcoholism, and thus, apparently, his behavior lacked the critical element of *mens rea*. Whatever may be the merits of such a doctrine of criminal responsibility, it surely cannot be said to follow from *Robinson*. The entire thrust of *Robinson*'s interpretation of the Cruel and Unusual Punishment Clause is that criminal penalties may be inflicted only if the accused has committed some act, has engaged in some behavior, which society has an interest in preventing, or perhaps in historical common law terms, has committed some *actus reus*. * * *

Ultimately, then, the most troubling aspects of this case, were *Robinson* to be extended to meet it, would be the scope and content of what could only be a constitutional doctrine of criminal responsibility. In dissent it is urged that the decision could be limited to conduct which is "a characteristic and involuntary part of the pattern of the disease as it afflicts" the particular individual, and that "[it] is not foreseeable" that it would be applied "in the case of offenses such as driving a car while intoxicated, assault, theft, or robbery." That is limitation by fiat. In the first place, nothing in the logic of the dissent would limit its application to chronic alcoholics. If Leroy Powell cannot be convicted of public intoxication, it is difficult to see how a State can convict an individual for murder, if that individual, while exhibiting normal behavior in all other respects, suffers from a "compulsion" to kill, which is an "exceedingly strong influence," but "not completely overpowering." Even if we limit our consideration to chronic alcoholics, it would seem impossible to confine the principle within the arbitrary bounds which the dissent seems to envision. * * *

Traditional common-law concepts of personal accountability and essential considerations of federalism lead us to disagree with appellant. We are unable to conclude, on the state of this record or on the current state of medical knowledge, that chronic alcoholics in general, and Leroy Powell in particular, suffer from such an irresistible compulsion to drink and to get drunk in public that they are utterly unable to control their performance of either or both of these acts and thus cannot be deterred at all from public intoxication. * * *

Affirmed.

MR. JUSTICE FORTAS, with whom MR. JUSTICE DOUGLAS, MR. JUSTICE BRENNAN, and MR. JUSTICE STEWART join, dissenting.

* * * The sole question presented is whether a criminal penalty may be imposed upon a person suffering the disease of "chronic alcoholism" for a condition—being "in a state of intoxication" in public—which is a characteristic part of the pattern of his disease and which, the trial court found, was not the consequence of appellant's volition but of "a compulsion symptomatic of the disease of chronic alcoholism." We must consider whether the Eighth Amendment, made applicable to the States through the Fourteenth Amendment, prohibits the imposition of this penalty in these rather special circumstances as "cruel and unusual punishment." This case does not raise any question as to the right of the police to stop and detain those who are intoxicated in public, whether as a result of the disease or otherwise; or as to the State's power to commit chronic alcoholics for treatment. Nor does it concern the responsibility of an alcoholic for criminal *acts.* We deal here with the mere *condition* of being intoxicated in public. * * *

* * * *Robinson* stands upon a principle which, despite its subtlety, must be simply stated and respectfully applied because it is the foundation of individual liberty and the cornerstone of the relations between a civilized state and its citizens: Criminal penalties may not be inflicted upon a person for being in a condition he is powerless to change. In all probability, Robinson at some time before his conviction elected to take narcotics. But the crime as defined did not punish this conduct. The statute imposed a penalty for the offense of "addiction"—a condition which Robinson could not control. Once Robinson had become an addict, he was utterly powerless to avoid criminal guilt. He was powerless to choose not to violate the law.

In the present case, appellant is charged with a crime composed of two elements—being intoxicated and being found in a public place while in that condition. The crime, so defined, differs from that in *Robinson.* The statute covers more than a mere status. But the essential constitutional defect here is the same as in *Robinson,* for in both cases the particular defendant was accused of being in a condition which he had no capacity to change or avoid. The trial judge sitting as trier of fact found, upon the medical and other relevant testimony, that Powell is a "chronic alcoholic." He defined appellant's "chronic alcoholism" as "a disease which destroys the afflicted person's will power to resist the constant, excessive consumption of alcohol." He also found that "a chronic alcoholic does not appear in public by his own volition but under a compulsion symptomatic of the disease of chronic alcoholism." I read these findings to mean that appellant was powerless to avoid drinking; that having taken his first drink, he had "an uncontrollable compulsion to drink" to the point of intoxication; and that, once intoxicated, he could not prevent himself from appearing in public places. * * *

The findings in this case, read against the background of the medical and sociological data to which I have referred, compel the conclusion that the infliction upon appellant of a criminal penalty for being intoxicated in a public place would be "cruel and inhuman punishment" within the prohibition of the Eighth Amendment. This conclusion follows because appellant is a "chronic alcoholic" who, according to the trier of fact, cannot resist the "constant excessive consumption of alcohol" and does not appear in public by his own volition but under a "compulsion" which is part of his condition.

I would reverse the judgment below.

[MR. JUSTICE BLACK concurring opinion, with whom MR. JUSTICE HARLAN joins has been omitted.]

MR. JUSTICE WHITE, concurring in the result.

If it cannot be a crime to have an irresistible compulsion to use narcotics, I do not see how it can constitutionally be a crime to yield to such a compulsion. Punishing an addict for using drugs convicts for addiction under a different name. Distinguishing between the two crimes is like forbidding criminal conviction for being sick with flu or epilepsy but permitting punishment for running a fever or having a convulsion. Unless *Robinson* is to be abandoned, the use of narcotics by an addict must be beyond the reach of the criminal law. Similarly, the chronic alcoholic with an irresistible urge to consume alcohol should not be punishable for drinking or for being drunk.

Powell's conviction was for the different crime of being drunk in a public place. * * *

The sober chronic alcoholic has no compulsion to be on the public streets; many chronic alcoholics drink at home and are never seen drunk in public. Before and after taking the first drink, and until he becomes so drunk that he loses the power to know where he is or to direct his movements, the chronic alcoholic with a home or financial resources is as capable as the nonchronic drinker of doing his drinking in private, of removing himself from public places and, since he knows or ought to know that he will become intoxicated, of making plans to avoid his being found drunk in public. For these reasons, I cannot say that the chronic alcoholic who proves his disease and a compulsion to drink is shielded from conviction when he has knowingly failed to take feasible precautions against committing a criminal act, here the act of going to or remaining in a public place. * * *

* * * The fact remains that some chronic alcoholics must drink and hence must drink somewhere. Although many chronics have homes, many

others do not. For all practical purposes the public streets may be home for these unfortunates, not because their disease compels them to be there, but because, drunk or sober, they have no place else to go and no place else to be when they are drinking. This is more a function of economic station than of disease, although the disease may lead to destitution and perpetuate that condition. For some of these alcoholics I would think a showing could be made that resisting drunkenness is impossible and that avoiding public places when intoxicated is also impossible. As applied to them this statute is in effect a law which bans a single act for which they may not be convicted under the Eighth Amendment—the act of getting drunk. * * *

It is also possible that the chronic alcoholic who begins drinking in private at some point becomes so drunk that he loses the power to control his movements and for that reason appears in public. The Eighth Amendment might also forbid conviction in such circumstances, but only on a record satisfactorily showing that it was not feasible for him to have made arrangements to prevent his being in public when drunk and that his extreme drunkenness sufficiently deprived him of his faculties on the occasion in issue.

These prerequisites to the possible invocation of the Eighth Amendment are not satisfied on the record before us. * * * Powell had a home and wife, and if there were reasons why he had to drink in public or be drunk there, they do not appear in the record.

Because Powell did not show that his conviction offended the Constitution, I concur in the judgment affirming the Travis County court.

JONES V. CITY OF LOS ANGELES

Ninth Circuit Court of Appeals
444 F.3d 1118 (9th Cir. 2006)

WARDLAW, CIRCUIT JUDGE.

Six homeless individuals, unable to obtain shelter on the night each was cited or arrested, filed this Eighth Amendment challenge to the enforcement of a City of Los Angeles ordinance that criminalizes sitting, lying, or sleeping on public streets and sidewalks at all times and in all places within Los Angeles's city limits. Appellants seek limited injunctive relief from enforcement of the ordinance during nighttime hours, i.e., between 9:00 p.m. and 6:30 a.m., or at any time against the temporarily infirm or permanently disabled. We must decide whether the Eighth Amendment right to be free from cruel and unusual punishment prohibits enforcement of that law as applied to homeless individuals involuntarily sitting, lying, or sleeping on the street due to the unavailability of shelter in Los Angeles.

The facts underlying this appeal are largely undisputed. Edward Jones, Patricia Vinson, George Vinson, Thomas Cash, Stanley Barger, and Robert Lee Purrie ("Appellants") are homeless individuals who live on the streets of Los Angeles's Skid Row district. Appellees are the City of Los Angeles, Los Angeles Police Department ("L.A.P.D.") Chief William Bratton, and Captain Charles Beck ("Appellees" or "the City"). Federal law defines the term "homeless individual" to include

> (1) an individual who lacks a fixed, regular, and adequate nighttime residence; and
>
> (2) an individual who has a primary nighttime residence that is—
>
> > (A) a supervised publicly or privately operated shelter designed to provide temporary living accommodations (including welfare hotels, congregate shelters, and transitional housing for the mentally ill);
> >
> > (B) an institution that provides a temporary residence for individuals intended to be institutionalized; or
> >
> > (C) a public or private place not designed for, or ordinarily used as, a regular sleeping accommodation for human beings.

Stewart B. McKinney Homeless Assistance Act of 1987 § 103(a), 42 U.S.C. § 11302(a) (2000). Appellants are six of the more than 80,000 homeless individuals in Los Angeles County on any given night.

The term "Skid Row" derives from the lumber industry practice of building a road or track made of logs laid crosswise over which other logs were slid. By the 1930s, the term was used to describe the area of town frequented by loggers and densely populated with bars and brothels. Beginning around the end of the nineteenth century, the area now known as Los Angeles's Skid Row became home to a transient population of seasonal laborers as residential hotels began to develop. For decades Skid Row has been home for "the down and out, the drifters, the unemployed, and the chronic alcoholic[s]" of Los Angeles. Covering fifty city blocks immediately east of downtown Los Angeles, Skid Row is bordered by Third Street to the north, Seventh Street to the south, Alameda Street to the east, and Main Street to the west.

Los Angeles's Skid Row has the highest concentration of homeless individuals in the United States. According to the declaration of Michael Alvidrez, a manager of single-room-occupancy ("SRO") hotels in Skid Row owned by the Skid Row Housing Trust, since the mid-1970s Los Angeles has chosen to centralize homeless services in Skid Row. The area is now largely comprised of SRO hotels (multi-unit housing for very low income persons typically consisting of a single room with shared bathroom), shelters, and other facilities for the homeless.

Skid Row is a place of desperate poverty, drug use, and crime, where Porta-Potties serve as sleeping quarters and houses of prostitution. Recently, it has been reported that local hospitals and law enforcement agencies from nearby suburban areas have been caught "dumping" homeless individuals in Skid Row upon their release. This led Los Angeles Mayor Antonio Villaraigosa to order an investigation into the phenomenon in September 2005. L.A.P.D. Chief William Bratton, insisting that the Department does not target the homeless but only people who violate city ordinances (presumably including the ordinance at issue), has stated:

> If the behavior is aberrant, in the sense that it breaks the law, then there are city ordinances. . . . You arrest them, prosecute them. Put them in jail. And if they do it again, you arrest them, prosecute them, and put them in jail. It's that simple.

This has not always been City policy. The ordinance at issue was adopted in 1968. In the late 1980s, James K. Hahn, who served as Los Angeles City Attorney from 1985 to 2001 and subsequently as Mayor, refused to prosecute the homeless for sleeping in public unless the City provided them with an alternative to the streets.

For the approximately 11,000–12,000 homeless individuals in Skid Row, space is available in SRO hotels, shelters, and other temporary or transitional housing for only 9000 to 10,000, leaving more than 1000 people unable to find shelter each night. In the County as a whole, there are almost 50,000 more homeless people than available beds. In 1999, the fair market rent for an SRO room in Los Angeles was $379 per month. Yet the monthly welfare stipend for single adults in Los Angeles County is only $221. Wait-lists for public housing and for housing assistance vouchers in Los Angeles are three- to ten-years long.

The result, in City officials' own words, is that " '[t]he gap between the homeless population needing a shelter bed and the inventory of shelter beds is severely large.' " As Los Angeles's homeless population has grown, the availability of low-income housing in Skid Row has shrunk, according to the declaration of Alice Callaghan, director of a Skid Row community center and board member of the Skid Row Housing Trust. According to Callaghan's declaration, at night in Skid Row, SRO hotels, shelters, and other temporary or transitional housing are the only alternatives to sleeping on the street; during the day, two small parks are open to the public. Thus, for many in Skid Row without the resources or luck to obtain shelter, sidewalks are the only place to be.

As will be discussed below, Appellants' declarations demonstrate that they are not on the streets of Skid Row by informed choice. In addition, the Institute for the Study of Homelessness and Poverty reports that homelessness results from mental illness, substance abuse, domestic violence, low-paying jobs, and, most significantly, the chronic lack of affordable housing. It also reports that between 33% and 50% of the homeless in Los Angeles are mentally ill, and 76% percent of homeless adults in 1990 had been employed for some or all of the two years prior to becoming homeless.

Against this background, the City asserts the constitutionality of enforcing Los Angeles Municipal Code section 41.18(d) against those involuntarily on the streets during nighttime hours, such as Appellants. It provides:

> No person shall sit, lie or sleep in or upon any street, sidewalk or other public way.
>
> The provisions of this subsection shall not apply to persons sitting on the curb portion of any sidewalk or street while attending or viewing any parade * * *; nor shall the provisions of this subsection supply [sic] to persons sitting upon benches or other seating facilities provided for such purpose by municipal authority by this Code.

L.A., Cal., Mun.Code § 41.18(d) (2005). A violation of section 41.18(d) is punishable by a fine of up to $1000 and/or imprisonment of up to six months.

Section 41.18(d) is one of the most restrictive municipal laws regulating public spaces in the United States. The City can secure a conviction under the ordinance against anyone who merely sits, lies, or sleeps in a public way at any time of day. Other cities' ordinances similarly directed at the homeless provide ways to avoid criminalizing the status of homelessness by making an element of the crime some conduct in combination with sitting, lying, or sleeping in a state of homelessness. For example, Las Vegas prohibits standing or lying in a public way only when it obstructs pedestrian or vehicular traffic. Others, such as Portland, prohibit "camping" in or upon any public property or public right of way. Still others contain safe harbor provisions such as limiting the hours of enforcement. Other cities include as a required element sitting, lying, or sleeping in clearly defined and limited zones. As a result of the expansive reach of section 41.18(d), the extreme lack of available shelter in Los Angeles, and the large homeless population, thousands of people violate the Los Angeles ordinance every day and night, and many are arrested, losing what few possessions they may have.[1] Appellants are among them.

---

[1] During oral argument, the attorney for the City asserted that L.A.P.D. officers leaflet Skid Row the day before making their section 41.18(d) sweeps to warn the homeless, and do not cite or arrest people for violating section 41.18(d) unless there are open beds in homeless shelters at the time of the violations. No evidence in the record supports these assertions.

Robert Lee Purrie is in his early sixties. He has lived in the Skid Row area for four decades. Purrie sleeps on the streets because he cannot afford a room in an SRO hotel and is often unable to find an open bed in a shelter. Early in the morning of December 5, 2002, Purrie declares that he was sleeping on the sidewalk at Sixth Street and Towne Avenue because he "had nowhere else to sleep." At 5:20 a.m., L.A.P.D. officers cited Purrie for violating section 41.18(d). He could not afford to pay the resulting fine.

Purrie was sleeping in the same location on January 14, 2003, when police officers woke him early in the morning and searched, handcuffed, and arrested him pursuant to a warrant for failing to pay the fine from his earlier citation. The police removed his property from his tent, broke it down, and threw all of his property, including the tent, into the street. The officers also removed the property and tents of other homeless individuals sleeping near Purrie. After spending the night in jail, Purrie was convicted of violating section 41.18(d), given a twelve-month suspended sentence, and ordered to pay $195 in restitution and attorneys' fees. Purrie was also ordered to stay away from the location of his arrest. Upon his release, Purrie returned to the corner where he had been sleeping on the night of his arrest to find that all the belongings he had left behind, including blankets, clothes, cooking utensils, a hygiene kit, and other personal effects, were gone.

Stanley Barger suffered a brain injury in a car accident in 1998 and subsequently lost his Social Security Disability Insurance. His total monthly income consists of food stamps and $221 in welfare payments. According to Barger's declaration, he "want[s] to be off the street" but can only rarely afford shelter. At 5:00 a.m. on December 24, 2002, Barger was sleeping on the sidewalk at Sixth and Towne when L.A.P.D. officers arrested him. Barger was jailed, convicted of violating section 41.18(d), and sentenced to two days time served.

When Thomas Cash was cited for violating section 41.18(d), he had not worked for approximately two years since breaking his foot and losing his job, and had been sleeping on the street or in a Skid Row SRO hotel. Cash suffers from severe kidney problems, which cause swelling of his legs and shortness of breath, making it difficult for him to walk. At approximately noon on January 10, 2003, Cash tired as he walked to the SRO hotel where he was staying. He was resting on a tree stump when L.A.P.D. officers cited him.

Edward Jones's wife, Janet, suffers serious physical and mental afflictions. Edward takes care of her, which limits his ability to find full-time work, though he has held various minimum wage jobs. The Joneses receive $375 per month from the Los Angeles County General Relief program, enabling them to stay in Skid Row SRO hotels for the first two weeks of each month. Because shelters separate men and women, and

Janet's disabilities require Edward to care for her, the Joneses are forced to sleep on the streets every month after their General Relief monies run out. At 6:30 a.m. on November 20, 2002, Edward and Janet Jones were sleeping on the sidewalk at the corner of Industrial and Alameda Streets when the L.A.P.D. cited them for violating section 41.18(d).

Patricia and George Vinson, a married couple, were looking for work and a permanent place to live when they were cited for violating section 41.18(d). They use their General Relief payments to stay in motels for part of every month and try to stay in shelters when their money runs out. On the night of December 2, 2002, they missed a bus that would have taken them to a shelter and had to sleep on the sidewalk near the corner of Hope and Washington Streets instead. At 5:30 a.m. the next morning, L.A.P.D. officers cited the Vinsons for violating section 41.18(d).

The record before us includes declarations and supporting documentation from nearly four dozen other homeless individuals living in Skid Row who have been searched, ordered to move, cited, arrested, and/or prosecuted for, and in some cases convicted of, violating section 41.18(d). Many of these declarants lost much or all of their personal property when they were arrested.

On February 19, 2003, Appellants filed a complaint in the United States District Court for the Central District of California pursuant to 42 U.S.C. § 1983. They seek a permanent injunction against the City of Los Angeles and L.A.P.D. Chief William Bratton and Captain Charles Beck (in their official capacities), barring them from enforcing section 41.18(d) in Skid Row between the hours of 9:00 p.m. and 6:30 a.m. Appellants allege that by enforcing section 41.18(d) twenty-four hours a day against persons with nowhere else to sit, lie, or sleep, other than on public streets and sidewalks, the City is criminalizing the status of homelessness in violation of the Eighth [Amendment, as well as other claims under federal and state law] .* * * On cross-motions for summary judgment, the district court granted judgment in favor of the City. * * * [T]he district court held that enforcement of the ordinance does not violate the Eighth Amendment because it penalizes conduct, not status. This appeal timely followed. * * *

The City could not expressly criminalize the status of homelessness by making it a crime to be homeless without violating the Eighth Amendment, nor can it criminalize acts that are an integral aspect of that status. Because there is substantial and undisputed evidence that the number of homeless persons in Los Angeles far exceeds the number of available shelter beds at all times, including on the nights of their arrest or citation, Los Angeles has encroached upon Appellants' Eighth Amendment protections by criminalizing the unavoidable act of sitting, lying, or sleeping at night while being involuntarily homeless. A closer analysis of *Robinson* and *Powell* instructs that the involuntariness of the act or condition the City criminalizes is the critical factor delineating a constitutionally cognizable status, and incidental conduct which is integral to and an unavoidable result of that status, from acts or conditions that can be criminalized consistent with the Eighth Amendment. * * *

[F]ive Justices in *Powell* understood *Robinson* to stand for the proposition that the Eighth Amendment prohibits the state from punishing an involuntary act or condition if it is the unavoidable consequence of one's status or being. Although this principle did not determine the outcome in *Powell,* it garnered the considered support of a majority of the Court. Because the conclusion that certain involuntary acts could not be criminalized was not dicta, we adopt this interpretation of *Robinson* and the Cruel and Unusual Punishment Clause as persuasive authority. We also note that in the absence of any agreement between Justice White and the plurality on the meaning of *Robinson* and the commands of the Cruel and Unusual Punishment Clause, the precedential value of the *Powell* plurality opinion is limited to its precise facts. * * *

The *Robinson* and *Powell* decisions, read together, compel us to conclude that enforcement of section 41.18(d) at all times and in all places against homeless individuals who are sitting, lying, or sleeping in Los Angeles's Skid Row because they cannot obtain shelter violates the Cruel and Unusual Punishment Clause. As homeless individuals, Appellants are in a chronic state that may have been acquired "innocently or involuntarily." Whether sitting, lying, and sleeping are defined as acts or conditions, they are universal and unavoidable consequences of being human. It is undisputed that, for homeless individuals in Skid Row who have no access to private spaces, these acts can only be done in public. In contrast to Leroy Powell, Appellants have made a substantial showing that they are "unable to stay off the streets on the night[s] in question."

In disputing our holding, the dissent veers off track by attempting to isolate the supposed "criminal conduct" from the status of being involuntarily homeless at night on the streets of Skid Row. Unlike the cases the dissent relies on, which involve failure to carry immigration documents, illegal reentry, and drug dealing, the conduct at issue here is involuntary and inseparable from status—they are one and the same, given that human beings are biologically compelled to rest, whether by sitting, lying, or sleeping. * * * The City and the dissent apparently believe that Appellants can avoid sitting, lying, and sleeping for days, weeks, or months at a time to comply with the City's ordinance, as if human beings could remain in perpetual motion. That being an impossibility, by criminalizing sitting, lying, and sleeping, the City is in fact criminalizing Appellants' status as homeless individuals. * * *

Homelessness is not an innate or immutable characteristic, nor is it a disease, such as drug addiction or alcoholism. But generally one cannot become a drug addict or alcoholic, as those terms are commonly used, without engaging in at least some voluntary acts (taking drugs, drinking alcohol). Similarly, an individual may become homeless based on factors both within and beyond his immediate control, especially in consideration of the composition of the homeless as a group: the mentally ill, addicts, victims of domestic violence, the unemployed, and the unemployable. That Appellants may obtain shelter on some nights and may eventually escape from homelessness does not render their status at the time of arrest any less worthy of protection than a drug addict's or an alcoholic's.

Undisputed evidence in the record establishes that at the time they were cited or arrested, Appellants had no choice other than to be on the streets. Even if Appellants' past volitional acts contributed to their current need to sit, lie, and sleep on public sidewalks at night, those acts are not sufficiently proximate to the conduct at issue here for the imposition of penal sanctions to be permissible. In contrast, we find no Eighth Amendment protection for conduct that a person makes unavoidable based on their own immediately proximate voluntary acts, for example, driving while drunk, harassing others, or camping or building shelters that interfere with pedestrian or automobile traffic.

Our holding is a limited one. We do not hold that the Eighth Amendment includes a *mens rea* requirement, or that it prevents the state from criminalizing conduct that is not an unavoidable consequence of being homeless, such as panhandling or obstructing public thoroughfares. * * *

And we are not called upon to decide the constitutionality of punishment when there are beds available for the homeless in shelters.

We hold only that * * * the Eighth Amendment prohibits the City from punishing involuntary sitting, lying, or sleeping on public sidewalks that is an unavoidable consequence of being human and homeless without shelter in the City of Los Angeles.

We do not suggest that Los Angeles adopt any particular social policy, plan, or law to care for the homeless. * * * All we hold is that, so long as there is a greater number of homeless individuals in Los Angeles than the number of available beds, the City may not enforce section 41.18(d) at all times and places throughout the City against homeless individuals for involuntarily sitting, lying, and sleeping in public. Appellants are entitled at a minimum to a narrowly tailored injunction against the City's enforcement of section 41.18(d) at certain times and/or places. * * *

REVERSED AND REMANDED.

RYMER, J., dissenting:

* * * Los Angeles Municipal Code (LAMC) § 41.18(d) does not punish people simply because they are homeless. It targets *conduct*—sitting, lying or sleeping on city sidewalks—that can be committed by those with homes as well as those without. * * *

Here, the majority holds that the Eighth Amendment "prohibits the City from punishing involuntary sitting, lying, or sleeping on public sidewalks that is an unavoidable consequence of being human and homeless without shelter in the City of Los Angeles." In other words, the City cannot penalize the status of being homeless plus the condition of being without shelter that exists by virtue of the City's failure to provide sufficient housing on any given night. The ramifications of so holding are quite extraordinary. We do not—and should not—immunize from criminal liability those who commit an act as a result of a condition that the government's failure to provide a benefit has left them in.

Regardless, the challenge should fail even on the majority's view of the law because Jones has not shown that he was accused of being in an involuntary condition which he had no capacity to change or avoid. * * * Jones's theory (embraced by the majority) is that the City's failure to supply adequate shelter caused the six persons who pursue this action to commit the prohibited act, that is, the act of sleeping, sitting or lying on the streets. However, there is no showing in this case that shelter was unavailable on the night that any of the six was apprehended. * * *

Accordingly, I part company with the majority's expansive construction of the substantive limits on criminality. It exceeds the boundaries set by the Supreme Court on the *Robinson* limitation, and intrudes into the state's province to determine the scope of criminal responsibility. I would affirm.

CHAPTER 4

THE MENS REA REQUIREMENT

■ ■ ■

INTRODUCTION

The term mens rea has at least two different meanings. Mens rea is sometimes used in a broad sense to refer to culpability generally. In this sense, mens rea means the kind of moral blameworthiness that ought to make a person criminally responsible for his or her actions. When we use this broader meaning, we are often seeking to determine whether we, within the constraints of Western moral culture, feel comfortable blaming the defendant for what happened. This is a question of retribution: who deserves blame and punishment?

More often, however, mens rea in the criminal law context refers to "the particular mental state provided for in the definition of the offense."[a] This narrower definition of mens rea is sometimes referred to as the scienter or intent requirement. The subject of this chapter is mens rea in the narrow sense.

The study of mens rea reveals some dramatic differences between jurisdictions that primarily incorporate the English common law and jurisdictions that have incorporated the Model Penal Code (MPC). The English common law produced a wide variety of terms used to describe a person's mental state, including terms like "wilfully," "maliciously," "corruptly," "intentionally," "knowingly," "recklessly," and "negligently." Within the common law system, these terms have no necessary relationship to one another, and they do not even always mean the same thing from statute to statute. Judges working within the common law tradition also developed a distinction between "specific intent" and "general intent" crimes. Common law courts have defined the terms "specific intent" and "general intent" in different and sometimes conflicting ways.

The Model Penal Code, in contrast, recognizes only four mental states: (1) purposely, (2) knowingly, (3) recklessly, and (4) negligently. *See* MPC § 2.02(2). These terms—purpose, knowledge, recklessness, and negligence—are precisely defined, they have a logical relationship to one another, and they always mean the same thing wherever they appear. When no mental state is expressed in the statute, the mental state element is satisfied if the person acts purposely, knowingly, or recklessly.

---

[a] Joshua Dressler, UNDERSTANDING CRIMINAL LAW 10.02[C] (6th ed. 2012).

See MPC § 2.02(3). In other words, under the MPC, if no mens rea element is specified, the default rule is that "recklessness" is sufficient to prove the mental state element.

A. THE HISTORICAL DEVELOPMENT OF MENS REA

REGINA V. CUNNINGHAM

Court of Criminal Appeal, 1957
41 Crim.App. 155, 2 Q.B. 396, 2 All. Eng. Rep. 412

BYRNE, J. read the judgment of the court: * * *

The appellant was convicted * * * upon an indictment framed under section 23 of the Offences Against the Person Act, 1861, which charged that he unlawfully and maliciously caused to be taken by Sarah Wade a certain noxious thing, namely coal gas, so as thereby to endanger the life of the said Sarah Wade. The facts were that the appellant was engaged to be married, and Mrs. Wade, his prospective mother-in-law, [lived next to], No. 7a, Bakes Street, Bradford, which was unoccupied but which was to be occupied by the appellant after his marriage. Mrs. Wade and her husband, an elderly couple, lived in the house next door. At one time the two houses had been one, but when the building was converted into two houses a wall had been erected to divide the cellars of the two houses, and that wall was composed of rubble loosely cemented.

On the evening of Jan. 17 last, the appellant went to the cellar of No. 7a, Bakes Street, wrenched the gas meter from the gas pipes and stole it, together with its contents. * * * The facts were not really in dispute, and in a statement to a police officer the appellant said: 'All right I will tell you, I was short of money, I had been off work for three days, I got 8 shillings from the gas meter. I tore it off the wall and threw it away.' Although there was a stop tap within two feet of the meter, the appellant did not turn off the gas, with the result that a very considerable volume of gas escaped, some of which seeped through the wall of the cellar and partially asphyxiated Mrs. Wade, who was asleep in her bedroom next door, with the result that her life was endangered. * * *

The act of the appellant was clearly unlawful and, therefore, the real question for the jury was whether it was also malicious within the meaning of section 23 of the Offences Against the Person Act, 1861.

* * * Section 23 provides as follows:

> "Whosoever shall unlawfully and maliciously administer to or cause to be administered to or taken by any other person any poison or other destructive or noxious thing, so as thereby to endanger the life of such person, or so as thereby to inflict upon

> such person any grievous bodily harm, shall be guilty of felony . . ."

Counsel argued * * * that the learned judge misdirected the jury as to the meaning of the word "maliciously." * * *

* * * [T]he following principle * * * was propounded by the late Professor C.S. Kenny in the first edition of his Outlines of Criminal Law published in 1902 * * *: " * * * in any statutory definition of a crime, malice must be taken not in the old vague sense of 'wickedness' in general, but as requiring either (i) an actual intention to do the particular kind of harm that in fact was done, or (ii) recklessness as to whether such harm should occur or not (i.e. the accused has foreseen that the particular kind of harm might be done, and yet has gone on to take the risk of it). It is neither limited to, nor does it indeed require, any ill-will towards the person injured." * * *

In his summing-up, the learned judge directed the jury as follows: * * *

> 'Unlawful' does not need any definition. It is something forbidden by law. What about 'malicious'? 'Malicious' for this purpose means wicked—something which he has no business to do and perfectly well knows it. 'Wicked' is as good a definition as any other which you would get. * * *

With the utmost respect to the learned judge, we think it is incorrect to say that the word 'malicious' in a statutory offence merely means wicked. We think the learned judge was, in effect, telling the jury that if they were satisfied that the appellant acted wickedly—and he had clearly acted wickedly in stealing the gas meter and its contents—they ought to find that he had acted maliciously in causing the gas to be taken by Mrs. Wade so as thereby to endanger her life. In our view, it should have been left to the jury to decide whether, even if the appellant did not intend the injury to Mrs. Wade, he foresaw that the removal of the gas meter might cause injury to someone but nevertheless removed it. We are unable to say that a reasonable jury, properly directed as to the meaning of the word 'maliciously' in the context of section 23, would, without doubt, have convicted.

In these circumstances, this court has no alternative but to allow the appeal and quash the conviction.

B. PROBLEMS OF STATUTORY INTERPRETATION

Sometimes a statute expressly includes a mental state, but it is not clear which element or elements that mental state modifies. In such cases, the court must utilize canons of statutory construction to figure out the legislature's intent. The Supreme Court illustrates this process in *United States v. Yermian*. As you read the case, think about how the court would rule if operating under the Model Penal Code. The next case, *Holloway v. United States*, demonstrates that understanding what mental states are comprehended by the statute often requires a long, torturous trip into legislative history and precedent.

UNITED STATES V. YERMIAN

Supreme Court of the United States
468 U.S. 63, 104 S.Ct. 2936, 82 L.Ed.2d 53 (1984)

JUSTICE POWELL delivered the opinion of the Court.

It is a federal crime under 18 U.S.C. § 1001 to make any false or fraudulent statement in any matter within the jurisdiction of a federal agency. To establish a violation of § 1001, the Government must prove beyond a reasonable doubt that the statement was made with knowledge of its falsity. This case presents the question whether the Government also must prove that the false statement was made with actual knowledge of federal agency jurisdiction.

I

Respondent Esmail Yermian was convicted in the District Court of Central California on three counts of making false statements in a matter within the jurisdiction of a federal agency, in violation of § 1001. The convictions were based on false statements respondent supplied his employer in connection with a Department of Defense security questionnaire. Respondent was hired in 1979 by Gulton Industries, a defense contractor. Because respondent was to have access to classified material in the course of his employment, he was required to obtain a Department of Defense Security Clearance. To this end, Gulton's security officer asked respondent to fill out a "Worksheet For Preparation of Personnel Security Questionnaire."

In response to a question on the worksheet asking whether he had ever been charged with any violation of law, respondent failed to disclose that in 1978 he had been convicted of mail fraud. * * * In describing his employment history, respondent falsely stated that he had been employed by two companies that had in fact never employed him. The Gulton security officer typed these false representations onto a form entitled "Department of Defense Personnel Security Questionnaire." Respondent reviewed the typed document for errors and signed a certification stating that his answers were "true, complete, and correct to the best of [his] knowledge" and that he understood "that any misrepresentation or false statement . . . may subject [him] to prosecution under section 1001 of the United States Criminal Code." * * *

Government investigators subsequently discovered that respondent had submitted false statements on the security questionnaire. Confronted with this discovery, respondent acknowledged that he had responded falsely to questions regarding his criminal record and employment history. On the basis of these false statements, respondent was charged with three counts in violation of § 1001.

At trial, respondent admitted to having actual knowledge of the falsity of the statements he had submitted in response to the Department of Defense Security Questionnaire. He explained that he had made the false statements so that information on the security questionnaire would be consistent with similar fabrications he had submitted to Gulton in his employment application. Respondent's sole defense at trial was that he had no actual knowledge that his false statements would be transmitted to a federal agency.[2]

Consistent with this defense, respondent requested a jury instruction requiring the Government to prove not only that he had actual knowledge that his statements were false at the time they were made, but also that he had actual knowledge that those statements were made in a matter within the jurisdiction of a federal agency. The District Court rejected that request and instead instructed the jury that the Government must prove that respondent "knew or should have known that the information was to be submitted to a government agency." Respondent's objection to this instruction was overruled, and the jury returned convictions on all three counts charged in the indictment.

The Court of Appeals for the Ninth Circuit reversed, holding that the District Court had erred in failing to give respondent's requested instruction. The Court of Appeals read the statutory terms 'knowingly and willfully' to modify both the conduct of making false statements and the circumstance that they be made "in any matter within the jurisdiction of [a federal agency]." The court therefore concluded that "as an essential element of a section 1001 violation, the government must prove beyond a reasonable doubt that the defendant knew at the time he made the false statement that it was made in a matter within the jurisdiction of a federal agency." The Court of Appeals rejected the Government's argument that the "reasonably foreseeable" standard provided by the District Court's jury instructions satisfied any element of intent possibly associated with the requirement that false statements be made within federal agency jurisdiction.

---

[2] Respondent maintained this defense despite the fact that both the worksheet and the questionnaire made reference to the Department of Defense, and the security questionnaire signed by respondent was captioned 'Defense Department.' The latter document also contained a reference to the 'Defense Industrial Security Clearance Office,' stated that respondent's work would require access to 'secret' material, and informed respondent that his signature would grant 'permission to the Department of Defense to obtain and review copies of [his] medical and institutional records.' Nevertheless, respondent testified that he had not read the form carefully before signing it and thus had not noticed either the words 'Department of Defense' on the first page or the certification printed above the signature block.

The decision of the Court of Appeals for the Ninth Circuit conflicts with decisions by the three other Courts of Appeals that have considered the issue. We granted certiorari to resolve the conflict, and now reverse.

II

The only issue presented in this case is whether Congress intended the terms 'knowingly and willfully' in § 1001 to modify the statute's jurisdictional language, thereby requiring the Government to prove that false statements were made with actual knowledge of federal agency jurisdiction. The issue thus presented is one of statutory interpretation. Accordingly, we turn first to the language of the statute.

A

The relevant language of § 1001 provides:

> Whoever, in any matter within the jurisdiction of any department or agency of the United States knowingly and willfully . . . makes any false, fictitious or fraudulent statements or representations, . . . shall be fined. . . .

The statutory language requiring that knowingly false statements be made "in any matter within the jurisdiction of any department or agency of the United States" is a jurisdictional requirement. Its primary purpose is to identify the factor that makes the false statement an appropriate subject for federal concern. Jurisdictional language need not contain the same culpability requirement as other elements of the offense. Indeed, we have held that "the existence of the fact that confers federal jurisdiction need not be one in the mind of the actor at the time he perpetrates the act made criminal by the federal statute." Certainly in this case, the statutory language makes clear that Congress did not intend the terms "knowingly and willfully" to establish the standard of culpability for the jurisdictional element of § 1001. The jurisdictional language appears in a phrase separate from the prohibited conduct modified by the terms "knowingly and willfully." Any natural reading of § 1001, therefore, establishes that the terms "knowingly and willfully" modify only the making of "false, fictitious or fraudulent statements," and not the predicate circumstance that those statements be made in a matter within the jurisdiction of a federal agency. Once this is clear, there is no basis for requiring proof that the defendant had actual knowledge of federal agency jurisdiction. The statute contains no language suggesting any additional element of intent, such as a requirement that false statements be "knowingly made in a matter within federal agency jurisdiction," or "with the intent to deceive the Federal Government." On its face, therefore, § 1001 requires that the Government prove that false statements were made knowingly and willfully, and it unambiguously dispenses with any requirement that the Government also prove that those statements were made with actual knowledge of federal agency jurisdiction.[7] Respondent's argument that the legislative history of the statute supports a contrary interpretation is unpersuasive. * * *

III

Respondent argues that absent proof of actual knowledge of federal agency jurisdiction, § 1001 becomes a "trap for the unwary," imposing criminal sanctions on "wholly innocent conduct." Whether or not respondent fairly may characterize the intentional and deliberate lies prohibited by the statute (and manifest in this case) as "wholly innocent conduct," this argument is not sufficient to overcome the express statutory language of § 1001. Respondent does not argue that Congress lacks the power to impose criminal sanctions for deliberately false statements submitted to a federal agency, regardless of whether the person who made such statements actually knew that they were being submitted to the Federal Government. That is precisely what Congress has done here. In the unlikely event that § 1001 could be the basis for imposing an unduly harsh result on those who intentionally make false statements to the Federal Government, it is for Congress and not this Court to amend the criminal statute.

IV

Both the plain language and the legislative history establish that proof of actual knowledge of federal agency jurisdiction is not required under § 1001. Accordingly, we reverse the decision of the Court of Appeals to the contrary.

It is so ordered.

JUSTICE REHNQUIST, with whom JUSTICE BRENNAN, JUSTICE STEVENS, and JUSTICE O'CONNOR join, dissenting.

It is common ground that in a prosecution for the making of false statements the Government must prove that the defendant actually knew that the statements were false at the time he made them. The question presented here is whether the Government must also prove that the defendant actually knew that his statements were made in a matter within "the jurisdiction of any department or agency of the United States." The Court concludes that the plain language and the legislative history of 18 U.S.C. § 1001 conclusively establish that the statute is intended to reach false statements made without actual knowledge of federal involvement in the subject matter of the false statements. I cannot agree. * * *

I

I think that in this case, '[a]fter 'seiz[ing] everything from which aid can be derived,' we are left with an ambiguous statute.' Notwithstanding

[7] Because the statutory language unambiguously dispenses with an actual knowledge requirement, we have no occasion to apply the principle of lenity urged by the dissent.

the majority's repeated, but sparsely supported, assertions that the evidence of Congress' intent not to require actual knowledge is "convincing," and "unambiguou[s]," I believe that the language and legislative history of § 1001 can provide "no more than a guess as to what Congress intended." I therefore think that the canon of statutory construction which requires that "ambiguity concerning the ambit of criminal statutes . . . be resolved in favor of lenity," is applicable here. Accordingly, I would affirm the Court of Appeals' conclusion that actual knowledge of federal involvement is a necessary element for conviction under § 1001.

The federal false-statements statute, 18 U.S.C. § 1001, provides that

> [whoever], *in any matter within the jurisdiction of any department or agency of the United States* knowingly and willfully . . . makes any false, fictitious or fraudulent statements or representations, . . . shall be fined not more than $10,000 or imprisoned not more than five years, or both.

The majority correctly begins its analysis with the language of the statute, but in my view, it incorrectly concludes that the statutory language is unambiguous.

In drawing that conclusion, the Court does no more than point out that the "in any matter" language is placed at the beginning of the sentence in a phrase separate from the later phrase specifying the prohibited conduct. The Court then concludes that under any "natural reading' of the statute, it is clear that "knowingly and willfully" modify only the phrase specifying the prohibited conduct. Although 'there is no errorless test for identifying or recognizing 'plain' or 'unambiguous' language" in a statute, the Court's reasoning here amounts to little more than simply pointing to the ambiguous phrases and proclaiming them clear. In my view, it is quite impossible to tell which phrases the terms "knowingly and willfully" modify, and the magic wand of *ipse dixit* does nothing to resolve that ambiguity. * * *

[T]he fact that the Court's 'natural reading' has not seemed so natural to the judges of the Ninth and Fifth Circuits, nor for that matter to me, indicates that the Court's reading, though certainly a plausible one, is not at all compelled by the statutory language. * * *

I respectfully dissent.

HOLLOWAY V. UNITED STATES

Supreme Court of the United States
526 U.S. 1, 119 S.Ct. 966, 143 L.Ed.2d 1 (1999)

JUSTICE STEVENS delivered the opinion of the Court.

Carjacking "with the intent to cause death or serious bodily harm" is a federal crime.[1] The question presented in this case is whether that phrase requires the Government to prove that the defendant had an unconditional intent to kill or harm in all events, or whether it merely requires proof of an intent to kill or harm if necessary to effect a carjacking. * * *

I

A jury found petitioner guilty on three counts of carjacking, as well as several other offenses related to stealing cars. In each of the carjackings, petitioner and an armed accomplice identified a car that they wanted and followed it until it was parked. The accomplice then approached the driver, produced a gun, and threatened to shoot unless the driver handed over the car keys. The accomplice testified that the plan was to steal the cars without harming the victims, but that he would have used his gun if any of the drivers had given him a 'hard time.' When one victim hesitated, petitioner punched him in the face but there was no other actual violence.

The District Judge instructed the jury that the Government was required to prove beyond a reasonable doubt that the taking of a motor vehicle was committed with the intent "to cause death or serious bodily harm to the person from whom the car was taken." After explaining that merely using a gun to frighten a victim was not sufficient to prove such intent, he added the following statement over the defendant's objection:

> In some cases, intent is conditional. That is, a defendant may intend to engage in certain conduct only if a certain event occurs.
>
> In this case, the government contends that the defendant intended to cause death or serious bodily harm if the alleged

---

[1] As amended by the Violent Crime Control and Law Enforcement Act of 1994, § 60003(a)(14), 108 Stat. 1970, and by the Carjacking Correction Act of 1996, § 2, 110 Stat. 3020, the statute provides:

> Whoever, *with the intent to cause death or serious bodily harm* takes a motor vehicle that has been transported, shipped, or received in interstate or foreign commerce from the person or presence of another by force and violence or by intimidation, or attempts to do so, shall—
>
> (1) be fined under this title or imprisoned not more than 15 years, or both,
>
> (2) if serious bodily injury (as defined in section 1365 of this title, including any conduct that, if the conduct occurred in the special maritime and territorial jurisdiction of the United States, would violate section 2241 or 2242 of this title) results, be fined under this title or imprisoned not more than 25 years, or both, and
>
> (3) if death results, be fined under this title or imprisoned for any number of years up to life, or both, or sentenced to death.

victims had refused to turn over their cars. If you find beyond a reasonable doubt that the defendant had such an intent, the government has satisfied this element of the offense. . . .

In his post-verdict motion for a new trial, petitioner contended that this instruction was inconsistent with the text of the statute. The District Judge denied the motion, stating that there 'is no question that the conduct at issue in this case is precisely what Congress and the general public would describe as carjacking, and that Congress intended to prohibit it in § 2119.' Moreover, the judge determined that even though the issue of conditional intent has not been discussed very often, at least in the federal courts, it was a concept that scholars and state courts had long recognized.

* * * [T]he Court of Appeals affirmed. * * *

II

Writing for the Court in *United States v. Turkette,* Justice White reminded us that the language of the statutes that Congress enacts provides "the most reliable evidence of its intent." For that reason, we typically begin the task of statutory construction by focusing on the words that the drafters have chosen. In interpreting the statute at issue, "we consider not only the bare meaning" of the critical word or phrase "but also its placement and purpose in the statutory scheme."

The specific issue in this case is what sort of evil motive Congress intended to describe when it used the words "with the intent to cause death or serious bodily harm" in the 1994 amendment to the carjacking statute. More precisely, the question is whether a person who points a gun at a driver, having decided to pull the trigger if the driver does not comply with a demand for the car keys, possesses the intent, at that moment, to seriously harm the driver. In our view, the answer to that question does not depend on whether the driver immediately hands over the keys or what the offender decides to do after he gains control over the car. At the relevant moment, the offender plainly does have the forbidden intent.

The opinions that have addressed this issue accurately point out that a carjacker's intent to harm his victim may be either "conditional" or "unconditional." The statutory phrase at issue theoretically might describe (1) the former, (2) the latter, or (3) both species of intent. Petitioner argues that the "plain text" of the statute "unequivocally" describes only the latter: that the defendant must possess a specific and unconditional intent to kill or harm in order to complete the proscribed offense. To that end, he insists that Congress would have had to insert the words "if necessary" into the disputed text in order to include the conditional species of intent within the scope of the statute. Because Congress did not include those words, petitioner contends that we must assume that Congress meant to provide a federal penalty for only those carjackings in which the offender actually attempted to harm or kill the driver (or at least intended to do so whether or not the driver resisted).

We believe, however, that a commonsense reading of the carjacking statute counsels that Congress intended to criminalize a broader scope of conduct than attempts to assault or kill in the course of automobile robberies. As we have repeatedly stated, "the meaning of statutory language, plain or not, depends on context." "When petitioner's argument is considered in the context of the statute, it becomes apparent that his proffered construction of the intent element overlooks the significance of the placement of that element in the statute. The carjacking statute essentially is aimed at providing a federal penalty for a particular type of robbery. The statute *mens rea* component thus modifies the act of 'taking' the motor vehicle. It directs the factfinder's attention to the defendant's state of mind at the precise moment he demanded or took control over the car 'by force and violence or by intimidation." If the defendant has the proscribed state of mind at that moment, the statute's scienter element is satisfied. * * *

Two considerations strongly support the conclusion that a natural reading of the text is fully consistent with a congressional decision to cover both species of intent. First, the statute as a whole reflects an intent to authorize federal prosecutions as a significant deterrent to a type of criminal activity that was a matter of national concern. Because that purpose is better served by construing the statute to cover both the conditional and the unconditional species of wrongful intent, the entire statute is consistent with a normal interpretation of the specific language that Congress chose. Indeed, petitioner's interpretation would exclude from the coverage of the statute most of the conduct that Congress obviously intended to prohibit.

Second, it is reasonable to presume that Congress was familiar with the cases and the scholarly writing that have recognized that the 'specific intent' to commit a wrongful act may be conditional. The facts of the leading case on the point are strikingly similar to the facts of this case. In *People v. Connors*, the Illinois Supreme Court affirmed the conviction of a union organizer who had pointed a gun at a worker and threatened to kill him forthwith if he did not take off his overalls and quit work. The Court held that the jury had been properly instructed that the "specific intent to kill" could be found even though that intent was "coupled with a condition" that the defendant would not fire if the victim complied with his demand. That holding has been repeatedly cited with approval by other courts and by scholars. Moreover, it reflects the views endorsed by the authors of the Model [Penal] Code. The core principle that emerges from these sources is that a defendant may not negate a proscribed intent by requiring the victim to comply with a condition the defendant has no right to impose; "an intent to kill, in the alternative, is nevertheless an intent to kill." * * *

In short, we disagree with petitioner's reading of the text of the Act and think it unreasonable to assume that Congress intended to enact such a truncated version of an important criminal statute.[14] The intent requirement of § 2119 is satisfied when the Government proves that at the moment the defendant demanded or took control over the driver's automobile the defendant possessed the intent to seriously harm or kill the driver if necessary to steal the car (or, alternatively, if unnecessary to steal the car). Accordingly, we affirm the judgment of the Court of Appeals.

It is so ordered.

JUSTICE SCALIA, dissenting.

The issue in this case is the meaning of the phrase, in 18 U.S.C. § 2119, "with the intent to cause death or serious bodily harm." (For convenience' sake, I shall refer to it in this opinion as simply intent to kill.) As recounted by the Court, petitioner's accomplice, Vernon Lennon, 'testified that the plan was to steal the cars without harming the victims, but that he would have used his gun if any of the drivers had given him a 'hard time.' 'The District Court instructed the jury that the intent element would be satisfied if petitioner possessed this 'conditional' intent. Today's judgment holds that instruction to have been correct.

I dissent from that holding because I disagree with the following, utterly central, passage of the opinion:

> [A] carjacker's intent to harm his victim may be either 'conditional' or 'unconditional.' The statutory phrase at issue theoretically might describe (1) the former, (2) the latter, or (3) both species of intent.

I think, to the contrary, that in customary English usage the unqualified word "intent" does not usually connote a purpose that is subject to any conditions precedent except those so remote in the speaker's estimation as to be effectively nonexistent—and it *never* connotes a purpose that is subject to a condition which the speaker hopes will not occur. (It is this last sort of "conditional intent" that is at issue in this case, and that I refer to in my subsequent use of the term.) "Intent" is "[a] state of mind in which a person seeks to accomplish a given result through a course of action." Black's Law Dictionary 810 (6th ed. 1990). One can hardly "seek to accomplish" a result he hopes will not ensue. * * *

---

[14] We also reject petitioner's argument that the rule of lenity should apply in this case. We have repeatedly stated that "the rule of lenity applies only if, after seizing everything from which aid can be derived, . . . we can make no more than a guess as to what Congress intended."

If I have made a categorical determination to go to Louisiana for the Christmas holidays, it is accurate for me to say that I 'intend' to go to Louisiana. And that is so even though I realize that there are some remote and unlikely contingencies—"acts of God," for example—that might prevent me. (The fact that these remote contingencies are always implicit in the expression of intent accounts for the humorousness of spelling them out in such expressions as "if I should live so long," or 'the Good Lord willing and the creek don't rise." It is less precise, though tolerable usage, to say that I 'intend' to go if my purpose is conditional upon an event which, though not virtually certain to happen (such as my continuing to live), is reasonably likely to happen, and which I hope will happen. I might, for example, say that I 'intend' to go even if my plans depend upon receipt of my usual and hoped-for end-of-year bonus.

But it is *not* common usage—indeed, it is an unheard-of usage—to speak of my having an "intent" to do something, when my plans are contingent upon an event that is not virtually certain, and that I hope will not occur. When a friend is seriously ill, for example, I would not say that "I intend to go to his funeral next week." I would have to make it clear that the intent is a conditional one: "I intend to go to his funeral next week if he dies." The carjacker who intends to kill if he is met with resistance is in the same position: he has an "intent to kill if resisted"; he does not have an "intent to kill." No amount of rationalization can change the reality of this normal (and as far as I know exclusive) English usage. The word in the statute simply will not bear the meaning that the Court assigns. * * *

There are of course innumerable federal criminal statutes containing an intent requirement, ranging from intent to steal, to intent to defeat the provisions of the Bankruptcy Code, to intent that a vessel be used in hostilities against a friendly nation, to intent to obstruct the lawful exercise of parental rights. Consider, for example, 21 U.S.C. § 841, which makes it a crime to possess certain drugs with intent to distribute them. Possession alone is also a crime, but a lesser one. Suppose that a person acquires and possesses a small quantity of cocaine for his own use, and that he in fact consumes it entirely himself. But assume further that, at the time he acquired the drug, he told his wife not to worry about the expense because, if they had an emergency need for money, he could always resell it. If conditional intent suffices, this person, who has never sold drugs and has never 'intended' to sell drugs in any normal sense, has been guilty of possession with intent to distribute. * * *

The Court confidently asserts that "petitioner's interpretation would exclude from the coverage of the statute most of the conduct that Congress obviously intended to prohibit." It seems to me that one can best judge what Congress 'obviously intended' not by intuition, but by the words that Congress enacted, which in this case require intent (not conditional intent) to kill. Is it implausible that Congress intended to define such a narrow federal crime? Not at all. The era when this statute was passed contained well publicized instances of not only carjackings, and not only carjackings involving violence or the threat of violence (as of course most of them do); but also of carjackings in which the perpetrators senselessly harmed the car owners when that was entirely unnecessary to the crime. I have a friend whose father was killed, and whose mother was nearly killed, in just such an incident—after the car had already been handed over. It is not at all implausible that Congress should direct its attention to this particularly savage sort of carjacking—where killing the driver is part of the intended crime.

Indeed, it seems to me much more implausible that Congress would have focused upon the ineffable 'conditional intent' that the Court reads into the statute, sending courts and juries off to wander through 'would-a, could-a, should-a' land. It is difficult enough to determine a defendant's actual intent; it is infinitely more difficult to determine what the defendant planned to do upon the happening of an event that the defendant hoped would not happen, and that he himself may not have come to focus upon. There will not often be the accomplice's convenient confirmation of conditional intent that exists in the present case. Presumably it will be up to each jury whether to take the carjacker ("Your car or your life") at his word. Such a system of justice seems to me so arbitrary that it is difficult to believe Congress intended it. Had Congress meant to cast its carjacking net so broadly, it could have achieved that result—and eliminated the arbitrariness—by defining the crime as "carjacking under threat of death or serious bodily injury." Given the language here, I find it much more plausible that Congress meant to reach—as it said—the carjacker who intended to kill.

In sum, I find the statute entirely unambiguous as to whether the carjacker who hopes to obtain the car without inflicting harm is covered. Even if ambiguity existed, however, the rule of lenity would require it to be resolved in the defendant's favor. The Government's statement that the rule of lenity "has its *primary* application in cases in which there is some doubt whether the legislature intended to criminalize conduct that might otherwise appear to be innocent," is carefully crafted to conceal the fact that we have repeatedly applied the rule to situations just like this. For example, in *Ladner v. United States,* the statute at issue made it a crime to assault a federal officer with a deadly weapon. The defendant, who fired one shotgun blast that wounded two federal officers, contended that under this statute he was guilty of only one, and not two, assaults. The Court said, in an opinion joined by all eight Justices who reached the merits of the case:

> This policy of lenity means that the Court will not interpret a federal criminal statute so as to increase the penalty that it

> places on an individual when such an interpretation can be based on no more than a guess as to what Congress intended. If Congress desires to create multiple offenses from a single act affecting more than one federal officer, Congress can make that meaning clear. We thus hold that the single discharge of a shotgun alleged by the petitioner in this case would constitute only a single violation of § 254.

If the statute is not, as I think, clear in the defendant's favor, it is at the very least ambiguous and the defendant must be given the benefit of the doubt. * * *

[JUSTICE THOMAS' dissenting opinion has been omitted.]

C. INTENT

Under the common law, intent is defined in two ways. First, one acts with the requisite intent if it is his or her conscious object or purpose to cause a certain result or to engage in certain prohibited conduct. Alternatively, one "intends" a particular social harm if one knows to a virtual certainty that one's actions will cause that social harm. In other words, intent at common law is equated with either "conscious object" or "knowledge to a virtual certainty." The common law also distinguishes between specific intent and general intent crimes. The specific intent-general intent distinction is discussed below in Section E, subsection 2.

The Model Penal Code uses the term 'purposely' to reflect a mental state akin to the first common law definition of intent. Note, however, that 'intent' under the common law also encompasses something akin to, but not quite the same as, what the Model Penal Code calls "knowledge." *See* Model Penal Code § 2.02(2)(a).

Because of difficulties inherent in proving intent, courts have adopted legal shortcuts which allow the fact finder in a murder case to infer an intent to kill when absolute proof of such intent is lacking. One such shortcut is the "natural and probable consequences" doctrine explained in *State v. Fugate*.

STATE V. FUGATE

Court of Appeals of Ohio, Second District
36 Ohio App.2d 131, 303 N.E.2d 313 (2d Dist. 1973)

KERNS, J.

The defendant, Herbert Lee Fugate, appellant herein, was tried by a jury and convicted of armed robbery and first degree murder. From the judgment and sentence thereupon entered by the Court of Common Pleas of Montgomery County, Fugate has perfected an appeal to this court.

On April 15, 1971, the appellant entered the Point Garage located at the intersection of Hamilton and McLain Streets with a loaded sixteen-gauge shotgun. In the process of robbing the owner of the garage, Sylvester Leingang, Fugate struck him on two different occasions with the barrel of the shotgun, causing severe head wounds. He then ordered his victim, Mr. Leingang, into the basement of the garage where he shot and killed him.

At the time of the robbery and killing, Fugate was 19 years of age, weighed approximately 175, and was over 6 feet tall. The decedent was 66 years of age. The fatal wound extended laterally from the left rear toward the right front of the body of Leingang.

The first assignment of error is based upon the proposition that the killing was not done "purposely" as required by R.C. 2901.01, and in support of this alleged error the appellant has alluded to a number of cases which show that an intent to kill is essential to a conviction for first degree murder. The cited cases have little more than academic interest in this case unless the jury was required to accept the testimony of Fugate that the shooting was accidental to the exclusion of all other evidence presented at the trial.

But the jury was not so limited in its consideration of the evidence. The element of intent may be, and usually is, determined from attendant circumstances, and the composite picture developed by the evidence in this case is particularly suited to a reasonable finding that the killing was done purposely. As stated in *State v. Salter:* "intent is a mental phenomenon, and in order to determine whether an intent to do a certain act existed, the circumstances surrounding the act must be examined and the intent determined therefrom." Or as set forth in paragraph four of the syllabus in *State v. Huffman:* "The intent of an accused person dwells in his mind. Not being ascertainable by the exercise of any or all of the senses, it can never be proved by the direct testimony of a third person and it need not be." * * *

"It is the law of Ohio that an intent to kill may be presumed where the natural and probable consequence of a wrongful act is to produce death, and such intent may be deduced from all the surrounding circumstances, including the instrument used to produce death, and the manner of inflicting a fatal wound."

In the present case, the evidence, and the inferences reasonably deducible therefrom, amply support the jury findings as to every essential element of the crime. The first assignment of error is overruled. * * *

We find no prejudicial error in the record, and the judgment of the Court of Common Pleas will be affirmed.

Judgment affirmed.

D. KNOWLEDGE

Another mens rea term used in both common law and Model Penal Code jurisdictions is the mental state of "knowledge." Under the common law, a person knows of a fact if he either is aware of that fact or correctly believes the fact exists. Many jurisdictions recognize another way of proving knowledge: willful blindness or deliberate ignorance. The Ninth Circuit Court of Appeals discusses willful blindness in *United States v. Jewell*.

UNITED STATES V. JEWELL

United States Court of Appeals for the Ninth Circuit
532 F.2d 697 (9th Cir. 1976)

BROWNING, CIRCUIT JUDGE.

* * *

Appellant defines "knowingly" in 21 U.S.C. §§ 841 and 960 to require that positive knowledge that a controlled substance is involved be established as an element of each offense.[a] On the basis of this interpretation, appellant argues that it was reversible error to instruct the jury that the defendant could be convicted upon proof beyond a reasonable doubt that if he did not have positive knowledge that a controlled substance was concealed in the automobile he drove over the border, it was solely and entirely because of the conscious purpose on his part to avoid learning the truth. The majority concludes that this contention is wrong in principle, and has no support in authority or in the language or legislative history of the statute.

It is undisputed that appellant entered the United States driving an automobile in which 110 pounds of marihuana worth $6,250 had been concealed in a secret compartment between the trunk and rear seat. Appellant testified that he did not know the marihuana was present. There was circumstantial evidence from which the jury could infer that appellant had positive knowledge of the presence of the marihuana, and that his contrary testimony was false.[1] On the other hand there was

---

[a] 21 U.S.C. § 841 provides in part: "[I]t shall be unlawful for any person knowingly or intentionally—(1) to manufacture, distribute, or dispense, or possess with intent to manufacture, distribute, or dispense, a controlled substance * * *."

21 U.S.C. § 960 provides in part: "Any person who * * * knowingly or intentionally imports or exports a controlled substance, * * * shall be punished * * *."

[1] Appellant testified that a week before the incident in question he sold his car for $100 to obtain funds "to have a good time." He then rented a car for about $100, and he and a friend drove the rented car to Mexico. * * *

Their testimony regarding acquisition of the load car follows a pattern common in these cases: they were approached in a Tijuana bar by a stranger who identified himself only by his first name 'Ray.' He asked them if they wanted to buy marihuana, and offered to pay them $100 for driving a car north across the border. Appellant accepted the offer and drove the load car back, alone. Appellant's friend drove appellant's rented car back to Los Angeles.

evidence from which the jury could conclude that appellant spoke the truth that although appellant knew of the presence of the secret compartment and had knowledge of facts indicating that it contained marihuana, he deliberately avoided positive knowledge of the presence of the contraband to avoid responsibility in the event of discovery.[2] If the jury concluded the latter was indeed the situation, and if positive knowledge is required to convict, the jury would have no choice consistent with its oath but to find appellant not guilty even though he deliberately contrived his lack of positive knowledge. * * *

Appellant tendered an instruction that to return a guilty verdict the jury must find that the defendant knew he was in possession of marihuana. The trial judge rejected the instruction because it suggested that "absolutely, positively, he has to know that it's there." The court said, "I think, in this case, it's not too sound an instruction because we have evidence that if the jury believes it, they'd be justified in finding he actually didn't know what it was—he didn't because he didn't want to find it."

The court instructed the jury . . . that the government must prove beyond a reasonable doubt that the defendant "knowingly" brought the marihuana into the United States and that he "knowingly" possessed the marihuana. The court continued:

> The Government can complete their burden of proof by proving, beyond a reasonable doubt, that if the defendant was not

---

Appellant testified that the stranger instructed him to leave the load car at the address on the car registration slip with the keys in the ashtray. The person living at that address testified that he had sold the car a year earlier and had not seen it since. When the Customs agent asked appellant about the secret compartment in the car, appellant did not deny knowledge of its existence, but stated that it was in the car when he got it.

There were many discrepancies and inconsistencies in the evidence reflecting upon appellant's credibility. Taking the record as a whole, the jury could have concluded that the evidence established an abortive scheme, concocted and carried out by appellant from the beginning, to acquire a load of marihuana in Mexico and return it to Los Angeles for distribution for profit.

[2] Both appellant and his companion testified that the stranger identified as 'Ray' offered to sell them marihuana and, when they declined, asked if they wanted to drive a car back to Los Angeles for $100. Appellant's companion "wanted no part of driving the vehicle.' He testified, "It didn't sound right to me." Appellant accepted the offer. The Drug Enforcement Administration agent testified that appellant stated "he thought there was probably something wrong and something illegal in the vehicle, but that he checked it over. He looked in the glove box and under the front seat and in the trunk, prior to driving it. *He didn't find anything, and, therefore, he assumed that the people at the border wouldn't find anything either."* (emphasis added). Appellant was asked at trial whether he had seen the special compartment when he opened the trunk. He responded, "Well, you know, I saw a void there, but I didn't know what it was." He testified that he did not investigate further. The Customs agent testified that when he opened the trunk and saw the partition he asked appellant "when he had that put in." Appellant told the agent "that it was in the car when he got it."

The jury would have been justified in accepting all of the testimony as true and concluding that although appellant was aware of facts making it virtually certain that the secret compartment concealed marihuana, he deliberately refrained from acquiring positive knowledge of the fact.

actually aware that there was marijuana in the vehicle he was driving when he entered the United States his ignorance in that regard was solely and entirely a result of his having made a conscious purpose to disregard the nature of that which was in the vehicle, with a conscious purpose to avoid learning the truth.

The legal premise of these instructions is firmly supported by leading commentators here and in England. Professor Rollin M. Perkins writes, "One with a deliberate antisocial purpose in mind . . . may deliberately 'shut his eyes' to avoid knowing what would otherwise be obvious to view. In such cases, so far as criminal law is concerned, the person acts at his peril in this regard, and is treated as having 'knowledge' of the facts as they are ultimately discovered to be." J. Edwards, writing in 1954, introduced a survey of English cases with the statement, "For well-nigh a hundred years, it has been clear from the authorities that a person who deliberately shuts his eyes to an obvious means of knowledge has sufficient mens rea for an offence based on such words as . . . 'knowingly.'" "Professor Glanville Williams states, on the basis of both English and American authorities, 'To the requirement of actual knowledge there is one strictly limited exception. . . . (T)he rule is that if a party has his suspicion aroused but then deliberately omits to make further enquiries, because he wishes to remain in ignorance, he is deemed to have knowledge.'" Professor Williams concludes, "The rule that wilful blindness is equivalent to knowledge is essential, and is found throughout the criminal law."[7]

The substantive justification for the rule is that deliberate ignorance and positive knowledge are equally culpable. The textual justification is that in common understanding one "knows" facts of which he is less than absolutely certain. To act "knowingly," therefore, is not necessarily to act only with positive knowledge, but also to act with an awareness of the high probability of the existence of the fact in question. When such awareness is present, "positive" knowledge is not required.

This is the analysis adopted in the Model Penal Code. Section 2.02(7) states: "When knowledge of the existence of a particular fact is an element of an offense, such knowledge is established if a person is aware of a high probability of its existence, unless he actually believes that it

---

[7] Mr. Williams' concluding paragraph reads in its entirety:

The rule that wilful blindness is equivalent to knowledge is essential, and is found throughout the criminal law. It is, at the same time, an unstable rule, because judges are apt to forget its very limited scope. A court can properly find wilful blindness only where it can almost be said that the defendant actually knew. He suspected the fact; he realised its probability; but he refrained from obtaining the final confirmation because he wanted in the event to be able to deny knowledge. This, and this alone, is wilful blindness. It requires in effect a finding that the defendant intended to cheat the administration of justice. Any wider definition would make the doctrine of wilful blindness indistinguishable from the civil doctrine of negligence in not obtaining knowledge.

does not exist." As the Comment to this provision explains, "Paragraph (7) deals with the situation British commentators have denominated 'wilful blindness' or 'connivance,' the case of the actor who is aware of the probable existence of a material fact but does not satisfy himself that it does not in fact exist." * * *

There is no reason to reach a different result under the statute involved in this case. Doing so would put this court in direct conflict with Courts of Appeals in two other circuits that have approved "deliberate ignorance" instructions in prosecutions under 21 U.S.C. § 841(a), or its predecessor, 21 U.S.C. § 174. * * *

Appellant's narrow interpretation of 'knowingly' is inconsistent with the Drug Control Act's general purpose to deal more effectively "with the growing menace of drug abuse in the United States." Holding that this term introduces a requirement of positive knowledge would make deliberate ignorance a defense. It cannot be doubted that those who traffic in drugs would make the most of it. This is evident from the number of appellate decisions reflecting conscious avoidance of positive knowledge of the presence of contraband—in the car driven by the defendant or in which he is a passenger, in the suitcase or package he carries, in the parcel concealed in his clothing.

It is no answer to say that in such cases the fact finder may infer positive knowledge. It is probable that many who performed the transportation function, essential to the drug traffic, can truthfully testify that they have no positive knowledge of the load they carry. Under appellant's interpretation of the statute, such persons will be convicted only if the fact finder errs in evaluating the credibility of the witness or deliberately disregards the law.

It begs the question to assert that a "deliberate ignorance" instruction permits the jury to convict without finding that the accused possessed the knowledge required by the statute. Such an assertion assumes that the statute requires positive knowledge. But the question is the meaning of the term 'knowingly' in the statute. If it means positive knowledge, then, of course, nothing less will do. But if 'knowingly' includes a mental state in which the defendant is aware that the fact in question is highly probable but consciously avoids enlightenment, the statute is satisfied by such proof.

It is worth emphasizing that the required state of mind differs from positive knowledge only so far as necessary to encompass a calculated effort to avoid the sanctions of the statute while violating its substance. "A court can properly find wilful blindness only where it can almost be said that the defendant actually knew.' In the language of the instruction in this case, the government must prove, "beyond a reasonable doubt, that if the defendant was not actually aware . . . his ignorance in that regard was solely and entirely a result of . . . a conscious purpose to avoid learning the truth."

No legitimate interest of an accused is prejudiced by such a standard, and society's interest in a system of criminal law that is enforceable and that imposes sanctions upon all who are equally culpable requires it.

The conviction is affirmed.

[The dissenting opinion of JUDGE KENNEDY, with whom JUDGES ELY, HUFSTEDLER and WALLACE join, is omitted.]

NOTE

In a 2011 civil case, *Global-Tech Appliances, Inc. v. SEB S.A.*, the U.S. Supreme Court clarified the proof needed for a showing of willful blindness. The Court explained that when the government tries to prove knowledge through willful blindness, it must go beyond merely showing that the defendant was deliberately indifferent to a known risk. Willful blindness requires a showing that the defendant (1) subjectively believed there was a high probability that a fact existed, and (2) took deliberate actions to avoid learning that fact.

E. SPECIAL PROBLEMS IN INTENT

1. TRANSFERRING INTENT

One of the basic principles of criminal law is the idea that an intent to do one thing, such as intending to steal rum, cannot be used as a substitute for an intent to do another thing, such as intending to burn down a ship. *Regina v. Faulkner*, 13 Cox C.C. 550 (1877). If the statute requires an intent to burn down a ship, then the government must prove that the defendant's conscious object or purpose was to burn down the ship, or that the defendant knew to a virtual certainty that his actions would cause the ship to burn down. An intent to steal rum is not the same as an intent to burn down a ship. An intent to light a match in order to steal that rum is a far cry from purposefully burning down a ship or knowing that one's actions will burn down the ship. Similarly, an intent to injure a person is not the same thing as an intent to damage property.

What if an individual attempts to shoot and kill one person (X), misses, and instead kills another person (Y)? Can that individual be held criminally liable for intentionally murdering Y?

If an intent to do one thing cannot be used as proof of an intent to do another completely different thing, then one might surmise that an individual who intends to shoot and kill one person, but instead mistakenly shoots and kills another person, cannot be held criminally liable for intentionally killing that other person (although he might be liable for recklessly killing that individual). Under both the common law and the Model Penal Code, however, the shooter can be held criminally liable for intentionally killing the other person even if that other person was in fact an unintended victim. *See* Model Penal Code § 2.03(2), The court in *People v. Scott* explains why.

PEOPLE V. SCOTT

Supreme Court of California
14 Cal.4th 544, 927 P.2d 288, 59 Cal.Rptr.2d 178 (1996)

BROWN, J.

A jury convicted defendants Damien Scott and Derrick Brown of various crimes for their part in a drive-by shooting which resulted in the death of one person and injury to several others. We must decide in this case whether the doctrine of transferred intent may be used to assign criminal liability to a defendant who kills an unintended victim when the defendant is also prosecuted for the attempted murder of an intended victim.

Under the classic formulation of California's common law doctrine of transferred intent, a defendant who shoots with the intent to kill a certain person and hits a bystander instead is subject to the same criminal liability that would have been imposed had "the fatal blow reached the person for whom intended." "In such a factual setting, the defendant is deemed as culpable as if he had accomplished what he set out to do."

Here, it was established at trial that defendants fired an automatic weapon into a public park in an attempt to kill a certain individual, and fatally shot a bystander instead. The case presents the type of factual setting in which courts have uniformly approved reliance on the transferred intent doctrine as the basis of determining a defendant's criminal liability for the death of an unintended victim. Consistent with a line of decisions beginning with *Suesser* nearly a century ago, we conclude that the jury in this case was properly instructed on a transferred intent theory of liability for first degree murder. * * *

I. BACKGROUND

In May 1991, Calvin Hughes became the target of a family vendetta. While Hughes and Elaine Scott were romantically involved, Hughes and his sister, Eugenia Griffin, shared Scott's apartment. After the bloom faded from the romance, relations between Hughes and Scott became increasingly acrimonious and one night Hughes and Scott got into a physical altercation. Defendant Damien Scott and codefendant Derrick Brown, Scott's adult sons, came to her aid and forced Hughes and Griffin out of the apartment.

A few days later, Hughes borrowed Griffin's car and, accompanied by his friend Gary Tripp, returned to Scott's place to retrieve his personal belongings. When Scott attempted to bar his entry, Hughes forced his way into the apartment and gathered his things. On his way out, he heard Scott threaten to page her sons.

Hughes and Tripp drove to Jesse Owens Park in South Los Angeles to meet Griffin. Nathan Kelley and his teenage son, Jack Gibson, had parked nearby. As Hughes stood beside Kelley's car, talking to him through the open window, three cars entered the park. Gunfire erupted. Defendant Scott and codefendant Brown, riding in the first car, sprayed the area with bullets. Hughes took cover behind the front bumper of Kelley's car. When there was a lull in the shooting, Hughes sprinted toward the park gym. A renewed hail of gunfire followed him. A bullet hit the heel of his shoe. The shooting stopped when Hughes took cover behind the gym. The gunmen left the park.

In the aftermath, the victims discovered both Kelley's and Griffin's vehicles had been riddled with bullets; Gary Tripp had been shot in the leg and buttocks; and Jack Gibson had been killed when a bullet struck him in the head.

In an amended multi[illegible]on, defendant Scott and codefendant Bro[illegible] the murder of Jack Gibson [and] attempted [illegible] Gary Tripp. * * *

At a second [illegible] mistrial due to a deadlocked jury, the prosecutor sought to establish that Jack Gibson was the unintended victim of defendants' premeditated and deliberate intent to kill Calvin Hughes. At the prosecution's request, the trial court instructed the jury on transferred intent using a modified version of CALJIC No. 8.65. The court stated as follows: "As it relates to the charge of murder, where one attempts to kill a certain person, but by mistake or inadvertence kills a different person, the crime, if any, so committed is the same as though the person originally intended to be killed, had been killed." The jury was also instructed on second degree express malice and implied malice murder.

The jury convicted both defendants of second degree murder [and] two counts of attempted murder. * * *

Defendants appealed their convictions and, in a published decision, the Court of Appeal modified and affirmed the judgments of conviction. In relevant part, the Court of Appeal rejected defendants' argument that a transferred intent instruction only applies when the prosecution elects to charge the defendant with first degree murder of the unintended victim, and not also with attempted murder of the intended victim.

We granted defendant Scott's petition for review.

The jury convicted defendants of second degree murder for fatally shooting the unintended victim. It cannot be determined from the verdicts, however, whether the jury relied on the transferred intent instruction to convict defendants of second degree murder on an express malice theory, or whether it reached that verdict through a finding of implied malice. Consequently, it is necessary to decide whether a transferred intent instruction was properly given in this case.

II. DISCUSSION

The common law doctrine of transferred intent was applied in England as early as the 16th century. The doctrine became part of the common law in many American jurisdictions, including that of California, and is typically invoked in the criminal law context when assigning criminal liability to a defendant who attempts to kill one person but accidentally kills another instead. Under such circumstances, the accused is deemed as culpable, and society is harmed as much, as if the defendant had accomplished what he had initially intended, and justice is achieved by punishing the defendant for a crime of the same seriousness as the one he tried to commit against his intended victim. Under the classic formulation of the common law doctrine of transferred intent, the defendant's guilt is thus "exactly what it would have been had the blow fallen upon the intended victim instead of the bystander."

In California, the transferred intent doctrine was first addressed in *Suesser*. The defendant in that case was convicted of first degree murder and sentenced to death for fatally shooting an individual under the erroneous belief he was firing at a different person named Allen, whom the defendant deliberately and with premeditation intended to kill. On appeal, the defendant argued the trial court erred in refusing his request to instruct the jury that malice must exist towards the person actually killed, and that if the defendant shot the deceased erroneously believing him to be Allen, he was guilty of only second degree murder. The trial court instructed instead in accordance with the common law doctrine of transferred intent, explaining to the jury that the defendant was guilty of the same degree of murder as if he had killed Allen instead of the deceased.

Persuaded by the reasoning of commentators and the weight of authority from other jurisdictions, *Suesser* held that the common law doctrine of transferred intent survived the enactment of California's murder statute. The opinion in *Suesser* does not expressly state the rationale behind the rule of transferred intent. One of the out-of-state decisions cited by the *Suesser* court did so succinctly, however. In *State v. Murray,* the defendant was convicted of first degree murder for killing a bystander in an attempt on the life of another person. The Oregon Supreme Court affirmed the judgment because the defendant "exhibited the same malignity and recklessness in the one event he would have displayed in the other, and the consequences to society are just as fearful."

Suesser and a number of other California decisions present the classic 'bad aim' cases in which a defendant who attempts to kill one individual and inadvertently kills a bystander instead is convicted of murder on the theory of transferred intent. Courts in these cases have uniformly rejected the defendants' argument that their convictions were based on insufficient evidence of intent to kill. * * *

Nor is application of the transferred intent doctrine under these circumstances foreclosed by the prosecutor having charged defendants with attempted murder of the intended victim. Contrary to what its name implies, the transferred intent doctrine does not refer to any actual intent that is capable of being "used up" once it is employed to convict a defendant of a specific intent crime against the intended victim.

Courts and commentators have long recognized that the notion of creating a whole crime by "transferring" a defendant's intent from the object of his assault to the victim of his criminal act is, as Dean Prosser aptly describes it, a "bare-faced" legal fiction. The legal fiction of transferring a defendant's intent helps illustrate why, as a theoretical matter, a defendant can be convicted of murder when she did not intend to kill the person *actually killed*. The transferred intent doctrine does not, however, denote an actual "transfer" of "intent" from the intended victim to the unintended victim. Rather, as applied here, it connotes a *policy*—that a defendant who shoots at an intended victim with intent to kill but misses and hits a bystander instead should be subject to the same criminal liability that would have been imposed had he hit his intended mark. It is the policy underlying the doctrine, rather than its literal meaning, that compels the conclusion that a transferred intent instruction was properly given in this case.

Conversely, reliance on a transferred intent theory of liability for the first degree murder of the unintended victim did not prevent the prosecutor from also charging defendants with attempted murder of the intended victim. As previously recounted, defendants shot at an intended victim, missed him, and killed another individual instead. In their attempt to kill the intended victim, defendants committed crimes against two persons. They may be held accountable for the death of the unintended victim on a theory of transferred intent. Their criminal liability for attempting to kill the intended victim is that which the law assigns, here, in accordance with the attempted murder statute.

Defendant Scott argues that when an accused is charged with attempted murder of the intended victim, and transferred intent is used to assign a defendant's liability for the killing of an unintended victim, the defendant is being prosecuted as if he intended to kill two people rather than one. Defendant asserts that, under these circumstances, transferred intent should not be applied. He finds support for this proposition in *People v. Birreuta*, where the court stated that a murderer who premeditates and deliberates two killings is more culpable, and should be punished more severely, than the murderer who intends to kill only one victim and inadvertently kills another.

In *Birreuta,* the defendant was convicted of two counts of first degree murder for fatally shooting both an intended and an unintended victim. The court reversed the conviction that was based on the theory of transferred intent, holding that when the intended victim is killed, it is unnecessary to rely on the fiction of transferred intent. According to the court, the defendant's premeditation and deliberation can be directly and fully employed in prosecuting the first degree murder of the intended victim.

The *Birreuta* court viewed killers who premeditatedly and deliberately kill two people as more culpable than those who only intend to kill one person and mistakenly kill another in the attempt. The court noted that when the transferred intent doctrine is applied to hold the latter accountable for the accidental killing as a first degree murder, this distinction in culpability disappears.

We observe that although application of the transferred intent doctrine in the classic bad aim cases has been consistent, in cases involving crimes relating to both intended and unintended victims, reliance on the doctrine to assign criminal liability has led to mixed results. Some courts simply apply the rule of *Suesser* without addressing the question whether the death of, or injury to, the intended as well as the unintended victim requires a different analysis. Other courts acknowledge the potential for analytical distinctions but reach conflicting resolutions. The court in *People v. Carlson* stated, in dictum, that transferred intent "applies even though the original object of the assault is killed as well as the person whose death was the accidental or the unintended result of the intent to kill the former." The court in *Birreuta* expressed a contrary view, holding the transferred intent doctrine did not apply when both intended and unintended victims are killed.

Because the facts of the case presented here do not involve the fatal shooting of both an intended and unintended victim, we have no occasion to determine whether *Birreuta*'s reasoning or its conclusion is correct, and we decline to express a view on that decision.[a] As previously discussed, the evidence at trial in this case was that defendants' attempt to kill one person resulted in the killing of an innocent bystander. Under these circumstances, *Suesser* and its progeny have uniformly applied the

---

[a] In a later case, the California Supreme Court expressed its view that *Birreuta* was incorrectly decided. People v. Bland, 28 Cal. 4th 313 (2002). Notably, the *Bland* Court held that the transferred intent doctrine does not apply to attempted murder, explaining "Someone who in truth does not intend to kill a person is not guilty of that person's attempted murder even if the crime would have been murder—due to transferred intent—if the person were killed. To be guilty of attempted murder, the defendant must intend to kill the alleged victim, not someone else." *Id.* at 328.

common law doctrine of transferred intent to assign a defendant's criminal liability for the killing of the unintended victim. Consistent with the line of decisions beginning with *Suesser* nearly a century ago, because defendants shot at one person with an intent to kill, missed him, and killed a bystander instead, they may be held accountable for a crime of the same seriousness as the one they would have committed had they hit their intended target. * * *

III. DISPOSITION

The judgment of the Court of Appeal affirming the judgments of conviction is affirmed.

NOTE

Joshua Dressler argues that in the classic "bad aim" case, the fiction of transferred intent is unnecessary:

> [T]he transferred intent doctrine is unnecessary and, if invoked without great care, misleading. Consider the typical "bad aim" case: *A* intends to kill *B*, but instead kills *C*, and is prosecuted for intent-to-kill murder. In this case, there is no need to transfer *A*'s intention to kill *B* to unintended victim *C*; *A* has the requisite intent *without* the doctrine. There is no need to think in terms of *A*'s *mens rea* following a bullet to its eventual victim. One need only look at the definition of criminal homicide to see this: The social harm of murder is the "killing of a human being by another human being." The requisite intent, therefore, is the intent to kill *a*, not a specific, human being. In the present case, *A* intended to kill *a* human being (*B*), so the *mens rea* is satisfied; and he did in fact kill *a* human being (*C*), so the *actus reus* is proven. Thus, the elements of murder are proved without invoking the legal fiction of transferred intent.

Joshua Dressler, UNDERSTANDING CRIMINAL LAW § 10.04(A)(3)(b) (6th ed. 2012).

2. THE SPECIFIC INTENT/GENERAL INTENT DISTINCTION

The common law draws a distinction between specific intent and general intent crimes. Although the distinction is better understood as the product of history than of logic, it is important for students and practitioners to be familiar with it because different legal rules apply depending on whether the defendant is charged with a specific intent or a general intent crime. *People v. Atkins* explains how to determine whether an offense is a specific intent or a general intent crime and why it matters to the defendant who wishes to present evidence of voluntary intoxication in his defense.

PEOPLE V. ATKINS

Supreme Court of California
25 Cal.4th 76, 18 P.3d 660, 104 Cal.Rptr.2d 738 (2001)

CHIN, J.

Is evidence of voluntary intoxication admissible, under Penal Code section 22, on the issue of whether defendant formed the required mental state for arson? We conclude that such evidence is not admissible because arson is a general intent crime. Accordingly, we reverse the judgment of the Court of Appeal.

FACTS AND PROCEDURAL HISTORY

On September 26, 1997, defendant told his friends that he hated Orville Figgs and was going to burn down Figgs's house.

On the afternoon of September 27, defendant and his brother David drove by Figgs's home on the Ponderosa Sky Ranch. Defendant 'flipped the bird' at Figgs as they passed by.

Later that day, around 5:00 p.m., a neighbor saw David drive a white pickup truck into the Ponderosa Sky Ranch canyon, but could not tell if he had a passenger. Around 9:00 p.m., the same neighbor saw the pickup truck drive out of the canyon at a high rate of speed. A half-hour later, a fire was reported. Shortly after 10:00 p.m., Figgs was awakened by a neighbor. Because the fire was rapidly approaching his house, Figgs set up a fire line. The fire came within 150 feet of his house.

At 9:00 or 9:30 p.m., one of defendant's friends saw defendant at David's apartment. He was angrily throwing things around. When asked if defendant was heavily intoxicated, the friend replied, "Yes. Agitated, very agitated."

The county fire marshall, Alan Carlson, responded to the fire around 1:30 a.m. and saw a large fire rapidly spreading in the canyon below the ranch. He described fire conditions on that night as 'extreme.' Both the weather and the vegetation were particularly dry. The wind was blowing from 12 to 27 miles per hour, with gusts up to 50 miles per hour. The canyon had heavy brush, trees, grass, and steep sloping grades. The fire could not be controlled for three days and burned an area from 2.5 to 2.8 miles long.

The fire marshall traced the origin of the fire to an approximately 10-foot square area that was completely burned and smelled of 'chainsaw mix,' a combination of oil and gasoline. A soil sample taken from that area tested positive for gasoline. About 40 feet away, the marshall found defendant's wallet, which was near a recently opened beer can, and tire tracks. He also found a disposable lighter nearby and two more beer cans in other parts of the canyon. All the cans had the same expiration date.

Several days later, defendant spoke with the fire marshall. After waiving his *Miranda* rights, defendant told the marshall that he and his brother had spent much of the day drinking. They then drove in David's white pickup to the Ponderosa Sky Ranch canyon, where they drank some more and stayed between three and one-half to five hours. Defendant saw that the area was in poor condition and decided to burn some of the weeds. His family had once lived there. He pulled out the weeds, placed them in a small pile in a cleared area, retrieved a plastic gasoline jug from David's truck, and from the jug poured 'chainsaw mix' on the pile of weeds. Defendant put the jug down a few feet away and lit the pile of weeds with a disposable lighter. The fire quickly spread to the jug and got out of hand. He and David tried to put the fire out, unsuccessfully. They panicked and fled while the jug was still burning. Defendant told the marshall that he meant no harm, claimed the fire was an accident, but admitted that he and his family had hard feelings with the Figgs family.

The marshall testified that the fire had not been started in a cleared area. The area was covered with vegetation, and there was no evidence that the fire started accidentally during a debris burn or that someone had tried to put it out. The marshall opined that the fire was intentionally set.

An information charged defendant with arson of forest land. The trial court instructed on arson[2] and on the lesser offenses of arson to property, unlawfully causing a fire of forest land, and misdemeanor unlawfully causing a fire of property. It described arson and all lesser offenses as general intent crimes and further instructed that voluntary intoxication is not a defense to arson and the lesser crimes and does not relieve defendant of responsibility for the crime. The jury found defendant guilty as charged.

Defendant appealed, arguing that evidence of voluntary intoxication was admissible to show that he lacked the requisite mental state for arson. The Court of Appeal agreed. It reasoned that, as defined in its prior decisions of *In re Stonewall F.*, the mens rea for arson is the intent to set fire to or burn or cause to be burned forest land, a specific mental state, as to which voluntary intoxication evidence is admissible under section 22, subdivision (b). The court reversed because the instruction that voluntary intoxication was not a defense to arson "denied defendant the opportunity to prove he lacked the required mental state."

We granted the People's petition for review on the issue of whether evidence of voluntary intoxication is admissible, under section 22, to negate the required mental state for arson.

---

[2] The trial court defined arson, in the language of CALJIC No. 14.80, as follows: "Any person who willfully and maliciously sets fire to or burns or causes to be burned any forest land is guilty of arson in violation of [section 451, subdivision (c)]. * * * The word 'willfully' means intentionally. * * * "

DISCUSSION

Section 22 provides, as relevant:

> (a) No act committed by a person while in a state of voluntary intoxication is less criminal by reason of his or her having been in that condition. * * *
>
> (b) Evidence of voluntary intoxication is admissible solely on the issue of whether or not the defendant actually formed a required specific intent, or, when charged with murder, whether the defendant premeditated, deliberated, or harbored express malice aforethought.

Evidence of voluntary intoxication is inadmissible to negate the existence of general criminal intent. In *People v. Hood*, * * * we held that intoxication was relevant to negate the existence of a specific intent, but not a general intent, and that assault is a general intent crime for this purpose. We stated:

> The distinction between specific and general intent crimes evolved as a judicial response to the problem of the intoxicated offender. That problem is to reconcile two competing theories of what is just in the treatment of those who commit crimes while intoxicated. On the one hand, the moral culpability of a drunken criminal is frequently less than that of a sober person effecting a like injury. On the other hand, it is commonly felt that a person who voluntarily gets drunk and while in that state commits a crime should not escape the consequences.
>
> Before the nineteenth century, the common law refused to give any effect to the fact that an accused committed a crime while intoxicated. The judges were apparently troubled by this rigid traditional rule, however, for there were a number of attempts during the early part of the nineteenth century to arrive at a more humane, yet workable, doctrine. The theory that these judges explored was that evidence of intoxication could be considered to negate intent, whenever intent was an element of the crime charged. As Professor Hall notes, however, such an exculpatory doctrine could eventually have undermined the traditional rule entirely, since some form of *mens rea* is a requisite of all but strict liability offenses. To limit the operation of the doctrine and achieve a compromise between the conflicting feelings of sympathy and reprobation for the intoxicated offender, later courts both in England and this country drew a distinction between so-called specific intent and general intent crimes.

Although we noted in *Hood* that specific and general intent have been notoriously difficult terms to define and apply, we set forth a general definition distinguishing the two intents: "When the definition of a crime consists of only the description of a particular act, without reference to intent to do a further act or achieve a future consequence, we ask whether the defendant intended to do the proscribed act. This intention is deemed to be a general criminal intent. When the definition refers to defendant's intent to do some further act or achieve some additional consequence, the crime is deemed to be one of specific intent." The basic framework that *Hood* established in designating a criminal intent as either specific or general for purposes of determining the admissibility of evidence of voluntary intoxication has survived.

Defendant argues that arson requires the specific intent to burn the relevant structure or forest land, a mental state that may be negated by evidence of voluntary intoxication. The People argue that arson is a general intent crime with a mental state that cannot be negated by such evidence. The Courts of Appeal have disagreed on the intent requirement for arson. * * *

We agree with the People that arson requires only a general criminal intent and that the specific intent to set fire to or burn or cause to be burned the relevant structure or forest land is not an element of arson. * * *

As relevant here, the proscribed acts within the statutory definition of arson are to (1) set fire to; (2) burn; or (3) cause to be burned, any structure, forest land, or property. Language that typically denotes specific intent crimes, such as "with the intent" to achieve or "for the purpose of" achieving some further act, is absent from section 451." "A crime is characterized as a 'general intent' crime when the required mental state entails only an intent to do the act that causes the harm; a crime is characterized as a 'specific intent' crime when the required mental state entails an intent to cause the resulting harm." The statute does not require an additional specific intent to burn a "structure, forest land, or property," but rather requires only an intent to do the act that causes the harm. * * * Thus, the intent requirement for arson fits within the *Hood* definition of general intent, i.e., the description of the proscribed act fails to refer to an intent to do a further act or achieve a future consequence. * * *

Finally, we reject defendant's argument that the withholding of voluntary intoxication evidence to negate the mental state of arson violates his due process rights by denying him the opportunity to prove he did not possess the required mental state. (*Montana v. Egelhoff*, 518 U.S. 37 (1996)).[a]

[a] We will study *Montana v. Egelhoff* in Chapter 10.

CONCLUSION

We reverse the judgment of the Court of Appeal and remand the case to the Court of Appeal for further proceedings consistent with this opinion.

NOTE

Atkins explains the most common way common law courts distinguish between specific intent and general intent crimes. In addition, a crime that requires a mental state of recklessness or negligence is generally regarded as a general intent crime. As *Atkins* suggests, the specific intent/general intent distinction evolved as a pragmatic strategy to deal with the problem of the intoxicated offender. Over time, however, courts began to rely upon the distinction in other areas of criminal law jurisprudence. We will encounter it again, for example, when we study the law of mistake. The Model Penal Code does not employ the specific intent/general intent distinction.

F. STRICT LIABILITY CRIMES

Some statutes do not include a mental state element. In such cases, the court must determine whether the legislature purposely left out a mental state element because it wanted to treat the crime as one of strict liability (one for which the government need not prove any mental state) or whether the omission was inadvertent. In *Morissette v. United States*, the Supreme Court explains that when a statute is silent as to mens rea, the ordinary presumption is that a mental state is required for criminal liability.

MORISSETTE V. UNITED STATES

Supreme Court of the United States
342 U.S. 246, 72 S.Ct. 240, 96 L.Ed. 288 (1952)

MR. JUSTICE JACKSON delivered the opinion of the Court.

This would have remained a profoundly insignificant case to all except its immediate parties had it not been so tried and submitted to the jury as to raise questions both fundamental and far-reaching in federal criminal law, for which reason we granted certiorari.

On a large tract of uninhabited and untilled land in a wooded and sparsely populated area of Michigan, the Government established a practice bombing range over which the Air Force dropped simulated bombs at ground targets. These bombs consisted of a metal cylinder about forty inches long and eight inches across, filled with sand and enough black powder to cause a smoke puff by which the strike could be located. At various places about the range signs read "Danger—Keep Out—Bombing Range." Nevertheless, the range was known as good deer country and was extensively hunted.

Spent bomb casings were cleared from the targets and thrown into piles 'so that they will be out of the way.' They were not stacked or piled in any order but were dumped in heaps, some of which had been accumulating for four years or upwards, were exposed to the weather and rusting away.

Morissette, in December of 1948, went hunting in this area but did not get a deer. He thought to meet expenses of the trip by salvaging some of these casings. He loaded three tons of them on his truck and took them to a nearby farm, where they were flattened by driving a tractor over them. After expending this labor and trucking them to market in Flint, he realized $84.

Morissette, by occupation, is a fruit stand operator in summer and a trucker and scrap iron collector in winter. An honorably discharged veteran of World War II, he enjoys a good name among his neighbors and has had no blemish on his record more disreputable than a conviction for reckless driving.

The loading, crushing and transporting of these casings were all in broad daylight, in full view of passers-by, without the slightest effort at concealment. When an investigation was started, Morissette voluntarily, promptly and candidly told the whole story to the authorities, saying that he had no intention of stealing but thought the property was abandoned, unwanted and considered of no value to the Government. He was indicted, however, on the charge that he "did unlawfully, wilfully and knowingly steal and convert" property of the United States of the value of $84, in violation of 18 U.S.C. § 641, which provides that "whoever embezzles, steals, purloins, or knowingly converts" government property is punishable by fine and imprisonment. Morissette was convicted and sentenced to imprisonment for two months or to pay a fine of $200. The Court of Appeals affirmed, one judge dissenting.

On his trial, Morissette, as he had at all times told investigating officers, testified that from appearances he believed the casings were cast-off and abandoned, that he did not intend to steal the property, and took it with no wrongful or criminal intent. The trial court, however, was unimpressed, and ruled: "He took it because he thought it was abandoned and he knew he was on government property. . . . That is no defense. . . . I don't think anybody can have the defense they thought the property was abandoned on another man's piece of property." * * * The court refused to submit or to allow counsel to argue to the jury whether Morissette acted with innocent intention. * * * [The court told the jury] "[t]hat if this young man took this property (and he says he did), without any permission (he says he did), that was on the property of the United States Government (he says it was), that it was of the value of one cent or more (and evidently it was), that he is guilty of the offense charged here. If you believe the government, he is guilty. . . . The question on intent is whether or not he intended to take the property. He says he did. Therefore, if you believe either side, he is guilty. * * *

The Court of Appeals * * * affirmed the conviction . . . , rul[ing] that this particular offense requires no element of criminal intent. This conclusion was thought to be required by the failure of Congress to express such a requisite and this Court's decisions in *United States v. Behrman* and *United States v. Balint*.[a]

I.

In those cases this Court did construe mere omission from a criminal enactment of any mention of criminal intent as dispensing with it. If they be deemed precedents for principles of construction generally applicable to federal penal statutes, they authorize this conviction. Indeed, such adoption of the literal reasoning announced in those cases would do this and more—it would sweep out of all federal crimes, except when expressly preserved, the ancient requirement of a culpable state of mind. We think * * * an effect has been ascribed to them more comprehensive than was contemplated and one inconsistent with our philosophy of criminal law.

The contention that an injury can amount to a crime only when inflicted by intention is no provincial or transient notion. It is as universal and persistent in mature systems of law as belief in freedom of the human will and a consequent ability and duty of the normal individual to choose between good and evil. A relation between some mental element and punishment for a harmful act is almost as instinctive as the child's familiar exculpatory 'But I didn't mean to,' and has afforded the rational basis for a tardy and unfinished substitution of deterrence and reformation in place of retaliation and vengeance as the motivation for public prosecution. Unqualified acceptance of this doctrine by English common law in the Eighteenth Century was indicated by Blackstone's sweeping statement that to constitute any crime there must first be a 'vicious will.' * * *

Crime, as a compound concept, generally constituted only from concurrence of an evil-meaning mind with an evil-doing hand, was congenial to an intense individualism and took deep and early root in American soil.[9] As the states codified the common law of crimes, even if their enactments were silent on the subject, their courts assumed that the

---

[a] In *United States v. Behrman,* the Court held that the Anti–Narcotic Act of 1914 which made it a crime to sell, barter, exchange or give away certain drugs could be applied to a physician who prescribed large amounts of heroin and cocaine to a known addict regardless of the doctor's intent or knowledge. In *United States v. Balint,* the Court held that a New York anti-narcotic statute did not make knowledge an element of the offense, and therefore the indictment did not have to charge that the defendants sold the prescribed drugs knowing them to be prohibited.

[9] Holmes, The Common Law, considers intent in the chapter on The Criminal Law, and earlier makes the pithy observation: 'Even a dog distinguishes between being stumbled over and being kicked.'

omission did not signify disapproval of the principle but merely recognized that intent was so inherent in the idea of the offense that it required no statutory affirmation. Courts, with little hesitation or division, found an implication of the requirement as to offenses that were taken over from the common law. The unanimity with which they have adhered to the central thought that wrongdoing must be conscious to be criminal is emphasized by the variety, disparity and confusion of their definitions of the requisite but elusive mental element. However, courts of various jurisdictions, and for the purposes of different offenses, have devised working formulae, if not scientific ones, for the instruction of juries around such terms as 'felonious intent,' 'criminal intent,' 'malice aforethought,' 'guilty knowledge,' 'fraudulent intent,' 'wilfulness,' '*scienter*,' to denote guilty knowledge, or '*mens rea*,' to signify an evil purpose or mental culpability. By use or combination of these various tokens, they have sought to protect those who were not blameworthy in mind from conviction of infamous common-law crimes.

However, the *Balint* and *Behrman* offenses belong to a category of another character, with very different antecedents and origins. The crimes there involved depend on no mental element but consist only of forbidden acts or omissions. This, while not expressed by the Court, is made clear from examination of a century-old but accelerating tendency, discernible both here and in England, to call into existence new duties and crimes which disregard any ingredient of intent. The industrial revolution multiplied the number of workmen exposed to injury from increasingly powerful and complex mechanisms, driven by freshly discovered sources of energy, requiring higher precautions by employers. Traffic of velocities, volumes and varieties unheard of came to subject the wayfarer to intolerable casualty risks if owners and drivers were not to observe new cares and uniformities of conduct. Congestion of cities and crowding of quarters called for health and welfare regulations undreamed of in simpler times. Wide distribution of goods became an instrument of wide distribution of harm when those who dispersed food, drink, drugs, and even securities, did not comply with reasonable standards of quality, integrity, disclosure and care. Such dangers have engendered increasingly numerous and detailed regulations which heighten the duties of those in control of particular industries, trades, properties or activities that affect public health, safety or welfare.

While many of these duties are sanctioned by a more strict civil liability, lawmakers, whether wisely or not, have sought to make such regulations more effective by invoking criminal sanctions to be applied by the familiar technique of criminal prosecutions and convictions. This has confronted the courts with a multitude of prosecutions, based on statutes or administrative regulations, for what have been aptly called 'public welfare offenses.' These cases do not fit neatly into any of such accepted classifications of common-law offenses, such as those against the state, the person, property, or public morals. Many of these offenses are not in the nature of positive aggressions or invasions, with which the common law so often dealt, but are in the nature of neglect where the law requires care, or inaction where it imposes a duty. Many violations of such regulations result in no direct or immediate injury to person or property but merely create the danger or probability of it which the law seeks to minimize. While such offenses do not threaten the security of the state in the manner of treason, they may be regarded as offenses against its authority, for their occurrence impairs the efficiency of controls deemed essential to the social order as presently constituted. In this respect, whatever the intent of the violator, the injury is the same, and the consequences are injurious or not according to fortuity. Hence, legislation applicable to such offenses, as a matter of policy, does not specify intent as a necessary element. The accused, if he does not will the violation, usually is in a position to prevent it with no more care than society might reasonably expect and no more exertion than it might reasonably exact from one who assumed his responsibilities. Also, penalties commonly are relatively small, and conviction does no grave damage to an offender's reputation. Under such considerations, courts have turned to construing statutes and regulations which make no mention of intent as dispensing with it and holding that the guilty act alone makes out the crime. This has not, however, been without expressions of misgiving.

The pilot of the movement in this country appears to be a holding that a tavernkeeper could be convicted for selling liquor to an habitual drunkard even if he did not know the buyer to be such. Later came Massachusetts holdings that convictions for selling adulterated milk in violation of statutes forbidding such sales require no allegation or proof that defendant knew of the adulteration. Departures from the common-law tradition, mainly of these general classes, were reviewed and their rationale appraised by Chief Justice Cooley, as follows:

> I agree that as a rule there can be no crime without a criminal intent; but this is not by any means a universal rule. . . . Many statutes which are in the nature of police regulations, as this is, impose criminal penalties irrespective of any intent to violate them; the purpose being to require a degree of diligence for the protection of the public which shall render violation impossible.

* * * It was not until recently that the Court took occasion more explicitly to relate abandonment of the ingredient of intent, not merely with considerations of expediency in obtaining convictions, nor with the *malum prohibitum* classification of the crime, but with the peculiar nature and quality of the offense. We referred to '. . . a now familiar type of legislation whereby penalties serve as effective means of regulation,' and continued, 'such legislation dispenses with the conventional requirement for criminal conduct—awareness of some wrongdoing. In the

interest of the larger good it puts the burden of acting at hazard upon a person otherwise innocent but standing in responsible relation to a public danger.' But we warned: 'Hardship there doubtless may be under a statute which thus penalizes the transaction though consciousness of wrongdoing be totally wanting.'

Neither this Court nor, so far as we are aware, any other has undertaken to delineate a precise line or set forth comprehensive criteria for distinguishing between crimes that require a mental element and crimes that do not. We attempt no closed definition, for the law on the subject is neither settled nor static. * * *

Stealing, larceny, and its variants and equivalents, were among the earliest offenses known to the law that existed before legislation; they are invasions of rights of property which stir a sense of insecurity in the whole community and arouse public demand for retribution, the penalty is high and, when a sufficient amount is involved, the infamy is that of a felony, which, says Maitland, is '. . . as bad a word as you can give to man or thing.' State courts of last resort, on whom fall the heaviest burden of interpreting criminal law in this country, have consistently retained the requirement of intent in larceny-type offenses. If any state has deviated, the exception has neither been called to our attention nor disclosed by our research.

Congress, therefore, omitted any express prescription of criminal intent from the enactment before us in the light of an unbroken course of judicial decision in all constituent states of the Union holding intent inherent in this class of offense, even when not expressed in a statute. Congressional silence as to mental elements in an Act merely adopting into federal statutory law a concept of crime already so well defined in common law and statutory interpretation by the states may warrant quite contrary inferences than the same silence in creating an offense new to general law, for whose definition the courts have no guidance except the Act. * * *

We hold that mere omission from § 641 of any mention of intent will not be construed as eliminating that element from the crimes denounced.

Reversed.

COMMONWEALTH V. BARONE

Superior Court of Pennsylvania
276 Pa.Super. 282, 419 A.2d 457 (1980)

CERCONE, PRESIDENT JUDGE.

The Commonwealth brings the instant appeal from the trial court's order granting of appellee's demurrer to the charge of homicide by vehicle, Motor Vehicle Code, 75 Pa.C.S. § 3732 (1977). Ms. Barone filed a cross-appeal challenging an earlier order of court dismissing various of her earlier petitions and motions attacking the constitutionality of this statute. Albeit for different reasons, the majority of this Court agree that the order of the trial court discharging appellant should be affirmed.

(1) Section 3732 of the Motor Vehicle Code provides:

> Any person who unintentionally causes the death of another person while engaged in the violation of any law of this Commonwealth or municipal ordinance applying to the operation or use of a vehicle or to the regulation of traffic is guilty of homicide by vehicle, a misdemeanor of the first degree, when the violation is the cause of death.

The Commonwealth argues and the Dissent agrees that the words of this provision are precise and unambiguous. From this the Commonwealth further reasons that this statute unequivocally evidences a legislative intent to impose the severe penal sanctions of up to five years imprisonment and a possible fine, on drivers who, no matter how unintentionally, cause a death while operating a vehicle in violation of any statewide or municipal rule regulating operation or use of an auto. In our opinion, the above language is not susceptible to such a 'plain meaning' approach. After having examined the legislative history of this enactment, we would hold that the legislature intended to select culpable negligence as defined in the Crimes Code * * * as its touchstone for punishment. * * *

Section 305 provides in pertinent part:

> (a) The requirements of culpability prescribed by . . . Section 302 of this title . . . do not apply to:
>
> (2) offenses defined by statutes other than this title, insofar as a legislative purpose to impose absolute liability for such offenses or with respect to any material element thereof plainly appears.

This section of the Crimes Code is essentially identical to the parallel provision of the Model Penal Code, § 205(1)(b) (1962). The Comments to this proviso expressly observe "(t)hat this section makes a frontal attack on absolute or strict liability in penal law, whenever the offense carries a possibility of sentence of imprisonment." Implementation of this strong common law tradition against strict penal responsibility is found in the Code's commandment that legislation should not be found to impose strict liability unless a legislative intent to do so "plainly appears." With this in mind, our Court should not liberally apply this 'plainly appears' test, but rather should carefully scrutinize the legislature's use of any settled terms which have heretofore been commonly associated with "fault."

The above approach, however, is not novel to Pennsylvania appellate courts. Our courts, as the Dissent correctly points out, have customarily adhered to the following principles of statutory construction 1) When the legislature employs language which is plain and unambiguous, there is no longer justification to resort to the rules of statutory construction; 2) In deciding whether a word or phrase is plain and unambiguous within the meaning of the above principle, an appellate court is to construe the word or phrase in accordance with its common and approved usage and; 3) If our legislature has utilized a word or phrase which is centuries old in our common law jurisprudence, we must interpret it consistently with its heritage in our legal traditions.

I begin with the words that are used to delineate the offense in this case. The critical word in the title is "homicide." In this Commonwealth, our court has uniformly interpreted enactments which carry this solemn title as requiring that the voluntary act which caused the death be done with some degree of fault, that is, intentionally, knowingly, recklessly, or more recently negligently. The legislature has further provided that the 'homicide' which is punishable is that which is caused 'unintentionally' while operating a motor vehicle. Taken in context, "unintentional" plainly means only that the conduct causing the death was not done purposely or with design. It neither plainly negatives the above understanding of the term "homicide" nor does it modify the phrase "while engaged in the violation of any law of this Commonwealth or municipal ordinance applying to the operation or use of a vehicle or to the regulation of traffic" in such an unambiguous manner as to preclude a judgment that the violation must still be "negligent." Viewed from this perspective, the above words and phrases could be read as either evidencing a legislative purpose to impose strict criminal responsibility or to fix accountability only for negligent violations. In our opinion, the plain meaning analysis of both the Dissent and Judge Spaeth's Concurring Opinion have obscured a simple fact. In civil law, the dual purpose for employing criminal statutory violations as standards is both to compensate the innocent victim and to deter the actor from repeating the harm causing act or omission. The criminal statute which serves as the index, however, does not share this compensation function, but rather is customarily drafted to protect the public at large from the conduct it prohibits. Underlying the criminal statute is the notion that punishment is necessary in order to reform or teach the accused not to repeat the offense and to deter others from imitating him. With regard to this particular statute, if the ultimate goal is to protect the public from imprudent driver conduct, then what purpose is to be served by punishing an operator who may have acted reasonably and prudently under the circumstances. To demonstrate, failing to adhere to the left-right-left rule when merging into traffic involves more risk to others; however, in a civil action a jury of the defendant's peers may find that it was not unreasonable to omit to observe this rule when the defendant is rushing an injured person to a hospital. To hold, as the Dissent does, that this same defendant may be criminally punished without reference to his state of mind simply does not make sense. If, with reference to the accused's evaluation of and perception of the operative factors, his conduct conforms to what is socially acceptable under the same or similar circumstances, how does this mark him as one who needs to suffer punishment? Does this statute envision punishing such an operator or separating him from his family and the remainder of society for five years? Does it seek to reduce traffic fatalities by deterring operators from exercising such care in the future? We surmise that it does not. Accordingly, we must reject the Dissent's plain meaning analysis. * * *

a.

Where, as here, we determine that the words or phrases of an act are equivocal or ambiguous, legislative intention may be ascertained by examining the circumstances which surrounded enactment, the harm sought to be regulated and prevented, the object sought to be obtained, the consequences of any particular construction, and the germane legislative history.

Circumstances Surrounding Enactment

[Regarding the circumstances surrounding the enactment of the statute, the court found that "the vehicular homicide proviso was but one aspect of a massive overhauling of all Pennsylvania rules of the road," required by a new federal transportation policy. The harm sought to be regulated and prevented was "highway accidents and delays * * * due in large degree to both Pennsylvania and non-resident operators proceeding on the highways on the basis of different and obsolete rules of driver conduct."]

Other Statutes

Nor do the supposed shortcomings of our involuntary manslaughter statute alone justify a determination that the vehicular homicide proviso was intended to create strict criminal responsibility. This Court has recently ruled that the convenience of investigation and prosecution is not the polestar in ascertaining what the essential elements of an offense are or what degree of culpability must accompany them. We concede that the history of this proviso confirms a legislative judgment that a distinct offense was needed due to the reluctance of juries to convict for involuntary manslaughter in fatal traffic accident cases; however, we dispute that this history supports the further proposition that as a result of this difficulty the legislature threw in the proverbial towel and deemed it essential to punish every violator no matter how reasonable his conduct. Faced with this difficulty, we reason that the legislature intended to adopt an intermediate response.

It is true that under the present involuntary manslaughter statute a negligent operator completely escapes any criminal punishment unless the violation which precipitated death was perpetrated 'in a reckless or grossly negligent manner.' We suggest that the legislature intended to fill this void not by punishing every death causing violation, but rather only intended to reach those violations in which there has been a 'gross deviation' from the required standard of care. To hold otherwise is to completely confuse and obscure the distinctions between legality, justification, excuse, and culpability in the law of vehicular homicide. In passing this statute, we do not discern that the legislature abandoned its heretofore sensitive approach to the law of homicide generally. We read the subject provision as merely supplementing the already existing law as relates to deaths caused by Motor Vehicle Code violations. Thus, this provision being within this general conceptual framework, it continues to recognize that Motor Vehicle Code violations may involve[26] differing species of culpability. For example, it is more aggravating to cause a death through an intentional violation rather than reckless, and worse to bring it about through reckless violation than negligent violation. In the past, Pennsylvania law punished the former two, it did not punish the latter. The latter until now has been an innocent homicide. Accordingly, as the Dissent concedes there was a need for a new offense governing deaths resulting from negligent violations of the rules of the road. This is that measure and we would so hold.

IV.

The only remaining question is whether the trial court properly sustained Ms. Barone's demurrer to the charge. In reviewing the propriety of this action, "the test to be applied . . . is whether the evidence of record and the inferences reasonably drawn therefrom would support a guilty verdict, and in making our determination we must read the evidence in the light most favorable to the Commonwealth." Instantly, the focus of our inquiry is whether the Commonwealth's evidence was sufficient to prove beyond a reasonable doubt that Ms. Barone's conduct amounted to "a gross deviation from the standard of care that a reasonable person would observe in (her) situation."

Thus viewed, the Commonwealth adduced the following. On September 14, 1977, Ms. Barone was on route to her place of employment in a two-door, brown Toyota. At approximately 8:00 a.m. she arrived at the intersection of Bethel Grant Road and Morris Road in Upper Gwynedd Township, Montgomery County. The weather was clear and the roadways dry. As she approached the intersection, she observed a stop sign and initially obeyed its command to come to a complete stop. As is often the case at a major thoroughfare during this time of day, traffic was heavy. She observed this traffic for approximately two to three minutes

[26] We are not unmindful of the difficulty of the jury's discriminating between recklessness and negligence when both of the above statutory offenses are submitted for its consideration. We are, however, confident that our lower courts are capable of devising formulations which clarify the distinctions between the two mental states. See Model Penal Code, § 2.02, Comment at 124–28.

waiting for an opportunity to safely cross the intersection. Subsequently, Ms. Barone apparently either failed to look to her right or misjudged the distance and rate of speed of the oncoming traffic and proceeded into the intersection. While in the intersection her auto was struck by a motorcycle resulting in the motorcycle operator's death. Commonwealth witnesses also testified that prior to impact Ms. Barone neither sounded her horn nor did she apply her brakes in an effort to avoid the collision. We are persuaded that based upon the above the jury could not have properly found that Ms. Barone's actions amounted to "a gross deviation from the standard of care that a reasonable person would observe in (her) situation." We are convinced that no jury of reasonable men and women could have found a gross deviation from the applicable standard of care in light of the undisputed fact that Ms. Barone waited patiently at the stop sign for several minutes before proceeding into the intersection. Under these circumstances, such conduct could not have established a violation of section 3732.

Accordingly, we would affirm the lower court's determination that the above evidence was not sufficient to go to the jury.

Order affirmed and defendant discharged.

SPAETH, JUDGE, concurring:

* * * The dissent has concluded that section 3732 should be construed to create strict criminal liability, and I agree (although I regard the issue as exceedingly close, and respect the President Judge's contrary conclusion).[2] The dissent has also concluded, however, that as so construed, section 3732 is constitutional, and as to this, I disagree; in my opinion, section 3732 represents a violation of due process, perhaps not under the federal constitution, but certainly under our state constitution.

I

Statutes creating, or arguably creating, strict criminal liability have required the courts to engage in a distinctive analysis, not usual in the criminal law. Before examining the statute involved in the present case, therefore, it is important to review the cases, so that one may understand how this analysis has developed and what its distinctive features are. In conducting this review, it will be convenient to look first at the federal cases, and then at the cases decided by our Supreme Court and by this court.

---

[2] An argument may be made that section 3732 does not, by the Commonwealth construction, impose strict liability but liability for negligence, the theory being that it is negligent for someone to violate a traffic law. However, a mere violation of a traffic law may not constitute even civil negligence, and definitely will not constitute criminal negligence as defined under section 302(b)(4) of the Crimes Code. See 18 Pa.C.S. § 302(b)(4) (criminal negligence is conduct that 'involves a gross deviation from the standard of care that a reasonable person would use in the actor's situation'). Accordingly, if the Commonwealth's construction of section 3732 is correct, the section must be labelled a strict criminal liability section.

A

The Federal Cases

"The existence of mens rea is the rule of, rather than the exception to, the principles of Anglo-American criminal jurisprudence." "The contention that an injury can amount to a crime only when inflicted by intention is no provincial or transient notion. It is as universal and persistent in mature systems of law as belief in freedom of the human will and a consequent ability and duty of the normal individual to choose between good and evil." The concept of strict criminal liability is apparently of relatively recent origin in our system of law, and has been the subject of Supreme Court scrutiny on only a very few occasions. In only one case, *Morissette*, has the Court undertaken a full discussion of the problems presented by a statute creating, or arguably creating, a strict liability crime. * * *

Two important principles may be derived from *Morissette*; it is these principles that render distinctive the analysis to be employed when examining a statute creating, or arguably creating, strict criminal liability. The first principle is that in determining whether the imposition of strict criminal liability is consistent with due process, several factors, including the policy and intent of the legislature, the origins of the offense, the reasonableness of the standards imposed, and the punishment and stigma attached to a conviction, must be considered. The second principle is that in considering these several factors, a court must shuttle back and forth, between the question whether the statute can be construed as not requiring proof of criminal intent, and the question whether, if so construed, the statute will violate due process; the answer to one of these questions will color, or affect, the answer to the other. Thus in *Morissette* the Court was persuaded to construe the statute as not creating strict criminal liability but instead as requiring proof of intent. * * *

II

It is now in order to apply the * * * analysis to the present case. The first step will be to determine whether, in enacting section 3732, the legislature intended to make homicide by vehicle a strict liability crime. If it appears that the legislature did so intend, the second step will be to determine whether the section violates due process. If it appears that it does, the third, and last, step will be to re-examine the section, to determine whether it may be saved, or whether it must be declared unconstitutional.

[After analyzing the legislative history, the concurrence concludes that the legislature intended to make this crime one of strict liability.]

* * * [I]f the legislature had intended to limit criminal violations under section 3732 to reckless or negligent defendants, it need not have

enacted the section at all, for those defendants were already subject to prosecution for involuntary manslaughter under section 2504 of the Crimes Code. Indeed, a consideration of the crime of involuntary manslaughter provides what seems to me a probably correct explanation of why the legislature intended to create strict criminal liability under section 3732. The cases demonstrate that the Commonwealth has had difficulty in obtaining convictions for involuntary manslaughter, for proof of a traffic violation may not be proof of recklessness or gross negligence. It seems probable that in enacting section 3732, the legislature intended to overcome this difficulty by broadening the scope of liability to include those persons who merely violated traffic ordinances. * * *

B

When construed to create strict criminal liability, does section 3732 violate due process?

In testing the constitutionality of a statute creating strict criminal liability, the two most important considerations are the severity of the possible punishment and the moral stigma that may be attached to a conviction. As the Sixth Circuit stated in *United States v. Heller*, "Certainly if Congress attempted to define a (strict liability) offense that placed an onerous stigma on an offender's reputation and that carried a severe penalty, the Constitution would be offended."

1

Appellee's conviction under section 3732 of homicide by vehicle places a most onerous stigma on her reputation.

The Commentary, Homicide by Vehicle, states that the use of the term "homicide by vehicle," as compared with the term "manslaughter," "lessen(s) the stigma attached to convictions." If this be so, the stigma attached nevertheless remains most onerous. As Henry Hart has observed, one cannot truthfully say to any defendant that there is nothing wrong with being labeled a criminal. Especially is this so when the crime is "homicide by vehicle." Labels may not be ignored. To be labeled a rapist or murderer places a far more onerous stigma on a person than to be labeled as someone convicted of misbranding a drug. While the word "homicide," by itself, means only the killing of a human being, included within this definition are the terms "murder" and "manslaughter." Indeed, the Crimes Code defines the term "criminal homicide" so as to include "murder" and "manslaughter." Adding the phrase "by vehicle" does little to lessen the stigma attached to the word "homicide," except perhaps among lawyers. In popular parlance, "homicide" is usually equated with "murder." * * *

While there apparently has been no case holding what type of a conviction does such grave damage to reputation as to violate the federal due process clause, it must be noted that the stigma attached to 'homicide by vehicle' is different from, and far more serious than, the stigma attached to such crimes as the fishing violation considered in *United States v. Ayo-Gonzalez* * * *. This court has been extremely concerned with the unfair effects that a criminal record may have upon a defendant's future. Indeed, it is not an overstatement to say that to saddle appellee in this case with a homicide record might result in more damage to her future than even the imprisonment she may receive for her conviction. * * *

I acknowledge that despite the foregoing scholarly commentary, the federal courts have held that a sentence of imprisonment may be imposed for conviction of a strict liability crime. *United States v. Balint* (five years); *United States v. Freed* (ten years); *United States v. Mowat* (six months imprisonment); *United States v. Ayo-Gonzalez* (one year imprisonment). *But see United States v. Heller* (possible twenty year term is too severe for a strict liability crime). It is because of these cases that I said at the beginning of this opinion that "perhaps" section 3732 did not violate federal due process. It very well may violate federal due process, for in addition to carrying a sentence of imprisonment, conviction "gravely besmirch(es)" the defendant's reputation. However, I know of no federal case resting a finding of violation of due process on damage to reputation alone.

How the federal courts would decide such a case need not concern us, for under the decisions of our Supreme Court and of this court, it is settled that imposition of imprisonment upon conviction of a strict liability crime does constitute a violation of due process under our State constitution.

In *Commonwealth v. Koczwara*, the defendant was convicted of violating the Pennsylvania Liquor Code by serving alcohol to minors. The evidence established that an employee of the defendant's served the minors when the defendant was not present and without the defendant knowledge. Nevertheless the defendant was convicted, fined, and sentenced to three months imprisonment. On appeal the Supreme Court noted that the crime was a violation of a mere "regulatory provision," "generally enforceable by light penalties, and although violations are labelled crimes, the considerations applicable to them are totally different from those applicable to true crimes, which involve moral delinquency and which are punishable by imprisonment or another serious penalty." Although concluding that the legislature could create such strict criminal liability, the Court held that to imprison the defendant violated due process under the Pennsylvania Constitution.

While *Koczwara* involved vicarious liability, it is nevertheless controlling on the issue presented in this case because of the distinction made by the Court between, on the one hand, true crimes, and on the other hand, strict liability (including vicarious liability) crimes. The Court made it clear that to imprison someone for anything other than a true crime was unconstitutional; and it defined a true crime as one that involves both "moral delinquency" and "personal causation." From this distinction the conclusion followed that since strict liability (including vicarious liability) crimes are not true crimes, they may not constitutionally be punished by imprisonment. Thus in *Koczwara* our Supreme Court went beyond *Balint*, and the federal cases following it, and gave judicial recognition to the views of Sayre and the other commentators, that since strict liability crimes are not true crimes they should not be punished like true crimes.

C

Is it possible to save section 3732?

Since, when construed to create strict criminal liability, section 3732 violates due process, both because conviction too gravely besmirches the defendant's reputation and because the punishment is too severe, it is necessary to proceed to the third, and final, step of the * * * analysis, and re-examine the section to determine whether after all it may be construed so that it will not violate due process. Two possible constructions suggest themselves.

1

The first possible construction would be to construe section 3732 as not imposing strict criminal liability. * * * Nevertheless, the difficulty, which I find insuperable, would be that then we should have to answer the question if section 3732 does not create strict criminal liability, what sort of conduct does it make culpable? By its own terms section 3732 does not refer to intentional conduct. The only remaining forms of culpable conduct would seem to be either recklessness or negligence. However, if section 3732 is construed to require proof of either of these, it becomes a duplicate of section 2504 of the Crimes Code, which defines involuntary manslaughter as a crime:

> (a) General rule. A person is guilty of involuntary manslaughter when as a direct result of the doing of an unlawful act in a reckless or grossly negligent manner, or the doing of a lawful act in a reckless or grossly negligent manner, he causes the death of another person.

It would be to some extent absurd to have two different criminal statutes apply to the same conduct. * * *

2

The second possible construction would be to construe section 3732 as creating strict criminal liability, but to save it by removing that part or parts that result in a violation of due process. That is what the Supreme Court did in *Commonwealth v. Koczwara*, where instead of striking down the section of the Liquor Code involved, the Court merely removed from the section the sanction of imprisonment. To save section 3732, however, one would have to remove from it not only the sanction of imprisonment but also the label "homicide by vehicle"; for as discussed above, what renders the section a violation of due process is the combination of a too severe penalty and a too onerous stigma. Removing both the sanction of imprisonment and creating a new name for the crime would amount to re-writing the section and would be an encroachment upon the legislative function.

3

I am thus left with the conclusion that rather than attempt to save section 3732, it should be declared unconstitutional. The legislature would then be free to produce a constitutional version of the section, if it should so desire.

I should affirm the decision of the lower court.

WIEAND, JUDGE, dissenting:

I respectfully dissent.

* * *

The language of the section defining homicide by vehicle is precise and unambiguous. As it pertains to the facts of the instant case, the only culpability required is a violation of a law "applying to the operation or use of a vehicle or to the regulation of traffic." Highway safety and the means for achieving it are legitimately, even uniquely, within the legislature's area of concern. Because automobiles are potentially hazardous instrumentalities, the legislature, in the public interest, may adopt traffic regulations and rules of the road reasonably calculated to promote care on the part of those who use its highways. Apparently alarmed by the deplorable carnage on our highways, the legislature determined that potential prosecution for involuntary manslaughter was an inadequate response. Motorists are generally reputable citizens. When one of them is involved in an automobile accident resulting in death to another person, the cause frequently is a negligent violation of a rule of the road or speed limit. A reckless disregard for the safety of others is frequently absent, and when it is present, it is often difficult to prove beyond a reasonable doubt. Therefore, the legislature determined to make criminal responsibility dependent upon violation of a traffic law and not necessarily on culpable or criminal negligence. * * *

Homicide by vehicle, as I have observed, is the legislature's response to a high fatality rate on the public highways. The standard adopted to define the offense, i.e., a violation of a traffic law that causes a death, is not unreasonable. Motorists cannot justly complain that they will be held criminally accountable for the consequences if they violate the Vehicle

Code. These factors, I believe, are controlling. Contrary to appellee's argument, the classification of the offense as a misdemeanor of the first degree and the fixing of a maximum sentence equivalent to that prescribed for involuntary manslaughter are not determinative. These considerations must yield to the paramount interest of the legislature in establishing laws which regulate the operation of vehicles on the highways of the Commonwealth. In previous due process challenges to motor vehicle regulations, Pennsylvania courts have invariably upheld statutes that evidenced a reasonable relation to the legislative purpose and were not arbitrary or capricious. I conclude that the offense of homicide by vehicle is not an unreasonable method to effectuate a legitimate state safety policy. * * *

CHAPTER 5

MISTAKE AND IGNORANCE

■ ■ ■

INTRODUCTION

We have already seen how the criminal law deals with one kind of mistake when we studied the doctrine of transferred intent in Chapter 4. In "transferred intent" cases, the defendant mistakenly hurts a different victim than the one intended. Suppose, in contrast, the defendant commits the prohibited act with some kind of belief that turns out to have been wrong? How should the criminal law respond? These questions are the subject of this chapter.

The law of mistake and ignorance can be very confusing, but you will not go wrong if you remember one simple point: as a general rule, mistake is the flip side of mens rea. That is, the question of whether the defendant's ignorance or mistaken belief is a defense can usually be answered if one understands what mental state the statute requires.

It is important to know whether you are interpreting a penal code that relies primarily on the common law or one that relies on the Model Penal Code when considering questions of mistake. The common law approach to mistake and ignorance relies on the distinction we examined in Chapter 4 between specific intent and general intent crimes. The common law approach also incorporates a second distinction: between mistakes of fact and mistakes of law. The Model Penal Code does not observe the specific intent/general intent distinction; nor does it distinguish between mistakes of fact and mistakes of law. *See* Model Penal Code § 2.04.

We have observed that the main thing to keep in mind when considering whether mistake or ignorance is a defense is what mental state the statute requires. This is another way of saying that mistake and ignorance are usually case-in-chief defenses. However, there are some situations, both in common law-based and MPC-based penal codes, where the defendant's mistake of law is an affirmative defense.

A. MISTAKES OF FACT

The common law rules regarding mistakes of fact are fairly simple, turning on the distinction between specific intent and general intent crimes. If one is charged with a specific intent crime, an honest mistake that negates the specific intent required for commission of the offense is a complete defense. The mistake need not be reasonable as long as it is in good faith.[a]

If one is charged with a general intent crime, a mistake of fact that negates an element of the crime must be both honest and reasonable to exculpate. A minority of common law jurisdictions subject the general intent defendant's mistake-of-fact claim to even further scrutiny, employing either a moral wrong or legal wrong test. These doctrines are explained in *Bell v. State.*

The next two cases both involve claims of mistake of fact. *People v. Navarro* provides a clear explanation of the common law rules for mistakes of fact. *Bell v. State* examines whether a state legislature can, consistent with due process, preclude a mistake of age defense to a charge of promoting prostitution in the first degree.

PEOPLE V. NAVARRO

Appellate Department, Superior Court of California, Los Angeles
99 Cal. App. 3d Supp. 1, 160 Cal.Rptr. 692 (Super. 1979)

DOWDS, J.

Defendant, charged with a violation of Penal Code section 487, subdivision 1, grand theft, appeals his conviction after a jury trial of petty theft, a lesser but necessarily included offense. His contention on appeal is that the jury was improperly instructed. The only facts set forth in the record on appeal are that defendant was charged with stealing four wooden beams from a construction site and that the state of the evidence was such that the jury could have found that the defendant believed either (1) that the beams had been abandoned as worthless and the owner had no objection to his taking them or (2) that they had substantial value, had not been abandoned and he had no right to take them.

The court refused two jury instructions proposed by defendant reading as follows:

Defendant's A

> If one takes personal property with the good faith belief that the property has been abandoned or discarded by the true owner, he is not guilty of theft. This is the case even if such good faith belief is unreasonable. The prosecutor must prove beyond a

[a] For example, let's say Sally is charged with larceny—a specific intent crime which is defined as the taking and carrying away of another's personal property with intent to permanently deprive the possessor of such property—after mistakenly taking Robert's black umbrella believing it was her own. Sally can argue mistake of fact as a defense and will likely be acquitted if the jury believes that Sally honestly thought Robert's black umbrella was her own. Even if Sally's mistake was unreasonable—Sally's umbrella was blue, so she should have known that Robert's black umbrella was not her umbrella—Sally will be exonerated because if she honestly believed the umbrella was her own, then she lacked the specific intent to permanently deprive Robert of his umbrella.

reasonable doubt that the defendant did not so believe for you to convict a defendant of theft.

Defendant's B

If one takes personal property with the good faith belief that he has permission to take the property, he is not guilty of theft. This is the case even if such good faith belief is unreasonable. The prosecutor must prove beyond a reasonable doubt that the defendant did not so believe for you to convict a defendant of theft.

Instead, the court instructed the jury in the words of the following modified instructions:

Modified-Defendant's A

If one takes personal property in the reasonable and good faith belief that the property has been abandoned or discarded by the true owner, he is not guilty of theft.

Modified-Defendant B

If one takes personal property in the reasonable and good faith belief that he has the consent or permission of the owner to take the property, he is not guilty of theft.

If you have a reasonable doubt that the defendant had the required criminal intent as specified in these instructions, the defendant is entitled to an acquittal.

Accordingly, the question for determination on appeal is whether the defendant should be acquitted if there is a reasonable doubt that he had a good faith belief that the property had been abandoned or that he had the permission of the owner to take the property or whether that belief must be a reasonable one as well as being held in good faith. * * *

Evidence was presented * * * from which the jury could have concluded that defendant believed that the wooden beams had been abandoned and that the owner had no objection to his taking them, i.e., that he lacked the specific criminal intent required to commit the crime of theft (intent permanently to deprive an owner of his property).

* * *

The proper rule, it seems to us, is set forth in Perkins on Criminal Law: "If no specific intent or other special mental element is required for guilt of the offense charged, a mistake of fact will not be recognized as an excuse unless it was based upon reasonable grounds. . . . [On the other hand, because] of the requirement of a specific intent to steal there is no such thing as larceny by negligence. One does not commit this offense by carrying away the chattel of another in the mistaken belief that it is his own, no matter how great may have been the fault leading to this belief, if the belief itself is genuine."

La Fave and Scott, Handbook on Criminal Law sets forth at page 357 what the authors call the ". . . rather simple rule that an honest mistake of fact or law is a defense when it negates a required mental element of the crime . . . " As an example they refer to the crime of receiving stolen property, stating ". . . if the defendant by a mistake of either fact or law did not know the goods were stolen, even though the circumstances would have led a prudent man to believe they were stolen, he does not have the required mental state and thus may not be convicted of the crime."

In the instant case the trial court in effect instructed the jury that even though defendant in good faith believed he had the right to take the beams, and thus lacked the specific intent required for the crime of theft, he should be convicted unless such belief was reasonable. In doing so it erred. It is true that if the jury thought the defendant's belief to be unreasonable, it might infer that he did not in good faith hold such belief. If, however, it concluded that defendant in good faith believed that he had the right to take the beams, even though such belief was unreasonable as measured by the objective standard of a hypothetical reasonable man, defendant was entitled to an acquittal since the specific intent required to be proved as an element of the offense had not been established.

* * *

The judgment is reversed.

BELL V. STATE

Court of Appeals of Alaska
668 P.2d 829 (Alaska Ct. App. 1983)

BRYNER, CHIEF JUDGE.

Willie B. Bell appeals his convictions for promoting prostitution in the first degree in violation of AS 11.66.110(a)(2) and managing a prostitution enterprise in violation of AS 11.66.120(a)(1). He also appeals the sentence imposed. We affirm.

Bell was a twenty-nine-year-old army sergeant when he procured two sixteen-year-old girls, C.R. and M.J., and one fourteen-year-old girl, D.W., for prostitution. C.R. began living with Bell and engaging in prostitution after Bell promised to marry her and to buy her a new car and new clothing. At Bell's direction, D.W. and M.J. worked as prostitutes in May, 1980. On May 22, 1980, Bell assaulted M.J., claiming that she had been drinking instead of "working." Fearing that Bell would harm them, C.R. and M.J. left him and contacted police, who obtained a search warrant to record conversations between M.J., C.R. and Bell. A telephone conversation between Bell and C.R. and a conversation involving Bell,

M.J. and C.R. were recorded pursuant to the warrant and used as evidence against Bell.

The indictment returned against Bell charged two counts of promoting prostitution in the first degree, alleging that he induced D.W. to engage in prostitution when she was under the age of sixteen (Count I), and that he induced C.R. to engage in prostitution by means of force (Count II). Count III of the indictment, as it went to the jury, alleged that Bell was guilty of attempted promotion of prostitution in the first degree, regarding M.J. The indictment also alleged that Bell managed, supervised, controlled or owned a prostitution enterprise other than a house of prostitution (Count IV). Bell was convicted of Counts I and IV. On Count II, Bell was acquitted of the charge but convicted of the lesser-included offense of promoting prostitution in the third degree. On Count III, Bell was found not guilty of the charge but guilty of the lesser-included offense of attempted promotion of prostitution in the third degree. Bell was not sentenced on Counts II and III. Superior Court Judge Milton M. Souter sentenced Bell to a five-year term with two years suspended on Count I, and a four-year term with three years suspended on Count IV. The sentences for these offenses were to run concurrently. Subsequently, Judge Souter refused to reduce the sentence.

On appeal, Bell argues that: (1) he should have been allowed to present a reasonable mistake of age defense to the charge contained in Count I * * *.

I. MISTAKE OF AGE

Bell asserts that the trial court erred in refusing to give a proposed jury instruction providing for a reasonable mistake of age defense to the charge of inducing a person under the age of sixteen to engage in prostitution in violation of AS 11.66.110(a)(2).[1] Bell argues that AS

[1] AS 11.66.110 provides:

PROMOTING PROSTITUTION IN THE FIRST DEGREE.

(a) A person commits the crime of promoting prostitution in the first degree if he

(1) induces or causes a person to engage in prostitution through the use of force;

(2) as other than a patron of a prostitute, induces or causes a person under 16 years of age to engage in prostitution; or

(3) induces or causes a person in his legal custody to engage in prostitution.

(b) In a prosecution under (a)(2) of this section, it is not a defense that the defendant reasonably believed that the person he induced or caused to engage in prostitution was 16 years of age or older.

(c) Promoting prostitution in the first degree is a class B felony.

The jury was instructed on the elements of this offense. The court then instructed that:

> It is not a defense to the crime charged in Count I of the Indictment that the defendant reasonably believed that the person he induced or caused to engage in prostitution was 16 years of age or older.

The instruction proposed by Bell stated:

> It is a defense to Count I of the indictment, Inducing a Person Under 16 Years of Age to Engage in Prostitution, that the defendant reasonably and in good faith believed that the female person was of the age of sixteen years or older, even though, in fact, she was under the age of sixteen years. If from all the evidence you have a reasonable

11.66.110(b) violates his due process rights under the United States and Alaska constitutions by expressly precluding mistake of age as a defense to the charge of violating AS 11.66.110(a)(2). We find this argument unpersuasive and conclude that the legislature may, consistent with the requirements of constitutional due process, preclude mistake of age from constituting a defense to the crime of promoting prostitution in the first degree.

It is apparent that the legislature considered procurement of a person under sixteen to be an aggravated form of promoting prostitution. The commentary to the Revised Criminal Code, 2 Senate Journal, Supplement No. 47, at 109 (1978), states that by denying a defendant the defense of reasonable mistake as to age, creation of strict liability was intended as to the element of the offense involving age of the victim. * * *

Bell correctly states the well-recognized rule in this jurisdiction that criminal intent is a necessary ingredient of criminal liability and that one charged with criminal conduct must have an awareness or consciousness of wrongdoing. *Speidel v. State,* 460 P.2d 77, 78 (Alaska 1969). In *Speidel,* the awareness of wrongdoing was in the context of a larceny-type crime, for which courts have historically required a specific intent to wrongfully deprive. In *Alex v. State,* 484 P.2d 677 (Alaska 1971), the supreme court discussed the intent required for non-larceny crimes:

> However, as applied to crimes generally, what is imperative, is that an accused's act be other than simply inadvertent or neglectful. What is essential is not an awareness that a given conduct is a "wrongdoing" in the sense that it is proscribed by law, but rather, an awareness that one is committing the specific acts which are defined by law as a "wrongdoing." It is, however, no defense that one was not aware that his acts were wrong in the sense that they were proscribed by law. So long as one acts intentionally, with cognizance of his behavior, he acts with the requisite awareness of wrongdoing.

We believe this language is applicable to Bell's actions, since he was consciously committing the acts proscribed by law. As an element of this offense, Bell was required to be aware that he was procuring women to engage in acts of prostitution. Indeed, the jurors in this case were instructed that they must be convinced beyond a reasonable doubt that the defendant engaged in conduct which caused or induced [D.W.] to engage in prostitution; [and] that the defendant engaged in said conduct with the specific intent to cause or induce [D.W.] to engage in prostitution.

---

doubt as to the question whether defendant reasonably and in good faith believed that she was sixteen years of age or older, you must give the defendant the benefit of that doubt and find him not guilty.

Thus, while Bell was not required to know the age of those whom he procured, this is not to say that the offense did not require *mens rea* or a culpable mental state.

We also note that AS 11.66.110(b) is in accord with the common law view that there should be no exculpation for mistake where, if the facts had been as the actor believed them to be, his conduct would still be illegal or immoral.[4] As Bell recognizes on appeal, his conduct would still have been illegal even if D.W. had been sixteen or over. AS 11.66.130(a)(2).[5] * * *

In continuing to press his claim that AS 11.66.110(b) imposes an unconstitutional standard, Bell relies upon *State v. Guest,* 583 P.2d 836 (Alaska 1978), in which the supreme court upheld a trial court's decision to instruct the jury on a defense of reasonable mistake of age in a statutory rape case. Following the reasoning of *Speidel* and *Alex,* the court stated that an intent requirement must be read into former AS 11.15.120 to save it from unconstitutionality. To refuse a defense of mistake of age in a statutory rape case, according to the *Guest* court, would be to impose significant criminal liability without any criminal mental element.

Bell relies most heavily upon the following language in *Guest:*

> It has been urged in other jurisdictions that where an offender is aware he is committing an act of fornication he therefore has sufficient criminal intent to justify a conviction for statutory rape because what was done would have been unlawful under the facts as he thought them to be. We reject this view. While it is true that under such circumstances a mistake of fact does not serve as a complete defense, we believe that it should serve to reduce the offense to that which the offender would have been guilty of had he not been mistaken. Thus, if an accused had a reasonable belief that the person with whom he had sexual intercourse was sixteen years of age or older, he may not be convicted of statutory rape. If, however, he did not have a reasonable belief that the victim was eighteen years of age or

---

[4] In the landmark case of *Regina v. Prince,* L.4., 2 Cr.Cas.Res. 154 (1875), the defendant was convicted of taking a girl under sixteen years of age from under the care of her father, even though the defendant reasonably believed she was older. The defense of mistake of age was disallowed on the ground that removal of an unmarried girl from the lawful custody of her parents would have been a crime even had she been as old as he believed. Hence, the defendant acted at his peril.

[5] AS 11.66.130 provides, in relevant part:

(a) A person commits the crime of promoting prostitution in the third degree if, with intent to promote prostitution, he . . .

(2) as other than a patron of a prostitute, induces or causes a person 16 years of age or older to engage in prostitution. . . .

(b) Promoting prostitution in the third degree is a class A misdemeanor.

> older, he may still be criminally liable for contribution to the delinquency of a minor.

The court cited in support of its position section 2.04(2) of the Model Penal Code (Proposed Official Draft 1962), which provides:

> Although ignorance or mistake would otherwise afford a defense to the offense charged, the defense is not available if the defendant would be guilty of another offense had the situation been as he supposed. In such case, however, the ignorance or mistake of the defendant shall reduce the grade and degree of the offense of which he may be convicted to those of the offense of which he would be guilty had the situation been as he supposed.

We believe the problem addressed in *Guest* is distinguishable from the issue at hand. As we have stated, Bell did not lack criminal intent; he intended to promote prostitution. The court in *Guest* was careful to point out that fornication was not itself a crime, so that it could not have been considered as a lesser-included offense of statutory rape. Also, although the court went on to observe that Guest *might* still have been guilty of contributing to the delinquency of a minor under former AS 11.40.130 if he did not have a reasonable belief that his partner was under eighteen, it is clear that Bell was *necessarily* guilty of promoting prostitution in the third degree if the facts were as he supposed them to be.

* * *

We hold that AS 11.66.110(b), which expressly dispenses with mistake of age as a defense to promoting prostitution in the first degree, does not violate due process of law. We therefore conclude that the trial court did not err in rejecting Bell's challenge to the instruction on mistake of age. * * *

The conviction and sentence are AFFIRMED.

NOTE

Regina v. Prince, mentioned in *Bell*, is usually cited for the principle that even if a defendant charged with a general intent crime was honestly and reasonably mistaken about a fact that negates the mens rea required for commission of the offense, the defendant can still be held liable for the charged offense if the defendant's conduct was immoral. In addition to this "moral wrong" doctrine, courts in jurisdictions that incorporate the common law sometimes articulate a "legal wrong" doctrine: even if a defendant charged with a general intent crime was laboring under an honest and reasonable mistake of fact that negated the mental state required for commission of the offense, she will not be exculpated if, had the facts been as the defendant believed them to be, she would have been be guilty of some other crime.

The Model Penal Code does not distinguish between specific intent and general intent crimes. Under the MPC, a mistake of fact is a defense if it negates the mental state required for commission of the offense. *See* Model Penal Code § 2.04(1). The MPC, however, also applies a rule that is similar to the common law's legal wrong doctrine. Under the MPC, even if the defendant's mistake negates the mental state required for commission of the offense, if the defendant would be guilty of another offense if the facts were as he believed them to be, then he will be found guilty of the charged offense. *See* Model Penal Code § 2.04(2). The MPC, however, in contrast to the common law legal wrong doctrine, allows the defendant to be punished only at the penalty set for the other, lesser crime, not the charged offense.

B. MISTAKES OF LAW

Under both the common law and the Model Penal Code, the general rule regarding mistakes of law is that ignorance of the law is no excuse. Except in certain limited circumstances described below, a person cannot defend against a crime by claiming that he did not know what he was doing was unlawful.

There are three exceptions to the general rule that ignorance of the law is no excuse. First, a person who reasonably relies on an official interpretation of the law that turns out to be erroneous can be exonerated. This defense is often called "official interpretation of the law" and is also known as "entrapment by estoppel." Second, ignorance of the law can be a defense to a crime if knowledge that the prohibited conduct is unlawful is an element of the crime. In such a case, the defendant's lack of knowledge will negate the mens rea required for commission of the offense. Third, the U.S. Supreme Court has held that under certain limited circumstances, the prosecution of a person who lacks fair notice of a legal duty imposed by law can violate due process. We will study each of these three exceptions in the cases below.

Should courts recognize a fourth exception to the general rule that ignorance of the law is no excuse when the defendant is a recent immigrant to the United States, unfamiliar with United States laws or mores, and the behavior that constituted the crime was appropriate behavior in light of the immigrant's own culture? The "cultural defense" is examined in Chapter 10.

1. OFFICIAL INTERPRETATION OF THE LAW

Although the law in this area is very confused and uncertain, jurisdictions whose penal codes primarily incorporate the common law have sometimes acknowledged an affirmative defense to defendants who commit crimes upon reliance on official statements of the law, whether set forth in judicial rulings or in oral or written statements by officials.

The *Marrero* case discusses the requirements of this defense. Section 2.04(3) of the Model Penal Code codifies this affirmative defense.

PEOPLE V. MARRERO

Court of Appeals of New York
69 N.Y.2d 382, 507 N.E.2d 1068, 515 N.Y.S.2d 212 (1987)

BELLACOSA, J.

The defense of mistake of law is not available to a Federal corrections officer arrested in a Manhattan social club for possession of a loaded .38 caliber automatic pistol who claimed he mistakenly believed he was entitled, pursuant to the interplay of CPL 2.10, 1.20 and Penal Law § 265.20, to carry a handgun without a permit as a peace officer. * * *

On the trial of the case, the court rejected the defendant's argument that his personal misunderstanding of the statutory definition of a peace officer is enough to excuse him from criminal liability under New York's mistake of law statute (Penal Law § 15.20). The court refused to charge the jury on this issue and defendant was convicted of criminal possession of a weapon in the third degree. We affirm the Appellate Division order upholding the conviction.

Defendant was a Federal corrections officer in Danbury, Connecticut, and asserted that status at the time of his arrest in 1977. He claimed at trial that there were various interpretations of fellow officers and teachers, as well as the peace officer statute itself, upon which he relied for his mistaken belief that he could carry a weapon with legal impunity.

The starting point for our analysis is the New York mistake statute as an outgrowth of the dogmatic common-law maxim that ignorance of the law is no excuse. The central issue is whether defendant's personal misreading or misunderstanding of a statute may excuse criminal conduct in the circumstances of this case. * * *

The [common law rule], which was to encourage the societal benefit of individuals' knowledge of and respect for the law, is underscored by Justice Holmes' statement: "It is no doubt true that there are many cases in which the criminal could not have known that he was breaking the law, but to admit the excuse at all would be to encourage ignorance where the law-maker has determined to make men know and obey, and justice to the individual is rightly outweighed by the larger interests on the other side of the scales." (Holmes, The Common Law, at 48 [1881]).

The revisors of New York's Penal Law intended no fundamental departure from this common-law rule in Penal Law § 15.20, which provides in pertinent part:

§ 15.20. *Effect of ignorance or mistake upon liability.*

* * *

2. A person is not relieved of criminal liability for conduct because he engages in such conduct under a mistaken belief that it does not, as a matter of law, constitute an offense, unless such mistaken belief is founded upon an official statement of the law contained in (a) a statute or other enactment * * *[; or] (d) an interpretation of the statute or law relating to the offense, officially made or issued by a public servant, agency, or body legally charged or empowered with the responsibility or privilege of administering, enforcing or interpreting such statute or law.

This section was added to the Penal Law as part of the wholesale revision of the Penal Law in 1965. When this provision was first proposed, commentators viewed the new language as codifying "the established common law maxim on mistake of law, while at the same time recognizing a defense when the erroneous belief is founded upon an 'official statement of the law.' "

The defendant claims as a first prong of his defense that he is entitled to raise the defense of mistake of law under section 15.20 (2) (a) because his mistaken belief that his conduct was legal was founded upon an official statement of the law contained in the statute itself.[a] Defendant argues that his mistaken interpretation of the statute was reasonable in view of the alleged ambiguous wording of the peace officer exemption statute, and that his "reasonable" interpretation of an "official statement" is enough to satisfy the requirements of subdivision (2) (a). However, the whole thrust of this exceptional exculpatory concept, in derogation of the traditional and common-law principle, was intended to be a very narrow escape valve. Application in this case would invert that thrust and make mistake of law a generally applied or available defense instead of an unusual exception which the very opening words of the mistake statute make so clear, i.e., "A person is not relieved of criminal liability for conduct * * * unless" (Penal Law § 15.20). * * *

The prosecution further counters defendant's argument by asserting that one cannot claim the protection of mistake of law under section 15.20 (2) (a) simply by misconstruing the meaning of a statute but must instead establish that the statute relied on actually permitted the conduct in question and was only later found to be erroneous. To buttress that argument, the People analogize New York's official statement defense to the approach taken by the Model Penal Code (MPC). Section 2.04 of the MPC provides:

---

[a] Under New York Penal Law § 265.02, a person is guilty of criminal possession of a weapon in the third degree when "[s]uch person possesses any loaded firearm." N.Y. PENAL LAW § 265.02 (McKinney 2004). New York Penal Law § 265.20 (exemptions) states that section 265.02 shall not apply to possession of any weapons by "peace officers as defined in subdivision thirty-three of section 1.20 of the criminal procedure law." N.Y. PENAL LAW § 265.20. New York's Criminal Procedure Law § 1.20(33) defines "peace officer" as including "[a]n attendant, or an official, or guard of any state prison *or of any penal correctional institution*." N.Y. CRIM. PROC. LAW § 1.20 (emphasis added).

Section 2.04. *Ignorance or Mistake.*

* * *

> (3) A belief that conduct does not legally constitute an offense is a defense to a prosecution for that offense based upon such conduct when * * * (b) he acts in reasonable reliance upon an official statement of the law, *afterward determined to be invalid or erroneous*, contained in (i) a statute or other enactment.

Although the drafters of the New York statute did not adopt the precise language of the Model Penal Code provision with the emphasized clause, it is evident and has long been believed that the Legislature intended the New York statute to be similarly construed. In fact, the legislative history of section 15.20 is replete with references to the influence of the Model Penal Code provision. * * *

The "official statement" component in the mistake of law defense in both paragraphs (a) and (d) adds yet another element of support for our interpretation and holding. Defendant tried to establish a defense under Penal Law § 15.20 (2) (d) as a second prong. But the interpretation of the statute relied upon must be "officially made or issued by a public servant, agency or body legally charged or empowered with the responsibility or privilege of administering, enforcing or interpreting such statute or law." We agree with the People that the trial court also properly rejected the defense under Penal Law § 15.20 (2) (d) since none of the interpretations which defendant proffered meets the requirements of the statute. * * *

Strong public policy reasons underlie the legislative mandate and intent which we perceive in rejecting defendant's construction of New York's mistake of law defense statute. If defendant's argument were accepted, the exception would swallow the rule. Mistakes about the law would be encouraged, rather than respect for and adherence to law. There would be an infinite number of mistake of law defenses which could be devised from a good-faith, perhaps reasonable but mistaken, interpretation of criminal statutes, many of which are concededly complex. Even more troublesome are the opportunities for wrongminded individuals to contrive in bad faith solely to get an exculpatory notion before the jury. * * *

Accordingly, the order of the Appellate Division should be affirmed.

HANCOCK, JR., J. [dissenting.]

The rule adopted by the majority prohibiting the defense of mistake of law under Penal Law § 15.20 (2) (a) in the circumstances here is directly contrary to the plain dictates of the statute and a rejection of the jurisprudential reforms and legislative policies underlying its enactment. For these reasons, as more fully explained herein, we cannot agree with this decision. * * *

II

Penal Law § 15.20 (effect of ignorance or mistake upon liability), in pertinent part, provides: "2. A person is not relieved of criminal liability for conduct because he engages in such conduct under a mistaken belief that it does not, as a matter of law, constitute an offense, unless such mistaken belief is founded upon an official statement of the law contained in (a) a statute or other enactment."

It is fundamental that in interpreting a statute, a court should look first to the particular words of the statute in question, being guided by the accepted rule that statutory language is generally given its natural and most obvious meaning. Here, there is but one natural and obvious meaning of the statute: that if a defendant can establish that his mistaken belief was "founded upon" his interpretation of "an official statement of the law contained in * * * [a] statute," he should have a defense. No other natural and obvious meaning has been suggested.

It is difficult to imagine a case more squarely within the wording of Penal Law § 15.20 (2) (a) or one more fitted to what appears clearly to be the intended purpose of the statute than the one before us. For this reason it is helpful to discuss the statute and its apparent intended effect in the light of what defendant contends was his mistaken belief founded on an official statement of the law contained in a statute. * * *

Defendant's mistaken belief that, as a Federal corrections officer, he could legally carry a loaded weapon without a license was based on the express exemption from criminal liability under Penal Law § 265.02 accorded in Penal Law § 265.20 (a) (1) (a) to "peace officers" as defined in the Criminal Procedure Law and on his reading of the statutory definition for "peace officer" in CPL 2.10 (25) as meaning a correction officer "of *any* penal correctional institution," including an institution not operated by New York State. Thus, he concluded erroneously that, as a corrections officer in a Federal prison, he was a "peace officer" and, as such, exempt by the express terms of Penal Law § 265.20 (a) (1) (a). This mistaken belief, based in good faith on the statute defining "peace officer" is, defendant contends, the precise sort of "mistaken belief * * * founded upon an official statement of the law contained in * * * a statute or other enactment" which gives rise to a mistake of law defense under Penal Law § 15.20 (2) (a). He points out, of course, that when he acted in reliance on his belief he had no way of foreseeing that a court would eventually resolve the question of the statute's meaning against him and rule that his belief had been mistaken, as three of the five-member panel at the Appellate Division ultimately did in the first appeal.

The majority, however, has accepted the People's argument that to have a defense under Penal Law § 15.20 (2) (a) "a defendant must show that the statute *permitted his conduct*, not merely that he believed it did." Here, of course, defendant cannot show that the statute permitted his conduct. To the contrary, the question has now been decided by the Appellate Division and it is settled that defendant was not exempt under Penal Law § 265.20 (a) (1) (a). Therefore, the argument goes, defendant can have no mistake of law defense. * * *

Nothing in the statutory language suggests the interpretation urged by the People and adopted by the majority: that Penal Law § 15.20 (2) (a) is available to a defendant *not* when he has mistakenly read a statute *but only* when he has correctly read and relied on a statute which is later invalidated. Such a construction contravenes the general rule that penal statutes should be construed against the State and in favor of the accused and the Legislature's specific directive that the revised Penal Law should not be strictly construed but "must be construed according to the fair import of [its] terms to promote justice and effect the objects of the law."

More importantly, the construction leads to an anomaly: only a defendant who is *not mistaken* about the law when he acts has a mistake of law defense. In other words, a defendant can assert a defense under Penal Law § 15.20 (2) (a) only when his reading of the statute is *correct—not mistaken.* Such construction is obviously illogical; it strips the statute of the very effect intended by the Legislature in adopting the mistake of law defense. * * * An interpretation of a statute which produces an unreasonable or incongruous result and one which defeats the obvious purpose of the legislation and renders it ineffective should be rejected.

Finally, the majority's disregard of the natural and obvious meaning of Penal Law § 15.20 (2) (a) so that a defendant mistaken about the law is deprived of a defense under the statute amounts, we submit, to a rejection of the obvious legislative purposes and policies favoring jurisprudential reform underlying the statute's enactment. It is self-evident that in enacting Penal Law § 15.20 (2) as part of the revision and modernization of the Penal Law the Legislature intended to effect a needed reform by abolishing what had long been considered the unjust archaic common-law rule totally prohibiting mistake of law as a defense. Had it not so intended it would simply have left the common-law rule intact. In place of the abandoned "*ignorantia legis*" common-law maxim the Legislature enacted a rule which permits *no defense for ignorance of law* but *allows a mistake of law defense* in specific instances, including the one presented here: when the defendant's erroneous belief is founded on an "official statement of the law." * * *

Although expressing its evident conviction that the statute should be treated as an "exceptional exculpatory concept * * * intended to be a very narrow escape valve," the majority cites no language in the statute or in the legislative history supporting its views or the construction of Penal Law § 15.20 (2) (a) which seems so contrary to the statute's plain language and evident purpose. Despite the assertion that such construction reflects "appropriate precedential awareness" the majority cites no precedential authority.

Instead, the majority bases its decision on an analogous provision in the Model Penal Code and concludes that despite its totally different wording and meaning Penal Law § 15.20 (2) (a) should be read as if it were Model Penal Code § 2.04 (3) (b) (i). But New York in revising the Penal Law did not adopt the Model Penal Code. As in New Jersey, which generally adopted the Model Penal Code but added one section which is substantially more liberal, New York followed parts of the Model Penal Code provisions and rejected others. In *People v Goetz,* we said that the Legislature's rejection of the verbatim provisions of the Model Penal Code was crucial in determining its intent in drafting the statute. The significance of the alterations here can be no different.

While Penal Law § 15.20 (2) and Model Penal Code § 2.04 are alike in their rejection of the strict common-law rule, they are not alike in wording and differ significantly in substance. * * * In respect to the defense based upon an actor's reliance on an official statement of law contained in a statute the Model Penal Code and the New York statute are totally dissimilar. The Model Penal Code *does not* permit a defense for someone who acts in good faith upon a *mistaken belief* that a specific statute authorizes his conduct. The defense is limited to an act in reliance on an official statement of law in a statute "afterward determined to be *invalid or erroneous*." The New York statute, in contrast, specifically *permits* the defense when the actor proceeds under "a *mistaken belief*" that his conduct does not "constitute an offense" when that "*mistaken belief* is founded upon an official statement of the law contained in * * * a statute."

Thus, the precise phrase in the Model Penal Code limiting the defense under section 2.04 (3) (b) (i) to reliance on a statute "afterward determined to be invalid or erroneous" which, if present, would support the majority's narrow construction of the New York statute, is omitted from Penal Law § 15.20 (2) (a). How the Legislature can be assumed to have enacted the very language which it has specifically rejected is not explained. * * *

III

Any fair reading of the majority opinion, we submit, demonstrates that the decision to reject a mistake of law defense is based on considerations of public policy and on the conviction that such a defense would be bad, rather than on an analysis of CPL 15.20 (2) (a) under the usual principles of statutory construction. The majority warns, for example, that if the defense were permitted "the exception would swallow the rule" that "[mistakes] about the law would be encouraged" that an "infinite number of mistake of law defenses * * * could be devised" and that "wrongminded individuals [could] contrive in bad faith solely to get an exculpatory notion before the jury." * * *

It is no answer to protest that the defense may become a "false and diversionary stratagem[ ]" or that "wrongminded individuals [could] contrive" an "infinite number of mistake of law defenses" for it is the very business of the courts to separate the true claims from the false. * * * Justice Holmes wrote in commenting on John Austin's argument that permitting the mistake of law defense would present courts with problems they were not prepared to solve: "If justice requires the fact to be ascertained, the difficulty of doing so is no ground for refusing to try."

IV

* * * There should be a reversal and defendant should have a new trial in which he is permitted to assert a defense of mistake of law under Penal Law § 15.20 (2) (a).

NOTE

Apparently, Marrero purchased his .38 caliber pistol from a gun dealer in New York who told him that he didn't need a permit for the gun because federal corrections officers are considered "peace officers" under New York law. Paul H. Robinson, CRIMINAL LAW CASE STUDIES 33 (2d ed. 2002); Dan M. Kahan, *Ignorance of the Law Is an Excuse—But Only for the Virtuous*, 96 MICH. L. REV. 127, 131 (1997) (suggesting that local gun dealers "routinely sold weapons to federal prison guards without demanding proof that the guards were licensed to carry such weapons."). Marrero also spoke to the instructor of a local criminal justice course, who supported this interpretation of the law. Kahan, *supra* at 131.

The trial judge in Marrero's case initially agreed with Marrero's reading of the law and granted his motion to dismiss the indictment. *Id.* at 131–32. The state appealed, and the appellate court voted 3–2 to reverse the trial court's ruling and reinstate the indictment. *Id.* at 132. Are any of these facts relevant to Marrero's mistake of law claim? Should they be?

UNITED STATES V. CLEGG

United States Court of Appeals for the Ninth Circuit
846 F.2d 1221 (9th Cir. 1988)

PER CURIAM.

Eugene Ray Clegg is charged with exporting firearms in violation of 18 U.S.C. § 922(a)(1) (1982) and 22 U.S.C. § 2778(b)(2), (c) (1982). * * *

Facts

Prior to his arrest in September 1982, Clegg taught at an American school in Islamabad, Pakistan. According to Clegg, United States officials, affiliated with various agencies of our government, solicited, encouraged and assisted his efforts to supply weapons to Afghan rebels resisting Soviet occupation of their country. Believing that this solicitation, encouragement, and assistance constituted official permission to transport arms, Clegg smuggled arms through Pakistan to the Afghan rebels. He was arrested in Pakistan, where he was imprisoned. Upon his release, United States marshals escorted him back to this country. He returned home facing charges of exporting firearms in violation of federal law. In defending against these charges, Clegg seeks to prove that he acted in reasonable good-faith reliance on statements of United States officials that led him to believe he was lawfully transporting guns.

The acts on which Clegg claims to have relied include the following alleged events, occurrence of which Clegg proposes to prove at trial: (1) that Lieutenant Colonel Durham of the United States Army, second in command in Pakistan, informed Clegg that the United States supplied arms to Afghan rebels, and that the United States wanted Clegg to smuggle arms to the rebels; (2) that Durham offered to put Clegg in contact with the rebels, that he later became aware of Clegg's smuggling, that he helped Clegg to plan a large secret arms shipment which never took place, and that he supplied Clegg with arms for resale to Afghan rebels on one occasion; (3) that Colonel Maugher of the United States Army, who was director of military intelligence for the United States in Pakistan, knew of Clegg's activities, and that Maugher once sold ammunition to Clegg with the understanding that it was destined for resale to the rebels; and (4) that several other individual government officials, whose positions led Clegg to believe that they had power to authorize arms shipments to the rebels, knew of Clegg's shipments and on at least one occasion assisted Clegg in shipping arms. * * *

Discussion

A. This case is controlled by our recent decision in *United States v. Tallmadge*. In *Tallmadge*, we reviewed a conviction for violation of 18 U.S.C. § 922(h)(1) (1982), which prohibits convicted felons from receiving firearms. Tallmadge defended on the ground that his state felony conviction had been reduced to a misdemeanor. While that fact alone did not bring him outside the sweep of section 922, we exonerated Tallmadge because he had disclosed these facts to a licensed firearm dealer and the dealer had sold him the weapon anyway. In reaching this conclusion, we reasoned as follows:

> In the matter before us, the uncontradicted evidence established that Tallmadge received and possessed firearms in reliance upon the representation of a federally licensed gun dealer that a person convicted of a felony in a state court could purchase firearms if the offense had subsequently been reduced to a misdemeanor. We have no doubt that under the doctrine of entrapment by estoppel a person could not be prosecuted under

> 18 U.S.C. §§ 922(h)(1) and 1202(a)(1) if an ATF official had represented that a person convicted of a felony can purchase firearms after the charge has been reduced to a misdemeanor. Here, the misleading statement regarding the lawfulness of Tallmadge's proposed conduct was made by a licensee of the federal government. * * *
>
> The Department of the Treasury requires a licensed firearms dealer and a prospective buyer to fill out a form entitled Firearms Transaction Record to permit the licensee to determine if he may lawfully sell a firearm to such person. The form also requires the firearms dealer "to alert the transferee [buyer] of certain restrictions on the receipt and possession of arms." The form further provides that "[t]he transferor [seller] of the firearm is responsible for determining the lawfulness of the transaction. . . . " To fulfill this duty the form provides that the firearms dealer "should be familiar with the Gun Control Act of 1968 and Title VII, Unlawful Possession or Receipt of Firearms, and 27 CFR Part 178 (Commerce in Firearms and Ammunition)." Thus, Congress has not only granted certain persons the exclusive right to engage in the business of selling firearms, it has also given them the [a]ffirmative duty of inquiring of a prospective buyer whether he has a criminal record that would make it unlawful for him to purchase a firearm. In addition, the Treasury Department requires licensees to inform buyers concerning the restrictions imposed by Congress on the purchase of firearms. Clearly, the United States Government has made licensed firearms dealers federal agents in connection with the gathering and dispensing of information on the purchase of firearms. Under these circumstances, we believe that a buyer has the right to rely on the representations of a licensed firearms dealer, who has been made aware of all the relevant historical facts, that a person may receive and possess a weapon if his felony conviction has been reduced to a misdemeanor.

We view this as an a fortiori case. Tallmadge was dealing with a licensed firearm dealer, a private party. Clegg alleges that he dealt not merely with government officials, but with officials of the highest rank. Moreover, Clegg, unlike Tallmadge, was operating far from the territory of the United States, in a place not obviously covered by American law. If Tallmadge was entitled to rely upon the representations of the gun dealer as a complete defense, we can hardly deny the same defense to Clegg. Whatever our disagreements may be with the court's ruling in *Tallmadge*, it is the law of the circuit and we are bound to follow it. * * *

The judgment of the district court is AFFIRMED.

SKOPIL, CIRCUIT JUDGE, dissenting.

I dissent from the majority's holding that Clegg is entitled to assert a mistake of law defense to the charges of exporting firearms without a license. Generally, ignorance of the law or a mistake as to the law's requirements cannot be a defense in a criminal prosecution. An exception has been created to provide for the legitimate reliance on an official interpretation of law. * * *

Nothing in my search of the record in this case discloses the requisite reliance on an official interpretation of the law. Even assuming that Clegg dealt with officials possessing the requisite authority[1] to suspend the law, Clegg never alleges these officials authorized the unlawful conduct or told him that his activities were lawful. In fact, Clegg admits that he was involved in gun running [activities] before he ever became acquainted with these officials. As the majority notes in its summary of Clegg's allegations, various officials of the United States may have become aware of Clegg's activities. Moreover, several officials may have actually helped Clegg in his quest to supply arms to Afghan rebels. Liberally construed, the officials' conduct may amount to what the majority terms "solicitation, encouragement, and assistance" to Clegg. Nevertheless, in my opinion, there is still lacking any allegation of an official representation that Clegg's conduct was lawful. Hence, Clegg may well have had the aid of various United States officials. This does not make his conduct lawful. I would reverse the district court's ruling that Clegg is entitled to assert the defense.

STATE V. FRIDLEY

Supreme Court of North Dakota
335 N.W.2d 785 (N.D. 1983)

PAULSON, JUSTICE.

Gaylord Duane Fridley [Fridley] appeals from a judgment of conviction entered in the Stark County Court of Increased Jurisdiction on September 23, 1982, upon a jury's verdict finding him guilty of driving while his license was revoked. We affirm.

On the evening of April 1, 1982, Fridley was stopped for speeding in Dickinson by two auxiliary police officers of the Dickinson Police

---

[1] The majority does not specifically address the issue of what authority the official must possess. In *United States v. Barker*, 546 F.2d 940, 946–49 (D.C.Cir.1976), Judge Wilkey approved the use of a mistake of law defense for someone who relied on the "apparent authority" of a government official. Other circuits have adopted a stricter standard by requiring that the government official have actual authority. *See United States v. Duggan*, 743 F.2d 59, 84 (2d Cir.1984). In *Tallmadge*, we seemed to conclude that a licensed firearms dealer is an agent of the United States empowered by statute to interpret the law. *See Tallmadge*, 829 F.2d at 774. Here, the majority simply notes that Clegg dealt with "officials of the highest rank" but does not decide whether such officials are empowered either to provide Clegg with a license to export arms or to suspend the license requirement.

Department. A routine driver license check revealed that Fridley's driver's license had been revoked. Fridley was subsequently arrested and cited for driving while his license was revoked, in violation of § 39–06–42 of the North Dakota Century Code.

Fridley demanded a jury trial. [The state made a motion in limine to prevent Fridley from introducing evidence in support of his mistake argument on the ground that it was irrelevant and would only confuse the jury.] Fridley resisted the State's motion in limine on the grounds that his defense to the charge would rest upon the statutorily defined defense of excuse based upon mistake of law, pursuant to §§ 12.1–05–08 and 12.1–05–09, N.D.C.C., respectively. Fridley said his defense would be based on his mistaken assumption that he was legally authorized to drive at the time he was arrested.

The State's motion *in limine* was heard by the court on the same day as the trial. Fridley contended during his offer of proof that after he received notice of his license revocation, he contacted by telephone, in March of 1982, a person named "Debbie" of the Drivers License Division in regard to the procedures necessary for obtaining a work permit to drive. According to Fridley, "Debbie" told him that he must take a driver's test, that he must forward $10.00 along with his "SR-22 Form," and that he should send his driver's license with his application for a work permit to the Drivers License Division. Fridley stated that he was told he would then be without a driver license for seven days. Fridley testified that he interpreted the substance of his conversation with "Debbie" to mean that his driver's license would be revoked for a period of seven days commencing only when these requested materials "hit the Bismarck office." * * *

In response to the State's motion in limine, Fridley also requested the following jury instruction based upon §§ 12.1–05–08 and 12.1–05–09, N.D.C.C.:

> Gaylord Fridley's conduct may be excused if he believe [sic] the facts were such that his conduct was necessary because of an official interpretation by the Drivers License Division. If you find that this belief is negligently or recklessly held, you may find that Gaylord Fridley was not justified in relying upon the interpretation by the personnel at the Drivers License Division. However, if you find that Gaylord Fridley, in good faith, relied upon the interpretation of the personnel at the Drivers License Division, and it is proved to your satisfaction by a preponderance of the evidence, then you should find Gaylord Fridley not guilty.

The court refused Fridley's requested jury instruction and granted the State's motion in limine prohibiting the defendant "from making any reference to contacts made through the Drivers License Division after the official written decision by the hearing officer" revoking his license. The court determined that any reference to statements made by "Debbie" at the Drivers License Division would constitute hearsay. * * * The trial court also determined that, under § 12.1–05–09, N.D.C.C., the statements purportedly made by "Debbie" concerning the procedures for obtaining a work permit did not qualify as an "official interpretation" of the law defining driving while one's license is revoked. The court also concluded that there was no basis for granting the defendant's requested jury instruction because, as a matter of law, there had been no showing of "reasonable reliance" on an official statement or interpretation of the law. * * *

The jury found Fridley guilty of driving while his license was revoked on September 13, 1982. The court fined Fridley $400.00 and sentenced him to serve 30 days in jail, with 15 days suspended on the condition that he have no moving traffic violations for a period of one year. Fridley appeals.

In his appeal Fridley contends that the trial court erred in granting the State's motion in limine, thus precluding him from presenting evidence to establish his defense of excuse based upon mistake of law. We hold that the trial court properly granted the State's motion in limine—not on the basis of the reasons given by the trial court for its decision—but on the basis that, as a matter of law, the defense of excuse, based upon mistake of law, is not applicable to prosecutions under § 39–06–42, N.D.C.C., a strict liability offense for which proof of culpability is not required. * * *

Section 39–06–42(1), N.D.C.C., under which Fridley was convicted, provides in pertinent part as follows:

> 39–06–42. Penalty for driving while license suspended or revoked—Impoundment of vehicle number plates—Authority of cities.
>
> 1. Except as provided in chapters 39–16 and 39–16.1, and in section 39–06.1–11, any person who drives a motor vehicle on any public highway of this state at a time when his license or privilege so to do is suspended or revoked shall be guilty of a class B misdemeanor. . . .

It is evident that § 39–06–42(1), N.D.C.C., does not contain a mental culpability requirement. Although § 12.1–02–02(2), N.D.C.C., provides that if a statute defining a crime does not specify any culpability requirement and does not provide explicitly that a person may be guilty without culpability, the culpability that is required is "willfully," past decisions of our court have restricted the application of § 12.1–02–02(2), N.D.C.C., to offenses defined in Title 12.1, N.D.C.C., alone. In addition, we have previously pointed out that § 39–06–42, N.D.C.C., is one of several strict liability offenses found throughout our Century Code. * * *

Section 12.1–05–09, N.D.C.C., provides:

> 12.1–05–09. Mistake of law.—Except as otherwise expressly provided, a person's good faith belief that conduct does not constitute a crime is an affirmative defense if he acted in reasonable reliance upon a statement of the law contained in:
>
> 1. A statute or other enactment.
>
> 2. A judicial decision, opinion, order, or judgment.
>
> 3. An administrative order or grant of permission.
>
> 4. An official interpretation of the public servant or body charged by law with responsibility for the interpretation, administration, or enforcement of the law defining the crime.

Chapter 12.1–05 of the North Dakota Century Code "is an almost complete adoption of Chapter 6 of the Proposed [Federal Criminal] Code dealing with defenses involving justification and excuse." The language of § 12.1–05–09, N.D.C.C., is identical to § 609 of the Proposed Federal Criminal Code. It is therefore helpful, as an aid to interpreting the North Dakota mistake of law statute, to examine the Comments of the draftsmen of the Proposed Federal Criminal Code.

The Final Report, supra at page 53, contains, in relevant part, the following Comment regarding § 609:

> This section sets forth those circumstances under which a person is excused from criminal liability for his conduct because he mistakenly believed his conduct did not constitute a crime. *The defense is not available for infractions where proof of culpability is generally not required.* [Emphasis added.]

Although the above-quoted Comment indicates that the defense of mistake of law is not applicable to "infractions" where proof of culpability is not required, we believe the same holds true in regard to § 39–06–42, N.D.C.C., a class B misdemeanor for which proof of culpability is not required. * * *

In the instant case, allowing the assertion of the mistake of law defense, which rests upon a defendant's "good faith belief" that his conduct does not constitute a crime, is difficult to reconcile with the concept of a strict liability offense for which proof of a culpable state of mind is not required. * * *

For the reasons stated in this opinion, the judgment of conviction is affirmed.

2. IGNORANCE OR MISTAKE THAT NEGATES THE MENS REA

If one is charged with an offense and knowledge that the prohibited conduct is unlawful an element of that offense, then one can argue that one's lack of knowledge as to the unlawfulness of one's conduct negates an essential element of the crime. This type of mistake is a complete defense. In *Cheek v. United States* and *Bryan v. United States*, the U.S. Supreme Court discusses and explains this type of mistake of law defense.

CHEEK V. UNITED STATES

Supreme Court of the United States
498 U.S. 192, 111 S.Ct. 604, 112 L.Ed.2d 617 (1991)

JUSTICE WHITE delivered the opinion of the Court.

Title 26, § 7201 of the United States Code provides that any person "who willfully attempts in any manner to evade or defeat any tax imposed by this title or the payment thereof" shall be guilty of a felony. Under 26 U.S.C. § 7203, "any person required under this title . . . or by regulations made under authority thereof to make a return . . . who willfully fails to . . . make such return" shall be guilty of a misdemeanor. This case turns on the meaning of the word "willfully" as used in §§ 7201 and 7203.

I

Petitioner John L. Cheek has been a pilot for American Airlines since 1973. He filed federal income tax returns through 1979 but thereafter ceased to file returns. He also claimed an increasing number of withholding allowances—eventually claiming 60 allowances by mid-1980—and for the years 1981 to 1984 indicated on his W-4 forms that he was exempt from federal income taxes. In 1983, petitioner unsuccessfully sought a refund of all tax withheld by his employer in 1982. Petitioner's income during this period at all times far exceeded the minimum necessary to trigger the statutory filing requirement.

As a result of his activities, petitioner was indicted for 10 violations of federal law. He was charged with six counts of willfully failing to file a federal income tax return for the years 1980, 1981, and 1983 through 1986, in violation of 26 U.S.C. § 7203. He was further charged with three counts of willfully attempting to evade his income taxes for the years 1980, 1981, and 1983 in violation of § 7201. In those years, American Airlines withheld substantially less than the amount of tax petitioner owed because of the numerous allowances and exempt status he claimed on his W-4 forms. The tax offenses with which petitioner was charged are specific intent crimes that require the defendant to have acted willfully.

At trial, the evidence established that between 1982 and 1986, petitioner was involved in at least four civil cases that challenged various aspects of the federal income tax system. In all four of those cases, the plaintiffs were informed by the courts that many of their arguments, including that they were not taxpayers within the meaning of the tax laws, that wages are not income, that the Sixteenth Amendment does not authorize the imposition of an income tax on individuals, and that the Sixteenth Amendment is unenforceable, were frivolous or had been repeatedly rejected by the courts. During this time period, petitioner also attended at least two criminal trials of persons charged with tax offenses. In addition, there was evidence that in 1980 or 1981 an attorney had advised Cheek that the courts had rejected as frivolous the claim that wages are not income.[4]

Cheek represented himself at trial and testified in his defense. He admitted that he had not filed personal income tax returns during the years in question. He testified that as early as 1978, he had begun attending seminars sponsored by, and following the advice of, a group that believes, among other things, that the federal tax system is unconstitutional. Some of the speakers at these meetings were lawyers who purported to give professional opinions about the invalidity of the federal income tax laws. Cheek produced a letter from an attorney stating that the Sixteenth Amendment did not authorize a tax on wages and salaries but only on gain or profit. Petitioner's defense was that, based on the indoctrination he received from this group and from his own study, he sincerely believed that the tax laws were being unconstitutionally enforced and that his actions during the 1980–1986 period were lawful. He therefore argued that he had acted without the willfulness required for conviction of the various offenses with which he was charged.

In the course of its instructions, the trial court advised the jury that to prove "willfulness" the Government must prove the voluntary and intentional violation of a known legal duty, a burden that could not be proved by showing mistake, ignorance, or negligence. The court further advised the jury that an objectively reasonable good-faith misunderstanding of the law would negate willfulness, but mere disagreement with the law would not. The court described Cheek's beliefs about the income tax system and instructed the jury that if it found that Cheek "honestly and reasonably believed that he was not required to pay income taxes or to file tax returns," a not guilty verdict should be returned.

After several hours of deliberation, the jury sent a note to the judge that stated in part:

> We have a basic disagreement between some of us as to if Mr. Cheek honestly & reasonably believed that he was not required

---

[4] The attorney also advised that despite the Fifth Amendment, the filing of a tax return was required and that a person could challenge the constitutionality of the system by suing for a refund after the taxes had been withheld, or by putting himself "at risk of criminal prosecution."

to pay income taxes. . . . Page 32 [the relevant jury instruction] discusses good faith misunderstanding & disagreement. Is there any additional clarification you can give us on this point?

The District Judge responded with a supplemental instruction containing the following statements:

[A] person's opinion that the tax laws violate his constitutional rights does not constitute a good faith misunderstanding of the law. Furthermore, a person's disagreement with the government's tax collection systems and policies does not constitute a good faith misunderstanding of the law.

At the end of the first day of deliberation, the jury sent out another note saying that it still could not reach a verdict because "we are divided on the issue as to if Mr. Cheek honestly & reasonably believed that he was not required to pay income tax." When the jury resumed its deliberations, the District Judge gave the jury an additional instruction. This instruction stated in part that "an honest but unreasonable belief is not a defense and does not negate willfulness," and that "advice or research resulting in the conclusion that wages of a privately employed person are not income or that the tax laws are unconstitutional is not objectively reasonable and cannot serve as the basis for a good faith misunderstanding of the law defense." The court also instructed the jury that "persistent refusal to acknowledge the law does not constitute a good faith misunderstanding of the law." Approximately two hours later, the jury returned a verdict finding petitioner guilty on all counts.[6]

Petitioner appealed his convictions, arguing that the District Court erred by instructing the jury that only an objectively reasonable misunderstanding of the law negates the statutory willfulness requirement. The United States Court of Appeals for the Seventh Circuit rejected that contention and affirmed the convictions. * * * Because the Seventh Circuit's interpretation of "willfully" as used in these statutes conflicts with the decisions of several other Courts of Appeals, we granted certiorari.

II

The general rule that ignorance of the law or a mistake of law is no defense to criminal prosecution is deeply rooted in the American legal system. Based on the notion that the law is definite and knowable, the common law presumed that every person knew the law. This common-law

---

[6] A note signed by all 12 jurors also informed the judge that although the jury found petitioner guilty, several jurors wanted to express their personal opinions of the case and that notes from these individual jurors to the court were "a complaint against the narrow & hard expression under the constraints of the law." At least two notes from individual jurors expressed the opinion that petitioner sincerely believed in his cause even though his beliefs might have been unreasonable.

rule has been applied by the Court in numerous cases construing criminal statutes.

The proliferation of statutes and regulations has sometimes made it difficult for the average citizen to know and comprehend the extent of the duties and obligations imposed by the tax laws. Congress has accordingly softened the impact of the common-law presumption by making specific intent to violate the law an element of certain federal criminal tax offenses. Thus, the Court almost 60 years ago interpreted the statutory term "willfully" as used in the federal criminal tax statutes as carving out an exception to the traditional rule. This special treatment of criminal tax offenses is largely due to the complexity of the tax laws. In *United States v. Murdock,* the Court recognized that:

> Congress did not intend that a person, by reason of a bona fide misunderstanding as to his liability for the tax, as to his duty to make a return, or as to the adequacy of the records he maintained, should become a criminal by his mere failure to measure up to the prescribed standard of conduct.

The Court held that the defendant was entitled to an instruction with respect to whether he acted in good faith based on his actual belief. * * *

Subsequent decisions have refined this proposition. In *United States v. Bishop,* we described the term "willfully" as connoting "a voluntary, intentional violation of a known legal duty," and did so with specific reference to the "bad faith or evil intent" language employed in *Murdock.* Still later, *United States v. Pomponio* addressed a situation in which several defendants had been charged with willfully filing false tax returns. * * * Taken together, *Bishop* and *Pomponio* conclusively establish that the standard for the statutory willfulness requirement is the "voluntary, intentional violation of a known legal duty."

III

Cheek accepts the *Pomponio* definition of willfulness, but asserts that the District Court's instructions and the Court of Appeals' opinion departed from that definition. In particular, he challenges the ruling that a good-faith misunderstanding of the law or a good-faith belief that one is not violating the law, if it is to negate willfulness, must be objectively reasonable. We agree that the Court of Appeals and the District Court erred in this respect.

A

Willfulness, as construed by our prior decisions in criminal tax cases, requires the Government to prove that the law imposed a duty on the defendant, that the defendant knew of this duty, and that he voluntarily and intentionally violated that duty. We deal first with the case where the issue is whether the defendant knew of the duty purportedly imposed by the provision of the statute or regulation he is accused of violating, a case in which there is no claim that the provision at issue is invalid. In such a case, if the Government proves actual knowledge of the pertinent legal duty, the prosecution, without more, has satisfied the knowledge component of the willfulness requirement. But carrying this burden requires negating a defendant's claim of ignorance of the law or a claim that because of a misunderstanding of the law, he had a good-faith belief that he was not violating any of the provisions of the tax laws. This is so because one cannot be aware that the law imposes a duty upon him and yet be ignorant of it, misunderstand the law, or believe that the duty does not exist. In the end, the issue is whether, based on all the evidence, the Government has proved that the defendant was aware of the duty at issue, which cannot be true if the jury credits a good-faith misunderstanding and belief submission, whether or not the claimed belief or misunderstanding is objectively reasonable.

In this case, if Cheek asserted that he truly believed that the Internal Revenue Code did not purport to treat wages as income, and the jury believed him, the Government would not have carried its burden to prove willfulness, however unreasonable a court might deem such a belief. Of course, in deciding whether to credit Cheek's good-faith belief claim, the jury would be free to consider any admissible evidence from any source showing that Cheek was aware of his duty to file a return and to treat wages as income, including evidence showing his awareness of the relevant provisions of the Code or regulations, of court decisions rejecting his interpretation of the tax law, of authoritative rulings of the Internal Revenue Service, or of any contents of the personal income tax return forms and accompanying instructions that made it plain that wages should be returned as income.[8]

We thus disagree with the Court of Appeals' requirement that a claimed good-faith belief must be objectively reasonable if it is to be considered as possibly negating the Government's evidence purporting to show a defendant's awareness of the legal duty at issue. Knowledge and belief are characteristically questions for the factfinder, in this case the jury. Characterizing a particular belief as not objectively reasonable transforms the inquiry into a legal one and would prevent the jury from considering it. * * *

It was therefore error to instruct the jury to disregard evidence of Cheek's understanding that, within the meaning of the tax laws, he was not a person required to file a return or to pay income taxes and that

---

[8] Cheek recognizes that a "defendant who knows what the law is and who disagrees with it . . . does not have a bona fide misunderstanding defense," but asserts that "a defendant who has a bona fide misunderstanding of [the law] does not 'know' his legal duty and lacks willfulness." The Reply Brief for Petitioner, at 13, states: "We are in no way suggesting that Cheek or anyone else is immune from criminal prosecution if he knows what the law is, but believes it should be otherwise, and therefore violates it."

wages are not taxable income, as incredible as such misunderstandings of and beliefs about the law might be. Of course, the more unreasonable the asserted beliefs or misunderstandings are, the more likely the jury will consider them to be nothing more than simple disagreement with known legal duties imposed by the tax laws and will find that the Government has carried its burden of proving knowledge.

B

Cheek asserted in the trial court that he should be acquitted because he believed in good faith that the income tax law is unconstitutional as applied to him and thus could not legally impose any duty upon him of which he should have been aware. Such a submission is unsound. * * *

Claims that some of the provisions of the tax code are unconstitutional are submissions of a different order. They do not arise from innocent mistakes caused by the complexity of the Internal Revenue Code. Rather, they reveal full knowledge of the provisions at issue and a studied conclusion, however wrong, that those provisions are invalid and unenforceable. Thus in this case, Cheek paid his taxes for years, but after attending various seminars and based on his own study, he concluded that the income tax laws could not constitutionally require him to pay a tax.

We do not believe that Congress contemplated that such a taxpayer, without risking criminal prosecution, could ignore the duties imposed upon him by the Internal Revenue Code and refuse to utilize the mechanisms provided by Congress to present his claims of invalidity to the courts and to abide by their decisions. There is no doubt that Cheek, from year to year, was free to pay the tax that the law purported to require, file for a refund and, if denied, present his claims of invalidity, constitutional or otherwise, to the courts. Also, without paying the tax, he could have challenged claims of tax deficiencies in the Tax Court, § 6213, with the right to appeal to a higher court if unsuccessful. Cheek took neither course in some years, and when he did was unwilling to accept the outcome. As we see it, he is in no position to claim that his good-faith belief about the validity of the Internal Revenue Code negates willfulness or provides a defense to criminal prosecution under §§ 7201 and 7203. Of course, Cheek was free in this very case to present his claims of invalidity and have them adjudicated, but like defendants in criminal cases in other contexts, who "willfully" refuse to comply with the duties placed upon them by the law, he must take the risk of being wrong.

We thus hold that in a case like this, a defendant's views about the validity of the tax statutes are irrelevant to the issue of willfulness and need not be heard by the jury, and, if they are, an instruction to disregard them would be proper. For this purpose, it makes no difference whether the claims of invalidity are frivolous or have substance. It was therefore not error in this case for the District Judge to instruct the jury not to consider Cheek's claims that the tax laws were unconstitutional. However, it was error for the court to instruct the jury that petitioner's asserted beliefs that wages are not income and that he was not a taxpayer within the meaning of the Internal Revenue Code should not be considered by the jury in determining whether Cheek had acted willfully.

IV

For the reasons set forth in the opinion above, the judgment of the Court of Appeals is vacated, and the case is remanded for further proceedings consistent with this opinion.

It is so ordered.

JUSTICE SOUTER took no part in the consideration or decision of this case.

JUSTICE SCALIA, concurring in the judgment.

I concur in the judgment of the Court because our cases have consistently held that the failure to pay a tax in the good-faith belief that it is not legally owing is not "willful." I do not join the Court's opinion because I do not agree with the test for willfulness that it directs the Court of Appeals to apply on remand.

As the Court acknowledges, our opinions from the 1930's to the 1970's have interpreted the word "willfully" in the criminal tax statutes as requiring the "bad purpose" or "evil motive" of "intentionally violating a known legal duty." It seems to me that today's opinion squarely reverses that long-established statutory construction when it says that a good-faith erroneous belief in the unconstitutionality of a tax law is no defense. It is quite impossible to say that a statute which one believes unconstitutional represents a "known legal duty." * * *

I find it impossible to understand how one can derive from the lonesome word "willfully" the proposition that belief in the nonexistence of a textual prohibition excuses liability, but belief in the invalidity (*i.e.*, the legal nonexistence) of a textual prohibition does not. One may say, as the law does in many contexts, that "willfully" refers to consciousness of the act but not to consciousness that the act is unlawful. Or alternatively, one may say, as we have said until today with respect to the tax statutes, that "willfully" refers to consciousness of both the act *and* its illegality. But it seems to me impossible to say that the word refers to consciousness that some legal text exists, without consciousness that that legal text is binding, *i.e.*, with the good-faith belief that it is not a valid law. Perhaps such a test for criminal liability would make sense (though in a field as complicated as federal tax law, I doubt it), but some text other than the mere word "willfully" would have to be employed to describe it—and that text is not ours to write.

Because today's opinion abandons clear and longstanding precedent to impose criminal liability where taxpayers have had no reason to expect it, because the new contours of criminal liability have no basis in the statutory text, and because I strongly suspect that those new contours make no sense even as a policy matter, I concur only in the judgment of the Court.

[JUSTICE BLACKMUN's dissenting opinion has been omitted.]

BRYAN V. UNITED STATES

Supreme Court of the United States
524 U.S. 184, 118 S.Ct. 1939, 141 L.Ed.2d 197 (1998)

JUSTICE STEVENS delivered the opinion of the Court.

Petitioner was convicted of "willfully" dealing in firearms without a federal license. The question presented is whether the term "willfully" in 18 U.S.C. § 924(a)(1)(D) requires proof that the defendant knew that his conduct was unlawful, or whether it also requires proof that he knew of the federal licensing requirement.

I

In 1968 Congress enacted the Omnibus Crime Control and Safe Streets Act. 82 Stat. 197–239. In Title IV of that Act Congress made findings concerning the impact of the traffic in firearms on the prevalence of lawlessness and violent crime in the United States and amended the Criminal Code to include detailed provisions regulating the use and sale of firearms. As amended, 18 U.S.C. § 922 defined a number of "unlawful acts"; subsection (a)(1) made it unlawful for any person except a licensed dealer to engage in the business of dealing in firearms.[1] Section 923 established the federal licensing program and repeated the prohibition against dealing in firearms without a license, and § 924 specified the penalties for violating "any provision of this chapter." Read literally, § 924 authorized the imposition of a fine of up to $5,000 or a prison sentence of not more than five years, "or both," on any person who dealt in firearms without a license even if that person believed that he or she was acting lawfully.[2] As enacted in 1968, § 922(a)(1) and § 924 omitted an express scienter requirement and therefore arguably imposed strict criminal liability on every unlicensed dealer in firearms. The 1968 Act also omitted

---

[1] 82 Stat. 228. The current version of this provision, which is substantially the same as the 1968 version, is codified at 18 U.S.C. § 922(a)(1)(A). It states:

(a) It shall be unlawful—

(1) for any person—

(A) except a licensed importer, licensed manufacturer, or licensed dealer, to engage in the business of importing, manufacturing, or dealing in firearms, or in the course of such business to ship, transport, or receive any firearm in interstate or foreign commerce.

[2] § 924. Penalties

(a) Whoever violates any provision of this chapter . . . shall be fined not more than $5,000 or imprisoned not more than five years, or both.

any definition of the term "engaged in the business" even though that conduct was an element of the unlawful act prohibited by § 922(a)(1).

In 1986 Congress enacted the Firearms Owners' Protection Act (FOPA), in part, to cure these omissions. The findings in that statute explained that additional legislation was necessary to protect law-abiding citizens with respect to the acquisition, possession, or use of firearms for lawful purposes.[3] FOPA therefore amended § 921 to include a definition of the term "engaged in the business,"[4] and amended § 924 to add a scienter requirement as a condition to the imposition of penalties for most of the unlawful acts defined in § 922. For three categories of offenses the intent required is that the defendant acted "knowingly"; for the fourth category, which includes "any other provision of this chapter," the required intent is that the defendant acted "willfully."[5] The § 922(a)(1)(A) offense at issue in this case is an "other provision" in the "willfully" category.

II

The jury having found petitioner guilty, we accept the Government's version of the evidence. That evidence proved that petitioner did not have a federal license to deal in firearms; that he used so-called "straw purchasers" in Ohio to acquire pistols that he could not have purchased

---

[3] The Congress finds that—. . . .

(b)(2) additional legislation is required to reaffirm the intent of the Congress, as expressed in section 101 of the Gun Control Act of 1968, that 'it is not the purpose of this title to place any undue or unnecessary Federal restrictions or burdens on law-abiding citizens with respect to the acquisition, possession, or use of firearms appropriate to the purpose of hunting, trapshooting, target shooting, personal protection, or any other lawful activity, and that this title is not intended to discourage or eliminate the private ownership or use of firearms by law-abiding citizens for lawful purposes.

[4] Section 921 of title 18, United States Code, is amended—. . . .

(21) The term 'engaged in the business' means—. . . .

(C) as applied to a dealer in firearms, as defined in section 921(a)(11)(A), a person who devotes time, attention, and labor to dealing in firearms as a regular course of trade or business with the principal objective of livelihood and profit through the repetitive purchase and resale of firearms, but such term shall not include a person who makes occasional sales, exchanges, or purchases of firearms for the enhancement of a personal collection or for a hobby, or who sells all or part of his personal collection of firearms. . . .

[5] Title 18 U.S.C. § 924(a)(1) currently provides:

Except as otherwise provided in this subsection, subsection (b), (c), or (f) of this section, or in section 929, whoever—

(A) knowingly makes any false statement or representation with respect to the information required by this chapter to be kept in the records of a person licensed under this chapter or in applying for any license or exemption or relief from disability under the provisions of this chapter;

(B) knowingly violates subsection (a)(4), (f), (k), (r), (v), or (w) of section 922;

(C) knowingly imports or brings into the United States or any possession thereof any firearm or ammunition in violation of section 922(*l*); or

(D) willfully violates any other provision of this chapter,

shall be fined under this title, imprisoned not more than five years, or both.

himself; that the straw purchasers made false statements when purchasing the guns; that petitioner assured the straw purchasers that he would file the serial numbers off the guns; and that he resold the guns on Brooklyn street corners known for drug dealing. The evidence was unquestionably adequate to prove that petitioner was dealing in firearms, and that he knew that his conduct was unlawful.[8] There was, however, no evidence that he was aware of the federal law that prohibits dealing in firearms without a federal license.

Petitioner was charged with a conspiracy to violate 18 U.S.C. § 922(a)(1)(A), by willfully engaging in the business of dealing in firearms, and with a substantive violation of that provision. After the close of evidence, petitioner requested that the trial judge instruct the jury that petitioner could be convicted only if he knew of the federal licensing requirement,[10] but the judge rejected this request. Instead, the trial judge gave this explanation of the term "willfully":

> A person acts willfully if he acts intentionally and purposely and with the intent to do something the law forbids, that is, with the bad purpose to disobey or to disregard the law. Now, the person need not be aware of the specific law or rule that his conduct may be violating. But he must act with the intent to do something that the law forbids.

Petitioner was found guilty on both counts. On appeal he argued that the evidence was insufficient because there was no proof that he had knowledge of the federal licensing requirement, and that the trial judge had erred by failing to instruct the jury that such knowledge was an essential element of the offense. The Court of Appeals affirmed. It concluded that the instructions were proper and that the Government had elicited "ample proof" that petitioner had acted willfully.

Because the Eleventh Circuit has held that it is necessary for the Government to prove that the defendant acted with knowledge of the licensing requirement, we granted certiorari to resolve the conflict.

III

The word "willfully" is sometimes said to be "a word of many meanings" whose construction is often dependent on the context in which

---

[8] Why else would he make use of straw purchasers and assure them that he would shave the serial numbers off the guns? Moreover, the street corner sales are not consistent with a good-faith belief in the legality of the enterprise.

[10] KNOWLEDGE OF THE LAW

The Federal Firearms Statute which the Defendant is charged with, conspiracy to violate and with allegedly violated *[sic]*, is a specific intent statute. You must accordingly find, beyond a reasonable doubt, that Defendant at all relevant times charged, acted with the knowledge that it was unlawful to engage in the business of firearms distribution lawfully purchased by a legally permissible transferee or gun purchaser.... You must be persuaded that with the actual knowledge of the federal firearms licensing laws Defendant acted in knowing and intentional violation of them.

it appears. Most obviously it differentiates between deliberate and unwitting conduct, but in the criminal law it also typically refers to a culpable state of mind. As we explained in *United States v. Murdock*, a variety of phrases have been used to describe that concept.[12] As a general matter, when used in the criminal context, a "willful" act is one undertaken with a "bad purpose." In other words, in order to establish a "willful" violation of a statute, "the Government must prove that the defendant acted with knowledge that his conduct was unlawful."

Petitioner argues that a more particularized showing is required in this case for two principal reasons. First, he argues that the fact that Congress used the adverb "knowingly" to authorize punishment of three categories of acts made unlawful by § 922 and the word "willfully" when it referred to unlicensed dealing in firearms demonstrates that the Government must shoulder a special burden in cases like this. This argument is not persuasive because the term "knowingly" does not necessarily have any reference to a culpable state of mind or to knowledge of the law. As Justice Jackson correctly observed, "the knowledge requisite to knowing violation of a statute is factual knowledge as distinguished from knowledge of the law." Thus, in *United States v. Bailey*, we held that the prosecution fulfills its burden of proving a knowing violation of the escape statute "if it demonstrates that an escapee knew his actions would result in his leaving physical confinement without permission." And in *Staples v. United States,* we held that a charge that the defendant's possession of an unregistered machine gun was unlawful required proof "that he knew the weapon he possessed had the characteristics that brought it within the statutory definition of a machine gun." It was not, however, necessary to prove that the defendant knew that his possession was unlawful. Thus, unless the text of the statute dictates a different result, the term "knowingly" merely requires proof of knowledge of the facts that constitute the offense.

With respect to the three categories of conduct that are made punishable by § 924 if performed "knowingly," the background presumption that every citizen knows the law makes it unnecessary to adduce specific evidence to prove that "an evil-meaning mind" directed the "evil-doing hand." More is required, however, with respect to the conduct in the fourth category that is only criminal when done "willfully." The jury must find that the defendant acted with an evil-meaning mind, that is to say, that he acted with knowledge that his conduct was unlawful.

---

[12] The word often denotes an act which is intentional, or knowing, or voluntary, as distinguished from accidental. But when used in a criminal statute it generally means an act done with a bad purpose. The word is also employed to characterize a thing done without ground for believing it is lawful or conduct marked by careless disregard whether or not one has the right so to act.

Petitioner next argues that we must read § 924(a)(1)(D) to require knowledge of the law because of our interpretation of "willfully" in two other contexts. In certain cases involving willful violations of the tax laws, we have concluded that the jury must find that the defendant was aware of the specific provision of the tax code that he was charged with violating. Similarly, in order to satisfy a willful violation in *Ratzlaf*, we concluded that the jury had to find that the defendant knew that his structuring of cash transactions to avoid a reporting requirement was unlawful. Those cases, however, are readily distinguishable. Both the tax cases and *Ratzlaf* involved highly technical statutes that presented the danger of ensnaring individuals engaged in apparently innocent conduct. As a result, we held that these statutes "carve out an exception to the traditional rule" that ignorance of the law is no excuse and require that the defendant have knowledge of the law. The danger of convicting individuals engaged in apparently innocent activity that motivated our decisions in the tax cases and *Ratzlaf* is not present here because the jury found that this petitioner knew that his conduct was unlawful.

Thus, the willfulness requirement of § 924(a)(1)(D) does not carve out an exception to the traditional rule that ignorance of the law is no excuse; knowledge that the conduct is unlawful is all that is required. * * *

Accordingly, the judgment of the Court of Appeals is affirmed.

It is so ordered.

JUSTICE SCALIA, with whom THE CHIEF JUSTICE and JUSTICE GINSBURG join, dissenting.

Petitioner Sillasse Bryan was convicted of "willfully" violating the federal licensing requirement for firearms dealers. The jury apparently found, and the evidence clearly shows, that Bryan was aware in a general way that some aspect of his conduct was unlawful. The issue is whether that general knowledge of illegality is enough to sustain the conviction, or whether a "willful" violation of the licensing provision requires proof that the defendant knew that his conduct was unlawful specifically because he lacked the necessary license. On that point the statute is, in my view, genuinely ambiguous. Most of the Court's opinion is devoted to confirming half of that ambiguity by refuting Bryan's various arguments that the statute clearly requires specific knowledge of the licensing requirement. The Court offers no real justification for its implicit conclusion that either (1) the statute unambiguously requires only general knowledge of illegality, or (2) ambiguously requiring only general knowledge is enough. Instead, the Court curiously falls back on "the traditional rule that ignorance of the law is no excuse" to conclude that "knowledge that the conduct is unlawful is all that is required." In my view, this case calls for the application of a different canon—"the familiar rule that, 'where there is ambiguity in a criminal statute, doubts are resolved in favor of the defendant.' "

Title 18 § 922(a)(1)(A) makes it unlawful for any person to engage in the business of dealing in firearms without a federal license. That provision is enforced criminally through § 924(a)(1)(D), which imposes criminal penalties on whoever "willfully violates any other provision of this chapter." The word "willfully" has a wide range of meanings, and " 'its construction [is] often . . . influenced by its context.' " In some contexts it connotes nothing more than "an act which is intentional, or knowing, or voluntary, as distinguished from accidental." In the present context, however, inasmuch as the preceding three subparagraphs of § 924 specify a *mens rea* of "knowingly" for *other* firearms offenses, see §§ 924(a)(1)(A)–(C), a "willful" violation under § 924(a)(1)(D) must require some mental state more culpable than mere intent to perform the forbidden act. The United States concedes (and the Court apparently agrees) that the violation is not "willful" unless the defendant knows in a general way that his conduct is unlawful.

That concession takes this case beyond any useful application of the maxim that ignorance of the law is no excuse. Everyone agrees that § 924(a)(1)(D) requires some knowledge of the law; the only real question is *which* law? The Court's answer is that knowledge of *any* law is enough—or, put another way, that the defendant must be ignorant of *every* law violated by his course of conduct to be innocent of willfully violating the licensing requirement. The Court points to no textual basis for that conclusion other than the notoriously malleable word "willfully" itself. Instead, it seems to fall back on a presumption (apparently derived from the rule that ignorance of the law is no excuse) that even where ignorance of the law *is* an excuse, that excuse should be construed as narrowly as the statutory language permits.

I do not believe that the Court's approach makes sense of the statute that Congress enacted. I have no quarrel with the Court's assertion that "willfully" in § 924(a)(1)(D) requires only "general" knowledge of illegality—in the sense that the defendant need not be able to recite chapter and verse from Title 18 of the United States Code. It is enough, in my view, if the defendant is generally aware that the *actus reus* punished by the statute—dealing in firearms without a license—is illegal. But the Court is willing to accept a *mens rea* so "general" that it is entirely divorced from the *actus reus* this statute was enacted to punish. That approach turns § 924(a)(1)(D) into a strange and unlikely creature. Bryan would be guilty of "willfully" dealing in firearms without a federal license even if, for example, he had never heard of the licensing requirement but was aware that he had violated the law by using straw purchasers or filing the serial numbers off the pistols. The Court does not even limit (for there is no rational basis to limit) the universe of relevant laws to federal *firearms* statutes. Bryan would also be "acting with an evil-meaning mind," and hence presumably be guilty of "willfully" dealing in firearms without a license, if he knew that his street-corner transactions violated

New York City's business licensing or sales tax ordinances. (For that matter, it ought to suffice if Bryan knew that the car out of which he sold the guns was illegally double-parked, or if, in order to meet the appointed time for the sale, he intentionally violated Pennsylvania's speed limit on the drive back from the gun purchase in Ohio.) Once we stop focusing on the conduct the defendant is actually charged with (*i.e.*, selling guns without a license), I see no principled way to determine *what* law the defendant must be conscious of violating.

Congress is free, of course, to make criminal liability under one statute turn on knowledge of another, to use its firearms dealer statutes to encourage compliance with New York City's tax collection efforts, and to put judges and juries through the kind of mental gymnastics described above. But these are strange results, and I would not lightly assume that Congress intended to make liability under a federal criminal statute depend so heavily upon the vagaries of local law—particularly local law dealing with completely unrelated subjects. If we must have a presumption in cases like this one, I think it would be more reasonable to presume that, when Congress makes ignorance of the law a defense to a criminal prohibition, it ordinarily means ignorance of the unlawfulness of the specific conduct punished *by that criminal prohibition*.

That is the meaning we have given the word "willfully" in other contexts where we have concluded it requires knowledge of the law. *See, e.g., Ratzlaf*, 510 U.S. at 149 ("To convict Ratzlaf of the crime with which he was charged, . . . the jury had to find he knew the structuring in which he engaged was unlawful"); *Cheek v. United States*, 498 U.S. 192, 201 ("The standard for the statutory willfulness requirement is the 'voluntary, intentional violation of a known legal duty.' . . . The issue is whether the defendant knew of the duty purportedly imposed by the provision of the statute or regulation he is accused of violating"). The Court explains these cases on the ground that they involved "highly technical statutes that presented the danger of ensnaring individuals engaged in apparently innocent conduct." That is no explanation at all. The complexity of the tax and currency laws may explain why the Court interpreted "willful" to require some awareness of illegality, as opposed to merely "an act which is intentional, or knowing, or voluntary, as distinguished from accidental." But it *in no way* justifies the distinction the Court seeks to draw today between knowledge of the law the defendant is actually charged with violating and knowledge of *any* law the defendant could conceivably be charged with violating. * * *

* * * It is common ground that the statutory context here requires some awareness of the law for a § 924(a)(1)(D) conviction, but the statute is simply ambiguous, or silent, as to the precise contours of that *mens rea* requirement. In the face of that ambiguity, I would invoke the rule that

" 'ambiguity concerning the ambit of criminal statutes should be resolved in favor of lenity.' "

> The rule that penal laws are to be construed strictly, is, perhaps, not much less old than construction itself. It is founded on the tenderness of the law for the rights of individuals; and on the plain principle that the power of punishment is vested in the legislative, not in the judicial department.

In our era of multiplying new federal crimes, there is more reason than ever to give this ancient canon of construction consistent application: by fostering uniformity in the interpretation of criminal statutes, it will reduce the occasions on which this Court will have to produce judicial havoc by resolving in defendants' favor a circuit conflict regarding the substantive elements of a federal crime.

I respectfully dissent.

3. FAIR NOTICE AND DUE PROCESS (THE *LAMBERT* EXCEPTION)

LAMBERT V. CALIFORNIA

Supreme Court of the United States
355 U.S. 225, 78 S.Ct. 240, 2 L.Ed.2d 228 (1957)

MR. JUSTICE DOUGLAS delivered the opinion of the Court.

Section 52.38 (a) of the Los Angeles Municipal Code defines "convicted person" as follows:

> Any person who, subsequent to January 1, 1921, has been or hereafter is convicted of an offense punishable as a felony in the State of California, or who has been or who is hereafter convicted of any offense in any place other than the State of California, which offense, if committed in the State of California, would have been punishable as a felony.

Section 52.39 provides that it shall be unlawful for "any convicted person" to be or remain in Los Angeles for a period of more than five days without registering; it requires any person having a place of abode outside the city to register if he comes into the city on five occasions or more during a 30-day period; and it prescribes the information to be furnished the Chief of Police on registering. Section 52.43 (b) makes the failure to register a continuing offense, each day's failure constituting a separate offense.

Appellant, arrested on suspicion of another offense, was charged with a violation of this registration law. The evidence showed that she had been at the time of her arrest a resident of Los Angeles for over seven years. Within that period she had been convicted in Los Angeles of the crime of forgery, an offense which California punishes as a felony. Though convicted of a crime punishable as a felony, she had not at the time of her arrest registered under the Municipal Code. At the trial, appellant asserted that § 52.39 of the Code denies her due process of law and other rights under the Federal Constitution, unnecessary to enumerate. The trial court denied this objection. The case was tried to a jury which found appellant guilty. The court fined her $250 and placed her on probation for three years. * * * The case is here on appeal. * * * [W]e now hold that the registration provisions of the Code as sought to be applied here violate the Due Process requirement of the Fourteenth Amendment.

The registration provision, carrying criminal penalties, applies if a person has been convicted "of an offense punishable as a felony in the State of California" or, in case he has been convicted in another State, if the offense "would have been punishable as a felony" had it been committed in California. No element of willfulness is by terms included in the ordinance nor read into it by the California court as a condition necessary for a conviction.

We must assume that appellant had no actual knowledge of the requirement that she register under this ordinance, as she offered proof of this defense which was refused. The question is whether a registration act of this character violates due process where it is applied to a person who has no actual knowledge of his duty to register, and where no showing is made of the probability of such knowledge.

We do not go with Blackstone in saying that "a vicious will" is necessary to constitute a crime, for conduct alone without regard to the intent of the doer is often sufficient. There is wide latitude in the lawmakers to declare an offense and to exclude elements of knowledge and diligence from its definition. But we deal here with conduct that is wholly passive—mere failure to register. It is unlike the commission of acts, or the failure to act under circumstances that should alert the doer to the consequences of his deed. The rule that "ignorance of the law will not excuse" is deep in our law, as is the principle that of all the powers of local government, the police power is "one of the least limitable." On the other hand, due process places some limits on its exercise. Engrained in our concept of due process is the requirement of notice. Notice is sometimes essential so that the citizen has the chance to defend charges. Notice is required before property interests are disturbed, before assessments are made, before penalties are assessed. Notice is required in a myriad of situations where a penalty or forfeiture might be suffered for mere failure to act. * * *

Registration laws are common and their range is wide. Many such laws are akin to licensing statutes in that they pertain to the regulation of business activities. But the present ordinance is entirely different. Violation of its provisions is unaccompanied by any activity whatever, mere presence in the city being the test. Moreover, circumstances which might move one to inquire as to the necessity of registration are completely lacking. At most the ordinance is but a law enforcement technique designed for the convenience of law enforcement agencies through which a list of the names and addresses of felons then residing in a given community is compiled. The disclosure is merely a compilation of former convictions already publicly recorded in the jurisdiction where obtained.

Nevertheless, this appellant on first becoming aware of her duty to register was given no opportunity to comply with the law and avoid its penalty, even though her default was entirely innocent. She could but suffer the consequences of the ordinance, namely, conviction with the imposition of heavy criminal penalties thereunder. We believe that actual knowledge of the duty to register or proof of the probability of such knowledge and subsequent failure to comply are necessary before a conviction under the ordinance can stand. As Holmes wrote in The Common Law, "A law which punished conduct which would not be blameworthy in the average member of the community would be too severe for that community to bear." Its severity lies in the absence of an opportunity either to avoid the consequences of the law or to defend any prosecution brought under it. Where a person did not know of the duty to register and where there was no proof of the probability of such knowledge, he may not be convicted consistently with due process. Were it otherwise, the evil would be as great as it is when the law is written in print too fine to read or in a language foreign to the community.

Reversed.

MR. JUSTICE FRANKFURTER, whom MR. JUSTICE HARLAN and MR. JUSTICE WHITTAKER join, dissenting.

The present laws of the United States and of the forty-eight States are thick with provisions that command that some things not be done and others be done, although persons convicted under such provisions may have had no awareness of what the law required or that what they did was wrongdoing. The body of decisions sustaining such legislation, including innumerable registration laws, is almost as voluminous as the legislation itself. The matter is summarized in *United States v. Balint*: "Many instances of this are to be found in regulatory measures in the exercise of what is called the police power where the emphasis of the statute is evidently upon achievement of some social betterment rather than the punishment of the crimes as in cases of *mala in se*."

Surely there can hardly be a difference as a matter of fairness, of hardship, or of justice, if one may invoke it, between the case of a person wholly innocent of wrongdoing, in the sense that he was not remotely conscious of violating any law, who is imprisoned for five years for conduct relating to narcotics, and the case of another person who is placed on probation for three years on condition that she pay $250, for failure, as a local resident, convicted under local law of a felony, to register under a law passed as an exercise of the State's "police power." * * *

STATE V. BRYANT

Supreme Court of North Carolina
614 S.E.2d 479 (N.C. 2005)

BRADY, JUSTICE.

Convicted sex offenders " 'are a serious threat in this Nation. The victims of sex assault are most often juveniles,' and 'when convicted sex offenders reenter society, they are much more likely than any other type of offender to be rearrested for a new rape or sexual assault.' " Because of this public safety concern North Carolina, like every other state in the nation, enacted a sex offender registration program to protect the public from the unacceptable risk posed by convicted sex offenders. In the case *sub judice*, this Court must specifically determine whether N.C.G.S. § 14–208.11, which criminalizes a convicted sex offender's failure to register, violates the notice requirement of the Due Process Clause of the United States Constitution, either facially or as applied. Because we find no such constitutional violation, we reverse the Court of Appeals.

FACTUAL AND PROCEDURAL BACKGROUND

* * *

The evidence adduced at trial established that on 20 March 2000, defendant was serving an active sentence in the custody of the South Carolina Department of Corrections. That day, defendant was notified by prison personnel of his duty to register with the State of South Carolina as a convicted sex offender upon his release from custody. Specifically, defendant was informed that he was required to register as a result of his 20 March 1996 convictions in Pickens County South Carolina for "criminal sexual conduct with a minor first degree and assault with intent to commit criminal sexual conduct." In conjunction with this notification, defendant signed a form entitled "South Carolina Department of Corrections Notice of Sex Offender Registry," acknowledging that he had been notified, orally and in writing, of his lifelong duty to register with the State of South Carolina. This form specifically notified defendant that:

> Pursuant to Section 23–3–430 of Code of Laws of South Carolina, any person who has been convicted, pled guilty or nolo contendere of offenses deemed sexual in nature must register with the Sheriff's Office in their county of residence. All offenses described in Section 23–3–430 *or similar offenses from other jurisdictions* are included, to include both current commitments and prior convictions. . . .

> *If an inmate who is required to register moves out of the State of South Carolina, s/he is required to provide written notice to the county sheriff where s/he was last registered in South Carolina within 10 days of the change of address to a new state.*
>
> *A person must send written notice of change of address to the county Sheriff's Office in the new county and the county where s/he previously resided within 10 days of moving to a new residence.* Any person required to register under this program shall be required to register annually for life.

(emphasis added). Defendant also indicated, by filling out the appropriate portions of the aforementioned form, that he would be residing in Greenville, South Carolina upon his release.

On 17 August 2000, several months after defendant was released from prison, he completed yet another registration form indicating that he had moved to Pickens County, South Carolina. However, in October 2000 defendant traveled to North Carolina, as a worker with the Dixie Classic Fair. While at the fair in Winston-Salem, North Carolina, defendant met Crystal Sunshine Miller.

At trial, Ms. Miller testified that defendant approached her and one of her daughters while they were waiting in line for an amusement ride. Defendant offered to get Ms. Miller and her daughter on the ride if she let him accompany them. Ms. Miller testified that this encounter "proceeded into me and him talking the rest of the time that the fair was here. [Defendant] decided that he had finally found somewhere and something worth staying for, so he decided to stay." * * *

On or about 1 November 2000, defendant moved in with Ms. Miller, who lived at 4373 Grove Avenue in Winston-Salem, North Carolina. Thus, defendant came to reside in the home that Ms. Miller shared with her two young daughters, who at the time of defendant's trial were five and two years old, respectively, and other members of her family. Over the next few months, defendant cooked, cleaned and stayed at home with Ms. Miller's children while she worked. Then, on 7 December 2000, defendant proposed marriage to Ms. Miller, and she accepted. Throughout the time defendant lived at 4373 Grove Avenue, he received mail addressed to him at Ms. Miller's home, including hospital bills, letters from his mother, and Christmas presents. Defendant continued living at 4373 Grove Avenue until 30 March 2001, when his relationship with Ms. Miller soured. Thus, defendant does not dispute that he was a resident of North Carolina at the time of his arrest.

At defendant's trial, Detective Kelly Wilkinson, of the Winston-Salem Police Department testified that he had occasion to interview defendant on 30 March 2001. Before this interview Detective Wilkinson had performed a "criminal history check" on defendant, which revealed that although defendant had registered as a convicted sex offender in South Carolina, he had failed to register upon establishing residency in North Carolina. During this interview, defendant indicated to Detective Wilkinson that he had come to North Carolina in October 2000 and that his current residence was 4373 Grove Avenue. We note that there is no indication in the record that, upon establishing a new residence in North Carolina, defendant notified the appropriate South Carolina authorities of his out-of-state move, in spite of his duty to do so. Moreover, during his interview with Detective Wilkinson, defendant acknowledged that he was required to register as a sex offender in South Carolina and admitted that he was also a convicted sex offender in the State of Florida.

Additionally, Deputy Reid, whose duties include maintaining the sex offender registry for Forsyth County, testified that North Carolina has a statutory equivalent to the South Carolina offense of criminal sexual conduct with a minor. Thus, as in South Carolina, defendant was required to register as a sex offender in the state of North Carolina. However, Deputy Reid stated that, as of the date of her testimony, defendant still had not registered as a convicted sex offender in this State.

On 21 February 2002, a Forsyth County jury found defendant guilty of failing to register as a sex offender and having attained the status of habitual felon. The trial judge determined that defendant had a prior record level of IV due in part to his eight prior convictions, four of which were felony convictions for sexual crimes. The trial court then sentenced defendant in the presumptive range for his habitual felon and failure to register as a sex offender convictions to a total minimum term of 133 months and a total maximum term of 169 months imprisonment.

Defendant entered notice of appeal on 22 February 2002, and the Court of Appeals heard oral argument on 3 December 2003. On 6 April 2004, the Court of Appeals held that "North Carolina's sex offender registration statute is unconstitutional as applied to an out-of-state offender who lacked notice of his duty to register upon moving to North Carolina." * * *

On 15 April 2004, the State filed petitions for writ of supersedeas and discretionary review with this Court, which this Court allowed on 12 August 2004. * * *

THE NORTH CAROLINA SEX OFFENDER REGISTRATION PROGRAM

In 1994, Congress enacted legislation that conditioned continued federal funding of state law enforcement on state adoption of sex offender registration laws and set minimum standards for such state programs. * * * A year later, the North Carolina General Assembly enacted legislation requiring convicted sex offenders to register with local law enforcement agencies in compliance with the Jacob Wetterling Act and in recognition that convicted sex offenders pose an unacceptable risk to the public. And, as the United States Supreme Court recently acknowledged, "by 1996, every State, the District of Columbia, and the Federal Government had enacted some variation of [a sex offender registration and community notification program]." Moreover, the Federal Bureau of Prisons is required to inform every sex offender incarcerated in federal penal and correctional institutions that the individual "shall be subject to a registration requirement as a sex offender in any State in which the person resides, is employed, . . . or is a student."

Thus, convicted sex offenders had been subject to registration throughout the fifty states for approximately six years when, in 2001, defendant was arrested for failing to register as a convicted sex offender in North Carolina. * * *

The North Carolina Sex Offender and Public Protection Registration Program is a public safety measure specifically designed "to assist law enforcement agencies' efforts to protect communities." With the creation of this program, the General Assembly explicitly recognized that "sex offenders often pose a high risk of engaging in sex offenses even after being released from incarceration or commitment and that protection of the public from sex offenders is of paramount governmental interest." Later amendments to the registration program were adopted, further recognizing that individuals who commit certain types of offenses against minors, "such as kidnapping, pose significant and unacceptable threats to the public safety and welfare of the children in this State and that the protection of those children is of great governmental interest." Thus the twin aims of the North Carolina Sex Offender and Public Protection Registration Program, public safety and protection, are clearly legitimate and of great importance to the State.

To accomplish these goals, the North Carolina Sex Offender and Public Protection Registration Program requires every individual having a reportable conviction as defined by N.C.G.S. § 14–208.6, which includes offenses against minors and "sexually violent offenses," to register as a convicted sex offender with the sheriff of the county in which the person resides. If an individual convicted of such a crime moves to North Carolina "from outside this State, the person shall register within 10 days of establishing residence in this State, or whenever the person has been present in the State for 15 days, whichever comes first." Additionally, non-resident workers and students who have reportable convictions or are required to register as sex offenders in their resident state must also register as a convicted sex offender in the county in which they are employed or attend school.

By statute each sheriff of North Carolina's one hundred counties is required to obtain certain information from registering sex offenders, including the individual's full name, physical description accompanied by a current photograph and fingerprints, driver's license number, home address, and the "type of offense for which the person was convicted, the date of conviction, and the sentence imposed." Much of this information then becomes public record and "shall be available for public inspection." To better serve the public, information regarding sex offenders is now available via the Internet as part of the North Carolina Sex Offender & Public Protection Registry at http://sbi.jus.state.nc.us/DOJHAHT/SOR/. Additionally, "the sheriff shall release any other relevant information that is necessary to protect the public concerning a specific person, but shall not release the identity of the victim of the offense that required registration." * * *

Of particular importance to our analysis is a 1997 amendment to this provision deleting the statutory *mens rea* requirement, which provided that only those offenders "who, knowingly and with the intent to violate" the registration provisions of N.C.G.S. § 14–208.11 were subject to conviction and punishment under the Sex Offender Registration Program. "In construing a statute with reference to an amendment, the presumption is that the legislature intended to change the law. This is especially so, in our view, when the statutory language is so drastically altered by the amendment." By deleting the original mens rea requirement in N.C.G.S. § 14–208.11, the General Assembly clearly expressed its intent to make failure to register as a sex offender a strict liability offense under North Carolina law. Thus, due to the clear legislative intent and the rule of law that "due process does not require every regulatory provision to contain a state-of-mind element," no showing of knowledge or intent is necessary to establish a violation of N.C.G.S. § 14–208.11.

Accordingly, a defendant who has committed a registerable offense but fails to comply with the registration requirements discussed above is guilty of a Class F felony. Although a defendant's term of imprisonment will necessarily vary under North Carolina's Structured Sentencing Act, we note that a defendant convicted of failing to register as a convicted sex offender with a prior record level of I could be subject to a potential minimum presumptive term of 13 to 16 months imprisonment. Here, defendant had a prior record level of IV; thus, the minimum possible presumptive sentence for failing to register as a sex offender carried with it a minimum term of 20 months to a maximum term of 24 months imprisonment.

THE CONSTITUTIONALITY OF N.C.G.S. § 14–208.11

This Court must now address whether N.C.G.S. § 14–208.11 violates the Due Process Clause of the United States Constitution. * * * The Due Process Clause of the Fifth Amendment to the United States Constitution guarantees that "No person shall be . . . deprived of life, liberty, or property without due process of law." A similar requirement, that no "State [shall] deprive any person of life, liberty, or property without due process of law" is also contained in the Fourteenth Amendment to the federal constitution. Due process has come to provide two types of protection for individuals against improper governmental action, substantive and procedural due process. Substantive due process ensures that the government does not engage in conduct that "shocks the conscience," or hinder rights "implicit in the concept of ordered liberty." In the event that the legislation in question meets the requirements of substantive due process, procedural due process "ensures that when government action deprive[s] a person of life, liberty, or property . . . that action is implemented in a fair manner." And it is the latter of the two, procedural due process, that defendant relies upon here. Specifically, defendant seeks to have N.C.G.S. § 14–208.11 declared unconstitutional based on allegedly insufficient notice of the existence of the criminal statute itself.

Defendant, relying almost exclusively on *Lambert v. California*, asserts that the State must prove "actual or probable notice of the duty to register in order to satisfy due process." Defendant contends that "the Court of Appeals rightly dismissed the 'osmosis' defense in light of Congress' express requirements that state registration programs incorporate detailed notification procedures." According to defendant, "those statutes conclusively rebut the notion that states can rely on convicted sex offenders to divine their registration duties through mental telepathy or the exercise of moral imagination." Defendant's arguments reflect a clear misunderstanding of due process jurisprudence. * * *

With respect to whether N.C.G.S. § 14–208.11 is unconstitutional as applied to defendant, a convicted sex offender in another jurisdiction who subsequently moved to North Carolina, defendant argues that the State must prove actual or probable notice of his duty to register to satisfy the due process notice requirement of *Lambert v. California*. Defendant argues that although he registered as a convicted sex offender in South Carolina, "nothing in the registration form or the statutes mentioned any duty to register outside of South Carolina." Thus, defendant alleges, due to his lack of actual notice, his convictions for failure to register as a sex offender and for having attained the status of habitual felon were obtained in violation of the Due Process clause of the United States Constitution. We find defendant's arguments wholly unpersuasive. We first note that the United States Supreme Court has acknowledged:

> The general rule that ignorance of the law or a mistake of law is no defense to criminal prosecution is deeply rooted in the American legal system. Based on the notion that the law is definite and knowable, the common law presumed that every

> person knew the law. This common-law rule has been applied by the Court in numerous cases construing criminal statutes.

Cheek v. United States, 498 U.S. 192, 199 (1991).

However, more than three decades before *Cheek*, the United States Supreme Court created a narrow exception to the general rule that ignorance of the law is no excuse, holding that "actual knowledge of the duty to register or proof of the probability of such knowledge and subsequent failure to comply are necessary" before a conviction under a general criminal registration act can stand. In *Lambert*, a provision of the City of Los Angeles, California Municipal Code required that all persons convicted of a felony, whether that conviction occurred in California or another state and was punishable as a felony in California, who remained in Los Angeles more than five days register as a felon with the Chief of Police. The police discovered, upon defendant's arrest for "suspicion of another offense," that defendant, a resident of Los Angeles for more than seven years, had been convicted of a felony but had not registered with the Chief of Police. After being convicted for failing to register, defendant appealed to the United States Supreme Court, arguing that the municipal code, as applied, denied her due process of law.

On appeal, the United States Supreme Court held that Lambert's conviction did indeed violate due process because her conduct in failing to register was "wholly passive" and "at most the ordinance is but a law enforcement technique designed for the convenience of law enforcement agencies." However, in so holding, the Supreme Court emphasized that in *Lambert*, "circumstances which might move one to inquire as to the necessity of registration [were] completely lacking." Of note, however, is the marked difference between the registration ordinance in *Lambert* and modern sex offender registration statutes.

In *Lambert*, the registration requirement was a general municipal ordinance, whereas the sex offender registration statutes enacted in North Carolina and all other states are statewide registration programs. Unlike the registration requirement in *Lambert*, these programs are directed at a narrow class of defendants, convicted sex offenders, rather than all felons. And, perhaps most crucially, rather than serving as a general law enforcement device, as the United States Supreme Court found the city of Los Angeles' felon registration ordinance, modern sex offender registration programs were specifically enacted as public safety measures based on legislative determinations that convicted sex offenders pose an unacceptable risk to the general public once released from incarceration.

Moreover, *Lambert's* "application has been limited, lending some credence to Justice Frankfurter's colorful prediction in dissent that the case would stand as 'an isolated deviation from the strong current of precedents—a derelict on the waters of the law.'" Thus, it is clear that the legal maxim *ignorantia juris non excusat* remains the general rule. Therefore, to be entitled to relief under the decidedly narrow *Lambert* exception, a defendant must establish that his conduct was "wholly passive" such that "*circumstances which might move one to inquire as to the necessity of registration are completely lacking*" and that defendant was ignorant of his duty to register and there was no reasonable probability that defendant knew his conduct was illegal.

We find this case rich with circumstances that would move the reasonable individual to inquire of his duty to register in North Carolina such that defendant's conduct was not wholly passive and *Lambert* is not controlling. First, defendant had actual notice of his *lifelong duty* to register with the State of South Carolina as a convicted sex offender. Second, defendant had actual notice that he must register as a convicted sex offender in South Carolina for "similar offenses from other jurisdictions" and had a duty to inform South Carolina officials of a move out of state "within 10 days of the change of address to a new state," which defendant failed to do. Third, defendant himself informed law enforcement authorities that he had been convicted of a sex offense in Florida. These circumstances coupled with the pervasiveness of sex offender registration programs certainly constitute circumstances which would lead the reasonable individual to inquire of a duty to register in *any* state upon relocation.

Simply put, a convicted sex offender's failure to inquire into a state's laws on registration requirement is neither entirely innocent nor wholly passive, particularly when combined with that sex offender's violation of his previous resident state's sex offender registration laws. Furthermore, as all fifty states and the District of Columbia had enacted sex offender registration programs in compliance with federal law by 1996, approximately four years before defendant's release from prison, it would be nonsensical to allow sex offenders to escape their duty to register by moving to a state that has not provided them with actual notice of their duty to register, and then claim ignorance of the law.

We find the case *sub judice* overflowing with circumstances "which might move one to inquire as to the necessity of registration." Accordingly, we hold that defendant's case does not fall within the narrow *Lambert* exception to the general rule that ignorance of the law is no excuse. Thus, because "generally a legislature need do nothing more than enact and publish the law, and afford the citizenry a reasonable opportunity to familiarize itself with its terms and to comply," we are bound by the rule that "all citizens are presumptively charged with knowledge of the law."

We conclude that defendant, a convicted sex offender, was provided actual notice by South Carolina of his duty to register as a convicted sex offender. This notice was sufficient to put defendant on notice to inquire into the applicable law of the state to which he relocated, in this instance North Carolina. Therefore, defendant's conviction for failure to register as a sex offender under N.C.G.S. § 14–208.11 does not violate due process.

CONCLUSION

N.C.G.S. § 14–208.11 is constitutional on its face and as applied to defendant, an out-of-state registered sex offender who failed to register in North Carolina. Accordingly, the decision of the Court of Appeals is reversed and this case is remanded to that court for consideration of the remainder of defendant's assignments of error not previously addressed.

REVERSED and REMANDED.

CHAPTER 6

CAUSATION AND CONCURRENCE

■ ■ ■

A. CAUSATION

The third basic element of a crime is the causation requirement.[a] Causation is actually part of the actus reus requirement. Recall that the actus reus consists of (1) a voluntary act (or omission when the defendant has a legal duty to act) that (2) causes (3) the social harm. Because causation analysis can become quite complicated, courts tend to treat causation as a separate element of the crime.

It is important not to confuse causation as it is defined and dealt with in tort law with causation as it is defined and dealt with in criminal law. "Because of the higher stakes in the criminal law, and its especially strong commitment to personal, rather than vicarious, responsibility, some courts expressly provide that a tort conception of causation is insufficient to impose criminal responsibility. Instead, a stricter test, requiring a closer connection between the defendant's conduct and the resulting harm, may be applied."[b]

Two types of causation must be proven to establish criminal liability. First, the defendant's conduct must be an actual or but-for cause of the social harm. Second, the defendant's conduct must be the proximate or legal cause of the social harm.

1. ACTUAL (OR "BUT FOR") CAUSATION

The first inquiry a court makes is whether the defendant is an actual cause (a.k.a. cause-in-fact or "but for" cause) of the social harm. Many different factors may have caused the social harm. The actual cause inquiry determines whether the defendant's voluntary act or omission is one of those causal factors. It does not show that the defendant is the primary cause of the social harm. It merely narrows down the field of actors who might be held criminally liable for the social harm.

---

[a] As mentioned in an earlier chapter, not all crimes require a causal link between the actus reus and the social harm. Causation is namely required for result crimes (crimes which are defined in terms of a prohibited result), but not for conduct crimes (crimes which are defined in terms of prohibited conduct). JOSHUA DRESSLER, UNDERSTANDING CRIMINAL LAW § 9.10[D] (6th ed. 2012). For example, proof that the defendant's act or omission caused the social harm is required for the crime of murder which is defined in terms of a prohibited result (the death of a human being). Causation, however, is not an element of the crime of speeding, which is defined in terms of prohibited conduct (driving over the speed limit).

[b] JOSHUA DRESSLER, UNDERSTANDING CRIMINAL LAW § 14.01[C] (6th ed. 2012).

In order to determine whether the defendant is an actual cause of the social harm, courts apply the "but for" test. Under this test, the court asks, "But for D's voluntary act (or omission where D had a duty to act), would the social harm have occurred *when it did*?" If the answer to this question is "no" (without D's conduct, the social harm would not have occurred when it did), then D is an actual cause.

2. PROXIMATE CAUSATION

The second inquiry a court makes is whether the defendant was the proximate cause of the social harm. The defendant must be both an actual cause and the proximate cause (and perform a voluntary act with the requisite mens rea) in order to be found criminally liable.

At base, the proximate cause inquiry is an examination into the question whether it is fair and just to hold the defendant criminally liable. There are no hard and fast rules governing this inquiry. Generally speaking, when the defendant's conduct is the direct cause of the social harm (when there are no intervening causes), courts tend to find that it is fair and just to hold the defendant criminally liable for the resulting harm. When intervening causes (acts or events that come after the defendant's act but before the social harm and also contribute causally to the social harm) are present, many courts apply intervening cause analysis to decide whether to hold the defendant criminally liable.

Intervening cause analysis differs depending on whether the intervening cause is characterized as a dependent (or responsive) intervening cause or an independent (or coincidental) intervening cause. A dependent intervening cause is one that is dependent upon or responsive to the defendant's voluntary act. An independent intervening cause is one that is independent of or coincidental to the defendant's voluntary act. If the intervening cause is dependent, the general rule is that the defendant is the proximate cause unless the intervening cause is extremely unusual or bizarre. If the intervening cause is independent, the defendant is generally relieved of criminal liability (i.e., not the proximate cause) unless the intervening cause is foreseeable. Sometimes courts simply focus on the foreseeability of the social harm, as opposed to the foreseeability of the intervening cause.

When courts are uncomfortable with the result obtained through intervening cause analysis, they may rely on other factors when deciding whether to hold the defendant criminally liable as the proximate cause. As you read the cases in this chapter, think about what other factors seem to influence courts deciding causation cases.

COMMONWEALTH V. REMENTER

Superior Court of Pennsylvania
410 Pa.Super. 9, 598 A.2d 1300 (1991)

BECK, J.

On April 19, 1989, the decedent Mary Berry was crushed to death beneath the wheels of a passer-by's automobile while attempting to escape from an ongoing assault by her boyfriend, appellant Charles Rementer. Appellant was charged with having caused the death of Mary Berry and was convicted of murder in the third degree[a] at a non-jury trial. He appeals from the judgment of sentence which was imposed after the denial of post-verdict motions. He raises two primary challenges to his conviction. Appellant first argues that the evidence at trial was insufficient to prove that his conduct caused the death of the victim. He also alleges that the Commonwealth failed to prove malice, an essential element of third degree murder. We affirm.

Appellant's conviction for third degree murder arose from events which occurred during the early evening hours of April 19, 1989 in Philadelphia. On that evening, at about 6:30 p.m., the decedent Berry and appellant entered a bar together at 7th and Oregon. The bartender serving them, who had known Berry for many years, noted that Berry and appellant were arguing, although the bartender could not discern the substance of the argument. During the argument Berry became "very upset" and was "crying hysterical[ly]."

Shortly thereafter, Berry left the bar and got into her cab, which was parked outside and which she drove for a living. A moment later, appellant followed her, got into the driver's side where Berry was sitting, shoved her into the passenger's seat and drove away.

An out-of-town trucker, Brent Murphy, was taking a break from loading his truck a few blocks from the bar when he saw Berry's cab. Berry was hanging out of the passenger window, screaming "Help me, he's trying to kill me." The driver of the cab, identified as appellant, was holding on to Berry, beating her and pulling her hair. Berry, by "fighting and kicking," had managed to get one leg out of the passenger window, but all the while appellant was "trying to pull her back in by her hair."

While Murphy watched, Berry struggled away from appellant and fell out of the passenger window. Appellant also left the car and continued the assault on Berry, beating her "with his fists in the face" while she was lying on the ground. Murphy ran into a nearby supermarket and told somebody to call the police. When he emerged from the store, appellant

[a] Under Pennsylvania law, murder in the first degree is an intentional killing, punishable by death or life imprisonment. Murder in the second degree is one committed while the defendant is engaged in the perpetration of a felony (i.e., the felony murder rule) and is punishable by life imprisonment. Murder in the third degree encompasses all other kinds of murder, and is punishable by up to 40 years in prison. *See* 18 Pa. Cons. Stat. §§ 1102, 2502.

was holding Berry against the cab while he continued to beat her. Murphy heard Berry say, "Don't hurt me, Charlie." Appellant pulled Berry into the cab, held her down, shut the door and drove away. About ten minutes later, a short distance away, Murphy saw the police. Berry was dead and the police had been summoned. Murphy explained to the police what he had witnessed moments earlier.

Meanwhile, three young men were standing at a nearby intersection. One of them, David Brotnitsky, saw appellant and Berry standing and arguing under the bridge of the I-95 on-ramp. Berry's cab was parked nearby on Water Street. Appellant punched Berry in the face and Berry ran away from him. Appellant pursued her, grabbed her and dragged her back to the cab. At first, appellant threw Berry in the back seat but she again managed to escape. Appellant then "got out after her and threw her in the front seat." Thinking that the fight was over, Brotnitsky stopped paying attention. The next thing he noticed was that the police had arrived on Water Street to investigate Berry's death.

Another witness, John Smith, was driving towards Water Street when he saw Berry's cab moving slow[ly] along the curb with the passenger door open. Smith yelled and asked the occupants what was going on. Just then, Berry ran from the cab towards Smith's car shouting unintelligible pleas for help. Another occupant of Smith's car suggested finding a police officer. As he pulled away Smith saw Berry in the rear view mirror. She was lying on the street and a station wagon was driving away "from her body."

Joseph Campbell was also in the vicinity when he saw "Charlie," whom he recognized from the neighborhood, and Berry fighting and arguing. Berry was shouting for help and running from appellant. Campbell saw appellant punch Berry in the head. Berry then ran towards oncoming cars, finally stopping at a station wagon. From where he was standing a short distance away, Campbell saw Berry grab on to the window of the station wagon and then fall. No more than two minutes passed from the time Campbell saw appellant strike Berry in the face to the time she fell beneath the wheels of the station wagon to her death.

The station wagon referred to by Smith and Campbell was driven by Vito Michielli. Michielli and his wife and two small children were on Water Street that evening driving home from a shopping trip. Berry and appellant approached his car forcing him to stop. Berry was screaming "help me" and "let me in" and attempted to open the back door of the station wagon. Michielli and his wife were frightened and the children began to cry. The Michiellis' reaction was to lock all the doors and attempt to close the windows of the car. Mr. Michielli reached out of his window, pushed Berry away and sped off. Not until several days later, when a local newspaper reported the incident and Berry's tragic death, did Michielli realize that in leaving the scene his car had run over Berry.

Michielli's wife also testified. She said that she first saw Berry running up the middle of the street toward their car. Mrs. Michielli stated that appellant was chasing her and that when they reached the Michiellis' car, he was "right behind her." Berry went over to the driver's side of the station wagon and appellant went to the passenger side. Mrs. Michielli saw Berry reach in to open the rear door of the car and heard her scream, "Help me, Help me, please let me in." Mr. Michielli pushed Berry away from the car and immediately drove off. Mrs. Michielli was also unaware at the time that the incident had ended with Berry's death.

The medical examiner's report revealed that Berry had suffered "blunt head trauma consistent with direct blows to the face, recent contusions to the chin, right and left cheeks near the nose and contused lacerations to the upper and lower lips, on the inside of the mouth." The medical examiner also found that Berry sustained a crush injury of the chest, "consistent with a motor vehicle passing over the body." There were also fractures of the skull and of the ribs. The coroner's report, as stipulated to by the parties at trial, concluded that the crush injury was the cause of death. Finally, the Mobile Crime Unit discovered a large clump of Berry's hair inside the cab, which had been forcibly pulled from Berry's head.

At trial, appellant testified on his own behalf. He stated that both he and Berry had injected cocaine earlier on the day of her death. He testified that they were arguing and that they had also been drinking. Appellant stated that he drove Berry's cab out of concern for her welfare because she was "acting schizy from the cocaine." According to appellant, Berry's pleas for help were entirely unprovoked by him. He said that he pulled her back into the cab to prevent her from hurting herself and from "making a scene." Appellant admitted striking Berry but claimed that he did so out of anger because his attempts to calm her down by talking rationally had failed. He also claimed that he hit her only once, did not mean to hurt her and did not intend to kill her.

The trial court found appellant guilty of murder in the third degree. Following the denial of post-trial motions, appellant was sentenced to a term of imprisonment of four to twelve years. On appeal he argues that the Commonwealth failed to present sufficient evidence to establish two essential elements of third degree murder, i.e., causation and malice. We will address each challenge separately. * * *

[I]t is undisputed that causation constitutes an essential element of the offense of murder which the Commonwealth must prove beyond a reasonable doubt. * * * The issue regarding causation plainly arises in the instant case because the immediate cause of Berry's death was the crushing blow received under the wheels of Michielli's station wagon. Appellant argues that by the time Berry ran over to Michielli's car the "unfortunate domestic dispute" had ended and that therefore Berry's death had an accidental and intervening cause. Thus, according to appellant, the chain of causation between his assault on Berry and her resulting death had been broken. As such, he argues, his actions did not constitute a sufficiently direct cause of Berry's death. Moreover, appellant argues that Berry's death was not foreseeable and stemmed not from his assault but from independent actions by Berry for which he, appellant, cannot be held culpable. We reject these claims.

Certain fundamental principles guide our inquiry. First, it is well established that the tort theory of causation will not suffice to impose criminal responsibility. This principle was first explicitly adopted by the supreme court in *Commonwealth v. Root* which held that ". . . the accused is not guilty unless his conduct was a cause of death sufficiently direct as to meet the requirements of the *criminal*, and not the *tort*, law." The *Root* court explained: "Legal theory which makes guilt or innocence of criminal homicide depend upon such accidental and fortuitous circumstances as are now embraced by modern tort law's encompassing concept of proximate cause is too harsh to be just." Thus, a "more direct causal connection is required for conviction."

It is difficult to draw a bright line between causation in the criminal law and in the tort law. Certain principles can, however, be ascertained. In order to impose criminal liability, causation must be direct and substantial. Defendants should not be exposed to a loss of liberty based on the tort standard which only provides that the event giving rise to the injury is a substantial factor. Although typically the tort context refers only to substantial and not to direct and substantial as in the criminal context, the additional language in the criminal law does not provide much guidance. Therefore, criminal causation has come to involve a case-by-case social determination; i.e., is it just or fair under the facts of the case to expose the defendant to criminal sanctions. In other words, was the defendant's conduct so directly and substantially linked to the actual result as to give rise to the imposition of criminal liability or was the actual result so remote and attenuated that it would be unfair to hold the defendant responsible for it?

Many cases have grappled with the concept of what constitutes a legally sufficient causal connection where, as here, the immediate cause of death was not the blow dealt by the defendant's hand. We have concluded, from a careful reading of these cases and from analysis provided by criminal law commentators, that the resolution of the causation issue here and in analogous cases involves a two part inquiry. The first part of the inquiry requires us to decide whether the defendant's conduct was an operative cause of the victim's death. With respect to establishing a causal relationship between conduct and result, our crimes code poses a threshold factual requirement and that is, the conduct must be "an antecedent but for which the result in question would not have occurred." Thus, if the victim's death is attributable *entirely* to other factors and not at all brought about by the defendant's conduct, no causal connection exists and no criminal liability for the result can attach. The second part of the test raises the question of whether the result of defendant's actions were so extraordinarily remote or attenuated that it would be unfair to hold the defendant criminally responsible.

In discussing the first part of the test we point out that the defendant's conduct need not be the sole cause of the victim's death in order to establish causal connection. In *Commonwealth v. Skufca,* a parent left two small children trapped inside a locked apartment while she went out for the evening. A fire started which suffocated the children who were impossible to rescue due to their mother's action in locking them inside an unattended apartment. Suffocation through smoke inhalation was the immediate medical cause of death. In upholding the involuntary manslaughter conviction of the parent, the supreme court emphasized:

> [I]t has never been the law of this Commonwealth that criminal responsibility must be confined to a sole or immediate cause of death. . . . Criminal responsibility is properly assessed against one whose conduct was a direct and substantial factor in producing the death even though other factors combined with that conduct to achieve the result.

* * * In *Commonwealth v. Cheeks,* the victim was stabbed in the abdomen by the defendant during a robbery. The stabbing necessitated an operation which resulted in complications including abdominal distention. As a result of the victim's post-operative condition, tubes were inserted through the victim's nostrils and into his stomach. The victim was disoriented, uncooperative and confused and pulled out the tubes on several occasions. Finally, he pulled out a tube, gagged and asphyxiated. The defendant in *Cheeks* argued that the stab wound was not the cause of death and that the victim's own actions had intervened as an independent act of causation. The supreme court disagreed. The court found that "the fact that the stabbing was not the immediate cause of death is not controlling." The stabbing was an operative link in a chain of events which resulted in the victim's death. The court saw defendant's conduct as the cause which necessarily triggered the series of events which ended in the victim's death.

However, causation-in-fact, the "but for" element of assessing the causal connection, alone will not necessarily determine criminal culpability.[4] If it did, little would distinguish tort liability from criminal

---

[4] In explaining the inadequacy of the but-for inquiry in assessing ultimate criminal liability, the comments to the Model Penal Code use the following illustration to demonstrate a causal connection which might satisfy the but-for test but which, due to remoteness of result, would not constitute legally sufficient causation:

liability. Our cases emphasize that a criminal conviction requires "a more direct causal connection" than tort concepts. Thus not only do we demand that the defendant's conduct actually cause the victim's death in that "it is an antecedent but for which the result in question would not have occurred," we also question, in cases such as the instant one, whether the fatal result was so extraordinary, remote or attenuated that it would be unfair to hold the defendant criminally responsible for it.

In our view, it is this second prong of the causation inquiry which is in fact at issue when our cases impose a "stricter" or "more direct" test for criminal causation than is needed for tort liability. Thus, the defendant's conduct must bear a direct and substantial relationship to the fatal result in order to impose criminal culpability. Put another way, if the fatal result was an unnatural or obscure consequence of the defendant's actions, our sense of justice would prevent us from allowing the result to impact on the defendant's guilt.

This concept is often addressed in terms of foreseeability. For instance, in *Commonwealth v. Skufca*, in which a parent was held to have legally caused the death of her children who died of smoke inhalation after being trapped in a room by their mother, the court noted: "Although suffocation due to the fire was the immediate cause of the children's death, appellant's unlawful conduct in leaving them locked in the room, without supervision, for several hours, susceptible to numerous foreseeable dangers, was the legal cause of their death." * * *

In *Commonwealth v. Lang*, this court found that a police officer's death during a high speed pursuit of a fleeing defendant on a motorcycle was a "foreseeable" and direct consequence of the defendant's conduct and "not a fortuitous or coincidental event." In *Lang*, we found that the "[defendant] knew or should have known that his actions, speeding and attempting to elude arrest, were likely to result in injury to someone: either to himself, to some innocent third party, or to the pursuing police officer."

In contrast to the above-cited and similar cases, is *Commonwealth v. Colvin* wherein the actual result was so remote and fortuitous that it must be said to have no bearing on the defendant's culpability. In *Colvin*, this court reversed an involuntary manslaughter conviction due to insufficiency of evidence on causation. In that case, the defendant threw a stone at a house, breaking a window. The noise the mischief made was heard by only one member of the household. That person immediately informed his mother, who had not heard the stone hit the house, about

---

For example, if the defendant attempted to shoot his wife, with the result that she retired to her parents' country home and died there from falling off a horse, no one would think that he should be held guilty for murder, though he did intend her death and his attempt to kill her was a but-for cause of her encounter with the horse. * * *

what had just happened and the mother collapsed and died. Implicit in the court's finding that the causal connection was not "direct" enough, is an appreciation that the fatal result was so remote and attenuated from the risks hazarded by the defendant's unlawful conduct in throwing the stone, that it had no "bearing on the liability of the actor or on the gravity of his offense."

In light of the foregoing principles, we examine appellant's claim that the evidence at trial was insufficient to establish the necessary causal connection between his conduct and Berry's resulting death. Appellant first contends that the argument he was having with Berry was over by the time she approached Michielli's car for aid and that, therefore, her actions in seeking refuge in the station wagon cannot be attributed to him. Berry's actions were not provoked by his assault but were spontaneous and unrelated to the "earlier dispute," appellant argues, and therefore, his conduct cannot be said to have caused her death.

This argument that there was no dispute occurring at the time Berry ran to Michielli's car is belied by considerable evidence which, when viewed in the light most favorable to the Commonwealth, establishes quite the contrary. As described above, several witnesses testified to the ferocity and tenacity of appellant's assault on Berry and all the observations attested to occurred within minutes of Berry's death. Campbell testified that he saw Berry shouting and running for help. He said appellant punched Berry in the head no more than two minutes before she fell to her death beneath the wheels of the car. Smith, Campbell and the Michiellis all testified that Berry's actions right up until the instant of her death were accompanied by cries for help, a fact which completely refutes appellant's claim that her actions were not taken in response to his conduct. Finally, Mrs. Michielli stated that when Berry approached their car, appellant was chasing her and was right behind her. Appellant's contention that the "dispute" had ended is wholly without support in the record.

Appellant further argues that Berry's death occurred through such an unforeseeable chain of events that his conduct cannot be said to have caused the fatal result. We disagree. The evidence at trial plainly established that appellant subjected Berry to a brutal and persistent assault from which she continually attempted to escape. In the first place, it is completely natural and foreseeable that any victim of an assault would respond to the danger by trying to escape it. In fact, it is difficult to imagine behavior which is more responsive or more predictable than fleeing from a deadly assault. Moreover, Berry's actions were particularly likely in the context of the instant case. Berry was clearly intent upon escaping her assailant at any cost and attempted to do so repeatedly. She tried climbing out of the car window, only to be beaten and pulled back into the car. She ran away from appellant twice after that and each time was violently forced back into the car by appellant. Just before Berry escaped for the last, and fatal, time, the cab was seen moving along the street with the passenger door open. The risk that Berry might suffer serious injury or death either during the assault or in her attempt to avoid it, was inherent in the situation appellant's attack created. In our view, the fatal result of appellant's assault is not rendered unforeseeable merely because the precise agency of death, i.e. the Michielli's station wagon, could not have been foretold. Appellant perpetrated a deadly assault on the decedent in and around an automobile on a public street with other moving vehicles in close proximity. It is absurd to argue that the fatal result was so extraordinary or accidental that appellant should not be held criminally liable for the consequences of his conduct. We find that more than sufficient evidence was adduced at trial from which the factfinder could conclude that appellant's conduct was the legal cause of Berry's death. * * *

Judgment of sentence affirmed.

STATE V. GOVAN

Court of Appeals of Arizona, Division One, Department B
154 Ariz. 611, 744 P.2d 712 (Ct. App. 1987)

GREER, J.

On May 13, 1985, appellant was indicted on one count of second degree murder. Following a jury trial, he was convicted on October 18, 1985, of the lesser-included offense of manslaughter. He was sentenced to a mitigated term of imprisonment of six years.

The incident which gave rise to the criminal charges in this case occurred on April 5, 1980. The appellant and Ms. Sharon Keeble, with whom he had been living for three years, argued over the appellant's alleged molestation of the victim's teenage daughter. The victim eventually fired a shot at the appellant. The appellant then left the scene, but later that day returned and was observed again arguing with the victim. The victim borrowed a neighbor's telephone and attempted to call the police. While the victim was attempting to dial the phone, the appellant pulled a gun out of his pocket and shot at the victim, striking her in the neck. As a result she was paralyzed from the neck down. The appellant told police that he had not intended to shoot the victim, but had drawn his gun and fired behind him without taking aim.

On May 1, 1980, the state charged appellant with aggravated assault for shooting Ms. Keeble. During Ms. Keeble hospitalization, appellant visited her and they were subsequently married. The aggravated assault charge was dismissed without prejudice on March 11, 1981. Due to her quadriplegia Ms. Keeble suffered from several ailments and needed constant care. In January, 1985, the victim contracted pneumonia and died. Appellant was subsequently charged with second degree murder and convicted of manslaughter. * * *

The appellant argues that he cannot be convicted of anything because there was no evidence to show that the shot he fired caused the quadriplegia of the victim. Defense counsel argued that the state needed to bring in a doctor from every institution that treated Ms. Keeble to show that the quadriplegia was the direct result of the gunshot wound. He then concluded that, "as to the rest of it, I would just say there is insufficient evidence." In denying the motion, the trial court properly noted that there was uncontroverted evidence that the victim had been taken immediately to a hospital in the Phoenix area and remained a quadriplegic until her death. In addition, both of the doctors who testified at trial said, without objection, that the cause of death was pneumonia stemming from the quadriplegia, which was caused by a gunshot wound to the neck.

In this case, there was substantial, if not overwhelming, evidence that the gunshot to the victim's neck resulted in her immediate paralysis and quadriplegia. It was not error to deny the motion for judgment of acquittal.

The appellant also argues, based on *State v. Hall,* that the death was not the natural result of his having shot the victim. In *Hall*, the court first distinguished between cases where an intervening event was a coincidence and those where it was a response to the defendant's prior actions. It then stated that,

> A defendant's actions may still be a proximate cause of death regardless of the type of intervening act that occurred, but as 'common sense would suggest, the perimeters of legal cause are more closely drawn when the intervening cause was a matter of coincidence rather than response.'

Thus, an intervening cause that was a coincidence will be a superseding cause when it was unforeseeable. Alternatively, an intervening cause that was a response will be a superseding cause only where it was abnormal and unforeseeable. Appellant's action would not be a proximate cause of Ms. Keeble's death if the chain of natural effects and causes was either non-existent because of or broken by intervening events which were unforeseeable and hence were superseding events. Here there were no intervening events which could be characterized as superseding. In this case, it is clear that the gunshot wound resulted in the quadriplegia. Furthermore, medical testimony proved that the quadriplegia, including the complications caused by the tracheostomy, eventually resulted in a "response" to that condition, which resulted in the victim's death. Thus, the appellant's conduct was a proximate cause of the victim's death and he is criminally liable for it.

The appellant refines his argument on appeal to contend that the victim simply gave up her will to live, and this broke the chain of causation between the shooting and her death. He points out that the victim did not seek medical attention for at least two weeks after she knew that she was ill.

This argument was never presented to the trial court. Ordinarily we would not review a matter not argued below, but to allow a conviction to stand that is not supported by the evidence would be fundamental error. However, we do not find appellant's argument persuasive. Although a victim may break the chain of causation by voluntarily doing harm to himself, this should not be so when an individual causes the victim to commit suicide or lose the will to live because of extreme pain from wounds inflicted by the appellant, or when the wound has rendered the victim irresponsible. The impact of quadriplegia on a person's physical and mental well-being may be equated with the effects of extreme pain. Thus, the rationale in *Hall* applies also to the relationship between the gunshot wound and the alleged loss of will to live. The appellant's conduct could be regarded as a proximate cause of the victim's death, and he would still be criminally liable for it.

Judgment and sentence affirmed.

HENDERSON V. KIBBE

Supreme Court of the United States
431 U.S. 145, 97 S.Ct. 1730, 52 L.Ed.2d 203 (1977)

STEVENS, J.

Respondent is in petitioner's custody pursuant to a conviction for second-degree murder. The question presented to us is whether the New York State trial judge's failure to instruct the jury on the issue of causation was constitutional error requiring a Federal District Court to grant habeas corpus relief. Disagreeing with a divided panel of the Court of Appeals for the Second Circuit, we hold that it was not.

On the evening of December 30, 1970, respondent and his codefendant encountered a thoroughly intoxicated man named Stafford in a bar in Rochester, N. Y. After observing Stafford display at least two $100 bills, they decided to rob him and agreed to drive him to a nearby town. While in the car, respondent slapped Stafford several times, took his money, and, in a search for concealed funds, forced Stafford to lower his trousers and remove his boots. They then abandoned him on an unlighted, rural road, still in a state of partial undress, and without his coat or his glasses. The temperature was near zero, visibility was obscured by blowing snow, and snow banks flanked the roadway. The time was between 9:30 and 9:40 p.m.

At about 10 p.m., while helplessly seated in a traffic lane about a quarter mile from the nearest lighted building, Stafford was struck by a speeding pickup truck. The driver testified that while he was traveling 50 miles per hour in a 40-mile zone, the first of two approaching cars flashed its lights—presumably as a warning which he did not understand. Immediately after the cars passed, the driver saw Stafford sitting in the road with his hands in the air. The driver neither swerved nor braked his vehicle before it hit Stafford. Stafford was pronounced dead upon arrival at the local hospital.

Respondent and his accomplice were convicted of grand larceny, robbery, and second-degree murder. Only the conviction of murder, as defined in N. Y. Penal Law § 125.25 (2), is now challenged. That statute provides that "[a] person is guilty of murder in the second degree" when "[under] circumstances evincing a depraved indifference to human life, he recklessly engages in conduct which creates a grave risk of death to another person, *and thereby causes the death of another person.*" (Emphasis added.)

Defense counsel argued that it was the negligence of the truckdriver, rather than the defendants' action, that had caused Stafford's death, and that the defendants could not have anticipated the fatal accident.[4] On the other hand, the prosecution argued that the death was foreseeable and would not have occurred but for the conduct of the defendants who therefore were the cause of death.[5] Neither party requested the trial judge to instruct the jury on the meaning of the statutory requirement that the defendants' conduct "thereby cause[d] the death of another person," and no such instruction was given. * * *

---

[4] ". . . [Y]ou are going to have to honestly come to the conclusion that here is three people, all three drinking, and that these two, or at least my client were in a position to perceive this grave risk, be aware of it and disregard it. Perceive that Mr. Stafford would sit in the middle of the northbound lane, that a motorist would come by who was distracted by flashing lights in the opposite lane, who then froze at the wheel, who then didn't swerve, didn't brake, and who was violating the law by speeding, and to make matters worse, he had at that particular time, because of what the situation was, he had low beams on, that is a lot of anticipation. That is a lot of looking forward. Are you supposed to anticipate that somebody is going to break the law when you move or do something? I think that is a reasonable doubt."

[5] "As I mentioned not only does the first count contain reference to and require proof of a depraved indifference to a human life, it proves that the defendant recklessly engaged in conduct which created a risk of death in that they caused the death of George Stafford. Now, I very well know, members of the jury, you know, that quite obviously the acts of both of these defendants were not the only the direct or the most preceding cause of his death. If I walked with one of you downtown, you know, and we went across one of the bridges and you couldn't swim and I pushed you over and you drowned because you can't swim, I suppose you can say, well, you drowned because you couldn't swim. But of course, the fact is that I pushed you over. The same thing here. Sure, the death, the most immediate, the most preceding, the most direct cause of Mr. Stafford's death was the motor vehicle. . . . But how did he get there? Or to put it differently, would this man be dead had it not been for the acts of these two defendants? And I submit to you, members of the jury, that the acts of these two defendants did indeed cause the death of Mr. Stafford. He didn't walk out there on East River Road. He was driven out there. His glasses were taken and his identification was taken and his pants were around his ankles."

The Appellate Division of the New York Supreme Court affirmed respondent's conviction. Although respondent did not challenge the sufficiency of the instructions to the jury in that court, Judge Cardamone dissented on the ground that the trial court's charge did not explain the issue of causation or include an adequate discussion of the necessary mental state. That judge expressed the opinion that "the jury, upon proper instruction, could have concluded that the victim's death by an automobile was a remote and intervening cause."

The New York Court of Appeals also affirmed. It identified the causation issue as the only serious question raised by the appeal, and then rejected the contention that the conduct of the driver of the pickup truck constituted an intervening cause which relieved the defendants of criminal responsibility for Stafford's death. The court held that it was "not necessary that the ultimate harm be intended by the actor. It will suffice if it can be said beyond a reasonable doubt, as indeed it can be here said, that the ultimate harm is something which should have been foreseen as being reasonably related to the acts of the accused."[7] The court refused to consider the adequacy of the charge to the jury because that question had not been raised in the trial court.

Respondent then filed a petition for a writ of habeas corpus in the United States District Court for the Northern District of New York. The District Court held that the respondent's attack on the sufficiency of the charge failed to raise a question of constitutional dimension and that, without more, "the charge is not reviewable in a federal habeas corpus proceeding."

The Court of Appeals for the Second Circuit reversed * * * On the merits, the court held that since the Constitution requires proof beyond a reasonable doubt of every fact necessary to constitute the crime, the failure to instruct the jury on an essential element as complex as the

---

[7] The New York court added:

We subscribe to the requirement that the defendants' actions must be a *sufficiently direct cause* of the ensuing death before there can be any imposition of criminal liability, and recognize, of course, that this standard is greater than that required to serve as a basis for tort liability. Applying these criteria to the defendants' actions, we conclude that their activities on the evening of December 30, 1970 were a sufficiently direct cause of the death of George Stafford so as to warrant the imposition of criminal sanctions. In engaging in what may properly be described as a despicable course of action, Kibbe and Krall left a helplessly intoxicated man without his eyeglasses in a position from which, because of these attending circumstances, he could not extricate himself and whose condition was such that he could not even protect himself from the elements. The defendants do not dispute the fact that their conduct evinced a depraved indifference to human life which created a grave risk of death, but rather they argue that it was just as likely that Stafford would be miraculously rescued by a good [S]amaritan. We cannot accept such an argument. There can be little doubt but that Stafford would have frozen to death in his state of undress had he remained on the shoulder of the road. The only alternative left to him was the highway, which in his condition, for one reason or another, clearly foreboded the probability of his resulting death.

causation issue in this case created an impermissible risk that the jury had not made a finding that the Constitution requires.

Because the Court of Appeals decision appeared to conflict with this Court's holding in *Cupp v. Naughten*, we granted certiorari. * * *

I

The Court has held "that the Due Process Clause protects the accused against conviction except upon proof beyond a reasonable doubt of every fact necessary to constitute the crime with which he is charged." One of the facts which the New York statute required the prosecution to prove is that the defendants' conduct caused the death of Stafford. As the New York Court of Appeals held, the evidence was plainly sufficient to prove that fact beyond a reasonable doubt. It is equally clear that the record requires us to conclude that the jury made such a finding.

There can be no question about the fact that the jurors were informed that the case included a causation issue that they had to decide. The element of causation was stressed in the arguments of both counsel. The statutory language, which the trial judge read to the jury, expressly refers to the requirement that defendants' conduct "cause[d] the death of another person." The indictment tracks the statutory language; it was read to the jurors and they were given a copy for use during their deliberations. The judge instructed the jury that all elements of the crime must be proved beyond a reasonable doubt. Whether or not the arguments of counsel correctly characterized the law applicable to the causation issue, they surely made it clear to the jury that such an issue had to be decided. It follows that the objection predicated on this Court's holding in *Winship* is without merit.

II

* * * The New York Court of Appeals concluded that the evidence of causation was sufficient because it can be said beyond a reasonable doubt that the "ultimate harm" was "something which should have been foreseen as being reasonably related to the acts of the accused." It is not entirely clear whether the court's reference to "ultimate harm" merely required that Stafford's death was foreseeable, or, more narrowly, that his death by a speeding vehicle was foreseeable.[14] In either event, the court was satisfied that the "ultimate harm" was one which "should have been foreseen." Thus, an adequate instruction would have told the jury that if the ultimate harm should have been foreseen as being reasonably related to defendants' conduct, that conduct should be regarded as having caused the death of Stafford.

---

[14] The passage of the opinion quoted in n. 7, *supra,* emphasizes the obvious risk of death by freezing, suggesting that defendants need not have foreseen the precise manner in which the death did occur.

The significance of the omission of such an instruction may be evaluated by comparison with the instructions that were given. One of the elements of respondent's offense is that he acted "recklessly." By returning a guilty verdict, the jury necessarily found, in accordance with its instruction on recklessness, that respondent was "aware of and consciously disregard[ed] a substantial and unjustifiable risk" that death would occur. A person who is "aware of and consciously disregards" a substantial risk must also foresee the ultimate harm that the risk entails. Thus, the jury's determination that the respondent acted recklessly necessarily included a determination that the ultimate harm was foreseeable to him.

In a strict sense, an additional instruction on foreseeability would not have been cumulative because it would have related to an element of the offense not specifically covered in the instructions given. But since it is logical to assume that the jurors would have responded to an instruction on causation consistently with their determination of the issues that were comprehensively explained, it is equally logical to conclude that such an instruction would not have affected their verdict.[16] Accordingly, we reject the suggestion that the omission of more complete instructions on the causation issue "so infected the entire trial that the resulting conviction violated due process." Even if we were to make the unlikely assumption that the jury might have reached a different verdict pursuant to an additional instruction, that possibility is too speculative to justify the conclusion that constitutional error was committed.

The judgment is reversed.

It is so ordered.

B. CONCURRENCE

The final basic element of a crime is the concurrence requirement which mandates a connection between the *actus reus* and the *mens rea.* Two types of concurrence must be present. First, the defendant must possess the requisite *mens rea* at the same time she engages in the *actus reus.* Joshua Dressler, UNDERSTANDING CRIMINAL LAW § 15.01 (6th ed. 2012). This is called temporal concurrence because the focus is on whether the required *mens rea* was present at the same time that the

---

[16] In fact, it is not unlikely that a complete instruction on the causation issue would actually have been favorable to the prosecution. For example, an instruction might have been patterned after the following example given in W. LaFave & A. Scott, CRIMINAL LAW 260 (1972):

> *A,* with intent to kill *B,* only wounds *B,* leaving him lying unconscious in the unlighted road on a dark night, and then *C,* driving along the road, runs over and kills *B.* Here *C*'s act is a matter of coincidence rather than a response to what *A* has done, and thus the question is whether the subsequent events were foreseeable, as they undoubtedly were in the above illustration.

Such an instruction would probably have been more favorable to the prosecution than the instruction on recklessness which the court actually gave.

defendant performed the *actus reus*. Second, the mens rea must be the motivating force behind the *actus reus*. This is called motivational concurrence. As you read the following case, decide for yourself whether the concurrence requirement was satisfied.

THABO MELI V. REGINAM

Privy Council
[1954] 1 All E.R. 373

Jan. 13. LORD REID: The four appellants in this case were convicted of murder after a trial before Sir Walter Harragin, judge of the High Court of Basutoland, in March, 1953. The appeal which has been heard by this Board dealt with two matters: first, whether the conclusions of the learned judge on questions of fact were warranted: and secondly, whether, on a point of law, the accused are entitled to have the verdict quashed.

On the first matter, there really is no ground for criticizing the learned judge's treatment of the facts. It is established by evidence, which was believed and which is apparently credible, that there was a preconceived plot on the part of the four accused to bring the deceased man to a hut and there to kill him, and then to fake an accident, so that the accused should escape the penalty for their act. The deceased man was brought to the hut. He was there treated to beer and was at least partially intoxicated; and he was then struck over the head in accordance with the plan of the accused. Witnesses say that while the deceased was seated and bending forward he was struck a heavy blow on the back of the head with a piece of iron like the instrument produced at the trial. But a post-mortem examination showed that his skull had not been fractured and medical evidence was to the effect that a blow such as the witness described would have produced more severe injuries than those found at the post-mortem examination. There is at least doubt whether the weapon which was produced as being like the weapon which was used could have produced the injuries that were found, but it may be that this weapon is not exactly similar to the one which was used, or it may be that the blow was a glancing blow and produced less severe injuries than those which one might expect. In any event, the man was unconscious after receiving the blow, but he was not then dead. There is no evidence that the accused then believed that he was dead, but their Lordships are prepared to assume from their subsequent conduct that they did so believe; and it is only on that assumption that any statable case can be made for this appeal. The accused took out the body, rolled it over a low krantz or cliff, and dressed up the scene to make it look like an accident. Obviously, they believed at that time that the man was dead, but it appears from the medical evidence that the injuries which he received in the hut were not sufficient to cause the death and that the final cause of his death was exposure when he was left unconscious at the foot of the krantz.

The point of law which was raised in this case can be simply stated. It is said that two acts were done: —first, the attack in the hut; and, secondly, the placing of the body outside afterwards—and that they were separate acts. It is said that, while the first act was accompanied by mens rea, it was not the cause of death; but that the second act, while it was the cause of death, was not accompanied by mens rea; and on that ground, it is said that the accused are not guilty of murder, though they may have been guilty of culpable homicide. It is said that the mens rea necessary to establish murder is an intention to kill, and that there could be no intention to kill when the accused thought that the man was already dead, so their original intention to kill had ceased before they did the act which caused the man death. It appears to their Lordships impossible to divide up what was really one series of acts in this way. There is no doubt that the accused set out to do all these acts in order to achieve their plan, and as parts of their plan; and it is much too refined a ground of judgment to say that, because they were under a misapprehension at one stage and thought that their guilty purpose had been achieved before, in fact, it was achieved, therefore they are to escape the penalties of the law. Their Lordships do not think that this is a matter which is susceptible of elaboration. There appears to be no case, either in South Africa or England, or for that matter elsewhere, which resembles the present. Their Lordships can find no difference relevant to the present case between the law of South Africa and the law of England; and they are of the opinion that by both laws there can be no separation such as that for which the accused contend. Their crime is not reduced from murder to a lesser crime merely because the accused were under some misapprehension for a time during the completion of their criminal plot.

Their Lordships must, therefore, humbly advise Her Majesty that this appeal should be dismissed.

Appeal dismissed.

CHAPTER 7

CRIMINAL HOMICIDE

■ ■ ■

INTRODUCTION

The term "criminal homicide" encompasses a host of different crimes, all involving the unlawful killing of a human being by another human being. Criminal homicide can be divided into two main categories: murder and manslaughter. Under both the common law and contemporary penal codes, murder is broadly defined as the unlawful killing of a human being by another human being with malice aforethought. Manslaughter is traditionally defined as the unlawful killing of a human being by another human being without malice aforethought.

The law of homicide has changed very slowly in the last few centuries. Even the Model Penal Code drafters, who sought to update the criminal law in many ways, altered the common law of homicide very little. So in this area the content of the law is fairly clear and well-settled. The interesting issues with respect to homicide involve policy—the "goodness of fit" between the criminal law and the society to which it applies. Two issues in this regard are whether the law of homicide should change more than it has, and whether the law we have is applied fairly.

Should the law of homicide change? Homicide is generally considered reprehensible but, as we will see, some kinds of homicides have traditionally been considered more heinous than other kinds. As times change, cultural assessments of the relative seriousness of various homicide crimes may change as well. As you read the materials in this chapter, consider whether the assessments of relative evil made by the common law structure still fit contemporary American life and, if not, how the law ought to change.

A second issue in the law of homicide, one particularly relevant for practitioners of criminal law, is how to ensure that prosecutors, defense counsel, judges, and fact-finders fairly apply settled law. Even if the law reflects a cultural consensus in terms of categorizing homicides, jury members, judges, and attorneys may consciously or unconsciously bring conflicting assumptions and even prejudices to the table. As you read the materials in this chapter, consider whether and how this kind of "bad discretion" to apply the law unequally can be curbed.

A third policy problem that arises in the law of homicide is one we first examined when we studied the doctrine of transferred intent: the tension between a "culpability" approach and a "social harm" approach to criminal punishment. When a person has died, does it make more sense to inquire into the badness of the perpetrator or to focus on punishing the bad result? Is there a way that the criminal law can do both?

A. DEFINITIONAL ISSUES

Homicide law makes unlawful the unexcused, unjustified killing of a human. But what constitutes "killing" and what constitutes "a human"? Two definitional issues—one that pertains to the beginning of the human life cycle and one to the end of the human life cycle—should be mentioned before we proceed.

With respect to the beginning of the human life cycle, under English common law the prohibition on homicide applied as soon as a person was "born alive." Thus, the seventeenth-century English jurist Edward Coke wrote: "If a woman be quick with child [a fetus has "quickened" when the mother can feel its movements], and by a potion or otherwise killeth it in her wombe, or if a man beat her, whereby the childe dyeth in her body, and she is delivered of a dead childe, this is a great misprision [misdemeanor], and no murder; but if the childe be born alive and dyeth of the potion, battery, or other cause, this is murder; for in law it is accounted a reasonable creature, *in rerum natura*, when it is born alive." 3 COKE, INSTITUTES 58 (1648). Some contemporary American penal codes that incorporate the common law have been interpreted to incorporate this "born alive" rule. *See, e.g.*, *Keeler v. Superior Court*, 2 Cal.3d 619 (1970).

At the same time, United States constitutional law protects a woman's right to choose an abortion by balancing the woman's interest in bodily autonomy with the state's interest in protecting human life. In *Roe v. Wade*, 410 U.S. 113, 93 S.Ct. 705, 35 L.Ed.2d 147 (1973), and again in *Planned Parenthood of Southeastern Pennsylvania v. Casey*, 505 U.S. 833, 112 S.Ct. 2791, 120 L.Ed.2d 674 (1992), the Court identified "viability"—the ability of a fetus to live outside the womb—as the fulcrum of this balance. In these cases, the Court set out three principles:

> First is a recognition of the right of the woman to choose to have an abortion before viability and to obtain it without undue interference from the State. * * * Second is a confirmation of the State's power to restrict abortions after fetal viability, if the law contains exceptions for pregnancies which endanger the woman's life or health. And third is the principle that the State has legitimate interests from the outset of the pregnancy in protecting the health of the woman and the life of the fetus that may become a child.

Casey, 505 U.S. at 846. Based on these principles, a state may criminalize the killing of a fetus as long as the law contains exceptions that protect the mother's constitutional rights.

The states have incorporated the common law tradition, constitutional requirements, and moral values in different ways in their penal codes. For instance, Section 210.0(1) of the Model Penal Code incorporates the common law's "born alive" rule, defining "human being" for the purposes of homicide law as "a person who has been born and is alive." Some states specifically criminalize the death or injury of a viable fetus. *See, e.g.*, Ind. Code Ann. § 35–42–1–1 (defining the killing of a viable fetus as murder); *State v. Ard*, 505 S.E.2d 328 (S.C. 1998) (permitting the death penalty to be imposed for the killing of a fetus). Other states criminally punish the death or injury of a "quick" fetus, even if it is not viable. *See* Ark. Code Ann. § 5–1–102(13)(B) (Supp. 1999) (including a fetus twelve weeks or older in the definition of a "person"); *People v. Davis*, 872 P.2d 591 (Cal. 1994) (holding that a murder prosecution is permissible when a fetus is seven to eight weeks old); 720 Ill. Comp. Stat. 5/9–1.2,–2.1,–3.2, 5/12–3.1,–4.4 (permitting homicide prosecutions for the killing of a fetus at any stage of development). Finally, a few states punish the injury or death of a fetus by amplifying the penalties against killing or harming a pregnant woman. *See, e.g.*, Kan. Stat. Ann. §§ 21–3440,–3441 (1995) (creating heightened penalties for felonies and misdemeanors resulting in a miscarriage).

At the other end of the human life cycle, advances in medicine have made it possible for people to be kept alive much longer after a severe injury than was possible at English common law. Contemporary American criminal codes have adapted to this new reality in several ways. First, all fifty states and the District of Columbia now interpret "death" to include "brain death," in which respiration and heartbeat continue but the person has no brain function left. A majority of these jurisdictions have adopted the Uniform Determination of Death Act (UDDA) promulgated by the National Conference of Commissioners on Uniform State Laws. According to the UDDA, "An individual who has sustained either (1) irreversible cessation of circulatory or respiratory functions, or (2) irreversible cessation of all functions, including the brain stem, is dead. A determination of death must be made in accordance with accepted medical standards." Uniform Determination of Death Act § 1. The UDDA seeks both to shield physicians who follow accepted medical practice from liability, and to facilitate organ transplant. Thus, recognizing "brain death" means that the actions of physicians in turning off life support or engaging in transplant surgery after brain death do not break the chain of causation, and the person who originally caused the fatal injury can be criminally prosecuted. *See, e.g.*, *People v. Eulo*, 472 N.E.2d 286 (N.Y. 1984); *Commonwealth v. Golston*, 366 N.E.2d 744 (Mass. 1977).

B. CATEGORIZING HOMICIDES

Although the common law and Model Penal Code approaches to homicide share the central distinction between murder and manslaughter, these terms are differently defined under the two systems. Thus, an overview will be useful.

As a point of departure, it may be useful to know that under both the common law approach and the Model Penal Code, "malice" and "malice aforethought" have lost their everyday meaning. Thus, "malice" no longer means meanness or evil, and "aforethought" no longer refers to premeditation. "Malice aforethought" should rather be understood as a legal term of art or technical label for the mens rea of murder.

In penal codes that primarily rely on the common law, an unlawful killing of a human being is committed with "malice aforethought" and constitutes murder when any one of four conditions are present:

1. An intent to kill;
2. An intent to commit serious bodily injury;[a]
3. An "abandoned and malignant heart" or "depraved heart" (a.k.a. depraved heart murder); or
4. The felony murder rule applies.

If the defendant intends to kill, he acts with express malice. If malice aforethought is shown in any other way, it is considered implied malice.

When proof of murder depends on proof of malice aforethought, what kind of evidence will be sufficient? As we have seen, intent to kill may be inferred from circumstantial evidence. Another evidentiary rule typically observed in jurisdictions that have incorporated the common law is the "deadly weapon rule," which permits (but does not require) the jury to infer intent to kill when the defendant has used a deadly weapon[b] aimed at a vital part of the human body. When attempting to infer an intent to kill or seriously injure, the jury is also permitted to rely on the "natural and probable consequences" doctrine introduced in Chapter 4.

Manslaughter is defined under the common law approach as the unlawful killing of a human being by another human being without

---

[a] Not all jurisdictions recognize intent to commit serious bodily injury as a means of proving malice aforethought. Where it is recognized, the rule reflects a desire to prevent defendants charged with murder from simply arguing, "But I didn't mean to kill," and in that way creating a reasonable doubt. States differ in how they define serious bodily injury. Some define "serious bodily injury" as injury that imperils human life while others define it as injury that seriously interferes with one's health and comfort.

[b] States are not in agreement about what constitutes a "deadly weapon." In some states, a "deadly weapon" is an instrument designed for the purpose of causing death or serious bodily injury. Some states define a "deadly weapon" as anything likely to produce death or serious bodily injury. Yet other states follow the Model Penal Code and define the term "deadly weapon" as anything that, as used or intended, is capable of causing death or serious bodily injury. *See* Model Penal Code § 210.0(4).

malice aforethought. Most common law-based jurisdictions recognize two types of manslaughter: voluntary manslaughter and involuntary manslaughter.

Voluntary manslaughter, the more serious type of manslaughter, is an intentional killing that would normally qualify as second degree murder, but which is reduced to the lesser crime of voluntary manslaughter through the application of a partial defense, such as provocation (also known as heat of passion), imperfect self defense, or diminished capacity. We will study the doctrine of provocation later in this chapter. Imperfect self-defense and diminished capacity are discussed in Chapter 10. A typical sentence for voluntary manslaughter might run from three to eleven years in prison.

Involuntary manslaughter is the least serious form of criminal homicide in many jurisdictions, carrying penalties from two to five years in prison. Generally speaking, a defendant may be charged with involuntary manslaughter if he or she brought about the death of another human being through "criminal negligence," a legal term of art that is defined sometimes as gross negligence and sometimes as recklessness. As you will see in this chapter, states are not consistent regarding the mental state required for involuntary manslaughter.

Some states that follow the common law recognize an additional homicide crime: vehicular manslaughter. Where vehicular manslaughter is recognized, it often carries penalties even lower than those for involuntary manslaughter. In California, for example, a conviction for involuntary manslaughter may be punished with imprisonment for two, three, or four years, whereas a conviction for vehicular manslaughter may result in less than a year in jail. *See* Cal. Penal Code § 193.

Section 210.1 of the Model Penal Code (MPC) defines criminal homicide as the purposeful, knowing, reckless, or negligent death of another human being, thus calling into play the four mens rea elements defined in § 2.02. Criminal homicide is murder when it is committed purposely or knowingly, or when it is committed recklessly "under circumstances manifesting extreme indifference to the value of human life." *See* § 210.2. This recklessness and indifference is presumed if the actor is engaged in or is an accomplice to the commission of, attempt to commit, or flight after committing or attempting to commit, certain other crimes. This formulation represents the MPC drafters' response to the common law doctrines of depraved heart murder and felony murder. The Model Penal Code does not recognize degrees of murder.

Section 210.3 of the MPC defines manslaughter as criminal homicide (1) when it is committed recklessly (but without circumstances manifesting extreme indifference to the value of human life), and (2) when a homicide that would otherwise be murder "is committed under the influence of extreme mental or emotional disturbance for which there is reasonable explanation or excuse." This latter formulation represents the MPC's response to the common law doctrine of heat of passion.

C. DEGREES OF MURDER (FIRST DEGREE VS. SECOND DEGREE MURDER)

Many jurisdictions divide common law murder into two degrees, an approach initiated by Pennsylvania over two centuries ago and widely copied by other states. In these jurisdictions, a murder charge will be raised to first degree murder upon proof that (1) the murder involved "premeditation and deliberation," (2) the murder was committed using a means specified in the first degree murder statute, such as lying in wait, poison, or torture, or (3) the murder occurred during the commission or attempted commission of an enumerated felony (namely rape, robbery, kidnaping, burglary, or arson).

Although the words "premeditation" and "deliberation" are often treated as synonyms, they are not one and the same. Premeditation generally means that the killer must have reflected upon and thought about the killing in advance. No particular length of time is required for premeditation. Indeed, some jurisdictions observe the "wink of an eye" doctrine, under which premeditation can occur in an instant. Deliberation refers to the *quality* of the accused's thought processes. In general, a killing that is deliberate is one that is undertaken with a cool head.

A recurring question in the courts is how fact-finders ought to interpret circumstantial evidence of premeditation and deliberation. How, for example, should evidence of multiple blows be interpreted—as evidence of deliberation, or as evidence of an unthinking frenzy? How should fact-finders interpret situations in which the victim took a long time to die? In each of the following cases, the court had to decide whether there was sufficient evidence of premeditation and deliberation to sustain a first degree murder conviction. Do the opinions set out logical and usable guidelines for finding premeditation and deliberation? Does the requirement of premeditation and deliberation itself make sense as a way of isolating the very worst homicides, or should other factors be equally or more important?

STATE V. BROWN

Supreme Court of Tennessee
836 S.W.2d 530 (Tenn. 1992)

DAUGHTREY, JUSTICE.

This capital case arose from the death of four-year-old Eddie Eugene Brown and the subsequent conviction of his father for first-degree murder, as well as for child neglect.[1] After careful review, we have reached the conclusion that the evidence introduced at trial is not sufficient to support a conviction for first-degree murder. We therefore hold that the defendant's conviction must be reduced to second-degree murder.

1. Factual Background

The victim in this case, Eddie Eugene Brown, was born in early February 1982, the son of defendant Mack Edward Brown and his co-defendant, Evajean Bell Brown, who were not living together at the time of Eddie's birth and were later divorced. * * *

Mack had been living with his wife and his son for less than a year when Eddie died. The Brown's next-door neighbor testified that, at around 3:40 a.m. on April 10, 1986, she heard yelling and screaming in their apartment. She distinctly heard a man's voice say, "Shut up. Get your ass over here. Sit down. Shut up. I know what I'm doing." She also heard a woman's voice say, "Stop, don't do that. Leave me alone. Stop don't do that. She testified that the fight went on for 30 minutes and that she heard a sound which she described as a "thump, like something heavy hit the wall." The only other evidence introduced concerning the events of that morning was the tape of Evajean's call for an ambulance. At 8:59 a.m. she telephoned for help for her son, stating that he "fell down some steps and he's not breathing."

The paramedics who answered the call tried to revive Eddie but were unsuccessful. His heartbeat was reestablished at the hospital, but as it turned out, he was already clinically brain-dead. One of the treating nurses later testified that at that point, Eddie was being kept alive only for purposes of potential organ donation.

Various examinations indicated that the child had suffered two, and possibly three, skull fractures. * * * The CT scan showed a cerebral edema, or swelling of the brain, which was more pronounced on the right side of the brain than the left, and which had shifted the midline of Eddie's brain toward the left. The pathologist who performed the autopsy noted the presence of vomit in Eddie's lungs and explained that swelling in the brain can cause vomiting. He theorized that repeated blows to Eddie's head caused cerebral hemorrhages and swelling. According to the expert, this pressure in the skull resulted in Eddie's aspiration of his own vomit and his ultimate death. He testified further that the swelling process could have taken as long as four or five hours to a day, or as little as 15 minutes.

[1] Eddie's mother was charged as well, but her trial ended in a mistrial and because of double jeopardy considerations, she cannot be retried.

A neurological surgeon testified that Eddie's brain injuries were, at least in part, consistent with contrecoup[4] injuries, which occur when the head is violently shaken back and forth. The surgeon explained that there is a limited amount of fluid between the brain and the skull. That fluid generally serves as a shock absorber, but when the skull and brain are moving at a sufficient velocity and the skull suddenly stops, the fluid is not an adequate buffer between the delicate brain tissue and the hard skull surface. As he described this phenomenon at trial, "when the skull stops the brain slaps up against it," resulting in severe bruising and swelling of the brain.

In addition to his cranial and cerebral injuries, Eddie had several internal injuries. When Eddie's internal organs were removed for donation, the county medical examiner observed hemorrhaging in the duodenum section of his intestine. He testified that such localized hemorrhaging was consistent with a blow by a fist to the upper portion of the abdomen. Additionally, blood was found in the child's stool and urine, and his liver enzymes were elevated. There was testimony to the effect that these conditions may have resulted from cardiac arrest, but that they are also consistent with blows to the abdomen, liver, and kidneys.

Finally, Eddie had bruises of varying ages on his face, scalp, ears, neck, chest, hips, legs, arms, buttocks, and scrotum. He had a large abrasion on his shoulder, scratches on his neck and face, and a round, partially healed wound on his big toe which, according to one of his treating nurses, was consistent with a cigarette burn.[5] He had lacerations on both his ears at the scalp. He had linear bruises consistent with being struck with a straight object. The autopsy revealed an old lesion at the base of his brain which was evidence of a head injury at least two weeks before his death. X-rays revealed a broken arm which had not been treated and which had occurred three to five weeks before his death. The injury to his arm was confirmed by a witness who had noticed his arm hanging limply and then later noticed it in a homemade sling. * * *

Brown's statement indicates that around two or three o'clock on the morning of April 10, 1986, he and his wife both spanked Eddie because Eddie had urinated and defecated on the floor. The defendant admitted to another spanking, after he had sent Eddie to bed, and after he and his wife had a fight over money. As the defendant described it, it was during this spanking that his "mood began to kind of snap and let go." He said that he remembered going to Eddie's bedroom and remembered ordering Evajean out of the room. Although he denied remembering anything other than spanking Eddie's bottom with the open part of his hand, he stated that he was afraid he had beaten Eddie during the time that everything "went blank." The only thing he clearly recalled before that point was

[4] The neurological surgeon testified that "contrecoup" is French for "back and forth."

[5] There was testimony that Mack Brown smoked cigarettes but Evajean did not. * * *

Eddie "staring at [him] mean" and saying, "I hate you! I hate you!" He stated that his next memory was of going downstairs and hearing Eddie behind him, falling onto the landing and into the door.

When the police questioned the defendant, his right hand was badly swollen. He explained that several days prior to April 10, he had injured his hand while working on his car and had sought medical treatment at Fort Sanders Hospital. They put a splint on his hand and gave him pain medication. He denied having struck Eddie with his right hand, stating that "[i]t hurts so bad there ain't no way." The hospital's records indicate that on April 3, the defendant's hand was x-rayed and splinted. The records do not indicate that there was any break in the skin on the hand.

With the consent of the defendant, the police searched the apartment and recovered numerous items stained with blood consistent with Eddie's blood type, including an adult pajama top, a brown paper bag from the living room floor, and several towels and wash cloths. Police also found a bandage under the kitchen sink which was stained with blood consistent with Eddie's blood type. The blood on this bandage material was on the outside near the adhesive tape, not on the inner surface, which would have been next to the skin of the person wearing the bandage. The pants the defendant was wearing at the time of his arrest also had blood stains on them that were consistent with Eddie's blood type. A number of other items collected from the apartment tested positive for human blood, but the type of blood could not be determined because there was too little blood or they had been washed. These items included the couch cover, a pillow case and sheets taken from Eddie's bed, paint chips from the wall in Eddie's room, a child's undershirt and socks, and a three-by-five inch section of the living room rug. * * *

2. Sufficiency of the Evidence

We are asked first to decide whether the evidence was sufficient to support the verdict of first-degree murder. The defendant argues principally that premeditation was not shown. * * *

* * * The statute in effect at the time of the homicide in this case defined first-degree murder as follows:

> Every murder perpetrated by means of poison, lying in wait, or by other kind of willful, deliberate, malicious, and premeditated killing, or committed in the perpetration of, or attempt to perpetrate, any murder in the first degree, arson, rape, robbery, burglary, larceny, kidnapping, aircraft piracy, or the unlawful throwing, placing or discharging of a destructive device or bomb, is murder in the first degree.

T.C.A. § 39–2–202(a) (1982).

Based upon our review of the record, we conclude that the evidence in this case is insufficient to establish deliberation and premeditation. Hence, the defendant's conviction for first-degree murder cannot stand. However, we do find the evidence sufficient to sustain a conviction of second-degree murder.

At common law, there were no degrees of murder, but the tendency to establish a subdivision by statute took root relatively early in the development of American law. The pattern was set by a 1794 Pennsylvania statute that identified the more heinous kinds of murder as murder in the first degree, with all other murders deemed to be murder in the second degree. Some states have subdivided the offense into three or even four degrees of murder, but since the enactment of the first such statute in 1829, Tennessee has maintained the distinction at two. It is one which this Court has found to be "not only founded in mercy and humanity, but . . . well fortified by reason."[8]

* * * Because conviction of second-degree murder also requires proof of intent and malice, the two distinctive elements of first-degree murder are deliberation and premeditation.

* * * [P]erhaps the two most oft-repeated propositions with regard to the law of first-degree murder, that the essential ingredient of first-degree murder is premeditation and that premeditation may be formed in an instant, are only partially accurate, because they are rarely quoted in context. In order to establish first-degree murder, the premeditated killing must also have been done deliberately, that is, with coolness and reflection. As noted in *Rader v. State*:

> When the murder is not committed in the perpetration of, or attempt to perpetrate any of the felonies named in the [statute], then, in order to constitute murder in the first degree, it must be perpetrated by poison or lying in wait, or some other kind of willful, deliberate, malicious, and premeditated killing; that is to say, the deliberation and premeditation must be akin to the deliberation and premeditation manifested where the murder is by poison or lying in wait. * * *

The obvious point to be drawn from this discussion is that even if intent (or "purpose to kill") and premeditation ("design") may be formed in an instant, deliberation requires some period of reflection, during which the mind is "free from the influence of excitement, or passion."

Despite admonitions in the opinions of the Tennessee Supreme Court during the nineteenth century and early part of the twentieth century regarding the necessity of maintaining a clear line of demarcation

---

[8] At common law and in Tennessee prior to 1829, the only penalty provided for murder was death; the creation of second-degree murder introduced the possibility of a life sentence upon conviction.

between first- and second-degree murder, that line has been substantially blurred in later cases. The culprit appears to be the shortcutting of analysis, commonly along three or four different tracks.

One of those has been the same error decried by Justice Turney in 1872, i.e., the use of the terms "premeditation" and "deliberation" interchangeably, or sometimes collectively, to refer to the same concept. * * *

Another weakness in our more recent opinions is the tendency to overemphasize the speed with which premeditation may be formed. The cases convert the proposition that no specific amount of time between the formation of the design to kill and its execution is required to prove first-degree murder, into one that requires virtually no time lapse at all, overlooking the fact that while intent (and perhaps even premeditation) may indeed arise instantaneously, the very nature of deliberation requires time to reflect, a lack of impulse, and, as the older cases had held at least since 1837, a "cool purpose." * * *

A more recent version of Wharton's Criminal Law, however, returns the discussion of premeditation and deliberation to its roots:

> Although an intent to kill, without more, may support a prosecution for common law murder, such a murder ordinarily constitutes murder in the first degree only if the intent to kill is accompanied by premeditation and deliberation. 'Premeditation' is the process simply of thinking about a proposed killing before engaging in the homicidal conduct; and 'deliberation' is the process of carefully weighing such matters as the wisdom of going ahead with the proposed killing, the manner in which the killing will be accomplished, and the consequences which may be visited upon the killer if and when apprehended. 'Deliberation' is present if the thinking, i.e., the 'premeditation,' is being done in such a cool mental state, under such circumstances, and for such a period of time as to permit a 'careful weighing' of the proposed decision.

C. Torcia, Wharton's Criminal Law § 140 (14th ed. 1979). * * *

Logically, of course, the fact that repeated blows (or shots) were inflicted on the victim is not sufficient, by itself, to establish first-degree murder. Repeated blows can be delivered in the heat of passion, with no design or reflection. Only if such blows are inflicted as the result of premeditation and deliberation can they be said to prove first-degree murder. * * *

This discussion leads us inevitably to the conclusion that Mack Brown's conviction for first-degree murder in this case cannot be sustained. The law in Tennessee has long recognized that once the homicide has been established, it is presumed to be murder in the second degree. The state bears the burden of proof on the issue of premeditation and deliberation sufficient to elevate the offense to first-degree murder.

Here, there simply is no evidence in the record that in causing his son's death, Mack Brown acted with the premeditation and deliberation required to establish first-degree murder. There is proof, circumstantial in nature, that the defendant acted maliciously toward the child, in the heat of passion or anger, and without adequate provocation—all of which would make him guilty of second-degree murder. The only possible legal basis upon which the state might argue that a first-degree conviction can be upheld in this case is the proof in the record that the victim had sustained "repeated blows." It was on this basis, and virtually no other, that we upheld a similar first-degree murder conviction for the death of a victim of prolonged child abuse in *State v. LaChance*. In view of our foregoing discussion concerning the shortcomings of such an analysis, we find it necessary to depart from much of the rationale underlying that decision.

In abandoning *LaChance*, we are following the lead of a sister state. In *Midgett v. State*, the Arkansas Supreme Court was asked to affirm the first-degree murder conviction of a father who had killed his eight-year-old son by repeated blows of his fist. As was the case here, there was a shocking history of physical abuse to the child, established both by eyewitness testimony and by proof of old bruises and healed fractures.

* * * [T]he *Midgett* court noted:

> The appellant argues, and we must agree, that in a case of child abuse of long duration the jury could well infer that the perpetrator comes not to expect death of the child from his action, but rather that the child will live so that the abuse may be administered again and again. Had the appellant planned his son's death, he could have accomplished it in a previous beating. . . . The evidence in this case supports only the conclusion that the appellant intended not to kill his son but to further abuse him or that his intent, if it was to kill the child, was developed in a drunken, heated, rage while disciplining the child. Neither of those supports a finding of premeditation or deliberation.

The Arkansas court, in strengthening the requirements for proof of premeditation and deliberation in a first-degree murder case involving a victim of child abuse, found it necessary to overrule prior case law to the extent that it was inconsistent with the opinion in *Midgett*. We do the same here. Like the *Midgett* court, we do not condone the homicide in this case, or the sustained abuse of the defenseless victim, Eddie Brown. We simply hold that in order to sustain the defendant's conviction, the proof must conform to the statute. Because the state has failed to establish sufficient evidence of first-degree murder, we reduce the defendant's

conviction to second-degree murder and remand the case for resentencing.
* * *

STATE V. BINGHAM

Supreme Court of Washington
105 Wash.2d 820, 719 P.2d 109 (1986)

GOODLOE, J.

In this case, we review the sufficiency of the evidence of the premeditation element in an aggravated first degree murder conviction. The Court of Appeals found the evidence insufficient and reversed and remanded for resentencing for second degree murder. We affirm the Court of Appeals decision.

On February 18, 1982, the raped and strangled body of Leslie Cook, a retarded adult, was found in a pasture in Sequim. Cook was last seen alive on February 15, 1982, with respondent Charles Dean Bingham. The Clallam County Prosecutor, by amended information, charged Bingham with aggravated first degree (premeditated) murder, rape being the aggravating circumstance. The prosecutor also notified Bingham that the State would seek the death penalty.

The evidence presented at trial showed that on February 15, Cook and Bingham got off a bus together in Sequim about 6 p.m. There was no evidence that they knew each other before this time. They visited a grocery store and two residences. Cook was last seen at the residence of Wayne Humphrey and Enid Pratt where Bingham asked for a ride back to Port Angeles. When he was told no, Bingham said they would hitchhike. They left together heading toward the infrequently traveled Old Olympic Highway. None of the witnesses who saw the two heard any argument or observed any physical contact between them. Three days later, Cook's body was found in a field about a quarter mile from the Humphrey-Pratt residence.

At trial, King County Medical Examiner Reay described the results of the autopsy he performed on Cook's body. The cause of death was "asphyxiation through manual strangulation," accomplished by applying continuous pressure to the windpipe for approximately 3 to 5 minutes. Cook had a bruise on her upper lip, more likely caused by a hand being pressed over her mouth than by a violent blow. Tears were found in Cook's vaginal wall and anal ring. Spermatozoa were present. These injuries were inflicted antemortem. Also, there was a bite mark on each of Cook's breasts. Reay testified that these occurred perimortem or postmortem.

Two forensic odontologists testified that the bite mark on one breast matched Bingham's teeth. No conclusive determination could be made with respect to the other bite mark.

The prosecutor's theory, as revealed in both his opening statement and closing argument, was that Bingham wanted to have sex with Cook and that he had to kill her in order to do so. The prosecutor hypothesized that Bingham had started the act while Cook was alive, and that he put his hand over her mouth and then strangled her in order to complete the act. The prosecutor also told the jury that the murder would be premeditated if Bingham had formed the intent to kill when he began to strangle Cook, and thought about that intent for the 3 to 5 minutes it took her to die.

The court instructed the jury on aggravated first degree murder and on the lesser included offenses of first and second degree murder and first degree manslaughter. The court also gave Bingham's proposed instruction on voluntary intoxication.

The jury found Bingham guilty of aggravated first degree murder. The jury also found, in the penalty phase, that the State had failed to prove that there were insufficient mitigating circumstances to warrant leniency. The trial court therefore sentenced Bingham to life imprisonment without the possibility of release or parole. * * *

We must determine whether evidence of premeditation was sufficiently demonstrated in order for the issue to go to the jury and in order to sustain a finding of premeditated killing. * * *

Bingham was charged with first degree murder pursuant to RCW 9A.32.030(1)(a), which requires for conviction "a premeditated intent to cause the death of another." The element of premeditation distinguishes first and second degree murder. Section (1)(a) of the second degree murder statute, RCW 9A.32.050, requires for conviction "intent to cause the death of another person but without premeditation."

The only statutory elaboration on the meaning of premeditation is found in RCW 9A.32.020(1), which states that premeditation "must involve more than a moment in point of time." Washington case law further defines premeditation as "the mental process of thinking beforehand, deliberation, reflection, weighing or reasoning for a period of time, however short." We recently approved an instruction which defined premeditation as "the deliberate formation of and reflection upon the intent to take a human life."

Premeditation may be shown by direct or circumstantial evidence. Circumstantial evidence can be used where the inferences drawn by the jury are reasonable and the evidence supporting the jury's verdict is substantial. In this case, the State presented no direct evidence. The issue thus becomes whether sufficient circumstantial evidence of premeditation was presented. Bingham was not charged with felony murder.[a]

---

[a] Apparently, the prosecutor did not charge Bingham with felony murder because he thought felony murder was a lesser included offense of aggravated first degree murder, and that

To show premeditation, the State relied on the pathologist's testimony that manual strangulation takes 3 to 5 minutes. The State argues this time is an appreciable amount of time in which Bingham could have deliberated. Bingham argues that time alone is not enough and that other indicators of premeditation must be shown. * * *

We agree with the Court of Appeals majority that to allow a finding of premeditation only because the act takes an appreciable amount of time obliterates the distinction between first and second degree murder. Having the opportunity to deliberate is not evidence the defendant did deliberate, which is necessary for a finding of premeditation. Otherwise, any form of killing which took more than a moment could result in a finding of premeditation, without some additional evidence showing reflection. Holding a hand over someone's mouth or windpipe does not necessarily reflect a decision to kill the person, but possibly only to quiet her or him. Furthermore, here a question of the ability to deliberate or reflect while engaged in sexual activity exists. * * *

The facts of a savage murder generate a powerful drive, almost a juggernaut for jurors, and indeed for judges, to crush the crime with the utmost condemnation available, to seize whatever words or terms reflect maximum denunciation, to cry out murder "in the first degree." But it is the task and conscience of a judge to transcend emotional momentum with reflective analysis. The judge is aware that many murders most brutish and bestial are committed in a consuming frenzy or heat of passion, and that these are in law only murder in the second degree. * * *

Exercising our responsibility, we find manual strangulation alone is insufficient evidence to support a finding of premeditation. We affirm the Court of Appeals decision.

CALLOW, J. (dissenting).

I would reinstate the aggravated first degree murder conviction of defendant. Sufficient evidence was presented on premeditation for that issue to be submitted to the jury. The decision on that issue is the function of the jury; not to be taken away. * * *

The rule announced by the majority seems to be that premeditation must take place *before the commencement* of the act that results in death. Take the farmer's son who begins to fill the bin with wheat as a joke on his brother sleeping at its bottom. Then, realizing that he will inherit the whole farm if he persists, he does so and causes his brother's death. He

---

the jury would be instructed on felony murder before deliberations. The trial court, however, rejected the prosecutor's proposed instruction on felony murder. The Court of Appeals of Washington upheld the trial court's decision on this issue, stating: "We believe the evidence also would have supported a finding of felony murder . . . However, the State did not charge Bingham with felony murder. The trial judge correctly refused to instruct the jury that felony murder was a lesser included offense of the crime as charged." *State v. Bingham*, 40 Wash. App. 553, 699 P.2d 262 (1985).

had time to premeditate and did so in the middle of the act. He has committed aggravated first degree murder. That a murderer originally commenced an act without intending death does not grant him a carte blanche to persist when he realizes that to do so will kill his victim. * * *

The testimony of Dr. Donald Reay, Chief Medical Examiner for King County, who performed the autopsy on Leslie Cook, is illuminating as to what is necessary to effect death by manual strangulation. * * *

> Q. Doctor, when you say manual strangulation, you mean the hands?
>
> A. Yes, correct.
>
> Q. Okay, now how long does it take someone to die by manual strangulation, doctor?
>
> A. Ordinarily the process will take three to five minutes.
>
> Q. And what sort of force or what sort of action is required during that three to five minutes period?
>
> A. The requirement is to stop the blood flow to the brain and at the same time prevent a person from breathing. The result is that they become oxygen deficient and the heart is sensitive over a period of time and leads to lack of oxygen that develops an abnormal rhythm which proceeds to death.
>
> Q. Doctor, does unconsciousness come before death in a case of manual strangulation?
>
> A. Oh, yes. Yes.
>
> Q. And how long does it take before someone is unconscious, do you know?
>
> A. If a well placed hold about the neck, it can take a matter of seconds. We have done some tests where a person becomes unconscious in a matter of six to seven seconds, if the vessels are pinched in a very quick fashion.
>
> Q. And death ensues within three to five minutes?
>
> A. Yes, that may be unconsciousness, but if the pressure is released the person will wake up. It's a hold that sometimes is used by law enforcement, but if the pressure is sustained then the brain goes without oxygen and in addition the airways collapse over the lungs and heart go without oxygen and there are deficits building up which affect the heart and it starts to develop abnormal beats or rhythms and eventually leads to death.

Q. Doctor, does this sort of asphyxiation by manual strangulation in this instance, does it take a steady pressure for that three to five minute period?

A. Yes, the pressure can vary, certainly, but the important thing is to include the airway and the arterial supply. One or the other will effectively do it.

* * *

If one sits quietly and watches the clock for 3 to 5 minutes, an appreciation of the fullness of that length of time pervades one's thoughts. The jury was entitled to put itself in the shoes of the victim and the murderer. The victim would have gone from apprehension to fear, terror, and then lapsed into unconsciousness. During this time the victim, in all likelihood, would have struggled and the defendant would have watched all of this in the eyes of his victim. As to the defendant, the continued, deliberate exertion of strength required for that length of time was substantial. By the fact of death, we know that not once during all that it took to effect death did he desist from accomplishing his purpose. * * *

The State presented substantial circumstantial evidence on the issue of premeditation. The trial court properly left that issue to the jury. The jury found that the defendant did premeditate. I would reinstate the first degree murder conviction of the defendant.

NOTE

Judge Goodloe, writing for the majority in *State v. Bingham*, questions whether a man can "deliberate or reflect while engaged in sexual activity." Do you find this reason in support of the majority's finding that there was insufficient evidence of premeditation persuasive?

GILBERT V. STATE

Court of Appeals of Florida, Fourth District
487 So.2d 1185, 11 Fla. L. Weekly 1007 (Fla. Dist. Ct. App. 1986)

WALDEN, J.

Upon trial by jury, Roswell Gilbert was found guilty of the premeditated murder of his wife, Emily, in contravention of section 782.04(1)(a)1, Florida Statutes (1981). He, at age 75, was sentenced to life imprisonment. Under section 775.082, Florida Statutes (1981), there is a mandatory minimum sentence of 25 years. Thus, Mr. Gilbert would be incarcerated until he reached the age of 100 years before he would be eligible for release.

Mr. and Mrs. Gilbert lived together in a Fort Lauderdale condominium. They had been married for 51 years. Emily suffered from osteoporosis and Alzheimer's Disease. Her physician, Dr. Hidalgo, had prescribed Percodan to help alleviate the pain of the arthritis. The dosage was for moderate pain. There is no doubt that she was in pain because of the osteoporosis and sometimes confused because of the Alzheimer's.

At trial, appellant's attorney called a couple of Emily's friends, in addition to Dr. Hidalgo, to testify as to her physical and emotional condition before her death.

On direct examination Lillian Irvin testified that Emily was in a lot of pain because of the arthritis. One day, while Lillian was in her condominium office, Emily came in looking for appellant. She was upset and crying. He was in a condominium meeting, so Lillian called him out of the meeting to come and attend to his wife. When he arrived Emily said, "I'm so sick, I want to die, I'm so sick . . . Ros I want to die, I want to die."

On cross-examination Lillian testified that Emily would come down from her tenth floor apartment every day to either look for appellant or walk around the condominium pool. The couple also went out to lunch every day.

Jacqueline Rhodes also testified for the defense. She stated that Emily had deteriorated during the last two years of their acquaintance. She was forgetful at times and in pain because of her back. In Jacqueline's opinion appellant had always been very kind and attentive to his wife.

On one particular occasion, Jacqueline went to the Gilberts' apartment and saw Emily lying on the sofa crying and looking very sick. This struck Jacqueline as particularly indicative of Emily's condition.

Appellant testified in his own defense. He recounted their lives together from the first incident of osteoporosis, which was approximately eight years before her death. As time progressed the arthritis worsened and then Emily began to lose her memory. This was diagnosed as Alzheimer's Disease. The manifestation of Emily's illness which appeared to bother appellant the most was her increased dependence on him.

Appellant then described the events which led up to Emily's death. On March 2, Emily had another bout with osteoporosis. The next day he took her to the hospital. Emily did not want to stay there and became uncooperative and insisted on going home. Finally, appellant decided it was best to take her home. This made Emily feel better.

On March 4, the day of the killing, appellant took Emily out to lunch as usual. When they got back he gave her four Percodan tablets, put her on the sofa and went to a condominium meeting. A few minutes later Emily followed him down to the meeting. Appellant left the meeting and took Emily back to their apartment. As she lay on the sofa, she said,

"Please, somebody help me. Please, somebody help me." In his own words this is how appellant killed Emily:

> Who's that somebody but me, you know, and there she was in pain and all this confusion and I guess if I got cold as icewater that's what had happened. I thought to myself, I've got to do it, it got to be mine, I've got to end her suffering, this can't go on.
>
> I went in. The gun was up on the top shelf with a clip in it. I loaded it with one shell, pulled the clip out. I don't like to leave loaded guns laying around.
>
> Well, then I shot her in the head. I felt her pulse, I could still feel it. I thought, Oh, my God, I loused it up.
>
> I went back to the shop. This time I was shaking. I wasn't cold as ice at all. Back to the shop, put another round in the gun, came back, put another bullet in her head.
>
> The only comforting thing, the first shot there was no convulsive reaction, just her right hand shook like that fast and her head went over the impacted bullet and it slowly came down, didn't make any noise except her mouth just opened slowly like that and then, you know, I thought it hit so fast she didn't know what happened. Then I felt her pulse. It turned out I was wrong. The pulse keeps going after this episode for a few minutes anyway. I didn't know that. I just thought I had, you know—and the second time I fired I felt the pulse seemed to be gone. So I somehow got to the telephone and called the security guard downstairs and I said, "I just killed my wife," and—

His attorney continued the questioning:

> [Mr. Varon:] Ros, why did you use a gun?
>
> [Appellant:] I think poison is a horrible way to die. There's no such thing as instantaneous death with poison. I know nothing about poisons but I know that and I know nothing about poisons, I didn't have any. If I did have any, I wouldn't know how to use it. I'd probably louse it up, just get her terribly sick and that's not going to do any—
>
> Q. Ros—
>
> A Firing a shot in the head will cause cessation of all consciousness in one millisecond, one thousandth of a second. I'm sure she didn't even hear the gun go off and I've been asked that question.
>
> . . .
>
> Q. Why did you think that or did you feel that you're the only one that could have ended her suffering?

A. Natural conclusion. I can't go to the medical people. They have no cure for Alzheimer's. The osteoporosis was getting worse slowly in time. Everything looked like it was converging to a climax.

Q. Ros—

A. I couldn't see any other end than her dying. If I put her in a nursing home, well, after that hospital thing I don't think a nursing home would take her. The hospital certainly wouldn't take her.

So I put her in a nursing home and they won't let me stay there and she's separated from me. It would be a horrible death for her. She would die.

Then I can't confide in my friends without getting them involved, you know, in this sort of thing that I did. I couldn't go to the doctor. He is a professional. He is duly bound to report it to the authorities and they would pull me out of the picture.

The whole thing was a mess and the only solution to me was to terminate her suffering. That's all.

Q. Now, Ros—

A. If I could continue?

Q. Yes, please.

A. I didn't consider what would happen to me at all. The only important thing was to terminate her suffering. I could take care of whatever happens to me and it's happening right now and that was of no consequence to me.

Sure, I know I was breaking the law but there seems to be things more important than the law, at least to me in my private tragedy. So it's murder. So what?

On cross-examination appellant testified that he had never talked with Emily about killing her and had decided to shoot her from behind so she would not see the gun.

The record reveals that up until the time of her death, Emily was always neat and well-dressed, wearing makeup, jewelry, and coordinated outfits. She also went to the hairdresser every two weeks up until the last week of her life.

Her doctor testified that Emily could have lived for another five to ten years. She was never bedridden or completely incapacitated. * * *

In the case at hand there was no evidence that Emily left a mercy will. It is ridiculous and dangerous to suggest, as appellant does, that a constructive mercy will was left when Emily (or anyone else who is sick) said/says, "I'm so sick I want to die." Such a holding would judicially sanction open season on people who, although sick, are also chronic complainers. Because there was no mercy will, appellant's good faith intentions do not come into play. "Good faith" is not a legal defense to first degree murder. * * *

Finally, this court notices that this aged defendant has been a peaceful, law-abiding and respected citizen up until this time. No one has suggested that he will again kill someone or enter upon a criminal career. However, the absolute rigidity of the statutory mandatory minimum sentences do not permit consideration of these factors or, for that matter, they, different from the sentencing guidelines, do not take into account any mitigating circumstances. Whether such sentences should somehow be moderated so as to allow a modicum of discretion and whether they should allow distinctions to be made in sentencing between different kinds of wrongdoers, for instance, between a hired gangster killer and one, however misguided, who kills for love or mercy, are all questions which, under our system, must be decided by the legislature and not by the judicial branch. We leave it there.

Having completely considered the written and oral appellate presentation, the judgment of conviction is

AFFIRMED.

GLICKSTEIN, J., concurring specially.

I agree in general with the reasoning of the majority, and entirely concur in the result. * * *

I have some concern, [however], about the hint in the main opinion that trial courts should be enabled to vary minimum mandatory sentences according to the "kind" of wrongdoer; e.g., hired killer versus misguided mercy killer. I do not favor opening the door to such distinctions.

My thoughts lie with the victim, who was silenced forever by appellant's criminal act. She would be no more dead if a hired gangland killer had pulled the trigger.

Can it be that we feel more comfortable about imposing severe punishment on persons we perceive to belong to a separate tribe, whom we label criminals, than on those we see as members of our own tribe? In fact, we are all members of a common humanity.

The Decalogue states categorically, "Thou shalt not murder." It draws no distinction between murder by members of the middle class and murder by members of an underclass. It draws no distinction between murder by a family member and murder by a stranger. It draws no distinction between murder out of a misguided notion of compassion and murder for hire.

The victims in all such cases are equally dead. If the act was deliberate, the minimum penalty should not vary with the actor's purported motivation.

The concept of permissive mitigation of the minimum penalty based upon a claim the motive for the killing was compassion is even more difficult to accept when the offender is sophisticated, educated and mature, and has enjoyed opportunities in life to make choices.

NOTE

Cases posing issues similar to the issues in *Gilbert* continue to occur. On August 4, 2012, 66-year-old John Wise walked into the intensive care unit room at the Akron General Medical Center in Cleveland, Ohio, where his wife of 45 years lay bedridden and unable to speak after suffering a stroke the week before. Wise fired a single shot into his wife's head, killing her. Wise told a friend that he and his wife had agreed long ago that they did not want to live if bedridden and disabled. Thomas J. Sheeran & John Seewer, *Ohio Hospital Shooting: Mercy Killing or Murder?*, ASSOCIATED PRESS, Aug. 12, 2012. According to Donna Cohen, head of the Violence and Injury Prevention Program at the University of Florida, "Seeing a dying or disabled spouse suffering can be enough to push someone over the edge." *Id.* Cohen worries that these types of incidents will occur more often with longer life expectancies and a continuing shortage of mental health services for older people. *Id.* According to Cohen, two in five homicides in the state of Ohio involve people 55 and older. *Id.*

Under both the common law tradition and the Model Penal Code, suicide (killing oneself) and active euthanasia (killing another out of mercy rather than ill-will) are illegal.[a] Several states have passed statutes explicitly criminalizing physician-assisted suicide. However, one jurisdiction in the United States—Oregon—has gone against this trend, legalizing physician-assisted suicide through passage of the Oregon Death with Dignity Act, adopted by voters in 1994. As one commentator describes its provisions:

> The Death with Dignity Act specifically permits competent, terminally ill adult Oregon residents to obtain prescriptions from their doctors for the purpose of lethal self-administration. * * * The attending physician is assigned specific responsibilities under the Act, including to determine whether the patient has a terminal disease, whether the patient is competent, whether the patient is a resident of Oregon, and, perhaps most importantly, to ensure that

---

[a] Euthanasia is commonly divided into two types, active and passive. "*Active* euthanasia involves prescribing medication or treatments aimed at shortening a person's life and alleviating his or her suffering. * * * *Passive* euthanasia . . . may take two forms: one is abstention from performing acts that prolong the patient's life. An example may be refraining from connecting a patient to a respirator or to a resuscitation machine. The other form involves discontinuation of actions designed to sustain life. This means withdrawing machines to which the patient has already been connected." Raphael Cohen-Almagor, *Euthanasia and Physician-Assisted Suicide in the Democratic World: A Legal Overview*, 16 N.Y. INT'L L. REV. 1, 2–3 (2003).

> the patient has made an informed decision. Before a patient may qualify to end his or her life under the Act, a consulting physician must also confirm the attending physician's diagnosis that the patient has a terminal disease and independently determine that the patient is competent and has made a voluntary and informed decision. The attending or consulting physician must also refer the patient to a psychological counselor if either doctor believes that the patient "may be suffering from a psychiatric or psychological disorder or depression causing impaired judgment." In such a case, the Act specifically prohibits the prescription of medication for the purpose of ending the patient's life until the counselor determines that the patient is not suffering from depression or any other psychological disorder. The patient is also encouraged to notify family members of his decision, and the Act requires a waiting period between the patient's request and physician's prescription of the medication.

Comment, *The Oregon Death with Dignity Act: A Successful Model or a Legal Anomaly Vulnerable To Attack?*, 40 HOUS. L. REV. 1387, 1391–92 (2004).

How often has the Act been utilized? The Comment continues:

> During the five-year period from 1998 through 2002, 198 prescriptions of lethal doses were written in accordance with the Death with Dignity Act. Of these 198 prescription recipients, 129 died after ingesting the medication; the remaining patients either died from their underlying disease or were still alive at the time the fifth-year data was compiled. Moreover, the 129 PAS [physician-assisted suicide] deaths in Oregon during the five-year study comprise less than one-eighth of one percent of Oregon resident deaths.

Id. at 1392.

Although Oregon is the only United States jurisdiction that formally allows assisted suicide, even in jurisdictions where euthanasia is a crime juries sometimes refuse to apply the law. Raphael Cohen-Almagor reports on the strange career of Dr. Jack Kevorkian, nicknamed "Dr. Death," who reportedly helped more than 130 terminal patients to die, some with the aid of a machine he invented to help people commit suicide by automatically injecting first a narcotic and then a lethal dose of potassium chloride.

> In Michigan, a special statute was passed in 1993 to stop Dr. Jack Kevorkian from assisting patients to die. However, Dr. Kevorkian stood trial several times and in all instances the juries refused to convict him of violating that statute, although Kevorkian admitted he had assisted people to commit suicide. Kevorkian was acquitted on the grounds that his main intent was to relieve pain, not to cause death. In November 1998, he actively performed euthanasia on Thomas Youk, stood trial and was convicted of second-degree murder and of delivering a controlled substance for the purpose of

> injecting Youk with lethal drugs. Kevorkian was given a jail sentence of 10 to 25 years on the second-degree murder conviction, and 3 to 7 years on the "controlled substance" conviction.

Raphael Cohen-Almagor, *Euthanasia and Physician-Assisted Suicide in the Democratic World: A Legal Overview*, 16 N.Y. INT'L L. REV. 1, 19–20 (2003).

Should the law recognize a constitutionally-protected liberty interest in an individual's right to take her own life, and if so, should that right encompass the right to involve others, such as physicians, in implementing the patient's decision? In *Washington v. Glucksberg*, 521 U.S. 702, 117 S.Ct. 2258, 138 L.Ed.2d 772 (1997), the Supreme Court held that the right to commit suicide was *not* a liberty interest protected by the Due Process Clause of the Fourteenth and Fifth Amendments. Moreover, the Court held that state governments have a legitimate government interest in prohibiting suicide and euthanasia, including the preservation of human life; the protection of the integrity and ethics of the medical profession; the protection of vulnerable groups from abuse, neglect, and mistake; and the protection of disabled and terminally ill people from prejudice, negative and inaccurate stereotypes, and societal indifference. *Glucksberg*, 521 U.S. at 703. Therefore, the state of Washington was free to enforce a statute banning physician-assisted suicide.

On the same day that the Court handed down *Glucksberg*, it also decided *Vacco v. Quill*, 521 U.S. 793, 117 S.Ct. 2293, 138 L.Ed.2d 834 (1997). In that case, physicians had asked for a judgment that New York's laws prohibiting physician-assisted suicide were unconstitutional under the Equal Protection Clause, given that New York permitted competent patients to refuse life-saving medical treatment. The physicians argued that such a refusal is practically equivalent to a physician-assisted suicide, so the law should not allow the former while criminalizing the latter. The Court rejected the equal protection challenge, asserting that "[t]he distinction between letting a patient die and making that patient die is important, logical, rational, and well established: It comports with fundamental legal principles of causation . . ." *Vacco v. Quill*, 521 U.S. at 793–94. Do you agree with the Court?

D. THE DOCTRINE OF PROVOCATION (VOLUNTARY MANSLAUGHTER)

One of the ways an intentional killing can be mitigated from murder to voluntary manslaughter is through the doctrine of provocation, also known as the heat of passion defense. Under this doctrine, one who kills in response to legally adequate provocation is treated as having acted without malice aforethought, the mens rea required for murder. In reality, however, the defendant who claims provocation often acts with an intent to kill or an intent to grievously injure, two means of proving malice aforethought. The better way to think about provocation is that the defendant's culpability is mitigated, not because of the absence of malice aforethought, but because of culturally-sanctioned sympathy with his or her loss of self control. Thus, the provocation defense is often described as a concession to human weakness.

Over the years, American jurisdictions have embraced three different approaches to determining whether a defendant charged with murder is entitled to a voluntary manslaughter instruction: (1) the early common law (categorical) test; (2) the modern "reasonable man" (later "reasonable person" test; and (3) the Model Penal Code's extreme mental or emotional disturbance defense. These different approaches are discussed in greater detail below.

Historically, the provocation defense developed through the desire of common law judges to align the dictates of the criminal law with Anglo-American cultural mores. One note-writer observes that the cultural notion of "honor" had much to do with the emergence of provocation doctrine:

> In English society, a man was bound by a code of honor that strictly defined the parameters of appropriate behavior during particular forms of social intercourse. Since the protection of a man's "natural honor" was contingent on his conformity to this behavior, the honor code was much more pervasive and influential than the loose rules of etiquette that structure modern society. "Men of honour"—men who took their natural honor seriously—were expected to retaliate swiftly and forcefully in the face of an affront. The act of retaliation, regardless of the consequences, would negate the threat to honor. "What is more," explains [Jeremy Horder], "[the man of honor] was not expected to retaliate reluctantly. . . . He was expected to resent the affront, and to retaliate in anger." [Jeremy Horder, PROVOCATION AND RESPONSIBILITY 25–30 (1992).]
>
> Anger, rage, and retaliatory measures, then, were culturally programmed reactions, "implanted" in the psyches of sixteenth-century English males as not only justifiable, but also obligatory courses of action. To the extent that men of honor believed retaliatory actions were the direct functions of courage, retaliatory "boxes on the ear," fist fights, and even duels were encouraged in English society. Moreover, the code of honor did not simply dictate that men were obliged to engage in some form of ambiguous "angered retaliation"; the form of retaliation was strictly regulated by culturally defined principles of proportionality. These rules of proportionality, as well as the principle of natural honor they reflected, were explicitly embodied in early-modern manslaughter laws.

Note, James J. Sing, *Culture as Sameness: Toward a Synthetic View of Provocation and Culture in the Criminal Law*, 108 YALE L.J. 1845, 1867 (1999).

Sing argues further that understood from this perspective, the doctrine of heat of passion as originally developed was not a concession to human frailty (and thus a type of excuse), but rather a recognition that anger and passion are in some circumstances justified by the prevailing culture (and thus a type of justification). As you read the cases below, consider whether in the context of contemporary Anglo-American culture heat of passion is conceptualized as a justification, an excuse, or a little of both.[a]

1. THE EARLY COMMON LAW'S CATEGORICAL APPROACH TO PROVOCATION

The first approach to provocation, which emerged in the 1700s, was called the early common law or categorical test. Under this approach, one could claim the provocation mitigation if and only if one killed in response to: (1) an aggravated assault or battery, (2) the observation of a serious crime against a close relative, (3) an illegal arrest, (4) mutual combat, or (5) catching one's wife in the act of adultery. Only these categories of provocative acts were recognized at early common law as adequate provocation, and judges themselves created and applied these categories. Provocation was considered a question of "law," rather than "fact."

One categorical rule which has survived throughout the years even in modern jurisdictions is the "mere words" rule. Under this rule, mere words are never enough to constitute legally adequate provocation. The mere words rule made sense under the early common law categorical approach, when judges strictly controlled the kinds of situations subject to the provocation doctrine, but makes less sense under the modern trend which allows the jury to decide on a case by case basis whether there was adequate provocation.

Even though the mere words rule has been observed as a general matter, courts have made exceptions in certain situations. The next case, *People v. Ambro*, illustrates one long-standing exception to the mere words rule.

PEOPLE V. AMBRO

Appellate Court of Illinois, Second District
153 Ill.App.3d 1, 505 N.E.2d 381 (1987)

NASH, J.

After a jury trial, defendant, George Ambro, was convicted of murdering his wife, Ruth Ambro, and sentenced to a term of 20 years' imprisonment. On appeal, defendant contends . . . the trial court erred in

---

[a] For further discussion regarding the distinction between justifications and excuses, *see* the Introduction to Chapter 10.

refusing to instruct the jury on the offense of voluntary manslaughter based on provocation. * * *

Defendant and Ruth Ambro were married on May 25, 1974, and, at the time of the killing on March 28, 1985, the couple had two children, Jocelyn and Bethany, ages six and two years old. In 1978, the couple began experiencing marital difficulties and Ruth attempted suicide. In June 1984, the couple separated until Ruth returned to their Elgin residence two weeks later. During late 1984 and early 1985, the couple's marital problems worsened. Defendant testified that the couple did not have marital relations until after December 1984, and Ruth would stay out at night until 4:30 a.m. without explanation. He stated he became suspicious of her activities when he observed that Ruth was wearing different types of underwear and discovered she had purchased birth control pills.

In January 1985, the couple joined a marital counselling [sic] group, and on March 20, 1985, Ruth informed the group that she no longer loved defendant and was going to divorce him. Defendant stated that he attempted suicide shortly thereafter. On March 26, 1985, Ruth met with an attorney and scheduled a meeting for March 29, 1985, to sign a petition for dissolution of the marriage.

Defendant testified that he returned home from work on the evening of March 28, 1985, at approximately 5:30 p.m. and Ruth immediately began bickering. * * * [T]he couple had dinner and argued about Ruth's treatment of the children. Defendant accused Ruth of mistreating Bethany by hitting her and not feeding her properly and asked Ruth if she was taking her frustration toward defendant out on the child. Defendant stated that when Ruth picked up Bethany's high chair and threw it back about three feet, he became very upset and confused. * * *

After Bethany was put to bed, the couple continued their argument. Defendant stated he was cleaning the kitchen counter and was holding two knives in his hand when his wife, who was on the living room sofa, told him that he had no right to complain about her handling of the children because he "had no right to the children." She then called defendant an alcoholic and told him that he did not love the children and that she was going to take them away from him. Defendant testified he could not describe his feelings at that point and had never had such feelings before. He went to the living room, kneeled beside Ruth and asked her what he could do to restore their relationship. Ruth said, "I have another man and when we make love I feel like it was." She then said, "I know you want to kill me. Pull that knife and make it easy for me." Defendant then stabbed Ruth with a knife, testifying that he had no conscious knowledge of doing so or an intent to stab her. He immediately called the police, but Ruth never regained consciousness and died soon after being brought to the hospital. At trial, medical testimony established that the wife died from a single stab wound through the heart. * * *

Defendant tendered a jury instruction defining the offense of manslaughter based on provocation, but the trial court sustained an objection by the State and refused to submit it to the jury, which was instructed only on the charge of murder. After deliberations, the jury convicted defendant of murder and he was sentenced to a term of 20 years' imprisonment.

We consider first defendant's contention that the trial court erred in refusing to instruct the jury on the offense of voluntary manslaughter based on provocation. Defendant argues that it was error to refuse his tendered instruction based on section 9–2(a) of the Criminal Code of 1961 (Code) (Ill. Rev. Stat. 1985, ch. 38, par. 9–2(a)), which defines voluntary manslaughter. That section states:

> A person who kills an individual without lawful justification commits voluntary manslaughter if at the time of the killing he is acting under a sudden and intense passion resulting from serious provocation by:
>
> (1) The individual killed * * *.
>
> * * * Serious provocation is conduct sufficient to excite an intense passion in a reasonable person.

Defendant asserts that the evidence warranted submission of the manslaughter instruction to the jury. In resolving this issue, we must first determine whether the evidence relating to the conduct of Ruth Ambro prior to the killing is, if believed by the jury, the type of provocation contemplated under section 9–2(a) of the Code. In *People v. Matthews*, the court characterized this requirement by stating:

> Passion on the part of the slayer, no matter how violent will not relieve him from liability for murder unless it is engendered by a provocation which the law recognizes as being reasonable and adequate. If the provocation is not sufficient the crime is murder.

The general rule in Illinois is that the only categories of provocation which are considered sufficiently serious to reduce the crime of murder to voluntary manslaughter are substantial physical injury or assault, mutual quarrel or combat, illegal arrest, and adultery with the offender's spouse.[a] Mere words, however aggravated, abusive, opprobrious, or indecent, are not sufficient provocation. Moreover, adultery by a spouse

---

[a] Under the early common law's categorical approach to provocation, this last category of legally adequate provocation was limited to husbands who caught their wives in the act of adultery. Wives who caught their husbands in the act were not considered adequately provoked to merit a reduction in the charge from murder to manslaughter. *See* CYNTHIA LEE, MURDER AND THE REASONABLE MAN: PASSION AND FEAR IN THE CRIMINAL COURTROOM 22-23, 46-52 (NYU Press 2003).

has generally been limited to those instances where the parties were discovered in the act of adultery or immediately before or after its commission.

An apparent exception to these general rules, based on verbal revelations of infidelity and other conduct, has been recognized in two Illinois cases in which convictions for voluntary manslaughter were affirmed. In *People v. Ahlberg,* the defendant's killing of his wife was the culmination of a series of events. In that case, defendant's wife moved out of the house with the children without informing her husband, and he looked for her for several days. When the victim finally contacted him, she informed the defendant that she was getting a divorce because she was tired of "being the nice school teacher's wife," that he had never satisfied her sexually, and that she had found an older man who could love her and her two children more than he could. Under these circumstances, the reviewing court considered that it would be a "direct refutation of logic and a miscarriage of justice" to follow the rule that mere words are insufficient to cause provocation serious enough to support a conviction for manslaughter.

In *People v. Carr*, defendant and his wife had engaged in frequent arguments in the six months preceding the shooting, most of them over the husband's suspicions of infidelity by her. Defendant's wife then moved out of their home, and defendant informed a cousin of the victim that he would kill his wife if she tried to remove any furniture from their home. The wife returned two weeks later to remove some furniture. The couple began arguing, and, when the wife told him, "At least now I have a real man," defendant shot her. The appellate court cited *Ahlberg* with approval and concluded that the evidence was sufficient to support defendant's conviction for voluntary manslaughter.

In *People v. Harris*, the court reviewed the two cases and noted that both *Ahlberg* and *Carr* involved situations where the revelation of adultery was one of a series of provoking statements or circumstances. The court then determined that "these cases do not support the proposition that Illinois has adopted the more liberal approach concerning verbal communication of the fact of adultery as provocation." We agree with that conclusion, since neither *Ahlberg* nor *Carr* were based on mere verbal conduct. In both cases, there was a history of ongoing marital discord, a wife who evidenced an intent to permanently leave her husband, insulting remarks concerning the husband's masculinity, and an announcement of adultery by the wife.

In the present case, defendant and his wife had been experiencing marital difficulties for seven years and, as in *Carr*, defendant began to suspect her of infidelity shortly before he killed her. One week before her death, Ruth told the couple's marital-counselling group and defendant that she no longer loved her husband and was going to seek a divorce. She then contacted an attorney to draft a petition for dissolution of the marriage and informed defendant of her actions. On the evening of the killing, defendant became upset over his wife's treatment of Bethany and her threats of seeking a divorce, and the couple engaged in repeated arguments during which the wife implied that defendant was not the father of her children, called him an alcoholic, and told him she was going to take the children when she left him. When defendant knelt beside his wife and asked how he could restore their relationship, she informed him of her adultery and then goaded him to kill her.

These facts closely parallel the series of events found to constitute serious provocation in *Ahlberg* and *Carr* and, in our view, go beyond the provocation elements in those cases, since the victim here goaded defendant to kill her. On these facts, we conclude the present case falls within the exception recognized in *Ahlberg* and *Carr* and find that the wife's conduct was the type of provocation which Illinois law recognizes as sufficiently serious, if believed by the jury, to reduce the crime of murder to voluntary manslaughter. * * *

Accordingly, the judgment of the trial court is reversed and the cause remanded for a new trial.

Reversed and remanded.[b]

NOTE

Courts have made exceptions to the mere words rule in a few other situations. For example, in *State v. Tackett*, 8 N.C. 210 (1820), the Supreme Court of North Carolina ordered a new trial for a white man who was convicted of murdering a slave, suggesting that a white man who kills another man's slave in response to words of reproach uttered by that slave is entitled to claim provocation. In explaining why a new trial was in order, the court noted that the trial court's instruction to the jury (that the case was to be determined by the same rules and principles of law as if the deceased, a slave, had been a white man) was in error. According to the court, it was appropriate to grant more leniency to a white man who kills a slave than to a white man who kills another white man because:

> It exists in the nature of things, that where slavery prevails, the relation between a white man and a slave differs from that, which subsists between free persons; and every individual in the community feels and understands, that the homicide of a slave may be extenuated by acts which would not produce a legal provocation if done by a white person. * * *
>
> It is a rule of law, that neither words of reproach, insulting gestures, nor a trespass against goods or land, are provocations

---

[b] In 1989, the Supreme Court of Illinois overruled *People v. Ambro*, *People v. Ahlberg*, and *People v. Carr*, holding that a wife's confession of adultery, no matter how insulting, does not constitute legally adequate provocation. *People v. Chevalier*, 544 N.E.2d 942 (Ill. 1989).

> sufficient to free the party killing from the guilt of murder, where he made use of a deadly weapon. But it cannot be laid down as a rule, that some of these provocations, if offered by a slave, well known to be turbulent and disorderly, would not extenuate the killing, if it were instantly done under the heat of passion, and without circumstances of cruelty.

Should courts recognize an exception to the mere words rule for persons of color who kill in response to a racist epithet? Professor Camille Nelson argues that the doctrine of provocation should be expanded to include an appreciation of serial or cumulative provocation. Under her proposal, a black man who has suffered countless acts of racism would be able to claim provocation from being called the "N word." She explains:

> Such recognition of "serial provocation" would better appreciate the reality of racist abuses. Unlike the case of the battered woman who might be in a longstanding relationship with her abuser, victims of racism are bombarded by various abuses from many different persons and sources. If the accused is a black person who has been the victim of routine racist microaggressions, the racist act or racist insult should be situated in the context of such racism. Psychiatrists who have studied black populations view such microaggressions as "incessant and cumulative" assaults on black self-esteem. Racism affects mental well-being, in addition to causing stress, by compromising the self-concept of the person subjected to racial abuses.

Camille A. Nelson, *(En)raged or (En)gaged: The Implications of Racial Context to the Canadian Provocation Defence*, 35 U. RICH. L. REV. 1007, 1051 (2002).

2. THE MODERN "REASONABLE PERSON" TEST

In the late 1800s, many American jurisdictions began to abandon the categorical approach to provocation in favor of an approach that utilized a reasonableness requirement to determine which types of behavior could be considered legally adequate provocation. Under the modern test for provocation in jurisdictions that have incorporated the common law, the jury must find: (1) the defendant acted in a heat of passion; (2) the defendant was reasonably provoked into a heat of passion; (3) the defendant did not have sufficient time to "cool off" between the provocative act or event and the killing; and (4) a reasonable person in the defendant's shoes would not have had sufficient time to cool. Additionally, there must be a causal connection between the provocation, the passion, and the killing, meaning that the provocation must be what actually provoked the killing. Some jurisdictions also embrace what is called the misdirected retaliation rule, requiring that the person killed must be the provoker in order for a defendant to be able to claim the provocation defense.

Although the modern test for provocation gives more decision-making power to the jury than the early common law approach, courts in jurisdictions following the common law continue to differ with respect to how much of provocation doctrine should be implemented by the judge and how much should be left to the jury. In some jurisdictions, judges continue to impose rules on what situations may legally constitute adequate provocation. In other jurisdictions, the jury is given virtually free rein to hear the facts and decide whether the alleged provocation was adequate. *People v. Berry*, which follows, is an example of the latter approach.

PEOPLE V. BERRY

Supreme Court of California
18 Cal.3d 509, 556 P.2d 777, 134 Cal.Rptr. 415 (1976)

SULLIVAN, J.

Defendant Albert Joseph Berry was charged by indictment with one count of murder and one count of assault by means of force likely to produce great bodily injury. The assault was allegedly committed on July 23, 1974, and the murder on July 26, 1974. In each count, the alleged victim was defendant's wife, Rachel Pessah Berry. A jury found defendant guilty as charged and determined that the murder was of the first degree. Defendant was sentenced to state prison for the term prescribed by law. He appeals from the judgment of conviction.

Defendant contends that there is sufficient evidence in the record to show that he committed the homicide while in a state of uncontrollable rage caused by provocation and flowing from a condition of diminished capacity and therefore that it was error for the trial court to fail to instruct the jury on voluntary manslaughter as indeed he had requested. He claims: (1) that he was entitled to an instruction on voluntary manslaughter as defined by statute since the killing was done upon a sudden quarrel or heat of passion; and (2) that he was also entitled to an instruction on voluntary manslaughter in the context of a diminished capacity defense since malice was negatived by mental defect or disease. We agree with defendant as to the first instruction, but not as to the second.

Defendant, a cook, 46 years old, and Rachel Pessah, a 20-year-old girl from Israel, were married on May 27, 1974. Three days later Rachel went to Israel by herself, returning on July 13, 1974. On July 23, 1974, defendant choked Rachel into unconsciousness. She was treated at a hospital where she reported her strangulation by defendant to an officer of the San Francisco Police Department. On July 25, Inspector Sammon, who had been assigned to the case, met with Rachel and as a result of the interview a warrant was issued for defendant's arrest.

While Rachel was at the hospital, defendant removed his clothes from their apartment and stored them in a Greyhound Bus Depot locker. He stayed overnight at the home of a friend, Mrs. Jean Berk, admitting to her that he had choked his wife. On July 26, he telephoned Mrs. Berk and informed her that he had killed Rachel with a telephone cord on that morning at their apartment. The next day Mrs. Berk and two others telephoned the police to report a possible homicide and met Officer Kelleher at defendant's apartment. They gained entry and found Rachel on the bathroom floor. A pathologist from the coroner's office concluded that the cause of Rachel's death was strangulation. Defendant was arrested on August 1, 1974, and confessed to the killing.

At trial defendant did not deny strangling his wife, but claimed through his own testimony and the testimony of a psychiatrist, Dr. Martin Blinder, that he was provoked into killing her because of a sudden and uncontrollable rage so as to reduce the offense to one of voluntary manslaughter. He testified that upon her return from Israel, Rachel announced to him that while there she had fallen in love with another man, one Yako, and had enjoyed his sexual favors, that he was coming to this country to claim her and that she wished a divorce. Thus commenced a tormenting two weeks in which Rachel alternately taunted defendant with her involvement with Yako and at the same time sexually excited defendant, indicating her desire to remain with him. Defendant's detailed testimony, summarized below, chronicles this strange course of events.

After their marriage, Rachel lived with defendant for only three days and then left for Israel. Immediately upon her return to San Francisco she told defendant about her relationship with and love for Yako. This brought about further argument and a brawl that evening in which defendant choked Rachel and she responded by scratching him deeply many times. Nonetheless they continued to live together. Rachel kept taunting defendant with Yako and demanding a divorce. She claimed she thought she might be pregnant by Yako. She showed defendant pictures of herself with Yako. Nevertheless, during a return trip from Santa Rosa, Rachel demanded immediate sexual intercourse with defendant in the car, which was achieved; however upon reaching their apartment, she again stated that she loved Yako and that she would not have intercourse with defendant in the future.

On the evening of July 22nd defendant and Rachel went to a movie where they engaged in heavy petting. When they returned home and got into bed, Rachel announced that she had intended to make love with defendant, "But I am saving myself for this man Yako, so I don't think I will." Defendant got out of bed and prepared to leave the apartment whereupon Rachel screamed and yelled at him. Defendant choked her into unconsciousness.

Two hours later defendant called a taxi for his wife to take her to the hospital. He put his clothes in the Greyhound bus station and went to the home of his friend Mrs. Berk for the night. The next day he went to Reno and returned the day after. Rachel informed him by telephone that there was a warrant for his arrest as a result of her report to the police about the choking incident. On July 25th defendant returned to the apartment to talk to Rachel, but she was out. He slept there overnight. Rachel returned around 11 a.m. the next day. Upon seeing defendant there, she said, "I suppose you have come here to kill me." Defendant responded, "yes," changed his response to "no," and then again to "yes," and finally stated "I have really come to talk to you." Rachel began screaming. Defendant grabbed her by the shoulder and tried to stop her screaming. She continued. They struggled and finally defendant strangled her with a telephone cord.

Dr. Martin Blinder, a physician and psychiatrist, called by the defense, testified that Rachel was a depressed, suicidally inclined girl and that this suicidal impulse led her to involve herself ever more deeply in a dangerous situation with defendant. She did this by sexually arousing him and taunting him into jealous rages in an unconscious desire to provoke him into killing her and thus consummating her desire for suicide. Throughout the period commencing with her return from Israel until her death, that is from July 13 to July 26, Rachel continually provoked defendant with sexual taunts and incitements, alternating acceptance and rejection of him. This conduct was accompanied by repeated references to her involvement with another man; it led defendant to choke her on two occasions, until finally she achieved her unconscious desire and was strangled. Dr. Blinder testified that as a result of this cumulative series of provocations, defendant at the time he fatally strangled Rachel, was in a state of uncontrollable rage, completely under the sway of passion.

We first take up defendant's claim that on the basis of the foregoing evidence he was entitled to an instruction on voluntary manslaughter as defined by statute which is "the unlawful killing of a human being, without malice . . . upon a sudden quarrel or heat of passion." In *People v. Valentine*, this court, in an extensive review of the law of manslaughter, specifically approved the following quotation from *People v. Logan* as a correct statement of the law: "In the present condition of our law it is left to the jurors to say whether or not the facts and circumstances in evidence are sufficient to lead them to believe that the defendant did, or to create a reasonable doubt in their minds as to whether or not he did, commit his offense under a heat of passion. The jury is further to be admonished and advised by the court that this heat of passion must be such a passion as would naturally be aroused in the mind of an ordinarily reasonable person under the given facts and circumstances, and that, consequently, no defendant may set up his own standard of conduct and justify or excuse himself because in fact his passions were aroused, unless further the jury believe that the facts and circumstances were sufficient to arouse the passions of the ordinarily reasonable man.... For the fundamental of the inquiry is whether or not the defendant's reason was, at the time of his act, so disturbed or obscured by some passion—not necessarily fear and never, of course, the passion for revenge—to such an extent as would render ordinary men of average disposition liable to act rashly or without due deliberation and reflection, and from this passion rather than from judgment."

We further held in *Valentine* that there is no specific type of provocation required by section 192 and that verbal provocation may be sufficient. In *People v. Borchers,* in the course of explaining the phrase "heat of passion" used in the statute defining manslaughter we pointed out that "passion" need not mean "rage" or "anger" but may be any "(v)iolent, intense, high-wrought or enthusiastic emotion" and concluded there "that defendant was aroused to a heat of 'passion' by a series of events over a considerable period of time . . . " Accordingly we there declared that evidence of admissions of infidelity by the defendant's paramour, taunts directed to him and other conduct, "supports a finding that defendant killed in wild desperation induced by (the woman's) long continued provocatory conduct." We find this reasoning persuasive in the case now before us. Defendant's testimony chronicles a two-week period of provocatory conduct by his wife Rachel that could arouse a passion of jealousy, pain and sexual rage in an ordinary man of average disposition such as to cause him to act rashly from this passion. It is significant that both defendant and Dr. Blinder testified that the former was in the heat of passion under an uncontrollable rage when he killed Rachel.

The Attorney General contends that the killing could not have been done in the heat of passion because there was a cooling period, defendant having waited in the apartment for 20 hours. However, the long course of provocatory conduct, which had resulted in intermittent outbreaks of rage under specific provocation in the past, reached its final culmination in the apartment when Rachel began screaming. Both defendant and Dr. Blinder testified that defendant killed in a state of uncontrollable rage, of passion, and there is ample evidence in the record to support the conclusion that this passion was the result of the long course of provocatory conduct by Rachel, just as the killing emerged from such conduct in Borchers. * * *

[A]s we have already explained, the court did commit error in refusing to instruct on voluntary manslaughter based on sudden quarrel or heat of passion.

HEAT OF PASSION AND WIFE KILLING: MEN WHO BATTER/MEN WHO KILL

Donna K. Coker

2 S. Cal. Rev. L. & Women's Stud. 71 (1992)[a]

* * * [H]omicide law divides sane individuals who intentionally kill into two major categories: those who premeditate murder and those who act in the heat of passion. Social stereotypes of wife-killing that characterize the killer as a previously non-violent man who "snapped" under pressure, roughly parallel the understandings which underlie heat-of-passion doctrine. However, this social stereotype is grossly inaccurate when applied to men who are identified as "batterers" and when applied to the general category of husband-wife killings. Violence perpetrated by abusive men is purposeful, not spontaneous; the majority of men who kill their wives have a documented history of violent assaults. Furthermore, one would expect to find empirical evidence of wife-killers who fit the stereotype of the heat-of-passion killer in those reports of forensic psychiatrists whose job it is to aid defense counsel, yet these reports seem to confirm that men who kill and men who batter have remarkably similar personality traits and similar motivations. While further research is needed before we can determine whether or not the "impassioned" wife-killer exists, if he does exist, he is apparently part of a very small group of wife-killers.

* * * The case of *People v. Berry* appears in many criminal law textbooks as well as legal treatises, generally for the proposition that the question of "cooling off" is a jury question. * * *

At his trial, Berry offered only two defense witnesses: himself and a psychiatrist, Dr. Martin Blinder. Dr. Blinder testified that

> [Rachel] was a depressed, suicidally inclined girl [sic] and . . . this suicidal impulse led her to involve herself even more deeply in a dangerous situation with defendant. She did this by sexually arousing him and taunting him into jealous rages in an unconscious desire to provoke him into killing her and thus consummating her desire for suicide.

The defense needed Blinder's testimony for two different, but equally critical, reasons. First, the fact that Berry had a prior conviction for stabbing and injuring his second wife had already been ruled admissible. Blinder's testimony was required to neutralize this damaging fact, but, in fact, Blinder went one step better by explaining that Berry's past violence resulted from his repeated emotional victimization at the hands of women. Second, Blinder's testimony was needed most obviously in order to cast the killing as a heat of passion killing and, in particular, to explain

[a] Reprinted with the permission of the *Southern California Review of Law and Women's Studies.*

the 20-hour wait in Rachel's apartment as a result of *cumulative* passion and not premeditation and lying-in-wait. The result was psychiatric testimony that brilliantly—if tautologically—turned facts about Berry that suggested the antithesis to a "heat of passion killer"—i.e., a proclivity for violence, a history of serious prior assaults on the victim identical in kind to the fatal assault, Berry's stabbing of his ex-wife under remarkably similar circumstances, and a psychological profile fitting that of an abuser-into evidence of Berry's increasing provocation as the result of Rachel's relentless "taunting." * * *

In essence, Berry's defense was that he *was* the sort of man who abused women—but the twist was [Dr. Martin] Blinder's psychiatric explanation that Berry's violence was a result of his choosing women who enraged him and provoked him to violence. The fact that Berry had a prior conviction for assaulting his ex-wife with a butcher knife, that in past relationships with other women he had destroyed their property, forcing former girlfriends to "put him out of the house, locking the door," indicated to Blinder the personality of the *women* with whom Berry involved himself, more than it demonstrated Berry's dangerous and abusive nature. Blinder testified that these women "offer[ed] him the promise of comfort but ultimately deliver[ed] . . . emotional pain." Yet Blinder's testimony provides a classic portrait of an abuser. Berry was *most* dangerous when women threatened to leave him. Berry was "emotionally dependent" on wives and girlfriends; he threatened physical violence in order to control women; he destroyed women's property; and he had a history of violent relationships with wives and lovers. The Supreme Court's opinion read Dr. Blinder's testimony to focus narrowly on the effect of *Rachel's* "provocative" behavior on Berry's mental state. Dr. Blinder's testimony, however, refers to a cumulative rage resulting from the provocation of *all* the women in Berry's entire life.

> Q: . . . How would you characterize [Berry's] state of mind . . . [at the time of the homicide]?
>
> A: . . . I would say that he was in a state of uncontrollable rage which was a product of having to contend with what seems to me an incredibly provacative [sic] situation, an incredibly provacative [sic] young woman, and *that this immediate situation was superimposed upon Mr. Berry having encountered the situation time and time again. So that we have a cumulative effect dating back to the way his mother dealt with him.*
>
> . . .
>
> Q: . . . [Y]ou say that the situation involving Rachel Berry and Albert Berry . . . was the product of . . . cumulative . . . provocations. Now, specifically, what would you base your opinion as to provocations on?

. . .

A: . . . We have two factors here. . . . The past history, that is, the history of this man well in advance of his meeting the deceased. And then the history of his relationship with her. And I think the two go together. . . . After 15 years [of marriage to his second wife] and five children, his wife leaves him for . . . another man. . . . They continued to live together, during which time his wife taunted him about her boyfriend. . . .

One night while they were having sex, his wife [calls him by the name of her boyfriend.] Despondent and enraged at the same time, he went into the kitchen, obtained a knife, and stabbed his wife in the abdomen. And she was not serious. He only got to spend a year in jail for that. . . .

So we have this pattern of enormous dependency on these women and then rupture of the relationship with tremendous rage, almost uncontrollable. I think in one instance he put his foot through the stereo . . . he had purchased for one of these girls [sic]. . . .

So we see a succession of women, beginning with his mother, who offer the promise of comfort but ultimately deliver indifference and emotional pain.

The irony of this defense testimony is found in its confirmation that Berry had a *propensity* to assault wives and lovers under circumstances in which he claimed the woman's infidelity provoked him. Rachel, then, became the recipient of Berry's cumulative rage against *all* the past women in his life. * * * The District Attorney attempted to highlight Blinder's complete reliance on Berry for his clinical assessment of Rachel and Berry's former lovers:

Q: . . . Really, everything that you have [about Rachel] basically is what Mr. Berry tells you about her?

A: . . . Well, let's put it this way, Mr. Winkler. . . . We're looking at a man who's had a series of relationships which have been in the same pattern time after time and which have all ended in much the same way, not perhaps the violent outcome but at least psychologically the same kind of outcome. It would be very surprising if Mr. Berry did any better in this relationship than he did with all the others.

Q: . . . You are basing your opinion that [Berry] had these types of relationships primarily on what Mr. Berry tells you, is that correct . . . ?

A: . . . Well, in part. I think I am basing it primarily on my ability to detect, identify familiar clinical patterns and some of

> the data that Mr. Berry gives me fits into this clinical pattern. . . . When you get a total longitudinal history of this man, *one can almost draw up the nature of his relationships with women* without his telling you a great deal about them.

* * *

Indicia of premeditation of the obsessive, brooding kind characteristic of batterers is clear in *Berry*. Berry himself said in his police statement, "I deliberately waited to kill her. No pretense, no bullshi[t], no nothing." Berry's long wait for Rachel to return home provides further evidence. His two prior assaults on Rachel also suggest premeditation, but the court's failure to understand the escalating, obsessive nature of wife battering prevents its recognition. The opinion relies on Blinder's explanation that the two prior assaults were evidence of Berry's increasingly provoked state. In fact, prior assaults just as easily support a "rehearsal" model or provide evidence of Berry's resort to increasingly dangerous tactics in order to control Rachel. Berry's ambivalence—his uncertainty about whether or not he intended to kill Rachel—and the fact that his two prior assaults of Rachel were similar in kind though not in severity, strongly point to the kind of "locked-in"—"it all depends on what *she* does"—sense of causality that mark the most dangerous of abusive men. Berry's confession evidences this kind of ambivalence. He requests to go back on the record to say, "I knew damn well when I was waiting for her, I'd probably kill her" but at trial testified that when Rachel asked if he'd come to kill her, he first said "yes" then "no" then "yes" again. While Berry admits that he knew he would "*probably* kill her," he also states that his intent was to make her stop screaming: "She come in the door. She started screaming. I told her to shut up. All I wanted to do was talk. She kept screaming at me. I grabbed her and we wrestled . . . and I tried to shut her up. She wouldn't stop screaming. I wrapped the phone cord around her [neck]." * * *

Time and again the court identifies Rachel as the actor and Berry as the one who is acted upon. The violence "results," a brawl is "brought about" by Rachel's behavior, and Berry is therefore "led" to choke her. * * *

* * * Berry portrayed himself, and likely believed himself to be, the real victim. When asked by the police why he didn't just leave Rachel—"[w]hat made you want to take her life first?" he responded:

> I had so much planned in the future, everything. We were going to open up a restaurant when she came back [from Israel]. Had it all planned we were going to move, we were going to get out of that apartment because of bad memories. . . . I never denied her anything. She could have anything—as a matter of fact, when she was in Israel I sent her my last God damn hundred dollars.

This testimony portrays a man who is feeling great disappointment and loss. It also portrays a man wholly captured by his own perspective of reality—unable to imagine what was motivating Rachel. Berry's pain, no doubt, was genuine, but it was not his pain that killed Rachel. * * *

Though Blinder's testimony focused on Rachel's "provocative" sexual behavior, the truth is that Berry didn't kill Rachel until it appeared that she might make good on her threat to leave him. * * * Of course, a defense witness tells it from the perspective of the accused, but in this circumstance, the defendant's perspective is largely that of the Court and that of the Law, as well. That perspective, * * * suggests that a woman's "abandonment" of a husband is provocative—and that a woman's preference of another lover is provocation of the worst sort.

PROVOKED REASON IN MEN AND WOMEN: HEAT-OF-PASSION MANSLAUGHTER AND IMPERFECT SELF-DEFENSE

Laurie J. Taylor
33 UCLA L. Rev. 1679 (1986)

* * * Women are almost always killed by men, often by those with whom they have had an intimate relationship. Therefore, it is not surprising that in heat-of-passion killings of women, the passion often is connected to the victim's sexuality. Many defendants in the early English cases that define voluntary manslaughter were men who had killed their wives or their wives' lovers upon discovering them in the act of adultery. The earliest case specifying that provocation, not revenge, must be the cause of a killing for it to be considered manslaughter involved the prosecution of a defendant for killing his wife's lover. The court ordered that the defendant be burned in the hand and "directed the executioner to burn him gently, because there could not be greater provocation than this." The case that first enumerated the categories of adequate provocation involved a man who killed another man in a quarrel, but the court was especially solicitous of one category: "Jealousy is the rage of a man, and adultery is the highest invasion of property. . . . a man cannot receive a higher provocation." The court lamented that killing the lover was merely partially excused and not justifiable. One writer maintains that "the pre-statutory English law of provocation amounted to little more than a re-statement of the established rule which admitted the defence where one spouse [sic] discovered the other in the act of adultery."

This writer's use of the term "spouse" is misleading: for almost three centuries only husbands could invoke the defense of provocation when they killed after witnessing adultery. While the law sympathized with the jealous rage of men, it assumed that wives did not experience similar rage. In 1946, 275 years after a court first announced the defense of provocation, an English court finally stated that wives who killed their husbands or their husbands' lovers could also avail themselves of the defense.

Adultery evoked a similar response from United States courts. The case some consider the first American use of the reasonable man standard for provocation focused on whether assault with intent to murder after learning of adultery justified a finding of heat of passion. The "honor defense" or "unwritten" law that allowed a court to acquit a defendant entirely when he killed to protect his honor (i.e., his exclusive right to possess the sexuality of his wife and his female relatives) had supporters in the legal community as recently as fifty years ago. Until the 1960s and 1970s, statutes in four states made it justifiable for the husband to kill his wife's lover.[87] * * *

Historically, when a defendant claimed adultery as provocation, courts lessened traditional requirements for adequate provocation. From 1871 to 1946, a line of English cases held that words alone could sufficiently provoke if those words confessed adultery. American courts have held that discovery of a letter revealing completed adultery could sufficiently provoke a defendant, and that learning in other ways of a wife's infidelity sufficed as well. Some courts have even held that killing to prevent adultery justifies acquittal, and that a man coming upon his wife and her lover in the act of adultery can claim self-defense if he kills the lover.

Partially excusing homicide because the discovery of adultery provides adequate provocation effectively sends a message to a defendant that although his act was wrong, he is not entirely blameworthy. Acquitting a defendant who kills to prevent or in reaction to adultery, * * * implies societal approval of the act itself and tells the defendant that there has been no social harm. The quality of the relationship between the defendant and the victim is irrelevant, except that the law recognizes the defense only when the relationship is legal marriage. The law of provocation endorses men's ownership of women's sexuality by expressly sanctioning violent reactions by husbands to their wives' infidelity.

Although the defense of provocation upon the discovery of adultery now applies to women as well as to men, it is a shallow concession to equality that bears little legitimacy or meaning. Cases and social studies show that women rarely react to their husband's infidelity with deadly violence. In contrast, men who kill their wives or lovers frequently act after accusing them of infidelity.

---

87 * * * These states were Georgia, New Mexico, Texas, and Utah. In *Reed v. State*, 123 Tex. Crim. 348, 59 S.W.2d 122 (1933), the court held that a wife who killed a woman committing adultery with her husband was not justified by the Texas statute [even though that statute provided that a husband who killed his wife's lover would be completely justified if he caught them in the act of adultery]. *See also Scroggs v. State*, 94 Ga. App. 28, 93 S.E.2d 583 (1956) (wife killing to prevent adultery is justified, but were she to kill in the heat of passion upon discovering commission of husband's adultery, she would be guilty of manslaughter).

NOTE

Laurie Taylor argues that "[f]emale homicide is so different from male homicide that women and men may be said to live in two different cultures, each with its own 'subculture of violence.'" Laurie J. Taylor, *Provoked Reason in Men and Women: Heat-of-Passion Manslaughter and Imperfect Self-Defense*, 33 UCLA L. REV. 1679, 1681 (1986). Statistics compiled by the United States Bureau of Justice Statistics support Taylor's claim that homicide is highly gendered. First, men commit far more homicides than women in general. For example, in 2008, men were 7 times more likely than females to commit murder.[a] Second, women are significantly more likely than men to be the victims of intimate homicide. In 2008, 45 percent of the female victims of homicide were killed by an intimate partner, whereas only 4.9 percent of the male victims of homicide were killed by an intimate partner.[b]

Finally, although statistics on this point are difficult to find, the data appear to indicate that women are disproportionately the killers of infants and children. *See, e.g.*, Lynne Marie Kohm and Thomas Scott Liverman, *Prom Mom Killers: The Impact of Blame Shift and Distorted Statistics on Punishment for Neonaticide*, 9 WM. & MARY J. WOMEN & L. 43, 53–54 (2002) (according to a study by the Centers for Disease Control, 89 percent of infants killed on the day of their birth were killed by their mothers; according to a report by the Department of Human Health and Services, mothers perpetrate 78 percent of fatal child abuse); *see generally* Michelle Oberman, *Mothers Who Kill: Coming to Terms with Modern American Infanticide*, 34 AM. CRIM. L. REV. 1 (1996). If Taylor's assertion that there are gendered "subcultures of violence" is correct, how should the law respond? If men tend to kill their wives, ex-wives, and girlfriends and women tend to kill their babies and children, what might sex equality require?

Taylor argues that "cumulative rage," as exemplified in *Berry*, should not be recognized as an emotion adequate for mitigation to voluntary manslaughter, but that "cumulative terror" should be, recognizing that many women kill their male partners in response to physical and/or psychological abuse. Is this a fair result? As we will see when we study the doctrine of self-defense, battered women who kill their abusers are not always able to meet the requirements for a valid claim of self-defense. For such women, provocation may be the only defense available to avoid a murder conviction.

3. WHO IS "THE REASONABLE PERSON"

In jurisdictions that follow the common law, a determination that the defendant's homicide should be treated as voluntary manslaughter rather than murder requires a determination that the defendant was reasonably provoked into a heat of passion. Courts often interpret this

[a] U.S. Bureau of Justice Statistics, "Homicide Trends in the U.S., 1980–2008" at 9, *available at* http://www.bjs.gov/content/pub/pdf/htus8008.pdf (last visited October 1, 2013).

[b] U.S. Bureau of Justice Statistics, "Homicide Trends in the U.S., 1980–2008" at 18, *available at* http://www.bjs.gov/content/pub/pdf/htus8008.pdf (last visited October 1, 2013).

reasonableness requirement to mean that a "*reasonable person*" in the defendant's situation would have been provoked to act in the heat of passion. Even the Model Penal Code, which instructs jurors to consider the situation from the point of view of the actor (i.e. defendant), requires jurors to find that the defendant's explanation for his mental or emotional disturbance is a *reasonable* one. Thus reasonableness is a key component of the provocation defense in both common law and Model Penal Code jurisdictions.

The reasonable person test raises several questions. Does a reasonable person ever kill in the heat of passion? Isn't this a contradiction in terms? If so, why are we using the reasonable person as a standard for judging unreasonable behavior? Moreover, who is the reasonable person? Is the reasonable person the average person or the ideal person? Does the reasonable person look like the defendant, and if so to what extent? Does the reasonable person carry all the beliefs and assumptions of her culture, including its prejudices?

One of the classic discussions of the reasonable person rule took place in a 1978 English case, *Director of Public Prosecutions v. Camplin*. The defendant was a 15-year-old boy who killed an older man by splitting his skull with a chapati pan after they had sex, allegedly against the boy's will, subsequent to which the victim laughed at him. At trial, the defense suggested to the jury that they should take his age into account and judge his actions by the standard of a reasonable 15-year-old boy. The trial judge rejected this idea and instructed the jury to judge Camplin by the standard of a reasonable adult. Camplin was found guilty of murder.

The question certified for appeal to the House of Lords was whether the standard should have been that of the reasonable adult or a reasonable boy. The Lords wrote several opinions. Lord Diplock suggested that "the public policy that underlay the adoption of the 'reasonable man' test in the common law doctrine of provocation was to reduce the incidence of fatal violence by preventing a person relying on his own exceptional pugnacity or excitability as an excuse for loss of self control." Lord Simon added that "it would be unjust that the drunk man or one exceptionally pugnacious or bad-tempered or over-sensitive should be able to claim that these matters rendered him peculiarly susceptible to the provocation offered, where the sober and even-tempered man would hang for his homicide." The Lords appeared to agree, in light of these considerations, that the reasonable person is "[a]n ordinary person of either sex, not exceptionally excitable or pugnacious, but possessed of such powers of self-control as everyone is entitled to expect that his fellow citizens will exercise in society as it is today." Furthermore, the Lords held that the trial judge erred in instructing the jury to hold the 15-year-old defendant to the standard of an adult man; rather, "the reasonable man referred to in the [standard] is a person having the power of self-control to be expected of an ordinary person of the ... age of the [defendant]...."

The common law thus seems to draw a line between physical or demographic characteristics that might be pertinent to the gravity of the provocation and the defendant's reaction to it, and characteristics pertaining purely to the defendant's powers of judgment or self-control, such as drunkenness or ill-temper. In its application, however, the operation of the reasonable person standard has been less than clear. This is particularly true with respects to situations that inflame some people but not others in the same society. Consider the following excerpts by Robert Mison and Joshua Dressler on the reasonable person in a society where men and boys equate masculine identity with not being gay. *See* Angela P. Harris, *Gender, Violence, Race and Criminal Justice*, 52 STAN. L. REV. 777 (2000) (noting that masculine identity in the United States is tied to not being a woman and not being gay).

The Mison and Dressler excerpts on what used to be called the "non-violent homosexual advance defense," a.k.a. the "gay panic defense," are particularly noteworthy in light of the killing of Larry King, a gender-non-conforming fifteen-year-old who was shot in the back of his head in Oxnard, California on February 12, 2008 by his fourteen-year-old classmate Brandon McInerney. King started wearing makeup and high heel stiletto shoes to school in the weeks before he was killed. A few days before he was killed, King allegedly asked McInerney in front of McInerney's friends whether McInerney would be his Valentine. One day before the killing, King and McInerney passed each other in the hallway at school, and King allegedly said something like, "What's up, baby?" to McInerney. After this incident, McInerney told one of King's friends to say farewell to King because she would never see him again. The next day, McInerney brought a loaded gun concealed in his backpack to school. McInerney went to the computer lab, walked up behind King, and shot him twice in the back of the head before walking out of the room. At trial, McInerney claimed that King's sexually flirtatious and deviant behavior provoked him into a heat of passion. McInerney claimed that when he heard King telling a female classmate that he was going to change his name from Larry to Leticia, he snapped and lost his self-control. The jury deadlocked, with seven in favor of finding McInerney guilty of voluntary manslaughter and five in favor of finding him guilty of murder. McInerney ultimately pled guilty to second degree murder and voluntary manslaughter, and was sentenced to 21 years in prison.

HOMOPHOBIA IN MANSLAUGHTER: THE HOMOSEXUAL ADVANCE AS INSUFFICIENT PROVOCATION

Robert B. Mison
80 Cal. L. Rev. 133 (1992)[a]

INTRODUCTION

The question is simple: Should a nonviolent sexual advance in and of itself constitute sufficient provocation to incite a reasonable man to lose his self-control and kill in the heat of passion? If so, the defendant will be guilty of voluntary manslaughter, not murder. This sexual-advance defense could be used by a male or a female who claims that he or she killed in reaction to the victim's sexual advance. As the law now stands, however, only a homosexual advance can mitigate murder to manslaughter.

Consider the following story[5] in which the defendant successfully raised the homosexual-advance defense to mitigate his crime. A young man is out drinking heavily with his friends. His car breaks down and he hitches a ride from another man, the victim. Together they drive around looking for women for sex. After a while, the young man asks, "Where can I get a blow job?" The victim-to-be responds, "I can handle that." They continue to drive around, stopping at a convenience store for some cigarettes before going to a baseball field at a local school. They wander into the shadows where the victim pulls down his pants and underwear and attempts to embrace the young man. But the young man kicks him, stomps on him, takes his money, and leaves the victim to die on the isolated field. Before leaving the scene, the young man returns to the victim's car and carefully wipes it clean of his fingerprints.

At his trial, the young man claims that the victim's homosexual overture provoked him to lose his self-control and kill. He took the money and wiped his fingerprints from the car only as an afterthought. Defense counsel argues that a reasonable jury could find the victim's homosexual advance sufficient provocation for the defendant's acts and requests the judge to instruct the jury on the lesser included offense of voluntary manslaughter. The prosecution does not object. The judge, satisfied that a reasonable jury could find the victim's sexual advance adequate provocation, permits defense counsel to argue provocation and agrees to instruct the jury on voluntary manslaughter. The jury finds the young man guilty—of voluntary manslaughter.

So unfolds a homosexual-advance case. Regardless of the ultimate verdict, allowing the defense to argue provocation and instructing the jury on the reduced charge of voluntary manslaughter in cases such as

---

[5] This story is a retelling of *Schick v. State,* 570 N.E.2d 918, 921–22 (Ind. Ct. App. 1991).

the foregoing is both immoral and inconsistent with the goals of modern criminal jurisprudence. Although the sufficiency of provocation is normally a question for the fact finder, judges may decide as a matter of law that no rational jury could find an alleged homosexual advance sufficient provocation to kill. With few exceptions, however, trial courts have permitted juries to make that decision as a matter of fact. The continued use and acceptance of this defense sends a message to juries and the public that if someone makes a homosexual overture, such an advance may be sufficient provocation to kill that person. This reinforces both the notions that gay men are to be afforded less respect than heterosexual men, and that revulsion and hostility are natural reactions to homosexual behavior. * * *

WHEN "HETEROSEXUAL" MEN KILL "HOMOSEXUAL" MEN: REFLECTIONS ON PROVOCATION LAW, SEXUAL ADVANCES, AND THE "REASONABLE MAN" STANDARD

Joshua Dressler
85 J. Crim. L. & Criminology 726 (1995)[a]

* * * In a recent article, Robert Mison asked the following "simple" question: "Should a nonviolent homosexual advance in and of itself constitute sufficient provocation to incite a reasonable man to lose his self-control and kill in the heat of passion" and, as a consequence, be convicted of manslaughter, rather than murder? Mison's answer was that it should not. Although trial courts almost always instruct juries on the provocation defense in homosexual-advance cases, Mison concluded that "judges should hold, as a matter of law, that a homosexual advance alone is not sufficient provocation to incite a 'reasonable man' to kill." * * *

As Mison claims, discrimination against gay men and lesbians is a serious legal problem, in part due to public (and judicial) ignorance regarding homosexuals and homosexuality. Nonetheless, Mison fails to make the case for a blanket rejection of the provocation defense in NHA [non-violent homosexual advance] prosecutions. One reason he fails is that he oversimplifies the motivations underlying the violence perpetrated in such cases. The primary reason he fails, however, is that he misapprehends the rationale of the provocation defense and the character of the Reasonable Man in provocation law. * * *

Mison * * * errs in his description of the Reasonable Man who should serve as the objective standard in heat-of-passion cases. Mison writes:

> The reasonable man is an ideal, reflecting the standard to which society wants its citizens and system of justice to aspire. It is an "entity whose life is said to be the public embodiment of rational

[a] Reprinted by special permission of Northwestern University School of Law, *Journal of Criminal Law and Criminology*.

behavior." If the reasonable man is the embodiment of both rational behavior and the idealized citizen, a killing based simply on a homosexual advance reflects neither rational nor exemplary behavior. The argument is not that the ordinary person would not be provoked by a homosexual advance, but rather that a reasonable person should not be provoked to kill by such an advance.

* * *

In the provocation area, the law does not deal with an idealized human being, because an ideal Reasonable Man, by definition, would never become angry enough that he would lose his self-control and kill solely on the basis of passion, rather than reason. Instead, the provocation defense is based on the principle that the defendant is, unfortunately, just like other ordinary human beings. That is why the defense represents a "concession to human weakness."

The Reasonable Man in the context of provocation law, therefore, is more appropriately described as the Ordinary Man (i.e., a person who possesses ordinary human weaknesses). There is more to be said on this subject, but it is sufficient for immediate purposes to emphasize that the Ordinary Man is someone far less praiseworthy than the Reasonable Man that Mison has in mind. * * *

Mison would probably argue that the law is wrong to justify or even to excuse homophobic-based anger; therefore, the actor's out-of-control reaction is wholly unjustifiable and inexcusable. But this argument goes too far. It is not necessarily the case that a person who kills after a NHA does so as the result of intolerance, bigotry, or homophobia.

It is true, of course, that a person who responds to a homosexual advance acts with knowledge of the provoker's sexual orientation, but the victim's status as a homosexual is not necessarily a motivation for the killing. Consider, again, the NHA cases that have found their way to the appellate courts. Most men—including non-homophobic heterosexuals and gay men—would justifiably become indignant if a stranger nonconsensually touched their genitals, fondled their buttocks, or committed a sexual act upon them while they slept. Certainly a woman would become outraged if a man touched her breasts, patted her on the buttocks, or had sexual relations with her while she was asleep. In such circumstances, no one would characterize her indignant response as heterophobic or anti-male in nature. And although a woman in such circumstances would probably not become angry enough to kill in response to the male's conduct (whereas a man might kill in a similar case of a homosexual advance), this difference in response is not necessarily the result of the man's homophobia and the woman's nonheterophobia. Instead, the difference may be that he is a he and she is a she.

The point is that an unwanted sexual advance is a basis for justifiable indignation. The reason it is far more likely that a man would kill under such circumstances than a woman, is that women rarely kill when provoked, but men frequently do. As noted, the provocation defense partially excuses what is primarily male behavior. However, heterosexual and homosexual advance cases are alike in certain key regards: (1) indignation in response to a violation of one's sexual privacy or autonomy is justifiable; (2) anger, one possible manifestation of such indignation, is justifiable or excusable; (3) any resulting killing is wholly unjustifiable; but (4) if the invasion of privacy is significant, ordinary, fallible human beings might become so upset that their out-of-control reaction deserves mitigated punishment. Thus, in short, there is a valid, non-homophobic basis for recognizing a partial excuse in many sexual-advance cases.

This is not meant to suggest that a heterosexual man on the receiving end of a homosexual advance is responding to the violation of his sexual privacy in a sexual-orientation-neutral way. While a sexual advance may be unwanted because the recipient does not have a sexual interest in the particular individual who is acting aggressively, if the sexual advance is homosexual in nature, and the recipient of the advance is exclusively heterosexual, the fact that the advance is homosexual in character will be a reason for the recipient's angry reaction.

Nor is this meant to suggest that the displeasure with which the heterosexual recipient reacts—enough anger that he might ultimately lose self-control—is not often aggravated by the fact that, for some men, the thought of participating in a homosexual act is physically (as distinguished from morally) repulsive. Human sexual desires are profoundly complicated and inherently personal. Consequentially, a person's distaste for a particular type of sexual act is, in a significant sense, a natural reaction of that person. Unless one assumes that people freely choose their sexual orientation and freely decide which sexual acts will give them pleasure, it is impossible to fairly condemn those heterosexual or homosexual males or females who find some sexual acts—including some sexual activities with persons of their own orientation—extremely distasteful and, therefore, emotionally upsetting.

A heterosexual person's repulsion at the thought of participating in a homosexual act is not always evidence of homophobia. A person may find homosexual conduct distasteful, but not hate homosexuals or want harm to befall them in their personal lives. Indeed, few human actions, especially those related to sexual feelings, are the result of a single motive or emotional strain. When a woman is angered because a man touches her against her will, her emotions may have multiple explanations: anger at the invasion of her sexual privacy; hatred of such "piggish" behavior; fear of another, perhaps greater, invasion of her autonomy. All that the law realistically can do in NHA cases is measure the actor's response—which might, but need not, have homophobic qualities to it—against the standard of the Ordinary Man in the actor's situation. * * *

NOTE

How can the criminal law respond to the concerns raised by Mison and Dressler? On August 12, 2013, the House of Delegates of the American Bar Association (ABA) unanimously passed a resolution to curtail the availability and effectiveness of gay panic and trans panic defenses. Gay panic refers to the nonviolent homosexual advance defense strategy discussed above. Trans panic refers to a similar defense strategy wherein a man charged with murdering a transgender woman claims he was provoked into a heat of passion upon discovering that an individual with whom he had engaged in sexual relations was biologically male, not female. *See* Cynthia Lee, *The Gay Panic Defense*, 42 U.C. DAVIS L. REV. 471, 513–517 (2008). The ABA Resolution urges federal, state, local and territorial governments to take the following legislative action:

> (a) Requiring courts in any criminal trial or proceeding, upon the request of a party, to instruct the jury not to let bias, sympathy, prejudice, or public opinion influence its decision about the victims, witnesses, or defendants based upon sexual orientation or gender identity, and
>
> (b) Specifying that neither a nonviolent sexual advance, nor the discovery of a person's sex or gender identity, constitutes legally adequate provocation to mitigate the severity of any non-capital crime.

See ABA Res. 113A (2013), *available at* http://www.americanbar.org/content/dam/aba/directories/policy/2013_hod_annual_meeting_113A.docx (last visited September 4, 2013).

Is categorical preclusion of a defense argument—even an argument that many find obnoxious—a good idea? Which institutional actor (legislature, judge, or jury) is the most appropriate body to decide whether the defendant has been provoked into a heat of passion by legally adequate provocation?

COMMONWEALTH V. CARR

Superior Court of Pennsylvania
398 Pa.Super. 306, 580 A.2d 1362 (1990)

WIEAND, J.

In this appeal from a sentence of life imprisonment imposed for murder of the first degree, the principal issue is whether the trial court erred when it disallowed evidence of the defendant's psychosexual history to show the likelihood of a killing in the heat of passion aroused by defendant's observation of two women engaged in homosexual lovemaking.

On May 13, 1988, Claudia Brenner and Rebecca Wight were hiking along the Appalachian Trail in Adams County, when they found an appropriate campsite and stopped for the night. There, they were resting and engaging in lesbian lovemaking when Claudia Brenner was shot in the right arm. After a short pause, additional shots were fired, as a result of which Brenner was struck four additional times in and about her face, neck and head. Rebecca Wight ran for cover behind a tree and was shot in the head and back. Brenner attempted to help Wight, who was unable to walk, but was unable to rouse her. Brenner thereupon went for help, but by the time help arrived, Wight was dead. Suspicion subsequently focused on Stephen Roy Carr. He was arrested and taken into custody on a fugitive warrant from the State of Florida and made statements which incriminated himself in the shooting. He was subsequently tried non-jury before the Honorable Oscar Spicer and found guilty of murder in the first degree.

Carr defended at trial on grounds, inter alia, that he had shot Brenner and Wight in the heat of passion caused by the serious provocation of their nude homosexual love-making. In support of this defense and to show the existence of passion, Carr offered to show a history of constant rejection by women, including his mother who may have been involved in a lesbian relationship, sexual abuse while in prison in Florida, inability to hold a job, and retreat to the mountains to avoid further rejection. This was relevant, he contended, to show that he was impassioned when provoked by the "show" put on by the women, including their nakedness,[a] their hugging and kissing and their oral sex. The trial court refused to allow evidence of Carr's psychosexual history, finding it irrelevant.

The crime of voluntary manslaughter is defined by the Pennsylvania Crimes Code as follows:

> A person who kills an individual without lawful justification commits voluntary manslaughter if at the time of the killing he is acting under a sudden and intense passion resulting from serious provocation. . . .

In *Commonwealth v. Copeland,* the Court said:

> The passion which will reduce an unlawful killing to voluntary manslaughter must be caused by legally adequate provocation.

[a] In *Eight Bullets: One Woman's Story of Surviving Anti–Gay Violence*, Claudia Brenner explains that she was partially dressed and Rebecca was fully dressed when the shooting happened.

The test for determining the existence of legally adequate provocation is an objective test.

In making the objective determination as to what constitutes sufficient provocation reliance may be placed upon the cumulative impact of a series of related events. The ultimate test for adequate provocation remains whether a reasonable man, confronted with this series of events, [would have become] impassioned to the extent that his mind was "incapable of cool reflection." * * *

If sufficient provocation exists, the fact finder must also determine whether the defendant actually acted in the heat of passion when he committed the homicide and thus whether the provocation led directly to the killing or whether there was sufficient "cooling" period so that a reasonable man would have regained his capacity to reflect.

The sight of naked women engaged in lesbian lovemaking is not adequate provocation to reduce an unlawful killing from murder to voluntary manslaughter. It is not an event which is sufficient to cause a reasonable person to become so impassioned as to be incapable of cool reflection. A reasonable person would simply have discontinued his observation and left the scene; he would not kill the lovers. Whatever a person's views about homosexuality, the law does not condone or excuse the killing of homosexuals any more than it condones the killing of heterosexuals. Similarly, it does not recognize homosexual activity between two persons as legal provocation sufficient to reduce an unlawful killing of one or both of the actors by a third person from murder to voluntary manslaughter.

A trial court must make an initial determination whether sufficient evidence has been presented of serious provocation. In the instant case, the judge was both court and jury. Appellant was permitted to show the nature of the activities in which his victims were engaged when he came upon them in the woods. "In a provocation defense, the actions of the victim establishing provocation are relevant. Those are the victim's actions on the [day] in question because the provocation must lead *directly* to the killing." After it had been determined that these activities were inadequate to provoke a heat of passion response, however, appellant's rejection by women and his mother's sexual preference were irrelevant. Appellant's history of misfortunes are not events which are in any way related to the events which he claims provoked him on May 13, 1988. An accused cannot, by recalling some past injury or insult, establish a foundation for a manslaughter verdict. The trial court did not err when it excluded evidence of appellant's psychosexual history. * * *

The judgment of sentence is affirmed.

4. THE MODEL PENAL CODE'S EXTREME MENTAL OR EMOTIONAL DISTURBANCE TEST

The Model Penal Code's provocation doctrine is found in § 210.3(1)(b), which permits a homicide that would otherwise be murder to be considered manslaughter when it is committed "under the influence of extreme mental or emotional disturbance for which there is reasonable explanation and excuse." This provision further provides that "The reasonableness of such explanation or excuse shall be determined from the viewpoint of a person in the actor's situation under the circumstances as he believes them to be." The MPC approach, therefore, appears much more "subjective" than the common law approach.

When you read *State v. Dumlao*, think about how the Model Penal Code's approach to provocation differs from both the early common law approach and the modern test for provocation. Is the Model Penal Code approach an improvement on these other approaches? How would *Berry* and *Ambro* be decided under the MPC?

STATE V. DUMLAO

Intermediate Court of Appeals of Hawaii
6 Haw.App. 173, 715 P.2d 822 (1986)

HEEN, J.

Defendant Vidado B. Dumlao (Dumlao) appeals from his conviction of murder. He argues on appeal that the trial court erred in refusing to give his requested manslaughter instruction. Relying on *State v. O'Daniel,* he contends there was sufficient evidence that he shot his mother-in-law, Pacita M. Reyes (Pacita), while "under the influence of extreme mental or emotional disturbance for which there [was] a reasonable explanation" to support an instruction under HRS § 707–702(2) (1976).[2] We agree and reverse. * * *

Since HRS § 707–702(2) is derived from MPC § 210.3,[9] we may look to the commentaries and cases from other jurisdictions explaining and

---

[2] HRS § 707–702(2) reads as follows:

Manslaughter. * * *

(2) In a prosecution for murder it is a defense, which reduces the offense to manslaughter, that the defendant was, at the time he caused the death of the other person, under the influence of extreme mental or emotional disturbance for which there is a reasonable explanation. The reasonableness of the explanation shall be determined from the view-point of a person in the defendant's situation under the circumstances as he believed them to be. * * *

[9] Section 210.3 states in pertinent part as follows:

Manslaughter

(1) Criminal homicide constitutes manslaughter when:

* * *

(b) a homicide which would otherwise be murder is committed under the influence of extreme mental or emotional disturbance for which there is reasonable explanation construing that section for insight into the meaning of the language of our statute. We will examine the first element of § 707–702 first.

A.

"Extreme mental or emotional disturbance" sometimes is, but should not be, confused with the "insanity" defense. The point of the extreme emotional disturbance defense is to provide a basis for mitigation that differs from a finding of mental defect or disease precluding criminal responsibility. The disturbance was meant to be understood in relative terms as referring to a loss of self-control due to intense feelings. * * *

An explanation of the term "extreme emotional disturbance" which reflects the situational or relative character of the concept was given in *People v. Shelton,* as follows:

> [T]hat extreme emotional disturbance is the emotional state of an individual, who: (a) has no mental disease or defect that rises to the level established by Section 30.05 of the Penal Law; and (b) is exposed to an extremely unusual and overwhelming stress;[a] and (c) has an extreme emotional reaction to it, as a result of which there is a loss of self-control and reason is overborne by intense feelings, such as passion, anger, distress, grief, excessive agitation or other similar emotions.[12]

It is clear that in adopting the "extreme mental or emotional disturbance" concept, the MPC intended to define the provocation element of manslaughter in broader terms than had previously been

---

> or excuse. The reasonableness of such explanation or excuse shall be determined from the viewpoint of a person in the actor's situation under the circumstances as he believes them to be.

[a] In *State v. Seguritan*, the Hawaii Supreme Court held that it was reversible error to instruct the jury that EMED manslaughter requires that the defendant "be exposed to an extremely unusual and overwhelming stress" because this language does not appear in the statute and focuses on the quality of the stress rather than on the defendant's reaction. 70 Haw. 173, 174 (1988). The remainder of *Dumlao*'s analysis of EMED manslaughter remains good law.

[12] The extreme emotional disturbance defense is also broader than the heat of passion doctrine which it replaced, in that a cooling off period intervening between the fatal act and the disturbance does not negate the defense. "A spontaneous explosion is not required." Rather, "a significant mental trauma" could have "affected a defendant's mind for a substantial period of time, simmering in the unknown subconscious and then inexplicably coming to the fore."

The drafters of the Model Penal Code (MPC) found it "shocking" that the common law disregarded the fact that the passage of time sometimes served only to increase rather than diminish outrage. MPC § 201.3 at 48, Comments (Tent. Draft No. 9, 1959). They said:

> Though it is difficult to state a middle ground between a standard which ignores all individual peculiarities and one which makes emotional distress decisive regardless of the nature of its cause, we think that such a statement is essential. For surely if the actor had just suffered a traumatic injury, if he were blind or were distraught with grief, if he were experiencing an unanticipated reaction to a therapeutic drug, it would be deemed atrocious to appraise his crime for purposes of sentence without reference to any of these matters. They are material because they bear upon the inference as to the actor's character that it is fair to draw upon the basis of his act. So too . . . where lapse of time increased rather than diminished the extent of the outrage perpetrated on the actor, . . . it was shocking in our view to hold this vital fact to be irrelevant.

done. It is equally clear that our legislature also intended the same result when it adopted the language of the MPC.

We turn then to the second prong of our analysis, the test to determine the reasonableness of the explanation for the mental or emotional disturbance. It is here that the most significant change has been made in the law of manslaughter.

B.

The anomaly of the reasonable person test was corrected by the drafters of the MPC through the development of an objective/subjective test of reasonableness. Dressler explains that,

> [I]t makes the test more, although not entirely, subjective, by requiring the jury to test the reasonableness of the actor's conduct, "from the viewpoint of a person in the actor's situation." Thus, the actor's sex, sexual preference, pregnancy, physical deformities, and similar characteristics are apt to be taken into consideration in evaluating the reasonableness of the defendant's behavior.

This more subjective version of the provocation defense goes substantially beyond the common law by abandoning preconceptions of what constitutes adequate provocation, and giving the jury wider scope.

Under the prior law of provocation, personal characteristics of the defendant were not to be considered. Under the MPC a change from the old provocation law and the reasonable person standard has been effected by requiring the factfinder to focus on a person in the defendant's situation. Thus, the MPC, while requiring that the explanation for the disturbance must be reasonable, provides that the reasonableness is determined from the defendant's viewpoint. The phrase "actor's situation," as used in § 210.3(b) of the MPC, is designedly ambiguous and is plainly flexible enough to allow the law to grow in the direction of taking account of mental abnormalities that have been recognized in the developing law of diminished responsibility.

Moreover, the MPC does not require the provocation to emanate from the victim as was argued by the State here.

In light of the foregoing discussion and the necessity of articulating the defense in comprehensible terms, we adopt the test enunciated by the New York Court of Appeals in *People v. Casassa:*

> [W]e conclude that the determination whether there was reasonable explanation or excuse for a particular emotional disturbance should be made by viewing the subjective, internal situation in which the defendant found himself and the external circumstances as he perceived them at the time, however inaccurate that perception may have been, and assessing from

that standpoint whether the explanation . . . for his emotional disturbance was reasonable, so as to entitle him to a reduction of the crime charged from murder . . . to manslaughter. . . .

The language of HRS § 707–702(2) indicates that the legislature intended to effect the same change in the test for manslaughter in Hawaii's law as was made by the MPC. Therefore, we hold that under HRS § 707–702(2) the broader sweep of the emotional disturbance defense applies when considering whether an offense should be reduced from murder to manslaughter. To hold that the pre-penal code law of provocation continues to hold sway would be to render the language of § 707–702(2) meaningless.

Thus, we hold in the instant case that the trial court was required to instruct the jury as requested by Dumlao, if there was any evidence to support a finding that at the time of the offense he suffered an "extreme mental or emotional disturbance" for which there was a "reasonable explanation" when the totality of circumstances was judged from his personal viewpoint.

We turn now to the question of whether there was evidence to support the proffered instruction.

II.

In the instant case, there was evidence of the following:

Arthur Golden, M.D., Dumlao's expert witness, stated at trial that his diagnosis of Dumlao was one of "paranoid personality disorder," which is a "long range, almost lifetime or certainly over many, many years, emotional or mental disorder. It is almost a way of functioning."

Dr. Golden diagnosed Dumlao as having unwarranted suspiciousness, one of the basic indicators of the "paranoid personality disorder." That unwarranted suspiciousness included pathological jealousy, which Dumlao suffered throughout his ten-year marriage. Dumlao harbored the belief that other males, including his wife's relatives, were somehow sexually involved with her. He could never figure out exactly who or where or how, yet this extreme suspiciousness persisted.

Dr. Golden described the second major sign of Dumlao's paranoid personality disorder as hypersensitivity, characterized by being easily slighted or quick to take offense, and a readiness to counterattack when a threat was perceived. For example, when somebody glanced or gazed at his wife, he would consider it a personal affront and could well believe that a sexual overture had been made to her. Dr. Golden believed that at the time of the offense Dumlao felt the need to counterattack because Dumlao perceived a very substantial threat. Dr. Golden stated that "[p]erhaps an ordinary individual in his situation would not have. He did."

Dr. Golden gave other examples from Dumlao's history, illustrating his extreme and irrational reactions to outwardly normal events.

Dr. Golden's observations were supported by the testimony of the State's witnesses Eduardo, Agapito and Pedrito Reyes, his brothers-in-law, as well as Florentina, his wife, and Gaudencio Dumlao, his father. For example, according to Florentina, during their entire marriage Dumlao's extreme jealousy had caused him to beat and kick her, throw a knife at her, [and] threaten her with his gun. He threatened on numerous occasions to beat or kill her. Dumlao accused her of having sexual relations with her brothers. Moreover, he would get angry for no more reason than that she might be behind some man in the checkout line at the store, and Dumlao would conclude that she was "talking to him or whatever, like that" and become jealous.

Dumlao's extreme and irrational jealousy concerning his wife was known to all the family members. According to Agapito, they couldn't even talk to their sister in Dumlao's presence. "If we have to talk to her, we have to talk from a distance because he suspects us." Furthermore, Dumlao "never allowed us to talk in a group."

Dumlao's testimony, describing his own perceptions of the night in question, further confirms the nature of his extreme jealousy. Dumlao described how he became suspicious and jealous of his wife that night because of the way that Agapito looked at him:

> A. I had this feeling that something going to happen when I leave because the action that I seen—Agapito.
>
> Q. What action? * * *
>
> A. He look at me on, the kine. He make sure—he make sure that—I don't know, making sure if I stay—if I leave the house or I don't know so I got the bad feeling so I never leave. * * *
>
> Q. Why did you have this feeling that he would go into your wife's bedroom?
>
> A. Jealousy arose. * * *
>
> Q. What did you do? Did you do anything after you went back to your bedroom?
>
> A. I wake up my wife, questioned her. * * *
>
> A. If he—if she had something to do with my brother-in-law, Agapito.
>
> Q. What do you mean, had something to do with your brother-in-law, Agapito? * * *

A. Sexual relation. * * *

Q. What happened after you insisted on her answering you?

A. She got up so I lay down—I laid down on the bedroom so I—I kick or push her on the side over there.

Dumlao went on to describe how, after his father had counseled him and he went back in the room, he could hear the voices of the others talking in the living room. He thought that they were talking about him. He then came out to "investigate" with his gun in his waistband. He saw "Pedrito with his eyes at me, burning eye, angry eye, angry," and he saw Eduardo and Agapito alongside Pedrito. Dumlao testified that Pedrito rushed at him holding a knife in his hand, saying, "My sister suffer ten years. You going to pay. Now you going to pay." He testified that when he pulled his gun to "try and scare [Pedrito]," the gun went off, firing the bullet that struck and killed Pacita.

CONCLUSION

Reviewing the evidence within the context of the meaning of HRS § 707–702(2), we conclude that it was sufficient to require the trial court to give Dumlao's requested instruction on manslaughter. There was evidence, "no matter how weak, inconclusive or unsatisfactory," that Dumlao killed Pacita while under the influence of "extreme emotional disturbance." Whether a jury will agree that there was such a disturbance or that the explanation for it was reasonable we cannot say. However, Dumlao was entitled to have the jury make that decision using the objective/subjective test.

The fact that the other witnesses contradicted his testimony concerning an attack by Pedrito, and that his testimony that he was only trying to scare Pedrito does not comport with the manslaughter defense, does not detract from Dumlao's right to the instruction based on the above evidence. Dumlao was entitled to an instruction on every theory of defense shown by the evidence. It was the jury's province to determine the weight and credibility of that evidence.

Reversed and remanded for new trial.

NOTE

Victoria Nourse undertook a study of intimate murder cases involving claims of provocation to see what kinds of claims were being deemed legally adequate by judges. Nourse found that in Model Penal Code jurisdictions (which Nourse calls "reform jurisdictions"), a frequent factual scenario in the intimate murder cases in which a male defendant was allowed to argue provocation to the jury involved departure, attempted separation, or rejection by the female partner. In many of these cases, the fatal violence that resulted in the female partner's death was preceded by her act of filing for divorce, attempting to end a casual dating relationship, breaking off an engagement, or trying to enforce a protective stay away order. Nourse reports:

> Departure is not an official category in the law of murder, but it is a frequent factual scenario in intimate murder cases in reform jurisdictions. In my study, over one-quarter of the MPC claims (twenty-six percent) that reached juries involved what I classify as a departure. By contrast, in common law jurisdictions, no departure claim in this category reached a jury. In none of these departure claims did the court report that the defendant acted because the victim was having an affair. In each, there was evidence that the "provoking" party sought to leave the relationship and that the parties' relationship was over, ending, or about to end. In all but one case, the provoking party was a woman. * * *
>
> The MPC asks juries to consider the defendant's "situation," and sometimes those situations include not only the defendant's perception of the situation but also his perception of the equities of the situation. For example, the defendant in [a case summarized earlier] came from his girlfriend's home to kill his wife, who wanted a divorce. If the law asks us to adopt the defendant's perspective, we must put on the shoes of one who is himself unfaithful to a relationship. Or consider the defendant in the *Perry* case. In that case, the defendant became enraged when a sheriff sought to execute a court order requiring him to leave his house. If we must adopt the defendant's perspective, we must put on the shoes of one claiming that a lawful court order (obtained upon representations that the defendant had refused to leave the home and was feared by his wife) entitled him to our compassion. In both of these cases, * * * juries were permitted by law to conclude that manslaughter was the appropriate verdict based on an EED theory. That the triers of fact in these cases returned murder verdicts does not diminish the fact that the law permitted these cases to come out quite differently, allowing defendants with essentially "unclean hands" to claim the law's leniency.

Victoria Nourse, *Passion's Progress: Modern Law Reform and the Provocation Defense*, 106 YALE L.J. 1331, 1354–55 (1997). Do these findings suggest that the MPC was a step backward rather than a step forward for women?

Just because a defendant is permitted to assert a defense does not mean the jury will agree to mitigate the charges. *See* Stuart M. Kirschner, et al., *The Defense of Extreme Emotional Disturbance: A Qualitative Analysis of Cases in New York County*, 10 PSYCH., PUBLIC POL'Y & L. 102 (2004) (finding that two-thirds of the *unsuccessful* claims of extreme emotional disturbance in New York County over a ten year period between 1988 to 1997 were by men who had killed their wives, girlfriends, former wives, former girlfriends, or fiancées).

Some states, such as Maryland, have attempted a compromise reform. Rather than completely abolishing the doctrine of provocation, Maryland bars the use of the provocation defense when a person kills in response to discovering his or her spouse in the act of adultery. Are categorical exclusions (like the Maryland statute reprinted below) a good idea? If the legislature creates a categorical exclusion for spousal adultery, might this open the door to the legislature creating other categorical exclusions, narrowing the types of cases for which a defendant can claim provocation? Is a categorical exclusion sufficiently attentive to context? Does it allow the jury to adequately consider the particular facts and circumstances of the individual defendant's case?

MARYLAND CRIMINAL LAW CODE § 2–207

Md. Code Ann., Crim. Law § 2–207

§ 2–207. Manslaughter

(b) Spousal adultery not a mitigating factor.—The discovery of one's spouse engaged in sexual intercourse with another does not constitute legally adequate provocation for the purpose of mitigating a killing from the crime of murder to voluntary manslaughter even though the killing was provoked by that discovery.

E. DEPRAVED HEART MURDER

When an individual acts with an intent to kill another human being, that individual is said to have acted with "express malice." Malice may be implied where the defendant intended to commit grievous bodily injury or killed during the commission or attempted commission of a qualifying felony. Malice is also implied when the individual who kills acts with "an abandoned and malignant heart." This type of murder is called depraved heart murder and is usually treated as murder in the second degree.

How does the prosecutor go about proving an abandoned and malignant heart? Although different jurisdictions have different names for this concept—"depraved heart," "abandoned and malignant heart," "wantonness," "extreme indifference to human life"—the common law approach has been fairly well settled. Malice will be implied in a homicide case if it can be shown that the defendant acted with gross recklessness and manifested an extreme indifference to human life, meaning that the defendant realized that his actions created a substantial and unjustified risk of death and yet went ahead and committed the actions anyway. It is important to distinguish this kind of unintentional killing from a death that follows from the defendant's grossly negligent or even reckless behavior. Homicides that involve a "depraved heart" shown by gross recklessness can be punished as second-degree murder. Unintentional killings that involve simple recklessness or gross negligence generally can only be punished as involuntary manslaughter. The following cases explore the ways courts and juries distinguish between those they believe are so morally blameworthy that they deserve a murder conviction and those they believe are less culpable, and therefore should be found guilty of involuntary manslaughter.

COMMONWEALTH V. MALONE

Supreme Court of Pennsylvania
354 Pa. 180, 47 A.2d 445 (1946)

MAXEY, CHIEF JUSTICE.

This is an appeal from the judgment and sentence under a conviction of murder in the second degree. William H. Long, age 13 years, was killed by a shot from a 32-caliber revolver held against his right side by the defendant, then aged 17 years. These youths were on friendly terms at the time of the homicide. The defendant and his mother, while his father and brother were in the U. S. Armed Forces, were residing in Lancaster, Pa., with the family of William H. Long, whose son was the victim of the shooting.

On the evening of February 26th, 1945, when the defendant went to a moving picture theater, he carried in the pocket of his raincoat a revolver which he had obtained at the home of his uncle on the preceding day. In the afternoon preceding the shooting, the decedent procured a cartridge from his father's room and he and the defendant placed it in the revolver.

After leaving the theater, the defendant went to a dairy store and there met the decedent. Both youths sat in the rear of the store ten minutes, during which period the defendant took the gun out of his pocket and loaded the chamber to the right of the firing pin and then closed the gun. A few minutes later, both youths sat on stools in front of the lunch counter and ate some food. The defendant suggested to the decedent that they play 'Russian Poker.'[1] Long replied; 'I don't care; go ahead.' The defendant then placed the revolver against the right side of Long and pulled the trigger three times. The third pull resulted in a fatal wound to Long. The latter jumped off the stool and cried: 'Oh! Oh! Oh!' and Malone said: 'Did I hit you, Billy? Gee, Kid, I'm sorry.' Long died from the wounds two days later.

The defendant testified that the gun chamber he loaded was the first one to the right of the firing chamber and that when he pulled the trigger he did not 'expect to have the gun go off.' He declared he had no intention of harming Long, who was his friend and companion. The defendant was indicted for murder, tried and found guilty of murder in the second degree and sentenced to a term in the penitentiary for a period not less than five

[1] It has been explained that 'Russian Poker' is a game in which the participants, in turn, place a single cartridge in one of the five chambers of a revolver cylinder, give the latter a quick twirl, place the muzzle of the gun against the temple and pull the trigger, leaving it to chance whether or not death results to the trigger puller.

years and not exceeding ten years. A new trial was refused and after sentence was imposed, an appeal was taken.

Appellant alleges certain errors in the charge of the court and also contends that the facts did not justify a conviction for any form of homicide except involuntary manslaughter. This contention we overrule.... At common law, the 'grand criterion' which 'distinguished murder from other killing' was malice on the part of the killer and this malice was not necessarily 'malevolent to the deceased particularly' but 'any evil design in general; the dictate of a wicked, depraved and malignant heart.' Among the examples that Blackstone cites of murder is 'coolly discharging a gun among a multitude of people,' causing the death of someone of the multitude. * * *

When an individual commits an act of gross recklessness for which he must reasonably anticipate that death to another is likely to result, he exhibits that "wickedness of disposition, hardness of heart, cruelty, recklessness of consequences, and a mind regardless of social duty" which proved that there was at that time in him "the state or frame of mind termed malice." This court has declared that if a driver "wantonly, recklessly, and in disregard of consequences" hurls "his car against another, or into a crowd" and death results from that act "he ought * * * to face the same consequences that would be meted out to him if he had accomplished death by wantonly and wickedly firing a gun."

In *Com. v. Hillman*, the charge of the court below was approved by this court. In that charge appears this statement: "Malice in law means a depraved and wicked heart that is reckless and disregards the rights of others. Reckless conduct that results in the death of another is malice. To illustrate that: If a man fires a gun into a crowd and kills another it is murder, because the fact of the reckless shooting of a gun into a crowd is malice in law. That wicked and depraved disposition and that recklessness and disregard of human life is malice."

In *Com. v. Knox*, the following instructions by the trial judge in a murder case was held by this court not to be error: "When a man uses a gun loaded with powder and shot and aimed at a vital part of the body of another and discharges it, he must be presumed to know that death is likely to follow." * * *

The killing of William H. Long by this defendant resulted from an act intentionally done by the latter, in reckless and wanton disregard of the consequences which were at least sixty per cent certain from his thrice attempted discharge of a gun known to contain one bullet and aimed at a vital part of Long's body. This killing was, therefore, murder, for malice in the sense of a wicked disposition is evidenced by the intentional doing of an uncalled-for act in callous disregard of its likely harmful effects on others. The fact that there was no motive for this homicide does not exculpate the accused. In a trial for murder proof of motive is always relevant but never necessary.

All the assignments of error are overruled and the judgment is affirmed. The record is remitted to the court below so that the sentence imposed may be carried out.

PEOPLE V. KNOLLER

Supreme Court of California
41 Cal.4th 139, 158 P.3d 731 (2007)

KENNARD, J.

I. FACTS AND PROCEEDINGS

In 1998, Pelican Bay State Prison inmates Paul Schneider and Dale Bretches, both members of the Aryan Brotherhood prison gang, sought to engage in a business of buying, raising, and breeding Presa Canario dogs. This breed of dog tends to be very large, weighing over 100 pounds, and reaching over five feet tall when standing on its hind legs. A document found in defendants' apartment describes the Presa Canario as "a gripping dog . . . always used and bred for combat and guard . . . [and] used extensively for fighting. . . . "

Prisoners Schneider and Bretches relied on outside contacts, including Brenda Storey and Janet Coumbs, to carry out their Presa Canario business. Schneider told Coumbs that she should raise the dogs.

As of May 1998, Coumbs possessed four such dogs, named Bane, Isis, Hera, and Fury. * * * Hera and Fury broke out of their fenced yard and attacked Coumbs's sheep. Hera killed at least one of the sheep and also a cat belonging to Coumbs's daughter. Coumbs acknowledged that Bane ate his doghouse and may have joined Fury in killing a sheep.

Defendants Knoller and Noel, who were attorneys representing a prison guard at Pelican Bay State Prison, met inmate Schneider at the prison sometime in 1999. In October 1999, defendants filed a lawsuit on behalf of Brenda Storey against Coumbs over the ownership and custody of the four dogs. Coumbs decided not to contest the lawsuit and to turn the dogs over to defendants. Coumbs warned Knoller that the dogs had killed Coumbs's sheep, but Knoller did not seem to care.

Defendant Knoller thereafter contacted Dr. Donald Martin, a veterinarian for 49 years, and on March 26, 2000, he examined and vaccinated the dogs. With his bill to Knoller, Dr. Martin included a letter, which said in part: "I would be professionally amiss [*sic*] if I did not mention the following, so that you can be prepared. These dogs are huge, approximately weighing in the neighborhood of 100 pounds each. They have had no training or discipline of any sort. They were a problem to even get to, let alone to vaccinate. You mentioned having a professional hauler gather them up and taking them.... Usually this would be done in crates, but I doubt one could get them into anything short of a livestock trailer, and if let loose they would have a battle. To add to this, these animals would be a liability in any household, reminding me of the recent attack in Tehama County to a boy by large dogs. He lost his arm and disfigured his face. The historic romance of the warrior dog, the personal guard dog, the gaming dog, etc. may sound good but hardly fits into life today." Knoller thanked Dr. Martin for the information and said she would pass it on to her client.

On April 1, 2000, both defendants and a professional dog handler took custody of the dogs from Coumbs. Bane then weighed 150 pounds and Hera 130 pounds. Coumbs told both defendants that she was worried about the dogs, that Hera and Fury should be shot, and that she was also concerned about Bane and Isis.

Hera remained for a short time at a kennel in San Mateo County while Bane was sent to a facility in Los Angeles County. Both defendants soon became concerned for the health of the two dogs. On April 30, 2000, defendants brought Hera to their sixth-floor apartment at 2398 Pacific Avenue in San Francisco. Bane arrived in September 2000. Codefendant Noel purchased dog licenses, registering himself and Knoller as the dogs' owners. * * *

A later search of defendants' apartment showed that they frequently exchanged letters with Pelican Bay inmates Schneider and Bretches. Over 100 letters were sent and received between March and December 2000, apparently under the guise of attorney-client correspondence. In the letters, defendants discussed a commercial breeding operation, considering various names such as GuerraHund Kennels, Wardog, and finally settling on Dog-O-War. Prisoners Schneider and Bretches' notes on a Web site for the business described Bane as "Wardog," and "Bringer of Death: Ruin: Destruction."

Between the time defendants Noel and Knoller brought the dogs to their sixth-floor apartment in San Francisco and the date of the fatal mauling of Diane Whipple on January 26, 2001, there were about 30 incidents of the two dogs being out of control or threatening humans and other dogs. Neighbors mentioned seeing the two dogs unattended on the sixth floor and running down the hall. Codefendant Noel's letters to prisoner Schneider confirmed this, mentioning one incident when defendant Knoller had to let go of the two dogs as they broke from her grasp and ran to the end of the hall. Noel described how the dogs even pushed past him and "took off side by side down the hall toward the elevator in a celebratory stampede" 240 lbs. of Presa wall to wall moving at top speed. In a letter to inmate Schneider, defendant Knoller admitted not having the upper body strength to handle Bane and having trouble controlling Hera.

When neighbors complained to defendants Noel and Knoller about the two dogs, defendants responded callously, if at all. In one incident, neighbors Stephen and Aimee West were walking their dog in a nearby park when Hera attacked their dog and "latched on" to the dog's snout. Noel was unable to separate the dogs, but Aimee threw her keys at Hera, startling Hera and causing Hera to release her grip on the Wests' dog. On another day, Stephen West was walking his dog when he encountered Noel with Bane. Bane lunged toward West's dog, but Noel managed to pull Bane back. When Stephen West next saw Noel, West suggested that Noel muzzle the dogs and talk to dog trainer Mario Montepeque about training them; Noel replied there was no need to do so. Defendants Knoller and Noel later encountered Montepeque, who advised defendants to have their dogs trained and to use a choke collar. Defendants disregarded this advice. On still another occasion, when dog walker Lynn Gaines was walking a dog, Gaines told Noel that he should put a muzzle on Bane; Noel called her a "bitch" and said the dog Gaines was walking was the problem.

There were also instances when defendants' two dogs attacked or threatened people. David Moser, a fellow resident in the apartment building, slipped by defendants Knoller and Noel in the hallway only to have their dog Hera bite him on the "rear end." When he exclaimed, "Your dog just bit me," Noel replied, "Um, interesting." Neither defendant apologized to Moser or reprimanded the dog. Another resident, Jill Cowen Davis, was eight months pregnant when one of the dogs, in the presence of both Knoller and Noel, suddenly growled and lunged toward her stomach with its mouth open and teeth bared. Noel jerked the dog by the leash, but he did not apologize to Davis. Postal carrier John Watanabe testified that both dogs, unleashed, had charged him. He said the dogs were in a "snarling frenzy" and he was "terrified for [his] life." When he stepped behind his mail cart, the dogs went back to Knoller and Noel. On still another occasion, the two dogs lunged at a six-year-old boy walking to school; they were stopped less than a foot from him.

One time, codefendant Noel himself suffered a severe injury to his finger when Bane bit him during a fight with another dog. The wound required surgery, and Noel had to wear a splint on his arm and have two steel pins placed in his hand for eight to 10 weeks.

Mauling victim Diane Whipple and her partner Sharon Smith lived in a sixth-floor apartment across a lobby from defendants. Smith encountered defendants' two dogs as often as once a week. In early December 2000, Whipple called Smith at work to say, with some panic in her voice, that one of the dogs had bitten her. Whipple had come upon codefendant Noel in the lobby with one of the dogs, which lunged at her and bit her in the hand. Whipple did not seek medical treatment for three deep, red indentations on one hand. Whipple made every effort to avoid defendants' dogs, checking the hallway before she went out and becoming anxious while waiting for the elevator for fear the dogs would be inside. She and Smith did not complain to apartment management because they wanted nothing to do with defendants Knoller and Noel.

On January 26, 2001, Whipple telephoned Smith to say she was going home early. At 4:00 p.m., Esther Birkmaier, a neighbor who lived across the hall from Whipple, heard dogs barking and a woman's "panic-stricken" voice calling, "Help me, help me." Looking through the peephole in her front door, Birkmaier saw Whipple lying facedown on the floor just over the threshold of her apartment with what appeared to be a dog on top of her. Birkmaier saw no one else in the hallway. Afraid to open the door, Birkmaier called 911, the emergency telephone number, and at the same time heard a voice yelling, "No, no, no" and "Get off." When Birkmaier again approached her door, she could hear barking and growling directly outside and a banging against a door. She heard a voice yell, "Get off, get off, no, no, stop, stop." She chained her door and again looked through the peephole. Whipple's body was gone and groceries were strewn about the hallway. Birkmaier called 911 a second time.

At 4:12 p.m., San Francisco Police Officers Sidney Laws and Leslie Forrestal arrived in response to Birkmaier's telephone calls. They saw Whipple's body in the hallway; her clothing had been completely ripped off, her entire body was covered with wounds, and she was bleeding profusely. Defendant Knoller and the two dogs were not in sight.

The officers called for an ambulance. Shortly thereafter, defendant Knoller emerged from her apartment. She did not ask about Whipple's condition but merely told the officers she was looking for her keys, which she found just inside the door to Whipple's apartment.

An emergency medical technician administered first aid to Whipple, who had a large, profusely bleeding wound to her neck. The wound was too large to halt the bleeding, and Whipple's pulse and breathing stopped as paramedics arrived. She was revived but died shortly after reaching the hospital.

An autopsy revealed over 77 discrete injuries covering Whipple's body "from head to toe." The most significant were lacerations damaging her jugular vein and her carotid artery and crushing her larynx, injuries typically inflicted by predatory animals to kill their prey. The medical examiner stated that although earlier medical attention would have increased Whipple's chances of survival, she might ultimately have died anyway because she had lost one-third or more of her blood at the scene. Plaster molds of the two dogs' teeth showed that the bite injuries to Whipple's neck were consistent with Bane's teeth.

Animal control officer Andrea Runge asked defendant Knoller to sign over custody of the dogs for euthanasia. Knoller, whom Runge described as "oddly calm," agreed to sign over Bane, but she refused to sign over Hera for euthanasia and she refused to help the animal control officers with the animals, saying she was "unable to handle the dogs." * * *

[At trial,] Noel did not testify, but he presented evidence of positive encounters between the two dogs and veterinarians, friends, and neighbors. Defendant Knoller did testify in her own defense. * * * She denied reading literature in the apartment referring to the vicious nature of the dogs. She thought the dogs had no personality problems requiring a professional trainer. She denied receiving or otherwise discounted any warnings about the two dogs' behavior and she maintained that virtually all the witnesses testifying to incidents with the dogs were lying. * * * She said she had just returned from walking Bane on the roof of the apartment building, and had opened the door to her apartment while holding Bane's leash, when Bane dragged her back across the lobby toward Whipple, who had just opened the door to her own apartment. The other dog, Hera, left defendants' apartment and joined Bane, who attacked Whipple. Knoller said she threw herself on Whipple to save her. She denied that Hera participated in the attack. She acknowledged not calling 911 to get help for Whipple.

Asked whether she denied responsibility for the attack on Whipple, Knoller gave this reply: "I said in an interview that I wasn't responsible but it wasn't for the-it wasn't in regard to what Bane had done, it was in regard to knowing whether he would do that or not. And I had no idea that he would ever do anything like that to anybody. How can you anticipate something like that? It's a totally bizarre event. I mean how could you anticipate that a dog that you know that is gentle and loving and affectionate would do something so horrible and brutal and disgusting and gruesome to anybody? How could you imagine that happening?" * * *

In rebuttal, the prosecution presented evidence that the minor character of defendant Knoller's injuries—principally bruising to the hands—indicated that she had not been as involved in trying to protect mauling victim Whipple as she had claimed. Dr. Randall Lockwood, the prosecution's expert on dog behavior, testified that good behavior by a dog on some occasions does not preclude aggressive and violent behavior on other occasions, and he mentioned the importance of training dogs such as Bane and Hera *not* to fight.

The jury found Knoller guilty of second degree murder; it also found * * * Noel guilty of involuntary manslaughter and owning a mischievous animal that caused the death of a human being. Both defendants moved for a new trial. The trial court denied Noel's motion. We quote below the pertinent statements by the trial court in granting Knoller's motion for a new trial on the second degree murder count.

The trial court observed: "The law requires that there be a subjective understanding on the part of the person that on the day in question—and I do not read that as being January 26th, 2001 because by this time, with all of the information that had come out dealing with the dogs, the defendants were fully on notice that they had a couple of wild, uncontrollable and dangerous dogs that were likely going to do something bad. Is the 'something bad' death? That is the ultimate question in the case. There is no question but that the something bad was going to be that somebody was going to be badly hurt. I defy either defendant to stand up and tell me they had no idea that those dogs were going to hurt somebody one day. *But can they stand up and say that they knew subjectively—not objectively and that's an important distinction—that these dogs were going to stand up and kill somebody?*" (Italics added.)

The trial court continued: "I am guided by a variety of principles. One of them is that public emotion, public outcry, feeling, passion, sympathy do not play a role in the application of the law. The other is that I am required to review all of the evidence and determine independently rather than as a jury what the evidence showed. I have laid out most of the evidence as it harms the defendants in this case. Their conduct from the time that they got the dogs to the time—to the weeks after Diane Whipple's death was despicable.

"There was one time on the stand, Ms. Knoller, when I truly believed what you said. You broke down in the middle of a totally scripted answer and you actually, instead of crying, you actually got mad and you said you had no idea that this dog could do what he did and pounded the table. I believed you. That was the only time, but I did believe you." The court then described the definition of second degree murder as requiring that one "*subjectively knows, based on everything, that the conduct that he or she is about to engage in has a high probability of death to another human being.*" (Italics added.)

The trial court went on: "What we have in this case as it relates to Ms. Knoller is the decision to take the dog outside, into the hallway, up to the roof, go to the bathroom, bring it back down and put it in the apartment. There was no question but that taking the dog out into the hallway by that very act exposed other people in the apartment, whether they are residents there or guests, invitees to what might happen with the dog. When you take everything as a totality, *the question is whether or not as a subjective matter and as a matter of law Ms. Knoller knew that there was a high probability that day, or on the day before on the day after,*—I reject totally the argument of the defendants that she had to know when she walked out the door—*she was going to kill somebody that morning. The Court finds that the evidence does not support it.*" (Italics added.)

The trial court concluded it had "no choice, ... taking the Legislature's scheme, the evidence that was received, as despicable as it is, but to determine not that [defendant Knoller] is acquitted of second degree murder but to find that on the state of the evidence, *I cannot say as a matter of law that she subjectively knew on January 26th that her conduct was such that a human being was likely to die.*" (Italics added.)

The trial court mentioned another consideration: "The Court also notes a great troubling feature of this case that Mr. Noel was never charged [with murder] as Ms. Knoller was. In the Court's view, given the evidence, Mr. Noel is more culpable than she. * * * Equality of sentencing and the equal administration of justice is an important feature in any criminal court. That played a role as well." The trial court then granted defendant Knoller's motion for a new trial on the second degree murder count.

As noted earlier, both defendants as well as the prosecution appealed. The Court of Appeal reversed the trial court's order granting Knoller's motion for a new trial on the second degree murder count. It disagreed with the trial court that a second degree murder conviction, based on a theory of implied malice, required that Knoller recognized "her conduct was such that a human being was likely to die." The Court of Appeal held that a second degree murder conviction can be based simply on a defendant's "subjective appreciation and conscious disregard of a likely risk of . . . serious bodily injury." In all other respects, the Court of Appeal affirmed both defendants' convictions.

II. THE ELEMENTS OF IMPLIED MALICE

Murder is the unlawful killing of a human being, or a fetus, with malice aforethought. Malice may be express or implied. At issue here is the definition of "implied malice."

Defendant Knoller was convicted of second degree murder as a result of the killing of Diane Whipple by defendant's dog, Bane. Second degree murder is the unlawful killing of a human being with malice aforethought but without the additional elements, such as willfulness, premeditation, and deliberation, that would support a conviction of first degree murder. Section 188 provides: "[M]alice may be either express or implied. It is express when there is manifested a deliberate intention to take away the life of a fellow creature. It is implied, when no considerable provocation appears, or when the circumstances attending the killing show an abandoned and malignant heart."

The statutory definition of implied malice, a killing by one with an "abandoned and malignant heart," is far from clear in its meaning. Indeed, an instruction in the statutory language could be misleading, for it "could lead the jury to equate the malignant heart with an evil disposition or a despicable character" instead of focusing on a defendant's awareness of the risk created by his or her behavior. "Two lines of decisions developed, reflecting judicial attempts 'to translate this amorphous anatomical characterization of implied malice into a tangible standard a jury can apply.'" Under both lines of decisions, implied malice requires a defendant's awareness of the risk of death to another.

III. THE COURT OF APPEAL'S TEST FOR IMPLIED MALICE

As discussed in the preceding part, the great majority of this court's decisions establish that a killer acts with implied malice only when acting with an awareness of *endangering human life.* This principle has been well settled for many years, and it is embodied in the standard jury instruction given in murder cases, including this one. The Court of Appeal here, however, held that a second degree murder conviction, based on a theory of implied malice, can be based simply on a defendant's awareness of the risk of causing *serious bodily injury* to another. * * *

We conclude that a conviction for second degree murder, based on a theory of implied malice, requires proof that a defendant acted with conscious disregard of the danger to human life. In holding that a defendant's conscious disregard of the risk of serious bodily injury suffices to sustain such a conviction, the Court of Appeal erred.

IV. THE TRIAL COURT'S GRANT OF A NEW TRIAL ON THE SECOND DEGREE MURDER CHARGE

We now turn to the second issue raised by the petition for review—whether the trial court abused its discretion in granting defendant Knoller a new trial on the second degree murder charge. Such an abuse of discretion arises if the trial court based its decision on impermissible factors or on an incorrect legal standard.

In granting Knoller a new trial, the trial court properly viewed implied malice as requiring a defendant's awareness of the danger that his or her conduct will result in another's *death* and not merely in serious bodily injury. But the court's ruling was legally flawed in other respects. As we explain below, the trial court based its ruling on an inaccurate definition of implied malice, and it inappropriately relied on the prosecutor's failure to charge codefendant Noel with murder.

As discussed earlier * * *, this court * * * had defined implied malice in two similar but somewhat different ways. Under the *Thomas* test, malice is implied when "the defendant for a base, antisocial motive and with wanton disregard for human life, does an act that involves a high degree of probability that it will result in death." Under the *Phillips* test, malice is implied when the killing is proximately caused by "an act, the natural consequences of which are dangerous to life, which act was deliberately performed by a person who knows that his conduct endangers the life of another and who acts with conscious disregard for life." In *People v. Dellinger*, we observed that although these two tests

"articulated one and the same standard," the *Thomas* test contained "obscure phraseology" and had "become a superfluous charge," so that the "better practice in the future" would be for trial courts to instruct juries in the straightforward language" of the *Phillips* test.

Here, the trial court properly instructed the jury in accordance with the *Phillips* test. But when the court evaluated defendant Knoller's new trial motion, it relied on language from the *Thomas* test, and as explained below, its description of that test was inaccurate. The court stated that a killer acts with implied malice when the killer "*subjectively knows,* based on everything, that the conduct that he or she is about to engage in has a *high probability of death* to another human being" and thus the issue in this case was "whether or not as a *subjective* matter and as a matter of law Ms. Knoller *knew* that there was a *high probability* "that her conduct would result in someone's death. (Italics added.) But * * * the *Phillips* test [does not] require a defendant's awareness that his or her conduct has a *high probability* of causing death. Rather, it requires only that a defendant acted with a "conscious disregard for human life." * * *

In ruling on Knoller's motion for a new trial, the trial court also commented that, in its view, codefendant Noel was more culpable than defendant Knoller, and that the district attorney's failure to charge Noel with murder was a "troubling feature of this case" that "played a role as well" in the court's decision to grant Knoller a new trial on the second degree murder charge. Dissimilar charging of codefendants, however, is not among the grounds for a new trial in section 1181. * * *

* * * Even assuming a new trial could be granted on such a ground, it is not justified here. Defendant Knoller and codefendant Noel were not similarly situated with regard to their dog Bane's fatal mauling of Whipple in the hallway of the apartment building where they all lived. The immediate cause of Whipple's death was Knoller's own conscious decision to take the dog Bane unmuzzled through the apartment building, where they were likely to encounter other people, knowing that Bane was aggressive and highly dangerous and that she could not control him. Bringing a more serious charge against the person immediately responsible for the victim's death was a permissible exercise of prosecutorial discretion, not grounds for a new trial.

V. CONCLUSION AND DISPOSITION

* * *

The Court of Appeal's judgment is reversed and the matter is remanded to that court, with directions to return the case to the trial court for reconsideration of defendant Knoller's new trial motion in accord with the views expressed in this opinion.

NOTE

When the case was remanded to the trial court, the judge who had originally heard the Knoller case had retired. A new judge reinstated the original murder conviction. Upon sentencing, Knoller (who was on parole after serving about three years in prison) requested probation, pointing to her lack of prior offenses. The trial judge, however, sentenced her to 15 years to life (reduced by the time already served). The judge also fined Knoller $10,000 and ordered her to pay $6,800 out of her prison earnings in restitution to Smith. Knoller's husband, Robert Noel, who was found guilty of involuntary manslaughter and sentenced to four years in prison, was paroled in 2003, after serving a little more than half his sentence.

Did the State provide sufficient evidence that Knoller was aware of the risk of death posed by her dogs and consciously disregarded this risk? Or did the State succeed only in proving that Knoller was a self-absorbed person who ignored a risk she *should* have recognized?

F. INVOLUNTARY MANSLAUGHTER

Generally speaking, there are two ways a prosecutor can secure an involuntary manslaughter conviction. First, the prosecutor can prove that the defendant had the requisite mens rea for involuntary manslaughter. Many jurisdictions use the term "criminal negligence" to describe the mental state necessary for an involuntary manslaughter conviction. "Criminal negligence," like the term "malice aforethought," is a legal term of art which has been defined in different ways. In most jurisdictions, something more than ordinary civil negligence is required; this state of mind is sometimes described as "gross negligence" and sometimes even "recklessness." However, a minority of courts, like the Court of Appeals of Washington in *State v. Williams*, have held that simple negligence is all that is required for an involuntary manslaughter conviction.

Since the difference between a reckless state of mind and a negligent state of mind (whether ordinary or gross) turns on whether the defendant was aware of a substantial and unjustifiable risk and chose to disregard it (recklessness requiring awareness of the risk and negligence not requiring such awareness), the mental state required and how it is defined can make a significant difference in the odds of conviction. In the following cases, the courts take different views on the mental state required for an involuntary manslaughter conviction. Pay careful attention to the terminology used to describe the required mental state and the definitions of these terms that the courts provide. Some of these definitions conflict with the usual meanings of the terms defined.

A second way one can be convicted of involuntary manslaughter is through application of the misdemeanor manslaughter rule. Because this doctrine can be understood as a kind of mini-felony murder rule, we will examine it in more detail after we have studied felony murder.

COMMONWEALTH V. WELANSKY

Supreme Judicial Court of Massachusetts
316 Mass. 383, 55 N.E.2d 902 (1944)

LUMMUS, J.

On November 28, 1942, and for about nine years before that day, a corporation named New Cocoanut Grove, Inc., maintained and operated a "night club" in Boston, having an entrance at 17 Piedmont Street, for the furnishing to the public for compensation of food, drink, and entertainment consisting of orchestra and band music, singing and dancing. It employed about eighty persons. The corporation, its officers and employees, and its business, were completely dominated by the defendant Barnett Welansky. * * * He owned, and held in his own name or in the names of others, all the capital stock. He leased some of the land on which the corporate business was carried on, and owned the rest, although title was held for him by his sister. He was entitled to, and took, all the profits. Internally, the corporation was operated without regard to corporate forms, as though the business were that of the defendant as an individual. It was not shown that responsibility for the number or condition of safety exits had been delegated by the defendant to any employee or other person.

The defendant was accustomed to spend[ing] his evenings at the night club, inspecting the premises and superintending the business. On November 16, 1942, he became suddenly ill, and was carried to a hospital, where he was in bed for three weeks and remained until discharged on December 11, 1942. During his stay at the hospital, although employees visited him there, he did not concern himself with the night club, because, as he testified, he "knew it would be all right" and that "the same system . . . [he] had would continue" during his absence. There is no evidence of any act, omission or condition at the night club on November 28, 1942, (apart from the lighting of a match hereinafter described), that was not within the usual and regular practice during the time before the defendant was taken ill when he was at the night club nearly every evening. * * *

* * * A little after ten o'clock on the evening of Saturday, November 28, 1942, the night club was well filled with a crowd of patrons. It was during the busiest season of the year. An important football game in the afternoon had attracted many visitors to Boston. Witnesses were rightly permitted to testify that the dance floor had from eighty to one hundred persons on it, and that it was "very crowded." Witnesses were rightly permitted to give their estimates, derived from their observations, of the number of patrons in various parts of the night club. Upon the evidence it could have been found that at that time there were from two hundred fifty to four hundred persons in the Melody Lounge, from four hundred to

five hundred in the main dining room and the Caricature Bar, and two hundred fifty in the Cocktail Lounge. * * *

A bartender in the Melody Lounge noticed that an electric light bulb which was in or near the cocoanut husks of an artificial palm tree in the corner had been turned off and that the corner was dark. He directed a sixteen year old bar boy who was waiting on customers at the tables to cause the bulb to be lighted. A soldier sitting with other persons near the light told the bar boy to leave it unlighted. But the bar boy got a stool, lighted a match in order to see the bulb, turned the bulb in its socket, and thus lighted it. The bar boy blew the match out, and started to walk away. Apparently the flame of the match had ignited the palm tree and that had speedily ignited the low cloth ceiling near it, for both flamed up almost instantly. The fire spread with great rapidity across the upper part of the room, causing much heat. The crowd in the Melody Lounge rushed up the stairs, but the fire preceded them. People got on fire while on the stairway. The fire spread with great speed across the foyer and into the Caricature Bar and the main dining room, and thence into the Cocktail Lounge. Soon after the fire started the lights in the night club went out. The smoke had a peculiar odor. The crowd were panic stricken, and rushed and pushed in every direction through the night club, screaming, and overturning tables and chairs in their attempts to escape.

The door at the head of the Melody Lounge stairway was not opened until firemen broke it down from outside with an axe and found it locked by a key lock, so that the panic bar could not operate. Two dead bodies were found close to it, and a pile of bodies about seven feet from it. The door in the vestibule of the office did not become open, and was barred by the clothing rack. The revolving door soon jammed, but was burst out by the pressure of the crowd. The head waiter and another waiter tried to get open the panic doors from the main dining room to Shawmut Street, and succeeded after some difficulty. The other two doors to Shawmut Street were locked, and were opened by force from outside by firemen and others. Some patrons escaped through them, but many dead bodies were piled up inside them. A considerable number of patrons escaped through the Broadway door, but many died just inside that door. Some employees, and a great number of patrons, died in the fire. Others were taken out of the building with fatal burns and injuries from smoke, and died within a few days.

I. *The pleadings, verdicts, and judgments.*

The defendant, his brother James Welansky, and Jacob Goldfine, were indicted for manslaughter in sixteen counts of an indictment numbered 413, each count for causing the death of a person described as "Jane Doe," "John Doe," or the like. The first six counts were quashed, leaving the last ten counts. Later a motion by the Commonwealth was allowed, substituting in each of the last ten counts the real name of a victim. Voluntarily the Commonwealth filed specifications as to those counts, by which it specified among other things that the alleged misconduct of the defendant consisted in causing or permitting or failing reasonably to prevent defective wiring, the installation of [flammable] decorations, the absence of fire doors, the absence of "proper means of egress properly maintained" and "sufficient proper" exits, and overcrowding. Some other specifications—such as failure to prevent the unlawful employment of minors—plainly had little or no relation to any wanton or reckless conduct that might result in manslaughter. * * * Another indictment numbered 414 in sixteen counts was returned against the same three persons. * * *

The defendant was found guilty upon counts 7 to 16 inclusive of indictment 413 and upon counts 7 to 15 inclusive of indictment 414. He was sentenced to imprisonment in the State prison upon each count for a term of not less than twelve years and not more than fifteen years, the first day of said term to be in solitary confinement and the residue at hard labor, the sentences to run concurrently. * * *

II. *The principles governing liability.*

The Commonwealth disclaimed any contention that the defendant intentionally killed or injured the persons named in the indictments as victims. It based its case on involuntary manslaughter through wanton or reckless conduct. The judge instructed the jury correctly with respect to the nature of such conduct.

Usually wanton or reckless conduct consists of an affirmative act, like driving an automobile or discharging a firearm, in disregard of probable harmful consequences to another. But where, as in the present case, there is a duty of care for the safety of business visitors invited to premises which the defendant controls, wanton or reckless conduct may consist of intentional failure to take such care in disregard of the probable harmful consequences to them or of their right to care.

To define wanton or reckless conduct so as to distinguish it clearly from negligence and gross negligence is not easy. * * * The words "wanton" and "reckless" are practically synonymous in this connection, although the word "wanton" may contain a suggestion of arrogance or insolence or heartlessness that is lacking in the word "reckless." * * *

The standard of wanton or reckless conduct is at once subjective and objective, as has been recognized ever since *Commonwealth v. Pierce.* Knowing facts that would cause a reasonable man to know the danger is equivalent to knowing the danger. The judge charged the jury correctly when he said, "To constitute wanton or reckless conduct, as distinguished from mere negligence, grave danger to others must have been apparent, and the defendant must have chosen to run the risk rather than alter his conduct so as to avoid the act or omission which caused the harm. If the grave danger was in fact realized by the defendant, his subsequent voluntary act or omission which caused the harm amounts to wanton or reckless conduct, no matter whether the ordinary man would have realized the gravity of the danger or not. But even if a particular defendant is so stupid [or] so heedless . . . that in fact he did not realize the grave danger, he cannot escape the imputation of wanton or reckless conduct in his dangerous act or omission, if an ordinary normal man under the same circumstances would have realized the gravity of the danger. A man may be reckless within the meaning of the law although he himself thought he was careful." * * *

The words "wanton" and "reckless" are thus not merely rhetorical or vituperative expressions used instead of negligent or grossly negligent. They express a difference in the degree of risk and in the voluntary taking of risk so marked, as compared with negligence, as to amount substantially and in the eyes of the law to a difference in kind. For many years this court has been careful to preserve the distinction between negligence and gross negligence, on the one hand, and wanton or reckless conduct on the other. In pleadings as well as in statutes the rule is that "negligence and wilful and wanton conduct are so different in kind that words properly descriptive of the one commonly exclude the other."

Notwithstanding language used commonly in earlier cases, and occasionally in later ones, it is now clear in this Commonwealth that at common law conduct does not become criminal until it passes the borders of negligence and gross negligence and enters into the domain of wanton or reckless conduct. There is in Massachusetts at common law no such thing as "criminal negligence." * * *

To convict the defendant of manslaughter, the Commonwealth was not required to prove that he caused the fire by some wanton or reckless conduct. Fire in a place of public resort is an ever present danger. It was enough to prove that death resulted from his wanton or reckless disregard of the safety of patrons in the event of fire from any cause. * * *

Judgment affirmed.

NOTE

The fire at the New Coconut Grove stirred up a torrent of angry emotions which may have encouraged the prosecution of Mr. Welansky who was ill in the hospital at the time of the fire. Professor Phillip Johnson comments on the *Welansky* case:

> It appears that the public of Boston and the newspapers felt an enormous psychological need to find a scapegoat for the Coconut Grove fire, in which hundreds of people died horribly. Initially, there was a call for prosecution of the 16-year-old busboy who apparently started the fire. He seems to have been a model youth from an impoverished background, however, and public opinion

soon turned towards more suitable scapegoats. There were attacks in the newspapers upon a variety of public officials who were responsible in varying degrees for failing to require that the unsafe conditions be rectified. A fire inspector had reported on conditions at the nightclub just eight days before the fire, and had found them to be fairly acceptable. Eventually, the newspaper attacks came to center on the owners of the club, and Welansky was indicted.

In fact, the cause of the fire was never satisfactorily explained and the degree to which any negligence on the part of Welansky contributed to it remained highly speculative. In 1970, the Boston Fire Department concluded a renewed investigation of the case and found that the cause of the fire could not be determined. At that time, the busboy who had supposedly started the fire, now 44 years old, was still receiving abusive telephone calls blaming him for the fire.

PHILLIP JOHNSON, TEACHER'S MANUAL for CRIMINAL LAW: CASES, MATERIALS AND TEXT (4th ed. 1990), *citing* GOLDSTEIN, DERSHOWITZ, AND SCHWARZ, CRIMINAL LAW: THEORY AND PROCESS (1974).

In 1993, the city's fire department reopened its investigation into the fire and found new evidence that the club's air conditioning system was filled with methyl chloride on the night of the fire. Methyl chloride is a flammable alternative to the usual coolants. *New Theory Offered on Deadly 1942 Blaze*, LAS VEGAS REVIEW JOURNAL, Sept. 25, 1993, at 8A.

STATE V. WILLIAMS

Court of Appeals of Washington
4 Wash.App. 908, 484 P.2d 1167 (1971)

HOROWITZ, C.J.

Defendants, husband and wife, were charged by information filed October 3, 1968, with the crime of manslaughter for negligently failing to supply their 17-month child with necessary medical attention, as a result of which he died on September 12, 1968. Upon entry of findings, conclusions and judgment of guilty, sentences were imposed on April 22, 1969. Defendants appeal.

The defendant husband, Walter Williams, is a 24-year-old full-blooded Sheshont Indian with a sixth-grade education. His sole occupation is that of laborer. The defendant wife, Bernice Williams, is a 20-year-old part Indian with an 11th grade education. At the time of the marriage, the wife had two children, the younger of whom was a 14-month son. Both parents worked and the children were cared for by the 85-year-old mother of the defendant husband. The defendant husband assumed parental responsibility with the defendant wife to provide clothing, care and medical attention for the child. Both defendants possessed a great deal of love and affection for the defendant wife's young son.

The court expressly found:

> That both defendants were aware that William Joseph Tabafunda was ill during the period September 1, 1968 to September 12, 1968. The defendants were ignorant. They did not realize how sick the baby was. They thought that the baby had a toothache and no layman regards a toothache as dangerous to life. They loved the baby and gave it aspirin in hopes of improving its condition. They did not take the baby to a doctor because of fear that the Welfare Department would take the baby away from them. They knew that medical help was available because of previous experience. They had no excuse that the law will recognize for not taking the baby to a doctor.
>
> The defendants Walter L. Williams and Bernice J. Williams were negligent in not seeking medical attention for William Joseph Tabafunda.
>
> That as a proximate result of this negligence, William Joseph Tabafunda died.

From these and other findings, the court concluded that the defendants were each guilty of the crime of manslaughter as charged.

Defendants take no exception to [these] findings but contend that the findings do not support the conclusions that the defendants are guilty of manslaughter as charged. The contentions raise two basic issues, (1) the existence of the duty to furnish medical aid charged by the information to be violated and the seriousness of the breach required; and (2) the issue of proximate cause, *i.e.*, whether defendants were put on notice, in time to save the child's life, that medical care was required. Because the nature of the duty and the quality or seriousness of the breach are closely interrelated, our discussion of the first issue involved will embrace both matters.

Parental duty to provide medical care for a dependent minor child was recognized at common law and characterized as a natural duty. In Washington, the existence of the duty is commonly assumed and is stated at times without reference to any particular statute. * * * On the question of the quality or seriousness of breach of the duty, at common law, in the case of involuntary manslaughter, the breach had to amount to more than mere ordinary or simple negligence—gross negligence was essential. In Washington, however, RCW 9.48.060 (since amended by Laws of 1970, ch. 49, § 2) and RCW 9.48.150 supersede both voluntary and involuntary manslaughter as those crimes were defined at common law. Under these statutes the crime is deemed committed even though the death of the victim is the proximate result of only simple or ordinary negligence.

The concept of simple or ordinary negligence describes a failure to exercise the "ordinary caution" necessary to make out the defense of excusable homicide. Ordinary caution is the kind of caution that a man of reasonable prudence would exercise under the same or similar conditions. If, therefore, the conduct of a defendant, regardless of his ignorance, good intentions and good faith, fails to measure up to the conduct required of a man of reasonable prudence, he is guilty of ordinary negligence because of his failure to use "ordinary caution." If such negligence proximately causes the death of the victim, the defendant, as pointed out above, is guilty of statutory manslaughter. * * *

The remaining issue of proximate cause requires consideration of the question of when the duty to furnish medical care became activated. If the duty to furnish such care was not activated until after it was too late to save the life of the child, failure to furnish medical care could not be said to have proximately caused the child's death. Timeliness in the furnishing of medical care also must be considered in terms of "ordinary caution." The law does not mandatorily require that a doctor be called for a child at the first sign of any indisposition or illness. The indisposition or illness may appear to be of a minor or very temporary kind, such as a toothache or cold. If one in the exercise of ordinary caution fails to recognize that his child's symptoms require medical attention, it cannot be said that the failure to obtain such medical attention is a breach of the duty owed. In our opinion, the duty as formulated in *People v. Pierson*, properly defines the duty contemplated by our manslaughter statutes. The court there said:

> We quite agree that the Code does not contemplate the necessity of calling a physician for every trifling complaint with which the child may be afflicted which in most instances may be overcome by the ordinary household nursing by members of the family; that a reasonable amount of discretion is vested in parents, charged with the duty of maintaining and bringing up infant children; and that the standard is at what time would an ordinarily prudent person, solicitous for the welfare of his child and anxious to promote its recovery, deem it necessary to call in the services of a physician.

It remains to apply the law discussed to the facts of the instant case. * * *

Dr. Gale Wilson, the autopsy surgeon and chief pathologist for the King County Coroner, testified that the child died because an abscessed tooth had been allowed to develop into an infection of the mouth and cheeks, eventually becoming gangrenous. This condition, accompanied by the child's inability to eat, brought about malnutrition, lowering the child's resistance and eventually producing pneumonia, causing the death. Dr. Wilson testified that in his opinion the infection had lasted for approximately 2 weeks, and that the odor generally associated with gangrene would have been present for approximately 10 days before death. He also expressed the opinion that had medical care been first obtained in the last week before the baby's death, such care would have been obtained too late to have saved the baby's life. Accordingly, the baby's apparent condition between September 1 and September 5, 1968 became the critical period for the purpose of determining whether in the exercise of ordinary caution defendants should have provided medical care for the minor child.

The testimony concerning the child's apparent condition during the critical period is not crystal clear, but is sufficient to warrant the following statement of the matter. The defendant husband testified that he noticed the baby was sick about 2 weeks before the baby died. The defendant wife testified that she noticed the baby was ill about a week and a half or 2 weeks before the baby died. The evidence showed that in the critical period the baby was fussy; that he could not keep his food down; and that a cheek started swelling up. The swelling went up and down, but did not disappear. In that same period, the cheek turned "a bluish color like." The defendants, not realizing that the baby was as ill as it was or that the baby was in danger of dying, attempted to provide some relief to the baby by giving the baby aspirin during the critical period and continued to do so until the night before the baby died. The defendants thought the swelling would go down and were waiting for it to do so; and defendant husband testified, that from what he had heard, neither doctors nor dentists pull out a tooth "when it's all swollen up like that." There was an additional explanation for not calling a doctor given by each defendant. Defendant husband testified that "the way the cheek looked, . . . and that stuff on his hair, they would think we were neglecting him and take him away from us and not give him back." Defendant wife testified that the defendants were "waiting for the swelling to go down," and also that they were afraid to take the child to a doctor for fear that the doctor would report them to the welfare department, who, in turn, would take the child away. "It's just that I was so scared of losing him." They testified that they had heard that the defendant husband's cousin lost a child that way. The evidence showed that the defendants did not understand the significance or seriousness of the baby's symptoms. However, there is no evidence that the defendants were physically or financially unable to obtain a doctor, or that they did not know an available doctor, or that the symptoms did not continue to be a matter of concern during the critical period. Indeed, the evidence shows that in April 1968 defendant husband had taken the child to a doctor for medical attention.

In our opinion, there is sufficient evidence from which the court could find, as it necessarily did, that applying the standard of ordinary caution, *i.e.,* the caution exercisable by a man of reasonable prudence under the same or similar conditions, defendants were sufficiently put on notice concerning the symptoms of the baby's illness and lack of improvement in the baby's apparent condition in the period from September 1 to September 5, 1968 to have required them to have obtained medical care for the child. The failure so to do in this case is ordinary or simple negligence, and such negligence is sufficient to support a conviction of statutory manslaughter.

The judgment is affirmed.

NOTE

The Court of Appeals of Washington was unmoved by the defendants' claim that the reason they did not take the baby to the doctor was because they were afraid the doctor would report them to the welfare department, which would then take the baby away. Whether the defendants acted negligently turns on the reasonableness or unreasonableness of their actions. The question of reasonableness depends in turn on the fact finder's construction of the reasonable person. Who is the "reasonable person" against whom these American Indian parents should be compared? Should the fact finder consider race, ethnicity, class, age, gender, or level of education? Consider that the Indian Child Welfare Act of 1978, excerpted below, "was passed in response to rising concern in the mid-1970s over the consequences to Indian children, Indian families, and Indian tribes of abusive child welfare practices that resulted in the separation of large numbers of Indian children from their families and tribes through adoption or foster care placement, usually in non-Indian homes." Adoptive Couple v. Baby Girl, 133 S. Ct. 2552 (2013). Despite passage of this Act, Native American children are still being taken from their parents and placed into non-Native American foster homes at alarming rates. According to a 2011 investigation by National Public Radio, nearly 700 Native American children in South Dakota are removed from their Native American parents each year. Laura Sullivan & Amy Walters, *Native Foster Care: Lost Children, Shattered Families*, NATIONAL PUBLIC RADIO, Oct. 25, 2011, *available at* http://www.npr.org/2011/10/25/141672992/native-foster-care-lost-children-shattered-families (last visited Nov. 10, 2013). Native American children make up less than 15 percent of the state's child population, but represent more than half of the children in foster care. *Id.* Approximately 90 percent of the Native children are removed into non-Native foster homes or group care. *Id.*

INDIAN CHILD WELFARE ACT OF 1978

P.L. 95–608 HOUSE REPORT NO. 95–1386
July 24, 1978

* * * The wholesale separation of Indian children from their families is perhaps the most tragic and destructive aspect of American Indian life today.

Surveys of states with large Indian populations conducted by the Association of American Indian Affairs (AAIA) in 1969 and again in 1974 indicate that approximately 25–35 percent of all Indian children are separated from their families and placed in foster homes, adoptive homes, or institutions. In some states the problem is getting worse: in Minnesota, one in every eight Indian children under 18 years of age is living in an adoptive home; and, in 1971–72, nearly one in every four Indian children under 1 year of age was adopted.

The disparity in placement rates for Indians and non-Indians is shocking. In Minnesota, Indian children are placed in foster care or in adoptive homes at a per capita rate five times greater than non-Indian children. In Montana, the ratio of Indian foster-care placement is at least 13 times greater. In South Dakota, 40 percent of all adoptions made by the State's Department of Public Welfare since 1967–68 are of Indian children, yet Indians make up only 7 percent of the juvenile population. The number of South Dakota Indian children living in foster homes is per capita, nearly 16 times greater than the non-Indian rate. In the state of Washington, the Indian adoption rate is 19 times greater and the foster care rate 10 times greater. In Wisconsin, the risk run by Indian children of being separated from their parents is nearly 1,600 percent greater than it is for non-Indian children. Just as Indian children are exposed to these great hazards, their parents are too. * * *

The Indian child welfare crisis will continue until the standards for defining mistreatment are revised. Very few Indian children are removed from their families on the grounds of physical abuse. One study of a North Dakota reservation showed that these grounds were advanced in only 1 percent of the cases. Another study of a tribe in the Northwest showed the same incidence. The remaining 99 percent of the cases were argued on such vague grounds as "neglect" or "social deprivation" and on allegations of the emotional damage the children were subjected to by living with their parents. Indian communities are often shocked to learn that parents they regard as excellent caregivers have been judged unfit by non-Indian social workers.

In judging the fitness of a particular family, many social workers, ignorant of Indian cultural values and social norms, make decisions that are wholly inappropriate in the context of Indian family life and so they frequently discover neglect or abandonment where none exists.

For example, the dynamics of Indian extended families are largely misunderstood. An Indian child may have scores of, perhaps more than a hundred, relatives who are counted as close, responsible members of the family. Many social workers, untutored in the ways of Indian family life or assuming them to be socially irresponsible, consider leaving the child with persons outside the nuclear family as neglect and thus as grounds for terminating parental rights. * * *

One of the grounds most frequently advanced for taking Indian children from their parents is the abuse of alcohol. However, this standard is applied unequally. In areas where rates of problem drinking among Indians and non-Indians are the same, it is rarely applied against non-Indian parents. Once again cultural biases frequently affect decision making. * * *

NOTE

What about class? Could the fact that Walter and Bernice Williams were not wealthy, white collar professionals have influenced the legal decision-makers responsible for deciding their fate? Professor Jennifer Collins studied a number of fatal neglect cases brought against parents or guardians and found that class status seemed to affect which parents were prosecuted. Preferential treatment was given to parents who were middle or upper class over those who were unemployed or in blue collar positions. Only 23.3 percent of parents who were identifiable as either white collar professionals or married to a white collar professional were prosecuted compared to 85.7 percent of parents who were blue collar workers, unemployed, or had some other indicator of lower socioeconomic status. Parents in blue collar professions or unemployed were four times more likely to be prosecuted for child neglect than parents from wealthier socioeconomic groups. Jennifer M. Collins, *Crime and Parenthood: The Uneasy Case for Prosecuting Negligent Parents*, 100 NW. U. L. REV. 807, 809, 831–32 (2006).

G. THE FELONY MURDER RULE

Under the common law felony murder rule (also known as the second degree felony murder rule), a person who kills during the commission or attempted commission of a qualifying felony has committed second degree murder. The felon's accomplices may also be convicted of second degree murder. (We will explore the question of what makes a person an accomplice in Chapter 12.)

In addition to the common law doctrine of felony murder, many jurisdictions that follow the common law also elevate, by statute, certain homicides to first-degree murder status if the killing occurred during the perpetration or attempted perpetration of an enumerated felony (i.e., a felony specified in the first degree murder statute). The felonies that are typically enumerated are rape, robbery, arson, burglary, and kidnaping.

In *People v. Aaron*, the Supreme Court of Michigan describes the history of the felony murder rule:

> Felony murder has never been a static, well-defined rule at common law, but throughout its history has been characterized by judicial reinterpretation to limit the harshness of the application of the rule. Historians and commentators have concluded that the rule is of questionable origin and that the

reasons for the rule no longer exist, making it an anachronistic remnant, "a historic survivor for which there is no logical or practical basis for existence in modern law." * * *

At early common law, the felony-murder rule went unchallenged because at that time practically all felonies were punishable by death. It was, therefore, "of no particular moment whether the condemned was hanged for the initial felony or for the death accidentally resulting from the felony." Thus . . . no injustice was caused directly by application of the rule at that time. * * *

Case law of Nineteenth-Century England reflects the efforts of the English courts to limit the application of the felony-murder doctrine. In [a] case involving a death resulting from arson, Judge Stephen instructed the jury as follows:

> [Instead] of saying that any act done with intent to commit a felony and which causes death amounts to murder, it should be reasonable to say that any act known to be dangerous to life and likely in itself to cause death, done for the purpose of committing a felony which causes death, should be murder.

In this century, the felony-murder doctrine was comparatively rarely invoked in England and in 1957 England abolished the felony-murder rule. * * *

Felony murder is often described as a strict liability crime because under the felony murder rule, a person may be convicted of murder even if she had no intent to kill and was not reckless or negligent with respect to the risk of death. That is to say, accidental deaths that occur in the commission of or attempt to commit a felony are covered by the felony murder rule. Because of its relative indifference to mens rea, the felony murder rule is in tension with the rest of homicide law, which focuses, as we have seen, on the actor's culpability as the primary way of meting out punishment.

One example of the broad reach of the felony murder rule comes from a newspaper report involving the death of an 87-year-old man who was accidentally shoved during an altercation between a security guard and a shoplifter:

> * * * JC Penney security guard Harry Delatorre, 20, and [Jesse] Rhodes were wrestling over a pair of women's acidwash Levi Jeans [which Delatorre thought Rhodes was attempting to steal] when they accidentally shoved [Stanley Dollin], who was slowly strolling down the crowded avenue in the afternoon, Berkeley Homicide Inspector Bob Maloney said. [Dollin sustained head injuries and died three days later. Rhodes was charged with first degree murder.]

> If convicted, Rhodes will be sentenced to 25 years in state prison.
>
> "Maybe there is some humanity in the system for this poor, humble and physically weak woman," McWilliams said. "This doesn't make sense to her, she's not a killer. She has a long history of petty theft, but she is not a killer."

Patricia Jacobus, *Rash of Unrelated August Killings Plagues Berkeley*, THE DAILY CALIFORNIAN, August 16, 1989, p. 1.

Courts troubled by the spectacle of accidental deaths being treated as murders have attempted to limit the operation of the felony murder rule with additional rules. Four such limiting rules are found in many jurisdictions that recognize felony murder. These are: (1) the inherently dangerous felony limitation, (2) the "res gestae" requirement, (3) the merger doctrine, and (4) the agency rule. The cases in this section outline these limitations on the felony murder rule.

1. THE INHERENTLY DANGEROUS FELONY LIMITATION

PEOPLE V. JAMES

Court of Appeal of California, Fourth Appellate District, Division 2
62 Cal.App.4th 244, 74 Cal.Rptr.2d 7 (1998)

RICHLI, J.

While defendant Kathey Lynn James (defendant) was manufacturing methamphetamine, one of the volatile chemicals she was using in the process caught fire; a conflagration followed in which her home was destroyed and three of her children killed.

A jury found defendant guilty on three counts of second degree murder, one count of manufacturing methamphetamine, and one count of conspiracy to manufacture methamphetamine; the jury expressly based each of the murder verdicts on both implied malice and second degree felony murder. Defendant was sentenced to 45 years to life in prison.

In the published portion of this opinion, we hold (1) manufacturing methamphetamine is an inherently dangerous felony for purposes of the second degree felony-murder rule. * * *

Factual Background

In August 1995, defendant rented a mobilehome (or trailer) in the Aguanga area of Riverside County. She lived there with her four children: Jimmy, who was seven; Deon, three; Jackson, two; and Megan, one. Two other adults, Richard Jones, and his girlfriend Kristy Barton, also lived in the mobilehome. Jones and Barton looked after the children and kept house. Michael Talbert lived elsewhere, but he, too, stayed in the mobilehome from time to time. Defendant owned a camper, which was kept next to the mobile home. Harry "Happy" Jensen lived in the camper. In exchange for room and board, he acted as handyman.

Defendant supported the entire household by manufacturing methamphetamine. All the adults were methamphetamine users; none of them had any other source of income. Defendant made a batch of methamphetamine about once a week. * * *

Jensen and Talbert, and, to a lesser extent, Jones and Barton, all saw defendant manufacturing methamphetamine. She began with "Mini-Thin" tablets, an over-the-counter medicine containing pseudoephedrine. First, she dissolved the tablets in hot water; then she added Coleman fuel, acetone, and/or lye, and "boil[ed] them down" to extract the ephedrine. Next, she "gassed" the solution. That is, she combined salt and sulfuric acid to make hydrochloric gas; when she applied the gas to the solvent, solid pseudoephedrine dropped out. Next, she put the pseudoephedrine into a Pyrex coffeepot, added red phosphorus and iodine, and heated the mixture on a hot plate. She wrapped the coffeepot with tape so that, if it blew up, pieces of Pyrex would not fly around the room. Finally, she cleaned the methamphetamine with acetone. The acetone dissolved the methamphetamine, leaving any impurities behind. Then she removed and evaporated the acetone. This left pure methamphetamine. Sometimes defendant would speed up the evaporation process by putting the acetone in the oven, on the stove top, or in the microwave.

At any given time, defendant had on hand 1 or 2 five-gallon drums of acetone, up to 30 to 40 one-gallon cans of Coleman fuel, and up to 20 cans of lye. The acetone was kept in a shed and brought inside, as needed, in a smaller jar or can. The lye was kept both in the kitchen and in the back bathroom. It was also used to clean out clogged drains. Defendant kept red phosphorus in glass jars under her bed. She kept iodine crystals in a plastic jar. She kept muriatic and/or sulfuric acid under the bathroom sink.

Theresa Kloos, who bought methamphetamine from defendant, once saw defendant "cooking" methamphetamine in the kitchen. She also saw her use a microwave to dry some freshly made drugs. Two small children, in diapers, were nearby. * * *

On December 26, 1995, about 3:15 p.m., a fire broke out in the mobilehome and burned it to the ground. Defendant escaped through the window of the front bathroom. Her oldest son, Jimmy, also escaped through a window. Deon, Jackson, and Megan died in the fire.

During the fire, defendant was crying and screaming, "The kids are in the house. My babies. My babies." She told a neighbor, "I tried to get them out but got burned."

Defendant sustained burns to her face, her right hand, the front of both calves, and the back of her right thigh. The burns to her calves stopped at a line at the level of her bike pants. Similarly, the burns to her hands stopped at a line on her wrist. * * *

After the fire, Barton and Jones took Jimmy to the home of a neighbor, Kim Hartigan. Jimmy told Hartigan "his mother was cooking white stuff on the stove. . . . [W]hile she was pouring the white stuff in the pan, . . . it caught on fire." Police officers came to Hartigan's house and asked Jimmy what had happened. Jimmy said his mother put a pan on the stove and poured some "white stuff" into it. An officer asked, "What white stuff?" Jimmy answered, "The stuff you put in the toilet." * * *

At trial, Jimmy testified that when the fire started, he was in the living room. The three younger children were in the kitchen. Jensen was resting on a couch in the living room. At first, Jimmy testified defendant was in the bathroom. However, after listening to a tape of his previous statements to police, he testified she was in the kitchen, cooking something at the stove. He described it as drain cleaner and as "white medicine." "She cooks it and she sells it." Jensen was also cooking. * * *

Defendant testified she had made some 300 batches of methamphetamine over a 10-year period and had never had an explosion or a fire. She "cooked" in the back bathroom, with the door locked, or in the camper; she never "cooked" in the kitchen, or in the presence of her children. She admitted using Coleman fuel in the manufacturing process, but she denied using acetone, except for using a small quantity of it to purify the methamphetamine she made for her personal use. Aside from her red phosphorous and her iodine crystals, which she buried off her property, she kept her chemicals and equipment in a locked cabinet in the back bathroom.

Defendant claimed she manufactured methamphetamine "in the safest way as possible." She manufactured "[o]ne step at a time, which made it a lot more safe and clean." She tried to avoid adding any heat to the process, although, when she needed to, she used a lukewarm heating plate. She had hired Barton and Jones to take care of her children so they would not be around when she was "cooking." * * *

I. The Felony of Manufacturing Methamphetamine Is Inherently Dangerous to Human Life

Defendant contends manufacturing methamphetamine cannot be used to support a murder conviction under the second degree felony-murder rule, because it is not an inherently dangerous felony.

A. *The Second Degree Felony-murder Rule.*

Murder is defined as the "unlawful killing of a human being . . . with malice aforethought." Malice "may be express or implied." Express malice murder requires an intent to kill. * * *

Murder also may be committed, even in the absence of actual malice, under the felony-murder rule. "The felony-murder rule 'artificially imposes malice as to one crime because of defendant's commission of another' and thereby satisfies the standard of culpability necessary to raise a homicide to murder." "The felony-murder rule applies to both first and second degree murder." Under the first degree felony-murder rule, a homicide is first degree murder if it is committed in the perpetration or attempted perpetration of statutorily specified felonies (including arson, robbery and rape). Under the second degree felony-murder rule, a homicide is second degree murder if it is committed in the perpetration or attempted perpetration of any felony that is inherently dangerous to human life.

"[T]he justification for the imputation of implied malice under these circumstances is that, 'when society has declared certain inherently dangerous conduct to be felonious, a defendant should not be allowed to excuse himself by saying he was unaware of the danger to life. . . . ' . . . [A]lso . . . , ' "[i]f the felony is not inherently dangerous, it is highly improbable that the potential felon will be deterred; he will not anticipate that any injury or death might arise solely from the fact that he will commit the felony." ' Thus, under the latter circumstances the commission of the felony could not serve logically as the basis for imputation of malice."

"In determining whether a felony is inherently dangerous, the court looks to the elements of the felony in the abstract, 'not the "particular" facts of the case,' i.e., not to the defendant's specific conduct." " 'This form of [viewed-in-the-abstract] analysis is compelled because there is a killing in every case where the rule might potentially be applied. If in such circumstances a court were to examine the particular facts of the case prior to establishing whether the underlying felony is inherently dangerous, the court might well be led to conclude the rule applicable despite any unfairness which might redound to the defendant by so broad an application: the existence of the dead victim might appear to lead inexorably to the conclusion that the underlying felony is exceptionally hazardous.' "

For many years, the California Supreme Court found it unnecessary to define "inherently dangerous felony." In *People v. Burroughs*, however, it referred to an inherently dangerous felony as one which "by its very nature, . . . cannot be committed without creating a substantial risk that someone will be killed. . . . " Later, in *People v. Patterson*, it defined an inherently dangerous felony as "an offense carrying 'a high probability' that death will result." Most recently, the court reaffirmed both of these definitions, treating them as if they were equivalent and interchangeable.

B. *The Propriety of Considering Evidence.*

Whether a felony is inherently dangerous for purposes of the second degree felony-murder rule is a question of law, or, at a minimum, a mixed question of law and fact, which we review de novo. In applying this standard of review, however, we face a difficult threshold question: What evidence—if any—may we look to?

In every relevant California case we have found—with two significant exceptions, which we will discuss in due course—the reviewing court decided whether the felony at issue was inherently dangerous without considering any evidence at all. This is consistent with the requirement that the court must view the elements of the felony in the abstract. * * *

The first case which suggested a court may consider evidence on this question was *People v. Patterson*. There, the trial court initially dismissed a murder charge against the defendant, on the ground that the underlying felony of furnishing cocaine was not inherently dangerous. The People appealed, but the Court of Appeal affirmed. * * * The Supreme Court reversed. It held: "In determining whether defendant had committed an inherently dangerous felony, the court should have considered only the particular crime at issue, namely, furnishing cocaine, and not the entire group of offenses included in the statute but not involved here."

The Supreme Court then went on to state: "Defendant . . . argues that even the more narrow offense of furnishing cocaine is not an inherently dangerous felony and therefore the trial court acted correctly in dismissing the murder charge, despite its faulty analysis. In countering that argument, the People have asked us to take judicial notice of various medical articles and reports that assertedly demonstrate that the offense of furnishing cocaine is sufficiently dangerous to life to constitute an inherently dangerous felony. *The task of evaluating the evidence on this issue is most appropriately entrusted to the trial court, subject, of course, to appellate review. We therefore direct the Court of Appeal to remand the matter to the trial court for further proceedings in light of this opinion.*"

The second case was *People v. Taylor*. There, the defendant furnished phencyclidine (PCP) to the victim, who drowned while under its influence. The defendant was charged with furnishing PCP, and with murder. At trial, both sides presented expert testimony with respect to whether furnishing PCP is inherently dangerous. The trial court ruled that furnishing PCP was an inherently dangerous felony. The jury found the defendant guilty of murder on that theory. * * *

The appellate court began by holding the issue was subject to de novo review. It analogized it to an issue of statutory interpretation. The court then added: "[T]he determination of a 'high probability of death' depends, at least somewhat, on evidence as to the dangerousness of the underlying felony in the abstract, evidence which is best garnered from testimony by experts. Appellate courts have often used evidence gathered by trial courts and referees as the basis for de novo legal rulings." Ultimately, the court held, based on "the record provided," that furnishing PCP is not inherently dangerous.

Patterson and *Taylor* thus permit a court to consider evidence of whether a felony is inherently dangerous. This is a practical necessity when the danger claimed to be inherent in the elements of a felony is a matter of scientific, medical or technological expertise, rather than common knowledge. The status of a felony may even change over time, as the state of the art changes. * * *

The trial court still must determine whether a felony is inherently dangerous based on the elements of the felony in the abstract. However, it may, in its discretion, hear proffered evidence that is relevant to that determination. Such evidence ordinarily will consist of expert testimony and scientific or technical literature. The trial court must be careful not to transgress the prohibition against considering the defendant's specific conduct—or, most of all, the fact that that specific conduct happened to cause death. * * *

E. *Analysis.*

Manufacturing methamphetamine demands the use of hazardous materials. Acetone, Coleman fuel and ether, in particular, are highly volatile and extremely flammable. Their vapors can be ignited by almost any ignition source, including a hot plate or a pilot light. The very process of "cooking" methamphetamine demands the presence of some heat source; and pilot lights are ubiquitous, not only in homes, but also in businesses and motel rooms—though their presence is all too easy to forget. The red phosphorus, iodine, and various acids involved also are extremely hazardous. * * *

Defendant relies on the evidence that only a small minority of methamphetamine labs are actually associated with a fatality. However, "we do not understand the term 'high probability' to mean greater than 50 percent. Very few activities in life, even noncriminal conduct, carry such a risk." "[C]ourts have hesitated to turn the law into a pure statistical analysis." We dare say only a small minority of simple kidnappings actually result in death. Nevertheless, simple kidnapping has repeatedly been held to be inherently dangerous. * * *

Defendant also relies on the evidence that a skilled person can manufacture methamphetamine "relatively" safely. A similar argument, however, was rejected in *People v. Morse*. There, the issue was whether reckless or malicious possession of a destructive device is inherently dangerous felony." * * *

The dangers of manufacturing methamphetamine are closely analogous to the dangers of possessing a destructive device, as in *Morse*. Both felonies involve a dangerous instrumentality; its maker often loses control over it; it may wreak enormous havoc on persons and property; the victims are often unintended sufferers; and, considering its destructive potential, the dangerous instrumentality is susceptible of fairly easy concealment.

In some ways, manufacturing methamphetamine is *more* dangerous than possessing a destructive device. One can commit the felony of possessing a destructive device even if the device has been rendered inoperable. However, one cannot commit the felony of manufacturing methamphetamine without possessing at least some hazardous substances; without using, pouring and mixing those substances; or without applying heat. Thus, manufacturing methamphetamine "by its very nature, . . . cannot be committed without creating a substantial risk that someone will be killed. . . . "

We conclude the trial court correctly ruled that manufacturing methamphetamine is inherently dangerous to human life for purposes of the second degree felony-murder rule. * * *

HINES V. STATE

Supreme Court of Georgia
276 Ga. 491, 578 S.E.2d 868 (2003)

FLETCHER, C.J.

While hunting, Robert Lee Hines mistook his friend Steven Wood for a turkey and shot him dead. A jury convicted Hines of felony murder based on the underlying crime of possession of a firearm by a convicted felon, but acquitted him of felony murder based on the underlying felony of misuse of a firearm while hunting. * * *

Taken in the light most favorable to the jury's verdict of guilty, the evidence at trial showed that, late in the afternoon of April 8, 2001, Hines and some of his friends and relatives went turkey hunting. They split into two groups, with Hines and his friend Randy Stoker hunting together in one area, and the victim, the victim's wife, and Hines's son hunting in a different area, approximately one-fourth mile away. As the sky was growing dark, Hines heard a turkey gobble, "saw it fan out and shot." Hines's shot went through heavy foliage and hit the victim approximately eighty feet away. Immediately thereafter, the victim's wife screamed, "You shot Wood." Hines and his son went for help, but the victim died before help could arrive.

On his return, Hines tried to convince his son and Stoker to take responsibility for the shooting. They both refused. The entire group, however, agreed to say that they did not know who had shot Wood. Hines removed his camouflage clothing and hid his shotgun and hunting gear before the police arrived.

Two days later, Hines admitted he had shot Wood and showed the police where he had hidden his shotgun. Hines's son showed the police where he had hidden Hines's hunting clothing and gear, which included unopened cans of beer. An open beer can and foam insulation wrap that belonged to Hines were found near where Hines had fired the fatal shot.

We conclude that the evidence at trial was sufficient for a reasonable trier of fact to have found Hines guilty beyond a reasonable doubt of the crimes for which he was convicted. * * *

Hines contends that a convicted felon's possession of a firearm while turkey hunting cannot be one of the inherently dangerous felonies required to support a conviction for felony murder. "The only limitation on the type of felony that may serve as an underlying felony for a felony murder conviction is that the felony must be inherently dangerous to human life." A felony is "inherently dangerous" when it is " 'dangerous per se' " or " 'by its circumstances creates a foreseeable risk of death.' " Depending on the facts, possession of a firearm by a convicted felon can be an inherently dangerous felony.

In *Ford v. State*, the defendant was a convicted felon who was unloading a handgun when it accidentally discharged, went through the floor, and killed an occupant of the apartment below. A jury convicted Ford for felony murder based on his felonious possession of a firearm. This Court reversed, finding that, because no evidence showed the defendant knew there was an apartment below him or that the victim was present, his possession of a firearm could not support a conviction for felony murder.

In contrast to *Ford*, Hines intentionally fired his shotgun intending to hit his target. He had been drinking before he went hunting, and there was evidence that he had been drinking while hunting. He knew that other hunters were in the area and was unaware of their exact location. He also knew that other people visited the area in which he was hunting. He took an unsafe shot at dusk, through heavy foliage, at a target eighty feet away that he had not positively identified as a turkey. Under these circumstances, we conclude that Hines's illegal possession of a firearm created a foreseeable risk of death. Accordingly, Hines's violation of the prohibition against convicted felons possessing firearms was an inherently dangerous felony that could support a felony murder conviction. * * *

Judgment affirmed. All the Justices concur, except Sears, P. J., who dissents.

SEARS, PRESIDING JUSTICE, dissenting.

Because I conclude that circumstances surrounding Hines's commission of the status felony of possessing a firearm were not inherently dangerous within the meaning of our decision in *Ford v. State*, I dissent to the majority's affirmance of Hines's conviction of felony murder.

In *Ford*, this Court held that for a felony to serve as the basis for a felony murder conviction, it had to be inherently dangerous by its very nature or had to be committed under circumstances creating a foreseeable risk of death. We also held that the imputation of malice that justifies the felony murder rule is dependent on the "perpetrator's life-threatening state of mind accompanying [the] commission [of the underlying felony]." In *Ford*, however, we did not specify how to determine whether a particular felony, either by its nature or as it was committed, was inherently dangerous to human life. Because of the severe punishments that accompany a conviction of murder and because it is illogical to impute malice for purposes of felony murder ' "from the intent to commit a felony not [foreseeably] dangerous to human life," ' I conclude that for purposes of our felony-murder doctrine, a felony is inherently dangerous per se or as committed if it carries " 'a high probability' that [a human] death will result." This standard will ensure that our felony murder rule is not inappropriately expanded by "reducing the seriousness of the act which a defendant must commit in order to be charged with murder."

In the present case, I conclude that the possession of a firearm by Hines was not committed in a fashion that was inherently dangerous and that carried a high probability that death would result. The fact that Hines was hunting, a dangerous sport; the fact that he had been drinking before he went hunting; the fact that he was hunting at dusk; and the fact that he fired a shot when he knew other hunters were in the general area in which he was hunting may establish that Hines was negligent, but do not establish that his acts created a high probability that death to a human being would result, or that he had a "life-threatening state of mind." Moreover, as for the fatal shot, Hines testified that he heard a turkey gobble, that he "saw it fan out," and that he then fired at the object. Even though Hines may not, as stated by the majority, have positively identified his target as a turkey, he had to make a split-second decision regarding his target and concluded, based on hearing a gobble and seeing something "fan out," that the object was a turkey. I cannot conclude that, under these circumstances, the failure of the hunter to identify his target beyond doubt carried a high probability that a human being would be killed or that he acted with a "life-threatening state of mind." The death in this case is clearly a tragic incident, and Hines's conduct before and after the shooting was reprehensible. But the sanction of life in prison for murder should be reserved for cases in which the defendant's moral failings warrant such punishment. Here, the application of the felony murder statute to Hines's actions punishes him more severely than his culpability merits. In this regard, Hines will be serving the same punishment—life in prison—as an arsonist convicted of felony murder who firebombed an apartment that he knew was occupied, causing the death of two young children, and the same punishment as an armed robber convicted of felony murder who entered a store with a firearm and shot and killed a store employee. This result is unwarranted and unnecessary, as Hines could be prosecuted and convicted of an appropriate lesser crime, such as involuntary manslaughter or the misuse of a firearm while hunting.[13]

One final note. Hunting is a time-honored recreational activity encouraged by the State of Georgia and enjoyed by many of our State's citizens. No doubt a number of hunters have probably engaged in negligent hunting practices similar to those in this case. Although I do not condone such careless practices, neither can I agree with subjecting so many hunters to the possibility of spending life in prison when they do not fastidiously follow proper hunting procedures and accidentally shoot a fellow hunter.

For the foregoing reasons, I dissent to the majority opinion.

2. THE RES GESTAE REQUIREMENT

A second consideration in the application of the felony murder rule is the res gestae requirement. The res gestae requirement has two parts. First, the felony and the homicide must be close in time and distance. In other words, there must be both temporal and geographical proximity between the homicide and the felony. Recall that in order for the felony murder rule to apply, the killing must occur "during the commission or attempted commission" of a felony. Clearly, the felony murder rule does not apply if the killing occurs *before* the felony. One might also presume that the felony murder rule does not apply if the killing occurs *after* the commission of the felony. Courts, however, have expanded the time period during which the felony is said to be occurring by holding that felony murder liability continues until the felon reaches a place of temporary safety. The first case in this section, *People v. Bodely*, discusses this "place of temporary safety" rule.

Second, the res gestae requirement demands a causal connection between the felony and the homicide. Courts, however, are not in agreement regarding how much of a causal connection is required. Some courts, like the court in *People v. Stamp*, merely require a but-for causal

[13] Hines was in fact convicted of this crime in the present case.

connection. Others, like the court in *King v. Commonwealth*, require a greater causal connection between the felonious conduct and the death.

PEOPLE V. BODELY

Court of Appeal of California, Sixth Appellate District
32 Cal.App.4th 311, 38 Cal.Rptr.2d 72 (1995)

MIHARA, J.

The question presented by this case is whether a killing which occurs during the perpetrator's flight from a burglary[a] occurs "in the perpetration" of the burglary and therefore is felony murder. We conclude that such a killing is felony murder and affirm the judgment.

FACTS

Defendant entered a supermarket, grabbed $75 out of a cash register and ran. Several supermarket employees pursued him. He ran out of the supermarket into the parking lot and got into his car. Joseph Andre, who was in the parking lot at the time, joined in the chase. Andre ran in front of defendant's car and put his hands on the hood as if to stop the car. Andre then went to the driver's side window of defendant's car, put his arm inside the car and told defendant to stop. Defendant drove away, jerking the car sharply to the left. Defendant's car hit Andre, knocking Andre onto the hood of the car. Andre then fell off of the hood and struck the back of his head on the pavement. This impact resulted in Andre's death. Defendant sped up and drove away. Defendant was convicted of first degree murder, burglary and an unrelated robbery and committed to state prison. On appeal, he challenges only the murder conviction.

ANALYSIS

"All murder . . . which is committed in the perpetration of, or attempt to perpetrate . . . burglary . . . is murder of the first degree." Defendant claims that Andre's death did not occur "in the perpetration of . . . burglary" because defendant had already left the burglarized structure when he caused Andre's death. Defendant concedes that felony-murder liability continues throughout the flight of a perpetrator from the scene of a *robbery*[b] until the perpetrator reaches a place of temporary safety. However, he claims that the perpetration of burglary "is over" when the burglar leaves the structure, because burglary, unlike robbery, does not require the perpetrator to asport any loot.[c] Hence, in defendant's view, the flight of the perpetrator from a burglary is not part of the

[a] Under California Penal Code § 459, the offense of burglary requires entrance into "any structure which has walls on all sides and is covered by a roof" (*People v. Stickman,* 34 Cal. 242 (1867) with "intent to commit grand or petit larceny or any felony."

[b] California Penal Code § 211 defines robbery as "the felonious taking of personal property in the possession of another, from his person or immediate presence, and against his will, accomplished by means of force or fear."

[c] "Asportation" is the technical term for "taking and carrying away" in the law of theft.

perpetration of the offense. The only authority on point is *People v. Fuller,* which resolved this precise issue against defendant. Defendant asks us not to follow *Fuller.*[d]

The Attorney General asks us to follow *Fuller* and hold that the perpetration of a felony does not end for purposes of felony-murder liability until the perpetrator has "reached a place of temporary safety." Numerous California Supreme Court decisions hold that the perpetration of a *robbery* continues, for felony-murder liability purposes, so long as the robbers are in flight from the scene of the crime and have not reached a place of temporary safety. While this so-called "escape rule" was originally justified by an analysis based on when the crime of robbery was "complete," the California Supreme Court has more recently explained that the duration of felony-murder liability is not determined by considering whether the felony itself has been completed. Instead, "the homicide is committed in the perpetration of the felony if the killing and the felony are *parts of one continuous transaction.*"

If we apply this "one continuous transaction" analysis, no rationale supports limiting the escape rule exclusively to robbery. The perpetrator's immediate escape from the scene of a crime is no less a part of the same continuous transaction which includes the crime when the crime is burglary than when the crime is robbery. Burglary and robbery, like many other crimes, are generally technically "complete" for purposes of criminal liability prior to the escape of the perpetrator. However, "the escape rule serves the legitimate public policy considerations of deterrence and culpability" by extending felony-murder liability beyond the technical completion of the crime. While the California Supreme Court has never actually decided the precise issue raised here, its various statements on this subject reflect that the escape rule is not limited to the crime of robbery. In *People v. Bigelow,* the California Supreme Court explained that "the test used in felony-murder cases to determine when a killing is so closely related to an underlying felony as to justify an enhanced punishment for the killing" is that ". . . the crime continues until the criminal has reached a place of temporary safety." In *People v. Cooper,* the California Supreme Court mentioned that ". . . the potential of felony-murder liability of *burglars* continues through the escape until the perpetrators reach a place of temporary safety" and cited *Fuller* for this proposition. * * *

Since the application of the escape rule to burglary is consistent with the "one continuous transaction" test, we conclude that felony-murder liability continues during the escape of a burglar from the scene of the burglary until the burglar reaches a place of temporary safety.

---

[d] In *People v. Fuller*, the Court of Appeal for the Fifth District of California held that flight following a burglary is considered part of the same transaction as long as the felon has not yet reached a place of temporary safety. The court also held that the felony murder rule applies to both escaping robbers and escaping burglars. 86 Cal. App. 3d 618 (1978).

CONCLUSION

The judgment is affirmed.

COTTLE, P.J., and WUNDERLICH, J., concurred.

PEOPLE V. STAMP

Court of Appeal of California, Second Appellate District, Division Three
2 Cal.App.3d 203, 82 Cal.Rptr. 598 (1969)

COBEY, ACTING P.J.

These are appeals by Jonathan Earl Stamp, Michael John Koory and Billy Dean Lehman, following jury verdicts of guilty of robbery and murder, both in the first degree. Each man was given a life sentence on the murder charge together with the time prescribed by law on the robbery count.

Defendants appeal their conviction of the murder of Carl Honeyman who, suffering from a heart disease, died between 15 and 20 minutes after Koory and Stamp held up his business, the General Amusement Company, on October 26, 1965, at 10:45 a.m. * * *

On this appeal appellants primarily rely upon their position that the felony-murder doctrine should not have been applied in this case due to the unforeseeability of Honeyman's death. * * *

Defendants Koory and Stamp, armed with a gun and a blackjack, entered the rear of the building housing the offices of General Amusement Company, ordered the employees they found there to go to the front of the premises, where the two secretaries were working. Stamp, the one with the gun, then went into the office of Carl Honeyman, the owner and manager. Thereupon Honeyman, looking very frightened and pale, emerged from the office in a "kind of hurry." He was apparently propelled by Stamp who had hold of him by an elbow.

The robbery victims were required to lie down on the floor while the robbers took the money and fled out the back door. As the robbers, who had been on the premises 10 to 15 minutes, were leaving, they told the victims to remain on the floor for five minutes so that no one would "get hurt."

Honeyman, who had been lying next to the counter, had to use it to steady himself in getting up off the floor. Still pale, he was short of breath, sucking air, and pounding and rubbing his chest. As he walked down the hall, in an unsteady manner, still breathing hard and rubbing his chest, he said he was having trouble "keeping the pounding down inside" and that his heart was "pumping too fast for him." A few minutes later, although still looking very upset, shaking, wiping his forehead and rubbing his chest, he was able to walk in a steady manner into an employee's office. When the police arrived, almost immediately thereafter, he told them he was not feeling very well and that he had a pain in his chest. About two minutes later, which was 15 or 20 minutes after the robbery had occurred, he collapsed on the floor. At 11:25 he was pronounced dead on arrival at the hospital. The coroner's report listed the immediate cause of death as heart attack.

The employees noted that during the hours before the robbery Honeyman had appeared to be in normal health and good spirits. The victim was an obese, 60-year-old man, with a history of heart disease, who was under a great deal of pressure due to the intensely competitive nature of his business. Additionally, he did not take good care of his heart.

Three doctors, including the autopsy surgeon, Honeyman's physician, and a professor of cardiology from U.C.L.A., testified that although Honeyman had an advanced case of atherosclerosis, a progressive and ultimately fatal disease, there must have been some immediate upset to his system which precipitated the attack. It was their conclusion in response to a hypothetical question that but for the robbery there would have been no fatal seizure at that time. The fright induced by the robbery was too much of a shock to Honeyman's system. There was opposing expert testimony to the effect that it could not be said with reasonable medical certainty that fright could ever be fatal. * * *

Appellant's contention that the evidence was insufficient to prove that the robbery factually caused Honeyman's death is without merit. The test on review is whether there is substantial evidence to uphold the judgment of the trial court, and in so deciding this court must assume in the case of a jury trial the existence of every fact in favor of the verdict which the jury could reasonably have deduced from the evidence. A review of the facts as outlined above shows that there was substantial evidence of the robbery itself, that appellants were the robbers, and that but for the robbery the victim would not have experienced the fright which brought on the fatal heart attack. * * *

Appellant's contention that the felony-murder rule is inapplicable to the facts of this case is also without merit. Under the felony-murder rule of section 189 of the Penal Code, a killing committed in either the perpetration of or an attempt to perpetrate robbery is murder of the first degree. This is true whether the killing is wilfull, deliberate and premeditated, or merely accidental or unintentional, and whether or not the killing is planned as a part of the commission of the robbery.

The doctrine presumes malice aforethought on the basis of the commission of a felony inherently dangerous to human life. This rule is a rule of substantive law in California and not merely an evidentiary shortcut to finding malice as it withdraws from the jury the requirement that they find either express malice or the implied malice which is manifested in an intent to kill. Under this rule no intentional act is necessary other than the attempt to or the actual commission of the robbery itself. When a robber enters a place with a deadly weapon with the intent to commit robbery, malice is shown by the nature of the crime. * * *

The doctrine is not limited to those deaths which are foreseeable. Rather a felon is held strictly liable for *all* killings committed by him or his accomplices in the course of the felony. As long as the homicide is the direct causal result of the robbery the felony-murder rule applies whether or not the death was a natural or probable consequence of the robbery. So long as a victim's predisposing physical condition, regardless of its cause, is not the *only* substantial factor bringing about his death, that condition, and the robber's ignorance of it, in no way destroys the robber's criminal responsibility for the death. So long as life is shortened as a result of the felonious act, it does not matter that the victim might have died soon anyway. In this respect, the robber takes his victim as he finds him. * * *

The judgment is affirmed.

KING V. COMMONWEALTH

Court of Appeals of Virginia
6 Va.App. 351, 368 S.E.2d 704 (1988)

COLEMAN, J.

* * * Nelson James King appeals his conviction of second degree murder under the statute. He argues that he could not be convicted of second degree murder for the accidental death of a cofelon occurring during the commission of a felony. He also argues that the trial court erred in instructing the jury on the elements of the offense. We hold that because the death was not caused by an act of the felons in furtherance of the felony, appellant is not criminally liable for the death.

On October 17, 1984, King and his copilot, Mark Lee Bailey, were flying a Beechcraft Bonanza airplane carrying over five hundred pounds of marijuana to the New River Valley airport in Dublin, Virginia. They were flying for Wallace Thrasher, who owned the airplane and ran the drug smuggling operation. King was a licensed pilot; Bailey was not. The two encountered heavy cloud cover and fog near Mt. Airy, North Carolina and apparently became lost. In an effort to navigate through the cloud cover and fog, they flew the plane to a lower altitude in order to follow U.S. Route 52. Bailey was piloting the plane at this time. As Bailey flew, King was examining navigation maps in an attempt to determine the plane's whereabouts. The airplane crashed into Fancy Gap Mountain killing Bailey almost instantly. King was thrown from the plane and survived. King was charged with felony homicide under Code § 18.2–33 for Bailey's death. A jury convicted King of second degree murder under the statute and recommended a six-year penitentiary sentence.

Code § 18.2–33 defines second degree felony homicide: "The killing of one accidentally, contrary to the intention of the parties, while in the prosecution of some felonious act other than those specified in §§ 18.2–31 and 18.2–32, is murder of the second degree and is punishable as a Class 3 felony." This statute and its companion, § 18.2–32, defining first degree felony-murder, codify the common law doctrine of felony-murder. The doctrine was developed to elevate to murder a homicide committed during the course of a felony by imputing malice to the killing. The justification for imputing malice was the theory that the increased risk of death or serious harm occasioned by the commission of a felony demonstrated the felon's lack of concern for human life. The doctrine was originally limited, therefore, to felonies that were inherently or foreseeably dangerous. The purpose of the doctrine was to deter inherently dangerous felonies by holding the felons responsible for the consequences of the felony, whether intended or not. While the range of felonies which may be a predicate for the felony-murder conviction has changed, the function of the doctrine is still to elevate to murder a homicide resulting from a felony by imputing malice. * * *

The second degree felony-murder statute in Virginia contemplates a killing with malice. Indeed, "the commission of *any* felonious act . . . supplies the malice which raises the incidental homicide to the level of second-degree murder." It does not follow, however, that any death of any person which occurs during the period in which a felony is being committed will subject the felon to criminal liability under the felony-murder rule. To construe our statute to encompass every accidental death occurring during the commission of a felony, regardless of whether it causally relates to or results from the commission of the felony, is to make felons absolutely liable for the accidental death of another even though such death is fortuitous and the product of causes wholly unrelated to the commission of the felony. Recognizing the potentially harsh and far reaching effects of such a construction of the felony-murder doctrine, the Virginia courts, as well as others, have limited its application. In order for the incidental accidental killing to be murder, the homicide must be criminal in nature and must contain the elements or attributes of criminal homicide cognizable at common law.

One of the most significant factors in defining the scope of the felony-murder doctrine involves the causation required between the felony and the death. Previous decisions of the Virginia Supreme Court have found it unnecessary to decide whether "a mere nexus" between the death and predicate felony is sufficient to satisfy the statute or whether a more direct causal relationship is required. We must address that issue at this time.

In Virginia, it is clear when the homicide is within the *res gestae* of the initial felony and emanates therefrom, it is committed in the perpetration of that felony. The Court explained that "the felony-murder statute applies where the killing is so closely related to the felony in time, place, and causal connection as to make it a part of the same criminal enterprise." * * *

In a leading case involving the felony-murder doctrine, which the Virginia Supreme Court has cited with approval, the Pennsylvania Supreme Court addressed the causation problem at length. Rejecting their previous standard of proximate cause, the court stated:

> In adjudging a felony-murder, it is to be remembered at all times that the thing which is imputed to a felon for a killing incidental to his felony is *malice* and *not the act of killing*. The mere coincidence of homicide and felony is not enough to satisfy the requirements of the felony-murder doctrine. . . . "Death must be a consequence of the felony . . . and not merely coincidence."

The court noted further: "[T]he 'causation' requirement for responsibility in a felony-murder is that the homicide stem from the commission of the felony." The *Redline* court noted that the malice of the underlying felony attaches to whatever else the criminal may do in connection with the felony. Therefore, "the killing must have been done by the defendant or by an accomplice or confederate or by one acting in furtherance of the felonious undertaking."

The implications of this reasoning are threefold. First, only acts causing death which are committed by those involved in the felony can be the basis for a conviction. Second, the act causing death must result from some effort to further the felony before malice can be imputed to that act. Third, there must be some act attributable to the felons which causes death. It is not sufficient that death be only temporally related to commission of the felony. Death must be directly related in time, place, and causal connection to the commission of the felony; the felony or acts in furtherance thereof must contribute to cause the death to constitute a "killing" within the felony-murder statute. * * *

In the present case, King and Bailey were in the airplane to further the felony of possession of marijuana with the intent to distribute. They were flying over the mountains while committing the felony. The time and the place of the death were closely connected with the felony. However, no causal connection exists between the felony of drug distribution and the killing by a plane crash. Thus, no basis exists to find that the accidental death was part or a result of the criminal enterprise. In the felony-murder cases cited above, death, to be considered an "accidental killing" within the statute, has resulted from a particular act which was an integral part of the felony or an act in direct furtherance of the felony—shooting a gun, striking a match, distributing cocaine. In this case, there is no such act which caused the death. Thus, there has been no homicide, or unlawful killing by another, for which a cofelon can be held accountable. Bailey, who was flying the plane at the time of the crash, was not killed by King or by any act of King which was in furtherance of the felony. We see no "act of killing" which we can attribute to King or to the felony. The felony-murder rule does not exist to enable courts to impute "the act of killing" where an accidental death results from fortuitous circumstances and the only connection with the felony is temporal. The cause of Bailey's death was Bailey's piloting and adverse weather conditions. The accident stemmed not from the possession or distribution of drugs, but from fog, low cloud cover, pilot error, and inexperience. Had Bailey and King been transporting drugs in an automobile when they encountered heavy fog and Bailey, not seeing a curve, had driven off the mountain, the legal consequences would be the same. The commission of the felony merely accounted for their presence at the location of the accident, and nothing directly related to the commission of the felony caused the accident. Thus, flying into the mountain was not a direct consequence of the felony. Had the plane been flying low or recklessly to avoid detection, for example, the crash would be a consequence or action which was directly intended to further the felony and a different result might obtain. * * *

The Commonwealth argues that the jury could infer that King's conduct in the commission of the underlying felony was inherently dangerous to human life and that his action of putting the plane in a dangerous position and allowing an unlicensed pilot to fly caused the crash. Accepting without comment the Commonwealth's argument that the evidence established involuntary manslaughter based on King's antecedent negligence, the evidence still establishes no causal relationship between the felony of possession of marijuana and the death by plane crash. If King and Bailey had been transporting legal cargo that day, the crash would still have occurred. It is true, of course, that but for the felony, King and Bailey probably would not have been in the plane. However, criminal liability for felony-murder requires more than a finding that "but for" the felony the parties would not have been present at the time and location of the accidental death. The act or acts causing death must have been directly calculated to further the felony or necessitated by the commission of the felony. Such a causal connection is absent in this case.

Because we reverse the conviction on the grounds stated above, we do not address the issue of the trial judge's jury instructions.

Reversed and dismissed.

3. THE MERGER DOCTRINE

Another limitation on the felony murder rule is the merger doctrine. Under this doctrine, felonies that are assaultive in nature "merge" with the homicide and cannot serve as the basis for a felony murder conviction.

In other words, if the underlying felony is deemed to be assaultive, the felony murder rule is inapplicable and the government must prove malice aforethought some other way than through the felony murder rule. *Rose v. State* explains and applies the merger doctrine.

ROSE V. STATE

Supreme Court of Nevada
255 P.3d 291 (2011)

DOUGLAS, C.J.

In this appeal, we address whether a charge of assault with a deadly weapon merges with a charged homicide so that it cannot be used as the basis for second-degree felony murder. * * *

Facts

Appellant Brian Rose was convicted of second-degree murder with the use of a deadly weapon for shooting his girlfriend, Jackie Watkins, in the head. On the day of the killing, Rose and his friend, Jake Timms, went target shooting in the desert with Rose's .40 caliber Smith & Wesson semiautomatic handgun. Afterwards, they picked up Watkins and went to a barbeque at the home of another friend, Julius Castano. Rose brought the gun inside the house and placed it in the family room because he claimed he feared someone might break into his car and steal his registered gun.

Throughout the evening, Rose, Timms, and Julius handled the gun. At one point, Rose took the magazine out of the gun and pulled the slide back to make sure the chamber was empty. Timms took the gun and put it in a holster on his hip. After eating dinner and drinking, Rose, Watkins, Timms, and Julius retired to the living room. Timms eventually fell asleep on the couch with the gun still in the holster around his waist. At some point Rose took the gun from the sleeping Timms and placed it in his waistband.

Later in the evening, Rose shot Watkins in the head while she spoke on the phone to her friend Erin Fragoso. * * * According to Rose's voluntary statement to police, he aimed the gun at or near Watkins while she was talking to Fragoso and told her to get off the phone. He then shot a single round from his gun and hit the top of Watkins's head. * * *

Officers arrived quickly at the home and noted that Watkins was positioned as if she was still talking on the phone. Medical personnel took Watkins to the hospital where she died from deprivation of blood to the brain. At the Castano home, officers found an ejected cartridge on the floor against the wall, behind a couch. Officers also found Rose's loaded Smith & Wesson handgun upstairs in a bedroom.

A police officer located Rose, who was driving at speeds approaching 100 miles per hour, and followed him but did not pull him over. Rose pulled over voluntarily, exited his car, and was taken into custody. Upon his arrest, the police read Rose his *Miranda* rights, and he was interviewed by Las Vegas Metropolitan Police Department homicide detectives. Rose admitted to knowing how to use his gun and knowing that the gun had no hammer. Rose told the detectives that he did not know his gun was loaded and that he accidentally shot Watkins. He also told them that he considered fleeing to Mexico. When the detectives asked Rose if he intended to shoot Watkins, he responded, "God no."

Rose acknowledged that he must have pulled the trigger when he turned, but there was no witness testimony presented that Rose purposefully aimed and fired at Watkins. In his voluntary statement to detectives, Rose claimed that he had pointed the gun at the chair next to Watkins to be "a dick." He said he gave Watkins "a squinted look" and smiled to let her know he was playing around. Rose stated that he "looked back the other way and, and then when [he] looked back, that's when it actually went off." Rose asserted that he did not care whether Watkins got off the phone or not, and, at the time, he believed the gun was empty. At the end of the interrogation, the detectives told Rose that Watkins died, and Rose became very upset and cried.

Rose was charged with one count of murder with use of a deadly weapon. * * * Rose filed a pretrial motion asking the district court to strike the second-degree felony murder theory and disallow the State from presenting any instructions on such a charge. Specifically, Rose asked the court to apply the merger doctrine, arguing that "assault with a deadly weapon cannot support a murder conviction under the second-degree felony murder rule because to allow that would alleviate the State from ever having to prove intent to kill in all cases wherein a killing results from a felonious assault." The district court denied Rose's motion and permitted the State to argue this theory.

Ultimately, the jury returned a general verdict finding Rose guilty of second-degree murder with the use of a deadly weapon. Rose filed a motion to set aside the guilty verdict or, in the alternative, for a new trial. The district court denied Rose's motion, * * * Rose was sentenced to 10 to 25 years in prison, plus an equal and consecutive term for the use of a deadly weapon. Rose now appeals from his judgment of conviction.

Discussion

The record indicates that the State relied on the felony murder rule as one of its theories for second-degree murder. During closing argument, the State argued that malice could be established in four ways: (1) express malice (intent to kill), (2) implied malice (reckless disregard of consequences and social duty), (3) felony murder based on assault with a deadly weapon, and (4) commission of an unlawful act that naturally tends to destroy the life of a human being. It argued that if the killing occurred during "the prosecution of committing a felony," specifically, assault with a deadly weapon, the crime was second-degree murder. This argument was consistent with the jury instruction the district court gave regarding * * * second-degree murder.

On appeal, Rose contends that assault with a deadly weapon cannot be used as a predicate felony to obtain a second-degree murder conviction under the felony murder rule because it merges with the homicide and thus is barred by the merger doctrine. He contends that the State's reliance on this theory, and the concomitant instructions given regarding second-degree felony murder, were therefore improper. * * *

Second-degree felony murder

The felony murder rule makes a killing committed in the course of certain felonies murder, without requiring the State to present additional evidence as to the defendant's mental state. The rule takes two forms in Nevada: first-degree felony murder and second-degree felony murder. The Legislature has specified the felonies that provide the malicious intent necessary to characterize a killing as first-degree murder. In contrast, there are no statutorily enumerated felonies with respect to second-degree felony murder[.] * * * [The relevant] statutes broadly provide that killings occurring in the commission of an unlawful act that naturally tends to destroy human life or committed in the "prosecution of a felonious intent" are murder and, unless the murder is committed in a manner that satisfies the first degree murder statute are murder of the second degree. Despite that broad language, this court has placed restrictions on the use of the felony murder rule to establish second-degree murder in order to avoid the potential for "untoward" prosecutions that a broad application of the felony murder rule would allow. In particular, we have required that "two elements [be] satisfied: (1) . . . 'the [predicate] felony [must be] inherently dangerous, * * * 'and (2) . . . 'there [must be] an immediate and direct causal relationship—without the intervention of some other source or agency—between the actions of the defendant and the victim's death.' " The question presented by Rose is whether we should further narrow the use of the felony murder rule to establish second-degree murder by applying the merger doctrine.

Application of the merger doctrine

The merger doctrine developed in the felony murder context as a means of restricting the scope of the felony murder rule, particularly when it is used to support a second-degree murder conviction. "The merger doctrine developed due to the understanding that the underlying felony must be an independent crime and not merely the killing itself. Thus, certain underlying felonies 'merge' with the homicide and cannot be used for purposes of felony murder."

This court has considered the merger doctrine in the context of first-degree felony murder. In *Contreras,* * * * we declined to apply the merger doctrine to first-degree felony murder when the underlying felony was burglary with the intent to commit battery. In doing so, we emphasized the fact that the Legislature had specifically included burglary as a felony that supports first-degree felony murder regardless of the intent underlying the burglary, and that we were reluctant to depart from the Legislature's intent in that respect. However, *Contreras* did not address the merger doctrine in the context of second-degree felony murder. We do so now.

The merger doctrine was first articulated and applied to second-degree felony murder in California in *People v. Ireland,* in response to a trial court instruction allowing second-degree felony murder based on assault with a deadly weapon as the predicate felony. The California Supreme Court held that such an instruction was improper because "[t]o allow such use of the felony murder rule would effectively preclude the jury from considering the issue of malice aforethought in all cases wherein homicide has been committed as a result of a felonious assault—a category which includes the great majority of all homicides."

Recently, in *Sarun Chun,* the California Supreme Court further clarified when an underlying felony merges with murder in the context of second-degree felony murder. It plainly stated that an underlying felony that is assaultive in nature necessarily merges with the homicide and cannot be the basis for a second-degree felony murder instruction. The court went on to define an assaultive felony as any felony that involves a threat of immediate violent injury. "Accordingly, if the elements of the crime have an assaultive aspect, the crime merges with the underlying homicide even if the elements also include conduct that is not assaultive." The *Sarun Chun* court declined to enumerate which felonies are assaultive but held that shooting at an occupied vehicle is assaultive and cannot be used as the underlying felony to support a second-degree felony murder charge; therefore, it concluded that the trial court erred in instructing the jury on second-degree felony murder. * * *

We are persuaded by the California Supreme Court's reasoning that allowing assaultive-type felonies to form the basis for a second-degree murder conviction based on the felony murder rule would mean that virtually every homicide would occur in the commission of a felony and therefore be murder. * * *

Under our decision today, the application of the merger doctrine turns on a determination of whether the underlying felony is assaultive in nature. We therefore also must determine whether that question presents a factual determination for the jury or a legal determination for the trial court. We faced a similar decision as to the question of whether a felony is inherently dangerous for purposes of second-degree felony murder.

Recently, in *Ramirez v. State,* we abandoned earlier cases that had suggested that that question is a legal one to be determined in the abstract based on the elements of the underlying felony; we instead held that the jury must determine whether the felony underlying a second-degree felony murder charge is inherently dangerous based on the manner in which the felony was committed. In applying the merger doctrine, we are similarly persuaded that the jury should determine whether the underlying felony is assaultive—*i.e.,* involves a threat of immediate violent injury—based on the manner in which the felony was committed.

In the present case, the predicate felony for the second-degree felony murder theory was assault with a deadly weapon. At the time that Rose shot Watkins, NRS 200.471 defined assault as "[u]lawfully attempting to use physical force against another person" or "[i]ntentionally placing another person in reasonable apprehension of immediate bodily harm." The offense was a felony if the assault was made with the use of a deadly weapon. The assault here is based on Rose's act of aiming the gun at or near Watkins and telling her to get off the phone. The conduct could be viewed as using a deadly weapon to intentionally place the victim in reasonable apprehension of immediate bodily harm by threatening her with immediate violent injury. A jury therefore could find that the felony was assaultive and merged with the homicide. Alternatively, a properly instructed jury could have found implied malice based on the circumstances of the killing, and still convicted Rose of second-degree murder. But based on the facts of this case and the conflicting evidence as to Rose's state of mind, we cannot conclude beyond a reasonable doubt that a rational jury would have found Rose guilty of second-degree murder absent the omitted instruction.

Accordingly, we reverse the judgment of conviction and remand to the district court for further proceedings consistent with this opinion.

NOTE

In *Rose v. State*, the Supreme Court of Nevada noted that whether the underlying felony is assaultive and therefore merges with the homicide is a question of fact for the jury to decide. In contrast, the Supreme Court of California in *People v. Chun*, 45 Cal.4th 1172, 203 P.3d 425, 91 Cal.Rptr.3d 106 (2009), found that the judge, as opposed to the jury, should decide whether the felony merges with the homicide by considering the elements of the felony in the abstract, not the facts of the case. The *Chun* court explained, "In determining whether a crime merges, the court looks to its elements and not the facts of the case." The *Chun* court also abandoned an approach it had previously utilized to decide questions of merger under which assaultive crimes for which the court could discern an "independent felonious purpose" did not merge, thus permitting application of the felony murder rule.

4. THIRD PARTY KILLINGS: THE AGENCY RULE

Another limitation on the felony murder rule recognized in most jurisdictions is the third party killing rule. Under this rule, if a third party, i.e. someone other than the felon or one of his agents, is responsible for the killing, the felony murder rule does not apply and the prosecutor seeking a murder conviction must prove malice aforethought using some other theory of malice aforethought (other than the felony murder rule). This rule, as explained in *State v. Canola*, is based on principles of agency. A minority of jurisdictions permit felony murder liability even if the killing was by a third party, relying on principles of proximate causation.

STATE V. CANOLA

Supreme Court of New Jersey
73 N.J. 206, 374 A.2d 20 (1977)

CONFORD, J.

Defendant, along with three confederates, was in the process of robbing a store when a victim of the robbery, attempting to resist the perpetration of the crime, fatally shot one of the cofelons. The sole issue for our resolution is whether, under N.J.S.A. 2A:113–1, defendant may be held liable for felony murder. A divided part of the Appellate Division determined the question in the affirmative. Because of the dissent, the appeal is here as of right.

The facts of this case * * * may be summarized as follows. The owner of a jewelry store and his employee, in an attempt to resist an armed robbery, engaged in a physical skirmish with one of the four robbers. A second conspirator, called upon for assistance, began shooting, and the store owner returned the gunfire. Both the owner and the felon, one Lloredo, were fatally shot in the exchange, the latter by the firearm of the owner.

Defendant and two others were indicted on two counts of murder, one count of robbery and one count of having been armed during the robbery. The murder counts were based on the deaths, respectively, of the robbery victim and the co-felon. After trial on the murder counts defendant was found guilty on both and was sentenced to concurrent terms of life imprisonment. The Appellate Division unanimously affirmed the conviction for the murder of the robbery victim, and this court denied a petition for certification addressed thereto. However, when the Appellate Division majority upheld the trial court's denial of a motion to dismiss the count addressed to the homicide of the co-felon, Judge Handler dissented.

Conventional formulations of the felony murder rule would not seem to encompass liability in this case. * * * A recent study of the early formulations of the felony murder rule by such authorities as Lord Coke,

Foster and Blackstone and of later ones by Judge Stephen and Justice Holmes concluded that they were concerned solely with situations where the felon or a confederate did the actual killing. Contrary to the division of view in the modern American cases on the point, it has been observed that the English courts never applied the felony murder rule to hold a felon guilty of the death of his co-felon at the hands of the intended victim.

The precise issue in the present case is whether a broader concept than the foregoing—specifically, liability of a felon for the death of a co-felon effected by one resisting the felony—is required by the language of our statute applicable to the general area of felony murder. N.J.S.A. 2A:113–1. This reads:

> If any person, in committing or attempting to commit arson, burglary, kidnapping, rape, robbery, sodomy or any unlawful act against the peace of this State, of which the probable consequences may be bloodshed, kills another, *or if the death of anyone ensues from the committing or attempting to commit any such crime or act . . . then such person so killing is guilty of murder*. (emphasis added).

* * * The Appellate Division majority was of the view that the above-emphasized portion of the statute, referred to by it as the "ensues clause," compelled the result it arrived at. It said:

> * * * In our view the statute indicates an intention on the part of the Legislature to extend criminal responsibility beyond that imposed upon a felon at common law and to hold liable all participants in an armed robbery for deaths which occur during the commission of the crime.

Judge (now Justice) Handler, in dissenting, cited the decisions representing the majority view in those other jurisdictions which had considered the general question, and said they hold that "a felon cannot be found guilty for the death of an accomplice occurring during the commission of the felony." * * * For reasons to be more fully explicated, we are in accord with the conclusion arrived at in the dissent. * * *

It is clearly the majority view throughout the country that, at least in theory, the doctrine of felony murder does not extend to a killing, although growing out of the commission of the felony, if directly attributable to the act of one other than the defendant or those associated with him in the unlawful enterprise. This rule is sometimes rationalized on the "agency" theory of felony murder.[2]

---

[2] The classic statement of the theory is found in an early case applying it in a context pertinent to the case at bar, *Commonwealth v. Campbell*, as follows:

> No person can be held guilty of homicide unless the act is either actually or constructively his, and it cannot be his act in either sense unless committed by his

A contrary view, which would attach liability under the felony murder rule for *any* death proximately resulting from the unlawful activity—even the death of a co-felon—notwithstanding the killing was by one resisting the crime, does not seem to have the present allegiance of any court.

At one time the proximate cause theory was espoused by the Pennsylvania Supreme Court. The reasoning of the *Almeida* decision, involving the killing of a policeman shot by other police attempting to apprehend robbers, was distinctly circumvented when the question later arose whether it should be applied to an effort to inculpate a defendant for the killing of his co-felon at the hands of the victim of the crime. *Commonwealth v. Redline.* The court there held against liability. Examining the common-law authorities relied upon by the *Almeida* majority, the *Redline* court concluded:

> As already indicated, *Almeida* was, itself, an extension of the felony-murder doctrine by judicial decision and is not to be extended in its application beyond facts such as those to which it was applied.

The court then held that "in order to convict for felony murder, *the killing must have been done by the defendant or by an accomplice or confederate or by one acting in furtherance of the felonious undertaking.*" The court refused, however, actually to overrule the *Almeida* decision, thereby creating a distinction (although the opinion indicates it was a half-hearted one) between the situation in which the victim was an innocent party and the killing therefore merely "excusable" and that in which the deceased was a felon and the killing thus "justifiable." Twelve years later the Pennsylvania court did overrule *Almeida* in a case involving Almeida's companion, Smith. The court noted, *inter alia*, the harsh criticism leveled against the common-law felony rule, its doubtful deterrent effect, the failure of the cases cited in *Almeida* to support the conclusions reached therein, the inappropriateness of tort proximate-cause principles to homicide prosecution, and the "will-of-the-wisp" distinction drawn by the *Almeida* court between justifiable and excusable homicides. * * *

The California cases have taken a wholly unique course in this area of the criminal law. The Court of Appeal, influenced by the early Pennsylvania cases, first adopted the proximate cause theory. In *People v. Harrison,* the court held the defendants guilty of first degree murder when the owner of a store being robbed exchanged gunfire with the robbers and killed an employee. But in *People v. Washington,* the Supreme Court refused to hold a surviving felon liable for the death of a

---

own hand or by someone acting in concert with him or in furtherance of a common object or purpose.

co-felon, instead reverting to the common law view of *Campbell, supra,* and overruling *People v. Harrison*. It said:

> Accordingly, for a defendant to be guilty of murder under the felony-murder rule the act of killing must be committed by the defendant or by his accomplice acting in furtherance of their common design.

In *dicta,* however, the court stated that it was not necessary to invoke the felony murder rule in order to imply the malice requisite for murder and that such malice is evident when the defendant does an act (*apart* from the felony) "that involves a high degree of probability that it will result in death." Accordingly, in *People v. Gilbert,* while adhering to the notion that for the strict liability of the felony murder rule to apply the felon or his accomplice must do the killing, the court recognized the implication of *Washington* that "entirely apart from the felony murder rule, malice may be established when a defendant initiates a gun battle, and that under such circumstances he may be convicted of murder for a killing committed by another." * * *

To be distinguished from the situation before us here, and from the generality of the cases discussed above, are the so-called "shield" cases. The first of these were the companion cases of *Taylor v. State,* and *Keaton v. State*. In attempting to escape after robbing a train, defendants thrust the brakeman in front of them as a shield, as a result of which he was fatally shot by law officers. The court had no difficulty in finding defendants guilty of murder. The court in *Taylor* noted the correctness of the *Campbell* case doctrine that a person could not be held liable for homicide unless the act is either actually or constructively committed by him, but indicated it was inapplicable to a case where defendants forced deceased to occupy a place of danger in order that they might carry out the crime. In *Keaton,* the court said defendant would be responsible for the "reasonable, natural and probable result of his act" of placing deceased in danger of his life. The conduct of the defendants in cases such as these is said to reflect "express malice," justifying a murder conviction. * * *

Reverting to our immediate task here, it is to determine whether our own statute necessarily mandates the proximate cause concept of felony murder, as thought by the Appellate Division majority. It is fair to assume, initially, that the Legislature had no special reason in 1796 to ordain a rule of felony murder beyond that generally accepted in Anglo-American jurisprudence at the end of the eighteenth century. As above noted, there was then no precedent, either English or American, for holding the felon for killings at the hands of others than the felon himself or those confederated with him—that is to say, the so called agency rule held sway. But as seen above, the view of the Appellate Division was that the "ensues clause" of N.J.S.A. 2A:113–1 must be deemed to have expanded the culpability of the felon to killings by others not confederated with him, if proximately related to the felonious enterprise, else the clause would be meaningless surplusage in the act. However, other plausible motivations for the ensues clause can be postulated consistent with a legislative intent to adhere to the traditional limitations of the felony murder doctrine. * * *

[I]t is inescapable that the ensues clause is connected with the conclusion of the section, "then such person so killing is guilty of murder." This fortifies the view that even as to a death which "ensues" from the commission or attempt to commit the felony, liability for murder is intended to be restricted to the person "so killing," *i.e.*, the felon or his agents, not third persons, conformably with the limitation of the Pennsylvania *Redline* doctrine. * * *

With such background, and assuming the statute is facially susceptible of the interpretation here advocated by the State, it is appropriate to consider the public policy implications of the proposed doctrine as an extension of prior assumptions in this State as to the proper limitations of the felony murder rule.

Most modern progressive thought in criminal jurisprudence favors restriction rather than expansion of the felony murder rule. A leading text states: "The felony murder rule is somewhat in disfavor at the present time. The courts apply it when the law requires, but they do so grudgingly and tend to restrict its application where the circumstances permit." It has frequently been observed that although the rule was logical at its inception, when all felonies were punishable by death, its survival to modern times when other felonies are not thought to be as blameworthy as premeditated killings is discordant with rational and enlightened views of criminal culpability and liability. * * *

The final report of the New Jersey Criminal Law Revision Commission was, however, unwilling totally to reject the felony murder rule, concluding instead:

> It is true that we have no way of knowing how many of the homicides resulting in felony murder convictions were committed purposefully, knowingly or recklessly and how many were negligent or accidental. But it is our belief that this rule of law does lead some to refuse to assume a homicidal risk in committing other crimes.

The proposed New Jersey Penal Code does nevertheless offer limited defenses not hitherto available under the felony murder rule, and it confines the rule to deaths caused by the felon or his co-felons "in the course of and in furtherance of [the felony]." This is standard "agency theory" formulation and would seem intended to exclude liability for acts of persons other than felons or co-felons though generally arising out of the criminal episode.

In view of all of the foregoing, it appears to us regressive to extend the application of the felony murder rule beyond its classic common-law limitation to acts by the felon and his accomplices, to lethal acts of third persons not in furtherance of the felonious scheme. The language of the statute does not compel it, and, as indicated above, is entirely compatible with the traditional limitations of the rule. Tort concepts of foreseeability and proximate cause have shallow relevance to culpability for murder in the first degree. Gradations of criminal liability should accord with the degree of moral culpability for the actor's conduct. * * *

It is our judgment that if the course of the law as understood and applied in this State for almost 200 years is to be altered so drastically, it should be by express legislative enactment.

The judgment of the Appellate Division is modified so as to strike the conviction and sentencing of defendant for murder of the co-felon Lloredo.

SULLIVAN, J. (concurring in result only).

The practical result of the majority holding is that even though some innocent person or a police officer be killed during the commission of an armed robbery, the felon would bear no criminal responsibility of any kind for that killing as long as it was not at the hand of the felon or a confederate. The legislative intent, as I see it, is otherwise.

The thrust of our felony murder statute, N.J.S.A. 2A:113–1, is to hold the criminal liable for any killing which ensues during the commission of a felony, even though the felon, or a confederate, did not commit the actual killing. The only exception I would recognize would be the death of a co-felon, which could be classified as a justifiable homicide and not within the purview of the statute.

The Legislature should act promptly to clarify the situation resulting from the majority opinion. If it does not extend the felony murder statute to encompass a killing during the commission of a felony not at the hand of the felon or confederate, it should, at least, provide that the felon be chargeable with manslaughter for such killing (in addition to liability for the felony).

I therefore concur in the result but only for the reason stated above.

[C.J. HUGHES dissent has been omitted.]

NOTE

Following the decision in *State v. Canola*, the New Jersey legislature seemed to take Justice Sullivan's advice, amending its Penal Code to provide that "criminal homicide constitutes murder when: * * * the actor * * * is engaged in the commission of, or an attempt to commit, or flight after committing or attempting to commit [a designated felony], and * * * any person causes the death of a person other than one of the participants." N.J. Stat. Ann. § 2C:11–3(a)(1)(3) (2004).

In California, a new theory of second-degree murder has emerged: "provocative act murder." Under this theory, when a defendant or his accomplice commits a "provocative act" and his victim or a police officer kills in reasonable response to that act, the defendant can be found guilty of murder.

Does this doctrine violate the agency rule? The California courts have said no: provocative act murder is based on an expansion of the so-called "gun battle rule," under which an actor who initiates a gun battle with law enforcement can be held guilty of second-degree murder on a depraved heart murder theory. Provocative act murder, therefore, is not a species of felony murder.

H. THE MISDEMEANOR MANSLAUGHTER DOCTRINE

Under the misdemeanor manslaughter doctrine, a homicide that occurs during the commission of (1) a misdemeanor (an unlawful act not amounting to a felony), or (2) a felony that cannot serve as the underlying felony for a felony murder conviction constitutes involuntary manslaughter. Courts have placed various limitations on the application of the misdemeanor manslaughter doctrine, just as they have on felony murder. For instance, in some jurisdictions the doctrine only applies to deaths that occur during the commission of a misdemeanor that is *malum in se* (evil in and of itself). In these jurisdictions, a *malum prohibitum* offense (an act or omission that does not carry any particular moral opprobrium) cannot serve as the trigger for a misdemeanor manslaughter conviction. Some states apply an "inherently dangerous" restriction, holding that the underlying misdemeanor must be inherently dangerous to life or safety. Some states will not apply the doctrine if the underlying crime is a strict liability crime (one which requires no mens rea at all). Other states place no limitations on the type of act that can serve as the underlying misdemeanor or unlawful act. Some states require that the misdemeanor be the actual and proximate cause of the death. Other states do not require any causal relationship between the commission of the misdemeanor and the death. In *Todd v. State*, the Court of Appeal of Florida discusses the requirements for an involuntary manslaughter conviction under the misdemeanor manslaughter doctrine as it is applied in Florida.

TODD V. STATE

Court of Appeal of Florida, Fifth District
594 So.2d 802, 17 Fla. L. Weekly D 369 (Ct. App. 1992)

GRIFFIN, J.

On March 18, 1990, appellant entered the Lighthouse Church and stole $110 from the collection plate. The theft was witnessed by several members of the congregation, one of whom, Richard Voegltin, took off in his car in pursuit of appellant. During the pursuit, Mr. Voegltin, who had a preexisting heart condition, began to experience cardiac dysrhythmia. He lost control of his vehicle, collided with a tree at low speed and died of cardiac arrest.

The state charged appellant with manslaughter, alleging that he caused the death of Mr. Voegltin by committing the misdemeanor offense of petty theft which caused Voegltin to pursue him in order to recover the stolen property. Appellant filed a motion to dismiss, asserting that, because it cannot be said with any reasonable degree of medical certainty that Mr. Voegltin died as a result of chasing appellant, because Mr. Voegltin was at high risk of having a heart attack due to his preexisting medical condition, and because the appellant had no knowledge of this preexisting medical condition, the manslaughter charge should be dismissed. The trial court denied the motion to dismiss. We reverse.

The issue, as presented to us, is whether Florida recognizes the misdemeanor manslaughter rule. Reduced to basics, the misdemeanor manslaughter rule is that an unintended homicide which occurs during the commission of an unlawful act not amounting to a felony constitutes the crime of involuntary manslaughter. It is sometimes referred to more broadly as "unlawful act manslaughter." * * *

The misdemeanor manslaughter rule has been the subject of surprisingly little analysis, although in their Handbook on Criminal Law, LaFave and Scott have included a detailed discussion and critique of this theory of criminal responsibility. They suggest that "the trend today, barely underway, is to abolish altogether this type of involuntary manslaughter. . . . " The authors posit that to punish as homicide the result of an unlawful act that is unintended and produced without any consciousness of the risk of producing it is "too harsh" and "illogical."

One of the few secondary sources cited by LaFave and Scott on this topic is a 1939 law review article by I. Wilner entitled *Unintentional Homicide In the Commission of an Unlawful Act*. In this article the author argues that the principal historic purpose of this rule was not, in fact, punishment of the homicide but vigorous punishment of the underlying "unlawful act," which in most cases was a violation of some property right.

Because of the facial simplicity of the misdemeanor manslaughter rule, its application by courts has led to some rather extraordinary findings of criminal liability for homicide. For example, in 1926 a Texas court found liability for manslaughter on the following facts: The victim discovered the defendant committing adultery with the victim's wife. Adultery was a misdemeanor in Texas. The victim made a murderous attack on the defendant. In defending himself against the murderous attack, the defendant killed the victim. The court decided that since the victim's murderous attack was a foreseeable reaction to the defendant's criminal misconduct, the defendant was guilty of manslaughter. In *Commonwealth v. Mink,* the defendant was attempting to commit suicide, but her fiancee [sic] intervened to try to stop her and was accidentally killed by the defendant. Because suicide was an unlawful act *malum in se,* the court found defendant guilty of manslaughter.

Over time, this theory of criminal responsibility has developed many complexities. Courts differ about whether the unlawful act must amount to a criminal offense and whether different standards should apply for *malum in se* or *malum prohibitum* offenses. In this case, neither of these issues is of concern. The offense in this case is a *malum in se* misdemeanor offense under the criminal law of Florida. However, the other principal point of divergence in the development of the misdemeanor manslaughter rule—the issue of causation—is critical to this case.

The views on the requirement of causation in unlawful act manslaughter differ widely among the various jurisdictions. In some instances, no causal relationship at all has been required. At the other extreme is the requirement that there be not only a direct causal relationship between the unlawful act and the death, but that the death must be a natural and probable consequence of the offense. An example cited by Wilner is the case of *Votre v. State,* where, contrary to statute, the defendant gave whiskey to the victim, who was a minor. Consumption of the alcohol caused the victim to suffer a heart attack of which he died. The Indiana court held that the defendant was not guilty of manslaughter because the homicide must follow both as a part of the perpetration of the unlawful act and as a natural and probable consequence of it. * * *

Florida courts, by simply interpreting the statutory definition of manslaughter ("the killing of a human being by the act, procurement, or culpable negligence of another, without lawful justification . . . "), appear always to have understood the importance of causation as an element of this type of homicide. Our courts also have appreciated the foreseeability element of causation. * * *

In this case, even if it were assumed that the stress of pursuit brought on the heart attack, it cannot be said that the petty theft was the legal cause of Mr. Voegltin's death. The crime itself was a minor property offense. There is no suggestion of any touching or any threat to anyone's person. This is not even a case, like a purse snatching, where violence was necessary to produce the theft. Nor is it asserted that Mr. Voegltin died from fright or horror at witnessing the crime. The state's traverse specifically asserts that it was the pursuit that caused the fatal heart attack. Although the petty theft did trigger a series of events that concluded in the death of Mr. Voegltin and was, in that sense, a "cause" of the death, the petty theft did not encompass the kind of direct, foreseeable risk of physical harm that would support a conviction of manslaughter. The relationship between the unlawful act committed (petty theft) and the result effected (death by heart attack during pursuit in an automobile) does not meet the test of causation historically or currently required in Florida for conviction of manslaughter.

REVERSED.

CHAPTER 8

SEXUAL OFFENSES

■ ■ ■

INTRODUCTION

In 1961, when the Model Penal Code was promulgated, American law closely reflected the Anglo-American common law, which recognized three basic sexual offenses: forcible rape, statutory rape, and sodomy. Forcible rape was typically defined as "the carnal knowledge of a woman, not the perpetrator's wife, forcibly and against her will." Statutory rape was typically defined as sexual intercourse with a female under the age of consent, where the age of consent varied from age 18 to age 10.

Statutory and forcible rape shared some common features. First, neither crime contained an explicit mens rea as an essential element of the crime. Statutory rape, however, is often described as a strict liability crime, meaning the defendant can be found guilty of the crime even if he did not know that the victim was under the age of consent. Forcible rape, in contrast, is considered to be a general intent crime. Second, both kinds of rape, forcible and statutory, assumed that the victim would be a woman and the perpetrator would be a man, requiring vaginal intercourse as the actus reus element of the crime. Under this definition, forcible sexual intercourse without the consent of a male child by a male adult would not constitute rape, nor would oral or anal intercourse, whether by force or with a child. The vaginal intercourse requirement also meant that an assault in which an object other than a penis was put into the victim's vagina did not fall within the traditional definition of forcible rape. Finally, the penalties for forcible rape and statutory rape were similar: for both crimes the range of possible punishments was extremely broad, from as low as three years in prison, to as high as the death penalty. This wide range of penalties gave enormous discretion to the sentencing judge.

In addition to statutory and forcible rape, the American criminal law of a generation ago punished sodomy, ominously and ambiguously defined in many statutes as "the crime against nature." *See Wainwright v. Stone*, 414 U.S. 21, 94 S.Ct. 190, 38 L.Ed.2d 179 (1973) (upholding, against a void-for-vagueness charge, a Florida statute that punished "the abominable and detestable crime against nature, either with mankind or beast"). Under English common law as originally adopted by the United States, sodomy always included anal intercourse between men. It also sometimes included any sexual contact with an animal, and sometimes both same-sex and cross-sex oral sex. Although same-sex relations between men were uniformly criminalized within the common law tradition, same-sex relations between women were more ambiguously treated. Lesbian relations might or might not be a crime, depending on the jurisdiction. At English common law, sodomy was a capital offense. Even after sodomy stopped being a capital offense, the penalties were quite high, with 10 or 20 year maximums being common.

Unlike forcible rape, the crime of sodomy did not require either force or non-consent. The absence of a force element meant that the defendant could not win an acquittal by questioning whether the victim really resisted or whether his or her resistance was adequate, questions that traditionally lay at the center of many forcible rape prosecutions. The absence of a non-consent element in sodomy law meant that married men could be convicted of sodomy against their wives, even in states where marital rape was not a crime. More importantly, the absence of a non-consent element meant that prosecutors could convict consenting adults, such as gay and lesbian couples, of sodomy.

In contrast to rape and sodomy, prostitution was not a crime at common law. In the United States, prostitution was not widely criminalized until the Progressive Era (roughly 1880 to 1920), when a moral panic about the social evils of prostitution and the "white slave trade" it engendered took hold of the public. By 1961, the vast majority of United States jurisdictions punished prostitution and related crimes such as owning a brothel.

Since 1961, courts and legislatures have changed many aspects of the law of sexual offenses. The law of forcible rape has changed the most dramatically. The law seems to be moving to reconceptualize forcible rape not as a crime against a woman's honor, but as a crime against a person's sexual autonomy.[a] The law of sodomy has similarly been drastically altered by judicial recognition of the liberty interests of consenting, adult same-sex partners. In contrast, the law of statutory rape and the law of prostitution have remained relatively stable since 1961.

A. FORCIBLE RAPE

In contrast to homicide law in the United States, the law of forcible rape has changed in fundamental ways since the founding of the nation. First, the states have gone in different directions in reforming their laws. Some states, like Michigan, have followed the MPC in trying to create a unified body of sexual assault law with many different gradations. Other states have been more haphazard. For example, California has simply created more sex crimes whenever there is a public outcry, without trying

[a] In recognition of the need to reassess the law regarding sexual offenses as expressed in the original Model Penal Code, the American Law Institute began a new project in 2013, entitled the Model Penal Code: Sexual Assault and Related Offenses.

to integrate them into a coherent whole. The California Penal Code has separate provisions criminalizing forcible rape, sodomy, oral copulation, penetration with an object, lewd and lascivious acts with a child under 14, spousal rape, sexual assault of an animal, and many other crimes. Therefore, although the law of homicide is easy to categorize into a generic "common law approach" and "MPC approach," forcible rape law is much more varied.

Second, and more importantly, the basic purposes of forcible rape law are being rethought in contemporary times as Western culture regarding sexuality and gender undergoes rapid changes. Some of the changes in forcible rape doctrine are a direct result of feminist activism. Other changes have occurred as norms concerning sexuality have changed drastically in the last couple of generations.

As you read the materials on forcible rape, keep in the back of your mind some policy questions upon which we as a society have yet to reach consensus. First, what is the harm caused by rape? Are there analogies to other crimes that are useful in answering this question? Is rape a type of violence like assault and battery? Is it a forcible taking of sex? (Some commentators have suggested, for example, that rape should be analogized to armed robbery.) Or, are the harms of rape sui generis?

The second policy question to keep in mind is a corollary of the first. What interests does rape law protect, and what interests should it protect? Does it (and should it) protect male access to female bodies? Does it (and should it) protect people's sexual autonomy? Does it (and should it) protect people against bad sex?

Third, is all rape equal, or are there good reasons to treat different kinds of rape differently? If we do want to separate out certain rapes as deserving of more punishment than others, how do we identify those rapes? Several possible criteria are suggested by existing doctrine: (1) mens rea (should rape be punished more harshly when the perpetrator intentionally has sexual intercourse without the victim's consent than when the perpetrator is merely reckless or negligent as to whether the victim is consenting?); (2) the presence or absence of a relationship between the perpetrator and the victim (is stranger rape worse than acquaintance rape, or the other way around?); (3) the presence or absence of violence (is a rape at gunpoint worse than being raped while drunk or unconscious?); and (4) the presence or absence of meaningful consent (is the rape of a mentally retarded victim or a victim who is comatose more or less heinous than the rape of someone clearly able to say "no"?). Consider whether and how these various sorting criteria might be reflected in the law.

Fourth, what kinds of doctrinal rules will both further the goals of preventing and redressing rape and protecting the rights of defendants?

As you will see in the materials that follow, the cultural context of rape law enforcement is pervaded with class and race bias.

Finally, do we need to look beyond the criminal justice system to solve the problem of rape? Should we look to mediation and the tort system? Should we look to social education?

1. THE ELEMENT OF FORCE OR THREAT OF FORCE

In many forcible rape cases, the critical question is whether the defendant used force or threat of force to accomplish the sexual intercourse. At one time, many states required proof of physical resistance by the victim in cases where the defendant used or threatened force not amounting to deadly force. In such cases, a woman claiming she was raped had to resist her attacker "to her utmost" in order to prove the sexual intercourse was by force or threat of force and without her consent. Most (though not all) jurisdictions have eliminated the resistance requirement for the reasons offered in Justice Wilner's dissenting opinion in *Rusk v. State*. Even without an explicit resistance requirement, however, evidence of resistance plays an important role in establishing the elements of force and non-consent. Judges and jurors often look for evidence of resistance by the victim and may be skeptical of the victim's claim of rape if the victim did not physically resist. The next several cases focus on whether there was sufficient evidence of force or threat of force to support a rape conviction. Even when proof of resistance is not explicitly required, the question of resistance remains just below the surface.

RUSK V. STATE

Court of Special Appeals of Maryland
43 Md.App. 476, 406 A.2d 624 (1979)

THOMPSON, J.

* * * Edward Salvatore Rusk, the appellant, was convicted in the Criminal Court of Baltimore of rape in the second degree and of assault. He was sentenced to concurrent terms of ten years for the rape and five years for the assault. The appellant does not challenge the conviction for assault but only for the rape. We will, therefore, affirm the assault conviction.

The prosecutrix was a twenty-one year old mother of a two-year old son. She was separated from her husband but not yet divorced. Leaving her son with her mother, she attended a high school reunion after which she and a female friend, Terry, went bar hopping in the Fells Point area of Baltimore. They drove in separate cars. At the third bar the prosecutrix met appellant. * * *

They had a five or ten minute conversation in the bar; at the end of which the prosecutrix said she was ready to leave. Appellant requested a ride home and she agreed. When they arrived at appellant's home, the prosecutrix parked at the curb on the side of the street opposite his rooming house but did not turn off the ignition. She put the car in park and appellant asked her to come up to his apartment. She refused. He continued to ask her to come up, and she testified she then became afraid. While trying to convince him that she didn't want to go to his apartment she mentioned that she was separated and if she did, it might cause her marital problems particularly if she were being followed by a detective. The appellant then took the keys out of the car and walked over to her side of the car, opened the door and said, "Now will you come up?" The prosecutrix then told him she would. She stated:

> At that point, because I was scared, because he had my car keys. I didn't know what to do. I was someplace I didn't even know where I was. It was in the city. I didn't know whether to run. I really didn't think, at that point, what to do. Now, I know that I should have blown the horn. I should have run. There were a million things I could have done. I was scared, at that point, and I didn't do any of them.

The prosecutrix followed appellant into the rowhouse, up the stairs, and into the apartment. When they got into appellant's room, he said that he had to go to the bathroom and left the room for a few minutes. The prosecutrix made no attempt to leave. When appellant came back, he sat on the bed while she sat on the chair next to the bed. He turned the light off and asked her to get on the bed with him. He started to pull her onto the bed and also began to remove her blouse. She stated she took off her slacks and removed his clothing because "he asked [her] to do it." After they both undressed, prosecutrix stated:

> I was still begging him to please let, you know, let me leave. I said, 'you can get a lot of other girls down there, for what you want,' and he just kept saying, 'no,' and then I was really scared, because I can't describe, you know, what was said. It was more the look in his eyes; and I said, at that point—I didn't know what to say; and I said, 'If I do what you want, will you let me go without killing me?' Because I didn't know, at that point, what he was going to do; and I started to cry; and when I did, he put his hands on my throat, and started lightly to choke me; and I said, 'If I do what you want, will you let me go?' And he said, yes, and at that time, I proceeded to do what he wanted me to.

She stated that she performed oral sex and they then had sexual intercourse.[1]

---

[1] If we could say at this point that there is enough evidence for a reasonable fact finder to say such threat of force is solely that which overcame her will to resist, the conduct of both following intercourse would belie that conclusion:

* * *

The Court of Appeals of Maryland last spoke on the amount of force required to support a rape conviction in *Hazel v. State,* when the Court said:

"Force is an essential element of the crime and to justify a conviction, the evidence must warrant a conclusion either that the victim resisted and her resistance was overcome by force or that she was prevented from resisting by threats to her safety."[2]

In all of the victim's testimony we have been unable to see any resistance on her part to the sex acts and certainly can we see no fear as would overcome her attempt to resist or escape as required by *Hazel.* Possession of the keys by the accused may have deterred her vehicular escape but hardly a departure seeking help in the rooming house or in the street. We must say that "the way he looked" fails utterly to support the fear required by *Hazel.* * * *

As we said in *Winegan v. State*:

> [Where] the victim's story could not be corroborated by wounds, bruises or disordered clothing, the lack of consent could be shown by fear based upon reasonable apprehension. * * *

The State argues * * * that the evidence that the accused "started lightly to choke me" as well as the circumstances of being in a somewhat strange part of town late at night were sufficient to overcome the will of a normal twenty-one year old married woman. We are not impressed with the argument. * * *

"Q. All right. Now, after the sexual intercourse came to a conclusion, what is the very next thing that took place?

A. I asked him if I could leave now, and he said, 'Yes;' and I got up and got dressed; and he got up and got dressed; and he walked me to my car, and asked if he could see me again; and I said, 'Yes;' and he asked me for my telephone number; and I said, 'No, I'll see you down [at] Fell's Point sometime,' just so I could leave.

Q. What is the reason that you said that you would meet him the next day?

A. I didn't say the next day, and I just said I would see him down there only so I could leave. I didn't know what else to say. I had no intention of meeting him again."

After arriving home she said:

"I sat in the car, thinking about it a while, and I thought I wondered what would happen if I hadn't of done what he wanted me to do. So I thought the right thing to do was to go report it, and I went from there to Hillendale to find a police car."

If, in quiet contemplation after the act, she had to wonder what would have happened, her submission on the side of prudence seems hardly justified. Indeed, if she had to wonder afterward, how can a fact finder reasonably conclude that she was justifiably in fear sufficient to overcome her will to resist, at the time.

2 Since *Hazel*, the Maryland Legislature has codified extensively the law pertaining to sexual offenses providing in Md. Code, Art. 27, § 463 as follows: "(a) What constitutes.—A person is guilty of rape in the second degree if the person engages in vaginal intercourse with another person: (1) By force or threat of force against the will and without the consent of the other person. . . . " The statute has made no change in the force as required by *Hazel.*

[W]e find the evidence legally insufficient to warrant a conclusion that appellant's words or actions created in the mind of the victim a reasonable fear that if she resisted, he would have harmed her, or that faced with such resistance, he would have used force to overcome it. The prosecutrix stated that she was afraid, and submitted because of "the look in his eyes." After both were undressed and in the bed, and she pleaded to him that she wanted to leave, he started to lightly choke her. At oral argument it was brought out that the "lightly choking" could have been a heavy caress. We do not believe that "lightly choking" along with all the facts and circumstances in the case, were sufficient to cause a reasonable fear which overcame her ability to resist. In the absence of any other evidence showing force used by appellant, we find that the evidence was insufficient to convict appellant of rape.

Judgment on the rape conviction reversed. * * *

WILNER, J. [dissenting].

With the deepest respect for the generally superior wisdom of colleagues who authored or endorsed the majority Opinion, but with the equally profound conviction that, in this case, they have made a serious mistake, I record this dissent.

The majority's error, in my judgment, is not in their exposition of the underlying principles of law that must govern this case, but rather in the manner that they have applied those principles. The majority have trampled upon the first principle of appellate restraint. Under the guise of judging the sufficiency of the evidence presented against appellant, they have tacitly—perhaps unwittingly, but nonetheless—effectively substituted their own view of the evidence (and the inferences that may fairly be drawn from it) for that of the judge and jury. In so doing, they have not only improperly invaded the province allotted to those tribunals, but, at the same time, have perpetuated and given new life to myths about the crime of rape that have no place in our law today. * * *

Md. Annot. Code art. 27, § 463(a) considers three types of conduct as constituting second degree rape. We are concerned only with the first: a person is guilty of rape in the second degree if he (1) engages in vaginal intercourse with another person, (2) by force or threat of force, (3) against the will, and (4) without the consent of the other person. There is no real question here as to the first, third, or fourth elements of the crime. The evidence was certainly sufficient to show that appellant had vaginal intercourse with the victim, and that such act was against her will and without her consent. The point at issue is whether it was accomplished by force or threat of force; and I think that in viewing the evidence, that point should remain ever clear. Consent is not the issue here, only whether there was sufficient evidence of force or the threat of force.

Unfortunately, courts, including in the present case a majority of this one, often tend to confuse these two elements—force and lack of consent—and to think of them as one. They are not. They mean, and require, different things. What seems to cause the confusion—what, indeed, has become a common denominator of both—elements is the notion that the victim must actively resist the attack upon her. If she fails to offer sufficient resistance (sufficient to the satisfaction of the judge), a court is entitled, or at least presumes the entitlement, to find that there was no force or threat of force, or that the act was not against her will, or that she actually consented to it, or some unarticulated combination or synthesis of these elements that leads to the ultimate conclusion that the victim was not raped. Thus it is that the focus is almost entirely on the extent of resistance—the victim's acts, rather than those of her assailant. Attention is directed not to the wrongful stimulus, but to the victim's reactions to it. Right or wrong, that seems to be the current state of the Maryland law; and, notwithstanding its uniqueness in the criminal law, and its illogic, until changed by statute or the Court of Appeals, I accept it as binding.

But what is required of a woman being attacked or in danger of attack? How much resistance must she offer? Where is that line to be drawn between requiring that she either risk serious physical harm, perhaps death, on the one hand, or be termed a willing partner on the other? Some answers were given in *Hazel v. State,* although, as in so many cases, they were stated in the context of both the requirement of force and the lack of consent. * * *

From these pronouncements in *Hazel*, this Court has articulated what the majority refers to as a "rule of reason"—i.e., that "where the victim's story could not be corroborated by wounds, bruises or disordered clothing, the lack of consent could be shown by fear based upon reasonable apprehension." As so phrased, I do not consider this to be a rule of reason at all; it is highly unreasonable, and again mixes the element of consent with that of force. But what I do accept is what the Court of Appeals said in Hazel: (1) if the acts and threats of the defendant were reasonably calculated to create in the mind of the victim—having regard to the circumstances in which she was placed—a real apprehension, due to fear, of imminent bodily harm, serious enough to impair or overcome her will to resist, then such acts and threats are the equivalent of force; (2) submission is not the equivalent of consent; and (3) the real test is whether the assault was committed without the consent and against the will of the prosecuting witness.

Upon this basis, the evidence against appellant must be considered. Judge Thompson recounts most, but not quite all, of the victim's story. The victim—I'll call her Pat—attended a high school reunion. She had arranged to meet her girlfriend Terry there. The reunion was over at

9:00, and Terry asked Pat to accompany her to Fell's Point. Pat had gone to Fell's Point with Terry on a few prior occasions, explaining in court: "I've never met anybody [there] I've gone out with. I met people in general, talking in conversation, most of the time people that Terry knew, not that I have gone down there, and met people as dates." She agreed to go, but first called her mother, who was babysitting with Pat's two-year old son, to tell her that she was going with Terry to Fell's Point, and that she would not be home late. It was just after 9:00 when Pat and Terry, in their separate cars, left for Fell's Point, alone.

They went to a place called Helen's and had one drink. They stayed an hour or so and then walked down to another place (where they had another drink), stayed about a half hour there, and went to a third place. Up to this point, Pat conversed only with Terry, and did not strike up any other acquaintanceships. Pat and Terry were standing against a wall when appellant came over and said hello to Terry, who was conversing with someone else at the time. Appellant then began to talk with Pat. They were both separated, they both had young children; and they spoke about those things. Pat said that she had been ready to leave when appellant came on the scene, and that she only talked with him for five or ten minutes. It was then about midnight. Pat had to get up with her baby in the morning and did not want to stay out late.

Terry wasn't ready to leave. As Pat was preparing to go, appellant asked if she would drop him off on her way home. She agreed because she thought he was a friend of Terry's. She told him, however, as there walked to her car, "I'm just giving a ride home, you know, as a friend, not anything to be, you know, thought of other than a ride." He agreed to that condition.

Pat was completely unfamiliar with appellant's neighborhood. She had no idea where she was. When she pulled up to where appellant said he lived, she put the car in park, but left the engine running. She said to appellant "Well, here, you know, you are home." Appellant then asked Pat to come up with him and she refused. He persisted in his request, as did she in her refusal. She told him that even if she wanted to come up, she dared not do so. She was separated and it might cause marital problems for her. Finally, he reached over, turned off the ignition, took her keys, got out of the car, came around to her side, opened the door, and said to her, "Now, will you come up?"

It was at this point that Pat followed appellant to his apartment, and it is at this point that the majority of this Court begins to substitute its judgment for that of the trial court and jury. We know nothing about Pat and appellant. We don't know how big they are, what they look like, what their life experiences have been. We don't know if appellant is larger or smaller than she, stronger or weaker. We don't know what the inflection was in his voice as he dangled her car keys in front of her. We can't tell whether this was in a jocular vein or a truly threatening one. We have no idea what his mannerisms were. The trial judge and the jury could discern some of these things, of course, because they could observe the two people in court and could listen to what they said and how they said it. But all we know is that, between midnight and 1:00 a.m., in a neighborhood that was strange to Pat, appellant took her car keys, demanded that she accompany him, and most assuredly implied that unless she did so, at the very least, she might be stranded.

Now, let us interrupt the tale for a minute and consider the situation. Pat did not honk the horn; she did not scream; she did not try to run away. Why, she was asked. "I was scared. I didn't think at the time what to do." Later, on cross-examination: "At that point, because I was scared, because he had my car keys. I didn't know what to do. I was someplace I didn't even know where I was. It was in the city. I didn't know whether to run. I really didn't think, at that point, what to do. Now, I know that I should have blown the [h]orn. I should have run. There were a million things I could have done. I was scared, at that point, and I didn't do any of them." What, counsel asked, was she afraid of? "Him," she replied. What was she scared that he was going to do? "Rape me, but I didn't say that. It was the way he looked at me, and said, 'Come on up, come on up;' and when he took the keys, I knew that was wrong. I just didn't say, are you going to rape me." * * *

How does the majority opinion view these events? It starts by noting that Pat was a 21-year old mother who was separated from her husband but not yet divorced, as though that had some significance. To me, it has none, except perhaps (when coupled with the further characterization that Pat and Terry had gone "bar hopping") to indicate an underlying suspicion, for which there is absolutely no support in the record, that Pat was somehow "on the make." Even more alarming, and unwarranted, however, is the majority's analysis of Pat's initial reflections on whether to report what had happened. Ignoring completely her statement that she "didn't want to go through what I'm going through now," the majority, in footnote 1, cavalierly and without any foundation whatever, says:

> If, in quiet contemplation after the act, she had to wonder what would have happened, her submission on the side of prudence seems hardly justified. Indeed, if she had to wonder afterward, how can a fact finder reasonably conclude that she was justifiably in fear sufficient to overcome her will to resist, at the time.

It is this type of reasoning—if indeed "reasoning" is the right word for it—that is particularly distressing. The concern expressed by Pat, made even more real by the majority opinion of this court, is one that is common among rape victims, and largely accounts for the fact that most incidents of forcible rape go unreported by the victim. If appellant had desired, and Pat had given, her wallet instead of her body, there would be no question about appellant's guilt of robbery. Taking the car keys under those circumstances would certainly have supplied the requisite threat of force or violence and negated the element of consent. No one would seriously contend that because she failed to raise a hue and cry she had consented to the theft of her money. Why then is such life-threatening action necessary when it is her personal dignity that is being stolen?

Rape has always been considered a most serious crime, one that traditionally carried the heaviest penalty. But until recently, it remained shrouded in the taboos and myths of a Victorian age, and little real attention was given to how rapes occur, how they may be prevented, and how a victim can best protect herself from injury when an attack appears inevitable. The courts are as responsible for this ignorance and the misunderstandings emanating from it as any other institution in society, and it is high time that they recognize reality.

Rape is on the increase in the United States. The Uniform Crime Reports compiled by the F.B.I show more than a doubling in both the absolute number of forcible rapes and in the rate per 100,000 population between 1965 and 1974. Between 1973 and 1977, forcible rape has increased 19%. As the result of the Battelle Study, we now know some things about this crime that we could only guess at before. Nearly half of the rapes occur when this one did, between 8:00 p.m. and 2:00 a.m., and, as in this case, approximately one-third of rape victims had come into contact with their assailants voluntarily, under circumstances other than hitchhiking. Physical force is absent in over half of reported cases and, in a third of the cases, no weapon is involved. * * *

Of particular significance is what was learned about resistance. The most common type of resistance offered by victims is verbal. Note: verbal resistance is resistance! In cases arising in the large cities, only 12.7% of the victims attempted flight, and only 12% offered physical resistance. The reason for this is apparent from the next thing learned: that "[rape] victims who resisted were more likely to be injured than ones who did not." The statistics showed, for rapes in large cities, that, where physical resistance was offered, over 71% of the victims were physically injured in some way, 40% requiring medical treatment or hospitalization.

Said the Report: "These results indicate one possible danger of the popular notion (and some statutory requirements) that a victim of an attack should resist to her utmost."

In a second volume of the Report, intended for prosecutors, some of the social attitudes about rape were discussed. With respect to resistance, it was noted:

> Perhaps because most women's experience and expertise with violence tends to be minimal, they are unlikely to engage in

> physical combat or succeed when they do. Many women employ what is referred to as 'passive resistance.' This can include crying, being slow to respond, feigning an inability to understand instructions or telling the rapist they are pregnant, diseased or injured. While these techniques may not always be successful, their use does suggest that the victim is surely not a willing partner.

In contrast to some of the inferences sought to be drawn by the majority from Pat's reactions, the Report further points out:

> Rather than expressing their emotions, some victims respond to a rape with a calm, composed demeanor or 'controlled reaction.' These victims do not wish to exhibit emotions, especially in front of a stranger or authority figure like the prosecutor. Psychologically it is important for these victims to demonstrate that they can handle stress in a mature and adult manner. The appearance of casualness hides and may avoid true and often intense emotions. This 'control' may result in victim responses which are considered inappropriate such as giggling, smiling or even laughing. Unfortunately this type of response can cause others to doubt the victim's account of the rape.

Finally, perhaps in response to the oft-quoted comment of Matthew Hale that still pervades societal thinking about rape ("[Rape] is an accusation easily to be made and hard to be proved, and harder to be defended by the party accused, tho never so innocent"), the Report observes:

> On a national average, 15 percent of all forcible rapes reported to the police were 'determined by investigation' to be unfounded. Given the inherent skepticism of many criminal justice personnel to rape victims and the harassment and invasion of privacy that a reporting victim is likely to confront, it is doubtful that many false accusations proceed past the initial report. Curtis (1974) asserts that 'contrary to widespread opinion, there is in fact little hard empirical evidence that victims in rape lie more than, say victims in robbery.' Undoubtedly, there are false reports. However, the danger posed by the myth that women 'cry rape' is that police officers and prosecutors will believe it and then place the burden on the victims to prove the contrary. * * *

Where does this leave us but where we started? A judge and a jury, observing the witnesses and hearing their testimony, concluded without dissent that there was sufficient evidence to find beyond a reasonable doubt that appellant had sexual intercourse with Pat by force or threat of force against her will and without her consent; in other words, that the extent of her resistance and the reasons for her failure to resist further were reasonable. No claim is made here that the jury was misinstructed on the law of rape. Yet a majority of this Court, without the ability to see and hear the witnesses, has simply concluded that, in their judgment, Pat's fear was not a reasonable one, or that there was no fear at all (a point that appellant conceded at oral argument before the Court en banc). In so doing, they have ignored the fact of a young woman alone in a strange neighborhood at 1:00 in the morning with a man who had taken her keys and was standing at her open car door demanding that she come with him; they have ignored that she offered the very type of verbal resistance that is prudent, common, and recommended by law enforcement agencies; they have ignored that the reasonableness of Pat's apprehension is inherently a question of fact for the jury to determine. Brushing all of this aside, they have countermanded the judgment of the trial court and jury and declared Pat to have been, in effect, an adulteress. * * *

NOTE

The government appealed the decision you just read, and in 1981, the Court of Appeals of Maryland (Maryland's highest court) reversed the intermediate court of appeals, holding that the reversal of Rusk's rape conviction was in error because the reasonableness of Pat's fear was a question of fact for the jury, not the appellate court, to decide. *State v. Rusk*, 424 A.2d 720 (Md. 1981). Three judges vigorously dissented, however, on the ground that "there is no evidence to support the majority's conclusion that the prosecutrix was forced to submit to sexual intercourse, certainly not fellatio." Continued the dissent:

> While courts no longer require a female to resist to the utmost or to resist where resistance would be foolhardy, they do require her acquiescence in the act of intercourse to stem from fear generated by something of substance. She may not simply say, "I was really scared," and thereby transform consent or mere unwillingness into submission by force. These words do not transform a seducer into a rapist. She must follow the natural instinct of every proud female to resist, by more than mere words, the violation of her person by a stranger or an unwelcomed friend. She must make it plain that she regards such sexual acts as abhorrent and repugnant to her natural sense of pride. She must resist unless the defendant has objectively manifested his intent to use physical force to accomplish his purpose. The law regards rape as a crime of violence. The majority today attenuates this proposition. It declares the innocence of an at best distraught young woman. It does not demonstrate the defendant's guilt of the crime of rape.

424 A.2d, at 733.

Professor Susan Estrich notes that "*State v. Rusk* is one of the most vigorously debated rape cases in recent volumes of the case reporters." SUSAN ESTRICH, REAL RAPE 63 (1987). "All told, twenty-one judges, including the trial judge, reviewed the sufficiency of evidence. Ten concluded that Rusk was a rapist; eleven that he was not." *Id.*

Dissenting Justice Wilner references statistics that indicate victims of rape who resist are more likely to be injured than those who do not resist. Relying on such statistics, authorities often encourage women to refrain from resisting a sexual assault in order to avoid physical injury. Sarah E. Ullman, *Review and Critique of Empirical Studies of Rape Avoidance*, 24 CRIM. J. & BEHAVIOR 177, 181 (1997). Most of the studies on victim resistance to rape, however, have shown that forceful physical resistance, such as punching, kicking, biting, scratching, using a weapon, or martial arts techniques, and forceful verbal resistance, such as screaming for help or yelling to scare the offender, are effective at avoiding rape. Rob T. Guerette & Shannon A. Santana, *Explaining Victim Self-Protective Behavior Effects in Crime Incident Outcomes: A Test of Opportunity Theory*, 56 CRIM & DELINQUENCY 198, 200 (2010). Studies indicate that non-forceful verbal resistance, such as trying to reason with the rapist, pleading, begging, and crying, are ineffective at avoiding rape, except perhaps in acquaintance rape cases. *Id.* at 200–201. One study found that physical force was the only strategy that significantly helped avoid rape. Jody Clay-Warner, *Avoiding Rape: The Effects of Protective Actions and Situational Factors on Rape Outcome*, 17 VIOLENCE AND VICTIMS 691, 697 (2002). This study found an 81 percent reduction in the likelihood of rape for women who physically resisted. *Id.*

STATE V. ALSTON

Supreme Court of North Carolina
310 N.C. 399, 312 S.E.2d 470 (1984)

MITCHELL, JR. A.J.

The defendant raises on appeal the question whether the evidence of his guilt of kidnapping and second degree rape was sufficient to support his convictions of those crimes. For reasons discussed herein, we conclude the evidence was insufficient to support his conviction of either crime.

The State's evidence tended to show that at the time the incident occurred the defendant and the prosecuting witness in this case, Cottie Brown, had been involved for approximately six months in a consensual sexual relationship. During the six months the two had conflicts at times and Brown would leave the apartment she shared with the defendant to stay with her mother. She testified that she would return to the defendant and the apartment they shared when he called to tell her to return. Brown testified that she and the defendant had sexual relations throughout their relationship. Although she sometimes enjoyed their sexual relations, she often had sex with the defendant just to accommodate him. On those occasions, she would stand still and remain entirely passive while the defendant undressed her and had intercourse with her.

Brown testified that at times their consensual sexual relations involved some violence. The defendant had struck her several times throughout the relationship when she refused to give him money or refused to do what he wanted. Around May 15, 1981, the defendant struck her after asking for money that she refused to give him. Brown left the apartment she shared with the defendant and moved in with her mother. She did not have intercourse with the defendant after May 15 until the alleged rape on June 15. After Brown left the defendant, he called her several times and visited her at Durham Technical Institute where she was enrolled in classes. When he visited her they talked about their relationship. Brown testified that she did not tell him she wanted to break off their relationship because she was afraid he would be angry.

On June 15, 1981, Brown arrived at Durham Technical Institute by taxicab to find the defendant standing close to the school door. The defendant blocked her path as she walked toward the door and asked her where she had moved. Brown refused to tell him, and the defendant grabbed her arm, saying that she was going with him. Brown testified that it would have taken some effort to pull away. The two walked toward the parking lot and Brown told the defendant she would walk with him if he let her go. The defendant then released her. She testified that she did not run away from him because she was afraid of him. She stated that other students were nearby.

Brown stated that she and the defendant then began a casually paced walk in the neighborhood around the school. They walked, sometimes side by side, sometimes with Brown slightly behind the defendant. As they walked they talked about their relationship. Brown said the defendant did not hold her or help her along in any way as they walked. The defendant talked about Brown's "dogging" him and making him seem a fool and about Brown's mother's interference in the relationship. When the defendant and Brown left the parking lot, the defendant threatened to "fix" her face so that her mother could see he was not playing. While they were walking out of the parking lot, Brown told the defendant she wanted to go to class. He replied that she was going to miss class that day.

The two continued to walk away from the school. Brown testified that the defendant continually talked about their relationship as they walked, but that she paid little attention to what he said because she was preoccupied with her own thoughts. They passed several people. They walked along several streets and went down a path close to a wooded area where they stopped to talk. The defendant asked again where Brown had moved. She asked him whether he would let her go if she told him her address. The defendant then asked whether the relationship was over and Brown told him it was. He then said that since everyone could see her but him he had a right to make love to her again. Brown said nothing.

The two turned around at that point and began walking towards a street they had walked down previously. Changing directions, they walked in the same fashion they had walked before—side by side with Brown sometimes slightly behind. The defendant did not hold or touch Brown as they walked. Brown testified that the defendant did not say where they were going but that, when he said he wanted to make love, she knew he was going to the house of a friend. She said they had gone to the house on prior occasions to have sex. The defendant and Brown passed the same group of men they had passed previously. Brown did not ask for assistance because some of the men were friends of the defendant, and she assumed they would not help. The defendant and Brown continued to walk to the house of one of the defendant's friends, Lawrence Taylor.

When they entered the house, Taylor was inside. Brown sat in the living room while the defendant and Taylor went to the back of the house and talked. When asked why she did not try to leave when the defendant and Taylor were in the back of the house, Brown replied, "[There] was nowhere to go. I don't know. I just didn't." The defendant returned to the living room area and turned on the television. He attempted to fix a broken fan. Brown asked Taylor for a cigarette, and he gave her one.

The defendant began talking to Brown about another man she had been seeing. By that time Taylor had gone out of the room and perhaps the house. The defendant asked if Brown was "ready." The evidence tended to show that she told him "no, that I wasn't going to bed with him." She testified that she did not want to have sex with the defendant and did not consent to do so at any time on June 15.

After Brown finished her cigarette, the defendant began kissing her neck. He pulled her up from the chair in which she had been sitting and started undressing her. He noticed that she was having her menstrual period, and she sat down pulling her pants back up. The defendant again took off her pants and blouse. He told her to lay down on a bed which was in the living room. She complied and the defendant pushed apart her legs and had sexual intercourse with her. Brown testified that she did not try to push him away. She cried during the intercourse. Afterwards they talked. The defendant told her he wanted to make sure she was not lying about where she lived and that he would not let her up unless she told him.

After they dressed they talked again about the man Brown had been seeing. They left the house and went to the defendant's mother's house. After talking with the defendant's mother, Brown took a bus home. She talked with her mother about taking out a complaint against the defendant but did not tell her mother she and the defendant had had sex. Brown made a complaint to the police the same day.

The defendant continued to call Brown after June 15, but she refused to see him. One evening he called from a telephone booth and told her he had to talk. When he got to her apartment he threatened to kick her door down and Brown let him inside. Once inside he said he had intended merely to talk to her but that he wanted to make love again after seeing her. Brown said she sat and looked at him, and that he began kissing her. She pulled away and he picked her up and carried her to the bedroom. He performed oral sex on her and she testified that she did not try to fight him off because she found she enjoyed it. The two stayed together until morning and had sexual intercourse several times that night. Brown did not disclose the incident to the police immediately because she said she was embarrassed.

The defendant put on no evidence and moved at the close of the State's evidence for dismissal of both charges based on insufficiency of evidence. The trial court denied the motions and the majority in the Court of Appeals affirmed the trial court.

Upon the defendant's motion to dismiss, the question for the court is whether substantial evidence was introduced of each element of the offense charged and that the defendant was the perpetrator. Substantial evidence is "such relevant evidence as a reasonable mind might accept as adequate to support a conclusion." The issue of substantiality is a question of law for the court. If the evidence is sufficient only to raise a suspicion or conjecture as to either the commission of the offense or the identity of the perpetrator, the motion to dismiss should be allowed. This is true even though the suspicion is strong.

The court is to consider the evidence in the light most favorable to the State in ruling on a motion to dismiss. The State is entitled to every reasonable intendment and inference to be drawn from the evidence; contradictions and discrepancies do not warrant dismissal—they are for the jury to resolve. * * *

In his second assignment of error the defendant contends there was no substantial evidence that the sexual intercourse between Brown and him was by force and against her will. He argues that the evidence was insufficient to allow the trial court to submit the issue of his guilt of second degree rape to the jury. After a review of the evidence, we find this argument to have merit.

Second degree rape involves vaginal intercourse with the victim both by force and against the victim's will. Consent by the victim is a complete defense, but consent which is induced by fear of violence is void and is no legal consent.

A defendant can be guilty of raping even his mistress or a "common strumpet." This is so because consent to sexual intercourse freely given can be withdrawn at any time prior to penetration. If the particular act of intercourse for which the defendant is charged was both by force and against the victim's will, the offense is rape without regard to the victim's consent given to the defendant for prior acts of intercourse.

Where as here the victim has engaged in a prior continuing consensual sexual relationship with the defendant, however, determining the victim's state of mind at the time of the alleged rape obviously is made more difficult. Although inquiry in such cases still must be made into the victim's state of mind at the time of the alleged rape, the State ordinarily will be able to show the victim's lack of consent to the specific act charged only by evidence of statements or actions by the victim which were clearly communicated to the defendant and which expressly and unequivocally indicated the victim's withdrawal of any prior consent and lack of consent to the particular act of intercourse.

In the present case the State introduced such evidence. It is true, of course, that Brown gave no physical resistance to the defendant. Evidence of physical resistance is not necessary to prove lack of consent in a rape case in this jurisdiction. Brown testified unequivocally that she did not consent to sexual intercourse with the defendant on June 15. She was equally unequivocal in testifying that she submitted to sexual intercourse with the defendant only because she was afraid of him. During their walk, she told the defendant that their relationship was at an end. When the defendant asked her if she was "ready" immediately prior to having sexual intercourse with her, she told him "no, that I wasn't going to bed with him." Even in the absence of physical resistance by Brown, such testimony by her provided substantial evidence that the act of sexual intercourse was against her will.

The State did not offer substantial evidence, however, of the element of force. As we have stated, actual physical force need not be shown in order to establish force sufficient to constitute an element of the crime of rape. Threats of serious bodily harm which reasonably induce fear thereof are sufficient. In the present case there was no substantial evidence of either actual or constructive force.

The evidence in the present case tended to show that, shortly after the defendant met Brown at the school, they walked out of the parking lot with the defendant in front. He stopped and told Brown he was going to "fix" her face so that her mother could see he was not "playing." This threat by the defendant and his act of grabbing Brown by the arm at the school, although they may have induced fear, appeared to have been unrelated to the act of sexual intercourse between Brown and the defendant. More important, the record is devoid of evidence that Brown was in any way intimidated into having sexual intercourse with the defendant by that threat or any other act of the defendant on June 15. Brown said she did not pay a lot of attention to what the defendant said because she was thinking about other things. She specifically stated that her fear of the defendant was based on an experience with him prior to June 15 and that on June 15 he did not hold her down or threaten her with what would happen if she refused to submit to him. The State failed to offer substantial evidence of force used or threatened by the defendant on June 15 which related to his desire to have sexual intercourse on that date and was sufficient to overcome the will of the victim.

We note that the absence of an explicit threat is not determinative in considering whether there was sufficient force in whatever form to overcome the will of the victim. It is enough if the totality of the circumstances gives rise to a reasonable inference that the unspoken purpose of the threat was to force the victim to submit to unwanted sexual intercourse. The evidence introduced in the present case, however, gave rise to no such inference. Under the peculiar facts of this case, there was no substantial evidence that threats or force by the defendant on June 15 were sufficiently related to sexual conduct to cause Brown to believe that she had to submit to sexual intercourse with him or suffer harm. Although Brown's general fear of the defendant may have been justified by his conduct on prior occasions, absent evidence that the defendant used force or threats to overcome the will of the victim *to resist the sexual intercourse alleged to have been rape*, such general fear was not sufficient to show that the defendant used the force required to support a conviction of rape.

In summary, we think that the State's evidence was sufficient to show that the act of sexual intercourse in question was against Brown's will. It was not sufficient, however, to show that the act was accomplished by actual force or by a threat to use force unless she submitted to sexual intercourse. Since the State did not introduce substantial evidence of the element of force required to sustain a conviction of rape, the trial court erred in denying the defendant's motion to dismiss the case against the defendant for second degree rape.

For the foregoing reasons, we reverse the opinion of the Court of Appeals holding that there was no error in the defendant's trial for kidnapping and second degree rape and remand this action to the Court of Appeals for its further remand to the Superior Court, Durham County, for the entry of directed verdicts in favor of the defendant.

NOTE

Professor Lynne Henderson argues that "a primary impediment to recognition that rape is a real and frequent crime is a widely accepted cultural 'story' of heterosexuality that results in an unspoken 'rule' of male innocence and female guilt in law." Lynne Henderson, *Rape and Responsibility*, 11 LAW & PHIL. 127 (1992). Henderson explains:

> * * * We as a society still see women as responsible for "controlling" heterosexuality, and blame them when they do not, despite a

concomitant belief that emphasizes male initiation and persistence in sexual matters. In bourgeois culture, in a bizarre distortion of causality, girls are raised to believe that their dress, makeup, hairstyle, walk, and talk determine male reactions. As Susan Estrich noted in 1985, Ann Landers, the popular advice columnist wrote, "the woman who 'repairs to some private place for a few drinks and a little shared affection' has, by her acceptance of such a cozy invitation, given the man reason to believe she is a candidate to whatever he might have in mind." Landers doesn't seem to have changed her mind in the intervening years, despite feminist efforts to combat the ideology of female responsibility for rape. Landers published the following letter in 1991:

> Dear Ann Landers: I hope I can put into words my personal theory on date rape . . . There is no hiding a man's arousal. Usually, the female enjoys bringing it on every bit as much as the man enjoys the experience. It is all part of human nature.
>
> The problem is that for many men, there is only one way to end arousal and that is ejaculation. At the height of ecstasy, does the female partner think the man is going to excuse himself, go . . . and take a cold shower? No way. *He wants the final act.*
>
> . . . If the female partner has made up her mind that there is NOT going to be penetration, she should put a stop to the proceedings at the very first sign of male arousal. A female who doesn't want the total [sic] sexual experience should have healthy respect for a flashing red warning light. If she goes beyond this point she could be in trouble.

Here, women control sex, but men lose control, and it is "only natural." Males are incapable of being aroused and then going without intercourse. Heterosexual contact or play inevitably requires intercourse. Men are entitled if women lead them on. Landers seemingly approves this vision, responding "I see a great deal of logic in what you have said" and ending her commentary with the statement that "The female who agrees to hours of petting but does not want to complete the sex act is asking for trouble and she will probably get it." Thus, because women are expected to control sexual activity, perversely they become responsible for rape.

Id. at 138–39.

As we have seen, at early common law forcible rape was generally defined as "the carnal knowledge of a woman, not the perpetrator's wife, forcibly and against her will," where "carnal knowledge" meant penetration by a penis. Under this definition, men could not be victims of forcible rape. Today, most sexual assault statutes in the United States are formally gender-neutral, so that both men and women can be victims of rape. However, a cultural norm lingers in American society that it is shameful for a man to be the victim of a rape. The result is that male rape is underreported and seldom discussed. As I. Bennett Capers points out:

> As a society, we rarely think of male-victim rape. On the few occasions that we do, we assume male rape victimization occurs only in prisons. That assumption is wrong. In fact, even outside of prisons, males are victims of rape. A study conducted by the Bureau of Justice Statistics, based on surveys of households, estimated that more than 36,000 males age twelve and over were victims of completed rape or attempted rape during 2008 alone and that one in thirty-three men in the United States has been the victim of rape or attempted rape. Again, this number probably underestimates the frequency of male-victim rape. Even more than female victims, male rape victims are likely to encounter disbelief or derision when they report their victimization. In addition, male victims, both straight and gay, face the added risk of homophobia. Indeed, prior to the U.S. Supreme Court's 2003 decision in *Lawrence v. Texas* invalidating sodomy laws, those who came forward as rape victims risked being prosecuted as criminals in many states.

I. Bennett Capers, *Real Rape Too*, 99 CAL. L. REV. 1259, 1261–62 (2011).

A Pentagon study released in 2013 found that 53 percent of unwanted sexual contact in the military in 2012 involved attacks on men, mostly by other men. See James Dao, "*In Debate Over Military Sexual Assault, Men Are Overlooked Victims,*" N.Y. TIMES, June 23, 2013, *available at* http://www.nytimes.com/2013/06/24/us/in-debate-over-military-sexual-assault-men-are-overlooked-victims.html?pagewanted=all & _r=0. The New York Times reported: "In interviews, nearly a dozen current and former service members who said they were sexually assaulted in the military described fearing that they would be punished, ignored or ridiculed if they reported the attacks. Most said that before 2011, when the ban on openly gay service members was repealed, they believed they would have been discharged if they admitted having sexual contact—even unwanted contact—with other men." *Id.*

Capers argues that "we might make significant progress toward eliminating rape" if men understood themselves as possible victims as well as perpetrators. Capers, *Real Rape Too*, 99 CAL. L. REV. at 1306. Capers also argues that acknowledging the prevalence of male victims exposes the missteps of second-wave feminist activism against rape:

> In their efforts to eradicate one type of sexism—i.e., the sexism inherent in rape laws that treated women as naturally unreliable and thus required corroboration—feminists inadvertently entrenched another type of sexist thinking: the weak female victim, incapable of resisting, and requiring special patriarchal protections.

Id. at 1306–07. Is the contemporary dominant cultural narrative about sexual assault still a story of "male innocence and female guilt," or is it now a story about female innocence and male guilt? Consider the following case, which was decided in the early 1990s. Do you think the case would come out the same way if decided today?

COMMONWEALTH V. BERKOWITZ

Superior Court of Pennsylvania
415 Pa.Super. 505, 609 A.2d 1338 (1992)

PER CURIAM.

Appellant appeals from judgment of sentence imposed following convictions of rape and indecent assault. We are called upon to determine the degree of physical force necessary to complete the act of rape in Pennsylvania. We find that under the totality of the circumstances, evidence of sufficient force was not adduced herein. * * * Accordingly, we discharge appellant on the rape conviction. * * *

I. FACTS AND PROCEDURAL HISTORY

In the spring of 1988, appellant and the victim were both college sophomores at East Stroudsburg State University, ages twenty and nineteen years old, respectively. They had mutual friends and acquaintances. On April nineteenth of that year, the victim went to appellant's dormitory room. What transpired in that dorm room between appellant and the victim thereafter is the subject of the instant appeal.

During a one day jury trial held on September 14, 1988, the victim gave the following account during direct examination by the Commonwealth. At roughly 2:00 on the afternoon of April 19, 1988, after attending two morning classes, the victim returned to her dormitory room. There, she drank a martini to "loosen up a little bit" before going to meet her boyfriend, with whom she had argued the night before. Roughly ten minutes later she walked to her boyfriend's dormitory lounge to meet him. He had not yet arrived.

Having nothing else to do while she waited for her boyfriend, the victim walked up to appellant's room to look for Earl Hassel, appellant's roommate. She knocked on the door several times but received no answer. She therefore wrote a note to Mr. Hassel, which read, "Hi Earl, I'm drunk. That's not why I came to see you. I haven't seen you in a while. I'll talk to you later, [victim's name]." She did so, although she had not felt any intoxicating effects from the martini, "for a laugh."

After the victim had knocked again, she tried the knob on the appellant's door. Finding it open, she walked in. She saw someone lying on the bed with a pillow over his head, whom she thought to be Earl Hassel. After lifting the pillow from his head, she realized it was appellant. She asked appellant which dresser was his roommate's. He told her, and the victim left the note.

Before the victim could leave appellant's room, however, appellant asked her to stay and "hang out for a while." She complied because she "had time to kill" and because she didn't really know appellant and wanted to give him "a fair chance." Appellant asked her to give him a back rub but she declined, explaining that she did not "trust" him. Appellant then asked her to have a seat on his bed. Instead, she found a seat on the floor, and conversed for a while about a mutual friend. No physical contact between the two had, to this point, taken place.

Thereafter, however, appellant moved off the bed and down on the floor, and "kind of pushed [the victim] back with his body. It wasn't a shove, it was just kind of a leaning-type of thing." Next appellant "straddled" and started kissing the victim. The victim responded by saying, "Look, I gotta go. I'm going to meet [my boyfriend]." Then appellant lifted up her shirt and bra and began fondling her. The victim then said "no."

After roughly thirty seconds of kissing and fondling, appellant "undid his pants and he kind of moved his body up a little bit." The victim was still saying "no" but "really couldn't move because [appellant] was shifting at [her] body so he was over [her]." Appellant then tried to put his penis in her mouth. The victim did not physically resist, but rather continued to verbally protest, saying "No, I gotta go, let me go," in a "scolding" manner.

Ten or fifteen more seconds passed before the two rose to their feet. Appellant disregarded the victim's continual complaints that she "had to go," and instead walked two feet away to the door and locked it so that no one from the outside could enter.

Then, in the victim's words, "[appellant] put me down on the bed. It was kind of—like he didn't throw me on the bed. It's hard to explain. It was kind of like a push but no. . . . " She did not bounce off the bed. "It wasn't slow like a romantic kind of thing, but it wasn't a fast shove either. It was kind of in the middle."

Once the victim was on the bed, appellant began "straddling" her again while he undid the knot in her sweatpants. He then removed her sweatpants and underwear from one of her legs. The victim did not physically resist in any way while on the bed because appellant was on top of her, and she "couldn't like go anywhere." She did not scream out at anytime because, "[i]t was like a dream was happening or something."

Appellant then used one of his hands to "guide" his penis into her vagina. At that point, after appellant was inside her, the victim began saying "no, no to him softly in a moaning kind of way . . . because it was just so scary." After about thirty seconds, appellant pulled out his penis and ejaculated onto the victim stomach.

Immediately thereafter, appellant got off the victim and said, "Wow, I guess we just got carried away." To this the victim retorted, "No, we didn't get carried away, you got carried away." The victim then quickly dressed, grabbed her school books and raced downstairs to her boyfriend who was by then waiting for her in the lounge.

Once there, the victim began crying. Her boyfriend and she went up to his dorm room where, after watching the victim clean off appellant's semen from her stomach, he called the police.

Defense counsel's cross-examination elicited more details regarding the contact between appellant and the victim before the incident in question. The victim testified that roughly two weeks prior to the incident, she had attended a school seminar entitled, "Does 'no' sometimes means 'yes'?" Among other things, the lecturer at this seminar had discussed the average length and circumference of human penises. After the seminar, the victim and several of her friends had discussed the subject matter of the seminar over a speaker-telephone with appellant and his roommate Earl Hassel. The victim testified that during that telephone conversation, she had asked appellant the size of his penis. According to the victim, appellant responded by suggesting that the victim "come over and find out." She declined.

When questioned further regarding her communications with appellant prior to the April 19, 1988 incident, the victim testified that on two other occasions, she had stopped by appellant's room while intoxicated. During one of those times, she had laid down on his bed. When asked whether she had asked appellant again at that time what his penis size was, the victim testified that she did not remember.

Appellant took the stand in his own defense and offered an account of the incident and the events leading up to it which differed only as to the consent involved. According to appellant, the victim had begun communication with him after the school seminar by asking him of the size of his penis and of whether he would show it to her. Appellant had suspected that the victim wanted to pursue a sexual relationship with him because she had stopped by his room twice after the phone call while intoxicated, laying down on his bed with her legs spread and again asking to see his penis. He believed that his suspicions were confirmed when she initiated the April 19, 1988 encounter by stopping by his room (again after drinking), and waking him up.

Appellant testified that, on the day in question, he did initiate the first physical contact, but added that the victim warmly responded to his advances by passionately returning his kisses. He conceded that she was continually "whispering . . . no's," but claimed that she did so while "amorously . . . passionately" moaning. In effect, he took such protests to be thinly veiled acts of encouragement. When asked why he locked the door, he explained that "that's not something you want somebody to just walk in on you [doing.]"

According to appellant, the two then laid down on the bed, the victim helped him take her clothing off, and he entered her. He agreed that the victim continued to say "no" while on the bed, but carefully qualified his agreement, explaining that the statements were "moaned passionately." According to appellant, when he saw a "blank look on her face," he immediately withdrew and asked "is anything wrong, is something the matter, is anything wrong." He ejaculated on her stomach thereafter because he could no longer "control" himself. Appellant testified that after this, the victim "saw that it was over and then she made her move. She gets right off the bed . . . she just swings her legs over and then she puts her clothes back on." Then, in wholly corroborating an aspect of the victim's account, he testified that he remarked, "Well, I guess we got carried away," to which she rebuked, "No, we didn't get carried, you got carried away.' "

After hearing both accounts, the jury convicted appellant of rape and indecent assault. . . . Appellant was then sentenced to serve a term of imprisonment of one to four years for rape and a concurrent term of six to twelve months for indecent assault. Post-trial bail was granted pending this timely appeal. * * *

II. SUFFICIENCY OF THE EVIDENCE

Appellant's argument in this regard was well summarized by appellant's counsel in his brief.

> * * * Mr. Berkowitz prays that this Court overturns his rape conviction. He asks that this Court define the parameters between what may have been unacceptable social conduct and the criminal conduct necessary to support the charge for forcible rape.
>
> We contend that upon review, the facts show no more than what legal scholars refer to as "reluctant submission." The complainant herself admits that she was neither hurt nor threatened at any time during the encounter. She admits she never screamed or attempted to summon help. The incident occurred in a college dormitory in the middle of the afternoon.
>
> There has never been an affirmed conviction for forcible rape under similar circumstances. Not one factor which this Court has considered significant in prior cases, exists here. The uncontroverted evidence fails to establish forcible compulsion.
>
> The Commonwealth counters:
>
> Viewing the evidence and its inferences in the light most favorable to the Commonwealth, the jury's conclusion that the Defendant's forcible conduct overcame [the victim's] will is reasonable. The assault was rapid and the victim was physically

> overcome. Because she was acquainted with the Defendant, [the victim] had no reason to be fearful or suspicious of him and her resorting to verbal resistance only is understandable. More importantly, perhaps, it is only her lack of consent that is truly relevant. It is entirely reasonable to believe that the Defendant sat on her, pushed her on the bed and penetrated her before she had time to fully realize her plight and raise a hue and cry. If the law required active resistance, rather [than] the simple absence of consent, speedy penetration would immunize the most violent attacks and the goal-oriented rapist would reap an absurd reward. Certainly a victim must communicate her objections. But, contrary to the Defendant's arguments, Pennsylvania law says she can "just say no." [The victim] said "no." She said it repeatedly, clearly and sternly. She was rapidly, forcibly raped and deserves the protection of the law.
>
> With the Commonwealth position, the trial court agreed. We cannot.

In viewing the evidence, we remain mindful that credibility determinations were a matter solely for the fact finder below. On appeal, we must examine the evidence in the light most favorable to the Commonwealth drawing all reasonable inferences therefrom. If a jury could have reasonably determined from the evidence adduced that all of the necessary elements of the crime were established, then the evidence will be deemed sufficient to support the verdict.

> In Pennsylvania, the crime of rape is defined by statute as follows:
>
> A person commits a felony of the first degree when he engages in sexual intercourse with another person not his spouse:
>
> (1) by forcible compulsion;
>
> (2) by threat of forcible compulsion that would prevent resistance by a person of reasonable resolution;
>
> (3) who is unconscious; or
>
> (4) who is so mentally deranged or deficient that such person is incapable of consent.

18 Pa.C.S.A. § 3121. A statutory caveat to this rule may be found in section 3107 of title 18.

> Resistance Not Required
>
> The alleged victim need not resist the actor in prosecution under this chapter: Provided, however, that nothing in this section shall be construed to prohibit a defendant from introducing evidence that the alleged victim consented to the conduct in question.

The contours of Pennsylvania's rape statute, however, are not immediately apparent. As our Supreme Court explained in the landmark case, *Commonwealth v. Rhodes*:

> "[F]orcible compulsion" as used in section 3121(1) includes not only physical force or violence but also moral, psychological or intellectual force used to compel a person to engage in sexual intercourse against that person's will.

Closely related to section 3121(1) is section 3121(2) which applies to the situation where "forcible compulsion" is not actually used but is threatened. That section uses the phrase "by threat of forcible compulsion that would prevent resistance by a person of reasonable resolution." The Model Penal Code used the terminology "compels her to submit by any threat that would prevent resistance by a woman of ordinary resolution" and graded that offense as gross sexual imposition, a felony of the third degree. The Pennsylvania legislature rejected the concept that sexual intercourse compelled by "gross imposition" should be graded as a less serious offense and, therefore, enacted section 3121(2). By use of the phrase "person of reasonable resolution," the legislature introduced an objective standard regarding the use of *threats* of forcible compulsion to prevent resistance (as opposed to actual application of "forcible compulsion.").

The determination of whether there is sufficient evidence to demonstrate beyond a reasonable doubt that an accused engaged in sexual intercourse by forcible compulsion (which we have defined to include "not only physical force or violence, but also moral, psychological or intellectual force used to compel a person to engage in sexual intercourse against that person's will"), or by the threat of such forcible compulsion that would prevent resistance by a person of reasonable resolution *is, of course, a determination that will be made in each case based upon the totality of the circumstances that have been presented to the fact finder.* Significant factors to be weighed in that determination would include the respective ages of the victim and the accused, the respective mental and physical conditions of the victim and the accused, the atmosphere and physical setting in which the incident was alleged to have taken place, the extent to which the accused may have been in a position of authority, domination or custodial control over the victim, and whether the victim was under duress. This list of possible factors is by no means exclusive.

Before us is not a case of mental coercion. There existed no significant disparity between the ages of appellant and the victim. They were both college sophomores at the time of the incident. Appellant was age twenty; the victim was nineteen. The record is devoid of any evidence suggesting that the physical or mental condition of one party differed from the other in any material way. Moreover, the atmosphere and physical setting in which the incident took place was in no way coercive.

The victim walked freely into appellant's dorm room in the middle of the afternoon on a school day and stayed to talk of her own volition. There was no evidence to suggest that appellant was in any position of authority, domination or custodial control over the victim. Finally, no record evidence indicates that the victim was under duress. Indeed, nothing in the record manifests any intent of appellant to impose "moral, psychological or intellectual" coercion upon the victim.

Nor is this a case of a threat of forcible compulsion. When asked by defense counsel at trial whether appellant had at any point threatened her in any manner, the victim responded, "No, he didn't." Moreover, careful review of the record fails to reveal any express or even implied threat that could be viewed as one which, by the objective standard applicable herein, "would prevent resistance by a person of reasonable resolution."

Rather, the Commonwealth contends that the instant rape conviction is supported by the evidence of actual physical force used to complete the act of intercourse. Essentially, the Commonwealth maintains that, viewed in the light most favorable to it, the record establishes that the victim did not consent to engage in the intercourse, and thus, any force used to complete the act of intercourse thereafter constituted "forcible compulsion."

In response, appellant urges that the victim's testimony itself precludes a finding of "forcible compulsion." Appellant essentially argues that the indisputable lack of physical injuries and physical resistance proves that the evidence was insufficient to establish rape.

In beginning our review of these arguments, it is clear that any reliance on the victim's absence of physical injuries or physical resistance is misplaced. Although it is true that the instant victim testified that she was not "physically hurt in any fashion," and that it was "possible that [she] took no physical action to discourage [appellant]," such facts are insignificant in a sufficiency determination. As our Supreme Court has made clear, " 'rape . . . is defined, not in terms of the physical injury to the victim, but in terms of the effect it has on the victim's volition.' " Similarly, our legislature has expressly commanded that the "victim *need not resist* the actor in prosecutions under" Chapter 31. As the *Rhodes* Court observed, this legislative mandate was intended to make it clear that "lack of consent is not synonymous with lack of resistance." Thus, while the *presence* of actual injury or physical resistance might well indicate "forcible compulsion," we are compelled to conclude that the absence of either or both is not fatal to the Commonwealth's case.

What is comparatively uncertain, however, in the absence of either an injury or resistance requirement, is the precise degree of actual physical force necessary to prove "forcible compulsion." As the *Rhodes*

Court has made clear, no precise definition of the term "forcible compulsion" may be found.

The "force necessary to support convictions for rape and involuntary deviate sexual intercourse *need only be such as to establish lack of consent and to induce the woman to submit without additional resistance* . . . The degree of force required to constitute rape [or involuntary deviate sexual intercourse] is *relative* and *depends upon the facts and particular circumstances of the case.*"

The *Rhodes* Court specifically refused to "delineate all of the possible circumstances that might tend to demonstrate that sexual intercourse was engaged in by forcible compulsion or by threat of forcible compulsion within the meaning of [title 18] section 3121(1) and (2)." Rather, the Court left that delineation to evolve "in the best tradition of the common law—by development of a body of case law. . . . [W]hether there is sufficient evidence to demonstrate . . . that an accused engaged in sexual intercourse by forcible compulsion . . . is, of course, a determination that will be made in each case based on the *totality of the circumstances. . . .* " Thus, the ultimate task for the fact finder remains the question of whether, under the totality of circumstances, "the victim . . . was forced to . . . engage in sexual intercourse . . . *against his or her will.*"

Here, the victim testified that the physical aspects of the encounter began when appellant "kind of pushed me back with his body. It wasn't a shove, it was just kind of a leaning-type thing." She did not testify that appellant "pinned" her to the floor with his hands thereafter; she testified that he "started kissing me . . . [and] lift[ing] my shirt [and] bra . . . straddling me kind of . . . shifting at my body so that he was over me." When he attempted to have oral sex with her, appellant "knelt up straight . . . [and] tried to put his penis in my mouth . . . and after he obviously couldn't . . . he, we got up." Although appellant then locked the door, his act cannot be seen as an attempt to imprison the victim since she knew and testified that the type of lock on the door of appellant's dorm room simply prevented those on the outside from entering but could be opened from the inside without hindrance. Appellant did not push, shove or throw the victim to his bed; he "put" her on the bed, not in a "romantic" way, but not with a "fast shove either." Once on the bed, appellant did not try to restrain the victim with his hands in any fashion. Rather, while she was "just kind of laying there," he "straddled" her, "quick[ly] undid" the knot in her sweatpants, "took off" her sweatpants and underwear, placed the "weight of his body" on top of her and "guided" his penis inside her vagina.

Even in the light most favorable to the Commonwealth, the victim's testimony as to the physical aspects of the encounter cannot serve as a basis to prove "forcible compulsion." The cold record is utterly devoid of any evidence regarding the respective sizes of either appellant or the victim. As such, we are left only to speculate as to the coercive effect of such acts as "leaning" against the victim or placing the "weight of his body" on top of her. This we may not do. Moreover, even if the record indicated some disparity in the respective weights or strength of the parties, such acts are not themselves inconsistent with consensual relations. Except for the fact that appellant was on top of the victim before and during intercourse, there is no evidence that the victim, if she had wanted to do so, could not have removed herself from appellant's bed and walked out of the room without any risk of harm or danger to herself whatsoever. These circumstances simply cannot be bootstrapped into sexual intercourse by forcible compulsion.

Similarly inconclusive is the fact that the victim testified that the act occurred in a relatively brief period of time. The short time frame might, without more, indicate that the victim desired the sexual encounter as easily as it might that she didn't, given the fact that no threats or mental coercion were alleged. At most, therefore, the physical aspects of the encounter establishes that appellant's sexual advances may have been unusually rapid, persistent and virtually uninterrupted. However inappropriate, undesirable or unacceptable such conduct may be seen to be, it does not, standing alone, prove that the victim was "forced to engage in sexual intercourse against her will."

The only evidence which remains to be considered is the fact that both the victim and appellant testified that throughout the encounter, the victim repeatedly and continually said "no." Unfortunately for the Commonwealth, under the existing statutes, this evidence alone cannot suffice to support a finding of "forcible compulsion."

Evidence of verbal resistance is unquestionably relevant in a determination of "forcible compulsion." At least twice previously this Court has given weight to the failure to heed the victim's oral admonitions. In each such case, however, evidence of verbal resistance was only found sufficient where coupled with a sufficient threat of forcible compulsion, mental coercion, or actual physical force of a type inherently inconsistent with consensual sexual intercourse. Thus, although evidence of verbal protestations may be relevant to prove that the intercourse was against the victim's will, it is not dispositive or sufficient evidence of "forcible compulsion."

If the legislature had intended to define rape, a felony of the first degree, as non-consensual intercourse, it could have done so. It did not do this. It defined rape as sexual intercourse by "forcible compulsion." If the legislature means what it said, then where as here no evidence was adduced by the Commonwealth which established either that mental coercion, or a threat, or force inherently inconsistent with consensual intercourse was used to complete the act of intercourse, the evidence is insufficient to support a rape conviction. Accordingly, we hold that the trial court erred in determining that the evidence adduced by the Commonwealth was sufficient to convict appellant of rape. * * *

IV. CONCLUSION

For the foregoing reasons, we conclude that the evidence adduced by the Commonwealth was insufficient to convict appellant of rape. * * * The remaining issues appellant raises need not be addressed in view of this disposition. Accordingly, we *discharge* appellant as to the rape conviction. * * *

[There were no dissenting opinions.]

NOTE

After *Berkowitz* was decided, the Pennsylvania Senate unanimously approved legislation that would have eliminated the force or the threat of force requirement for a rape conviction. In other words, sexual intercourse without the victim's consent and against the victim's will would have been sufficient for rape under the proposed legislation. *"No" Enough in State's Rape Bill*, S.D. UNION TRIB., June 15, 1994, at A–6. The Senate's action, however, did not carry the day. The Pennsylvania rape statute today still requires "forcible compulsion" or a "threat of forcible compulsion that would prevent resistance by a person of reasonable resolution." 18 PA. CRIM. STAT. ANN. § 3121 (2013).

Should the crime of rape be redefined to eliminate the force or threat of force element? In *State of New Jersey in the Interest of M.T.S.*, the Supreme Court of New Jersey does not formally eliminate the force requirement, but accomplishes almost the same result by suggesting that the requirement is satisfied simply by the act of sexual penetration without the permission of the victim.

STATE OF NEW JERSEY IN THE INTEREST OF M.T.S.

Supreme Court of New Jersey
129 N.J. 422, 609 A.2d 1266 (1992)

HANDLER, J.

Under New Jersey law a person who commits an act of sexual penetration using physical force or coercion is guilty of second-degree sexual assault. The sexual assault statute does not define the words "physical force." The question posed by this appeal is whether the element of "physical force" is met simply by an act of non-consensual penetration involving no more force than necessary to accomplish that result.

That issue is presented in the context of what is often referred to as "acquaintance rape." The record in the case discloses that the juvenile, a seventeen-year-old boy, engaged in consensual kissing and heavy petting with a fifteen-year-old girl and thereafter engaged in actual sexual penetration of the girl to which she had not consented. There was no evidence or suggestion that the juvenile used any unusual or extra force or threats to accomplish the act of penetration.

The trial court determined that the juvenile was delinquent for committing a sexual assault. The Appellate Division reversed the disposition of delinquency, concluding that non-consensual penetration does not constitute sexual assault unless it is accompanied by some level of force more than that necessary to accomplish the penetration.

We granted the State's petition for certification.

I

The issues in this case are perplexing and controversial. We must explain the role of force in the contemporary crime of sexual assault and then define its essential features. We then must consider what evidence is probative to establish the commission of a sexual assault. The factual circumstances of this case expose the complexity and sensitivity of those issues and underscore the analytic difficulty of those seemingly-straightforward legal questions.

On Monday, May 21, 1990, fifteen-year-old C.G. was living with her mother, her three siblings, and several other people, including M.T.S. and his girlfriend. A total of ten people resided in the three-bedroom town-home at the time of the incident. M.T.S., then age seventeen, was temporarily residing at the home with the permission of C.G.'s mother; he slept downstairs on a couch. C.G. had her own room on the second floor. At approximately 11:30 p.m. on May 21, C.G. went upstairs to sleep after having watched television with her mother, M.T.S., and his girlfriend. When C.G. went to bed, she was wearing underpants, a bra, shorts, and a shirt. At trial, C.G. and M.T.S. offered very different accounts concerning the nature of their relationship and the events that occurred after C.G. had gone upstairs. The trial court did not credit fully either teenager's testimony.

C.G. stated that earlier in the day, M.T.S. had told her three or four times that he "was going to make a surprise visit up in [her] bedroom." She said that she had not taken M.T.S. seriously and considered his comments a joke because he frequently teased her. She testified that M.T.S. had attempted to kiss her on numerous other occasions and at least once had attempted to put his hands inside of her pants, but that she had rejected all of his previous advances.

C.G. testified that on May 22, at approximately 1:30 a.m., she awoke to use the bathroom. As she was getting out of bed, she said, she saw M.T.S., fully clothed, standing in her doorway. According to C.G., M.T.S. then said that "he was going to tease [her] a little bit." C.G. testified that she "didn't think anything of it"; she walked past him, used the bathroom, and then returned to bed, falling into a "heavy" sleep within fifteen minutes. The next event C.G. claimed to recall of that morning was waking up with M.T.S. on top of her, her underpants and shorts removed. She said "his penis was into [her] vagina." As soon as C.G. realized what had happened, she said, she immediately slapped M.T.S. once in the face, then "told him to get off [her], and get out." She did not scream or cry out. She testified that M.T.S. complied in less than one minute after being struck; according to C.G., "he jumped right off of [her]." She said she did not know how long M.T.S. had been inside of her before she awoke.

C.G. said that after M.T.S. left the room, she "fell asleep crying" because "[she] couldn't believe that he did what he did to [her]." She explained that she did not immediately tell her mother or anyone else in the house of the events of that morning because she was "scared and in shock." According to C.G., M.T.S. engaged in intercourse with her "without [her] wanting it or telling him to come up [to her bedroom]." By her own account, C.G. was not otherwise harmed by M.T.S.

At about 7:00 a.m., C.G. went downstairs and told her mother about her encounter with M.T.S. earlier in the morning and said that they would have to "get [him] out of the house." While M.T.S. was out on an errand, C.G.'s mother gathered his clothes and put them outside in his car; when he returned, he was told that "[he] better not even get near the house." C.G. and her mother then filed a complaint with the police.

According to M.T.S., he and C.G. had been good friends for a long time, and their relationship "kept leading on to more and more." He had been living at C.G.'s home for about five days before the incident occurred; he testified that during the three days preceding the incident they had been "kissing and necking" and had discussed having sexual intercourse. The first time M.T.S. kissed C.G., he said, she "didn't want him to, but she did after that." He said C.G. repeatedly had encouraged him to "make a surprise visit up in her room."

M.T.S. testified that at exactly 1:15 a.m. on May 22, he entered C.G.'s bedroom as she was walking to the bathroom. He said C.G. soon returned from the bathroom, and the two began "kissing and all," eventually moving to the bed. Once they were in bed, he said, they undressed each other and continued to kiss and touch for about five minutes. M.T.S. and C.G. proceeded to engage in sexual intercourse. According to M.T.S., who was on top of C.G., he "stuck it in" and "did it [thrust] three times, and then the fourth time [he] stuck it in, that's when [she] pulled [him] off of her." M.T.S. said that as C.G. pushed him off, she said "stop, get off," and he "hopped off right away."

According to M.T.S., after about one minute, he asked C.G. what was wrong; she replied with a back-hand to his face. He recalled asking C.G. what was wrong a second time, and her replying, "how can you take advantage of me or something like that." M.T.S. said that he proceeded to get dressed and told C.G. to calm down, but that she then told him to get away from her and began to cry. Before leaving the room, he told C.G.,

"I'm leaving . . . I'm going with my real girlfriend, don't talk to me . . . I don't want nothing to do with you or anything, stay out of my life . . . don't tell anybody about this . . . it would just screw everything up." He then walked downstairs and went to sleep.

On May 23, 1990, M.T.S. was charged with conduct that if engaged in by an adult would constitute second-degree sexual assault of the victim, contrary to N.J.S.A. 2C:14–2c(1). * * * Following a two-day trial on the sexual assault charge, M.T.S. was adjudicated delinquent. After reviewing the testimony, the court concluded that the victim had consented to a session of kissing and heavy petting with M.T.S. The trial court did not find that C.G. had been sleeping at the time of penetration, but nevertheless found that she had not consented to the actual sexual act. Accordingly, the court concluded that the State had proven second-degree sexual assault beyond a reasonable doubt. On appeal, following the imposition of suspended sentences on the sexual assault and the other remaining charges, the Appellate Division determined that the absence of force beyond that involved in the act of sexual penetration precluded a finding of second-degree sexual assault. It therefore reversed the juvenile's adjudication of delinquency for that offense.

II

The New Jersey Code of Criminal Justice, N.J.S.A. 2C:14–2c(1), defines "sexual assault" as the commission "of sexual penetration" "with another person" with the use of "physical force or coercion."[1] An unconstrained reading of the statutory language indicates that both the act of "sexual penetration" and the use of "physical force or coercion" are separate and distinct elements of the offense. Neither the definitions section of N.J.S.A. 2C:14–1 to –8, nor the remainder of the Code of Criminal Justice provides assistance in interpreting the words "physical force." The initial inquiry is, therefore, whether the statutory words are

[1] The sexual assault statute, N.J.S.A.: 2C:14–2c(1), reads as follows:

c. An actor is guilty of sexual assault if he commits an act of sexual penetration with another person under any one of the following circumstances:

(1) The actor *uses physical force or coercion,* but the victim does not sustain severe personal injury;

(2) The victim is one whom the actor knew or should have known was physically helpless, mentally defective or mentally incapacitated;

(3) The victim is on probation or parole, or is detained in a hospital, prison or other institution and the actor has supervisory or disciplinary power over the victim by virtue of the actor's legal, professional or occupational status;

(4) The victim is at least 16 but less than 18 years old and:

(a) The actor is related to the victim by blood or affinity to the third degree; or

(b) The actor has supervisory or disciplinary power over the victim; or

(c) The actor is a foster parent, a guardian, or stands in loco parentis within the household;

(5) The victim is at least 13 but less than 16 years old and the actor is at least 4 years older than the victim.

Sexual assault is a crime of the second degree.

unambiguous on their face and can be understood and applied in accordance with their plain meaning. The answer to that inquiry is revealed by the conflicting decisions of the lower courts and the arguments of the opposing parties. The trial court held that "physical force" had been established by the sexual penetration of the victim without her consent. The Appellate Division believed that the statute requires some amount of force more than that necessary to accomplish penetration.

The parties offer two alternative understandings of the concept of "physical force" as it is used in the statute. The State would read "physical force" to entail any amount of sexual touching brought about involuntarily. A showing of sexual penetration coupled with a lack of consent would satisfy the elements of the statute. The Public Defender urges an interpretation of "physical force" to mean force "used to overcome lack of consent." That definition equates force with violence and leads to the conclusion that sexual assault requires the application of some amount of force in addition to the act of penetration.

Current judicial practice suggests an understanding of "physical force" to mean "any degree of physical power or strength used against the victim, even though it entails no injury and leaves no mark." Resort to common experience or understanding does not yield a conclusive meaning. The dictionary provides several definitions of "force," among which are the following: (1) "power, violence, compulsion, or constraint exerted upon or against a person or thing," (2) "a general term for exercise of strength or power, esp. physical, to overcome resistance," or (3) "strength or power of any degree that is exercised without justification or contrary to law upon a person or thing." *Webster's Third New International Dictionary* 887 (1961). Thus, as evidenced by the disagreements among the lower courts and the parties, and the variety of possible usages, the statutory words "physical force" do not evoke a single meaning that is obvious and plain. Hence, we must pursue avenues of construction in order to ascertain the meaning of that statutory language. Those avenues are well charted. When a statute is open to conflicting interpretations, the court seeks the underlying intent of the legislature, relying on legislative history and the contemporary context of the statute. * * *

The provisions proscribing sexual offenses found in the Code of Criminal Justice, N.J.S.A. 2C:14–2c(1), became effective in 1979, and were written against almost two hundred years of rape law in New Jersey. The origin of the rape statute that the current statutory offense of sexual assault replaced can be traced to the English common law. Under the common law, rape was defined as "carnal knowledge of a woman against her will." American jurisdictions generally adopted the English view, but over time states added the requirement that the carnal knowledge have been forcible, apparently in order to prove that the act was against the victim's will. As of 1796, New Jersey statutory law defined rape as "carnal knowledge of a woman, forcibly and against her will." Those three elements of rape—carnal knowledge, forcibly, and against her will—remained the essential elements of the crime until 1979.

Under traditional rape law, in order to prove that a rape had occurred, the state had to show both that force had been used and that the penetration had been against the woman's will. Force was identified and determined not as an independent factor but in relation to the response of the victim, which in turn implicated the victim's own state of mind. Thus, the perpetrator's use of force became criminal only if the victim's state of mind met the statutory requirement. The perpetrator could use all the force imaginable and no crime would be committed if the state could not prove additionally that the victim did not consent. Although the terms "non-consent" and "against her will" were often treated as equivalent, under the traditional definition of rape, both formulations squarely placed on the victim the burden of proof and of action. * * *

The presence or absence of consent often turned on credibility. To demonstrate that the victim had not consented to the intercourse, and also that sufficient force had been used to accomplish the rape, the state had to prove that the victim had resisted. According to the oft-quoted Lord Hale, to be deemed a credible witness, a woman had to be of good fame, disclose the injury immediately, suffer signs of injury, and cry out for help. Courts and commentators historically distrusted the testimony of victims, "assuming that women lie about their lack of consent for various reasons: to blackmail men, to explain the discovery of a consensual affair, or because of psychological illness." Evidence of resistance was viewed as a solution to the credibility problem; it was the "outward manifestation of nonconsent, [a] device for determining whether a woman actually gave consent." * * *

In many jurisdictions the requirement was that the woman have resisted to the utmost. "Rape is not committed unless the woman oppose the man to the utmost limit of her power." * * *

Critics of rape law agreed that the focus of the crime should be shifted from the victim's behavior to the defendant's conduct, and particularly to its forceful and assaultive, rather than sexual, character. Reformers also shared the goals of facilitating rape prosecutions and of sparing victims much of the degradation involved in bringing and trying a charge of rape. There were, however, differences over the best way to redefine the crime. Some reformers advocated a standard that defined rape as unconsented-to sexual intercourse; others urged the elimination of any reference to consent from the definition of rape. Nonetheless, all proponents of reform shared a central premise: that the burden of showing non-consent should not fall on the victim of the crime. In dealing with the problem of consent the reform goal was not so much to purge the entire concept of consent from the law as to eliminate the burden that had been placed on victims to prove they had not consented.

Similarly, with regard to force, rape law reform sought to give independent significance to the forceful or assaultive conduct of the defendant and to avoid a definition of force that depended on the reaction of the victim. Traditional interpretations of force were strongly criticized for failing to acknowledge that force may be understood simply as the invasion of "bodily integrity." In urging that the "resistance" requirement be abandoned, reformers sought to break the connection between force and resistance. * * *

III

* * * The reform statute defines sexual assault as penetration accomplished by the use of "physical force" or "coercion," but it does not define either "physical force" or "coercion" or enumerate examples of evidence that would establish those elements. Some reformers had argued that defining "physical force" too specifically in the sexual offense statute might have the effect of limiting force to the enumerated examples. The task of defining "physical force" therefore was left to the courts. * * *

[T]he New Jersey Code of Criminal Justice does not refer to force in relation to "overcoming the will" of the victim, or to the "physical overpowering" of the victim, or the "submission" of the victim. It does not require the demonstrated non-consent of the victim. As we have noted, in reforming the rape laws, the Legislature placed primary emphasis on the assaultive nature of the crime, altering its constituent elements so that they focus exclusively on the forceful or assaultive conduct of the defendant. * * *

The intent of the Legislature to redefine rape consistent with the law of assault and battery is further evidenced by the legislative treatment of other sexual crimes less serious than and derivative of traditional rape. The Code redefined the offense of criminal sexual contact to emphasize the involuntary and personally-offensive nature of the touching. Sexual contact is criminal under the same circumstances that render an act of sexual penetration a sexual assault, namely, when "physical force" or "coercion" demonstrates that it is unauthorized and offensive. Thus, just as any unauthorized touching is a crime under traditional laws of assault and battery, so is any unauthorized sexual contact a crime under the reformed law of criminal sexual contact, and so is any unauthorized sexual penetration a crime under the reformed law of sexual assault.

The understanding of sexual assault as a criminal battery, albeit one with especially serious consequences, follows necessarily from the

Legislature's decision to eliminate non-consent and resistance from the substantive definition of the offense. Under the new law, the victim no longer is required to resist and therefore need not have said or done anything in order for the sexual penetration to be unlawful. The alleged victim is not put on trial, and his or her responsive or defensive behavior is rendered immaterial. We are thus satisfied that an interpretation of the statutory crime of sexual assault to require physical force in addition to that entailed in an act of involuntary or unwanted sexual penetration would be fundamentally inconsistent with the legislative purpose to eliminate any consideration of whether the victim resisted or expressed non-consent. * * *

Because the statute eschews any reference to the victim's will or resistance, the standard defining the role of force in sexual penetration must prevent the possibility that the establishment of the crime will turn on the alleged victim's state of mind or responsive behavior. We conclude, therefore, that any act of sexual penetration engaged in by the defendant without the affirmative and freely-given permission of the victim to the specific act of penetration constitutes the offense of sexual assault. Therefore, physical force in excess of that inherent in the act of sexual penetration is not required for such penetration to be unlawful. The definition of "physical force" is satisfied under N.J.S.A. 2C:14–2c(1) if the defendant applies any amount of force against another person in the absence of what a reasonable person would believe to be affirmative and freely-given permission to the act of sexual penetration. * * *

Under the reformed statute, permission to engage in sexual penetration must be affirmative and it must be given freely, but that permission may be inferred either from acts or statements reasonably viewed in light of the surrounding circumstances. Persons need not, of course, expressly announce their consent to engage in intercourse for there to be affirmative permission. Permission to engage in an act of sexual penetration can be and indeed often is indicated through physical actions rather than words. Permission is demonstrated when the evidence, in whatever form, is sufficient to demonstrate that a reasonable person would have believed that the alleged victim had affirmatively and freely given authorization to the act. * * *

Today the law of sexual assault is indispensable to the system of legal rules that assures each of us the right to decide who may touch our bodies, when, and under what circumstances. The decision to engage in sexual relations with another person is one of the most private and intimate decisions a person can make. Each person has the right not only to decide whether to engage in sexual contact with another, but also to control the circumstances and character of that contact. No one, neither a spouse, nor a friend, nor an acquaintance, nor a stranger, has the right or the privilege to force sexual contact.

We emphasize as well that what is now referred to as "acquaintance rape" is not a new phenomenon. Nor was it a "futuristic" concept in 1978 when the sexual assault law was enacted. Current concern over the prevalence of forced sexual intercourse between persons who know one another reflects both greater awareness of the extent of such behavior and a growing appreciation of its gravity. Notwithstanding the stereotype of rape as a violent attack by a stranger, the vast majority of sexual assaults are perpetrated by someone known to the victim. One respected study indicates that more than half of all rapes are committed by male relatives, current or former husbands, boyfriends or lovers. Similarly, contrary to common myths, perpetrators generally do not use guns or knives and victims generally do not suffer external bruises or cuts. Although this more realistic and accurate view of rape only recently has achieved widespread public circulation, it was a central concern of the proponents of reform in the 1970s.

The insight into rape as an assaultive crime is consistent with our evolving understanding of the wrong inherent in forced sexual intimacy. It is one that was appreciated by the Legislature when it reformed the rape laws, reflecting an emerging awareness that the definition of rape should correspond fully with the experiences and perspectives of rape victims. Although reformers focused primarily on the problems associated with convicting defendants accused of violent rape, the recognition that forced sexual intercourse often takes place between persons who know each other and often involves little or no violence comports with the understanding of the sexual assault law that was embraced by the Legislature. Any other interpretation of the law, particularly one that defined force in relation to the resistance or protest of the victim, would directly undermine the goals sought to be achieved by its reform. * * *

Accordingly, we reverse the judgment of the Appellate Division and reinstate the disposition of juvenile delinquency for the commission of second-degree sexual assault.

2. WHAT COUNTS (OR SHOULD COUNT) AS CONSENT?

Forcible rape generally requires proof that the sexual intercourse was without the consent of the victim. What if a woman initially consents to sexual intercourse, but then changes her mind? Should a man who persists in having sexual intercourse under such circumstances be found guilty of rape? The California Supreme Court provides its answers to these questions in *In re John Z.*

What if the victim said "no," but the defendant honestly believed she meant "yes"? Should a man who honestly but mistakenly believed his female partner was consenting, even though she said no, be absolved of liability for rape? One famous English case held that a defendant can defend against a rape charge by claiming that he honestly believed the victim was consenting. *See Regina v. Morgan*, 1976 A.C. 182, 214. According to the *Morgan* court, such a defendant may be acquitted even if his belief is completely unreasonable.

In the United States, most jurisdictions require that the rape defendant's mistake as to the victim's consent must be honest *and reasonable* in order to constitute a successful defense to a forcible rape charge. Note that asserting an honest and reasonable belief in consent is different from a claim that the victim was actually consenting.

What constitutes a reasonable belief in consent? If a substantial percentage of women say "no" when they really mean "yes," is it reasonable for a man to think that a woman who says "no" is in fact consenting? Several studies indicate that many women and some men say "no" when they actually want to engage in sexual intercourse. Charlene L. Muehlenhard, *Examining Stereotypes about Token Resistance to Sex*, 35 PSYCHOLOGY OF WOMEN QUARTERLY 676 (2011).

When juries assess whether the complaining witness consented or whether the defendant reasonably believed the complaining witness was consenting, it appears that cultural attitudes may matter more than gender. In 2009, law professor Dan Kahan provided 1500 Americans aged eighteen years or older (average age of 46) with a written summary of the facts in *Berkowitz*. Dan Kahan, *Culture, Cognition, and Consent: Who Perceives What, and Why, in Acquaintance Rape Cases*, 158 U. PA. L.REV. 729, 765 (2010). The summary presented the facts as told by the defendant and the complainant, who were called "Dave" and "Lucy," and described them as agreeing that the complainant had repeatedly said "no" both before and during sexual intercourse. Kahan asked participants to indicate the intensity of their agreement or disagreement with a number of statements, including whether Lucy consented to sexual intercourse with Dave, whether Dave honestly believed Lucy was consenting, whether it was reasonable for Dave to have believed Lucy was consenting, and whether it would be unfair to convict Dave of rape. Kahan also measured participants' cultural values to see how closely they aligned with either a hierarchical, individualist, or communitarian world view.

Kahan found that gender mattered less than cultural attitudes. "Overall, women were no more or less likely to favor conviction than were men." *Id.* at 733. Older women who held hierarchical attitudes, however, were more inclined than others to form a pro-defendant view of the facts. *Id.* at 794. Kahan's findings suggest that the debate over whether "no" means "no" in acquaintance rape cases is less about differences between the way men and women see the world and more about differences in cultural attitudes. Kahan also found that variations in legal definitions of rape had either a small or no impact on the likelihood that participants would support or oppose conviction. This suggests that changing people's cultural attitudes may be have more of an impact on verdicts in rape cases than law reform.

The next case, *In re John Z.*, examines the question of whether consent to sexual intercourse once given can be withdrawn. Reasonable minds can and do disagree over whether the law should consider the non-consent element of rape satisfied when the victim initially consents and then changes her mind. The courts are split on how to resolve this question.

IN RE JOHN Z.

Supreme Court of California
29 Cal.4th 756, 60 P.3d 183, 128 Cal.Rptr.2d 783 (2003)

CHIN, J.

We granted this case to settle a conflict in Court of Appeal decisions as to whether the crime of forcible rape (Pen. Code, § 261, subd. (a)(2)) is committed if the female victim consents to an initial penetration by her male companion, and then withdraws her consent during an act of intercourse, but the male continues against her will. (*Compare People v. Vela* (1985) 172 Cal. App. 3d 237, 218 Cal.Rptr. 161 (*Vela*) [no rape committed] *with People v. Roundtree* (2000) 77 Cal.App.4th 846, 91 Cal.Rptr.2d 921 (*Roundtree*) [rape committed].) We agree with *Roundtree* and the Court of Appeal in the present case that a withdrawal of consent effectively nullifies any earlier consent and subjects the male to forcible rape charges if he persists in what has become nonconsensual intercourse.

The juvenile court * * * found that [the defendant] committed forcible rape. * * * He was committed to Crystal Creek Boys Ranch. On appeal, defendant contends the evidence is insufficient to sustain the finding that he committed forcible rape. We disagree.

FACTS

The following facts are largely taken from the Court of Appeal opinion in this case. During the afternoon of March 23, 2000, 17-year-old Laura T. was working at Safeway when she received a call from Juan G., whom she had met about two weeks earlier. Juan wanted Laura to take him to a party at defendant's home and then return about 8:30 p.m. to pick him up. Laura agreed to take Juan to the party, but since she planned to attend a church group meeting that evening she told him she would be unable to pick him up.

Sometime after 6:00 p.m., Laura drove Juan to defendant's residence. Defendant and Justin L. were present. After arranging to have Justin L.'s stepbrother, P. W., buy them alcohol, Laura picked up P. W. and drove him to the store where he bought beer. Laura told Juan she would stay until 8:00 or 8:30 p.m. Although defendant and Juan drank the beer, Laura did not.

During the evening, Laura and Juan went into defendant's parents' bedroom. Juan indicated he wanted to have sex but Laura told him she was not ready for that kind of activity. Juan became upset and went into the bathroom. Laura left the bedroom and both defendant and Justin asked her why she "wouldn't do stuff." Laura told them that she was not ready.

About 8:10 p.m., Laura was ready to leave when defendant asked her to come into his bedroom to talk. She complied. Defendant told her that Juan had said he (Juan) did not care for her; defendant then suggested that Laura become his girlfriend. Juan entered the bedroom and defendant left to take a phone call.

When defendant returned to the bedroom, he and Juan asked Laura if it was her fantasy to have two guys, and Laura said it was not. Juan and defendant began kissing Laura and removing her clothes, although she kept telling them not to. At some point, the boys removed Laura's pants and underwear and began "fingering" her, "playing with [her] boobs" and continued to kiss her. Laura enjoyed this activity in the beginning, but objected when Juan removed his pants and told defendant to keep fingering her while he put on a condom. Once the condom was in place, defendant left the room and Juan got on top of Laura. She tried to resist and told him she did not want to have intercourse, but he was too strong and forced his penis into her vagina. The rape terminated when, due to Laura's struggling, the condom fell off. Laura told Juan that "maybe it's a sign we shouldn't be doing this," and he said "fine" and left the room. (Although Juan G. was originally a codefendant, at the close of the victim's testimony he admitted amended charges of sexual battery and unlawful sexual intercourse, a misdemeanor.)

Laura rolled over on the bed and began trying to find her clothes; however, because the room was dark she was unable to do so. Defendant, who had removed his clothing, then entered the bedroom and walked to where Laura was sitting on the bed and "he like rolled over [her] so [she] was pushed back down to the bed." Laura did not say anything and defendant began kissing her and telling her that she had "a really beautiful body." Defendant got on top of Laura, put his penis into her vagina "and rolled [her] over so [she] was sitting on top of him." Laura testified she "kept . . . pulling up, trying to sit up to get it out . . . and he grabbed my hips and pushed me back down and then he rolled me back over so I was on my back . . . and . . . kept saying, will you be my girlfriend." Laura "kept like trying to pull away" and told him that "if he really did care about me, he wouldn't be doing this to me and if he did want a relationship, he should wait and respect that I don't want to do this." After about 10 minutes, defendant got off Laura, and helped her dress and find her keys. She then drove home.

On cross-examination, Laura testified that when defendant entered the room unclothed, he lay down on the bed behind her and touched her shoulder with just enough pressure to make her move, a nudge. He asked her to lie down and she did. He began kissing her and she kissed him back. He rolled on top of her, inserted his penis in her and, although she resisted, he rolled her back over, pulling her on top of him. She was on top of him for four or five minutes, during which time she tried to get off, but he grabbed her waist and pulled her back down. He rolled her over and continued the sexual intercourse. Laura told him that she needed to go home, but he would not stop. He said, "just give me a minute," and she said, "no, I need to get home." He replied, "give me some time" and she repeated, "no, I have to go home." Defendant did not stop, "he just stayed inside of me and kept like basically forcing it on me." After about a "minute, minute and [a] half," defendant got off Laura.

Defendant testified, admitting that he and Juan were kissing and fondling Laura in the bedroom, but claimed it was with her consent. He also admitted having sexual intercourse with Laura, again claiming it was consensual. He claimed he discontinued the act as soon as Laura told him that she had to go home.

DISCUSSION

Although the evidence of Laura's initial consent to intercourse with John Z. was hardly conclusive, we will assume for purposes of argument that Laura impliedly consented to the act, or at least tacitly refrained from objecting to it, until defendant had achieved penetration. (But see § 261.6 [defining the type of consent at issue under section 261 as "positive cooperation in act or attitude pursuant to an exercise of free will"].) As will appear, we conclude that the offense of forcible rape occurs when, during apparently consensual intercourse, the victim expresses an objection and attempts to stop the act and the defendant forcibly continues despite the objection.

Vela held that where the victim consents to intercourse at the time of penetration but thereafter withdraws her consent, any use of force by her assailant past that point is not rape. The court in *Vela* found "scant authority" on point, relying on two out-of-state cases which had held that if consent is given prior to penetration, no rape occurs despite the withdrawal of consent during intercourse itself. According to *Vela*, these cases held that "the presence or absence of consent at the moment of initial penetration appears to be the crucial point in the crime of rape."

Vela agreed with these cases, reasoning that "the essence of the crime of rape is the outrage to the person and feelings of the female resulting from the nonconsensual violation of her womanhood. When a female willingly consents to an act of sexual intercourse, the penetration by the male cannot constitute a violation of her womanhood nor cause outrage to her person and feelings. If she withdraws consent during the act of sexual intercourse and the male forcibly continues the act without interruption, the female may certainly feel outrage because of the force applied or because the male ignores her wishes, but the sense of outrage to her person and feelings could hardly be of the same magnitude as that resulting from an initial nonconsensual violation of her womanhood. It would seem, therefore, that the essential guilt of rape as stated in . . . section 263 is lacking in the withdrawn consent scenario."

With due respect to *Vela* and the two sister state cases on which it relied, we find their reasoning unsound. First, contrary to *Vela*'s assumption, we have no way of accurately measuring the level of outrage the victim suffers from being subjected to continued forcible intercourse following withdrawal of her consent. We must assume the sense of outrage is substantial. More importantly, section 261, subdivision (a)(2), defines rape as "an act of sexual intercourse accomplished with a person not the spouse of the perpetrator. . . . where it is accomplished against a person's will by means of force, violence, duress, menace, or fear of immediate and unlawful bodily injury on the person or another." Nothing in section 261 conditions the act of rape on the degree of outrage of the victim. Section 263 states that "the essential guilt of rape consists in the outrage to the person and feelings of the victim of the rape. Any sexual penetration, however slight, is sufficient to complete the crime." But no California case has held that the victim's outrage is an element of the crime of rape. * * *

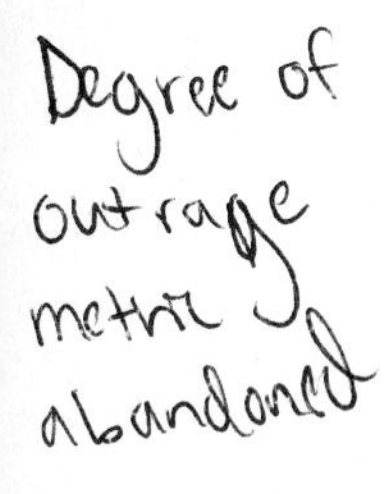

As the Court of Appeal in this case stated, "while outrage of the victim may be the cause for criminalizing and severely punishing forcible rape, outrage by the victim is not an element of forcible rape. Pursuant to section 261, subdivision (a)(2), forcible rape occurs when the act of sexual intercourse is accomplished against the will of the victim by force or threat of bodily injury and it is immaterial at what point the victim withdraws her consent, so long as that withdrawal is communicated to the male and he thereafter ignores it."

In the present case, assuming arguendo that Laura initially consented to, or appeared to consent to, intercourse with defendant, substantial evidence shows that she withdrew her consent and, through her actions and words, communicated that fact to defendant. Despite the dissent's doubt in the matter, no reasonable person in defendant's position would have believed that Laura continued to consent to the act. As the Court of Appeal below observed, "Given [Laura's testimony], credited by the court, there was nothing equivocal about her withdrawal of any initially assumed consent."

Vela appears to assume that, to constitute rape, the victim's objections must be raised, or a defendant's use of force must be applied, *before* intercourse commences, but that argument is clearly flawed. One can readily imagine situations in which the defendant is able to obtain penetration before the victim can express an objection or attempt to resist. Surely, if the defendant thereafter ignores the victim's objections and forcibly continues the act, he has committed "an act of sexual intercourse accomplished . . . against a person's will by means of force. . . ."

Defendant, candidly acknowledging *Vela*'s flawed reasoning, contends that, in cases involving an initial consent to intercourse, the male should be permitted a "reasonable amount of time" in which to withdraw, once the female raises an objection to further intercourse. As defendant argues, "By essence of the act of sexual intercourse, a male's primal urge to reproduce is aroused. It is therefore unreasonable for a female and the law to expect a male to cease having sexual intercourse immediately upon her withdrawal of consent. It is only natural, fair and just that a male be given a reasonable amount of time in which to quell his primal urge. . . ."

We disagree with defendant's argument. Aside from the apparent lack of supporting authority for defendant's "primal urge" theory, the principal problem with his argument is that it is contrary to the language of section 261, subdivision (a)(2): Nothing in the language of section 261 or the case law suggests that the defendant is entitled to persist in intercourse once his victim withdraws her consent.

In any event, even were we to accept defendant's "reasonable time" argument, in the present case he clearly was given ample time to withdraw but refused to do so despite Laura's resistance and objections. Although defendant testified he withdrew as soon as Laura objected, for purposes of appeal we need not accept this testimony as true in light of Laura's contrary testimony. As noted above, Laura testified that she struggled to get away when she was on top of defendant, but that he grabbed her waist and pushed her down onto him. At this point, Laura told defendant that if he really cared about her, he would respect her wishes and stop. Thereafter, she told defendant *three* times that she needed to go home and that she did not accept his protestations he just needed a "minute." Defendant continued the sex act for at least four or five minutes after Laura *first* told him she had to go home. According to Laura, after the *third* time she asked to leave, defendant continued to insist that he needed more time and "just stayed inside of me and kept like basically forcing it on me," for about a "minute, minute and [a] half." Contrary to the dissent's concerns, the force defendant exerted in resisting Laura attempts to stop the act was clearly ample to satisfy section 261, subdivision (a)(2). * * *

We disapprove *Vela*, to the extent that decision is inconsistent with our opinion. The judgment of the Court of Appeal is affirmed.

BROWN, J. (dissenting).

A woman has an absolute right to say "no" to an act of sexual intercourse. After intercourse has commenced, she has the absolute right to call a halt and say "no more," and if she is compelled to continue, a forcible rape is committed. Although California's rape statutes are gender neutral, the criminalization of more subtle forms of sexual violence reflects a new view of women as "responsible, autonomous beings who possess the right to personal, sexual, and bodily self-determination." Thus, both courts and legislatures have expanded the concept of rape to include spousal rape, lesser degrees of rape, and what has been characterized as postpenetration rape.

To the extent the majority holds the clear withdrawal of consent nullifies any earlier consent and forcible persistence in what then becomes nonconsensual intercourse is rape, not assault and battery as the Court of Appeal held in *People v. Vela*, I concur in that portion of its reasoning. However, because the majority ignores critical questions about the nature and sufficiency of proof in a postpenetration rape case, I cannot concur in the rest of the majority opinion. The majority opinion is deficient in several respects. First, the opinion fails to consider whether the victim's statements in this case clearly communicated her withdrawal of consent. Second, there is no attempt to define what constitutes force in this context. Finally, questions about wrongful intent are given short shrift.

The People must prove the elements of a crime beyond a reasonable doubt. As relevant to this case, "Rape is an act of sexual intercourse . . . with a person not the spouse of the perpetrator" "accomplished against a person's will by means of force, violence, duress, menace, or fear of immediate and unlawful bodily injury on the person or another." Presumably, in a postpenetration rape case, the prosecution still has the burden of showing, beyond a reasonable doubt, that the victim clearly communicated withdrawal of consent and the defendant exercised some degree of force to continue. Moreover, a defendant's reasonable and good faith mistake of fact regarding a person's consent to sexual intercourse is a defense to rape. To be acquitted, a defendant need only raise a reasonable doubt as to his reasonable and honest belief in consent. Thus, to convict in such a case, the People must prove the absence of such a belief *beyond a reasonable doubt*.

Ordinarily, these cases involve a credibility contest in which the victim tells one story, the defendant another. The trial judge in this juvenile matter relied primarily on Laura's testimony and rejected John Z.'s testimony in its entirety. Even so, "assuming arguendo that Laura initially consented to, or appeared to consent to, intercourse with defendant," the facts in this case, as described solely by the prosecution witness, create doubt both about the withdrawal of consent and the use of force.

This is a sordid, distressing, sad little case. From any perspective, its facts are appalling. Laura T., a 17-year-old girl, finds herself alone in a house with four young men, ranging in age from 16 to 21. One of them, Juan, is "sort of" her boyfriend. Laura and Juan met at a bus stop near her workplace and had known each other for about two weeks when they arrived at the "party" at John Z.'s house on March 23, 2000. Laura drove to the party in her own vehicle. She planned to drop Juan off and leave. The other partygoers were unknown to Laura. John Z. was introduced to her after they arrived. Instead of leaving, Laura remained at John Z.'s house for several hours. During the evening she was openly affectionate with Juan, and sporadically engaged in some mutual kissing with John Z.-in the kitchen and later in the master bedroom when Juan was sulking in the bathroom.

This is how she described subsequent events:

Around 8:00 p.m., Laura decided she was ready to leave. Before she walked out the door, John asked if he could talk to her. She walked back into the house and went into his bedroom, which was completely dark. She did not ask to turn on the light. She entered the room willingly and was not restrained from leaving. They sat in the dark, talking. John told her Juan never cared about her, was only "using [her] and anyone else could use [her] too." John said he really liked her; she should dump Juan and become John's girlfriend. When Juan came into the bedroom, Laura confronted him with what John had said. He denied it. The boys asked if she had ever fantasized about having "two guys." Laura said she had not, but she continued to sit on the bed in John's darkened bedroom with both Juan and John while one or both of them removed various items of her clothing. At first, she tried to replace her clothing, but after pulling her bra back into place a couple of times, she made no further efforts to retrieve her clothes. Asked why she did not leave, she responded: "There is no reason. I just didn't. I didn't think about it. I had already tried to leave once, and they asked me to go in the bedroom and talk."

Feeling there was "no point in fighting" because there was nothing she could do about it anyway, she laid back on the bed, with Juan on one side of her and John on the other. She did not say anything and she was not fighting or resisting while the rest of her clothing was removed. The boys were "fingering" her and playing with her "boobs" and kissing her and "like just trying to like keep me satisfied type of thing." She acknowledged that she enjoyed these activities, enjoyed it "because it was like a threesome" she was laughing and liked being the center of attention.

After that prelude and after she had intercourse with Juan, which ended when the condom kept falling off and she told him perhaps that was a sign they "shouldn't be doing this," we come to the facts which form the basis of John Z.'s adjudication. According to Laura, she was sitting on the bed naked when John Z. came into the room, naked or partially unclothed. She had been unable to find her clothes in the dark. John sat on the bed behind her and touched her with one hand on her shoulder. He did not pull or push her backward. He nudged her with one hand. His left hand was in a cast. She laid back down on the bed. John began kissing her. She kissed him back. He climbed on top of her and achieved penetration. She did not say anything. She did not push him away, slap him or strike him. He made no threats and he did not hurt her. John asked her repeatedly "will you be my girlfriend?"

He rolled over so she was on top. She remained in that position for four to five minutes. Although he held her only with one hand on her waist-not hard enough for her to feel the pressure or to create a bruise-she was unable to extricate herself or break the connection. There was no conversation when intercourse began and she said nothing while she was on top of him. When she found herself on the bottom again, she said: "If he really did care about me, he wouldn't be doing this to me and if he really did want a relationship, he should wait and respect that I don't want to do this." John responded: "I really do care about you." She never "officially" told him she did not want to have sexual intercourse.

Sometime later she said: "I should be going now." "I need to go home." John said: "Just give me a minute." Several minutes later, she said again: "I need to get home." He said: "G]ive me some time." She said: "No. I have to go home." The third time she told him she had to go home she was a little more urgent. She never "officially" cried, but she was starting to. When asked if at anytime while having intercourse with John Z., she had told him "no," Laura answers: "No," and repeats her contingent statement. Calling a halt, her answers suggest, was entirely John Z.'s responsibility. He said he cared about her, "but he still just let it happen."

The majority finds Laura's "actions and words" clearly communicated withdrawal of consent in a fashion "no reasonable person in defendant's position" could have mistaken. But, Laura's silent and ineffectual movements could easily be misinterpreted. And, none of her statements are unequivocal. While Laura may have felt these words clearly conveyed her unwillingness, they could reasonably be understood as requests for reassurance or demands for speed. And, Laura's own testimony demonstrates that is precisely how John Z. interpreted what she said. Indeed, Laura demonstrates a similar ambivalence. When asked if she had made it clear to John that she didn't want to have sex, Laura says "I thought I had," but she acknowledges she "never officially told him" she did not want to have sexual intercourse. When asked by the prosecutor on redirect why she told John "I got to go home," Laura answers: "Because I had to get home so my mom wouldn't suspect anything."

Furthermore, even if we assume that Laura's statements evidenced a clear intent to withdraw consent, sexual intercourse is not transformed into rape merely because a woman changes her mind. As the majority acknowledges, by reason of Penal Code sections 261 and 263, " '[t]he crime of rape therefore is necessarily committed when a victim withdraws her consent during an act of sexual intercourse but is *forced* to complete the act. The statutory requirements of the offense are met as the act of sexual intercourse is *forcibly* accomplished against the victim's will.' " In other words, an act of sexual intercourse becomes rape under these circumstances if all the elements of rape are present. Under the facts of this case, however, it is not clear that Laura was forcibly compelled to continue. All we know is that John Z. did not instantly respond to her statement that she needed to go home. He requested additional time. He did not demand it. Nor did he threaten any consequences if Laura did not comply.

The majority relies heavily on John Z.'s failure to desist immediately. But, it does not tell us how soon would have been soon enough. Ten seconds? Thirty? A minute? Is persistence the same thing as force? And even if we conclude persistence should be criminalized in this situation, should the penalty be the same as for forcible rape? Such questions seem inextricably tied to the question of whether a reasonable person would know that the statement "I need to go home" should be interpreted as a demand to stop. Under these circumstances, can the withdrawal of consent serve as a proxy for both compulsion and wrongful intent?

The majority finds these deficiencies insignificant because this is a juvenile adjudication. But, if John Z. is convicted of a felony as an adult, the same juvenile adjudication will qualify as a strike.[a] * * *

I respectfully dissent.

NOTE

Should the law require an affirmative "yes" as evidence of consent? In 1996, Antioch College implemented a new Sexual Offense Prevention Policy (reprinted below) requiring men and women engaging in sexual activity to acquire willing and verbal consent for each individual sex act. The policy met with a firestorm of controversy.

---

[a] Justice Brown is referring to California's Three Strikes law which mandates 25 years to life for an individual with two strikes, i.e. two prior serious or violent felonies, who is convicted of a third felony which does not have to be serious or violent.

THE ANTIOCH COLLEGE SEXUAL OFFENSE PREVENTION POLICY

Approved by the Board of Trustees on June 8, 1996

* * *

CONSENT

1. For the purpose of this policy, "consent" shall be defined as follows: the act of willingly and verbally agreeing to engage in specific sexual behavior. See (4) below when sexual behavior is mutually and simultaneously initiated.

Because of the importance of communication and the potential dangers when misunderstanding exists in a sexual situation, those involved in any sexual interaction need to share enough of a common understanding to be able to adequately communicate: 1) requests for consent; and, 2) when consent is given, denied or withdrawn.

Note: Recognized American and international sign languages are considered a form of verbal language for the purpose of this policy.

2. When sexual behavior is not mutually and simultaneously initiated, then the person who initiates sexual behavior is responsible for verbally asking for the consent of the other individual(s) involved.

3. The person with whom sexual contact/conduct is initiated shall verbally express his/her willingness or must verbally express consent, and/or express his/her lack of willingness by words, actions, gestures, or any other previously agreed upon communication. Silence and/or non-communication must never be interpreted as consent.

4. When sexual behavior is mutually and simultaneously initiated, then the persons involved share responsibility for getting/giving or refusing/denying consent by words, actions, gestures or by any other previously agreed upon communication.

5. Obtaining consent is an on-going process in any sexual interaction. Verbal consent should be obtained with each new level of physical and/or sexual behavior in any given interaction, regardless of who initiates it. Asking "Do you want to have sex with me?" is not enough. The request for consent must be specific to each act.

6. If someone has initially consented but then stops consenting during a sexual interaction, she/he should communicate withdrawal of consent verbally (example: saying "no" or "stop") and/or through physical resistance (example: pushing away). The other individual(s) must stop immediately.

7. In order for consent to be meaningful and valid under this policy:

a) the person not initiating must have judgment and control unimpaired by any drug or intoxicant administered to prevent her/his resistance, and/or which has been administered surreptitiously, by force or threat of force, or by deception;

b) the person not initiating must have judgment and control unimpaired by mental dysfunction which is known to the person initiating;

c) the person not initiating must not be asleep or unconscious;

d) the person initiating must not have forced, threatened, coerced, or intimidated the other individual(s) into engaging in sexual behavior.

8. To knowingly take advantage of someone who is under the influence of alcohol, drugs, prescribed or over-the-counter medication is not acceptable behavior in the Antioch community.

3. TOWARD A RIGHT OF SEXUAL AUTONOMY?

NEGOTIATING SEX

Michelle J. Anderson
78 S. Cal. L. Rev. 1401 (2005)

INTRODUCTION

Adrienne had just turned thirteen. Late one autumn night, after her siblings and parents had fallen asleep, she crawled out of bed, walked downstairs to the basement, unlocked and opened the sliding glass door, and slipped outside.

It was Mike's idea. He was a varsity basketball player from a nearby high school. Mike proposed they both sneak out and meet on the street halfway between their houses. Wanting Mike to like her, Adrienne agreed.

Mike never showed.

At that hour, the suburban streets were still. Adrienne walked three miles to Mike's house, where she found him waiting in his front yard. He signaled for her to come into the house. "Don't make any noise because my parents are asleep," he said. "They'd kill me if they found us in here." So throughout the night, Adrienne remained silent.

Mike led her downstairs into the family room. Now that she was inside his house, a deep fear set in, and Adrienne panicked. In her words, "I just completely left my body." She does not know how her clothes came off. All she remembers is coming back to the intense pain of Mike ramming inside her. He was ripping her apart. She blacked out.

The next thing she remembers is being in another room. Mike was lying on a beanbag chair, her face was in his crotch, and he was palming her head like a basketball. Trapped and gagging, Adrienne thought she was going to choke to death. She blacked out again.

It was early in the morning when Adrienne walked home alone, slid through the basement door, crawled into bed, and wept herself to sleep before anyone in our house stirred. Five years passed before my sister ended her silence and told someone what had happened that night.

Adrienne suffered flashbacks and acute psychological distress. For a while, she was suicidal. Her reactions are not unique. Many people respond to sexual trauma at the time it occurs with physical paralysis and mental dissociation. Such trauma leaves many with fragmented memories. Nearly a third of rape victims develop rape-related post traumatic stress disorder ("PTSD"). Approximately twenty-eight percent of rape victims experience suicidal ideation.

Rape, particularly acquaintance rape, is so common today that most people are likely to have a family member or a friend who suffered something similar to what Adrienne experienced. Despite the fact that Adrienne's story is in this sense ordinary, it is extraordinary to read because silence still tends to shroud the issue of sexual assault—we rarely hear such stories in legal scholarship or in the broader world. In this Article, Adrienne's experience will therefore stand for many others like it that remain unspoken.

The common law has historically defined rape as a man obtaining sexual intercourse with a woman by force and without her consent. In his Commentaries on the Laws of England, William Blackstone explained that rape was the "carnal knowledge of a woman forcibly and against her will." "Forcibly" meant that the man used physical force or the threat of physical force to obtain sexual intercourse. "Against her will" meant that the woman did not consent to having sexual intercourse with him, and the common law required that she resist him to the utmost of her physical capacity to express her nonconsent.

The abuse Adrienne suffered would not be considered rape under the common law. Mike did not have to employ physical force to penetrate her vaginally and orally. He never beat her or threatened her with a knife. Moreover, Adrienne did not resist Mike to the utmost of her physical capacity to express that his actions were against her will.

Despite some legislative and judicial tinkering at the margins, the statutes in the vast majority of states and the District of Columbia continue to reflect the requirements of the common law. Rape statutes no longer formally require that victims resist their assailants to the utmost of their physical capacities to express lack of consent. Nevertheless, statutes still overwhelmingly require both the defendant's force and the victim's nonconsent before an act of sexual penetration becomes a felony, and the way courts interpret these terms usually requires the victim's "reasonable resistance." Although states have slightly broadened the kinds of coercion that they are willing to recognize as unlawful force, what Mike did to Adrienne still would not qualify within the current definition of force.

Academic proposals for rape law reform have moved well beyond where state laws linger. Arguing that requirements of a defendant's force and a victim's resistance are archaic and unfair, legal scholars have asserted that the crux of the crime of rape is sex without consent. Scholars have offered two interpretive models for understanding nonconsent as the crux of rape. I will call the first the "No Model" and the second the "Yes Model."

Under the No Model, when a woman says "no" to a man's sexual advances, she does not consent, and courts should recognize that sexual penetration after that point is rape. In feminist lingo, "no means no." Without a "no," the law presumes the woman consents, and sexual penetration therefore is not rape. The No Model breaks from the common law in that it does not require the man to employ physical force to obtain sex, nor does it require the woman to physically resist her attacker to prove her nonconsent. Instead, it requires her to verbally express her refusal.

The trouble with the No Model is that it cannot account for the ways victims frequently react to sexual trauma. Like Adrienne, many respond with mental dissociation and physical paralysis. Just as the trauma of the situation can obliterate the power to resist physically, it can obliterate the ability to say "no." Adrienne did not physically resist or verbally express her refusal to Mike's sexual advances. He penetrated her while she remained profoundly passive, a mental runaway from pain she could not bear. Under the No Model, she thereby consented.

Under the Yes Model, by contrast, a man must obtain affirmative permission from his partner before he penetrates her. If the woman does not express a "yes" of some kind, the law presumes the woman does not consent, and sexual penetration is rape.

Defenders of the Yes Model make two important points. First, they emphasize that a woman's silence alone cannot mean "yes." This is the Yes Model's attempt to break from both the common law and the No Model. Second—and in some tension with the first tenet—they underscore that a woman can express a "yes" through her nonverbal behavior. Stephen Schulhofer, architect of the Yes Model, argues that engaging in "sexual petting," for example, can express a "yes" to sexual penetration. "If she doesn't say 'no,' and if her silence is combined with passionate kissing, hugging, and sexual touching, it is usually sensible to infer actual willingness." When things heat up, then, the Yes Model melts into the No Model, in which silence constitutes consent.

How does the Yes Model interpret what Mike did to Adrienne? Mike could not presume consent to penetration from Adrienne's silence alone, to be sure. He had to obtain a "yes" to penetration from her words or nonverbal behavior. Because Adrienne never uttered a word, Mike was left to parse the tacit implications of her actions. Adrienne snuck out and walked three miles to his house late at night to see him. She followed him into his house alone. Although he informed her that his parents were within earshot, she did not call out to them. Her clothes came off in an isolated room. Her passive silence was combined with his "passionate kissing, hugging, and sexual touching." Could Mike sensibly "infer actual willingness"?

At its core, the Yes Model relies on a man's ability to infer actual willingness from a woman's body language. Yet study after study indicate that men consistently misinterpret women's nonverbal behavior. They impute erotic innuendo and sexual intent where there is none. Any theory that relies on a man's ability to intuit a woman's actual willingness allows him to construct consent out of stereotype and hopeful imagination.

Moreover, the Yes Model assumes that consent to sexual petting implies consent to sexual penetration. Because unprotected sexual penetration spreads sexually transmitted diseases ("STDs"), including the human immunodeficiency virus ("HIV") that causes the acquired immunodeficiency syndrome ("AIDS"), people often engage in petting instead of penetration in order to minimize the potential health consequences associated with penetration. Even if someone actively engages in "passionate kissing, hugging, and sexual touching," it would therefore not be, as Schulhofer claims, "sensible to infer actual willingness" to penetration without a verbal objection. If two people are engaged in petting and one escalates the situation, mental dissociation and frozen fright can occur, paralyzing the victim's ability to resist or say "no."

Under the two main proposals for legal reform in rape law, what happened to Adrienne and so many others like her was probably just bad sex—an unfortunate misunderstanding that could have been avoided only if she had done something differently. Maybe she should have told him that she only wanted to spend time with him and kiss. Maybe she should have emphasized, "I do not want you to interpret my actions as actual permission for sexual penetration." Maybe she should have yelled "no" and awoken Mike's parents or, better yet, kicked him in the shins. Under either the No or Yes Model, the onus was on her to say and do more.

The fundamental problem with both the No and Yes Models of rape law reform is in the notion of consent itself. Traditionally, sexual consent has meant a woman's passive acquiescence to male sexual initiative.

Recently, many legal scholars have fought for a "refurbished version of consent." If the No and Yes Models are the result of those efforts, it is time to give up that fight. Not only must rape law abolish the force and resistance requirements, it must also abolish the nonconsent requirement.

This Article defines and defends a new model of rape law reform. It argues that the law should eliminate the requirement of nonconsent. In its place, the law should recognize the centrality of negotiation, in which individuals would be required to consult with their partners before sexual penetration occurs. Negotiation would not require a verbal contract for penetration. Instead, it would require only what conscientious and humane partners already have: a communicative exchange, before penetration occurs, about whether they want to engage in sexual intercourse.

Specifically, the law should define "rape" as engaging in an act of sexual penetration with another person when the actor fails to negotiate the penetration with the partner before it occurs. The law should define "negotiation" as an open discussion in which partners come to a free and autonomous agreement about the act of penetration. Negotiations would have to be verbal unless the partners had established a context in which they could reliably read one another's nonverbal behavior to indicate free and autonomous agreement. Force, coercion, or misrepresentations by the actor would be evidence of a failure to negotiate.

The Negotiation Model would protect the values that rape law should be designed to protect. It would maximize autonomy and equality and minimize coercion and subordination. It would require people to treat their sexual partners with respect and humanity. * * *

NOTE

How would *Berkowitz* come out under Anderson's "Negotiation Model?" How would *M.T.S.* come out? Would Anderson's model impose new and unfamiliar sexual norms upon the unwary? Anderson suggests that "[t]o maximize fair notice, before or once a rape law based on the Negotiation Model is passed in a jurisdiction, there must be widespread public education on television, in schools, and in the media about the ethical and legal importance of negotiating sexual penetration." 78 S. CAL. L. REV. at 1433.

Professor Stephen Schulhofer, whose proposed sexual assault scheme is discussed in Anderson's article, argues that the law of sexual assault should protect a broad right of sexual autonomy.

> [T]he law of sexual abuse should be reorganized around two . . . distinct groups of offenses, with one or two degrees of each. "Rape" should reach intercourse by force, in the sense of actual or threatened physical violence. A new offense, "sexual abuse" or "sexual misconduct" would reach nonviolent interference with

> freedom of choice. To restrain the impact of cultural inertia on interpretation of the latter offense, it might even be named "nonviolent sexual abuse" or "sexual misconduct without force."

Stephen J. Schulhofer, *Taking Sexual Autonomy Seriously*, 11 LAW & PHIL. 35, 74 (1992). Is Schulhofer's approach preferable to Anderson's "Negotiation Model?" Note that Schulhofer's "sexual misconduct" would include consensual sexual interactions when that consent was obtained under constraints that in our culture would be perceived as illegitimate. Schulhofer explains:

> One example is sexual harassment in the workplace. This looks like an area that is hardly ripe for criminal sanctions. But if a supervisor tries to get sexual favors by offering a promotion (or by threatening to veto one), he is confronting the employee with alternatives (no matter whether we call them offers or threats) that his position gives him no right to impose. If the supervisor used his position to get an economic payoff from the employee, he would be guilty of extortion. If a professor threatened to withhold a good grade or a good recommendation until he got some cash from a student, again he would be guilty of extortion.
>
> The worker or student should have the same right to control her sexuality that she has to control her wages or her bank account. What makes the woman's consent invalid is not that the supervisor's act involves too much pressure. What makes the consent invalid is that rules already settled in our culture deny the supervisor the right to require an employee to choose between her promotion and her legally protected interests. One of those interests should be—and is—her sexual independence. For the same reason, the high school principal who allegedly obtained sex from a student by threatening to block her graduation should certainly be guilty of a crime.

Stephen J. Schulhofer, *The Feminist Challenge in Criminal Law*, 143 U. PA. L. REV. 2151 (1995). Schulhofer argues that a film director who imposes a "casting couch" requirement on an aspiring actress is also committing extortion (and thus presumably would be guilty of sexual assault under Schulhofer's autonomy model). Do you agree?

4. NON-FORCIBLE RAPE

Today, many states punish more than just forcible rape. Sexual intercourse with a person who is unconscious or mentally or developmentally challenged and sexual intercourse procured by some types of fraud are examples of sexual offenses that do not involve the element of force or threat of force, yet are defined as rape in some jurisdictions. Do such crimes reflect Schulhofer's concept of a right of sexual autonomy?

In the next case, *State v. Scherzer*, the court examines a case involving apparently consensual and nonforcible intercourse with a mentally disabled girl.

STATE V. SCHERZER

Superior Court of New Jersey
301 N.J. Super. 363, 694 A.2d 196 (1997)

SHEBELL, P.J.

In May 1990, defendants, Kevin Scherzer and Kyle Scherzer, twin brothers, were indicted, along with three co-defendants, Peter Quigley, Richard Corcoran, Jr., and John Maher, on various sexual assault charges allegedly committed against a mentally defective victim, M.G. In September 1990, the prosecutor's application to have three juveniles, Christopher Archer, his brother Paul Archer, and Bryant Grober, tried as adults was granted. Therefore, in September 1991, a superseding indictment was obtained charging all eight defendants with second degree conspiracy to commit aggravated sexual assault (Count One); two counts of first degree aggravated sexual assault (sexual penetration of mentally defective person) (Counts Two and Four); two counts of first degree aggravated sexual assault (sexual penetration using physical force or coercion) (Counts Three and Five); and four counts of third degree aggravated criminal sexual contact (Counts Six, Seven, Eight, and Nine). * * *

* * * The three appellants, Kevin Scherzer, Kyle Scherzer and Christopher Archer, were convicted of second degree conspiracy to commit aggravated sexual assault (Count One), and first degree aggravated sexual assault by force or coercion (Count Three). They were acquitted of Counts Four through Nine. In addition, Christopher Archer and Kevin Scherzer were convicted of first degree aggravated sexual assault upon a mentally defective person (Count Two), and Kyle Scherzer was convicted of the lesser included offense of second degree attempted aggravated sexual assault. * * *

Kyle and Kevin Scherzer and Christopher Archer, appeal. * * *

FACTS

M.G. lived in Glen Ridge most of her life, where she attended special education classes at the elementary and middle schools. In 1989, when seventeen years of age, she attended classes for the "educably mentally retarded" at West Orange High School. She participated in athletics programs, such as softball and basketball, at Glen Ridge High School. Defendants were also Glen Ridge residents and M.G. had known them since grade school.

At trial M.G. testified that on the afternoon of March 1, 1989, she went to Carteret Park in Glen Ridge, to play basketball. There she saw the Archer brothers, Corcoran, and another boy. While she was shooting baskets, Christopher Archer, Grober, Quigley, and two other boys greeted her. In her direct testimony, M.G. said that Grober told her that if she went to the Scherzers' basement with them she would get to go out with

Paul. However, on cross-examination she said that she went up to Grober, placed her hand on his crotch, and said something to the effect of "Nice package you have there. Would you like a blow job?" On redirect, she stated the latter testimony was a lie, as she did not want to hurt people.

She said she walked to the Scherzers' house with Christopher Archer, who put his arm around her shoulders. She viewed this as "romantic." When they arrived, there were already "a lot of people" on the stairs and in the basement. Others started setting up chairs near the couch, while she and Grober sat on the couch. M.G. said that when some of the boys asked her to, she took off her sweat pants and T-shirt. Thereafter, at the urging of the boys, sexual activity occurred beginning with M.G. inserting her fingers in her vagina, her masturbating and performing fellatio on five of the young men, permitting Kevin to insert a broomstick and Christopher to insert the handle of a baseball bat into her vagina. She said she permitted Corcoran to put a small stick in her vagina. Four of the boys also sucked on her breasts. Before she left, some of the boys told her "not to tell anybody" or they would tell her mother and she would "get in trouble."

Paul Archer, called on behalf of the defense, testified to a different account of the events. He said he and Quigley went to the park because he had heard some baseball players would be throwing the ball around. When they arrived, they went over to talk to the Scherzer brothers and some other friends who were on the basketball court. Soon afterward, Grober and Christopher arrived. Then M.G. arrived carrying a basketball and went directly to Grober. Paul overheard M.G. say, "Bryant, you're really hot. You're sexy. I like your bod[y]. You have a nice package." Grober appeared startled. Paul said that in all the years he had known Grober, he had never before seen him engage in conversation with M.G. After M.G. made these comments to Grober, Paul saw her reach for Grober's crotch, and Grober lunged back. M.G. then asked if Grober wanted a "blow job." At first Grober did not take her seriously, but after they talked, he asked if she meant it.

Paul and Quigley walked to the Scherzers' house, where there were "a couple of guys" playing Nintendo in the basement. Soon, Grober and M.G. appeared. Paul observed Grober drop his pants, and M.G. kneel down and perform fellatio. After a while, he saw Grober rest his hand on M.G.'s shoulder, but did not observe him exert pressure. Grober then moved his hand to the top of M.G.'s head, but once again no pressure was exerted. He did not hear M.G. say any words of resistance. According to Paul, the entire act took about thirty seconds. Grober then sat down and did not participate in any other sexual activity with M.G.

According to Paul, M.G., who was "totally in control" of the events, then said that "that blow job just got me so horny, I want to have sex with someone." When no one responded, she stood up, pulled down her pants, and then laid down on the couch. He said she then placed her fingers followed by the other objects into her vagina voluntarily. Kevin and Christopher helped her move the broomstick in and out. On cross-examination, Paul admitted that he had testified, when the judge was taking his guilty plea, that his brother and Kevin had inserted the broomstick into M.G., but said that testimony was a mistake.

He said that as people started to leave, M.G. walked to him, pulled up her shirt and bra, and said, "Paul, don't you like my breasts?" She asked him to touch them, but he refused. He said no one else touched her breasts, nor did he observe M.G. masturbating any of the boys or anyone doing anything with a stick. When M.G. asked if the boys wanted to "come back another day and do it again," no one responded. Some of the boys said, "[Y]ou're not going to say anything about this?" and she said no. He said that the entire incident, from the time M.G. first walked up to Grober at the park until she left the basement, lasted about twenty minutes.

Three boys who said they left the basement soon after the sexual activity began testified for the State. They agreed that M.G.'s activities with Grober, which is all they witnessed, appeared to be voluntary, as they did not see Grober use any force.

The first adult to whom M.G. related the incident was her swimming instructor, who testified that on March 3, 1989, after the swim class, M.G. came to talk to her, but seemed hesitant. M.G. said she had gone to a party during the week, that there were boys there, and that "something had happened." When asked what happened, M.G. said she did not want to talk about it now. The next day the instructor talked to M.G. in the locker room. M.G. told her she had gone to someone's basement and the boys asked her to "suck their dicks" and "stuck something up [her] butt." The instructor told M.G.'s classroom teacher at West Orange High School about the incident. The teacher informed M.G.'s parents about a week after the incident occurred. When M.G. learned that the instructor had told others about the incident, she was angry and said that it was her own fault that the "boys got in trouble" and that "she was going to lie."

M.G.'s mother took her to a gynecologist on March 14, 1989, however, a pelvic examination showed nothing abnormal. Her mother first met with the Glen Ridge police on March 22, 1989, and on March 27, 1989, M.G. and her mother met with Detective Sheila Byron. They brought a stick M.G. had brought home after the incident. Detective Byron became the principal investigator on the case.

M.G. gave the prosecution four statements—on April 7, May 5, May 18, and August 3, 1989. In the third statement the word "forced" in the phrase "additional acts were forced upon me" was crossed out and changed to "done." The investigator who took the statement from M.G. testified that he made the change because he did not think she knew "what the concept of the word force was." However, under cross-examination, M.G. testified that she requested the change because the acts were not forced on her. * * *

The State presented numerous witnesses who testified concerning M.G.'s personality, mental acuity, and the way she was perceived by others. A teacher who taught M.G. and other educable mentally retarded students at West Orange High School, said that M.G. functioned verbally on a second-grade level, had poor self-esteem, and was "very easily led" by people whom she hoped would like her. An instructor, who in 1982 taught tennis to a group of children that included M.G. and the Archers, all about eleven or twelve at the time, testified that the other children, including the Archers, would call M.G. "stupid" and "a retard." He said that when he offered M.G. the opportunity to be in a different group, she said those boys were her friends and she wanted to be with them.

Dawn Lipinski, the sister of M.G.'s friend Jennifer Lipinski, testified that "everyone knows that [M.G.] is different." She also said that M.G. would "do anything that she's asked to do" and that she had never heard her say no to any request. M.G.'s sister also said that everybody knew that M.G. was different. She testified that M.G. talks as if she is five or six years old, cannot follow simple instructions, and does not understand money. As an example of how easily led M.G. was, her sister said that when M.G. was five years old, a group of children, including Kyle and Kevin, persuaded her to eat dog feces.

M.G.'s mother testified about the social problems that emerged when M.G. was attending Columbia High School in Maplewood in 1987. She said M.G. would act the part of the class clown, setting herself up for ridicule. M.G.'s teachers at Columbia were concerned she might be raped. This led her mother to have her gynecologist prescribe birth control pills for her. M.G.'s mother also testified that, prior to the incident, M.G. had received sexual phone calls from Christopher Archer.

A guidance counselor at Columbia High School, testified about the sexual incidents in which M.G. was involved while at Columbia. M.G. told someone that "she wanted to be fucked," she would regularly exchange sexual comments with a group of football players in the cafeteria, and someone once touched her breast in health class. After these incidents, the guidance counselor claimed to have told M.G. that she had a right to refuse to allow someone to touch her body, but she could not understand this concept, especially when the person touching her was a friend.

The young men who testified at trial about the incident, three for the State and one for the defense, Paul Archer, all acknowledged it was common knowledge that M.G. was different. She was described as hard to communicate with, and as "slower, simple," something one could recognize after a few minutes of conversation. She associated mainly with younger children, was subjected to teasing, was the butt of jokes, was in special education classes, and was called "a retard."

The State presented three expert witnesses: Dr. Susan Esquilin, a psychologist specializing in the area of sexual abuse; Dr. Gerald Meyerhoff, a psychiatrist specializing in the field of child and adolescent psychiatry and mental retardation in children and adolescents; and Dr. Ann Burgess, a registered nurse with a doctorate in psychiatric mental health nursing and a specialist in the field of rape trauma.

Dr. Esquilin administered an I.Q. test on which M.G. scored 64, the mildly-mentally retarded range. On the adaptive behavior test, which measures daily living skills, M.G. scored in the top half, when compared to other retarded people. According to Esquilin, M.G. had a high risk of victimization because "she so focused on what somebody else wants and needs and not what she feels she wants and needs. . . . She's likely to do what anybody asks her to do." Esquilin expressed the opinion that M.G. is mentally defective, as she is incapable of exercising the right to refuse to engage in sexual conduct, and understands coercion only as the use of physical force. To M.G., her sexuality was a way of pleasing others. Esquilin's review of the Ferraez tapes strengthened her opinion that M.G. was susceptible to coercion and social pressure and that she had an immature concept of friendship.

Dr. Meyerhoff diagnosed M.G. as mildly-mentally retarded and suffering from attention-deficit hyperactivity disorder, residual state. * * * In his opinion, M.G. was "mentally defective" because although she understood that she was engaging in conduct of a sexual nature, she did not understand that she had the right to refuse to participate in the sexual activity. * * * Under cross-examination he acknowledged M.G. was at times sexually aggressive because sexual activity fulfilled her need for friendship, which "was an important part of her life." He also acknowledged that she was capable of lying and being deceptive.

Dr. Burgess, who had co-authored a pioneering study on rape trauma syndrome ("RTS") in 1974, testified about the kinds of reactions she had observed in rape victims and how her observations served to dispel such common myths as that victims immediately report a rape or that all victims display an emotional demeanor after an attack. She said that adolescent rape victims often do not disclose information about rape immediately, especially when the assailant is known to them, because they have divided loyalties about the assailant and fear retaliation. Recantation may be a way of protecting the assailant from getting into trouble or for the victim to deny that the rape occurred. * * *

Additionally, Burgess testified that M.G. suffered from RTS, as M.G. reported the incident only to people with whom she felt safe, and because of the type of friendship she desired with defendants. * * *

I

We first consider whether the judge erred in denying defendants' judgments of acquittal and whether the jury's verdicts were against the weight of evidence. * * *

[The court holds that there was sufficient evidence to support the defendants' conviction for conspiracy to commit aggravated sexual assault.]

The judge also denied defendants' motions for judgments of acquittal on the counts charging aggravated sexual assault under N.J.S.A. 2C:14–2a(5)(a) and (b). The offenses are defined by the Code as follows:

> a. An actor is guilty of aggravated sexual assault if he commits an act of sexual penetration with another person under any one of the following circumstances:
>
> . . . .
>
> (5) The actor is aided or abetted by one or more other persons and either of the following circumstances exists:
>
> (a) The actor uses *physical force or coercion,* or
>
> (b) The victim is one whom the actor knew or should have known was physically helpless, *mentally defective* or mentally incapacitated;. . . .

[Emphasis added.]

Under N.J.S.A. 2C:14–1c, "sexual penetration" can mean vaginal intercourse, fellatio, or insertion of fingers or objects into the vagina either by the actor or by the victim upon the actor's instruction, with depth of insertion irrelevant to whether the crime was committed. In *State in the Interest of M.T.S.,* the Supreme Court held that the definition of "physical force" in N.J.S.A. 2C:14–2a(5)(a) is satisfied "if the defendant applies any amount of force against another person in the absence of what a reasonable person would believe to be affirmative and freely-given permission to the act of sexual penetration." There need be no more physical force than that "inherent in the act of sexual penetration." * * *

Therefore, on the third count, the State had to prove that defendants engaged in an act of sexual penetration while aided or abetted by at least one other person and that defendants used force or coercion. Viewing the State's evidence as to defendants' use of force or coercion in a light most favorable to it * * *, we are convinced that the State failed to present enough evidence to prove to a reasonable jury that force or coercion were used against M.G. Her testimony and conduct clearly reflect that her engaging in the sexual activity in question was voluntary for purposes of N.J.S.A. 2C:14–2a(5)(a), and did not involve force or coercion.

M.G. never testified that the sexual activity was done without her consent. There was no evidence that physical force without permission, as defined by *M.T.S*, was used by defendants. Nor did we find it reasonable on the evidence presented to infer that force or coercion was engaged in by or on behalf of defendants. Persuasion is not coercion under N.J.S.A. 2C:14–2a(5)(a) merely because the victim is mentally defective, as such conduct is specifically covered under subsection (b). Nor is there any indication that M.G. was in any way intimidated by the size or number of the boys present.

In any event, even if a judgment of acquittal were denied, Count Three, charging penetration using physical force or coercion, must ultimately fail as a manifest denial of justice. Paul Archer and two other boys present testified to the absence of force and the voluntariness of M.G.'s actions in the Scherzer basement. M.G.'s own testimony fails to support a finding of force or coercion. She said on direct that she went to the basement because Grober said she would be able to go out with Paul Archer if she did. Even if defendants did lure her to the basement with promises of a date with Paul, the trial judge correctly instructed the jury that being promised a date with Paul was not enough to constitute criminal coercion. Moreover, on cross-examination she said that she went up to Grober at the park, placed her hand on his crotch, and asked him if he wanted her to give him a blow job. Although on redirect, she said that the latter testimony was a lie, Paul testified to substantially that account of the incident. M.G. also said that she did not try to leave the basement because she wanted to stay, and that she could have left if she wanted to. M.G. said she had the prosecutor change the word "forced" to "done" in her August 3, 1989 statement because the acts were not forced on her. * * * The jury also heard Dr. Meyerhoff describe M.G. as sexually aggressive. Under no proper theory of force or coercion could a reasonable jury find those elements of the offense beyond a reasonable doubt on the admissible facts and applicable law.

However, a different conclusion results as to Count Two. N.J.S.A. 2C:14–1(h) defines "mentally defective" as a condition that renders one "temporarily or permanently incapable of understanding the nature of [one's] conduct, including, but not limited to, being incapable of providing consent." The Supreme Court clarified this definition [in a case called *Olivio*] by specifying that the mentally defective person must be "unable to comprehend the distinctively sexual nature of the conduct, or incapable of understanding or exercising the right to refuse to engage in such conduct with another." Thus, as to this count, the inquiry is whether the State presented sufficient evidence for a reasonable jury to conclude that defendants, knowing that M.G. was mentally defective, purposely engaged in sexual penetration while aided or abetted by at least one other person.

The State presented two experts, Doctors Esquilin and Meyerhoff, who expressed their opinion that M.G. was mentally defective under the *Olivio* standard because, although M.G. understood that she was engaging in conduct of a sexual nature, she did not understand that she had the right to refuse. Defendants had known her since grade school, and thus it was reasonable to infer they were aware of this defect. M.G.'s tennis teacher testified that in 1982 the Archers were among those who called M.G. "stupid" and "a retard." M.G.'s sister and Dawn Lipinski both testified that everyone knew that M.G. was "different."

M.G.'s friends, family, and teachers testified to her inability to say no to any request because she wanted to please people and to her use of sexuality to make friends. Lipinski said she had never heard M.G. say no to any request. M.G.'s sister related an incident that occurred when M.G. was five years old—a group of children, including Kyle and Kevin, persuaded her to eat dog feces—as an example of how easily led she was. M.G.'s mother testified about phone calls of a sexual nature that M.G. received from Christopher Archer. M.G.'s high school guidance counselor testified that after she learned M.G. was engaging in sexual conversations with a group of football players in the cafeteria and had allowed someone to touch her breast in health class, she told M.G. that she had a right not to allow someone to touch her body, but that she did not appear to understand the concept, especially when the person touching her was someone she considered to be a friend.

The State presented ample evidence that all three defendants were aware of M.G.'s acquiescent nature in sexual and other matters and that they had taken advantage of that aspect of her personality in the past. Even if they could not be expected to have labeled her as "mentally defective," they, as reasonable young persons were shown under the circumstances presented to have known that M.G. did not understand that she could say no to a request. This we hold to be sufficient under N.J.S.A. 2C:14–2a(5)(b).

There was no dispute that vaginal penetration of M.G. occurred, and according to M.G.'s testimony, all three defendants were involved in either preparing, inserting, or trying to insert, either the broom handle or the bat into M.G. while she lay on the couch. That the bat may not have actually entered M.G. is irrelevant since it touched her vaginal area. * * *

* * * We conclude that as to the convictions on all counts other than Count Three, it does not appear "that there was a miscarriage of justice under the law."

Quite the contrary, the evidence weighed heavily in favor of the jury's verdicts. Only on the force or coercion count, was there insufficient evidence of the use of force or coercion. On the basis of the permissible evidence presented to the jury, we conclude that the jury could rationally have found that all the elements required to prove the remaining counts on which defendants were convicted were proved beyond a reasonable doubt and that the jury's verdicts were not against the weight of evidence. * * *

We vacate defendants' convictions only on Count Three. * * *

The judge on resentencing must note that defendants were not proved to have committed sexual assault by force or coercion and that consequently all have one less conviction. * * *

Affirmed in part and reversed in part. Remanded for resentencing.

NOTE

The next case, *Boro v. Superior Court*, discusses the common law distinction between fraud-in-the-factum and fraud-in-the-inducement. Under this distinction, if the sexual intercourse is procured by deceit or fraud about the nature of the act, i.e., fraud-in-the-factum, then the victim's consent is considered null and void and the defendant can be convicted of (non-forcible) rape. If, however, the victim is induced to engage in the sexual intercourse by a false promise or some other deceit, but knows she is engaging in sexual intercourse, i.e., fraud-in-the-inducement, then her consent is considered valid for purposes of rape law and a charge of (non-forcible) rape cannot be sustained.[a] Does this distinction in *Boro* make sense? Is it trying to do the work that a right to sexual autonomy might accomplish more straightforwardly?

Although the question is not presented by the facts before it, the *Boro* court also examines whether a woman having sexual intercourse with a man impersonating her husband constitutes fraud-in-the-factum or fraud-in-the-inducement, a question that has split the courts.

BORO V. SUPERIOR COURT

Court of Appeal of California, First Appellate District, Division One
163 Cal.App.3d 1224, 210 Cal.Rptr. 122 (1985)

NEWSOM, J.

By timely petition filed with this court, petitioner Daniel Boro seeks a writ of prohibition to restrain further prosecution of count II of the information on file against him in San Mateo County Superior Court No. C–13489 charging him with a violation of Penal Code section 261, subdivision (4), rape: "an act of sexual intercourse accomplished with a person not the spouse of the perpetrator, under any of the following circumstances: . . . (4) Where a person is at the time unconscious of the nature of the act, and this is known to the accused."[a]

[a] Although sexual intercourse achieved by fraud-in-the-inducement was not considered rape at common law, in some jurisdictions, it was deemed the lesser crime of seduction by statute.

[a] The District Attorney agreed to dismiss Count I which charged Boro with forcible rape.

Petitioner contends that his motion to dismiss should have been granted with regard to count II because the evidence at the preliminary hearing proved that the prosecutrix, Ms. R., was aware of the "nature of the act" within the meaning of section 261, subdivision (4). The Attorney General contends the opposite, arguing that the victim's agreement to intercourse was predicated on a belief—fraudulently induced by petitioner—that the sex act was necessary to save her life, and that she was hence unconscious of the *nature* of the act within the meaning of the statute.

In relevant part the factual background may be summarized as follows. Ms. R., the rape victim, was employed as a clerk at the Holiday Inn in South San Francisco when, on March 30, 1984, at about 8:45 a.m., she received a telephone call from a person who identified himself as "Dr. Stevens" and said that he worked at Peninsula Hospital.

"Dr. Stevens" told Ms. R. that he had the results of her blood test and that she had contracted a dangerous, highly infectious and perhaps fatal disease; that she could be sued as a result; that the disease came from using public toilets; and that she would have to tell him the identity of all her friends who would then have to be contacted in the interest of controlling the spread of the disease.

"Dr. Stevens" further explained that there were only two ways to treat the disease. The first was a painful surgical procedure—graphically described—costing $9,000, and requiring her uninsured hospitalization for six weeks. A second alternative, "Dr. Stevens" explained, was to have sexual intercourse with an anonymous donor who had been injected with a serum which would cure the disease. The latter, nonsurgical procedure would only cost $4,500. When the victim replied that she lacked sufficient funds the "doctor" suggested that $1,000 would suffice as a down payment. The victim thereupon agreed to the nonsurgical alternative and consented to intercourse with the mysterious donor, believing "it was the only choice I had."

After discussing her intentions with her work supervisor, the victim proceeded to the Hyatt Hotel in Burlingame as instructed, and contacted "Dr. Stevens" by telephone. The latter became furious when he learned Ms. R. had informed her employer of the plan, and threatened to terminate his treatment, finally instructing her to inform her employer she had decided not to go through with the treatment. Ms. R. did so, then went to her bank, withdrew $1,000 and, as instructed, checked into another hotel and called "Dr. Stevens" to give him her room number.

About a half hour later the defendant "donor" arrived at her room. When Ms. R. had undressed, the "donor," petitioner, after urging her to relax, had sexual intercourse with her.

At the time of penetration, it was Ms. R.'s belief that she would die unless she consented to sexual intercourse with the defendant: as she testified, "My life felt threatened, and for that reason and that reason alone did I do it."

Petitioner was apprehended when the police arrived at the hotel room, having been called by Ms. R.'s supervisor. Petitioner was identified as "Dr. Stevens" at a police voice lineup by another potential victim of the same scheme.

Upon the basis of the evidence just recounted, petitioner was charged [under] section 261, subdivision (4)—rape "[where] a person is at the time unconscious of the nature of the act, and this is known to the accused." * * *

The People's position is stated concisely: "We contend, quite simply, that at the time of the intercourse Ms. R., the victim, was 'unconscious of the nature of the act': because of [petitioner's] misrepresentation she believed it was in the nature of a medical treatment and not a simple, ordinary act of sexual intercourse." Petitioner, on the other hand, stresses that the victim was plainly aware of the *nature* of the act in which she voluntarily engaged, so that her motivation in doing so (since it did not fall within the proscription of section 261, subdivision (2)) is irrelevant.

Our research discloses sparse California authority on the subject. A victim need not be totally and physically unconscious in order that section 261, subdivision (4) apply. In *People v. Minkowski*, the defendant was a physician who "treated" several victims for menstrual cramps. Each victim testified that she was treated in a position with her back to the doctor, bent over a table, with feet apart, in a dressing gown. And in each case the "treatment" consisted of the defendant first inserting a metal instrument, then substituting an instrument which "felt different"—the victims not realizing that the second instrument was in fact the doctor's penis. The precise issue before us was never tendered in *People v. Minkowski* because the petitioner there *conceded* the sufficiency of evidence to support the element of consciousness.

The decision is useful to this analysis, however, because it exactly illustrates certain traditional rules in the area of our inquiry. Thus, as a leading authority has written, "if deception causes a misunderstanding as to the fact itself (fraud in the *factum*) there is no legally-recognized consent because what happened is not that for which consent was given; whereas consent induced by fraud is as effective as any other consent, so far as direct and immediate legal consequences are concerned, if the deception relates not to the thing done but merely to some collateral matter (fraud in the inducement)."

The victims in *Minkowski* consented, not to sexual intercourse, but to an act of an altogether different nature, penetration by medical instrument. The consent was to a pathological, and not a carnal, act, and the mistake was, therefore, in the *factum* and not merely in the inducement.

Another relatively common situation in the literature on this subject—discussed in detail by Perkins is the fraudulent obtaining of intercourse by impersonating a spouse. As Professor Perkins observes, the courts are not in accord as to whether the crime of rape is thereby committed. "[The] disagreement is not in regard to the underlying principle but only as to its application. Some courts have taken the position that such a misdeed is fraud in the inducement on the theory that the woman consents to exactly what is done (sexual intercourse) and hence there is no rape; other courts, with better reason it would seem, hold such a misdeed to be rape on the theory that it involves fraud in the *factum* since the woman's consent is to an innocent act of marital intercourse while what is actually perpetrated upon her is an act of adultery. Her innocence seems never to have been questioned in such a case and the reason she is not guilty of adultery is because she did not consent to adulterous intercourse. Statutory changes in the law of rape have received attention earlier and need not be repeated here."

In California, of course, we have by statute adopted the majority view that such fraud is in the *factum*, not the inducement, and have thus held it to vitiate consent. It is otherwise, however, with respect to the conceptually much murkier statutory offense with which we here deal, and the language of which has remained essentially unchanged since its enactment.

The language itself could not be plainer. It defines rape to be "an act of sexual intercourse" with a nonspouse, accomplished where the victim is "at the time unconscious of the nature of the act . . . . " Nor, as we have just seen, can we entertain the slightest doubt that the Legislature well understood how to draft a statute to encompass fraud in the *factum* and how to specify certain fraud in the inducement as vitiating consent. Moreover, courts of this state have previously confronted the general rule that fraud in the inducement does not vitiate consent. * * *[5]

[T]he Attorney General cites *People v. Howard.* There, the court dealt with section 288a, subdivision (f) and section 286, subdivision (f) making criminal oral copulation or sodomy between adults where one person is "unconscious of the nature of the act." But in *Howard, supra* the victim was a 19-year-old with the mental capacity of a 6- to-8-year-old, who "simply [did] not understand the nature of the act in which he [participated]." Whether or not we agree with the *Howard* court's

[5] It is not difficult to conceive of reasons why the Legislature may have consciously wished to leave the matter where it lies. Thus, as a matter of degree, where consent to intercourse is obtained by promises of travel, fame, celebrity and the like—ought the liar and seducer to be chargeable as a rapist? Where is the line to be drawn?

analysis, we note that here, in contrast, there is not a shred of evidence on the record before us to suggest that as the result of mental retardation Ms. R. lacked the capacity to appreciate the nature of the sex act in which she engaged. On the contrary, her testimony was clear that she precisely understood the "nature of the act," but, motivated by a fear of disease, and death, succumbed to petitioner's fraudulent blandishments.

To so conclude is not to vitiate the heartless cruelty of petitioner's scheme, but to say that it comprised crimes of a different order than a violation of section 261, subdivision (4).

Let a peremptory writ of prohibition issue restraining respondent from taking further action upon count II (a violation of Pen. Code, § 261, subd. (4)) in *People v. Daniel Kayton Boro* . . . other than dismissal. The stay of trial heretofore imposed shall remain in effect until the finality of this opinion.

NOTE

After getting his rape with an unconscious victim charge dismissed, Boro, believe it or not, did the same thing to another woman and was prosecuted again. *See* Patricia Falk, *Rape by Fraud and Rape by Coercion*, 64 BROOKLYN L. REV. 39, 57 (1998). This time, he was not able to escape criminal liability because in response to *Boro v. Superior Court*, the California legislature amended the Penal Code in 1985 to punish cases where a person induces someone to engage in sexual intercourse by false or fraudulent representation intended to create fear. *See* Cal. Penal Code § 266c.

5. RACE AND RAPE

THE SOCIAL CONSTRUCTION OF A RAPE VICTIM: STORIES OF AFRICAN-AMERICAN MALES ABOUT THE RAPE OF DESIRÉE WASHINGTON

Kevin Brown
in BLACK MEN ON RACE, GENDER, AND SEXUALITY: A CRITICAL READER (Carbado ed. 1999)

THE "VICTIMIZATION" OF MIKE TYSON: STORIES FROM THE HOME FRONT

As one might expect, from the time Tyson was accused of raping Desirée Washington until he was finally sentenced, the "accusation" was a hot topic of conversation. I had a number of discussions about the accusation with other African-American males living in Indianapolis. When the accusation was first made, I asked a lot of my friends what they thought. None of us seriously entertained the possibility that Mike Tyson might actually be convicted of rape; any doubt was resolved in favor of Mike Tyson. I do not remember a single male speaking up for Desirée Washington.

A typical discussion occurred at the barbershop in which I get my hair cut. Anyone familiar with the African-American male community knows that to really take the pulse of the community about a particular issue, you must discuss it at a barbershop. The barbershop is more than a place to get your haircut—it is also a cultural institution. The barbershop is a place where we (males) hang out and receive part of our initiation into the finer points of being a male.

I put the issue of Mike Tyson on the floor by asking a question for general discussion to anyone who was willing to take it up: "What do you think about the claim by Desirée Washington that she was raped by Mike Tyson?" Desirée had no supporters here. Among the comments that were fairly typical were: "Well, she got in his limousine, didn't she?" "His limousine showed up at her hotel room at 2:00 in the morning?" "What do you expect, if you go out with a man at 2:00 in the morning." "No doubt the reason that she is doing this is because, like he said, she was probably mad because he didn't walk her to the limousine." From these comments, an initial image of Desirée took shape. I thought to myself, it's obvious, she must have consented. Not only that, I thought this woman must be crazy. Imagine doing all this because someone would not walk her to the limousine. As for Mike, he was being victimized by a vindictive and unstable woman.

Another discussion that I had prior to the trial was with a friend of mine who was closely involved in organizing the boxing matches that took place during the Summer Celebration. Here was an opportunity for me to get an inside scoop on what had occurred. I asked my friend if he thought Mike had raped Desirée Washington. He responded, "[yeah] he did it, but we have got some things on her, too, she wasn't completely innocent." The confident tone in his voice and what he said implied that Desirée might have brought this on herself.

This kind of inside information was precisely what I had hoped to find when I called him—the real inside story that would give me the complete picture so that I could understand precisely what had happened. So I asked, "Oh, really? Well, what did she do?"

I assumed that he was about to divulge the damning piece of evidence. You know, the piece of evidence that Perry Mason always hit the murderer with when they were on the stand in the final ten minutes of an otherwise dull episode. As he gave his response, his voice suggested quiet confidence that this piece of information would be the deciding piece of evidence. "She violated curfew."

Hmmm, I thought, that is serious business. She broke a pageant rule that was there for her protection. No doubt these rules were, in part, to protect the contestants from this kind of situation. If only she had followed the rules, this would not have happened.

Prior to the trial, it was clear that all those I had discussed the rape with were resolving all doubt in favor of Mike Tyson. At least that view is consistent with the law; a person (man?) (white man?) accused of rape, especially date rape, is presumed innocent until proven guilty beyond a reasonable doubt.

No one I talked to believed that Tyson would or should be convicted. Therefore, the verdict by the Indianapolis jury had a profound effect on our image of the "victim" in the rape. After Mike was convicted, he did not appear to lose any support. Shortly after the verdict, I went back to the same barbershop and once again raised the issue. This time I sought to find out what people thought the appropriate punishment should be. I asked my barber, an older man whose judgment I have come to respect through our many conversations over the past ten years, for his opinion.

"Do you think Mike Tyson should go to jail?"

"If he did it, and I'm not saying he did," my barber responded, "but if he did, I think that, well, maybe you ought to be lenient here. Perhaps he needs counseling, if he did it. And in fact, you know, there was a White guy this past summer who was also convicted of rape, and he received a suspended sentence."

This was the beginning of the redefinition of Mike as the victim. Before the conviction, Mike was being victimized by an unbalanced and jealous woman. Now he was also being victimized by the "White" criminal justice system.

If he did it! Even though Mike Tyson had been convicted by a jury that had heard all of the legally admissible evidence and therefore was certainly more knowledgeable about the case than my barber, he (and now I) was not willing to accept that verdict as a pronouncement of what had actually occurred. Those unfamiliar with African-American culture may ask how my barber could now say, "If he did it." According to the Indianapolis poll, 67 percent of African-Americans polled believed that Tyson was unfairly convicted and another 11 percent believed that, although he was guilty, his sentence was unfair. Only 7 percent of the African-Americans polled believed that Tyson got what he deserved. The remaining 15 percent expressed no opinion on the issue. In contrast, 40 percent of the Whites polled believed that Tyson got what he deserved. Only 28 percent believed he was unfairly convicted, while an additional 10 percent believed that, though he was guilty, his sentence was unfair. The remaining 22 percent expressed no opinion.

My barber's response tapped into two dominant beliefs in African-American culture. First, Blacks, and particularly Black males, cannot expect fair treatment by America's White criminal justice system. The same poll also indicated that 37 percent of the Whites and 70 percent of the Blacks believed that the judicial system treats Blacks and Whites differently. In Tyson's prosecution, ten of the twelve jurors who voted for conviction were White, and both the judge and prosecutor were White. When African-Americans talk about racism in the criminal justice system, this is part of what we mean—prosecution, judgment, and convictions of African-Americans by Whites. Comparing the sentencing of Mike Tyson to that of some White person convicted of the same crime was also based upon this same notion. It becomes even easier to view Tyson's prosecution in a racial context when it is juxtaposed against the acquittal of William Kennedy for date rape.

Viewing Tyson as a victim of the White criminal justice system completely changes the interpretation and understanding of his prosecution, conviction, and punishment. Mike Tyson's conviction is not just his individual conviction. Rather, it is a symbolic of the American judicial system's harsh treatment of African-Americans, particularly males. To support Tyson, then, is to fight against racial domination of African-Americans.

The second belief that my barber tapped into was that the fight against racial subordination will usually trump the fight against the sexual subordination of African-American women in the Black community. Although it is true that a Sister had been raped by a Brother, Tyson was now a victim of racism in the criminal justice system. Despite the fact that Brothers certainly want to support Sisters, concerns about the Sisters must wait until after we have dealt with Man (resolved the racial issue). Let us not forget, we have been trying to resolve the racial issue for over 370 years.

After my barber responded, another Brother in the barbershop joined in and brought up the fact that Desirée had appeared on television the night before and told her side of the story. During this program, she made it clear she had not received any compensation for her appearance. One of the other barbers in the shop pointed out that, although it may be true that Desirée did not get any money before the program aired, she very well could have received payment right after the program was shown. Another patron, seizing on this possibility, responded, "You know that show was on at 7:00 or 8:00, that doesn't tell you what she got paid at 9:00 or 10:00." Another Brother said, "Even if she didn't get paid for this particular appearance, she is going to get money from the tabloids. She is going to sue, she is going to get plenty of money. This women is going to be set for the rest of her life. God damn! Some people are lucky."

Now the motives for Desirée's not toeing the traditional line—racism trumps sexism—were out in the open. Desirée was out for herself. This wily eighteen-year-old college freshman from Coventry, Rhode Island, was too sophisticated and worldly for Mike Tyson. She was doing all this for the money. Desirée had just hit the lottery and was going to cash in big. And the terrible thing about it was that this Sister, in conjunction with the White criminal justice system, had brought down another Brother in order to advance her own greedy self-interest. * * *

The next day, I happened to be flipping channels on the television and turned to a station delivering the Indianapolis news. I tuned in just in time to see a number of African-American ministers and community leaders pleading for leniency and mercy for Mike Tyson. One of the ministers pointed out that the Bible said, " 'blessed are the merciful' and we are simply asking for mercy for Mike Tyson." Just like that, the sentencing of Mike Tyson had become a religious issue. I thought, well, if God is on Mike's side, then he must be innocent.

One of the Black reporters at the news conference responded to this statement by asking the minister, "Doesn't the Bible also command that thou shalt not engage in fornication?" A split of religious authority had occurred, but this split was quickly resolved. The minister who had quoted the Bible retorted to this imprudent question by reminding the reporter that it was the Black community leaders who had gotten African-Americans hired at the local television stations: "It was from us pressuring the stations you work at that got you your job." So now the issue of leniency for Mike Tyson had become an issue of loyalty to the African-American community.

As I prepared my remarks for this Conference, I started to think about the mental images that were in my mind. I sensed my outrage about how Mike Tyson had been victimized. He had been victimized by a criminal justice system. He had been victimized by a woman who had consented to have sex with him. He was then victimized by her again when she decided to take him down to advance her own greedy self-interest. He was victimized by a lawyer who failed to provide him with an adequate defense. He had been victimized by a jury that had been pressured into returning a guilty verdict against him. He was victimized, victimized, victimized.

THE "DE-VICTIMIZATION" OF MIKE TYSON

In a few moments of quiet reflection about the Tyson-Washington incident, a number of things began to occur to me that were obvious in so many ways. Only two people actually know that happened that night in that hotel room. With the passage of time and the need to envision the incident in the way that supported their articulated versions, even Mike and Desirée may now have difficulty recalling exactly what happened. The others and I were collectively constructing a story of what happened, from bits and pieces of information and preexisting thought patterns. Like authors of books, makers of films, or writers of poetry, we were putting meaning into an otherwise meaningless situation. And once this was done, we acted as if our story was what actually happened.

Why was the view of Tyson as the victim so easy to formulate and to accept? The answer stared me in the face. Most of my construction of Tyson as the victim proceeded from one of the most fundamental beliefs in the African-American community. Justice is White. The postconviction redefinition of Tyson as a victim occurred because of the fundamental belief that a Black man could not expect justice within the American criminal justice system. Never mind the fact that Tyson could afford the best lawyer money can buy. Never mind the fact that there were (only) two African-Americans on the jury.

If Tyson had been convicted by an all-Black jury, with an African-American prosecutor and judge, my perception of the incident would have been significantly different. The ability to construct an image of Tyson as a victim of racism in the criminal justice system (defined in the African-American culture as the prosecution, judgment, and conviction of Blacks by Whites) would have almost completely disappeared. With racism substantially eliminated as a concern, I could have quickly focused on other aspects of this situation. My concern about racism and oppression, however, had controlled my interpretation of the rape of Desirée Washington.

I began to think more and more about how my desire to struggle against perceived racism was keeping me from understanding other aspects of this situation. For starters, I had not been able to see Desirée Washington as the victim, and yet this is precisely what the jury saw when it convicted Tyson. As I began to think about the possibility of Desirée Washington as the victim, a number of issues about her came quickly to mind. Before, I was willing to believe that an eighteen-year-old college freshman could be so sophisticated that she could hatch a plan to take down the former heavyweight champion of the world. This required me to believe that she could easily outsmart a man who was not only seven years her senior and had been heavyweight champion of the world but who also had experienced a rough divorce.

Desirée often talked about how terrified she was that night. "Terrified" cannot possibly describe what she must have felt. I tried to imagine being an eighteen-year-old, 108 pound woman in a hotel room with a person who could arguably be considered the best fighter of all time. I had seen Mike Tyson fight heavyweights such as Michael Spinks, Trevor Berbick, and Razor Ruddick. "Terrified" is the word I would use to describe how they appeared entering the ring to face Mike Tyson. Those men were heavyweight boxers, some even heavyweight champions at the time. They also had the safety and comfort of knowing that if things got out of hand, they could lay down on the canvas and take the ten count. At least for them, there was a referee who could stop the fight.

Then there were all of those who suggested that something was wrong because Desirée Washington might profit from being raped by

Mike Tyson. I thought of how many times I have heard people express sympathy for the men Tyson beat in the ring—men who were receiving millions of dollars for about two minutes worth of work. Fights that people personally paid thirty dollars or more to see. Unlike Desirée, however, these boxers had volunteered to give up their bodies to be abused by Mike Tyson.

Victimization, however, was not confined to Desirée. The implications for African-American women were victimizing as well: "Don't talk about date rape, because we won't believe you; you must have consented." "Don't cooperate with the Man in taking down a Brother, even if you think he is wrong, especially one who is a celebrity." "Your concern about your bodies and how males inflict pain on you has to be subordinated until the racial problem is resolved." Of course, I realized that African-Americans will never resolve the racial problem.

Then, finally, I realized that there was one last group of victims who were being obscured by the notion of Tyson as the victim: African-American males, including those who had to rallied to support, explain, and justify Mike Tyson's actions. In an effort to exonerate himself, Tyson used an explanation and defense of his conduct that drew on every negative stereotype about African-American males that exists. His defense portrayed black men as oversexed, prone to violent and aggressive behavior, and dumb as a brick wall. Tyson literally had been responsible for producing millions of dollars of negative publicity, reinforcing the very social construction of African-American men in dominant culture of which I had so often complained. As I was envisioning myself as fighting racism by supporting Tyson, I was also embracing and approving of the image of Black males against which I struggle so hard.

PATRIARCHAL STORIES I: CULTURAL RAPE NARRATIVES IN THE COURTROOM

Andrew E. Taslitz
5 S. Cal. Rev. L. & Women's Stud. 387 (1996)[a]

B. Mike Tyson: Embracing the Beast

1. Desiree's Tale

Mike Tyson embraced the image of the beast. He played directly into white tales of dangerous carnal black desires. His defense: he was so famous and such an animal that any woman who came up to his room, including Desiree Washington, the woman he was charged with raping, had to know precisely why she was there.

[a] Reprinted with the permission of the *Southern California Review of Law and Women's Studies*.

Washington's tale was of an innocent betrayed. She was a star high school student, stereotypically beautiful, attending the Miss Black America contest as a participant. Her dad had long been a huge Tyson fan. Consequently, when Tyson visited the contestants and asked Washington out, saying he liked her because she was a "nice, Christian girl," she jumped at it and said "yes." When he neither called nor showed, however, she got ready for bed. To her surprise, he finally called at about 1:30 a.m. She said it was too late, but he said that he would be gone in the morning, so she agreed to meet him at his limousine to go out.

When she got to the limo, however, he said he had to get something from his room, and encouraged her to accompany him for the brief stop. Once in the room, they chatted, and he was friendly. But he abruptly changed his tone, saying, "Oh, you're turning me on." She said that she did not do one night stands, and he said she was "just a baby." She was uncomfortable but did not sense danger.

She excused herself to use the bathroom. When she returned, he had stripped to his underpants. She went for her purse, saying it was time to go. But Tyson was much faster. He quickly stripped off her outer jacket, bustier, shorts, and underpants and told her not to fight. She told him to leave her alone, expressing fear she might get pregnant and saying again she did not do one night stands. She complained that he was not wearing a condom, but he said he did not need one; they would just make a baby.

He then tried putting his penis in her vagina, but it hurt, and she started crying. He then twisted her like a pretzel and licked her vagina for lubrication. She hit him, saying that Tyson had said he respected her and thought she was a good Christian girl. He ignored her, calling her "Oh, Mommy," and hurt her further. He asked whether she wanted to get on top, but when he moved to let her do so, she tried to flee. He resumed his original efforts, pulled out, and ejaculated outside of her.

When she got back to her room, she told her roommate that Tyson had "tried" to rape her, unable to admit to herself that she had been raped, and then cried. Within twenty-three hours, she had reported the rape to police and her parents. Shortly thereafter, she went to Methodist Hospital.

2. Tyson's Tart

There were several factors working in Tyson's favor. Most importantly, Washington was a black woman, invoking the theme of over-powering female lust. While Tyson, as a black male, might be viewed as a beast too, in the white stories such beasts only attack white women. What the beasts do to black women those women like anyway.

The theme of animal sexuality was reinforced by Washington's being young and attractive. Moreover, she went to a man's room at two o'clock in the morning, clearly invoking themes of breached silence. She had a motive to lie too: Tyson was wealthy, and crying rape might be a quick way to make some serious money. Moreover, Tyson had claimed Washington seemed fine until he brushed her off after the act. Angry at being treated like a one night stand, she cried rape. Indeed, had she really been raped, would she have had the strength to complete the pageant? Yet that is what she did. Furthermore, Tyson offered witnesses who testified that Washington had been friendly with Tyson before the rape. Moreover, Washington admitted she had taken the time to change her panty shield when she went to the bathroom in Tyson's hotel, hardly the behavior of a woman fearing rape. The picture seemed a clear one of the Lying Woman.

There were, however, two problems for Tyson: first, he warmly embraced, even magnified, his image as a lustful beast; and second, Washington's behavior, conduct, character, and background were radically disconnected from the image of a hypersexual whore.

3. The Beast Awakes

Even Tyson's defenders early on fed media images of Tyson as a quintessential black stud. One of the officers in charge of investigating Washington's charges put it this way:

> I've got an eighteen-year-old black victim who leading black spokesmen are trashing. I saw some professor from some small southern school on television explaining that what Mike Tyson did to Desiree was part of some black dating ritual. It's normal, he said, for black men to treat black women this way.

Tyson, rather than seek to overcome white cultural images of black men, sought, instead, to magnify them. His lawyer stressed repeatedly that Tyson was an octopus, publicly feeling female breasts and behinds everywhere he went, including at the Miss Black America contest. Every woman knew what he was about, and Washington was no exception.

Tyson's behavior before and at the trial matched this image. At a press conference, Tyson was heard saying to a friend, "I should have killed the bitch." On the stand, his usual soft-spoken manner snapped at least once, revealing an angry face on a large, powerful man. He was, testified one witness, routinely disrespectful of black women and black leaders. His testimony at trial, moreover, seemed scripted like an actor playing a role. This impression was reinforced when he became obviously rattled and uncomfortable once the prosecutor departed from the expected routine. Moreover, he admitted at trial that he had lied to the grand jury twice. At trial, he said he flatly asked Washington, "Want to screw?" as his way of asking for a date, something he had denied to the grand jury. He also told the grand jury that his bodyguard, Dale Edwards, had been in the adjacent room of Tyson's suite at the time of the rape and heard what really happened. At trial, however, he admitted this was not so and claimed he had just "assumed" Edwards had been there.

The physical evidence, moreover, seemed to confirm Tyson's bullying, something rare in a "date" rape. Washington had two small vaginal abrasions, one 1/8 of an inch wide and the other 3/8 of an inch long, making her wince with pain when the doctor inserted a speculum. Such injuries, testified a prosecution expert, are virtually unknown in consensual sex cases but occur in 10–20% of all rapes. Even the defense's own expert, called to say that such injuries can come from consensual sex, admitted he had seen such injuries only two to three times in 20,000 examinations. Her panties were also torn at the waistband, consistent with her testimony that Tyson ripped her clothes off. Additionally, blood on her panties matched the site of the injuries she described.

Tyson was, therefore, an admitted liar and beast. He reinforced, rather than re-thought, precisely those themes likely to lead to his conviction.

4. Captivated by Innocence

There was much about Desiree Washington that contradicted standard cultural tales. "Jurors were captivated by her beauty, innocence and integrity." She was small and slight next to the 260-pound Tyson. She bore the scars and blood of the bully. She was a good student and churchgoer, with a father who revered Mike Tyson. When she testified, she made clear that the thought of publicly attacking a black man in court troubled her deeply. Her image, then, was of a good, somewhat innocent kid misled. Except for her arguable lapse of judgment that night, she presented little apparent threat to the patriarchal order.

Moreover, her demeanor and relatively prompt reporting of the incident matched what was expected of a victim. She returned from Tyson's room to his limo. The limo driver had done a practicum at a mental health counseling center, where she attended women who had been raped and beaten. She thought Washington fit the profile, her eyes "frantic, dazed, and disoriented," her clothes and hair mussed, looking scared. And she kept repeating: "I don't believe him. I don't believe him. Who does he think he is?" She reported the rape quickly to her roommate (saying that he tried to rape her), 911, the hospital, and her family. Her 911 call, which was played for the jury, was powerful and fully consistent with her tale in court. It included her fears that no one would believe her or that they would think that she was just after money. Consistency, as we have seen, is something jurors expect if they are to convict in a rape case. Movingly for the jury, she explained how, like a little girl, she had to sleep with her mom many nights after the pageant to shield her from nightmares.

Greed rang hollow as a motivator as well. When Tyson had first called Washington, she had asked her roommate to come along, but the roommate had refused. It would be hard to set up a rape blackmail scheme if there had been an eyewitness. Moreover, Tyson had offered her a substantial sum of money to drop the charges, which she had refused. At trial, little more than speculation supported greed as a motivator, speculation that contradicted Washington's deeds and demeanor. However, some have argued that there were a host of procedural errors at trial that prevented Tyson from countering this image.

Once Tyson made the decision to embrace the image of the black beast, to go beyond that image and admit to, and even celebrate, abusive behavior toward black women, Washington's race began to matter less. At that point, her actions and injuries fit well the bullying theme to which Tyson was tethered, pushing the incident over the thin line from seduction to rape. Washington followed many, though not all, of the rules on silence too. By day's end, the jury decided there was a beast who needed caging, rare, very rare, where a black woman has cried pain.

B. STATUTORY RAPE

GARNETT V. STATE

Court of Appeals of Maryland
332 Md. 571, 632 A.2d 797 (1993)

MURPHY, J.

Maryland's "statutory rape" law prohibiting sexual intercourse with an underage person is codified in Maryland Code (1957, 1992 Repl.Vol.) Art. 27, § 463, which reads in full:

> Second degree rape.
>
> (a) *What constitutes.*—A person is guilty of rape in the second degree if the person engages in vaginal intercourse with another person:
>
> (1) By force or threat of force against the will and without the consent of the other person; or
>
> (2) Who is mentally defective, mentally incapacitated, or physically helpless, and the person performing the act knows or should reasonably know the other person is mentally defective, mentally incapacitated, or physically helpless; or
>
> (3) Who is under 14 years of age and the person performing the act is at least four years older than the victim.
>
> (b) *Penalty.*—Any person violating the provisions of this section is guilty of a felony and upon conviction is subject to imprisonment for a period of not more than 20 years.

Subsection (a)(3) represents the current version of a statutory provision dating back to the first comprehensive codification of the criminal law by the Legislature in 1809. Now we consider whether under the present statute, the State must prove that a defendant knew the complaining witness was younger than 14 and, in a related question, whether it was error at trial to exclude evidence that he had been told, and believed, that she was 16 years old.

I

Raymond Lennard Garnett is a young retarded man.[a] At the time of the incident in question he was 20 years old. He has an I.Q. of 52. His guidance counselor from the Montgomery County public school system, Cynthia Parker, described him as a mildly retarded person who read on the third-grade level, did arithmetic on the 5th-grade level, and interacted with others socially at school at the level of someone 11 or 12 years of age. Ms. Parker added that Raymond attended special education classes and for at least one period of time was educated at home when he was afraid to return to school due to his classmates' taunting. Because he could not understand the duties of the jobs given him, he failed to complete vocational assignments; he sometimes lost his way to work. As Raymond was unable to pass any of the State's functional tests required for graduation, he received only a certificate of attendance rather than a high-school diploma.

In November or December 1990, a friend introduced Raymond to Erica Frazier, then aged 13; the two subsequently talked occasionally by telephone. On February 28, 1991, Raymond, apparently wishing to call for a ride home, approached the girl's house at about nine o'clock in the evening. Erica opened her bedroom window, through which Raymond entered; he testified that "she just told me to get a ladder and climb up her window." The two talked, and later engaged in sexual intercourse. Raymond left at about 4:30 a.m. the following morning. On November 19, 1991, Erica gave birth to a baby, of which Raymond is the biological father.

---

[a] In *Atkins v. Virginia*, 536 U.S. 304 (2002), the Supreme Court held that the execution of a mentally retarded individual constitutes cruel and unusual punishment in violation of the Eighth Amendment. In reaching this conclusion, Justice Stevens, writing for the court, surveyed clinical definitions of mental retardation and found that most "require not only subaverage intellectual function, but also significant limitations in adaptive skills such as communication, self-care, and self-direction that become manifest before age 18. Mentally retarded persons frequently know the difference between right and wrong and are competent to stand trial. Because of their impairments, however, by definition they have diminished capacities to understand and process information, to communicate, to abstract from mistakes and learn from experience, to engage in logical reasoning, to control impulses, and to understand the reactions of others. There is no evidence that they are more likely to engage in criminal conduct than others, but there is abundant evidence that they often act on impulse rather than pursuant to a premeditated plan, and that in group settings they are followers rather than leaders. Their deficiencies do not warrant an exemption from criminal sanctions, but they do diminish their personal culpability." 536 U.S. at 318.

Raymond was tried before the Circuit Court for Montgomery County (Miller, J.) on one count of second degree rape under § 463(a)(3) proscribing sexual intercourse between a person under 14 and another at least four years older than the complainant. At trial, the defense twice proffered evidence to the effect that Erica herself and her friends had previously told Raymond that she was 16 years old, and that he had acted with that belief. The trial court excluded such evidence as immaterial, explaining:

> Under 463, the only two requirements as relate to this case are that there was vaginal intercourse, [and] that . . . Ms. Frazier was under 14 years of age and that . . . Mr. Garnett was at least four years older than she.
>
> In the Court's opinion, consent is no defense to this charge. The victim's representation as to her age and the defendant's belief, if it existed, that she was not under age, what amounts to what otherwise might be termed a good faith defense, is in fact no defense to what amount[s] to statutory rape.
>
> It is in the Court's opinion a strict liability offense.

The court found Raymond guilty. It sentenced him to a term of five years in prison, suspended the sentence and imposed five years of probation, and ordered that he pay restitution to Erica and the Frazier family. Raymond noted an appeal; we granted certiorari prior to intermediate appellate review by the Court of Special Appeals to consider the important issue presented in the case.

II

* * * Section 463(a)(3) does not expressly set forth a requirement that the accused have acted with a criminal state of mind, or mens rea. The State insists that the statute, by design, defines a strict liability offense, and that its essential elements were met in the instant case when Raymond, age 20, engaged in vaginal intercourse with Erica, a girl under 14 and more than 4 years his junior. Raymond replies that the criminal law exists to assess and punish morally culpable behavior. He says such culpability was absent here. He asks us either to engraft onto subsection (a)(3) an implicit mens rea requirement, or to recognize an affirmative defense of reasonable mistake as to the complainant's age. Raymond argues that it is unjust, under the circumstances of this case which led him to think his conduct lawful, to brand him a felon and rapist.

III

Raymond asserts that the events of this case were inconsistent with the criminal sexual exploitation of a minor by an adult. As earlier observed, Raymond entered Erica's bedroom at the girl's invitation; she directed him to use a ladder to reach her window. They engaged voluntarily in sexual intercourse. They remained together in the room for more than seven hours before Raymond departed at dawn. With an I.Q. of 52, Raymond functioned at approximately the same level as the 13-year-old Erica; he was mentally an adolescent in an adult's body. Arguably, had Raymond's chronological age, 20, matched his socio-intellectual age, about 12, he and Erica would have fallen well within the four-year age difference obviating a violation of the statute, and Raymond would not have been charged with any crime at all.

The precise legal issue here rests on Raymond's unsuccessful efforts to introduce into evidence testimony that Erica and her friends had told him she was 16 years old, the age of consent to sexual relations, and that he believed them. Thus the trial court did not permit him to raise a defense of reasonable mistake of Erica's age, by which defense Raymond would have asserted that he acted innocently without a criminal design. At common law, a crime occurred only upon the concurrence of an individual's act and his guilty state of mind. In this regard, it is well understood that generally there are two components of every crime, the *actus reus* or guilty act and the *mens rea* or the guilty mind or mental state accompanying a forbidden act. The requirement that an accused have acted with a culpable mental state is an axiom of criminal jurisprudence. Writing for the United States Supreme Court, Justice Robert Jackson observed:

> The contention that an injury can amount to a crime only when inflicted by intention is no provincial or transient notion. It is as universal and persistent in mature systems of law as belief in freedom of the human will and a consequent ability and duty of the normal individual to choose between good and evil.

* * *

To be sure, legislative bodies since the mid-19th century have created strict liability criminal offenses requiring no mens rea. Almost all such statutes responded to the demands of public health and welfare arising from the complexities of society after the Industrial Revolution. Typically misdemeanors involving only fines or other light penalties, these strict liability laws regulated food, milk, liquor, medicines and drugs, securities, motor vehicles and traffic, the labeling of goods for sale, and the like. Statutory rape, carrying the stigma of felony as well as a potential sentence of 20 years in prison, contrasts markedly with the other strict liability regulatory offenses and their light penalties.

Modern scholars generally reject the concept of strict criminal liability. Professors LaFave and Scott summarize the consensus that punishing conduct without reference to the actor's state of mind fails to reach the desired end and is unjust:

> It is inefficacious because conduct unaccompanied by an awareness of the factors making it criminal does not mark the actor as one who needs to be subjected to punishment in order to deter him or others from behaving similarly in the future, nor does it single him out as a socially dangerous individual who needs to be incapacitated or reformed. It is unjust because the actor is subjected to the stigma of a criminal conviction without being morally blameworthy. Consequently, on either a preventive or retributive theory of criminal punishment, the criminal sanction is inappropriate in the absence of *mens rea.* * * *

IV

The legislatures of 17 states have enacted laws permitting a mistake of age defense in some form in cases of sexual offenses with underage persons. * * * In some states, the defense is available in instances where the complainant's age rises above a statutorily prescribed level, but is not available when the complainant falls below the defining age. In other states, the availability of the defense depends on the severity of the sex offense charged to the accused.

In addition, the highest appellate courts of four states have determined that statutory rape laws by implication required an element of mens rea as to the complainant's age. In the landmark case of *People v. Hernandez*, the California Supreme Court held that, absent a legislative directive to the contrary, a charge of statutory rape was defensible wherein a criminal intent was lacking; it reversed the trial court's refusal to permit the defendant to present evidence of his good faith, reasonable belief that the complaining witness had reached the age of consent. In so doing, the court first questioned the assumption that age alone confers a sophistication sufficient to create legitimate consent to sexual relations: "the sexually experienced 15-year-old may be far more acutely aware of the implications of sexual intercourse than her sheltered cousin who is beyond the age of consent." The court then rejected the traditional view that those who engage in sex with young persons do so at their peril, assuming the risk that their partners are underage:

> [I]f [the perpetrator] participates in a mutual act of sexual intercourse, believing his partner to be beyond the age of consent, with reasonable grounds for such belief, where is his criminal intent? In such circumstances he has not consciously taken any risk. Instead he has subjectively eliminated the risk by satisfying himself on reasonable evidence that the crime cannot be committed. If it occurs that he has been mislead, we cannot realistically conclude for such reason alone the intent with which he undertook the act suddenly becomes more heinous. . . . [T]he courts have uniformly failed to satisfactorily

explain the nature of the criminal intent present in the mind of one who in good faith believes he has obtained a lawful consent before engaging in the prohibited act.

* * * Two-fifths of the states, therefore, now recognize the defense in cases of statutory sexual offenses.

V

We think it sufficiently clear, however, that Maryland's second degree rape statute defines a strict liability offense that does not require the State to prove mens rea; it makes no allowance for a mistake-of-age defense. The plain language of § 463, viewed in its entirety, and the legislative history of its creation lead to this conclusion. * * *

Section 463(a)(3) prohibiting sexual intercourse with underage persons makes no reference to the actor's knowledge, belief, or other state of mind. As we see it, this silence as to mens rea results from legislative design. First, subsection (a)(3) stands in stark contrast to the provision immediately before it, subsection (a)(2) prohibiting vaginal intercourse with incapacitated or helpless persons. In subsection (a)(2), the Legislature expressly provided as an element of the offense that "the person performing the act *knows or should reasonably know* the other person is mentally defective, mentally incapacitated, or physically helpless." In drafting this subsection, the Legislature showed itself perfectly capable of recognizing and allowing for a defense that obviates criminal intent; if the defendant objectively did not understand that the sex partner was impaired, there is no crime. That it chose not to include similar language in subsection (a)(3) indicates that the Legislature aimed to make statutory rape with underage persons a more severe prohibition based on strict criminal liability.

Second, an examination of the drafting history of § 463 during the 1976 revision of Maryland's sexual offense laws reveals that the statute was viewed as one of strict liability from its inception and throughout the amendment process. As originally proposed, Senate Bill 358 defined as a sexual offense in the first degree a sex act committed with a person less than 14 years old by an actor four or more years older. The Senate Judicial Proceedings Committee then offered a series of amendments to the bill. Among them, Amendment #13 reduced the stipulated age of the victim from less than 14 to 12 or less. Amendment #16 then added a provision defining a sexual offense in the second degree as a sex act with another "under 14 years of age, which age the person performing the sexual act knows or should know." These initial amendments suggest that, at the very earliest stages of the bill's life, the Legislature distinguished between some form of strict criminal liability, applicable to offenses where the victim was age 12 or under, and a lesser offense with a *mens rea* requirement when the victim was between the ages of 12 and 14.

Senate Bill 358 in its amended form was passed by the Senate on March 11, 1976. The House of Delegates' Judiciary Committee, however, then proposed changes of its own. It rejected the Senate amendments, and defined an offense of rape, without a *mens rea* requirement, for sexual acts performed with someone under the age of 14. The Senate concurred in the House amendments and S.B. 358 became law. Thus the Legislature explicitly raised, considered, and then explicitly jettisoned any notion of a *mens rea* element with respect to the complainant's age in enacting the law that formed the basis of current § 463(a)(3). In the light of such legislative action, we must inevitably conclude that the current law imposes strict liability on its violators.

This interpretation is consistent with the traditional view of statutory rape as a strict liability crime designed to protect young persons from the dangers of sexual exploitation by adults, loss of chastity, physical injury, and, in the case of girls, pregnancy. The majority of states retain statutes which impose strict liability for sexual acts with underage complainants. We observe again, as earlier, that even among those states providing for a mistake-of-age defense in some instances, the defense often is not available where the sex partner is 14 years old or less; the complaining witness in the instant case was only 13. The majority of appellate courts, including the Court of Special Appeals, have held statutory rape to be a strict liability crime.

VI

Maryland's second degree rape statute is by nature a creature of legislation. Any new provision introducing an element of *mens rea*, or permitting a defense of reasonable mistake of age, with respect to the offense of sexual intercourse with a person less than 14, should properly result from an act of the Legislature itself, rather than judicial fiat. Until then, defendants in extraordinary cases, like Raymond, will rely upon the tempering discretion of the trial court at sentencing.

JUDGMENT AFFIRMED, WITH COSTS.

STATE V. YANEZ

Supreme Court of Rhode Island
716 A.2d 759 (R.I. 1998)

GOLDBERG, JUSTICE.

The principal issue presented by this case is whether a reasonable mistake of fact concerning a complainant's age may be asserted as a defense to a charge of statutory-rape. For the reasons articulated in this opinion, we hold that with respect to the age requirement, first-degree child-molestation sexual assault is a strict-liability offense. Consequently a defendant charged with this offense may not introduce evidence that he or she was mistaken regarding the child's age, nor is a defendant entitled to a jury instruction regarding the same. * * *

Facts

The defendant, Alejandro Yanez (Yanez), was eighteen-years-old when he engaged in consensual sexual intercourse with Allison (a fictitious name), the victim in this case, who was thirteen-years-old at the time. The two were first introduced to each other, albeit ever so briefly, in August 1992, nearly a year before this incident. Allison testified that she was attending a Portuguese festival with a girlfriend when she saw her aunt's boyfriend, Victor Yanez (Victor), defendant's brother. According to Allison, who at that time was only twelve-years-old, Victor introduced her to Yanez. For the next eleven months Allison and Yanez had virtually no contact with each other except for the obligatory "Hello" in passing. Then one day in mid-July 1993, while Allison was walking to the local park to meet friends, she saw Yanez cruise by in his white Trans Am convertible with the top down. She testified that she waved to Yanez, who proceeded to turn the Trans Am around and offer her a ride. Since the park was only across the street, Allison declined Yanez's invitation, but when he persisted, Allison acceded. The two briefly talked during the quarter-mile trip. Yanez gave Allison his name and telephone number, and the two conversed again briefly that night on the telephone.

The next day Allison received a telephone message from either her mother or her sister that Yanez had called her and asked that she call him back. Allison returned Yanez's telephone call, and the two made arrangements to meet in the parking lot behind St. Joseph's Church in West Warwick. From the church the two left in Yanez's car and went for a ride. According to Allison, they proceeded to the home of a friend of Yanez's where they engaged in consensual sexual intercourse on the floor in a back bedroom.

Following the conclusion of their first "date" Allison returned home quite late. After entering the house, Allison proceeded directly to the bathroom to shower whereupon she was subsequently confronted by her mother. While in the bathroom, Allison's mother noticed her underwear on the floor and asked if she had engaged in sexual intercourse. Allison initially denied having had sexual intercourse that evening but later admitted the truth. Subsequently Allison's mother contacted the police, whereupon Allison admitted that she had engaged in sexual intercourse but named as her partner a person called Derek. Allison later explained that she had lied about Yanez's identity because she did not want her mother to know that she had engaged in sexual intercourse with Yanez. A subsequent police investigation revealed that Yanez admitted having had sexual intercourse with Allison but insisted that Allison had told him that she was sixteen-years-old. Allison denied having told Yanez that she was sixteen years of age and, in fact, testified that on the two or three occasions when Yanez had inquired about her age, she had responded that she was only thirteen.

Yanez was indicted on one count of first-degree child-molestation sexual assault in violation of G.L.1956 §§ 11–37–8.1 and 11–37–8.2, although the trial testimony would later reveal that this was not an isolated incident and that there were two more equally sordid, uncharged encounters.[1] At trial defense counsel made numerous attempts to introduce evidence not only demonstrating Yanez's mistaken belief concerning Allison's age but also evidence concerning Allison's apparent maturity in light of her appearance, physical development, and demeanor. The trial justice rejected this evidence and determined that in cases in which conduct is made criminal because the victim is a minor, the defense of ignorance or mistaken belief with respect to the victim's age is not available. The trial justice further indicated that he intended to charge the jury with respect to the unavailability of this defense and consequently declined to charge in accordance with Yanez's requested mistake of fact instructions. * * *

Following deliberations a Superior Court jury convicted Yanez of first-degree child-molestation sexual assault. The trial justice sentenced Yanez to the minimum twenty year sentence but suspended eighteen years of the sentence with probation. The trial justice also ordered that Yanez have no contact with Allison for twenty years and, as required by law, that Yanez register with the local police authorities as a convicted sex offender. Yanez was released on bail pending the outcome of this appeal. * * *

I

Mistake of Fact Defense

The crime of statutory-rape was legislatively created in England during the thirteenth century in order to afford special protection to those society had deemed too young to appreciate the consequences of their actions. Thus English courts, which had generally recognized the mistake of fact defense in criminal prosecutions since 1638, did not begin to discuss this defense in the context of statutory-rape cases until the later half of the nineteenth century. At that time, the mistake of fact defense was rejected by courts both in England and in the United States.

Characterizing statutory-rape as a strict-liability offense remained the law in every American jurisdiction until 1964. * * * [T]he majority of courts that have considered this issue continue to reject the reasonable mistake of a victim's age as a defense to statutory-rape and maintain their allegiance to the common law. * * *

[1] Far from the dissent's contention that the uncharged sexual encounters occurred before this charged incident and that Allison and Yanez were actually dating each other, the record simply does not contain this inference. * * *

A. Statutory Interpretation

* * *

Section 11–37–8.1 provides that:

> "[a] person is guilty of first degree child molestation sexual assault if he or she engages in sexual penetration with a person fourteen (14) years of age or under."

The term "sexual penetration" is defined in § 11–37–1(8) as follows:

" 'Sexual penetration'—sexual intercourse, cunnilingus, fellatio, and anal intercourse, or any other intrusion, however slight, by any part of a person's body or by any object into the genital or anal openings of another person's body, but emission of semen is not required."

Clearly the plain words and meaning of § 11–37–8.1 prohibit the sexual penetration of an underaged person and make no reference to the actor's state of mind, knowledge, or belief. In our opinion this lack of a *mens rea* results not from negligent omission but from legislative design. * * *

The Rhode Island General Assembly has divided sexual offenses into two main categories—sexual assault and child-molestation sexual assault. An examination of the pertinent provisions reveals that the Legislature has carefully distinguished between the two, explicitly requiring a *mens rea* for sexual assaults that were either unknown at common law or for those acts of sexual abuse that did not involve sexual intercourse, anal intercourse, cunnilingus, or fellatio while electing to maintain the common law's strict-liability for child-molestation sexual assault. * * *

It can be inferred from this statutory classification that the child-molestation sexual assault statutes' silence with regard to a *mens rea* "is designed to subserve the state interest of protecting female children from the severe physical and psychological consequences of engaging in coitus before attaining the age of consent in the statute." Had the Legislature intended not only to punish the act of child-molestation sexual assault but also to require a mental state, the Legislature could easily have provided for such an element. But its decision to include a *mens rea* requirement in the sexual assault statutes while declining to provide a *mens rea* requirement in the child-molestation sexual assault statutes, demonstrates that the Legislature's omission was intentional. This is a sensible and pragmatic objective with which we shall not interfere by engrafting a *mens rea* requirement where one was not intended.

B. Due Process Argument

Despite the Legislature's design Yanez nonetheless continues to argue that § 11–37–8.1 contains an implicit element that the accused must have knowledge that the victim is fourteen years of age or younger. Yanez suggests that § 11–37–8.1 violates his due-process rights because he had neither the opportunity to learn Allison's true age nor the opportunity to present a meaningful defense concerning his reasonable mistake. In support of this argument Yanez relies on *Morissette v. United States*, in which the Supreme Court observed "that intent was so inherent in the idea of the offense that it required no statutory affirmation." * * *

[I]n order for Yanez to prove that the Legislature's exercise of its power runs afoul of the protections guaranteed by the due-process clause, Yanez must demonstrate that this practice "offends some principle of justice so rooted in the traditions and conscience of our people as to be ranked as fundamental." Yanez cannot satisfy this test. * * *

We note that at the sentencing hearing the trial justice was fully cognizant of Yanez's favorable presentence report, his work history, his expressed remorse, and his supportive family. However, there is no escaping the fact that on their very first "date" following a brief encounter lasting only two or three minutes the previous day, this eighteen-year-old defendant engaged in sexual intercourse on the bedroom floor of his friend's house with this thirteen-year-old girl. The trial justice appropriately observed that there was some measure of planning involved in Yanez's encounters with Allison, which were aimed at avoiding detection by her mother. The trial justice further noted that the fact that Allison may have been "experienced" for someone her age or that her unfortunate past might have been somewhat unstable or troubled is not a defense. Indeed, the trial justice appropriately concluded that Allison is exactly the type of victim whose vulnerability the Legislature had intended to protect and that an offense perpetrated upon one in her circumstances "is more harmful than one committed upon someone who has a stable environment." Thus, although observing that "it is the public policy of this state * * * that those who engage in sexual intercourse with a person under 14, should be treated harshly," the trial justice nonetheless fashioned a compassionate sentence designed to promote not only rehabilitation but also deterrence. In the words of the trial justice, this sentence is "[n]ot only to deter this young man from committing similar crimes, but to discourage or deter others in the community; to let them know that if they're going to succumb to passion with someone under 14 years of age, there's a very high price to pay." We agree with the trial justice and find no error in his decision. * * *

Conclusion

For the reasons articulated, we deny the defendant's appeal and affirm the judgment of conviction. The papers in this case are hereby remanded to the Superior Court.

FLANDERS, JUSTICE, dissenting.

I respectfully dissent. I cannot believe that the Legislature intended that G.L.1956 § 11–37–8.1 (Rhode Island's statutory-rape law)—carrying a mandatory-minimum sentence of twenty years in jail—should be construed by the Judiciary to bar an accused teenager's reasonable mistake-of-age defense to charges based upon his engaging in consensual sexual acts with his teenaged girlfriend. The unavoidable result of such a draconian interpretation of this law is the imposition on this defendant, Alejandro Yanez (Alex)—a young man who was barely eighteen years old at the time of this incident—of an uncommonly brutal, harsh, and undeserved punishment that is so out of whack with reality that it is virtually without parallel in any jurisdiction of the United States.[10]

If any legislative intent is apparent in the language used in § 11–37–8.1 to criminalize sex with children, it is the intent manifest in its title to outlaw sexual abuse of children by adults and to punish severely those who commit such "child molestation." But there is a world of difference between a crime involving intentional child molestation and a situation like this one in which two teenage lovers engage in a fully consensual act (or acts) of sexual intercourse in the mistaken belief on the part of one of them that they are both of a legal age to do so. Although their exuberant sexual behavior may be sniffed at by a tongue-clucking majority as "sordid," it is certainly not "child molestation" within the meaning of Rhode Island's statutory-rape law.[11] Any criminal statute that carries a mandatory twenty-year jail sentence and imposes a lifelong stigma as a sexual predator on any violator should be rationally interpreted to draw a distinction between these two very different scenarios—especially when, as here, the sexual conduct in question would have been unquestionably legal if Alex's sexual partner had been sixteen years old, as she allegedly said she was.

In this case, two versions of what happened vie for acceptance. According to the defense, Alex, an eighteen-year-old (who was only six

---

[10] Although Alex received the minimum twenty-year sentence after the trial justice refused to consider his mistake-of-age defense, the trial justice ordered him to serve the first two years of his sentence in prison and suspended the remaining eighteen years while placing Alex on probation for this period. Thus, even after Alex finishes serving his prison sentence, he will be subject to re-imprisonment for up to eighteen years if he fails to keep the peace or engages in any other conduct that causes a hearing justice to be reasonably satisfied that he has violated the terms of his probation. Moreover, he will be required to register as a convicted sex offender and will be forever stigmatized as a convicted felon and child molester. Accordingly, in the circumstances of this case I disagree with the majority's conclusion that this outcome represents "a compassionate sentence."

[11] The uncharged sexual conduct alluded to by the majority relates to testimony by Allison that she and Alex had engaged in sexual activity on other occasions, apparently *before* the charged incident occurred at the house of Alex's friend. Thus, far from painting a picture of a "sordid" one-time tryst on the floor of a dingy back room, the evidence indicated that Allison and Alex had been dating each other and that the sexual activity that grew out of their relationship was no more sordid than any other case of premarital, teenage sex. Indeed, the trial justice himself noted at the sentencing hearing that the consensual sexual encounter for which Alex was charged was not a one-time affair: "[O]n the second date they're having sexual intercourse. Apparently times have changed."

months too old for participation in our juvenile court system), had been dating a mature-looking young woman whom he had met several times previously and who phoned him and asked him to go out on that fateful evening. Alex claims that the young woman told him she was sixteen when (unbeknownst to him) she was really a month and a half shy of her fourteenth birthday. Her deceit was made more credible Alex contends, by her mature and developed physical appearance, her poise, her association with older teenagers, and her evident sexual experience.[13] The defense was prepared to produce witnesses to corroborate the reasonableness of Alex's being taken in by these misrepresentations but the trial justice barred him from doing so. In any event, there is no dispute that Alex and his date engaged in fully consensual sexual relations with each other. The prosecution, on the other hand, paints Alex as a fully accountable eighteen-year-old adult who, after having been warned that the young woman was not old enough to be seeing him, nonetheless proceeded to take advantage of her, knowing full well that the allure of his relative sophistication—together with his ownership of a car and access to a friend's apartment—would work its magic on an impressionable thirteen-year-old. But because the trial justice prevented Alex from introducing any evidence concerning the reasonableness of his mistaken belief that his teenage girlfriend was of legal age to engage in consensual sex, the jury never got to hear any of this testimony.

I would hold that in this type of situation the General Assembly intended that a jury—not judges or prosecutors—is the appropriate body to sort out true cases of child molestation from those involving consensual premarital sex between teenagers based upon a mistaken but reasonably held belief that both were old enough to do so legally. To this end, a criminal defendant indicted under § 11–37–8.1 should be afforded the opportunity to defend against such charges by showing a reasonable and good-faith mistake concerning the age of his or her consenting sexual partner.

I am both surprised and disappointed that a majority of this Court believes otherwise and thinks that Rhode Island's statutory-rape law must be interpreted as a strict-liability crime when it comes to the age of the accused's sexual partner. * * *

It is true that over the last century and a half, many American jurisdictions have adopted so-called statutory-rape laws. And many of these statutes, like Rhode Island's, set out only two express elements—sexual penetration and age—and say nothing about a required mental state. This omission is not dispositive, however. Because "intent [is] so inherent in the idea of the [criminal] offense that it require[s] no

[13] Indeed, by the time of Alex's trial Allison had become pregnant by a different boyfriend, a condition which she initially and falsely blamed on Alex in order to conceal her sexual activity from her family.

statutory affirmation," *Morissette,* 342 U.S. at 252, most criminal statutes do not specify the mental state required for the forbidden acts to constitute a crime. Rather the common-law tradition mandates that the forbidden acts must be the result of intentional wrongdoing. * * *

Unlike regulatory prohibitions directed at *mala prohibita* offenses such as the sale of adulterated milk, child molestation does not naturally fall under the heading of statutorily prohibited public-welfare offenses. Child molestation is an inherently contemptible crime against an identifiable victim. To lump such a crime with petty gambling or commercial mislabeling belittles the gravity of intentional sexual-abuse crimes. Conversely, the degree of punishment and societal opprobrium befitting true sexual-abuse crimes cannot be so cavalierly imposed without regard to the culpable intention of the actor as can the light fines and slap-on-the-wrist penalties attached to typical public-welfare offenses. * * *

III

The Emerging Rule

The last of the triad of points I would make is that a growing number of American jurisdictions have now adopted a new and still emerging American rule that antiquates judicially imposed strict-liability schemes for statutory rape. The Model Penal Code of 1962 (MPC) expressly rejects strict liability in the rape or sexual-assault context. Section 213.3(1)(a) of that code, the rough equivalent of our § 11–37–8.1, would prohibit sexual intercourse with a female under the age of sixteen when the actor is at least four years older than the victim. But the MPC expressly allows a reasonable-mistake-of-fact defense when, as here, the alleged victim is at least ten years old, *see* 2 MPC § 213.6 cmt. 2, although the MPC does adopt an irrebuttable presumption that a child victim actually under the age of ten cannot be reasonably taken for a sixteen-year-old. The MPC approach thus has the effect of attaching a "*mens rea* of [at least] recklessness to the age element in statutory rape." 2 MPC, § 213.6 cmt.2 at 415.

Today some fifteen American states have adopted the MPC in some form. Some set a critical age higher than the MPC's common-law designation of ten (occasionally as high as fourteen or sixteen) for the no-credible-error presumption, but all these states establish penalties far more flexible than our rigid twenty-year minimum sentence—even for the most egregious type of forcible child molestation. Six additional states expressly provide for a mistake-of-fact defense without age limitation, and two states, California and New Mexico, have judicially recognized a mistake-of-age defense by construction of generic statutory provisions similar to ours. And Alaska, as noted, has held the defense to be constitutionally mandated.

In *Hernandez* the Supreme Court of California departed from its own prior decisional law that had rejected the mistake-of-fact defense in the statutory-rape context. California's statute, which punished underage intercourse as a mere misdemeanor, contained general language similar to that employed in our statute—that is language devoid of any explicit reference to an intent requirement or to strict liability. The *Hernandez* court decided that such a statute left no room for strict liability. In explaining its holding on this score, the California high court noted, "The severe penalty imposed for [statutory rape], the serious loss of reputation conviction entails, * * * and the fact that it has been regarded for centuries as a crime involving moral turpitude, make it extremely unlikely that the Legislature meant to include the morally innocent to make sure the guilty did not escape." * * *

With *Hernandez* and the MPC taking the lead, twenty-three American jurisdictions, nearly half, now explicitly recognize some form of the mistake-of-age defense. * * *

For the above-stated reasons I am unwilling to attribute to the General Assembly an unexpressed intention to place Rhode Island on the outermost fringes of current legal thinking and actual practice regarding the mistake-of-age defense, especially when virtually no other state in the whole country imposes such an inflexibly harsh penalty without regard to the defendant's true culpability. In my judgment the majority's conversion of § 11–37–8.1 into a strict-liability crime in mistake-of-age cases, coupled with the statute's mandatory minimum twenty-year prison sentence and convicted sex-offender status, creates an unparalleled and unjustified "double-whammy" that rains down its crushing blows indiscriminately upon innocently intentioned teenage lovers and heinous child molesters alike. Certainly the Legislature may enact strict measures to discourage sexual intercourse with minors or to avoid teenage pregnancy. But a mandatory twenty-years-to-life sentencing range is utterly out of proportion to this goal if mistake of age is not available as a defense.

Furthermore, the General Assembly's manifest aim to punish and to deter intentional sexual molestation of children does not require the judicial creation of strict liability in this situation. Allowing a criminal defendant accused of sexual assault upon a teenaged minor to claim mistake of age as a defense will neither burden prosecutors unduly nor insulate true child molesters from societal retribution. A jury can sort out a legitimate mistake-of-age defense in this context from fabricated excuses.

In sum, absent plain language in a statute that indicates otherwise, a teenaged boy's improvident participation in premarital sex with a teenaged girl that he reasonably believed was old enough to consent should not result in that teenager beginning his adult life in prison as a convicted child molester with a mandatory minimum term of twenty years in jail hanging over his head for the foreseeable future.

For these reasons I would reverse the trial court's conviction and remand this case for a new trial that would allow Alex to raise a reasonable-mistake-of-age defense to the charges.

STATUTORY RAPE LAWS: DOES IT MAKE SENSE TO ENFORCE THEM IN AN INCREASINGLY PERMISSIVE SOCIETY?

82 ABA J. 86 (1996)[a]

Statutory rape laws were enacted in the Middle Ages to protect the chastity of young women. Now they are emerging as the latest solution to the teen pregnancy problem, after a 1995 study by the Alan Guttmacher Institute found about two-thirds of teen mothers were impregnated by adult males.

In California, Gov. Pete Wilson announced in his 1996 state-of-the-state address that statutory rape is a crime that is going to be treated as such. The state allocated more than 82 million to 16 jurisdictions to step up enforcement. The highest priority for prosecution were cases resulting in pregnancies and those in which there was an age discrepancy of more than five years. Soon after, California passed a law stiffening penalties to include a $25,000 fine and nine-year prison sentence for second-time offenders.

Some call these laws a relic of an oppressive past, while others think they promote family values. The positions of law professors Michelle Oberman, DePaul University—Chicago, and Richard Delgado, University of Colorado—Boulder, are more nuanced. Oberman thinks the laws must be recast as a weapon against coerced sex, while Delgado believes they will always be subject to selective enforcement.

YES: THE RISK OF PSYCHOLOGICAL HARM TO GIRLS IS TOO GREAT

Michelle Oberman

In an era in which more than 50 percent of teens under age 18 are sexually active, it is inconceivable that we could incarcerate every person who has sex with a minor. Nonetheless, important reasons remain for enforcing, and even expanding, statutory rape laws.

These laws reflect a consensus that minors are not mature enough to make major decisions because they are vulnerable to coercion and exploitation. This concern permeates the law—minors may disaffirm their contracts, generally may not consent to their own health care, may not drink alcohol and cannot vote. Therefore, the real question facing those who see statutory rape laws as antiquated is whether minors are somehow better able to protect themselves in sexual encounters than they are in other adult endeavors. The answer from numerous sources is no.

Studies by the American Association for University Women demonstrate that, for girls in particular, adolescence is a time of acute crisis in which self-esteem, body image, academic confidence and the willingness to speak out decline precipitously. Psychologists studying girls' sexuality report that these combined sources of insecurity, coupled with the perceived importance of being attractive to males, lead many girls to look to males for validation. In short, they try to fulfill their emotional needs through sex.

What this means is that many girls consent to sexual relationships that we, as a society, can and should recognize as exploitative. Traditional rape laws, focusing on lack of consent, do nothing to combat the problem of the 14-year-old girl who says yes to a 33-year-old neighbor because sleeping with an adult makes her feel important, or who says yes to a classmate who threatens to spread rumors about her unless she sleeps with him, or who says yes to several boys because they took her out.

Such encounters often result in permanent harm to girls through depression, disease and pregnancy. The very real harms girls suffer by "consenting" to sexual exploitation provide ample justification for laws that penalize those who would prey upon them.

Most modern statutory rape laws are gender-neutral and impose criminal liability only if the "victim" is under the age of consent and the partner is older by anywhere from two to five years or more. Bright-line rules are a sensible, if imperfect, mechanism for protecting minors, since there are valid reasons to suspect coercion when a girl 15 or younger has a partner 18 or older.

However, despite their usefulness, these statutes ignore the many exploitative sexual encounters between minors of similar ages. Moreover, the failure to mention coercion, coupled with the fact that age—disparate sexual unions are commonplace, yields little guidance for enforcement. Absent an explicit focus on coercion, these laws invite selective, discriminatory enforcement.

Instead of abolishing statutory rape laws, we ought to consider how to refine them. In doing so, we must remain cognizant of the harm we seek to prevent. The "wrong" committed by coercing a minor exists independently of teen pregnancy. Although no legal solution will eliminate the risks inherent in sexual activity and allow girls to come of age safely, the law has a critical role to play in setting predatory sexual behavior off-limits.

NO: SELECTIVE ENFORCEMENT TARGETS 'UNPOPULAR' MEN

Richard Delgado

Except in the case of the very young, who of course should be protected from sexual predators, statutory rape laws are a bad idea. Most such laws provide that anyone who has sex with someone younger than a certain age—frequently 16—is guilty of the crime of rape, since an underage partner is unable to give valid consent. These laws can only be applied unevenly—and they are.

Consider: Recent surveys show the median age of first intercourse for women in the United States is 17 years and a few months; for boys, it is a little lower. This means that a high percentage of young women are victims of statutory rape, and a very large percentage of young men belong in jail. Laws that sweeping are out of touch with social norms and cannot be enforced, except selectively—and, indeed, statutory rape laws are.

Unable to prosecute the whole country, law enforcement officials apply the law principally against two groups: men, frequently older, who have sex with girls from "good homes"; and minority men, who are punished if they commit the crime of having sex with white women or impregnate a woman of color under circumstances that add to the welfare rolls.

Amending the laws, as some legislators want to do, so that they would apply with special force to men who have sex with women five or more years younger would help, but only a little: Prosecutors cannot possibly charge in every case of a 16-year-old girl who has sex with her 21-year-old boyfriend.

The laws would continue to be used as weapons to punish men who are politically unpopular, socially unacceptable, of the wrong color, or who make the mistake of having intercourse with a woman from a socially upstanding (and well-connected) family. These laws, then, uphold old notions of chastity and virginity, while providing a weapon against men from social groups we do not like.

They also deprive women in their mid-and late teens of choice under the guise of protecting that choice. In this respect, they are the modern descendants of Victorian and late medieval laws punishing the crime of seduction, which were used to protect noble families against the loss of a property right in their daughters' marriageability.

Punishments for pressured sex and sex with the very young—and even hardcore pornography, which glorifies and encourages brutal sex and rape—are socially imperative, and the same is true for sexual harassment in the workplace and elsewhere. But overbroad statutory rape laws are one of the worst ideas that the family-values crowd has produced in years.

Women rarely are charged for sex with younger men. This is perhaps as it should be—men and women stand on very different footings with respect to physical and social power. But this relative scarcity of reverse-enforcement cases should cause us to ask deeper questions: What is rape? What is consent? When is intercourse pressured, and when is it an expression of love between two autonomous individuals?

These are all important questions. But mechanistic laws, which contain overtones of Puritanism, can only impede us in addressing these matters. They are both paternalistic and patriarchal, and should be firmly resisted.

C. SODOMY

BOWERS V. HARDWICK

Supreme Court of the United States
478 U.S. 186, 106 S.Ct. 2841, 92 L.Ed.2d 140 (1986)

WHITE, JUSTICE, delivered the opinion of the Court, in which BURGER, C.J., and POWELL, REHNQUIST, and O'CONNOR, JJ. joined.

In August 1982, respondent Hardwick (hereafter respondent) was charged with violating the Georgia statute criminalizing sodomy by committing that act with another adult male in the bedroom of respondent's home. After a preliminary hearing, the District Attorney decided not to present the matter to the grand jury unless further evidence developed.

Respondent then brought suit in the Federal District Court, challenging the constitutionality of the statute insofar as it criminalized consensual sodomy.[2] He asserted that he was a practicing homosexual, that the Georgia sodomy statute, as administered by the defendants, placed him in imminent danger of arrest, and that the statute for several reasons violates the Federal Constitution. The District Court granted the defendants' motion to dismiss for failure to state a claim.

A divided panel of the Court of Appeals for the Eleventh Circuit reversed. Relying on our decisions in *Griswold v. Connecticut*, *Eisenstadt v. Baird*, *Stanley v. Georgia*, and *Roe v. Wade*,[a] the court went on to hold

---

[2] * * * The only claim properly before the Court, therefore, is Hardwick's challenge to the Georgia statute as applied to consensual homosexual sodomy. We express no opinion on the constitutionality of the Georgia statute as applied to other acts of sodomy.

[a] In *Griswold v. Connecticut*, 381 U.S. 479 (1965), the Court struck down a Connecticut statute forbidding the use of contraceptives, holding that the statute violated the right of marital privacy. In *Eisenstadt v. Baird*, 405 U.S. 438 (1972), the Court held that it was a violation of equal protection for the State to prohibit the distribution of contraceptives to unmarried persons while allowing such distribution to married couples. In *Stanley v. Georgia*, 394 U.S. 557 (1969), the Court invalidated a law that prohibited the knowing possession of obscene materials. In *Roe v. Wade*, 410 U.S. 113 (1973), the Court held that a woman has the right to choose whether to terminate her pregnancy at least during the first trimester of pregnancy.

that the Georgia statute violated respondent's fundamental rights because his homosexual activity is a private and intimate association that is beyond the reach of state regulation by reason of the Ninth Amendment and the Due Process Clause of the Fourteenth Amendment.

Because other Courts of Appeals have arrived at judgments contrary to that of the Eleventh Circuit in this case, we granted the Attorney General's petition for certiorari questioning the holding that the sodomy statute violates the fundamental rights of homosexuals. We agree with petitioner that the Court of Appeals erred, and hence reverse its judgment.

This case does not require a judgment on whether laws against sodomy between consenting adults in general, or between homosexuals in particular, are wise or desirable. It raises no question about the right or propriety of state legislative decisions to repeal their laws that criminalize homosexual sodomy, or of state-court decisions invalidating those laws on state constitutional grounds. The issue presented is whether the Federal Constitution confers a fundamental right upon homosexuals to engage in sodomy and hence invalidates the laws of the many States that still make such conduct illegal and have done so for a very long time. The case also calls for some judgment about the limits of the Court's role in carrying out its constitutional mandate.

We first register our disagreement with the Court of Appeals and with respondent that the Court's prior cases have construed the Constitution to confer a right of privacy that extends to homosexual sodomy and for all intents and purposes have decided this case. * * *

Accepting the decisions in these cases [dealing with child rearing and education, family relationships, procreation, marriage, contraception, and abortion], we think it evident that none of the rights announced in those cases bears any resemblance to the claimed constitutional right of homosexuals to engage in acts of sodomy that is asserted in this case. No connection between family, marriage, or procreation on the one hand and homosexual activity on the other has been demonstrated, either by the Court of Appeals or by respondent. * * *

Precedent aside, however, respondent would have us announce, as the Court of Appeals did, a fundamental right to engage in homosexual sodomy. This we are quite unwilling to do. It is true that despite the language of the Due Process Clauses of the Fifth and Fourteenth Amendments, which appears to focus only on the processes by which life, liberty, or property is taken, the cases are legion in which those Clauses have been interpreted to have substantive content, subsuming rights that to a great extent are immune from federal or state regulation or proscription. Among such cases are those recognizing rights that have little or no textual support in the constitutional language.

Striving to assure itself and the public that announcing rights not readily identifiable in the Constitution's text involves much more than the imposition of the Justices' own choice of values on the States and the Federal Government, the Court has sought to identify the nature of the rights qualifying for heightened judicial protection. In *Palko v. Connecticut*, it was said that this category includes those fundamental liberties that are "implicit in the concept of ordered liberty," such that "neither liberty nor justice would exist if [they] were sacrificed."

It is obvious to us that neither of these formulations would extend a fundamental right to homosexuals to engage in acts of consensual sodomy. Proscriptions against that conduct have ancient roots. Sodomy was a criminal offense at common law and was forbidden by the laws of the original thirteen States when they ratified the Bill of Rights. In 1868, when the Fourteenth Amendment was ratified, all but 5 of the 37 States in the Union had criminal sodomy laws. In fact, until 1961, all 50 States outlawed sodomy, and today, 24 States and the District of Columbia continue to provide criminal penalties for sodomy performed in private and between consenting adults. Against this background, to claim that a right to engage in such conduct is "deeply rooted in this Nation's history and tradition" or "implicit in the concept of ordered liberty" is, at best, facetious.

Nor are we inclined to take a more expansive view of our authority to discover new fundamental rights imbedded in the Due Process Clause. The Court is most vulnerable and comes nearest to illegitimacy when it deals with judge-made constitutional law having little or no cognizable roots in the language or design of the Constitution. * * *

Respondent, however, asserts that the result should be different where the homosexual conduct occurs in the privacy of the home. He relies on *Stanley v. Georgia*, where the Court held that the First Amendment prevents conviction for possessing and reading obscene material in the privacy of one's home: "If the First Amendment means anything, it means that a State has no business telling a man, sitting alone in his house, what books he may read or what films he may watch."

Stanley did protect conduct that would not have been protected outside the home, and it partially prevented the enforcement of state obscenity laws; but the decision was firmly grounded in the First Amendment. The right pressed upon us here has no similar support in the text of the Constitution, and it does not qualify for recognition under the prevailing principles for construing the Fourteenth Amendment. Its limits are also difficult to discern. Plainly enough, otherwise illegal conduct is not always immunized whenever it occurs in the home. Victimless crimes, such as the possession and use of illegal drugs, do not escape the law where they are committed at home. *Stanley* itself recognized that its holding offered no protection for the possession in the home of drugs, firearms, or stolen goods. And if respondent's submission is limited to the voluntary sexual conduct between consenting adults, it would be difficult, except by fiat, to limit the claimed right to homosexual conduct while leaving exposed to prosecution adultery, incest, and other sexual crimes even though they are committed in the home. We are unwilling to start down that road.

Even if the conduct at issue here is not a fundamental right, respondent asserts that there must be a rational basis for the law and that there is none in this case other than the presumed belief of a majority of the electorate in Georgia that homosexual sodomy is immoral and unacceptable. This is said to be an inadequate rationale to support the law. The law, however, is constantly based on notions of morality, and if all laws representing essentially moral choices are to be invalidated under the Due Process Clause, the courts will be very busy indeed. Even respondent makes no such claim, but insists that majority sentiments about the morality of homosexuality should be declared inadequate. We do not agree, and are unpersuaded that the sodomy laws of some 25 States should be invalidated on this basis.[8]

Accordingly, the judgment of the Court of Appeals is

Reversed.

[The opinion of CHIEF JUSTICE BURGER, concurring in the judgment is omitted.]

JUSTICE POWELL, concurring.

I join the opinion of the Court. I agree with the Court that there is no fundamental right—*i.e.,* no substantive right under the Due Process Clause—such as that claimed by respondent Hardwick, and found to exist by the Court of Appeals. This is not to suggest, however, that respondent may not be protected by the Eighth Amendment of the Constitution. The Georgia statute at issue in this case, Ga. Code Ann. § 16–6–2 (1984), authorizes a court to imprison a person for up to 20 years for a single private, consensual act of sodomy. In my view, a prison sentence for such conduct—certainly a sentence of long duration—would create a serious Eighth Amendment issue. Under the Georgia statute a single act of sodomy, even in the private setting of a home, is a felony comparable in terms of the possible sentence imposed to serious felonies such as aggravated battery, first-degree arson, and robbery.

In this case, however, respondent has not been tried, much less convicted and sentenced. Moreover, respondent has not raised the Eighth Amendment issue below. For these reasons this constitutional argument is not before us.

---

[8] Respondent does not defend the judgment below based on the Ninth Amendment, the Equal Protection Clause, or the Eighth Amendment.

JUSTICE BLACKMUN, with whom JUSTICE BRENNAN, JUSTICE MARSHALL, and JUSTICE STEVENS join, dissenting.

This case is no more about "a fundamental right to engage in homosexual sodomy," as the Court purports to declare, than *Stanley v. Georgia* was about a fundamental right to watch obscene movies, or *Katz v. United States* was about a fundamental right to place interstate bets from a telephone booth. Rather, this case is about "the most comprehensive of rights and the right most valued by civilized men," namely, "the right to be let alone."

The statute at issue, Ga. Code Ann. § 16–6–2 (1984), denies individuals the right to decide for themselves whether to engage in particular forms of private, consensual sexual activity. The Court concludes that § 16–6–2 is valid essentially because "the laws of . . . many States . . . still make such conduct illegal and have done so for a very long time." But the fact that the moral judgments expressed by statutes like § 16–6–2 may be " 'natural and familiar . . . ought not to conclude our judgment upon the question whether statutes embodying them conflict with the Constitution of the United States.' " Like Justice Holmes, I believe that "[i]t is revolting to have no better reason for a rule of law than that so it was laid down in the time of Henry IV. It is still more revolting if the grounds upon which it was laid down have vanished long since, and the rule simply persists from blind imitation of the past." I believe we must analyze Hardwick's claim in the light of the values that underlie the constitutional right to privacy. If that right means anything, it means that, before Georgia can prosecute its citizens for making choices about the most intimate aspects of their lives, it must do more than assert that the choice they have made is an " 'abominable crime not fit to be named among Christians.' "

I

In its haste to reverse the Court of Appeals and hold that the Constitution does not "confe[r] a fundamental right upon homosexuals to engage in sodomy," the Court relegates the actual statute being challenged to a footnote and ignores the procedural posture of the case before it. A fair reading of the statute and of the complaint clearly reveals that the majority has distorted the question this case presents.

First, the Court's almost obsessive focus on homosexual activity is particularly hard to justify in light of the broad language Georgia has used. Unlike the Court, the Georgia Legislature has not proceeded on the assumption that homosexuals are so different from other citizens that their lives may be controlled in a way that would not be tolerated if it limited the choices of those other citizens. Rather, Georgia has provided that "[a] person commits the offense of sodomy when he performs or submits to any sexual act involving the sex organs of one person and the mouth or anus of another." The sex or status of the persons who engage in the act is irrelevant as a matter of state law. In fact, to the extent I can discern a legislative purpose for Georgia's 1968 enactment of § 16–6–2, that purpose seems to have been to broaden the coverage of the law to reach heterosexual as well as homosexual activity. I therefore see no basis for the Court's decision to treat this case as an "as applied" challenge to § 16–6–2, or for Georgia's attempt, both in its brief and at oral argument, to defend § 16–6–2 solely on the grounds that it prohibits homosexual activity. Michael Hardwick's standing may rest in significant part on Georgia's apparent willingness to enforce against homosexuals a law it seems not to have any desire to enforce against heterosexuals. But his claim that § 16–6–2 involves an unconstitutional intrusion into his privacy and his right of intimate association does not depend in any way on his sexual orientation. * * *

II

"Our cases long have recognized that the Constitution embodies a promise that a certain private sphere of individual liberty will be kept largely beyond the reach of government." In construing the right to privacy, the Court has proceeded along two somewhat distinct, albeit complementary, lines. First, it has recognized a privacy interest with reference to certain *decisions* that are properly for the individual to make. Second, it has recognized a privacy interest with reference to certain *places* without regard for the particular activities in which the individuals who occupy them are engaged. The case before us implicates both the decisional and the spatial aspects of the right to privacy.

A

The Court concludes today that none of our prior cases dealing with various decisions that individuals are entitled to make free of governmental interference "bears any resemblance to the claimed constitutional right of homosexuals to engage in acts of sodomy that is asserted in this case." While it is true that these cases may be characterized by their connection to protection of the family, the Court's conclusion that they extend no further than this boundary ignores the warning in *Moore v. East Cleveland* against "clos[ing] our eyes to the basic reasons why certain rights associated with the family have been accorded shelter under the Fourteenth Amendment's Due Process Clause." We protect those rights not because they contribute, in some direct and material way, to the general public welfare, but because they form so central a part of an individual's life. "[T]he concept of privacy embodies the 'moral fact that a person belongs to himself and not others nor to society as a whole.' " And so we protect the decision whether to marry precisely because marriage "is an association that promotes a way of life, not causes; a harmony in living, not political faiths; a bilateral loyalty, not commercial or social projects." We protect the decision whether to have a child because parenthood alters so dramatically an individual's self-definition, not because of demographic considerations or the Bible's command to be fruitful and multiply. And we protect the family because it contributes so powerfully to the happiness of individuals, not because of a preference for stereotypical households. The Court recognized in *Roberts* that the "ability independently to define one's identity that is central to any concept of liberty" cannot truly be exercised in a vacuum; we all depend on the "emotional enrichment from close ties with others."

Only the most willful blindness could obscure the fact that sexual intimacy is "a sensitive, key relationship of human existence, central to family life, community welfare, and the development of human personality." The fact that individuals define themselves in a significant way through their intimate sexual relationships with others suggests, in a Nation as diverse as ours, that there may be many "right" ways of conducting those relationships, and that much of the richness of a relationship will come from the freedom an individual has to *choose* the form and nature of these intensely personal bonds.

In a variety of circumstances we have recognized that a necessary corollary of giving individuals freedom to choose how to conduct their lives is acceptance of the fact that different individuals will make different choices. For example, in holding that the clearly important state interest in public education should give way to a competing claim by the Amish to the effect that extended formal schooling threatened their way of life, the Court declared: "There can be no assumption that today's majority is 'right' and the Amish and others like them are 'wrong.' A way of life that is odd or even erratic but interferes with no rights or interests of others is not to be condemned because it is different." The Court claims that its decision today merely refuses to recognize a fundamental right to engage in homosexual sodomy; what the Court really has refused to recognize is the fundamental interest all individuals have in controlling the nature of their intimate associations with others.

B

The behavior for which Hardwick faces prosecution occurred in his own home, a place to which the Fourth Amendment attaches special significance. The Court's treatment of this aspect of the case is symptomatic of its overall refusal to consider the broad principles that have informed our treatment of privacy in specific cases. Just as the right to privacy is more than the mere aggregation of a number of entitlements to engage in specific behavior, so too, protecting the physical integrity of the home is more than merely a means of protecting specific activities that often take place there. Even when our understanding of the contours of the right to privacy depends on "reference to a 'place,' the essence of a Fourth Amendment violation is 'not the breaking of [a person's] doors, and the rummaging of his drawers,' but rather is 'the invasion of his indefeasible right of personal security, personal liberty and private property.' " * * *

III

The Court's failure to comprehend the magnitude of the liberty interests at stake in this case leads it to slight the question whether petitioner, on behalf of the State, has justified Georgia's infringement on these interests. I believe that neither of the two general justifications for § 16–6–2 that petitioner has advanced warrants dismissing respondent's challenge for failure to state a claim.

First, petitioner asserts that the acts made criminal by the statute may have serious adverse consequences for "the general public health and welfare," such as spreading communicable diseases or fostering other criminal activity. * * * [I]t is not surprising that the record before us is barren of any evidence to support petitioner's claim. In light of the state of the record, I see no justification for the Court's attempt to equate the private, consensual sexual activity at issue here with the "possession in the home of drugs, firearms, or stolen goods," to which *Stanley* refused to extend its protection. None of the behavior so mentioned in *Stanley* can properly be viewed as "[v]ictimless,": drugs and weapons are inherently dangerous, and for property to be "stolen," someone must have been wrongfully deprived of it. Nothing in the record before the Court provides any justification for finding the activity forbidden by § 16–6–2 to be physically dangerous, either to the persons engaged in it or to others.

The core of petitioner's defense of § 16–6–2, however, is that respondent and others who engage in the conduct prohibited by § 16–6–2 interfere with Georgia's exercise of the " 'right of the Nation and of the States to maintain a decent society.' " Essentially, petitioner argues, and the Court agrees, that the fact that the acts described in § 16–6–2 "for hundreds of years, if not thousands, have been uniformly condemned as immoral" is a sufficient reason to permit a State to ban them today.

I cannot agree that either the length of time a majority has held its convictions or the passions with which it defends them can withdraw legislation from this Court's scrutiny. As Justice Jackson wrote so eloquently for the Court in *West Virginia Board of Education v. Barnette,* "we apply the limitations of the Constitution with no fear that freedom to be intellectually and spiritually diverse or even contrary will disintegrate the social organization. . . . [F]reedom to differ is not limited to things that do not matter much. That would be a mere shadow of freedom. The test of its substance is the right to differ as to things that touch the heart of the existing order." It is precisely because the issue raised by this case touches the heart of what makes individuals what they are that we should be especially sensitive to the rights of those whose choices upset the majority.

The assertion that "traditional Judeo-Christian values proscribe" the conduct involved cannot provide an adequate justification for § 16–6–2. That certain, but by no means all, religious groups condemn the behavior at issue gives the State no license to impose their judgments on the entire citizenry. The legitimacy of secular legislation depends instead on whether the State can advance some justification for its law beyond its conformity to religious doctrine. A State can no more punish private behavior because of religious intolerance than it can punish such behavior because of racial animus . . . No matter how uncomfortable a certain group may make the majority of this Court, we have held that "[m]ere public intolerance or animosity cannot constitutionally justify the deprivation of a person's physical liberty." * * *

IV

* * * [D]epriving individuals of the right to choose for themselves how to conduct their intimate relationships poses a far greater threat to the values most deeply rooted in our Nation's history than tolerance of nonconformity could ever do. Because I think the Court today betrays those values, I dissent.

[The opinion of Mr. JUSTICE STEVENS, with whom JUSTICE BRENNAN and JUSTICE MARSHALL join dissenting, is omitted.]

NOTE

The decision in *Bowers v. Hardwick* was closely divided. Justice Lewis Powell provided the swing vote in favor of the Court's ruling that the State of Georgia did not violate Michael Hardwick's right of due process when it arrested him for committing sodomy with another adult male in the privacy of his own home. Apparently, Justice Powell had second thoughts about his decision. After his retirement, he told a group of students at NYU School of Law, "I think I probably made a mistake in that one," referring to his opinion in *Bowers*. Anand Agneshwar, *Ex-Justice Says He May Have Been Wrong*, NAT'L L.J., Nov. 5, 1990, at 3.

The next excerpt provides some interesting factual background not found in the Supreme Court's opinion.

BEYOND THE PRIVACY PRINCIPLE

Kendall Thomas

92 COLUM. L. REV. 1431 (1992)

A. *Trail of Blood: The Untold Story of* Bowers v. Hardwick

* * * Michael Hardwick's first encounter with the police power of the state of Georgia took place one morning a block away from the gay bar in Atlanta where he worked.[12] An Atlanta police officer named K.R. Torick

[12] This information is taken from Michael Hardwick's account of the case, which appears in Peter Irons, THE COURAGE OF THEIR CONVICTIONS, 392–403 (1988), and from Laurence Tribe's

stopped Hardwick after seeing him throw a beer bottle into a trashcan outside the bar. As Hardwick recounts the story, the officer "made me get in the car and asked me what I was doing. I told him that I worked there, which immediately identified me as a homosexual, because he knew it was a homosexual bar." Torick then issued Hardwick a ticket for drinking in public. Because of a discrepancy on the ticket between the day and the date he was to appear in court, Hardwick failed to appear. Within two hours of Hardwick's scheduled appearance, Torick went to Hardwick's house with a warrant for his arrest, only to find that he was not at home. When Hardwick returned to his apartment, his roommate told him of the police officer's visit. Hardwick then went to the Fulton County courthouse, where he paid a $50 fine. In Hardwick's words:

> I told the county clerk the cop had already been at my house with a warrant and he said that was impossible. He said it takes forty-eight hours to process a warrant. He wrote me a receipt just in case I had any problems with it further down the road. That was that, and I thought I had taken care of it and everything was finished, and I didn't give it much thought.

Three weeks later, Hardwick arrived home from work to find three men whom he did not know outside his house. In his account of the incident, Hardwick admits that he has no proof that these men were police officers, "but they were very straight, middle thirties, civilian clothes."

> I got out of the car, turned around, and they said 'Michael' and I said yes, and they proceeded to beat the hell out of me. Tore all the cartilage out of my nose, kicked me in the face, cracked about six of my ribs. I passed out. I don't know how long I was unconscious. . . . I managed to crawl up the stairs into the house, into the back bedroom. What I didn't realize was that I'd left a trail of blood all the way back.

A few days after this incident, and nearly a month after his first visit, Officer Torick again appeared at Hardwick's home. Torick found Hardwick in his bedroom having sex with another man.

> He said, My name is Officer Torick. Michael Hardwick, you are under arrest. I said, For what? What are you doing in my bedroom? He said, I have a warrant for your arrest. I told him the warrant isn't any good. He said, It doesn't matter, because I was acting under good faith.

Torick handcuffed Hardwick and his partner and took them to jail, where they were booked, fingerprinted, and photographed. As the two

---

discussion of *Hardwick* in Laurence H. Tribe, AMERICAN CONSTITUTIONAL LAW, 1424–25 (2d ed. 1988). Professor Tribe argued the case on Hardwick's behalf before the Supreme Court.

men were taken to a holding tank, Hardwick recalls that the arresting officer "made sure everyone in the holding cells and guards and people who were processing us knew I was in there for 'cocksucking' and that I should be able to get what I was looking for. The guards were having a real good time with that." Some hours later, Hardwick and his partner were transferred to another part of the building in which he was being held, in the course of which the jail officers made it clear to the other inmates that the men were gay, remarking "Wait until we put [him] into the bullpen. Well, fags shouldn't mind—after all, that's why they are here." Hardwick and his partner remained in jail for the greater part of the day, when friends were permitted to post bail for their release.

Shortly after his release, Hardwick accepted an offer from the Georgia affiliate of the American Civil Liberties Union to undertake his defense in the state courts. Hardwick and his attorneys planned to challenge the constitutionality of the state sodomy law's criminalization of the sexual conduct for which he had been arrested. Before the case came to trial, however, the Fulton County District Attorney declined to seek a grand jury indictment against Hardwick on the sodomy charges. In legal terms, this did not mean that the matter was at an end; the governing statute of limitations rendered Hardwick subject to indictment on the sodomy charges at any time within the next four years. In political terms, it meant that Hardwick (and gays and lesbians throughout the state) continued to be vulnerable to harassment and violence that would likely go unchecked and unchallenged so long as the sodomy statute remained in the Georgia criminal code. Faced with this prospect, Hardwick agreed to take his constitutional claim to the federal courts. * * *

LAWRENCE V. TEXAS

Supreme Court of the United States
539 U.S. 558, 123 S.Ct. 2472, 156 L.Ed.2d 508 (2003)

KENNEDY, J.

* * * The question before the Court is the validity of a Texas statute making it a crime for two persons of the same sex to engage in certain intimate sexual conduct.

In Houston, Texas, officers of the Harris County Police Department were dispatched to a private residence in response to a reported weapons disturbance. They entered an apartment where one of the petitioners, John Geddes Lawrence, resided. The right of the police to enter does not seem to have been questioned. The officers observed Lawrence and another man, Tyron Garner, engaging in a sexual act. The two petitioners were arrested, held in custody overnight, and charged and convicted before a Justice of the Peace.

The complaints described their crime as "deviate sexual intercourse, namely anal sex, with a member of the same sex (man)." The applicable state law is Tex. Penal Code Ann. § 21.06(a) (2003). It provides: "A person commits an offense if he engages in deviate sexual intercourse with another individual of the same sex." The statute defines "deviate sexual intercourse" as follows:

(A) any contact between any part of the genitals of one person and the mouth or anus of another person; or

(B) the penetration of the genitals or the anus of another person with an object.

The petitioners exercised their right to a trial *de novo* in Harris County Criminal Court. They challenged the statute as a violation of the Equal Protection Clause of the Fourteenth Amendment and of a like provision of the Texas Constitution. Those contentions were rejected. The petitioners, having entered a plea of *nolo contendere*, were each fined $200 and assessed court costs of $141.25.

The Court of Appeals for the Texas Fourteenth District considered the petitioners' federal constitutional arguments under both the Equal Protection and Due Process Clauses of the Fourteenth Amendment. After hearing the case en banc the court, in a divided opinion, rejected the constitutional arguments and affirmed the convictions. The majority opinion indicates that the Court of Appeals considered our decision in *Bowers v. Hardwick,* to be controlling on the federal due process aspect of the case. *Bowers* then being authoritative, this was proper.

We granted certiorari to consider three questions:

1. Whether Petitioners' criminal convictions under the Texas "Homosexual Conduct" law—which criminalizes sexual intimacy by same-sex couples, but not identical behavior by different-sex couples—violate the Fourteenth Amendment guarantee of equal protection of laws?

2. Whether Petitioners' criminal convictions for adult consensual sexual intimacy in the home violate their vital interests in liberty and privacy protected by the Due Process Clause of the Fourteenth Amendment?

3. Whether *Bowers v. Hardwick* should be overruled?

The petitioners were adults at the time of the alleged offense. Their conduct was in private and consensual.

II

We conclude the case should be resolved by determining whether the petitioners were free as adults to engage in the private conduct in the exercise of their liberty under the Due Process Clause of the Fourteenth

Amendment to the Constitution. For this inquiry we deem it necessary to reconsider the Court's holding in *Bowers*. * * *

The facts in *Bowers* had some similarities to the instant case. A police officer, whose right to enter seems not to have been in question, observed Hardwick, in his own bedroom, engaging in intimate sexual conduct with another adult male. The conduct was in violation of a Georgia statute making it a criminal offense to engage in sodomy. One difference between the two cases is that the Georgia statute prohibited the conduct whether or not the participants were of the same sex, while the Texas statute, as we have seen, applies only to participants of the same sex. Hardwick was not prosecuted, but he brought an action in federal court to declare the state statute invalid. He alleged he was a practicing homosexual and that the criminal prohibition violated rights guaranteed to him by the Constitution. The Court, in an opinion by Justice White, sustained the Georgia law. Chief Justice Burger and Justice Powell joined the opinion of the Court and filed separate, concurring opinions. Four Justices dissented.

The Court began its substantive discussion in *Bowers* as follows: "The issue presented is whether the Federal Constitution confers a fundamental right upon homosexuals to engage in sodomy and hence invalidates the laws of the many States that still make such conduct illegal and have done so for a very long time." That statement, we now conclude, discloses the Court's own failure to appreciate the extent of the liberty at stake. To say that the issue in *Bowers* was simply the right to engage in certain sexual conduct demeans the claim the individual put forward, just as it would demean a married couple were it to be said marriage is simply about the right to have sexual intercourse. The laws involved in *Bowers* and here are, to be sure, statutes that purport to do no more than prohibit a particular sexual act. Their penalties and purposes, though, have more far-reaching consequences, touching upon the most private human conduct, sexual behavior, and in the most private of places, the home. The statutes do seek to control a personal relationship that, whether or not entitled to formal recognition in the law, is within the liberty of persons to choose without being punished as criminals.

This, as a general rule, should counsel against attempts by the State, or a court, to define the meaning of the relationship or to set its boundaries absent injury to a person or abuse of an institution the law protects. It suffices for us to acknowledge that adults may choose to enter upon this relationship in the confines of their homes and their own private lives and still retain their dignity as free persons. When sexuality finds overt expression in intimate conduct with another person, the conduct can be but one element in a personal bond that is more enduring. The liberty protected by the Constitution allows homosexual persons the right to make this choice. * * *

At the outset it should be noted that there is no longstanding history in this country of laws directed at homosexual conduct as a distinct matter. Beginning in colonial times there were prohibitions of sodomy derived from the English criminal laws passed in the first instance by the Reformation Parliament of 1533. The English prohibition was understood to include relations between men and women as well as relations between men and men. Nineteenth-century commentators similarly read American sodomy, buggery, and crime-against-nature statutes as criminalizing certain relations between men and women and between men and men. The absence of legal prohibitions focusing on homosexual conduct may be explained in part by noting that according to some scholars the concept of the homosexual as a distinct category of person did not emerge until the late 19th century. Thus early American sodomy laws were not directed at homosexuals as such but instead sought to prohibit nonprocreative sexual activity more generally. * * *

It was not until the 1970's that any State singled out same-sex relations for criminal prosecution, and only nine States have done so. . . . Over the course of the last decades, States with same-sex prohibitions have moved toward abolishing them. * * *

It must be acknowledged, of course, that the Court in *Bowers* was making the broader point that for centuries there have been powerful voices to condemn homosexual conduct as immoral. The condemnation has been shaped by religious beliefs, conceptions of right and acceptable behavior, and respect for the traditional family. For many persons these are not trivial concerns but profound and deep convictions accepted as ethical and moral principles to which they aspire and which thus determine the course of their lives. These considerations do not answer the question before us, however. The issue is whether the majority may use the power of the State to enforce these views on the whole society through operation of the criminal law. "Our obligation is to define the liberty of all, not to mandate our own moral code." * * *

As an alternative argument in this case, counsel for the petitioners and some *amici* contend that *Romer* provides the basis for declaring the Texas statute invalid under the Equal Protection Clause. That is a tenable argument, but we conclude the instant case requires us to address whether *Bowers* itself has continuing validity. Were we to hold the statute invalid under the Equal Protection Clause some might question whether a prohibition would be valid if drawn differently, say, to prohibit the conduct both between same-sex and different-sex participants.

Equality of treatment and the due process right to demand respect for conduct protected by the substantive guarantee of liberty are linked in important respects, and a decision on the latter point advances both interests. If protected conduct is made criminal and the law which does so remains unexamined for its substantive validity, its stigma might remain even if it were not enforceable as drawn for equal protection reasons. When homosexual conduct is made criminal by the law of the State, that declaration in and of itself is an invitation to subject homosexual persons to discrimination both in the public and in the private spheres. The central holding of *Bowers* has been brought in question by this case, and it should be addressed. Its continuance as precedent demeans the lives of homosexual persons.

The stigma this criminal statute imposes, moreover, is not trivial. The offense, to be sure, is but a class C misdemeanor, a minor offense in the Texas legal system. Still, it remains a criminal offense with all that imports for the dignity of the persons charged. The petitioners will bear on their record the history of their criminal convictions. Just this Term we rejected various challenges to state laws requiring the registration of sex offenders. We are advised that if Texas convicted an adult for private, consensual homosexual conduct under the statute here in question the convicted person would come within the registration laws of at least four States were he or she to be subject to their jurisdiction. This underscores the consequential nature of the punishment and the state-sponsored condemnation attendant to the criminal prohibition. Furthermore, the Texas criminal conviction carries with it the other collateral consequences always following a conviction, such as notations on job application forms, to mention but one example. * * *

The doctrine of *stare decisis* is essential to the respect accorded to the judgments of the Court and to the stability of the law. It is not, however, an inexorable command. * * *

The rationale of *Bowers* does not withstand careful analysis. In his dissenting opinion in *Bowers* Justice Stevens came to these conclusions:

> Our prior cases make two propositions abundantly clear. First, the fact that the governing majority in a State has traditionally viewed a particular practice as immoral is not a sufficient reason for upholding a law prohibiting the practice; neither history nor tradition could save a law prohibiting miscegenation from constitutional attack. Second, individual decisions by married persons, concerning the intimacies of their physical relationship, even when not intended to produce offspring, are a form of "liberty" protected by the Due Process Clause of the Fourteenth Amendment. Moreover, this protection extends to intimate choices by unmarried as well as married persons.

Justice Stevens' analysis, in our view, should have been controlling in *Bowers* and should control here.

Bowers was not correct when it was decided, and it is not correct today. It ought not to remain binding precedent. *Bowers v. Hardwick* should be and now is overruled.

The present case does not involve minors. It does not involve persons who might be injured or coerced or who are situated in relationships where consent might not easily be refused. It does not involve public conduct or prostitution. It does not involve whether the government must give formal recognition to any relationship that homosexual persons seek to enter. The case does involve two adults who, with full and mutual consent from each other, engaged in sexual practices common to a homosexual lifestyle. The petitioners are entitled to respect for their private lives. The State cannot demean their existence or control their destiny by making their private sexual conduct a crime. Their right to liberty under the Due Process Clause gives them the full right to engage in their conduct without intervention of the government. "It is a promise of the Constitution that there is a realm of personal liberty which the government may not enter." The Texas statute furthers no legitimate state interest which can justify its intrusion into the personal and private life of the individual. * * *

The judgment of the Court of Appeals for the Texas Fourteenth District is reversed, and the case is remanded for further proceedings not inconsistent with this opinion.

It is so ordered.

O'CONNOR, J. (concurring).

The Court today overrules *Bowers v. Hardwick*. I joined *Bowers*, and do not join the Court in overruling it. Nevertheless, I agree with the Court that Texas' statute banning same-sex sodomy is unconstitutional. Rather than relying on the substantive component of the Fourteenth Amendment's Due Process Clause, as the Court does, I base my conclusion on the Fourteenth Amendment's Equal Protection Clause.

The Equal Protection Clause of the Fourteenth Amendment "is essentially a direction that all persons similarly situated should be treated alike." Under our rational basis standard of review, "legislation is presumed to be valid and will be sustained if the classification drawn by the statute is rationally related to a legitimate state interest."

Laws such as economic or tax legislation that are scrutinized under rational basis review normally pass constitutional muster, since "the Constitution presumes that even improvident decisions will eventually be rectified by the democratic processes." We have consistently held, however, that some objectives, such as "a bare . . . desire to harm a politically unpopular group," are not legitimate state interests. When a law exhibits such a desire to harm a politically unpopular group, we have applied a more searching form of rational basis review to strike down such laws under the Equal Protection Clause. * * *

The statute at issue here makes sodomy a crime only if a person "engages in deviate sexual intercourse with another individual of the same sex." Sodomy between opposite-sex partners, however, is not a crime in Texas. That is, Texas treats the same conduct differently based solely on the participants. Those harmed by this law are people who have a same-sex sexual orientation and thus are more likely to engage in behavior prohibited by § 21.06.

The Texas statute makes homosexuals unequal in the eyes of the law by making particular conduct—and only that conduct—subject to criminal sanction. It appears that prosecutions under Texas' sodomy law are rare. This case shows, however, that prosecutions under § 21.06 *do* occur. And while the penalty imposed on petitioners in this case was relatively minor, the consequences of conviction are not. As the Court notes, petitioners' convictions, if upheld, would disqualify them from or restrict their ability to engage in a variety of professions, including medicine, athletic training, and interior design. Indeed, were petitioners to move to one of four States, their convictions would require them to register as sex offenders to local law enforcement.

And the effect of Texas' sodomy law is not just limited to the threat of prosecution or consequence of conviction. Texas' sodomy law brands all homosexuals as criminals, thereby making it more difficult for homosexuals to be treated in the same manner as everyone else. Indeed, Texas itself has previously acknowledged the collateral effects of the law, stipulating in a prior challenge to this action that the law "legally sanctions discrimination against [homosexuals] in a variety of ways unrelated to the criminal law," including in the areas of "employment, family issues, and housing."

Texas attempts to justify its law, and the effects of the law, by arguing that the statute satisfies rational basis review because it furthers the legitimate governmental interest of the promotion of morality. In *Bowers*, we held that a state law criminalizing sodomy as applied to homosexual couples did not violate substantive due process. We rejected the argument that no rational basis existed to justify the law, pointing to the government's interest in promoting morality. The only question in front of the Court in *Bowers* was whether the substantive component of the Due Process Clause protected a right to engage in homosexual sodomy. *Bowers* did not hold that moral disapproval of a group is a rational basis under the Equal Protection Clause to criminalize homosexual sodomy when heterosexual sodomy is not punished.

This case raises a different issue than *Bowers:* whether, under the Equal Protection Clause, moral disapproval is a legitimate state interest to justify by itself a statute that bans homosexual sodomy, but not heterosexual sodomy. It is not. Moral disapproval of this group, like a bare desire to harm the group, is an interest that is insufficient to satisfy rational basis review under the Equal Protection Clause. Indeed, we have never held that moral disapproval, without any other asserted state interest, is a sufficient rationale under the Equal Protection Clause to justify a law that discriminates among groups of persons. * * *

Texas argues, however, that the sodomy law does not discriminate against homosexual persons. Instead, the State maintains that the law discriminates only against homosexual conduct. While it is true that the law applies only to conduct, the conduct targeted by this law is conduct that is closely correlated with being homosexual. Under such circumstances, Texas' sodomy law is targeted at more than conduct. It is instead directed toward gay persons as a class. "After all, there can hardly be more palpable discrimination against a class than making the conduct that defines the class criminal." When a State makes homosexual conduct criminal, and not "deviate sexual intercourse" committed by persons of different sexes, "that declaration in and of itself is an invitation to subject homosexual persons to discrimination both in the public and in the private spheres." * * *

That this law as applied to private, consensual conduct is unconstitutional under the Equal Protection Clause does not mean that other laws distinguishing between heterosexuals and homosexuals would similarly fail under rational basis review. Texas cannot assert any legitimate state interest here, such as national security or preserving the traditional institution of marriage. Unlike the moral disapproval of same-sex relations—the asserted state interest in this case—other reasons exist to promote the institution of marriage beyond mere moral disapproval of an excluded group.

A law branding one class of persons as criminal solely based on the State's moral disapproval of that class and the conduct associated with that class runs contrary to the values of the Constitution and the Equal Protection Clause, under any standard of review. I therefore concur in the Court's judgment that Texas' sodomy law banning "deviate sexual intercourse" between consenting adults of the same sex, but not between consenting adults of different sexes, is unconstitutional.

JUSTICE SCALIA, with whom THE CHIEF JUSTICE and JUSTICE THOMAS join, dissenting.

"Liberty finds no refuge in a jurisprudence of doubt." That was the Court's sententious response, barely more than a decade ago, to those seeking to overrule *Roe v. Wade*. The Court's response today, to those who have engaged in a 17-year crusade to overrule *Bowers v. Hardwick*, is very different. The need for stability and certainty presents no barrier.

Most of the rest of today's opinion has no relevance to its actual holding—that the Texas statute "furthers no legitimate state interest which can justify" its application to petitioners under rational-basis review. Though there is discussion of "fundamental propositions," and "fundamental decisions," nowhere does the Court's opinion declare that homosexual sodomy is a "fundamental right" under the Due Process Clause; nor does it subject the Texas law to the standard of review that would be appropriate (strict scrutiny) if homosexual sodomy *were* a "fundamental right." Thus, while overruling the *outcome* of *Bowers*, the Court leaves strangely untouched its central legal conclusion: "Respondent would have us announce . . . a fundamental right to engage in homosexual sodomy. This we are quite unwilling to do." Instead the Court simply describes petitioners' conduct as "an exercise of their liberty"—which it undoubtedly is—and proceeds to apply an unheard-of form of rational-basis review that will have far-reaching implications beyond this case.

I

I begin with the Court's surprising readiness to reconsider a decision rendered a mere 17 years ago in *Bowers* v. *Hardwick*. I do not myself believe in rigid adherence to *stare decisis* in constitutional cases; but I do believe that we should be consistent rather than manipulative in invoking the doctrine. * * *

Today's opinion is the product of a Court, which is the product of a law-profession culture, that has largely signed on to the so-called homosexual agenda, by which I mean the agenda promoted by some homosexual activists directed at eliminating the moral opprobrium that has traditionally attached to homosexual conduct. I noted in an earlier opinion the fact that the American Association of Law Schools (to which any reputable law school *must* seek to belong) excludes from membership any school that refuses to ban from its job-interview facilities a law firm (no matter how small) that does not wish to hire as a prospective partner a person who openly engages in homosexual conduct.

One of the most revealing statements in today's opinion is the Court's grim warning that the criminalization of homosexual conduct is "an invitation to subject homosexual persons to discrimination both in the public and in the private spheres." It is clear from this that the Court has taken sides in the culture war, departing from its role of assuring, as neutral observer, that the democratic rules of engagement are observed. Many Americans do not want persons who openly engage in homosexual conduct as partners in their business, as scoutmasters for their children, as teachers in their children's schools, or as boarders in their home. They view this as protecting themselves and their families from a lifestyle that they believe to be immoral and destructive. The Court views it as "discrimination" which it is the function of our judgments to deter. So imbued is the Court with the law profession's anti-anti-homosexual culture, that it is seemingly unaware that the attitudes of that culture are not obviously "mainstream"; that in most States what the Court calls "discrimination" against those who engage in homosexual acts is perfectly legal; that proposals to ban such "discrimination" under Title VII have repeatedly been rejected by Congress; that in some cases such "discrimination" is *mandated* by federal statute; and that in some cases such "discrimination" is a constitutional right. *See Boy Scouts of America v. Dale,* 530 U.S. 640 (2000).

Let me be clear that I have nothing against homosexuals, or any other group, promoting their agenda through normal democratic means. Social perceptions of sexual and other morality change over time, and every group has the right to persuade its fellow citizens that its view of such matters is the best. That homosexuals have achieved some success in that enterprise is attested to by the fact that Texas is one of the few remaining States that criminalize private, consensual homosexual acts. But persuading one's fellow citizens is one thing, and imposing one's views in [the] absence of democratic majority will is something else. I would no more *require* a State to criminalize homosexual acts—or, for that matter, display *any* moral disapprobation of them—than I would *forbid* it to do so. What Texas has chosen to do is well within the range of traditional democratic action, and its hand should not be stayed through the invention of a brand-new "constitutional right" by a Court that is impatient of democratic change. It is indeed true that "later generations can see that laws once thought necessary and proper in fact serve only to oppress;" and when that happens, later generations can repeal those laws. But it is the premise of our system that those judgments are to be made by the people, and not imposed by a governing caste that knows best.

One of the benefits of leaving regulation of this matter to the people rather than to the courts is that the people, unlike judges, need not carry things to their logical conclusion. The people may feel that their disapprobation of homosexual conduct is strong enough to disallow homosexual marriage, but not strong enough to criminalize private homosexual acts—and may legislate accordingly. The Court today pretends that it possesses a similar freedom of action, so that we need not fear judicial imposition of homosexual marriage, as has recently occurred in Canada (in a decision that the Canadian Government has chosen not to appeal). At the end of its opinion—after having laid waste the foundations of our rational-basis jurisprudence—the Court says that the present case "does not involve whether the government must give formal recognition to any relationship that homosexual persons seek to enter." Do not believe it. More illuminating than this bald, unreasoned disclaimer is the progression of thought displayed by an earlier passage in the Court's opinion, which notes the constitutional protections afforded to "personal decisions relating to *marriage*, procreation, contraception, family relationships, child rearing, and education," and then declares that "persons in a homosexual relationship may seek autonomy for these purposes, just as heterosexual persons do." Today's opinion dismantles the structure of constitutional law that has permitted a distinction to be made between heterosexual and homosexual unions, insofar as formal recognition in marriage is concerned. If moral disapprobation of homosexual conduct is "no legitimate state interest" for purposes of proscribing that conduct, and if, as the Court coos (casting aside all pretense of neutrality), "when sexuality finds overt expression in intimate conduct with another person, the conduct can be but one element in a personal bond that is more enduring," what justification could there possibly be for denying the benefits of marriage to homosexual couples exercising "the liberty protected by the Constitution?" Surely not the encouragement of procreation, since the sterile and the elderly are allowed to marry. This case "does not involve" the issue of homosexual marriage only if one entertains the belief that principle and logic have nothing to do with the decisions of this Court. Many will hope that, as the Court comfortingly assures us, this is so.

The matters appropriate for this Court's resolution are only three: Texas's prohibition of sodomy neither infringes a "fundamental right" (which the Court does not dispute), nor is unsupported by a rational relation to what the Constitution considers a legitimate state interest, nor denies the equal protection of the laws. I dissent.

NOTE

Should the Court have followed Justice O'Connor's suggestion, striking down Texas' sodomy statute as a violation of equal protection? In Lawrence v. Texas *as the Perfect Storm*, Professor Christopher Leslie explains "that if the Court had struck the statute on equal protection grounds, it would have left gender-neutral sodomy laws intact and those sodomy laws could then have been enforced primarily against gays and lesbians." Christopher R. Leslie, Lawrence v. Texas *as the Perfect Storm*, 38 UC DAVIS L. REV. 509 (2005).

Another question raised by *Lawrence v. Texas* involves the meaning of the following passage from the majority opinion:

> The present case does not involve minors. It does not involve persons who might be injured or coerced or who are situated in relationships where consent might not easily be refused. It does not involve public conduct or prostitution. It does not involve whether the government must give formal recognition to any relationship that homosexual persons seek to enter.

Professor Kelly Strader notes that one can interpret the above language as placing limits on *Lawrence*'s reach or as simply describing the case before the Court as a relatively easy case to decide. J. Kelly Strader, *Resurrecting*

Lawrence v. Texas *as a Basis for Challenging Criminal Prosecutions*, 25 CRIM. JUSTICE 30, 32 (2010). Strader notes that lower courts have relied on this language to limit *Lawrence*'s reach. J. Kelly Strader, Lawrence'*s Criminal Law*, 16 BERKELEY J. CRIM. L. 41, 58 (2011) (noting that lower courts have refused to apply *Lawrence v. Texas* to cases involving minors, coercion, police conduct, nonconsensual conduct and prostitution). Strader argues that these courts have misinterpreted *Lawrence*:

> In the context of the decision in its entirety, *Lawrence*'s "limiting" language—"[t]he present case does not involve . . . "—is simply another way of saying in effect, "This is a straightforward case involving no showing of harm. We are leaving harder cases, in which the state might well be able to prove harm, for another day."

Id. at 59.

D. PROSTITUTION

Prostitution was not a crime at English common law, and until the late nineteenth century prostitutes were usually punished criminally, if at all, under vagrancy, indecent exposure, and nuisance laws. In the late nineteenth and early twentieth century, however, an anti-prostitution movement emerged in the United States. This "abolitionist" movement was made up of feminists concerned with the economic, political and social subjugation of women; moral purists concerned about innocent women being dragooned into so-called "white slavery" and the sordid public spectacle of "red-light districts;" and physicians and other "social hygienists" concerned with the spread of venereal disease and other public health effects of prostitution. These reformers succeeded into whipping the public into a panic about prostitution, and at both the state and federal level both prostitution and its many manifestations were criminalized.

Although Progressive-Era reformists focused their disapproval on the procurers, pimps, and other male exploiters of prostitutes, the burden of the new criminalization largely fell on women. A Massachusetts study of the "white slave trade" published in 1914, for example, noted: "The police court records show that relatively few male patrons of prostitutes are arrested for their share in the offense involved. Just here there seems to be a lack of evenhanded justice. When men are found in a raided house they are not arrested unless taken in the act of fornication. The usual penalty for the offense for the man is a fine of $10. . . . Very rarely is even a short jail sentence imposed." Commission for the Investigation of the White Slave Traffic, So Called, Report of the Commission for the Investigation of the White Slave Traffic, H. Rep. N. 2281, at 60 (Mass. 1914).

Why the criminal law's relative lack of interest in johns as opposed to prostitutes? A commentator offers the following reasons:

> [T]he Victorian myth that men could not control their sex drives, while female sexuality was nonexistent, continued and persists today, affecting the way the justice system differentiates prostitutes and johns. Prostitutes were considered by some as a necessary evil, keeping male urges in check and preventing men from bothering other "respectable" women like their wives. In fact, many believed that [v]ice is one of the weaknesses of men; it cannot be extirpated; if repressed unduly at one point, it will break out more violently and bafflingly elsewhere; a segregated district is really a protection to the morality of the womanhood of the city, for without it rape would be common and clandestine immorality would increase.
>
> Therefore, men were not faulted for acting upon their irrepressible desires. This may help explain the justice system's hesitancy to punish them. In contrast, women were acting against their nature by acting sexually and society sought to separate them from respectable women. Thus, legislatures enacted laws "to control female sexuality and promiscuity, even though prostitution is considered a 'necessary evil' which must exist, albeit clandestinely, to serve the sexual freedom of men."
>
> Another reason for the vilification of prostitutes was the threat they posed to the existing patriarchal familial structure which guarded male dominance. Prostitutes asserted independence by not relying on married life as their sole source of support and by making more money than could be had in legitimate occupations. Thus, the nineteenth-century campaign to criminalize prostitution was part of a sometimes desperate attempt to enforce norms of marriage, chastity, and propriety on women—to keep women in the private sphere of home and family, to prevent them from supporting themselves independently of men, to encourage them to marry.

Julie Lefler, *Shining the Spotlight on Johns: Moving Toward Equal Treatment of Male Customers and Female Prostitutes*, 10 HASTINGS WOMEN'S L.J. 11, 14–15 (1999).

Today, should prostitution be a crime at all? What are the harms prostitution causes, and how can they be alleviated? Does the decision in *Lawrence* change the way we should think about prostitution? Consider these questions as you read the following case.

STATE V. ROMANO

Supreme Court of Hawai'i
155 P.3d 1102 (2007)

Opinion of the Court by ACOBA, J.

I

A

On January 18, 2003, Officer Jeffrey Tallion was on duty with the Narcotics/Vice Division of the Honolulu Police Department Morals Detail. He testified he was on assignment investigating prostitution in the Waik'ak'a area. Tallion related that the investigations involved "checking into hotel rooms and then . . . either go[ing] on to the street or . . . set[ting] up appointments either in the telephone book or 'Pennysaver,' 'Midweek,' or internet cases."

In preparation for his undercover operation, Tallion obtained a hotel room at the Aston Waikiki Beach Hotel and dressed in civilian clothes. He browsed through the "Pennysaver" newspaper and called the phone number on a massage advertisement. When Defendant answered the phone call, Tallion asked if she did "out calls." At this time, there was no discussion of any illicit conduct or sexual acts.

Tallion set up an appointment with Defendant and they met on the street in front of the Aston Waikiki Beach Hotel, but then moved to Tallion's hotel room. In court, Tallion positively identified Defendant as the individual he met outside on January 18, 2003.

Upon arriving in the room, Tallion confirmed that the price of an out call was $100 and then asked Defendant whether "she did anything else." Defendant responded, "Like what? Dance?" Tallion responded, "No," so Defendant asked, "Well, what do you have in mind?"

Tallion then answered, "Well, I was referring to a blowjob." Defendant replied, "No, hands only." Tallion clarified, "So no blowjob, so handjob." Defendant responded, "Yeah, I can do that." Tallion asked the cost and Defendant responded, "Add 20." Tallion reconfirmed with, "Oh, $20 for a handjob?" and Defendant replied, "Yes." Tallion testified that a handjob is street vernacular commonly used in prostitution for "assisted masturbation."

Following Defendant's reply, Tallion "gave a pre-determined signal" and the arrest team entered the hotel room. Tallion apprised Honolulu police officer William Lurbe of the facts and Lurbe placed Defendant under arrest.[1]

---

[1] HRS § 712–1200(1) states that "[a] person commits the offense of prostitution if the person engages in, or agrees or offers to engage in, sexual conduct with another person for a fee." HRS § 712–1200(2) defines "sexual conduct," inter alia, as "sexual contact." HRS § 707–700 (1993) defined sexual contact as:

Tallion testified that he had been with the Morals Detail for three years; he was involved in 400 prostitution cases in 2002 as either the undercover or arresting officer; maybe five of the prostitution cases were initiated from "Pennysaver" ads; and after the talk about "handjob," Defendant added $20.00 to her quoted $100.00 charge for the out-call service. On cross-examination, Tallion recounted that he found Defendant's advertisement in "Pennysaver's" Massage/Acupuncture Section and not the Adult Section. He also related that "hands only" could have meant what a masseuse actually does.

In his testimony, Lurbe testified that he arrested Defendant for prostitution on January 18, 2003, after being "informed by [Tallion] that he [had] obtained a prostitution violation from [Defendant], which was assisted masturbation for $20." * * *

B

On August 21, 2003, Defendant filed a "Motion to Dismiss." In the memorandum attached to the motion, Defendant asserted that *Lawrence [v. Texas]* "invalidate[d] Hawaii's prostitution statutes [and] thus[,] the [prosecution's] case [against Defendant] must necessarily fail." * * *

The court denied the motion, stating that it "[did] not agree with the applicability of [*Lawrence*] to the instant situation."

Defendant took the witness stand in her own defense and testified that she was a self-employed license massage therapist, she had been a licensed massage therapist for "19 years, going on 20" and her license was current and up-to-date on January 18, 2003. She testified that she placed her ad under the "Body, Mind and Spirit," "Massage," or "Health and Fitness" sections and not under the "Personal" or "Adult" sections.

Defendant also recounted that on January 18, 2003, Tallion immediately asked for a blow job when she entered the hotel room. She explained that she was "caught off guard" because she was "not the typical person that men want this from," as she was "overweight" and "old."

She reported that after Tallion asked for the "blow job," she put her hands up and stated, "Hey, I only do hands only." She also declared that she was shaking her head "no" at the same time. Defendant then indicated that Tallion repeated his question again and also asked how

---

[A]ny touching of the sexual or other intimate parts of a person not married to the actor, or of the sexual or other intimate parts of the actor by the person, whether directly or through the clothing or other material intended to cover the sexual or other intimate parts.

The definition of sexual contact in HRS § 707–700 was amended in 2004, see Haw. Sess. L. Act 61, § 3 at 303, by adding the phrase "other than acts of 'sexual penetration' " after "any touching" in the first sentence.

much it would cost. Defendant again said, "No, hands only." Defendant also maintained that Tallion was "loud," "demanding," and "boisterous."

After Defendant repeated "hands only" again, Tallion asked about handjobs. Defendant claims that she had no intent to commit any kind of sexual contact with Tallion. She explained that she only gave Tallion a figure of $20 because she felt threatened and because of Tallion's loud demands. She then testified about a 1983 incident where "[she] got beat up real bad by this person who [she] had gone to for a job for telephone soliciting."

On cross-examination, Defendant admitted that she "couldn't remember [the conversation between Tallion and herself] word for word." She also stated that Tallion did not block her way to the door leading to the hallway, Tallion did not tell her she could not leave the room, and she did not attempt to use the telephone or walk out of the room. Furthermore, Defendant indicated that she said "yes" when Tallion asked for a handjob, she knew that handjob could mean assisted masturbation, she told Tallion that the handjob would cost $20.00 extra, and she said "yes" when Tallion reiterated $20.00 for a handjob. On redirect examination, Defendant claimed that she felt trapped because it was not her room, the room "didn't have much room in it," and "she was within arm's reach of [Tallion]."

Following Defendant's testimony, the defense rested. The court found Defendant guilty of the charged offense. Defendant was sentenced to six months' probation and fined $500.00. * * *

VI

* * * [T]he dissent agrees with Defendant and argues that (1) "at the time of this court's holding in [*State v. Mueller,* 66 Haw. 616, 671 P.2d 1351 (1983)], there was no federal precedent addressing whether the criminalization of an utterly private sexual activity (and its associated monetary component) abridged an individual's right to privacy [but] *Lawrence* created just such a precedent, confirming that individual decisions by married and unmarried persons 'concerning the intimacies of their physical relationship . . . are a form of "liberty" protected by the Due Process Clause of the Fourteenth Amendment[,]' " and (2) "article I, section 6 does not abide the criminalization of wholly private, consensual sexual activity between adults without the state's having demonstrated a compelling interest by way of 'injury to a person or abuse of an institution the law protects.' " We must respectfully disagree with these propositions and discuss them herein.

VII

The dissent's first position is not tenable because it runs into the specific qualification in *Lawrence* that excludes prostitution as part of protected "liberty" under the federal due process clause.

> The present case does not involve minors. It does not involve persons who might be injured or coerced or who are situated in relationships where consent might not easily be refused. *It does not involve public conduct or prostitution.* It does not involve whether the government must give formal recognition to any relationship that homosexual persons seek to enter. *The case does involve two adults who, with full and mutual consent from each other, engaged in sexual practices common to a homosexual lifestyle.* The petitioners are entitled to respect for their private lives. The State cannot demean their existence or control their destiny by making their private sexual conduct a crime. Their right to liberty under the Due Process Clause gives them the full right to engage in their conduct without intervention of the government.

539 U.S. at 578, 123 S.Ct. 2472 (emphases added).

[D]espite this clear exclusion, the dissent argues that a logical extension of *Lawrence* precludes the states from exercising their police power to curb prostitution.

> [W]here two consenting adults swap money for sex in a transaction undertaken entirely in seclusion, the analysis of the *Lawrence* majority, *despite the majority's attempt to avoid the notion, leads inexorably to the conclusion that the state may not exercise its police power to criminalize a private decision between two consenting adults to engage in sexual activity, whether for remuneration or not.*

But, the dissent's position is not supportable on this premise. The Court has in the past drawn legal boundaries around its decisions, despite the fact that arguably logic would "lead[ ] inexorably" beyond such strictures. * * * Hence, although the Court's language may seemingly point to broader application, that does not portend an extension of a given proposition especially when, as here, the Court expressly limits the scope of the liberty interest protected.

Furthermore, the dissent misreads *Lawrence.* As mentioned above, prostitution, *i.e.,* "swap[ping] money for sex" is expressly rejected as a protected liberty interest under *Lawrence. Lawrence* did not involve an exchange of money for sexual relations but focused on the *specific sexual conduct,* i.e., sodomy, as being outside the scope of legitimate government concern. It is important to remember that "[t]he question before the Court [was] the validity of a Texas statute making it a crime for two persons of the same sex to engage in certain intimate sexual conduct[.]" * * * *Lawrence* thus contains a lengthy dissertation on homosexual conduct and sodomy dating back to 1533. * * *

IX

As to the dissent's second position, in our view *Lawrence* as construed above does not vitiate the holding in *Mueller*. In *Mueller*, the defendant was charged with "engag[ing] in, or agree[ing] to engage in, sexual conduct with another person, in return for a fee, in violation of [HRS §] 712–1200 [,]" as Defendant was so charged in the instant case. Somewhat similarly the question posed there was "whether the proscriptions of [HRS] § 712–1200 may be applied to an act of sex for a fee that took place in a private apartment." In affirming the conviction, this court said that "we are not convinced a decision to engage in sex for hire is a fundamental right in our scheme of ordered liberty, . . . [therefore] we affirm [the defendant's] conviction."

XI

Mueller acknowledged the resiliency of prostitution laws as noted by the drafters of the penal code. This court declared that "[t]he drafters of the Hawai'i Penal Code justified the enactment of HRS § 712–1200 on 'the need for public order.' [Thus this court] would not dispute that it was reasonable for the legislature to act on that basis." It was recognized that "[a] large segment of society undoubtedly regards prostitution as immoral and degrading, and the self-destructive or debilitating nature of the practice, at least for the prostitute, is often given as a reason for outlawing it. [Accordingly, w]e could not deem these views irrational."[14] * * *

Based on the foregoing, the * * * judgment is affirmed.

Dissenting Opinion by Levinson, J.

* * * I would reverse the district court's * * * judgment. * * *

---

[14] Relatedly, there is a general consensus in the international community that prostitution has negative consequences. The Convention for the Suppression of the Traffic in Person and the Exploitation of the Prostitution of Others states that "prostitution and the accompanying evil of the traffic in person for the purpose of prostitution are incompatible with the dignity and worth of the human person and endanger the welfare of the individual, the family and the community." Dec. 2, 1949, 96 U.N.T.S. 271 [hereinafter the Convention]. The parties to the Convention agree to punish any person who "[e]xploits the prostitution of another person, even with the consent of that person" and "to take or to encourage, through their public and private education, health, social, economic and other related services, measures for the prevention of prostitution and for the rehabilitation and social adjustment of the victims of prostitution and of the offences referred to in the present Convention." *Id.*

The United States has agreed to "take all appropriate measures, including legislation, to suppress all forms of traffic in women and exploitation of prostitution of women." Convention on the Elimination of All Forms of Discrimination against Women, Dec. 18, 1979, 1249 U.N.T.S. 13, 19 I.L.M. 33 (1980) [hereinafter the Convention on Discrimination]. The Convention on Discrimination was adopted in 1979 by the UN General Assembly and as of Nov. 2006, 185 countries (over 90% of the members of the UN) are parties to the Convention. Several of the countries that have ratified the treaty are Afghanistan, Australia, Austria, Cuba, China, Germany, Israel, Italy, Mexico, and Netherlands. *See* United Nations, Division on the Advancement of Women, http://www.un.org/womenwatch/daw/cedaw/states.htm (last visited Feb. 21, 2007).

The majority asserts that I argue "that a logical extension of *Lawrence* precludes the states from exercising their police power to curb prostitution." The majority mischaracterizes the import of my reasoning. My analysis draws a clear line between purely private behavior between consenting adults—requiring demonstration of a compelling state interest before *criminal* penalties may be imposed—and the public realm, where the state retains broad power to impose time/place/manner regulations. Adoption of my analysis by the majority, would not, therefore, compel the legalization of prostitution in its usual manifestations: streetwalking, escort services, or even hostess bars.

I merely assert that HRS § 712–1200(1) *as applied to Romano in the present matter* is unconstitutional. Romano's prosecution and conviction reflect an extraordinarily cramped application of HRS § 712–1200(1). The uncontroverted evidence in the present matter demonstrates that Romano was held criminally accountable for wholly private, though admittedly sexual, behavior with another consenting adult. As its majority noted, *Lawrence* presupposed *private* sexual activity between two adults fully capable of giving valid consent. Neither the present matter nor *Lawrence* concerned "persons who might be injured or coerced or who are situated in relationships where consent might not be easily refused." And, as I have emphasized, this case does not implicate public solicitation, streetwalking, or salacious advertising, which are not private activities. Rather, the present record reflects that the charged transaction could not conceivably have hurt anybody other than Romano, which renders her conviction under HRS § 712–1200(1)—absent a showing of a compelling interest from the prosecution—a violation of her federal and state constitutional rights to privacy as articulated in *Lawrence* and by the drafters of article I, section 6.

With regard to demonstrating the necessary compelling interest, at the hearing on Romano's motion to dismiss, the prosecution did speak generally to the state's interest "in making prostitution illegal," *e.g.*, avoiding the "disruption to the marital contract," and "any sexual diseases that might get passed through promiscuous sex." However, such concerns as moral depravity, the salacious reputation of a community, and disease and their attendant impact on productivity, tourism, etc., are commonly trotted out in the name of the "general welfare," are generally speculative and attenuated, and can be moderated through "less restrictive" time, place, and manner regulations. The prosecution's unelaborated theory does not constitute evidence at all, let alone proof of a compelling state interest and narrow tailoring justifying Romano's *criminal conviction.* As Justice Levinson wrote in his *Kantner* dissent, "it is self-evident that '[r]egulation and prohibition are not coextensive.' "

In light of the foregoing analysis, I would reverse the district court's * * * judgment.

CHAPTER 9

THEFT OFFENSES

■ ■ ■

INTRODUCTION

Like homicide law and rape law, the law of theft shows clearly the imprints of history and culture on law. Unlike those other crimes, however, the law of theft is deeply intertwined with economics and technology. The evolution of the law of theft in the English common law reflected the emergence of capitalism: from being a crime against the person, theft became a crime against property, and evolved as the concept of property itself evolved. As Professor Michael Tigar has stated, "There is no better way to understand the relation between the development of capitalist legal institutions and the changing contours of the right of property than by studying the cases of those charged with stealing." Theft law has evolved, as well, in response to new technological capacities. For instance, the advent of the computer and the World Wide Web expanded the capacities of thieves, in turn prompting a new wave of criminal law reforms.

Despite the dramatic changes in political economy and technological capacity from thirteenth-century England to the present-day United States, some basic questions have remained the same. What is the harm caused by theft? What sorts of things constitute "property" so that they can be stolen? Can rules developed in previous centuries be altered to address current problems, and if so, at what cost? If not, what might an entirely new structure of theft look like?

Section A of this chapter examines the law of theft from a historical perspective and introduces you to the basic theft crimes—larceny, embezzlement, and false pretenses. This section illustrates, as well, the point that to fully understand the doctrine, it is necessary to understand the cultural environment from which it emerged. Section B of the chapter addresses two "aggravated" forms of theft: burglary and robbery.

A. THEFT

The Anglo-American common law of theft began with the basic crime of larceny. Later, English judges created the related crime of larceny by trick through the common law process, and Parliament created two additional statutory theft crimes, embezzlement and false pretenses. When the United States was founded, American lawmakers incorporated into their penal codes the three basic theft crimes—larceny, embezzlement, and false pretenses. Eventually, however, reformers in many states incorporated all three into a single consolidated crime of theft, hoping to escape the procedural nightmares caused by doctrinal complexity. The consolidation approach is reflected, as well, in the Model Penal Code. *See* Model Penal Code § 223.1(1).

Even where the law of theft has been consolidated, the ghosts of the original common law crimes continue to haunt contemporary statutes. In order to understand the contemporary law of theft, it is necessary to understand the growth and development of the English common law of theft.

1. LARCENY

The most ancient of the basic theft crimes is larceny, which consists of (1) the trespassory "taking" and "carrying away" of personal property (2) from the possession of another (3) with the intent to permanently deprive the owner of it. The actus reus of larceny is the trespassory taking and carrying away of the personal property of another. The mens rea is the specific intent to permanently deprive the owner of that property.

a. The Taking Must Be "Trespassory"

The "taking" or "caption" of personal property must be "trespassory"—that is, the actor must have no right to use the property. A taking is considered "trespassory" if the actor takes possession of the property without the possessor's consent or other lawful justification.

b. The "Asportation" or "Carrying Away" Requirement

The "carrying away" element of larceny has a technical name: "asportation." Courts have held that asportation means the assertion of control over and some movement of the item contrary to the possession of the owner, no matter how slight. Thus, if I come across your laptop in the law library and, intending to steal it, I pick it up but then put it back because I realize I'm being watched, I have technically committed larceny. In contemporary law, there is some debate over whether the asportation requirement is met in the retail context, where people commonly pick up merchandise and move it around within the store. *See, e.g., Craig v. State*, 410 So.2d 449, 453 (Ala. Crim. App. 1981) ("it is clear that if a shopper moves merchandise from one place to another within a store with the intention to steal it, there has been asportation and the shopper may be found guilty of larceny"). *But see People v. Parrett*, 90 Misc.2d 541, 394 N.Y.S.2d 809 (N.Y. Dist. Ct. 1977) (reversing theft conviction when defendant concealed clothing in her purse, paid for other items, and was apprehended upon arriving to the second floor by escalator, on the ground that no asportation from the store had occurred).

c. Mens Rea: Specific Intent to Permanently Deprive

To be guilty of larceny, one must have the specific intent to permanently deprive another of the property. In other words, one must intend to steal the property. If an actor takes the personal property of another, honestly believing that he owns the property or has a right to possess it, he is not guilty of larceny because he lacks the specific intent to steal. This is true even if the actor unreasonably and mistakenly believes that he has a claim of right to the property.

d. Concurrence

In order for a taking of personal property to constitute larceny, there must also be concurrence between the mens rea and the actus reus. In other words, the taking and the specific intent to permanently deprive must occur at the same time. Therefore, for example, if you lend me your laptop and after I have borrowed it for a few days I decide to take it from you permanently, I have not committed larceny. Because my intent to permanently deprive you of the property did not occur at the same time as my initial taking, concurrence between the mens rea and the actus reus is lacking and my taking of your laptop would not be considered larceny.

e. Constructive Possession, Custody, and Larceny by Trick

In the 1779 English case of *Rex v. Pear*, a man named Pear rented a horse, telling the owner that he was going to Surrey with it. Instead, he rode to Smithfield and sold the horse. Although the written reports of the case are in disarray, the jury apparently found that Pear intended to sell the horse when he rented it, and that he had committed larceny. The rationale for this holding was that Pear's taking of the horse had been wrongful, and therefore void, from the very beginning because it had been achieved by deceit. Under conventional larceny law, Pear was not guilty of larceny because the initial taking was not trespassory. Pear took possession of the horse with the owner's consent. In order to make this idea fit the existing doctrinal structure of larceny, the court needed to invent a number of legal fictions. *Rex v. Pear* came to stand for the general principle that an employer or principal retains "constructive possession" of property when she entrusts it to an employee or agent; the employee or agent receives only "custody." Therefore, when an employee or agent obtains custody of a thing through *deceit*, and takes custody with the specific intent to permanently deprive the owner of it, she violates the owner's (constructive) possession, commits a trespassory taking, and has committed "larceny by trick."

The distinction between "custody" and "possession" remains important in contemporary law. If initially you are in lawful possession of the property of another, and later form the intent to steal that property, you are not guilty of larceny because you have not trespassorily taken property from the possession of another. On the other hand, if you merely have custody of property and decide to steal that property, at the moment you gain possession you are guilty of larceny because someone else had (constructive) possession of the property and you trespassorily took possession of the property from that person.

Joshua Dressler explains that "a person has *possession* of property when he has sufficient control over it to use it in a reasonably unrestricted manner." JOSHUA DRESSLER, UNDERSTANDING CRIMINAL LAW § 32.04[B][1] (6th ed. 2012). "A person has mere 'custody' of property if he has physical control over it, but his right to use it is substantially restricted by the person in constructive possession of the property." *Id.* Under contemporary law, "constructive possession" exists in three situations: (1) when a principal or employer delivers property to an agent or employee to use, keep, make a delivery for the principal; (2) when the owner of property loses it or misplaces it and someone else finds it; and (3) when a property owner delivers the property to another person as part of a transaction to be completed in the owner's presence. In any of these situations, if a person takes and carries away the property with the intent to permanently deprive the owner, the crime is larceny. This is because the owner at all times retained constructive possession of the property.

f. The "Breaking Bulk" Doctrine

Larceny as it existed in thirteenth-century England was not a crime against property but a crime against "the king's peace." That is, the harm to be avoided was the violence—disturbance of the peace—that might erupt when one person openly and deliberately committed an act contrary to the lawful right of possession of another.

As England evolved into a commercial society, common law judges began to expand the scope of larceny, in the process slowly transforming the harm punished by theft from the disturbance of the royal peace to the interference with an individual's right to control a movable object. One famous way-station in this process was the decision in *Carrier's Case.* A foreign merchant entrusted some bales of "woad"—a blue dye used in the woolen industry—to a carrier who was to bring them to Southampton. Somewhere along the way, the carrier broke the packages open and misappropriated the contents, finally abandoning the goods in London. Both the merchant and the Sheriff of London claimed the right to the bales, the sheriff on the theory (established by precedent) that goods taken feloniously and later abandoned belonged to the government.

The case was an important one politically: wool was a key industry in fifteenth-century England (even the king was a wool merchant), and the security of foreign merchants and their property was in question as well. Under existing law, however, the situation did not constitute larceny because the carrier's initial possession of the bales had been lawful. However, the judges of the Exchequer Chamber who took the case reported nevertheless that the carrier had committed larceny. Although the judges did not reach a consensus on the reason why, Lord Chokke's opinion came to be taken as the rule of the case. Chokke reasoned that while the carrier received possession of the packages (or bales), he was in mere custody of its contents. When the carrier broke the bales open, an unlawful taking of the contents occurred, constituting larceny.

This "breaking bulk" doctrine became incorporated into the law of larceny, and still survives in contemporary American law. For example, in *United States v. Mafnas*, the defendant, the employee of an armored car service, opened bags of money in his care and removed the cash. 701 F.2d 83 (9th Cir. 1983). The court held that Mafnas's crime was larceny rather than embezzlement, relying on the "breaking bulk" reasoning first publicly articulated in 1473.

2. EMBEZZLEMENT

The common law courts were not willing to extend the law of larceny infinitely, however, and the remaining key expansions of the law of theft were accomplished by statute. The crime of embezzlement is an example. Suppose I am the owner of a bank and I hire you as a teller to collect money from my customers. You accept all the deposits according to bank protocols, but you "cook the books" to make the deposits appear less than they are, and you keep the surplus money for yourself. Under the existing law of larceny, no crime has been committed. You have not committed larceny against me because I am not the owner of the money; the customers are. Neither have you committed larceny by trick against the customers because you lawfully received possession of the deposits and obtained (according to the courts) more than mere "custody."

Under contemporary statutes, embezzlement generally is defined as (1) the intentional conversion of (2) the property of another (3) by someone who is already in lawful possession of it (or by someone to whom it has been "entrusted"). "Conversion" means some act that seriously interferes with the owner's ability to use the property. Thus, the simple movement of an object in space—which would be enough to constitute "asportation" for the purpose of larceny—is not enough to constitute a conversion. Acts that would constitute conversion include using something up, selling it, using it as collateral for a loan, giving it away, inflicting serious damage to it, or delivering it to someone not entitled to it.

The distinction between "larceny by trick" and "embezzlement" is that under the doctrine of larceny by trick, the defendant's initial taking is achieved by deceit and is thus considered never to constitute possession, whereas in embezzlement, the defendant receives lawful possession of the property.

3. FALSE PRETENSES

The crime of false pretenses, like the crime of embezzlement, was created by statute to fill the gaps left by the expanded law of larceny. Under the doctrine of "larceny by trick," as we have seen, a person who gained possession of property through deception could be found guilty of larceny. But a person who gained both possession of and title to property through deception was not guilty of any crime. Parliament responded to the problem with a 1757 statute making it a crime to obtain property by "false pretense." Under that statute, any person who knowingly and designedly by false pretense obtained title to property from another was guilty of the crime of false pretenses.

In a commercial society where people commonly make representations intended to produce a transaction, the kind of deceit that constitutes false pretenses had to be distinguished from mere "puffing," or representations that everyone ought to recognize as exaggerated or possibly false. The defendant's intentions were made the key. As one commentator explains:

> To commit false pretenses, the perpetrator must have an "intent to defraud." . . . An omission, or silence . . . could be considered a "deceitful means or artful practice." "One who knew he was obtaining money or a chattel by his misrepresentation of fact and who received it with intent to take a fraudulent advantage of the other, has obtained it by fraud whether his original statement was made for this purpose or not." The silence, in light of full knowledge of the situation, was the equivalent of a repetition of the false statement at the moment of acquisition. An intent to defraud was also found where the person made an untrue statement innocently, but thereafter learned of the mistake before the property was received and fraudulently failed to disclose the information upon acquisition.
>
> False pretenses further required that the victim was deceived. Property is "not obtained by the untrue representation of fact if the real facts are known to the other. Hence it is essential to show that the owner was misled by the misrepresentation." It was also "not an indictable offense, under the statute, for one to obtain by false statements payment of a debt already due, or personal property to the possession of which he was entitled, because no injury was done."

Courtney Chetty Genco, *What Happened to* Durland*?: Mail Fraud, RICO, and Justifiable Reliance*, 68 NOTRE DAME L. REV. 333, 350 (1992).

Finally, the traditional law of false pretenses required that the misrepresentation pertain to some existing fact in the past or present, and not a "mere promise as to the future," such as the false promise to fulfill a contract. *See Durland v. United States*, 161 U.S. 306, 16 S.Ct. 508, 40 L.Ed. 709 (1896).

The modern crime of false pretenses requires: (1) a false statement of fact that (2) causes the victim (3) to pass title to the defendant. The defendant must: (4) know the statement is false; and (5) thereby intend to defraud the victim. The main difference between larceny by trick and the crime of false pretenses is "that a thief who uses trickery to secure title, and not simply possession, is guilty of false pretenses; one who merely secures possession through fraud is guilty of larceny by trick." JOSHUA DRESSLER, UNDERSTANDING CRIMINAL LAW § 32.10[B] (6th ed. 2012).

4. CONSOLIDATED THEFT STATUTES

Most American jurisdictions now have passed "consolidated theft statutes" which roll the three traditional theft crimes—larceny/larceny by trick, embezzlement, and false pretenses—into a single crime of theft. The existence of a consolidated theft statute means that prosecutors do not risk having their indictment dismissed if they charge the wrong crime. American legislatures have also created new theft crimes over the years to address specific threats. However, consolidated theft statutes and even many new theft crimes continue to rely on the old common law distinctions, and therefore it is important to understand those distinctions. The case that follows provides an example.

COMMONWEALTH V. MILLS

Supreme Judicial Court of Massachusetts
436 Mass. 387, 764 N.E.2d 854 (2002)

SPINA, J.

Following a jury trial, the defendant was found guilty of three counts of larceny from the city of Boston; two counts of larceny by false pretenses from the Committee for Public Counsel Services (CPCS); three counts of perjury; three counts of pension fraud; two counts of procurement fraud; two counts of making false claims; and four counts of failure to make tax returns. Based on the five larceny convictions, the judge adjudicated the defendant a "common and notorious thief" pursuant to G.L. c. 266, § 40,[2]

---

[2] General Laws c. 266, § 40, provides:

Whoever, having been convicted, upon indictment, of larceny or of being accessory to larceny before the fact, afterward commits a larceny or is accessory thereto before the fact, and is convicted thereof upon indictment, and whoever is convicted at the same sitting of the court, as principal or accessory before the fact, of three distinct and sentenced him to serve not less than eighteen and not more than twenty years in prison with various lesser concurrent sentences on the remaining charges. The defendant filed a timely notice of appeal. * * *

1. Background. The defendant retired in 1978 from the Boston police department after he was diagnosed with hypertensive heart disease. He applied for and received from the board a nontaxable accidental disability pension of approximately $15,500 per year. The defendant then began to run a private investigation business, Mills Investigations, Inc. (Mills Investigations), out of his home in New Hampshire.

During 1993, 1994, and 1995, the defendant spent every business day at the Middlesex Superior Court, either in the court room assigned to clerk-magistrate Joseph Marshall or in Marshall's office. Beginning in April, 1994, Marshall handled most of the appointments of counsel for indigent defendants and motions for investigation funds. When the designated bar advocate was not in the courtroom, Marshall would deviate from the master list and appoint one attorney from among a group of four who were typically in the courtroom. Those four attorneys moved for investigation funds in every one of their cases and always retained the services of Mills Investigations. Marshall "rubber-stamped" his allowance of these motions off the record and in his back office where the defendant usually spent three hours a day socializing with Marshall.

For fiscal year 1993, the defendant billed CPCS for approximately $107,000 for investigative services. For fiscal year 1994, the defendant billed CPCS for approximately $197,000, representing 5,483 hours of investigative services. On forty-four occasions, the defendant submitted bills with more than twenty-four hours of work attributed to a single day. For fiscal year 1995, the defendant billed CPCS for approximately $359,000, representing 10,057 hours of investigative services. The defendant submitted 211 bills in which he claimed to have worked well over twenty-four hours in a single day (with some days as long as seventy-two hours).

Between 1992 and 1994, the defendant received approximately $45,000 in nontaxable accidental disability benefits from the board. Once approved for a disability pension, the only limitation to keeping the full amount received each year is the amount of income the recipient earns, if any, during that same time period. Following receipt of pension benefits, every disability pensioner is required by statute to file with the board a yearly earnings report, signed under the pains and penalties of perjury. The board calculates an earned income limitation for each disability

---

larcenies, shall be adjudged a common and notorious thief, and shall be punished by imprisonment in the state prison for not more than twenty years or in jail for not more than two and one half years.

pensioner, and the pensioner must refund a dollar's worth of pension for each dollar of income over the established limit. To collect money owed as a refund, the board sends bills to pensioners requesting remittance of a check in the appropriate amount. If the pensioner does not respond, the board withholds the amount due from the current pension distribution as security until payment is properly received.

The board estimated that the defendant could earn up to $30,228 in 1992, $30,820 in 1993, and $32,484 in 1994 before being liable for any refunds. For 1992, the defendant withdrew $89,637 from the corporate account of Mills Investigations for his own personal use; he reported to the board that he had earned a total of $25,000. For 1993, the defendant withdrew $65,640 from the corporate account of Mills Investigations for his own personal use; he reported to the board that he had earned a total of $17,500. For 1994, the defendant withdrew $104,494 from the corporate account of Mills Investigations for his own personal use; he reported to the board that he had earned a total of $30,000. As a result of the defendant under-reporting his earnings, the board never sought a refund of any pension money.

2. Motion for required finding of not guilty. At the close of the Commonwealth's case, the defendant presented a general motion for required findings of not guilty. The motion was denied. The defense rested without presenting any evidence, the defendant renewed his motion, and it was again denied.

The defendant now asserts that the Superior Court judge erred in denying his motion for a required finding of not guilty with respect to the larceny indictment charging him with three counts of stealing the property of the city of Boston when he submitted false earnings reports to the board. He contends that while making such fraudulent statements would violate criminal statutes for perjury, and pension fraud, such conduct did not constitute larceny. The defendant argues that he obtained his accidental disability pension payments lawfully. What he did was make it unlikely that the board would demand a refund and hold his future pension payments as security therefor. The defendant also asserts that because the judge erred in denying his motion for required findings of not guilty, his adjudication as a common and notorious thief should be vacated because only two larceny convictions (from CPCS) would remain.

In his general motion for a required finding of not guilty, the defendant stated that the evidence produced by the Commonwealth was insufficient to prove beyond a reasonable doubt that he had committed the offenses as charged in the indictments. * * * The pertinent indictment herein, for three counts of larceny under G.L. c. 266, § 30,[3] charged the

[3] General Laws c. 266, § 30(1), states, in pertinent part, as follows:

Whoever steals, or with intent to defraud obtains by a false pretence, or whoever unlawfully, and with intent to steal or embezzle, converts, or secretes with intent to

defendant with stealing the property of the city of Boston, namely "money or a release of a claim to money, the value of which exceeded $250." "[T]he word 'steal' has become 'a term of art and includes the criminal taking or conversion' by way either of larceny, embezzlement or obtaining by false pretences." These three formerly separate crimes have been merged into the one crime of larceny as defined in G.L. c. 266, § 30. Larceny can be established by evidence that would have warranted a conviction upon any one of the three formerly separate charges. The purpose of the merger of these three common-law crimes of "stealing" into one statutory crime was to eliminate the possibility that a defendant indicted for one of the crimes would escape punishment if the proof at trial established another of the crimes.

General Laws c. 277, § 41, provides: "In an indictment for criminal dealing with personal property with intent to steal, an allegation that the defendant stole said property shall be sufficient; and such indictment may be supported by proof that the defendant committed larceny of the property, or embezzled it, or obtained it by false pretences." Thus, "[t]he statute explicitly permits convictions to be supported by evidence that the defendant's theft was committed in any manner condemned by the law."

The Commonwealth was not ordered to elect its theory of the manner in which the alleged larcenies were committed. To require the Commonwealth to elect a particular theory of larceny would be to continue to afford an opportunity to frustrate the ends of justice in derogation of the specific legislative intent to eliminate the merely technical differences between three cognate and similar offenses. Here, there was no restriction in the indictment as to what legal theory of the statutory crime of larceny would be established by the evidence. As such, the proof offered by the Commonwealth with respect to the three counts of "stealing" from the board could be used to support any of the theories of larceny.

Our well-established standard of review of the denial of a motion for a required finding of not guilty is "whether, after viewing the evidence in the light most favorable to the prosecution, any rational trier of fact could have found the essential elements of the crime beyond a reasonable doubt." Where, as here, a defendant submits a generally expressed motion for a required finding of not guilty, the motion applies to any offense properly charged in the indictment and is correctly denied when the evidence supports any such properly charged offense. Therefore, we examine whether the Commonwealth presented sufficient evidence to establish the essential elements of at least one form of "stealing," namely larceny, embezzlement, or larceny by false pretenses, beyond a reasonable

---

convert, the property of another as defined in this section, whether such property is or is not in his possession at the time of such conversion or secreting, shall be guilty of larceny. . . .

doubt. If so, then the Superior Court judge did not err in denying the defendant's motion for a required finding of not guilty.

"To support a conviction of larceny under G.L. c. 266, § 30, the Commonwealth is required to prove the 'unlawful taking and carrying away of the personal property of another with the specific intent to deprive the person of the property permanently.'" We agree with the well-reasoned analysis of the Appeals Court that filing false earnings reports with the board does not constitute a trespassory taking of money, and the "release of a claim to money" is not property within the meaning of G.L. c. 266, § 30(2), or the common law.

With respect to embezzlement, the evidence should establish that the defendant "fraudulently converted" to his personal use property that was under his control by virtue of a position of "trust or confidence" and did so with the intent to deprive the owner of the property permanently. Contrary to the Commonwealth's argument that the Appeals Court added a new element to the crime of embezzlement, the existence of a confidential or fiduciary relationship between the embezzler and the victim has always been at the heart of this crime. The fraudulent conversion of property by parties who merely have a debtor-creditor relationship does not constitute embezzlement.

The defendant's filing of false earnings reports with the board, conduct intended to eliminate the possibility that the board would demand a refund of a portion of his annual accidental disability pension because of his earned income, does not establish the essential elements of embezzlement. Pursuant to G.L. c. 32, § 13(1)(b), "[p]ayments under any annuity, pension or retirement allowance . . . shall be due and payable for the month on the last day of each month during the continuance of such annuity, pension or retirement allowance, as the case may be." General Laws c. 32, § 91A, provides that "[e]very person pensioned or retired under any general or special law for disability, including accidental disability, shall in each year on or before April fifteenth subscribe, under the penalties of perjury, and file with the [public employee retirement administration] commission a statement . . . certifying the full amount of his earnings from earned income during the preceding year." If such earnings exceed a predetermined amount, said person "shall refund the portion of his retirement allowance for such preceding year equal to such excess and until such refund is made, his pension or retirement allowance shall be held as security therefor." This procedure establishes a debtor-creditor relationship between the recipient of a disability retirement allowance and the board. The recipient is lawfully entitled to a specified amount on a monthly basis. If, after submitting an earned income statement, it is determined that the recipient should have received a smaller disability retirement allowance because of other earned income, the recipient then must refund a portion of it to the board and future distributions will be withheld until that debt has been satisfied.

At the time the defendant filed his annual earnings reports with the board on or about April 15, 1993, April 4, 1994, and April 28, 1995, he was not "fraudulently converting" money that was under his control by virtue of a position of "trust or confidence." The money he received was merely the distribution of a government benefit to which he was lawfully entitled each month for his own personal use and to which, at the time of receipt, he obtained complete title and possession. By filing false earnings reports, the defendant was ensuring that he would not have to pay a reimbursement to the board and would not be subjected to any subsequent withholdings. While such conduct certainly constitutes perjury, and pension fraud, it is not embezzlement.

The Commonwealth contends that the nature of the relationship between an alleged embezzler and a victim is one of fact that falls within the province of the jury to decide. This would ordinarily be true where, to establish the essential elements of embezzlement, the Commonwealth must show that the defendant acquired control of property through a position of "trust or confidence." In this case, the relationship between the defendant and the board is established, as a matter of law, to be that of debtor and creditor.

The final "stealing" offense that falls under the larceny statute is larceny by false pretenses. A prosecution for larceny by false pretenses requires proof that (1) a false statement of fact was made; (2) the defendant knew or believed that the statement was false when he made it; (3) the defendant intended that the person to whom he made the false statement would rely on it; and (4) the person to whom the false statement was made did rely on it and, consequently, parted with property.

Following his diagnosis of hypertensive heart disease, the defendant applied for, and the board made a determination that he was entitled to, an accidental disability retirement allowance. The Commonwealth has not contested the defendant's lawful entitlement to this benefit. However, when the defendant filed annual earnings reports with the board in 1993, 1994, and 1995, he stated that he had earned far less income than he had actually withdrawn from the corporate account of Mills Investigations for his own personal use. The evidence warrants a finding that the defendant knowingly made such false statements with the intent that the board would rely on them, would determine that he had not exceeded his annual earned income limitations, and, consequently, would continue to pay him the full amount of his accidental disability retirement allowance every year. This is exactly what happened; the defendant's expectations were fulfilled. The defendant's actions resulted in his receiving a greater allowance from the board than that to which he was lawfully entitled and constituted larceny by false pretenses.

We conclude that the judge did not err in denying the defendant's motion for required findings of not guilty with respect to the three counts of larceny from the board. After viewing the evidence in the light most favorable to the Commonwealth, a rational trier of fact could have found the essential elements of larceny by false pretenses beyond a reasonable doubt. * * *

B. AGGRAVATED THEFT

1. BURGLARY

UNITED STATES V. EICHMAN

United States District Court for the Southern District of New York
756 F.Supp. 143 (S.D.N.Y. 1991)

SAND, DISTRICT JUDGE.

This criminal case involves charges arising from acts allegedly committed by the defendants at the United States Armed Forces Recruiting Station at Times Square in New York City. Count three of the indictment * * * charges the defendants with burglary in the third degree in violation of N.Y. Penal Law § 140.20 (McKinney 1988). Presently before this Court are the defendants' motions to dismiss count three of the indictment, or, in the alternative, to permit an inspection of the grand jury minutes.

The issue raised by defendants' motions is what constitutes "enter[ing] . . . in a building with intent to commit a crime therein" under the burglary provisions of the New York Penal Law. * * *

I. BACKGROUND

The government and the defendants are in substantial agreement as to the facts of this case. On September 11, 1990, defendants Shawn Eichman and Joseph Urgo went to the Armed Forces Recruiting Station at Times Square and climbed onto the roof of the one story structure using a ladder. Once on the roof the defendants poured motor oil over the surface of the roof and onto the exterior signs of the building. The defendants then lowered the American flag flying over the building, doused it with lighter fluid and set it on fire. Defendants claim that their activities were acts of political protest symbolizing their objection to American policy in the Persian Gulf.

Shortly after they ignited the flag, defendants were arrested on the roof by New York City police officers. The next day they were arraigned on a complaint charging attempted arson of the recruiting station. The government subsequently decided not to pursue the arson charge. Instead, the indictment returned by the grand jury charged defendants with three other crimes: (1) injuring and committing depredations against property of the United States; (2) reckless endangerment; and (3) burglary in the third degree. * * *

On December 17, 1990, defendants moved to dismiss the burglary count of the indictment on the ground that absent an allegation that defendants entered within the four walls of the recruiting station, the government would be unable to prove the "entry" element of the burglary count at trial. * * * The government argues that the defendants' motions should be denied because the indictment pleads all the necessary elements of burglary under New York law. However, the government nonetheless asks this Court to reach the merits of defendants' argument regarding the entry element. * * *

II. DISCUSSION

* * * Defendants also argue for dismissal on the ground that the government indicted them on the burglary charge, which is the only felony count in the indictment, in order to punish them for expressing their political views. In response, the government maintains that it could have sought indictment on the charge of attempted arson, which carries a higher penalty than burglary, but did not do so because it thought that the burglary charge better fit the defendants' conduct. The decision whether to prosecute an individual, and for what crime, are matters resting in the sound discretion of the prosecuting authorities. This Court finds no reason to question the government's exercise of its prosecutorial discretion in this case. * * *

The underlying issue raised by defendants' motions is whether the defendants can be convicted of burglary under New York law if the government does not attempt to prove that they ever entered within the four walls or beneath the roof of the recruiting station. This court is convinced that they cannot.

Under New York law, a person must "enter or remain unlawfully in a building" in order to be guilty of burglary in the third degree. In defining unlawful entry the Penal Law focuses on the requirement of unlawfulness, defining it in terms of lack of license or privilege to be in a building. However, the Penal Law does not define the breadth of the concept of entering in a building.

In the absence of statutory guidance, the parties place their reliance on a recent Court of Appeals decision, *People v. King*. In *King*, the defendant appealed his conviction for attempted burglary of a jewelry store. The store was on the ground floor and had a metal security gate covering the display windows and the vestibule area which led past the display windows and into the interior of the store. The defendant was apprehended after he cut a small hole in the part of the security gate directly in front of the vestibule area.

The defendant's first contention in *King* was that he should not have been convicted because it would have been impossible for him to enter the store in that the hole was not big enough for his body to pass through. The Court rejected this contention, holding that because the Penal Law does not define "enter" the term retains its common law meaning, which is that entry is accomplished when a person "intrudes within a building, no matter how slightly." Because the defendant could have put a part of his body through the hole, the entry requirement was satisfied.

The defendant's second contention was that the vestibule area was not part of the "building" within the meaning of the statute, such that his attempt to enter it was not attempted burglary. The Court also rejected this contention, holding that the "existence of the security gate, which can be pulled down to completely enclose the vestibule area from public access, albeit with a temporary fourth wall, makes the vestibule functionally indistinguishable from the space inside the display cases or the rest of the store."

In this case, both parties focus on the part of the *King* opinion which discusses the vestibule area. The government reads that part as standing for the proposition that the element of entering is satisfied so long as the defendant goes into "an area of or related to a building to which the public has been or can be denied access." The defendants interpret *King* to mean that in order to be guilty of burglary, the defendant must intrude into some enclosed space in or connected to a building.

In deciding which view of *King* is correct, the appropriate starting point is the common law of burglary since, according to the *King* Court, the element of entry still retains its common law meaning in New York. At common law, burglary was the breaking and entering of a dwelling house at night with the intent to commit a felony therein. The predominate impetus of common law burglary was "to protect the security of the home, and the person within his home." The offense was directed at preserving the internal security of the dwelling; consequently, an entry into the structure itself was an essential element of the crime. The intrusion of any part of the defendant's body, or of an object held in his hand, was sufficient to establish the element of entry. Yet there had to be some movement by the defendant across the external boundaries of the structure, some breaking of the planes created by the threshold and the four walls. Activity conducted outside the external boundaries of a dwelling, no matter how felonious, was not burglary at common law.[2]

---

[2] Thus Lord Hale maintained that firing a gun into a house was not burglary unless some part of the weapon crossed the threshold.

The scope of common law burglary was expanded somewhat through the concept of curtilage. Curtilage was defined as the area within close proximity to the dwelling house. Outbuildings within the curtilage were deemed to be part of the dwelling house, such that an unlawful entry into the outbuilding was burglary. In essence, then, the effect of the concept of curtilage was to expand the definition of dwelling house; however, it did not alter the entry requirement. Thus a defendant might be convicted of burglary for stealing from a homeowner's barn, but only if he actually entered within the four walls of the barn.

Because the common law required that a defendant penetrate the exterior walls of a structure in order to be guilty of burglary, such penetration is required for the commission of statutory burglary in New York. Thus in this case, the defendants may be convicted of burglary only if the government can prove that they actually entered within the four walls or beneath the roof of the recruiting station.

This conclusion comports with the Court of Appeal's decision in *King* and the case law of New York's lower courts. In *King*, the vestibule of the jewelry store was within the planes created by the four exterior walls of the building. Thus the defendant was guilty of attempted burglary because he tried to gain entrance to the vestibule. * * *

In addition to its consonance with the caselaw of New York, the view of the entry requirement adopted by this Court comports with the restraints imposed by the rule of lenity. * * * Courts should decline to interpret a criminal statute to encompass situations which a reasonable layperson could not foresee as being within the ambit of the statute. In this case, there is little doubt but that the defendants knew that their actions on the rooftop of the recruiting station violated the law. Trespass, destruction of government property, reckless endangerment and perhaps even attempted arson were foreseeable charges stemming from their conduct. That the defendants could reasonably have foreseen the charge of burglary is, however, a much more doubtful proposition.

In sum, this Court is of the view that the New York Penal Law requires that a defendant actually enter within the four walls or beneath the roof of a building in order to be guilty of burglary in the third degree. At trial, the jury will be instructed that they may not convict the defendants of the burglary charge unless they find that such an entry occurred. Of course, if the government presents no evidence of such entry then the count will be dismissed.

STATE V. THIBEAULT

Supreme Judicial Court of Maine
402 A.2d 445 (Me. 1979)

DELAHANTY, JUSTICE.

A Superior Court jury, Penobscot County, found Dale Thibeault guilty of Class B burglary. 17–A M.R.S.A. § 401(B). On April 24, 1978, Thibeault was sentenced to a term of six years at the Maine State Prison. On appeal, the defendant attacks the legality of his conviction on numerous grounds. * * *

The prosecution introduced ample evidence tending to show that on the evening of December 9, 1977, the defendant entered an apartment leased by David and Debbie Gardner with the intent, later consummated, to abscond with certain valuables. On his case-in-chief, the defendant called one of the co-tenants, David Gardner, to the stand. Gardner testified that he had been friendly with the defendant for several years and that prior to the December 9 incident he had given the defendant blanket permission to enter his apartment at any time. On cross-examination, Gardner allowed that he had not given the defendant permission to remove any property from the apartment.

On appeal, as at his trial, the defendant directs his attack at that segment of the jury instructions in which the presiding Justice discussed the evidence pertinent to the "license or privilege" language found in Section 401.[1] The challenged passage reads as follows:

> Now as to the license and privilege. There's not much of a dispute that Mr. Gardner, one of the co-tenants, gave permission but it becomes your duty under the law and considering all the facts whether or not the State has sustained its burden which I have given you beyond a reasonable doubt that the Defendant, Mr. Thibeault, knew that he was not licensed and privileged or privileged to do so with the intent to commit this crime of theft which I have defined to you. Was that a license? Was it a privilege? Was it a qualified license or privilege? It's for you to say what was in the mutual contemplation of the parties when permission to enter was given by Mr. Gardner. There is no dispute that Mr. Gardner, himself, says, I never gave him consent to steal or to rip off the apartment, so the facts are not much in dispute. Therefore, you must decide whether or not from all the testimony, from all the facts, and under the law which I have given to you, whether or not the Defendant, in whatever

---

[1] The pertinent portion of Section 401 provides:

> A person is guilty of burglary if he enters or surreptitiously remains in a structure, knowing that he is not licensed or privileged to do so, with the intent to commit a crime therein.

> condition he was, knew that he was not licensed or privileged when he went in those premises to commit the crime of theft.
>
> * * *

The defendant argues that under Section 401 a person cannot validly be convicted of burglary if the individual rightfully in possession has given that person permission to enter the structure. He contends that the jury instruction was erroneous to the extent that it gave the jury the impression that if it found that the defendant had intended to commit a crime within the apartment that intention would negative, for the purposes of the burglary statute, Gardner's permission to enter.

At common law, consent to enter was a complete defense to a burglary prosecution. Burglary, like arson, was conceived of as an invasion of the "right of habitation." Thus, mere entry upon the dwelling of another in the nighttime with intent to commit a felony therein was insufficient to constitute the common-law crime of burglary. The prosecution additionally had to prove a "breaking": "the actual or constructive use of some force against a part of a building in effectuating an *unconsented* entry." That the initial entry must be trespassory was established in Maine in *State v. Newbegin*, where the defendant was convicted of burglarizing a dry goods store which, at the time in question, was open for trade. The defendant lifted an unlocked latch, opened a door, stole some cloth, and escaped all without attracting the attention of the store attendants. The Court reversed the burglary conviction finding that the State had failed to establish a breaking. * * *

Since the common law required a "violation of the security designed to exclude," it was axiomatic that a person entering with the permission of the lawful possessor could not be guilty of burglary. As one authority explains,

> (t)he law was not ready to punish one who had been "invited" in any way to enter the dwelling. The law sought only to keep out intruders, and thus anyone given authority to come into the house could not be committing a breaking when he so entered.

Although we have not had occasion to deal with a consent defense to a burglary prosecution since *Newbegin* was decided in 1846, it is nevertheless clear that consent remained a valid defense at least until such time as Maine's Criminal Code became effective in 1976. The former burglary statutes all included or incorporated by reference the familiar breaking element. Furthermore, our interpretations of that element were entirely consistent with the "security-designed-to-exclude" rationale put forth in *Newbegin*.[3]

---

[3] * * * In State v. Cookson, Me., 293 A.2d 780, 784–85 (1972), for example, Justice Weatherbee declared:

Although few quarreled with the logic of including the requirement of a trespassory entry for a law designed to protect the security of the habitation, judicial interpretations of the "force" aspect of the breaking element rightly attracted the criticism of reformers. In interpreting the "force" aspect, the judges of the common law perhaps wishing to constrict the application of what was then a capital crime, created a host of fine distinctions and bewildering qualifications.[4]

With burglary no longer a capital offense, the irrationality of these interpretations became manifest. Many state legislatures have reacted by excising the breaking element from their statutes entirely. In these jurisdictions, burglary has been reduced to a three-element crime: (1) entry (2) of a structure (3) with the intent to commit a crime. Under such a statute, it is clear that consent to enter is not a defense since, no vestige of the breaking element remaining, the entry need not be trespassory to be burglarious.

In other jurisdictions, Maine among them, the word "breaking" has been eliminated and a word or phrase such as "unlawful," "unauthorized," or "without license or privilege" has been inserted in the statute to qualify "entry." Where such language has been employed in a burglary statute, the result has generally been to retain so much of the breaking element as required a trespassory entry while at the same time eliminating the illogical rules stemming from the "force" aspect of breaking. Of course, where the statute requires a trespassory entry, the lawful possessor's consent is a complete defense.

New York's burglary statute and the judicial interpretations thereof are particularly instructive since that statute makes use of the same "license or privilege" language found in our Section 401.[5] The New York courts have held that the "license or privilege" language included in Section 140.00(5) requires a trespassory entry.

We hold that the "license or privilege" language in Maine's Section 401 requires a like construction. The portion of the statute relevant to this appeal provides that "(a) person is guilty of burglary if he enters . . . a structure, knowing that he is not licensed . . . to do so, with the intent to

---

> It appears clear that the offense of burglary is one primarily against the security of the habitation. It marks the state's determination to safeguard in his dwelling the homeowner, his family and guests from the dangers that accompany felonious invasions of their sanctuaries during the particularly vulnerable periods of darkness. (footnote omitted.)

[4] For example, if the defendant entered through an open door or window, no breaking occurred since no force was used: the occupant, it was said, had not sufficiently secured his dwelling and was therefore not entitled to the protection of the law. Worse still, courts were divided over the question of whether pushing open a partly open door or window was a sufficient use of force to satisfy the breaking element.

[5] Both New York and Maine appear to have adopted modified versions of the Model Penal Code's definition of burglary. Model Penal Code § 221.1(1974).

commit a crime therein." Breaking the statute down to its constituent parts, we discern four elements: (1) entry (2) of a structure (3) with the knowledge that the entry is not licensed and (4) with the intent to commit a crime within the structure. Obviously, the "license" referred to in the statute means the license to enter a particular structure. The "do so" clearly refers back to "enters." Accordingly, the prosecution must, as an independent proposition, prove beyond reasonable doubt that the accused knew that he was not "licensed" to enter the structure.

The State argues that since the defendant entered the Gardners' apartment for the unlawful purpose of stealing certain valuables, any permission he may have secured from Gardner would be negated. We find no room in Section 401 for this argument. Whether or not the defendant had permission to enter is a question that must be resolved without reference to his alleged intent, another separate and distinct element of the crime. The Louisiana Supreme Court, construing that state's "unauthorized entry" statute, responded to the same argument as follows:

> As we construe the burglary statute, the entry must be unauthorized and this must be determined as a distinct element of the offense separate and apart from the intent to steal. If the legislature desired that burglary consist only of an entry with intent to steal, they would have omitted the word *unauthorized.*

Much the same can be said of Maine's Section 401. If we construed the statute to allow the existence of a criminal intent upon entry to negate the permission of the lawful possessor, the result would be, for all practical purposes, the expungement of the "license" language from the statute. If the State's argument is accepted, a burglary defendant would have to prevail on the question of his intent to commit a crime in order to prevail on the "license or privilege" issue. The State's interpretation would thus render the "license or privilege" language mere surplusage, and Section 401 would be little more than a variation on the typical three-element statute discussed earlier. We have no reason to believe that the Legislature would inject unnecessary language into any of the Code's provisions. Indeed, our familiar rule has been to construe statutes, particularly criminal ones, as being free of superfluous language.

It is true that the Comment appended to Section 401 declares that the statute eliminates "the common law requirement . . . that there be a 'breaking.' " However, the next sentence, "(t)he crime loses nothing in seriousness if the burglar enters a door inadvertently left open, rather than through a door he breaks open," indicates that the revisers intended to draft the statute in such a way as to eliminate only the "force" aspect of breaking together with the irrational judicial interpretations that accompanied it. The "license or privilege" language inserted in the statute itself indicates that the trespassory aspect of the breaking element was retained.

Turning to the instruction given by the presiding Justice, we conclude that the jury was given the mistaken impression that it could find the defendant guilty of burglary whether or not David Gardner gave him permission to enter the apartment. "There's not much of a dispute," stated the court, "that Mr. Gardner, one of the co-tenants, gave permission. . . . " That being the case, the jury's function, according to the court, was to determine whether or not the defendant "knew that he was not licensed (to enter) with the intent to commit this crime of theft. . . . " The instruction invited the jury to consider whether, in the words of the presiding Justice, a "qualified license" existed. As our analysis here indicates, Section 401 does not contemplate the kind of qualification outlined by the presiding Justice. A remand will therefore be necessary. * * *

Judgment of conviction set aside.

Case remanded for a new trial.

2. ROBBERY

CROCKER V. STATE

Supreme Court of Mississippi
272 So.2d 664 (Miss. 1973)

INZER, JUSTICE:

Appellant George Leon Crocker was indicted, tried and convicted in the Circuit Court of Neshoba County for the crime of robbery. He was sentenced to serve a term of ten years in the State Penitentiary. From this conviction and sentence, he appeals. We reverse and remand.

The principal contention of appellant is that the trial court was in error in refusing to grant his request for a directed verdict at the close of the state's case.

The indictment in this case in effect charged that appellant committed an assault on one Jesse S. McKenzie and did thereby put him in bodily fear of immediate injury to his person and that appellant did take $500 from the person of Jesse S. McKenzie against his will, and did then and there feloniously and violently take, steal and carry away $500.

McKenzie testified that at approximately eleven o'clock on the morning of June 26, 1971, appellant came to his home and after they had a cup of coffee, he and appellant went to the store where they drank some beer and whiskey. When they returned McKenzie changed his clothes. He had his billfold containing $500 in the bib of his coveralls which he removed. He stated that he removed the billfold and put it in his pocket. It is unclear from his testimony whether he put the billfold in the pocket of the coveralls which he removed, or whether he put it in the pocket of the clothes he put on. Apparently, he left it on the bed because he stated appellant got the billfold, removed $500 therefrom, laid the billfold down and left. Although the state attempted to get him to say that the appellant took the money from his person by force or violence, he never would say that any force or violence was used. On cross examination he stated that appellant did not in any way use force, violence, or fear to get his money. He concluded his testimony by stating that his clothes were on the bed and his wallet was in his clothes, and that appellant took his money from his wallet and left. He also stated at one point in his testimony that appellant had been gone for about an hour before he missed his money.

It is well settled that the three essential elements of robbery are as follows: (1) felonious intent, (2) force or putting in fear as a means of effectuating the intent, and (3) by that means taking and carrying away the property of another from his person or in his presence. All these elements must occur in point of time. If force is relied upon as proof of the charge it must be force by which another is deprived of and the offender gains possession of the property. If putting in fear is relied upon, it must be the fear under duress of which the owner parts with possession. It is apparent that the state failed to prove the second necessary element of the crime of robbery and therefore, the trial court was in error in refusing to grant the appellant's motion for a directed verdict, insofar as the crime of robbery is concerned.

The state, while contending the evidence is sufficient to sustain the charge of robbery, urges that although we find the evidence of the charge of robbery was insufficient to sustain the conviction, it was sufficient to sustain a conviction of the lesser included offense of larceny, and that this Court should sustain the conviction insofar as the conviction includes larceny and remand the case for proper sentencing. The state cites Section 2523, Mississippi Code 1942 Annotated (1956), which reads as follows:

> On an indictment for any offense the jury may find the defendant guilty of the offense as charged, or of any attempt to commit the same offense, or may find him guilty of an inferior offense, or other offense, the commission of which is necessarily included in the offense with which he is charged in the indictment, whether the same be a felony or misdemeanor, without any additional count in the indictment for that purpose.

Under the provisions of this section the jury could have found appellant guilty of grand larceny instead of robbery, and in that event the conviction would be upheld. The difficulty here is that the state chose to rely upon the charge of robbery, and the trial court submitted the case to the jury on that charge, instead of submitting the case to the jury on the lesser included offense of grand larceny. Under these circumstances, this

Court cannot sustain a conviction of the constituent offense of grand larceny. * * *

Reversed and appellant ordered held for further action of the grand jury.

MILLER V. SUPERIOR COURT

Court of Appeal of California, 4th Appellate District, Division One
115 Cal.App.4th 216, 8 Cal.Rptr.3d 872 (2004)

MCINTYRE, J.

Penal Code section 211 defines a robbery as "the felonious taking of personal property in the possession of another, from his person or immediate presence, and against his will, accomplished by means of force or fear." * * * The issue presented in this case is whether the immediate presence requirement of a robbery charge is satisfied where the defendant, after stealing property belonging to the victim but not from the victim's presence, is confronted by the victim as he is attempting to carry the property to a place of temporary safety and uses forcible resistance to keep the property. We conclude that the immediate presence requirement is met under such circumstances and thus deny the defendant's petition for a writ of prohibition challenging the superior court's order denying his motion to dismiss the robbery charge.

FACTUAL AND PROCEDURAL BACKGROUND

On August 27, 2002, Jose Higareda went into the public restroom at La Jolla Cove to change into his swimming trunks. He went into one of the restroom's enclosed stalls and hung his pants, which contained his wallet (with more than $200 in cash), cellular telephone and keys, on a hook inside the stall door. As Higareda was changing, Miller walked into the restroom and entered the stall directly across from Higareda's. There was no one else in the restroom at the time.

After Higareda finished putting on his swimming trunks, he walked out of the restroom, inadvertently leaving his pants hanging inside the stall. After taking a few steps outside the restroom, Higareda realized his mistake and went back into the restroom. He checked the stall where he had left his pants and, after discovering the pants missing, began looking under the doors of the other stalls to try to locate them. Higareda heard the sound of someone opening Velcro coming from the stall directly across from the one where he had left his pants.

Because his wallet had a Velcro fastener, Higareda became suspicious, entered a stall adjacent to the one Miller was in and looked over the top into Miller's stall. Miller, who appeared to be shielding something from Higareda's view, inquired what Higareda was doing. Higareda responded that someone had taken his belongings and Miller told him to report the situation to a lifeguard. Higareda waited outside

Miller's stall for 15 to 20 minutes, expecting that Miller would come out. During that time, Miller repeatedly asked other persons who entered the restroom for toilet paper, but did not leave the stall.

Ultimately, Higareda's friend, Dennis O'Brien, entered the restroom looking for Higareda. Higareda told O'Brien that someone had taken his belongings and that he believed Miller had them. O'Brien knocked on the door of Miller's stall, demanding that Miller "give . . . the stuff back." Miller told O'Brien to leave him "the 'f' alone," but Higareda continued to demand that Miller return his property. After additional exchanges, O'Brien announced that he was going to get a lifeguard, although, at Higareda's request, he did not leave the restroom.

Five to ten seconds later, Miller came out of his stall and attempted to leave the restroom, saying "[l]et me out of here." Higareda and O'Brien blocked Miller from leaving and yelled for someone to get a lifeguard. Miller charged at the men, trying to push and shove his way out of the restroom. After a great deal of scuffling, O'Brien placed Miller in a headlock and Higareda demanded to see what Miller had in his pockets. Miller gave Higareda his wallet, which Higareda held until lifeguards arrived.

Police arrested Miller at the scene and found $241 in cash in his wallet, which did not fasten with Velcro, and 2.43 grams of methamphetamine in his shorts pocket. O'Brien told the officers that he found Higareda's pants and empty wallet underneath a tremendous mound of toilet paper in the stall Miller had occupied. Officers suspected that Miller was under the influence of a controlled substance at the time of his arrest; Miller subsequently tested positive for the presence of methamphetamine.

The district attorney charged Miller with one count each of robbery and possession of a controlled substance. * * *

Miller filed a section 995 motion to dismiss the robbery charge against him on the ground that the evidence did not establish that he took property from Higareda's person or immediate presence. The superior court concluded that, in accordance with *People v. Estes*, Miller's resistance to Higareda's attempt to regain the property was sufficient to establish the immediate presence requirement and that the evidence thus supported the robbery charge against Miller. Based on its findings, the court denied Miller's section 995 motion.

Miller filed the instant petition for writ of prohibition, challenging the denial order and reasserting his argument that because there is no evidence showing the property was taken from Higareda's person or immediate presence, the evidence admitted at his preliminary hearing is insufficient to support the robbery charge against him. We issued an order to show cause why the relief should not be granted and stayed further proceedings in the trial court.

DISCUSSION

* * *

2. Robbery

As noted above, a "robbery" is "the felonious taking of personal property in the possession of another, from his person or immediate presence, and against his will, accomplished by means of force or fear." (§ 211.) The crime is essentially a theft with two aggravating factors, that is, a taking (1) from victim's person or immediate presence, and (2) accomplished by the use of force or fear.

"The taking element of robbery itself has two necessary elements, gaining possession of the victim's property and asporting or carrying away the loot." "Immediate presence" is spatially, not temporally, descriptive and thus "refer[s] to the area from which the property is taken, not how far it is taken" or for what duration. "A thing is in the [immediate] presence of a person, in respect to robbery, which is so within his reach, inspection, observation or control, that he could, if not overcome by violence or prevented by fear, retain his possession of it." The "immediate presence" component focuses on whether the stolen property was located in an area in which the victim could have expected to take effective steps to retain control over his property. Traditionally, the "immediate presence" requirement has been described as relating to the "gaining possession" element of the taking rather than the "carrying away" element of a robbery charge.

To support a robbery charge, the taking must also be accomplished by force or fear. Circumstances otherwise constituting a mere theft will establish a robbery where the perpetrator peacefully acquires the victim's property, but then uses force to retain or escape with it. For example, in *People v. Anderson*, the California Supreme Court held that the defendant was properly convicted of robbery based on evidence that he examined a rifle and ammunition at a pawnshop under the guise of being interested in purchasing the items and while the pawnshop clerk was totaling the purchase price, he loaded the rifle and pointed it at the clerk to facilitate his escape.

The *Anderson* court stated "[i]n this state, it is settled that a robbery is not completed at the moment the robber obtains possession of the stolen property and that the crime of robbery includes the element of asportation, the robber's escape with the loot being considered as important in the commission of the crime as gaining possession of the property. . . . Accordingly, if one who has stolen property from the person of another uses force or fear in removing, or attempting to remove, the property from the owner's immediate presence, . . . the crime of robbery has been committed."

The *Anderson* court cited with approval *People v. Phillips*, in which the defendant had a gas station attendant pump gasoline into his car and then confronted the attendant with a rifle, refusing to pay for the gas. There, the appellate court affirmed the judgment of conviction based on the taking of the gasoline, upholding the jury's implicit finding that the defendant took the gasoline from the immediate presence of the attendant by means of force or fear.

Although these cases address the peaceful acquisition of property from the immediate presence of the victim, with force or fear arising only in an effort to carry the property away, subsequent authority establishes that the victim's presence after the taking is in progress is sufficient to establish the immediate presence element of a robbery charge. In *Estes*, a department store security guard saw the defendant shoplifting items of clothing inside the store and attempted to stop the defendant, who had left the store without paying for the items. The defendant pulled out a knife, swung it at the security guard and threatened to kill the guard.

The *Estes* court rejected the defendant's contention that the merchandise was not taken from the security guard's immediate presence, stating "[t]he evidence establishe[d] that [the defendant] forcibly resisted the security guard's efforts to retake the property and used that force to remove the items from the guard's immediate presence. By preventing the guard from regaining control over the merchandise, [the] defendant is held to have taken the property as if the guard had actual possession of the goods in the first instance." The *Estes* court also observed that a "[d]efendant's guilt is not to be weighed at each step of the robbery as it unfolds. The events constituting the crime of robbery, although they may extend over large distances and take some time to complete, are linked by a single-mindedness of purpose."

Miller and the dissent suggest that because the security guard in *Estes* observed the thief taking clothing from the store, the immediate presence element was otherwise satisfied in accordance with the standard set forth in *People v. Hayes*, *supra*, (to wit, that "[a] thing is in the [immediate] presence of a person, in respect to robbery, which is so within his reach, inspection, observation or control, that he could, if not overcome by violence or prevented by fear, retain his possession of it") and that the above-quoted language in *Estes* was merely dicta. We disagree. Although the *Estes* court could have found that the immediate presence element was satisfied based on the security guard's observation of the theft, the fact remains that it did not do so. Rather the court concluded that, as the use of force or fear only in carrying the stolen property away was sufficient to support a robbery charge, the victim's immediate presence during the asportation of the property was likewise sufficient. Courts and practitioners have widely accepted this analysis, such that robberies in which the victim only comes upon the defendant after the latter has gained possession of the stolen property are commonly referred to as "*Estes* robberies." * * *

Although the dissent credits us with "complet[ing] the transmogrification of the crime of robbery," in light of the widespread acceptance of the analysis of *Estes* and the fact that the California Supreme Court has not criticized or overruled *Estes* in the 20 years since that decision issued, we do not believe that our opinion expresses a change in the law, but instead reflects the current state of the law on the issue of what is sufficient to establish the immediate presence element of a robbery charge. We conclude from these authorities that, although the immediate presence and force or fear elements of robbery originally had to be satisfied at the time of the gaining possession aspect of a taking, the law has long since allowed these elements to be supplied after the defendant has initially gained possession of the victim's property.

Pursuant to the long-standing principles announced in *Estes*, Miller's use of force to retain the property after Higareda confronted him while he was attempting to get away with Higareda's money was sufficient to support the assertion of a robbery charge against him. In such circumstances, Higareda could reasonably "have expected to take effective steps to retain control over his property" and thus the immediate presence requirement is satisfied.

For the foregoing reasons, we conclude that the preliminary hearing evidence is sufficient to support the existence of a taking from Higareda's immediate presence and thus the trial court did not err in denying Miller's section 995 motion to dismiss the robbery charge against Miller. * * *

MCDONALD, J., dissenting.

The majority opinion completes the transmogrification of the crime of robbery from the offense defined in Penal Code section 211 as the "taking of personal property in the possession of another, from his person or immediate presence . . . , accomplished by means of force or fear" to the new offense of the taking or retaining personal property under those circumstances, a change accomplished by the court without legislative assistance.

Section 211 defines "robbery" as "the felonious taking of personal property in the possession of another, from his person or immediate presence, and against his will, accomplished by means of force or fear." The taking element of robbery itself has two necessary elements, gaining possession of the victim's property and asporting or carrying away the loot. However, *Cooper* further stated:

"Although the 'immediate presence' language comes directly from section 211, this language does not pertain to the duration of robbery.... Taking from the 'person' and from the 'immediate presence' [in section 211] are alternatives. These terms are spatially, rather than temporally, descriptive. They refer to the area from which the property is taken, not how far it is taken. [Citations.] Put another way, these limitations on the scope of the robbery statute relate to the 'gaining possession' component of the taking as distinct from the 'carrying away' component."

In *People v. Hayes*, the Supreme Court adopted the following definition of "immediate presence:" " '[a] thing is in the [immediate] presence of a person, in respect to robbery, which is so within his reach, inspection, observation or control, that he could, if not overcome by violence or prevented by fear, retain his possession of it.' "

"Immediate presence" means at least an area within which the victim could reasonably be expected to exercise some physical control over his or her property. Under the Supreme Court decisions in *Cooper*, *Hayes* and *Webster*, a necessary element of a section 211 robbery is the victim's presence in a location in which he or she could reasonably expect some physical control of the personal property at the time the perpetrator gained possession of the property. In this case, Higareda was not in that location; he was outside the public restroom at the time Miller gained possession of Higareda's trousers and the items contained in those trousers. An element of the charged robbery, as described by the Supreme Court, is absent in this case. Miller may have been guilty of burglary, assault, theft or other criminal offenses, but he was not guilty of robbery.

The majority opinion agrees that Miller did not gain possession of Higareda's personal property from either his person or from his immediate possession. It also concludes that Miller retained possession of Higareda's personal property in his immediate presence during the asportation phase of the incident, and that retention of the personal property during the asportation phase of the incident satisfied the taking "from the person or immediate presence" element of robbery.

The majority opinion's conclusion that the victim's presence during the asportation phase of the incident is sufficient to satisfy the elements of robbery is directly in conflict with language of the Supreme Court's opinion in *Cooper*. It seeks to obviate that conflict by describing the Supreme Court cases as representing the "traditional" view of robbery, which has evolved into a new and different rule creating a new and different offense known as an "*Estes* robbery." * * *

* * * The language from *Estes* quoted ante is effectively dicta because the guard was present and observed the defendant gain possession of the property; the defendant in *Estes* gained possession of the property in the guard's immediate presence under the *Hayes* test and *Estes* is factually

inapposite to this case. The court in *Estes* unnecessarily stated the element of "immediate presence" was satisfied retroactively by the defendant's use of force during the asportation phase of the incident after he gained possession of the property. To the extent *Estes* stated the element of immediate presence can be satisfied by a victim's presence during a defendant's asporting or carrying away of property, it is inconsistent with *Cooper*, which concluded immediate presence applies only to the gaining possession component and not to the asporting or carrying away component. *Estes* does not establish the immediate presence element was satisfied in this case. Rather, *Estes* under its facts, established only that the force or fear element of robbery could be satisfied if present during the asportation phase of the incident. * * *

The approval by *Cooper* of *Estes* was limited to the temporal aspect of the force or fear element of robbery and confirmed the holding of *Estes*, but not its dicta, that the force or fear element of robbery may be supplied by conduct during the asportation phase of the incident even if not present at the gaining possession phase of the incident. That is an *Estes* robbery. *Cooper* gave no approval to the language of *Estes*, which was unnecessary to its decision, that the immediate presence element of robbery could be satisfied during the asportation phase of the incident although not present at the gaining possession phase.

I do not agree with the majority opinion that the crime of robbery has evolved into a retention rather than a taking crime and, because bound by my understanding of *Cooper* and *Hayes*, I conclude the preliminary hearing evidence does not support a reasonable inference that the property was on Higareda's person or in his immediate presence at the time Miller gained possession of it. The trial court therefore erred by denying Miller's section 995 motion to dismiss the robbery charge against him. I would let a peremptory writ of prohibition issue restraining the San Diego County Superior Court from taking further action on the robbery charge against petitioner, other than to dismiss it.

NOTE

Where is the line between theft and robbery? *Rigell v. State*, 782 So.2d 440 (Fla. Dist. Ct. App. 2001), involved the following facts:

> [T]he victim and her husband were walking through a parking lot when the victim noticed a man ahead of them. After passing the man, the victim "felt two hands go on my shoulder bag—go on my purse, wrench downwards, a sharp pain in my right shoulder. My shoulder sort of gave way, and I screamed that he has got my bag." The purse strap broke. Although she felt pain, she had no physical injuries. She attempted to chase the assailant but fell to the ground.

Rigell, 782 So.2d 440, 441.

The defendant was convicted of robbery and appealed, arguing that there was insufficient evidence of force, a necessary element of robbery. The appellate court, however, affirmed the conviction, with the following explanation: "[T]he key distinction in determining the level of force necessary to distinguish theft from robbery is whether more force than was necessary to remove the property from the victim was used, or force enough to overcome victim resistance." 782 So.2d at 441.

CHAPTER 10

CRIMINAL LAW DEFENSES

■ ■ ■

INTRODUCTION

Criminal law defenses are traditionally divided into two categories: case-in-chief defenses (also known as failure of proof defenses or prima facie case defenses) and affirmative defenses. A case-in-chief defense is one in which the defendant attacks the prosecution's case in chief by arguing that the prosecutor has failed to meet its burden of proof on at least one essential element of the crime, such as the mens rea, the actus reus, causation, or concurrence. Since the government bears the burden of proving every element of the crime beyond a reasonable doubt, all the defendant has to do is raise a reasonable doubt as to the existence of one element to secure an acquittal. Unconsciousness and mistakes of fact, which we have already studied, are examples of case-in-chief defenses.

An affirmative defense is one in which the defendant admits that the government has met its burden of proof regarding its case in chief, but argues that he or she should be acquitted for some other reason. These "other reasons," when recognized by the law, are called affirmative defenses. The legislature can assign the burden of proving or disproving an affirmative defense to either the prosecution or the defense. Generally speaking, the legislature will make the defendant bear the burden of proving the requirements of an affirmative defense. The standard of proof necessary for a defendant to successfully carry off an affirmative defense can vary from defense to defense and jurisdiction to jurisdiction. Typically, however, the defendant must prove the elements of the affirmative defense by a preponderance of the evidence.[a]

Affirmative defenses are traditionally characterized as either justification defenses or excuse defenses.[b] A justification defense is one in which the defendant claims he did the right thing or took the most appropriate action under the circumstances. For example, self-defense is

---

[a] A legislature may require a higher standard of proof for a particular affirmative defense. For example, in *Leland v. Oregon*, 343 U.S. 790, 72 S.Ct. 1002, 96 L.Ed. 1302 (1952), the Supreme Court upheld Oregon's rule that a defendant bears the burden of proving the affirmative defense of insanity beyond a reasonable doubt.

[b] A third category of less common, crime-specific defenses also exists. For example, legal impossibility is recognized in some common law jurisdictions as a defense to the crime of attempt. Abandonment is recognized in some jurisdictions as a defense to the crime of attempt, and in some jurisdictions as a defense to the crime of conspiracy. We will study these crime-specific defenses in Chapters 11 (attempts) and 13 (conspiracy).

considered a justification defense. The defendant who claims self-defense argues that under the circumstances he did what society would have wanted him to do—kill his attacker rather than be killed himself. Justification defenses focus on the correctness or justness of the defendant's action.

Excuse defenses, in contrast, focus on the individual defendant and whether he is blameworthy or culpable. In other words, the defendant's act is presumed to have been wrongful, but the defendant asks us to excuse him for some other reason. For example, insanity is an excuse defense. The defendant who claims insanity admits that his act (e.g., killing an innocent person) was wrongful but asks for leniency on the ground that a defect in his mental condition prevented him from knowing right from wrong or being able to control his actions.

At early common law, the justification and excuse distinction was extremely important. A justification would result in a complete acquittal while an excuse defense could only help the capital defendant escape the death penalty. Today, the distinction is less critical because both justification and excuse defenses can lead to complete acquittals. Nonetheless, the justification-excuse distinction is still important in certain situations having to do with accomplice liability. For example, if a defendant is justified in violating the law, then that defendant's accomplices presumably are not guilty either, for there was no wrongdoing. Excuses, however, are considered personal to the actor. Therefore, if a defendant is acquitted on the basis of an excuse, her accomplices may still be found guilty of the crime. *See* JOSHUA DRESSLER, UNDERSTANDING CRIMINAL LAW § 17.05 [E] (6th ed. 2012).

Justification and excuse defenses, like substantive crimes, reflect their cultural context. The justification defenses, for instance, have emerged from a social consensus, influenced by the history and practices of Anglo-American culture, that in some situations breaking the law is more desirable than obeying the law. The excuse defenses, similarly, rest on culturally-shaped moral intuitions that some people are so lacking in personal responsibility that they should not be criminally punished. As you read these materials, consider whether the cultural bases for the justification and excuse defenses are solid. Are some defenses becoming obsolete? Should certain aspects of the existing law of defenses be updated? Should the law recognize new defenses to reflect changing social norms?

A. JUSTIFICATION DEFENSES

1. SELF-DEFENSE

Self-defense is usually considered a justification defense. When a defendant is successful at proving all the elements of a self-defense claim, her liability for the crime will be eliminated, and she will be acquitted. In some jurisdictions, even if the defendant is not able to convince the jury that all of the elements of self-defense were present, the defendant may be convicted of a lesser-included offense. This situation is referred to as imperfect self-defense and is discussed in more detail below.

A defendant claiming self-defense must have had an honest and reasonable belief that (1) he or she was threatened with an imminent threat of unlawful force, (2) the force he or she used was necessary to repel the threat, and (3) the force used was proportionate to the threatened force. In short, the defense of self-defense includes an imminence requirement, a necessity requirement, and a proportionality requirement. In addition to these requirements, the defendant must not have been the initial aggressor—that is, the one who started the affray.

The three requirements of imminence, necessity, and proportionality are not absolute requirements. The defendant does not have to be correct in her belief that force was necessary in order to defend against an imminent threat of unlawful force. Rather, the defendant can be acquitted as long as she *reasonably* believed in the need to act in self-defense, even if her belief was mistaken. Whether the defendant honestly and reasonably believed she was threatened with imminent unlawful force and whether the force the defendant used was reasonably necessary and proportional to the threat are questions for the fact-finder to decide. Trials involving self-defense, therefore, are highly fact-intensive, requiring both the prosecution and defense to present detailed and competing stories about what happened.

Trials involving self-defense also raise questions of cultural bias. For example, what constitutes a *reasonable* belief with respect to the threat of imminent, unlawful force? As we have seen in previous chapters, the answer may vary depending on whether certain characteristics of the defendant are factored into the reasonableness equation. The cases that follow examine whether the reasonableness requirement in self-defense doctrine reflects an objective or a subjective standard. These cases also allow us to revisit a question we encountered in our study of the doctrine of provocation: to what extent should the law employ a normative standard of reasonableness, and to what extent should it equate reasonableness with typicality?

PEOPLE V. GOETZ

Court of Appeals of New York

68 N.Y.2d 96, 497 N.E.2d 41, 506 N.Y.S.2d 18 (1986)

WACHTLER, C.J.

A Grand Jury has indicted defendant on attempted murder, assault, and other charges for having shot and wounded four youths on a New

York City subway train after one or two of the youths approached him and asked for $5. The lower courts, concluding that the prosecutor's charge to the Grand Jury on the defense of justification was erroneous, have dismissed the attempted murder, assault and weapons possession charges. We now reverse and reinstate all counts of the indictment.

I

The precise circumstances of the incident giving rise to the charges against defendant are disputed, and ultimately it will be for a trial jury to determine what occurred. We feel it necessary, however, to provide some factual background to properly frame the legal issues before us. Accordingly, we have summarized the facts as they appear from the evidence before the Grand Jury. We stress, however, that we do not purport to reach any conclusions or holding as to exactly what transpired or whether defendant is blameworthy. The credibility of witnesses and the reasonableness of defendant's conduct are to be resolved by the trial jury.

On Saturday afternoon, December 22, 1984, Troy Canty, Darryl Cabey, James Ramseur, and Barry Allen boarded an IRT express subway train in The Bronx and headed south toward lower Manhattan. The four youths[a] rode together in the rear portion of the seventh car of the train. Two of the four, Ramseur and Cabey, had screwdrivers inside their coats, which they said were to be used to break into the coin boxes of video machines.[b]

Defendant Bernhard Goetz boarded this subway train at 14th Street in Manhattan and sat down on a bench towards the rear section of the same car occupied by the four youths. Goetz was carrying an unlicensed

---

[a] Interestingly, the court omits mention of the fact that the four youths were Black and Goetz [the defendant] was White. This colorblind attitude was replicated at Goetz's trial to the detriment of the prosecution. Law professor George Fletcher, who sat through the trial, observed that race was never explicitly mentioned by either the prosecution or the defense, as if race was irrelevant. Instead, the defense covertly appealed to the Black-as-Criminal stereotype by referring to the four youths as "savages," "predators," and "vultures," terms which suggested that the teens were criminals and/or gang members preying on innocent law-abiding citizens like Goetz. Fletcher opines that "[t]he covert appeal to racial bias came out most dramatically in the recreation of the shooting, played out while Joseph Quirk was testifying. The defendant called in four props to stand in for the four victims Canty, Allen, Ramseur, and Cabey. The nominal purpose of the demonstration was to show the way in which each bullet entered the body of each victim. The defense's real purpose, however, was to recreate for the jury, as dramatically as possible, the scene that Goetz encountered when four young black passengers began to surround him. For that reason Barry Slotnick (Goetz's attorney) asked the Guardian Angels to send him the four young black men to act as the props in the demonstration. In came the four young black Guardian Angels, fit and muscular, dressed in T-shirts, to play the parts of the four victims in a courtroom minidrama." GEORGE P. FLETCHER, A CRIME OF SELF-DEFENSE: BERNHARD GOETZ AND THE LAW ON TRIAL 206–207 (1988).

[b] Some newspaper accounts of the shooting erroneously reported that the youths had threatened Goetz with sharpened screwdrivers. None of the youths, however, used screwdrivers to threaten Goetz. The two youths who did not approach Goetz had screwdrivers inside their jackets which they planned to use to break into the coin boxes on some video machines. GEORGE P. FLETCHER, A CRIME OF SELF–DEFENSE: BERNHARD GOETZ AND THE LAW ON TRIAL (1988).

.38 caliber pistol loaded with five rounds of ammunition in a waistband holster. The train left the 14th Street station and headed towards Chambers Street.

It appears from the evidence before the Grand Jury that Canty approached Goetz, possibly with Allen beside him, and stated "give me five dollars." Neither Canty nor any of the other youths displayed a weapon. Goetz responded by standing up, pulling out his handgun and firing four shots in rapid succession. The first shot hit Canty in the chest; the second struck Allen in the back; the third went through Ramseur's arm and into his left side; the fourth was fired at Cabey, who apparently was then standing in the corner of the car, but missed, deflecting instead off of a wall of the conductor's cab. After Goetz briefly surveyed the scene around him, he fired another shot at Cabey, who then was sitting on the end bench of the car. The bullet entered the rear of Cabey's side and severed his spinal cord.

All but two of the other passengers fled the car when, or immediately after, the shots were fired. The conductor, who had been in the next car, heard the shots and instructed the motorman to radio for emergency assistance. The conductor then went into the car where the shooting occurred and saw Goetz sitting on a bench, the injured youths lying on the floor or slumped against a seat, and two women who had apparently taken cover, also lying on the floor. Goetz told the conductor that the four youths had tried to rob him.

While the conductor was aiding the youths, Goetz headed towards the front of the car. The train had stopped just before the Chambers Street station and Goetz went between two of the cars, jumped onto the tracks and fled. Police and ambulance crews arrived at the scene shortly thereafter. Ramseur and Canty, initially listed in critical condition, have fully recovered. Cabey remains paralyzed, and has suffered some degree of brain damage.

On December 31, 1984, Goetz surrendered to police in Concord, New Hampshire, identifying himself as the gunman being sought for the subway shootings in New York nine days earlier. Later that day, after receiving *Miranda* warnings, he made two lengthy statements, both of which were tape recorded with his permission. In the statements, which are substantially similar, Goetz admitted that he had been illegally carrying a handgun in New York City for three years. He stated that he had first purchased a gun in 1981 after he had been injured in a mugging. Goetz also revealed that twice between 1981 and 1984 he had successfully warded off assailants simply by displaying the pistol.

According to Goetz's statement, the first contact he had with the four youths came when Canty, sitting or lying on the bench across from him, asked "how are you," to which he replied "fine." Shortly thereafter, Canty, followed by one of the other youths, walked over to the defendant and stood to his left, while the other two youths remained to his right, in the corner of the subway car. Canty then said "give me five dollars." Goetz stated that he knew from the smile on Canty's face that they wanted to "play with me." Although he was certain that none of the youths had a gun, he had a fear, based on prior experiences, of being "maimed."

Goetz then established "a pattern of fire," deciding specifically to fire from left to right. His stated intention at that point was to "murder [the four youths], to hurt them, to make them suffer as much as possible." When Canty again requested money, Goetz stood up, drew his weapon, and began firing, aiming for the center of the body of each of the four. Goetz recalled that the first two he shot "tried to run through the crowd [but] they had nowhere to run." Goetz then turned to his right to "go after the other two." One of these two "tried to run through the wall of the train, but * * * he had nowhere to go." The other youth (Cabey) "tried pretending that he wasn't with [the others]" by standing still, holding on to one of the subway hand straps, and not looking at Goetz. Goetz nonetheless fired his fourth shot at him. He then ran back to the first two youths to make sure they had been "taken care of." Seeing that they had both been shot, he spun back to check on the latter two. Goetz noticed that the youth who had been standing still was now sitting on a bench and seemed unhurt. As Goetz told the police, "I said '[you] seem to be all right, here's another,' " and he then fired the shot which severed Cabey's spinal cord. Goetz added that "if I was a little more under self-control * * * I would have put the barrel against his forehead and fired." He also admitted that "if I had had more [bullets], I would have shot them again, and again, and again." * * *

III

Penal Law article 35 recognizes the defense of justification, which "permits the use of force under certain circumstances." One such set of circumstances pertains to the use of force in defense of a person, encompassing both self-defense and defense of a third person. Penal Law § 35.15 (1) sets forth the general principles governing all such uses of force: "[a] person may * * * use physical force upon another person when and to the extent he *reasonably believes* such to be necessary to defend himself or a third person from what he *reasonably believes* to be the use or imminent use of unlawful physical force by such other person."

Section 35.15 (2) sets forth further limitations on these general principles with respect to the use of "deadly physical force": "A person may not use deadly physical force upon another person under circumstances specified in subdivision one unless (a) He *reasonably believes* that such other person is using or about to use deadly physical force * * * or (b) He *reasonably believes* that such other person is committing or attempting to commit a kidnapping, forcible rape, forcible sodomy or robbery."

Thus, consistent with most justification provisions, Penal Law § 35.15 permits the use of deadly physical force only where requirements as to triggering conditions and the necessity of a particular response are met. As to the triggering conditions, the statute requires that the actor "reasonably believes" that another person either is using or about to use deadly physical force or is committing or attempting to commit one of certain enumerated felonies, including robbery. As to the need for the use of deadly physical force as a response, the statute requires that the actor "reasonably believes" that such force is necessary to avert the perceived threat.

Because the evidence before the second Grand Jury included statements by Goetz that he acted to protect himself from being maimed or to avert a robbery, the prosecutor correctly chose to charge the justification defense in section 35.15 to the Grand Jury. The prosecutor properly instructed the grand jurors to consider whether the use of deadly physical force was justified to prevent either serious physical injury or a robbery, and, in doing so, to separately analyze the defense with respect to each of the charges. He elaborated upon the prerequisites for the use of deadly physical force essentially by reading or paraphrasing the language in Penal Law § 35.15. The defense does not contend that he committed any error in this portion of the charge.

When the prosecutor had completed his charge, one of the grand jurors asked for clarification of the term "reasonably believes." The prosecutor responded by instructing the grand jurors that they were to consider the circumstances of the incident and determine "whether the defendant's conduct was that of a reasonable man in the defendant's situation." It is this response by the prosecutor—and specifically his use of "a reasonable man"—which is the basis for the dismissal of the charges by the lower courts. As expressed repeatedly in the Appellate Division's plurality opinion, because section 35.15 uses the term "*he* reasonably believes," the appropriate test, according to that court, is whether a defendant's beliefs and reactions were "reasonable *to him*." Under that reading of the statute, a jury which believed a defendant's testimony that he felt that his own actions were warranted and were reasonable would have to acquit him, regardless of what anyone else in defendant's situation might have concluded. Such an interpretation defies the ordinary meaning and significance of the term "reasonably" in a statute, and misconstrues the clear intent of the Legislature, in enacting section 35.15, to retain an objective element as part of any provision authorizing the use of deadly physical force.

Penal statutes in New York have long codified the right recognized at common law to use deadly physical force, under appropriate circumstances, in self-defense. These provisions have never required that an actor's belief as to the intention of another person to inflict serious injury be correct in order for the use of deadly force to be justified, but they have uniformly required that the belief comport with an objective notion of reasonableness. * * *

Had the drafters of section 35.15 wanted to adopt a subjective standard, they could have simply used the language of [Model Penal Code] section 3.04 [which omits "any requirement of reasonableness"]. "Believes" by itself requires an honest or genuine belief by a defendant as to the need to use deadly force. Interpreting the statute to require only that the defendant's belief was "reasonable to *him*," as done by the plurality below, would hardly be different from requiring only a genuine belief; in either case, the defendant's own perceptions could completely exonerate him from any criminal liability.

We cannot lightly impute to the Legislature an intent to fundamentally alter the principles of justification to allow the perpetrator of a serious crime to go free simply because that person believed his actions were reasonable and necessary to prevent some perceived harm. To completely exonerate such an individual, no matter how aberrational or bizarre his thought patterns, would allow citizens to set their own standards for the permissible use of force. It would also allow a legally competent defendant suffering from delusions to kill or perform acts of violence with impunity, contrary to fundamental principles of justice and criminal law.

We can only conclude that the Legislature retained a reasonableness requirement to avoid giving a license for such actions. * * * Statutes or rules of law requiring a person to act "reasonably" or to have a "reasonable belief" uniformly prescribe conduct meeting an objective standard measured with reference to how "a reasonable person" could have acted. * * *

Goetz also argues that the introduction of an objective element will preclude a jury from considering factors such as the prior experiences of a given actor and thus, require it to make a determination of "reasonableness" without regard to the actual circumstances of a particular incident. This argument, however, falsely presupposes that an objective standard means that the background and other relevant characteristics of a particular actor must be ignored. To the contrary, we have frequently noted that a determination of reasonableness must be based on the "circumstances" facing a defendant or his "situation." Such terms encompass more than the physical movements of the potential assailant. As just discussed, these terms include any relevant knowledge the defendant had about that person. They also necessarily bring in the physical attributes of all persons involved, including the defendant. Furthermore, the defendant's circumstances encompass any prior experiences he had which could provide a reasonable basis for a belief that another person's intentions were to injure or rob him or that the use of deadly force was necessary under the circumstances.

Accordingly, a jury should be instructed to consider this type of evidence in weighing the defendant's actions. * * * The jury would have to determine, in light of all the "circumstances," as explicated above, if a reasonable person could have had these beliefs.

The prosecutor's instruction to the second Grand Jury that it had to determine whether, under the circumstances, Goetz's conduct was that of a reasonable man in his situation was thus essentially an accurate charge. * * *

Accordingly, the order of the Appellate Division should be reversed, and the dismissed counts of the indictment reinstated.

NOTE

At his subsequent criminal trial, Goetz claimed he acted in self-defense when he shot the four youths. He was found not guilty by a predominantly White jury on all counts except for the illegal possession of a handgun charge. GEORGE P. FLETCHER, A CRIME OF SELF-DEFENSE: BERNHARD GOETZ AND THE LAW ON TRIAL (U. of Chicago Press 1988).

Nine years later, Goetz was tried in a civil action brought by Darryl Cabey, the youth who was paralyzed after Goetz shot him in the spine. An all-minority six person civil jury found Goetz liable to Cabey, and ordered Goetz to pay Cabey $43 million in damages. Adam Nossiter, *Bronx Jury Orders Goetz to Pay Man He Paralyzed $43 Million*, N.Y. TIMES, Apr. 24, 1996; Joseph A. Kirby, *"Subway Vigilante" Case in Final Stage,* CHI. TRIB., Apr. 23, 1996, at 4. In 2000, the New York Times reported that Cabey still had not received any part of this $43 million judgment from Goetz, who subsequently filed for bankruptcy. Tina Kelley, *Following Up; Still Seeking Payment from Bernard Goetz*, N.Y. TIMES, Sept. 10, 2000, *available at* http://topics.nytimes.com/top/reference/timestopics/people/c/darrell_cabey/ (last visited Dec. 3, 2013).

Goetz ran for mayor of New York City in 2001, referring to himself on his campaign website, as "well known on crime issues." Jennifer Steinhauer, *Undaunted by Their Slim Prospects, Outsiders Crowd Mayoral Race*, N.Y. TIMES, Aug. 28, 2001, *available at* http://www.nytimes.com/2001/08/28/nyregion/undaunted-by-their-slim-prospects-outsiders-crowd-mayoral-race.html?pagewanted=all & src=pm (last visited Dec. 4, 2013) (noting that few of the outsider candidates for mayor hoped to win, except Mr. Goetz). In 2013, Goetz was arrested after trying to sell $30 worth of marijuana to an undercover police officer. Michael Schwirtz, *Bernard Goetz, Man in '84 Subway Shooting, Faces Marijuana Charges*, N.Y. TIMES, Nov. 2, 2013, *available at* http://www.nytimes.com/2013/11/03/nyregion/bernard-goetz-man-in–84–subway-shooting-faces-marijuana-charges.html?ref=bernhardhgoetz & _r=0 (last visited Dec. 4, 2013).

STATE V. SIMON

Supreme Court of Kansas
231 Kan. 572, 646 P.2d 1119 (1982)

MCFARLAND, J.

* * *

The issue presented in this appeal is whether the statutory justification for the use of deadly force in defense of a person contained in K.S.A. 21–3211 is to be determined by the trier of fact using a subjective standard (from the viewpoint of the accused's state of mind) or by using an objective standard (from the viewpoint of a reasonable man in the accused's position).

The instruction given herein on self-defense was PIK Crim. 54.17 as follows:

> A person is justified in the use of force to defend himself against an aggressor's imminent use of unlawful force to the extent it *appears reasonable to him* under the circumstances then existing.

The statutory authority for any instruction relative to use of force in defense of a person is K.S.A. 21–3211 which provides:

> A person is justified in the use of force against an aggressor when and to the extent it appears to him and *he reasonably believes* that such conduct is necessary to defend himself or another against such aggressor's imminent use of unlawful force.

The Judicial Council Comments to K.S.A. 21–3211 provide in relevant part:

> The section defines the right to defend one's person against unlawful aggression. It attempts to define the phrase 'reasonably believes.' A reasonable belief implies both a belief and the existence of facts that would persuade a reasonable man to that belief.

* * *

The State contends K.S.A. 21–3211 requires the trier of fact to determine the reasonableness of the accused's actions by an objective rather than a subjective standard. The State further contends PIK Crim. 54.17 improperly instructs the jury to utilize a subjective standard in determining the reasonableness of the accused's actions. We agree with both contentions.

We note that of all the times self-defense instructions have been involved in appeals before us, this is the first time this precise issue has been raised. * * *

Defendant is an elderly homeowner in Wichita. Steffen Wong, a young man of Oriental extraction, rented half of the duplex next door. By virtue of Mr. Wong's racial heritage, defendant assumed he was an expert in the martial arts.[a] Defendant was afraid of Steffen Wong, and heated words had been exchanged between the two. Defendant was fearful because more "Orientals" were moving into the neighborhood, and one had expressed interest in purchasing defendant's home.

On May 27, 1981, Mr. Wong was fired upon as he attempted to enter his own duplex. Shortly thereafter Rickey and Brenda Douglas, the residents of the other half of the duplex, pulled into their driveway and were fired upon by the defendant. Police officers arrived a few minutes later and defendant fired a number of shots at the officers who had previously identified themselves. Defendant was charged with two counts of aggravated assault for firing at Steffen Wong and Rickey Douglas. At trial defendant testified as to his general fear of Mr. Wong and that Mr. Wong had walked toward him cursing just before the incident started. The defense called a clinical psychologist who testified defendant was a "psychological invalid" who was very tense and fearful. The psychologist stated defendant's mental condition permitted him to "misjudge reality" and see himself under attack. The tentative diagnosis was "anxiety neurosis."

The jury was instructed:

> A person is justified in the use of force to defend himself against an aggressor's imminent use of unlawful force to the extent it appears reasonable to him under the circumstances then existing.

Defense counsel argued to the jury that the evidence showed defendant believed Mr. Wong was an imminent threat to him and that the firing of the gun appeared reasonable to the defendant. The jury acquitted defendant on both counts. Under the totality of the circumstances, one must assume the acquittals were occasioned in large measure by the improper instruction on self-defense.

We hereby disapprove the giving of PIK Crim. 54.17 as being an incorrect statement of the law of Kansas as set forth in K.S.A. 21–3211. * * * We conclude that the jury should properly have been instructed in the following language or its equivalent:

> A person is justified in the use of force against an aggressor when and to the extent it appears to him and he reasonably believes that such conduct is necessary to defend himself or

---

[a] It appears that Mr. Simon was relying on the Asian-as-Martial Artist Stereotype which links Asians to proficiency in Karate, Kung Fu, Tae Kwando, or some other martial art form from Asia. *See* Cynthia Lee, MURDER AND THE REASONABLE MAN: PASSION AND FEAR IN THE CRIMINAL COURTROOM (NYU Press 2003); Cynthia Kwei Yung Lee, *Race and Self-Defense: Toward a Normative Conception of Reasonableness*, 81 MINN. L. REV. 367, 438 (1996).

> another against such aggressor's imminent use of unlawful force. A reasonable belief implies both a belief and the existence of facts that would persuade a reasonable man to that belief.

This instruction combines the language of K.S.A. 21–3211 with the necessary definition set forth in the Judicial Council Comments following the statute, and results in setting forth the requisite objective standard.

The appeal is sustained.

MURDER AND THE REASONABLE MAN: PASSION AND FEAR IN THE CRIMINAL COURTROOM

Cynthia Lee, 2003[a]

THE ASIAN-AS-FOREIGNER STEREOTYPE

> Fear of the foreigner is sometimes a black streak that runs through America's political culture. We see instances of [this] when it involves hate crimes, not necessarily directed at black Americans, but at foreign Americans.
>
> —Mike McCurry, Former White House Press Secretary to President Bill Clinton

Even though it is oxymoronic to speak of "foreign" "Americans," the term "foreign Americans" conveys meaning. Asians and Latinos are usually considered foreign Americans. A person who asks an Asian American, "So, where are you from?" usually expects to hear, "I'm from Japan," or "I'm from China," or "I'm from Vietnam." If one answers, "I'm from Houston," or "I'm from New York," one is likely to be asked, "No, I mean, where are your parents from?" Even if true, it won't do to say, "My parents were also born in Houston," because the speaker is interested in finding out which foreign country the Asian person is from, even if she isn't from a foreign country.

The focus on the Asian in Asian American is deep-rooted. During World War II, when the United States was at war with Japan, hostility toward Japan extended to all persons of Japanese ancestry, even Japanese Americans born and raised in the United States for several generations. From 1942 to 1945, all persons of Japanese descent were forced to leave their homes and were incarcerated in internment camps because the American government viewed them as a potential threat.

In times of economic uncertainty, resentment and violence against Asian Americans seem to increase as individuals vent their frustrations on model-minority Asian Americans who are perceived as stealing valuable job opportunities from "real" Americans. Because many individuals can't tell Americans of Asian descent apart from Asian

---

[a] Reprinted with permission from NYU Press.

nationals, Asian Americans are mistaken for Asian nationals and then blamed for foreign imports that threaten domestic goods, such as American cars. In the film, *Who Killed Vincent Chin?* filmmakers Renee Tajima and Christine Choy illustrate the association between Asians and foreign car imports by juxtaposing the image of angry White[b] American autoworkers and their friends taking turns swinging a baseball bat as hard as possible at a Japanese economy car with the actual baseball bat beating of Vincent Chin, a Chinese American man who was mistaken for a Japanese. Around the time of Chin's death, a Detroit radio station hosted "Toyota parties," encouraging people to demolish Japanese autos with a sledgehammer, and a car dealership in Detroit ran television commercials that showed a battle tank crushing a Japanese car.

The Asian-as-Foreigner stereotype continues today, although it often takes more subtle forms. During the O.J. Simpson trial, for example, much of the racial joking that arose in connection with the case was directed at two prominent Asian Americans, the presiding judge, Lance Ito, and the criminalist, Dennis Fung. Ito and Fung, both of whom speak English without a noticeable accent, were portrayed by radio station disk jockeys, publishing houses, and even a United States senator as bumbling, heavily accented Asians who could barely speak English. The 1996 campaign finance scandal involving Johnny Huang and the Democratic National Party and the December 1999 arrest of scientist Wen Ho Lee on charges of illegally downloading nuclear secrets raised the specter of the evil Asian foreigner again, prompting Neil Gotanda to opine that "The Wen Ho Lee case and the campaign finance scandals are the most serious threat to Asian Pacific Americans since the end of the Vietnam war."

Another example of the Asian-as-Foreigner stereotype at work is reflected in crimes of violence against Asians and Asian Americans. Jerry Kang has noted that Asian and Asian Americans are often targeted by muggers who assume that all Asians carry a lot of cash. The fact that some individuals from certain Asian countries do carry a lot of cash contributes to this type of targeting. A mugger who sees someone who looks Asian is not likely to know whether the person was born and raised in the United States or is from another country, and is not likely to ask. The problem is compounded by stereotypes about Asians as "physically weak and culturally adverse to defending themselves."

The Asian-as-Foreigner stereotype is complicated by the fact that approximately two-thirds of all Asians in the United States are foreigners. Frank Wu cautions us not to use this statistical information to "justify the assumption that everyone with an Asian name is a guest or a

[b] The author purposely capitalizes the "W" in "White" to draw attention to the fact that Whiteness is a socially constructed racial category.

tourist," because such an assumption "leads to implications that the Asians are enjoying their sojourn and will ultimately return elsewhere."

Because of the constant conflation of Asian nationals and Asian Americans, symptomatic of the Asian-as-Foreigner stereotype, the tragic shooting of Yoshihiro Hattori, a Japanese foreign exchange student, has special significance for Asian Americans. Hattori died after being shot by a Louisiana homeowner who claimed he shot the unarmed Japanese teenager in self-defense.

> October 17, 1992. Two sixteen-year-old high school students, Webb Haymaker and Yoshihiro Hattori, were looking for a Halloween party in the suburbs of Baton Rouge, Louisiana, when they came across the home of Rodney and Bonnie Peairs. The home was decorated for Halloween, and was just a few doors away from the correct house. Hattori was a Japanese foreign exchange student, and Haymaker was a member of his host family. Haymaker was dressed as a car accident victim. Hattori was dressed as the character played by John Travolta in the movie "Saturday Night Fever." He wore a white tuxedo jacket and carried a small black camera. The boys rang the front doorbell. No one answered the door, but the boys heard the clinking of window blinds coming from the carport area. The boys walked around the house to the carport, Haymaker leading the way. A moment later, Bonnie Peairs opened the back door leading out to the carport. She saw Haymaker, who started to say, "We're here for the party." Then Hattori came around the corner. When Bonnie Peairs saw Hattori, she emitted a scream, slammed the door, and called for her husband to "get the gun." Without asking any questions, Rodney Peairs ran to the bedroom and grabbed a laser-scoped .44 magnum Smith and Wesson, one of a number of guns he owned.
>
> The two boys had walked away from the house and were on the sidewalk about ten yards from the house when Peairs rushed out of the house from the back door and into the carport area. The carport light and a street light in front of the house illuminated the carport and the sidewalk area. Hattori turned and approached Peairs, smiling and explaining in his broken English, "We are here for the party." Rather than telling Hattori that he had the wrong house, Peairs pointed his laser-scoped gun at Hattori and shouted, "Freeze." Hattori, who was from Japan, a country where firearms are prohibited, had never learned the English word "Freeze," so he continued to approach Peairs. Without waiting a second longer, Peairs fired one shot at Hattori's chest. Hattori collapsed and died on the spot. The entire incident—from the time Peairs opened his back door to

the time he fired his gun—took place in approximately three seconds.

Peairs was charged with manslaughter. At trial, Peairs asserted that he shot Hattori in self-defense. He claimed that Hattori was skipping or walking very fast toward him and looked very scary. Peairs said Hattori, the slight teenage boy, looked like a crazy man. When Hattori did not stop after Peairs shouted at him to freeze, Peairs claimed he was terrified and thought his life was in danger. Although Hattori was carrying a camera, Peairs did not claim that he thought the camera was a gun. In fact, Peairs later admitted, during the course of the civil wrongful death action filed by Hattori's parents, that he did not see a gun, knife, stick, or club in Hattori's hand that night.

The judge instructed the jury that in order to acquit Peairs, they had to find that Peairs *reasonably* believed he was imminent danger of losing his life or receiving great bodily harm and that the killing was necessary to save Peairs from the danger. After little more than three hours of deliberation, the jury found Peairs not guilty of manslaughter. Spectators in the courtroom applauded the verdict. In contrast to the public outrage over the short deliberation process in the *O.J. Simpson* case, in which jurors reached a verdict of acquittal in less than four hours, there was little public outrage over the shortness of deliberation time leading to Peairs' acquittal. In fact, the residents of the town of Baton Rouge felt so strongly that Peairs was justified in shooting Hattori that they loudly objected to plans to erect a memorial in honor of Hattori.

The key question in the *Peairs* case was whether it was *reasonable* for Peairs to believe (1) that he was in imminent danger of death or great bodily harm, and (2) that it was necessary to shoot Hattori to protect himself from such imminent death or great bodily harm. Reasonable minds can certainly disagree on this question. On the one hand, Peairs had pointed a gun at Hattori and shouted at him to freeze. Hattori kept approaching. Arguably, the average Louisiana homeowner in Peairs' situation could have thought Hattori posed a very real threat of death or great bodily injury. If Hattori wouldn't stop after being warned to stop, there was nothing left to do but shoot. Additionally, this shooting took place in Louisiana. * * * [P]lace (i.e., geographic location) has some influence over whether the use of deadly force is seen as reasonable. Studies have shown that men in Southern states are more prone to perceive nonthreatening insults as a threat to their honor and more prone to respond violently to threats of a nondeadly nature.

On the other hand, Peairs could have completely avoided the shooting tragedy by retreating into his house and locking the door. Once inside, Peairs could have called the police. There was little reason to think Hattori would try to follow Peairs inside the house and force the door open. Recall that by the time Peairs came outside with his gun, the two boys were already on the sidewalk, leaving the premises. They were not hanging around near the back door, waiting for someone to open it so they could enter. Moreover, Peairs did not have to go outside in the first place. When his wife screamed at him to get the gun, Peairs could have asked her why she was screaming. He could have quickly locked the doors and called the police. In fact, if Hattori and Haymaker had been robbers, it would have been much safer for Peairs to lock the doors right away (to prevent entry into the home), rather than rushing to get a gun. Any of these less fatal measures would have avoided the imagined danger poised by Hattori.

How did the Asian-as-Foreigner stereotype influence the verdict in this case? The fact that Hattori was in fact a foreigner, a Japanese citizen and not an American, simply made it easier for the Baton Rouge jury to empathize with Peairs. They could picture themselves in Peair's shoes. If an Asian teenager came onto their property and refused to freeze even with a gun pointed at his chest, that teenager was asking to be shot. Bonnie Peair's trial testimony is very revealing in this regard. When asked to describe Hattori, she responded, "I guess he appeared Oriental. He could have been Mexican or whatever." Mrs. Peairs was unable to tell whether Hattori was Asian or Mexican or neither. All she knew was that Hattori was different. He wasn't White like her.

Because of Hattori's nationality, the jurors couldn't see Hattori as one of their own sons. If Webb Haymaker, the boy from the neighborhood, had been the victim in this case, Peairs would have found it difficult to persuade the jury that he was terrified for his life and thought the boy looked like a crazy man. It would have been difficult for the defense to paint a credible picture of the victim as the bad guy. If Haymaker had been shot and killed, it is unlikely that the spectators in the courtroom would have applauded the not guilty verdict. Haymaker's parents and his siblings would have been in the courtroom, reminding the other members of that Baton Rouge community that the dead boy could have been their son. But it was a teenager from Japan who was shot and killed, and the sight of his grieving parents in the courtroom only served to remind the jurors that the victim was not one of the community's own. * * *

NOTE

The necessity requirement in self-defense doctrine suggests that the force the defendant used must have been reasonably necessary to thwart an imminent unlawful attack. If the defendant could have avoided the threatened force, then it is difficult to say that his use of force was really necessary. This raises the question of whether a person claiming self-defense has a duty to retreat. If the defendant could have retreated from the conflict instead of using force, one could argue that the defendant's use of force was not truly necessary.

At common law in England, an individual had a duty to retreat to the wall before using deadly force in self-defense. Many American states also impose a duty to retreat before an individual can justifiably use deadly force in self-defense, provided a safe retreat is available and known to the individual. However, even in states that require retreat, under what is known as the Castle Doctrine, one is not required to retreat before using deadly force if one is attacked in one's home. Some jurisdictions have extended the Castle Doctrine beyond the home to cover attacks when one is in one's car or workplace.

Before 2005, Florida was one of the states that required individuals to retreat before using deadly force in self-defense, except if they were attacked in their home. The next case, *Jenkins v. State,* examines the duty to retreat rule that applied in Florida before 2005.

JENKINS V. STATE

Florida Court of Appeals
942 So.2d 910 (Fla. App. 2006)

ALTENBERND, JUDGE.

Melvin Stacy Jenkins appeals his judgment and sentence for manslaughter. We conclude that Mr. Jenkins established his claim of self-defense and that the State failed to present legally sufficient evidence to overcome that defense. Accordingly, we reverse the judgment.

Mr. Jenkins is a forty-two-year-old roofer who lived in a run-down mobile home park in Hillsborough County. He and his family rented two small trailers that were divided by a narrow driveway between them. He lived in one trailer, and his wife, his daughter, and his son lived in the other. Mr. Jenkins was charged with manslaughter with a deadly weapon, arising out of an altercation with twenty-five-year-old Bryan Cerezo that occurred just outside of Mr. Jenkins' trailers. The altercation ended when Mr. Jenkins inflicted a single, fatal stab wound to Mr. Cerezo.

At trial, the State presented the evidence of three witnesses to this event, all of whom were neighboring residents in the same trailer park and were unrelated to Mr. Jenkins. * * * Much of the evidence presented by Mr. Jenkins and the State's witnesses was undisputed, although each witness provided a different perspective of the events.

On March 19, 2004, just before 3 p.m., Mr. Jenkins was in his trailer when his teenage daughter arrived and told him that she had just had a disagreement with a woman at a nearby apartment complex. The nature of this disagreement was never developed at trial. At about this same time, Mr. Jenkins heard someone banging on the door to his wife's trailer. The person banging on the door was Bryan Cerezo. Mr. Jenkins had never met Mr. Cerezo prior to this day, but apparently he learned from his daughter that this was the boyfriend of the woman involved in the disagreement.

Mr. Jenkins called out to Mr. Cerezo and told him that no one was home and that he should quit banging on the door and leave. Mr. Cerezo claimed he was looking for Mr. Jenkins' son and refused to leave, even though Mr. Jenkins asked him repeatedly to do so. Mr. Jenkins was preparing to go to work and had his six-inch sheath knife on his belt. Mr. Jenkins testified, and one of the State's witnesses confirmed, that Mr. Jenkins typically carried this knife on his belt for use in his work. His remaining roofing tools were located by the door.

While he was speaking to Mr. Cerezo, Mr. Jenkins came out of his trailer holding his hammer.[1] Mr. Cerezo continued to verbally confront Mr. Jenkins. The confrontation was loud enough to attract the attention of the three witnesses who testified for the State. These witnesses described Mr. Cerezo as "furious" and "a wild man." Mr. Jenkins testified that Mr. Cerezo was acting like "a lunatic."[2] One eyewitness indicated that Mr. Cerezo looked larger and stronger than Mr. Jenkins.[3] Mr. Cerezo claimed that he was a gang member and that he would come back to the mobile home park with "20 guns and silencers and kill everybody." One of the witnesses testified he heard Mr. Cerezo yelling, "I'm going to kill you. You're a dead man." Another witness heard Mr. Cerezo threaten to burn down Mr. Jenkins' trailer. This latter witness "thought" he heard Mr. Jenkins reply, "Come on." Mr. Jenkins testified that he told Mr. Cerezo "to take his gang banging ass out of there."

Mr. Cerezo told Mr. Jenkins to throw down the hammer and fight like a man. This statement was heard by one of the State's witnesses who saw Mr. Jenkins toss his hammer to the side. At this point, the two men were apparently on the edge or in the common driveway that essentially served as the street for the row of very small trailer lots.[4] According to Mr. Jenkins, he told Mr. Cerezo, "I didn't come down here to fight." Mr. Jenkins testified that Mr. Cerezo took a couple of steps as if he was going to leave and then "just ran right back to me and just blasted me on the side of my head." One witness described this punch as a left-handed one. Another witness saw Mr. Cerezo land this punch. Both of these witnesses saw the resulting cut to the left side of Mr. Jenkins' face, which began to bleed down his face. One of the State's witnesses testified that Mr.

---

1 Once Mr. Jenkins exited his trailer, it is unclear whether his daughter remained inside the trailer with him or whether she too was outside and witnessed the altercation.

2 A toxicology report performed on Mr. Cerezo after his death revealed that he was mildly intoxicated. There was, however, no other evidence that might have explained why Mr. Cerezo was acting the way the witnesses described.

3 The medical examiner testified that the victim was 5 feet 9 inches tall and weighed 157 pounds.

4 Although described in the testimony as a common "driveway," the aerial photographs of this area reveal a dirt road through and around the trailers in this area, not a road that terminates at one end.

Jenkins "just wobbled. His legs wobbled and he just stood there." Another said that Mr. Jenkins did not fall down, but his knees "buckled." One witness saw Mr. Jenkins step back. Mr. Cerezo also backed up after landing this punch.

Mr. Jenkins took out his sheath knife. Only one of the State's witnesses saw the knife, and this witness testified that Mr. Jenkins "showed [Mr. Cerezo] the knife." Mr. Jenkins and one of the other witnesses testified that Mr. Cerezo pulled his shirt open and pulled his arm back behind his body where Mr. Jenkins could not see it. According to Mr. Jenkins, Mr. Cerezo claimed that he had "a Glock" with which he was going to "cap" Mr. Jenkins. Mr. Cerezo then clenched his fist and charged at Mr. Jenkins again. Mr. Jenkins' knife entered the left side of Mr. Cerezo's chest, consistent with Mr. Jenkins raising it with his right hand into a defensive position in response to a left-handed punch. The only witness to actually see the stabbing testified that Mr. Jenkins did not swing the knife, but instead the knife appeared to "kick out" in reaction to the second punch.

Mr. Cerezo backed up, walked a short distance away, collapsed, and died. At this point, one of the witnesses called 911. The medical examiner confirmed that Mr. Cerezo died from a single knife wound that caused fatal injuries to his heart and liver. The six-inch wound was essentially level, with no apparent twisting, and primarily from the left side to the right without a hilt bruise, suggesting that the knife entered the body from a right-handed motion without enough force to thrust the hilt against or into the body.

When Mr. Cerezo collapsed, Mr. Jenkins approached one of the neighbors who had witnessed the event. He told the neighbor that he did not mean to stab Mr. Cerezo—he had intended only to "nick" him. Mr. Jenkins fled from the scene but turned himself in several days later when he knew that a warrant was outstanding.

The State presented several diagrams and witnesses to establish that the fight took place in the common driveway and not on "the premises" of either of the two trailer lots rented by the Jenkins family. The State also explored with the witnesses whether Mr. Jenkins might have been able to escape from the confrontation before acting in self-defense. The first witness was asked whether he saw Mr. Jenkins "walk away after the victim punched him," and responded, "He backed up, but the guy gave him another punch." This witness testified that Mr. Jenkins never took a step toward Mr. Cerezo. Another witness testified that Mr. Jenkins might have been able to retreat a couple of feet, but he did not get a chance to because Mr. Cerezo "[came] at him too fast." The prosecutor asked Mr. Jenkins if anyone stopped him from walking away after the first punch, and Mr. Jenkins replied, "Where was I going to walk to?"

Mr. Jenkins made a motion for judgment of acquittal at the end of the State's case and renewed the motion after he presented his defense. The jury was then instructed on the charge of manslaughter with a weapon and other lesser-included charges. The jury received instructions on self-defense. Because there was some question as to where this altercation occurred and whether that location would qualify as the curtilage of Mr. Jenkins' residence, the jury heard instructions on self-defense in general as well as self-defense for situations occurring in a defendant's home.

The jury deliberated more than six hours and asked questions along the way. Ultimately, they found Mr. Jenkins guilty of the lesser offense of manslaughter without a weapon, an apparent partial jury pardon. Mr. Jenkins was sentenced as a habitual offender to twenty-five years' imprisonment, followed by five years' probation.

Pursuant to section 776.012, Florida Statutes (2004), a "person is justified in the use of deadly force only if he or she reasonably believes that such force is necessary to prevent imminent death or great bodily harm to himself or herself or another or to prevent the imminent commission of a forcible felony." A person under attack has a duty to "retreat to the wall" before taking a life; the person must have used all reasonable means in his power, consistent with his own safety, to avoid the danger and to avert the necessity of taking human life.

When a person is attacked within his or her own home, however, a different standard applies.

> [W]hen a person is in his own home and he or the members of his family are assaulted or placed in apparent imminent danger of great personal injury, he has the right to stand his ground and meet force with force, even to the extent of taking life if he actually believes, and the circumstances and surrounding conditions are such that a reasonably cautious and prudent person would believe, danger of death or great personal injury to be imminent, at the hands of [the] assailant.

Harris v. State. In some cases, this "castle doctrine" is described as follows: [W]hen one is violently assaulted in his own house *or immediately surrounding premises,* he is not obliged to retreat. (emphasis added).

While the defendant may have the burden of going forward with evidence of self-defense, the burden of proving guilt beyond a reasonable doubt never shifts from the State, and this standard broadly includes the requirement that the State prove beyond a reasonable doubt that the defendant did not act in self-defense. If a defendant establishes a prima facie case of self-defense, the State must overcome the defense by rebuttal, or by inference in its case-in-chief. If the State fails to sustain this burden of proof, the trial court is duty-bound to grant a judgment of acquittal in favor of the defendant. Here, the State did not present evidence sufficient to overcome Mr. Jenkins' claim of self-defense; in fact, the testimony of the State's witnesses supported that defense.

We have struggled with this case nearly as hard as the jury struggled. If Mr. Jenkins had stayed inside his trailer or had returned to his trailer when Mr. Cerezo suggested that he throw down his hammer and fight like a man, and perhaps called the police, it is unlikely that Mr. Cerezo would have died. On the other hand, Mr. Cerezo refused to leave Mr. Jenkins' property and was loudly threatening Mr. Jenkins and his family. Mr. Jenkins' teenage daughter was nearby, and numerous people were apparently watching the altercation but offered no assistance.

Mr. Jenkins was not required to cower in his trailer while Mr. Cerezo threatened him and his family and tried to enter the trailer of Mr. Jenkins' wife and children. Mr. Jenkins was within his right to exit his trailer, stand on the common driveway of the neighboring trailers, and demand that Mr. Cerezo leave. Indeed, defusing such a situation without calling the police may have seemed wise in light of Mr. Cerezo's threats to return with gang members and burn down Mr. Jenkins' trailer or otherwise kill him and his family.

Thus, the issue of self-defense in this case did not arise at the beginning of the verbal confrontation because at that point Mr. Jenkins was not faced with the use of force. This was implicitly acknowledged by the prosecutor, whose questions of retreat focused on the brief moment in time after Mr. Cerezo landed the first punch and drew back. There was no dispute that at this point Mr. Jenkins reasonably believed he was at risk of great bodily harm. Mr. Cerezo had landed a left-handed punch to Mr. Jenkins' face, causing a gash below his eye. Mr. Jenkins "wobbled" from the impact. Nevertheless, Mr. Cerezo pulled back, continued to threaten to kill Mr. Jenkins, and prepared to charge Mr. Jenkins a second time. Even if the jury rejected Mr. Jenkins' testimony that Mr. Cerezo threatened to shoot him with a firearm, the State's witnesses all confirmed that Mr. Cerezo threatened to kill Mr. Jenkins and that he attacked Mr. Jenkins, cutting his face with the first punch.

Further, it was only upon the occurrence of this attack that any "duty to retreat" arose. The State failed to present evidence, however, that Mr. Jenkins could have reasonably retreated from this fight once it began. The State's witnesses testified that during this brief moment in time, there was no reasonable opportunity to retreat. Rather, the eyewitnesses saw [that] Mr. Jenkins "wobbled" and his knees "buckled," and testified that Mr. Jenkins had no time to retreat before Mr. Cerezo charged at him a second time.[6] It was only at this point—faced with a serious aggressor

[6] We are inclined to believe that the State's presentation on the location of the fight, whether on or off the Jenkins' property, was probably a distraction that may have confused the jury. The jury may have been left with the impression that it was required to convict Mr. Jenkins

and no avenue of retreat—that Mr. Jenkins pulled out his knife. Even then, there was no evidence that Mr. Jenkins did anything other than "show" Mr. Cerezo the knife until he was faced with a second attack by Mr. Cerezo. * * *

* * * The State's witnesses uniformly identified the victim as the aggressor who invited the fight and threw the first punch. The witnesses stated that Mr. Jenkins never moved toward the victim and was instead rushed by the victim and did not have time to retreat. * * *

Mr. Jenkins did not know Mr. Cerezo until Mr. Cerezo began pounding on the adjoining trailer. The evidence was undisputed that Mr. Jenkins repeatedly asked Mr. Cerezo to leave. Although Mr. Jenkins came out of the trailer holding a hammer and with a sheathed knife on his belt, the State's witnesses confirmed that these items were customary tools of Mr. Jenkins' trade, not weapons procured specifically to fight Mr. Cerezo. The State argued that Mr. Jenkins' throwing away his hammer in response to Mr. Cerezo's challenge was an act of aggression, but the witnesses agreed that Mr. Jenkins tossed the hammer to the side and did not move toward Mr. Cerezo. Mr. Jenkins testified that as he threw the hammer, he told Mr. Cerezo he did not want to fight. This gesture is equally indicative of a reasonable person assuming that he might defuse the tension by discarding the hammer. Mr. Cerezo landed a solid punch that "wobbled" Mr. Jenkins, backed up, and threatened to kill Mr. Jenkins again. Although Mr. Jenkins unsheathed and held his knife where Mr. Cerezo could see it, Mr. Cerezo drew his arm back and came at Mr. Jenkins for a second time. The State's witness who saw the single stab wound that killed Mr. Cerezo testified that Mr. Jenkins did not swing the knife out at Mr. Cerezo, and the resulting wound was consistent with this testimony.

Mr. Jenkins presented evidence sufficient to establish a prima facie issue of self-defense. It was the State's burden to overcome this defense and prove beyond a reasonable doubt that Mr. Jenkins was not acting in lawful self-defense. Here, the State was unable to present the competent, substantial evidence necessary to overcome Mr. Jenkins' defense and in fact presented evidence consistent with the defense. The trial court should have granted Mr. Jenkins' motion for judgment of acquittal.

Reversed and remanded for discharge.

---

if the fight occurred in a common roadway and not on the premises of his modest, mobile "castle." Even in the roadway, however, the jury was instructed that self-defense applied if Mr. Jenkins "reasonably believe[d] that such force [was] necessary to prevent imminent death or great bodily harm to himself or another." *See* Fla. Std. Jury Instr. (Crim.) 3.6(f). Even if the "castle" doctrine did not specifically apply, the proximity of this altercation to Mr. Jenkins' residence was relevant and telling. The "flight" potentially available to Mr. Jenkins was to retreat into the home despite the "wild man" threatening him outside of it, or to run away from his home, arguably leaving his teenage daughter behind. Whether the "castle doctrine" applied or not, the State failed to present evidence that Mr. Jenkins had a reasonable avenue of retreat; in fact its evidence suggested otherwise.

NOTE

In 2005, the Florida legislature amended its self-defense law, eliminating its previous duty to retreat requirement. An individual in Florida no longer has a duty to retreat before using deadly force in self-defense and can stand his ground if attacked in any place where he has a lawful right to be as long as the individual reasonably believes such force is necessary to prevent imminent death or great bodily harm. *See* Fla. Stat. § 776.012 & 776.013(3). States that do not require individuals to retreat before using deadly force in self-defense are often called "Stand Your Ground" or "Shoot First" jurisdictions. The rule that no retreat is required is also sometimes called the "True Man" rule. Does the no-duty-to-retreat rule reflect cultural preoccupations about masculinity? Is it peculiarly "American"?

Stand Your Ground laws became the subject of nationwide scrutiny following the fatal shooting of Trayvon Martin, an unarmed African American teenager, by George Zimmerman in February 2012. *See* Tamara F. Lawson, *A Fresh Cut in an Old Wound—A Critical Analysis of the Trayvon Martin Killing: The Public Outcry, the Prosecutor's Discretion, and the Stand Your Ground Law*, 23 U. FLA. J.L. & PUB. POL'Y 271 (2013). Zimmerman was the Neighborhood Watch Captain for the Retreat at Twin Lakes community in Florida, a state that had passed a Stand Your Ground law in 2005. Zimmerman thought Martin, who was walking on the street in a dark grey hoodie, looked suspicious and followed him, even after a 911 dispatcher told him it was not necessary to do so. A physical scuffle ensued, which ended when Zimmerman shot Martin. *See* Cynthia Lee, *Making Race Salient: Trayvon Martin and Implicit Bias in a Not Yet Post-Racial Society,* 91 N.C. L. REV. 1555 (2013).

At trial, Zimmerman claimed he shot Martin in self-defense when he was on the ground getting beaten by Martin after Martin started reaching for Zimmerman's gun. In July 2013, Zimmerman was found not guilty of murder or manslaughter by a predominantly white and all-female six person jury. After the Trayvon Martin shooting, there were renewed calls for the abolition of Stand Your Ground laws. On November 8, 2013, a panel of Florida lawmakers rejected a proposal to repeal Florida's Stand Your Ground law. *Florida Panel Rejects "Stand Your Ground" Law Repeal, Expands Its Scope Instead*, REUTERS, Nov. 8, 2013, *available at* http://rt.com/usa/florida-defends-stand-your-ground–458/ (last visited Dec. 4, 2013).

TRAYVON MARTIN KILLING IN FLORIDA PUTS 'STAND YOUR GROUND' LAW ON TRIAL

Patrik Jonsson

The Christian Science Monitor, Atlanta, March 16, 2012, at 10[a]

For many tuning in across the nation, the shooting late last month in Florida of an unarmed black teenager by a suspicious neighborhood watch captain looks like a racially motivated murder.

That's why the decision by the police not to arrest George Zimmerman for getting out of his car and shooting Trayvon Martin in the middle of a gated neighborhood in Sanford, Fla., on Feb. 26 has raised allegations of racial injustice and profiling.

The shooting has sparked a nationwide protest petition, the involvement of a black militia group, and, on Friday, a call by the parents of the slain teenager for the FBI to investigate the handling of the case, which police have handed off to state investigators.

The shooting also presents a tragic snapshot of so-called "Stand Your Ground" laws, what critics call "license-to-murder."

Such laws eliminate the English Law concept of a "duty to retreat" from dangerous situations outside the home. Without that, an armed citizen has no obligation to stand down in the face of a threat.

The problem, as the Martin case highlights, is that making the duty to retreat "totally irrelevant," as Stetson University law professor Robert Batey has said, means the law gives prosecutors fewer factors to consider when determining self-defense, including, potentially, the extent to which a person claiming self-defense may have aggravated the situation.

Florida became the first state to pass a specific Stand Your Ground law in 2005, essentially expanding self-defense zones from the home to most public places. Seventeen states now have such laws.

"It's hard to imagine that this couldn't have been resolved by [Mr. Zimmerman] leaving, so that no one would've gotten hurt, so this is a case where the Stand Your Ground law can actually make a legal difference," says former federal prosecutor Jeffrey Bellin, a law professor at Southern Methodist University, in Dallas.

"Even if you have suspicions about what motivated this, and you think there was a racial element and no justification for this shooting, the fact is he had no obligation to retreat under the law," he notes. "If prosecutors don't have the evidence to disprove the claim of self-defense, they won't be able to win."

---

[a] This article first appeared in *The Christian Science Monitor* on March 16, 2012, and is reproduced with permission.

But for the parents of the victim, and some 240,000 people who have signed a petition for a federal investigation on the Change.org website, the bare facts of the case suggest that Zimmerman was the aggressor and that the failure to arrest him points to covert racism and an abdication of authority by the local police department.

In a press conference Friday, Trayvon Martin's parents said they no longer had any faith in the Sanford Police Department and called on the FBI to take over the investigation.

"We're not getting any closure, any answers, and it's very disturbing," Tracy Martin, Trayvon's father, said. "As a father, I'm hurt. I feel betrayed by the Sanford Police Department."

Meanwhile, tensions are roiling in the area as several large rallies and protests are being planned and a black militia group has vowed to place the shooter under citizen's arrest. The state has said it may take several weeks to complete its review of the case.

On Feb. 26, Zimmerman, 28, a self-appointed block watch captain in The Retreat at Twin Lakes, a gated community in Sanford, just outside Orlando, called 911 from his car to report a suspicious person—a black man wearing a hoodie—walking slowly through the neighborhood. The 911 operator, according to police, told Zimmerman to wait for police to arrive. The man in the hoodie was Trayvon, returning to his family's house from buying Skittles and an iced tea at a local convenience store.

Instead of waiting for police, Zimmerman exited the car and shot Trayvon after a brief altercation. Trayvon, 17, had no previous criminal record, while Zimmerman recently had a 2005 felony arrest for assault on a police officer expunged by the courts.

"Had Trayvon Martin been the triggerman, they would have arrested him day one, hour one and he would be in jail with no bail," Ben Crump, a Tallahassee lawyer representing the family, told the Florida Courier.

"We have a murderer on the streets, walking around," Natalie Jackson, another lawyer representing the family, said on Friday.

Sanford Police Chief Bill Lee told the Orlando Sentinel that he had no grounds to arrest Zimmerman, and told reporters Thursday that that he has invited the US Department of Justice and the Florida Department of Law Enforcement to review the investigation. Florida officials confirmed they began an investigation on March 13.

"It's an open book," Mr. Lee said. "If they want to look at what we did and how we did it and what information we have, they're welcome to it."

Police have released little information, including the 911 tapes, about what happened that night and no details about how Trayvon and Zimmerman ended up grappling. What has been revealed is that before an officer arrived, Trayvon and Zimmerman got into a fight, according to police, witnesses heard one or both calling for help, and Zimmerman shot Trayvon once in the chest with a 9 mm handgun.

One witness said he came upon the scene and saw Zimmerman on his back on the ground, which jibes with statements by the police that he was covered in grass and blood. Another witness has said in a TV interview that "there was no punching, no hitting going on at the time, no wrestling," but police say that witness gave an official account to them that jibed with Zimmerman's story.

In a letter to the Orlando Sentinel on Friday, Zimmerman's father, Robert Zimmerman, wrote that his son is part-Hispanic "with many black family members and friends." He also pushed back at the idea that Zimmerman was the aggressor who instigated the altercation.

"At no time did George follow or confront Mr. Martin," he wrote. "When the true details of the event become public, and I hope that will be soon, everyone should be outraged by the treatment of George Zimmerman in the media."

The emotional stakes, racial backdrop, and the awkward position of the police department suggest how state laws broadening self-defense rights can backfire. But whether it's a prosecutor or a jury deciding the outcome of a case, self-defense arguments are often powerful and difficult to disprove beyond a reasonable doubt, even in jurisdictions without Stand Your Ground laws.

"This is a tragedy, and to the extent the law plays a role in encouraging this type of situation to happen, it calls into question the law," says Professor Bellin. "At the same time, it's not clear that if this happens in a jurisdiction where there isn't a Stand Your Ground law, that you necessarily get a different result."

NOTE

As a general rule, an initial aggressor has no right to claim self-defense unless he retreats or withdraws from the conflict and successfully communicates his withdrawal to the victim. Even in Stand Your Ground states that do not require retreat as a general matter, retreat is required of initial aggressors.

There is no universal definition for the term "initial aggressor." In some jurisdictions, one must engage in an unlawful act reasonably calculated to bring about a physical confrontation in order to be considered the initial aggressor. Other jurisdictions say that one who provokes an affray loses the right to claim self-defense. In yet other jurisdictions, one must be "free from fault," or one loses the right to claim self-defense. One does not have to be the first person to use force to be considered the initial aggressor. If A threatens to slap B and B responds by punching A, A is the initial aggressor even though B was the first person to actually use force.

What happens when the defendant begins a fist fight and the victim responds by pulling a gun or knife? May the defendant use deadly force to protect himself and still claim self-defense? The older common law rule was that an initial aggressor who provoked an affray whether with deadly or non-deadly force had to retreat if a safe retreat was available and known to him and could only use deadly force in self-defense if the victim pursued him as he retreated, using or threatening the defendant with deadly force. Many jurisdictions today will allow a non-deadly aggressor to use deadly force if the other person responds to his threat of non-deadly force with deadly force. In these jurisdictions, a non-deadly aggressor automoatically regains the right to act in self-defense if the other person responds with deadly force. The non-deadly initial aggressor who is threatened with deadly force does not have to retreat even if a safe retreat is available and known to him.

2. EXPANDING THE SCOPE OF SELF-DEFENSE

STATE V. STEWART

Supreme Court of Kansas
243 Kan. 639, 763 P.2d 572 (1988)

LOCKETT, J.

* * * Peggy Stewart fatally shot her husband, Mike Stewart, while he was sleeping. She was charged with murder in the first degree, K.S.A. 21–3401. Defendant pled not guilty, contending that she shot her husband in self-defense. Expert evidence showed that Peggy Stewart suffered from the battered woman syndrome. Based upon the battered woman syndrome, the trial judge instructed the jury on self-defense. The jury found Peggy Stewart not guilty.

The State stipulates that Stewart "suffered considerable abuse at the hands of her husband," but contends that the trial court erred in giving a self-defense instruction since Peggy Stewart was in no imminent danger when she shot her sleeping husband. We agree that under the facts of this case the giving of the self-defense instruction was erroneous.

* * *

Following an annulment from her first husband and two subsequent divorces in which she was the petitioner, Peggy Stewart married Mike Stewart in 1974. Evidence at trial disclosed a long history of abuse by Mike against Peggy and her two daughters from one of her prior marriages. Laura, one of Peggy's daughters, testified that early in the marriage Mike hit and kicked Peggy, and that after the first year of the marriage Peggy exhibited signs of severe psychological problems. Subsequently, Peggy was hospitalized and diagnosed as having symptoms of paranoid schizophrenia; she responded to treatment and was soon released. * * *

In 1977, two social workers informed Peggy that they had received reports that Mike was taking indecent liberties with her daughters. Because the social workers did not want Mike to be left alone with the girls, Peggy quit her job. In 1978, Mike began to taunt Peggy by stating that Carla, her 12-year-old daughter, was "more of a wife" to him than Peggy.

Later, Carla was placed in a detention center, and Mike forbade Peggy and Laura to visit her. When Mike finally allowed Carla to return home in the middle of summer, he forced her to sleep in an un-air conditioned room with the windows nailed shut, to wear a heavy flannel nightgown, and to cover herself with heavy blankets. Mike would then wake Carla at 5:30 a.m. and force her to do all the housework. Peggy and Laura were not allowed to help Carla or speak to her.

When Peggy confronted Mike and demanded that the situation cease, Mike responded by holding a shotgun to Peggy's head and threatening to kill her. Mike once kicked Peggy so violently in the chest and ribs that she required hospitalization. Finally, when Mike ordered Peggy to kill and bury Carla, she filed for divorce. Peggy's attorney in the divorce action testified in the murder trial that Peggy was afraid for both her and her children's lives. * * *

Mike's intimidation of Peggy continued to escalate. One morning, Laura found her mother hiding on the school bus, terrified and begging the driver to take her to a neighbor's home. That Christmas, Mike threw the turkey dinner to the floor, chased Peggy outside, grabbed her by the hair, rubbed her face in the dirt, and then kicked and beat her.

After [Mike threw Carla out of the house and] Laura moved away, Peggy's life became even more isolated. Once, when Peggy was working at a cafe, Mike came in and ran all the customers off with a gun because he wanted Peggy to go home and have sex with him right that minute. He abused both drugs and alcohol, and amused himself by terrifying Peggy, once waking her from a sound sleep by beating her with a baseball bat. He shot one of Peggy's pet cats, and then held the gun against her head and threatened to pull the trigger. Peggy told friends that Mike would hold a shotgun to her head and threaten to blow it off, and indicated that one day he would probably do it.

In May 1986, Peggy left Mike and ran away to Laura's home in Oklahoma. It was the first time Peggy had left Mike without telling him. Because Peggy was suicidal, Laura had her admitted to a hospital. There, she was diagnosed as having toxic psychosis as a result of an overdose of her medication. On May 30, 1986, Mike called to say he was coming to get her. Peggy agreed to return to Kansas. Peggy told a nurse she felt like she wanted to shoot her husband. At trial, she testified that she decided to return with Mike because she was not able to get the medical help she needed in Oklahoma.

* * * Peggy testified that Mike threatened to kill her if she ever ran away again. As soon as they arrived at the house, Mike forced Peggy into the house and forced her to have oral sex several times.

The next morning, Peggy discovered a loaded .357 magnum. She testified she was afraid of the gun. She hid the gun under the mattress of the bed in a spare room. Later that morning, as she cleaned house, Mike kept making remarks that she should not bother because she would not be there long, or that she should not bother with her things because she could not take them with her. She testified she was afraid Mike was going to kill her.

Mike's parents visited Mike and Peggy that afternoon. Mike's father testified that Peggy and Mike were affectionate with each other during the visit. Later, after Mike's parents had left, Mike forced Peggy to perform oral sex. After watching television, Mike and Peggy went to bed at 8:00 p.m. As Mike slept, Peggy thought about suicide and heard voices in her head repeating over and over, "kill or be killed." At this time, there were two vehicles in the driveway and Peggy had access to the car keys. About 10:00 p.m., Peggy went to the spare bedroom and removed the gun from under the mattress, walked back to the bedroom, and killed her husband while he slept. She then ran to the home of a neighbor, who called the police.

When the police questioned Peggy regarding the events leading up to the shooting, Peggy stated that things had not gone quite right that day, and that when she got the chance she hid the gun under the mattress. She stated that she shot Mike to "get this over with, this misery and this torment." When asked why she got the gun out, Peggy stated to the police:

> I'm not sure exactly what . . . led up to it . . . and my head started playing games with me and I got to thinking about things and I said I didn't want to be by myself again. . . . I got the gun out because there had been remarks made about me being out there alone. It was as if Mike was going to do something again like had been done before. He had gotten me down here from McPherson one time and he went and told them that I had done something and he had me put out of the house and was taking everything I had. And it was like he was going to pull the same thing over again.

Two expert witnesses testified during the trial. The expert for the defense, psychologist Marilyn Hutchinson, diagnosed Peggy as suffering from "battered woman syndrome," or post-traumatic stress syndrome. Dr. Hutchinson testified that Mike was preparing to escalate the violence in retaliation for Peggy's running away. She testified that loaded guns, veiled threats, and increased sexual demands are indicators of the escalation of the cycle.[a] Dr. Hutchinson believed Peggy had a repressed knowledge that she was in a "really grave lethal situation."

The State's expert, psychiatrist Herbert Modlin, neither subscribed to a belief in the battered woman syndrome nor to a theory of learned helplessness[b] as an explanation for why women do not leave an abusive relationship. Dr. Modlin testified that abuse such as repeated forced oral sex would not be trauma sufficient to trigger a post-traumatic stress disorder. He also believed Peggy was erroneously diagnosed as suffering from toxic psychosis. He stated that Peggy was unable to escape the abuse because she suffered from schizophrenia, rather than the battered woman syndrome.

At defense counsel's request, the trial judge gave an instruction on self-defense to the jury. The jury found Peggy not guilty. * * *

Although the State may not appeal an acquittal, it may reserve questions for appeal. We will not entertain an appeal by the prosecution merely to determine whether the trial court committed error. The appeal by the prosecution must raise a question of statewide interest, the answer to which is essential to the just administration of criminal law.

The question reserved is whether the trial judge erred in instructing on self-defense when there was no imminent threat to the defendant and no evidence of any argument or altercation between the defendant and the victim contemporaneous with the killing. We find this question [is] of statewide importance.

The State claims that under the facts the instruction should not have been given because there was no lethal threat to defendant contemporaneous with the killing. The State points out that Peggy's annulment and divorces from former husbands, and her filing for divorce after leaving Mike, proved that Peggy knew there were non-lethal methods by which she could extricate herself from the abusive relationship. * * *

In *State v. Rose*, we approved an instruction on self-defense which stated in part: "[B]efore a person can take the life of another, it must reasonably appear that his own life must have been in imminent danger, or that he was in imminent danger of some great bodily injury from the hands of the person killed. No one can attack and kill another because he may fear injury at some future time." The perceived imminent danger had to occur in the present time, specifically during the time in which the defendant and the deceased were engaged in their final conflict. * * *

---

[a] Dr. Hutchinson was referring to the "cycle of violence" in an abusive relationship which "begins with an initial building of tension and violence, culminates in an explosion, and end with a 'honeymoon.'" *State v. Stewart*, 243 Kan. 639 (1988) (J. Herd's dissent).

[b] According to Lenore Walker, "learned helplessness" refers to the fact that women in abusive relationships become conditioned to believe they are helpless to stop or escape the violence. LENORE E.A. WALKER, THE BATTERED WOMAN (1979).

The traditional concept of self-defense has posited one-time conflicts between persons of somewhat equal size and strength. When the defendant claiming self-defense is a victim of long-term domestic violence, such as a battered spouse, such traditional concepts may not apply. Because of the prior history of abuse, and the difference in strength and size between the abused and the abuser, the accused in such cases may choose to defend during a momentary lull in the abuse, rather than during a conflict. However, in order to warrant the giving of a self-defense instruction, the facts of the case must still show that the spouse was in imminent danger close to the time of the killing.

* * * A self-defense instruction must be given if there is any evidence to support a claim of self-defense, even if that evidence consists solely of the defendant's testimony.

Where self-defense is asserted, evidence of the deceased's long-term cruelty and violence towards the defendant is admissible. In cases involving battered spouses, expert evidence of the battered woman syndrome is relevant to a determination of the reasonableness of the defendant's perception of danger. Other courts which have allowed such evidence to be introduced include those in Florida, Georgia, Illinois, Maine, New Jersey, New York, Pennsylvania, Washington, and Wisconsin. However, no jurisdictions have held that the existence of the battered woman syndrome in and of itself operates as a defense to murder.

In order to instruct a jury on self-defense, there must be some showing of an imminent threat or a confrontational circumstance involving an overt act by an aggressor. There is no exception to this requirement where the defendant has suffered long-term domestic abuse and the victim is the abuser. * * *

Here, however, there [was] an absence of imminent danger to defendant: Peggy told a nurse at the Oklahoma hospital of her desire to kill Mike. She later voluntarily agreed to return home with Mike when he telephoned her. She stated that after leaving the hospital Mike threatened to kill her if she left him again. Peggy showed no inclination to leave. In fact, immediately after the shooting, Peggy told the police that she was upset because she thought Mike would leave her. Prior to the shooting, Peggy hid the loaded gun. The cars were in the driveway and Peggy had access to the car keys. After being abused, Peggy went to bed with Mike at 8 p.m. Peggy lay there for two hours, then retrieved the gun from where she had hidden it and shot Mike while he slept.

Under these facts, the giving of the self-defense instruction was erroneous. Under such circumstances, a battered woman cannot reasonably fear imminent life-threatening danger from her sleeping spouse. We note that other courts have held that the sole fact that the victim was asleep does not preclude a self-defense instruction. In *State v.*

Norman, cited by defendant, the defendant's evidence disclosed a long history of abuse. Each time defendant attempted to escape, her husband found and beat her. On the day of the shooting, the husband beat defendant continually throughout the day, and threatened either to cut her throat, kill her, or cut off her breast. In the afternoon, defendant shot her husband while he napped. The North Carolina Court of Appeals held it was reversible error to fail to instruct on self-defense. The court found that, although decedent was napping at the time defendant shot him, defendant's unlawful act was closely related in time to an assault and threat of death by decedent against defendant and that the decedent's nap was "but a momentary hiatus in a continuous reign of terror."

There is no doubt that the North Carolina court determined that the sleeping husband was an evil man who deserved the justice he received from his battered wife. Here, similar comparable and compelling facts exist. But, as one court has stated: "To permit capital punishment to be imposed upon the subjective conclusion of the [abused] individual that prior acts and conduct of the deceased justified the killing would amount to a leap into the abyss of anarchy." Finally, our legislature has not provided for capital punishment for even the most heinous crimes.[c] We must, therefore, hold that when a battered woman kills her sleeping spouse when there is no imminent danger, the killing is not reasonably necessary and a self-defense instruction may not be given. To hold otherwise in this case would in effect allow the execution of the abuser for past or future acts and conduct. * * *

The appeal is sustained.

HERD, J., dissenting:

The sole issue before us on the question reserved is whether the trial court erred in giving a jury instruction on self-defense. We have a well-established rule that a defendant is entitled to a self-defense instruction if there is any evidence to support it, even though the evidence consists solely of the defendant's testimony. It is for the jury to determine the sincerity of the defendant's belief she needed to act in self-defense, and the reasonableness of that belief in light of all the circumstances.

It is not within the scope of appellate review to weigh the evidence. An appellate court's function is to merely examine the record and determine if there is *any* evidence to support the theory of self-defense. If the record discloses any competent evidence upon which self-defense could be based, then the instruction must be given. In judging the evidence for this purpose, all inferences should be resolved in favor of the defendant. * * *

---

[c] Two years after the decision in this case, the Kansas legislature passed a capital punishment statute, authorizing imposition of the death penalty for certain heinous crimes.

It is evident from prior case law appellee met her burden of showing some competent evidence that she acted in self-defense, thus making her defense a jury question. She testified she acted in fear for her life, and Dr. Hutchinson corroborated this testimony. The evidence of Mike's past abuse, the escalation of violence, his threat of killing her should she attempt to leave him, and Dr. Hutchinson's testimony that appellee was indeed in a "lethal situation" more than met the minimal standard of "any evidence" to allow an instruction to be given to the jury.

Appellee introduced much uncontroverted evidence of the violent nature of the deceased and how he had brutalized her throughout their married life. * * * The evidence showed Mike had a "Dr. Jekyll and Mr. Hyde" personality. He was usually very friendly and ingratiating when non-family persons were around, but was belligerent and domineering to family members. He had a violent temper and would blow up without reason. * * *

Mike threw twelve-year-old Carla out of the house without resources, and Laura left home as soon as she could. Mike would not let appellee see her daughters and ran Laura off with a shotgun when she tried to visit. Appellee's life became even more isolated. Towards the end, both the phone and utilities were disconnected from the house.

Appellee finally took the car and ran away to Laura's home in Oklahoma. It was the first time she had ever left Mike without telling him. She was suicidal and again hearing voices, and Laura had her admitted to a hospital. * * * She soon felt better, but was not fully recovered, when Mike found out where she was and called her to say he was coming to get her. She told a nurse she felt like she wanted to shoot him, but the nurse noted her major emotion was one of hopelessness.

The hospital nevertheless released appellee to Mike's care, and he immediately drove her back to Kansas. * * * *He said if she ever ran away again, he would kill her.*

When they reached the house, Mike would not let appellee bring in her suitcases and forced her to have oral sex four or five times in the next 36 hours, with such violence that the inside of her mouth was bruised. The next morning, appellee found a box of bullets in the car that had not been there before. She then discovered a loaded .357 magnum. This frightened her, because Mike had promised to keep his guns unloaded. She did not know how to unload the gun, so she hid it under the mattress of the bed in a spare room. As she cleaned house, Mike remarked she should not bother, because she would not be there long. He told her she should not bother with her things, because she could not take them with her. She took these statements to mean she would soon be dead and she grew progressively more terrified. Throughout the day Mike continued to force her to have oral sex, while telling her how he preferred sex with other women.

The sexual abuse stopped when Mike's parents came to visit. Mike's father testified everything seemed normal during their stay. After the visit, Mike again forced appellee to perform oral sex and then demanded at 8:00 p.m. she come to bed with him. The cumulative effect of Mike's past history, coupled with his current abusive conduct, justified appellee's belief that a violent explosion was imminent. As he slept, appellee was terrified and thought about suicide and heard voices in her head repeating over and over, "kill or be killed." The voices warned her there was going to be killing and to get away.

She went to the spare bedroom and removed the gun from under the mattress, walked back to the bedroom, and fatally shot Mike. After the first shot, she thought he was coming after her so she shot again and fled wildly outside, barefoot, wearing only her underwear. Ignoring the truck and car outside, although she had the keys in her purse inside, she ran over a mile to the neighbors' house and pled with them to keep Mike from killing her. She thought she had heard him chasing her. The neighbor woman took the gun from appellee's hand and gave her a robe while her husband called the sheriff. The neighbor testified appellee appeared frightened for her life and was certain Mike was alive and looking for her. * * *

Dr. Hutchinson explained to the jury at appellee's trial the "cycle of violence" which induces a state of "learned helplessness" and keeps a battered woman in the relationship. She testified appellee was caught in a such a cycle. The cycle begins with an initial building of tension and violence, culminates in an explosion, and ends with a "honeymoon." The woman becomes conditioned to trying to make it through one more violent explosion with its battering in order to be rewarded by the "honeymoon phase," with its expressions of remorse and eternal love and the standard promise of "never again." After all promises are broken time after time and she is beaten again and again, the battered woman falls into a state of learned helplessness where she gives up trying to extract herself from the cycle of violence. She learns fighting back only delays the honeymoon and escalates the violence. If she tries to leave the relationship, she is located and returned and the violence increases. She is a captive. She begins to believe her husband is omnipotent, and resistance will be futile at best. * * *

It was Dr. Hutchinson's opinion Mike was planning to escalate his violence in retaliation against appellee for running away. She testified that Mike's threats against appellee's life, his brutal sexual acts, and appellee's discovery of the loaded gun were all indicators to appellee the violence had escalated and she was in danger. Dr. Hutchinson believed appellee had a repressed knowledge she was in what was really a gravely lethal situation. She testified appellee was convinced she must "kill or be killed." * * *

The majority claims permitting a jury to consider self-defense under these facts would permit anarchy. This underestimates the jury's ability to recognize an invalid claim of self-defense. * * *

The majority bases its opinion on its conclusion appellee was not in imminent danger, usurping the right of the jury to make that determination of fact. The majority believes a person could not be in imminent danger from an aggressor merely because the aggressor dropped off to sleep. This is a fallacious conclusion. For instance, picture a hostage situation where the armed guard inadvertently drops off to sleep and the hostage grabs his gun and shoots him. The majority opinion would preclude the use of self-defense in such a case. * * *

I would deny this appeal.

NOTE

Evidence of "battered women's syndrome" (BWS) has increasingly been admissible in court in civil and criminal cases involving domestic violence. The pioneering social science researcher in this area has been Lenore Walker, who treats BWS as a sub-category of post-traumatic stress syndrome, consisting of "a collection of thoughts, feelings, and actions that logically follow a frightening experience that one expects could be repeated." LENORE E.A. WALKER, *Battered Women Syndrome and Self-Defense*, 6 NOTRE DAME J. L., ETHICS & PUB. POL'Y 321, 327 (1992); *see also* LENORE E.A. WALKER, THE BATTERED WOMAN (1979) and LENORE E.A. WALKER, THE BATTERED WOMAN SYNDROME (2d ed. 1984).

Walker defines a battered woman as someone "in an intimate relationship with a man who repeatedly subjects * * * her to forceful physical and/or psychological abuse," where "repeatedly" is defined as "more than once" and "abuse" includes any of six categories of behavior, from life-threatening violence to "extreme verbal harassment and expressing comments of a derogatory nature with negative value judgments." WALKER, THE BATTERED WOMAN SYNDROME 203 (2d ed. 1984). In the courts, as the *Stewart* opinion indicates, Walker's theories are often reduced to two basic psychological concepts: the "cycle of violence" and "learned helplessness."

Recently, Walker's research and the concepts of learned helplessness, the cycle of violence, and even the term "battered woman's syndrome" itself have come under fire. David L. Faigman and Amy J. Wright, for example, question the evidence for both the "cycle of violence" and "learned helplessness." Reviewing Walker's research methods, Faigman and Wright note that Walker's technique allowed subjects to guess the answer the researchers were looking for, and that her theory relies heavily on the interviewers' interpretations of their subjects' responses. Moreover, Walker's own data indicate that not all subjects, or even most subjects, actually experience all three stages of the cycle of violence. *See* David L. Faigman & Amy J. Wright, *The Battered Woman Syndrome in the Age of Science*, 39 ARIZ. L. REV. 67, 77–78 (1997). Faigman and Wright are also critical of

Walker's use of the concept of learned helplessness, noting that it emerged from experiments with dogs and that, unlike dogs, women continue to resist their batterers in numerous ways rather than becoming completely passive and unable to respond. *Id.* at 79. Faigman and Wright conclude, "The battered woman syndrome illustrates all that is wrong with the law's use of science." *Id.* at 68.

Feminist activists and scholars, too, have been critical of the BWS concept and of Walker's theories. First, the name "battered women's syndrome" suggests that only women can be victims. Although the vast majority of intimate violence is in fact perpetrated on women by men, domestic violence exists in the gay, lesbian, bisexual, and transgender communities as well, and men may also be battered by women. Children and the elderly, as well, may suffer psychological and physical abuse from intimates. Moreover, BWS suggests that women who are abused are victims who lack agency. Elizabeth Schneider argues, in contrast, that survivors of domestic violence must be seen as exercising agency within social as well as psychological constraints. Elizabeth M. Schneider, *Particularity and Generality: Challenges of Feminist Theory and Practice in Work on Woman-Abuse*, 67 NYU L. REV. 520, 548–550 (1992).

Second, critics fear that too-rigid application of the cycle of violence and learned helplessness theories will cause some trial judges to deny the admission of expert testimony on BWS when the defendant does not exhibit all the symptoms identified by Walker or when the defendant seems insufficiently "sick" or psychologically disturbed. The psychological focus of BWS evidence arguably reinforces longstanding stereotypes about men and women, rather than combating them. The result of these combined pressures may be that in order to get their case to the jury, lawyers for battered women may have to paint their clients as passive, frightened, and mentally disturbed, and morally pure as well—a process that in itself may be a degrading experience for the defendant. As Michael Dowd comments:

> "Good" battered women are passive, loyal housewives, acting as loving companions to their abusers. These women must have flawless characters and continually appeal to the police and courts for help, regardless of the futility of their efforts. By contrast, the "bad" battered woman is one who fails to possess any of the virtues of the "good" woman, and who may have even obtained an education and pursued a career. This demonstration of control often operates to disqualify the "bad" battered woman from the group. Infidelity or abuse of drugs is equally discrediting.

Michael Dowd, *Dispelling the Myths About the "Battered Woman's Defense": Towards a New Understanding*, 19 FORDHAM URB. L.J. 567, 581 (1992). Sharon Angella Allard adds that Black women have particular difficulty being perceived by juries and judges as fitting into the "good" battered woman category. Sharon Angella Allard, *Rethinking Battered Woman Syndrome: A Black Feminist Perspective*, 1 UCLA WOMEN'S L.J. 191, 197

(1991) (arguing that Black women tend to be seen as acting out of revenge and anger rather than fear).

Third, the psychological focus of BWS evidence tends to obscure its relevance to the objective elements of a self-defense claim. For example, BWS evidence could be introduced to show that the defendant was correct in believing that she was facing a threat of death because of her long experience with the batterer and her ability to read even subtle physical and verbal cues. BWS evidence could also be introduced to show that escape is much less easy than it might appear to a jury, since batterers frequently go to great lengths to hunt down their partners and victims are most likely to be killed when they are attempting to leave the relationship.

Recent activism on battering has renamed the topic "battering and its effects," rather than the diagnosis of a particular "syndrome" particular to women. Recent social science, as well, emphasizes physical battering as one element of a larger pattern of control. One team of researchers describes the concept of a "culture of battering":

> The culture of battering refers to the relationship context of an abusive relationship. The first of the three elements of the culture of battering is the abuse, which includes at least one of the following types: physical, emotional, sexual, familial, and property. Professionals have increasingly recognized non-physical forms of abuse as harmful to domestic violence victims. The second element is the systematic pattern of domination and control that the batterer exerts over his victim. This pattern may be initiated by the batterer's gradual imposition of a series of rules that his victim must follow or be punished for violating. * * * The third element, hiding, denying, and minimizing the abuse, refers to typical coping strategies that battered women use to reduce the psychological impact of the abuse. Each of these elements to some degree must be present in order for a culture of battering to be established. * * *

Karla Fischer, Neil Vidmar & René Ellis, *The Culture of Battering and the Role of Mediation in Domestic Violence Cases*, 46 SMU L. REV. 2117, 2141, 2121–2122 (1993). How, if at all, does this expanded concept of "the culture of battering" fit legal concepts of self-defense?

JURIES AND EXPERT EVIDENCE: SOCIAL FRAMEWORK TESTIMONY

Neil Vidmar & Regina A. Schuller
52 Law & Contemp. Probs. 133 (1989)

During the past decade and a half, courts have been faced with an increasing number of attempts to have social science experts testify about such matters as eyewitness unreliability, post-traumatic stress disorders, or cross-cultural differences in the meaning of behavior. The purpose of the testimony, to which Walker and Monahan have given the generic label of "social framework evidence" in order to distinguish it from other forms of social science evidence, is to provide the factfinder, usually a jury, with information about the social and psychological context in which contested adjudicative facts occurred. It is presumed that knowledge about the context will help the factfinder interpret the contested adjudicative facts. * * *

A partial list of evidence that would qualify as social framework evidence would include testimony on eyewitness reliability, predictions of dangerousness, battered woman syndrome, rape trauma syndrome, behavioral and psychological symptoms of sexually abused children, battered child syndrome, "brainwashed" defendants, Vietnam veterans syndrome, discriminatory behavior, effects of cultural stress, and psycholinguistic meaning.

Despite the wide variety of substantive topics and the use of the evidence for different litigation goals, all this evidence shares the common characteristic of employing general conclusions drawn from social science research to help evaluate factual issues in a specific case. In each instance, the evidence involves general assertions about some aspect of human behavior that is intended to help the trier of fact, usually a jury, to interpret the meaning of some disputed fact or testimony at issue in the suit.

In theory, social framework testimony does not bear directly on the ultimate fact to be decided by the trier; rather, it provides a social and psychological context in which the trier can understand and evaluate claims about the ultimate fact. Thus, a psychologist called to testify about potential eyewitness unreliability does not assert that the eyewitness in the particular case is wrong, only that studies of perception and recall indicate that people in similar contexts are often wrong. To cite another example, an expert called to testify about rape trauma syndrome, in a case where the defendant disputes the complainant's testimony that she did not consent to sexual intercourse, describes studies on the characteristic reactions and behavior patterns of women who have been sexually assaulted. Although in some instances the expert may also be allowed to indicate that the complainant herself exhibits these characteristic symptoms, the testimony revolves around characteristics of a class of persons, sexual assault victims. The factfinder may then use this information to evaluate case-specific evidence. * * *

NOTE

The widespread acceptance of "battered women's syndrome" evidence in the courtroom is due to the activism of feminist lawyers in the 1970s and 1980s, and their sense that the law of self-defense as it stood disserved women. Another feminist criticism of the law of self-defense is that it assumes that the parties involved in a physical confrontation meet on more or less equal terms. The next case, *State v. Wanrow*, illustrates one court's sensitivity to this concern.

STATE V. WANROW

Supreme Court of Washington
88 Wash.2d 221, 559 P.2d 548 (1977)

UTTER, ASSOCIATE JUSTICE.

Yvonne Wanrow was convicted by a jury of second-degree murder and first-degree assault. She appealed her conviction to the Court of Appeals. The Court of Appeals reversed and remanded the case. * * * We granted review and affirm the Court of Appeals.

We order a reversal of the conviction on two grounds. The first is the ground stated by the Court of Appeals regarding the erroneous admission of the tape recording. The second ground is error committed by the trial court in improperly instructing the jury on the law of self-defense as it related to the defendant.

On the afternoon of August 11, 1972, defendant's (respondent's) two children were staying at the home of Ms. Hooper, a friend of defendant. Defendant's son was playing in the neighborhood and came back to Ms. Hooper's house and told her that a man tried to pull him off his bicycle and drag him into a house. Some months earlier, Ms. Hooper's 7-year-old daughter had developed a rash on her body which was diagnosed as venereal disease. Ms. Hooper had been unable to persuade her daughter to tell her who had molested her. It was not until the night of the shooting that Ms. Hooper discovered it was William Wesler (decedent) who allegedly had violated her daughter. A few minutes after the defendant's son related his story to Ms. Hooper about the man who tried to detain him, Mr. Wesler appeared on the porch of the Hooper house and stated through the door, 'I didn't touch the kid, I didn't touch the kid.' At that moment, the Hooper girl, seeing Wesler at the door, indicated to her mother that Wesler was the man who had molested her. Joseph Fah, Ms. Hooper's landlord, saw Wesler as he was leaving and informed Shirley Hooper that Wesler had tried to molest a young boy who had earlier lived in the same house, and that Wesler had previously been committed to the Eastern State Hospital for the mentally ill. Immediately after this revelation from Mr. Fah, Ms. Hooper called the police who, upon their arrival at the Hooper residence, were informed of all the events which had transpired that day. Ms. Hooper requested that Wesler be arrested then and there, but the police stated, 'We can't, until Monday morning.' Ms. Hooper was urged by the police officer to go to the police station Monday morning and 'swear out a warrant.' Ms. Hooper's landlord, who was present during the conversation, suggested that Ms. Hooper get a baseball bat located at the corner of the house and 'conk him over the head' should Wesler try to enter the house uninvited during the weekend.

To this suggestion, the policeman replied, 'Yes, but wait until he gets in the house.' (A week before this incident Shirley Hooper had noticed someone prowling around her house at night. Two days before the shooting someone had attempted to get into Ms. Hooper's bedroom and had slashed the window screen. She suspected that such person was Wesler.)

That evening, Ms. Hooper called the defendant and asked her to spend the night with her in the Hooper house. At that time she related to Ms. Wanrow the facts we have previously set forth. The defendant arrived sometime after 6 p.m. with a pistol in her handbag. The two women ultimately determined that they were too afraid to stay alone and decided to ask some friends to come over for added protection. The two women then called the defendant's sister and brother-in-law, Angie and Chuck Michel. The four adults did not go to bed that evening, but remained awake talking and watching for any possible prowlers. There were eight young children in the house with them. At around 5 a.m., Chuck Michel, without the knowledge of the women in the house, went to Wesler's house, carrying a baseball bat. Upon arriving at the Wesler residence, Mr. Michel accused Wesler of molesting little children. Mr. Wesler then suggested that they go over to the Hooper residence and get the whole thing straightened out. Another man, one David Kelly, was also present, and together the three men went over to the Hooper house. Mr. Michel and Mr. Kelly remained outside while Wesler entered the residence.

The testimony as to what next took place is considerably less precise. It appears that Wesler, a large man who was visibly intoxicated, entered the home and when told to leave declined to do so. A good deal of shouting and confusion then arose, and a young child, asleep on the couch, awoke crying. The testimony indicates that Wesler than approached this child, stating, 'My what a cute little boy,' or words to that effect, and that the child's mother, Ms. Michel, stepped between Wesler and the child. By this time Hooper was screaming for Wesler to get out. Ms. Wanrow, a 5′ 4″ woman who at the time had a broken leg and was using a crutch, testified that she then went to the front door to enlist the aid of Chuck Michel. She stated that she shouted for him and, upon turning around to reenter the living room, found Wesler standing directly behind her. She testified to being gravely startled by this situation and to having then shot Wesler in what amounted to a reflex action.

After Wesler was shot, Ms. Hooper called the police via a Spokane crime check emergency phone number, stating, 'There's a guy broke in, and my girlfriend shot him.' The defendant later took the phone and engaged in a conversation with the police operator. The entire conversation was tape recorded.

At trial, over defense counsel's objection, the tape was admitted into evidence. After presentation of the evidence, the jury was instructed on the law and commenced deliberations. Deliberations progressed for a time, and the jurors requested to hear the tape again. The request was granted. Not long after reviewing the tape, the jury reached its verdict of guilty as to both counts. * * *

[The court concludes that the tape recording should not have been admitted into evidence.]

Reversal of respondent's conviction is also required by a second serious error committed by the trial court. Instruction No. 10, setting forth the law of self-defense, incorrectly limited the jury's consideration of acts and circumstances pertinent to respondent's perception of the alleged threat to her person. * * *

In the opening paragraph of instruction No. 10, the jury, in evaluating the gravity of the danger to the respondent, was directed to consider only those acts and circumstances occurring 'at or immediately before the killing . . .' This is not now, and never has been, the law of self-defense in Washington. On the contrary, the justification of self-defense is to be evaluated in light of *all* the facts and circumstances known to the defendant, including those known substantially before the killing. * * *

The second paragraph of instruction No. 10 contains an equally erroneous and prejudicial statement of the law. That portion of the instruction reads:

> However, when there is no reasonable ground for the person attacked to believe that *his* person is in imminent danger of death or great bodily harm, and it appears to *him* that only an ordinary battery is all that is intended, and all that *he* has reasonable grounds to fear from *his* assailant, *he* has a right to stand *his* ground and repel such threatened assault, yet *he* has no right to repel a threatened assault with naked hands, by the use of a deadly weapon in a deadly manner, unless *he* believes, *and has reasonable grounds to believe*, that *he* is in imminent danger of death or great bodily harm.

(Italics ours.) In our society women suffer from a conspicuous lack of access to training in and the means of developing those skills necessary to effectively repel a male assailant without resorting to the use of deadly weapons. Instruction No. 12 does indicate that the 'relative size and strength of the persons involved' may be considered; however, it does not make clear that the defendant's actions are to be judged against her own subjective impressions and not those which a detached jury might determine to be objectively reasonable. * * *

The second paragraph of instruction No. 10 not only establishes an objective standard, but through the persistent use of the masculine gender leaves the jury with the impression the objective standard to be applied is that applicable to an altercation between two men. The impression created—that a 5′ 4″ woman with a cast on her leg and using a crutch must, under the law, somehow repel an assault by a 6′ 2″ intoxicated man without employing weapons in her defense, unless the jury finds her determination of the degree of danger to be objectively reasonable—constitutes a separate and distinct misstatement of the law and, in the context of this case, violates the respondent's right to equal protection of the law. The respondent was entitled to have the jury consider her actions in the light of her own perceptions of the situation, including those perceptions which were the product of our nation's 'long and unfortunate history of sex discrimination.' *Frontiero v. Richardson*, 411 U.S. 677, 684, 93 S.Ct. 1764, 1769, 36 L.Ed.2d 583 (1973). Until such time as the effects of that history are eradicated, care must be taken to assure that our self-defense instructions afford women the right to have their conduct judged in light of the individual physical handicaps which are the product of sex discrimination. To fail to do so is to deny the right of the individual woman involved to trial by the same rules which are applicable to male defendants. The portion of the instruction above quoted misstates our law in creating an objective standard of 'reasonableness.' It then compounds that error by utilizing language suggesting that the respondent's conduct must be measured against that of a reasonable male individual finding himself in the same circumstances.

We conclude that the instruction here in question contains an improper statement of the law on a vital issue in the case, is inconsistent, misleading and prejudicial when read in conjunction with other instructions pertaining to the same issue, and therefore is a proper basis for a finding of reversible error. * * *

In light of the errors in admission of evidence and instruction of the jury, the decision of the Court of Appeals is affirmed, the conviction reversed, and the case remanded for a new trial.

[The concurring opinion of WRIGHT, J., and the dissenting opinion of HAMILTON, J., have been omitted.]

NOTE

Donna Coker and Lindsay Harrison note that "Although Wanrow did not defend herself against an intimate abuser, the plurality opinion would ultimately provide a crucial tool for victims of domestic violence who act[ ] to defend themselves against their abusers." Donna Coker & Lindsay C Harrison, *The Story of* Wanrow*: The Reasonable Woman and the Law of Self-Defense*, *in* CRIMINAL LAW STORIES 213, 245 (Donna Coker & Robert Weisberg eds. 2013). The *Wanrow* decision made tremendous strides in recognizing the importance of gender in assessing the reasonableness of a female defendant's self-defense claim. While the case is well known for its contributions to the law of self-defense for women defendants, it is less well-known that Wanrow was a Native American activist on trial for murder of a White man at a time of strong anti-American Indian sentiment in Spokane County, Washington. *Id.* at 252. Despite this anti-American Indian sentiment, the trial court rejected Wanrow's attempt to proffer expert testimony on Native American culture. *Id.* at 253. Coker and Harrison explain that the expert witness would have testified "that within Indian culture . . . if 'an older person . . . would take advantage of a younger [child] or try to perform an unnatural sex act on that younger child, . . . [you would expect] a more severe reaction to such conduct . . . than there might be in the Anglo-Saxon culture.'" *Id.* The expert witness would have also testified that Native American mothers are more protective of their children than Anglo-Saxon mothers. *Id.* at 253-54. This testimony would have explained why Wanrow was especially fearful of Wesler and why it was reasonable for her to believe she needed to act in self-defense. *Id.* at 254.

3. IMPERFECT SELF-DEFENSE

What if you honestly believe that force is necessary on the present occasion, but your belief is unreasonable? Or, what if someone attacks you with nondeadly force, and you wrongfully escalate the conflict by using deadly force? Under the traditional common law approach, if the victim died you would be convicted of murder; you would not have a valid self-defense claim. However, in some states, your crime may be mitigated in a homicide prosecution from murder to voluntary manslaughter. This doctrine is called "imperfect self-defense." *See, e.g., In re Christian S.*, 7 Cal.4th 768, 30 Cal.Rptr.2d 33, 872 P.2d 574 (1994).

What is the rationale for this mitigation? The idea is that we need a middle ground between a complete defense and no defense. The person who honestly, even if wrongly and unreasonably, believes that force is necessary is not as culpable as someone who knows or believes that it is not necessary. Similarly, a nondeadly aggressor who then becomes the victim of deadly violence shares some fault with the defendant.

The mitigation principle incorporated in the doctrine of imperfect self-defense is incorporated, as well, in the justification defenses set out in the Model Penal Code. Section 3.09(2) provides that when the actor seeking an affirmative defense for the use of force is reckless or negligent in having a belief about the necessity of that force under the circumstances, or when the actor is reckless or negligent in acquiring or failing to acquire material knowledge concerning the justifiability of her use of force, she loses any justification defense as against prosecutions based on recklessness or negligence. The result, then, is similar to that achieved by the doctrine of imperfect self-defense. The actor who is acquitted of the charged offense on the ground of self-defense may be found guilty of a less serious crime which requires proof of recklessness or negligence as the mental state.

4. DEFENSE OF OTHERS

A close cousin of self-defense, defense of others is a justification defense used when a person uses force against another person to defend a third person he thinks is in imminent danger of unlawful attack. Like self-defense, defense of others includes an imminence requirement, a necessity requirement, and a proportionality requirement (deadly force may only be used to protect the third party from death or grievous bodily injury). Moreover, like self-defense, defense of others requires that the defendant honestly and reasonably believed the force he used was necessary to protect the third person from an imminent unlawful attack.

The older common law approach to defense of others diverged from self-defense doctrine in two ways. First, the older common law included an Act-at-Peril rule, which permitted the use of force in defense of a third person only if that person could legally use force in self-defense. In other words, the defendant who came to a third person's rescue did so at his peril. If it turned out that the third person had no right to use force in self-defense, then the defendant would have no defense. Second, under the older common law approach, the defense was only available if the defendant was in a particular status relationship with the person being protected. In other words, the third person being protected had to be a close relative or, in some cases, the servant or employee of the defendant.

Today, most jurisdictions have done away with both the Act-at-Peril rule and the status relationship limitation. When *People v. Young* was decided, however, the Act-at-Peril rule was the majority rule at the time. Note how the dissent tries to make use of the doctrine of mistake of fact in order to challenge the outcome.

PEOPLE V. YOUNG

Court of Appeals of New York
11 N.Y.2d 274, 183 N.E.2d 319 (1962)

PER CURIAM.

Whether one, who in good faith aggressively intervenes in a struggle between another person and a police officer in civilian dress attempting to effect the lawful arrest of the third person, may be properly convicted of assault in the third degree[a] is a question of law of first impression here.

---

[a] New York law as written when *Young* was decided, stated that a person is guilty of assault in the third degree, a class A misdemeanor, when he:

1. Commits an assault, or an assault and battery, not such as is specified in sections 240 [first degree assault] and 242 [second degree assault], or
2. Operates or drives or directs or knowingly and willfully permits any one subject to his commands to operate or drive any vehicle or any kind in a culpably negligent manner, whereby another suffers bodily injury, or

The opinions in the court below in the absence of precedents in this State carefully expound the opposing views found in other jurisdictions. The majority in the Appellate Division have adopted the minority rule in the other States that one who intervenes in a struggle between strangers under the mistaken but reasonable belief that he is protecting another who he assumes is being unlawfully beaten is thereby exonerated from criminal liability. The weight of authority holds with the dissenters below that one who goes to the aid of a third person does so at his own peril.

While the doctrine espoused by the majority of the court below may have support in some States, we feel that such a policy would not be conducive to an orderly society. We agree with the settled policy of law in most jurisdictions that the right of a person to defend another ordinarily should not be greater than such person's right to defend himself.[b] * * *

In this case there can be no doubt that the defendant intended to assault the police officer in civilian dress. The resulting assault was forceful. Hence motive or mistake of fact is of no significance as the defendant was not charged with a crime requiring such intent or knowledge. To be guilty of third degree assault "It is sufficient that the defendant voluntarily intended to commit the unlawful act of touching." Since in these circumstances the aggression was inexcusable the defendant was properly convicted.

Accordingly, the order of the Appellate Division should be reversed and the information reinstated.

FROESSEL, J., dissenting.

The law is clear that one may kill in defense of another when there is reasonable, though mistaken, ground for believing that the person slain is about to commit a felony or to do some great personal injury to the apparent victim; yet the majority now hold, for the first time, that in the event of a simple assault under similar circumstances, the mistaken belief, no matter how reasonable, is no defense.

Briefly, the relevant facts are these: On a Friday afternoon at about 3:40, Detectives Driscoll and Murphy, not in uniform, observed an argument taking place between a motorist and one McGriff in the street in front of premises 64 West 54th Street, in midtown Manhattan. Driscoll attempted to chase McGriff out of the roadway in order to allow traffic to

---

3. Strikes, beats, or willfully injures the person or apparatus of any news reporter or new photographer during the time when such reporter or photographer is engaged in the pursuit of his occupation or calling in any public place or gathering.

N.Y. Penal Law § 244 (1939).

[b] New York Penal Law § 35.27 states that "A person may not use physical force to resist an arrest, whether authorized or unauthorized, which is being effected or attempted by a police officer or peace officer when it would reasonably appear that the latter is a police officer or peace officer." N.Y. Penal Law § 35.27 (McKinney 1998).

pass, but McGriff refused to move back; his actions caused a crowd to collect. After identifying himself to McGriff, Driscoll placed him under arrest. As McGriff resisted, defendant "came out of the crowd" from Driscoll's rear and struck Murphy about the head with his fist. In the ensuing struggle Driscoll's right kneecap was injured when defendant fell on top of him. At the station house, defendant said he had not known or thought Driscoll and Murphy were police officers.

Defendant testified that while he was proceeding on 54th Street he observed two white men, who appeared to be 45 or 50 years old, pulling on a "colored boy" (McGriff), who appeared to be a lad about 18, whom he did not know. The men had nearly pulled McGriff's pants off, and he was crying. Defendant admitted he knew nothing of what had transpired between the officers and McGriff, and made no inquiry of anyone; he just came there and pulled the officer away from McGriff.

Defendant was convicted of assault [in the] third degree. In reversing upon the law and dismissing the information, the Appellate Division held that one is not "criminally liable for assault in the third degree if he goes to the aid of another whom he mistakenly, but *reasonably*, believes is being unlawfully beaten, and thereby injures one of the apparent assaulters" (emphasis supplied). While in my opinion the majority below correctly stated the law, I would reverse here and remit so that the Appellate Division may pass on the question of whether or not defendant's conduct was reasonable in light of the circumstances presented at the trial.

As the majority below pointed out, assault is a crime derived from the common law. Basic to the imposition of criminal liability both at common law and under our statutory law is the existence in the one who committed the prohibited act of what has been variously termed a guilty mind, a *mens rea* or a criminal intent.

Criminal intent requires an awareness of wrongdoing. When conduct is based upon mistake of fact reasonably entertained, there can be no such awareness and, therefore, no criminal culpability. In *People ex rel. Hegeman v. Corrigan* we stated: "it is very apparent that the innocence or criminality of the intent in a particular act generally depends on the knowledge or belief of the actor at the time. An honest and *reasonable* belief in the existence of circumstances which, if true, would make the act for which the defendant is prosecuted innocent, would be a good defense." (Emphasis supplied.)

It is undisputed that defendant did not know that Driscoll and Murphy were detectives in plain clothes engaged in lawfully apprehending an alleged disorderly person. If, therefore, defendant *reasonably* believed he was lawfully assisting another, he would not have been guilty of a crime. Subdivision 3 of section 246 of the Penal Law provides that it is not unlawful to use force "When committed either by the party about to be injured or *by another person in his aid or defense, in preventing or attempting to prevent an offense against his person,* * * * if the force or violence used is not more than sufficient to prevent such offense" (emphasis supplied). The law is thus clear that if defendant entertained an "honest and reasonable belief" that the facts were as he perceived them to be, he would be exonerated from criminal liability.

By ignoring one of the most basic principles of criminal law—that crimes *mala in se* require proof of at least general criminal intent—the majority now hold that the defense of mistake of fact is "of no significance." We are not here dealing with one of "a narrow class of exceptions" where the Legislature has created crimes which do not depend on *criminal* intent but which are complete on the mere intentional doing of an act *malum prohibitum*.

There is no need, in my opinion, to consider the law of other States, for New York policy clearly supports the view that one may act on appearances reasonably ascertained. * * * Our Penal Law, to which I have already alluded, is a statement of that policy. The same policy was expressed by this court in *People v. Maine*. There, the defendant observed his brother fighting in the street with two other men; he stepped in and stabbed to death one of the latter. The defense was justifiable homicide under the predecessor of section 1055. The court held it reversible error to admit into evidence the declarations of the defendant's brother, made before defendant happened upon the scene, which tended to show that the brother was the aggressor. We said: "Of course the acts and conduct of the defendant must be judged solely with reference to the situation as it was when he first and afterwards saw it." Mistake of relevant fact, reasonably entertained, is thus a defense to homicide under section 1055, and one who kills in defense of another and proffers this defense of justification is to be judged according to the circumstances as they appeared to him.

The mistaken belief, however, must be one which is reasonably entertained, and the question of reasonableness is for the trier of the facts. "The question is not merely what did the accused believe, but also, what did he have the right to believe?" Without passing on the facts of the instant case, the Appellate Division had no right to assume that defendant's conduct was reasonable, and to dismiss the information as a matter of law. Nor do we have the right to reinstate the verdict without giving the Appellate Division the opportunity to pass upon the facts.

Although the majority of our court are now purporting to fashion a policy "conducive to an orderly society," by their decision they have defeated their avowed purpose. What public interest is promoted by a principle which would deter one from coming to the aid of a fellow citizen who he has reasonable ground to apprehend is in imminent danger of personal injury at the hands of assailants? Is it reasonable to denominate, as justifiable homicide, a slaying committed under a mistaken but reasonably held belief, and deny this same defense of justification to one using less force? Logic, as well as historical background and related precedent, dictates that the rule and policy expressed by our Legislature in the case of homicide, which is an assault resulting in death, should likewise be applicable to a much less serious assault not resulting in death.

I would reverse the order appealed from and remit the case to the Appellate Division pursuant to section 543–b of the Code of Criminal Procedure "for determination upon the questions of fact raised in that court."

5. DEFENSE OF HABITATION

In contrast to the long acceptance in Anglo-American law of the right to use deadly force to defend oneself or another person from a deadly attack, it has long been recognized that deadly force is not permissible simply in defense of property. Between these two clear rules lies a gray area: the so-called "defense of habitation." Under what circumstances should the law permit the occupant of a dwelling to use deadly force against an intruder?

The original common law rule permitted an occupant of the dwelling to use any force necessary, including deadly force, if he reasonably believed the force was necessary to prevent an imminent, unlawful entry. In some jurisdictions that follow the common law, the original rule has been modified to restrict the use of deadly force to cases in which the occupant reasonably believes such force is necessary to prevent imminent, unlawful entry, *and* that the intruder intends to commit a felony or cause injury to any occupant of the dwelling. In other jurisdictions that incorporate the common law, the requirements are even more stringent. In these states, the occupant of a dwelling may use deadly force against an intruder only if he reasonably believes that such force is necessary to prevent imminent, unlawful entry, *and* that the intruder intends to commit a forcible felony or kill or cause grievous bodily injury to the occupant or another occupant of the dwelling. Note that in these jurisdictions, the defense of habitation can be described as a kind of "accelerated" self-defense or defense of others.

Some jurisdictions give the homeowner who uses deadly force against an intruder a huge advantage at trial in the form of a presumption. In these jurisdictions, the jury may presume that the homeowner's belief in the need to use deadly force to protect against an imminent threat of death or serious bodily injury was reasonable. In other words, the homeowner defendant does not have to prove that his or her belief in the need to use deadly force was reasonable. The defendant, however, must have used deadly force to prevent an entry into the home or residence. *People v. Brown* examines the question whether entry onto an unenclosed front porch constitutes an entry into the residence under California's defense of habitation.

PEOPLE V. BROWN

Court of Appeal of California, Third District
6 Cal.App.4th 1489, 8 Cal.Rptr.2d 513 (1992)

DAVIS, J.

A jury convicted defendant of assault with a deadly weapon and found he personally used a firearm, but did not personally inflict great bodily injury on the victim. There was evidence showing the victim entered defendant's front porch and advanced toward defendant with a hammer raised back at shoulder-height after the two had argued about a contract under which the victim was to perform landscaping work at defendant's house. At this point, defendant, standing in the doorway of his home, shot the victim in the leg. According to defendant he did so in fear for his life.

In the published portion of this opinion, we hold that defendant was not entitled to a requested instruction based on section 198.5, the "Home Protection Bill of Rights."[1] Although there was evidence that the victim's entry onto defendant's front porch was unlawful and forcible, an entry onto a front porch like defendant's does not constitute entry into a residence as required under section 198.5. The porch in this case is an unenclosed front porch, without any signs, gates or other indications that would tend to show the residential occupant did not expect intrusion into that area. The porch is connected to a walkway, which is connected to a driveway, which in turn is connected to a public sidewalk. There is a doorbell adjacent to the front door to signal the arrival of persons on the porch. * * * Using principles developed by this court in *People v. Nible,* we conclude that, under these circumstances, a residential occupant does not have a reasonable expectation of protection from unauthorized intrusion onto the porch and thus an entry there does not entitle a defendant occupant to an instruction based on section 198.5. In this situation, the occupant is left with the standard instructions on self-defense. * * *

Background

What began as a minor contract dispute between a homeowner and a bricklayer ended with the homeowner shooting the bricklayer in the leg.

---

[1] Section 198.5 [of the California Penal Code] provides:

> Any person using force intended or likely to cause death or great bodily injury within his or her residence shall be presumed to have held a reasonable fear of imminent peril of death or great bodily injury to self, family, or a member of the household when that force is used against another person, not a member of the family or household, who unlawfully and forcibly enters or has unlawfully and forcibly entered the residence and the person using the force knew or had reason to believe that an unlawful and forcible entry occurred. As used in this section, great bodily injury means a significant or substantial physical injury.

About a month before the incident in question, defendant, the homeowner, and Jason Neal, the bricklayer, entered into a contract. Neal was to lay a brick flower bed at defendant's home, and defendant was to pay for labor and certain materials. The contract was to be completed over a two-week period in April because defendant had guests arriving at the end of that time. Prior to April 14, defendant and Neal had some minor disagreement regarding Neal's performance, but Neal was to finish the job.

On April 14, Neal arrived at defendant's house around 11:30 a.m. to continue his work. This time he brought an acquaintance, Butler, to help him. Neal, Butler and defendant gave varying accounts of what happened next.

Neal's Testimony

As soon as Neal arrived at defendant's house on April 14, defendant came out of the garage and told Neal he thought Neal was going to be there earlier that morning. Defendant told Neal he should get his tools and leave without finishing the job. Defendant then said Neal could go ahead and finish, because he (defendant) had company arriving the next day. Defendant then changed his mind again and told Neal to get his tools from the porch; defendant also said he was keeping the tools Neal had stored in defendant's backyard because he had paid for them.

At this point, Neal acknowledges that defendant and he had a "disagreement." However, Neal maintained it never escalated to anything more than a "man-to-man discussion." After that, defendant shut the garage door and went into his house. Neal then took his tools from the porch, put them beside his car, and walked back toward the house with a hammer in his hand. When he reached the flower bed, he began knocking off the top layer of bricks because he was angry at being fired. Neal testified he was turned oblong with his back towards the front door of defendant's house, approximately seven feet from the door.

After defendant walked into the house, Neal did not see defendant again until after he heard the gun go off. He did not hear defendant say anything other than his name before he heard the gunshot. Neal denied threatening or attacking defendant.

Butler's Testimony

When Butler and Neal arrived at defendant's house on April 14, defendant told Neal to pack up his tools and go home, "he was through." Neal and defendant then had a "heated discussion." Neal got some tools from the porch and set them by his car, then walked back toward the porch with empty hands. After defendant went into the garage, Neal picked up the rest of his tools and starting hitting the bricks he had laid, saying, "he [defendant] wasn't going to pay him for it, so he [Neal] was going to take it out."

Neal was facing the front door while he was hitting the bricks. Defendant came to the screen door and told Neal "you better," then shot Neal in the leg. Neal never attempted to throw the hammer, attack defendant, or strike anything but the bricks in the flower bed. Neal never tried to enter the house. Butler testified he could not remember how high Neal swung the hammer, but Neal was intent on hammering the bricks.

Defendant's Testimony

On April 14, defendant reminded Neal their agreement was that the work would be finished within two weeks, which meant Neal had only until the next day to complete the job. Yet, Neal had just delivered the balance of the bricks the previous day. Defendant did not think Neal could finish in that short time, so he told Neal to get his tools and go, that he would find someone else to finish the job.

At this point Neal picked up a "brick carry," walked over to defendant and started waving it around. Defendant backed further into the garage and warned Neal he was going to close the garage door. When Neal left the garage and passed a stack of bricks, he angrily kicked the pile down. Once inside the house, defendant heard a "hammering noise." Defendant hurried to the front door and saw Neal hammering away at the flower bed; defendant then started out the screen door and said something like, "Cut it out! Stop! Stop! Stop!"

Once defendant opened the screen door and started out, Neal looked up and saw defendant. He raised up and swung back with the hammer, then came off the flower bed with the hammer in his right hand, raised to his shoulder. He whirled around and began moving towards defendant, "not fast, but deliberate." Defendant testified Neal was like a "raging" animal and was in a "very antagonistic mood."

When defendant realized that only the screen door stood between himself and Neal, he jumped back inside and tried closing the screen door. He was very afraid, and concerned only with how to stop Neal and protect himself. Because of some problem with the hydraulic on the screen door, defendant believed he had to hold onto it or else it would fly open. Defendant testified he could not reach around the wooden door, which was open and to his left, in time to shut it, without letting go of the screen door. So, while holding onto the screen door handle, defendant picked up a handgun, which was lying under a cloth on a room divider next to the door. By this time, Neal had stepped over the flower bed and had come up to the first level of the porch, approximately five feet from defendant. Defendant fired the gun through the screen door, hitting Neal in the leg.

Defendant was afraid and "knew [Neal] was going to attack [him] with that hammer. . . ." Defendant testified he intended to shoot down at

the ground and sidewalk. He wasn't trying to hit Neal, but rather to stop him. Neal's right leg was on the porch when defendant shot him.

Discussion

1. Defendant's Requested Jury Instruction on Section 198.5

Section 198.5, enacted in 1984 and entitled the "Home Protection Bill of Rights," creates a rebuttable presumption that a residential occupant has a reasonable fear of death or great bodily injury when he or she uses deadly force against an unlawful and forcible intruder into the residence. For section 198.5 to apply, four elements must be met. There must be an unlawful and forcible entry into a residence; the entry must be by someone who is not a member of the family or the household; the residential occupant must have used "deadly" force against the victim within the residence; and finally, the residential occupant must have had knowledge of the unlawful and forcible entry.

These four elements would comprise the heart of any instruction based on section 198.5. The trial court refused defendant's request to instruct under section 198.5 because the court found no evidence of "entry" into the "residence."

It is undisputed there was evidence showing that Neal's entry onto the porch was unlawful and forcible; that Neal was not a member of defendant's family or household; that defendant's firing of the gun constituted use of deadly force under section 198.5; and that defendant knew of Neal's unlawful and forcible entry, since he testified he ordered Neal off the property and then saw Neal approach menacingly with a hammer and told him to stop. The issue narrows to whether Neal's entry onto defendant's front porch constituted an entry into defendant's residence. In other words, is an entry onto an unenclosed front porch (a porch that has no access barriers from a public sidewalk) an entry into a residence, so that a residential occupant who uses deadly force against an unlawful and forcible intruder becomes entitled, upon request, to a jury instruction based on section 198.5? We conclude there was no residential entry here.

This issue requires us to examine the scope of the term "residence" in section 198.5 as it relates to a front porch. The plain language of section 198.5 shows the statute was intended to give residential occupants additional protection in situations where they are confronted in their own homes by unlawful intruders such as burglars. It is appropriate, therefore, to look at relevant burglary cases to determine whether there was an entry into a residence in this case.

Preliminarily, we note that California's statutory definition of burglary is broader than the common law definition. Under California law, a breaking is no longer required. Furthermore, California case law has expanded the definition of a burglarious entry into a building or

residence, to encompass situations where burglary would be inapplicable under the common law.

The California Courts of Appeal have formed various tests for determining the scope of the terms "residence" or "building" for burglarious entry. We conclude the reasonable expectation test this court formulated in *Nible* is the appropriate one to employ here. Since one of the purposes of the burglary statute is to protect against unauthorized entry and the attendant danger that the occupant will react violently to the intrusion, the reasonable expectation test focuses on the protection the inhabitants of a structure reasonably expect. In situations implicating this particular purpose, the proper question is whether the nature of a structure's composition is such that a reasonable person would expect some protection from unauthorized intrusions. In *Nible*, this court held that a reasonable person would believe a window screen provides some protection against unauthorized intrusions, noting that even an open door or window affords some expectation of such protection because reasonable persons understand the social convention that portals may not be crossed without permission from the structure's owner.

This safety-based reasonable expectation test is appropriate for the issue presented here involving section 198.5. This is because section 198.5 gives a defendant a rebuttable presumption that he was in reasonable fear of imminent danger when he used deadly force within his residence against an intruder (most likely a burglar) who unlawfully and forcibly entered the residence. As noted in *Owen*, section 198.5 establishes a presumption " 'that the very act of forcible entry entails a threat to the life and limb of the homeowner.' "

Applying this reasonable expectation test to the ordinary, unenclosed front porch at issue here, we conclude that Neal's entry onto the porch cannot constitute entry into defendant's residence for purposes of section 198.5. A reasonable person would not expect protection from unauthorized intrusion onto this kind of porch. Quite the contrary. Social convention dictates that anyone wishing to summon the occupant's presence or gain entry into the home must first enter the porch. The porch is not a portal. Absent "no soliciting" signs or a gate or some other barrier, Girl Scouts selling cookies, the person delivering the newspaper, the door-to-door salesperson or any stranger will likely come onto a front porch of this nature, without permission. The reasonable residential occupant would not react violently to this entry. We find that a residential occupant does not have a reasonable expectation of protection from unauthorized intrusion onto a front porch like the one involved in this case.

Defendant argues that a reasonable person would have an expectation of protection because of the threat of immediate access to the home. It is true that once on the porch, particularly if the front door is open (as it was in this case), an intruder would have ready access to the home. It is nonetheless a qualitatively lesser expectation of protection than that recognized in section 198.5, and a situation which is adequately covered by the self-defense doctrine. If a residential occupant reasonably believes that bodily injury is about to be inflicted upon him or her by the intruder's presence on the porch, then the occupant can use reasonable force to repel the intruder, and the occupant, if tried, would be entitled to self-defense instructions.

Defendant relies on *In re Christopher J.* That reliance is misplaced. There, the Fourth District held that entry into a carport with intent to commit theft constituted a burglary because the carport was "an integral part of the dwelling house." The carport was roofed and attached to the dwelling house on one side; also, it was enclosed in the rear with a half-wall and open on two sides. * * *

We hold that a residential occupant does not have a reasonable expectation of protection from unauthorized intrusion onto the kind of front porch involved in this case, and therefore entry onto such a porch does not constitute entry into a residence for section 198.5 purposes. The trial court correctly denied defendant's request for a jury instruction based on section 198.5, which would have given defendant a rebuttable presumption that he was in reasonable fear of imminent danger when he used deadly force against Jason Neal. * * *

6. DEFENSE OF PROPERTY

As a general matter, one is not allowed to use deadly force in defense of property. As we have seen, however, the existence of a "defense of habitation" or a privilege to use deadly force against home intruders, blurs the line between defense of property and defense of self and others. In *People v. Ceballos* and the article that follows, note the overlap in law, fact, and culture, between defending one's self and defending one's property. *Ceballos* also addresses the problems raised by the use of automatic protection devices.

PEOPLE V. CEBALLOS

Supreme Court of California
12 Cal.3d 470, 526 P.2d 241, 116 Cal.Rptr. 233 (1974)

BURKE, J.

Don Ceballos was found guilty by a jury of assault with a deadly weapon. Imposition of sentence was suspended and he was placed on probation. He appeals from the judgment, contending primarily that his conduct was not unlawful because the alleged victim was attempting to commit burglary when hit by a trap gun mounted in the garage of defendant's dwelling and that the court erred in instructing the jury. We have concluded that the former argument lacks merit, that the court did not commit prejudicial error in instructing the jury, and that the judgment should be affirmed.

Defendant lived alone in a home in San Anselmo. The regular living quarters were above the garage, but defendant sometimes slept in the garage and had about $2,500 worth of property there. In March 1970 some tools were stolen from defendant's home. On May 12, 1970, he noticed the lock on his garage doors was bent and pry marks were on one of the doors. The next day he mounted a loaded .22 caliber pistol in the garage. The pistol was aimed at the center of the garage doors and was connected by a wire to one of the doors so that the pistol would discharge if the door was opened several inches.

The damage to defendant's lock had been done by a 16-year-old boy named Stephen and a 15-year-old boy named Robert. On the afternoon of May 15, 1970, the boys returned to defendant's house while he was away. Neither boy was armed with a gun or knife. After looking in the windows and seeing no one, Stephen succeeded in removing the lock on the garage doors with a crowbar, and, as he pulled the door outward, he was hit in the face with a bullet from the pistol. Stephen testified: He intended to go into the garage "[for] musical equipment" because he had a debt to pay to a friend. His "way of paying that debt would be to take [defendant's] property and sell it" and use the proceeds to pay the debt. He "wasn't going to do it [i.e., steal] for sure, necessarily." He was there "to look around," and "getting in, I don't know if I would have actually stolen."

Defendant, testifying in his own behalf, admitted having set up the trap gun. He stated that after noticing the pry marks on his garage door on May 12, he felt he should "set up some kind of a trap, something to keep the burglar out of my home." When asked why he was trying to keep the burglar out, he replied, ". . . Because somebody was trying to steal my property . . . and I don't want to come home some night and have the thief in there . . . usually a thief is pretty desperate . . . and . . . they just pick up a weapon . . . if they don't have one . . . and do the best they can." When asked by the police shortly after the shooting why he assembled the trap gun, defendant stated that "he didn't have much and he wanted to protect what he did have."

As heretofore appears, the jury found defendant guilty of assault with a deadly weapon. An assault is "an unlawful attempt, coupled with a present ability, to commit a violent injury on the person of another."

Defendant contends that had he been present he would have been justified in shooting Stephen since Stephen was attempting to commit burglary, that * * * defendant had a right to do indirectly what he could have done directly, and that therefore any attempt by him to commit a violent injury upon Stephen was not "unlawful" and hence not an assault. The People argue that * * * as a matter of law a trap gun constitutes excessive force, and that in any event the circumstances were not in fact such as to warrant the use of deadly force.

The issue of criminal liability under statutes such as Penal Code section 245 where the instrument employed is a trap gun or other deadly mechanical device appears to be one of first impression in this state, but in other jurisdictions courts have considered the question of criminal and civil liability for death or injuries inflicted by such a device.

At common law in England it was held that a trespasser, having knowledge that there are spring guns in a wood, cannot maintain an action for an injury received in consequence of his accidentally stepping on the wire of such gun. That [rule] aroused such a protest in England that it was abrogated seven years later by a statute, which made it a misdemeanor to set spring guns with intent to inflict grievous bodily injury but excluded from its operation a spring gun set between sunset and sunrise in a dwelling house for the protection thereof.

In the United States, courts have concluded that a person may be held criminally liable under statutes proscribing homicides and shooting with intent to injure, or civilly liable, if he sets upon his premises a deadly mechanical device and that device kills or injures another. However, an exception to the rule that there may be criminal and civil liability for death or injuries caused by such a device has been recognized where the intrusion is, in fact, such that the person, were he present, would be justified in taking the life or inflicting the bodily harm with his own hands. The phrase "were he present" does not hypothesize the actual presence of the person, but is used in setting forth in an indirect manner the principle that a person may do indirectly that which he is privileged to do directly.

Allowing persons, at their own risk, to employ deadly mechanical devices imperils the lives of children, firemen and policemen acting within the scope of their employment, and others. Where the actor is present, there is always the possibility he will realize that deadly force is not necessary, but deadly mechanical devices are without mercy or discretion. Such devices "are silent instrumentalities of death. They deal death and destruction to the innocent as well as the criminal intruder without the slightest warning. The taking of human life [or infliction of great bodily injury] by such means is brutally savage and inhuman."

It seems clear that the use of such devices should not be encouraged. Moreover, whatever may be thought in torts, the foregoing rule setting forth an exception to liability for death or injuries inflicted by such devices "is inappropriate in penal law for it is obvious that it does not prescribe a workable standard of conduct; liability depends upon fortuitous results." We therefore decline to adopt that rule in criminal cases. * * *

Furthermore, even if that rule were applied here, * * * defendant was not justified in shooting Stephen. Penal Code section 197 provides: "Homicide is . . . justifiable . . . 1. When resisting any attempt to murder any person, or to commit a felony, or to do some great bodily injury upon any person; or, 2. When committed in defense of habitation, property, or person, against one who manifestly intends or endeavors, by violence or surprise, to commit a felony. . . . " Since a homicide is justifiable under the circumstances specified in section 197, *a fortiori* an attempt to commit a violent injury upon another under those circumstances is justifiable.

By its terms subdivision 1 of Penal Code section 197 appears to permit killing to prevent any "felony," but in view of the large number of felonies today and the inclusion of many that do not involve a danger of serious bodily harm, a literal reading of the section is undesirable. *People v. Jones* read into section 197, subdivision 1, the limitation that the felony be "some atrocious crime attempted to be committed by force." * * *

* * * [W]hatever may have been the very early common law, the rule developed at common law that killing or use of deadly force to prevent a felony was justified only if the offense was a forcible and atrocious crime. * * *

Examples of forcible and atrocious crimes are murder, mayhem, rape and robbery. In such crimes "from their atrocity and violent human life [or safety] either is, or is presumed to be, in peril."

Burglary has been included in the list of such crimes. However, in view of the wide scope of burglary under Penal Code section 459, as compared with the common law definition of that offense, in our opinion it cannot be said that under all circumstances burglary under section 459 constitutes a forcible and atrocious crime.[2]

Where the character and manner of the burglary do not reasonably create a fear of great bodily harm, there is no cause for exaction of human life, or for the use of deadly force. The character and manner of the burglary could not reasonably create such a fear unless the burglary threatened, or was reasonably believed to threaten, death or serious bodily harm.

In the instant case the asserted burglary did not threaten death or serious bodily harm, since no one but Stephen and Robert was then on the premises. A defendant is not protected from liability merely by the fact that the intruder's conduct is such as would justify the defendant, were

[2] At common law burglary was the breaking and entering of a mansion house in the night with the intent to commit a felony. Burglary under Penal Code section 459 differs from common law burglary in that the entry may be in the daytime and of numerous places other than a mansion house, and breaking is not required. For example, under section 459 a person who enters a store with the intent of committing theft is guilty of burglary. It would seem absurd to hold that a store detective could kill that person if necessary to prevent him from committing that offense.

he present, in believing that the intrusion threatened death or serious bodily injury. There is ordinarily the possibility that the defendant, were he present, would realize the true state of affairs and recognize the intruder as one whom he would not be justified in killing or wounding.

We thus conclude that defendant was not justified under Penal Code section 197, subdivisions 1 or 2, in shooting Stephen to prevent him from committing burglary. * * *

We recognize that our position regarding justification for killing under Penal Code section 197, subdivisions 1 and 2, differs from the position of section 143, subdivision (2), of the Restatement Second of Torts, regarding the use of deadly force to prevent a "felony . . . of a type . . . involving the breaking and entry of a dwelling place" but in view of the supreme value of human life we do not believe bodily force can be justified to prevent all felonies of the foregoing type, including ones in which no person is, or is reasonably believed to be, on the premises except the would-be burglar. * * *

Defendant also argues that had he been present he would have been justified in shooting Stephen under subdivision 4 of Penal Code section 197, which provides, "Homicide is . . . justifiable . . . 4. When necessarily committed in *attempting*, by lawful ways and means, *to apprehend* any person for any felony committed. . . ." (Italics added.) The argument cannot be upheld. The words "attempting . . . to apprehend" contain the idea of acting for the purpose of apprehending. * * * Here no showing was made that defendant's intent in shooting was to apprehend a felon. Rather it appears from his testimony and extrajudicial statement heretofore recited that his intent was to prevent a burglary, to protect his property, and to avoid the possibility that a thief might get into defendant's house and injure him upon his return. * * *

Defendant also does not, and could not properly, contend that the intrusion was in fact such that, were he present, he would be justified under Civil Code section 50 in using deadly force. That section provides, "Any necessary force may be used to protect from wrongful injury the person or property of oneself. . . ." This section also should be read in the light of the common law, and at common law in general deadly force could not be used solely for the protection of property. " 'The preservation of human life and limb from grievous harm is of more importance to society than the protection of property.' " * * *

At common law an exception to the foregoing principle that deadly force could not be used solely for the protection of property was recognized where the property was a dwelling house in some circumstances. * * * Also at common law if another attempted to burn a dwelling the owner was privileged to use deadly force if this seemed necessary to defend his "castle" against the threatened harm. Further, deadly force was privileged if it was, or reasonably seemed, necessary to protect the dwelling against a burglar.

Here we are not concerned with dispossession or burning of a dwelling, and, as heretofore concluded, the asserted burglary in this case was not of such a character as to warrant the use of deadly force. * * *

We conclude that as a matter of law the exception to the rule of liability for injuries inflicted by a deadly mechanical device does not apply under the circumstances here appearing. * * *

The judgment is affirmed.

KILLER OF THIEF WINS WIDE SUPPORT

Jeffrey Bair
The San Diego Union Tribune, Dec. 27, 1994, at A–8[a]

ERIE, Pa.—Barkeeper Thomas Radu shot an unarmed thief in the back of the head. That much is clear. The question is whether he had good reason.

The 70-year-old tavern owner is accused of killing James Blum after catching Blum with his hand in the till Nov. 4 in the latest in a series of robberies at what a neighbor called a workingman's bar. As Blum's partner watched, Radu grabbed his gun and fired, police said. Blum—who had been a suspect in some of the 10 robberies at the bar during the previous three months—fell near the door of the nearly empty tavern with a bullet in his brain and a wad of bills in his possession.

A prosecutor has been considering for nearly two months whether to drop a homicide charge against Radu, who has considerable support from friends and strangers. "He's no hero, but I think that he should be relieved of the whole thing," grocer Mike Dowd said. "Look at what he was facing. The only people in there were two baddy-bads, so to speak. And they had no intention of leaving. They had the intention of beating the hell out of him." Radu is free pending a hearing Jan. 6 and has been back at Radu's Tavern, which he has operated for 35 years. His lawyer, David Ridge, said Radu was defending himself. District Attorney Rusty Cunningham must determine whether Radu himself was threatened, as required by law for a finding of justifiable homicide.

History could be on Radu's side. In 1991, a jury in Erie needed only two hours to clear garage owner Daniel Strong of wounding two stereo thieves with a shotgun. "I hope the man gets off," Strong said about Radu. "If somebody is willing to take the risk of robbing somebody, of maybe doing harm, of being lazy and breaking the law to take what someone else like me has worked hard for, then he is taking the chance of losing his life, too."

---

[a] Reprinted with permission of The Associated Press.

When WLKK talk show host Barry Dain Steinhagen suggested Radu should be prosecuted because he was not in danger, callers overwhelmingly favored dropping the charge. "Some of them are saying, 'Enough is enough.' " Steinhagen said. "Sure, people are frustrated. But what I was saying was that Radu had no right to take matters into his own hands."

Radu's neighbors say he was frustrated with frequent robberies at the brick tavern where he was known to have a low tolerance for sloppy drunks and other troublemakers. He cherished the metal shop and paper mill workers who unwound at Radu's Tavern after their shifts—hard-working men like him. Radu has said he does not want to discuss the shooting.

NOTE

As indicated in *People v. Ceballos*, another situation in which force, including deadly force, may sometimes be justified is when a person is attempting to prevent the commission of a felony, or attempting to apprehend a fleeing felon. The older common law approach permitted any force, including deadly force, in both the prevention and the detention of felons, although in some jurisdictions the privilege to use deadly force to stop a fleeing felon was limited by a kind of Act-at-Peril rule under which the privilege was lost if the person killed or injured turned out to be an innocent bystander. *See, e.g., People v. Piorkowski*, 41 Cal.App.3d 324 (1974) (the use of deadly force by a private citizen in arresting a fleeing felon is only privileged if a felony was in fact committed and the defendant had reasonable cause for believing the person arrested to have committed it).

As *Ceballos* also suggests, whether and in what circumstances deadly force should be used to defend oneself against burglary remains a contested issue. Consider the case that follows.

PEOPLE V. QUESADA

Court of Appeal of California, First Appellate District, Division One
113 Cal.App.3d 533, 169 Cal.Rptr. 881 (1980)

GRODIN, J.

Defendant's house was burglarized during the night while no one was at home. Two days later, under circumstances we shall describe, defendant shot and killed the burglar. In response to charges of murder with use of a firearm, defendant claimed justification under Penal Code section 197, subdivision 4, which provides that "[h]omicide is . . . justifiable . . . When necessarily committed in attempting, by lawful ways and means, to apprehend any person for any felony committed, . . . " By case law, that justification exists "only where the felony committed is one which threatens death or great bodily harm." The trial court instructed the jury that it was its duty to determine whether the burglary met that description, taking into account the surrounding facts. The jury, apparently rejecting the asserted justification defense, found defendant guilty of involuntary manslaughter and found also that he used a firearm in the commission of that offense. The trial court suspended imposition of sentence, and defendant was admitted to probation conditioned on confinement in the county jail for one year.

On appeal, appellant contends that burglary at night is *necessarily* a felony which threatens death or bodily injury for purposes of determining the justifiability of deadly force used by a citizen to apprehend the burglar, and that the trial court erred in not so instructing the jury. Alternatively, he contends that the firearm use finding should be stricken because such use was an element of the involuntary manslaughter offense which he was found to have committed. We are not persuaded by either contention for the reasons which follow, and therefore affirm.

The Factual Setting. The following synopsis is based primarily on appellant's testimony at trial. In the evening of January 24, 1979, appellant left his apartment to go bowling. When he returned at 2 a.m. the following morning he found that it had been ransacked and that a number of valuable items, including his stereo, had been stolen. No one was in the apartment when the burglary occurred.

Later that day appellant told a neighbor, Art Sanchez, about the theft. The following day, January 26, Sanchez informed appellant that a person named Edie had asked Sanchez if he knew anyone who wanted to buy a stereo. Sanchez related to appellant Edie's description of the stereo and appellant concluded from the description that the stereo might be his.

Sanchez asked appellant not to contact the police, since Edie was married to a cousin of Sanchez and they were not positive that the stereo belonged to appellant. Accordingly, appellant devised a plan for recovering his property: Sanchez would have Edie bring the stereo to Sanchez' house for sale, appellant and some friends would grab Edie, and then they would notify the police. Sanchez warned appellant that Edie was dangerous and unpredictable: he was a narcotics addict usually "high" on drugs; he had just been released from prison, where he had been a member of a prison gang; he stole for a living; and he sometimes carried a gun.

That night, as planned, Sanchez and a companion, Cabrera, visited Edie, saw the stereo, agreed to purchase it for $400 (which appellant supplied), and returned to Sanchez' house to complete the transaction. There, Cabrera gave the $400 to Edie, who then helped to carry the stereo speakers into the house from his car, and left.

Meanwhile, appellant and friends were waiting in the bedroom. When Cabrera announced that Edie was leaving, appellant went to the kitchen, identified the stereo as his, and went outside, where he saw Edie in his car. Appellant tried to open the driver's door, but it was locked. Appellant told Edie to "freeze" and get out of the car. Cabrera opened the passenger door and tried to grab Edie, telling him to stop and get out. Edie then reached under his seat, causing both appellant and Cabrera to believe that he was reaching for a gun. They both stepped back and Edie accelerated, hitting two trees with his open passenger door. Appellant, who was armed with a loaded 9-mm. automatic pistol, then fired into the driver's door of the car. He feared, he testified, that Edie would run over him or Cabrera and get away. Edie then shifted forward and accelerated down the street, and appellant gave chase. Appellant testified that he saw the brake lights go on, and thought Edie was going to stop and shoot, so appellant fired at the car, emptying the gun. Edie died of a bullet wound in his chest.

I

As regards appellant's conviction for involuntary manslaughter, the sole issue is whether the trial court erred in refusing to give an instruction, which appellant's counsel requested, to the effect that homicide is justifiable "when necessarily committed in attempting, by lawful ways and means, to apprehend any person who has committed burglary of the first degree." * * *

In [*People v. Ceballos*] the defendant was convicted of assault with a deadly weapon after a trap gun, which he had mounted in the garage of his dwelling, fired and hit a person who entered the garage in an attempt to commit burglary. * * *

In considering whether the burglary in that case involved an "atrocious crime" within the meaning of the common-law (and therefore statutory) rule, the court in *Ceballos* stated: "Where the character and manner of the burglary do not reasonably create a fear of great bodily harm, there is no cause for exaction of human life, or for the use of deadly force. The character and manner of the burglary could not reasonably create such a fear unless the burglary threatened, or was reasonably believed to threaten, death or serious bodily harm. In the instant case the asserted burglary did not threaten death or serious bodily harm, since no one but [the burglars] was then on the premises."

Appellant characterizes this last quoted sentence from *Ceballos* as dictum, but clearly it is more than that. It is a necessary element of the court's analysis, supporting the conclusion that the use of deadly force to prevent the burglary of an unoccupied premises is not justified under Penal Code section 197. And since a burglary committed when no one is on the premises is not a crime which threatens death or serious bodily harm so as to justify the use of deadly force in preventing its occurrence, it would seem to follow that it is not, or at least not per se, the sort of crime which justifies the use of deadly force by a citizen in apprehending the criminal. In the latter case, as well as the former, the modern common law rule limits the use of deadly force to "dangerous" felonies: "The law does not permit the use of deadly force for the mere purpose of preventing a nondangerous felony, and a private person cannot defeat this restriction merely by saying his purpose is arrest rather than prevention."[3] Indeed, the court in *Piorkowski* expressly determined that "[t]he reasoning of the court in *Jones* [limiting subdivision 1 of section 197 to dangerous felonies on the basis of common law] applies with like force and effect in construing subdivision 4 of section 197." We conclude that the trial court did not err by refusing to give the instruction requested. * * *

The order granting probation is affirmed.

7. NECESSITY

The idea behind the necessity defense (also sometimes called the "choice of evils" defense) is that sometimes the greater good is served by breaking the law than by obeying it. In such circumstances, the defendant should not be criminally punished. Necessity therefore provides an affirmative defense to the actor in situations in which, from an objective perspective, the harm caused by breaking the law is less than the harm avoided by the action.

While the specific elements of the necessity defense vary from jurisdiction to jurisdiction, as a general matter, a defendant claiming necessity as a defense in jurisdictions incorporating the common law may be acquitted if:

1. The harm the defendant was seeking to avoid was greater than the harm the defendant would likely cause by breaking the law (the balance of harms inquiry);
2. The defendant was seeking to avoid a clear and imminent danger;
3. It was reasonable for the defendant to believe his illegal conduct would abate the threatened harm. In other words, there is a causal connection between the defendant's illegal act and the harm the defendant was seeking to avoid;
4. No effective legal alternatives were available to the defendant;

---

[3] Whether the common law has developed similar limitations upon the use of deadly force by police officers is more debatable. It is interesting to note that "[t]he privilege of using deadly force had its common-law development primarily in the areas of law enforcement and crime prevention, and the extent of the development is not surprising since all felonies were punishable by death in those early days. As the felon had forfeited his life by the perpetration of his crime, it was quite logical to authorize the use of deadly force if this reasonably seemed necessary to bring him to justice." Since escape from arrest is not a crime punishable by death, the justification for licensing a private citizen to impose capital punishment upon persons fleeing from crimes outside that category is not readily apparent. We do not, of course, reach that policy question.

5. The legislature has not determined the matter in a way that goes against the defendant (aka no legislative preclusion); and

6. The defendant was not at fault for creating the dangerous situation.

The Model Penal Code's version of the necessity defense is found in section 3.02, which provides:

> [C]onduct that the actor believes to be necessary to avoid a harm or evil to himself or others is justifiable provided that: (a) the harm or evil sought to be avoided by such conduct is greater than that sought to be prevented by the law defining the offense charged; and (b) neither the Code nor other law defining the offense provides exceptions or defenses dealing with the specific situation involved; and (c) a legislative purpose to exclude the justification claimed does not otherwise plainly appear.

Model Penal Code § 3.02.

Like the common law version of the necessity defense, the Model Penal Code focuses on a balancing of the relative harms. However, there are also some key differences. First, under the Model Penal Code, there is no imminence requirement. As long as the jury finds the harm avoided greater than the harm caused and the defendant believes the action was necessary, the harm need not be imminent. Second, the common law tradition suggests that necessity is not a defense to homicide on the theory that it can never constitute the greater good to kill an innocent person. (Recall the *Dudley & Stephens* case in Chapter 1.) Under the Model Penal Code, however, there is no such explicit limitation; it is possible, therefore, that under certain circumstances killing an innocent person could be successfully defended as necessary.

Most common law judges and the drafters of the Model Penal Code seem to have imagined the necessity defense being used in cases without broader social or political implications: for example, the person lost in a blizzard who breaks into a mountain cabin to stay alive, or the person who deliberately burns another's property in order to create a firebreak during a dangerous wildfire. As it happens, however, the necessity defense is also invoked in cases involving political protest. In such cases, judges are often reluctant to instruct juries on the defense and to admit evidence that might support the defense. Consider the case that follows.

UNITED STATES V. SCHOON

United States Court of Appeals for the Ninth Circuit
939 F.2d 826 (9th Cir. 1991)

BOOCHEVER, C.J.

Gregory Schoon, Raymond Kennon, Jr., and Patricia Manning appeal their convictions for obstructing activities of the Internal Revenue Service Office in Tucson, Arizona, and failing to comply with an order of a federal police officer. Both charges stem from their activities in protest of United States involvement in El Salvador. They claim the district court improperly denied them a necessity defense. Because we hold the necessity defense inapplicable in cases like this, we affirm.

I

On December 4, 1989, thirty people, including appellants, gained admittance to the IRS office in Tucson, where they chanted "keep America's tax dollars out of El Salvador," splashed simulated blood on the counters, walls, and carpeting, and generally obstructed the office's operation. After a federal police officer ordered the group, on several occasions, to disperse or face arrest, appellants were arrested.

At a bench trial, appellants proffered testimony about conditions in El Salvador as the motivation for their conduct. They attempted to assert a necessity defense, essentially contending that their acts in protest of American involvement in El Salvador were necessary to avoid further bloodshed in that country. While finding appellants motivated solely by humanitarian concerns, the court nonetheless precluded the defense as a matter of law, relying on Ninth Circuit precedent. The sole issue on appeal is the propriety of the court's exclusion of a necessity defense as a matter of law.

II

A district court may preclude a necessity defense where "the evidence, as described in the defendant's offer of proof, is insufficient as a matter of law to support the proffered defense." To invoke the necessity defense, therefore, the defendants colorably must have shown that: (1) they were faced with a choice of evils and chose the lesser evil; (2) they acted to prevent imminent harm; (3) they reasonably anticipated a direct causal relationship between their conduct and the harm to be averted; and (4) they had no legal alternatives to violating the law. We review *de novo* the district court's decision to bar a necessity defense.

The district court denied the necessity defense on the grounds that (1) the requisite immediacy was lacking; (2) the actions taken would not abate the evil; and (3) other legal alternatives existed. Because the threshold test for admissibility of a necessity defense is a conjunctive one, a court may preclude invocation of the defense if "proof is deficient with regard to any of the four elements. . . . "

While we could affirm substantially on those grounds relied upon by the district court, we find a deeper, systemic reason for the complete absence of federal case law recognizing a necessity defense in an indirect civil disobedience case. Indirect civil disobedience involves violating a law which is not, itself, the object of protest, whereas direct civil disobedience involves protesting the existence of a particular law by breaking that law. This case involves indirect civil disobedience because these protestors were not challenging the laws under which they were charged. In contrast, the civil rights lunch counter sit-ins, for example, constituted direct civil disobedience because the protestors were challenging the rule that prevented them from sitting at lunch counters.

While our prior cases consistently have found the elements of the necessity defense lacking in cases involving indirect civil disobedience, we have never addressed specifically whether the defense is available in cases of indirect civil disobedience. * * * Today, we conclude, for the reasons stated below, that the necessity defense is inapplicable to cases involving indirect civil disobedience.

III

Necessity is, essentially, a utilitarian defense. It therefore justifies criminal acts taken to avert a greater harm, maximizing social welfare by allowing a crime to be committed where the social benefits of the crime outweigh the social costs of failing to commit the crime. Pursuant to the defense, prisoners could escape a burning prison; a person lost in the woods could steal food from a cabin to survive; an embargo could be violated because adverse weather conditions necessitated sale of the cargo at a foreign port; a crew could mutiny where their ship was thought to be unseaworthy; and property could be destroyed to prevent the spread of fire.

What all the traditional necessity cases have in common is that the commission of the "crime" averted the occurrence of an even greater "harm." In some sense, the necessity defense allows us to act as individual legislatures, amending a particular criminal provision or crafting a one-time exception to it, subject to court review, when a real legislature would formally do the same under those circumstances. For example, by allowing prisoners who escape a burning jail to claim the justification of necessity, we assume the lawmaker, confronting this problem, would have allowed for an exception to the law proscribing prison escapes.

Because the necessity doctrine is utilitarian, however, strict requirements contain its exercise so as to prevent nonbeneficial criminal conduct. For example, " 'if the criminal act cannot abate the threatened harm, society receives no benefit from the criminal conduct.' " Similarly, to forgive a crime taken to avert a lesser harm would fail to maximize social utility. The cost of the crime would outweigh the harm averted by its commission. Likewise, criminal acts cannot be condoned to thwart threats, yet to be imminent, or those for which there are legal alternatives to abate the harm.

Analysis of three of the necessity defense's four elements leads us to the conclusion that necessity can never be proved in a case of indirect civil disobedience. We do not rely upon the imminent harm prong of the defense because we believe there can be indirect civil disobedience cases in which the protested harm is imminent.

A

1. Balance of Harms

It is axiomatic that, if the thing to be averted is not a harm at all, the balance of harms necessarily would disfavor any criminal action. Thus, if an insane person bombed a welfare office for "helping those who won't help themselves," that person should be prevented from claiming necessity because the operation of a welfare system is simply not a cognizable harm. Welfare cannot constitute a harm where society has expressed its preference for such a system. * * *

Just as welfare was not a cognizable harm in our hypothetical, the El Salvador policy has been chosen by society and, therefore, cannot be deemed a cognizable harm here. The El Salvador policy does not violate the Constitution. Appellants have never suggested as much. There is no evidence that the procedure by which the policy was adopted was in any way improper; nor is there any evidence that appellants were prevented systematically from participating in the democratic processes through which the policy was chosen.

Under these circumstances, as a matter of law, whenever Congress has decided a matter exclusively within its constitutionally-delineated realm of authority, its decision, be it in the form of policy or law, cannot constitute a cognizable harm. If there is no cognizable harm to prevent, the harm resulting from any criminal action taken to prevent it necessarily outweighs any benefit.

2. Causal Relationship Between Criminal Conduct and Harm to be Averted

This inquiry requires a court to judge the likelihood that an alleged harm will be abated by the taking of illegal action. In the sense that the likelihood of abatement is required in the traditional necessity cases, there will never be such likelihood in cases of indirect political protest. In the traditional cases, a prisoner flees a burning cell and averts death, or someone demolishes a home to create a firebreak and prevents the conflagration of an entire community. The nexus between the act undertaken and the result sought is a close one. Ordinarily it is the volitional illegal act alone which, once taken, abates the evil.

In political necessity cases involving indirect civil disobedience against congressional acts, however, the act alone is unlikely to abate the evil precisely because the action is indirect.[1] Here, the IRS obstruction, or the refusal to comply with a federal officer's order, are unlikely to abate the killings in El Salvador, or immediately change Congress's policy; instead, it takes another *volitional* actor not controlled by the protestor to take a further step; Congress must change its mind.

3. Legal Alternatives

A final reason the necessity defense does not apply to these indirect civil disobedience cases is that legal alternatives will never be deemed exhausted when the harm can be mitigated by congressional action. In *Dorrell*, which involved a protestor's trespass on Vandenburg Air Force Base to protest the MX missile program, we answered Dorrell's claims that legal alternatives, like lobbying Congress, were futile by noting that "he differed little from many whose passionate beliefs are rejected by the will of the majority legitimately expressed." The necessity defense as applied in the traditional context requires that one have no legal *alternative* to the illegal conduct contemplated *that would abate the evil*. For the existence of a legal alternative to preclude the taking of illegal action, it would necessarily have to be one which *would abate the evil*. Thus, a person fleeing a burning jail would not be asked either to perish or wait in his cell because someone might conceivably save him (both legal alternatives) because neither are well-suited to the purpose of avoiding death. In other words, a reasonableness requirement is implied into judging whether legal alternatives exist.

The legal alternatives requirement has been treated differently in the political context, however. *Dorrell* did not inquire into the "likelihood" that petitioning Congress would succeed. It merely assumed that the "possibility" of Congress changing its mind was sufficient. Yet, certainly an inquiry into the efficacy of legal alternatives available to a fleeing prisoner would have been undertaken. Without expressly saying so, *Dorrell* decided that petitioning Congress to change a policy is *always* a legal alternative, regardless of the likelihood of the plea's success.

Reading between the lines in *Dorrell*, it appears we took the reasonable position that, once Dorrell had a chance to convince Congress, the necessity defense became unavailable because otherwise he would be

[1] Obviously, the same may not be true of instances of direct civil disobedience. For example, if the evil to be abated was a particular shipment of weapons to El Salvador and the protestors hijacked the truck or destroyed those weapons, the precise evil would have been abated. Because our case does not involve direct civil disobedience, we do not address the applicability of the necessity defense to such incidents.

granted license to violate the law without the concomitant, and outweighing, benefit that the necessity doctrine envisions. That this is so in every indirect political protest does not change the fact that we failed to measure the reasonableness of the legal alternative of petitioning Congress. The cases involving protest of congressional policy have implicitly decided that, because Congress can change its mind at any time in response to citizen protest, petitioning Congress is always an adequate legal alternative. Thus there is never an absence of legal alternatives in cases where congressional action is the protest's aim.

B

As have courts before us, we could assume, as a threshold matter, that the necessity defense is conceivably available in these cases, but find the elements never satisfied. Such a decision, however, does not come without significant costs. First, the failure of the federal courts to hold explicitly that the necessity defense is unavailable in these cases results in district courts expending unnecessary time and energy trying to square defendants' claims with the strict requirements of the doctrine. Second, such an inquiry oftentimes requires the courts to tread into areas constitutionally committed to other branches of government. For example, in *May*, which involved trespass on a naval base to protest American nuclear weapons policy, we noted that, "to consider defendants' argument [that trespassing was justified by the nefariousness of the Trident missile] would put us in the position of usurping the functions that the Constitution has given to the Congress and to the President." Third, holding out the possibility of the defense's applicability sets a trap for the unwary civil disobedient, rather than permitting the individual to undertake a more realistic cost-benefit analysis before deciding whether to break the law in political protest. Fourth, assuming the applicability of the defense in this context may risk its distortion in traditional cases. Finally, some commentators have suggested that the courts have sabotaged the usually low threshold for getting a defense theory before the jury as a means of keeping the necessity defense from the jury.

The real problem here is that litigants are trying to distort to their purposes an age-old common law doctrine meant for a very different set of circumstances. What these cases are really about is gaining notoriety for a cause—the defense allows protestors to get their political grievances discussed in a courtroom. It is precisely this political motive that has left some courts, like the district court in this case, uneasy. Because these attempts to invoke the necessity defense "force the courts to choose among causes they should make legitimate by extending the defense of necessity," and because the criminal acts, themselves, do not maximize social good, they should be subject to a *per se* rule of exclusion.

Thus, we see the failure of any federal court to recognize a defense of necessity in a case like ours not as coincidental, but rather as the natural consequence of the historic limitation of the doctrine. Indirect protests of congressional policies can never meet all the requirements of the necessity doctrine. Therefore, we hold that the necessity defense is not available in such cases.

CONCLUSION

Because the necessity defense was not intended as justification for illegal acts taken in indirect political protest, we affirm the district court's refusal to admit evidence of necessity.

AFFIRMED.

COMMONWEALTH V. HUTCHINS

Supreme Judicial Court of Massachusetts, Essex
410 Mass. 726, 575 N.E.2d 741 (1991)

O'CONNOR, J.

The defendant was convicted of drug offenses at a bench trial in the District Court. He requested a jury trial de novo. Thus, any errors that may have occurred during the bench trial are without consequence. In a jury session of the District Court, the charges were first amended to charges of cultivation of THC (a chemical found in marihuana) and of marihuana, and of possession of both substances with intent to distribute. Subsequently, the charges were reduced to simple possession or cultivation of THC and marihuana, and the defendant waived trial by jury.

Before trial, the defendant filed a motion to dismiss the complaints "on the ground that any possession of controlled substances by the [d]efendant is within the [d]efense of [m]edical [n]ecessity." The motion states that counsel "wishes to present a clear record for the reviewing court," and therefore requests the court to "state that it is denying the [d]efendant the right to assert a defense of medical necessity as a matter of law." * * * After a hearing, a judge complied, and endorsed the motion. "10/24/85. Motion denied. Def[endant] will not be allowed to introduce [evidence] re defense of medical necessity." Following a bench trial, the defendant was convicted of both reduced charges, and appealed. * * * We now affirm the convictions.

In support of his motion, as an offer of proof, the defendant submitted affidavits, excerpts from his medical records, literature on a disease known as progressive systemic sclerosis (scleroderma) and on the medicinal uses of marihuana and other materials. Through these materials, the defendant offered to prove the following facts: The defendant is a forty-seven year old man who has been diagnosed as having scleroderma accompanied by Raynaud's phenomenon, related to his service in the Navy. Scleroderma is a chronic disease that results in the buildup of scar tissue throughout the body. The cause of scleroderma is not known and no effective treatment or cure has been discovered. In the most severe cases, scleroderma may result in death. The defendant's medical history includes episodes of fatigue, hypertension, loss of appetite, weight loss of up to twenty-five pounds, diarrhea, nausea, vomiting, reflux of food and stomach acid into the mouth, reduced motility and constriction of the esophagus, extreme difficulty and pain in swallowing, and swollen, painful joints and extreme sensitivity to the cold in his hands and feet. He also suffers from severe depression, related at least in part to his disease, and was briefly hospitalized after attempting suicide. As a result of his illness, the defendant has been unable to work since 1978.

According to the offer of proof, the defendant's medical condition has been unsuccessfully treated with numerous medications and therapies by physicians of the Veterans Administration. The constriction of his esophagus has been treated by dilation and in 1974 was so severe that his treating physician advised him to have his esophagus surgically removed and replaced with a piece of his own intestine. The defendant has informed his treating physicians that since 1975, with some success, he has used marihuana, in lieu of antidepressants and surgery, to alleviate certain symptoms of his illness including nausea, loss of appetite, difficulty in eating, drinking or swallowing, loss of motility of the esophagus, spasticity, hypertension, and anxiety. Two of his treating physicians state that, although they are unable to "confirm [the defendant's] claim that his use of mari[h]uana has caused his remarkable remission, . . . it does appear that his use of mari[h]uana does alleviate the previously mentioned symptoms." These two physicians also state that "there appears to be a sufficient basis to conduct a scientific and medical investigation into the possible use of mari[h]uana to treat the disease of scleroderma." A research study of its therapeutic potential and medical uses indicates that the use of marihuana, indeed, may be effective to treat loss of appetite, nausea, vomiting, and weight loss and may relieve severe anxiety and depression. One of the defendant's other treating physicians, however, does not find that marihuana "had any effect in [the defendant's] case" and that he is "unaware of any published or unpublished evidence of [a] beneficial effect of mari[h]uana in this condition." Through correspondence with his physicians, the Veterans Administration, and members of the Massachusetts Legislature and the United States Congress, the defendant has made numerous, albeit unsuccessful, attempts lawfully to obtain either a prescription for marihuana or permission to participate in a research study on the use of marihuana to treat scleroderma. The Massachusetts Legislature has considered a bill providing for the use of marihuana in therapeutic research on more than one occasion, but no such statute has been enacted in the Commonwealth. The Veterans Administration has determined that presently there is no research study on the use of marihuana to treat scleroderma and therefore will not dispense marihuana for the defendant's treatment.

In *Commonwealth v. Hood*, we said, "It is, perhaps, 'more prudent for the judge to follow the traditional, and constitutionally sounder, course of waiting until all the evidence has been introduced at trial before ruling on its sufficiency to raise a proffered defense. If, at that time, the defendant has failed to produce some evidence on each element of the defense, the judge should decline to instruct on it. . . . In that event, the judge, may if appropriate, give curative instructions to caution the jury against considering evidence not properly before them.' " However, the defendant cannot fairly complain about the procedure adopted by the judge in this case if, as the Commonwealth contends and the judge appears to have concluded, the proof offered would not support a necessity defense. Our question, then, is whether, if the defendant were able to prove by admissible evidence at trial the facts contained in the offer of proof, a properly instructed fact finder could determine that the defendant had established the defense which he asserts.

"Under the common law defense of justification by necessity, a crime committed under the pressure of imminent danger may be excused if the harm sought to be avoided far exceeds the harm resulting from the crime committed." "In essence, the 'competing harms' defense exonerates one who commits a crime under the 'pressure of circumstances' if the harm that would have resulted from compliance with the law significantly exceeds the harm actually resulting from the defendant's violation of the law." At its root is an appreciation that there may be circumstances where the value protected by the law is, as a matter of public policy, eclipsed by a superseding value which makes it inappropriate and unjust to apply the usual criminal rule.

"We have ruled that 'the application of the defense is limited to the following circumstances: (1) the defendant is faced with a clear and imminent danger, not one which is debatable or speculative; (2) the defendant can reasonably expect that his [or her] action will be effective as the direct cause of abating the danger; (3) there is [no] legal alternative which will be effective in abating the danger; and (4) the Legislature has not acted to preclude the defense by a clear and deliberate choice regarding the values at issue.' " It must be understood, however, that that oft-repeated principle, that the necessity defense is limited to certain specified circumstances, does not mean that, whenever those circumstances obtain, the defense automatically applies. Rather, the first question always is whether the harm that would have resulted from compliance with the law significantly outweighs the harm that reasonably could result from the court's acceptance of necessity as an excuse in the circumstances presented by the particular case. Only when a comparison of the "competing harms" in specific circumstances clearly favors excusing what would otherwise be punishable conduct, is it appropriate then to inquire whether the standards enumerated in the cases cited above, standards which themselves do not call for a comparison of competing harms, have been met.

We mention two illustrative cases. In *Commonwealth v. Thurber* the defendant was convicted of escape from the Massachusetts Correctional Institution at Concord. At the trial, the defendant presented evidence that he had escaped because his life was in imminent danger at the prison. In discussing the necessity defense we quoted with approval a statement in a California case of the circumstances in which an escape from prison might be excused, one of the circumstances being that the escape be accomplished without violence, and another being that "[t]he prisoner immediately reports to the proper authorities when he has attained a position of safety from the immediate threat." In *Thurber* we "[a]ssum[ed] that we would apply the doctrine [of necessity] as a justification for escape in a proper case." The extent of public harm likely to attend a peaceful escape from prison, followed by the prisoner's prompt submission to the authorities, would be minimal compared to the likely harm to the prisoner, as demonstrated by the defendant's evidence in *Thurber*, if he were to comply with the law. Common sense tells us that, in the absence of a clear and specific contrary statutory expression, the court would not frustrate legislative intent in a *Thurber*-type situation by recognizing a necessity defense.

Commonwealth v. Iglesia provides another illustration. There, the defendant was charged with unlawfully carrying a firearm. He testified that he was attacked by a man with a gun, that he wrested the gun from the man, and that he immediately went to the police station with it. Again, as we did in *Commonwealth v. Thurber*, we "assume[d] . . . that, when 'a defendant seizes a firearm from one who had expressed an immediate intention to use it, and flees to a place of safe-keeping,' such possession might be lawful." In *Iglesia*, as in *Thurber*, the likely harm to society that would be likely to result from recognition of a necessity defense, carefully limited as to circumstances, would be significantly outweighed by the potential harm to the defendant, if his evidence were to be believed, if he were to comply with the law. It is fair to assume, in the absence of a specifically expressed contrary legislative intent, that judicial recognition of a necessity defense in the circumstances of the *Iglesia* case would not contradict any legislative policy determination.

Accepting the defendant's offer of proof, and assuming, as we do without decision, that the circumstances referred to above as enumerated * * * obtain, nevertheless we rule that the defendant's proffered evidence does not raise the defense of necessity. In our view, the alleviation of the defendant's medical symptoms, the importance to the defendant of which we do not underestimate, would not clearly and significantly outweigh the potential harm to the public were we to declare that the defendant's cultivation of marihuana and its use for his medicinal purposes may not be punishable. We cannot dismiss the reasonably possible negative impact of such a judicial declaration on the enforcement of our drug laws, including but not limited to those dealing with marihuana, nor can we ignore the government's overriding interest in the regulation of such substances. Excusing the escaped prisoner in the circumstances presented by *Thurber,* or the carrier of a gun in the circumstances of *Iglesia,* is quite different from excusing one who cultivates and uses marihuana in the circumstances of this case.

Judgment affirmed.

LIACOS, C.J. (dissenting, with whom NOLAN, J., joins).

I believe that a jury, not a judge, ordinarily should be allowed to determine whether medical necessity is a defense to a charge of possession or cultivation of marihuana. "The defendant[ ] presented sufficient evidence to raise such a defense. Neither the judge below nor this court should substitute its judgment for the sound deliberations of the jury."

The court today engages in speculative judicial fact finding by concluding that "the alleviation of the defendant's medical symptoms, the importance to the defendant of which we do not underestimate, would not clearly and significantly outweigh the potential harm to the public were we to declare that the defendant's cultivation of marihuana and its use for his medicinal purposes may not be punishable. We cannot dismiss the reasonably possible negative impact of such a judicial declaration on the enforcement of our drug laws, including but not limited to those dealing with marihuana, nor can we ignore the government's overriding interest in the regulation of such substances." While I recognize that the public has a strong interest in the enforcement of drug laws and in the strict regulation of narcotics, I do not believe that the interest would be significantly harmed by permitting a jury to consider whether the defendant cultivated and used marihuana in order to alleviate agonizing and painful symptoms caused by an illness. The court seems to suggest that we should not condone the use of marihuana, regardless of a particular individual's reasons for using the drug. Although the court appears to recognize the defense by taking this position, it fails to give sufficient consideration to the rationale behind the common law defense of necessity. That rationale is based on the recognition that, under very limited circumstances, "the value protected by the law is, as a matter of public policy, eclipsed by a superseding value which makes it inappropriate and unjust to apply the usual criminal rule."

The superseding value in a case such as the present one is the humanitarian and compassionate value in allowing an individual to seek relief from agonizing symptoms caused by a progressive and incurable illness in circumstances which risk no harm to any other individual. In my view, the harm to an individual in having to endure such symptoms may well outweigh society's generalized interest in prohibiting him or her from using the marihuana in such circumstances. On a proper offer of proof I would recognize the availability of a necessity defense when marihuana is used for medical purposes.

To recognize a medical necessity defense based on the use of marihuana for medical purposes would not allow *every* defendant charged with possessing or cultivating marihuana to present such a defense to the jury. Instead, "the application of the defense [would be] limited to the following circumstances: (1) the defendant is faced with a clear and imminent danger, not one which is debatable or speculative; (2) the defendant can reasonably expect that his [or her] action will be effective as the direct cause of abating the danger; (3) there is [no] legal alternative which will be effective in abating the danger; and (4) the Legislature has not acted to preclude the defense by a clear and deliberate choice regarding the values at issue." The defendant's offer of proof satisfied all the elements of a necessity defense. The judge erred in not allowing the defendant to present evidence of medical necessity to a jury of his peers.

The defendant's offer of proof contained sufficient allegations that he faced a "clear and imminent danger." The defendant presented affidavits from two physicians who stated that the defendant's esophagus was dangerously constricted as a result of his illness, and that, without treatment, his esophagus would constrict to the point where the defendant would be unable to eat or drink without great difficulty and pain. The physicians also stated in the affidavits "that it does appear that [the defendant's] use of mari[h]uana does alleviate [his nausea, loss of appetite, difficulty in swallowing, spasticity, hypertension, and anxiety]." Thus, the defendant offered to prove the second element of a necessity defense by showing that he had a "reasonable expectation" that smoking marihuana would be effective in abating the danger. The third element was satisfied when the defendant offered to prove that he had unsuccessfully attempted to acquire marihuana legally by seeking authorization from the Federal government to use marihuana for medical research. Finally, the fourth element was satisfied in this case since the Legislature has not precluded the medical necessity defense by clearly and deliberately choosing among the values at stake.

Since the defendant's offer of proof satisfied the four elements of a necessity defense, the judge's refusal to allow the defendant to present evidence of medical necessity to the jury improperly prevented the jury from exercising their vital functions of "[1] temper[ing] the application of strict rules of law by bringing the common sense judgment of a group of laymen to the case [and] . . . [2] stand[ing] as a check on arbitrary enforcement of the law. 'Fear of unchecked power, so typical of our State and Federal Governments in other respects, found expression in the criminal law in this insistence upon community participation in the determination of guilt or innocence.'" The court today once again unnecessarily interferes with the proper functions of the jury. I dissent.

NOTE

When do legal alternatives exist? In *United States v. Arellano-Rivera*, 244 F.3d 1119 (9th Cir. 2001), *cert. denied*, 535 U.S. 976 (2002), the defendant was convicted of unlawfully reentering the United States after being deported in violation of a federal statute, 8 U.S.C. § 1326, and argued that he was wrongfully precluded from submitting evidence to support a necessity defense. Arellano-Rivera was detained, along with four other individuals, by a U.S. Border Patrol agent in the hills near Andrade, California, about two miles from the United States-Mexico border. He admitted that he was a citizen of Mexico and had no legal right to be in the United States. At trial, Arellano-Rivera offered to prove that he suffered from an advanced case of Acquired Immune Deficiency Syndrome (AIDS), along with related illnesses, and that he was entering the United States to receive treatment he was unable to obtain in Mexico. The Ninth Circuit, citing *Schoon*, held that the district court properly refused to allow Arellano-Rivera to submit his evidence because there was a legal alternative: Arellano-Rivera could have petitioned the United States Attorney General for temporary admission into the United States on the basis of his dire medical condition, but did not do so. The court held that this failure barred a necessity claim, even though it was extremely unlikely that the United States Attorney General would have granted such a claim. Indeed, the Ninth Circuit held that necessity would not have been a cognizable defense even if Arellano-Rivera had petitioned the Attorney General and his petition had been denied. According to the court, "an alien cannot lawfully overrule the Attorney General and parole himself as a matter of 'necessity.' " 244 F.3d 1119 at 1126.

IN RE EICHORN

Court of Appeal of California, Fourth Appellate District, Division Three
69 Cal.App.4th 382, 81 Cal.Rptr.2d 535 (1998)

CROSBY, J.

James Warner Eichorn was convicted of a misdemeanor violation of a City of Santa Ana ordinance banning sleeping in designated public areas. The appellate department affirmed his conviction and denied his request to transfer the cause. Eichorn thereafter petitioned for writ of habeas corpus in this court. We conclude his conviction must be set aside.

I

James Eichorn was cited for violation of the city's anticamping ordinance (Santa Ana Mun. Code, ch. 10, art. VIII, § 10–402) on the evening of January 25, 1993.[1] Following a detour to the Supreme Court that established the ordinance was facially constitutional, Eichorn's case eventually went to trial.

In a significant pretrial ruling, the court (Judge James M. Brooks) determined Eichorn could not present a necessity defense to a jury. Eichorn had offered to prove that on the night of the violation every shelter bed within the city that was available to a homeless single man with no children was occupied, and that he was involuntarily homeless, i.e., he had done everything he could to alleviate his condition. Due to circumstances beyond his control, defendant, a 14-year resident of Santa Ana, had been unable to find work as a manual laborer that paid enough to allow him to find an alternative place to sleep.

The court determined defendant had not made a sufficient showing to allow a jury to consider his necessity defense: "It appears that the defense of necessity is not supported by the offer of proof. The first element wasn't satisfied, in the court's view, no significant, imminent evil for this defendant or any other person."[2] Defendant objected that the court's ruling "not only goes against what we understand to have been the statements and admissions by the People and by [Judge Margines, who had previously handled the case] but undermines the whole reason why we were going forward at trial . . . it's clearly eviscerated our entire defense."

In light of Judge Brooks's ruling on the necessity defense, and noting there was no dispute Eichorn was in a sleeping bag in the civic center on the night in question, Eichorn's lawyer agreed to go forward without a jury on the constitutional issue whether the ordinance was unconstitutional as applied to him based on his alleged involuntary homelessness.

Trial commenced without a jury in May 1996. Officer Carol Craig testified defendant was in a sleeping bag on the ground about 10:30 p.m. outside a county office building in the civic center. He was using his clothes as a pillow. Craig asked (as she always did) why Eichorn wasn't at the National Guard Armory (a homeless shelter several miles away). A bus from the civic center to the armory usually picked up people between 5:00 and 6:00 p.m. According to Craig's police report, defendant replied he had tried "a while back." It was full, so he never returned. The court

---

[1] Section 10–402 reads as follows:

Unlawful Camping. It shall be unlawful for any person to camp, occupy camp facilities or use camp paraphernalia in the following areas, except as otherwise provided: (a) Any street; (b) Any public parking lot or public area, improved or unimproved." Camp paraphernalia included a sleeping bag.

[2] The court's questions and comments suggested it was not impressed with defendant's claim lack of sleep was a significant evil ("what do you mean 'bodily harm?' Like tired eyelids or blood?"; "[I]f he didn't sleep here, he'd lose sleep and this would be a horrible physical thing to impose on him?").

judicially noticed that the walk between the civic center and the armory was "through very dangerous areas of town." Police photographed and cited Eichorn, then asked him to move on. He complied.

James Meeker, a professor at the University of California, Irvine in the department of criminology, law and society, testified he had conducted a study on homelessness in January and February 1993. There were more than 3,000 homeless individuals in Orange County during this period. Most homeless were longtime residents of Orange County (average 14 years) who had lost jobs and could not afford housing. The county had relatively little affordable housing, and it had been decreasing. Single men had a particularly difficult time because they were less likely to receive the support from family, friends, or governmental agencies. Most were sleeping outdoors because they had no other choice. Homeless individuals were 10 times as likely to be victimized by crime than the average population. Many homeless stayed in urban areas because of proximity to assistance providers (food, clothing and shelter), day jobs (just 8 percent were unemployed and not looking for jobs), public facilities (restrooms, etc.) and the lack of transportation.

Timothy Shaw was the executive director of the Orange County Homeless Issues Task Force. He pegged the number of homeless in Santa Ana at about 1,500 persons in 1993. There were about 118 shelter beds available for single men like Eichorn, most available on a first-come, first-served basis. In addition, the armory could accommodate 125 persons during the winter (although it frequently exceeded its capacity). As was routine, these shelters were full on the night Eichorn was cited.

Maria Mendoza was the county's homeless coordinator and oversaw use of the armory as a shelter. The armory was available only on cold winter nights. She explained how the bus to the armory would leave from the civic center in the late afternoon. Those on the bus had priority at the armory. Eichorn had spent some 20 nights there in December and January. On January 25, the armory was 13 persons over capacity, which was not uncommon. That the armory would accept excess capacity was not a given. Usually, only those "at risk" (e.g., women and children) would be admitted after the maximum was reached, and generally only when it was raining.

Eichorn, 49 years old, testified he had moved to Costa Mesa in 1972, a few years after his discharge from the Marine Corps. The Vietnam veteran lost his job in a machine shop in 1980, and subsequently ended up without a place to live. He moved to Santa Ana because a friend told him about a job driving an ice cream truck. He sold ice cream for about a year and was able to afford a motel room. When he lost that job, he frequented the casual labor office in Santa Ana until it closed. When he worked and could save enough, he would live in a motel. He also relied on general relief and food stamps. However, general relief was no longer enough to secure affordable housing because most of the less expensive motels had been torn down. If he could not get into a shelter, Eichorn would sleep in the civic center, where he was close to services (including restrooms) and where there was "safety in numbers" (i.e., where it was less likely someone would steal or attack him while he slept). He loved to work and did so every chance he got. He did not like living outside. He had been turned away from the armory in the past and had a "nervous walk" back to the civic center. On January 25, he did not recall whether he had tried to find a spot at a shelter or whether he heard that the shelters were full. He recalled eating around 7:00 p.m. He was in his sleeping bag listening to his radio when Craig arrived around 10:30 p.m. Eichorn's mother and stepfather lived in Long Beach, but staying with them was not an option because he was "an adult responsible for" himself. Defendant denied a problem with alcohol or drugs.

June Marcott, program manager for food stamps and general relief of the County of Orange, testified Eichorn received food stamps on a regular basis from 1989 through 1993, except when he was employed in parts of 1991 and 1992. He was eligible for $307 monthly in general relief if he participated in a work program (working nine days a month) and looked for work (four job applications per day). He last received general relief in November 1990 and was terminated because he did not submit a job search report. He applied for relief in March and June 1992, but was denied.

The court found Eichorn had violated the camping ordinance and was not involuntarily homeless on the night in question, finding he chose not to go to the armory. He also suggested defendant should have sought out familial assistance and should have applied for general relief. The court ordered him to perform 40 hours of community service. By a two-to-one margin, the appellate department of the superior court affirmed the conviction without opinion and declined to certify the case to this court for direct review. Eichorn filed this petition for habeas corpus and seeks to set aside his conviction.

II

Eichorn makes a multipronged attack on his conviction. One of his contentions is that he was induced to waive his right to a jury trial by the court's pretrial ruling that he could not present a necessity defense. As noted above, the court ruled the defense's offer of proof was inadequate, i.e., defendant had not presented enough evidence to get to a jury on the issue of whether he violated the law to prevent a significant evil. This ruling was error, and we vacate the judgment accordingly.

California appellate courts have recognized the necessity defense "despite the absence of any statutory articulation of this defense and rulings from the California Supreme Court that the common law is not a part of the criminal law in California."

In *Tobe v. City of Santa Ana*, the Supreme Court, while holding the camping ordinance was facially valid, declined to decide whether and how it might be unconstitutionally applied. The court refused to assume that the ordinance would be enforced "against persons who have no alternative to 'camping' or placing 'camp paraphernalia' on public property." Indeed, the *Tobe* court was given assurances by the People "that a necessity defense might be available to 'truly homeless' persons and that prosecutorial discretion would be exercised." * * *

An instruction on the defense of necessity is required where there is evidence "sufficient to establish that defendant violated the law (1) to prevent a significant evil, (2) with no adequate alternative, (3) without creating a greater danger than the one avoided, (4) with a good faith belief in the necessity, (5) with such belief being objectively reasonable, and (6) under circumstances in which he did not substantially contribute to the emergency." * * *

Whether necessity exists is generally a question of fact.

At a minimum, reasonable minds could differ whether defendant acted to prevent a "significant evil." Sleep is a physiological need, not an option for humans. It is common knowledge that loss of sleep produces a host of physical and mental problems (mood irritability, energy drain and low motivation, slow reaction time, inability to concentrate and process information). Certainly, no one would suggest that a groggy truck driver who stops his rig on the side of a road rather than risk falling asleep at the wheel does not act to prevent a significant evil, i.e., harm to himself and others. Indeed, Judge Margines had denied Eichorn's request for funds to hire an expert to testify about the harmful effects of sleep loss: "I mean it doesn't take an expert to tell us that, to convince a person, that there are ill effects that arise from sleep [deprivation]."

The court must instruct if the evidence could result in a finding defendant's criminal act was justified by necessity. Eichorn's offer of proof was sufficient. There was substantial if not uncontradicted evidence that defendant slept in the civic center because his alternatives were inadequate and economic forces were primarily to blame for his predicament. Thus, whether denominated a denial of his right to jury trial or of his due process right to present a defense the court's error was clear, fundamental, and struck at the heart of the trial process. * * *

The writ is granted and the cause remanded to the former municipal court with directions to set aside the judgment of conviction and to proceed in conformity with this opinion.[a]

---

[a] According to Mr. Eichorn's appellate counsel, the District Attorney did not refile charges against Mr. Eichorn after the case was remanded.

NOTE

What does legislative preclusion mean when there is a conflict between sovereigns? In 1996, California voters enacted an initiative measure called the Compassionate Use Act, which created an exception to California drug laws for a patient, or his or her primary caregiver, who possesses or cultivates marijuana for the patient's medical purposes upon the recommendation or approval of a physician. In response to this new medical marijuana law, several "medical cannabis dispensaries" emerged to provide marijuana to qualified patients. One of these was the Oakland Cannabis Buyers' Cooperative. As the United States Supreme Court described it:

> The Cooperative is a not-for-profit organization that operates in downtown Oakland. A physician serves as medical director, and registered nurses staff the Cooperative during business hours. To become a member, a patient must provide a written statement from a treating physician assenting to marijuana therapy and must submit to a screening interview. If accepted as a member, the patient receives an identification card entitling him to obtain marijuana from the Cooperative.

United States v. Oakland Cannabis Buyers' Cooperative, 532 U.S. 483, 486, 121 S.Ct. 1711, 149 L.Ed.2d 722 (2001).

In 1998, the federal government sought an injunction against the Cooperative, arguing that even though the Cooperative's activities conformed to California law, they violated the federal Controlled Substances Act, which prohibits the manufacture and distribution of various drugs, including marijuana. In *United States v. Oakland Cannabis Buyers' Cooperative*, the Supreme Court agreed with the federal government and held that the Controlled Substances Act does not include a medical necessity exception. Justice Thomas wrote for the Court:

> Under any conception of legal necessity, one principle is clear: The defense cannot succeed when the legislature itself has made a "determination of values." In the case of the Controlled Substances Act, the statute reflects a determination that marijuana has no medical benefits worthy of an exception (outside the confines of a Government-approved research project). Whereas some other drugs can be dispensed and prescribed for medical use, the same is not true for marijuana. Indeed, for purposes of the Controlled Substances Act, marijuana has "no currently accepted medical use" at all.

Id. at 491.

B. EXCUSE DEFENSES

In contrast with the justification defenses, which share a common logical structure, the excuses developed under the common law and the Model Penal Code have various structures. What they share is the intuition that under some circumstances, even though the defendant broke the law and was not morally justified in doing so, the defendant should nevertheless not be punished because she lacks moral responsibility for her actions. Sometimes this lack of responsibility is situational: the defendant who acts under duress, for example, is conceived of as an ordinary, reasonable person caught in unreasonable circumstances. In other situations the defendant's lack of responsibility is rooted in her very personality: the criminal defendant who is insane, whose capacity is diminished, or who is a minor is conceived of as lacking full moral agency across the board.

1. DURESS

Duress, also known as coercion or compulsion, is an affirmative defense in which the defendant claims she was threatened by another person with physical force (either to herself or a third person) unless she committed a specific crime. While the elements of duress vary from jurisdiction to jurisdiction, the basic elements of the duress defense in jurisdictions that have incorporated the common law include the following:

Common Law

1. The defendant acted in response to an imminent threat of death or serious bodily injury;
2. The defendant had a well-grounded (or reasonable) fear that the threat would be carried out unless she committed a specified crime;
3. The defendant had no reasonable opportunity to escape the threatened harm.

See Alafair S. Burke, *Rational Actors, Self-Defense, and Duress: Making Sense, Not Syndromes, Out of the Battered Woman*, 81 N.C. L. REV. 211, 253 (2002).

There is often confusion in the courts about the difference between necessity and duress, and in some jurisdictions the judges use terms like "lesser evil," "choice of evils," "justification," "compulsion," "coercion," "duress," and "necessity" more or less interchangeably. The key difference between necessity and duress is that conduct under duress is a response to a threat from a specific individual to commit the acts that constitute the crime. Conduct under necessity, in contrast, involves a response to a dire situation.

At early common law, the duress defense was limited to cases in which the defendant or members of her family were threatened. Today, most jurisdictions that follow the common law allow a threat to kill or seriously injure the defendant or any other person to satisfy element one.

The imminence requirement in element one has been strictly construed in some cases. For example, in one case, a man agreed to cooperate with the government and testify against a defendant in a criminal trial. Right before trial, the man was threatened by armed assailants who nearly ran him over. The man gave false testimony at trial. At his subsequent trial for perjury, the man asserted duress as a defense. The court rejected his duress defense, concluding that the threat of death or serious bodily harm was not imminent or impending when he testified falsely at trial. *See State v. Rosillo*, 282 N.W.2d 872 (Minn. 1979).

Section 2.09 of the Model Penal Code, which sets out the defense of duress, excuses criminal conduct that was coerced by the use of, or threat to use, unlawful force against the actor's person or the person of another that a "person of reasonable firmness in his situation would have been unable to resist." Unlike the common law formulation, the Model Penal Code's duress defense is not limited to situations involving threats of death or great bodily harm. Nor is there any explicit imminence requirement, although the question of the imminence of the threat is relevant to the issue of whether a person of reasonable firmness would have been able to resist it. Finally, within the common law tradition the principle seems to have been accepted that duress can never be a defense to murder, at least where the defendant was the principal actor because it is wrong to kill an innocent person. Under the Model Penal Code, a duress defense to homicide is possible, even if the victim is an innocent.

UNITED STATES V. CONTENTO-PACHON

United States Court of Appeals for the Ninth Circuit
723 F.2d 691 (9th Cir. 1984)

BOOCHEVER, C.J.

This case presents an appeal from a conviction for unlawful possession with intent to distribute a narcotic controlled substance in violation of 21 U.S.C. § 841(a)(1). At trial, the defendant attempted to offer evidence of duress and necessity defenses. The district court excluded this evidence on the ground that it was insufficient to support the defenses. We reverse because there was sufficient evidence of duress to present a triable issue of fact.

I. FACTS

The defendant-appellant, Juan Manuel Contento-Pachon, is a native of Bogota, Colombia and was employed there as a taxicab driver. He asserts that one of his passengers, Jorge, offered him a job as the driver of a privately-owned car. Contento-Pachon expressed an interest in the job and agreed to meet Jorge and the owner of the car the next day.

Instead of a driving job, Jorge proposed that Contento-Pachon swallow cocaine-filled balloons and transport them to the United States. Contento-Pachon agreed to consider the proposition. He was told not to mention the proposition to anyone, otherwise he would "get into serious trouble." Contento-Pachon testified that he did not contact the police because he believes that the Bogota police are corrupt and that they are paid off by drug traffickers.

Approximately one week later, Contento-Pachon told Jorge that he would not carry the cocaine. In response, Jorge mentioned facts about Contento-Pachon's personal life, including private details which Contento-Pachon had never mentioned to Jorge. Jorge told Contento-Pachon that his failure to cooperate would result in the death of his wife and three year-old child.

The following day the pair met again. Contento-Pachon's life and the lives of his family were again threatened. At this point, Contento-Pachon agreed to take the cocaine into the United States.

The pair met two more times. At the last meeting, Contento-Pachon swallowed 129 balloons of cocaine. He was informed that he would be watched at all times during the trip, and that if he failed to follow Jorge's instruction he and his family would be killed.

After leaving Bogota, Contento-Pachon's plane landed in Panama. Contento-Pachon asserts that he did not notify the authorities there because he felt that the Panamanian police were as corrupt as those in Bogota. Also, he felt that any such action on his part would place his family in jeopardy.

When he arrived at the customs inspection point in Los Angeles, Contento-Pachon consented to have his stomach x-rayed. The x-rays revealed a foreign substance which was later determined to be cocaine.

At Contento-Pachon's trial, the government moved to exclude the defenses of duress and necessity. The motion was granted. We reverse.

A. DURESS

There are three elements of the duress defense: (1) an immediate threat of death or serious bodily injury, (2) a well-grounded fear that the threat will be carried out, and (3) no reasonable opportunity to escape the threatened harm. Sometimes a fourth element is required: the defendant must submit to proper authorities after attaining a position of safety.

Factfinding is usually a function of the jury, and the trial court rarely rules on a defense as a matter of law. If the evidence is insufficient as a matter of law to support a duress defense, however, the trial court should exclude that evidence.

The trial court found Contento-Pachon's offer of proof insufficient to support a duress defense because he failed to offer proof of two elements: immediacy and inescapability.[1] We examine the elements of duress.

Immediacy: The element of immediacy requires that there be some evidence that the threat of injury was present, immediate, or impending. "[A] veiled threat of future unspecified harm" will not satisfy this requirement. The district court found that the initial threats were not immediate because "they were conditioned on defendant's failure to cooperate in the future and did not place defendant and his family in immediate danger."

Evidence presented on this issue indicated that the defendant was dealing with a man who was deeply involved in the exportation of illegal substances. Large sums of money were at stake and, consequently, Contento-Pachon had reason to believe that Jorge would carry out his threats. Jorge had gone to the trouble to discover that Contento-Pachon was married, that he had a child, the names of his wife and child, and the location of his residence. These were not vague threats of possible future harm. According to the defendant, if he had refused to cooperate, the consequences would have been immediate and harsh.

Contento-Pachon contends that he was being watched by one of Jorge's accomplices at all times during the airplane trip. As a consequence, the force of the threats continued to restrain him. Contento-Pachon's contention that he was operating under the threat of immediate harm was supported by sufficient evidence to present a triable issue of fact.

Escapability: The defendant must show that he had no reasonable opportunity to escape. The district court found that because Contento-Pachon was not physically restrained prior to the time he swallowed the balloons, he could have sought help from the police or fled. Contento-Pachon explained that he did not report the threats because he feared that the police were corrupt. The trier of fact should decide whether one in Contento-Pachon's position might believe that some of the Bogota police were paid informants for drug traffickers and that reporting the matter to the police did not represent a reasonable opportunity of escape.

If he chose not to go to the police, Contento-Pachon's alternative was to flee. We reiterate that the opportunity to escape must be reasonable. To flee, Contento-Pachon, along with his wife and three year-old child, would have been forced to pack his possessions, leave his job, and travel to a place beyond the reaches of the drug traffickers. A juror might find that this was not a reasonable avenue of escape. Thus, Contento-Pachon presented a triable issue on the element of escapability.

---

[1] We believe that a triable issue was presented as to the [second] element, that the fear be well-grounded, based on the same facts that lead us to the conclusion as to the immediacy of the threats.

Surrender to Authorities: As noted above, the duress defense is composed of at least three elements. The government argues that the defense also requires that a defendant offer evidence that he intended to turn himself in to the authorities upon reaching a position of safety. Although it has not been expressly limited, this fourth element seems to be required only in prison escape cases. Under other circumstances, the defense has been defined to include only three elements.

The Supreme Court in *United States v. Bailey,* noted that "escape from federal custody. . . . is a continuing offense and. . . . an escapee can be held liable for failure to return to custody as well as for his initial departure." This factor would not be present in most crimes other than escape.

In cases not involving escape from prison there seems little difference between the third basic requirement that there be no reasonable opportunity to escape the threatened harm and the obligation to turn oneself in to authorities on reaching a point of safety. Once a defendant has reached a position where he can safely turn himself in to the authorities he will likewise have a reasonable opportunity to escape the threatened harm.

That is true in this case. Contento-Pachon claims that he was being watched at all times. According to him, at the first opportunity to cooperate with authorities without alerting the observer, he consented to the x-ray. We hold that a defendant who has acted under a well-grounded fear of immediate harm with no opportunity to escape may assert the duress defense, if there is a triable issue of fact whether he took the opportunity to escape the threatened harm by submitting to authorities at the first reasonable opportunity.

B. NECESSITY

The defense of necessity is available when a person is faced with a choice of two evils and must then decide whether to commit a crime or an alternative act that constitutes a greater evil. Contento-Pachon has attempted to justify his violation of 21 U.S.C. § 841(a)(1) by showing that the alternative, the death of his family, was a greater evil.

Traditionally, in order for the necessity defense to apply, the coercion must have had its source in the physical forces of nature. The duress defense was applicable when the defendant's acts were coerced by a human force. This distinction served to separate the two similar defenses. But modern courts have tended to blur the distinction between duress and necessity. * * *

The defense of necessity is usually invoked when the defendant acted in the interest of the general welfare. For example, defendants have asserted the defense as a justification for (1) bringing laetrile into the United States for the treatment of cancer patients; (2) unlawfully entering a naval base to protest the Trident missile system; (3) burning Selective Service System records to protest United States military action.

Contento-Pachon's acts were allegedly coerced by human, not physical forces. In addition, he did not act to promote the general welfare. Therefore, the necessity defense was not available to him. Contento-Pachon mischaracterized evidence of duress as evidence of necessity. The district court correctly disallowed his use of the necessity defense.

II. CONCLUSION

Contento-Pachon presented credible evidence that he acted under an immediate and well-grounded threat of serious bodily injury, with no opportunity to escape. Because the trier of fact should have been allowed to consider the credibility of the proffered evidence, we reverse. The district court correctly excluded Contento-Pachon's necessity defense.

REVERSED and REMANDED.

COYLE, DISTRICT JUDGE (dissenting in part and concurring in part):

In order to establish a defense of duress, the trial court in this case required Contento-Pachon to show (1) that he or his family was under an immediate threat of death or serious bodily injury; (2) that he had a well grounded fear that the threat would be carried out; and (3) that he had no reasonable opportunity to escape the threat. Applying this three-part test, the trial court found that the defendant's offer of proof was insufficient to support a defense of duress. The government argues that this holding should be affirmed and I agree. * * *

In granting the government's motion in limine excluding the defense of duress, the trial court specifically found Contento-Pachon had failed to present sufficient evidence to establish the necessary elements of immediacy and inescapability. In its Order the district court stated:

> The first threat made to defendant and his family about three weeks before the flight was not immediate; the threat was conditioned upon defendant's failure to cooperate in the future and did not place the defendant and his family in immediate danger or harm. Moreover, after the initial threat and until he went to the house where he ingested the balloons containing cocaine, defendant and his family were not physically restrained and could have sought help from the police or fled. No such efforts were attempted by defendant. Thus, defendant's own offer of proof negates two necessary elements of the defense of duress.

In cases where the defendant's duress has been raised, the courts have indicated that the element of immediacy is of crucial importance. The trial court found that the threats made against the defendant and his family lacked the requisite element of immediacy. This finding is adequately supported by the record. The defendant was outside the presence of the drug dealers on numerous occasions for varying lengths of time. There is no evidence that his family was ever directly threatened or even had knowledge of the threats allegedly directed against the defendant.

Moreover, the trial court found that the defendant and his family enjoyed an adequate and reasonable opportunity to avoid or escape the threats of the drug dealers in the weeks before his flight. Until he went to the house where he ingested the balloons containing cocaine, defendant and his family were not physically restrained or prevented from seeking help. The record supports the trial court's findings that the defendant and his family could have sought assistance from the authorities or have fled. Cases considering the defense of duress have established that where there was a reasonable legal alternative to violating the law, a chance to refuse to do the criminal act and also to avoid the threatened danger, the defense will fail. Duress is permitted as a defense only when a criminal act was committed because there was no other opportunity to avoid the threatened danger.

The district court is vested with broad discretion whether to admit or exclude proffered evidence and its rulings will not be overturned on review without a clear showing of abuse of discretion. Because the district court's decision granting the government's motion *in limine* is fully and adequately supported by the record, I cannot agree that the district court abused its discretion and I therefore respectfully dissent.

I agree with the majority, however, that the district court properly excluded Contento-Pachon's necessity defense.

STATE V. HUNTER

Supreme Court of Kansas
241 Kan. 629, 740 P.2d 559 (1987)

LOCKETT, J.

Compulsion

Defendant James C. Hunter appeals his convictions of two counts of felony murder, two counts of aggravated kidnapping, one count of aggravated robbery, one count of aggravated battery on a law enforcement officer, and one count of aggravated battery. Hunter raises numerous issues, among them that the trial judge committed reversible error by refusing Hunter's requested instruction on his defense of compulsion. We reverse and remand for a new trial.

In February 1985 James C. Hunter, a resident of Amoret, Missouri, was hitchhiking from Texas back to the Kansas City area. He arrived in Wichita on February 12, 1985. On February 13, Hunter hitched a ride with Mark Walters, Lisa Dunn, and Daniel Remeta. On the way north on I–135, Remeta displayed two weapons, a .357 Magnum and an inoperative .22 pistol. Hunter repaired the .22 and Remeta fired the .22

out of the car window several times. When they reached the intersection of I–135 and I–70, Hunter asked to be let off. At that point Remeta began talking about another hitchhiker he wished he had killed and also described prior crimes he had committed, including several murders.

At the Levant exchange on I–70, Dunn, Walters, Remeta, and the defendant were pulled over by a police car. The driver of the police car was Thomas County Undersheriff Benjamin F. Albright, who had been asked to investigate a vehicle matching the description of the car. Albright instructed the occupants to remain in the car and put their hands on the ceiling. One of the passengers exited the car and fired two shots through Albright's windshield. Albright identified the person who fired these shots as having shoulder-length brown hair and a full beard. This description matched that of the defendant. Immediately thereafter, Albright was shot by the same person in the arm and chest. At trial, Albright identified James Hunter as his assailant. Hunter, Dunn, and Remeta all testified that it was Remeta who shot Albright. Hunter testified that, after Albright was shot, he attempted to shoot Remeta with the .22 handgun but accidentally wounded Dunn. Dunn and Remeta corroborated this testimony.

Shortly after the Albright shooting, the Remeta vehicle reached the Bartlett Elevator in Levant, Kansas. There were eight individuals at the elevator: Maurice Christie, the elevator manager; Fred Sager, the assistant manager; and Dennis Tubbs, Raymond Haremza, Rick Schroeder, Glenn Moore, and two others. The testimony concerning Hunter's activities at the Levant elevator conflicted greatly. Christie testified that he observed "a bearded man," later identified as Hunter, holding a gun in the face of Rick Schroeder and forcing him into a pickup truck. Sager testified that he saw a bearded man with a gun in his hand and that Rick Schroeder got into the pickup by himself. Dennis Tubbs testified that Hunter held Schroeder's arm and told him to get into the pickup; he further testified he saw only one person with a gun. After Rick Schroeder and Glenn Moore were taken as hostages and loaded into Moore's pickup truck, Christie, while attempting to call the sheriff from the scale house, was shot by Remeta.

Following the shooting at the elevator, the hostages were driven to a point north of U.S. Highway 24 near Colby, Kansas. Remeta testified that he killed both Schroeder and Moore and left them at the side of the road. Police caught up with the pickup truck and forced it off the road at a farm. During an exchange of gunfire, Walters was killed. Subsequently, Remeta, Dunn, and Hunter were arrested.

Remeta, Dunn, and Hunter were formally charged on February 15, 1985. A preliminary hearing was held, after which all three defendants were bound over. At the arraignment, all defendants refused to enter a plea and the trial court entered pleas of not guilty on behalf of all three.

Prior to trial, Remeta entered a plea of guilty to all charges. Dunn and Hunter were tried by a jury, found guilty of all counts, and sentenced to consecutive terms. Hunter now appeals his conviction of two counts of felony murder (Schroeder and Moore), two counts of aggravated kidnapping (Schroeder and Moore), one count of aggravated battery on a law enforcement officer (Albright), one count of aggravated battery (Christie), and one count of aggravated robbery. * * *

COMPULSION

* * * Hunter contends that the trial court committed reversible error by refusing to instruct the jury on his defense of compulsion. We agree. K.S.A. 21–3209 provides for the defense of compulsion to crimes other than murder or manslaughter, stating:

> (1) A person is not guilty of a crime other than murder or voluntary manslaughter by reason of conduct which he performs under the compulsion or threat of the imminent infliction of death or great bodily harm, if he reasonably believes that death or great bodily harm will be inflicted upon him or upon his spouse, parent, child, brother or sister if he does not perform such conduct.
>
> (2) The defense provided by this section is not available to one who willfully or wantonly places himself in a situation in which it is probable that he will be subjected to compulsion or threat.
>
> Defendant's requested instruction, taken from PIK Crim. 2d 54.13, stated:
>
> It is a defense to the charges of Aggravated Battery Against a Law Enforcement Officer, Aggravated Robbery and Aggravated Kidnapping, if the defendant acted under compulsion or threat of immediate infliction of death or great bodily harm, and if said defendant reasonably believed that death or great bodily harm would have been inflicted upon said defendant had he or she not acted as he or she did.

The trial court refused to give the compulsion instruction because the defendant was charged with premeditated and felony murder. * * *

Whether the defense of compulsion is available to a criminal defendant charged with felony murder under K.S.A. 21–3401 is an issue of first impression. * * * [E]arly cases refused to recognize any compulsion as sufficient to excuse intentional killing.[a] The rationale is that, when

[a] The Model Penal Code, in contrast to the common law, allows a defendant charged with any offense, including murder, to argue duress. *See* Model Penal Code § 2.09(1) providing that "it is an affirmative defense that the actor engaged in the conduct charged . . . because he was coerced to do so by the use of, or a threat to use, unlawful force against his person . . . that a person of reasonable firmness in his situation would have been unable to resist." Model Penal Code § 2.09(1).

confronted by a choice between two evils of equal magnitude, the individual ought to sacrifice his own life rather than escape by the murder of an innocent.

A number of jurisdictions, including Kansas, have incorporated by statute the common-law denial of the compulsion defense in crimes of murder. While not all jurisdictions have considered the applicability of these statutes to crimes of felony murder, we note that both Arizona and Missouri have held that defendants are barred from claiming the compulsion defense in felony-murder cases. They reason that the person charged need only have the required intent to commit or participate in the underlying felony and no other mental state on his part need be demonstrated because of the strict liability imposed by the felony-murder rule.

We are not, however, persuaded by the reasoning of these decisions. The better view, consistently adhered to by commentators, is that any limitation to the defense of duress be confined to crimes of intentional killing and not to killings done by another during the commission of some lesser felony. As LaFave and Scott have explained:

> [I]f *A* compels *B* at gunpoint to drive him to the bank which *A* intends to rob, and during the ensuing robbery *A* kills a bank customer *C, B* is not guilty of the robbery (for he was justified by duress) and so is not guilty of felony murder of *C* in the commission of robbery. The law properly recognizes that one is justified in aiding a robbery if he is forced by threats to do so to save his life; he should not lose the defense because his threateners unexpectedly kill someone in the course of the robbery and thus convert a mere robbery into a murder.

* * *

There were three versions of the events at the grain elevator in Levant. First, State's witnesses Christie, Sager, and Tubbs all testified that Hunter had played an active role in the kidnapping of Schroeder and Moore and the theft of the pickup truck. Christie and Sager testified that Hunter had a weapon. Second, Hunter testified that he had no weapon at the elevator and that he was ordered by Remeta to go to the other end of the building to watch to see if anyone tried to exit through the back door. According to Hunter, he then walked around to the back of the building and stopped there to wait to see what happened, and Remeta then ordered him back around to the other side and into the pickup. Hunter testified that he never felt he had a chance to escape. Third, Remeta testified that he had both guns at all times. He further stated that he asked Hunter to watch Schroeder and Moore at the pickup truck and that he would have shot Hunter if he had not followed orders.

In order to constitute the defense of compulsion, the coercion or duress must be present, imminent, and impending, and of such a nature as to induce a well-grounded apprehension of death or serious bodily injury if the act is not done. The doctrine of coercion or duress cannot be invoked as an excuse by one who had a reasonable opportunity to avoid doing the act without undue exposure to death or serious bodily harm. In addition, the compulsion must be continuous and there must be no reasonable opportunity to escape the compulsion without committing the crime.

The only opportunity Hunter would have had for escape would have been when he was out of sight of Remeta at the point when he went around the north side of the building at the Levant elevator. Hunter testified that Remeta came around the building and ordered him to return to the pickup. There was testimony that the total time which elapsed at the grain elevator was approximately five minutes. From the record, it is impossible to tell how long Hunter remained out of sight of Remeta. Viewed in the light most favorable to Hunter, however, and particularly in light of the fact that it was undisputed that Remeta had possession of the .357 Magnum at all times, it cannot be said that Hunter had a reasonable opportunity to escape.

Although some of the evidence supporting Hunter's defense of compulsion came from Hunter's own testimony, this court has held that a defendant is entitled to an instruction on his or her theory of the case even though the evidence is slight and supported only by defendant's own testimony. In this case, evidence came not only from Hunter, but also from Remeta and the State's witnesses Christie, Sager, and Tubbs. There was ample evidence presented from which the jury could have concluded that Hunter's acts were justified by compulsion.

Here, the record is replete with testimony that Daniel Remeta was a person to be feared. It was the function of the jury as the exclusive trier of fact to determine if it was believable that Hunter was afraid for his life, if such fear was reasonable, and if such fear justified any criminal acts which Hunter may have performed. When the trial judge refused the requested compulsion instruction, he effectively prevented the jury from considering the evidence presented in Hunter's defense. This denial of the jury's right to determine the facts constitutes reversible error. We reverse and remand this case for a new trial in accordance with this opinion. Because the resolution of this issue is dispositive of this appeal, we do not reach the other issues raised.

NOTE

Professor Phillip Johnson reports that "[o]n retrial Hunter obtained a change of venue and was acquitted of all charges by the jury after almost 3 years in prison." PHILLIP E. JOHNSON, CRIMINAL LAW: CASES, MATERIALS AND TEXT (6th ed. 2000). He notes that after the acquittal:

> Asked if he was bitter, Hunter replied, "Yeah I'm bitter. Basically at Ben Albright. I know what happened that day. He (Albright) just freaked out and lost it. He never looked up from that car. I thought that idiot was going to save my life. He's a police officer and he can't admit he turned tail."
>
> * * * [Hunter] said he has often wished he had taken the advice he has heard throughout life—never hitchhike. "I wouldn't do it (now) unless I got to. If a car breaks down, I can understand," he said. "I had been told for years you shouldn't hitchhike, you shouldn't hitchhike. I just wish them folks there had never stopped and picked me up."
>
> Hunter died a week later of a heart attack at the age of 35.

Id.

Increasingly, courts have been asked to consider whether evidence of battered woman syndrome should be admitted in cases in which an abused woman defendant claims she committed the charged offense under duress from her abuser. A few courts have decided that such evidence is relevant and should be admitted. *See, e.g., People v. Romero*, 26 Cal.App.4th 315, 13 Cal.Rptr.2d 332 (1992). Most courts, however, have deemed battered woman syndrome evidence irrelevant to claims of duress on the ground that the defense of duress requires an objectively reasonable fear of imminent death or grievous bodily injury and evidence of battered woman syndrome supports only a subjective fear. Alafair S. Burke, *Rational Actors, Self-Defense, and Duress: Making Sense, Not Syndromes, Out of the Battered Woman*, 81 N.C. L. REV. 211, 265 (2002) (noting "although battered women who claim duress have had some success in relying upon the battered woman syndrome theory, they have enjoyed less success than battered women who claim self-defense."). If courts are willing to admit battered woman syndrome evidence as relevant to the reasonableness of the battered woman's belief in the need to use deadly force against her abuser in self-defense, shouldn't they also admit battered woman syndrome evidence in cases involving claims of duress?

2. INTOXICATION

The defense of intoxication is traditionally understood as comprising two distinct defenses: voluntary intoxication and involuntary intoxication. As we have seen in Chapter 4 (Mens Rea), in jurisdictions that follow the common law, the traditional rule has been that whether a defendant can argue voluntary intoxication as a defense turns on whether the crime with which she is charged is considered a specific intent crime or a general intent crime. If the charged offense is a general intent crime, then the defendant will not be permitted to introduce evidence of her intoxication. If the offense is a specific intent crime, the defendant will be allowed to present evidence of her voluntary intoxication. In order to secure an acquittal, however, the defendant must show that because of her intoxicated condition, she did not have the specific intent required for commission of the crime.

In recent years, common law courts have become increasingly hostile toward the defense of voluntary intoxication. For instance, some states have decided to abolish the defense of voluntary intoxication, disallowing evidence of voluntary intoxication in all cases regardless of whether the charged offense is a specific intent or general intent crime. In 1996, the U.S. Supreme Court was asked to decide whether a legislature's decision to abolish the defense of voluntary intoxication is consistent with a criminal defendant's constitutional right to present evidence in his or her behalf. The Court answers this question in *Montana v. Egelhoff*.

Involuntary intoxication has been treated very differently by courts that follow the common law. In some jurisdictions, evidence of involuntary intoxication is admissible to negate either specific or general intent (although since general intent is often treated as "intent to do the physical actions that constitute the crime," it is unlikely that one would ever be so intoxicated as to not have such intent unless comatose). In most jurisdictions, involuntary intoxication can be the basis for a temporary insanity claim. In this way, involuntary intoxication can be used as an affirmative defense. Some jurisdictions acknowledge only this second use of involuntary intoxication evidence, holding that involuntary intoxication is only a defense if it caused the defendant to become temporarily insane.

What constitutes involuntary intoxication? The court in *Commonwealth v. Smith* reviews the common law precedents, and ultimately concludes that Pennsylvania law has incorporated the Model Penal Code on this point.

MONTANA V. EGELHOFF

Supreme Court of the United States
518 U.S. 37, 116 S.Ct. 2013, 135 L.Ed.2d 361 (1996)

JUSTICE SCALIA announced the judgment of the Court and delivered an opinion, in which THE CHIEF JUSTICE, JUSTICE KENNEDY, and JUSTICE THOMAS join.

We consider in this case whether the Due Process Clause is violated by Montana Code Annotated § 45–2–203, which provides, in relevant part, that voluntary intoxication "may not be taken into consideration in determining the existence of a mental state which is an element of a criminal offense."

I

In July 1992, while camping out in the Yaak region of northwestern Montana to pick mushrooms, respondent made friends with Roberta Pavola and John Christenson, who were doing the same. On Sunday, July 12, the three sold the mushrooms they had collected and spent the rest of the day and evening drinking, in bars and at a private party in Troy, Montana. Some time after 9 p.m., they left the party in Christenson's 1974 Ford Galaxy station wagon. The drinking binge apparently continued, as respondent was seen buying beer at 9:20 p.m. and recalled "sitting on a hill or a bank passing a bottle of Black Velvet back and forth" with Christenson.

At about midnight that night, officers of the Lincoln County, Montana, sheriff's department, responding to reports of a possible drunk driver, discovered Christenson's station wagon stuck in a ditch along U.S. Highway 2. In the front seat were Pavola and Christenson, each dead from a single gunshot to the head. In the rear of the car lay respondent, alive and yelling obscenities. His blood-alcohol content measured .36 percent over one hour later. On the floor of the car, near the brake pedal, lay respondent's .38 caliber handgun, with four loaded rounds and two empty casings; respondent had gunshot residue on his hands.

Respondent was charged with two counts of deliberate homicide, a crime defined by Montana law as "purposely" or "knowingly" causing the death of another human being. A portion of the jury charge, uncontested here, instructed that "a person acts purposely when it is his conscious object to engage in conduct of that nature or to cause such a result," and that "a person acts knowingly when he is aware of his conduct or when he is aware under the circumstances his conduct constitutes a crime; or, when he is aware there exists the high probability that his conduct will cause a specific result." Respondent's defense at trial was that an unidentified fourth person must have committed the murders; his own extreme intoxication, he claimed, had rendered him physically incapable of committing the murders, and accounted for his inability to recall the events of the night of July 12. Although respondent was allowed to make this use of the evidence that he was intoxicated, the jury was instructed, pursuant to Mont. Code Ann. § 45–2–203 (1995), that it could not consider respondent's "intoxicated condition . . . in determining the existence of a mental state which is an element of the offense." The jury found respondent guilty on both counts, and the court sentenced him to 84 years' imprisonment.

The Supreme Court of Montana reversed. It reasoned (1) that respondent "had a due process right to present and have considered by the jury all relevant evidence to rebut the State's evidence on all elements of the offense charged," and (2) that evidence of respondent's voluntary intoxication was "clearly . . . relevant to the issue of whether respondent acted knowingly and purposely." Because § 45–2–203 prevented the jury from considering that evidence with regard to that issue, the court concluded that the State had been "relieved of part of its burden to prove beyond a reasonable doubt every fact necessary to constitute the crime charged," and that respondent had therefore been denied due process. We granted certiorari.

II

* * * Respondent . . . acknowledges that the right to present relevant evidence "has not been viewed as absolute." That is a wise concession, since the proposition that the Due Process Clause guarantees the right to introduce all relevant evidence is simply indefensible. As we have said: "The accused does not have an unfettered right to offer [evidence] that is incompetent, privileged, or otherwise inadmissible under standard rules of evidence." Relevant evidence may, for example, be excluded on account of a defendant's failure to comply with procedural requirements. And any number of familiar and unquestionably constitutional evidentiary rules also authorize the exclusion of relevant evidence. For example, Federal (and Montana) Rule of Evidence 403 provides: "*Although relevant,* evidence may be excluded if its probative value is substantially outweighed by the danger of unfair prejudice, confusion of the issues, or misleading the jury, or by considerations of undue delay, waste of time, or needless presentation of cumulative evidence." Hearsay rules similarly prohibit the introduction of testimony which, though unquestionably relevant, is deemed insufficiently reliable. * * *

Respondent's task, then, is to establish that a defendant's right to have a jury consider evidence of his voluntary intoxication in determining whether he possesses the requisite mental state is a "fundamental principle of justice."

Our primary guide in determining whether the principle in question is fundamental is, of course, historical practice. Here that gives respondent little support. By the laws of England, wrote Hale, the intoxicated defendant "shall have no privilege by this voluntary contracted madness, but shall have the same judgment as if he were in his right senses." * * * Blackstone, citing Coke, explained that the law viewed intoxication "as an aggravation of the offence, rather than as an excuse for any criminal misbehaviour." This stern rejection of inebriation as a defense became a fixture of early American law as well. The American editors of the 1847 edition of Hale wrote:

> Drunkenness, it was said in an early case, can never be received as a ground to excuse or palliate an offence. * * * [T]he uniform decisions of our own Courts from the first establishment of the government * * * constitute it now a part of the common law of the land. * * *

Against this extensive evidence of a lengthy common-law tradition decidedly against him, the best argument available to respondent is the one made by his *amicus* and conceded by the State: Over the course of the 19th century, courts carved out an exception to the common law's traditional across-the-board condemnation of the drunken offender, allowing a jury to consider a defendant's intoxication when assessing whether he possessed the mental state needed to commit the crime charged, where the crime was one requiring a "specific intent." * * *

[B]y the end of the 19th century, in most American jurisdictions, intoxication could be considered in determining whether a defendant was capable of forming the specific intent necessary to commit the crime charged.

* * * [E]ven assuming that when the Fourteenth Amendment was adopted the rule Montana now defends was no longer generally applied, this only cuts off what might be called an *a fortiori* argument in favor of the State. The burden remains upon respondent to show that the "new common-law" rule—that intoxication may be considered on the question of intent—was so deeply rooted at the time of the Fourteenth Amendment (or perhaps has become so deeply rooted since) as to be a fundamental principle which that Amendment enshrined.

That showing has not been made. Instead of the uniform and continuing acceptance we would expect for a rule that enjoys "fundamental principle" status, we find that fully one-fifth of the States either never adopted the "new common-law" rule at issue here or have recently abandoned it. * * *

It is not surprising that many States have held fast to or resurrected the common-law rule prohibiting consideration of voluntary intoxication in the determination of *mens rea*, because that rule has considerable justification—which alone casts doubt upon the proposition that the opposite rule is a "fundamental principle." A large number of crimes, especially violent crimes, are committed by intoxicated offenders; modern studies put the numbers as high as half of all homicides, for example. Disallowing consideration of voluntary intoxication has the effect of increasing the punishment for all unlawful acts committed in that state, and thereby deters drunkenness or irresponsible behavior while drunk. The rule also serves as a specific deterrent, ensuring that those who prove incapable of controlling violent impulses while voluntarily intoxicated go to prison. And finally, the rule comports with and implements society's moral perception that one who has voluntarily impaired his own faculties should be responsible for the consequences. * * *

* * * Although the rule allowing a jury to consider evidence of a defendant's voluntary intoxication where relevant to *mens rea* has gained considerable acceptance, it is of too recent vintage, and has not received sufficiently uniform and permanent allegiance, to qualify as fundamental,

especially since it displaces a lengthy common law tradition which remains supported by valid justifications today.

III

* * * *In re Winship* announced the proposition that the Due Process Clause requires proof beyond a reasonable doubt of every fact necessary to constitute the charged crime, and *Sandstrom v. Montana,* established a corollary, that a jury instruction which shifts to the defendant the burden of proof on a requisite element of mental state violates due process. These decisions simply are not implicated here because, as the Montana court itself recognized, "the burden is not shifted" under § 45–2–203. The trial judge instructed the jury that "the State of Montana has the burden of proving the guilt of the Defendant beyond a reasonable doubt," and that "[a] person commits the offense of deliberate homicide if he purposely or knowingly causes the death of another human being." Thus, failure by the State to produce evidence of respondent's mental state would have resulted in an acquittal. That acquittal did not occur was presumably attributable to the fact, noted by the Supreme Court of Montana, that the State introduced considerable evidence from which the jury might have concluded that respondent acted "purposely" or "knowingly." For example, respondent himself testified that, several hours before the murders, he had given his handgun to Pavola and asked her to put it in the glove compartment of Christenson's car. That he had to retrieve the gun from the glove compartment before he used it was strong evidence that it was his "conscious object" to commit the charged crimes; as was the execution-style manner in which a single shot was fired into the head of each victim. * * *

* * * The people of Montana have decided to resurrect the rule of an earlier era, disallowing consideration of voluntary intoxication when a defendant's state of mind is at issue. Nothing in the Due Process Clause prevents them from doing so, and the judgment of the Supreme Court of Montana to the contrary must be reversed.

It is so ordered.

JUSTICE O'CONNOR, with whom JUSTICE STEVENS, JUSTICE SOUTER, and JUSTICE BREYER join, dissenting.

* * *

I

This Court's cases establish that limitations placed on the accused's ability to present a fair and complete defense can, in some circumstances, be severe enough to violate due process. "The right of an accused in a criminal trial to due process is, in essence, the right to a fair opportunity to defend against the State's accusations." Applying our precedent, the Montana Supreme Court held that keeping intoxication evidence away from the jury, where such evidence was relevant to establishment of the requisite mental state, violated the due process right to present a defense and that the instruction pursuant to § 45–2–203 was not harmless error. In rejecting the Montana Supreme Court's conclusion, the Court emphasizes that "any number of familiar and unquestionably constitutional evidentiary rules" permit exclusion of relevant evidence. It is true that a defendant does not enjoy an absolute right to present evidence relevant to his defense. But none of the "familiar" evidentiary rules operates as Montana's does. The Montana statute places a blanket exclusion on a category of evidence that would allow the accused to negate the offense's mental-state element. In so doing, it frees the prosecution, in the face of such evidence, from having to prove beyond a reasonable doubt that the defendant nevertheless possessed the required mental state. In my view, this combination of effects violates due process. * * *

Meaningful adversarial testing of the State's case requires that the defendant not be prevented from raising an effective defense, which must include the right to present relevant, probative evidence. To be sure, the right to present evidence is not limitless. * * * Nevertheless, "an essential component of procedural fairness is an opportunity to be heard. That opportunity would be an empty one if the State were permitted to exclude competent, reliable evidence" that is essential to the accused's defense. Section 45–2–203 forestalls the defendant's ability to raise an effective defense by placing a blanket exclusion on the presentation of a type of evidence that directly negates an element of the crime, and by doing so, it lightens the prosecution's burden to prove that mental-state element beyond a reasonable doubt.

* * * A state legislature certainly has the authority to identify the elements of the offenses it wishes to punish, but once its laws are written, a defendant has the right to insist that the State prove beyond a reasonable doubt every element of an offense charged. "The Due Process Clause protects the accused against conviction except upon proof beyond a reasonable doubt of every fact necessary to constitute the crime with which he is charged." Because the Montana Legislature has specified that a person commits "deliberate homicide" only if he "purposely or knowingly causes the death of another human being," the prosecution must prove the existence of such mental state in order to convict. That is, unless the defendant is shown to have acted purposely or knowingly, *he is not guilty of the offense of deliberate homicide*. The Montana Supreme Court found that it was inconsistent with the legislature's requirement of the mental state of "purposely" or "knowingly" to prevent the jury from considering evidence of voluntary intoxication, where that category of evidence was relevant to establishment of that mental-state element.

Where the defendant may introduce evidence to negate a subjective mental-state element, the prosecution must work to overcome whatever doubts the defense has raised about the existence of the required mental state. On the other hand, if the defendant may *not* introduce evidence that might create doubt in the factfinder's mind as to whether that element was met, the prosecution will find its job so much the easier. A subjective mental state is generally proved only circumstantially. If a jury may not consider the defendant's evidence of his mental state, the jury may impute to the defendant the culpability of a mental state he did not possess. * * *

The plurality brushes aside this Court's precedents as variously fact bound, irrelevant, and dicta. I would afford more weight to principles enunciated in our case law than is accorded in the plurality's opinion today. It seems to me that a State may not first determine the elements of the crime it wishes to punish, and then thwart the accused's defense by categorically disallowing the very evidence that would prove him innocent.

II

The plurality does, however, raise an important argument for the statute's validity: the disallowance, at common law, of consideration of voluntary intoxication where a defendant's state of mind is at issue. Because this disallowance was permitted at common law, the plurality argues, its disallowance by Montana cannot amount to a violation of a "fundamental principle of justice."

From 1551 until its shift in the 19th century, the common-law rule prevailed that a defendant could not use intoxication as an excuse or justification for an offense, or, it must be assumed, to rebut establishment of a requisite mental state. "Early law was indifferent to the defence of drunkenness because the theory of criminal liability was then too crude and too undeveloped to admit of exceptions. . . . But with the refinement in the theory of criminal liability . . . a modification of the rigid old rule on the defence of drunkenness was to be expected." As the plurality concedes, that significant modification took place in the 19th century. Courts acknowledged the fundamental incompatibility of a particular mental-state requirement on the one hand, and the disallowance of consideration of evidence that might defeat establishment of that mental state on the other. In the slow progress typical of the common law, courts began to recognize that evidence of intoxication was properly admissible for the purpose of ascertaining whether a defendant had met the required mental-state element of the offense charged.

This recognition, courts believed, was consistent with the common-law rule that voluntary intoxication did not excuse commission of a crime; rather, an element of the crime, the requisite mental state, was not satisfied and therefore the crime had not been committed. As one influential mid-19th century case explained: "Drunkenness is no excuse for crime; yet, in that class of crimes and offences which depend upon guilty knowledge, or the coolness and deliberation with which they shall have been perpetrated, to constitute their commission . . . [drunkenness] should be submitted to the consideration of the Jury"; for, where the crime required a particular mental state, "it is proper to show any state or condition of the person that is adverse to the proper exercise of the mind" in order "to rebut" the mental state or "to enable the Jury to judge rightly of the matter."

Courts across the country agreed that where a subjective mental state was an element of the crime to be proved, the defense must be permitted to show, by reference to intoxication, the absence of that element. One court commented that it seemed "incontrovertible and to be universally applicable" that "where the nature and essence of the crime are made by law to depend upon the peculiar state and condition of the criminal's mind at the time with reference to the act done, drunkenness may be a proper subject for the consideration of the jury, not to excuse or mitigate the offence but to show that it was not committed."

With similar reasoning, the Montana Supreme Court recognized the incompatibility of a jury instruction pursuant to § 45–2–203 in conjunction with the legislature's decision to require a mental state of "purposely" or "knowingly" for deliberate homicide. It held that intoxication is relevant to formation of the requisite mental state. Unless a defendant is proved beyond a reasonable doubt to have possessed the requisite mental state, he did not commit the offense. Elimination of a critical category of defense evidence precludes a defendant from effectively rebutting the mental-state element, while simultaneously shielding the State from the effort of proving the requisite mental state in the face of negating evidence. It was this effect on the adversarial process that persuaded the Montana Supreme Court that the disallowance was unconstitutional.

The Due Process Clause protects those " 'principle[s] of justice so rooted in the traditions and conscience of our people as to be ranked as fundamental.' " At the time the Fourteenth Amendment was ratified, the common-law rule on consideration of intoxication evidence was in flux. The plurality argues that rejection of the historical rule in the 19th century simply does not establish that the " 'new common-law' " rule is a principle of procedure so "deeply rooted" as to be ranked "fundamental." But to determine whether a fundamental principle of justice has been violated here, we cannot consider only the historical disallowance of intoxication evidence, but must also consider the "fundamental principle" that a defendant has a right to a fair opportunity to put forward his defense, in adversarial testing where the State must prove the elements of the offense beyond a reasonable doubt. * * *

COMMONWEALTH V. SMITH

Superior Court of Pennsylvania
831 A.2d 636 (Pa. Super. 2003)

ORIE MELVIN, J.

Appellant, Karen Smith, appeals from the judgment of sentence of 48 hours to 18 months' incarceration imposed following her conviction of driving under the influence (DUI) and related summary offense. Appellant claims she established the affirmative defense of "involuntary intoxication" thereby negating the state of mind necessary to support a conviction of DUI. After review, we affirm.

The facts and procedural history of this matter may be summarized as follows. On March 29, 2002, Officer James E. Ott, of the Greenfield Township Police Department, observed Appellant driving a Ford truck on State Route 101 in Greenfield Township, Blair County, Pennsylvania. Officer Ott observed Appellant's vehicle drift completely into the oncoming lane and proceed to travel in the lane for oncoming traffic for one tenth of a mile until he activated his emergency lights. Appellant then pulled her vehicle to the side of the road, leaving a large portion of the vehicle protruding into the roadway, even though there was sufficient space to park the vehicle totally off of the roadway. Upon making contact with the Appellant, Officer Ott observed that her eyes were glassy and bloodshot and she emanated a strong odor of alcohol. When asked to exit her vehicle, Appellant stumbled and staggered numerous times. Appellant admitted to consuming beer earlier in the evening.

Officer Ott administered three field sobriety tests, all of which Appellant failed. Appellant was placed under arrest for DUI and transported to the hospital for a blood alcohol test, which she refused. On September 24, 2002, a bench trial was held. On direct examination, Appellant testified that she consumed alcohol while wearing a prescribed "duragesic" patch for pain. She testified that she did not realize that the patch would heighten the effects of alcohol. Appellant admitted that she did not read the directions or warnings for the patch. Moreover, Appellant offered no expert testimony whatsoever to support her allegation that the patch heightened the effects of the alcohol she consumed. The Honorable Thomas J. Peoples, Jr. found Appellant guilty and imposed sentence on October 17, 2002. Appellant filed a post sentence motion that was denied. This timely appeal followed.

Appellant's sole question on appeal reads as follows: I. IS THE DEFENSE OF INVOLUNTARY INTOXICATION OR INVOLUNTARY DRUGGED CONDITION A DEFENSE COGNIZABLE IN PENNSYLVANIA?

Initially, we note that Appellant was convicted of driving while under the influence of alcohol to a degree that rendered her incapable of safe driving. In order to prove a violation of this section, the Commonwealth must show: (1) that the defendant was the operator of a motor vehicle and (2) that while operating the vehicle, the defendant was under the influence of alcohol to such a degree as to render him or her incapable of safe driving. To establish the second element, it must be shown that alcohol has substantially impaired the normal mental and physical faculties required to safely operate the vehicle. Substantial impairment, in this context, means a diminution or enfeeblement in the ability to exercise judgment, to deliberate or to react prudently to changing circumstances and conditions. Evidence that the driver was not in control of himself, such as failing to pass a field sobriety test, may establish that the driver was under the influence of alcohol to a degree which rendered him incapable of safe driving, notwithstanding the absence of evidence of erratic or unsafe driving.

Appellant asserts that involuntary intoxication is a cognizable affirmative defense in a DUI prosecution. Specifically, she claims that "[i]n the pharmaceutical age, the labeling of drugs places on the physician in Pennsylvania, the duty to warn the patient of the side effects of drugs. When labeling is not on bold print but on minute instructions in tiny print inside of a box, it is not the consumer who is expected to be aware of the consequences, but the physician. Where testimony is offered, unrebutted, nor challenged, that the user was unaware of the polypharmacology of the drug a cognizable defense should be recognized in Pennsylvania." In effect, Appellant urges this Court to find that she was not criminally culpable for her conduct because she was unaware that the newly increased strength of the prescribed duragesic patch she was wearing would heighten the effects of the alcohol she voluntarily ingested. We are not persuaded.

Pennsylvania like many other jurisdictions, either by statute or caselaw, specifically limits the availability of a voluntary intoxication defense but does not specify whether an involuntary intoxication defense is available. In *Commonwealth v. Collins*, we recently noted that "the issue of whether involuntary intoxication is a defense to a DUI charge is unclear in Pennsylvania." Moreover, in the context of a DUI prosecution, assuming the defense applies, we have held that the defendant has the burden of proving the affirmative defense of involuntary intoxication by a preponderance of the evidence.

Generally speaking, many of the other jurisdictions that permit an accused to be completely relieved of criminal responsibility based on involuntary intoxication do so premised upon the notion that he or she was temporarily rendered legally insane at the time he or she committed the offense. The defense of involuntary intoxication has been recognized in other jurisdictions in four types of situations: (1) where the intoxication was caused by the fault of another (i.e., through force, duress, fraud, or contrivance); (2) where the intoxication was caused by an innocent mistake on the part of the defendant (i.e., defendant took hallucinogenic pill in reasonable belief it was aspirin or lawful tranquilizer); (3) where a defendant unknowingly suffers from a physiological or psychological condition that renders him abnormally susceptible to a legal intoxicant (sometimes referred to as pathological intoxication); and (4) where unexpected intoxication results from a medically prescribed drug. These widely varying circumstances make it difficult to formulate a comprehensive definition of the defense; nonetheless, it would appear that a key component is lack of culpability on the part of the defendant in causing the intoxication.

Instantly, Appellant's argument is most similar to the situation described above in type number four. This type is premised upon the notion that "because a patient is entitled to assume that an intoxicating dose would not be prescribed or administered by a physician, where intoxication results from medicine which has been prescribed (and taken as prescribed) or administered by a physician, such intoxication is generally considered involuntary." Significantly, Appellant's argument differs from a pure type four involuntary intoxication defense in that she does not claim that the patch alone caused an unknowing and unexpected intoxicating effect. Rather, she claims that a higher dose of the patch combined with her voluntary ingestion of an allegedly moderate amount of alcohol caused an unexpected intoxication. It would seem, however, that her intoxication was "self-induced" as defined by the Model Penal Code. Clearly, she "knowingly introduce[d]" a substance—alcohol—"the tendency of which to cause intoxication" she "ought to [have known]." Model Penal Code § 2.08(5)(b). In fact, this Court and our Supreme Court have previously rejected similar arguments in *Commonwealth v. Todaro* and *Commonwealth v. Hicks*.

In *Todaro*, the defendant was charged with involuntary manslaughter, recklessly endangering another person, and driving under the influence. This Court held that an instruction on involuntary intoxication was not required where the defendant inadvertently mixed alcoholic beverages with prescribed medication because there was no evidence to support a finding that defendant's intoxication was not voluntary. In *Hicks*, prior to the victim's murder the defendant had consumed a large quantity of alcohol and an amphetamine based diet pill. Defendant asserted that the record did not establish that he was sane so as to be criminally responsible for his conduct. He argued that his mental state was involuntarily induced from a mixture of the prescribed medication and alcohol because he was not warned of the possible effect of such combination. On appeal our Supreme Court held that the trial court properly weighed the evidence and found that defendant's behavior resulted from the voluntary ingestion of alcohol and not mental disease. * * *

Thus, it would appear that Pennsylvania law is consonant with the Model Penal Code's definition and would not characterize intoxication produced by the voluntary consumption of a prescription drug and alcohol as "involuntary" even if that consumption was without knowledge of a synergistic effect. Here, as in *Todaro* the evidence merely established that Appellant drank alcohol without regard to the effects of its combination with medication she was taking. Thus, even assuming the proffered defense is viable, these facts alone cannot establish involuntary intoxication.

Moreover, upon our careful review of the facts of this case even if we were to assume that such a defense is cognizable under Appellant's theory, she still cannot show that the trial court erred in rejecting this defense because she has failed to establish the necessary factual foundation to support her claimed defense. To absolve Appellant of criminal behavior by the complete defense of involuntary intoxication, she had the burden to show such intoxication by a preponderance of the evidence. If this defense is to be relied upon, Appellant must show that the combination is capable of causing the extreme intoxication which is alleged. The trial court cannot take judicial notice of this fact. Thus, at a minimum it will be necessary to present expert witnesses to establish this effect. Here, the only evidence of record is Appellant's self-serving statements that she had not read any of the labeling and was not told by her doctor of any possible side effects and thus was unaware of the alleged heightened effect of the patch when combined with alcohol consumption. Appellant did not present her physician or any other medical expert to establish that an increased inebriating effect was even possible. It follows that Appellant has not come close to putting the integrity of the conviction into question. Because Appellant was unable to establish the factual foundation for her proffered defense, * * * the trial court properly denied Appellant's motion in arrest of judgment.

Judgment of sentence affirmed.

3. INSANITY

The defendant's mental competency is a possible issue at three stages of the criminal proceeding. Before trial, the defense may argue that the defendant is incompetent to stand trial. The test for determining competency to stand trial is whether the defendant is capable of understanding the proceedings and assisting his counsel in presenting a defense. If the court decides that the defendant is incapable of understanding the proceedings or cannot assist in his defense, criminal proceedings are generally suspended until the defendant is deemed competent to stand trial.[a]

[a] The United States Supreme Court in 2003 held that the government may forcibly administer anti-psychotic drugs to render a mentally ill defendant competent to stand trial if the

Second, the defendant may put his mental competency into issue by claiming that he should be found not guilty by reason of insanity. Over the years, many different common law tests for determining whether a defendant is legally insane have been adopted. All of these tests examine the defendant's mental capacity at the time he or she committed the criminal act. The first case in this section, *United States v. Freeman*, discusses these various tests in detail and provides a cogent critique of the M'Naghten test, once the leading test for insanity. Under the M'Naghten Rule, an individual could be found not guilty by reason of insanity if:

> at the time of the committing of the act, the party accused was laboring under such a defect of reason, from disease of the mind as not to know the nature and quality of the act he was doing, or, if he did know it, that he did not know he was doing what was wrong.

Section 4.01 of the Model Penal Code provides an alternative definition of insanity. Section 4.01 provides:

> A person is not responsible for criminal conduct if at the time of such conduct as a result of mental disease or defect he lacks substantial capacity either to appreciate the wrongfulness of his conduct or to conform his conduct to the requirements of law.

As Christopher Slobogin notes:

> [The Model Penal Code] formulation works two changes in the M'Naghten Test. One is that, on its face, the ALI test does not require the black-or-white analysis that M'Naghten does. It speaks in terms of *substantial* lack of experience and capacity, as opposed to an *inability* to know the wrongfulness of the act. Second, the ALI test uses the word "appreciate" as opposed to the word "know." The latter modification was meant to provide an excuse to those who might "know" that the criminal act was wrong, but who are unable to internalize the wrongfulness of the act.

Christopher Slobogin, *The Integrationist Alternative to the Insanity Defense: Reflections on the Exculpatory Scope of Mental Illness in the Wake of the Andrea Yates Trial*, 30 AM. J. CRIM. L. 315, 318 (2003).

Well over half the states initially moved from the M'Naghten test to the Model Penal Code test. However, the 1982 acquittal of John Hinckley, who had tried to assassinate President Ronald Reagan, on insanity grounds under the Model Penal Code's test for insanity caused a public

---

treatment is (1) medically appropriate, (2) substantially unlikely to have side effects that may undermine the trial's fairness, and (3) necessary to significantly further important governmental interests. *Sell v. United States*, 539 U.S. 166 (2003).

outcry. In response, many jurisdictions, including the federal government, re-adopted some version of the stricter M'Naghten test. Today, most states use the M'Naghten test or some variation on M'Naghten. Clark v. Arizona, 548 U.S. 735, 750–51 (2006).[c]

One question that has split the courts is whether to construe the term "wrong" or "wrongfulness," which appears in both the M'Naghten test and the Model Penal Code's test for insanity, as "legal wrongfulness" (i.e., the defendant knew that he was acting illegally) or "moral wrongfulness" (i.e. the defendant knew that he was acting contrary to morality). The majority in *State v. Crenshaw* discusses the distinction between legal and moral wrongfulness.

Third, the mental capacity of a convicted defendant on death row may be an issue prior to execution. In *Ford v. Wainwright*, 477 U.S. 399 (1986), the United States Supreme Court ruled that the execution of an insane person constitutes cruel and unusual punishment in violation of the Eighth Amendment. Whether the state can forcibly medicate a defendant to make him sane for execution is an issue that has not yet been addressed by the high court.

UNITED STATES V. FREEMAN

United States Court of Appeals for the Second Circuit
357 F.2d 606 (2d Cir. 1966)

KAUFMAN, CIRCUIT JUDGE.

* * *

After a trial before Judge Tenney without a jury, Charles Freeman was found guilty on two counts of selling narcotics in violation of 21 U.S.C. §§ 173, 174, and sentenced to concurrent terms of five years on each count. Although Freeman denied commission of the substantive offense, his principal allegation at trial was that, at the time of the alleged sale of narcotics, he did not possess sufficient capacity and will to be held responsible for the criminality of his acts. In rejecting this contention, the District Court understandably relied upon the familiar *M'Naghten* Rules which, in their traditional formulation, permit acquittal only when it is proved that, "at the time of the committing of the act, the party accused was laboring under such a defect of reason, from disease of the mind as not to know the nature and quality of the act he was doing, or, if he did know it, that he did not know he was doing what was wrong." Since he could not find that Freeman's condition satisfied the rigid

[c] At least four states have abolished the insanity defense. In November 2012, the United States Supreme Court declined to consider whether abolishing the insanity defense comports with the Constitution. Robert Barnes, *The Supreme Court Won't Consider Insanity Challenge*, WASH. POST, Nov. 27, 2012, at A3.

requirements of this test, Judge Tenney had no alternative but to hold the defendant guilty as charged. * * *

THE EVIDENCE OF SALE

* * * The government's evidence established that on the evening of June 24, 1963, narcotics agents Coursey and Fluhr met one James Lockhart, an informant (or, in the more polite lexicon of the government, a "special employee"), in uptown Manhattan. After making the usual search of the informant in order to be sure he did not possess narcotics prior to contact with the suspect, Lockhart and Coursey walked to the corner of 110th Street and Broadway while Fluhr remained behind. Lockhart introduced Freeman to Coursey and, after some preliminary discussion, Freeman stated, "I hear you want to buy some heroin." When Coursey indicated that he did and inquired about the price, Freeman replied that it would be $230 a "piece." At Freeman's suggestion, the three men then proceeded to the close-by Gold Rail bar, where Freeman gave Coursey a sealed brown paper bag in return for which Coursey mistakenly paid the defendant $130 instead of the stipulated $230. Coursey then left the bar and met Agent Fluhr and Agent Casale. Together they performed a field test on the contents of the brown paper bag which revealed the presence of heroin. A chemical analysis subsequently confirmed this result.

Shortly thereafter, Coursey was notified by car radio that Lockhart had called him. Coursey returned to 110th Street and Broadway and entered a taxi in which Freeman and Lockhart had been riding. When Freeman asked if Coursey was trying to "beat" him out of $100, Coursey explained that the failure to make full payment in the bar had been a mistake and he turned over an additional $100.

On August 1, 1963, a second transaction took place; in many respects it was a sequel to the first. This time, Coursey and a different informant, Alfred Roach, entered Marvin's Bar on Broadway near 111th Street. Freeman, standing at the bar, said that he had been sick, but, nevertheless, had heard that Coursey had been buying large amounts of heroin and indicated that he would like to make another sale. A price of $235 per ounce was agreed upon and Freeman and Coursey adjourned to the men's room where Freeman handed Coursey another brown paper bag.[6] Coursey made payment, this time in the correct amount, and departed. A field test on the contents of the bag showed that it contained heroin and a chemical analysis confirmed the accuracy of this result.

While Freeman admitted taking part in the transactions of June 24 and August 1, he presented a different version of his participation. He

[6] Freeman apparently was uneasy in Marvin's Bar because he and the informant were the only Negroes present. Thus, Freeman hurrying to complete the transaction told Coursey, "Hurry up, man, because I got the stuff in my pocket and we look suspicious here because there is a whole lot of white people in here, we look suspicious in here."

testified that rather than being the culprit, he was merely a conduit being used by the informant to pass the brown paper packages to Agent Coursey. The money which the agent paid, Freeman said, was not his to keep, but was turned over to the informant who had furnished him in each instance with the brown paper bag. Judge Tenney chose to discredit Freeman's version of these transactions and we see no reason to disagree with his resolution of the credibility issue.

THE DEFENSE OF LACK OF RESPONSIBILITY

As is not uncommon in cases in which the defense is raised, the bulk of the evidence directly relating to the issue of criminal responsibility took the form of expert psychiatric testimony of witnesses called by both the government and the defense. Freeman's expert witness at trial was Dr. Herman Denber, Associate Professor of Clinical Psychiatry at New York Medical College and Director of Psychiatric Research at Manhattan State Hospital. Dr. Denber, who had examined the defendant on the previous afternoon, testified that Freeman was not only a narcotics addict, but also a confirmed alcoholic. * * *

* * * Describing his examination in some detail, Dr. Denber testified that Freeman displayed no depth or variation in his emotional reactions, spoke in a flat monotone and paused for excessively long periods before responding to questions. Dr. Denber also noted that as a result of taking impure narcotics for so long a time, Freeman suffered from frequent episodes of toxic psychosis[7] leading to a clouding of the sensorium (inability to know what one is doing or where one is) as well as delusions, hallucinations, epileptic convulsions and, at times, amnesia.[8] The witness testified, moreover, that Freeman had suffered "knock-outs" on three occasions while engaging in prize fighting, and that these had led to a general vagueness about details. Finally, Dr. Denber observed that Freeman had experienced "innumerable brain traumata" which produced such organic and structural changes as destroyed brain tissue.

---

[7] Dr. Denber defined a "psychosis" as "a disorder of the brain in which the individual's reality appreciation is altered and in which symptoms of thinking and feeling become abnormal." The term "toxic psychosis" refers to a "state of impaired mental functioning with clouding of the senses, non-awareness of time and place produced by some compound, usually medicinal, taken in excess over and above the usual requirements that are prescribed, and usually have been taken for a period of time by the individual."

[8] Dr. Denber testified that because of Freeman's extensive and prolonged use of narcotics such as heroin, cocaine, morphine, and benzedrine, amphetamines and sleeping pills, he did not derive satisfaction from the standard "fix" and was not, in any respect, just an ordinary drug addict. This massive infusion of drugs produced a condition which made Freeman at times, as he put it, so "messed up with the stuff" that he would fall "knocked cold in the street," with resultant head and other injuries. In addition, Freeman suffered from vomiting and chills and approximately twelve times a year for the last eight years, experienced auditory and visual hallucinations as well as paranoid delusions. For example, Freeman saw people in miniature and heard them call his name from under his bed. Indeed, Freeman told the Doctor, "At times I would think something was wrong with my head. I think the drugs I was using was eating up my brain."

Restricted to stating a conclusory opinion within the confines of *M'Naghten*, Dr. Denber initially averred that Freeman was incapable of knowing right from wrong, even under a strict interpretation of that limited test. However, upon amplifying this conclusion, the defense expert acknowledged that Freeman had an awareness of what he was doing on the nights of June 24 and August 1 in the sense that he possessed cognition that he was selling heroin. The Doctor also added that Freeman was not in "such a state of toxicity that he did not remember the dates. He told me the story [of the narcotics transactions] clearly, but it is my feeling about him, in particular, that as far as the social implications or the nature or meaning of what this meant to him at that moment he was not aware of it."

To respond to Dr. Denber's testimony, the government called on Dr. Robert S. Carson, a former staff physician at Payne-Whitney Clinic of The New York Hospital and Clinical Instructor in Psychiatry at Cornell University. Dr. Carson testified that Freeman was able to distinguish between right and wrong within the meaning of the *M'Naghten* test despite his heavy use of narcotics and alcohol. He noted that Freeman possessed the capacity to enter into purposeful activity such as the sale of narcotics, and he expressed the opinion that the defendant had been aware of the wrongfulness of his acts. In support of this view, Dr. Carson pointed to the fact that on the evening of August 1, 1963, Freeman had been sufficiently fearful of being apprehended that he had suggested that the transfer of narcotics take place in the privacy of the men's room of Marvin's Bar. In summary, Dr. Carson significantly acknowledged that Freeman had "some limitations" on his ability to distinguish right from wrong, but not to the degree required by the *M'Naghten* test. * * *

We are now concerned with whether the Court at trial should have applied a test less rigid than that provided by *M'Naghten*, so that the essential examination and psychiatric testimony could have been directed towards Freeman's capacity to exercise will or appreciate the wrongfulness of his conduct, rather than being confined to the relatively narrow inquiry required by *M'Naghten*. * * *

II.

We are here seeking a proper test of criminal responsibility. That we are not instead deciding the initial question—whether lack of such responsibility, however defined, should be a defense in criminal prosecutions—itself seems significant and worthy of at least some brief comment.

The criminal law, it has been said, is an expression of the moral sense of the community. The fact that the law has, for centuries, regarded certain wrong-doers as improper subjects for punishment is a testament to the extent to which that moral sense has developed. Thus, society has recognized over the years that none of the three asserted purposes of the criminal law—rehabilitation, deterrence and retribution—is satisfied when the truly irresponsible, those who lack substantial capacity to control their actions, are punished.

What rehabilitative function is served when one who is mentally incompetent and found guilty is ordered to serve a sentence in prison? Is not any curative or restorative function better achieved in such a case in an institution designed and equipped to treat just such individuals? And how is deterrence achieved by punishing the incompetent? Those who are substantially unable to restrain their conduct are, by definition, undeterrable and their "punishment" is no example for others; those who are unaware of or do not appreciate the nature and quality of their actions can hardly be expected rationally to weigh the consequences of their conduct. Finally, what segment of society can feel its desire for retribution satisfied when it wreaks vengeance upon the incompetent? Although an understandable emotion, a need for retribution can never be permitted in a civilized society to degenerate into a sadistic form of revenge.

A recognition that traditional notions of crime and punishment were inapplicable to the truly "irresponsible" hence came early to Anglo-American criminal law. We turn now to a consideration of those early stirrings.

III.

* * * Daniel M'Naghten suffered from what now would be described as delusions of persecution. Apparently, he considered his major persecutor to be Robert Peel, then Prime Minister of England, for M'Naghten came to London with the intention of assassinating the chief of the Queen's government. His plan would have succeeded but for the fact that Peel chose to ride in Queen Victoria's carriage because of her absence from the city, while Drummond, his secretary, rode in the vehicle which normally would have been occupied by Peel. M'Naghten, believing that the Prime Minister was riding in his own carriage, shot and killed Drummond in error.

After a lengthy trial in 1843, M'Naghten was found "not guilty by reason of insanity." M'Naghten's exculpation from criminal responsibility was most significant for several reasons. His defense counsel had relied in part upon Dr. Isaac Ray's historic work, MEDICAL JURISPRUDENCE OF INSANITY which had been published in 1838. This book, which was used and referred to extensively at the trial, contained many enlightened views on the subject of criminal responsibility in general and on the weaknesses of the right and wrong test in particular. Thus, for example, the jury was told that the human mind is not compartmentalized and that a defect in one aspect of the personality could spill over and affect other areas. As Chief Judge Biggs tells us in his Isaac Ray lectures compiled in THE GUILTY MIND, the court was so impressed with this and other medical evidence of M'Naghten's incompetency that Lord Chief Justice Tindal practically directed a verdict for the accused.

For these reasons, M'Naghten's case could have been the turning point for a new approach to more modern methods of determining criminal responsibility. But the Queen's ire was raised by the acquittal and she was prompted to intervene. Mid-19th Century England was in a state of social upheaval and there had been three attempts on the life of the Queen and one on the Prince Consort. Indeed, Queen Victoria was so concerned about M'Naghten's acquittal that she summoned the House of Lords to "take the opinion of the Judges on the law governing such cases." Consequently, the fifteen judges of the common law courts were called in a somewhat extraordinary session under a not too subtle atmosphere of pressure to answer five prolix and obtuse questions on the status of criminal responsibility in England. Significantly, it was Lord Chief Justice Tindal who responded for fourteen of the fifteen judges, and thus articulated what has come to be known as the *M'Naghten* Rules or *M'Naghten* test. Rather than relying on Dr. Ray's monumental work which had apparently impressed him at M'Naghten's trial, Tindal, with the Queen's breath upon him, reaffirmed the old restricted right-wrong test despite its 16th Century roots and the fact that it, in effect, echoed such uninformed concepts as phrenology and monomania. In this manner, Dr. Ray's insights were to be lost to the common law for over one hundred years except in the small state of New Hampshire. * * *

But the principal objection to *M'Naghten* is not that it was arrived at by this extraordinary process. Rather, the rule is faulted because it has several serious deficiencies which stem in the main from its narrow scope. Because *M'Naghten* focuses only on the cognitive aspect of the personality, i.e., the ability to know right from wrong, we are told by eminent medical scholars that it does not permit the jury to identify those who can distinguish between good and evil but who cannot control their behavior. The result is that instead of being treated at appropriate mental institutions for a sufficiently long period to bring about a cure or sufficient improvement so that the accused may return with relative safety to himself and the community, he is ordinarily sentenced to a prison term as if criminally responsible and then released as a potential recidivist with society at his mercy. To the extent that these individuals continue to be released from prison because of the narrow scope of *M'Naghten*, that test poses a serious danger to society's welfare.

Similarly, *M'Naghten*'s single track emphasis on the cognitive aspect of the personality recognizes no degrees of incapacity. Either the defendant knows right from wrong or he does not and that is the only choice the jury is given. But such a test is grossly unrealistic; our mental institutions, as any qualified psychiatrist will attest, are filled with people who to some extent can differentiate between right and wrong, but lack the capacity to control their acts to a substantial degree. As the commentary to the American Law Institute's Model Penal Code observes, "The law must recognize that when there is no black and white it must content itself with different shades of gray."

A further fatal defect of the *M'Naghten* Rules stems from the unrealistically tight shackles which they place upon expert psychiatric testimony. When the law limits a testifying psychiatrist to stating his opinion whether the accused is capable of knowing right from wrong, the expert is thereby compelled to test guilt or innocence by a concept which bears little relationship to reality. He is required thus to consider one aspect of the mind as a "logic-tight compartment in which the delusion holds sway leaving the balance of the mind intact. * * * "

* * * At bottom, the determination whether a man is or is not held responsible for his conduct is not a medical but a legal, social or moral judgment. Ideally, psychiatrists—much like experts in other fields—should provide grist for the legal mill, should furnish the raw data upon which the legal judgment is based. It is the psychiatrist who informs as to the mental state of the accused—his characteristics, his potentialities, his capabilities. But once this information is disclosed, it is society as a whole, represented by judge or jury, which decides whether a man with the characteristics described should or should not be held accountable for his acts. * * *

The true vice of *M'Naghten* is not, therefore, that psychiatrists will feel constricted in artificially structuring their testimony but rather that the ultimate deciders—the judge or the jury—will be deprived of information vital to their final judgment. For whatever the social climate of Victorian England, today's complex and sophisticated society will not be satisfied with simplistic decisions, based solely upon a man's ability to "know" right from wrong. * * *

IV.

Efforts to supplement or replace the *M'Naghten* Rules with a more meaningful and workable test have persisted for generations, with varying degrees of success. Perhaps the first to receive judicial approval, however, was more an added fillip to *M'Naghten* than a true substitute: the doctrine which permits acquittal on grounds of lack of responsibility when a defendant is found to have been driven by an "irresistible impulse" to commit his offense. * * *

As it has commonly been employed, however, we find the "irresistible impulse" test to be inherently inadequate and unsatisfactory. Psychiatrists have long questioned whether "irresistible impulses" actually exist; the more basic legal objection to the term "irresistible impulse" is that it is too narrow and carries the misleading implication that a crime impulsively committed must have been perpetrated in a sudden and explosive fit. Thus, the "irresistible impulse" test is unduly restrictive because it excludes the far more numerous instances of crimes committed after excessive brooding and melancholy by one who is unable to resist sustained psychic compulsion or to make any real attempt to control his conduct. * * *

In so many instances the criminal act may be the reverse of impulsive; it may be coolly and carefully prepared yet nevertheless the result of a diseased mind. * * *

With the exception of New Hampshire, American courts waited until 1954 and Judge Bazelon's opinion for the District of Columbia Circuit in *Durham v. United States*, for legal recognition that disease or defect of the mind may impair the whole mind and not a subdivided portion of it. The *Durham* court swept away the intellectual debris of a century and articulated a test which was as simple in its formulation as its sources were complex. A defendant is not criminally responsible, wrote Judge Bazelon, "if his unlawful act was the product of mental disease or mental defect."

The advantages of *Durham* were apparent and its arrival was widely hailed. The new test entirely eliminated the "right-wrong" dichotomy, and hence interred the overriding emphasis on the cognitive element of the personality which had for so long plagued *M'Naghten*. The fetters upon expert testimony were removed and psychiatrists were permitted and indeed encouraged to provide all relevant medical information for the common sense application of judge or jury.

Finally, *Durham* ended to a large degree the "professional perjury" decried by psychiatrists—the "juggling" of legal standards made inevitable by *M'Naghten* and rightly deplored by Justice Frankfurter. Too often, the unrealistic dogma of *M'Naghten* had compelled expert witnesses to "stretch" its requirements to "hard cases;" sympathetic to the plight of a defendant who was not, in fairness, responsible for his conduct, psychiatrists had found it necessary to testify that the accused did not know his act was "wrong" even when the defendant's words belied this conclusion. In its frank and express recognition that criminality resulting from mental disease or defect should not bring forth penal sanctions, *Durham* brought an end to this all too-frequent practice of "winking" at legal requirements, a practice which had contributed little to the self-respect and integrity of either medicine or the law.

In the aftermath of *Durham*, however, many students of the law recognized that the new rule, despite its many advantages, also possessed serious deficiencies. It has been suggested, for example, that *Durham's* insistence that an offense be the "product" of a mental disease or defect raised near-impossible problems of causation, closely resembling those encountered by the *M'Naghten* and irresistible impulse tests.

The most significant criticism of *Durham*, however, is that it fails to give the fact-finder any standard by which to measure the competency of the accused. As a result, psychiatrists when testifying that a defendant suffered from a "mental disease or defect" in effect usurped the jury's function. This problem was strikingly illustrated in 1957, when a staff conference at Washington's St. Elizabeth's Hospital reversed its previous determination and reclassified "psychopathic personality" as a "mental disease." Because this single hospital provides most of the psychiatric witnesses in the District of Columbia courts, juries were abruptly informed that certain defendants who had previously been considered responsible were now to be acquitted. It seems clear that a test which permits all to stand or fall upon the labels or classifications employed by testifying psychiatrists hardly affords the court the opportunity to perform its function of rendering an independent legal and social judgment.

V.

In 1953, a year before *Durham*, the American Law Institute commenced an exhaustive study of criminal conduct including the problem of criminal responsibility. In the ensuing months and years, under the scholarly direction of Professors Herbert Wechsler of Columbia University, its Chief Reporter, and Louis B. Schwartz of the University of Pennsylvania, Co-Reporter, the leading legal and medical minds of the country applied themselves to the task. Gradually and painstakingly a new definition of criminal responsibility began taking shape as Section 4.01 of the Model Penal Code was evolved. * * *

Section 4.01 provides that "A person is not responsible for criminal conduct if at the time of such conduct as a result of mental disease or defect he lacks substantial capacity either to appreciate the wrongfulness of his conduct or to conform his conduct to the requirements of law." For reasons which will be more fully set forth, we believe this test to be the soundest yet formulated and we accordingly adopt it as the standard of criminal responsibility in the Courts of this Circuit.

* * * The Model Penal Code formulation * * * recognizes that mental disease or defect may impair [the mind's] functioning in numerous ways. The rule, moreover, reflects awareness that from the perspective of psychiatry absolutes are ephemeral and gradations are inevitable. By employing the telling word "substantial" to modify "incapacity," the rule emphasizes that "any" incapacity is not sufficient to justify avoidance of criminal responsibility but that "total" incapacity is also unnecessary. The choice of the word "appreciate," rather than "know" in the first branch of the test also is significant; mere intellectual awareness that conduct is wrongful, when divorced from appreciation or understanding of the moral or legal import of behavior, can have little significance.

While permitting the utilization of meaningful psychiatric testimony, the American Law Institute formulation, we believe, is free of many of the defects which accompanied *Durham*. Although it eschews rigid classification, the Section is couched in sufficiently precise terms to provide the jury with a workable standard when the judge charges in terms comprehensible to laymen. Expert testimony, in short, will be admissible whenever relevant but always *as* expert testimony—and not as moral or legal pronouncement. Relieved of their burden of divining precise causal relationships, the judge or jury can concentrate upon the ultimate decisions which are properly theirs, fully informed as to the facts. * * *

We do not delude ourselves in the belief that the American Law Institute test is perfect. Perfection is unattainable when we are dealing with a fluid and evolving science. * * *

We believe, in sum, that the American Law Institute test—which makes no pretension at being the ultimate in faultless definition—is an infinite improvement over the *M'Naghten* Rules, even when, as had been the practice in the courts of this Circuit, those Rules are supplemented by the "irresistible impulse" doctrine. * * *

VI.

Since Freeman's responsibility was determined under the rigid standards of the *M'Naghten* Rules, we are compelled to reverse his conviction and remand the case for a new trial in which the criteria employed will be those provided by Section 4.01 of the Model Penal Code.

And lest our opinion be misunderstood or distorted, some additional discussion is in order. First, we wish to make it absolutely clear that mere recidivism or narcotics addiction will not *of themselves* justify acquittal under the American Law Institute standards which we adopt today. Indeed, the second clause of Section 4.01 explicitly states that "the terms 'mental disease or defect' do not include an abnormality manifested only by repeated criminal or otherwise anti-social conduct." We approve and adopt this important caveat. * * *

Secondly, in order to avoid any misapprehension as to the thrust of our opinion some mention should be made of the treatment to be afforded individuals found to lack criminal responsibility under the test we adopt. There is no question but that the security of the community must be the paramount interest. Society withholds criminal sanctions in cases of incompetence out of a sense of compassion and understanding. It would be obviously intolerable if those suffering from a mental disease or defect of such a nature as to relieve them from criminal responsibility were to be set free to continue to pose a threat to life and property.

* * * [W]e trust that Congress will explore its power to authorize commitment of those acquitted on these grounds. Such was the result of

Durham in the District of Columbia; shortly after that decision, Congress provided for mandatory post-trial commitment in all cases in the District resulting in acquittals on grounds of lack of responsibility. Pending Congressional action, however, we are confident that the several states will continue to step into the breach as they have in the past. Accordingly, we suggest that those adjudged criminally irresponsible promptly be turned over to state officials for commitment pursuant to state procedures.

Effective procedures for institutionalization and treatment of the criminally irresponsible are vital as an implementation to today's decision. Throughout our opinion, we have not viewed the choice as one between imprisonment and immediate release. Rather, we believe the true choice to be between different forms of institutionalization—between the prison and the mental hospital. Underlying today's decision is our belief that treatment of the truly incompetent in mental institutions would better serve the interests of society as well as the defendant's.

* * * Reversed and remanded.

STATE V. CRENSHAW

Supreme Court of Washington
98 Wash.2d 789, 659 P.2d 488 (1983)

BRACHTENBACH.

Rodney Crenshaw was convicted by a jury of first degree murder. Finding that the trial court committed no reversible error, we affirm the conviction.

Petitioner Rodney Crenshaw pleaded not guilty and not guilty by reason of insanity to the charge of first degree murder of his wife, Karen Crenshaw. A jury found him guilty. Petitioner appealed his conviction, assigning error to a number of the trial court's rulings. After the Court of Appeals affirmed the trial court in all respects, petitioner raised the same issues before this court. * * *

Before turning to the legal issues, the facts of the case must be recounted. While [petitioner] and his wife were on their honeymoon in Canada, petitioner was deported as a result of his participation in a brawl. He secured a motel room in Blaine, Washington, and waited for his wife to join him. When she arrived 2 days later, he immediately thought she had been unfaithful—he sensed "it wasn't the same Karen . . . she'd been with someone else."

Petitioner did not mention his suspicions to his wife; instead he took her to the motel room and beat her unconscious. He then went to a nearby store, stole a knife, and returned to stab his wife 24 times, inflicting a fatal wound. He left again, drove to a nearby farm where he had been employed and borrowed an ax. Upon returning to the motel room, he decapitated his wife with such force that the ax marks cut into the concrete floor under the carpet and splattered blood throughout the room.

Petitioner then proceeded to conceal his actions. He placed the body in a blanket, the head in a pillowcase, and put both in his wife's car. Next, he went to a service station, borrowed a bucket and sponge, and cleaned the room of blood and fingerprints. Before leaving, petitioner also spoke with the motel manager about a phone bill, then chatted with him for awhile over a beer.

When Crenshaw left the motel he drove to a remote area 25 miles away where he hid the two parts of the body in thick brush. He then fled, driving to the Hoquiam area, about 200 miles from the scene of the crime. There he picked up two hitchhikers, told them of his crime, and enlisted their aid in disposing of his wife's car in a river. The hitchhikers contacted the police and Crenshaw was apprehended shortly thereafter. He voluntarily confessed to the crime.

The defense of not guilty by reason of insanity was a major issue at trial. Crenshaw testified that he followed the Moscovite religious faith, and that it would be improper for a Moscovite not to kill his wife if she committed adultery. Crenshaw also has a history of mental problems, for which he has been hospitalized in the past. The jury, however, rejected petitioner's insanity defense, and found him guilty of murder in the first degree. * * *

Insanity is an affirmative defense the defendant must establish by a preponderance of the evidence.[a] Sanity is presumed, even with a history of prior institutional commitments from which the individual was released upon sufficient recovery.

The insanity defense is not available to all who are mentally deficient or deranged; legal insanity has a different meaning and a different purpose than the concept of medical insanity. A verdict of not guilty by reason of insanity completely absolves a defendant of any criminal responsibility. Therefore, "the defense is available only to those persons who have lost contact with reality so completely that they are beyond any of the influences of the criminal law."

Petitioner assigned error to insanity defense instruction 10 which reads:

> In addition to the plea of not guilty, the defendant has entered a plea of insanity existing at the time of the act charged.
>
> Insanity existing at the time of the commission of the act charged is a defense.

---

[a] States may choose to place the burden of proving sanity on the government, or they may place the burden of proving insanity on the defendant.

> For a defendant to be found not guilty by reason of insanity you must find that, as a result of mental disease or defect, the defendant's mind was affected to such an extent that the defendant was unable to perceive the nature and quality of the acts with which the defendant is charged or was unable to tell right from wrong with reference to the particular acts with which defendant is charged.
>
> What is meant by the terms "right and wrong" refers to knowledge of a person at the time of committing an act that he was acting contrary to the law.

But for the last paragraph, this instruction tracks the language of WPIC 20.01, which is the *M'Naghten* test. * * * Petitioner contends, however, that the trial court erred in defining "right and wrong" as legal right and wrong rather than in the moral sense.

We find this instruction was not reversible error on three alternative grounds: (1) The *M'Naghten* opinion amply supports the "legal" wrong definition as used in this case, (2) under these facts, "moral" wrong and "legal" wrong are synonymous, therefore the "legal" wrong definition did not alter the meaning of the test, and (3) because Crenshaw failed to prove other elements of the insanity defense, any error in the definition of wrong was harmless.

I

The definition of the term "wrong" in the *M'Naghten* test has been considered and disputed by many legal scholars. Courts from other jurisdictions are divided on the issue. In Washington, we have not addressed this issue previously. [The court concludes that the *M'Naghten* opinion supports the definition of "right and wrong" in Instruction 10, which referred to the defendant's knowledge of whether he was acting contrary to law.]

II

Alternatively, the statement in instruction 10 may be approved because, in this case, legal wrong is synonymous with moral wrong. This conclusion is premised on two grounds.

First, in discussing the term "moral" wrong, it is important to note that it is society's morals, and not the individual's morals, that are the standard for judging moral wrong under *M'Naghten.* If wrong meant moral wrong judged by the individual's own conscience, this would seriously undermine the criminal law, for it would allow one who violated the law to be excused from criminal responsibility solely because, in his own conscience, his act was not morally wrong. This principle was emphasized by Justice Cardozo:

> The anarchist is not at liberty to break the law because he reasons that all government is wrong. The devotee of a religious cult that enjoins polygamy or human sacrifice as a duty is not thereby relieved from responsibility before the law . . .

More recently the Arizona Supreme Court stated:

> We find no authority upholding the defendant's position that one suffering from a mental disease could be declared legally insane if he knew that the act was morally and legally wrong but he personally believed that act right. We believe that this would not be a sound rule, because it approaches the position of exonerating a defendant for his personal beliefs and does not take account of society's determination of defendant's capacity to conform his conduct to the law.

There is evidence on the record that Crenshaw knew his actions were wrong according to society's standards, as well as legally wrong. Dr. Belden testified:

> I think Mr. Crenshaw is quite aware on one level that he is in conflict with the law *and with people*. However, this is not something that he personally invests his emotions in.

We conclude that Crenshaw knew his acts were morally wrong from society's viewpoint and also knew his acts were illegal. His personal belief that it was his duty to kill his wife for her alleged infidelity cannot serve to exculpate him from legal responsibility for his acts.

A narrow exception to the societal standard of moral wrong has been drawn for instances wherein a party performs a criminal act, knowing it is morally and legally wrong, but believing, because of a mental defect, that the act is ordained by God: such would be the situation with a mother who kills her infant child to whom she is devotedly attached, believing that God has spoken to her and decreed the act. Although the woman knows that the law and society condemn the act, it would be unrealistic to hold her responsible for the crime, since her free will has been subsumed by her belief in the deific decree.

This exception is not available to Crenshaw, however. Crenshaw argued only that he followed the Moscovite faith and that Moscovites believe it is their duty to kill an unfaithful wife. This is not the same as acting under a deific command. Instead, it is akin to "[t]he devotee of a religious cult that enjoins . . . human sacrifice as a duty [and] is *not* thereby relieved from responsibility before the law." Crenshaw's personal "Moscovite" beliefs are not equivalent to a deific decree and do not relieve him from responsibility for his acts.

Once moral wrong is equated with society's morals, the next step, equating moral and legal wrong, follows logically. The law is, for the most part, an expression of collective morality. Most cases involving the insanity defense involve serious crimes for which society's moral judgment is identical with the legal standard. Therefore, a number of scholars have concluded that, as a practical matter, the way in which a court interprets the word "wrong" will have little effect on the eventual outcome of a case.

As one scholar explained:

> [S]ince by far the vast majority of cases in which insanity is pleaded as a defense to criminal prosecutions involves acts which are universally regarded as morally wicked as well as illegal, the hair-splitting distinction between legal and moral wrong need not be given much attention.

Society's morals and legal wrong are interchangeable concepts in the context of this case. Petitioner's crime, killing his wife by stabbing her 24 times then hacking off her head, is clearly contrary to society's morals as well as the law. Therefore by defining wrong in terms of legal wrong, the trial court did not alter the meaning of the *M'Naghten* test.

III

We also find that, under any definition of wrong, Crenshaw did not qualify for the insanity defense under *M'Naghten*; therefore, any alleged error in that definition must be viewed as harmless. * * *

* * * First, Crenshaw failed to prove an essential element of the defense because he did not prove his alleged delusions stemmed from a mental defect; second, he did not prove by a preponderance of the evidence that he was legally insane at the time of the crime.

In addition to an incapacity to know right from wrong, *M'Naghten* requires that such incapacity stem from a mental disease or defect. Assuming, arguendo, that Crenshaw did not know right from wrong, he failed to prove that a mental defect was the cause of this inability.

Petitioner's insanity argument is premised on the following facts: (1) he is a Moscovite and Moscovites believe it is their duty to assassinate an unfaithful spouse; (2) he "knew," without asking, that his wife had been unfaithful when he met her in Blaine and this was equivalent to an insane delusion; and (3) at other times in his life, he had been diagnosed as a paranoid personality and had been committed to mental institutions. A conscientious application of the *M'Naghten* rule demonstrates, however, that these factors do not afford petitioner the sanctuary of the insanity defense.

To begin, petitioner's Moscovite beliefs are irrelevant to the insanity defense, because they are not insane delusions. Some notion of morality, unrelated to a mental illness, which disagrees with the law and mores of our society is not an insane delusion.

Nor was petitioner's belief that his wife was unfaithful an insane delusion. Dr. Trowbridge, a psychiatrist, explained:

> A man suspects his wife of being unfaithful. Certainly such suspicions are not necessarily delusional, even if they're ill based. Just because he suspected his wife of being unfaithful doesn't mean that he was crazy.
>
> * * *
>
> Certainly when a man kills his wife he doesn't do it in a rational way. No one ever does that rationally. But that is not to suggest that every time a man kills his wife he was [*sic*] insane.

Finally, evidence of prior commitments to mental institutions is not proof that one was *legally* insane at the time the criminal act was committed. * * * Thus, petitioner does not establish the necessary connection between his criminal acts and his psychological problems to qualify for the insanity defense.

In addition, the preponderance of the evidence weighs against finding Crenshaw legally insane. All of the psychological experts, save one, testified that defendant was not insane at the time of the murder. The only doctor who concluded defendant (petitioner) was legally insane, Dr. Hunter, was a psychologist who had not examined petitioner for a year and a half.

Given the various qualifications of the experts, the time they spent with the petitioner, and the proximity in time of their examinations to the murder, the testimony does not establish by a preponderance of the evidence that petitioner was legally insane at the time of the murder.

Furthermore, in addition to the expert testimony, there was lay testimony that petitioner appeared rational at the time of the killing. After cleaning the motel room, Crenshaw resolved a phone bill dispute with the manager, then shared a beer with him without arousing any suspicion in the manager's mind. Also, the woman who gave him the ax testified as to his behavior the day before the murder:

> Well, he seemed very normal or I certainly wouldn't have handed him an ax or a hoe. He was polite, he done his work. He didn't, I wasn't afraid of him or anything. I mean we were just out there working and I certainly wouldn't have handed him an ax or anything like that if I would have thought that there was anything even remotely peculiar about him.

And, with specific reference to the time when petitioner borrowed the ax to decapitate his wife:

> Q. . . . did he seem rational to you?
>
> A. Oh, yes, he was very nice.

Q. Did he seem coherent when he spoke to you?

A. Oh, yes. . . .

. . .

Q. Did he appear to be sane to you then? . . .

A. Yes. . . .

Thus, at the same time that he was embroiled in the act of murdering his wife, he was rational, coherent, and sane in his dealings with others.

Finally, evidence of petitioner's calculated execution of the crime and his sophisticated attempts to avert discovery support a finding of sanity. Crenshaw performed the murder methodically, leaving the motel room twice to acquire the knife and ax necessary to perform the deed. Then, after the killing he scrubbed the motel room to clean up the blood and remove his fingerprints. Next, he drove 25 miles to hide the body in thick brush in a remote area. Finally, he drove several hundred miles and ditched the car in a river.

Such attempts to hide evidence of a crime manifest an awareness that the act was legally wrong. Moreover, petitioner testified that he did these things because he "didn't want to get caught."

To summarize thus far, we find no error in instruction 10 for the following reasons: (1) As we interpret the *M'Naghten* case, it was not improper for the trial court to instruct with reference to the law of the land, under the facts of this case; (2) because the concept of moral wrong refers to the mores of society and not to the individual's morals, "moral" wrong is synonymous with "legal" wrong with a serious crime such as this one, therefore, instructing in terms of legal wrong did not alter the meaning of the *M'Naghten* rule; (3) any error was harmless because (a) Crenshaw did not show that at the time of the crime his mind was affected as a result of a mental disease or defect and without this essential element the insanity defense was not available to him, and (b) an overwhelming preponderance of the evidence supports the finding that Crenshaw was not legally insane when he killed his wife. We thus conclude that the additional statement in instruction 10 was not improper, or, at the very least, that it was harmless error.

Nevertheless, we do not believe that, in the future, such a comment should be necessary. As the Legislature has chosen to codify the *M'Naghten* test in statutory form, it would be preferable to have this test presented to the jury without any elaboration. This would permit both parties to argue their theories of the case. * * * Thus, we hold prospectively that as a general rule no definition of wrong should accompany an insanity defense instruction. * * *

As stated above, we find that the Court of Appeals thoughtfully and correctly resolved the other assignments of error raised by petitioner, and we see no need to repeat their reasoning here. Finding no reversible error was committed by the trial court, we affirm the judgment.

DORE, J., dissenting.

The major issue of the subject appeal is whether the jury was properly instructed on insanity and, if not, whether this constituted prejudicial error.

The majority, in affirming the trial court and the Court of Appeals, upholds the validity of instruction 10, instructing the jurors the defendant would be "insane" only if he couldn't distinguish between *legal* right and wrong. The majority eliminated the *moral* right and wrong test by concluding that "moral" wrong and "legal" wrong are synonymous.

I disagree, for I believe that although at times moral and legal are "synonymous," sometimes they are distinguishable. This is a factual issue to be determined by the trier of the fact, and not by the courts as a matter of law. The submission of instruction 10 constituted prejudicial error. I would reverse for a new trial based on the instruction's erroneous statement of the law on insanity.

The majority has correctly set forth the facts, but I would like to supplement them by adding some pertinent information. Dr. Nathan Kronenberg, the psychiatrist who testified Crenshaw was competent to stand trial, added that in examining Crenshaw he noted tangentiality, loose associations, delusions of grandeur, religiosity (including a belief in his possession of special powers), auditory hallucinations, lack of insight, and extreme emotional liability on the part of the defendant. He further testified that the defendant's ability to assist in his defense was distorted by his paranoia.

Washington's test for insanity, a codification of *M'Naghten*'s rule, reads:

> To establish the defense of insanity, it must be shown that:
>
> (1) At the time of the commission of the offense, as a result of mental disease or defect, the mind of the actor was affected to such an extent that:
>
> (a) He was unable to perceive the nature and quality of the act with which he is charged; or
>
> (b) He was unable to tell right from wrong with reference to the particular act charged.
>
> (2) The defense of insanity must be established by a preponderance of the evidence.

The issue before us is whether the terms "right" and "wrong" as used in RCW 9A.12.010(1)(b) should be qualified for the jury. At trial, the jury was instructed the defendant would not be legally insane if he knew "legal right" from "legal wrong." Crenshaw contends the trial court erred in defining "right and wrong" as "legal right" and "legal wrong." The majority of the Court of Appeals held that

> If the accused knew his act was wrong—either legally or morally—then he cannot be excused for his crime by the insanity defense.

The Court of Appeals concluded that the trial court did not err in its instruction on insanity because, if the defendant knew his conduct was contrary to law, he could not be found legally insane even if he could not distinguish moral right from moral wrong. The majority avoids the problem by holding that legal right and moral right are "synonymous."

The defendant urges this court to define the terms solely as "moral right and wrong" or, alternatively, to leave the terms undefined for the jury, as does the pattern instruction. The Court of Appeals argued that if the moral sense of the terms becomes the standard, the defense would be broadened significantly. Anyone would be able to argue that his actions were justifiable by reference to his personal morality. * * *

The majority and the Court of Appeals miss the point. Of course, as they contend, the standard of right and wrong must be an objective one. That is not to say, however, that only the criminal code can provide that standard. I agree with the dissenting judge, Ringold, J., of the Court of Appeals, that if a defendant knows his acts are contrary to law, an inference may be drawn, *by a jury*, that defendant knew his acts were morally wrong. * * *

I do not believe that a jury's function in this regard should be usurped. As used in RCW 9A.12.010(1)(b), the terms "right" and "wrong" refer to their moral sense, and not to a defendant's knowledge that he has acted contrary to the law.

It is not the mere assertion by a defendant that he "thought" he committed no moral wrong which would excuse his otherwise criminal act. The statute requires that such belief be the result of mental disease or defect and that such defect existed at the time of the commission of the offense. * * *

This court has previously indicated that the *M'Naghten* test involved the moral definition of right and wrong. Prior to codification of the *M'Naghten* rule into our statutory scheme, we held that a jury was correctly instructed when it was told that the insanity defense would lie if defendant "was unable to perceive the *moral qualities*" of his act. The sole question is whether we want to hold a defendant answerable to our criminal law, notwithstanding the barbaric or cruel nature of the defendant's acts. A mind which cannot distinguish moral right from wrong cannot be held accountable for acts performed as a result of that illness and while suffering under that influence.

The majority * * * surprisingly seems to concede that at times there is a difference between legal right and wrong and moral right and wrong, stating:

> A narrow exception to the societal standard of moral wrong has been drawn for instances wherein a party performs a criminal act, knowing it is morally and legally wrong, but believing, because of a mental defect, that the act is ordained by God: such would be the situation with a mother who kills her infant child to whom she is devotedly attached, believing that God has spoken to her and decreed the act. Although the woman knows that the law and society condemn the act, it would be unrealistic to hold her responsible for the crime, since her free will has been subsumed by her belief in the deific decree.

This is exactly the point I wish to make in the subject case. Crenshaw knew if he killed his wife he was violating the law, but he believed he had a duty to do it under the teaching of his Moscovite "religious" beliefs. To determine his insanity under *M'Naghten*, as codified in RCW 9A.12.010, a determination must be made as to what was morally right and wrong. The jury had this duty and responsibility, but to do so it had to be properly instructed. Instruction 10 wrongly limited the jury to the *legal* right and wrong test and prevented it from determining whether Crenshaw knew the difference between *moral* right and wrong at the time he killed his wife. This constituted prejudicial error.

The majority concludes * * *, "Thus, we hold *prospectively* that as a general rule no definition of wrong should accompany an insanity defense instruction" (italics mine), impliedly admitting and agreeing that instruction 10 is defective and that the jury should be instructed under *both moral* and *legal* wrong in order to correctly determine insanity. Without saying so, the majority adopts WPIC 20.01 as a correct instruction on insanity. Crenshaw argued use of WPIC 20.01 would have permitted his lawyers to argue moral right and wrong as the true test of insanity in his case, and that his jury should have been so instructed. The majority holds that future defendants shall have the benefit of WPIC 20.01, but not defendant Crenshaw.

I would reverse and remand to the trial court for a new trial on the basis that instruction 10 was defective and constituted prejudicial error.

CLARK V. ARIZONA

Supreme Court of the United States
548 U.S. 735, 126 S.Ct. 2709, 165 L.Ed.2d 842 (2006)

JUSTICE SOUTER delivered the opinion of the Court. * * *

I

In the early hours of June 21, 2000, Officer Jeffrey Moritz of the Flagstaff Police responded in uniform to complaints that a pickup truck with loud music blaring was circling a residential block. When he located the truck, the officer turned on the emergency lights and siren of his marked patrol car, which prompted petitioner Eric Clark, the truck's driver (then 17), to pull over. Officer Moritz got out of the patrol car and told Clark to stay where he was. Less than a minute later, Clark shot the officer, who died soon after but not before calling the police dispatcher for help. Clark ran away on foot but was arrested later that day with gunpowder residue on his hands; the gun that killed the officer was found nearby, stuffed into a knit cap.

Clark was charged with first-degree murder under Ariz.Rev.Stat. Ann. § 13–1105(A)(3) (West Supp.2005) for intentionally or knowingly killing a law enforcement officer in the line of duty.[1] In March 2001, Clark was found incompetent to stand trial and was committed to a state hospital for treatment, but two years later the same trial court found his competence restored and ordered him to be tried. Clark waived his right to a jury, and the case was heard by the court.

At trial, Clark did not contest the shooting and death, but relied on his undisputed paranoid schizophrenia at the time of the incident in denying that he had the specific intent to shoot a law enforcement officer or knowledge that he was doing so, as required by the statute. Accordingly, the prosecutor offered circumstantial evidence that Clark knew Officer Moritz was a law enforcement officer. The evidence showed that the officer was in uniform at the time, that he caught up with Clark in a marked police car with emergency lights and siren going, and that Clark acknowledged the symbols of police authority and stopped. The testimony for the prosecution indicated that Clark had intentionally lured an officer to the scene to kill him, having told some people a few weeks before the incident that he wanted to shoot police officers. At the close of the State's evidence, the trial court denied Clark's motion for judgment of acquittal for failure to prove intent to kill a law enforcement officer or knowledge that Officer Moritz was a law enforcement officer.

In presenting the defense case, Clark claimed mental illness, which he sought to introduce for two purposes. First, he raised the affirmative

---

[1] Section 13–1105(A)(3) provides that "[a] person commits first degree murder if . . . [i]ntending or knowing that the person's conduct will cause death to a law enforcement officer, the person causes the death of a law enforcement officer who is in the line of duty."

defense of insanity, putting the burden on himself to prove by clear and convincing evidence, that "at the time of the commission of the criminal act [he] was afflicted with a mental disease or defect of such severity that [he] did not know the criminal act was wrong," § 13–502(A).[2] Second, he aimed to rebut the prosecution's evidence of the requisite *mens rea,* that he had acted intentionally or knowingly to kill a law enforcement officer.

The trial court ruled that Clark could not rely on evidence bearing on insanity to dispute the *mens rea.* The court cited *State v. Mott,* which "refused to allow psychiatric testimony to negate specific intent," and held that "Arizona does not allow evidence of a defendant's mental disorder short of insanity . . . to negate the *mens rea* element of a crime." As to his insanity, then, Clark presented testimony from classmates, school officials, and his family describing his increasingly bizarre behavior over the year before the shooting. Witnesses testified, for example, that paranoid delusions led Clark to rig a fishing line with beads and wind chimes at home to alert him to intrusion by invaders, and to keep a bird in his automobile to warn of airborne poison. There was lay and expert testimony that Clark thought Flagstaff was populated with "aliens" (some impersonating government agents), the "aliens" were trying to kill him, and bullets were the only way to stop them. A psychiatrist testified that Clark was suffering from paranoid schizophrenia with delusions about "aliens" when he killed Officer Moritz, and he concluded that Clark was incapable of luring the officer or understanding right from wrong and that he was thus insane at the time of the killing. In rebuttal, a psychiatrist for the State gave his opinion that Clark's paranoid schizophrenia did not keep him from appreciating the wrongfulness of his conduct, as shown by his actions before and after the shooting (such as circling the residential block with music blaring as if to lure the police to intervene, evading the police after the shooting, and hiding the gun).

At the close of the defense case consisting of this evidence bearing on mental illness, the trial court denied Clark's renewed motion for a directed verdict grounded on failure of the prosecution to show that Clark knew the victim was a police officer. The judge then issued a special verdict of first-degree murder, expressly finding that Clark shot and

[2] Section 13–502(A) provides in full that

> A person may be found guilty except insane if at the time of the commission of the criminal act the person was afflicted with a mental disease or defect of such severity that the person did not know the criminal act was wrong. A mental disease or defect constituting legal insanity is an affirmative defense. Mental disease or defect does not include disorders that result from acute voluntary intoxication or withdrawal from alcohol or drugs, character defects, psychosexual disorders or impulse control disorders. Conditions that do not constitute legal insanity include but are not limited to momentary, temporary conditions arising from the pressure of the circumstances, moral decadence, depravity or passion growing out of anger, jealousy, revenge, hatred or other motives in a person who does not suffer from a mental disease or defect or an abnormality that is manifested only by criminal conduct.

A defendant found "guilty except insane" is committed to a state mental health facility for treatment. See § 13–502(D).

caused the death of Officer Moritz beyond a reasonable doubt and that Clark had not shown that he was insane at the time. The judge noted that though Clark was indisputably afflicted with paranoid schizophrenia at the time of the shooting, the mental illness "did not . . . distort his perception of reality so severely that he did not know his actions were wrong." For this conclusion, the judge expressly relied on "the facts of the crime, the evaluations of the experts, [Clark's] actions and behavior both before and after the shooting, and the observations of those that knew [Clark]." The sentence was life imprisonment without the possibility of release for 25 years.

Clark moved to vacate the judgment and sentence, arguing, among other things, that Arizona's insanity test and its *Mott* rule each violate due process. * * *

D

Clark's argument that the *Mott* rule violates the Fourteenth Amendment guarantee of due process turns on the application of the presumption of innocence in criminal cases, the presumption of sanity, and the principle that a criminal defendant is entitled to present relevant and favorable evidence on an element of the offense charged against him.

1

The first presumption is that a defendant is innocent unless and until the government proves beyond a reasonable doubt each element of the offense charged, including the mental element or *mens rea*. Before the last century, the *mens rea* required to be proven for particular offenses was often described in general terms like "malice," but the modern tendency has been toward more specific descriptions, as shown in the Arizona statute defining the murder charged against Clark: the State had to prove that in acting to kill the victim, Clark intended to kill a law enforcement officer on duty or knew that the victim was such an officer on duty. As applied to *mens rea* (and every other element), the force of the presumption of innocence is measured by the force of the showing needed to overcome it, which is proof beyond a reasonable doubt that a defendant's state of mind was in fact what the charge states.

2

The presumption of sanity is equally universal in some variety or other, being (at least) a presumption that a defendant has the capacity to form the *mens rea* necessary for a verdict of guilt and the consequent criminal responsibility. This presumption dispenses with a requirement on the government's part to include as an element of every criminal charge an allegation that the defendant had such a capacity. * * *

3

The third principle implicated by Clark's argument is a defendant's right as a matter of simple due process to present evidence favorable to himself on an element that must be proven to convict him. * * * [E]vidence tending to show that a defendant suffers from mental disease and lacks capacity to form *mens rea* is relevant to rebut evidence that he did in fact form the required *mens rea* at the time in question; this is the reason that Clark claims a right to require the factfinder in this case to consider testimony about his mental illness and his incapacity directly, when weighing the persuasiveness of other evidence tending to show *mens rea,* which the prosecution has the burden to prove.

As Clark recognizes, however, the right to introduce relevant evidence can be curtailed if there is a good reason for doing that. * * * State law says that evidence of mental disease and incapacity may be introduced and considered, and if sufficiently forceful to satisfy the defendant's burden of proof under the insanity rule it will displace the presumption of sanity and excuse from criminal responsibility. But mental-disease and capacity evidence may be considered only for its bearing on the insanity defense, and it will avail a defendant only if it is persuasive enough to satisfy the defendant's burden as defined by the terms of that defense. The mental-disease and capacity evidence is thus being channeled or restricted to one issue and given effect only if the defendant carries the burden to convince the factfinder of insanity; the evidence is not being excluded entirely, and the question is whether reasons for requiring it to be channeled and restricted are good enough to satisfy the standard of fundamental fairness that due process requires. We think they are.

E

1

The first reason supporting the *Mott* rule is Arizona's authority to define its presumption of sanity (or capacity or responsibility) by choosing an insanity definition, and by placing the burden of persuasion on defendants who claim incapacity as an excuse from customary criminal responsibility. No one, certainly not Clark here, denies that a State may place a burden of persuasion on a defendant claiming insanity. And Clark presses no objection to Arizona's decision to require persuasion to a clear and convincing degree before the presumption of sanity and normal responsibility is overcome.

But if a State is to have this authority in practice as well as in theory, it must be able to deny a defendant the opportunity to displace the presumption of sanity more easily when addressing a different issue in the course of the criminal trial. Yet, as we have explained, just such an opportunity would be available if expert testimony of mental disease and incapacity could be considered for whatever a factfinder might think it was worth on the issue of *mens rea*. * * *

It is obvious that Arizona's *Mott* rule reflects such a choice. The State Supreme Court pointed out that the State had declined to adopt a defense of diminished capacity (allowing a jury to decide when to excuse a defendant because of greater than normal difficulty in conforming to the law).The court reasoned that the State's choice would be undercut if evidence of incapacity could be considered for whatever a jury might think sufficient to raise a reasonable doubt about *mens rea,* even if it did not show insanity. * * *

2

* * * An insanity rule gives a defendant already found guilty the opportunity to excuse his conduct by showing he was insane when he acted, that is, that he did not have the mental capacity for conventional guilt and criminal responsibility. But, as the dissent argues, if the same evidence that affirmatively shows he was not guilty by reason of insanity also shows it was at least doubtful that he could form *mens rea,* then he should not be found guilty in the first place; it thus violates due process when the State impedes him from using mental-disease and capacity evidence directly to rebut the prosecution's evidence that he did form *mens rea.*

Are there, then, characteristics of mental-disease and capacity evidence giving rise to risks that may reasonably be hedged by channeling the consideration of such evidence to the insanity issue on which, in States like Arizona, a defendant has the burden of persuasion? We think there are: in the controversial character of some categories of mental disease, in the potential of mental-disease evidence to mislead, and in the danger of according greater certainty to capacity evidence than experts claim for it.

To begin with, the diagnosis may mask vigorous debate within the profession about the very contours of the mental disease itself. And Members of this Court have previously recognized that the end of such debate is not imminent. * * *

Next, there is the potential of mental-disease evidence to mislead jurors (when they are the factfinders) through the power of this kind of evidence to suggest that a defendant suffering from a recognized mental disease lacks cognitive, moral, volitional, or other capacity, when that may not be a sound conclusion at all. Even when a category of mental disease is broadly accepted and the assignment of a defendant's behavior to that category is uncontroversial, the classification may suggest something very significant about a defendant's capacity, when in fact the classification tells us little or nothing about the ability of the defendant to form *mens rea* or to exercise the cognitive, moral, or volitional capacities that define legal sanity. The limits of the utility of a professional disease diagnosis are evident in the dispute between the two testifying experts in this case; they agree that Clark was schizophrenic, but they come to opposite conclusions on whether the mental disease in his particular case left him bereft of cognitive or moral capacity. * * *

There are, finally, particular risks inherent in the opinions of the experts who supplement the mental-disease classifications with opinions on incapacity: on whether the mental disease rendered a particular defendant incapable of the cognition necessary for moral judgment or *mens rea* or otherwise incapable of understanding the wrongfulness of the conduct charged. Unlike observational evidence bearing on *mens rea,* capacity evidence consists of judgment, and judgment fraught with multiple perils: a defendant's state of mind at the crucial moment can be elusive no matter how conscientious the enquiry, and the law's categories that set the terms of the capacity judgment are not the categories of psychology that govern the expert's professional thinking. * * * [T]hese empirical and conceptual problems add up to a real risk that an expert's judgment in giving capacity evidence will come with an apparent authority that psychologists and psychiatrists do not claim to have. We think that this risk, like the difficulty in assessing the significance of mental-disease evidence, supports the State's decision to channel such expert testimony to consideration on the insanity defense, on which the party seeking the benefit of this evidence has the burden of persuasion.

It bears repeating that not every State will find it worthwhile to make the judgment Arizona has made, and the choices the States do make about dealing with the risks posed by mental-disease and capacity evidence will reflect their varying assessments about the presumption of sanity as expressed in choices of insanity rules. The point here simply is that Arizona has sensible reasons to assign the risks as it has done by channeling the evidence.[45]

F

Arizona's rule serves to preserve the State's chosen standard for recognizing insanity as a defense and to avoid confusion and misunderstanding on the part of jurors. For these reasons, there is no violation of due process * * *, and no cause to claim that channeling

---

[45] Arizona's rule is supported by a further practical reason, though not as weighty as those just considered. As mentioned before, if substantial mental-disease and capacity evidence is accepted as rebutting mens rea in a given case, the affirmative defense of insanity will probably not be reached or ruled upon; the defendant will simply be acquitted (or perhaps convicted of a lesser included offense). If an acquitted defendant suffers from a mental disease or defect that makes him dangerous, he will neither be confined nor treated psychiatrically unless a judge so orders after some independent commitment proceeding. But if a defendant succeeds in showing himself insane, Arizona law (and presumably that of every other State with an insanity rule) will require commitment and treatment as a consequence of that finding without more. It makes sense, then, to channel capacity evidence to the issue structured to deal with mental incapacity when such a claim is raised successfully.

evidence on mental disease and capacity offends any " 'principle of justice so rooted in the traditions and conscience of our people as to be ranked as fundamental.' "

* * *

The judgment of the Court of Appeals of Arizona is, accordingly, affirmed.

It is so ordered.

[JUSTICE BREYER's opinion concurring in part and dissenting in part is omitted.]

JUSTICE KENNEDY, with whom JUSTICE STEVENS and JUSTICE GINSBURG join, dissenting.

* * *

II

Clark was charged with first-degree murder for the shooting of Officer Jeffrey Moritz. "A person commits first-degree murder if," as relevant here, "[i]ntending or knowing that the person's conduct will cause death to a law enforcement officer, the person causes the death of a law enforcement officer who is in the line of duty." Clark challenges the trial court's refusal to consider any evidence of mental illness, from lay or expert testimony, in determining whether he acted with the knowledge or intent element of the crime.

States have substantial latitude under the Constitution to define rules for the exclusion of evidence and to apply those rules to criminal defendants. This authority, however, has constitutional limits. " 'Whether rooted directly in the Due Process Clause of the Fourteenth Amendment or in the Compulsory Process or Confrontation Clauses of the Sixth Amendment, the Constitution guarantees criminal defendants "a meaningful opportunity to present a complete defense." ' " * * *

The central theory of Clark's defense was that his schizophrenia made him delusional. He lived in a universe where the delusions were so dominant, the theory was, that he had no intent to shoot a police officer or knowledge he was doing so. It is one thing to say he acted with intent or knowledge to pull the trigger. It is quite another to say he pulled the trigger to kill someone he knew to be a human being and a police officer. If the trier of fact were to find Clark's evidence sufficient to discount the case made by the State, which has the burden to prove knowledge or intent as an element of the offense, Clark would not be guilty of first-degree murder under Arizona law.

* * * The *mens rea* element of intent or knowledge may, at some level, comprise certain moral choices, but it rests in the first instance on a

factual determination. That is the fact Clark sought to put in issue. Either Clark knew he was killing a police officer or he did not.

The issue is not, as the Court insists, whether Clark's mental illness acts as an "excuse from customary criminal responsibility," but whether his mental illness, as a factual matter, made him unaware that he was shooting a police officer. If it did, * * * then he did not commit the crime as Arizona defines it. For the elements of first-degree murder, where the question is knowledge of particular facts—that one is killing a police officer—the determination depends not on moral responsibility but on empirical fact. Clark's evidence of mental illness had a direct and substantial bearing upon what he knew, or thought he knew, to be the facts when he pulled the trigger; this lay at the heart of the matter. * * *

The trial court's exclusion was all the more severe because it barred from consideration on the issue of *mens rea* all this evidence, from any source, thus preventing Clark from showing he did not commit the crime as defined by Arizona law. * * *

Arizona's rule is problematic because it excludes evidence no matter how credible and material it may be in disproving an element of the offense. * * *

This is not to suggest all general rules on the exclusion of certain types of evidence are invalid. If the rule does not substantially burden the defense, then it is likely permissible. Where, however, the burden is substantial, the State must present a valid reason for its *per se* evidentiary rule.

In the instant case Arizona's proposed reasons are insufficient to support its categorical exclusion. While the State contends that testimony regarding mental illness may be too incredible or speculative for the jury to consider, this does not explain why the exclusion applies in all cases to all evidence of mental illness. "A State's legitimate interest in barring unreliable evidence does not extend to *per se* exclusions that may be reliable in an individual case." * * *

The risk of jury confusion also fails to justify the rule. The State defends its rule as a means to avoid the complexities of determining how and to what degree a mental illness affects a person's mental state. The difficulty of resolving a factual issue, though, does not present a sufficient reason to take evidence away from the jury even when it is crucial for the defense. "We have always trusted juries to sort through complex facts in various areas of law." Even were the risk of jury confusion real enough to justify excluding evidence in most cases, this would provide little basis for prohibiting all evidence of mental illness without any inquiry into its likely effect on the jury or its role in deciding the linchpin issue of knowledge and intent. * * *

The Court undertakes little analysis of the interests particular to this case. By proceeding in this way it devalues Clark's constitutional rights. * * * The Court is correct that many mental diseases are difficult to define and the subject of great debate. Schizophrenia, however, is a well-documented mental illness, and no one seriously disputes either its definition or its most prominent clinical manifestations. The State's own expert conceded that Clark had paranoid schizophrenia and was actively psychotic at the time of the killing. The jury-confusion rationale, if it is at all applicable here, is the result of the Court's own insistence on conflating the insanity defense and the question of intent. Considered on its own terms, the issue of intent and knowledge is a straightforward factual question. A trier of fact is quite capable of weighing defense testimony and then determining whether the accused did or did not intend to kill or knowingly kill a human being who was a police officer. True, the issue can be difficult to decide in particular instances, but no more so than many matters juries must confront.

The Court says mental-illness evidence "can easily mislead," and may "tel[l] us little or nothing about the ability of the defendant to form *mens rea.*" These generalities do not, however, show how relevant or misleading the evidence in this case would be. As explained above, the evidence of Clark's mental illness bears directly on *mens rea,* for it suggests Clark may not have known he was killing a human being. It is striking that while the Court discusses at length the likelihood of misjudgment from placing too much emphasis on evidence of mental illness, it ignores the risk of misjudging an innocent man guilty from refusing to consider this highly relevant evidence at all. Clark's expert, it is true, said no one could know exactly what was on Clark's mind at the time of the shooting. The expert testified extensively, however, about the effect of Clark's delusions on his perceptions of the world around him, and about whether Clark's behavior around the time of the shooting was consistent with delusional thinking. This testimony was relevant to determining whether Clark knew he was killing a human being. * * *

The fact that mental-illness evidence may be considered in deciding criminal responsibility does not compensate for its exclusion from consideration on the *mens rea* elements of the crime. The evidence addresses different issues in the two instances. Criminal responsibility involves an inquiry into whether the defendant knew right from wrong, not whether he had the *mens rea* elements of the offense. While there may be overlap between the two issues, "the existence or nonexistence of legal insanity bears no necessary relationship to the existence or nonexistence of the required mental elements of the crime."

Even if the analyses were equivalent, there is a different burden of proof for insanity than there is for *mens rea.* Arizona requires the defendant to prove his insanity by clear and convincing evidence. The prosecution, however, must prove all elements of the offense beyond a reasonable doubt. The shift in the burden on the criminal responsibility issue, while permissible under our precedent, cannot be applied to the question of intent or knowledge without relieving the State of its responsibility to establish this element of the offense. * * * [W]here there is a right to have evidence considered on an element of the offense, the right is not respected by allowing the evidence to come in only on an issue for which the defendant bears the burden of proof.

* * * The State attempts to bring the instant case within the ambit of *Montana v. Egelhoff,* but in *Egelhoff* the excluded evidence concerned voluntary intoxication, for which a person can be held responsible. * * * [I]t was upheld because it "comports with and implements society's moral perception that one who has voluntarily impaired his own faculties should be responsible for the consequences." An involuntary mental illness does not implicate this justification. * * *

Future dangerousness is not, as the Court appears to conclude, a rational basis for convicting mentally ill individuals of crimes they did not commit. Civil commitment proceedings can ensure that individuals who present a danger to themselves or others receive proper treatment without unfairly treating them as criminals. The State presents no evidence to the contrary, and the Court ought not to imply otherwise. * * *

* * * It is unclear, moreover, what would have happened in this case had the defendant wanted to testify that he thought Officer Moritz was an alien. If disallowed, it would be tantamount to barring Clark from testifying on his behalf to explain his own actions. If allowed, then Arizona's rule would simply prohibit the corroboration necessary to make sense of Clark's explanation. In sum, the rule forces the jury to decide guilt in a fictional world with undefined and unexplained behaviors but without mental illness. This rule has no rational justification and imposes a significant burden upon a straightforward defense: He did not commit the crime with which he was charged.

These are the reasons for my respectful dissent.

4. DIMINISHED CAPACITY

Sometimes a defendant who cannot prove he was insane at the time of the crime will nevertheless seek to introduce evidence about his mental illness as a way of mitigating or eliminating his responsibility for the crime. The use of evidence of mental illness in this way is generally described as a "diminished capacity" defense.

In jurisdictions that follow the common law, diminished capacity defenses have been articulated in several different ways. One variant of the diminished capacity defense is called the "mens rea variant" of the defense. Under this variant, a defendant who can show that he was suffering from a mental disease or defect not amounting to insanity at the time he committed his crime and therefore lacked the mental state required for commission of the charged offense will be found not guilty of the charged offense. Diminished capacity of the mens rea variant is a case-in-chief defense because it attacks an element of the crime, the mens rea, and accordingly results in a complete acquittal. *Compare* Model Penal Code § 4.02 (permitting evidence of mental disease or defect to be admitted whenever relevant to prove that the defendant did or did not have a state of mind which is an element of the offense).

Another variant of the diminished capacity defense is the "partial responsibility variant." Under this variant, the defendant argues that because of some mental disease or defect not amounting to insanity, he (or she) is less blameworthy than others charged with the same offense. If the jury agrees, it can acquit him of the charged offense and find him guilty of a lesser offense. Before 1981, the California courts were receptive to this kind of claim. California's openness to claims of diminished capacity ended after the infamous Dan White case, in which a former police officer and City Supervisor named Dan White shot and killed former San Francisco Mayor George Moscone and then City Supervisor Harvey Milk (the first openly gay person to hold this office) in their offices in City Hall. White, who had resigned as a City Supervisor, was upset because Mayor Moscone refused to reappoint White to his position as a City Supervisor. At his 1979 trial, White successfully argued that he should be acquitted of murder and found guilty of voluntary manslaughter because he was suffering from diminished capacity. A prominent psychiatrist testified for the defense that one cause of White's outburst was high blood sugar caused by eating too much junk food, and the media dubbed the defense's argument the "Twinkie defense." The verdict in the case (seen as anti-gay by Milk's constituents) sparked rioting in the streets of San Francisco, and ultimately led the California legislature to abolish the defense of diminished capacity.[a]

[a] *See* Cal. Penal Code § 25(a) (West 2008) ("The defense of diminished capacity is hereby abolished."). Evidence of mental illness may still be used, however, to prove that the defendant lacked the mens rea required for the commission of the crime. *See* Miguel A. Mendez, *Diminished Capacity in California: Premature Reports of Its Demise*, 3 STAN. L. & POL'Y REV. 216 (1991). In other words, diminished capacity of the mens rea variant is still permitted in California.

5. INFANCY

IN RE DEVON T.

Court of Special Appeals of Maryland
85 Md.App. 674, 584 A.2d 1287 (1991)

MOYLAN, J.

The Present Case

The juvenile appellant, Devon T., was charged with committing an act which, if committed by an adult, would have constituted the crime of possession of heroin with intent to distribute. In the Circuit Court for Baltimore City, Judge Roger W. Brown found that Devon was delinquent. The heart of the case against Devon was that when on May 25, 1989, Devon was directed to empty his pockets by the security guard at the Booker T. Washington Middle School, under the watchful eye of the Assistant Principal, the search produced a brown bag containing twenty zip-lock pink plastic bags which, in turn, contained heroin. Upon this appeal, Devon raises the following contentions:

1. That the State did not offer legally sufficient evidence to rebut his presumptive incapacity because of infancy;

2. That the security guard's direction that he empty his pockets violated his Fourth Amendment right against unreasonable search and seizure. * * *

The Infancy Defense Generally

At the time of the offense, Devon was 13 years, 10 months, and 2 weeks of age. He timely raised the infancy defense. * * *

The case law and the academic literature alike conceptualize the infancy defense as but an instance of the broader phenomenon of a defense based upon lack of moral responsibility or capacity. The criminal law generally will only impose its retributive or deterrent sanctions upon those who are morally blameworthy—those who know they are doing wrong but nonetheless persist in their wrongdoing.

After several centuries of pondering the criminal capacity of children and experimenting with various cut-off ages, the Common Law settled upon its current resolution of the problem by late Tudor and early Stuart times. As explained by LaFave & Scott, *Criminal Law*, (2d ed. 1986), at 398, the resolution was fairly simple:

> At common law, children under the age of seven are conclusively presumed to be without criminal capacity, those who have reached the age of fourteen are treated as fully responsible, while as to those between the ages of seven and fourteen there is a rebuttable presumption of criminal incapacity.

The authors make clear that infancy was an instance of criminal capacity generally:

> The early common law infancy defense was based upon an unwillingness to punish those thought to be incapable of forming criminal intent and not of an age where the threat of punishment could serve as a deterrent.

* * *

Clark & Marshall, *A Treatise on the Law of Crimes*, emphasizes that the mental quality that is the *sine qua non* of criminal responsibility is the capacity to distinguish right from wrong:

> *Children Under the Age of Seven Years.*
>
> —Children under the age of seven years are, by an arbitrary rule of the common law, conclusively presumed to be *doli incapax*, or incapable of entertaining a criminal intent, and no evidence can be received to show capacity in" fact.
>
> *Children Between the Ages of 7 and 14.*
>
> —Children between the ages of 7 and 14 are presumed to be incapable of entertaining a criminal intent, but the presumption is not conclusive, as in the case of children under the age of 7. It may be rebutted by showing in the particular case that the accused was of sufficient intelligence to distinguish between right and wrong, and to understand the nature and illegality of the particular act, or, as it is sometimes said, that he was possessed of 'a mischievous discretion.' (footnotes omitted).

The reasoning behind the rule is made very clear, at 391:

> A child is not criminally responsible unless he is old enough, and intelligent enough, to be capable of entertaining a criminal intent; and to be capable of entertaining a criminal intent he must be capable of distinguishing between right and wrong as to the particular act.

Walkover, *The Infancy Defense in the New Juvenile Court*, distills the rationale to a single sentence:

> The infancy defense was an essential component of the common law limitation of punishment to the blameworthy.

* * *

What is Criminal Capacity in an Infant?

Before the juvenile master, the appellant timely raised the infancy defense. One party or the other (it matters not which) introduced the undisputed fact (it would not have mattered if the fact had been disputed) that at the time of the allegedly delinquent act, Devon was 13 years, 10 months, and 2 weeks of age. Thus, the issue of mental incapacity due to infancy was properly generated and before the court.

On that issue, Devon initially had the benefit of presumptive incapacity. The presumption having been generated, the State had the burdens (of both production and persuasion) of rebutting that presumption. * * * To overcome the presumption of incapacity, then, what precisely was that quality of Devon's mind as to which the State was required to produce legally sufficient evidence? It was required to produce evidence permitting the reasonable inference that Devon—the Ghost of *M'Naghten* speaks:—"at the time of doing the act knew the difference between right and wrong." * * *

In short, when Devon walked around the Booker T. Washington Middle School with twenty zip-lock bags of heroin, apparently for sale or other distribution, could Devon pass the *M'Naghten* test? Was there legally sufficient data before him to permit Judge Brown to infer that Devon knew the difference between right and wrong and knew, moreover, that what he was doing was wrong?

The Legal Sufficiency of the Evidence to Prove Devon's Knowledge of Right and Wrong

As we turn to the legal sufficiency of the evidence, it is important to know that the only mental quality we are probing is the cognitive capacity to distinguish right from wrong. Other aspects of Devon's mental and psychological make-up, such as his scholastic attainments, his I.Q., his social maturity, his societal adjustment, his basic personality, etc., might well require evidentiary input from psychologists, from parents, from teachers or other school authorities, etc. On knowledge of the difference between right and wrong, however, the general case law, as well as the inherent logic of the situation, has established that that particular psychic phenomenon may sometimes permissibly be inferred from the very circumstances of the criminal or delinquent act itself. * * *

Before looking at the circumstances of the delinquent act in this case, as well as at other data pointing toward Devon's awareness that he was doing wrong, a word is in order about the quantity of proof required. *In re William A*, quotes with approval from *Adams v. State,* in pointing out:

> It is generally held that the presumption of *doli incapax* is 'extremely strong at the age of seven and diminishes gradually until it disappears entirely at the age of fourteen. . . .' Since the strength of the presumption of incapacity decreases with the increase in the years of the accused, the quantum of proof necessary to overcome the presumption would diminish in substantially the same ratio.

That kind of a sliding standard of proof or inverse proportion is relatively rare in law. * * * Some analysis may be helpful as to how a presumption "diminishes gradually until it disappears entirely," as to how "incapacity decreases" as age increases, and as to how "the quantum of proof . . . diminish[es] in substantially the same ratio." * * *

The applicable common law on *doli incapax* with relation to the infancy defense establishes that on the day before their seventh birthday, no persons possess cognitive capacity. (0 per cent). It also establishes that on the day of their fourteenth birthday, all persons (at least as far as age is concerned) possess cognitive capacity. (100 per cent). On the time scale between the day of the seventh birthday and the day before the fourteenth birthday, the percentage of persons possessing such capacity steadily increases. The statistical probability is that on the day of the seventh birthday, at most a tiny fraction of one per cent will possess cognitive capacity. Conversely, on the day before the fourteenth birthday, only a tiny fraction of one per cent will lack such cognitive capacity. Assuming a steady rate of climb, the mid-point where fifty per cent of persons will lack cognitive capacity and fifty per cent will possess it would be at 10 years and 6 months of age. That is the scale on which we must place Devon.

We stress that the burden in that regard, notwithstanding the probabilities, was nonetheless on the State. The impact of the allocation of the burden of proof to the State is that the infant will enjoy the benefit of the doubt. The fact that the quantum of proof necessary to overcome presumptive incapacity diminishes in substantially the same ratio as the infant's age increases only serves to lessen the State's burden, not to eliminate it. The State's burden is still an affirmative one. It may not, therefore, passively rely upon the mere absence of evidence to the contrary.

We hold that the State successfully carried that burden. A minor factor, albeit of some weight, was that Devon was essentially at or near grade level in school. The report of the master, received and reviewed by Judge Brown, established that at the time of the offense, Devon was in middle school, embracing grades 6, 7, and 8. The report of the master, indeed, revealed that Devon had flunked the sixth grade twice, with truancy and lack of motivation as apparent causes. That fact nonetheless revealed that Devon had initially reached the sixth grade while still eleven years of age. That would tend to support his probable inclusion in the large majority of his age group rather than in a small and subnormal minority of it.

We note that the transcript of the hearing before the juvenile master shows that the master was in a position to observe first-hand Devon's receiving of legal advice from his lawyer, his acknowledgment [sic] of his understanding of it, and his acting upon it. His lawyer explained that he had a right to remain silent and that the master would not infer guilt from his exercise of that right. He acknowledged understanding that right. His lawyer also advised him of his right to testify but informed him that both the assistant state's attorney and the judge might question him about the delinquent act. Devon indicated that he wished to remain silent and say nothing. Although reduced to relatively simple language, the exchange with respect to the risk of self-incrimination and the privilege against self-incrimination forms a predicate from which an observer might infer some knowledge on Devon's part of the significance of incrimination.

The exchange, moreover, might have significance in two distinct evidentiary regards. It suggests that Devon's lawyer, who presumably had significant opportunity to talk to him before the hearing, concluded that Devon understood the significance of criminality and incrimination. * * *

The significance of the colloquy in this case, moreover, is far more direct. Here, the master was in a position to observe Devon closely throughout the exchange. It does, to be sure, require us to extrapolate that Devon's mental capacity on the day of the hearing, July 20, reflected his mental capacity two months earlier on May 25. * * *

We turn, most significantly, to the circumstances of the criminal act itself. As we do so, we note the relevance of such circumstances to the issue at hand. R. Perkins & R. Boyce, CRIMINAL LAW, (3d ed. 1982), point out, at 938:

> The prosecution, in brief, cannot obtain the conviction of such a person without showing that he had such maturity in fact as to have a guilty knowledge that he was doing wrong. Conduct of the defendant such as concealing himself or the evidence of his misdeed may be such under all the circumstances as to authorize a finding of such maturity.

W. LaFave & A. Scott, CRIMINAL LAW, (2d ed. 1986), speak to the same effect, at 399–400:

> Conduct of the defendant relating to the acts charged may be most relevant in overcoming the presumption. Thus hiding the body, inquiry as to the detection of poison, bribery of a witness, or false accusation of others have all been relied upon in finding capacity.

* * * Just such a use of a secluded location or concealment was present in this case. The case broke when a grandmother, concerned enough to have had her own live-in grandson institutionalized, complained to the authorities at Booker T. Washington Middle School that several of her grandson's classmates were being truant on a regular basis and were using her home, while she was out working, as the "hide

out" from which to sell drugs. Although the initial suspicion was directed toward Edward, it ultimately appeared that Edward and Devon were in the enterprise together. Children who are unaware that what they are doing is wrong have no need to hide out or to conceal their activities.

The most significant circumstance was the very nature of the criminal activity in which Devon engaged. It was not mere possession of heroin. It was possession of twenty packets of heroin with the intent to distribute. This was the finding of the court and it was supported by the evidence. There were no needle marks or other indications of personal use on Devon's body. Nothing in the information developed by the Juvenile Services Agency on Devon and his family gave any indication that this sixth grader, directly or indirectly, had the affluence to purchase drugs for himself in that amount. Indeed, a statement he gave to the interviewer from the Juvenile Services Agency acknowledged that he had been selling drugs for two days when the current offense occurred. His motivation was "that he just wanted something to do."

The evidence in this case affirmatively indicated that Devon and Edward and several other students had been regularly using the absent grandmother's home as a base from which to sell drugs. The circumstances clearly indicated that Devon and his companions were not innocent children unaware of the difference between games and crimes but "street wise" young delinquents knowingly involved in illicit activities. Realistically, one cannot engage in the business of selling drugs without some knowledge as to sources of supply, some pattern for receiving and passing on the money, some network of potential customers, and some *modus operandi* to avoid the eye of the police and of school authorities. It is almost inconceivable that such a crime could be engaged in without the drug pusher's being aware that it was against the law. That is, by definition, criminal capacity.

We hold that the surrounding circumstances here were legally sufficient to overcome the slight residual weight of the presumption of incapacity due to infancy.

JUDGMENT AFFIRMED; COSTS TO BE PAID BY APPELLANT.

6. CONSENT

As a general rule, consent is not recognized as a defense to a crime of violence. Courts, however, recognize one exception to this general rule. A defendant charged with a crime of violence may be exonerated based on the defense of consent where the defendant and victim were engaged in a contact sport, such as football or boxing. The rationale for this exception is that individuals involved in contact sports assume the risk of bodily injury.

In *People v. Samuels*, a court was asked to extend this exception for contact sports to a situation involving two individuals involved in the production of a sadomasochistic film. The defendant in this case claimed that the victim consented to being bound and struck when he volunteered to appear in the film.

PEOPLE V. SAMUELS

Court of Appeals of California, First Appellate District, Division Two
250 Cal.App.2d 501, 58 Cal.Rptr. 439 (1967)

SHOEMAKER, P.J.

Defendant Marvin Samuels was charged by indictment with two counts of conspiracy to violate Penal Code, section 311.2 (preparing and distributing obscene matter); two counts of assault by means of force likely to cause great bodily injury; and a final count of sodomy. Defendant pleaded not guilty to all charges.

The jury acquitted defendant of sodomy but found him guilty on both charges of conspiracy, one charge of aggravated assault and the offense of simple assault included in the other charge of aggravated assault. The simple assault conviction was subsequently dismissed. The court suspended the imposition of sentence, fined defendant $3,000 and placed him on probation for a period of 10 years.

Defendant appeals from the order granting probation and from an order denying his motion for new trial as to the conspiracy and aggravated assault charges. The latter order is nonappealable.

Defendant Samuels, an opthalmologist, testified that he recognized the symptoms of sadomasochism in himself, and his primary concern became to control and release his sadomasochistic urges in ways which were harmless. Through his hobby of photography, he participated in the production of several films on the [E]ast [C]oast. Three of these films depicted bound individuals being whipped. Defendant wielded the whip in two of the films and acted as the cameraman, producer and director for the third film. He testified that the apparent force of the whippings was "faked" and that cosmetics were used to supply the marks of the apparent beating. Defendant produced one of these films at the trial.

In early September 1964, defendant met Kenneth Anger in San Francisco. Anger was a self-employed film director who had made such films as "Fireworks" and "Scorpio Rising." He had also been a close friend of Dr. Kinsey from the institute by that name, had been a buyer for the institute for a period of seven years, and had an authorization to send material through the mails.

On the night of their initial meeting, Anger introduced himself to defendant and inquired whether defendant had seen "Scorpio Rising." Defendant replied that he had not. Defendant had seen "Fireworks," however, and considered it the most sadomasochistic film he had ever seen. He told Anger that he himself had made two or three rolls of film dealing with sadomasochistic activity and was interested in having them developed. Anger volunteered to have the films developed and also told defendant that he believed that the Kinsey Institute would be very interested in examining the footage and might want the films for their collection, since they were then studying the subject of sadomasochism. Defendant agreed to mail the films to Anger's Hollywood address. There was no discussion of having the films developed at an ordinary camera store.

In the middle of September, defendant mailed the three rolls of film to Anger in Hollywood. Anger sent the rolls to a local film service laboratory, and picked up the developed film several days later. One of the rolls was badly underexposed and nearly black. The other two rolls were visible, although slightly underexposed. Anger mailed the latter two films to Dr. Gebhardt of the Kinsey Institute, having previously written him and informed him that he was on the trail of footage which he thought would interest the institute. Anger mailed the underexposed roll to defendant.

Dr. Gebhardt returned the films to Anger, who mailed them to defendant.

Anger's next contact with defendant occurred in early November. The two men dined at a San Francisco restaurant and defendant stated during the course of the dinner that he had edited the films which Anger had developed for him, and he also stated that he intended to make more films of a sadomasochistic nature. Anger again volunteered to have them developed, and told defendant to mail them to Anger's San Francisco address. Defendant indicated that an individual who would play the role of the masochist in a future film was coming from out of state. When Anger again stated that the Kinsey Institute would be interested in the films, defendant expressed a willingness to donate to the institute both the films he had already made and those he intended to make. There was never any discussion of making the films available to the general public or to anyone other than the Kinsey Institute.

After dinner, defendant and Anger went to defendant's home, where the two rolls of film which he had edited were projected. Anger saw that the two rolls had been spliced together and that a shot of a solitary figure wielding a whip had been taken from the end of one roll, where it had previously appeared, and had been cut into several pieces and reinserted at various places in the two combined rolls. This film constitutes the basis for the second conspiracy count and will hereafter be referred to as the "horizontal" film.

At the trial Anger identified defendant as the man wielding the whip.

Anger's next contact with defendant occurred in mid-November, when he received two rolls of film from him. Anger deposited the films at Schaefer's Camera Store in San Francisco, using the fictitious name of "Jackson" and giving a false address. He subsequently returned to the camera shop and was told that only one of the films had thus far been developed and returned to the shop. He paid the developing fee and picked up the film.

The other roll of film had been sent by the camera shop to the Eastman Kodak Company in Palo Alto for processing. The company contacted the Palo Alto Police Department and projected the film for certain police officers and prosecuting attorneys, who confiscated the film.

A dummy roll of film was left at Schaefer's Camera Store. On November 20, Anger picked up this film and was apprehended by the police of San Francisco. Anger was taken to the Hall of Justice where he was questioned concerning the defendant and the films.

Later that day, the Santa Clara County district attorney's office obtained a warrant authorizing a search of defendant's home for whips and other instruments of torture.

Anger and several police officers of San Francisco then drove to the Santa Clara County district attorney's office, arriving there about 7:30 p.m. They viewed the film which Inspector Nieto of San Francisco had obtained from Eastman.

This film, which will henceforth be referred to as the "vertical" film, constituted the basis for the first conspiracy count and the aggravated assault charge. It shows a gagged and naked man strung up in an unfinished room, receiving a beating with whips and lashes administered by a man whom Anger identified as defendant. There are marks on the victim's buttocks, the small of his back and further up on his body. The film contained no splices.

After viewing the film, all of the officers proceeded to defendant's Sunnyvale residence, arriving there at approximately 9 p.m. When defendant opened the door, he was informed of the search warrant, it was read to him and then handed to him. The officers then entered the house and observed that the living room was in semi-darkness and that a movie screen was set up in the living room, and a projector was on the dining room table. Two canisters of film were on the table by the projector. One canister contained the "horizontal" film, and the other contained a travelogue entitled "Fire Island," which defendant had made on the [E]ast [C]oast.

Nieto accompanied defendant into the bedroom and was subsequently joined by Logan of the district attorney's office, who advised defendant of his rights to counsel and to remain silent. Logan then asked defendant the name of the individual who was strung from the beam in the "vertical" film. Defendant replied that he did not know his name and that he had met him in a San Francisco bar. In response to further questioning, defendant said that the film had been made in an unfinished room in the Sunnyvale house. He further stated that no third party was present when the film was made, and automatic camera settings were used. He then refused to say anything further until he had consulted an attorney.

Defendant was subsequently questioned by Nieto. The man in the "vertical" film was an individual whom he had met either at a "gay" bar or at Foster's. Defendant thought his name was "George," but did not know his present whereabouts. The man approached him and stated that he was an "M" looking for an "S." The man thereafter came to defendant's home and voluntarily submitted to the beating. Defendant admitted that he was a well-known sadist and stated that he was one of the best in the business. When asked about the white substance on the face of the victim in the film, defendant stated that it was adhesive tape. He subsequently accompanied Nieto into the unfinished room in his house and identified the studs to which the victim's feet had been anchored during the filming.

Lowell Bradford, Director of the Santa Clara County Laboratory of Criminalistics and a qualified expert, testified that he had extracted certain sections from the "vertical" film by way of color slides which were then made into prints. This film, as above noted, contained no splices. His examination of the prints taken from a "representative area" of the film led him to the conclusion that the camera could not have been stopped so as to allow for the application of cosmetics and that the marks and welts which appeared on the victim during this portion of the film occurred progressively from frame to frame in slow development and were not the result of any retouching. Bradford had made a similar examination of a representative area of the "horizontal" film and had concluded that the welts on the victim had progressively developed during uninterrupted sections of the film without any indication of camera stops during which cosmetics could have been applied. There was no evidence that either the "vertical" or "horizontal" films had been retouched and Bradford was of the opinion that both films truly and correctly represented what was before the camera at the time. Edward Chong, senior county photographer, and Rudolph Stohr of the Eastman Kodak Company, were of the same opinion as to the absence of retouching and the accurate depiction of the scene before the camera.

On cross-examination, Bradford admitted that he had never examined defendant's camera, a Bolex, and was generally unfamiliar with that type of camera. With the exception of one stop early in the film, his notes indicated no other distinct stops in the "vertical" film. He saw no interruption in the continuity of action and did not know whether the clear frames were actual stops or were attributable to a shutter fault.

Since he had not examined the camera, he did not know whether it had any such defect.

Bradford had also performed a laboratory examination of the riding crop, belt, cane and lash used to strike the victims in the two films and had been unable to detect any traces of blood or cosmetics.

Defendant testified on his own behalf and admitted making both films in his home. The man who had been strung up in the "vertical" film had telephoned defendant after he had let it be known in the San Francisco "underground" that he wanted volunteers for sadomasochistic films to be sent to the Kinsey Institute. Defendant arranged to meet him at the San Jose bus depot and drove him to his Sunnyvale home. After the filming had been completed, defendant drove him back to the bus depot in the "same condition he came in." During the course of the filming, which took some four hours, defendant strung the man up with hospital restraints and struck him lightly with a riding crop, pulling his punches just before striking the man's body. He stopped the camera periodically and applied cosmetics. Defendant had coached the man to move violently so as to make the film seem realistic. * * *

Dr. Robert Malone, a surgeon and physician whose practice included serving as team physician for a high school football team for a period of 10 years, was of the opinion that the marks on the victims in the "vertical" and "horizontal" films could have been caused only in part by the blows inflicted during the course of said films; that as to the "vertical" film, the dark coloration which appeared after the initial redness would not show up until at least 12 hours after the blow or trauma and certainly not within a period of a few minutes, as depicted in the film. The doctor testified at length as to the effect of the body being struck a violent blow in support of his opinion. If he were to assume that the marks did accurately depict the victim's reaction to the blows depicted in the film, his medical opinion would be that there would of necessity have been a breaking of the skin and some bleeding, which would be detectable on the instruments used to inflict the beating. He could conceive of no physiological or medical explanation for this change and believed that cosmetics must have been applied to the surface of the skin.

Defendant challenges the validity of his conviction of conspiracy and assault on numerous and diverse grounds. * * *

Defendant also contends that the consent of the victim is an absolute defense to the charge of aggravated assault and that the trial court erred in instructing the jury to the contrary. This argument cannot be sustained.

Although both parties concede that they were unable to find any California case directly in point, consent of the victim is not generally a defense to assault or battery, except in a situation involving ordinary physical contact or blows incident to sports such as football, boxing or wrestling. It is also the rule that the apparent consent of a person without legal capacity to give consent, such as a child or insane person, is ineffective.

It is a matter of common knowledge that a normal person in full possession of his mental faculties does not freely consent to the use, upon himself, of force likely to produce great bodily injury. Even if it be assumed that the victim in the "vertical" film did in fact suffer from some form of mental aberration which compelled him to submit to a beating which was so severe as to constitute an aggravated assault, defendant's conduct in inflicting that beating was no less violative of a penal statute obviously designed to prohibit one human being from severely or mortally injuring another. It follows that the trial court was correct in instructing the jury that consent was not a defense to the aggravated assault charge. * * *

The attempted appeal from the order denying a new trial is dismissed. The conviction as to aggravated assault is affirmed. The trial court is directed to vacate and set aside the convictions of conspiracy and the order of probation is vacated with directions to the trial court to reconsider the same in the light of our determination.

7. ENTRAPMENT

The defense of entrapment suggests the defendant should be acquitted because law enforcement officials inappropriately lured him into engaging in criminal activity. The courts have been divided over how best to conceptualize entrapment. Is it more like the lack of voluntary action defense discussed in *Martin v. State*, where the criminal act does not really "belong" to the defendant at all because of the police involvement? If so, it perhaps should be thought of as a case-in-chief defense. Or is it more like duress, in which it is said that the defendant did commit the crime but should not be punished because he was coerced by the police into doing so? If so, then it should be placed with other affirmative defenses. In *People v. Jamieson,* Justice Brickley describes these different approaches to entrapment as "objective" and "subjective," and explains why in the Supreme Court of Michigan's view the objective approach is better. In *United States v. Jacobson*, a U.S. Supreme Court decision, both the majority and the dissent employ the subjective approach to entrapment, but divide over what it means to say that the defendant was "predisposed" to commit the crime.

PEOPLE V. JAMIESON

Supreme Court of Michigan
436 Mich. 61, 461 N.W.2d 884 (1990)

BRICKLEY, JUSTICE.

We granted leave in this case to consider whether the trial court clearly erred in dismissing on the basis of entrapment the charges of unlawful delivery of controlled substances that were brought against defendants. * * *

I

Defendants, all Wayne County Jail guards, were charged with delivery of cocaine following an undercover operation in which the delivery was made to an informant. The Wayne County Sheriff's Department was contacted by a juvenile inmate at Wayne County Jail, Quinton Varner, concerning deputy sheriffs smuggling narcotics to inmates. While the testimony suggests that Varner furnished the government with a couple of names, he did not provide information which would allow the Sheriff's Department to accumulate a list of specific targets.

Following discussions with the jail administrator and the Wayne County Prosecutor's Office, Sergeant Booth was allowed ten days to work a scheme that would unveil guards who were participating in the unlawful delivery of narcotics into the jail. After considering other alternatives, the operation was instituted. Varner offered to cooperate with the Sheriff's Department in exchange for a thirty-day reduction in his sentence.

Sergeant Booth obtained a supply of cocaine and money from the United States Government Drug Enforcement Administration. The drugs and money were delivered to an undercover police officer who would deliver these items to the particular guard who would in turn deliver the items to the juvenile inside the jail.[2] When the transaction was completed the drugs and money were returned to Sergeant Booth. The targets of the operation were to be chosen by inmate Varner and instructed by him when and where to meet the outside contact in order to obtain the cocaine.

The trial judge found that, as a matter of law, defendants were entrapped and accordingly dismissed the charges against defendants * * *

The Court of Appeals * * * affirmed the trial court's holding, concluding that it was not clearly erroneous. * * *

---

[2] This type of operation has been referred to as a take-back sales operation or a reverse sting operation.

II

In order to reexamine the viability of the objective test for determining entrapment, we will first examine the development of the doctrine of entrapment and its evolution into two principal tests.

A

Although the doctrine of entrapment has a popular following, even extending, in the minds of speeders, to the motorcycle policeman hiding behind a billboard, the precise parameters of this defense and the standards for its application have not emerged without some struggle—a struggle that has manifested itself in the differences between the so-called objective and subjective tests.

Entrapment has been defined as the "conception and planning of an offense by an officer, and his procurement of its commission by one who would not have perpetrated it except for trickery, persuasion, or fraud of the officer." To determine whether entrapment has been established, a distinction is made between a trap for the "unwary innocent" and a trap for the "unwary criminal." There is no entrapment if a policeman merely furnishes an opportunity for the commission of a crime by one ready and willing to commit the activity. The mere fact of deceit will not defeat prosecution. The purpose of the defense of entrapment is to at least prevent unlawful government activity in instigating criminal activity. "The function of law enforcement is the prevention of crime and the apprehension of criminals.... [T]hat function does not include the manufacturing of crime."

The United States Supreme Court's rationale for an entrapment defense is grounded in an implied exception to criminal statutes. It is based on the assumption that Congress could not have intended that its statutes be enforced for criminal punishment of a defendant who has committed all the elements of a prescribed offense, but was tempted into violation of that statute by the government.

The United States Supreme Court first recognized and applied the defense of entrapment in *Sorrells v. United States*. In *Sorrells,* the Court held that the defendant, who had sold a half-gallon of whiskey to a United States government probation officer, was entitled to a defense of entrapment because of the "repeated and persistent solicitation" by the agent. The Court noted that "artifice and stratagem may be employed to catch those engaged in criminal enterprises, but that government may not implant in the mind of an innocent person the disposition to commit the alleged offense and induce its commission in order that they may prosecute." The controlling question is "whether the defendant is a person *otherwise innocent* whom the Government is seeking to punish for an alleged offense which is the product of the creative activity of its own officials." (emphasis added).

Sherman v. United States involved the selling of narcotics to a government informer who was being treated for narcotics addiction. The informant gained the trust of Sherman by sharing mutual experiences and problems in their attempt to overcome the apparent drug addiction. Because the informant was not responding to treatment, he asked Sherman to supply him with narcotics. Sherman tried to avoid the issue, but after repeated requests and the presumed suffering by the informant, Sherman agreed to supply him with narcotics. The United States Supreme Court concluded that entrapment was established as a matter of law.

> The case at bar illustrates an evil which the defense of entrapment is designed to overcome. The government informer entices someone attempting to avoid narcotics not only into carrying out an illegal sale but also into returning to the habit of use.... Thus the Government plays on the weaknesses of an innocent party and beguiles him into committing crimes which he otherwise would not have attempted.

Again, the United States Supreme Court focused on the state of mind of the offender. A different question is presented when the criminal design originates with the officials of the government, and they implant in the mind of an innocent person the disposition to commit the alleged offense and induce its commission in order that they may prosecute. * * *

In *United States v. Russell*, the * * * Court stated that in drug-related offenses law enforcement personnel have turned to one of the only practicable means of detection: the infiltration of drug rings and limited participation in their unlawful present practices. Such infiltration is a recognized and a permissible means of investigation.... The Court refused to extend the doctrine of entrapment beyond the majority opinions of *Sorrells* and *Sherman* holding that the principal element in the defense of entrapment [is] the defendant's predisposition to commit the crime. In *Russell*, the undercover agent supplied the defendant with an essential ingredient in the manufacture of speed. The Court concluded that the defendant was predisposed because he was involved in the enterprise prior to the agent's involvement. "[I]n the words of *Sherman*, "[he] was not an unwary innocent but an unwary criminal."

The decisions of *Sorrells*, *Sherman*, and *Russell* were reaffirmed in *Hampton v. United States*. * * * It is only when the Government's deception actually implants the criminal design in the mind of the defendant that the defense of entrapment comes into play."

In each of these four cases, the dissenters advocated an objective approach which shifts its focus from the defendant's state of mind to the conduct of the law enforcement officers. The rationale behind this test is that since the purpose of an entrapment defense is to prohibit reprehensible governmental methods and practices in the obtaining of a conviction, it should do so directly rather than indirectly. A defense under the objective approach is grounded on " 'whether the police conduct revealed in a particular case falls below the standards, to which the common feelings respond, for the proper use of governmental power.' "

The defense of entrapment and the public policy supporting the rule has long been recognized in Michigan jurisprudence. However, in *People v. Turner*, this Court renounced the subjective test followed by the United States Supreme Court and a majority of states, reasoning that the objective test is preferable because:

> [B]y definition, the entrapment defense cannot arise unless the defendant actually committed the proscribed act, that defendant is manifestly covered by the terms of the criminal statute involved.
>
> Furthermore, to say that such a defendant is otherwise innocent or not predisposed to commit the crime is misleading, at best. The very fact that he has committed an act that Congress has determined to be illegal demonstrates conclusively that he is not innocent of the offense. . . .
>
> The purpose of the entrapment defense, then, cannot be to protect persons who are otherwise innocent. Rather, it must be to prohibit unlawful governmental activity in instigating crime.

The *Turner* Court held that the defendant was entrapped as a matter of law. It stated that the agent engaged in overreaching conduct by pursuing the defendant after the first investigation did not turn up any evidence. Turner was not a drug dealer, and the agent played upon Turner's sympathy as a friend. The law enforcement officer went beyond merely creating an opportunity for the commission of a crime.

A California case, *People v. Barraza*, also provides a rationale for adopting the objective approach instead of the subjective test. The *Barraza* court stated:

> [A] test that looks to the character and predisposition of the defendant rather than the conduct of the police loses sight of the underlying reason for the defense of entrapment. No matter what the defendant's past record and present inclinations to criminality, or the depths to which he has sunk in the estimation of society, certain police conduct to ensnare him into further crime is not to be tolerated by an advanced society. . . . Human nature is weak enough . . . and sufficiently beset by temptations without government adding to them and generating crime.

Further the *Barraza* court gives examples of impermissible police conduct which would constitute entrapment under the objective test. The court listed as examples the following: (1) an appeal by police because of friendship or sympathy rather than for personal gain; (2) inducement that would make the commission of crime unusually attractive to a normal law-abiding person, (3) a guarantee that the act was not illegal; (4) an offer of exorbitant consideration or similar enticement.

> [W]hile the inquiry must focus primarily on the conduct of the law enforcement agent, that conduct is not to be viewed in a vacuum. . . . We reiterate, however, that under this test such matters as the character of the suspect, his predisposition to commit the offense, and his subjective intent are irrelevant.

As a matter of practicality, in many instances the application of the two theories overlap. When applying the subjective test, to determine if the accused is predisposed, the court must consider the official's conduct. Predisposition is linked to the amount of inducement and pressure offered by an agent as well as how long the agent persisted before commission of the illegal act. Similarly, courts applying the objective approach use the state of mind of the accused as a factor. When applying the objective test, consideration is given to the willingness of the accused to commit the act weighed against how a normally law-abiding person would react in similar circumstances. Under either approach, courts adhere to the fact that the function of law enforcement is to deter crime and not to manufacture it. * * *

In our view, each test has its flaws. The objective test has two. First, it encourages the courts to play a supervisory role over another branch of government, not to determine whether there has been illegal or unconstitutional practices engaged in by law enforcement, but, as will be seen in the case before us, whether the law enforcement technique was reprehensible. This often requires the courts to second-guess investigative techniques and law enforcement alternatives for which they obviously do not have expertise. Secondly, it sacrifices the conviction of an offender who is very much disposed toward the crime committed, but was fortunate enough to be snared by judicially disfavored law enforcement measures.

By the same token, the subjective test, in focusing on the predisposition of the defendant, suffers, theoretically at least, in going beyond the statutory requirement of guilt to find mitigating circumstances (not otherwise guilty) that logically speaking should not interfere with a finding of guilt. The subjective test also has the flaw of all subjective tests: attempting to determine the workings of the human mind in an individual situation. * * *

It is not necessary for us to announce today what we would do if we were operating on a clean slate, because we are not. Under the doctrine of stare decisis, principles of law deliberately examined and decided by a court of competent jurisdiction become precedent which should not be lightly departed. * * * We have been persuaded by the arguments on rehearing and by our own review of the law that stare decisis should carry the day.

III

We now turn to the application of the objective test to these cases.

When an accused claims entrapment, the trial court must conduct a separate evidentiary hearing to resolve the issue. The defendant bears the burden of proving by a preponderance of the evidence that law enforcement officials engaged in reprehensible behavior to obtain a conviction. The facts of each case must be examined to determine whether, under the circumstances, the governmental activity would induce a hypothetical person not ready and willing to commit the crime to engage in criminal activity. The trial judge's findings on the issue are subject to appellate review under the clearly erroneous standard.

In these cases the trial court found, as a matter of law, that the police conduct was outrageous and reprehensible because:

(1) the state supplied the narcotics which became the subject of the prosecution;

(2) the state considered no alternative plans;

(3) the state, in fact, designed the very plan in question, there being no evidence that the scheme was suggested by an individual suspect guard;

(4) the state determined no specific targets by name prior to execution of the plan;

(5) the state made no determination that any particular guard was involved in any ongoing illicit activity; and finally,

(6) the state violated its public trust and abrogated its responsibility to properly supervise a criminal investigation by permitting the operation to be produced, directed and choreographed by a teenaged felon.

* * *

In this case, the Wayne County Sheriff's Department was approached by an inmate who informed it of criminal activity at the jail involving prison guards. The evidence disclosed that the informant had witnessed ongoing criminal activity, observed contraband coming into the jail, and had been approached by some of the guards about delivery of drugs to him inside the jail. It was the informant who approached the Sheriff's Department, hoping for a reduction in his sentence—not the police who sought out informants for the purpose of developing criminal activity. The government did not, as the dissent suggests, invent[ ] the crime. Rather, the Sheriff's Department merely decided to act upon information received from an inmate.

The defendants and the dissent assert that it was error to use an "adolescent" informant who lacked maturity in the undercover operation. We do not see the error in allowing a sixteen-year-old who was convicted as an adult and incarcerated in an adult prison to participate as an informer in the investigation. Drug trafficking investigation as a general rule requires the use of informers with contacts in the drug culture. "These informers are commonly drug offenders who have been promised leniency in return for cooperation." Because of their status, generally they are always going to be of questionable character and stability.

The transaction involved very limited contact and was a one-time occurrence resulting in the arrest of defendants. The informer was not called upon to repeatedly solicit the targets in order to complete the transaction. The facts do not suggest that the government used friendship or sympathy to lure defendants into criminal activity. The inmate, although allowed to select the individuals to be targeted, was anything but in control of the activity. The formulation of the plan occurred outside the county jail and outside the control and influence of the informant.

In fact it was the police who secured the drugs, money, and outside contacts. The informant's only discretion and role was to inquire of his guards whether they would serve as couriers for his purported drug need. The defendants are all prison guards with control over inmates, not vice versa. If correctional officials play the role we all expect of them, then defendants were under no pressure to please inmates under their charge. On the record before us, the case simply cannot be made that this sixteen-year-old inmate preyed upon the weaknesses of his captors to the extent that they would be induced beyond a readiness to make contact with an alleged drug supplier outside the jail and to transport drugs inside the jail to such an inmate. Opportunity, yes, seduction, no.

Some emphasis was placed on the fact that the juvenile informer was left unprotected and unsupervised. We know of no rule of law or prison administration which would require that the government provide protection or supervision for those who volunteer to act as informants for the government. * * *

A review of the common law of this state shows that discretionary investigative enforcement measures extend beyond a tolerable level when by design the government uses continued pressure, appeals to friendship or sympathy, threats of arrest, an informant's vulnerability, sexual favors, or procedures which escalate criminal culpability. All of these traditional inducements are absent from the facts of this case.

Finally, the trial judge expressed concern over the fact that there was insufficient police control over the entire operation. He specifically stated that the state violated its public trust and abrogated its responsibility to properly supervise a criminal investigation by permitting the operation to be produced, directed and choreographed by a teenaged felon. However this factor only suggests that the criminal enterprise was not manufactured by the government officials. * * *

The targets were not unwary or vulnerable. To the contrary, they were trained in law enforcement, sworn to uphold the law, and spent their working days in a most controlled environment in which they were in charge. The plan to uncover the reported source of drugs in the jail did not prey on human weakness (it is hoped that transporting drugs into a jail by correction officers is not seen as a normal human weakness) or friendship or the use of authority to intimidate. Law enforcement corruption is not, and should not be, taken lightly when reported, and more often than not requires painstaking investigation to uncover. As has been noted by many courts and observers of the entrapment phenomenon, it is difficult to set forth precisely a definition of the kind of law enforcement measures that shock the sensibilities of the courts. But whatever it may be, this case does not present it.

ARCHER, JUSTICE (dissenting).

* * * I concur in the Court's affirmation of our adherence to the objective theory of entrapment, but I dissent from the majority's application of that test to the facts of this case. I do not believe the trial court clearly erred in ruling that the police officer's conduct entrapped these defendants. * * *

In today's climate, the unchecked fury of a vital war on drugs creates many incentives for police to sacrifice individual liberty in an effort to catch criminals, particularly drug traffickers we can call predisposed. Now, more than ever, our courts need a mechanism by which they can assure that law enforcement conduct does not "fall [ ] below standards, to which common feelings respond, for the proper use of governmental power."

The task of destroying illicit narcotics trade obviously requires not only artifice and police deception, but continuous law enforcement creativity. It is indisputable, however, that in a society which cherishes freedom, there must be limits on how far police may go in order to capture wrongdoers. Unless the courts in this society establish those limits, there is no disincentive to police overreaching, only the powerful incentive to stem the tide of drugs at whatever cost. * * *

II

I agree with the lead opinion that the major thrust of the entrapment defense in Michigan is to discourage police misconduct which creates the risk that otherwise reasonable, law-abiding citizens will be enticed into violating the law. The government "may not provoke or create a crime and then punish the criminal, its creature." It is under this definition of entrapment that I believe entrapment occurred in this case. By supplying the scheme, the means, the opportunity, and the controlled substance, the police manufactured a crime here where none had likely existed before. * * *

The bottom line in all these cases is the government manufacture of crime. This government manufacture of crime violates objective entrapment principles because it creates the substantial risk that persons uninvolved in criminal activity and otherwise unwilling to engage in criminal activity will be enticed into playing a role in a governmentally instigated crime. When Quinton Varner was turned loose in the Wayne County Jail, the government created the risk that sheriff's deputies who had never engaged in the jailhouse drug trade or contemplated doing so might be enticed to violate the law. * * *

The lead opinion ignores the element of government instigation when it equates the undercover scheme in this case with an ordinary drug transaction. In an ordinary drug transaction, an undercover officer purchases narcotics from a person who is already in illegal possession of the drugs or, in some instances, undercover officers might sell actual or facsimile narcotics to a person in the illicit business of purchasing those narcotics. In the undercover scheme in this case, however, there was never an actual purchase or sale. Although jail officials had reason to believe that an uncertain number of unidentified guards were engaged in the drug trade, it sought out particular individuals whom they had no reason to believe were already engaged in narcotics trafficking and convinced them to transfer the drugs from one police agent to another. * * *

While I agree * * * that not all undercover schemes in which the government is both the supplier and recipient of contraband are entrapment per se, there are three elements to the scheme employed here which the trial court correctly identified as * * * making this scheme reprehensible.

First, in the name of stemming the flow of narcotics into the Wayne County Jail, the police officers sent actual narcotics into the jail when a facsimile of the drug would have been sufficient. Allowing actual narcotics to travel into the jail and remain for a period of time in the possession of a sixteen-year-old inmate was a risk not justified, given the obvious reason for using actual drugs: The police wished to catch the guards committing the greater felony of delivery, rather than the lesser felony of attempt.

Second, and more important, it was unreasonable for the police officers in charge of this investigation to vest in Quinton Varner, a sixteen-year-old felon, the unfettered power to choose the targets of the operation. The lead opinion is correct in pointing out that the informers upon whom the police necessarily depend are seldom model citizens. However, in this undercover operation, Quinton Varner was far more than an informer. * * *

As an adolescent, Quinton Varner lacked the maturity that would justify giving him the ability to select which individuals he would try to subject to prosecution for a felony carrying a twenty-year penalty. Nor should he have been trusted to approach his targets in a manner mindful of the rights of those individuals.

It was particularly unreasonable to allow an inmate to select the targets of an undercover operation inside a penal institution. The society inside a jail or a prison is highly fractured; individuals within such institutions, particularly individuals engaged in illicit activities, often develop intense loyalties for those whom they consider friends, and strong distrust and dislike for those perceived as enemies. When the police officers allowed Quinton Varner to select the targets of the operation, they must have recognized the probability that Quinton Varner would be selective in his work. Rather than constructing an operation that would capture those guards already engaged in illicit drug trade and, it would be hoped, those at the center of that trade, the police officers created a situation in which Quinton Varner was allowed to set up any individual he wished, without regard to that individual's previous involvement in the drug trade. Meanwhile, Quinton Varner was free to leave untouched those individuals whom he chose not to see arrested, regardless of whether those individuals were amongst those most responsible for the presence of drugs in the Wayne County Jail. * * *

The trial court found that the defendants were entrapped in a scheme in which they were merely conduits for drugs supplied by and delivered to the government, in which the police introduced actual narcotics into the Wayne County Jail, and in which a sixteen-year-old felon was allowed to select the targets of the scheme regardless of the absence of any reasonable suspicion with regard to any particular defendant. * * * This decision was scarcely clearly erroneous; I believe it was clearly correct. I would affirm.

JACOBSON V. UNITED STATES

United States Supreme Court

503 U.S. 540, 112 S.Ct. 1535, 118 L.Ed.2d 174 (1992)

JUSTICE WHITE delivered the opinion of the Court.

On September 24, 1987, petitioner Keith Jacobson was indicted for violating a provision of the Child Protection Act of 1984 (Act), Pub.L. 98–292, 98 Stat. 204, which criminalizes the knowing receipt through the mails of a visual depiction [that] involves the use of a minor engaging in sexually explicit conduct. Petitioner defended on the ground that the Government entrapped him into committing the crime through a series of communications from undercover agents that spanned the 26 months preceding his arrest. Petitioner was found guilty after a jury trial. The Court of Appeals affirmed his conviction, holding that the Government had carried its burden of proving beyond reasonable doubt that petitioner was predisposed to break the law and hence was not entrapped.

I

In February 1984, petitioner, a 56-year-old veteran-turned-farmer who supported his elderly father in Nebraska, ordered two magazines and a brochure from a California adult bookstore. The magazines, entitled Bare Boys I and Bare Boys II, contained photographs of nude preteen and teenage boys. The contents of the magazines startled petitioner, who testified that he had expected to receive photographs of young men 18 years or older. On cross-examination, he explained his response to the magazines:

> [PROSECUTOR]: [Y]ou were shocked and surprised that there were pictures of very young boys without clothes on, is that correct?
>
> [JACOBSON]: Yes, I was.
>
> [PROSECUTOR]: Were you offended?
>
> . . . . .
>
> [JACOBSON]: I was not offended because I thought these were a nudist type publication. Many of the pictures were out in a rural or outdoor setting. There was—I didn't draw any sexual connotation or connection with that.

The young men depicted in the magazines were not engaged in sexual activity, and petitioner's receipt of the magazines was legal under both federal and Nebraska law. Within three months, the law with respect to child pornography changed; Congress passed the Act illegalizing [sic] the receipt through the mails of sexually explicit depictions of children. In the very month that the new provision became law, postal inspectors found petitioner's name on the mailing list of the California bookstore that had mailed him Bare Boys I and II. There followed over the next 2 1/2 years repeated efforts by two Government agencies, through five fictitious organizations and a bogus pen pal, to explore petitioner's willingness to break the new law by ordering sexually explicit photographs of children through the mail.

The Government began its efforts in January 1985 when a postal inspector sent petitioner a letter supposedly from the American Hedonist Society, which in fact was a fictitious organization. The letter included a membership application and stated the Society's doctrine: that members had the right to read what we desire, the right to discuss similar interests with those who share our philosophy, and finally that we have the right to seek pleasure without restrictions being placed on us by outdated puritan morality. Petitioner enrolled in the organization and returned a sexual attitude questionnaire that asked him to rank on a scale of one to four his enjoyment of various sexual materials, with one being really enjoy, two being enjoy, three being somewhat enjoy, and four being do not enjoy. Petitioner ranked the entry [p]re-teen sex as a two, but indicated that he was opposed to pedophilia.

For a time, the Government left petitioner alone. But then a new prohibited mailing specialist in the Postal Service found petitioner's name in a file, and in May 1986, petitioner received a solicitation from a second fictitious consumer research company, Midlands Data Research, seeking a response from those who believe in the joys of sex and the complete awareness of those lusty and youthful lads and lasses of the neophite [sic] age. The letter never explained whether neophite referred to minors or young adults. Petitioner responded: Please feel free to send me more information, I am interested in teenage sexuality. Please keep my name confidential.

Petitioner then heard from yet another Government creation, Heartland Institute for a New Tomorrow (HINT), which proclaimed that it was an organization founded to protect and promote sexual freedom and freedom of choice. We believe that arbitrarily imposed legislative sanctions restricting your sexual freedom should be rescinded through the legislative process. The letter also enclosed a second survey. Petitioner indicated that his interest in [p]reteen sex-homosexual material was above average, but not high. In response to another question, petitioner wrote: Not only sexual expression but freedom of the press is under attack. We must be ever vigilant to counter attack right wing fundamentalists who are determined to curtail our freedoms.

HINT replied, portraying itself as a lobbying organization seeking to repeal all statutes which regulate sexual activities, except those laws which deal with violent behavior, such as rape. HINT is also lobbying to eliminate any legal definition of the age of consent. These lobbying efforts were to be funded by sales from a catalog to be published in the future offering the sale of various items which we believe you will find to be both interesting and stimulating. HINT also provided computer matching of group members with similar survey responses; and, although petitioner was supplied with a list of potential pen pals, he did not initiate any correspondence.

Nevertheless, the Government's prohibited mailing specialist began writing to petitioner, using the pseudonym Carl Long. The letters employed a tactic known as mirroring, which the inspector described as reflect[ing] whatever the interests are of the person we are writing to. Petitioner responded at first, indicating that his interest was primarily in male-male items. Inspector Long wrote back:

> My interests too are primarily male-male items. Are you satisfied with the type of VCR tapes available? Personally, I like the amateur stuff better if its [sic] well produced as it can get

more kinky and also seems more real. I think the actors enjoy it more.

Petitioner responded:

As far as my likes are concerned, I like good looking young guys (in their late teens and early 20's) doing their thing together.

Petitioner's letters to Long made no reference to child pornography. After writing two letters, petitioner discontinued the correspondence.

By March 1987, 34 months had passed since the Government obtained petitioner's name from the mailing list of the California bookstore, and 26 months had passed since the Postal Service had commenced its mailings to petitioner. Although petitioner had responded to surveys and letters, the Government had no evidence that petitioner had ever intentionally possessed or been exposed to child pornography. The Postal Service had not checked petitioner's mail to determine whether he was receiving questionable mailings from persons—other than the Government—involved in the child pornography industry.

At this point, a second Government agency, the Customs Service, included petitioner in its own child pornography sting, Operation Borderline, after receiving his name on lists submitted by the Postal Service. Using the name of a fictitious Canadian company called Produit Outaouais, the Customs Service mailed petitioner a brochure advertising photographs of young boys engaging in sex. Petitioner placed an order that was never filled.

The Postal Service also continued its efforts in the Jacobson case, writing to petitioner as the Far Eastern Trading Company Ltd. The letter began:

As many of you know, much hysterical nonsense has appeared in the American media concerning pornography and what must be done to stop it from coming across your borders. This brief letter does not allow us to give much comments; however, why is your government spending millions of dollars to exercise international censorship while tons of drugs, which makes yours the world's most crime ridden country are passed through easily.

The letter went on to say:

[W]e have devised a method of getting these to you without prying eyes of U.S. Customs seizing your mail. . . . After consultations with American solicitors, we have been advised that once we have posted our material through your system, it cannot be opened for any inspection without authorization of a judge.

The letter invited petitioner to send for more information. It also asked petitioner to sign an affirmation that he was not a law enforcement officer or agent of the U.S. Government acting in an undercover capacity for the purpose of entrapping Far Eastern Trading Company, its agents or customers. Petitioner responded. A catalog was sent, and petitioner ordered Boys Who Love Boys, a pornographic magazine depicting young boys engaged in various sexual activities. Petitioner was arrested after a controlled delivery of a photocopy of the magazine.

When petitioner was asked at trial why he placed such an order, he explained that the Government had succeeded in piquing his curiosity:

> Well, the statement was made of all the trouble and the hysteria over pornography and I wanted to see what the material was. It didn't describe the—I didn't know for sure what kind of sexual action they were referring to in the Canadian letter.

In petitioner's home, the Government found the Bare Boys magazines and materials that the Government had sent to him in the course of its protracted investigation, but no other materials that would indicate that petitioner collected, or was actively interested in, child pornography.

Petitioner was indicted for violating 18 U.S.C. § 2252(a)(2)(A). The trial court instructed the jury on the petitioner's entrapment defense, petitioner was convicted, and a divided Court of Appeals for the Eighth Circuit, sitting en banc, affirmed, concluding that Jacobson was not entrapped as a matter of law. We granted certiorari.

II

There can be no dispute about the evils of child pornography or the difficulties that laws and law enforcement have encountered in eliminating it. Likewise, there can be no dispute that the Government may use undercover agents to enforce the law. "It is well settled that the fact that officers or employees of the Government merely afford opportunities or facilities for the commission of the offense does not defeat the prosecution. Artifice and stratagem may be employed to catch those engaged in criminal enterprises."

In their zeal to enforce the law, however, Government agents may not originate a criminal design, implant in an innocent person's mind the disposition to commit a criminal act, and then induce commission of the crime so that the Government may prosecute. Where the Government has induced an individual to break the law and the defense of entrapment is at issue, as it was in this case, the prosecution must prove beyond reasonable doubt that the defendant was disposed to commit the criminal act prior to first being approached by Government agents.

This long-established standard in no way encroaches upon Government investigatory activities. Indeed, the Government's internal guidelines for undercover operations provide that an inducement to commit a crime should not be offered unless:

> (a) [T]here is a reasonable indication, based on information developed through informants or other means, that the subject is engaging, has engaged, or is likely to engage in illegal activity of a similar type; or
>
> (b) The opportunity for illegal activity has been structured so that there is reason for believing that persons drawn to the opportunity, or brought to it, are predisposed to engage in the contemplated illegal activity.

Thus, an agent deployed to stop the traffic in illegal drugs may offer the opportunity to buy or sell drugs and, if the offer is accepted, make an arrest on the spot or later. In such a typical case, or in a more elaborate sting operation involving government-sponsored fencing where the defendant is simply provided with the opportunity to commit a crime, the entrapment defense is of little use because the ready commission of the criminal act amply demonstrates the defendant's predisposition. Had the agents in this case simply offered petitioner the opportunity to order child pornography through the mails, and petitioner—who must be presumed to know the law—had promptly availed himself of this criminal opportunity, it is unlikely that his entrapment defense would have warranted a jury instruction.

But that is not what happened here. By the time petitioner finally placed his order, he had already been the target of 26 months of repeated mailings and communications from Government agents and fictitious organizations. Therefore, although he had become predisposed to break the law by May 1987, it is our view that the Government did not prove that this predisposition was independent and not the product of the attention that the Government had directed at petitioner since January 1985.

The prosecution's evidence of predisposition falls into two categories: evidence developed prior to the Postal Service's mail campaign, and that developed during the course of the investigation. The sole piece of preinvestigation evidence is petitioner's 1984 order and receipt of the Bare Boys magazines. But this is scant if any proof of petitioner's predisposition to commit an illegal act, the criminal character of which a defendant is presumed to know. It may indicate a predisposition to view sexually oriented photographs that are responsive to his sexual tastes; but evidence that merely indicates a generic inclination to act within a broad range, not all of which is criminal, is of little probative value in establishing predisposition.

Furthermore, petitioner was acting within the law at the time he received these magazines. Receipt through the mails of sexually explicit depictions of children for noncommercial use did not become illegal under federal law until May 1984, and Nebraska had no law that forbade petitioner's possession of such material until 1988. Evidence of predisposition to do what once was lawful is not, by itself, sufficient to show predisposition to do what is now illegal, for there is a common understanding that most people obey the law even when they disapprove of it. This obedience may reflect a generalized respect for legality or the fear of prosecution, but for whatever reason, the law's prohibitions are matters of consequence. Hence, the fact that petitioner legally ordered and received the Bare Boys magazines does little to further the Government's burden of proving that petitioner was predisposed to commit a criminal act. This is particularly true given petitioner's unchallenged testimony that he did not know until they arrived that the magazines would depict minors.

The prosecution's evidence gathered during the investigation also fails to carry the Government's burden. Petitioner's responses to the many communications prior to the ultimate criminal act were at most indicative of certain personal inclinations, including a predisposition to view photographs of preteen sex and a willingness to promote a given agenda by supporting lobbying organizations. Even so, petitioner's responses hardly support an inference that he would commit the crime of receiving child pornography through the mails. Furthermore, a person's inclinations and "fantasies . . . are his own and beyond the reach of government. . . ."

On the other hand, the strong arguable inference is that, by waving the banner of individual rights and disparaging the legitimacy and constitutionality of efforts to restrict the availability of sexually explicit materials, the Government not only excited petitioner's interest in sexually explicit materials banned by law but also exerted substantial pressure on petitioner to obtain and read such material as part of a fight against censorship and the infringement of individual rights. For instance, HINT described itself as an organization founded to protect and promote sexual freedom and freedom of choice and stated that the most appropriate means to accomplish [its] objectives is to promote honest dialogue among concerned individuals and to continue its lobbying efforts with State Legislators. These lobbying efforts were to be financed through catalog sales. Mailings from the equally fictitious American Hedonist Society, and the correspondence from the nonexistent Carl Long, endorsed these themes.

Similarly, the two solicitations in the spring of 1987 raised the spectre of censorship while suggesting that petitioner ought to be allowed to do what he had been solicited to do. The mailing from the Customs Service referred to the worldwide ban and intense enforcement on this type of material, observed that what was legal and commonplace is now an underground and secretive service, and emphasized that [t]his environment forces us to take extreme measures to ensure delivery. The Postal Service solicitation described the concern about child pornography as hysterical nonsense, decried international censorship, and assured petitioner, based on consultation with American solicitors, that an order that had been posted could not be opened for inspection without authorization of a judge. It further asked petitioner to affirm that he was not a Government agent attempting to entrap the mail order company or its customers. In these particulars, both Government solicitations suggested that receiving this material was something that petitioner ought to be allowed to do.

Petitioner's ready response to these solicitations cannot be enough to establish beyond reasonable doubt that he was predisposed, prior to the Government acts intended to create predisposition, to commit the crime of receiving child pornography through the mails. The evidence that petitioner was ready and willing to commit the offense came only after the Government had devoted 2 1/2 years to convincing him that he had or should have the right to engage in the very behavior proscribed by law. Rational jurors could not say beyond a reasonable doubt that petitioner possessed the requisite predisposition prior to the Government's investigation and that it existed independent of the Government's many and varied approaches to petitioner. * * *

Law enforcement officials go too far when they implant in the mind of an innocent person the disposition to commit the alleged offense and induce its commission in order that they may prosecute. * * * When the Government's quest for convictions leads to the apprehension of an otherwise law-abiding citizen who, if left to his own devices, likely would have never run afoul of the law, the courts should intervene.

Because we conclude that this is such a case and that the prosecution failed, as a matter of law, to adduce evidence to support the jury verdict that petitioner was predisposed, independent of the Government's acts and beyond a reasonable doubt, to violate the law by receiving child pornography through the mails, we reverse the Court of Appeals' judgment affirming the conviction of Keith Jacobson.

It is so ordered.

JUSTICE O'CONNOR, with whom THE CHIEF JUSTICE and JUSTICE KENNEDY join, and with whom JUSTICE SCALIA joins except as to Part II, dissenting.

Keith Jacobson was offered only two opportunities to buy child pornography through the mail. Both times, he ordered. Both times, he asked for opportunities to buy more. He needed no Government agent to coax, threaten, or persuade him; no one played on his sympathies, friendship, or suggested that his committing the crime would further a greater good. In fact, no Government agent even contacted him face to face. The Government contends that from the enthusiasm with which Mr. Jacobson responded to the chance to commit a crime, a reasonable jury could permissibly infer beyond a reasonable doubt that he was predisposed to commit the crime. I agree.

The first time the Government sent Mr. Jacobson a catalog of illegal materials, he ordered a set of photographs advertised as picturing young boys in sex action fun. He enclosed the following note with his order: I received your brochure and decided to place an order. If I like your product, I will order more later. For reasons undisclosed in the record, Mr. Jacobson's order was never delivered.

The second time the Government sent a catalog of illegal materials, Mr. Jacobson ordered a magazine called Boys Who Love Boys, described as: 11 year old and 14 year old boys get it on in every way possible. Oral, anal sex and heavy masturbation. If you love boys, you will be delighted with this. Along with his order, Mr. Jacobson sent the following note: Will order other items later. I want to be discreet in order to protect you and me.

Government agents admittedly did not offer Mr. Jacobson the chance to buy child pornography right away. Instead, they first sent questionnaires in order to make sure that he was generally interested in the subject matter. Indeed, a cold call in such a business would not only risk rebuff and suspicion, but might also shock and offend the uninitiated, or expose minors to suggestive materials. Mr. Jacobson's responses to the questionnaires gave the investigators reason to think he would be interested in photographs depicting preteen sex. * * *

The rule that preliminary Government contact can create a predisposition has the potential to be misread by lower courts as well as criminal investigators as requiring that the Government must have sufficient evidence of a defendant's predisposition before it ever seeks to contact him. Surely the Court cannot intend to impose such a requirement, for it would mean that the Government must have a reasonable suspicion of criminal activity before it begins an investigation, a condition that we have never before imposed. The Court denies that its new rule will affect run-of-the-mill sting operations, and one hopes that it means what it says. Nonetheless, after this case, every defendant will claim that something the Government agent did before soliciting the crime created a predisposition that was not there before. For example, a bribetaker will claim that the description of the amount of money available was so enticing that it implanted a disposition to accept the bribe later offered. A drug buyer will claim that the description of the drug's purity and effects was so tempting that it created the urge to try it for the first time. In short, the Court's opinion could be read to prohibit the Government from advertising the seductions of criminal activity as part of its sting operation, for fear of creating a predisposition in its suspects. That limitation would be especially likely to hamper sting operations such as this one, which mimic the advertising done by genuine purveyors of pornography. No doubt the Court would protest that its opinion does not stand for so broad a proposition, but the apparent lack of a principled basis for distinguishing these scenarios exposes a flaw in the more limited rule the Court today adopts.

The Court's rule is all the more troubling because it does not distinguish between Government conduct that merely highlights the temptation of the crime itself, and Government conduct that threatens, coerces, or leads a suspect to commit a crime in order to fulfill some other obligation. For example, in *Sorrells*, the Government agent repeatedly asked for illegal liquor, coaxing the defendant to accede on the ground that one former war buddy would get liquor for another. In *Sherman*, the Government agent played on the defendant's sympathies, pretending to be going through drug withdrawal and begging the defendant to relieve his distress by helping him buy drugs.

The Government conduct in this case is not comparable. * * *

C. OTHER DEFENSE THEORIES

In this last section, we consider a few less traditional criminal law defenses (or, more accurately, defense theories), such as "black rage," the "cultural defense," and "rotten social background." While these defense theories are not widely accepted by the courts, sometimes these theories are allowed to the defendant's great benefit.

1. BLACK RAGE

BLACK RAGE CONFRONTS THE LAW

Paul Harris, 1997[a]

What is the black rage defense? It is a legal strategy that centers on the racial oppression experienced by the defendant. It is an attempt to explain to the judge and jury how the defendant's environment contributed to his or her crime. It shows how concrete instances of racial discrimination impacted on the mental state of the defendant.

It is essential to understand that the black rage defense is not an independent, freestanding defense. That is, one cannot argue that a defendant should be acquitted of murdering his boss because the boss fired him out of racial prejudice. The innovation inherent in the black rage defense is that it merges racial oppression with more conventional criminal defenses.

---

[a] Reprinted with permission from NYU Press.

The law has always recognized state-of-mind defenses. For example, if a person is insane at the time of the criminal act, he can raise his mental condition as a defense. So if, in the above example, the white boss's racist behavior caused the black worker to lose the ability to control himself, a defense of diminished capacity would be allowed. Such a defense would reduce first-degree murder to second-degree murder or manslaughter. Another example is a young African American surrounded by three skinheads wearing Nazi symbols and calling him "nigger." If he pulls a gun and shoots one of them, he can raise a self-defense claim. As part of the defense he would be allowed to argue that given his experience with racists it was "reasonable" for him to assume that he was in danger of serious bodily injury, and therefore it was legally justifiable to shoot before he was actually attacked.

State-of-mind defenses allow us to bring the racial reality of America into the court by presenting "social context" or "social framework" evidence. I have also described it to judges as "social reality" or "racial reality" evidence. The phrase "black rage defense" describes a lawyer's gestalt, a theory of the case, an all-encompassing strategy that uses racial reality evidence to establish self-defense, diminished capacity, insanity, mistake of fact, duress, or other state-of-mind defenses allowed by the criminal law.

In a larger sense, the black rage defense educates the judge and jury about society's role in contributing to the criminal act. It is part of a growing body of recognized criminal defenses that have forced the courts to consider the effects of environmental hardship. The Vietnam Vet Syndrome and post-traumatic stress disorder used to defend veterans scarred by the war in Vietnam and African American teenagers scarred by the war in urban America illustrates state-of-mind defenses rooted in social reality. The battered woman defense parallels the black rage defense, in introducing evidence of gender oppression in defense of women charged with crimes of violence against their abusive husbands and boyfriends. The cultural defense, another rapidly growing legal strategy, uses evidence of a defendant's culture (e.g., Laotian and Vietnamese refugees, Chinese immigrants, or Native Americans) to explain his or her state-of-mind in defense or mitigation of criminal charges. * * *

* * * In a riot situation where a defendant injures someone and is charged with attempted murder, a traditional defense is to argue that the defendant did not have the "specific intent to kill." In these situations attorneys have presented evidence of racial tension leading up to the riot in order to show that their clients were caught up in the violence, and that although they attacked people they did not intend to kill anyone. Therefore, they argue, the defendants may be guilty of assault but not attempted murder. The epitome of this type of case took place during the 1992 riot that rocked Los Angeles after the Rodney King verdicts. It

involved the prosecution of a young African American man named Damian Williams for smashing a brick into the head of a white truck driver Reginald Denny, an incident videotaped by a local news helicopter and shown on television in every city in America. The South-Central Los Angeles riots were black rage in action. Williams was consumed by that anger and his defense team took on the task of making that rage understandable to a jury.

The fires of 1992 find their kindling in the economic hopelessness and political resignation that is daily reality for residents in South-Central. They were fueled by institutional racism and continual acts of police misconduct. In 1990 alone, the City of Los Angeles paid victims of police abuse over a million dollars. Those who did not believe the police were capable of systematic unconstitutional behavior were shocked on March 3, 1991, to see a videotape of policemen repeatedly clubbing and kicking Rodney King. Two weeks later, a fifteen-year-old African American girl, Latasha Harlins, was shot to death by a middle-aged Korean American woman grocer, Soon Ja Du, after a dispute in a South Los Angeles grocery store. In November 1991 Soon Ja Du, convicted of manslaughter, was given probation, community service, and a five thousand dollar fine. California State Senator Diane Watson responded to the extremely lenient sentence by saying, "This might be the time bomb that explodes." Two weeks later, Los Angeles police officers fatally shot a twenty-eight-year-old black man, Henry Peco, causing a standoff with more than a hundred residents of the Imperial Court housing project in Watts. Two months later, the trial of the four policemen charged with assaulting King began, after the case was moved from Los Angeles to the primarily white, conservative venue of Simi Valley.

On April 29, 1992, a jury devoid of African Americans returned a verdict of not guilty on all charges except one count of excessive force against officer Lawrence Powell. The verdict was announced on live television. More than two thousand people gathered for a peaceful rally at the First African Methodist Episcopal Church in South-Central. But other residents took to the streets. There was a small confrontation between police and angry people at the intersection of Florence and Normandie in South-Central. The police left and a mob furious at the not guilty verdicts poured into the area. Reginald Denny was driving his large truck through the intersection. Bricks were thrown into his windows. As he came to a stop he was pulled from the truck and beaten. A television helicopter videotaped the scene. Twenty-nine-year-old Henry Watson was seen with his foot on Denny's neck as he lay on the ground. Nineteen-year-old Damian Williams was videotaped as he smashed a brick against Denny's head and strutted away in celebration. Denny managed to crawl back into his truck, where sympathetic blacks climbed into the cab of the vehicle to help him. One person held him in her arms while another man drove the truck to a hospital, saving Denny's life.

The riots swept through Los Angeles and nearby areas. Fifty-eight people were reported killed. There were more than two thousand injuries, more than seven thousand fires, $3 billion worth of damage, and 12,111 arrests. Though at least as many Latinos as blacks were arrested, the events were perceived nationally as a black riot. Many, if not most, of the participants were burning and looting out of economic envy and class rage, but there is no question that the injustice of the not guilty verdicts was the catalyst.

Williams and Watson were charged with the beatings of Denny and seven other motorists. Included in the charges were attempted murder and aggravated mayhem, both of which carry life imprisonment. A defense committee called "Free the LA Four" was formed for them and two other defendants. Williams was fortunate to obtain the services of an outstanding lawyer, Edi M.O. Faal. Faal was born in Gambia, West Africa, and trained at Middle Temple Inn of Court in London, where he became a barrister. A dignified-looking man in his late thirties, he was highly regarded among his peers for both his legal ability and his political acumen. His primary strategy was to show that any criminal acts Williams committed were a result of the unthinking emotion generated by the riot.

In early 1993 the four police officers who beat King were tried in federal court for violating his civil rights. Two were acquitted, but Officer Powell and Sergeant Stacy Koon were convicted. Facing a maximum of ten years and a $250,000 fine, they each received a thirty-month sentence. Two weeks later, Williams and Watson went to trial in front of a racially mixed jury consisting of four blacks, four Latinos, three whites, and one Asian.

Faal, with the aid of Wilma Shanks and David Lynn, attempted a two-pronged strategy that can be described as "he didn't do it, but if he did, he didn't do what the prosecutor is charging him with." Once in a while, a jury will accept this defense when they recognize that the defendant has committed a crime, but that the district attorney is guilty of overcharging. In Williams's case, Faal argued that Williams was mistakenly identified as the perpetrator. However, even if the jury believed that his client was the perpetrator, he argued that they should still find him not guilty of the two most serious crimes because he did not specifically intend to kill or permanently disfigure Denny.

Faal delivered a six-hour closing argument over two days. He had to go over all the evidence regarding each of the people Williams had been charged with assaulting. The *Los Angeles Times* described his closing as one that combined "sarcasm, eloquence, indignation and wit." After putting forth the weak defense of mistaken identification, Faal began a persuasive discussion of the riot and how the collective frenzy of the group was responsible for his client's acts. His legal point was quite clear:

in order to convict Williams of attempted murder and aggravated mayhem, the jury had to find premeditation and specific intent. Faal had presented as an expert witness a local sociologist named Armando Morales. Morales testified to the phenomenon of mob psychology, in which individuals are caught up in the "mass hysteria and mass convulsions" of the crowd. People act without reflection, without rationally considering what they are doing; they act impulsively, unpredictably. Faal tied Morales's testimony to the riot and put it all in the social context of a community's frustrated and indignant reaction to the not guilty verdicts of the four police officers.

> We know that on April 29, 1992, many people in many communities; Black, White, Hispanic, experienced tremendous disappointment from the verdicts that came down from Simi Valley. I'm talking about the acquittal of the police officers that were accused of beating Rodney King.
>
> People near Florence and Normandie congregated to grieve together or to express their disappointments together. The police came, there was a slight confrontation, the police left. A mob developed. The mob, true to its name which is a mob, got into a frenzy. People started acting in manners that they would not act otherwise and that whole situation became the 1992 riots, the L.A. Riots.
>
> People caught up in that frenzy were acting out their frustration, their anger, their disappointment. They were so consumed with emotions that they could not have rationally been entertaining the type of reflective thought which gives rise to specific intent to kill or to disfigure.

The defense was in the favorable situation of being able to contrast the injustice of the Simi Valley verdicts on assault charges against the police with the more serious charges of attempted murder and mayhem against their clients. Earl Broady, counsel for codefendant Watson, specifically told the jury that the defendants were in court because four L.A. policemen had been found not guilty of beating Rodney King. This was strongly contested by prosecutor Janet Moore:

> I say Mr. Faal and Mr. Broady are dead wrong. We are in court because of what these two men chose to do on April 29, 1992. They have no one else to blame but themselves.
>
> They are here because they acted in a violent and unconscionable way. They are not here because we are holding them responsible for the entire Los Angeles riot.

Faal was sophisticated in his concluding words. Instead of referring specifically to the Simi Valley verdict he talked about "justice," and he urged the racially mixed jury to rely on their personal experiences in coming to a fair result. His underlying theme was that the riot was caused by an injustice, and that by their verdict they could balance the scales of justice.

> Ladies and gentlemen, before I conclude the closing argument that I am giving on behalf [of] Mr. Damian Monroe Williams I have to remind you of a few things: number one, that justice does not exist in a vacuum. It's not a concept that you say justice and just put it in isolation.
>
> Justice exists in the real world. The court has given you the law to evaluate and the law to apply, and you are to evaluate the facts of this case. And in evaluating the facts and coming to your determination as to what facts have been proven and what facts have not been proven, you are not relying on the law alone, you are relying on your common sense. You are relying on your personal experiences and you are relying on your sense of fairness and justice in evaluating the facts of this case.

At the end of Faal's closing argument, supporters in the courtroom stood and applauded, some even wept. As Faal left the courtroom, he was embraced. People appreciated that throughout the long trial he had consciously articulated the frustration and rage of the African American community.

The jury deliberated for more than two weeks. They acquitted Williams of attempted murder and aggravated mayhem, the two charges that carried life imprisonment. They also acquitted him of all the other felonies except one—simple mayhem. He was also convicted of four misdemeanor assaults. Williams was sentenced to eight years in prison. As of 1995, he was in Pelican Bay—California's notorious high-tech, maximum security prison where conditions are so bad that a federal judge held that it had violated the cruel and unusual punishment prohibitions of the Constitution.

Reginald Denny seemed to understand the social context of the crimes against him. He said, "Things could have been a lot worse. I mean the next step for me would have been death. But I've been given a chance, and so I'm gonna extend that courtesy towards some guys who obviously were a little bit confused."

One woman, Cynthia Henry, who lived near the now infamous intersection, spoke for many people when she said, "I'm happy with the verdicts. I know that what they did was wrong, but it was in the heat of passion. I was watching what happened [in the King trial] on TV, and it hurt me to see that. But I could understand because I was angry too."

NOTE

Arguing black rage may lead to favorable results for individual black defendants, but do such arguments harm the greater Black community by perpetrating negative stereotypes about Blacks as deviant criminals? Anthony Alfieri argues that criminal defense attorneys should forego racialized narratives like the group contagion theory used by Edi Faal, lead counsel for Damian Williams, because such narratives harm the greater Black community by reinforcing negative stereotypes. Anthony V. Alfieri, *Defending Racial Violence*, 95 COLUM. L. REV. 1301 (1995). Alfieri grounds his argument in legal ethics, arguing that "criminal defense lawyers representing Black males in cases of racially-motivated violence bear a race-conscious responsibility to forego narratives or stories that construct racial identity in terms of individual, group, or community deviance." *Id.* at 1306. Abbe Smith disagrees, arguing that the rules of professional responsibility require criminal defense attorneys to zealously represent their clients. Abbe Smith, *Burdening the Least of Us: "Race-Conscious" Ethics in Criminal Defense*, 77 TEX. L. REV. 1585 (1999). Smith explains that a criminal defense attorney who puts the interests of the Black community over the interests of his or her client violates this duty. *Id.* at 1601.

Paul Harris explains that the black rage "defense" is not really a new defense but is a strategy that simply uses "social framework" evidence to support traditional criminal defenses, such as self-defense, diminished capacity, insanity, mistake, and duress. Social framework evidence is used in many other contexts as explained in the excerpt by Neil Vidmar and Regina Schuller, *supra*.

2. THE "CULTURAL DEFENSE"

PEOPLE V. APHAYLATH

Court of Appeals of New York
68 N.Y.2d 945, 502 N.E.2d 998, 510 N.Y.S.2d 83 (1986)

Defendant, a Laotian refugee living in this country for approximately two years, was indicted and tried for the intentional murder of his Laotian wife of one month. At trial, defendant attempted to establish the affirmative defense of extreme emotional disturbance to mitigate the homicide on the theory that the stresses resulting from his status of a refugee caused a significant mental trauma, affecting his mind for a substantial period of time, simmering in the unknowing subconscious and then inexplicably coming to the fore. Although the immediate cause for the defendant's loss of control was his jealousy over his wife's apparent preference for an ex-boyfriend, the defense argued that under Laotian culture the conduct of the victim wife in displaying affection for another man and receiving phone calls from an unattached man brought shame on defendant and his family sufficient to trigger defendant's loss of control.

The defense was able to present some evidence of the Laotian culture through the cross-examination of two prosecution witnesses and through the testimony of defendant himself, although he was hampered by his illiteracy in both his native tongue and English. Defendant's ability to adequately establish his defense was impermissibly curtailed by the trial court's exclusion of the proffered testimony of two expert witnesses concerning the stress and disorientation encountered by Laotian refugees in attempting to assimilate into the American culture. It appears from the record before us that the sole basis on which the court excluded the expert testimony was because "neither one * * * was going to be able to testify as to anything specifically relating to this defendant." It is unclear from this ruling whether the Trial Judge determined that she had no discretion to allow the testimony because the experts had no knowledge of this particular defendant or that she declined to exercise her discretion because of the experts' lack of knowledge of the defendant or his individual background and characteristics. Under either interpretation, however, the exclusion of this expert testimony as a matter of law was erroneous because the admissibility of expert testimony that is probative of a fact in issue does not depend on whether the witness has personal knowledge of a defendant or a defendant's particular characteristics. Whether or not such testimony is sufficiently relevant to have probative value is a determination to be made by the Trial Judge in the exercise of her sound discretion.

Accordingly, because the court's ruling was not predicated on the appropriate standard and the defendant may have been deprived of an opportunity to put before the jury information relevant to his defense, a new trial must be ordered.

CULTURAL EVIDENCE AND MALE VIOLENCE: ARE FEMINIST AND MULTICULTURALIST REFORMERS ON A COLLISION COURSE IN CRIMINAL COURTS?

Holly Maguigan
70 N.Y.U. L. Rev. 36 (1995)

Introduction

The American criminal justice system faces an important question: Can the courts permit defendants to introduce evidence of cultural background without condoning violence by men against women and children? In those trials in which cultural evidence is received, is the information entitled to such unquestioning deference that its receipt signals the recognition of a "cultural defense" to male violence? Two cases illustrate the problem.

At his 1988 murder trial in Brooklyn, Chinese immigrant Dong Lu Chen did not deny that he had killed his wife, also an immigrant from China, by bludgeoning her with a claw hammer. Instead, he offered evidence that he had killed her after learning of her infidelity. The trial court admitted defense testimony from an anthropologist that Chen's rage and violent impulses were normal in his culture of origin. The cultural expert testified that in Chen's village in China others would have intervened before the event resulted in a killing, and that in his new country Chen was removed from the moderating influences that would have prevented the homicide. Largely on the basis of the cultural evidence, the defendant was convicted of manslaughter, rather than murder, and sentenced to probation.

Similarly, at his 1981 rape trial in Los Angeles, African American Jacinto Rhines did not deny that he had had intercourse with the complainant, who was also African American and who testified that the defendant raped her by using physical force and an intimidating tone of voice. Instead, the defense contended that Rhines made a reasonable mistake about the complainant's consent. The defendant proffered testimony from a psychologist that there are cultural differences among races and that Black people speak to each other very loudly. In this case, however, the trial court excluded the proffered cultural information. The defendant was convicted of rape and the exclusion of the cultural evidence was upheld on appeal.

Chen and Rhines frame this Article's inquiry: whether the work of some reformers—toward increasing judicial responsiveness to claims of pluralism raised by defendants who are not part of the dominant culture—conflicts with the goals of other reformers, who focus their efforts on increasing the court's vigor in prosecuting crimes of family and anti-woman violence. Some observers see multiculturalist and feminist values on a collision course in the criminal courts. The perceived risk is that two overlapping groups of outsider voices—those of people not from the dominant culture (including women) and those of women (including women not from the dominant culture)—cannot be heard simultaneously in this country's criminal courts. * * *

I. The Misplaced Focus on a Separate Cultural Defense as the Cause of Tension Between Feminist and Multiculturalist Reform Goals

Advocates of a new, separately defined defense argue that its recognition is necessary to overcome the injustice of holding defendants from different cultures to the monolithic standards of the dominant one. Some opponents of the creation of a separate defense argue that recognition of pluralism, at the expense of the presumption that all know the law's requirements, would lead to relativism and chaos. Others, including some feminists scholars, argue that such a defense has already been recognized, but should be rejected because it condones violence against women.

Discussion of these issues is not, in fact, joined in any other than a purely theoretical fashion. There is not and will not be a separate cultural defense because as a practical matter such a defense can be neither defined nor implemented. In short, debate over a new cultural defense is misguided because the use of cultural information is not new, a workable legal definition of culture is impossible to develop, and the information is not being offered in court to create a separate defense. The current separate-defense debate obscures the real, practical problems of accomplishing reform goals that appear to be in competition with each other.

The multiculturalist reform goal is a system that takes a more pluralistic approach to the assessment of blame and the imposition of punishment. The operation of the current criminal justice system results in higher conviction rates and longer sentences for outsider defendants than for defendants who are part of the dominant culture. Scholars have suggested that at least part of the explanation for those disparities is that the present system does not reflect the shared values of a multicultural society but instead reinforces the white, traditionally male-identified values of the dominant culture. * * *

In apparent tension with a multiculturalist reform agenda is the feminist goal of vigilant protection of a value only recently and tentatively recognized by this criminal justice system: the right of women to be free from physical violence at the hands of men. Some observers believe that courts' receipt of cultural information, when offered to excuse or mitigate responsibility for violence against women, leads to dispositions that condone that violence. Simply admitting the evidence is seen as tantamount to excusing the criminal conduct. Some authors suggest that a cultural defense, if it were used to excuse or mitigate punishment for male violence against women and children, would violate international human rights norms. In this theoretical debate, a cultural defense is seen both as a quick-fix solution to the problem of pluralistic ignorance and as anathema to feminist reform goals. * * *

Many observers, both advocates and opponents of a formal "cultural defense," share the belief that increasing numbers of people accused of crime in this country are asserting such a defense. They view the phenomenon as a by-product of a recent "influx" of immigrants, mainly Asians, to this country. Some observers incorrectly posit a situation in which defendants use "cultural defenses" primarily in family violence cases. In fact, the use of cultural information is not a new phenomenon. It is not limited to immigrants. It does not occur primarily in cases involving violence against women or children. Finally, most culturally different defendants who try to introduce background evidence do not assert a freestanding cultural defense. * * *

For many years, cultural background evidence has been proffered to challenge the sufficiency of prosecution evidence regarding a defendant's state of mind. In guilty pleas, the information has been used to convince prosecutors and courts that, because they lacked the mens rea necessary for a conviction on the top count charged, defendants should be permitted to plead to lesser offenses or should receive lighter sentences than would seem warranted in the absence of cultural information. In trials, the information—often in the form of both lay and expert testimony—has been offered for a similar purpose: to demonstrate that the defendant's mens rea differed from that required for conviction. The information has been proffered in connection with both excuse and justification defenses.

The necessity of introducing evidence of a defendant's background results from the reality that individuals with decisionmaking roles in the American criminal courts are often culturally different from those accused of crime. A study of courtroom dynamics in the 1960s yielded the following conclusion:

> Examination of the courtroom culture . . . indicates that several factors work to the disadvantage of the culturally different in the trial process. These factors are: the value system of the legal profession, the procedures by which juries are selected, the value system of the jurors, the lack of articulation in communication between the culturally different and the professionals and nonprofessionals composing the court, and the negative stereotypes of cultural minorities held by the professionals.

In order to overcome "the lack of . . . communication between the culturally different and the professionals and nonprofessionals composing the court," defendants offer information about their backgrounds. This information, sometimes called "social framework evidence," is meant to maximize the information available to those charged with adjudication:

> The purpose of "social framework evidence" . . . is to provide the fact-finder, usually a jury, with information about the social and psychological context in which contested adjudicative facts occurred. It is presumed that knowledge about the context will help the fact-finder interpret the contested adjudicative facts.

Defendants use cultural evidence to give dominant-culture courts an information framework within which to assess questions of individual culpability under existing criminal law definitions. * * *

It is when "social framework" evidence, in the form of cultural information, is offered by men accused of family or anti-woman violence that there appears to be competition between feminist and multiculturalist values. The theoretical debate about recognition of a formal cultural defense misses that point. A separate cultural defense is not the cause of a conflict between multiculturalism and women's rights in criminal trials. Nor is it the answer to the current problems defendants face when trying to use cultural information. The real issue facing the courts is the adequacy of the current mechanisms to receive cultural information and to do so without endorsing family violence.

(MIS)IDENTIFYING CULTURE: ASIAN WOMEN AND THE "CULTURAL DEFENSE"

Leti Volpp
17 Harv. Women's L.J. 57 (1994)[a]

I. INTRODUCTION

The "cultural defense" is a legal strategy that defendants use in attempts to excuse criminal behavior or to mitigate culpability based on a lack of requisite mens rea. Defendants may also use "cultural defenses" to present evidence relating to state of mind when arguing self defense or mistake of fact. The theory underlying the defense is that the defendant, usually a recent immigrant to the United States, acted according to the dictates of his or her "culture," and therefore deserves leniency. There is, however, no formal "cultural defense"; individual defense attorneys and judges use their discretion to present or consider cultural factors affecting the mental state or culpability of a defendant. In my discussion of this strategy, I focus on the significance of its use for Asian women.

When examining the "cultural defense" and its effect on Asian women, I write from the subject position of an Asian American woman. I also write with the benefit of collective insight of Asian American women working with the Asian Women's Shelter in San Francisco, who created the "Cultural Defense" Study Group. The Study Group arose from concern about the use of the "cultural defense" and from the pressing need for Asian American women to articulate a position on its use.

The "cultural defense" presents several complex problems inherent in essentializing a culture and its effect on a particular person's behavior. I analyze the use of the defense in two cases in order to illustrate problems with the defense and situations in which allowing cultural information into the courtroom might be appropriate. I argue that any testimony about a defendant's cultural background must embody an accurate and personal portrayal of cultural factors used to explain an individual's state of mind and should not be used to fit an individual's behavior into perceptions about group behavior. * * *

II. INVISIBLE WOMAN: THE PEOPLE V. DONG LU CHEN

In 1989, Brooklyn Supreme Court Justice Edward Pincus sentenced Chinese immigrant Dong Lu Chen to five years probation for using a claw hammer to smash the skull of his wife, Jian Wan Chen. The defense sought to demonstrate that the requisite state of mind was lacking by introducing evidence about Chen's cultural background. After listening to a white anthropologist "expert," Burton Pasternak, provide a "cultural defense" for Dong Lu Chen, Pincus concluded that traditional Chinese values about adultery and loss of manhood drove Chen to kill his wife.

The defense introduced most of the information about Dong Lu Chen's cultural background through Pasternak's expert testimony. Defense Attorney Stewart Orden presented Pasternak with a lengthy hypothetical designed to evoke a response about the "difference" between how an "American" and a "Mainland Chinese individual" might respond to a particular set of events. This hypothetical was in fact a history of Dong Lu Chen and provided the defense's explanation for why he killed Jian Wan Chen. * * *

In September, 1986, the Chen family immigrated to the United States. While Dong Lu Chen worked as a dish washer in Maryland, Jian Wan Chen and the three children stayed in New York. During a visit when Jian Wan Chen refused to have sex with him and "became abusive," Dong Lu Chen became suspicious she was having an affair. He returned to Maryland, burdened with the stress of his wife's assumed infidelity.

In June, 1987, Dong Lu Chen moved to New York. On August 24 he rushed into his wife's bedroom and grabbed her breasts and vaginal area. They felt more developed to him and he took that as a sign she was having affairs. When he confronted her the next day, she said she was seeing another man. On September 7, when he again confronted her and said he wanted to have sex, "she said I won't let you hold me because I have other guys who will do this." His head felt dizzy, and he "pressed her down and asked her for how long had this been going on. She responded, for three months." Confused and dizzy, he picked something up and hit her a couple of times on the head. He passed out.

After presenting the above "facts" as part of his hypothetical, Orden asked Pasternak if this history was consistent with reactions "under normal conditions for people from Mainland China." Pasternak responded:

> Yes. Well, of course, I can't comment on the mental state of this particular person. I am not a psychiatrist. I don't know this particular person. But the events that you have described, the reactions that you have described would not be unusual at all for Chinese in that situation, for a normal Chinese in that situation. Whether this person is normal or not I have no idea. . . . If it was a normal person, it's not the United States, they would react very violently. They might very well have confusion. It would be very likely to be a chaotic situation. I've witnessed such situations myself.

Orden also asked Pasternak to verify that a "normal Chinese person from Mainland China" would react in a more extreme and much quicker way than an "American" to the history as given in the hypothetical. Pasternak answered:

> In general terms, I think that one could expect a Chinese to react in a much more volatile, violent way to those circumstances than someone from our own society. I think there's no doubt about it.

This initial testimony highlights some important issues. First, the distinction Orden and Pasternak draw between "American," "someone from our own society," and "Chinese" implies that "Chinese" and "American" are two utterly distinct categories: "American" does not encompass immigrant Chinese. This dichotomy rests on the lingering perception of Asians in America as somehow "foreign," as existing in "America" while not being "American." Importantly, the perspective that Chinese living in the United States are not "American" is the very basis for the assertion of the "cultural defense," on the grounds that someone from a distinctly "non-American" culture should not be judged by "American" standards. * * *

After dichotomizing "American" and "Chinese," Orden and Pasternak's second step in creating a "cultural defense" was to assert that a man considered "normal" in the category "Chinese" would react very differently from someone in the category "American" to the belief that his wife was having an affair. Their third step collapsed the history of a particular person with specific mental problems into the category "normal person from Mainland China." * * *

Continuing his description of Chinese familial life and values, Pasternak asserted that "casual sex, adultery, which is an even more extreme violation, and divorce" are perceived as deviations from these social mores. "In the Chinese context," adultery by a woman was considered a kind of "stain" upon the man, indicating that he had lost "the most minimal standard of control" over her. Pasternak contrasted the condemnation of adultery in China with the United States, "where we take this thing normally in the course of an event." He claimed that the Chinese woman was likely to be "thrown out" and that both parties would have difficulty remarrying. * * *

Pasternak's bizarre portrayal of divorce and adultery in China in fact had little basis in reality. When Assistant District Attorney Arthur Rigby pressed Pasternak for his sources during cross-examination, Pasternak mentioned fieldwork he did between the 1960s and 1988 (he could not remember the title of his own article), incidents he saw, such as a man chasing a woman with a cleaver, and stories he heard. He admitted he could not recall a single instance in which a man in China killed his wif or having ever heard about such an event, yet he suggested that this w accepted in China. Pasternak's description of "Chinese society" thus neither substantiated by fact nor supported by his own testimon description was in fact his own American fantasy.

During his cross-examination of Pasternak, Rigby attempted to undermine Chen's "cultural defense" by deconstructing Pasternak's identification of "American," his description of Chinese as insulated from Western influence and his depiction of Chinese Americans as completely non-assimilated. Rigby began his questioning by asking, "What would you consider your average American?" Pasternak responded, "I think you are looking at your average American."

With this statement Pasternak situated his own subjective position as the definition of the "average American." In other words, Pasternak defined the "average American" to be a white, professional male. By situating himself as the "average American," Pasternak exposed his subjective identification as the "average American" against whom the "foreigner," Dong Lu Chen, was to be compared.

* * * Justice Pincus was swayed by the "persuasiveness" of Pasternak's testimony about the "cultural" roots of Dong Lu Chen's actions. He held:

> Were this crime committed by the defendant as someone who was born and raised in America, or born elsewhere but primarily raised in America, even in the Chinese American community, the Court [*sic*] would have been constrained to find the defendant guilty of manslaughter in the first degree. But, this Court [*sic*] cannot ignore . . . the very cogent forceful testimony of Doctor Pasternak, who is, perhaps, the greatest expert in America on China and interfamilial relationships.

Pincus specifically found significant Pasternak's testimony that Chen lacked a Chinese community to act as a "safety valve" to keep Chen from killing his wife. Yet the alleged motivation for Chen's actions was his "shame" and humiliation before this very same community. The inconsistency in this reasoning is self-evident. * * *

In his decision to grant probation rather than impose a jail sentence, Pincus also took other unrelated "cultural" considerations into account. Pincus believed that the possible effect of Chen's incarceration on his ~hters' marriage prospects should be a factor in determining Chen's ... Pincus told a reporter, "Now there's a stigma of shame on the ... have young, unmarried daughters. To make them ... they must make sure he succeeds so they ... olloquy Pincus indicated that he also learned ... victim":

> ... background of this individual he has also ... ly destroying his family and his family's ... e are victims in this case: The deceased is a ... g is over. The defendant is a victim, a victim

that fell through the cracks because society didn't know where or how to respond in time.

Thus Pincus was able to justify his probationary sentencing: Dong Lu Chen did not serve time for killing his wife because in balancing this action and the surrounding circumstances he was just as much a "victim" as she was.

But where was Jian Wan Chen in this story? The defense strategy rendered her invisible. She was most notably present in the testimony as a dead body and as a reputed "adulteress," bringing a "stain" upon her husband. Jian Wan Chen did not exist as a multi-faceted person but was instead flattened into the description "adulteress." Any discussion of her at trial was premised upon her characterization as a woman who provoked her husband into jealousy. How should this flattening be interpreted? This invisibility and erasure of the woman, Jian Wan Chen?

Jian Wan Chen's invisibility involved more than the disappearance of a victim in a trial focused on the guilt or innocence of a defendant. The defense presented a narrative that relied on her invisibility as an Asian woman for its logical coherence. This invisibility was manifest through the absence of Jian Wan Chen as a subject, a void that was filled only by stereotypes of the sexual relationships of "Chinese women" and an image of her silent physicality. She appeared as an object, whose silence devalued her humanity to the extent that the taking of her life did not merit a prison sentence.

Jian Wan Chen's invisibility is a legacy of an intersection of race and gender that erases the existence of women of color from the popular consciousness. Because white male citizens personify what is considered "normal" in the United States, a status as "other" that is more than one deviation away from the "norm" rarely exists in popular consciousness. The exclusion of Jian Wan Chen exemplifies the difficulty that women of color have when attempting to express themselves as holistic subjects, as Asian women whose identity lies at the intersection of multiple forms of subordination.

Applying an intersectional analysis, it is clear that what Pasternak presented as "Chinese culture" privileged race over any consideration of gender oppression. Pasternak's perspective was "male," obviating the possibility that a woman, and specifically a Chinese immigrant woman, might describe divorce, adultery and male violence within "Chinese culture" very differently. The perspective, was, of course, also "white." The "whiteness" of Pasternak's perspective allowed him to situate Dong Lu Chen in a category labelled "Chinese" diametrically opposite to Pasternak's own "average," white, male citizen position. Yet this placement ignored that Jian Wan Chen was, in fact, the person categorically opposite to Pasternak: she was Chinese, immigrant and female. Thus, the "cultural defense" served in this case to legitimize male violence against women by glossing over the gendered aspects of Pasternak's testimony about "culture."

The Chen trial suffered from a complete absence of any female perspective: Dong Lu Chen, Pasternak, Orden, Rigby and Pincus were all male. Jian Wan Chen was dead, symbolizing how ideologies that subordinate groups of people literally transpire over the body of an "other." Thus, Jian Wan Chen's invisibility is not only the product of the racist notion that "Asian life is cheap," it also is a remnant of the indifference with which many in the United States treat the epidemic of violence against women. Furthermore, the complete disregard for her life also reflected the way racism and sexism intersect to render insignificant violence against women of color, and here specifically, Asian immigrant women.

The impact of the trial and probationary sentencing resonated beyond the courtroom, sending a message to the wider community. Jian Wan Chen's life was not valued; her life was worth less than other lives; her murderer did not deserve punishment in jail. Other Chinese immigrant women living with abuse at the hand of their partners and husbands identified with Jian Wan Chen and clearly understood that violence against them by their partners and husbands had the implicit approval of the state.

The Chen decision sent a message to battered immigrant Asian women that they had no recourse against domestic violence. One battered Chinese woman told a worker at the New York Asian Women's Center, "Even thinking about that case makes me afraid. My husband told me: 'If this is the kind of sentence you get for killing your wife, I could do anything to you. I have the money for a good attorney.' " In other words, her husband could afford to hire someone to testify as an expert to bolster a "cultural defense" that legitimized his violence. * * *

INDIVIDUALIZING JUSTICE THROUGH MULTICULTURALISM: THE LIBERALS' DILEMMA[a]

Doriane Lambelet Coleman
96 Colum. L. Rev. 1093 (1996)

Introduction

In California, a Japanese-American mother drowns her two young children in the ocean at Santa Monica and then attempts to kill herself; rescuers save her before she drowns. The children's recovered bodies bear deep bruises where they struggled as their mother held them under the water. The mother later explains that in Japan, where she is from, her actions would be understood as the time-honored, customary practice of

[a] This article originally appeared at 96 Colum. L. Rev. 1093 (1996). Reprinted by permission.

parent-child suicide. She spends only one year in jail—the year she is on trial.

In New York, a Chinese-American woman is bludgeoned to death by her husband. Charged with murder, her husband explains that his conduct comports with a Chinese custom that allows husbands to dispel their shame in this way when their wives have been unfaithful. He is acquitted of murder charges.

Back in California, a young Laotian-American woman is abducted from her place of work at Fresno State University and forced to have sexual intercourse against her will. Her Hmong immigrant assailant explains that, among his tribe, such behavior not only is accepted, but expected—it is the customary way to choose a bride. He is sentenced to 120 days in jail, and his victim receives $900 in reparations.

A Somali immigrant living in Georgia allegedly cuts off her two-year old niece's clitoris, partially botching the job. The child was cut in accordance with the time-honored tradition of female circumcision; this custom attempts to ensure that girls and women remain chaste for their husbands. The State charges the woman with child abuse, but is unable to convict her.

In these cases, the defense presented, and the prosecutor or court accepted, cultural evidence as an excuse for the otherwise criminal conduct of immigrant defendants. These official decisions appear to reflect the notion that the moral culpability of an immigrant defendant should be judged according to his or her own cultural standards, rather than those of the relevant jurisdiction. Although no state has formally recognized the use of exonerating cultural evidence, some commentators and judges have labelled this strategy the "cultural defense."

The cultural defense (and the issues it raises about the rights of immigrants to retain aspects of their cultures when they come to the United States) is an important part of the larger debate about multiculturalism which currently is prominent in academic, social, and political circles. In particular, this larger debate concerns whether there is and should be a unifying American culture that guides our institutions, including the justice system, or whether the United States is and should be a culturally pluralistic nation in all respects, including in the law.

The introductory illustrations exemplify this debate in the legal arena with an unusual clarity, because they pit foreign customs and cultural practices directly against essential elements of contemporary American legal culture, including the antidiscrimination principle that is central to equal protection doctrine and related principles of universal rights that are at the foundation of feminist legal doctrine.

Allowing sensitivity to a defendant's culture to inform the application of laws to that individual is good multiculturalism. It also is good progressive criminal defense philosophy, which has as a central tenet the idea that the defendant should get as much individualized (subjective) justice as possible. The illustrations that introduce this Article may be interpreted as reflecting this sort of sensitivity on the part of some prosecutors and judges.

For legal scholars and practitioners who believe in a progressive civil and human rights agenda, these illustrations also raise an important question: What happens to the victims—almost always minority women and children—when multiculturalism and individualized justice are advanced by dispositive cultural evidence? The answer, both in theory and in practice, is stark: They are denied the protection of the criminal laws because their assailants generally go free, either immediately or within a relatively brief period of time. More importantly, victims and potential victims in such circumstances have no hope of relief in the future, either individually or as a group, because when cultural evidence is permitted to excuse otherwise criminal conduct, the system effectively is choosing to adopt a different, discriminatory standard of criminality for immigrant defendants, and hence, a different and discriminatory level of protection for victims who are members of the culture in question. This different standard may defeat the deterrent effect of the law, and it may become precedent, both for future cases with similar facts, and for the broader position that race- or national origin-based applications of the criminal law are appropriate. Thus, the use of cultural defenses is anathema to another fundamental goal of the progressive agenda, namely the expansion of legal protections for some of the least powerful members of American society: women and children.

Margaret Fung, Executive Director of the Asian-American Defense and Education Fund, provided what is perhaps the best evidence of the tension that is created for progressives by these cases. When Ms. Fung first publicly addressed the decision in *People v. Chen*, the New York spousal killing case described above, she is reported to have expressed her concern that the result was bad for Asian women and for the image of Asian-Americans: "You don't want to import [immigrant] cultural values into our judicial system . . . We don't want women victimized by backward customs . . . We don't want so-called cultural experts perpetuating certain stereotypes that may not be accurate, . . . and putting that out to the American public." Later, however, Ms. Fung was reported to have reformulated her position on the use of cultural evidence by criminal defendants: To bar the cultural defense "would promote the idea that when people come to America, they have to give up their way of doing things. That is an idea we cannot support."

In addition to highlighting the dilemma posed by these cases, Margaret Fung's reactions highlight the two-fold discriminatory effect of the cultural defense. First, to the extent that cultural evidence is used to determine the outcome of criminal cases and to excuse some perpetrators of crimes, it results in disparate treatment of immigrants and other members of American society. Second, the particular cultural norms at issue in these cases are also inherently discriminatory in that they incorporate values about the lesser status of women and children; these values are contrary to those the contemporary international progressive agenda embraces. When the American legal system chooses to recognize such traditions in the context of pursuing individualized justice for the defendant, it condones the chauvinism that is at the core of these traditions.

The question of how to resolve the competing interests that Margaret Fung's turnaround so clearly sets out—a question that I call the "Liberals' Dilemma"—is the focus of this Article. Unlike existing scholarship in the area, most of which does not appear to recognize this dilemma, it is my premise that the answer for legal (rather than moral) purposes should not be made in an ad hoc fashion, based on political and professional affiliations. Rather, I believe the law must reflect a broader, more considered resolution of this question, and that this resolution can be accomplished only by engaging in a balancing of the two substantial and conflicting interests. Thus, the defendant's interest in using cultural evidence that incorporates discriminatory norms and behaviors must be weighed against the victims' and potential victims' interests in obtaining protection and relief through a non-discriminatory application of the criminal law. Contemporary jurisprudence favors just this sort of balancing, which considers the interests of the two parties in a given case, as well as those of society generally, in determining the outcome. Using this approach, I conclude that victims' interests in this area are more compelling than those of defendants. In the process, I acknowledge that my position is contrary to that pure vein of multiculturalism that decries ethnocentrism in any form; and I agree that it also is contrary to those aspects of the liberal agenda that traditionally have sought to embrace (at least in theory) simultaneously both cultural pluralism and individual rights, including the rights of defendants and of the women and children who are often their victims. In this context, I believe that there are several reasons for choosing rights over culture.

First, the criminal justice system already affords defendants substantial opportunities to raise established, nondiscriminatory arguments in support of their innocence or of a reduced sentence.

Second, permitting the use of culture-conscious, discriminatory evidence as part of the defendant's case-in-chief distorts the substantive criminal law and affords little or no protection to victims, whose assailants are left, as a result of this distortion, relatively free from broader societal strictures. There presently is no acceptable alternative to cure this deficiency.

Third, the use of cultural evidence risks a dangerous balkanization of the criminal law, where non-immigrant Americans are subject to one set of laws and immigrant Americans to another. This is a prospect that is inconsistent not only with one of the law's most fundamental objectives, the protection of society and all of its members from harm, but also with the important human and civil rights doctrines embodied in the Equal Protection Clause. Thus, society as a whole is best served by a balance that avoids the use of discriminatory cultural evidence.

Fourth, despite the benevolent interpretation I earlier afforded the modern acceptance of immigrant cultural evidence by some prosecutors and judges, there also is the substantial concern that culture consciousness—at least of the sort that leads to discriminatory results—may not be a good thing for a judicial system that is already plagued by a racist and sexist history. As Justice Brennan commented in his dissenting opinion in *McCleskey v. Kemp*, "formal dual criminal laws may no longer be in effect, and intentional discrimination may no longer be prominent. Nonetheless . . . subtle, less consciously held racial attitudes' continue to be of concern." It is at best ironic that progressive forces would purposefully give back to the system a new and lawful opportunity to treat immigrant women, children, and other minority victims of crimes as less valuable. At worst, this trend may foreshadow a return to overtly racist decisionmaking by some prosecutors and judges. * * *

A JUSTIFICATION OF THE CULTURAL DEFENSE AS PARTIAL EXCUSE

Alison Dundes Renteln[1]

2 S. Cal. Rev. L. & Women's Stud. 437 (1993)

In pluralistic societies, culture conflict is inevitable. When some of these conflicts reach the legal system, the question arises whether the cultural background of the defendant should be admissible as evidence in a court of law. The issue is not simply whether cultural evidence can be introduced, but whether such evidence can function to exonerate a defendant.

Necessarily, cultural data is admitted into courtrooms whenever a ...re conflict case occurs—it would be impossible to exclude it entirely. ... absence of any official policy guidelines, the cultural evidence ...ifferently from one case to the next, and from one court to the ...n lead to gross injustices, in which one defendant who ... goes free, while another defendant who commits a less ...eives too harsh a punishment.

...mission of the author. For further analysis, see ALISON DUNDES ... DEFENSE (Oxford 2004).

The purpose of this essay is to offer arguments in favor of the establishment of an official "cultural defense." A cultural defense is a defense asserted by immigrants, refugees, and indigenous people based on their customs or customary law. A successful cultural defense would permit the reduction (and possible elimination) of a charge, with a concomitant reduction in punishment. The rationale behind such a claim is that an individual's behavior is influenced to such a large extent by his or her culture that either (i) the individual simply did not believe that his or her actions contravened any laws (cognitive case), or (ii) the individual was compelled to act the way he or she did (volitional case). In both cases the individual's culpability is lessened.

The reason for admitting a cultural defense lies not so much in a desire to be culturally sensitive, although that is surely a large part of it, but rather in a desire to ensure equal application of the law to all citizens. By equality I mean, not merely the desire to treat all culture conflict cases in a more uniform manner, but also the desire to treat all individuals in society as equals. As I shall argue, individual justice demands that the legal system focus on the actor as well as the act, on motive as well as intent. This, in turn, necessitates the introduction of cultural information into the courtroom. Oftentimes cultural information is brought into the courtroom by defense attorneys in the context of a pre-existing defense, such as provocation or insanity. For many reasons, however, this strategy is unsatisfactory for the generic culture conflict case. The most salient drawback is that the standards against which a defendant's actions are judged are those of "the reasonable person." But it is precisely this idea of reasonableness that lies at the heart of the conflict. As I shall argue, the actions of defendants should be judged against behavioral standards that are reasonable for a person of that culture in the context of this culture. This would balance the requirements of individual justice and cultural accommodation with the competing demands of social order and the rule of law.

It must be emphasized from the outset that the consideration of cultural evidence in no way requires that it be dispositive. A common fear is that the establishment of a cultural defense may force us to condone practices which contravene the rights of historically disenfranchised groups, including women and children. The argument seems to be that, although human rights are respected in the United States, the rest of the world is still barbaric. Ignoring the culturally patronizing overtones of such an argument, I should like to point out that sometimes it is women (and children) who benefit from the existence of cultural defenses.

More importantly, as I shall explain in more detail below, the sort of cultural defense I advocate is one which functions as a partial excuse. The advantage of such a formulation is that a demonstration of cultural influence is not sufficient to acquit. Juries must decide whether cultural factors were determinative in a defendant's behavior, and, if so, whether that is sufficient to warrant either a lesser charge or complete acquittal. By employing the cultural defense as a partial excuse, courts would be better able to fit the punishment to the crime, which is surely one of the goals of the criminal justice system. * * *

There have been some cases in which the defense counsel has advanced a defense combining the mental illness and cultural considerations all in one. Under some circumstances this approach may be necessary, because the defendant suffers from some sort of mental trauma related to his or her culture. The case of *People v. Kimura* is one such example. It provides an illustration of a case in which the cognitive insanity defense was successfully employed. The other case I shall consider, *People v. Metallides*, is an illustration of the use of the volitional insanity defense.

3. *People v. Kimura*

When Fumiko Kimura, a Japanese American living in Santa Monica, California, learned of the infidelity of her husband, she attempted oyako-shinju, parent-child suicide, by wading into the Pacific Ocean with her two children. The two children died, but she survived and was charged with first-degree murder with special circumstances which could have brought the death penalty. Oyako-shinju, while illegal in Japan, is not unheard of as a means by which a family can avoid an otherwise unacceptable social predicament. The Japanese-American community gathered a petition with over 25,000 signatures appealing to the Los Angeles County district attorney not to prosecute her, arguing that her actions were based on a different worldview. According to this worldview, it is more cruel to leave the children behind with no one to look after them than it is for the mother to take them with her to the afterlife.

Six psychiatrists testified that Kimura was suffering from temporary insanity. Some based their conclusion on her failure to distinguish between her own life and the lives of her children. Through a plea bargain her homicide charge was reduced to voluntary manslaughter and she was sentenced to one year in county jail (which she had already served), five years probation, and psychiatric counseling. She was subsequently reunited with her husband(!).

Though her attorney, Mr. Klausner, claimed that his argument relied on psychiatric testimony, commentators believe that cultural factors played a role in the process. It is worth pointing out that Kimura appears to have benefitted from a cultural defense though she had resided in the United States for several years. As she had remained culturally isolated, she had not become assimilated. This suggests that assimilation often does not occur as rapidly as many believe.

Another important point is that the children's rights dimension of this case has hardly been discussed in the literature. While the court may have been correct in considering the cultural aspects of the case, it is arguable that probation was an unjustifiably light sentence to impose.

4. *People v. Metallides*

In the Miami, Florida case of *People v. Metallides* a Greek immigrant, Kostas Metallides, killed his best friend when he found out that he had raped Kostas' daughter. Metallides' attorney, a public defender, used a temporary insanity argument based on culture. Though not recognized as a defense in Florida, the attorney relied on the "irresistible impulse" test. Metallides' attorney constructed an argument around the cultural idea that the "law of the old country" is that "you do not wait for the police if your daughter has been raped." Though the jury was given temporary insanity as the official issue to decide, apparently it recognized that honor was a cultural concept. Metallides was acquitted because the jury technically found him not guilty by reason of temporary insanity, but those involved say it was because of arguments based on Greek culture. The defense attorney said that the judge may have allowed the cultural evidence because the judge's wife was Greek.

It seems unfair that it was possible to introduce the cultural defense only surreptitiously. Had the judge been unwilling to consider the irresistible impulse test, due to the absence of statutory authorization, or to interpret the cultural evidence as relevant, Metallides would not have had the benefit of a cultural defense. Moreover, the accuracy of the claims made concerning Greek culture could have been questioned, considering that no expert witness was consulted on this point.

While it was appropriate to allow the cultural argument to be heard, it appears that the jury gave excessive weight to it. Although one can only speculate about the jury's reasoning, it may have been that the jury felt that a vote to convict would lead to an excessive punishment under the circumstances, and so the preferred option was acquittal. One of the reasons for instituting the cultural defense as a separate defense is to avoid such artificial dichotomies.

Under the current system, a defendant's fate would appear to hinge upon the attitude of the judge to the relevancy of the cultural evidence and on the availability of particular insanity tests. Although Metallides was able to escape punishment by relying on the irresistible impulse test, other defendants may not have such good fortune. Another reason for adopting a cultural defense is to achieve a greater degree of uniformity in the handling of such cases. * * *

The major obstacle to the use of the provocation defense by defendants in cultural defense cases is judicial adherence to the "objective" reasonable person standard. Critics contend that it is absurd to judge whether an "objective" reasonable person would have been provoked, when the reality is that this "objective" being is simply the persona of the dominant culture. Their position is that the court should modify the standard, so that the application of the test evaluates whether the reasonable person from the defendant's culture would have been provoked. Whether or not the cultural defense can be effectively raised through the provocation defense depends entirely upon the judge's interpretation of the reasonable person standard: if the test is "objective," almost invariably no provocation will be found; if the test is "subjective," then ordinarily provocation will be found. This controversy is well illustrated in the cases of *People v. Aphaylath*, *Regina v. Ly*, and *People v. Chen*.

1. *People v. Aphaylath*

In 1982, May Aphaylath, a Laotian refugee residing in Rochester, New York stabbed his wife to death in a jealous rage when she received a phone call from a former boyfriend. The public defender tried to argue that Aphaylath's loss of self control was culturally based: "under Laotian culture the conduct of the victim wife in displaying affection for another man and receiving phone calls from an unattached man brought shame on defendant and his family sufficient to trigger defendant's loss of control." Defense counsel sought to introduce expert witnesses to establish that: (1) Aphaylath was suffering from culture shock or extreme disorientation and (2) the infidelity of one's wife brings great shame on the family. The public defender attempted to construct an argument that in Laotian culture the combination of the disgrace of his wife's conduct and the stress of resettlement could have triggered his disproportionate rage.

The judge disallowed the testimony of experts on the cultural issues because they had not evaluated the defendant and could, therefore, only testify about Laotian culture and refugee problems generally. The court took the view that jealousy was not a subject beyond the comprehension of the jury for which expert evidence was needed.

Aphaylath was convicted of murder in the second degree. The Supreme Court, Appellate division, denied the appeal based on the exclusion of expert evidence because it found the trial court's judgment appropriate with respect to excluding cultural evidence. The dissenting judge would have granted a new trial because the excluded testimony would have been "highly probative of whether there was a reasonable explanation for defendant's conduct from the perspective of his internal point of view." In his view, the evidence might have established extreme emotional disturbance that could serve as a mitigating factor.

The Court of Appeals of New York held that it was reversible error to exclude the testimony of expert witnesses concerning culture shock suffered by Laotian refugees. As a result the Court of Appeals ordered that the lower court decision be reversed and the case remanded for a new trial. This was not necessary because the prosecutor negotiated a plea bargain whereby an admission of guilt would lead to a conviction of manslaughter. Since the reduction in sentence from 15 years to life to 8 1/3 years to 25 years in prison was precisely what the public defender sought, the plea bargain was accepted.

Although this might have been a major coup for advocates of the relevance of culture for judicial decision-making, the opinion left much to be desired. Only four paragraphs long, the memorandum of the court gives little guidance as to when culture is relevant and how the ascertainment of culture should proceed. The public defender had hoped for a landmark decision and was bitterly disappointed.

2. *Regina v. Ly*

The relevance of culture for a defense of provocation was the central issue in the Canadian case of *Regina v. Ly*. The facts resemble those in *Aphaylath*. A Vietnamese refugee became suspicious that his common-law wife was no longer faithful to him. When he confronted her about this initially, explaining that he felt he had lost face in the eyes of the community, he spoke of committing suicide which his wife supposedly encouraged him to do. He took some pills but was treated in a hospital and survived. On one particular night he expected his wife home early and when she returned at two o'clock in the morning, he questioned her again. After she told him that where she had been was none of his business, he strangled her and tried again to kill himself.

At the trial he tried to emphasize the cultural significance of his wife's conduct, testifying that: "his wife's infidelity had caused him to lose 'face' and 'honour' and this had special importance to him because of his Vietnamese upbringing." The chairman of a Vietnamese refugee association corroborated the cultural argument. But the trial judge's instruction to the jury on provocation diminished the power of the cultural argument.

According to the Criminal Code of Canada, reducing a murder charge to manslaughter requires passing a two-pronged test. First, there must be a determination that the wrongful act or insult was of such a nature that it would deprive an ordinary person of self control. Second, the accused must have reacted to provocation, promptly before there was time for his passion to cool. One rationale for combining an "objective" reasonable person test and a "subjective" test of actual provocation is that an ordinary person might be provoked by something even though the accused was not.

The crux of the appeal was based on the trial judge's instruction that the jury not consider culture in assessing the first part of the test, namely whether the "ordinary person" would have been sufficiently provoked. As far as the judge was concerned, culture only goes to the question of whether the accused was actually provoked. But the defendant contended that the insult "could only be properly measured against the cultural background of the appellant." As the jury did not evaluate the reaction of an average Vietnamese male, Ly was convicted of second degree murder. The three judges of the British Columbia Court of Appeal affirmed the decision of the lower court.

Until the Canadian judiciary clarifies the nature of the test for provocation, the relevance of culture arguments will be ambiguous. In *Regina v. Ly* the judges followed precedent and took an unduly narrow view of provocation, one based almost exclusively on racial slurs. It is hard to fathom their reasoning. It is also curious that American and Canadian appellate courts came to diametrically opposed conclusions in similar cases within a year of each other.

3. *People v. Chen*

Dong Lu Chen, a Chinese born man living in New York, bludgeoned his wife to death after she confessed to adultery. A professor of anthropology at Hunter College, Burton Pasternak, testified that in China women are sometimes severely punished for adultery. He said that it is viewed as an "enormous stain" that reflects not only on the husband but "is a reflection on his ancestors and his progeny." Pasternak also observed that adultery rarely ends in a wife's murder in China. In China when irate husbands confront wives suspected of infidelity, the community normally intervenes to prevent any acts of violence. In fact, Pasternak could not cite any cases where Chinese men had killed adulterous wives, though he did know of beatings. Nor did he present evidence to show that a jealousy killing would go unpunished under either customary or modern Chinese law. It seems that no effort was made to discover what punishment would be imposed in the case of a husband who murders an adulterous wife, either under traditional or modern Chinese law. Some commentators have pointed out that at least under modern law such a husband would be punished.

Nevertheless, after a non-jury trial New York State Supreme Court Judge Edward Pincus relied heavily on Pasternak's testimony when he found Chen guilty of second degree manslaughter and decided to sentence him to only five years probation. This "sentence" of five years probation essentially represented a complete defense rather than mitigation.

Women's organizations, Asian-American groups, and Elizabeth Holtzman condemned the decision. They even went so far as to file a complaint with the State of New York Commission on Judicial Conduct asking for an investigation into the judge's decision.

4. What is Reasonable About Provocation?

The notion of an "objective" test of what an ordinary person believes is fraught with perils. The concept masks the subjective biases of the culture of the dominant group. In many cases throughout the world the application of the ordinary or reasonable person test has meant the forceful imposition of one set of values upon individuals whose own value system differs. * * *

* * * [R]etention of the "objective" reasonable person standard is grossly unfair because it means that the provocation defense, which is supposed to be available to all, is a defense only for those who belong to the dominant culture. There are two reasonable responses. Either the provocation defense should be abandoned altogether or the standard should be that of the culture to which the defendant belongs. After all, different things provoke different people. The purpose of the provocation defense is to hold less culpable those individuals who cannot control their actions. If the reasonable defendant from another culture cannot control his or her actions in the face of a certain provocation, what is the basis for holding that individual guilty of first-degree (premeditated) murder? * * *

A[ ] * * * practical query is what groups would be entitled to raise cultural defenses. There is realistically no way to limit their use, nor would it be fair to do so. However, to ensure that the defense not be subject to abuse, statutory authorization of cultural arguments should require that the defendant prove the authenticity of the tradition in question. The defendant would have the burden of proving that: (1) the group to which the defendant belongs remains committed to the cultural practice, and (2) the defendant was, in fact, motivated by the tradition.

One of the most vexing questions is how to limit the use of the cultural defense to bona fide ethnic minority groups and to prevent its use by sub-cultures. The reason why subcultures should not be entitled to use a cultural defense is that their worldview is not radically different from the rest of society. For example, gang members do not believe in witchcraft, coining, or other customs integral to a markedly different conceptual system. It may well be that the social and economic background of sub-cultural defendants should be raised in some cases. The suitable defense for this purpose is not the cultural defense but what has been called the "rotten social background" defense.

The sub-cultural defense has more to do with class differences than cultural differences. If individuals who come from lower socio-economic backgrounds were to rely on the cultural defense, then there would be nothing to prevent aristocrats from raising a "Great Gatsby" defense when they drive while intoxicated. Use of the rotten social background defense ensures that only those who have experienced life in the ghetto, or something akin to it, are entitled to a criminal defense. In reality it may not be possible to thwart the use of the cultural defense by subcultures. However, just because a cultural argument is advanced does not obligate a judge or jury to accept the argument.

Courts may be reluctant to allow cultural defenses because they fear that it will be difficult to ascertain the validity of the practice in question. Invoking a cultural defense might be unjustifiable because the practice may never have existed, may be considerably different from that described by a defendant * * * or may have ceased to exist * * *. One real danger of allowing cultural defenses might be the unwarranted assumption on the part of lawyers and judges that traditions do not change. Of course, cultures evolve, and so courts must guard against basing decisions on information that is anachronistic.

Some may object to a formal cultural defense on the grounds that putting the culture on trial may have adverse consequences for members of the group. There is concern that decisions based on group characteristics may lead to the reinforcement of social stereotypes. But it is important to recognize that members of groups do share common characteristics, and the desire to obliterate prejudice and hatred should not lead to the unfair treatment of individuals. That is, individualized justice based on group traits may be necessary to safeguard the rights of individual defendants and thus be more important than the promotion of a progressive social policy. Furthermore, since the cultural defense will only serve as a partial, rather than complete, excuse, this will ensure that the rights of children and other vulnerable groups are not violated in deference to culture.

The law must make many difficult determinations, e.g., questions of insanity and causation. There is no reason to suppose than cultural evidence is any more difficult to interpret than any other data. If it turns out to be the case that the process of verifying the cultural claim demonstrates its falsity, then it should obviously be rejected.

ON CULTURE, DIFFERENCE, AND DOMESTIC VIOLENCE

Leti Volpp

11 Am. U. J. Gender, Soc. Pol'y & Law 393 (2003)[1]

How should we consider cultural difference when we think about domestic violence? Elizabeth Schneider's path-breaking representation of Yvonne Wanrow, described in her book, Battered Women and Feminist Lawmaking, gives us an important example of how one can contemplate this question in the context of legal representation. In arguing that Yvonne Wanrow's perspective as a Native American woman had been excluded from her claim of self defense, Elizabeth Schneider and other attorneys at the Center for Constitutional Rights successfully asserted that the way one's specific identity shapes experiences must be factored

[1] Reprinted with permission.

into the consideration of a defendant's state of mind. What was missing, they argued, was evidence that would have explained why Yvonne Wanrow would react as she did when an uninvited white man, who she believed had tried to molest one of her children, entered her babysitter's home. This evidence included information as to the general lack of police protection in such situations, the pervasiveness of violence against women and children, Wanrow's belief that the man was a child molester, Wanrow's lack of trust in the police, and her belief that she could successfully defend herself only with a weapon.

But I fear that this representation was exceptional in its careful attention to particularized detail. I am concerned that when attempts to represent a woman's difference are less careful, what can accompany or underlie culturally based advocacy can be quite problematic. Very often, discussions of cultural alterity rely upon invocations of culture that are little more than crass, group based stereotypes that may, in fact, be quite remote from the individual experiences at issue. Moreover, unlike in Wanrow's case where the failures of the police were pivotal to the argument, invocations of culture often suggest that culture somehow exists apart from the state.

This reflects outmoded, although popular, perceptions of culture. Culture is still fused with ethnicity, and not understood as a descriptor explaining all kinds of social interactions. Moreover, culture is generally thought of as a noun, a fixed and static thing, rather than conceived as an adjective modifying particular practices. Discussions of the way culture can shape domestic violence occur in a broader context of already existing stereotypes about culture, that reflect problematic notions as to how culture is believed to link to race.

Despite the valiant attempts of organizations such as the Family Violence Prevention Fund to inform the American public that domestic violence in the United States is a universal phenomenon occurring at epidemic rates, behavior that we condemn, such as domestic violence, is more often conceptualized as cultural for nonwhite communities. In fact, some have argued that it appears that many feminists and battered women's advocates suspect that "other" cultures actually support domestic violence—without turning to ask whether this may also be the case in their own communities. This tendency to describe domestic violence as "cultural" when occurring in communities of color, and not through the language of power and control used to describe domestic violence in "mainstream" communities, is linked to the uninterrogated assumption that devalued and less powerful groups are somehow more culturally determined. This description suggests that members of communities of color behave in certain ways, because they follow cultural dictates, as if they are encoded with culture.

We can see this in the reaction to the case of Andrea Yates. Her killing of her five children was primarily explained as a result of mental illness, with a diagnosis of postpartum psychosis. While there was some discussion suggesting Andrea Yates inhabited a particular cultural location due to her family's Christian beliefs, that engendered their living in a school bus left by a traveling preacher, or that led her to keep having children without using birth control because the children came from God, the primary lens through which her behavior was understood was psychological. We thus heard about her experience with the mental health system, medications she had stopped taking, and suicide attempts.

Psychology is used to explain why people positioned as Western subjects act irrationally. In contrast, culture is used to explain why those considered non-Western subjects act irrationally. We could thus compare the coverage of Andrea Yates with other cases involving mothers who killed their children. One such case involved Khoua Her, a Hmong immigrant, who in Minnesota in 1998 strangled her six children and then hanged herself in a failed suicide attempt. Police had been called to the family's home at least sixteen times in the previous two years, and there was a long history of domestic violence. In searching for explanations, the media invoked a "cultural clash," and "the American pull to be an individual versus the Hmong orientation of putting the group first." Described as the worst mass murder in Minnesota memory, the Her case was invoked—along with tales of animal cruelty, religious sacrifice of small dogs, the statistic that nearly half of the Hmong community was on state welfare, a string of gang rapes, and a thirteen year old who smothered her newborn—by a popular radio talk show host who said, "Those people should either assimilate or hit the road."

We see here the process of selective blaming of culture. The same act is understood as the product of Hmong culture in one case, but not white American culture in the other. Rather, Andrea Yates, whether she is condemned or pitied, is primarily depicted as a mother under enormous pressure, her life uninflected [*sic*] by a racialized culture. Khoua Her, in contrast, is described as if her life is completely circumscribed by a racialized culture.

A particular academic description of culture that reflects some of these problems is an article which appeared in a symposium issue of the Stanford Law Review, authored by Nilda Rimonte, who was once the director of a battered women's shelter in Los Angeles that serves Asian women and children. In the article, Rimonte points to a number of reasons for domestic violence in Asian immigrant communities: the Pacific-Asian family's traditionally patriarchal system and the attendant belief in the supremacy of the male; the socialization goals and processes which favor the family and community over the individual; the cultural emphasis on silent suffering versus open communication of needs and feelings; and the enormous adjustment pressures which test the limits of immigrants' and refugees' survival skills. Rimonte also suggests that few Asian countries have woman's rights movements whose energy and goals might significantly influence the women in their society, asserts that Asians have a different sense of time, claims that the idea of choices and rights may not be appropriate for Asians, and states that, unlike the Western ideal of the healthy family, the Asian family is structured around male privilege, authority, and superiority. The article presents a frozen, monolithic description of culture for an enormous region of the world that elides any difference or heterogeneity. Rimonte's sweeping and inaccurate generalizations have allowed other writers to make blanket statements about gender subordination in "Asian cultures" and to assert that there is something more misogynistic about Asian immigrant communities than "our own."

In the face of this selective stereotyping, the appeal of universalist descriptions of domestic violence, to suggest that specific cultural formations have no impact, is understandable. Two examples that surfaced in discussions I recently had with Asian American and Pacific Islander domestic violence advocates come to mind. The first was the response of one advocate to the query of a "mainstream" women's shelter (meaning one not serving diverse populations), that inquired for advice about the "cultural shame" of an Indian immigrant who had been sexually assaulted; this cultural shame, said the shelter staff, prohibited the woman from using the shelter's public shower. The response of the advocate was to tell the shelter that any woman who had been sexually assaulted would have issues around privacy and bodily integrity. The second was the response of another advocate to the question as to what, specifically, were the issues for battered lesbians. The advocate's response was that a battered lesbian's experience of domestic violence will reflect her class position, whether she is disabled, whether she is an immigrant, or whether she lives in a rural area, like any other woman in those situations. She then reflected that perhaps the fear of being outed by the abusive partner, if the battered woman was not already out, was specific to lesbians—but then reflected that any battered woman fears being outed, as battered. This kind of approach, to shift attention away from a focus on particular assumptions about how cultural identities shape domestic violence, to examining how experiences are similar, seems necessary.

Yet I would agree with Sherene Razack, who, in examining narratives of sexual violence against South Asian women, cautions against a simple turn to universalist narratives. She argues that there are three problems with reacting against culturalist stereotypes through using universal arguments. Razack asserts that deculturalized narratives rarely have enough traction to displace orientalist fantasies that are believed in mainstream communities, are too abstract to use in conversations within communities that are the subject of description, and lastly, fail to grapple with the fact that violent acts are committed in culturally specific ways.

But then how do we describe the specifics of culture? One important shift would be to understand that cultural practices are imbricated with material and political forces. Usually when cultural explanations are given, a static and insular culture is blamed, detracting attention away from one's limited access to services, or from the policies of the state. Thus, part of what I am arguing for here is an understanding of culture that does not strip away the economic and the political from its content. Take, for example, the idea that Asian immigrants have difficulty gaining access to the Violence Against Women Act ("VAWA") self-petitioning process. When this is blamed on "cultural limitations" of Asian communities—such as passivity, or shame—it removes the onus from agencies or the government to try to make services more accessible. Thus, invocations of culture can erase the racism of agencies and entities that fail to provide appropriate services to battered women by hiring diverse staff who speak relevant languages or translate materials. Further, invocations of culture can detract attention away from the policies of the state: VAWA self-petitioning was only required as a remedy to fix U.S. immigration laws that gave batterers tools with which they could abuse partners, after Congress enacted the Marriage Fraud Act. For an example that foregrounds the importance of economic concerns, we could return to the case of Khoua Her. Recently, an article in the Hmong Times suggested that Her strangled her six children because she saw death as the only means of saving them from poverty, after she lost the low-paying job that had provided food and benefits for her family. Understanding Her's acts as solely the product of "Hmong culture" completely subsumes the role material forces may have played in shaping her perceptions.

Another important shift was evident in the second advocate's response, described above, when she insisted on invoking class, disability, immigrant status, and geographical location as relevant to any particular battered lesbian's experience. Identities and experiences do shape perspectives, but we must be attentive to the way in which this transpires through a complex process that reflects an individual's specific position. Essentializing narratives about particular cultures can often serve to mask reality. For example, a battered woman who is an immigrant may have failed to call the police, not because her culture condones passivity on the part of women, but because her partner was a police officer in her country of origin, because she has witnessed a failure of police protection and practices of police brutality, and because the police in her present location do not speak her language. Granting explanatory power to essentialized depictions of "culture," as purportedly made up of unchanging rituals that cement the subordinate location of women in a fixed system of social practices, will inevitably fail to accurately describe the relationship of culture, difference, and domestic violence.

3. ROTTEN SOCIAL BACKGROUND

"ROTTEN SOCIAL BACKGROUND": SHOULD THE CRIMINAL LAW RECOGNIZE A DEFENSE OF SEVERE ENVIRONMENTAL DEPRIVATION?

Richard Delgado
3 Law & Inequality J. 9 (1985)

Introduction

No jurisdiction in the United States or elsewhere recognizes a criminal defense based on socioeconomic deprivation *simpliciter*. Is this refusal principled and justified, or only a timid response to the prospect of changing to accommodate that which appears alien? That environment plays a significant role in shaping an individual's values and behavior is beyond dispute. For over two decades preferential treatment and affirmative action have been incorporated within our liberal-democratic heritage as means of compensating for unequal opportunity resulting from discrimination, inadequate education and material deprivation.

There is also a strong relationship between environmental adversity and criminal behavior. Of course, not all poor persons violate the law and not all those from privileged backgrounds are law-abiding; it remains, however, that of more than one million offenders entangled in the correctional system, the vast majority are members of the poorest class. Unless we are prepared to argue that offenders are poor because they are criminal, we should be open to the possibility that many turn to crime because of their poverty—that poverty is, for many, a determinant of criminal behavior.

Assuming that socioeconomic deprivation causes criminal behavior rather than the converse, should that mitigate criminal responsibility? * * *

Judge Bazelon first raised the possibility that extreme poverty might give rise to an RSB defense in *United States v. Alexander*, a 1973 opinion by the D.C. Circuit Court of Appeals. In *Alexander*, one of the defendants shot and killed a marine in a tavern after the marine called him a "black bastard." The defense attempted to show that the youth's action stemmed from an irresistible impulse to shoot, which they, in turn, traced to an emotionally and economically deprived childhood in Watts, California. The defendant reported that when he was young, his father deserted the family and the boy grew up with little money or attention. He was subjected to racist treatment and learned to fear and hate white persons.

A psychiatrist testified that the defendant suffered from impaired behavior controls rooted in his "rotten social background." The psychiatrist refused to label the defendant insane, however. The trial judge instructed the jury to disregard the testimony about the defendant's deprived background and to consider only whether or not his mental condition met the legal standard of insanity. The jury found him sane and the defendant was sentenced to twenty years to life.

The court of appeals affirmed. In a lengthy, troubled opinion that concurred in part and dissented in part, Judge Bazelon laid out his early thoughts on the RSB defense. For Bazelon, the trial judge erred in instructing the jury to disregard the testimony about defendant's social and economic background. That testimony might well have persuaded the jury that the defendant's behavioral controls were so impaired as to require acquittal, even though that impairment might not render him clinically insane. Apart from this, exposure to the testimony would benefit society. As a result of learning about the wretched conditions in which some of its members live, society would presumably decide to do something about them.

Nevertheless, Bazelon was not prepared to abandon all the trappings of the "disease" model. Among other things, that model provides a rationale for detaining dangerous persons following acquittal. Bazelon reviewed other possible dispositions for the RSB defendant—outright release, preventive detention, and psychological reprogramming—finding each unacceptable. According to Bazelon, the ultimate solution to the problem of violent crime in our society is some form of income redistribution coupled with other social reform measures. The current narrow insanity test conceals the need for such reform and thus should be broadened, although disposition of offenders not "sick" in any classic sense remained a problem for Bazelon.

Judge Bazelon further developed his views on an RSB defense in his Hoover lecture and in a reply article. In his Hoover address, Bazelon declared that "law's aims must be achieved by a moral process cognizant of the realities of social injustice." Persons must obey the law not out of fear, but because they personally believe its commands to be just. Punishment is justified only when inflicted upon persons whose actions are morally condemnable. This, in turn, requires that society's conduct in relation to the defendant entitle it to sit in condemnation, and that the defendant's mental, emotional, and behavioral controls were intact at the time of the crime. Citing the example of the defendant in *United States v. Alexander*, Bazelon urged that when these two conditions are not met, society is not entitled to inflict punishment.

In a response to Judge Bazelon and a short rejoinder, Professor Stephen Morse argued against Judge Bazelon's position. For Morse, all environments affect choice, making some choices easy and others hard.

Rarely, however, will environmental adversity completely eliminate a person's power of choice. Poor persons are free to choose or not choose to commit crimes, and the criminal law may justifiably punish them when they give in to temptation and break the law. Although he conceded a statistical correlation between poverty and crime, Morse denied that poverty causes crime. He pointed out that some poor persons are law-abiding, while some wealthy persons break the law, and that economic improvements often result in more, not less, crime. Moreover, Bazelon's social-welfare suggestions would be impractical because there is not enough money to eradicate all poverty; giving money to the poor would entail higher taxation, thus endangering such goals as free accumulation and disposition of wealth; and though eradicating poverty may eliminate some crime, it is a wasteful way to do it. Consequently, Bazelon's broadened inquiry into culpability could exonerate dangerous criminals without generating socially useful knowledge or experience. Indeed, Bazelon's defense skirts paternalism. When an individual has freely broken the law, respect for that individual's personhood *demands* punishment; any other treatment demeans the defendant, and treats him or her as something less than an autonomous individual.

The Bazelon-Morse debate thus raises, but does not answer, a number of key questions concerning a "rotten social background" defense. Does economic and cultural disadvantage impair controls or otherwise cause crime, and if so, how? If severe impairment can be shown in a particular case, what effect should this have on criminal responsibility? What should be done with the successful RSB defendant? The remainder of this article explores these and related questions. * * *

IV. A New Defense

An environment of extreme poverty and deprivation creates in individuals a propensity to commit crimes. In some cases, a defendant's impoverished background so greatly determines his or her criminal behavior that we feel it unfair to punish the individual. This sense of unfairness arises from the morality of the criminal law itself, in that "our collective conscience does not allow punishment where it cannot impose blame." And blame is inappropriate when a defendant's criminal behavior is caused by extrinsic factors beyond his or her control.

Still, the criminal law does not recognize a rotten social background, as such, as relevant to the issue of guilt. Commentators have noted this seeming inconsistency. For example, Professor Packer observes:

> If a person engages in criminal conduct while in an epileptic fit, we say that he was incapable of performing a voluntary act and we acquit. . . . At the other extreme, we recognize that cultural deprivation of a kind associated with urban poverty may in a very real sense restrict the individual's capacity to choose and make him more susceptible to engaging in antisocial conduct

> than the "average" member of society. However, we regard those constraints as too remote to justify an excuse on the ground that the person could not have helped acting as he did.

Professor Norval Norris, in commenting on the insanity defense, argues:

> Why not permit the defense of dwelling in a Negro ghetto? Such a defense would not be morally indefensible. Adverse social and subcultural background is statistically *more* criminogenic than is psychosis; like insanity, it also severely circumscribes the freedom of choice.... You argue that insanity destroys, undermines, diminishes a man's capacity to reject what is wrong and adhere to what is right. So does the ghetto—more so.

Indeed, why *not* permit a defense of dwelling in a ghetto? I have two purposes in this part of the article: (1) to analyze the legal and moral arguments for a new defense of rotten social background; and (2) to suggest possible models for such a defense. * * *

B. Possible Models.

Evidence of a rotten social background could be introduced in criminal trials in various ways. It could be relevant to a defense of excuse or justification, to a public policy defense relating to a society's responsibility for the rotten social background, or to considerations in the sentencing stage. In any of these ways, information about extreme poverty and deprivation can have the beneficial effect hoped for by Judge Bazelon in "compell[ing] us to explore these problems, and thereby offer[ing] some slight hope that we will learn, in the course of deciding individual cases, something about the causes of crime."

1. Excuses.

The previous discussion suggested a number of possible excuse defenses; the particular circumstances of each case would determine the appropriateness of each approach.

a. Involuntary rage.

Under this model, the RSB defendant would argue that a precipitating event evoked rage so powerful as to block his or her consciousness, rendering subsequent actions involuntary. Studies of repressed anger reviewed in part II indicate that long-term exposure to environmental insult can make an individual a virtual "time bomb." Such a person may react to a seemingly minor provocation with a violent response of which he or she is scarcely aware. Professor Hart summarizes the conventional theory of cases of automatic behavior as follows:

> What is missing in these cases appears to most people as a vital link between mind and body; and both the ordinary man and the lawyer might well insist on this by saying that in these cases

> there is not "really" a human action at all and certainly nothing for which anyone should be made criminally responsible. . . .

What extreme environmental deprivation causes the type of physical disorder required by the conventional defense, then the RSB person should be exculpated. The defense, however, should not be limited to cases of physical disorder, like epilepsy or brain tumor. The kind of pent-up rage and despair that can result from living in a crowded, violent neighborhood can cause an explosion of violence just as disordered brain circuitry can. When this occurs, a defense should be available. The defense would require proving: (i) that the defendant was acting automatically; and (ii) that the automatic state was caused by the extreme deprivation of a rotten social background.

b. Isolation from dominant culture.

The theory underlying this model of the defense is that some urban ghettos are social and cultural islands unto themselves, with their own rules, norms and values. A person who has lived since birth in such an environment may be so strongly socialized by it that he or she has little sense of the values of the larger society or opportunity to acquire the norms necessary to function responsibly in that society. This defense would be particularly appropriate for a younger defendant who has had little or no exposure to life outside the ghetto, and for whom acquiescence to ghetto norms was required to survive. It would require a psychological and sociological analysis of the defendant's development, and proof that the defendant did not adequately internalize the values of the larger society, while in fact living by ghetto norms endorsing violence and other criminal behavior.

c. Inability to control conduct.

This model assumes that a rotten social background can cause inability to control conduct, as insanity does. This defense would require a broad definition of disability, for instance, that proposed by Judge Bazelon in *Alexander*: that at the time of the defendant's unlawful conduct his or her mental or emotional processes or behavioral controls were impaired to such an extent that he or she cannot justly be held responsible for his or her act. This test is an advancement over the current medical-model tests for responsibility in that it allows for broad, socioeconomic explanations for loss of control. To a greater extent, it also preserves the dignity of an RSB defendant by not forcing him or her to opt, for strategic purposes, for a plea of insanity when he or she is not insane. * * *

4. Mitigation of sentence.

Evidence of rotten social background should be admissible during sentencing as a special circumstance which made conforming to the law especially difficult. When this is shown, the sentence should be reduced accordingly.

Sentence mitigation is probably appropriate for any RSB defendant:

> The special features of mitigation are that a good reason for administering a less severe penalty is made out if the situation or mental state of the convicted criminal is such that he was exposed to an unusual or specially great temptation, or his ability to control his actions is thought to have been impaired or weakened otherwise than by his own action, so that conformity to the law which he has broken was a matter of special difficulty for him as compared with normal persons normally placed.

When a defendant could not be acquitted on the basis of rotten social background, consideration of his or her background is still relevant to sentencing.

C. Summary.

From both individual and societal perspectives, a strong case can be made for new defenses for the criminal defendant whose crime stems from poverty, mistreatment, or a legitimate and frustrated desire for self-respect. Destitution and neglect affect individual behavior and choice; they are thus highly relevant to issues of criminal responsibility. Broader considerations favor a new defense, as well. If the criminal law reflects and reinforces a system of morality, then a criminal trial is an obvious and appropriate place to apply, test, and develop that morality. As Judge Bazelon observed: "We cannot rationally decry crime and brutality and racial animosity without at the same time struggling to enhance the fairness and integrity of the criminal justice system. That system has first-line responsibility for probing and coping with these complex problems." The simplest meaning of fairness in criminal trials is that no one should be punished without first having the opportunity to argue the issue of his or her culpability. The best reason for a defense acknowledging a rotten social background is that it is unfair to ignore it. * * *

CHAPTER 11

ATTEMPTS

■ ■ ■

INTRODUCTION

At common law, an attempt was defined as "an act, done with intent to commit a crime, and tending but failing to effect its commission." *People v. Rizzo*, 246 N.Y. 334 (1927). Most attempts were classified as misdemeanors regardless of the seriousness of the target offense. Today, most jurisdictions classify an attempt to commit a felony as a felony and an attempt to commit a misdemeanor as a misdemeanor. Generally speaking, the attempt in either case is treated as a less serious crime than the target offense.

The first three cases in this chapter, *People v. Rizzo*, *People v. Staples*, and *State v. Latraverse*, discuss the actus reus of an attempt. As will become evident from the cases, there is no single common law test for determining whether and when a defendant's acts go beyond mere preparation and become sufficient for an attempt. Instead, there are many tests, most of which focus on how much (or how little) remains to be done in order to complete the target offense. The Model Penal Code's provision on attempt, in contrast, requires a "substantial step" towards the culmination of the commission of the targeted offense. The Model Penal Code focuses on what the defendant has done, rather than on what remains to be done, and whether the defendant's acts or omissions are strongly corroborative of his criminal purpose.

The mens rea of an attempt is the specific intent to commit the targeted offense. *People v. Harris* explains how the mental state required for commission of an attempt can be narrower than the mental state or mental states required for commission of the target offense. *State v. Hinkhouse* provides an interesting fact pattern to test your understanding of the mens rea required for an attempt.

The law of attempt recognizes two defenses specific to attempts: the defense of impossibility and the defense of abandonment. *State v. LaTraverse* (the third case in this section) discusses the elements of the defense of abandonment. The last case in this chapter, *United States v. Thomas*, discusses the defense of impossibility.

A. THE ACTUS REUS REQUIREMENT

PEOPLE V. RIZZO

Court of Appeals of New York
246 N.Y. 334, 158 N.E. 888 (1927)

CRANE, J.

The police of the city of New York did excellent work in this case by preventing the commission of a serious crime. It is a great satisfaction to realize that we have such wide-awake guardians of our peace. Whether or not the steps which the defendant had taken up to the time of his arrest amounted to the commission of a crime, as defined by our law, is, however, another matter. He has been convicted of an attempt to commit the crime of robbery in the first degree and sentenced to State's prison. There is no doubt that he had the intention to commit robbery if he got the chance. An examination, however, of the facts is necessary to determine whether his acts were in preparation to commit the crime if the opportunity offered, or constituted a crime in itself, known to our law as an attempt to commit robbery in the first degree. Charles Rizzo, the defendant, appellant, with three others, Anthony J. Dorio, Thomas Milo and John Thomasello, on January 14th planned to rob one Charles Rao of a payroll valued at about $1,200 which he was to carry from the bank for the United Lathing Company. These defendants, two of whom had firearms, started out in an automobile, looking for Rao or the man who had the payroll on that day. Rizzo claimed to be able to identify the man and was to point him out to the others who were to do the actual holding up. The four rode about in their car looking for Rao. They went to the bank from which he was supposed to get the money and to various buildings being constructed by the United Lathing Company. At last they came to One Hundred and Eightieth street and Morris Park avenue. By this time they were watched and followed by two police officers. As Rizzo jumped out of the car and ran into the building all four were arrested. The defendant was taken out from the building in which he was hiding. Neither Rao nor a man named Previti, who was also supposed to carry a payroll, were at the place at the time of the arrest. The defendants had not found or seen the man they intended to rob; no person with a payroll was at any of the places where they had stopped and no one had been pointed out or identified by Rizzo. The four men intended to rob the payroll man, whoever he was; they were looking for him, but they had not seen or discovered him up to the time they were arrested.

Does this constitute the crime of an attempt to commit robbery in the first degree? The Penal Law, section 2, prescribes, "An act, done with intent to commit a crime, and tending but failing to effect its commission, is 'an attempt to commit that crime.'" The word "*tending*" is very indefinite. It is perfectly evident that there will arise differences of opinion as to whether an act in a given case is one *tending* to commit a crime. "Tending" means to exert activity in a particular direction. Any act in preparation to commit a crime may be said to have a tendency towards its accomplishment. The procuring of the automobile, searching the streets looking for the desired victim, were in reality acts tending toward the commission of the proposed crime. The law, however, has recognized that many acts in the way of preparation are too remote to constitute the crime of attempt. The line has been drawn between those acts which are remote and those which are proximate and near to the consummation. The law must be practical, and, therefore, considers those acts only as tending to the commission of the crime which are so near to its accomplishment that in all reasonable probability the crime itself would have been committed but for timely interference. The cases which have been before the courts express this idea in different language, but the idea remains the same. The act or acts must come or advance very near to the accomplishment of the intended crime. In *People v. Mills* it was said: "Felonious intent alone is not enough, but there must be an overt act shown in order to establish even an attempt. An overt act is one done to carry out the intention, and it must be such as would naturally effect that result, unless prevented by some extraneous cause." In *Hyde v. U. S.* it was stated that the act amounts to an attempt when it is so near to the result that the danger of success is very great. "There must be dangerous proximity to success." Halsbury in his "Laws of England" says: "An act, in order to be a criminal attempt, must be immediately, and not remotely, connected with and directly tending to the commission of an offence." *Commonwealth v. Peaslee* refers to the acts constituting an attempt as coming *very near* to the accomplishment of the crime.

The method of committing or attempting crime varies in each case so that the difficulty, if any, is not with this rule of law regarding an attempt, which is well understood, but with its application to the facts. As I have said before, minds differ over proximity and the nearness of the approach.

How shall we apply this rule of immediate nearness to this case? The defendants were looking for the payroll man to rob him of his money. This is the charge in the indictment. Robbery is defined in section 2120 of the Penal Law as "the unlawful taking of personal property, from the person or in the presence of another, against his will, by means of force, or violence, or fear of injury, immediate or future, to his person;" and it is made robbery in the first degree by section 2124 when committed by a person aided by accomplices actually present. To constitute the crime of robbery the money must have been taken from Rao by means of force or violence, or through fear. The crime of attempt to commit robbery was committed if these defendants did an act tending to the commission of this robbery. Did the acts above describe[d] come dangerously near to the taking of Rao's property? Did the acts come so near the commission of robbery that there was reasonable likelihood of its accomplishment but for the interference? Rao was not found; the defendants were still looking for him; no attempt to rob him could be made, at least until he came in sight; he was not in the building at One Hundred and Eightieth street and Morris Park avenue. There was no man there with the payroll for the United Lathing Company whom these defendants could rob. Apparently no money had been drawn from the bank for the payroll by anybody at the time of the arrest. In a word, these defendants had planned to commit a crime and were looking around the city for an opportunity to commit it, but the opportunity fortunately never came. Men would not be guilty of an attempt at burglary if they had planned to break into a building and were arrested while they were hunting about the streets for the building not knowing where it was. Neither would a man be guilty of an attempt to commit murder if he armed himself and started out to find the person whom he had planned to kill but could not find him. So here these defendants were not guilty of an attempt to commit robbery in the first degree when they had not found or reached the presence of the person they intended to rob.

For these reasons, the judgment of conviction of this defendant, appellant, must be reversed and a new trial granted. * * *

PEOPLE V. STAPLES

Court of Appeal of California, Second District, Division 5
6 Cal.App.3d 61, 85 Cal.Rptr. 589 (1970)

REPPY, J.

Defendant was charged in an information with attempted burglary. Trial by jury was waived, and the matter submitted on the testimony contained in the transcript of the preliminary hearing together with exhibits. Defendant was found guilty. * * *

I. The Facts

In October 1967, while his wife was away on a trip, defendant, a mathematician, under an assumed name, rented an office on the second floor of a building in Hollywood which was over the mezzanine of a bank. Directly below the mezzanine was the vault of the bank. Defendant was aware of the layout of the building, specifically of the relation of the office he rented to the bank vault. Defendant paid rent for the period from October 23 to November 23. The landlord had 10 days before commencement of the rental period within which to finish some interior repairs and painting. During this prerental period defendant brought into the office certain equipment. This included drilling tools, two acetylene gas tanks, a blow torch, a blanket, and a linoleum rug. The landlord observed these items when he came in from time to time to see how the repair work was progressing. Defendant learned from a custodian that no one was in the building on Saturdays. On Saturday, October 14, defendant drilled two groups of holes into the floor of the office above the mezzanine room. He stopped drilling before the holes went through the floor. He came back to the office several times thinking he might slowly drill down, covering the holes with the linoleum rug. At some point in time he installed a hasp lock on a closet, and planned to, or did, place his tools in it. However, he left the closet keys on the premises. Around the end of November, apparently after November 23, the landlord notified the police and turned the tools and equipment over to them. Defendant did not pay any more rent. It is not clear when he last entered the office, but it could have been after November 23, and even after the landlord had removed the equipment. On February 22, 1968, the police arrested defendant. After receiving advice as to his constitutional rights, defendant voluntarily made an oral statement which he reduced to writing.

Among other things which defendant wrote down were these:

> Saturday, the 14th . . . I drilled some small holes in the floor of the room. Because of tiredness, fear, and the implications of what I was doing, I stopped and went to sleep.
>
> At this point I think my motives began to change. The actual [*sic*] commencement of my plan made me begin to realize that even if I were to succeed a fugitive life of living off of stolen money would not give the enjoyment of the life of a mathematician however humble a job I might have.
>
> I still had not given up my plan however. I felt I had made a certain investment of time, money, effort and a certain psychological commitment to the concept.
>
> I came back several times thinking I might store the tools in the closet and slowly drill down (covering the hole with a rug of linoleum square. As time went on (after two weeks or so), my wife came back and my life as bank robber seemed more and more absurd.

II. Discussion of Defendant's Contentions

Defendant's position in this appeal is that, as a matter of law, there was insufficient evidence upon which to convict him of a criminal attempt under Penal Code section 664. Defendant claims that his actions were all preparatory in nature and never reached a stage of advancement in relation to the substantive crime which he concededly intended to commit (burglary of the bank vault) so that criminal responsibility might attach.

In order for the prosecution to prove that defendant committed an attempt to burglarize as proscribed by Penal Code section 664, it was required to establish that he had the specific intent to commit a burglary of the bank and that his acts toward that goal went beyond mere preparation.

The required specific intent was clearly established in the instant case. Defendant admitted in his written confession that he rented the office fully intending to burglarize the bank, that he brought in tools and equipment to accomplish this purpose, and that he began drilling into the floor with the intent of making an entry into the bank.

The question of whether defendant's conduct went beyond "mere preparation" raises some provocative problems. The briefs and the oral argument of counsel in this case point up a degree of ambiguity and uncertainty that permeates the law of attempts in this state. Each side has cited us to a different so-called "test" to determine whether this defendant's conduct went beyond the preparatory stage. Predictably each respective test in the eyes of its proponents yielded an opposite result. * * *

We suggest that the confusion in this area is a result of the broad statutory language of section 664, which reads in part: "Any person who attempts to commit any crime, but fails, or is prevented or intercepted in the perpetration thereof, is punishable. . . . " This is a very general proscription against all attempts not specifically made a crime. The statute does not differentiate between the various types of attempts which may be considered culpable. Reference must be made to case law in order to determine precisely what conduct constitutes an attempt. However, the statute does point out by the words "fails," "prevented," and "intercepted," those *conditions* which separate an attempt from the substantive crime. * * *

Our courts have come up with a variety of "tests" which try to distinguish acts of preparation from completed attempts. "The preparation consists in devising or arranging the means or measures necessary for the commission of the offense; the attempt is the direct movement toward the commission after the preparations are made." " '[The] act must reach far enough towards the accomplishment of the desired result to amount to the commencement of the consummation.' " "[Where] the intent to commit the substantive offense is . . . clearly established . . . [,] acts done toward the commission of the crime may constitute an attempt, where the same acts would be held insufficient to constitute an attempt if the intent with which they were done is equivocal and not clearly proved."

None of the above statements of the law applicable to this category of attempts provide a litmus-like test, and perhaps no such test is achievable. Such precision is not required in this case, however. There was definitely substantial evidence entitling the trial judge to find that defendant's acts had gone beyond the preparation stage. Without specifically deciding where defendant's preparations left off and where his activities became a completed criminal attempt, we can say that his "drilling" activity clearly was an unequivocal and direct step toward the completion of the burglary. It was a fragment of the substantive crime contemplated, i.e., the beginning of the "breaking" element. Further, defendant himself characterized his activity as the *actual commencement of his plan*. The drilling by defendant was obviously one of a series of acts which logic and ordinary experience indicate would result in the proscribed act of burglary. * * *

The order is affirmed.

STATE V. LATRAVERSE

Supreme Court of Rhode Island
443 A.2d 890 (R.I. 1982)

KELLEHER, J.

The defendant, Paul A. Latraverse (Latraverse), was found guilty by a Superior Court justice, after a jury-waived trial, of attempting knowingly and maliciously to dissuade a Woonsocket police officer from giving testimony before a grand jury, a violation of * * * the Anti-intimidation of Witnesses and Crime Victims statute.

Salvatore Lombardi (Lombardi) is a member of the Woonsocket police department. As a member of the detective division, he has done undercover work numerous times using the name Frank Torro. As Frank Torro, he had purchased four stolen cars from Latraverse, who owns and operates a Woonsocket used-car dealership. Following the sale, Latraverse was arrested and arraigned in the District Court on several charges of receiving stolen goods. At the time of the incident we are about to describe, Latraverse was free on bail while awaiting the grand jury's consideration of his dealings with "Torro."

On June 26, 1980, Lombardi arrived at his Morton Avenue home sometime between 11 p.m. and midnight after completing a tour of duty. At approximately 1:40 a.m. on June 27, he and his wife were watching a television program when a car with a faulty muffler passed by. The resulting noise caused Lombardi to look out the front window. There on the street he observed a late-model Ford Thunderbird bearing a license plate assigned to Latraverse's automobile agency. Lombardi was aware that the "T-bird" belonged to Latraverse. Once the vehicle had passed by, Lombardi took his walkie-talkie, went outside his home, and secreted himself in the darkness. Lombardi told the trial justice that he kept a vigilant eye on the early-morning traffic passing by his house because he had received threats as a result of his undercover work. He also testified that on one occasion while working under cover he was asked by Latraverse if his real name was "Salvatore Lombardi."

Lombardi watched the T-bird as it proceeded along Morton Avenue and then took a left onto Bellevue Street, and within a matter of twenty to thirty seconds, he observed the T-bird coming "down" Harrison Avenue. When the vehicle came to a halt, it was parked in front of 203 Harrison Avenue. Its lights were then extinguished. Harrison Avenue runs perpendicular to Morton Avenue and is almost directly across the street from the Lombardi residence. After a wait of a minute or so, Lombardi radioed headquarters for a "backup" because, in his words, he "wasn't going to take any chances" and he "felt" that Latraverse wanted to see him injured. As the backup vehicle came onto Morton Avenue from Hamlet Avenue, its lights were on, and the vehicle was proceeding at forty miles per hour toward the Harrison Avenue-Morton Avenue intersection. As the backup headed toward the intersection, the T-bird backed up on Harrison, made a U-turn, and headed away from the Morton Avenue area toward Park Place. The backup caught up with the darkened T-bird in front of 138 Harrison Avenue.

When the police looked at the interior of the car, they saw the following items: a can of gasoline; a rag; matches; an aluminum baseball bat; a wire coat hanger that had been stretched out so that it could be used to open a car door; and a note that read, "Hi, Sal, know [sic][1] it's my turn asshole."

After the defense had rested without presenting any evidence, Latraverse moved for a judgment of acquittal. Thereafter, the trial justice gave a bench decision in which, after first noting that this court had yet to express itself on the subject of criminal liability for attempting to commit a crime, he referred to several cases in which various courts in Connecticut, the District of Columbia, Maine, and Maryland had had their say in regard to whether an accused's conduct fell within the parameters of each jurisdiction's definition of what constituted criminal attempt.

Since the issues presented by Latraverse are those of first impression for this court, we shall briefly detail the evolution of the law of criminal attempt, noting as we proceed the differing views expressed through the years about what are the essential elements of the crime.

Although the criminal law is of ancient origin, the concept that there could be criminal liability for an attempt, even if ultimately unsuccessful, is of comparatively recent origin, beginning with *Rex v. Scofield*, Cald 397 (1784). In *Scofield*, Lord Mansfield observed:

> The *intent* may make an act, innocent in itself, criminal; nor is the *completion* of an act, criminal in itself, necessary to constitute criminality. Is it no offence to set fire to a train of

1 In order to appreciate the full flavor of the note, the word "know" must be read as "now" because the intended reading was, "Hi, Sal, now it's my turn asshole."

> gunpowder with intent to burn a house, because by accident, or the interposition of another, the mischief is prevented?

The classic elements of a common-law attempt are an intent to commit a crime, the execution of an overt act in furtherance of the intention, and a failure to consummate the crime. However, this common-law view fails to indicate how far the accused's conduct must proceed toward the actual consummation of the crime in order to be considered an attempt to commit that crime. It is generally agreed that neither the intent to commit a crime nor mere preparation in and of itself constitutes an attempt. The difficulty is to establish a standard that excludes preparation prior to the actual attempt to commit the crime while including as punishable those acts which have reached the point where intervention by the police is justified.

In looking to the tests formulated by the various courts that have sought to distinguish preparation from perpetration, we first look to our northern New England neighbor, Vermont, where "attempt" is defined as an act which "must reach far enough towards the accomplishment of the desired result to amount to the commencement of the consummation." Again, shortly before the turn of the century in Massachusetts, Mr. Justice Oliver Wendell Holmes, in considering an appeal involving an attempted poisoning, observed that "the act done must come pretty near to accomplishing that result before the law will notice it." A few years later, when the question was attempted arson, he said:

> Preparation is not an attempt. But some preparations may amount to an attempt. It is a question of degree. If the preparation comes very near to the accomplishment of the act, the intent to complete it renders the crime so probable that the act will be a misdemeanor * * *.

The learned jurist also stressed that the arson attempt was complete even though an accused had an opportunity to experience a change of mind. Twenty-four years later Mr. Justice Cardozo in *People v. Werblow,* expressed the belief that acts performed in furtherance of a criminal project do not reach the stage of attempt unless "they carry the project forward within dangerous proximity to the criminal end to be attained * * *."

Later, in *United States v. Coplon*, Judge Learned Hand, in considering whether the defendant's claim that her conduct "remained in the zone of 'preparation' and that the evidence did not prove an 'attempt,'" rejected a suggested doctrine whereby the crime of attempt would be proved by a showing that the accused had done all that was in his power to do but had been prevented from proceeding further by outside intervention. Judge Hand noted that there were many decisions in the United States in which the accused had passed beyond preparation even though he had been interrupted before taking the last of his intended steps. This noted jurist found the notion that the instant of consummation could serve as the dividing line between the areas of preparation and attempt to be most unpersuasive.

It should be obvious by now that much has been written trying to establish the exact placement of the dividing line where preparation ends and attempt begins, and we have no intention of contributing one whit to what has been described as the preparation-attempt "quagmire." Instead, we adopt the sensible approach to the question now before us embodied in § 5.01 of the American Law Institute's Model Penal Code, which reads in part as follows:

> Criminal Attempt.
>
> 1) *Definition of Attempt.* A person is guilty of an attempt to commit a crime if, acting with the kind of culpability otherwise required for commission of the crime, he:
>
> (a) purposely engages in conduct which would constitute the crime if the attendant circumstances were as he believes them to be; or
>
> (b) when causing a particular result is an element of the crime, does or omits to do anything with the purpose of causing or with the belief that it will cause such result without further conduct on his part; or
>
> (c) purposely does or omits to do anything which, under the circumstances as he believes them to be, is an act or omission constituting a substantial step in a course of conduct planned to culminate in his commission of the crime.
>
> (2) *Conduct Which May Be Held Substantial Step Under Subsection (1)(c).* Conduct shall not be held to constitute a substantial step under Subsection (1)(c) of this Section unless it is strongly corroborative of the actor's criminal purpose. Without negativing the sufficiency of other conduct, the following, if strongly corroborative of the actor's criminal purpose, shall not be held insufficient as a matter of law:
>
> (a) lying in wait, searching for or following the contemplated victim of the crime;
>
> (b) enticing or seeking to entice the contemplated victim of the crime to go to the place contemplated for its commission;
>
> (c) reconnoitering the place contemplated for the commission of the crime;
>
> (d) unlawful entry of a structure, vehicle or enclosure in which it is contemplated that the crime will be committed;

(e) possession of materials to be employed in the commission of the crime, which are specially designed for such unlawful use or which can serve no lawful purpose of the actor under the circumstances;

(f) possession, collection or fabrication of materials to be employed in the commission of the crime, at or near the place contemplated for its commission, where such possession, collection or fabrication serves no lawful purpose of the actor under the circumstances;

(g) soliciting an innocent agent to engage in conduct constituting an element of the crime. * * *

(4) *Renunciation of Criminal Purpose.* When the actor's conduct would otherwise constitute an attempt under Subsection (1)(b) or (1)(c) of this Section, it is an affirmative defense that he abandoned his effort to commit the crime or otherwise prevented its commission, under circumstances manifesting a complete and voluntary renunciation of his criminal purpose. The establishment of such defense does not, however, affect the liability of an accomplice who did not join in such abandonment or prevention.

Within the meaning of this Article, renunciation of criminal purpose is not voluntary if it is motivated, in whole or in part, by circumstances, not present or apparent at the inception of the actor's course of conduct, which increase the probability of detection or apprehension or which make more difficult the accomplishment of the criminal purpose. Renunciation is not complete if it is motivated by a decision to postpone the criminal conduct until a more advantageous time or to transfer the criminal effort to another but similar objective or victim."

In taking this approach, we follow the path previously taken by our appellate colleagues in the Second and Fifth Federal Circuit Courts of Appeals as well as the Supreme Courts of the States of Ohio and Washington.

It is obvious from a reading of the code that the intent of the drafters was to extend criminal responsibility for attempted criminal behavior by * * * drawing the line between attempt and noncriminal preparation further away from the final act so as to make the crime essentially one of criminal purpose implemented by an overt act strongly corroborative of such purpose. * * *

More to the point, however, is the substantial-step clause. Under § 5.01(1)(c) of the code, an attempt occurs when one "purposely does or omits to do anything which * * * is an act or omission constituting a substantial step in a course of conduct planned to culminate in his commission of the crime." To constitute a substantial step, the conduct must be "strongly corroborative of the actor's criminal purpose." The application of this standard will, of course, depend upon the nature of the intended crime and the facts of the particular case. A substantial step in the commission of robbery may be quite different from that in arson, rape, or some other crime, but this standard properly directs attention to overt acts of the defendant which convincingly demonstrate a firm purpose to commit a crime. In subscribing to the substantial-step doctrine, we endorse the sentiments expressed by Chief Judge Kaufman in *United States v. Stallworth*, in which the court, in rejecting the defendants' contention that they could not be convicted of an attempted bank robbery because they neither entered the bank nor brandished weapons, said:

> We reject this wooden logic. Attempt is a subtle concept that requires a rational and logically sound definition, one that enables society to punish malefactors who have unequivocally set out upon a criminal course without requiring law enforcement officers to delay until innocent bystanders are imperiled.

The code's requirement of a substantial step shifts the emphasis from what remains to be done to what already has been done. Thus, liability for a relatively remote preparatory act is precluded, but at the same time dangerous individuals may be lawfully apprehended at an earlier stage of their nefarious enterprises than would be possible under the [common law]. * * *

Having made our choice concerning the pertinent legal principles, we now turn to the merits of Latraverse's appeal. His argument is simple and straightforward. He argues that in taking the evidence adduced by the state in its best light, his actions in the early-morning hours of June 27, 1980, add up to nothing more than pure preparations that, in turn, must be considered abandoned by his decision to turn around on Harrison Avenue and leave the area.

With all due deference to Latraverse's claim of preparation and/or abandonment, the code's requirement of proof (1) that Latraverse must have been acting with the kind of culpability otherwise required for the commission of the crime he is charged with attempting and (2) that he must have been engaged in conduct which constituted a substantial step toward the commission of the crime emphasizes the importance of the necessity of encouraging early police intervention when a suspect is clearly bent on the commission of crime. There is no necessity that the police had to wait until Latraverse poured the gasoline or struck the match.

The evidence presented before the trial justice indicates that Latraverse had indeed taken substantial steps to effectuate his effort to intimidate Lombardi. There is no question that at 1:40 a.m. on the morning in question he was reconnoitering Lombardi's neighborhood and in the process continued his observation while parked in a darkened automobile 100 feet from the Lombardi household. No one disputes the fact that Latraverse carried with him a homemade tool for unlocking a motor vehicle as well as material that could cause an incendiary episode, and, the most persuasive evidence of Latraverse's intentions to enter Lombardi's property in the early-morning hours of June 27, 1980, his "billet-doux" to Lombardi in which he reminded "Sal" that it was now Latraverse's turn. We have no hesitancy whatsoever in holding that Latraverse's conduct constituted a substantial step in his endeavor to give Lombardi something to think about as the officer awaited his summons to appear before the grand jury.

The trial justice, rejecting Latraverse's abandonment defense, relied on *Wiley v. State,* in which the Maryland Court of Appeals observed that a voluntary abandonment of a criminal attempt that had proceeded beyond mere preparation into an overt act or acts in furtherance of the commission of the attempt does not serve as a defense because the crime has already been committed. We cannot fault the trial justice for his reliance on the legal principles expressed in the *Wiley* case. There is a divergence of opinion about whether or not a defendant can rely upon the doctrine of abandonment after he or she has gone so far as to commit a criminal attempt. The *Wiley* case represents one side. The code expresses a different point of view in that it recognizes as a defense to an attempted crime the abandonment of efforts to commit the crime when circumstances manifest a complete and voluntary renunciation of criminal purpose.

The code stresses that abandonment or renunciation is not complete and voluntary if it is motivated because either (*a*) the defendant has failed to complete the attempt because of unanticipated difficulties, unexpected resistance, or circumstances that increase the probability of detection or apprehension or (*b*) the defendant fails to consummate the attempted offense after deciding to postpone his endeavors until another time or to substitute another victim or another but similar objective. * * *

Since abandonment is an affirmative defense, Latraverse, if he wishes, has the opportunity and the burden of establishing by a preponderance of the evidence that he in fact voluntarily and completely abandoned his nefarious efforts on the evening in question when he turned around on Harrison Avenue and drove away from Lombardi's home toward Park Place. In placing the burden of abandonment upon the defendant, we perceive no constitutional limitations. Voluntary abandonment, as we view the doctrine, does not negate any element of the offense. Our adoption of the code's approach to abandonment is motivated solely by our belief that our actions are consonant with the purpose of the substantial-step rationale, which recognizes the desirability of early preventive action by the police before a defendant comes dangerously close to committing the intended crime. In like manner, the sole motivation for our recognition of an abandonment defense is the hope that individuals will desist from pursuing their criminal designs, thereby reducing the risk that the intended substantive crime will be accomplished.

Having recognized the abandonment defense, we now afford Latraverse the opportunity to establish by the fair preponderance of the evidence that his departure from Lombardi's neighborhood constituted a voluntary and complete abandonment of his criminal purposes on the evening in question. If this evidentiary hearing is not commenced within ten days of the filing date of this opinion, an order will be entered affirming the judgment of conviction entered in the Superior Court. If he accepts this mandate, the record in this case will be remanded to the Superior Court for a hearing so that the evidence may be presented forthwith to the trial justice for his evaluation. Jurisdiction will be retained by us for further appellate review if such is required.

B. THE MENS REA REQUIREMENT

PEOPLE V. HARRIS

Supreme Court of Illinois
72 Ill.2d 16, 377 N.E.2d 28 (1978)

WARD, C.J.

* * *

[T]he defendant was convicted on a charge, made by information, of the attempted murder of Joyce Baker on the night of November 18, 1975, in a country area east of Champaign. * * *

The alleged murder attempt took place while Miss Baker was sitting inside her car and the defendant was standing behind the car with a pistol in his hand. The defendant and Miss Baker had been keeping company. For much of the evening they had been engaged in an argument in which the defendant accused the victim of infidelity. As the argument became more heated, the defendant, who was driving, reached down and picked up a revolver from the floor of the car and placed it in his lap with the barrel pointed toward Miss Baker. He made several remarks which Miss Baker interpreted as threats to kill her.

Alarmed, she opened the door on her side of the car, got out and began to run away, but ran into a barbed wire fence, injuring her leg. The defendant also got out of the car. He did not pursue her, but remained standing by the car. After her collision with the fence, Miss Baker returned to the car, and made an unsuccessful attempt to capture the gun, which the defendant was holding in his hand and pointing in her general direction. Miss Baker then got into the car on the driver's side, and drove off toward a nearby farmhouse. She testified that as she drove off she looked in the rear vision mirror and saw the defendant standing behind the car. He was holding the gun with both hands, and pointing it at her. Then she heard something strike the rear window, and the broken pane of glass in the rear window fell out of its frame. There were no other witnesses, but following this episode the police were summoned, and they found the defendant walking down the road near the scene of the episode just described. When the car was located, the police officers testified, the rear glass was broken, and a bullet fragment was found on the left side of the rear seat.

The jury returned a verdict of guilty on the charge of attempted murder * * *. The defendant was sentenced to serve a term of not less than 4 years and not more than 12 years. * * *

The following instructions to the jury were tendered by the State and were given, over the objection of the defendant:

> A person commits the crime of attempt who, with intent to commit the crime of murder, does any act which constitutes a substantial step toward the commission of the crime of murder. The crime attempted need not have been committed.
>
> To sustain the charge of attempt, the State must prove the following propositions:
>
> *First*: That the defendant performed an act which constituted a substantial step toward the commission of the crime of murder; and
>
> *Second*: That the defendant did so with intent to commit the crime of murder.
>
> A person commits the crime of murder who kills an individual if, in performing the acts which cause the death, he *intends to kill or do great bodily harm to that individual.* (emphasis added).

The defendant objected to the last of the instructions on the ground that it told the jury it could find him guilty of attempted murder if the jury found that he had acted only with the intent to do great bodily harm and did not have the intent to cause death. * * *

The central difficulty * * * arises out of the difference between the elements of the offense of attempt and those of the specific offense attempted, murder. The definition of attempt, contained in section 8—4(a) of the Criminal Code of 1961, is:

> A person commits an attempt when, *with intent to commit a specific offense*, he does any act which constitutes a substantial step toward the commission of that offense. (emphasis added).

The statutory definition of murder is found in section 9–1(a) of the Code, and reads:

> A person who kills an individual without lawful justification commits murder if, in performing the acts which cause the death:
>
> (1) He either intends to kill or do great bodily harm to that individual or another, or knows that such acts will cause death to that individual or another; or
>
> (2) He knows that such acts create a strong probability of death or great bodily harm to that individual or another; or
>
> (3) He is attempting or committing a forcible felony other than voluntary manslaughter.

The crime of murder is thus committed not only when a person intends to kill another individual, but also when he intends to do great bodily harm, or when he knows that his acts create a strong probability of death or great bodily harm, or when he is attempting or committing a forcible felony. * * *

[In this case] the third instruction states that a person is guilty of the crime of murder "if, in performing the acts which cause the death, he intends to kill or do great bodily harm to that individual." * * * [T]his instruction * * * permits the jury to return a verdict of guilty upon evidence that the defendant intended only to cause great bodily harm short of death. An instruction must make it clear that to convict for attempted murder nothing less than a criminal intent to kill must be shown. * * *

Observations of LaFave and Scott are representative of authority that it is not sufficient to prove attempted murder to show that the accused intended to cause serious bodily harm:

> Some crimes, such as murder, are defined in terms of acts causing a particular result plus some mental state which need not be an intent to bring about that result. Thus, if A, B, and C have each taken the life of another, A acting with intent to kill, B with an intent to do serious bodily injury, and C with a reckless disregard of human life, all three are guilty of murder because the crime of murder is defined in such a way that any one of these mental states will suffice. However, if the victims do not die from their injuries, then only A is guilty of attempted murder; on a charge of attempted murder it is not sufficient to show that the defendant intended to do serious bodily harm or that he acted in reckless disregard for human life. Again, this is because intent is needed for the crime of attempt, so that

attempted murder requires an intent to bring about that result described by the crime of murder (*i.e.*, the death of another). * * *

Reversed and remanded.

STATE V. HINKHOUSE

Court of Appeals of Oregon
139 Or.App. 446, 912 P.2d 921 (1996)

LANDAU, J.

Defendant is infected with the human immunodeficiency virus (HIV). He was convicted of ten counts of attempted murder and ten counts of attempted assault I, based on his conduct of engaging in unprotected sexual intercourse with a number of victims without disclosing his medical condition. On appeal, he argues that the convictions must be set aside, because the evidence is insufficient to establish that he intended to cause the death of or serious physical injury to any of his several victims. The state argues that the evidence is sufficient to support the convictions. We agree with the state and affirm.

We state the facts in the light most favorable to the state. Defendant learned that he had tested positive for HIV in 1989. That year, he began a sexual relationship with P.B., who was 15 years old at the time. At the end of the summer, defendant moved to California, but he returned six months later and renewed his sexual relationship with P.B. During that relationship, defendant refused to use condoms, saying that he did not like them. He and P.B. did not discuss HIV. In July 1990, defendant again left. P.B. asked defendant why he was leaving. In the course of his explanation, defendant told P.B. that she might want to get tested for HIV. P.B. was tested and, in August 1990, she learned that she was HIV-positive. A few months later, defendant called P.B. and said that he wanted to meet with her. When they met, defendant asked whether she had been tested. P.B. responded, "Well, you should know my status because you gave it to me." Defendant did not deny the accusation, but just "brushed it off."

On November 3, 1990, defendant told his probation officer, Bill Carroll, that defendant was HIV-positive. Carroll immediately advised defendant of the implications of his HIV status, explaining the seriousness of the disease and the manner in which it is transmitted. Carroll explained that using a condom limits the risks of transmitting the virus, but he also explained that it would not eliminate the risk entirely. He told defendant that if he passed the virus to another person, "he would be killing someone." Over the next several months, Carroll and defendant continued to have conversations about HIV and the need to take precautions to avoid transmitting the virus. In a telephone conversation in 1991, Carroll again cautioned defendant: "If you infect anyone, that is murder." Defendant said that he understood and agreed that he would take appropriate precautions.

In 1992, defendant was taken into custody on a probation violation. He and Carroll continued their conversations about the danger defendant posed by continuing to engage in sexual relationships. According to Carroll, defendant said that he understood the situation and that "he would cease and desist from any kind of [sexual] activity." Nevertheless, defendant continued to engage in sexual relations with a number of women. When he was taken into custody again for another probation violation later that year, he was heard bragging about his sexual prowess with women, expressing neither concern nor remorse for the people whom he might have exposed to HIV. As a condition of his release, however, he signed a probation agreement that included a commitment not to engage in any unsupervised contact with women without express permission from his parole officer.

In 1993, defendant began several sexual relationships without notifying Carroll. In each case, he refused to use a condom during sex and failed to disclose his HIV status. In May of that year, he began a sexual relationship with P.D. He never used a condom and said nothing about HIV.

In June of 1993, defendant began having sex with L.K. She demanded that defendant use a condom, and he did so for three or four weeks. On one occasion, he promised to use a condom, but then he penetrated her without one, in spite of L.K.'s protests. L.K. and defendant then had a long talk about safe sex, in which defendant told her that he had just ended a long-term relationship, that he had not engaged in any risky behavior since then, and that he had recently tested negative for HIV. Defendant and L.K. resumed their sexual relationship. Defendant, however, persisted in failing to use a condom. When L.K. expressed concern about his behavior, defendant replied that there was no need to wear condoms, because, if either of them had HIV, the other already had been exposed. Defendant agreed to be tested for HIV, but never followed through.

After a brief hiatus, defendant and L.K. continued their sexual relationship. Defendant's sexual behavior became very rough. He would engage in intercourse so vigorously that L.K. would bleed. When L.K. complained, defendant's attitude was "very casual," even proud. Defendant also insisted on engaging in anal intercourse, and, although L.K. said that she was "dead set" against it, defendant attempted anal sex several times. She complained that, although at times he could be gentle, he was becoming "very rough and very rude," and that he would be "mean and spiteful and try[ ] to be hurtful." L.K. ended her relationship with defendant in August of 1993.

The following month, defendant began a sexual relationship with R.L. She suggested that defendant buy condoms, but he told her, "I don't believe in them." R.L. suggested that defendant might have HIV, but he denied that, saying, "I don't have it, and whoever is telling you is lying."

Throughout 1993, defendant continued to meet with his probation officer on a weekly basis. During that time they would discuss defendant's HIV status. At no time did defendant mention P.D., L.K. or R.L.

Around the same time that defendant began seeing R.L., he also began a romantic relationship with M.S. Defendant hopes that he and M.S. will marry someday. M.S. was aware of his HIV status, and defendant always wore condoms when he had sexual intercourse with her.

At trial, Dr. Beers explained that HIV is transmitted through bodily fluids, including semen. He said that even nontraumatic sexual intercourse is an effective method of transmitting the disease and that more violent sex or anal sex increases the risk of transmission, because of the increased likelihood that tears in tissue break down the body's barriers to the virus. He explained that a person may be infected after a single sexual exposure.

Defendant's psychologist, Dr. Norman, testified that defendant had a long history of acting out sexually and that he suffered from attention deficit disorder. He opined that defendant understood how HIV is transmitted and that it is a fatal disease. Norman also testified that, although defendant had reportedly threatened in 1991 to "go out and spread" HIV, he did not lend much credence to such threats. According to Norman, defendant simply did not think about the consequences of his behavior.

The state's expert, Dr. Johnson, agreed that defendant suffers from attention deficit disorder. Johnson testified that defendant also suffers from a borderline personality disorder and is antisocial. He recounted that defendant had acknowledged that his parole officer had warned him not to infect other people, and that defendant had responded that "he was going to do whatever he wanted, whenever he wanted." Johnson also thought that it was significant that defendant agreed to use, and in fact used, condoms when having intercourse with a woman for whom he expressed affection, but he did not use condoms with the other women with whom he had sex. Johnson also reported a conversation with another of defendant's former sexual partners, who said that, although defendant had denied that he was HIV-positive, he said that if he were positive, he would spread the virus to other people. In Johnson's opinion, such statements, coupled with defendant's behavior, showed intentional, deliberate conduct. Particularly in the light of the pattern of systematically recruiting and exploiting multiple partners over a long period of time, Johnson said, he found no evidence to suggest that defendant was acting impulsively or without the intent to harm.

Defendant moved for a judgment of acquittal, which the trial court denied. On appeal, defendant argues that the trial court erred in denying his motion, because the evidence is insufficient to support convictions for either attempted murder or attempted assault. He argues that there is no evidence that he intended to cause death or serious bodily injury, only evidence that—at most—he acted in reckless disregard of the consequences of his conduct. The state contends that the evidence is sufficient to support the convictions on both sets of charges, based on the undisputed evidence that defendant concealed or lied about his HIV status, refused to wear condoms, and intentionally had unprotected sex with a number of women, while fully aware of the fact that he was exposing them to the virus.

We review a denial of a motion for judgment of acquittal to determine whether, viewing the evidence in the light most favorable to the state, a rational trier of fact could have found the essential elements of the crime beyond a reasonable doubt. We must give the state the benefit of all reasonable inferences that properly may be drawn. A person is guilty of attempting to commit a crime "when the person intentionally engages in conduct which constitutes a substantial step toward commission of the crime." A person commits assault in the first degree when "the person intentionally causes serious physical injury to another by means of a deadly or dangerous weapon."

A person commits attempted murder when he or she attempts, without justification or excuse, intentionally to cause the death of another human being. To act "intentionally" is to "act[ ] with a conscious objective to cause the result or to engage in the conduct so described."

Viewing the evidence in the light most favorable to the state, we conclude that there is sufficient evidence for a rational trier of fact to find that defendant intended to cause both physical injury and death. He knew that he was HIV positive and that his condition was terminal. He knew that if he transmitted the virus to another person, that person eventually would die as well. He understood that having unprotected sex would expose his sexual partners to the virus and that a single sexual encounter could transmit the virus. He had been told, and he acknowledged, that having unprotected sex and transmitting the disease was "murder." He even signed an agreement that he would refrain from any unsupervised contact with women without the approval of his probation officer.

In spite of that awareness, defendant engaged in a persistent pattern of recruiting sexual partners over a period of many months. He consistently concealed or lied about his HIV status. He refused to wear condoms, or pretended to wear them, penetrating women without protection and against their protestations. He engaged in unprotected sex, including rough and violent intercourse, which increased the chances of passing the virus to his partners. He bragged about his sexual prowess, even after acknowledging his HIV status, and told at least one person that he intended to spread the disease to others by such conduct.

Defendant insists that he meant only to satisfy himself sexually, and that that is insufficient to prove intent to harm or to cause death. His conduct, however, demonstrates that his objective was more than mere sexual gratification. When he engaged in sexual intercourse with the woman he hoped to marry, he consistently wore condoms and made no attempt to conceal his HIV status. When he had sex with others, in contrast, he concealed or lied about his condition and refused any protection. Particularly in the light of the pattern of exploitation over a long period of time, a rational fact finder could conclude beyond a reasonable doubt that defendant did not act impulsively merely to satisfy his sexual desires, but instead acted deliberately to cause his victims serious bodily injury and death. The trial court did not err in denying defendant's motion for a judgment of acquittal.

Affirmed.

C. THE DEFENSE OF IMPOSSIBILITY

UNITED STATES V. THOMAS

United States Court of Military Appeals
32 C.M.R. 278, 13 U.S.C.M.A. 278 (1962)

KILDAY, JUDGE:

The accused herein, Thomas and McClellan, were tried in common by general court-martial. Separate charges against the pair alleged the offenses of conspiracy to commit rape, rape, and lewd and lascivious conduct, in violation of Articles 81, 120, and 134, Uniform Code of Military Justice, 10 USC §§ 881, 920, and 934, respectively. Upon arraignment, both men entered pleas of not guilty. Each was acquitted of rape, but the court-martial found them guilty of attempted rape, * * * and likewise convicted them of the other two charges upon which they were brought to trial. Both received identical sentences to dishonorable discharge, confinement at hard labor for three years, forfeiture of all pay and allowances for a like period, and reduction to the grade of airman recruit.

Thereafter, the findings and sentences adjudged by the trial court were approved by the officer exercising general court-martial jurisdiction. The board of review, however, set aside the findings of guilty of attempted rape and conspiracy as to both accused. * * *

The evidence adduced at the trial presents a sordid and revolting picture which need not be discussed in detail other than as necessary to decide the certified issues. In brief, both these young accused—Thomas being twenty years of age, and McClellan only nineteen, at the time of the instant offenses—started their fateful evening on a "bar hopping" spree. They were accompanied by an eighteen-year-old companion, Abruzzese, who, like both accused, held the grade of airman in the Navy. The latter was a co-actor in these offenses, but was granted immunity from prosecution for his criminality in the incidents, and testified as a witness for the Government.

After several stops the trio entered a tavern known as "Taylor's Place" where McClellan began dancing with a girl. Almost at once she collapsed in McClellan's arms. Thereafter, he, with his two companions, volunteered to take her home. They placed the apparently unconscious female in McClellan's car and left. Abruzzese was seated beside McClellan, who drove; Thomas was in the left rear seat next to the girl. Before they had proceeded very far McClellan, in frank, expressive language, suggested that this was a good chance for sexual intercourse as apparently this woman was just drunk and would never know the difference. Each of the three subsequently did or attempted to consummate this act and then started their return to town. The three became concerned as the woman had not regained consciousness.

In the meantime they dropped Abruzzese off at the USO. The accused, unable to find the female's home and becoming more concerned about her condition, stopped at a service station seeking help. The attendant called the police who, upon arriving at the service station, examined the girl and determined she was dead. An ambulance was called and she was taken to a hospital for further examination. An autopsy, later performed, revealed that she apparently died of "acute interstitial myocarditis." In general terms this is a weakening of the heart muscles with edema and inflammation which occurs more in young people without its presence being suspected. It was the general undisputed opinion that her death probably occurred at the time she collapsed on the dance floor at Taylor's Place or very shortly thereafter. Apparently, in deaths of this type, rigor mortis does not usually begin for some time and as a result the accused were unaware of the fact she was dead.

The chief witness for the prosecution was the co-actor Abruzzese who, as we have noted, had been granted immunity. He implicated himself and both accused in his testimony. A written statement by McClellan concerning the alleged offenses was introduced through an agent of the Office of Naval Intelligence, a witness for the prosecution. The accused Thomas discussed the alleged incident with this same Office of Naval Intelligence agent, but no statement by Thomas was introduced into evidence. Numerous other witnesses testified, including medical experts, and the record of trial and exhibits in this case are voluminous. However, as the board of review stated, no factual dispute exists as to the death of the female involved and the cause thereof. It is clear, as that appellate body concluded, the victim was dead at the time she was removed from the tavern or relatively shortly thereafter, and the prosecution adduced no convincing evidence that she was alive at the time the offenses were committed. * * *

Despite the fact that defense counsel at trial vigorously urged to the law officer that the offenses of attempt and conspiracy could not be found validly if the victim's death occurred prior to the commission of the alleged acts, the law officer ruled otherwise. He instructed the court that to find the accused guilty of rape, * * * it must be shown beyond a reasonable doubt that the victim was alive at the time of the alleged acts. Otherwise, he admonished the court members, the accused must be acquitted of [that] offense[ ]. The law officer then continued, and instructed the court on the elements of attempt as an included lesser crime to rape. However, unlike the instructions given as to rape * * *, the law officer did not instruct that being alive was essential to a finding of attempt. That clearly drawn distinction is illuminated by the following colloquy which subsequently ensued between a member of the court and the law officer:

> Cdr. Carpenter: I don't remember you pointing this out in your instructions—you said the woman must be alive if raped but you didn't say whether she had to be alive for attempted rape, although I think you implied it.
>
> LO: Yes, sir. There is no requirement under the instructions which I have given you that there be a finding she be alive before the accused may be convicted of attempted rape. * * *

Before the board of review, appellate defense counsel contended that the law officer erred in his instructions to the court on the attempt and conspiracy offenses. In support of that position, the defense argued that where circumstances beyond the accused's control make it legally impossible to commit a crime, as distinguished from factual impossibility to do so, there can be no attempt nor can there be a conspiracy to commit the substantive offense.

The board of review held that an attempt to commit a crime must be directed to an object on which it is possible to commit the crime. Reasoning that a corpse is not a person, the board of review determined that the law officer erred in his instruction that there was no requirement that the victim be alive before the accused could be convicted of attempted rape. Thus, the board stated, "If the consummation was not an offense, the attempt herein was not an offense," and concluded, "Legally under the facts and law before us the offense of rape and the lesser included offenses including attempts were impossible of commission." * * *

The rules of law applying to attempts and those applying to conspiracies are very closely related. Our principal discussion shall be confined to attempts. However, we shall, in essence, treat of the two certified issues together. * * *

In all candor we must confess that we claim no particular expertise as to the question of attempts as they have troubled our brothers on the bench of tribunals in the civilian community. We profess no mastery of the subject and do not purport to be more competent than other judges to resolve the conflicts in the civilian authorities which trouble them. However, as shall later be developed, we do not consider it necessary to evaluate the civilian decisions ourselves, nor to take a stand with or opposed to any one or group thereof. Nevertheless, as a backdrop against which to consider the problem, we deem it appropriate to explore the intricacies of the civilian holdings in the area. * * *

In practically all of the * * * texts [on the defense of impossibility], the specific question involved in this case—impossibility of completion of the substantive crime—is discussed at very considerable length. The two reasons for "impossibility" are treated in this connection: (1) If the intended act is not criminal, there can be no criminal liability for an attempt to commit the act. This is sometimes described as a "legal impossibility."[a] (2) If the intended substantive crime is impossible of accomplishment because of some physical impossibility unknown to the accused, the elements of a criminal attempt are present. This is sometimes described as "impossibility in fact."

The authorities seem to be in fair accord that (1), above, is not punishable as an attempt. There is some considerable conflict of authority as to whether (2), above, is punishable as an attempt, but the preponderance seems to be that such instances do constitute attempts. What is abundantly clear, however, is that it is most difficult to classify any particular state of facts as positively coming within one of these categories to the exclusion of the other.

Practically all writers on this subject, whether in law journal articles, texts, or judicial opinions, cite and discuss the same relatively limited number of decisions. These decisions are generally placed in the two following categories:

1. "Legal impossibility" in which attempt convictions have been set aside on the ground that it was legally impossible for

[a] The court is incomplete in its explanation of the defense of impossibility. What it describes as "legal impossibility" is also known as "pure legal impossibility." The court fails to explain that another form of legal impossibility called "hybrid legal impossibility" was recognized at common law. Under hybrid legal impossibility, the defendant is not guilty of an attempt if he was mistaken about a fact related to the legal status of an attendant circumstance in the definition of the offense. Most of the examples of legal impossibility listed by the court are cases of "hybrid legal impossibility" not "pure legal impossibility."

the accused to have committed the crime contemplated. These are as follows:

(a) A person accepting goods which he believed to have been stolen, but which were not then "stolen goods," was not guilty of an attempt to receive stolen goods.

(b) An accused who offered a bribe to a person believed to be a juror, but who was not a juror, could not be said to have attempted to bribe a juror.

(c) An official who contracted a debt which was unauthorized and a nullity, but which he believed to be valid, could not be convicted of an attempt to illegally contract a valid debt.

(d) A hunter who shot a stuffed deer believing it to be alive had not attempted to take a deer out of season.

(e) It is not an attempt to commit subornation of perjury where the false testimony solicited, if given, would have been immaterial to the case at hand and hence not perjurious.

2. Instances in which a claim of impossibility has been rejected and convictions sustained, are included below. Apparently these can all be classified as "impossibility in fact." These decisions are:

(a) It is now uniformly held that one is guilty if he attempts to steal from an empty pocket. The same is true as to an empty receptacle, and an empty house. The rule is applied whether the attempt is to commit burglary, robbery, extortion, or obtaining by false pretenses.

(b) One can attempt to possess narcotics, even though accused obtained possession of talcum believing it to be narcotics. And, one can be convicted of attempted use of a narcotic drug even though there is a reasonable doubt as to whether the substance was a narcotic.

(c) An accused may be guilty of attempted murder who, suspecting that a policeman on the roof was spying upon him through a hole, but ignorant that the policeman was then upon another part of the roof, fired at the hole with intent to kill. It is attempted murder to shoot into the intended victim's bed believing he is there asleep when in fact he is some place else. An accused is not absolved from the charge of attempted murder when he points an unloaded gun at his wife's head and pulls the trigger, if he actually thought at the time that it was loaded.

(d) In attempted abortion cases an accused may be guilty in the absence of proof that the woman was pregnant. Where the statute refers to "any woman," it is immaterial whether she was pregnant or not if the defendant believed she was.

* * *

The lack of logic between some of the holdings, the inherent difficulty in assigning a given set of facts to a proper classification; the criticism of existing positions in this area; and, most importantly, the denial of true and substantial justice by these artificial holdings have led, quite naturally, to proposals for reform in the civilian legal concepts of criminal attempts.

In addition to a progressive and modern view now evident in some judicial decisions and writings, The American Law Institute in its proposal of a "Model Penal Code" defines Criminal Attempts, in Article 5.01, as follows:

> (1) Definition of attempt. A person is guilty of an attempt to commit a crime if, acting with the kind of culpability otherwise required for commission of the crime, he:
>
> (a) purposely engages in conduct which would constitute the crime if the attendant circumstances were as he believes them to be; or
>
> (b) when causing a particular result is an element of the crime, does or omits to do anything with the purpose of causing or with the belief that it will cause such result, without further conduct on his part; or
>
> (c) purposely does or omits to do anything which, under the circumstances as he believes them to be, is a substantial step in a course of conduct planned to culminate in his commission of the crime."
>
> The import of that suggested statute is made clear in Tentative Draft No. 10 of the Model Penal Code of The American Law Institute, supra, at page 25, where it is stated:
>
> . . . It should suffice, therefore, to indicate at this stage what we deem to be the major results of the draft. They are:
>
> (a) to extend the criminality of attempts by sweeping aside the defense of impossibility (including the distinction between so-called factual and legal impossibility) and by drawing the line between attempt and non-criminal preparation further away from the final act; the crime becomes essentially one of criminal purpose implemented by an overt act strongly corroborative of such purpose; . . .

After having given this entire question a great deal more than casual attention and study, we are forced to the conclusion that the law of attempts in military jurisprudence has tended toward the advanced and modern position, which position will be achieved for civilian jurisprudence if The American Law Institute is completely successful in its advocacy of this portion of the Model Penal Code.

Because of the legal acumen of the law officer of this general court-martial, the trial was conducted in accordance with this approach. We conclude that his instructions to the court-martial with reference to the offense of rape, the lesser included offenses thereto, including attempt to rape, and conspiracy, furnished correct advice on impossibility insofar as the same is affected by the death of the victim. * * *

We hold, therefore, in accordance with the foregoing authorities, that in this instance the fact that the female, upon whom these detestable acts were performed, was already dead at the time of their commission, is no bar to conviction for attempted rape. * * *

For the above stated reasons, we hold that the law officer did not err in the instructions given to the court-martial in connection with attempted rape and conspiracy to commit rape.

It is clear from this record, by the findings of the court-martial and the facts as sustained by the board of review, that each of these appellants was guilty of each element necessary to the crime of attempted rape. That is, each of the appellants did:

1. A certain overt act.[b]

2. The act was done with the specific intent to commit the offense of rape; that is, each intended to have sexual intercourse with a female not his wife by force and without her consent.

3. The act amounted to more than mere preparation.

4. It apparently tended to effect the commission of the intended offense, even though

5. The intended offense failed of completion because, unknown to either appellant and as a matter beyond their control, their victim was already dead.

Likewise, all of the necessary elements of conspiracy to commit the offense of rape are present. That is:

1. Each of these accused and their co-actor Abruzzese mutually entered into an agreement to commit rape on the female alleged.

[b] The court here conflates the elements of an attempt under the Model Penal Code with the elements of a conspiracy. Under the Model Penal Code's definition of an attempt, a defendant must take a "substantial step" towards the commission of the offense, not merely an overt act. The Model Penal Code requires an "overt act" for conspiracy liability.

2. Thereafter, while the agreement continued in existence and while each of appellants remained a party thereto, each performed an overt act to effect the object of the agreement.

All the elements of both attempted rape and conspiracy to commit rape are present and were returned by the members of the court-martial under correct standards set out in the law officer's instructions. The board of review, therefore, erred in holding to the contrary.

The certified issues are answered in the negative, and the decision of the board of review is reversed. This case is returned to The Judge Advocate General of the Navy for action not inconsistent with this opinion.

[The opinion of FERGUSON, JUDGE, concurring in part and dissenting in part, has been omitted.]

CHAPTER 12

ACCOMPLICE LIABILITY (COMPLICITY)

■ ■ ■

INTRODUCTION

One who intentionally assists another in the commission of a crime can be convicted of that offense as an accomplice. At common law, the different parties involved were divided into principals and accessories. These distinctions were extremely important at common law. For example, the charging document had to state correctly whether the defendant was a principal or an accessory. If the indictment said the defendant was a principal and it turned out that the defendant was only an accessory, the indictment would be dismissed. These distinctions were also important in terms of timing. An accessory could not be tried before the principal in the first degree, and an accessory could not be convicted unless the principal in the first degree was convicted first. Additionally, principals had to be prosecuted in the jurisdiction in which the crime was perpetrated, while accessories could only be prosecuted in the jurisdiction in which their acts of assistance occurred. Although these common law rules have largely been abandoned, many courts still use the terminology of principal in the first degree, principal in the second degree, accessory before the fact, and accessory after the fact.

The "principal in the first degree" is the person who actually commits the acts constituting the offense or uses an "innocent instrumentality" to commit the crime. The innocent instrumentality can either be a non-culpable person, such as a mentally incompetent person, or a non-human agent, such as a trained animal.

The "principal in the second degree" is the person who intentionally assists the principal in the first degree and is present during the commission of the crime. The presence requirement can be satisfied by actual or constructive presence. An accomplice is constructively present if close enough to render assistance to the principal in the first degree during the commission of the crime. For example, an accomplice just outside a bank watching for police officers is constructively present at the scene of a bank robbery even though he is not inside the bank (not actually present) during the robbery because he is close enough to assist the principal in the first degree during the commission of the robbery.

An "accessory before the fact" is a person who intentionally assists in the commission of the crime, but is not present when the crime is being committed. For example, the person who buys the guns used to rob the bank but who does not accompany the others to the bank is an accessory before the fact.

An "accessory after the fact" is a person who helps the principal in the first degree and his or her accomplices avoid arrest, trial or conviction. While as a general rule, accomplices are held liable for the same crime as the principal in the first degree, an accessory after the fact is treated less harshly than a principal in the second degree and an accessory before the fact.

Accomplice liability today has both an actus reus requirement and a mens rea requirement. The actus reus requirement is satisfied by assisting the principal in the first degree in the commission of a crime. The mens rea requirement has two elements, which are discussed later in this chapter. Keep in mind that accomplice liability is derivative. The defendant who satisfies both the actus reus and the mens rea requirements for complicity is not guilty of "complicity." Rather, the defendant is guilty of the substantive crime—the crime with which the principal in the first degree has been charged.

A. THE ACTUS REUS REQUIREMENT

To satisfy the actus reus requirement for accomplice liability, an accomplice must assist the principal in the first degree in committing a crime. Some assistance, no matter how trivial, is required. Mere presence ordinarily is not sufficient for accomplice liability. *Pace v. State* addresses whether and when presence is sufficient to constitute the assistance required for accomplice liability.

PACE V. STATE

Supreme Court of Indiana
248 Ind. 146, 224 N.E.2d 312 (1967)

HUNTER, JUDGE.

This is an appeal from a jury finding and judgment of conviction of the defendant for the crime of accessory before the fact of robbery by placing in fear.

The defendant was charged by an affidavit filed in the St. Joseph Superior Court No. 2, May 26, 1964, with the crime of Accessory Before the Fact to Robbery by Putting in Fear, to-wit:

Arthur Madaras, being first duly sworn upon his oath, deposes and says:

> That on or about the 23rd day of May, 1964, at and in the County of St. Joseph, State of Indiana, one William Eugene Rootes did then and there unlawfully, feloniously and forcibly

> and by putting Richard Leon Reppert in fear, rob, take and steal from the said Richard Leon Reppert Two ($2.00) Dollars in good and lawful currency of the United States of America, belonging to the said Richard Leon Reppert, and one Benrus wrist watch with gold band valued in the sum of Fifty ($50.00) Dollars belonging to the said Richard Leon Reppert, and the said Carl Lemual Pace, Jr., at and in the County and State aforesaid, did then and there unlawfully and feloniously aid and abet, counsel and encourage the said William Eugene Rootes to do and commit the said felony in the manner and form aforesaid, contrary to the form of Statutes in such cases made and provided and against the peace and dignity of the State of Indiana.

The appellant waived arraignment and entered a plea of not guilty and was represented by [a] court appointed public defender. Trial was to a jury. At the close of State's evidence, defendant filed [a] written motion for directed verdict which was overruled. The jury rendered its verdict against the defendant and found him guilty as charged.

Thereafter on April 6, 1964 the court sentenced the defendant to the Indiana Reformatory for a period of not less than ten (10) or more than twenty-five (25) years. On April 23, 1965 a motion for new trial was filed which was overruled by the trial court. In the assignment of errors, the principal point urged is that the verdict of the jury is not sustained by sufficient evidence and the verdict of the jury is contrary to law. We are of the opinion that the principal ground for reversal presented by the assignment of errors which questions the sufficiency of the evidence to sustain the jury's finding of guilty is determinative of this case.

Viewing the evidence most favorable to the State, the record shows the following: appellant, his wife and two infant children were in a car driving from South Bend to LaPorte. Eugene Rootes was riding with them. The appellant was driving with his wife and one child in the front seat. Rootes and appellant's other child were in the back seat. While in South Bend, appellant after asking his wife for permission stopped to pick up a hitchhiker, Mr. Reppert, who sat next to Rootes in the back seat with one of appellant's infant children. Later Rootes pulled a knife and took Reppert's wallet. After driving further, Reppert got out of the car, Rootes then took his watch. The appellant said nothing during the entire period and they continued driving to LaPorte. This is all of the evidence presented by the record which would have any bearing on the crime charged, i.e., accessory before the fact of robbery by placing in fear.

The main question presented in the facts at bar is what evidence beyond the mere presence of a person at the scene of a crime is sufficient to sustain a conviction as an accessory before the fact? This court has previously stated that negative acquiescence is not enough to constitute a person guilty of aiding and abetting the commission of a crime.

Consequently, this court has always looked for affirmative conduct either in the form of acts or words from which reasonable inferences of a common design or purpose to effect the commission of a crime might be drawn. However, it has been further stated by this court in *Mobley v. State*:

> . . . in the absence of anything in his conduct showing a design to encourage, incite, aid, abet or assist in the crime, the trier of the facts may consider failure of such person to oppose the commission of the crime in connection with other circumstances and conclude therefrom that he assented to the commission of the crime, lent his countenance and approval thereto and thereby aided and abetted it . . .

It should be noted that the court in *Mobley*, in stating that a failure to oppose the commission of a crime may be considered as aiding and abetting, impliedly qualified this statement wherein the Court stated at p. 343:

> This, it seems to us, is particularly true when the person who fails to interfere owes a duty to protect as a parent owes to a child.

In other cases relying on *Mobley*, there has normally been some course of conduct of an affirmative nature to connect the defendant with the crime.

In the facts at bar we have found no evidence or reasonable inferences therefrom which might demonstrate that the appellant aided and abetted in the alleged crime. While he was driving the car, nothing was said nor did he act in any manner to indicate his approval or countenance of the robbery. While there is evidence from which a jury might reasonably infer that he knew the crime was being committed, his situation was not one which would demonstrate a duty to oppose it. We do not intend to draw any hard and fast rules in this area of the law. Each case must be reviewed on its own facts; in so doing we hold that the verdict is not sustained by substantial evidence of probative value and is therefore contrary to law.

We hold that the appellant's (defendant's) motion for a directed verdict should have been sustained by the trial court. Now, therefore, the judgment of the trial court should be reversed.

Judgment reversed.

B. THE MENS REA REQUIREMENT

Like the law of attempt and conspiracy, the law of complicity has a dual intent requirement. As a general rule, to be held liable as an accomplice, the defendant must have: (1) the intent to do the acts that assist the principal in the first degree in the commission of a crime, and (2) the intent that the principal in the first degree commit that crime. What if the crime in question can be committed unintentionally? *State v. Foster* indicates that courts are not as strict with regard to the second intent requirement in complicity law as they are when dealing with attempts and conspiracy.

What happens when an individual feigns his complicity, but provides the principal in the first degree with assistance in committing the crime? Can the feigning accomplice be found liable for the crime that the principal in the first degree commits? *Wilson v. People* addresses this question.

STATE V. FOSTER

Supreme Court of Connecticut
202 Conn. 520; 522 A.2d 277 (1987)

SANTANIELLO, J.

In June, 1982, the defendant was living with his girlfriend and their child in an apartment near the Martin Luther King School in Hartford. At approximately 7:30 p.m. in the evening of June 16, 1982, while walking near the school, the defendant's girlfriend was robbed and raped by a young black male who held a straight-edged razor to her throat. During the one half hour encounter, she observed her attacker's features and later that night described him and the clothes he was wearing to the police. She also described the assailant, with specific identifiable features, to the defendant.

The defendant, who was "bitter" about the attack, purposely went looking for his girlfriend's attacker. On June 22, 1982, the defendant and a friend, Otha Cannon, after visiting with the defendant's girlfriend for a short period of time, went walking in the vicinity where the rape and robbery had occurred. Near the Martin Luther King School, the defendant saw a man he thought matched the description of the assailant. After telling Cannon "[t]his is the guy who raped my lady," the defendant and Cannon confronted the suspected rapist, later identified as William Jack Middleton, in an alleyway next to the school. Upon being approached, Middleton became frightened and denied any involvement in the robbery or rape. He attempted to flee and a fight ensued; the defendant beat Middleton about the face, eye, chest and head with his fist and a blunt instrument, knocking him to the ground. The defendant, desiring to bring his girlfriend to the scene to make an identification, told Middleton to "wait here" while he left to get her. Although Middleton agreed to wait, the defendant, suspecting that he might flee, gave a knife to Cannon and told him to stay with Middleton to prevent his escape. Thereafter, while waiting for the defendant to return, Middleton, as he was reaching for something in his pocket, apparently charged at Cannon. As Middleton ran toward him, Cannon held out the knife that the defendant had given him and fatally stabbed Middleton. The victim had a straight-edged razor in his pocket which was later identified by the defendant's girlfriend as the one wielded by her assailant during the rape incident. * * *

The jury found the defendant guilty of kidnapping in the second degree, assault in the third degree * * *, and being an accessory to criminally negligent homicide in violation of General Statutes §§ 53a–8 and 53a–58 * * *. Thereafter, the defendant filed motions for acquittal * * * claiming, inter alia, that there was no such crime as being an accessory to criminally negligent homicide. The trial court denied both motions. The defendant appealed. * * *

General Statutes § 53a–8 provides in relevant part that "[a] person, acting with the mental state required for the commission of an offense, who . . . intentionally aids another person to engage in conduct which constitutes an offense shall be criminally liable for such conduct . . . as if he were the principal offender." We have previously stated that a conviction under § 53a–8 requires proof of a dual intent, i.e., "that the accessory have the intent to aid the principal and that in so aiding he intend to commit the offense with which he is charged."

Citing this "dual intent" requirement, and relying on *State v. Almeda* and *State v. Beccia,* cases which held that persons cannot attempt or conspire to commit an offense that requires an unintended result, the defendant argues that a person cannot be convicted as an accessory to criminally negligent homicide. He reasons that because accessorial liability requires an accused, in aiding a principal, to "intend to commit the offense with which he is charged" and because criminally negligent homicide requires that an unintended death occur, the crime of being an accessory to criminally negligent homicide is a logical impossibility in that it would require a defendant, in aiding another, to intend to commit a crime in which an unintended result occurs.

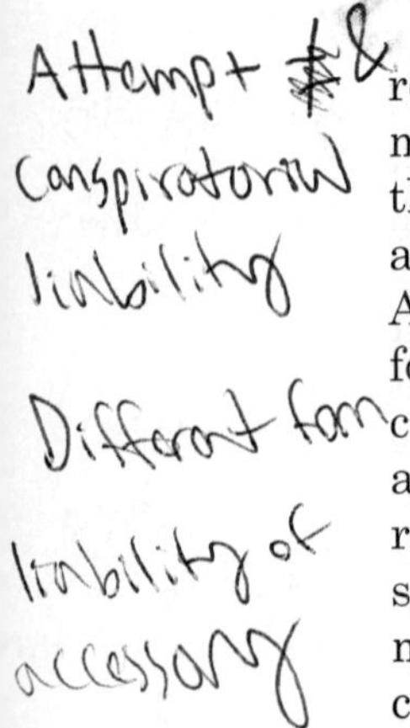

We find the defendant's argument unpersuasive. The defendant's reliance upon *Almeda* and *Beccia*, and the concept of "dual intent," is misplaced. Attempt and conspiratorial liability differ substantially from the liability imposed on an accessory. First, both attempt and conspiracy are offenses in and of themselves, while accessorial liability is not. Attempt is a distinct, inchoate offense and a defendant may be punished for attempting to commit a substantive offense without actually committing the crime. Likewise, conspiracy has been recognized as being a crime distinct from the commission of the substantive offense. "We have repeatedly held that conspiracy is a common-law crime and punishable as such under the statutes relating to the punishment of high crimes and misdemeanors. The commission of the substantive offense and a conspiracy to commit it are separate and distinct crimes . . . The crime of argument concerning the watch was resumed until Pierce, as he testified, thought they would be thrown out there.

While drinking the liquor at the Johnson Cafe, Pierce first commenced to talk about jobs that he had done and specifically mentioned his burglary of the Wheat Growers Cafe. This talk came up in connection with the disappearance of Wilson's wrist watch. Finally they reached the Commercial Hotel, where Pierce was a janitor, and in the furnace room the conversation about burglaries continued between them. There also was some talk concerning tools, and Pierce procured a piece of paper and wrote down a list of tools that would be needed, not that night, but at some future time, and Wilson said that he could get them for him. The subject of the watch again came up in the furnace room, and Pierce again denied taking it. Wilson suggested that they go to his father's office, to which he had the keys, to start on the jobs, and they there conceived the idea of breaking into Hecker Brothers' Drugstore. Wilson did not first propose the burglarizing, the idea originating with Pierce, and after the latter had told Wilson that he had burglarized the Wheat Growers Cafe several days before. There is some conflict in the evidence as to who first suggested breaking into Hecker Brothers' Drugstore, but they proceeded to the building in which it was located, tried several doors, finally going outside, and effecting an entry through the front transom. After Wilson had boosted Pierce up so that he could break the glass in the transom, and after looking around to see if anyone had heard them, Wilson again lifted Pierce and the latter handed the broken glass to Wilson, who dropped it on the cement. Thereupon Wilson again lifted Pierce up so that he could crawl through the transom. Pierce then proceeded to the cash register. Immediately after Pierce was inside the store Wilson ran to his father's office and telephoned the police to come to Hecker Brothers' Drugstore. He then returned to where the entry had been effected, and a few moments before the police arrived, Pierce handed to Wilson, through the transom, two or three bottles of liquor which he placed on the cement. Pierce noticed after he entered the store that Wilson had disappeared. Immediately after arrival of the police Wilson told them that Pierce was inside, designating him as "that guy from the Commercial Hotel." The police officer asked him how he knew, and he replied, "I boosted him in." Pierce escaped through the back door and Wilson immediately volunteered to track him down, and did so by going to Pierce's room at the Commercial Hotel, where he identified Pierce as the burglar in the presence of the police authorities. Wilson told the police, shortly after the apprehension of Pierce, that his connection with the burglary was for the purpose of getting even with Pierce for taking his watch, and that that was the only way he hoped to recover it. He also stated later that evening that he wanted to apprehend Pierce and turn him over to the authorities—he wanted to catch him in the act.

conspiracy is dependent on clear principles, and has characteristics and ingredients which separate it from all other crimes."

There is, however, no such crime as "being an accessory." The defendant is charged with committing one substantive offense; "[t]he accessory statute merely provides alternate means by which a substantive crime may be committed."

Second, the intent required for attempt or conspiratorial liability is distinguishable from the requisite intent for accessorial liability. * * *

Intentional conduct is defined as conduct "with respect to a result or to conduct described by a statute defining an offense when [a person's] conscious objective is to cause such a result or to engage in such conduct." Thus, to be guilty of attempt, a defendant's conscious objective must be to cause the result which would constitute the substantive crime. A person cannot attempt to commit a crime which requires that an unintended result occur, such as involuntary manslaughter, because it is logically impossible for one to intend to bring about an unintended result. *State v. Almeda, supra.* Similarly, to be guilty of conspiracy, the defendant, upon entering an agreement, must intend that his conduct achieve the requisite criminal result. When the substantive crime requires an unintended result, a person cannot conspire to commit that crime because it is logically impossible to agree to achieve a specific result unintentionally. *State v. Beccia, supra.*

Contrary to the defendant's assertions, and unlike attempt or conspiratorial liability, accessorial liability does not require that a defendant act with the conscious objective to cause the result described by a statute. Although we have stated that the defendant, in intentionally aiding another, must have the intent to commit the substantive offense; this language must be read in context. All the cases which speak of this "dual intent" involve crimes that require a defendant to act with a specific intent to commit the crime. Because the substantive crime with which the person was charged in those cases required that the accessory specifically intend to act or bring about a result, it is logical to state that the accessory, in aiding another, must have "intend[ed] to commit the offense with which he is charged."

Section 53a–8, however, is not limited to cases where the substantive crime requires the specific intent to bring about a result. General Statutes § 53a–8 merely requires that a defendant have the mental state required for the commission of a crime while intentionally aiding another. "When the commission of an offense . . . or some element of an offense, requires a particular mental state, such mental state is ordinarily designated . . . by the use of the terms intentionally, 'knowingly,' 'recklessly,' or 'criminal negligence'" General Statutes § 53a–5. Accordingly, an accessory may be liable in aiding another if he acts intentionally, knowingly, recklessly or with criminal negligence toward the result, depending on the mental state required by the substantive crime. When a crime requires that a person act with criminal negligence, an accessory is liable if he acts "with respect to a result or to a circumstance described by a statute defining an offense when he fails to perceive a substantial and unjustifiable risk that such result will occur or that such circumstance exists."

This interpretation is consistent with the underlying principles of accessorial liability. Such liability is designed to punish one who intentionally aids another in the commission of a crime and not one whose innocent acts in fact aid one who commits an offense. "Mere presence as an inactive companion, passive acquiescence, or the doing of innocent acts which may in fact aid the one who commits the crime must be distinguished from the criminal intent and community of unlawful purpose shared by one who knowingly and wilfully assists the perpetrator of the offense in the acts which prepare for, facilitate or consummate it."

Thus, accessorial liability is predicated upon the actor's state of mind at the time of his actions, and whether that state of mind is commensurate to the state of mind required for the commission of the offense. If a person, in intentionally aiding another, acts with the mental culpability required for the commission of a crime—be it "intentional" or "criminally negligent"—he is liable for the commission of that crime.

Moreover, because accessorial liability is not a distinct crime, but only an alternative means by which a substantive crime may be committed, it would be illogical to impose liability on the perpetrator of the crime, while precluding liability for an accessory, even though both possess the mental state required for the commission of the crime. * * *

Therefore, a person may be held liable as an accessory to a criminally negligent act if he has the requisite culpable mental state for the commission of the substantive offense, and he intentionally aids another in the crime. For the above reasons, we find that being an accessory to criminally negligent homicide is a cognizable crime under Connecticut law. Accordingly, the trial court did not err either in instructing the jury with respect to the crime or in denying the defendant's post-trial motions. * * *

The defendant next contends that even if the crime of being an accessory to criminally negligent homicide does exist, there was insufficient evidence to support a verdict of guilty and therefore the trial court erred in denying his motion for judgment of acquittal. We disagree. * * *

To establish the crime of being an accessory to criminally negligent homicide, it is incumbent that the state prove beyond a reasonable doubt that the defendant, in intentionally aiding another to engage in the commission of the offense, failed to perceive a substantial and

unjustifiable risk that death will occur, and that such death did occur. * * *

From the evidence presented, the jury could reasonably have found that the defendant intentionally had aided Cannon by giving him the knife. Additionally, the jury could reasonably have inferred that, in handing Cannon the knife to prevent Middleton from escaping, the defendant had failed to perceive a substantial and unjustifiable risk that death would occur. Contrary to the defendant's claim, there was sufficient evidence to support the conviction. Because the jury could have found the defendant guilty beyond a reasonable doubt if it found the state's evidence credible, the trial court did not err in denying the defendant's motion for judgment of acquittal. * * *

WILSON V. PEOPLE

Supreme Court of Colorado, en banc
103 Colo. 441, 87 P.2d 5 (1939)

MR. JUSTICE BOCK delivered the opinion of the court.

PLAINTIFF in error was charged and convicted under two counts of having unlawfully and feloniously aided, abetted and assisted one Dwight J. Pierce in the commission of a burglary and larceny. One of his defenses was the absence of felonious intent on his part to commit the crimes in question, because he acted solely as a decoy to detect the commission of the crime and to report it to the proper officers, so that Pierce might be apprehended. Plaintiff in error will hereinafter be referred to as Wilson.

The facts, substantially, are as follows: On the night of February 19, 1938, Wilson, son of the deputy district attorney of the thirteenth judicial district, and employed by him for several months prior thereto, was in Johnson's Cafe in Sterling, Colorado. Some time after 10 o'clock p.m. Pierce entered. Pierce had been drinking and was looking for a place where he could purchase more liquor. Without previous arrangement, Pierce approached Wilson and prevailed upon him to make an effort to find such a place. The two left the cafe and went to the Commercial Hotel, where Pierce borrowed some money. Wilson left and came back to repor to Pierce that no whiskey could be had, but he could get a pint of sloe gi This was satisfactory to Pierce, and Wilson procured a bottle of the which he delivered to Pierce, and both returned to the Johnson C where they drank some of the liquor. During that time a wrist w which Wilson had been wearing disappeared while he was in the co of Pierce. When Wilson missed his watch he immediately accused of taking it. He continued to make the accusation through the and at one time threatened to fight Pierce because of the alle Pierce denied the theft. The argument about the wrist watch noisy that the participants were asked to leave the cafe. The to another cafe and Wilson bought Pierce a cup of cof

The record indicates that Wilson was sincere in his belief that Pierce had taken his watch. Moreover, there is evidence in the people's case that tends to support his defense that he acted only as a decoy to apprehend Pierce in the act of committing the crime. Wilson's testimony at the trial substantially supported his defense that he had no criminal intent to feloniously burglarize or steal.

Plaintiff in error classifies his assignments of error under two headings: 1. That the court erred in giving to the jury Instruction No. 10. 2. That the court erred in not sustaining the defendant's motion for a nonsuit at the conclusion of the people's testimony, and that it again erred in not directing a verdict of not guilty at the conclusion of all of the evidence.

Taking up first the second ground of error, we are of the opinion that the evidence was sufficient to warrant the trial court's submission of the case to the jury. The motions for nonsuit, and for a directed verdict of not guilty, were properly denied.

Instruction No. 10, to the giving of which defendant assigns error, reads as follows: "One may not participate in the commission of a felony and then obtain immunity from punishment on the ground that he was a mere detective or spy. One who attempts to detect the commission of crime in others must himself stop short of lending assistance, or participation in the commission of the crime."

Defendant contends that this instruction is erroneous because it left no question of fact for the determination of the jury on his defense of decoy and detection. Wilson did assist Pierce in entering the drugstore. This he never denied and immediately revealed to the police his part in the transaction when they arrived in response to his call. The instruction inferentially placed guilt upon Wilson, because he did not "stop short of lending assistance," but actually gave assistance.

We find the following language in 16 Corpus Juris at page 128, section 115: "For one to be guilty as principal in the second degree, it is essential that he share in the criminal intent of the principal in the first degree; the same criminal intent must exist in the minds of both." And on page 129: "One who participates in a felony as a feigned accomplice, in order to entrap the other, is not criminally liable, and he need not take an officer of the law into his confidence to avoid an imputation of criminal intent."

In *Price v. People* the Supreme Court of the state of Illinois had before it an issue similar to the one here presented. There Price, with two others, was convicted of the crime of burglary. It appears the defendant in that case accompanying two others went to Milroy's house for the purpose of robbing him. He, with the others, entered the house where the holdup was committed, carried a gun, which he displayed, but which was not loaded, and did assist to a far greater extent than did Wilson in the instant case. Because of an interruption, the crime of robbery was not carried to a successful conclusion. Price testified that on the previous day he had talked to a constable about the matter and to an ex-sheriff. The evidence whether or not he did so was conflicting. Price insisted that his object in accompanying the other two was to expose the contemplated crime and to bring the real perpetrators to justice. We quote from the language of the court: "Waiving all controverted questions, the undisputed facts, as appears from the foregoing, are, that the accused, on the day of the attempted robbery, went deliberately to a constable of the town in which he lived and told him all about the contemplated crime, giving the true names of the parties, and telling him when and where it was to take place, and the name of the intended victim; that the attempt was made at the very time and place, and by the parties, stated by him, and that on the following morning he, in like manner, went to a justice of the peace and told him all about what had been done, and furnished him with the true names of the parties implicated, by means of which, on the same day, they were brought to trial, and were subsequently convicted of the crime. That a sane person, really guilty of committing so grave a crime as the one imputed to the accused, would thus act, is so inconsistent with all human experience as not to warrant the conviction of any one under the circumstances shown." The judgment of conviction was reversed.

In the case of *State v. Bigley*, the defendant, who with others was charged with committing a burglary, made substantially the same defense as did Wilson in the instant case. The assistance rendered by Bigley was to a greater degree than by Wilson here. In reversing the conviction the Supreme Court of Idaho uses the following language at page 640: "The defect in this reasoning is that Bigley can only be held responsible for his intent at the time the crime was committed, that is, the entering into the bank and taking of the money, and the only evidence in the record of his intent at that time was that while he desired the crime to be fully consummated by Coppinger and Lawley, his intention was not that he should be a participant therein with the intent of permanently depriving the bank of the money to be taken." * * *

Counsel for the people contend that the principle involved here has been set at rest by the opinion in *Connor v. People*. In that case we sustained the defense of entrapment and reversed the judgment of conviction. In the instant case we have the defense of detection and not entrapment, and any language relating to the defense of Connor is not applicable here.

In this connection we cite also Wharton's Criminal Law (12th ed.), volume 1, section 271, which reads in part as follows: "A detective entering apparently into a criminal conspiracy already formed for the purpose of exploding it is not an accessory before the fact. For it should be remembered that while detectives, when acting as decoys, may apparently provoke the crime, the essential element of *dolus,* or malicious determination to violate the law, is wanting in their case. And it is only the formal, and not the substantive, part of the crime that they provoke. They provoke, for instance, in larceny, the asportation of the goods, but not the ultimate loss by the owner. They may be actuated by the most unworthy of motives, but the *animus furandi* in larceny is not imputable to them; and it is in larcenous cases or cheats that they are chiefly employed."

It may be that the jury in the instant case placed more stress on the motives that actuated Wilson in his participation in the transaction than they did on the necessity of determining his felonious intent under the circumstances.

Reverting to Instruction No. 10, by judicial fiat this instruction makes any assistance in the perpetration of an offense criminal, whether felonious or not. The determination of whether the assistance by Wilson under the evidence in this case was given with felonious intent was solely the province of the jury, and this instruction erroneously invaded that province. There may be offenses and circumstances when any assistance rendered may make a participant guilty of a criminal offense; but here we are concerned only with the facts, circumstances and defenses in this case. Forfeiture of individual liberty through criminal procedure, by courts, must on our part meet all the demands of impartial justice. The giving of Instruction No. 10 constituted prejudicial error.

The judgment is reversed and the cause remanded for new trial.

MR. JUSTICE BAKKE and MR. JUSTICE BURKE not participating.

C. THE NATURAL AND PROBABLE CONSEQUENCES DOCTRINE

Many common law jurisdictions hold an accomplice liable not only for the crime he assisted, but also for any other crime that was the natural and probable consequence of the crime he assisted. Under this natural and probable consequences doctrine (not to be confused with the natural and probable consequences doctrine used to infer an intent to kill), the other crime must have been the reasonably foreseeable consequence of the intended crime. The next case discusses the natural and probable consequences doctrine in complicity law.

ROY V. UNITED STATES

District of Columbia Court of Appeals
652 A.2d 1098; 1995 D.C. App. LEXIS 6 (1994)

SCHWELB, J.

Nakia A. (Tony) Roy and Steve B. Ross were convicted at a joint trial of armed robbery, * * * and carrying a pistol without a license (CPWOL). * * * On appeal, Roy contends that the trial judge erred in denying his motion for judgment of acquittal (MJOA) on all charges, and he alleges related instructional error. * * *

We hold that the evidence was insufficient as a matter of law to support Roy's conviction [] of armed robbery. * * * We affirm Roy's CPWOL conviction and all of Ross' convictions.

I.

THE EVIDENCE

A. The Robbery.

This case had its genesis in an attempt by law enforcement officers to purchase a handgun through the use of a paid informant. The proposed undercover buy went awry when the prospective purchaser was robbed of his money instead.

On October 8, 1991, Peppi Miller, who was later to become the principal prosecution witness, was arrested on 10th Place in southeast Washington, D.C. and charged with possession of cocaine with intent to distribute it. Six weeks later, on November 20, 1991, Miller was working as an informant for Agent Mark Potter of the Bureau of Alcohol, Tobacco and Firearms (BATF). With Potter's advance knowledge, Miller undertook to arrange the undercover buy which generated the events underlying this case.

Miller testified that during the mid-afternoon of November 20, on 10th Place, S.E., he met with Tony Roy, whom he had known for several years, to discuss the purchase of a handgun and ammunition. Roy told Miller that he should come back later with $400, and that Roy would then have the weapon and two ammunition clips. Miller left the scene and met with Potter and two FBI agents. These men gave him $400 in bills and equipped him with a tape recorder and a transmitter.

At approximately 6:40 p.m., Miller returned to the scene and found Roy, who was with several other people. Miller activated his tape recorder and approached Roy to discuss the proposed purchase. Roy asked Miller if he had brought the money, and Miller showed him the bills. Roy then explained that Miller would have to wait for "Steve" [Ross], who was to bring the handgun.

Ross arrived some 45 minutes later, but he and Roy left with another man, apparently to remedy problems with Ross' car. The three men subsequently returned, and Miller asked Roy "what was up." Ross, meanwhile, walked towards the grounds of a nearby school. Roy told Miller that Steve had brought the handgun and that Miller should "go talk to Steve and get it from Steve."

Miller followed Ross through a gate into the school yard and down some steps to a location approximately thirty yards from the entrance. Roy remained in the vicinity of a blue trash can which was near the gate. Miller caught up with Ross, and at trial he described the ensuing events as follows:

> He [Ross] said, "What's up?" I said, "What's up?" He said, "you got the money?" I said, "Yes, I have the money." And then, I pulled the money out [of] my pocket, and he said, "Is it 350?" I said "No, it's 400." And then he said, "Count it," so I started counting it, and then he gave me the gun, and when he gave me the gun, I got ready to give him the money, and then he asked for the gun back. So, right then and there, I gave the gun back, and he said, "I really don't want to sell it right now."
>
> So, then, I was, like you know, "Tony,"[6] you know. I was calling him, "Tony" you know, to see what was going on, and then he put the clip into the chamber, pulled the round back, pointed the gun in my face and said for me to drop the money.
>
> . . . I asked him why he was doing this.
>
> . . . Then he said that he felt as though I had stuck up his people, and that he didn't want to tell me this. He said, "Motherfucker, you stuck my peoples up."
>
> . . . Then I said, "No I didn't do that—" I had, ". . . I never had a gun to do that."
>
> . . . And then he told me to run.
>
> . . . At that time, he had told me to put the money on the ground.
>
> . . . Then I started to back up, and then he said, "I'm not playing with you, I told you." He said, "Better yet, jump the fence," so I jumped the fence.
>
> . . . Then I gave off the distress signal . . . Ace of Spades . . . and gave a description of the clothes that he was wearing.
>
> At that point, I started walking toward Tenth Place by the back of the school.

---

[6] Presumably, Miller meant to say "Steve" [Ross], not "Tony" [Roy]. There is no evidence that Roy was on the scene or personally participated in this conversation or the robbery that followed.

Officers promptly responded to Miller's distress signal. Within two minutes, they had apprehended Roy, Ross, and several other individuals who were in the area. Roy and Ross were standing approximately five feet apart near the entrance to the school at the time of their capture. The officers recovered $600 in cash from Ross' front pants pocket; bills totaling $400 were bundled separately from the other money, and a BATF agent testified that these bills were in the same denominations as those which had been provided to Miller earlier.[7] A loaded handgun bearing Ross' fingerprint was found near the gate. * * *

II.

ROY'S APPEAL

A. The Trial Court's Rulings.

At the conclusion of the prosecution's case, Roy's attorney made an oral motion for judgment of acquittal (MJOA). She argued that

> my client is not charged with selling of the gun, or even planning to sell a gun; he's charged with an armed robbery of Peppi Miller, and I think, based on the evidence . . . that a reasonable juror could not conclude that he participated, in any fashion, with a person by the name of Steve Ross in this alleged armed robbery.

Counsel renewed her MJOA at the conclusion of the evidence. The trial judge denied each MJOA without elaboration, but his views are readily discernible from his thoughtful discussion of related instructional and other issues.

The judge stated that

> it seems to me there are two separate and distinct theories of aiding and abetting that may enable a factfinder to find Mr. Roy guilty, beyond a reasonable doubt, of the armed robbery.
>
> The first is, if a factfinder could find from that evidence, beyond a reasonable doubt, that he actually aided and abetted the armed robbery; that is, he knowingly and intentionally participated with Mr. Ross in the armed robbery . . . That's one theory.
>
> There is another theory. There is a separate and more difficult theory of vicarious aider and abettor liability that would hold Mr. Roy liable for armed robbery if he knowingly and intentionally aided and abetted Mr. Ross in an illegal act; that is, the sale of a gun; and whether he intended it or not, the armed robbery by Mr. Ross was the natural and probable

[7] The serial numbers of the bills had not been pre-recorded.

> consequence in the ordinary course of things, of the act that he, Mr. Roy, aided and abetted and set in motion.

For the convenience of the reader, we will refer to the "knowingly and intentionally participated" theory as "Theory A," and the "natural and probable consequences" theory as "Theory B."

During preliminary discussions which preceded the presentation of the evidence, the judge indicated an inclination to limit the prosecution to Theory A—"they're either going to prove that Mr. Roy was knowingly and intentionally involved in [the armed robbery] or they are not." Returning to the issue during the presentation of the evidence, the judge reaffirmed his preliminary impression:

> I tend to think . . . if all the jury could find is that Mr. Roy arranged for the sale of a gun, and that's all he intended to arrange, and there's no evidence from which a jury could infer that he had knowledge and intention that this was going to evolve into an armed robbery, that that might not be sufficient to prove his liability for armed robbery as an aider and abettor.
>
> . . . I doubt whether I'm going to conclude that it goes so far as to say, if you plan and participate in the sale of the gun, and whatever happens, no matter how much it was part of the original plan, is something for which you're held criminally accountable.

The prosecution, however, asked the judge to instruct the jury on both theories, and the judge attempted conscientiously to analyze the reach of Theory B:

> The case law that I've seen so far does not define very precisely what, in the ordinary course of things, natural and probable consequences means. And as I think of the facts of this case, in the context of the facts of the cases that I've looked at, in my view, this one is on the edge. So much so that I'm not even certain, at this point, whether I'll let this second theory be submitted to the jury and argued by the Government.
>
> As I see it, what the criminal law is trying to do in these cases is to draw a line to serve two different policies that are incompatible, or inconsistent with each other. On the one hand, there's clearly a policy in the criminal law not to hold people responsible for things that they did not intend to do, and there has to be some mens rea element for any criminal offense. On the other hand, there is a competing policy that says, if you put criminal conduct in motion, or you intentionally assist in the commission of a crime, then you are held responsible for the natural and probable consequences of that crime, even if they go beyond what you put in motion . . . Some where between those

> two things, the law draws a line in what you can be held liable for, and what you can't.

The judge ultimately ruled as follows:

> The conclusion I've reached is [that] . . . the alternative doctrine of aiding and abetting on which the government is relying in the case of Mr. Roy is * * * law that ought to be examined again by our Court of Appeals in my opinion. * * *
>
> In my opinion this case represents the outer reaches of the permissible use of the doctrine that a person can be criminally liable for an offense which he himself did not intend but which is arguably a natural and probable consequence of an offense which he did intend and which he did aid and abet the commission of by another.

In conformity with the foregoing analysis, the judge denied Roy's MJOA and instructed the jury both as to Theory A and as to Theory B. * * *

C. Theory A.

There was ample evidence that, while armed with a handgun, Steve Ross robbed Peppi Miller of his money. The prosecution's testimony, if credited, also established that Tony Roy participated in the planning of an illegal sale of a handgun to Miller. The question presented under the rubric of Theory A is whether the evidence, viewed in the light most favorable to the prosecution, was sufficient to support a finding that Roy knowingly and intentionally aided and abetted the armed robbery.

To establish aiding and abetting, the prosecution was obliged to prove that Roy "in some sort associated himself with the venture, that he participated in it as something that he wished to bring about, that he seek by his action to make it succeed." In order for one to be an accomplice [or an aider or abettor], he must be concerned in the commission of the specific crime with which the [principal] defendant is charged, he must be an associate in guilt of that crime, a participant in that offense as principal or accessory.

There was no direct evidence that Roy planned the robbery or, indeed, that he had any advance knowledge that a robbery would occur. Indeed, if Miller's account is credited, then Ross' decision to rob him appears to have been improvised at the last moment, and not planned in advance. According to Miller, Ross actually gave him the handgun. Although it may theoretically be possible that a man intent on robbing another would place the weapon (loaded or not) in his prospective victim's physical possession, we do not believe that an impartial jury could rationally conclude beyond a reasonable doubt that this is what occurred here. If, as Miller's testimony suggests, Ross did not decide to rob Miller until after both men had arrived at the scene of the crime, then the theory that Roy helped to plan the robbery in advance cannot reasonably be reconciled with the record.

D. Theory B.

The trial judge, as we have seen, expressed serious reservations regarding the applicability to the facts of record of the government's "natural and probable consequences" theory. Although the judge's initial leaning was to restrict the prosecution to Theory A, and although he recognized that the present case took him to the "outer reaches" of Theory B, the judge ultimately allowed the case to go to the jury on both theories, while expressly inviting this court to clarify the legal principles applicable to Theory B. We share the trial judge's initial reservations, and now conclude that the evidence was insufficient as a matter of law to support Roy's conviction pursuant to Theory B.

By invoking the "natural and probable consequences" theory, the government insists that we sustain Roy's convictions of armed robbery and PFCV without requiring a showing that Roy intended to participate in the robbery of Miller or in any other crime of violence. Armed robbery is a felony punishable by life imprisonment; selling a handgun, on the other hand, constitutes CPWOL, a misdemeanor of which Roy has been independently convicted. The government's application of the "natural and probable consequences" doctrine would thus dramatically expand Roy's exposure even where (as postulated here for purposes of Theory B) he did not intend that a crime of violence be committed.

This court has stated that "an accessory is liable for any criminal act which *in the ordinary course of things* was the *natural and probable* consequence of the crime that he advised or commanded, although such consequence may not have been intended by him." The italicized words place a number of obvious restrictions on the reach of Theory B. The phrase "in the ordinary course of things" refers to what may reasonably ensue from the planned events, not to what might conceivably happen, and in particular suggests the absence of intervening factors. "Natural" has many meanings, but the most apposite dictionary definition is "in accordance with or determined by nature." A natural consequence is thus one which is within the normal range of outcomes that may be expected to occur if nothing unusual has intervened. We need not define "probable," except to note that, even standing alone, this adjective sets a significantly more exacting standard than the word "possible." Accordingly, if we accord to the words of our cases their ordinary everyday meaning, it is not enough for the prosecution to show that the accomplice knew or should have known that the principal might conceivably commit the offense which the accomplice is charged with aiding and abetting. Without inserting additional phrases or adjectives into the calculus, we think that our precedents require the government to prove a good deal more than that. A "natural and probable" consequence in the "ordinary course of things" presupposes an outcome within a reasonably predictable range.

We turn to the facts at hand. We stated in *Hordge v. United States* that "one who aids and abets a felony is legally responsible for all acts of the other persons which are in furtherance of the common purposes, design, or plan to commit the felony." The government contends that the armed robbery of Miller was in furtherance of the common purpose because it resulted in the defendants' obtaining Miller's money—an achievement which, according to the government, was the defendant's prime design and plan in the first place. In our view, however, an exchange of a handgun for $400 is qualitatively different from an armed robbery in which Ross stole $600 and retained for himself the object which, in Roy's contemplation, was supposed to be sold. Not the least of the differences is that violence directed to the intended buyer may ricochet against the seller-turned-assailant. To suggest that a sale and an armed robbery have a common purpose is to exaggerate their similarities and to understate their differences.

The government argues that Peppi Miller was a logical target of a robbery because, "given the illegal nature of the activity in which he was involved, [he] was unlikely to file a complaint with the police about the robbery." This reasoning, however, recognizes no apparent limiting principle. If we were to accept the government's position, then the robbery of any buyer or seller in a drug or unlicensed pistol sale would be viewed as the "natural and probable consequence" of that transaction, for a participant in any illegal project may well be reluctant to invoke the aid of the constabulary. Moreover, as Roy points out, the buyer may be as likely to rob the seller as the seller is to rob the buyer; the government's reasoning would arguably sustain prosecution of Roy as an aider and abettor of armed robbery even if Miller had robbed Ross, rather than the other way around.

In this case, in our view, no impartial jury could rationally conclude, beyond a reasonable doubt, that Roy "crossed a moral divide by setting out on a project involving either the certain or contingent" commission of a robbery. Viewed in the light most favorable to the prosecution, the evidence would perhaps support a finding that Roy should have known that it was conceivable that Ross might rob Miller. The evidence was insufficient, however, to show that a robbery would follow in the "ordinary course of events," or that it was a "natural and probable consequence" of the activities in which Roy was shown to have engaged. We must therefore reverse for evidentiary insufficiency Roy's conviction for armed robbery. * * *

CHAPTER 13

CONSPIRACY

■ ■ ■

INTRODUCTION

In Chapter 12 we examined the law of complicity, which provides rules for holding more than one person responsible for a given crime. This chapter considers a different but related question: criminal behavior that is the product of collective action.

One response to such criminal behavior is the law of conspiracy. Conspiracy is a crime that is frequently charged by prosecutors, particularly under federal law. Indeed, Judge Learned Hand famously called conspiracy "the darling of the modern prosecutor's nursery." Harrison v. United States, 7 F.2d 259 (2d Cir. 1925). The idea of conspiracy liability, however, raises a number of new questions. What distinguishes liability for a conspiracy from accomplice liability? Who counts as a member of a conspiracy? Is a co-conspirator responsible for crimes that were not part of the original agreement but are committed by other members of the conspiracy?

The common law tradition understood collective criminality to pose special dangers, and thus made an agreement to commit a crime itself criminal. At early common law, a conspiracy was committed as soon as two persons formed an agreement to commit a crime or immoral act.

The crime of conspiracy was and continues to be the subject of sharp criticism for several reasons. First, under the early common law definition of a conspiracy, the scope of conduct that could be punished was very broad. The traditional common law definition of conspiracy was an agreement by two or more persons to commit either one or more criminal acts, or one or more acts that may not constitute a crime but are "corrupt, dishonest, fraudulent, immoral, and in that sense illegal." *See* State v. Burnham, 15 N.H. 396 (1844). Many commentators attacked the early common law notion that a person could be convicted of conspiracy to commit a legal act merely because that act was immoral or dishonest. Responding to this critique, most jurisdictions today require an agreement to commit a crime.

Second, the common law tradition of punishing an agreement to commit a crime without any acts beyond that agreement came dangerously close to violating the prohibition on thought crimes. In response to this concern, most jurisdictions today require proof of some "overt act" in furtherance of the conspiracy in order to demonstrate the existence of the conspiracy. This overt act need not be illegal or even central to accomplishing the ultimate goal of the conspiracy. A telephone call or meeting will satisfy the overt act requirement so long as done for the purpose of furthering the conspiracy.

Third, there are significant procedural consequences of charging defendants with conspiracy that tend to benefit the prosecution. For example, the trial of a conspiracy case may be held in any locale where any overt act by any of the conspirators took place. *See* Wayne R. LaFave and Austin Scott, Jr., CRIMINAL LAW § 12.1(b)(2) (5th ed. 2010). Accused co-conspirators may be tried together, increasing the possibility that the jury will transfer suspicions of guilt from one defendant to another. *Id.* § 12.1(b)(5). The law of evidence contains special accommodations for conspiracy cases, including exceptions to the rule against hearsay evidence. *Id.* § 12.1(b)(3). Finally, given the subjective nature of an "agreement," judges are often liberal in permitting the admission of circumstantial evidence to prove guilt. *Id.* § 12.1(b)(4).

Finally, certain substantive characteristics of conspiracy law make it a useful tool for prosecutors. Like attempt, conspiracy is an "inchoate" or incomplete crime. In contrast to the law of attempt, however, in conspiracy law there is no need to prove that the defendant ever came close to actually committing the target crime. Moreover, in common law jurisdictions, conspiracy does not "merge" into the target crime as attempt does. Rather, a defendant can be convicted of both the target crime and the conspiracy to commit that crime.

Because of the broad scope of conspiracy law and the favorable procedural consequences for the government, many scholars have commented on—and objected to—the potential abuses of conspiracy law. Others, however, defend conspiracy law, pointing to the inherent difficulty of proving something as ephemeral as an "agreement," as well as the difficulty of investigating and proving very complex criminal behavior involving many actors. Most significantly, commentators who defend the law of conspiracy point to the special dangers of collective action.

The Model Penal Code diverges from the common law approach to conspiracy in some important ways. Conceptually, the drafters of the Model Penal Code saw conspiracy as worthy of punishment for a different reason than the common law judges. The drafters of the Model Penal Code felt that a person who has entered into a conspiracy has demonstrated a firm commitment to criminal activity, and therefore poses a greater threat of actual social harm than a person who has not so agreed. Another difference is that under the Model Penal Code the crime of conspiracy "merges" with the completed crime; consequently, the actor cannot be punished for both a conspiracy and the target crime. *See* Model Penal Code 1.07(1)(b).

The Model Penal Code also diverges from the common law in its approach to feigning co-conspirators. The first case in this chapter, *United States v. Pacheco*, illuminates the difference between the common law's bilateral approach and the Model Penal Code's unilateral approach.

A. THE AGREEMENT

STATE V. PACHECO

Supreme Court of Washington
882 P.2d 183 (Wash. 1994)

JOHNSON, J.

The Defendant, Herbert Pacheco, appeals his convictions for conspiracy to commit first degree murder and conspiracy to deliver a controlled substance. He contends he did not commit conspiracy within the meaning of RCW 9A.28.040 because no genuine agreement existed between him and his sole coconspirator, an undercover police agent. We hold RCW 9A.28.040 and RCW 69.50.407 require an actual agreement between two coconspirators, and, therefore, reverse his convictions for conspiracy to commit murder in the first degree and conspiracy to deliver a controlled substance.

FACTS

Herbert Pacheco met Thomas Dillon in 1985, when Pacheco worked about 2 months for Dillon's private investigation firm. Pacheco bragged to Dillon about his involvement in illegal activities, including enforcement, collecting debts, procuring weapons, providing protection, and performing "hits."

In 1989, Dillon learned that Pacheco was a Clark County deputy sheriff. Dillon contacted the FBI and volunteered to inform on Pacheco. The FBI began an investigation of Pacheco. The Clark County Sheriff's office joined, and later directed the investigation. * * *

On March 26, 1990, according to a plan designed by the sheriff's office and the FBI, Dillon called Pacheco and told him he would like to meet to discuss a possible deal. Dillon and Pacheco met at a restaurant. Dillon said he had ties to the "Mafia" and offered Pacheco $500 in exchange for protection during a cocaine deal. Dillon told Pacheco that a buyer (an undercover FBI agent) would arrive shortly, and Pacheco was to protect Dillon during the transaction. Pacheco agreed. The undercover agent arrived and the purported drug transaction took place. Afterward, Dillon paid Pacheco $500.

The same scenario was replayed at a second purported drug transaction on April 2, 1990. Dillon again paid Pacheco $500. Later that night Dillon called Pacheco and pretended he had been shortchanged $40,000 in that afternoon's drug transaction. Dillon said he had been given $10,000 by his superiors to take care of the situation. Dillon agreed to meet Pacheco at a convenience store. At the store, Pacheco offered to kill the drug buyer for $10,000. Pacheco indicated if he had to kill anyone else, it would cost more. Pacheco proposed he go get his gun while Dillon located the drug buyer at his motel.

Dillon and Pacheco met at a lounge near the motel. They decided Pacheco would go to the lobby of the motel, call the buyer and convince him to come down to the lobby where Pacheco would then shoot him. Pacheco went to the lobby with a loaded gun, but he did not call the buyer's room. As Pacheco left the lobby, sheriff's deputies arrested him. Pacheco contended he was collecting evidence to build a case against Dillon and he thought he was following police procedures.

Pacheco was charged with conspiracy to commit first degree murder, attempted first degree murder, [and other offenses]. * * * The jury found Pacheco not guilty of attempted first degree murder, but convicted him on all other counts.

The Court of Appeals affirmed the convictions. We accepted review of the conspiracy convictions, limited to the issue of whether a conspiracy exists when the sole coconspirator is an undercover agent.

ANALYSIS

The Defendant contends he did not commit conspiracy within the meaning of RCW 9A.28.040 because his sole coconspirator was an undercover police agent who never "agreed" to commit the crime of murder in the first degree.

The Defendant argues the statute retains the common law, bilateral approach to conspiracy, which requires an actual agreement to commit a crime between the defendant and at least one other. Therefore, a government agent feigning agreement with the defendant does not constitute a conspiracy under the common law approach because no genuine agreement is reached. The Defendant asserts Washington is among those states whose statutes are patterned after the Model Penal Code but have been interpreted as adopting only a limited form of the code's unilateral approach, and retaining the requirement of a bilateral underlying agreement.

The State contends RCW 9A.28.040 follows the code's purely unilateral approach. Under the code, actual agreement is not required as long as the defendant believes another is agreeing to commit the criminal act. Therefore, a purported agreement between a government agent and a defendant would satisfy the code's unilateral conspiratorial agreement approach.

Adopted in 1975, as a part of the overhaul of the criminal code, RCW 9A.28.040 provides in part:

> (1) A person is guilty of criminal conspiracy when, with intent that conduct constituting a crime be performed, he agrees with one or more persons to engage in or cause the performance of such conduct, and any one of them takes a substantial step in pursuance of such agreement.
>
> (2) It shall not be a defense to criminal conspiracy that the person or persons with whom the accused is alleged to have conspired:
>
> (a) Has not been prosecuted or convicted; or
>
> (b) Has been convicted of a different offense; or
>
> (c) Is not amenable to justice; or
>
> (d) Has been acquitted; or
>
> (e) Lacked the capacity to commit an offense.

In construing a statute, our primary objective is to carry out the intent of the Legislature. When a term is not defined in a statute, the court may look to common law or a dictionary for the definition. As a general rule, we presume the Legislature intended undefined words to mean what they did at common law.

Subsection (1) of RCW 9A.28.O40 expressly requires an *agreement*, but does not define the term. Black's Law Dictionary defines *agreement as*, "[a] meeting of two or more minds; a coming together in opinion or determination; the coming together in accord of two minds on a given proposition." Similarly, *agreement* is defined in *Webster*'s as "a: the act of agreeing or coming to a mutual agreement . . . b: oneness of opinion. . . ." The dictionary definitions thus support the Defendant's argument.

Likewise, the common law definition of the agreement required for a conspiracy is defined not in unilateral terms but rather as a confederation or combination of minds. A conspiratorial agreement necessarily requires more than one to agree because it is impossible to conspire with oneself. We conclude that by requiring an agreement, the Legislature intended to retain the requirement of a genuine or bilateral agreement.

Subsection (2) provides the conspiratorial agreement may still be found even though the coconspirator cannot be convicted. In this sense, the statute incorporates a limited form of the code's unilateral conspiracy in that it is no longer necessary that agreement be proved against both conspirators. Thus, under subsection (2)'s unilateral approach, the failure to convict an accused's sole coconspirator will not prevent proof of the conspiratorial agreement against the accused. However, this does not indicate the Legislature intended to abandon the traditional requirement of two criminal participants reaching an underlying agreement.

Our case law supports this interpretation of RCW 9A.28.040. In *State v. Valladares*, two codefendants were charged with conspiracy to deliver cocaine. In a joint trial, one defendant was acquitted and the other, Valladares, was found guilty.

On appeal, the court held acquittal of Valladares' only alleged coconspirator mandated reversal of Valladares' conviction because the two outcomes were logically inconsistent. The inconsistent verdicts to the charge of conspiracy in the same trial nullified the possibility that the two coconspirators reached an agreement, a necessary element of the conspiracy. * * *

Valladares thus makes clear the Legislature adopted the unilateral approach to the limited extent set out in RCW 9A.28.040(2). However, the element of the "requisite corrupt agreement," or the bilateral agreement, is still necessary as set out in RCW 9A.28.040(1). Indeed, the essence of a conspiracy is the agreement to commit a crime. We will not presume the Legislature intended to overturn this long-established legal principle unless that intention is made very clear.

Additionally, the unilateral approach fails to carry out the primary purpose of the statute. The primary reason for making conspiracy a separate offense from the substantive crime is the increased danger to society posed by group criminal activity. However, the increased danger is nonexistent when a person "conspires" with a government agent who pretends agreement. In the feigned conspiracy there is no increased chance the criminal enterprise will succeed, no continuing criminal enterprise, no educating in criminal practices, and no greater difficulty of detection.

Indeed, it is questionable whether the unilateral conspiracy punishes criminal activity or merely criminal intentions. The "agreement" in a unilateral conspiracy is a legal fiction, a technical way of transforming nonconspiratorial conduct into a prohibited conspiracy. When one party merely pretends to agree, the other party, whatever he or she may believe about the pretender, is in fact not conspiring with anyone. Although the deluded party has the requisite criminal intent, there has been no criminal act.

The federal courts agree. In *Sears v. United States*, the Court of Appeals established the rule that "as it takes two to conspire, there can be no indictable conspiracy with a government informer who secretly intends to frustrate the conspiracy." Every federal court which has since considered the issue has adopted this approach.

Another concern with the unilateral approach is its potential for abuse. In a unilateral conspiracy, the State not only plays an active role in creating the offense, but also becomes the chief witness in proving the crime at trial. We agree with the Ninth Circuit this has the potential to put the State in the improper position of manufacturing crime. At the same time, such reaching is unnecessary because the punishable conduct in a unilateral conspiracy will almost always satisfy the elements of either solicitation or attempt. The State will still be able to thwart the activity and punish the defendant who attempts agreement with an undercover police officer.

* * * [T]he State has not persuaded us the Legislature intended to abandon the traditional requirement of an actual agreement. We hold RCW 9A.28.040 and RCW 69.50.407 require the defendant to reach a genuine agreement with at least one other coconspirator. The Defendant's convictions for conspiracy to commit murder in the first degree and conspiracy to deliver a controlled substance are reversed.

DURHAM, J. [dissenting].

The jury found that Herbert Pacheco, an aspiring hit man, planned a murder for money. Moreover, he took a substantial step toward that objective. Yet the majority overturns his conviction for conspiracy to commit murder solely because he conspired with a government agent rather than with another hit man. The Washington conspiracy statute does not require a co-conspirator to be a nongovernment actor. In fact, the statute explicitly envisages so-called unilateral conspiracies, as the majority admits. Because neither our case law, the statute, nor the rationale of conspiracy crimes compel the result arrived at by the majority, I dissent.

We accepted review solely to determine whether Washington's conspiracy statute countenances unilateral conspiracies. Yet the majority fails to provide even a cursory analysis of the essential differences between the bilateral and unilateral approaches to conspiracy. The bilateral approach asks whether there is an agreement between two or more persons to commit a criminal act. Its focus is on the content of the agreement and whether there is a shared understanding between the conspirators. The unilateral approach is not concerned with the content of the agreement or whether there is a meeting of minds. Its sole concern is whether the agreement, shared or not, objectively manifests the criminal intent of at least one of the conspirators. The majority does not even mention this crucial difference, and instead merely assumes that all conspiracies must be bilateral. In other words, the majority assumes precisely what it is supposed to prove; it begs the question. * * *

[T]he majority portrays the unilateral approach to conspiracy as an outdated relic from a bygone era. The Model Penal Code endorses unilateral conspiracies, the majority admits, but "every federal court, which has since considered the issue" has adopted the bilateral approach. The majority neglects to mention that all the federal courts adopting bilateral conspiracy are construing a different statute, one whose language requires bilateral conspiracies. In contrast, the Model Penal Code defines conspiracy "in terms of one person's agreeing with another, rather than in terms of an agreement among or between two or more people."

The code embodies a significant change in emphasis. In its view, the major basis of conspiratorial liability is not the group nature of the activity but the firm purpose of an individual to commit a crime which is objectively manifested in conspiring. The Washington conspiracy statute tracks the Model Penal Code's language rather than the "two or more persons" language of the general federal conspiracy statute. In any event, far from being antiquated or obsolete, the "movement toward a unilateral theory of the crime is the modern trend in conspiracy law."

A comparison of the revised Washington conspiracy statute with its predecessor is far more revealing of legislative intent than the majority's simplistic and premature resort to dictionary definitions. The predecessor statute used the phrase "whenever two or more persons shall conspire" which parallels the federal conspiracy statute and clearly requires bilateral conspiracy. The revised statute, in contrast, tracks the definitional language of the Model Penal Code, which adopts unilateral conspiracy.

Under a unilateral formulation, the crime of conspiracy is committed when a person agrees to proceed in a prohibited manner; under a bilateral formulation, the crime of conspiracy is committed when two or more persons agree to proceed in such manner. * * * The contrast between the prior and the present statute is clear, precise, and determinative.

Next, the majority constructs a straw man by claiming that the primary purpose of conspiracy is "the increased danger to society posed by group criminal activity." Preventing group criminal activity is the rationale behind bilateral conspiracy, but that rationale was decisively rejected by the Model Penal Code. At best, controlling group criminal activity is only one rationale for conspiracy statutes.

> A bilateral theory of conspiracy and the rigid standard of mutuality that it demands . . . are inconsistent with the recognition of an independent rationale for conspiracy law based on a conspirator's firm expectation of committing a crime.

Broderick, 94 Yale L.J. at 906 n.64. * * *

Finally, I share the majority's concern about the potential for abuse of unilateral conspiracy. However, the majority fails to take into consideration the effect of the entrapment defense. The potential for abuse is further restricted by the statute itself, which requires not only an agreement to engage in criminal conduct but also "a substantial step in pursuance of such agreement." In the end, the majority succeeds only in providing a superfluous protection to criminal defendants at the price of hamstringing government attempts to nip criminal acts in the bud.

B. THE MENS REA OF CONSPIRACY

In jurisdictions that have incorporated the common law, conspiracy is usually considered a specific intent crime. This required specific intent involves two elements: (1) the intent to enter into an agreement; and (2) the intent to commit, or aid in the commission of, the act or acts constituting the target crime. *People v. Swain* examines these two requirements in the context of a conspiracy to commit second degree murder.

Despite the designation of conspiracy as a specific intent crime, on occasion convictions for conspiracy have been permitted based not on evidence of what under the Model Penal Code would be called "purpose," but rather on some form of what the Model Penal Code calls "knowledge." *People v. Lauria* and *United States v. Lanza* explore the limits of conspiracy responsibility based on knowledge.

Under section 5.03 of the Model Penal Code, to be convicted of conspiracy the actor must have the purpose to promote or facilitate the target offense, or to aid others in committing, attempting, or soliciting the action that constitutes the crime.

PEOPLE V. SWAIN

Supreme Court of California
12 Cal.4th 593, 909 P.2d 994, 49 Cal.Rptr.2d 390 (1996)

BAXTER, ASSOCIATE JUSTICE.

Defendants Jamal K. Swain and David Chatman were each convicted of conspiracy to commit murder and other crimes, stemming from the drive-by shooting death of a 15-year-old boy. As we shall explain, we hold that intent to kill is a required element of the crime of conspiracy to commit murder. In light of the jury instructions given, and general verdicts returned, we cannot determine beyond a reasonable doubt whether the jury found that the defendants conspired with an intent to kill. That conclusion requires us to reverse defendants' conspiracy convictions.

FACTS AND PROCEDURAL BACKGROUND

The question before us is one of law; the facts found by the Court of Appeal, summarized below, are not disputed.

Prosecution evidence established that a brown van passed through the Hunter's Point neighborhood of San Francisco about 2:00 a.m. on January 13, 1991. It slowed down near the spot where the young victim, who was of Samoan descent, and his friends were listening to music on the street.

A young Black male who appeared to have no hair was driving the van. Suddenly several shots were fired from the front of the van. Defendant Chatman and another young man also fired guns from the rear of the van. One of the intended victims had yelled out "drive-by" as a warning of the impending shooting, so most of the people on the street ducked down. The 15-year-old victim, Hagbom Saileele, who was holding the radio from which music was playing, was shot twice from behind. He later died in surgery.

Afterward, defendant Swain was in jail and boasted to jailmates about what good aim he had with a gun: "He was talking about what a good shot he was. He was saying he had shot that Samoan kid when they were in the van going about 30 miles an hour up a hill." The area where the shooting occurred is hilly; the van would have had to have been traveling uphill as it passed by the scene of the shooting. * * *

The abandoned brown van was recovered by police; in the van and nearby were found surgical gloves, expended cartridges, a hooded ski mask, and two handguns: a .380-caliber semi-automatic and a .25-caliber automatic. Defendant Swain's fingerprint was on the inside of the driver's side window. The forensic evidence established that whoever had used the .380-caliber semi-automatic handgun, from which the fatal shots were fired, had been sitting in the driver's side front seat of the van.

The .380-caliber gun was traced, through a series of owners and transactions involving narcotics, to defendant Chatman. Chatman was interrogated by police; he denied any knowledge of the van and claimed he had not purchased the gun. When this story proved false, Chatman admitted he had bought the gun, but claimed it had been stolen from him. Still later, he claimed he had sold it to someone else.

A warrant was obtained for Chatman's arrest. After waiving his rights, Chatman told police he and two other people, not including Swain, had driven the van to the crime scene in order to get revenge for a car theft by a rival gang. Chatman insisted, to the police and at trial, that Swain had not been in the van. He could not, however, explain Swain's fingerprint inside the van.

The owner of the van testified Swain had never been inside his van prior to the incident, but that Swain had intimidated him into telling police he (Swain) had previously been inside the vehicle, since otherwise "he was going to have something done to him."

At trial, Chatman admitted he had been in the van, which was driven to Hunter's Point to retaliate for a car theft attributed to a neighborhood youth who was not the victim of the shooting. The original plan was allegedly to steal the car of the thief. Chatman admitted he had fired shots, but claimed he fired wildly and only in self-defense. In support of this self-defense theory, he testified he heard an initial shot and thought it was fired by someone outside the van shooting at him, so he returned the fire. As noted, Chatman claimed Swain was not in the van.

Swain testified he was not in the van during the shooting and did not do any shooting. He claimed he had entered the van earlier in the evening, but had left because "the smell of marijuana bothered him." He claimed he took BART (Bay Area Rapid Transit) to Berkeley, where he spent the evening at a relative's home. He denied boasting about shooting the victim and denied having threatened any witnesses.

The jury first returned a verdict finding defendant Chatman guilty of second degree murder and conspiracy. As instructed, the jury also made a finding that the target offense of the conspiracy was murder in the second degree. Several days later, the jury returned verdicts against defendant Swain, finding him not guilty of murder or its lesser included offenses, but guilty of conspiracy and of attempting to dissuade a witness from testifying by threats. Once again, the jury made a finding under the conspiracy count that the target offense of the conspiracy was murder in the second degree. * * *

Both defendants appealed on several grounds, including the question of whether intent to kill is a required element of the crime of conspiracy to commit murder. More particularly, where, as here, the target offense is determined to be murder in the second degree, does conviction of conspiracy to commit murder necessarily require proof of express malice—the functional equivalent of intent to kill—or can one conspire to commit implied malice murder? * * *

DISCUSSION

Defendants contend the jury should have been instructed that proof of intent to kill is required to support a conviction of conspiracy to commit murder, whether the target offense of the conspiracy—murder—is determined to be in the first or second degree. More particularly, defendants assert it was error to instruct the jury on the principles of implied malice second degree murder in connection with the determination of whether they could be found guilty of conspiracy to commit murder, since implied malice does not require a finding of intent to kill. As we shall explain, we agree.

We commence our analysis with a brief review of the elements of the crime of conspiracy, and of murder, the target offense of the conspiracy here in issue.

Conspiracy is an inchoate crime. It does not require the commission of the substantive offense that is the object of the conspiracy. "As an inchoate crime, conspiracy fixes the point of legal intervention at [the time of] agreement to commit a crime," and "thus reaches further back into preparatory conduct than attempt. . . . "

The crime of conspiracy is defined in the Penal Code as "two or more persons conspir[ing]" "[t]o commit any crime," together with proof of the commission of an overt act "by one or more of the parties to such agreement" in furtherance thereof. "Conspiracy is a 'specific intent' crime. . . . The specific intent required divides logically into two elements: (a) the intent to agree, or conspire, and (b) the intent to commit the offense which is the object of the conspiracy. . . . * * *

Turning next to the elements of the target offense of the conspiracy here in issue, Penal Code section 187 defines the crime of murder as the "unlawful killing of a human being . . . with malice aforethought." Malice aforethought "may be express or implied." "It is express when there is manifested a deliberate intention unlawfully to take away the life of a fellow creature. It is implied, when no considerable provocation appears, or when the circumstances attending the killing show an abandoned and malignant heart."

This court has observed that proof of unlawful "intent to kill" is the functional equivalent of express malice. * * *

As noted, the jury in this case was instructed on the elements of murder, including principles of implied malice second degree murder. Under the instructions given, the jury could have based its verdicts finding defendants guilty of conspiracy to commit murder in the second degree on a theory of implied malice murder. * * *

We have noted that conspiracy is a specific intent crime requiring an intent to agree or conspire, and a further intent to commit the target crime, here murder, the object of the conspiracy. Since murder committed with intent to kill is the functional equivalent of express malice murder, conceptually speaking, no conflict arises between the specific intent element of conspiracy and the specific intent requirement for such category of murders. Simply put, where the conspirators agree or conspire with specific intent to kill and commit an overt act in furtherance of such agreement, they are guilty of conspiracy to commit express malice murder. The conceptual difficulty arises when the target offense of murder is founded on a theory of implied malice, which requires no intent to kill.

Implied malice murder, in contrast to express malice, requires instead an intent to do some act, the natural consequences of which are dangerous to human life. * * * In such circumstances, ". . . it is not necessary to establish that the defendant intended that his act would result in the death of a human being." Hence, under an implied malice theory of second degree murder, the requisite mental state for murder—malice aforethought—is by definition "implied," as a matter of law, from the specific intent to do some act dangerous to human life together with the circumstance that a killing has resulted from the doing of such act. * * *

The element of malice aforethought in implied malice murder cases is therefore derived or "implied," in part through hindsight so to speak, from (i) proof of the specific intent to do some act dangerous to human life and (ii) the circumstance that a killing has resulted therefrom. It is precisely due to this nature of implied malice murder that it would be illogical to conclude one can be found guilty of conspiring to commit murder where the requisite element of malice is implied. Such a construction would be at odds with the very nature of the crime of conspiracy—an "inchoate" crime that "fixes the point of legal intervention at [the time of] agreement to commit a crime," and indeed "reaches further back into preparatory conduct than [the crime of] attempt"—precisely because commission of the crime could never be established, or deemed complete, unless and until a killing actually occurred.

By analogy, we have reached similar conclusions respecting the nature of proof of the element of malice required to establish the inchoate crimes of assault with intent to commit murder and attempted murder. * * *

We conclude that a conviction of conspiracy to commit murder requires a finding of intent to kill, and cannot be based on a theory of implied malice. * * *

That portion of the Court of Appeal's judgment affirming [defendants'] convictions of conspiracy to commit murder must therefore be reversed.

[The concurring opinion of Justice Mosk has been omitted.]

PEOPLE V. LAURIA

Court of Appeal, Second District, Division 2, California
251 Cal.App.2d 471 (1967)

FLEMING, J.

In an investigation of call-girl activity the police focused their attention on three prostitutes actively plying their trade on call, each of whom was using Lauria's telephone answering service, presumably for business purposes.

On January 8, 1965, Stella Weeks, a policewoman, signed up for telephone service with Lauria's answering service. Mrs. Weeks, in the course of her conversation with Lauria's office manager, hinted broadly that she was a prostitute concerned with the secrecy of her activities and their concealment from the police. She was assured that the operation of the service was discreet and "about as safe as you can get." It was arranged that Mrs. Weeks need not leave her address with the answering service, but could pick up her calls and pay her bills in person.

On February 11, Mrs. Weeks talked to Lauria on the telephone and told him her business was modelling and she had been referred to the answering service by Terry, one of the three prostitutes under investigation. She complained that because of the operation of the service she had lost two valuable customers, referred to as tricks. Lauria defended his service and said that her friends had probably lied to her about having left calls for her. But he did not respond to Mrs. Weeks's hints that she needed customers in order to make money, other than to invite her to his house for a personal visit in order to get better acquainted. In the course of his talk he said "his business was taking messages."

On February 15, Mrs. Weeks talked on the telephone to Lauria's office manager and again complained of two lost calls, which she described as a $50 and a $100 trick. On investigation the office manager could find nothing wrong, but she said she would alert the switchboard operators about slip-ups on calls.

On April 1 Lauria and the three prostitutes were arrested. Lauria complained to the police that this attention was undeserved, stating that Hollywood Call Board had 60 to 70 prostitutes on its board while his own service had only 9 or 10, that he kept separate records for known or suspected prostitutes for the convenience of himself and the police. When asked if his records were available to police who might come to the office to investigate call girls, Lauria replied that they were whenever the police had a specific name. However, his service didn't "arbitrarily tell the police about prostitutes on our board. As long as they pay their bills we tolerate them." In a subsequent voluntary appearance before the grand jury Lauria testified he had always cooperated with the police. But he admitted he knew some of his customers were prostitutes, and he knew Terry was a prostitute because he had personally used her services, and he knew she was paying for 500 calls a month.

Lauria and the three prostitutes were indicted for conspiracy to commit prostitution, and nine overt acts were specified. Subsequently the trial court set aside the indictment as having been brought without reasonable or probable cause. The People have appealed, claiming that a sufficient showing of an unlawful agreement to further prostitution was made.

To establish agreement, the People need show no more than a tacit, mutual understanding between coconspirators to accomplish an unlawful act. Here the People attempted to establish a conspiracy by showing that

Lauria, well aware that his codefendants were prostitutes who received business calls from customers through his telephone answering service, continued to furnish them with such service. This approach attempts to equate knowledge of another's criminal activity with conspiracy to further such criminal activity, and poses the question of the criminal responsibility of a furnisher of goods or services who knows his product is being used to assist the operation of an illegal business. Under what circumstances does a supplier become a part of a conspiracy to further an illegal enterprise by furnishing goods or services which he knows are to be used by the buyer for criminal purposes?

The two leading cases on this point face in opposite directions. In *United States v. Falcone*, the sellers of large quantities of sugar, yeast, and cans were absolved from participation in a moonshining conspiracy among distillers who bought from them, while in *Direct Sales Co. v. United States*, a wholesaler of drugs was convicted of conspiracy to violate the federal narcotic laws by selling drugs in quantity to a codefendant physician who was supplying them to addicts. The distinction between these two cases appears primarily based on the proposition that distributors of such dangerous products as drugs are required to exercise greater discrimination in the conduct of their business than are distributors of innocuous substances like sugar and yeast.

In the earlier case, *Falcone*, the [sellers'] knowledge of the illegal use of the goods was insufficient by itself to make the sellers participants in a conspiracy with the distillers who bought from them. Such knowledge fell short of proof of a conspiracy, and evidence on the volume of sales was too vague to support a jury finding that respondents knew of the conspiracy from the size of the sales alone.

In the later case of *Direct Sales*, the conviction of a drug wholesaler for conspiracy to violate federal narcotic laws was affirmed on a showing that it had actively promoted the sale of morphine sulphate in quantity and had sold codefendant physician, who practiced in a small town in South Carolina, more than 300 times his normal requirements of the drug, even though it had been repeatedly warned of the dangers of unrestricted sales of the drug. The court contrasted the restricted goods involved in *Direct Sales* with the articles of free commerce involved in *Falcone*: "All articles of commerce may be put to illegal ends," said the court. "But all do not have inherently the same susceptibility to harmful and illegal use. . . . This difference is important for two purposes. One is for making certain that the seller knows the buyer's intended illegal use. The other is to show that by the sale he intends to further, promote, and cooperate in it. This intent, when given effect by overt act, is the gist of conspiracy. While it is not identical with mere knowledge that another purposes unlawful action it is not unrelated to such knowledge. . . . The step from knowledge to intent and agreement may be taken. There is more than suspicion, more than knowledge, acquiescence, carelessness, indifference, lack of concern. There is informed and interested cooperation, stimulation, instigation. And there is also a 'stake in the venture' which, even if it may not be essential, is not irrelevant to the question of conspiracy."

While *Falcone* and *Direct Sales* may not be entirely consistent with each other in their full implications, they do provide us with a framework for the criminal liability of a supplier of lawful goods or services put to unlawful use. Both the element of *knowledge* of the illegal use of the goods or services and the element of *intent* to further that use must be present in order to make the supplier a participant in a criminal conspiracy.

Proof of *knowledge* is ordinarily a question of fact and requires no extended discussion in the present case. The knowledge of the supplier was sufficiently established when Lauria admitted he knew some of his customers were prostitutes and admitted he knew that Terry, an active subscriber to his service, was a prostitute. In the face of these admissions he could scarcely claim to have relied on the normal assumption an operator of a business or service is entitled to make, that his customers are behaving themselves in the eyes of the law. Because Lauria knew in fact that some of his customers were prostitutes, it is a legitimate inference he knew they were subscribing to his answering service for illegal business purposes and were using his service to make assignations for prostitution. On this record we think the prosecution is entitled to claim positive knowledge by Lauria of the use of his service to facilitate the business of prostitution.

The more perplexing issue in the case is the sufficiency of proof of *intent* to further the criminal enterprise. The element of intent may be proved either by direct evidence, or by evidence of circumstances from which an intent to further a criminal enterprise by supplying lawful goods or services may be inferred. Direct evidence of participation, such as advice from the supplier of legal goods or services to the user of those goods or services on their use for illegal purposes, such evidence as appeared in a companion case we decide today, *People v. Roy, ante*, provides the simplest case. When the intent to further and promote the criminal enterprise comes from the lips of the supplier himself, ambiguities of inference from circumstance need not trouble us. But in cases where direct proof of complicity is lacking, intent to further the conspiracy must be derived from the sale itself and its surrounding circumstances in order to establish the supplier's express or tacit agreement to join the conspiracy.

In the case at bench the prosecution argues that since Lauria knew his customers were using his service for illegal purposes but nevertheless continued to furnish it to them, he must have intended to assist them in carrying out their illegal activities. Thus through a union of knowledge and intent he became a participant in a criminal conspiracy. Essentially, the People argue that knowledge alone of the continuing use of his telephone facilities for criminal purposes provided a sufficient basis from which his intent to participate in those criminal activities could be inferred.

In examining precedents in this field we find that sometimes, but not always, the criminal intent of the supplier may be inferred from his knowledge of the unlawful use made of the product he supplies. Some consideration of characteristic patterns may be helpful.

1. Intent may be inferred from knowledge, when the purveyor of legal goods for illegal use has acquired a stake in the venture. For example, in *Regina v. Thomas*, a prosecution for living off the earnings of prostitution, the evidence showed that the accused, knowing the woman to be a convicted prostitute, agreed to let her have the use of his room between the hours of 9 p.m. and 2 a.m. for a charge of 3 a night. The Court of Criminal Appeal refused an appeal from the conviction, holding that when the accused rented a room at a grossly inflated rent to a prostitute for the purpose of carrying on her trade, a jury could find he was living on the earnings of prostitution.

In the present case, no proof was offered of inflated charges for the telephone answering services furnished the codefendants.

2. Intent may be inferred from knowledge, when no legitimate use for the goods or services exists. * * *

In *Shaw v. Director of Public Prosecutions*, the defendant was convicted of conspiracy to corrupt public morals and of living on the earnings of prostitution, when he published a directory consisting almost entirely of advertisements of the names, addresses, and specialized talents of prostitutes. Publication of such a directory, said the court, could have no legitimate use and serve no other purpose than to advertise the professional services of the prostitutes whose advertisements appeared in the directory. The publisher could be deemed a participant in the profits from the business activities of his principal advertisers.

Other services of a comparable nature come to mind: the manufacturer of crooked dice and marked cards who sells his product to gambling casinos; the tipster who furnishes information on the movement of law enforcement officers to known lawbreakers. In such cases the supplier must necessarily have an intent to further the illegal enterprise since there is no known honest use for his goods.

However, there is nothing in the furnishing of telephone answering service which would necessarily imply assistance in the performance of illegal activities. Nor is any inference to be derived from the use of an answering service by women, either in any particular volume of calls, or outside normal working hours. Night-club entertainers, registered nurses, faith healers, public stenographers, photographic models, and freelance substitute employees, provide examples of women in legitimate occupations whose employment might cause them to receive a volume of telephone calls at irregular hours.

3. Intent may be inferred from knowledge, when the volume of business with the buyer is grossly disproportionate to any legitimate demand, or when sales for illegal use amount to a high proportion of the seller's total business. In such cases an intent to participate in the illegal enterprise may be inferred from the quantity of the business done. For example, in *Direct Sales,* the sale of narcotics to a rural physician in quantities 300 times greater than he would have normal use for provided potent evidence of an intent to further the illegal activity. In the same case the court also found significant the fact that the wholesaler had attracted as customers a disproportionately large group of physicians who had been convicted of violating the Harrison Act. In *Shaw v. Director of Public Prosecutions*, almost the entire business of the directory came from prostitutes.

No evidence of any unusual volume of business with prostitutes was presented by the prosecution against Lauria.

Inflated charges, the sale of goods with no legitimate use, sales in inflated amounts, each may provide a fact of sufficient moment from which the intent of the seller to participate in the criminal enterprise may be inferred. In such instances participation by the supplier of legal goods to the illegal enterprise may be inferred because in one way or another the supplier has acquired a special interest in the operation of the illegal enterprise. His intent to participate in the crime of which he has knowledge may be inferred from the existence of his special interest.

Yet there are cases in which it cannot reasonably be said that the supplier has a stake in the venture or has acquired a special interest in the enterprise, but in which he has been held liable as a participant on the basis of knowledge alone. * * * In *Regina v. Bainbridge*, a supplier of oxygen-cutting equipment to one known to intend to use it to break into a bank was convicted as an accessory to the crime. In *Sykes v. Director of Public Prosecutions*, one having knowledge of the theft of 100 pistols, 4 submachine guns, and 1,960 rounds of ammunition was convicted of misprision of felony for failure to disclose the theft to the public authorities. It seems apparent from these cases that a supplier who furnishes equipment which he *knows* will be used to commit a serious crime may be deemed from that knowledge alone to have intended to produce the result. * * *

Logically, the same reasoning could be extended to crimes of every description. Yet we do not believe an inference of intent drawn from knowledge of criminal use properly applies to the less serious crimes classified as misdemeanors. The duty to take positive action to dissociate oneself from activities helpful to violations of the criminal law is far stronger and more compelling for felonies than it is for misdemeanors or petty offenses. In this respect, as in others, the distinction between felonies and misdemeanors, between more serious and less serious crime, retains continuing vitality. In historically the most serious felony, treason, an individual with knowledge of the treason can be prosecuted for concealing and failing to disclose it. In other felonies, both at common law and under the criminal laws of the United States, an individual knowing of the commission of a felony is criminally liable for concealing it and failing to make it known to proper authority. But this crime, known as misprision of felony, has always been limited to knowledge and concealment of felony and has never extended to misdemeanor. A similar limitation is found in the criminal liability of an accessory, which is restricted to aid in the escape of a principal who has committed or been charged with a *felony*. We believe the distinction between the obligations arising from knowledge of a felony and those arising from knowledge of a misdemeanor continues to reflect basic human feelings about the duties owed by individuals to society. Heinous crime must be stamped out, and its suppression is the responsibility of all. Venial crime and crime not evil in itself present less of a danger to society, and perhaps the benefits of their suppression through the modern equivalent of the posse, the hue and cry, the informant, and the citizen's arrest, are outweighed by the disruption to everyday life brought about by amateur law enforcement and private officiousness in relatively inconsequential delicts which do not threaten our basic security. * * *

With respect to misdemeanors, we conclude that positive knowledge of the supplier that his products or services are being used for criminal purposes does not, without more, establish an intent of the supplier to participate in the misdemeanors. With respect to felonies, we do not decide the converse, viz., that in all cases of felony knowledge of criminal use alone may justify an inference of the supplier's intent to participate in the crime. The implications of *Falcone* make the matter uncertain with respect to those felonies which are merely prohibited wrongs. But decision on this point is not compelled, and we leave the matter open.

From this analysis of precedent we deduce the following rule: the intent of a supplier who knows of the criminal use to which his supplies are put to participate in the criminal activity connected with the use of his supplies may be established by (1) direct evidence that he intends to participate, or (2) through an inference that he intends to participate based on, (a) his special interest in the activity, or (b) the aggravated nature of the crime itself.

When we review Lauria's activities in the light of this analysis, we find no proof that Lauria took any direct action to further, encourage, or direct the call-girl activities of his codefendants and we find an absence of circumstance from which his special interest in their activities could be inferred. Neither excessive charges for standardized services, nor the furnishing of services without a legitimate use, nor an unusual quantity of business with call girls, are present. The offense which he is charged with furthering is a misdemeanor, a category of crime which has never been made a required subject of positive disclosure to public authority. Under these circumstances, although proof of Lauria's knowledge of the criminal activities of his patrons was sufficient to charge him with that fact, there was insufficient evidence that he intended to further their criminal activities, and hence insufficient proof of his participation in a criminal conspiracy with his codefendants to further prostitution. Since the conspiracy centered around the activities of Lauria's telephone answering service, the charges against his codefendants likewise fail for want of proof.

In absolving Lauria of complicity in a criminal conspiracy we do not wish to imply that the public authorities are without remedies to combat modern manifestations of the world's oldest profession. Licensing of telephone answering services under the police power, together with the revocation of licenses for the toleration of prostitution, is a possible civil remedy. The furnishing of telephone answering service in aid of prostitution could be made a crime. * * * Other solutions will doubtless occur to vigilant public authorities if the problem of call-girl activity needs further suppression.

The order is affirmed.

NOTE

What mens rea is required as to attendant circumstances when one is charged with the crime of conspiracy? In *United States v. Feola*, two drug dealers agreed to attack a third person, who turned out to be a federal officer working undercover. 420 U.S. 671 (1975). Were they guilty of conspiracy to commit simple assault or the more serious crime of conspiracy to commit assault on a federal officer in the performance of his official duties? Arguably, the two men were guilty of a conspiracy to commit a simple assault since they did not agree to assault a federal officer. The United States Supreme Court, however, held that the defendants could be convicted of the more serious crime, even though they did not know at the time that the victim was a federal officer. The Court explained:

> This interpretation poses no risk of unfairness to defendants. It is no snare for the unsuspecting. Although the perpetrator of a narcotics [offense], such as the one involved here, may be surprised to find that his intended victim is a federal officer in civilian apparel, he nonetheless knows from the very outset that his planned course of conduct is wrongful.

420 U.S. at 685.

Feola represents the Court's interpretation of a particular statute, and thus does not constitute precedent on the broader point of the mens rea for attendant circumstances of a crime for purposes of conspiracy liability. Other courts have disagreed with *Feola*'s reasoning. Consider the criticism of one judge in the Southern District of New York:

> The trouble with *Feola* as a guiding precedent is that it purported to treat the statute as both "an aggravated assault statute," and as one involving a federal provision that was "jurisdictional only." But the Court did not acknowledge that some mens rea requirement is necessary with respect to the officers' status in order to effectuate Congress' intent to punish assaults upon federal officers more severely. At a minimum, the defendant must know that the assault victim is some kind of official, whether federal or state, or such a provision has no additional deterrent effect beyond the existing general laws prohibiting assaults. The contention that the defendants knew their conduct was criminal is no answer where the legislature is interested in punishing a particular form of assault more severely. * * *

United States v. Cordoba-Hincapie, 825 F. Supp. 485, 511 (E.D.N.Y. 1993).

C. THE PINKERTON RULE

When two or more people agree with another to commit a crime, what is their responsibility for ancillary crimes committed that promote their agreement? Applying agency law to the offense of conspiracy, in 1946 the Supreme Court announced what has come to be known as the "Pinkerton rule" of vicarious liability. *Pinkerton v. United States*, 328 U.S. 640 (1946), involved two brothers, Daniel and Walter Pinkerton, who were indicted for bootlegging on ten substantive counts and one conspiracy count of Internal Revenue Code violations. Although there was no evidence to show that Daniel had participated directly in the commission of all the substantive offenses (since he was in prison during some of them), the Supreme Court upheld his conviction for those offenses. The Court commented: "A different case would arise if the substantive offense committed by one of the conspirators was not in fact done in furtherance of the conspiracy, did not fall within the scope of the unlawful project, or was merely a part of the ramifications of the plan which could not be reasonably foreseen as a necessary or natural consequence of the unlawful agreement. But as we read this record, that is not this case." In dissent, Justice Rutledge objected that principles of vicarious liability taken from commercial law and tort law were inappropriate in the context of criminal responsibility.

The Pinkerton rule has come to stand for the proposition that a conspirator may be held liable for a crime committed by another member of the conspiracy even if that other crime was not part of the original agreement as long as the unintended crime was: (1) in furtherance of the conspiracy, (2) within the scope of the conspiracy, and (3) a reasonably foreseeable consequence of the original agreement. The case that follows illustrates the outer limits of the *Pinkerton* rule as interpreted by one federal circuit. The Model Penal Code rejects the Pinkerton rule.

UNITED STATES V. MOTHERSILL

U.S. Court of Appeals for the Eleventh Circuit
87 F.3d 1214 (11th Cir. 1996)

JOHN H. MOORE, II, SENIOR DISTRICT JUDGE:

On February 1, 1992, on a highway located in Jefferson County, Florida, Florida Highway Patrol Trooper James Fulford observed a car exceeding the speed limit and made a routine traffic stop. After making the usual inquiries, he discovered the car was a rental, and the driver was without a license; he arrested the driver of the vehicle for operating a vehicle without a license. After the driver consented, and while waiting for the car to be impounded, Trooper Fulford opened a gift-wrapped package found in the truck of the vehicle, purportedly containing a microwave oven. Unfortunately, there was a homemade pipe bomb inside the microwave oven, which was triggered to explode when the microwave was opened. Trooper Fulford died from the extensive injuries he received from the blast.

After law enforcement conducted a thorough investigation, the government indicted several individuals, ultimately filing a third superseding indictment on October 16, 1992, which included charges ranging from drug and RICO conspiracies to felony murder and the murder of a law enforcement officer. On March 9, 1993, after an eight-week criminal jury trial, Appellants were convicted of several counts.

Appellants Patrick and Paul Howell, Michael Morgan, Patricia Clarke, Norris Mothersill, Egnatius Johnson, and Errol Morrison were all found guilty of either Counts I or III, which alleged a conspiracy to commit racketeering pursuant to 18 U.S.C. § 1962(d) and conspiracy to traffic in controlled substances pursuant to 21 U.S.C. § 846, respectively. For purposes of the discussion below, it is noteworthy that Appellants Patrick and Paul Howell, Morgan, Clarke, Mothersill, and Johnson were all found guilty of Count XXVIII of the Third Superseding Indictment.[1] Count XXVIII dealt with Trooper Fulford's death, and Appellants Morgan, Clarke, Johnson and Mothersill were found guilty under the co-conspirator liability theory outlined in *Pinkerton v. United States*, 328

---

[1] Count XXVIII, in pertinent part, alleged Appellants:

did maliciously damage and destroy by means of fire and explosive materials property which was used in interstate or foreign commerce and in activities affecting interstate or foreign commerce, that is: a Sharpe microwave . . . and a 1991 Mitsubishi Galant . . . and as a direct and proximate result did cause the death of Florida Highway Patrol Trooper James Fulford, a public safety officer in the performance of his duties, in violation of Title 18, United States Code, Sections 844(I) and 2.

U.S. 640 (1946). Defendant Paul Howell was convicted * * * for his role in the creation of the bomb that led to Trooper Fulford's death. Patrick Howell was convicted under *Pinkerton* liability and for aiding and abetting the crime.[2]

After the district court sentenced Appellants to life or "life-plus" terms of imprisonment, Appellants appealed their convictions to this Court. * * * Appellants raise several issues, only one of which merits discussion, namely, the imposition of *Pinkerton* co-conspirator liability. * * * We affirm. * * *

II. DISCUSSION

a. Background Facts

Patrick Howell, Michael Morgan and Egnatius Johnson, among others, were the principal leaders of an elaborate drug operation, dating back to 1988, that supplied, distributed and sold crack cocaine throughout Florida, Alabama, Mississippi, Georgia, and North and South Carolina. * * * Patrick's brother, Paul Howell, Johnson's former girlfriend and Morgan's sister, Patricia Clarke, Norris Mothersill and Errol Morrison were also major players in the sophisticated and expansive operation. For purposes of our discussion, the precise scope and history of the conspiracy need not be recited; however, certain events and individuals, pertinent to the issue examined below, warrant mentioning. * * *

In August of 1991, Patrick Howell and Michael Morgan were plotting to rob a Ft. Lauderdale drug dealer named Alfonso Tillman. With Clarke and Johnson present, Howell and Morgan obtained a car rented by Paul Howell, and Morgan secured a weapon. Morgan, while Patrick Howell drove, shot and killed Tillman. After the shooting, the inside of the car needed extensive cleaning, and Clarke and Patrick and Paul Howell commenced the clean-up efforts. Tammie Bailey and Yolanda McCalister were the girlfriends of Michael Morgan and Patrick Howell respectively. Patrick Howell had informed McCalister of the murder, and warned her if she told anybody, he would kill her and her family. McCalister and Bailey ultimately rode in the rental car, noticing blood and bullet holes in the interior, and blood on Patrick Howell's shorts.

In October of 1991, after returning from a trip to Jamaica, Patrick Howell was detained by immigration officials and ultimately arrested. While Patrick was incarcerated, Paul took over the supervisory role in their drug operation. During this time, law enforcement officials were progressing in the investigation of the Tillman murder. In the wake of the Tillman murder, appellant Paul Howell, concerned about the possibility of

[2] "A defendant charged with conspiracy and the substantive offense 'normally will be responsible for the substantive crime under the *Pinkerton* theory and also may be responsible for the substantive crime under an aiding and abetting theory.'" *United States v. Meester*, 762 F.2d 867, 878 (11th Cir.1985) (quoting *United States v. Monaco*, 702 F.2d 860, 881 (11th Cir.1983)).

Ms. Bailey "straying" and turning to the authorities, constructed a pipe bomb with the intention of killing her in an apparent attempt to ensure she would not talk. To that end, he ordered the delivery of a gift-wrapped package containing a microwave oven to Ms. Bailey; inside the oven was the homemade pipe bomb that took Trooper Fulford's life.

b. *Pinkerton/Alvarez* co-conspirator liability

Basic to criminal law principles is the concept that the "commission of a substantive offense and a conspiracy to commit it are separate and distinct offenses." Each party to a continuing conspiracy may be vicariously liable for substantive criminal offenses committed by a co-conspirator during the course and in the furtherance of the conspiracy, notwithstanding the party's non-participation in the offenses or lack of knowledge thereof. Liability will not lie, however, if the substantive crime "did not fall within the scope of the unlawful project, or was merely a part of the ramifications of the plan which could not be reasonably foreseen as a necessary or natural consequence of the unlawful agreement." *Pinkerton,* 328 U.S. at 647–48. Hence, a court need not assess the individual culpability of a particular conspirator provided the "substantive crime was a reasonably foreseeable consequence of the conspiracy."

Generally, *Pinkerton* co-conspirator liability applies in two situations. First, where the substantive crime is also a goal of the conspiracy, e.g., where there is a narcotics conspiracy and a corresponding substantive crime of possession or distribution of cocaine. The second scenario is where the substantive offense differs from the precise nature of the ongoing conspiracy, but facilitates the implementation of its goals. For example, a particular co-conspirator, found guilty of conspiring to distribute drugs, may also be held liable for the substantive crime of possession of a firearm.

In *Alvarez*, this circuit expanded the breadth of *Pinkerton* liability to include reasonably foreseeable but originally unintended substantive crimes, in other words, embracing substantive crimes occurring "as a result of an unintended turn of events." Despite the fact that murder was not within the originally intended scope of the conspiracy in that case, the *Alvarez* Court found individual culpability of the defendants sufficient to support their murder convictions pursuant to the *Pinkerton* co-conspirator doctrine. * * *

The Court in *Alvarez* focused on two factors in finding that there was sufficient evidence to support the jury's conclusion that murder was a reasonably foreseeable consequence of the conspiracy. The first was the substantial amount of drugs and money involved in the drug conspiracy; as that court states, it was not a "nickel-and-dime" operation. The second involved the jury's ability to infer—given the amount of drugs and money involved in the operation—that the conspirators must have been aware of the likelihood that another member of their coterie would be using or carrying weapons and that, if necessary, deadly force would be used to protect the conspirators' interests. We find both factors are present in this case.

Appellants argue that the bombing was an attenuated, unintended act, and that it does not compare, for example, to the use of firearms for stealing or protecting drugs and monies derived from a conspiracy to distribute drugs. Appellants also maintain that Trooper Fulford's death was the result of an irrational act by Paul Howell which could not have been reasonably foreseen as a natural and probable consequence of the alleged conspiracy. The government, conversely, argues that deadly force and violence were more than peripheral possibilities; rather, they were routine practices and central to the goals and implementation of the conspiracy. A review of the record supports the government's position.

When viewed in light of the *Alvarez* theory of co-conspirator liability, it is clear that the trial court did not err by submitting the *Pinkerton* issue to the jury. There was sufficient evidence for a reasonable jury to have concluded beyond a reasonable doubt that the murder was a reasonably foreseeable consequence of the drug conspiracy. We further find that the court's jury instructions are sound and without error. We therefore find that *Pinkerton* liability was properly imposed on Appellants. * * *

An exhaustive examination of the record reveals abundant evidence supporting the jury's conclusion that the killing of individuals was a reasonably foreseeable consequence of the ongoing conspiracy, especially given the frequency with which weapons and violence, actual or threatened, were used in order to further the interests of the conspiracy. One need not look further than the Tillman murder to support its conclusion. Moreover, the record is replete with references to the conspirators being continuously armed and using such weapons either to protect or advance their interest, most notably by armed robberies. * * *

* * * Therefore, we hold that the imposition of *Pinkerton* liability on Appellants Morgan, Clarke, Johnson, Mothersill and Patrick Howell for the death of Trooper Fulford was proper, and hence, reject Appellants' attempts to reverse their convictions on this ground.

AFFIRMED.

D. WHARTON'S RULE

A doctrinal corollary of the idea that the collective decision to commit a crime merits punishment distinct from punishment for the crime itself is represented by the common law doctrine called Wharton's Rule. Under Wharton's Rule, certain crimes—among them adultery, incest, bigamy, and dueling—cannot be the subject of a conspiracy conviction because they are crimes that by their very definition require an agreement between two persons to commit the offense. Presumably, the legislature has already taken the collective character of the crime into account.

Wharton's Rule does not apply, however, if more than the minimum number of persons necessary to commit the offense agree to commit the crime. This rule is known as the "third party exception" to Wharton's Rule:

> For example, while the two persons who commit adultery cannot normally be prosecuted both for that offense and for conspiracy to commit it, the third-party exception would permit the conspiracy charge where a "matchmaker"—the third party—had conspired with the principals to encourage commission of the substantive offense. The rationale supporting this exception appears to be that the addition of a third party enhances the dangers presented by the crime. Thus, it is thought that the legislature would not have intended to preclude punishment for a combination of greater dimension than that required to commit the substantive offense.

Iannelli v. United States, 420 U.S. 770 (1975).

E. THE SHAPE AND BOUNDARIES OF CONSPIRACIES

KOTTEAKOS V. UNITED STATES

Supreme Court of the United States
328 U.S. 750, 66 S.Ct. 1239, 90 L.Ed. 1557 (1946)

MR. JUSTICE RUTLEDGE delivered the opinion of the Court.

The only question is whether petitioners have suffered substantial prejudice from being convicted of a single general conspiracy by evidence which the Government admits proved not one conspiracy but some eight or more different ones of the same sort executed through a common key figure, Simon Brown. Petitioners were convicted under the general conspiracy section of the Criminal Code, 18 U. S. C. § 88, of conspiring to violate the provisions of the National Housing Act, 12 U. S. C. § 1702, 1703, 1715, 1731. The judgments were affirmed by the Circuit Court of Appeals. We granted certiorari because of the importance of the question for the administration of criminal justice in the federal courts.

The indictment named thirty-two defendants, including the petitioners. The gist of the conspiracy, as alleged, was that the defendants had sought to induce various financial institutions to grant credit, with the intent that the loans or advances would then be offered to the Federal Housing Administration for insurance upon applications containing false and fraudulent information.

Of the thirty-two persons named in the indictment nineteen were brought to trial and the names of thirteen were submitted to the jury. Two were acquitted; the jury disagreed as to four; and the remaining seven, including petitioners, were found guilty.

The Government's evidence may be summarized briefly, for the petitioners have not contended that it was insufficient, if considered apart from the alleged errors relating to the proof and the instructions at the trial.

Simon Brown, who pleaded guilty, was the common and key figure in all of the transactions proven. He was president of the Brownie Lumber Company. Having had experience in obtaining loans under the National Housing Act, he undertook to act as broker in placing for others loans for modernization and renovation, charging a five per cent commission for his services. Brown knew, when he obtained the loans, that the proceeds were not to be used for the purposes stated in the applications.

In May, 1939, petitioner Lekacos told Brown that he wished to secure a loan in order to finance opening a law office, to say the least a hardly auspicious professional launching. Brown made out the application, as directed by Lekacos, to state that the purpose of the loan was to modernize a house belonging to the estate of Lekacos' father. Lekacos obtained the money. Later in the same year Lekacos secured another loan through Brown, the application being in the names of his brother and sister-in-law. Lekacos also received part of the proceeds of a loan for which one Gerakeris, a defendant who pleaded guilty, had applied.

In June, 1939, Lekacos sent Brown an application for a loan signed by petitioner Kotteakos. It contained false statements.[5] Brown placed the loan, and Kotteakos thereafter sent Brown applications on behalf of other persons. Two were made out in the names of fictitious persons. The proceeds were received by Kotteakos and petitioner Regenbogen, his partner in the cigarette and pinball machine business. Regenbogen, together with Kotteakos, had indorsed one of the applications. Kotteakos also sent to Brown an application for a loan in Regenbogen's name. This was for modernization of property not owned by Regenbogen. The latter, however, repaid the money in about three months after he received it.

The evidence against the other defendants whose cases were submitted to the jury was similar in character. They too had transacted business with Brown relating to National Housing Act loans. But no connection was shown between them and petitioners, other than that Brown had been the instrument in each instance for obtaining the loans.

---

[5] The application stated that the house on which the loan was sought was bought in 1936 rather than in 1938, that the purchase price was $8500 rather than $7200, and that the assessed valuation was $9500 rather than $6500. The application further stated that among the repairs contemplated was a repainting of the house, whereas in fact only the basement hallway and garage were repainted.

In many cases the other defendants did not have any relationship with one another, other than Brown's connection with each transaction. As the Circuit Court of Appeals said, there were "at least eight, and perhaps more, separate and independent groups, none of which had any connection with any other, though all dealt independently with Brown as their agent." As the Government puts it, the pattern was "that of separate spokes meeting in a common center," though, we may add, without the rim of the wheel to enclose the spokes.

The proof therefore admittedly made out a case, not of a single conspiracy, but of several, notwithstanding only one was charged in the indictment. The Court of Appeals aptly drew analogy in the comment, "Thieves who dispose of their loot to a single receiver—a single 'fence'—do not by that fact alone become confederates: they may, but it takes more than knowledge that he is a 'fence' to make them such." It stated that the trial judge "was plainly wrong in supposing that upon the evidence there could be a single conspiracy; and in the view which he took of the law, he should have dismissed the indictment." Nevertheless the appellate court held the error not prejudicial, saying among other things that "especially since guilt was so manifest, it was 'proper' to join the conspiracies," and "to reverse the conviction would be a miscarriage of justice." This is indeed the Government's entire position. It does not now contend that there was no variance in proof from the single conspiracy charged in the indictment. Admitting that separate and distinct conspiracies were shown, it urges that the variance was not prejudicial to the petitioners.

In *Berger v. United States*, this Court held that in the circumstances presented the variance was not fatal where one conspiracy was charged and two were proved, relating to contemporaneous transactions involving counterfeit money. One of the conspiracies had two participants; the other had three; and one defendant, Katz, was common to each. "The true inquiry," said the Court, "is not whether there has been a variance in proof, but whether there has been such a variance as to 'affect the substantial rights' of the accused."

The Court held the variance not fatal, resting its ruling on what has become known as "the harmless error statute," § 269 of the Judicial Code, as amended (28 U. S. C. § 391), which is controlling in this case and provides:

> On the hearing of any appeal, certiorari, writ of error, or motion for a new trial, in any case, civil or criminal, the court shall give judgment after an examination of the entire record before the court, without regard to technical errors, defects, or exceptions which do not affect the substantial rights of the parties.

* * * The question we have to determine is whether the same ruling may be extended to a situation in which one conspiracy only is charged and at least eight having separate, though similar objects, are made out

by the evidence, if believed; and in which the more numerous participants in the different schemes were, on the whole, except for one, different persons who did not know or have anything to do with one another.

The salutary policy embodied in § 269 was adopted by the Congress in 1919 (Act of February 26, 1919, c. 48, 40 Stat. 1181) after long agitation under distinguished professional sponsorship, and after thorough consideration of various proposals designed to enact the policy in successive Congresses from the Sixtieth to the Sixty-fifth. It is not necessary to review in detail the history of the abuses which led to the agitation or of the progress of the legislation through the various sessions to final enactment without debate. But anyone familiar with it knows that § 269 and similar state legislation grew out of widespread and deep conviction over the general course of appellate review in American criminal causes. This was shortly, as one trial judge put it after § 269 had become law, that courts of review "tower above the trials of criminal cases as impregnable citadels of technicality." So great was the threat of reversal, in many jurisdictions, that criminal trial became a game for sowing reversible error in the record, only to have repeated the same matching of wits when a new trial had been thus obtained.

In the broad attack on this system great legal names were mobilized, among them Taft, Wigmore, Pound and Hadley, to mention only four. The general object was simple: To substitute judgment for automatic application of rules; to preserve review as a check upon arbitrary action and essential unfairness in trials, but at the same time to make the process perform that function without giving men fairly convicted the multiplicity of loopholes which any highly rigid and minutely detailed scheme of errors, especially in relation to procedure, will engender and reflect in a printed record.

The task was too big, too various in detail, for particularized treatment. The effort at revision therefore took the form of the essentially simple command of § 269. It comes down on its face to a very plain admonition: "Do not be technical, where technicality does not really hurt the party whose rights in the trial and in its outcome the technicality affects." It is also important to note that the purpose of the bill in its final form was stated authoritatively to be "to cast upon the party seeking a new trial the burden of showing that any technical errors that he may complain of have affected his substantial rights, otherwise they are to be disregarded." But that this burden does not extend to all errors appears from the statement which follows immediately. "The proposed legislation affects only technical errors. If the error is of such a character that its natural effect is to prejudice a litigant's substantial rights, the burden of sustaining a verdict will, notwithstanding this legislation rest upon the one who claims under it." * * *

If, when all is said and done, the conviction is sure that the error did not influence the jury, or had but very slight effect, the verdict and the judgment should stand, except perhaps where the departure is from a constitutional norm or a specific command of Congress. But if one cannot say, with fair assurance, after pondering all that happened without stripping the erroneous action from the whole, that the judgment was not substantially swayed by the error, it is impossible to conclude that substantial rights were not affected. The inquiry cannot be merely whether there was enough to support the result, apart from the phase affected by the error. It is rather, even so, whether the error itself had substantial influence. If so, or if one is left in grave doubt, the conviction cannot stand. * * *

The Government's theory seems to be, in ultimate logical reach, that the error presented by the variance is insubstantial and harmless, if the evidence offered specifically and properly to convict each defendant would be sufficient to sustain his conviction, if submitted in a separate trial. For reasons we have stated and in view of the authorities cited, this is not and cannot be the test under § 269. But in apparent support of its view the Government argues that there was no prejudice here because the results show that the jury exercised discrimination as among the defendants whose cases were submitted to it. As it points out, the jury acquitted some, disagreed as to others, and found still others guilty. From this it concludes that the jury was not confused and, apparently, reached the same result as would have been reached or would be likely, if the convicted defendants had been or now should be tried separately.

One difficulty with this is that the trial court itself was confused in the charge which it gave to guide the jury in deliberation. The court instructed:

> The indictment charges but one conspiracy, and to convict each of the defendants of a conspiracy the Government would have to prove, and you would have to find, that each of the defendants was a member of that conspiracy. You cannot divide it up. It is one conspiracy, and the question is whether or not each of the defendants, or which of the defendants, are members of that conspiracy.

On its face, as the Court of Appeals said, this portion of the charge was plainly wrong in application to the proof made; and the error pervaded the entire charge, not merely the portion quoted. The jury could not possibly have found, upon the evidence, that there was only one conspiracy. The trial court was of the view that one conspiracy was made out by showing that each defendant was linked to Brown in one or more transactions, and that it was possible on the evidence for the jury to conclude that all were in a common adventure because of this fact and the similarity of purpose presented in the various applications for loans.

This view, specifically embodied throughout the instructions, obviously confuses the common purpose of a single enterprise with the several, though similar, purposes of numerous separate adventures of like character. It may be that, notwithstanding the misdirection, the jury actually understood correctly the purport of the evidence, as the Government now concedes it to have been; and came to the conclusion that the petitioners were guilty only of the separate conspiracies in which the proof shows they respectively participated. But, in the face of the misdirection and in the circumstances of this case, we cannot assume that the lay triers of fact were so well informed upon the law or that they disregarded the permission expressly given to ignore that vital difference.

As we have said, the error permeated the entire charge, indeed the entire trial. Not only did it permit the jury to find each defendant guilty of conspiring with thirty-five other potential co-conspirators, or any less number as the proof might turn out for acquittal of some, when none of the evidence would support such a conviction, as the proof did turn out in fact. It had other effects. One was to prevent the court from giving a precautionary instruction such as would be appropriate, perhaps required, in cases where related but separate conspiracies are tried together under § 557 of the Code, namely, that the jury should take care to consider the evidence relating to each conspiracy separately from that relating to each other conspiracy charged. The court here was careful to caution the jury to consider each defendant's case separately, in determining his participation in "the scheme" charged. But this obviously does not, and could not, go to keeping distinct conspiracies distinct, in view of the court's conception of the case.

Moreover, the effect of the court's misconception extended also to the proof of overt acts. Carrying forward his premise that the jury could find one conspiracy on the evidence, the trial judge further charged that, if the jury found a conspiracy, "then the acts or the statements of any of those whom you so find to be conspirators between the two dates that I have mentioned, may be considered by you in evidence as against all of the defendants whom you so find to be members of the conspiracy." The instructions in this phase also declared:

> It is not necessary, as a matter of law, that an overt act be charged against each defendant. It is sufficient if the conspiracy be established and the defendant be found to be a member of the conspiracy—it is sufficient to allege overt acts on the part of any others who may have been members of the conspiracy, if those acts were done in furtherance of, and for the purpose of accomplishing the conspiracy.

On those instructions it was competent not only for the jury to find that all of the defendants were parties to a single common plan, design and scheme, where none was shown by the proof, but also for them to impute to each defendant the acts and statements of the others without reference to whether they related to one of the schemes proven or another, and to find an overt act affecting all in conduct which admittedly could only have affected some.

* * * Guilt with us remains individual and personal, even as respects conspiracies. It is not a matter of mass application. There are times when of necessity, because of the nature and scope of the particular federation, large numbers of persons taking part must be tried together or perhaps not at all, at any rate as respects some. When many conspire, they invite mass trial by their conduct. Even so, the proceedings are exceptional to our tradition and call for use of every safeguard to individualize each defendant in his relation to the mass. Wholly different is it with those who join together with only a few, though many others may be doing the same and though some of them may line up with more than one group.

Criminal they may be, but it is not the criminality of mass conspiracy. They do not invite mass trial by their conduct. Nor does our system tolerate it. That way lies the drift toward totalitarian institutions. True, this may be inconvenient for prosecution. But our Government is not one of mere convenience or efficiency. It too has a stake, with every citizen, in his being afforded our historic individual protections, including those surrounding criminal trials. About them we dare not become careless or complacent when that fashion has become rampant over the earth.

Here toleration went too far. We do not think that either Congress, when it enacted § 269, or this Court, when deciding the *Berger* case, intended to authorize the Government to string together, for common trial, eight or more separate and distinct crimes, conspiracies related in kind though they might be, when the only nexus among them lies in the fact that one man participated in all. * * *

Reversed.

UNITED STATES V. BRUNO

Circuit Court of Appeals, Second Circuit
105 F.2d 921 (2d Cir. 1939)

Before L. HAND, AUGUSTUS N. HAND, and CLARK, CIRCUIT JUDGES.

PER CURIAM.

Bruno and Iacono were indicted along with 86 others for a conspiracy to import, sell and possess narcotics; some were acquitted; others, besides these two, were convicted, but they alone appealed. They complain [inter alia] that if the evidence proved anything, it proved a series of separate conspiracies, and not a single one, as alleged in the indictment. * * *

The first point was made at the conclusion of the prosecution's case: the defendants then moved to dismiss the indictment on the ground that several conspiracies had been proved, and not the one alleged. The evidence allowed the jury to find that there had existed over a substantial period of time a conspiracy embracing a great number of persons, whose object was to smuggle narcotics into the Port of New York and distribute them to addicts both in this city and in Texas and Louisiana. This required the cooperation of four groups of persons; the smugglers who imported the drugs; the middlemen who paid the smugglers and distributed to retailers; and two groups of retailers—one in New York and one in Texas and Louisiana—who supplied the addicts. The defendants assert that there were, therefore, at least three separate conspiracies; one between the smugglers and the middlemen, and one between the middlemen and each group of retailers. The evidence did not disclose any cooperation or communication between the smugglers and either group of retailers, or between the two groups of retailers themselves; however, the smugglers knew that the middlemen must sell to retailers, and the retailers knew that the middlemen must buy of importers of one sort or another. Thus the conspirators at one end of the chain knew that the unlawful business would not, and could not, stop with their buyers; and those at the other end knew that it had not begun with their sellers. That being true, a jury might have found that all the accused were embarked upon a venture, in all parts of which each was a participant, and an abettor in the sense that the success of that part with which he was immediately concerned, was dependent upon the success of the whole. That distinguishes the situation from that in *United States v. Peoni*, where Peoni, the accused, did not know that Regno, his buyer, was to sell the counterfeit bills to Dorsey, and had no interest in whether he did, since Regno might equally well have passed them to innocent persons himself. It might still be argued that there were two conspiracies; one including the smugglers, the middlemen and the New York group, and the other, the smugglers, the middlemen and the Texas & Louisiana group, for there was apparently no privity between the two groups of retailers. That too would be fallacious. Clearly, quoad the smugglers, there was but one conspiracy, for it was of no moment to them whether the middlemen sold to one or more groups of retailers, provided they had a market somewhere. So too of any retailer; he knew that he was a necessary link in a scheme of distribution, and the others, whom he knew to be convenient to its execution, were as much parts of a single undertaking or enterprise as two salesmen in the same shop. We think therefore that there was only one conspiracy. * * *

F. SPECIAL DEFENSES TO CONSPIRACY

As Chapter 11 explains, certain special defenses are available to those charged with attempts, namely abandonment under the Model

Penal Code and impossibility under the common law. Depending on the jurisdiction, these special defenses may also be available to persons charged with conspiracy.

The Model Penal Code recognizes the defense of abandonment (also known as renunciation or withdrawal) for persons charged with conspiracy. As with attempts, the defendant who asserts an abandonment defense must voluntarily and completely renounce his criminal purpose. Additionally, however, the Model Penal Code requires that the defendant thwart the success of the conspiracy. Section 5.03(6) provides:

> *Renunciation of Criminal Purpose.* It is an affirmative defense that the actor, after conspiring to commit a crime, thwarted the success of the conspiracy, under circumstances manifesting a complete and voluntary renunciation of his criminal purpose.

Model Penal Code § 5.03(6).

While the common law ostensibly rejects the defense of abandonment in the conspiracy context just as it rejects this defense in the attempts context, withdrawal from a conspiracy may nonetheless benefit a defendant in a common law jurisdiction because the statute of limitations for conspiracy begins to run as soon as the defendant withdraws from the conspiracy. The next case, *United States v. Read*, explains how an individual's withdrawal from a conspiracy interacts with statute of limitations rules. *Read* illustrates that the common law requirements for withdrawal are a lot less stringent than the requirements for abandonment under the Model Penal Code. *Read* also examines an issue that has divided the lower courts: which party bears the burden of proving or disproving the defense of withdrawal.

What about the defense of impossibility? Just as it rejects this defense in the context of attempts, the Model Penal Code rejects the defense of impossibility in the conspiracy context. It appears that most common law courts reject impossibility as a defense to conspiracy as well. In *United States v. Recio*, the Supreme Court considers whether the defense of impossibility should apply to a case where the government seizes the drugs that members of a drug conspiracy have agreed to distribute, making the object of the conspiracy impossible to achieve.

UNITED STATES V. READ

United States Court of Appeals, Seventh Circuit
658 F.2d 1225 (7th Cir. 1981)

BAUER, CIRCUIT JUDGE.

Defendants-appellants Ralph Read, Ronald E. Spiegel, and Howard Swiger appeal their convictions for conspiracy, mail fraud, and securities fraud. We affirm the judgments of conviction entered for Ralph Read and Howard Swiger in Nos. 80–1017 and 80–1019. We reverse Ronald

Spiegel's conviction for conspiracy in No. 80–1018 and remand for a new trial. We affirm Spiegel's conviction on the substantive counts.

I

The indictment charged a scheme to artificially inflate the year-end inventory of Cenco Medical Health Supply Corporation ("CMH") and thus increase its reported profits. The defendants-appellants were officers of CMH and Cenco, CMH's parent corporation. Ralph Read was president of Cenco and a member of its board of directors; Ronald Spiegel was a vice-president of Cenco, and president of CMH; Howard Swiger was also a vice-president of Cenco and comptroller of CMH. Other defendants Russell Rabjohns, Bernard Magdovitz, and Jack Carlson pled guilty to two counts and testified for the government. Another defendant, Robert Smith, was acquitted.

We need only briefly outline the evidence at trial showing defendants' massive manipulation of CMH's finances from 1970 to 1975. The greatest amount of the fraud was accomplished by overstating CMH's inventory. During annual inventory, each CMH branch recorded the amount of every item in stock on computer cards. When the cards were returned to the central Chicago office for processing, some of the defendants, at Spiegel's direction, increased the numbers on the cards. Thousands of cards were altered in this fashion; defendants made additional changes in the computer listings of the inventory that CMH submitted to its auditors. In 1970, defendants increased the reported inventory of CMH by 3.5 million dollars. In each succeeding year, defendants increased the inventory by several millions more and carried the previous years' inflation forward. The overstatement of inventory decreased CMH's cost of sales, which in turn produced greater reported profits, dollar-for-dollar. This practice continued until 1975. Estimates of the total fraud ranged from 20 to 25 million dollars. * * *

In 1974, Curtiss-Wright Corporation, a large conglomerate, purchased five percent of Cenco's shares. Curtiss-Wright's accountants, while examining Cenco's finances for a possible loan, found discrepancies in Cenco's inventory records. Alarmed, the defendants sought to create the appearance of $10 million of non-existent inventory should Curtiss-Wright's auditors physically check the inventory. In order to do so, they ordered the repacking of obsolete inventory in boxes of expensive products. Finally, in 1975, the defendants implemented an inventory destruction program to cover up the fraud. The defendants persuaded Cenco's board of directors to approve the destruction of $16 million of obsolete inventory as part of a supposed tax savings program. Almost all of the "destroyed" inventory existed only on paper.

The ultimate result of the fraud was to overstate the profitability of Cenco, thereby defrauding its board, its stockholders, and the SEC. The prosecution also showed that Read's compensation was linked to the company's profits.

The indictment charged the defendants with conspiracy, mail fraud, and securities fraud. On September 6, 1979, the case proceeded to trial against Read, Spiegel, Swiger, and Smith. On October 29, 1979, following almost eight weeks of testimony, the jury returned guilty verdicts on all counts as to Read, Spiegel, and Swiger. Smith was acquitted. Read, Spiegel, and Swiger appeal their convictions. * * *

III

Ronald Spiegel's main defense at trial was that he withdrew from the conspiracy more than five years before the indictment was filed. He argued that his prosecution therefore was barred by the statute of limitations. 18 U.S.C. § 3282. Spiegel argues on appeal that the trial court gave erroneous instructions on the issue of withdrawal.

The trial court instructed the jury:

> Now, we talked about withdrawal. How does a person withdraw from a conspiracy? A person can withdraw from a conspiracy, and in such a case he is not liable for the acts of his former co-conspirators after his withdrawal. A defendant may withdraw by notifying co-conspirators that he will no longer participate in the undertaking. A defendant may also withdraw from a conspiracy by engaging in acts inconsistent with the objects of the conspiracy. These acts or statements need not be known or communicated to all other co-conspirators as long as they are communicated in a manner reasonably calculated to reach some of them. To withdraw from a conspiracy there is no requirement that a conspirator try to convince the other co-conspirators to abandon their undertaking or that he go to public authorities or others to expose the conspiracy or to prevent the carrying out of an act involved in the conspiracy. But a withdrawal defense requires that a defendant completely abandon the conspiracy and that he do so in good faith. If you find that a defendant completely withdrew from the conspiracy before the 24th of April, 1974, you should acquit him. If you find that he was a member on April 24, 1974, and that an overt act was committed while he was still a member, his later withdrawal, if any, standing alone, is not a defense.
>
> Why do we pick the date "April 24th, 1974"? We do that because the indictment in this case, as you will see, bears a stamp, the Clerk's stamp that it was filed on April 24th, 1979. There is a five year statute of limitations for criminal conspiracy and the charge and the five year statute of limitations runs from the date of the last overt act in the indictment to the date of the filing of

the indictment. Accordingly, if you find that an overt act was committed within five years before April 24, 1979 another way of saying that is that if you find that an overt act was committed between April 24th, 1974 and August of 1975, the conspiracy count in its entirety may be considered by you, going all the way back to 1970 or earlier.

Spiegel objected to the above instructions. He claimed before the trial court, and here, that the instructions put the burden of proving withdrawal on Spiegel and failed to put the burden of disproving withdrawal beyond a reasonable doubt on the government. * * *

We agree that the instructions concerning withdrawal were erroneous and require a remand for a new trial on the conspiracy charge. We disagree, however, that withdrawal is a defense to the substantive crimes, and affirm Spiegel's conviction on those counts.

A

Due process requires that the prosecution prove beyond a reasonable doubt every fact necessary to constitute the crime charged. *In re Winship*, 397 U.S. 358, 364 (1970); *Mullaney v. Wilbur*, 421 U.S. 684, 685 (1975); *Patterson v. New York*, 432 U.S. 197 (1977). The prosecution's burden often includes disproving defenses because they bring into question facts necessary for conviction. This rule has been well-settled with regard to some defenses.

Patterson requires us to inquire whether the particular defense negates an essential element of the offense as defined by the legislature. As held in *Holloway v. McElroy*, 632 F.2d 605, 625 (5th Cir. 1980), the government "may not place the burden of persuasion on (an) issue upon the defendant if the truth of the 'defense' would necessarily negate an essential element of the crime charged."

18 U.S.C. § 371 provides: If two or more persons conspire either to commit any offense against the United States, or to defraud the United States, or any agency thereof in any manner or for any purpose, and one or more of such persons do any act to effect the object of the conspiracy, each shall be fined not more than $10,000 or imprisoned not more than five years, or both.

The statute, as long construed, requires the prosecution to prove (1) that the alleged conspiracy existed; (2) that an overt act was committed in furtherance of the conspiracy; and (3) that the defendant knowingly and intentionally became a member of the conspiracy.

Prosecution for conspiracy is also subject to a five-year statute of limitations, which runs from the date of the last overt act. In practice, to convict a defendant the prosecution must prove that the conspiracy existed and that each defendant was a member of the conspiracy at some point in the five years preceding the date of the indictment.

Withdrawal marks a conspirator's disavowal or abandonment of the conspiratorial agreement. By definition, after a defendant withdraws, he is no longer a member of the conspiracy and the later acts of the conspirators do not bind him. The defendant is still liable, however, for his previous agreement and for the previous acts of his co-conspirators in pursuit of the conspiracy. Withdrawal is not, therefore, a complete defense to the crime of conspiracy. Withdrawal becomes a complete defense only when coupled with the defense of the statute of limitations. A defendant's withdrawal from the conspiracy starts the running of the statute of limitations as to him. If the indictment is filed more than five years after a defendant withdraws, the statute of limitations bars prosecution for his actual participation in the conspiracy. He cannot be held liable for acts or declarations committed in the five years preceding the indictment by other conspirators because his withdrawal ended his membership in the conspiracy. It is thus only the interaction of the two defenses of withdrawal and the statute of limitations which shields the defendant from liability.[4]

Withdrawal, then, directly negates the element of membership in the conspiracy during the period of the statute of limitations. Under *Patterson*, *Mullaney*, and *Winship*, the government should disprove the defense of withdrawal beyond a reasonable doubt.

The government, however, insists that *Hyde v. United States*, 225 U.S. 347 (1912), a long-established Supreme Court case, placed the burden of proving withdrawal on the defendant. Indeed, *Hyde* has often been cited for that proposition in the courts of appeals. Almost every case we researched holds that the burden is on the defendant to "prove" or "establish" withdrawal. Within this Circuit, we recently held that it "is well-settled (that) this burden of establishing withdrawal lies on the defendant."

We have, however, reexamined *Hyde*. Our research convinces us that the cases, including our own, have misinterpreted *Hyde*. According to our interpretation, *Hyde* placed only the burden of going forward on the defendant. * * *

As withdrawal negates the essential element of membership, it must be disproved beyond a reasonable doubt by the government. We therefore overrule those cases imposing the burden of proving withdrawal on the defendant. We hold today that the burden of going forward with evidence of withdrawal and with evidence that he withdrew prior to the statute of limitations remains on the defendant. However, once he advances

4 Dropping out during the limitations period does not absolve a defendant. He is still liable for the agreement and acts committed before he withdraws. * * *

sufficient evidence, the burden of persuasion is on the prosecution to disprove the defense of withdrawal beyond a reasonable doubt. As in the cases of other defenses, once the jury has been instructed on the withdrawal defense, the jury should be instructed that the government bears the burden of disproving withdrawal beyond a reasonable doubt. * * *

UNITED STATES V. RECIO

Supreme Court of the United States
537 U.S. 270, 123 S.Ct. 819, 154 L.Ed.2d 744 (2003)

JUSTICE BREYER delivered the opinion of the Court.

We here consider the validity of a Ninth Circuit rule that a conspiracy ends automatically when the object of the conspiracy becomes impossible to achieve—when, for example, the Government frustrates a drug conspiracy's objective by seizing the drugs that its members have agreed to distribute. In our view, conspiracy law does not contain any such "automatic termination" rule.

I

In *United States v. Cruz*, 127 F.3d 791, 795 (9th Cir.1997), the Ninth Circuit, following the language of an earlier case, *United States v. Castro*, 972 F.2d 1107, 1112 (9th Cir. 1992), wrote that a conspiracy terminates when " 'there is affirmative evidence of abandonment, withdrawal, disavowal *or defeat of the object of the conspiracy*.' " (Emphasis added.) It considered the conviction of an individual who, the Government had charged, joined a conspiracy (to distribute drugs) after the Government had seized the drugs in question. The Circuit found that the Government's seizure of the drugs guaranteed the "defeat" of the conspiracy's objective, namely, drug distribution. The Circuit held that the conspiracy had terminated with that "defeat," i.e., when the Government seized the drugs. Hence the individual, who had joined the conspiracy after that point, could not be convicted as a conspiracy member.

In this case the lower courts applied the *Cruz* rule to similar facts: On November 18, 1997, police stopped a truck in Nevada. They found, and seized, a large stash of illegal drugs. With the help of the truck's two drivers, they set up a sting. The Government took the truck to the drivers' destination, a mall in Idaho. The drivers paged a contact and described the truck's location. The contact said that he would call someone to get the truck. And three hours later, the two defendants, Francisco Jimenez Recio and Adrian Lopez-Meza, appeared in a car. Jimenez Recio drove away in the truck; Lopez-Meza drove the car away in a similar direction. Police stopped both vehicles and arrested both men.

A federal grand jury indicted Jimenez Recio, Lopez-Meza, and the two original truck drivers, charging them with having conspired, together and with others, to possess and to distribute unlawful drugs. A jury convicted all four. But the trial judge then decided that the jury instructions had been erroneous in respect to Jimenez Recio and Lopez-Meza. The judge noted that the Ninth Circuit, in *Cruz*, had held that the Government could not prosecute drug conspiracy defendants unless they had joined the conspiracy before the Government seized the drugs. That holding, as applied here, meant that the jury could not convict Jimenez Recio and Lopez-Meza unless the jury believed they had joined the conspiracy before the Nevada police stopped the truck and seized the drugs. The judge ordered a new trial where the jury would be instructed to that effect. The new jury convicted the two men once again.

Jimenez Recio and Lopez-Meza appealed. They pointed out that, given *Cruz*, the jury had to find that they had joined the conspiracy before the Nevada stop, and they claimed that the evidence was insufficient at both trials to warrant any such jury finding. The Ninth Circuit panel, by a vote of 2 to 1, agreed. All three panel members accepted *Cruz* as binding law. Two members concluded that the evidence presented at the second trial was not sufficient to show that the defendants had joined the conspiracy before the Nevada drug seizure. One of the two wrote that the evidence at the first trial was not sufficient either, a circumstance she believed independently warranted reversal. The third member, dissenting, believed that the evidence at both trials adequately demonstrated preseizure membership. He added that he, like the other panel members, was bound by *Cruz*, but he wrote that in his view *Cruz* was "totally inconsistent with long established and appropriate principles of the law of conspiracy," and he urged the Circuit to overrule it en banc "at the earliest opportunity."

The Government sought certiorari. It noted that the Ninth Circuit's holding in this case was premised upon the legal rule enunciated in *Cruz*. And it asked us to decide the rule's validity, i.e., to decide whether "a conspiracy ends as a matter of law when the government frustrates its objective." We agreed to consider that question.

II

In *Cruz*, the Ninth Circuit held that a conspiracy continues " 'until there is affirmative evidence of abandonment, withdrawal, disavowal or defeat of the object of the conspiracy.' " The critical portion of this statement is the last segment, that a conspiracy ends once there has been " 'defeat of [its] object.' " The Circuit's holdings make clear that the phrase means that the conspiracy ends through "defeat" when the Government intervenes, making the conspiracy's goals impossible to achieve, even if the conspirators do not know that the Government has intervened and are totally unaware that the conspiracy is bound to fail. In our view, this statement of the law is incorrect. A conspiracy does not automatically terminate simply because the Government, unbeknownst to some of the conspirators, has "defeat[ed]" the conspiracy's "object."

Two basic considerations convince us that this is the proper view of the law. First, the Ninth Circuit's rule is inconsistent with our own understanding of basic conspiracy law. The Court has repeatedly said that the essence of a conspiracy is "an agreement to commit an unlawful act." That agreement is "a distinct evil," which "may exist and be punished whether or not the substantive crime ensues." The conspiracy poses a "threat to the public" over and above the threat of the commission of the relevant substantive crime—both because the "[c]ombination in crime makes more likely the commission of [other] crimes" and because it "decreases the probability that the individuals involved will depart from their path of criminality." Where police have frustrated a conspiracy's specific objective but conspirators (unaware of that fact) have neither abandoned the conspiracy nor withdrawn, these special conspiracy-related dangers remain. *Cf.* 2 W. LaFave & A. Scott, SUBSTANTIVE CRIMINAL LAW § 6.5, p. 85 (1986) ("[i]mpossibility" does not terminate conspiracy because "criminal combinations are dangerous apart from the danger of attaining the particular objective"). So too remains the essence of the conspiracy—the agreement to commit the crime. That being so, the Government's defeat of the conspiracy's objective will not necessarily and automatically terminate the conspiracy.

Second, the view we endorse today is the view of almost all courts and commentators but for the Ninth Circuit. No other Federal Court of Appeals has adopted the Ninth Circuit's rule. Three have explicitly rejected it. * * * One treatise, after surveying lower court conspiracy decisions, has concluded that "[i]mpossibility of success is not a defense." 2 LaFave & Scott, SUBSTANTIVE CRIMINAL LAW § 6.5, at 85; see also *id.*, § 6.5(b), at 90–93. And the American Law Institute's Model Penal Code § 5.03, p. 384 (1985), would find that a conspiracy "terminates when the crime or crimes that are its object are committed" or when the relevant "agreement . . . is abandoned." It would not find "impossibility" a basis for termination. * * *

The *Cruz* majority argued that the more traditional termination rule threatened "endless" potential liability. To illustrate the point, the majority posited a sting in which police instructed an arrested conspirator to go through the "telephone directory . . . [and] call all of his acquaintances" to come and help him, with the Government obtaining convictions of those who did so. The problem with this example, however, is that, even though it is not necessarily an example of entrapment itself, it draws its persuasive force from the fact that it bears certain resemblances to entrapment. The law independently forbids convictions that rest upon entrapment. And the example fails to explain why a different branch of the law, conspiracy law, should be modified to forbid entrapment-like behavior that falls outside the bounds of current entrapment law. At the same time, the *Cruz* rule would reach well beyond arguable police misbehavior, potentially threatening the use of properly run law enforcement sting operations. *See Lewis v. United States*, 385 U.S. 206, 208–09 (1966) (Government may "use decoys" and conceal agents' identity); *see also* M. Lyman, CRIMINAL INVESTIGATION 484–485 (2d ed. 1999) (explaining the importance of undercover operations in enforcing drug laws). * * *

III

We conclude that the Ninth Circuit's conspiracy-termination law holding set forth in *Cruz* is erroneous in the manner discussed. We reverse the present judgment insofar as it relies upon that holding. Because Jimenez Recio and Lopez-Meza have raised other arguments not here considered, we remand the case, specifying that the Court of Appeals may consider those arguments, if they were properly raised.

The judgment of the Ninth Circuit is reversed, and the case is remanded for further proceedings consistent with this opinion.

It is so ordered.

[JUSTICE STEVENS' opinion concurring in part and dissenting in part is omitted.]

CHAPTER 14

CRIME AND PUNISHMENT

■ ■ ■

INTRODUCTION

In Chapter 1, we saw that criminal law seeks to answer the question, What level of punishment does the person who has committed a crime deserve? This question may have raised other questions in your mind about punishment. In this chapter, we provide a brief look at the mechanics, consequences, and cultural contexts of criminal punishment in the United States. Specialized courses, such as upper-division courses on sentencing and on prison law, delve further into the technical and administrative rules and practices surrounding punishment.

How did incarceration become the punishment of choice in the United States, and which actors within the criminal justice system exercise power over an offender's sentence? Section A puts the American penitentiary into historical context, and traces the shift from "indeterminate" to "determinate" sentencing and the rise of mass incarceration. The section also provides some commentary on petty offense convictions in the United States, on the death penalty in the United States, and some implications of our reliance on mass incarceration.

What level of punishment is appropriate for a particular offense, or a particular offender? Throughout this book, we have seen how Anglo-American criminal law reflects Anglo-American moral culture, and how moral debates sometimes find their way into the law. In Section B, we look at a new view of adolescent criminality emerging in U.S. constitutional jurisprudence. This section addresses the following questions: Are young people responsible for their crimes? How can we tell? Should juvenile criminal justice look like adult criminal justice? Can recent advances in neuroscience answer these questions, or are they purely moral questions? The section also gives students a brief introduction to the juvenile justice system.

Finally, what are some of the contemporary consequences of punishment? The excerpt by Robert Blecker in Chapter 1 provided a glimpse into the world of prison, pointing to a gap between theories of punishment and the offender's actual experience on punishment. Section C of this chapter examines other tensions between the way our criminal justice system works in theory and in the real world. Do all criminal defendants get the quality of lawyering they are entitled to by law? How do so-called "collateral" consequences of punishment, such as deportation and sex offender registration, interact with incarceration? What have been the effects of mass incarceration on our society in the last few decades?

Section C ends with a look at alternatives to incarceration. The theory of restorative justice attempts to substitute "making things right" for "punishment" as the ultimate goal of the criminal justice system. New institutions, such as problem-solving courts, seek to change our legal culture's dependency on incarceration as the primary tool of criminal justice. These new frameworks and institutions may ultimately reshape the roles of key actors in the criminal justice system.

A. THE HISTORY AND TRENDS OF PUNISHMENT IN THE UNITED STATES

THE CRIME OF PUNISHMENT

David J. Rothman
The New York Review of Books

February 17, 1994

* * * In the 1820s and 1830s, American state governments were pioneers in prison design; they built huge and expensive institutions that provided each inmate with his own private cell, and sometimes, as in the Pennsylvania Penitentiary, his own private exercise yard. The prison, by excluding all corrupting influences and subjecting the inmate to steady labor and a quasi-military routine * * *, would reform the deviant and eradicate crime from the society. That this simplistic and utopian mission failed to achieve its aims is not nearly as surprising as the influence it exerted abroad. Alexis de Toqueville, it should be remembered, came to the United States not to write *Democracy in America* but to report on American prisons for the French assembly.

A second phase of prison reform took place in the opening decades of the twentieth century. American states were the first to introduce indeterminate sentences, under which the inmate was to serve, say, one to five years; the actual time of release depended on the parole board's estimate of whether the offender had been rehabilitated. The prisons introduced educational programs and psychological counseling and dropped the insistence on isolation; ostensibly, life behind walls would prepare inmates for life outside. Once more, European criminologists and legislators came to study American methods and generally admired the new measures.

But again the realities of prison life contradicted the reformers' hopes. Indeterminate sentences did not lead to "rehabilitation," and visitors to prisons could not ignore the overcrowding and brutality they found there or the periodic riots that took place in them. * * * [L]eading reformers * * * attributed these failures not to an inherent flaw in the design of the system but to the incompetence of administrators, the ignorance of the guards, and the stinginess of the legislators. For the reformers, rehabilitation and education continued to be altogether feasible goals of the prison system.

Beginning in the 1970s, and continuing to this day, an impressive literature has discredited each component of this inherited prison system. Foreign observers are appalled by current American prison conditions and sentencing practices; they cannot believe that we could be so retrogressive. * * * Human Rights Watch, having investigated prison conditions throughout the world, found in the US "numerous human rights abuses and frequent violations of the UN Standard Minimum Rules for the Treatment of Prisoners."

The most conspicuous sign of failure * * * is the heavy American reliance on keeping people in prison. * * * [Rothman describes how by the mid-1990s, the United States was the world leader in incarceration; moreover, the prison population was growing at the fastest rate in the world, states were spending more and more of their budgets on building new prisons, and still the new capacity could not keep up with the demand, resulting in vastly overcrowded conditions.]

The justice system is most troubling in its impact on minorities, particularly on African Americans. [Rothman notes that by 1994, 57 percent of black men in Baltimore between the ages of eighteen and thirty-five were either in prison or on probation or parole, out on bail, or being sought on an arrest warrant. Blacks made up 48 percent of prison inmates, as against 12 percent of the population.] * * *

Among the many reasons why so many blacks are in prison—including high rates of unemployment and inadequate urban schools—none is more decisive than the changes in the administration of criminal justice, particularly the sentencing practices that have been adopted since the 1980s. During the 1970s, liberal reformers—myself among them—became disillusioned with the principle that indeterminate sentences would encourage greater justice in punishment. The dominant view, expressed in many reports and studies, was that open-ended sentences adapted to the personal characteristics of the offender—his education, jobs, marital state, and so on—gave judges and parole boards the discretion to penalize blacks and lower-class offenders more heavily than white, middle-class ones. The reports also argued that rehabilitation programs were a sham. Not only were they ineffectual, but they made imprisonment seem legitimate and desirable. * * * Fostering the illusion that inmates were locked up for their own good, rehabilitation made sentences of five, ten, and fifteen years appear benevolent.

From this diagnosis came a proposed cure: encourage legislators to enact fixed sentences, reduce the discretion of the judge to set the penalty, and restrict, or even eliminate, the power of the parole board to determine the moment of release. The aim was to let the crime and the previous criminal record of the offender dictate the punishment, without any reference to the social characteristics of the criminal, including race, gender, occupation, work history, etc. Sentencing guidelines, drawn up in advance, would set the punishment within narrow ranges. In this way, virtually all first-time burglars would get, for example, a sentence between twelve and eighteen months, regardless of whether the burglar was white or black, male or female, from the urban or rural part of the state, or standing before a judge with a reputation for leniency or harshness.

The reformers were aware of the possibility that fixed sentences might turn out to be even longer than indeterminate ones. They recognized that longer sentences were the goal of the conservative and right-wing thinkers who also advocated fixed sentences. Such conservatives argued * * * that indeterminate sentences put offenders back on the streets too quickly. Since the actual time served almost always turned out to be less than the maximum provided in the original sentence, the criminal, they said, was being prematurely released and allowed to return to a life of crime. When "twenty-five years to life" turned out to be eight years, because parole boards often released inmates at one-third the minimum sentence, conservatives warned that the safety of society was being compromised. Thus fixed sentences represented a long overdue return to "truth in sentencing" which would make offenders serve out their time.

The oddness of the alliance did not weaken liberals' enthusiasm. They fully expected that the sentences indicated in guidelines would reduce the severity of penalties, starting with less serious crimes, and they believed that the number of prison cells available would limit the numbers put in prison. * * *

Reformers also expected their legislators to vote in ways that would cost the taxpayers less. Since prisons were expensive and becoming more so because of court-ordered improvements, politicians, they believed, would welcome a reduction in the number of prisoners.

Finally, reformers were attracted by the prospect that appointed commissions, not individual judges or parole boards, would be setting the scale of penalties. The advocates of commissions, it must be said, did not spend much time discussing who would actually serve on them or how their decisions would be translated into law or practice. Rather, they were convinced that sentencing decisions should be removed from politics and the criminal justice system insulated from popular pressures. Sentencing commissions, like other administrative bodies (most notably, the

Securities Exchange Commission and the Food and Drug Administration), would, it was thought, bring expertise and rational decisionmaking into bitterly contested disputes over sentences. Once decisions on punishment were removed from arbitrary judges, from overly conservative parole boards, and from legislators trying to please constituents, prison time would be doled out more sparingly and alternatives to prison would be used more frequently.

The reformers proved wrong on all counts. Fixed sentences were introduced in the 1980s, both in the federal system and in roughly one third of the states. But apart from a few jurisdictions (most notably Minnesota), sentencing guidelines have increased the time served and have relatively little effect on disparity in sentences. They have promoted prison overcrowding and reduced the importance of judges in sentencing, while giving more discretion to prosecutors. The distaste for rehabilitation has also contributed to making prisons into human warehouses. If educational and training programs are seen as futile, why should the state spend money on them?

Hostility to indeterminate sentences also made it easier for the federal government and the states to enact mandatory minimum statutes, which inevitably increase the time to be served. Once decisions about punishment became more mechanical—a matter of consulting a chart—and less concerned about what would be a just sentence for a particular criminal, mandatory minimum sentences seemed to have their own logic. * * * Moreover, mandatory minimum sentences have greatly increased the authority of prosecutors. In return for a guilty plea, they will indict on a lesser offense which does not carry a minimum. And prosecutors continue their discriminatory practices: far more often than blacks, whites get the chance to plead guilty to lesser crimes and thereby receive sentences below the mandatory minimums.

Why did the good intentions of the reformers lead to such punitive results? Part of the answer is the changed political environment of the 1980s. Reagan and Bush were able to make crime and sentencing procedures an issue that middle-class Americans could use to express their frustrations not only with unsafe streets but with affirmative action and the costs of welfare. Reformers also forgot * * * that many bond holders see prisons not as a drain upon public resources but as a sound investment, while some job seekers see them as a source of employment.

More important, reformers were wrong to think that sentencing commissions would be insulated from politics. * * *

[T]ransferring authority from judges and parole boards to a commission may make sentencing more of a political issue than it was before. Outrageous crimes can be used as evidence to support long-term changes in penal codes. In the past, a public outcry often affected a judge's behavior, and when there was a rash of robberies or a vicious child-abuse case, the next person to commit such a crime often received a harsher sentence in the hope of deterring future crimes. But when sentencing commissioners and legislators feel they must show they are tough, the repercussions go beyond an increased sentence for one highly publicized case and result, for years to come, in harsher penalties for entire categories of crimes. The real problem * * * is that once sentencing becomes "a tool in the hands of politicians," we get "democratic crime control." That is, there are no limits to punishment so long as those limits do not adversely affect the majority.

Probably the most serious drawback of the 1970s reform program was the failure to anticipate the prominence that would be given drug control, the issue that now dominates criminal justice procedures. * * *

What is clear is that arrests, convictions, and imprisonment for drug offenses, as distinguished from other crimes, have risen sharply, while everyone agrees that the increases reflect a change not in street behavior but in patterns of enforcement and punishment. Marc Mauer, the assistant director of Washington, D.C.'s Sentencing Project, calculates that drug arrests increased during the 1980s by 88 percent, and that [by the mid-1990s] one out of every four prison inmates [was] serving time or awaiting trial for a drug offense. * * * In New York City offenders sentenced for possession or sale of drugs increased over 600 percent between 1983 and 1989, notwithstanding the increasing severity of prison sentences for drug offenders during this period.

Drug law enforcement and punishment are aimed mostly at minorities, and the "war on drugs" is in large part a war on blacks. [Rothman reviews statistics under which, by the mid-1990s, despite similar levels of drug use across racial groups, blacks were five times more likely than whites to be arrested for drug offenses and among juveniles, blacks were ten times more likely.] * * *

[The federal sentencing guidelines bill] that was signed into law by President Reagan in 1984 had none of the nuances of the original proposal. The earlier instructions to the commission to decrease the amount of time served and not to overcrowd prisons were weakened. More important, the commissioners were appointed by the President with William Wilkens, a federal appeals court judge from South Carolina and a close associate of Senator Strom Thurmond, as chairman. Under Wilkens' leadership the commission adopted Reagan's rhetoric about "law and order" and "getting tough with the criminal." Its interpretations of the statute consistently curtailed judicial discretion and made penalties more severe. The commissioners ruled, for example, that sentences were to be meted out on the basis of "real offense"—that is, what the offender had presumably done, not what he had pleaded guilty to in bargaining with the prosecutor or been convicted for in court.

In day-to-day practice, * * * the judge must consult a set schedule to reach his sentence. He starts at the "base offense level," say, burglary, which has a score of 20, and then adds points to it on the basis of how the crime was carried out. If the offender discharged a gun, he adds seven points. If the crime resulted in bodily injury, he adds two; if it was serious bodily injury, another two. If $10,000 or less was stolen in the burglary, he adds nothing. But if the sum was between $10,000 and $50,000, he adds two, if more than $250,000 he adds three, and so on.

The judge then adds up the points and consults the guideline chart, which has the offense level scores running down the left, and, running across the top, six columns scoring the offender on the basis of his past criminal record. So if the burglar fired a gun, caused serious bodily injury, and made off with $300,000, he gets a score of 34; if this was his first offense, his sentence must fall between 151 and 188 months. If he has a long record, let us say IV on the scale of VI, his sentence must fall between 210 and 262 months.

The only two factors a judge may use to reduce the guideline's sentence are the offender's "acceptance of responsibility," i.e., by pleading guilty, which can bring a modest reduction, and his willingness to provide "substantial assistance" to the government, i.e., by turning state's evidence and implicating others, which can bring a major reduction. The judge may not reduce sentence time because of the offender's age, his employment record, his having a stable family life, the fact that he has children at home to support, or any other personal characteristic.

The impact of these guidelines [was] to increase the prison population and the average time served * * * Sentences of probation have declined. The guidelines have clearly elevated the prosecutor over the judge. Because sentences are severe, offenders may be tempted to go to trial rather than to plea bargain; to make certain this does not happen, prosecutors define the "base offense" downward to bring about a reduction in penalty, and hide their action so that the "real offense" on which the guidelines are set cannot be known. Thus in return for a guilty plea, the prosecutor will agree to charge the defendant with robbery without the use of a weapon, although he carried a pistol. Defendants and their lawyers understand that judges no longer control sentencing, bound as they are to the guidelines.[a] All the real bargaining has to be done with the prosecutors.

---

[a] In 2005, the Supreme Court ruled in *United States v. Booker*, 543 U.S. 220, 125 S. Ct. 738, 160 L. Ed. 2d 621 (2005), that the federal sentencing guidelines did not bind judges, but were only advisory. For an examination of sentencing outcomes in this post-*Booker* period, see, e.g., Amy Baron-Evans and Kate Stith, Booker Rules, 160 U. PA. L. REV. 1631 (2012). Baron-Evans and Stith argue that the new discretion afforded judges under *Booker* has reduced racialized sentencing disparities: "The gap in time served between black and white offenders was largest in 1994, at 37.7 months. It narrowed to 25.4 months in 2010, the smallest since 1992." *Id.* at 1690.

MISDEMEANORS

Alexandra Natapoff
85 S. Cal. L. Rev. 1313 (2012)

It has become a truism that the U.S. criminal system is too big. With an incarcerated population surpassing two million—more than all of Europe combined—the American penal behemoth is a target for widespread and bipartisan criticism. Prominent institutions from the Economist to the Cato Institute to the Heritage Foundation lament the immensity of the American prison population and the sprawl of U.S. criminal law. The Supreme Court recently ordered the state of California to reduce prison overcrowding. * * * Whatever work the criminal process is supposed to do—deter, rehabilitate, incapacitate, or vindicate—a growing consensus concludes that it cannot do it properly given its current scale.

This consensus significantly understates the problem. The U.S. criminal system is far larger and less principled than even the incarceration critique suggests because the prison population accounts mainly for felony offenders. Approximately one million felony convictions are entered in the U.S. each year; most of the aforementioned two million prisoners are serving felony sentences. But they are only the tip of the iceberg. An estimated ten million misdemeanor cases are filed annually, flooding lower courts, jails, probation offices, and public defender offices. While these individuals are largely ignored by the criminal literature and policymakers, they are nevertheless punished, stigmatized, and burdened by their convictions in many of the same ways as their felony counterparts.

In effect, the felony-centric view misapprehends the sprawling reality of the American criminal process. Most U.S. convictions are misdemeanors, and they are generated in ways that baldly contradict the standard due process model of criminal adjudication. Massive, underfunded, informal, and careless, the misdemeanor system propels defendants through in bulk with scant attention to individualized cases and often without counsel. By contrast, serious felonies get closer to the ideals of due process, where issues of law, evidence, and procedure are attended to in ways that embody basic legitimizing features of the criminal process. Standard doctrinal and scholarly descriptions of the criminal system tend to treat serious cases as paradigmatic but this can be misleading. Serious cases are exceptional both in number and in the resources they command, while misdemeanor cases comprise the bulk of the justice process. Far from accidental, the slipshod quality of petty offense processing is a dominant systemic norm that competes vigorously with and sometimes overwhelms foundational values of due process and adversarial adjudication. * * *

The scale and poverty of petty offense processing have created a world that often lacks the evidentiary and procedural protections that are supposed to ensure the guilt of the accused. As a result, every year the criminal system punishes thousands of petty offenders who are not guilty. Misdemeanants routinely plead to low-level crimes for which there is little or no evidence, without assistance of counsel or any other meaningful adversarial process. In some cases, defendants are demonstrably innocent. In others, the process is so lax that we cannot say with any certainty whether defendants are guilty or not. Moreover, because many of these underprocessed convictions are for urban disorder offenses, the phenomenon disproportionately affects minority and other heavily policed groups.

As innocence scholar, Samuel Gross, has candidly remarked, "we rarely even think about wrongful convictions for misdemeanors" * * *. But this inattention is undeserved. First, while a felony prison sentence is a uniquely corrosive experience, misdemeanants can also be significantly harmed by their convictions. Their criminal records deprive them of employment, as well as educational and social opportunities. They are routinely incarcerated—despite the absence of a prison sentence—as they wait in jail for their cases to be adjudicated. A petty conviction can affect eligibility for professional licenses, child custody, food stamps, student loans, health care, or lead to deportation. In many cities, misdemeanants are ineligible for public housing. The stigma of a misdemeanor conviction heightens the chances of subsequent arrest, and can ensure a longer felony sentence later on. In sum, misdemeanor convictions have become significant long-term burdens on individual defendants even though the processes by which such convictions are generated fall far short of minimum legal and evidentiary standards taken for granted in the felony world.

More broadly, misdemeanor processing reveals the deep structure of the criminal system: as a pyramid that functions relatively transparently and according to legal principle at the top, but in an opaque and unprincipled way for the vast majority of cases at the bottom. At the top, where cases are serious or defendants are well represented, procedures are enforced by judges, prosecutors and defense counsel. As a result, law and evidence matter: convictions must conform to the dictates of the code and there must be evidence to support them. The resulting convictions are as close as we get to ideals of legal substance and procedural legitimacy. By contrast, at the bottom where offenses are petty and procedures are weak, law and evidence hold little sway over outcomes. Instead, convictions are largely a function of being selected for arrest; this is because vulnerable, underrepresented defendants tend to plead guilty even in the absence of evidence. At the extreme, innocent people are wrongly convicted, but this is just the most dramatic manifestation of a larger state of affairs: the waning authority of law and evidence—and the correlatively heightened influence of law-enforcement discretion—as offenses get pettier and defendants grow poorer. * * *

[M]isdemeanors offer new insights into two of the system's most infamous dysfunctions: inaccuracy and the racialization of crime. First, the lack of procedural integrity in petty offense processing generates wrongful convictions, and it does so in ways that reveal the deepest sources of systemic inaccuracy. At bottom, those procedural weaknesses represent a philosophical abdication of a core requirement, namely, the need for evidence of individual fault as the basis for legitimate punishment. Second, that procedural abdication means that despite black-letter doctrine to the contrary, police are effectively empowered to decide not only who will be arrested but who will be convicted. In the context of urban policing, this de facto delegation of legal authority translates into the mass criminalization of young minority men.

TURNING THE CORNER ON MASS INCARCERATION?

David Cole

9 Ohio St. J. Crim. L. 27 (2011)

It is an old story by now. For the past forty years, the American criminal justice system has seen unremitting growth in the number of people behind bars. Over this period, about the only constant has been that the incarcerated population grew. It rose when crime rates decreased as well as when they increased, in lean times as well as prosperous times, under Democratic and Republican administrations, in federal and state institutions, and in red and blue states. But it seems the old story may now need revising. For the first time in forty years, the national incarceration rate is flattening out, even falling in state prisons. For the first time in three decades, the number of adults under any kind of correctional supervision—in prison or jail or on probation or parole—fell in 2009. At the same time, legal reforms that might have seemed impossible in former years have increasingly been adopted, reducing penalties for certain crimes, eliminating mandatory sentencing for others, and increasing expenditures for reintegration of prisoners into society. And racial disparities, a persistent and deep-rooted problem in the American criminal justice system, after rising for decades, have begun to drop from their highest levels.

Make no mistake—the United States still incarcerates at levels unheard of for any other nation, and the brunt of this policy still rests on the black and Latino population. It is, of course, too early to gauge how far any reversal might ultimately go. But these developments raise new and intriguing questions: is the United States in the midst of a transformation in criminal justice? What might explain the changes? And what can be done to accelerate the trends—if they are trends—toward a less harsh and more humane criminal justice approach?

The story of America's boom in incarceration is a familiar one, at least to criminal justice scholars and practitioners, if not necessarily to the general public * * *. For the first three-quarters of the twentieth century, the United States was on par with its Western counterparts in terms of incarceration rates, as the United States and much of Europe incarcerated approximately 100 persons per 100,000. Since the mid-1970s, however, the U.S. incarceration rate has skyrocketed, while those of our counterparts have either stayed relatively constant or increased at a much slower rate. As a result, we are now the world's undisputed leader in incarceration. On any given day, we have locked up approximately 700 persons per 100,000, or more than 2.3 million people.

* * * Now that the rate has increased steadily for two generations, criminologists have sought to explain the rise. They have looked to the appeal of "tough on crime" politics, the influence of the "prison-industrial complex," the rise in crime rates, the war on drugs, and other factors. I have argued elsewhere that a crucial piece of the puzzle is the extreme racial disparity in the incarcerated population. According to this theory, one reason that the majority can tolerate such high rates of incarceration is that most of those incarcerated are seen as "the other"—African Americans, Latinos, and/or the poor. African Americans, for example, make up about 13% of the general population but about half of the incarcerated population. The per capita incarceration rate among black males was 3161 per 100,000 in 2008, which is six-and-a-half times the rate for white males. * * * I have argued that if one in three *white* male babies born today could expect to spend time in prison during his life, rather than one in three *black* male babies, the politics of crime would look dramatically different. Instead of demanding harsher penalties, more prisons, and mandatory minimums, politicians would likely be calling for increased investment in education, after-school programs, and job training; expanded alternatives to incarceration; reductions in the severity of criminal sentences; and improved rehabilitation services. * * *

Today, however, it appears that politicians *are* increasingly demanding precisely these types of reforms. Although it is too early to be sure, there are signs that we may be in the midst of another transformative period in American criminal justice. The national incarceration rate, while still rising, has been rising more slowly since 2000 and is now virtually flat. * * *

Meanwhile, the "tough on crime" politics of the 1980s and 1990s seem to have abated significantly. Instead of enacting harsh mandatory sentences, Congress and the states have increasingly begun to study and adopt sentencing and criminal law reforms aimed at *reducing* incarceration. Many states have softened or repealed mandatory minimum sentences. * * *

Some states have begun to move toward a public health approach to nonviolent drug offending, providing enhanced substance abuse treatment and offering diversion to treatment as an alternative to incarceration. * * * In 2010, a referendum that would have legalized marijuana possession in California failed but received more than 46% of the vote. Drug courts, devoted to overseeing, guiding, inspiring, and enforcing coerced drug treatment as an alternative to conviction and incarceration, have proliferated dramatically in the last decade, from a rare curiosity to a regular fixture in many state legal systems; there are over 2500 such courts nationwide today.

States are also reforming probation, parole, and alternative sentencing, simultaneously seeking to make community supervision more effective and to reduce reliance on incarceration as a response to technical violations of probation and parole. * * *

Stretched by budgetary crises, states have also begun to ask whether they are expending unnecessary funds keeping individuals behind bars who would not pose a significant risk of committing serious crime if released. Several states have undertaken studies or adopted programs that seek to identify candidates for early release from prison. * * *

Many states * * * have consolidated or closed prisons and/or halted new prison construction. Other states and the federal government, however, continue to build prisons—in some instances, driven by overcrowding in their existing prisons.

Finally, states have shown increased interest in and directed increased resources toward reentry and reintegration programs. Realizing that something must be done to address the more than 700,000 people being released from prison each year, states are resurrecting rehabilitation under the name of reentry. * * *

[D]evelopments in recent years have resulted not merely in across-the-board reductions in incarceration for African Americans, Latinos, and whites, but also in a modest reduction in the racial disparities that plague the criminal justice system. The past decade saw a widespread campaign against "racial profiling," which included lawsuits, legislation, and increased public advocacy, education, and training. Perhaps as a result, racial disparities in both *incarceration* and criminal law *enforcement* have begun to diminish. * * *

Vast disparities remain, to be sure. While African Americans are 13% of the general population and roughly the same percentage of those who use and sell drugs, they are still 35% of those arrested on drug charges and 53.5% of those entering prison for a drug conviction. * * * Nearly one in four young black male high school dropouts is in prison or jail, as compared to about one in fourteen young white, Asian, or Hispanic male dropouts. Still, in the last decade, racial disparities in criminal law enforcement have fallen. As a result, the "costs" of criminal law enforcement, in terms of arrests, prosecutions, convictions, and sentences, are today at least marginally more fairly shared than they were a decade ago. * * *

A number of factors seem likely candidates. Perhaps most prominent at the moment are the serious budgetary crises afflicting nearly all states and the federal government. * * * Incarcerating a young man costs about $24,000 a year in direct costs, a tremendous drain on the public fisc. Nationwide, total state spending on corrections has increased from $12 billion in 1987 to $49 billion in 2007. The indirect and long-term costs are far greater, as incarceration has deep and wide ripple effects on the employment opportunities and likely criminal conduct of not only the incarcerated themselves, but their children and other members of the community.

Moreover, without significant efforts to rehabilitate, incarceration breeds recidivism, and with more than 700,000 prisoners released from prison each year, we can expect that two-thirds of them will be re-arrested and more than half back in prison within three years, once again costing the state more than $24,000 a year. * * *

Second, the violent crime rate has dropped significantly over the past twenty years, from 666.9 violent crimes per 100,000 people in 1989 to 454.5 per 100,000 in 2008. Cities, streets, and parks feel significantly safer in many parts of the country. This reduces public fear and alleviates political pressure to adopt "tough on crime" measures. * * *

Third, the war on drugs, responsible for much of the rise in incarceration, is increasingly acknowledged to be a failure. Drugs are as widely available and used today as when the war on drugs began. * * * The political culture is more open than ever to reforming out approach to the war on drugs. Nationwide polls show that the share of Americans favoring legalization of marijuana has grown from just 12% in 1969 to 46% today. * * * Several states * * * have decriminalized altogether or reduced penalties associated with possessions of small amounts of marijuana. * * *

Fourth, states have begun to recognize that many of those imprisoned need not be. Much of the rise in incarceration over the past forty years has been fueled by locking up hundreds of thousands of nonviolent offenders. In addition, overly harsh sentences have resulted in the incarceration of many older prisoners who, after spending years in prison, are well beyond the age when most criminal conduct occurs. * * *

Fifth, it is possible (though certainly too early to tell) that we have reached a limit to the incarceration levels that the majority will tolerate. Regardless of one's political inclinations, the fact that the United States incarcerates many more people per capita than any other nation in the world can hardly be a point of pride. * * * In 2009, there were an astonishing 7,225,800 adults in the United States in prison or jail or on probation or parole, a number close to the population of New York City (8.4 million) and constituting 2.4% of the nation's population. The declining incarceration rate may reflect popular sentiment that enough is enough.

Sixth, the "war on terror" may have, ironically, created space for more sensible reform in the criminal justice system. * * * [E]ver since 9/11, public fear of terrorism seems to have supplanted public fear of crime—even though the likelihood that a citizen will be the victim of ordinary crime is much higher than the likelihood that he will be a victim of a terrorist attack. A politician who establishes his bona fides by supporting tough policies in the "war on terror" may feel more leeway to support ameliorative reforms in criminal justice. And a populace focused on the "enemy" without may be less likely to focus on "enemies" within.

Finally, a number of factors may have coalesced to make Americans more likely to identify with those behind bars: (1) the large number of incarcerated persons; (2) the recent revelations, fueled by DNA evidence, that demonstrably innocent people have been incarcerated and even sentenced to death; and (3) the reduction, albeit minor, in racial disparities in criminal justice detailed above. Each of these developments might have the effect of increasing public sympathy for those behind bars. * * *

The critical question going forward is how to take what could be a turning point in incarceration trends and make it a major transformation. What is ultimately needed is substantial reform of sentencing practices, reduced reliance on incarceration, especially for drug crimes and other nonviolent offenses, and shortened criminal sentences for many crimes, including serious offenses. But reform cannot be limited to the criminal justice system itself; it must be accompanied by real investments in poverty alleviation in inner-city communities to ensure that those born and raised there have meaningful opportunities to pursue productive, law-abiding lives. * * *

If true reform is ever to take hold, the biggest hurdle to overcome may be the empathy gap that exists between the law-abiding and the criminally convicted, and, in particular, between the white majority and the inner-city communities from which so many of America's prisoners come. * * *

If Americans were to come to view those behind bars as part of our community, indeed our family, mass incarceration would no longer be tolerated.

NOTE

The history of the death penalty in the United States is also marked by racial disparities. According to historian James Acker, before Americans began to build prisons as part of the criminal justice system at the end of the 18th century, the sentencing options available to judges were limited to fines, short-term incarceration in local jails, corporal punishment (such as public humiliation in the stocks), and capital punishment. *See* James R. Acker, *The Death Penalty: An American History,* 6 CONTEMP. JUST. REV. 169, 170 (2003) (reviewing STUART BANNER, THE DEATH PENALTY: AN AMERICAN HISTORY (2003)). While each of these penalties served society's retributive and expressive needs, only a death sentence could provide long-term incapacitation of a particularly dangerous or habitual offender. *Id.* at 170. Thus, "capital punishment was the criminal law's principal defense against repeat offenders and other criminals who threatened individual safety and the social order." *Id.* American colonists applied the death penalty to crimes such as murder, adultery, sodomy, rape, bestiality, and some property crimes. *Id.*

Acker observes that the eighteenth-century American death penalty was disproportionately applied to slaves, whose potential insurrection posed a constant threat to the new settlements. *Id.* at 170-71. For instance, after a slave revolt in 1712, the colony of New York made attempted rape and attempted murder punishable by death only when perpetrated by slaves. *Id.* at 170. In this way, "race-based application of the death penalty took early root throughout the south." *Id.*

The racially disproportionate application of the death penalty survived the Civil War. For instance, in 1856 Virginia "counted 66 capital crimes for slaves . . . against only one (murder) for whites." STUART BANNER, THE DEATH PENALTY: AN AMERICAN HISTORY 141 (2002). Popular distaste for the death penalty after the Civil War led many state legislatures to apply it sparingly to only the worst offenses, such as murder and treason. Acker at 171. Many Southern states also granted juries the discretion to sentence offenders to death or life imprisonment, rather than having the death sentence mandatory for certain crimes. *Id.* Although after the passage of the Fourteenth Amendment the states could not formally apply the death penalty according to race, de facto discrimination was still alive and well. For example, in practice, rape in the South was only punished by death when a black man was convicted of raping a white woman. *Id.* at 172. Widespread racial discrimination in the composition of juries allowed all-white juries to routinely consider the defendant's race in sentencing, with the result that "throughout the South, for all crimes, black defendants were executed in numbers far out of proportion to their population. The death penalty was a means of racial control." STUART BANNER, THE DEATH PENALTY at 230.

In the present day, studies find that blacks disproportionately receive capital sentences, suggesting that race "operates as an extralegal factor" in prosecuting and sentencing. *Id.* at 172. In *McCleskey v. Kemp*,[b] the Supreme Court rejected the use of statistical regression analyses to prove racial discrimination in a black death-row inmate's claim that Alabama's application of the death penalty violated the Eighth and Fourteenth Amendments. Nonetheless, social scientists continue to find disturbing disparities. Criminologists Mona Lynch and Craig Haney, for instance, discovered in their research "a tendency for White jurors—especially White male jurors—to interpret many common penalty phase facts and circumstances as potentially mitigating for a White defendant but to see those same things as irrelevant or even aggravating for a defendant who is Black." Mona Lynch and Craig Haney, *Looking Across the Empathic Divide: Racialized Decision Making on the Capital Jury*, 2011 MICH. ST. L.REV. 573, 574. Indeed, reviewing the available research, Lynch and Haney conclude that "regression analysis has enabled researchers to make a strong case that all stages of the capital trial process—from charging decision to jury penalty phase verdicts—are influenced by racial factors." *Id.* at 575. They argue that the psychological mechanism of this racial bias is an "empathic divide" in which white decisionmakers identify with other whites but not with blacks. *Id.*

B. PUNISHMENT AS A CULTURAL PRACTICE

PUNISHING CHILDREN IN THE CRIMINAL LAW[c]

Cynthia V. Ward
82 Notre Dame L. Rev. 429 (2006)

Consider the facts in this attempted murder case, which California prosecutors filed in 1996:

Defendant told a witness that the victim's family "looked at him wrong," and that in return he, Defendant, "had to kill the baby." Defendant and two acquaintances then went to the victim's apartment when the victim's parents were out grocery shopping and had left their infant son with his eighteen-year-old stepsister, who was in the bathroom and did not hear Defendant and his friends enter the house. Defendant went to the baby's bedroom, took the baby, four-week-old Ignacio Bermudez, out of his bassinet, dropped him on the floor, and proceeded to beat the infant in the head with his fists, feet, and a stick. Defendant and his accomplices then stole property from the house and departed. After the assault, Defendant threatened a female witness with harm if she reported the incident. Defendant then told a family member about the attack; the family member reported him to the authorities. Questioned about the attack, Defendant first lied about it, then eventually re-enacted the assault in a videotaped interview with police.

---

[b] *McCleskey v. Kemp*, 481 U.S. 279 (1987) (excerpted in Chapter 2).

[c] The publisher bears responsibility for any errors which have occurred in reprinting or editing.

Doctors determined that Ignacio Bermudez had suffered "global" brain damage from the attack. Eighteen months after the assault, the baby was unable to see, walk, or make intelligible sounds. According to a media report at the time, "Doctors say nothing less than a miracle will restore Ignacio to health." California prosecutors described Defendant as the "ringleader" in the attack and charged him with attempted murder. The defense did not dispute the essential facts.

Is Defendant guilty?

Now consider one additional fact: at the time of his assault on Ignacio Bermudez, Defendant was six years old. Should the single circumstance of age make a difference to Defendant's guilt or punishment?

For most of the twentieth century the law's answer was "yes." Pre-adolescent offenders, even violent ones, were routinely found not responsible and were instead routed through the non-punitive juvenile system, which emphasized treatment and rehabilitation over blame. But the "youth excuse" has come under strong attack in response to high levels of public concern over the violent and harmful actions of young defendants. Over the past two decades the states have significantly revamped their criminal codes to make it easier to punish children who commit violent offenses. The fact that a six-year-old was actually charged with attempted murder reflects the change in attitude that underlies this trend: twenty years ago even the most serious cases involving children under seven were adjudicated in juvenile court, and in a non-punitive fashion. The law has changed dramatically, to the point where some states now allow judicial waiver of children into adult court at any age, at least when the child is charged with a serious offense. And in a small but growing number of cases, adult-sized punishment is in fact being inflicted—even when it involves a sentence of life without parole. * * *

The law itself has moved strongly and consistently in the direction of convicting and punishing juveniles who commit violent offenses. Politicians speak loudly in favor of "send[ing] a message to violent criminals of all ages" and of " 'putting these juvenile criminals where they need to be—behind bars in the adult prisons.' " Although legislators often cite the values of deterrence and public protection as reasons for the punitive turn toward juveniles, the angry tone of the debate also signals the presence of a strong retributive impulse.

But the punitive turn toward young offenders conflicts head-on with the received view of legal scholars that important differences between children and adults—and even between older adolescents and adults—mandate separate, and gentler, treatment of juveniles who commit serious crimes.

Considerable irony attends this debate. In the 1970s and 1980s, a vocal "Children's Rights" movement argued passionately for the proposition that adolescents were as competent as adults to make many important life decisions, including the decisions to drink alcohol, to consent to medical treatment, and to have an abortion without consulting a parent. Accompanying this movement were behavioral studies purporting to discover that, in important and legally relevant respects, the cognitive capacities of adolescents equal those of adults * * *.

[A] number of psychologists supported the adolescent autonomy position. In its amicus brief in the Supreme Court case of Hodgson v. Minnesota, for example, the American Psychological Association (APA) cited abundant studies supporting the claim that juveniles possess sufficient maturity to decide, without adult consultation, whether or not to have an abortion. "[B]y middle adolescence (age 14–15)," the APA report concluded, "young people develop abilities similar to adults in reasoning about moral dilemmas, understanding social rules and laws, [and] reasoning about interpersonal relationships and interpersonal problems. . . . "

When, in the 1990s, such research formed the basis for the argument that adolescents ought not only to be accorded rights, but also assigned responsibility (including criminal responsibility) for their behavior, the children's movement found that studies demonstrating the substantially equal capacities of adolescents and adults proved to be a double-edged sword. How could adolescents be mature enough to make their own decisions about abortion, but not mature enough to face the consequences of committing armed robbery or using marijuana? The very existence of a separate justice system for juveniles is predicated in part on the assumption that the basic competencies of adolescents and adults differ in fundamental ways that affect judgment. If adolescents and adults are equally capable decision-makers, the argument that adolescents suffer from "diminished responsibility" is called into question. Indeed, the very same evidence that had been used to advocate for young people's autonomy in medical decision-making could provide—and has provided for recent calls to treat juvenile delinquents as adults within our legal and penal systems.

The argument against juvenile liability becomes even more difficult when one considers that the threshold capacities required for criminal responsibility may well be lower than those required competently to exercise some rights for which children's advocates have fought. As Professor Stephen Morse has insightfully explained, the crimes for which children are subject to punishment as adults are almost always intentional crimes involving the knowing infliction of serious harm on a victim. Adolescents as well as adult offenders know that the acts do inflict such harm. It seems facially incoherent to argue (1) that the adolescent who intentionally shoots and kills his teacher should not be held responsible because he lacks even the fundamental capacity to realize that shooting someone will inflict serious harm, and (2) that adolescents as a class have sufficient maturity and judgment to decide whether or not to have an abortion. * * *

* * * In 2005 the United States Supreme Court entered the fray, holding in the case of *Roper v. Simmons* that a defendant who was not yet eighteen at the time he committed intentional murder could not constitutionally be executed for his crime because, in large part, relevant differences between juveniles and adults make the former less culpable for crime. To the extent that the Court's rationale transcends the specific context of capital punishment, the Court has joined forces with the scholarly wing of the debate and, in a meaningful sense, divided the law from itself.

In general, the "difference" scholars have limited their discussion to comparing adolescents with adults. Most take as a starting assumption that young children should not be held criminally responsible under any circumstances. Thus, in general the debate in the literature focuses on whether offenders of age fourteen or older ought to be excluded from criminal liability as a class.

But this age-circumscribed discussion, while important in some ways, ultimately fails to engage either the dimensions or the nationwide attraction of the punitive turn toward children in the criminal law. As noted above, that move toward punishing children as adults does not merely address the question of whether the age of criminal responsibility should be lowered to fifteen or fourteen. In at least twenty-eight states, the minimum age at which a child can be transferred to adult court is under fourteen, and in some states there is no lower limit at least for the most serious offenses. Indeed, the most controversial cases in recent years involve serious crimes committed by much younger children who, like Ignacio Bermudez's attacker, seem at the time of their acts to "know what they are doing." Increasingly the law allows such cases to be prosecuted, and such defendants to be punished, in the criminal system. * * *

I. Brandon T. and the Elements of Criminal Responsibility

Suppose that when you first read the description of the attack on Ignacio Bermudez you agreed that the perpetrator was guilty of a serious crime, that the charge of attempted murder seemed appropriate in the case. How did you then react when you read that Brandon was six years old at the time of the attack? Was your reaction the same as that of Harold Jewett, the California prosecutor who brought the attempted murder charge against Brandon? "It doesn't matter whether you're 6 or you're 106," said Jewett in an interview. "If you do something that hurts someone else, with knowledge of the wrongfulness of it, you're responsible for it, period." Or did the single fact of Brandon's age make you hesitate? If the latter, why? Did Brandon's age give you pause because you think it should matter to his criminal liability; or because you think that regardless of liability he should not be criminally punished; or for some other, independent reason? * * *

A. The Liability Thesis: Mens Rea in Children

One reason offered in favor of exempting children from criminal liability is that they lack the capacity to be mentally culpable. Young children in particular, according to this argument, are not capable of forming the requisite intent, or mens rea, to be responsible even for their otherwise criminal acts. This view has a long history. Even before the creation of separate juvenile courts in the late-nineteenth century, children younger than seven at the time of their acts were treated as not responsible for crime, largely on the theory that young children lack the capacity to form mens rea, or culpable intent. The assumption that juveniles lack the requisite mens rea for criminal responsibility was also a core reason for removing them from the criminal justice system entirely and creating a separate, non-punitive adjudication structure for dealing with juvenile crime. But what does it mean to say that a person lacks the capacity to form mens rea? To answer that we need to work from a theory of what mens rea is and what capacities it requires. * * *

2. Do Children as a Class Lack the Capacities Required for Criminal Liability?

a. Brandon T. and Threshold Culpability

[T]he law assumes the presence of three threshold capacities when a person is charged with a crime. These are (1) instrumental rationality, which in turn requires the capacity to form the conscious purpose to do a thing, to correlate that intent with actions capable of achieving it, and to follow through by performing those actions which cause the criminal harm; (2) the capacity to understand the difference between acting rightfully and acting wrongfully; and (3) the capacity to refrain from acting wrongfully which essentially assumes that defendant did not act under overpowering compulsion (from inside or outside) that left him with no choice but to do wrong.

Is it true that, as a class and by definition, children lack the threshold level of these capacities required for criminal liability? Consider, again, the case of Brandon T. Evidence in that case indicated that Brandon (1) held a grudge against the parents of Ignacio Bermudez; (2) determined to kill Ignacio in order to revenge himself on the baby's parents for "harassing him;" (3) recruited accomplices; (4) waited until Ignacio's parents were out of the house; and (5) went to the baby's room where he brutally beat Ignacio, inflicting enormous and irreparable damage. After the attack, Brandon T. (1) stole a very popular "Big Wheel" tricycle from the Bermudez house; (2) warned a potential witness, a little girl, "You better not tell anybody what I did;" (3) initially lied to police by saying that he didn't do it; and (4) eventually confessed and reenacted the entire event on videotape.

It seems clear from the facts that at the time he attacked Ignacio Bermudez, Brandon T. (1) intended to perform the acts that harmed Ignacio (he did not accidentally knock the baby out of its bassinet; he intentionally threw the baby on the floor); (2) did those intentional actions with the conscious purpose of harming the baby (when he took the baby out of the bassinet and dropped him, he did not think that Ignacio would fly out of the room; he knew the baby would fall to the floor and that the fall would harm him); (3) knew that if he were caught by authorities he would get into trouble; and (4) took precautions to prevent this from happening. On its face, Brandon's act was intentional and premeditated—not compelled or coerced—and the acts were done with the knowledge that if he were caught he would probably be punished. * * *

The result of making empathetic capacity a necessary component of normative competence would be that those offenders * * * who lack remorse and fellow feeling would be excused from criminal liability and punishment on those grounds. And this would be a pernicious result, for at least three reasons.

First, while it seems to be the case that many violent criminals are psychopaths, it is not the case that all psychopaths are criminals. * * * Since, by definition, they do not obey the law because they respect other people or because breaking the law would make them feel guilty, presumably they obey it for other reasons. Among those reasons are the costs associated with being criminally prosecuted and punished for committing a crime. Excusing psychopaths from criminal punishment would dramatically reduce the strength of this disincentive, and therefore dramatically reduce the psychopath's interest in remaining law-abiding. * * *

It may of course be true that lack of empathic ability makes it more difficult for a psychopath to obey the law, in the sense that one barrier to law-breaking—what we call "conscience"—is missing from the psychopath's mental toolkit. But * * * the fact that some people find it more difficult to obey the law than others is not, and should not be, valid grounds for an excuse from criminal responsibility.

But what if children as a group lack empathic capacity, or have less of it than adults? Shouldn't such a (temporary) disability absolve, or at least reduce, their liability for crime, on the grounds that this lack makes it more difficult for them to obey the law? As a normative matter this is an interesting question—but it requires an additional argument explaining why children should be excused on those grounds although adults possessing the same defect are not. Beyond that, and as a descriptive matter, it strikes me as quite implausible to say that children, even children as young as six, lack a threshold level of empathy as a group. * * *

B. The Relevance of Facts and Contact

* * *

If a defendant really believes that when you kill someone they come back to life the next day, it would be wrong to hold him guilty of murder or attempted murder since he doesn't comprehend an essential fact about the harm resulting from his purpose and his actions. At a minimum, understanding the "essential facts" about killing someone requires the knowledge that when someone dies they are gone for good. The younger children are, the less likely they are to understand such facts, and—the argument might go—this lack of understanding should render young children non-culpable for homicide or attempted homicide.

In the case of Brandon T., the evidence conflicted on the question of whether he understood what it means to kill or to die. On the one hand, Brandon's own father had been murdered when the child was four. Brandon knew that his father had died violently and the child was given to fantasizing about the event. On the other hand, Brandon's defense attorney and at least one court appointed expert concluded that the boy did not understand what it meant to kill a person, and on the basis of those opinions the court ultimately amended the criminal charge from attempted murder to assault with intent to commit bodily harm. Thus, the case offers no convincing argument that six-year-olds as a class must be exempted from liability for homicide. * * *

* * * Defendant must at least understand (1) the fact of the injury, (2) its permanence, and (3) that inflicting this loss is considered wrong. There was some evidence that Brandon T. did in fact understand all these things, and under such a standard he could therefore be held responsible. * * *

C. Other Differences as Basis for the Youth Excuse

* * *

[T]he scholarship focuses on differences between adolescents and adults, attempting to demonstrate that adolescents are less averse to risk, more likely to value short-term benefits over long-term costs, and more likely to be influenced by their social environment than adults, and that these differences ought to serve either as a complete bar to criminal liability for juveniles, or as a partial bar to such liability. The scholarship usually draws on behavioral studies demonstrating that adolescents as a class have weaker future-orientation than do adults as a class; that they take more health and safety risks than do adults as a class; and that they are more impulsive than adults as a class. These differences, the argument concludes, reduce adolescent blameworthiness and (thus) criminal culpability. * * *

However, * * * the legal relevance of such information is far from clear. First, this very same brain research indicates that brain maturation peaks at least several years beyond age eighteen, the legal age of majority. A possible implication of this finding is that the legal age of majority should be raised, say to twenty-two or twenty-five, by which time the brain is more fully developed. Even further, the studies now trumpeted as demonstrating "stark differences" between adolescent and adult brains also show that brain development continues well into a person's forties and fifties. At what point in a person's brain development does (s)he become criminally responsible? The studies themselves cannot answer that question. Instead, they simply expose us to the truth that ultimately, criminal responsibility is a matter of moral judgment rather than of scientific fact-finding. * * *

Of course, it may be the case that some, many, or even most children lack the necessary capacities to be held guilty of crime. But if this is true, it serves only as an argument for evaluating juvenile defendants individually (as we do all other defendants) for the purpose of deciding whether or not they meet the test of criminal responsibility. This question is usually decided during the criminal adjudication process rather than by a bright-line a priori rule that bars, or even presumptively bars, children from criminal responsibility. * * *

Finally, consider the argument that adolescents may be more susceptible to environmental influence, from peers and surrounding social pressures, and are therefore more likely to feel pressured into criminal acts than are adults. From the perspective of culpability for crime, this argument seems to cut both ways. If juveniles are more likely to be influenced by the signals from their environment, and they otherwise possess the threshold capacities for criminal responsibility, then perhaps the law should focus on sending strong anti-"criminogenic" signals to the class of potential juvenile offenders. In this connection, evidence indicates that juvenile offenders are often well aware that the law treats them more leniently than it does adults, and that some are quite willing to take advantage of this fact. [Ward notes that Christopher Simmons, whose murder prosecution was the basis for the Supreme Court's decision in *Roper v. Simmons*, "had confidently informed his friends that they could 'get away with it' because they were juveniles."] * * *

II. The Redemption Thesis: Punishment and Rehabilitation

* * *

A. Culpability v. Corrigibility

* * * [T]o a significant degree, our uneasiness about punishing children for crime rests not on the intuition that children are incapable of

intentional action, but on the intuitive judgment that children are more easily reformed than adults—that to send someone to prison for life for an act, even a monstrous act, committed while a juvenile is to waste a life that might well have been productive if allowed to grow to adulthood outside of prison. * * *

C. Age and Corrigibility

* * * But is it true that children as a class do, in fact, have more redemptive potential than do adults as a class? Some recent research indicates that this intuition may be baseless—that some youthful offenders, particularly those who begin committing serious crimes as young children, may be quite difficult, or even impossible, to rehabilitate. As one recent article summarized the problem:

> Numerous researchers have reported a robust inverse relation between the age of a youth's first conviction and his or her total number of convictions through early adulthood. Youths who are first convicted earlier are convicted more times not only because they began their "criminal careers" earlier but also because they are convicted at higher rates at all ages into early adulthood. * * *

Such findings, indicating "an inverse relation between age of onset and the frequency, seriousness, and persistence of delinquency," reinforce one intuition that seems to fuel the punitive turn of the criminal law toward juveniles—that there are in fact "Bad Seeds," who show their criminal proclivities early, have little or no capacity for remorse or reform, and who will continue to inflict harm on society until the criminal law puts them out of commission. Individual cases in which very young children commit atrocious crimes may reinforce this impression.

According to psychiatrist Martin Blinder, six-year-old Brandon T. was clearly in danger of becoming a "life-course persistent" offender. For Dr. Blinder—who evaluated Brandon to determine his competency to stand trial for the assault on Ignacio Bermudez—the signs were so marked in Brandon that, despite his youth, Blinder felt confident in diagnosing him as a "psychopath in the making." * * *

It may, in short, be true that at least some juvenile offenders—those who begin committing serious crimes while children and who demonstrate neither empathy toward others nor remorse for the harm they inflict—may be difficult or impossible to rehabilitate. * * *

Conclusion

* * * Why, then, do most of us still cringe at the thought of sending a six-year-old to prison, or to execution—even for an admittedly horrendous and intentional act? * * *

Consider, on the one hand, the law's general attitude toward the rights and status of children. Although the law of crime prohibits adults from torturing children or subjecting them to abuse, the law also affirmatively, and vigorously, enforces the rights of parents to direct the rearing, physical care, education, discipline, and external environment of their children. Thus, assuming no evidence of parental abuse, children normally have no legal recourse when their parents decide to divorce, move, change their children's school, discipline their children, direct their religious education, or monitor their social lives. The law—the United States Constitution itself—defends parents' rights to make such decisions, and thus enforces the confinement of children to their families until the age of majority. No other group of (unconvicted and uncommitted) persons is thus involuntarily subordinated, by law, to the power and authority of other individuals.

At the same time it enforces the control of children by the family, the law * * * increasingly treats children as autonomous adults for the purposes of criminal conviction and punishment. A strong argument can be made that this is both profoundly contradictory and patently unjust. Substantial empirical evidence supports the widespread intuition that most children who commit violent crimes come from backgrounds featuring core environmental and resource deficits as well as serious abuse and/or deprivation within their families. As noted, absent evidence of serious abuse, the law enforces the confinement of children to those families. Unlike adult criminals who, whatever their sufferings as children are not, by definition, living in legally-enforced subjection to their parents at the time of their crimes, children of poverty—that is, most children who commit violent offenses—have been prematurely and often continuously exposed to environments that make it all but impossible for such children to internalize the values implicit in the criminal law and to adopt those values as their own. It seems unjust, in that context, to hold children—especially young children who have had the least opportunity to perceive and make use of any exit options available—fully responsible as criminals, even for violent acts that inflict significant harm.

* * * Holding such children criminally responsible is not unjust because of any innate internal differences between children and adults—but because of the different treatment of children by the law, the law's confinement of children to criminogenic situations from which those children, unlike adults, have little or no opportunity to escape. The law contributes to the predicament in which they grow up, and the law, therefore, should acknowledge that contribution by making it relevant to the question of criminal responsibility when the defendant is a child.

THE IMPOSSIBLE PREDICAMENT OF GINA GRANT

Carrie T. Hollister
44 UCLA L. Rev. 913 (1997)

In April 1995, Harvard University rescinded its offer to Gina Grant of a much-coveted position in its 1995 freshman class. While refusing to provide details surrounding its decision, Harvard claimed that the rescission had less to do with the fact that, at age fourteen, she bludgeoned her mother to death with a crystal candlestick than with the fact that she failed to be forthcoming about the incident and its repercussions on her university application and in her admissions interview. To an application question that asked if she had "ever been dismissed, suspended or separated from school [or] placed on probation," Grant responded "no." When asked in an admissions interview about her mother's death, Grant responded that her mother had died "in an accident."

The details of Grant's case come not from her juvenile record or the trial transcript, but rather from local press accounts of the incident and the subsequent proceedings. Reports stated that before Grant admitted to committing the killing in self-defense, she first attempted to make her mother's death look like a suicide, then she briefly tried to place the blame on her hoodlum boyfriend. Whatever Grant's story, at the root of the incident was a stormy relationship between an admittedly troubled teen and an abusive parent. Because Grant was under sixteen and had no prior contacts with law enforcement, the South Carolina juvenile court had exclusive jurisdiction over her case. Though Grant pleaded no contest to voluntary manslaughter, her sentence was relatively short: one year (including her pretrial detention time) with the remainder to be served in a detention facility run by the South Carolina Department of Youth Services.

Eight months into her stay at the detention facility, Grant was released and placed on probation until her eighteenth birthday. Leaving behind the South Carolina community that knew about her past, she moved to Massachusetts, lived briefly in a center for girls "considered dangerous to themselves or to others," and then settled with relatives. Grant was determined to build a new life, and her hard work resulted in the type of all-around excellence that earned her an acceptance to Harvard University. She was at the top of her high school class, captain of the tennis team, community volunteer, and tutor.

In her admissions application and interview, Grant did not tell Harvard about her involvement in her mother's death or her adjudication because, as advised by her lawyers, she believed she was under no obligation to do so. Grant, who served her sentence and probationary period without problem, believed she was protected by a South Carolina statute that rendered sealed and confidential all of the arrest, court, and probation records associated with her case. In effect, Gina Grant's contact with the South Carolina juvenile court system was erased.

The State may have erased her official records, but because of an imperious South Carolina sheriff, Gina Grant's name was a household word at the time of her arrest and hearing. Ignoring South Carolina law which protects the identity of youthful offenders, Lexington County sheriff James Metts gave Grant's name to the press. " 'I was agitated,' he explained, . . . 'and I think that the juvenile-justice system makes a mockery of justice.' " Moreover, some of her court proceedings were open to the public, and her case made daily headlines.

In fact, it was through an anonymous delivery of newspaper clippings from Grant's detention and hearing that Harvard discovered the details of her past.

Harvard's decision to rescind its offer to Grant did not go unnoticed or unreported. An outpouring of sympathy for Grant came from attorneys and judges specializing in juvenile cases. The sentiment was clear: Grant was a juvenile justice success story. She was a product of that system's rehabilitative ideal, and proof that the "system can turn around even a deeply troubled child." Support came as well from the student body at Harvard and other colleges and universities and from high school friends and administrators.

There were many, however, who felt that social condemnation of Gina Grant was proper, and that Harvard had made the right decision. Grant's supporters were lambasted as having "twisted values" about crime, punishment, and rehabilitation. Indeed, the South Carolina parole board that reviewed Grant's case saw her "superior intelligence and the community support she had received to be aggravating rather than mitigating circumstances." The board's chairwoman remarked that "with the resources and intelligence she had, I have to believe she could have found other solutions." And while the rehabilitative ideal was one thing, attending Harvard was yet another; some felt that Gina Grant had come far enough. Despite her achievements, Grant was still an "ex offender," occupying "an anomalous position . . . somewhere between the poles of social acceptance and social condemnation, though obviously closer to the latter."

The controversy over the collision of Gina Grant's past with her future highlights a debate involving the juvenile justice system in general. Many of the basic tenets of the juvenile justice system that rely on confidentiality and judicial discretion—closed hearings, nondisclosure of names of delinquents to the press, sentencing practices, sealed records—are under fire as legislators and academics wrestle with th rising tide of serious and violent juvenile crime, overcrowded deten facilities, and a public that is increasingly demanding retributior accountability from juveniles who commit violent or serious crimes

I. The Juvenile Justice System

The juvenile justice system, while distinct from the adult criminal system, shares similar functions and goals. Both systems "serve the reconstruction of the offender, the incapacitation of the intractable criminal, the deterrence of others from criminal conduct, and the exaction of retribution and expiation for the offense." In the juvenile justice context, the weight given the specific functions—reconstruction, incapacitation, deterrence, and retribution—has changed dramatically throughout United States history. A complete divergence from the English justice system that was its predecessor, the current United States juvenile court system was the result of a nineteenth-century social science experiment with rehabilitation, refined by the recognition of juvenile rights in the 1960s. More recently, the juvenile justice system is under a potentially crippling siege that has resulted in an emphasis on the goals of incapacitation and deterrence, and a retraction from the goal of rehabilitation.

A. History of the Juvenile Justice System: The Rehabilitative Ideal

The manner of dealing with juveniles in seventeenth-and eighteenth-century America can be traced to medieval English chancery courts, in which children under seven were believed to be incapable of forming criminal intent, and those over seven who committed crimes were treated like adults. That system, brought to this country by the colonists, provided that children over seven would be "arrested, prosecuted, punished and housed in the same manner as adults." One of the early nineteenth-century reforms, the New York House of Refuge, was established in 1824. The House of Refuge provided for detention of juveniles who committed less-serious crimes away from adult prisoners. The House of Refuge and other nineteenth-century reforms were prompted by more protective attitudes and a clear sense that "troubled children should be removed from the fate that awaited them in adult prisons." The idea that children were "on some level, fundamentally different than adults," was beginning to take hold.

By the end of the nineteenth century, this notion of difference was [illegible] entrenched due to the efforts of reformers committed to a [illegible]de of progressive institutions, not the least of which was the [illegible]nent of a juvenile justice system based on treatment and [illegible]tion rather than retribution or deterrence. The movement was [illegible]ested in the criminal than in the crime, and adopted the spirit [illegible]eer rather than that of the detached observer." Based on [illegible] theories and imbued with compassion, these reformers [illegible]unishment was obsolete and the criminal sick," and that, [illegible]to youths who violated the laws, "sin" translated into

In an effort to devise a juvenile system that would at once train and control society's children and mold them into model citizens, Illinois adopted the Juvenile Court Act of 1899. The Act provided that when a child was determined to be at risk, public schools and public and voluntary agencies were "to ensure that 'the care, custody and discipline of the child shall approximate . . . that which should be given by its parents.'" When the schools and agencies failed adequately to extricate the child from the grips of peril, the juvenile court would intervene. Following the enactment of the Juvenile Court Act by Illinois, virtually every state, the District of Columbia, and Puerto Rico followed suit.

At its inception and well into the twentieth century, discretion on the part of the judge and informality of the process were the precepts of the juvenile court. Although the classic adult punishment-oriented system was built on "impartial and impersonal justice," judicial discretion as to the child's fate was paramount in this new system in which the particular circumstances of each child were to be examined. Because "each child's 'real needs' differed . . . no limits could be defined in advance."

The language employed by this new discretion-based juvenile justice system was, not surprisingly, ambiguous. Emphasizing the distinction between juvenile and criminal proceedings, court personnel adopted "a euphemistic vocabulary to eliminate any stigma or implication of a criminal proceeding." Children were not convicted, they were adjudicated; they were not arrested, they were detained. And "since no children were to be punished, there was no need to distinguish between criminal and noncriminal acts in designating a child as 'delinquent.'" In addition, a veil of secrecy was erected that denied lawyers and the press access to the courts and their charges; traditional rules of evidence were discarded; an constitutional safeguards were eliminated. The children were trea according to their needs, with the "rehabilitative goal applied equal juveniles charged with the most serious offenses as to those charge minor offenses."

The combination of a new vocabulary and a new way of tr miscreant amounted to what was in fact a revolution in the justice. A 1909 writing by Judge Julian Mack lauded the r purposes of the juvenile court as "not so much to punish as to degrade but to uplift, not to crush but to develop, not criminal but a worthy citizen." Despite these lofty prom discretion-based system would soon surface.

B. The Retreat: Procedural Due Process Rears It Vow to Get Tough on Crime

By the middle of the twentieth century, the accepted avenue for dealing with juvenile delin in practice, the mainstay of the juvenil discretion—was not necessarily in the int judicial discretion more often meant that the offender was denied basic due process guaranteed by the Constitution. As a result of this denial, a series of cases decided in the late 1960s and 1970s instituted many, but not all, of the due process protections that were absent from the original juvenile justice system, in many ways blurring the once-obvious distinctions between juvenile and adult courts. A second wave of reform began in the 1980s and continues today, aimed at taking discretion away from the judge in the form of get-tough legislation that directs transfer of certain offenders directly to adult criminal courts, that allows media and public access to the proceedings of certain offenders, and that imposes mandatory sentences. These reforms have also provided a forum for those promoting complete elimination of a separate juvenile justice system, as well as for those proposing a more intermediate solution, such as establishing a court midway between juvenile and adult courts to exclusively handle the repeat or serious offenders. * * *

In *In re Winship*, the Supreme Court recognized that juvenile court is a quasi-criminal court, and ruled that the appropriate standard of proof should be the criminal standard of "beyond a reasonable doubt," rather than the civil standard of "by a preponderance of the evidence."[c] Thus, by [...]970s, limited procedural due process rights had become an integral [...]he juvenile justice system.

[...]gh Legislation

[...]mal procedural safeguards in place, the juvenile court [...]he 1980s. The limp was aggravated by underfunding, [...]g crime rates, and a growing opinion that the [...]as a joke and a failure. The media's coverage of [...]ffenders committing horrifically violent crimes [...]tlight, focused attention on the juvenile justice [...]omings, and provided a springboard for what [...]le of renewed public and legislative interest in [...]udicial discretion was seen as a major culprit [...]nd the answer was to "get tough on crime" [...]e system, substituting the more traditional an[...]f incarceration and retribution for the laws[...] courts[...]

[...]on that juvenile involvement in serious [...]ular, juvenile homicide has increased [...]s a result, most of the get-tough [...]mmitted the most serious offenses [...]ny state legislatures have enacted [...]erious juvenile offenders in adult [...] on incarceration. An analysis of

[c] *In re W*[...]

this legislation reveals a variety of approaches to get-tough statutory change:

> (1) making it easier to prosecute juvenile offenders in adult courts (California and Florida), (2) lowering the age of judicial waiver (Tennessee, Kentucky, and South Carolina), and (3) excluding certain offenses from juvenile court jurisdiction (Illinois, Indiana, Oklahoma, and Louisiana). In addition, a number of states have attempted to stiffen juvenile court penalties for serious juvenile offenders through (1) mandating minimum terms of incarceration (Colorado, New York, and Idaho), or (2) enacting a comprehensive system of sentencing guidelines (Washington).

* * *

Still, the same public that is demanding stiffer penalties and harsher treatment is not willing to go all the way. Public polls indicate that despite a punitive push, the majority of people do not want juveniles incarcerated with adults after being tried in adult courts, and most do not support the death penalty for juveniles. Even though some states have embraced the get-tough approach, "the fact that a significant number of jurisdictions has chosen [an] integrated approach [i.e., distinct juvenile system with punitive provisions aimed at serious offenders] suggests that society is not yet prepared to reject fully the rehabilitative philosophy of the juvenile court."

C. Sealed-Record Statutes: An Essential Component of the Juvenile Justice System

* * *

In theory, a sealed record is the final reward for good behavior, providing the former offender with the proverbial clean slate. For those who earn it, a sealed or expunged record may translate into a legally sanctioned lie; that is, depending on the wording of the applicable statute, the subject of that record can confidently respond in the negative to any questions concerning involvement in an incident that is the subject of a sealed record.

As a tool of correction, the key to the sealed-record statute is the motivation and incentive it provides to young offenders. In a model statute proposal, Aidan Gough suggested that

> [O]ur penal law, in its present state, is one-sided, providing only negative motivation for reform—the avoidance of future incarceration. If the offender is provided with a positive stimulus and is given an initiating role in the process by which the readjustment of status is achieved, it is likely that he will regard it as more meaningful. As a means of social control, reward for

achievement of the conduct which punishment was designed to attain is more effective than punishment alone.

In addition, sealed-record statutes provide necessary protection for children involved in a less-than-perfect juvenile justice system. The problems stemming from judicial discretion as well as the near total confidentiality of juvenile proceedings, although important components of the juvenile system itself, have led to well-documented variations and disparities of treatment of similar cases. These "concerns about the quality of procedural justice and the reliability of delinquency adjudications" underscore the problems of relying too heavily on juvenile court records in many cases.

The ethical dilemma that arises from sanctioned dishonesty is not easily reconciled. "It is perhaps hard to articulate but there is . . . something objectionable about legalized prevarication even though one can rationalize the point by the worthiness of the end." * * *

[E]ducation attorney Alan Rose believes that the rehabilitative principles of the juvenile justice system are not binding on any institution, including Harvard. According to Rose, "Harvard is entitled to establish rules about who should go to school there. . . . And on the top of the list of applicants you'd screen out are any who have directed bodily harm at anyone else."

* * *

For Gina Grant, whose past "was never more than a Nexis search away from revelation," only the most inclusive sealed-record statute would have helped. A one-time offender who had done more than make good according to the rehabilitative ideal of the juvenile justice system, Grant was painted into a corner by the questions asked in Harvard's application and admissions interview. If her juvenile record was indeed sealed, then Harvard should not have had the right to inquire about it, and more importantly, to label her a liar for not telling them about it.

C. LEGAL AND SOCIAL CONTEXTS OF PUNISHMENT

COLLATERAL CONSEQUENCES OF CRIMINAL CONVICTIONS: CONFRONTING ISSUES OF RACE AND DIGNITY

Michael Pinard
85 N.Y.U. L. Rev. 457 (2010)

* * * Three decades after its incarceration explosion began, the United States is now experiencing a post-incarceration crisis: Record numbers of individuals—recently eclipsing 700,000 per year—are now exiting U.S. correctional facilities and returning to communities across the country. These individuals must confront a wide range of collateral

consequences stemming from their convictions, including ineligibility for federal welfare benefits, public housing, student loans, and employment opportunities, as well as various forms of civic exclusion, such as ineligibility for jury service and felon disenfranchisement. * * *

a. Housing

The U.S. federal government imposes restrictions on individuals with certain criminal records from receiving public housing assistance. For instance, federal law bans registered sex offenders and convicted methamphetamine producers from obtaining government-assisted housing for life. Federal law also grants local public housing authorities broad discretion to determine the scope of other criminal activity that will disqualify individuals from public housing. Local housing authorities across the United States have expanded the types of conduct that will preclude individuals from obtaining public housing. * * * In addition, several housing authorities ban individuals whose conduct did not lead to a conviction, such as individuals who received violations or other noncriminal dispositions. While some jurisdictions * * * allow otherwise ineligible individuals to reside in public housing or receive housing assistance within the exclusionary period upon a showing of rehabilitation, other jurisdictions provide no exceptions, and individuals must wait out the entire exclusionary period before becoming eligible for public housing.

b. Employment

"In most jurisdictions, the stigma [of a criminal record] takes on a legal significance" in the employment context. Individuals with criminal records confront numerous federal and state employment restrictions in both the public and private sectors. Federal and state laws and regulations impose collateral employment consequences through various mechanisms, including statutory prohibitions, licensing provisions, and statutorily required background checks.

For example, an individual with a criminal conviction will no longer be eligible for numerous categories of employment. Additional employment consequences are enforced by licensing agencies. Scores of jobs require occupational licenses, and state and municipal licensing agencies often have authority to conduct background checks with discretion to deny licenses based on an applicant's criminal history.

Theoretically, these consequences should be attenuated by federal and, in some cases, state antidiscrimination statutes, which afford statutory antidiscrimination protections to individuals with criminal records. While many of these statutes only pertain to public employment or licensing authorities, a few extend to the private sector as well. However, as some commentators have observed, these laws generally have weak enforcement mechanisms. As a result, despite these statutory protections, criminal records often bar individuals with criminal records from meaningful employment opportunities.

c. Public Benefits

Most criminal convictions do not have an effect on an individual's eligibility for federal welfare benefits. However, since 1996, federal law has denied welfare benefits assistance (cash assistance and food stamps) to individuals convicted of felony drug offenses. States can opt out of this law, and many have. Currently, fourteen states have adhered to the federal ban and as a result completely exclude individuals convicted of felony drug offenses from these benefits; twenty-two states enforce the ban in part; and fourteen states and the District of Columbia have opted out of the ban entirely.

d. Voting

The U.S. Supreme Court has declared voting restrictions based on convictions permissible under Section 2 of the Fourteenth Amendment. Such restrictions, both with respect to federal and state elections, are matters of state law. Forty-eight states and the District of Columbia ban individuals who are incarcerated for felony offenses from voting; thirty-five states ban individuals on parole for a felony offense from voting; and thirty states ban individuals on felony probation from voting. Two states, Virginia and Kentucky, impose lifetime exclusions for individuals convicted of felony offenses.

* * *

[T]here are no general federal expungement or sealing provisions in the United States. As a result, federal convictions remain on an individual's criminal record forever, unless he or she receives a presidential pardon, which is exceedingly rare. At the state level, gubernatorial pardons are technically available in every jurisdiction and are the most powerful tools "to avoid or mitigate conviction-related disabilities and disqualifications affecting employment, housing, and a myriad of other benefits and opportunities." However, like the presidential pardon, state pardons are very rare.

While most states have expungement or sealing provisions for state offenses, these mechanisms are generally limited to relatively narrow circumstances and cannot be applied to federal offenses. Expungements are usually restricted to certain types of offenses, such as misdemeanors, to individuals with certain types of criminal records, and/or to first offenders. Only a few states have expungement or sealing provisions for adults convicted of felony offenses. Moreover, there are often limits on the number of convictions a person can expunge, and there are usually waiting periods before a person is eligible for expungement. Furthermore, a state pardon or expungement, even if obtained, can be relatively limited because it "may have no effect upon disabilities imposed under federal law." Some states also have administrative restoration policies. However, commentators have noted the inconsistency and limited scope of these provisions, as well as the burdensome logistical obstacles to obtaining relief. * * *

Collateral consequences have always attached to criminal records in the United States. Scholars have explained that these consequences descend from England's notion of "civil death," which historically accompanied convictions. These consequences became less severe over time, particularly in the 1960s and 1970s, but they expanded dramatically in the 1980s and 1990s as part of the "war on drugs" and "tough on crime" movements. * * *

Scholars have * * * argued that the growth of collateral consequences, like the incarceration explosion, has been rooted in race. The role of race is particularly evident when it comes to felon disenfranchisement, where contemporary policies follow a long historical pattern of racial exclusion. Criminal disenfranchisement laws reach back to colonial times in the United States and were extended in original state constitutions. Even with the adoption of the Fifteenth Amendment in 1870, African American disenfranchisement continued in the South. After Reconstruction, disenfranchisement laws were retooled specifically to exclude African Americans from voting. Several "southern states tailored their disenfranchisement laws" to crimes purportedly committed primarily by African Americans, "while excluding crimes purportedly committed primarily by whites." Others imposed poll taxes, literacy tests, and grandfather clauses. Along with these measures, "the explicit use of felon disenfranchisement contributed to preventing African Americans . . . from voting." * * *

For example, "13 percent of African-American men have lost the right to vote, a rate that is seven times the national average."

The other collateral consequences discussed in this Article do not share similar records of explicit racial targeting. However, these consequences expanded dramatically in the 1980s and 1990s as part of the "war on drugs." To help fight this "war," Congress created several collateral consequences that disqualify drug offenders from various federal aid programs. For example, Congress passed laws that disqualify those convicted of felony drug offenses from receiving specific public benefits, including food stamps; that make individuals convicted of distribution or possession of controlled substances ineligible for a variety of federal benefits; that disqualify individuals convicted of specific drug offenses from federal health care programs; and that disqualify, for certain periods of time, students convicted of any drug offense (including misdemeanors) from receiving federal student loans.

Unlike felon disenfranchisement laws, these consequences did not explicitly target African Americans. However, at the very least, the decisionmakers who enacted these consequences ignored both the racial history of drug criminalization and the predictably disproportionate impact that these consequences would have on people of color. * * *

[Pinard argues that felon disenfranchisement policies in the United States are harsher than those extant in Canada, the United Kingdom, and South Africa—the "Comparison Countries."]

The United States should draw lessons from the Comparison Countries * * * and reshape its web of collateral consequences. The overall goal of collateral consequences in any country should be to best position formerly incarcerated individuals to become productive contributors to their families and communities. * * *

D. Analyze the Racially Disproportionate Impact of Collateral Consequences

The United States should draw lessons from Canada, which took steps in 1996 to ease its disproportionate incarceration of Aborigines. As explained above, African Americans and Latinos * * * are uniquely burdened by collateral consequences. * * *

Iowa, Connecticut, and Wisconsin have recently taken affirmative steps to address the disproportionate impact of criminal justice policies on people of color. A study by The Sentencing Project found that in 2005 Iowa had the highest ratio of African American to White prisoners in the United States, at nearly fourteen to one. In response to these findings, Iowa enacted legislation in April 2008 that requires that any "propose[d] . . . change in the law which creates a public offense . . . or changes existing sentencing, parole or probation procedures" be accompanied by a correctional impact statement. This statement "shall include information concerning . . . the impact of the legislation on minorities."

Connecticut, which had the fourth highest ratio of African American to White prisoners in the United States, followed Iowa in June 2008 by enacting legislation requiring that "a racial and ethnic impact statement . . . be prepared with respect to certain bills and amendments that could, if passed, increase or decrease the pretrial or sentenced population of the correctional facilities in [Connecticut]."

In 2008, Wisconsin's governor issued an executive order "[d]irect[ing] all state agencies with relevant information and capability . . . to develop reporting mechanisms to track traffic citation, arrest, charging, sentencing and revocation patterns by jurisdiction and race." The executive order also called for the creation of the Racial Disparities Oversight Commission, which was to "exercise oversight and advocacy concerning programs and policies to reduce disparate treatment of people of color across the spectrum of the criminal justice system." As in Iowa, the efforts that led to this executive order began with a national study on racial disparities in the juvenile justice system. That report found that, in

2003, youth of color in Wisconsin were ten times more likely to be detained than White youth—the highest ratio in the country. * * *

Similar studies should examine the extent to which people of color are disproportionately impacted by collateral consequences throughout the United States. Federal legislation passed in 2008 required that data on the collateral consequences in all fifty states, "each territory of the United States, and the District of Columbia" be studied and compiled. This will lead to a more complete understanding of these consequences, which are now extraordinarily difficult to quantify. However, fact-finding bodies, such as sentencing commissions or other government agencies, should also be formed to study the disproportionate impact of these consequences. These bodies should be established in each state, with the goal of compiling a thorough state-by-state measure of racial disparities in collateral consequences.

Moreover, racial and ethnic impact statements, similar to those that are now required in Iowa, Connecticut, and Wisconsin, should accompany any proposed expansion of federal or state collateral consequences. The statements would recognize and examine any proposed expansion's racial impact. * * *

Public rhetoric in the United States has long embraced the notion that a person who completes his or her sentence for a criminal offense has paid his or her debt to society and is allowed to start anew. However, the collateral consequences described above, as well as the countless others that exist at the federal, state, and local levels, prove that actual practice does not align with this rhetoric. The reality is that it is nearly impossible for individuals convicted of criminal offenses to move past their criminal records because collateral consequences continue to punish them long after the completion of their sentences.

NOTE

In *Padilla v. Kentucky*, 130 S. Ct. 1473 (2010), the Supreme Court held in a 7–2 decision that defense counsel has a Sixth Amendment obligation to inform a noncitizen client regarding the risk of deportation associated with a guilty plea. Finding that deportation has become unique in its severity and relationship to the criminal process because modern immigration law has made deportation "virtually inevitable for a vast number of noncitizens convicted of crimes," the majority found that "deportation is a particularly severe 'penalty' " and "intimately related to the criminal process."

Padilla, a licensed commercial truck driver, was driving his tractor-trailer through Hardin County, Kentucky, and was arrested at a weigh station after authorities found over 1,000 pounds of marijuana in the vehicle. Padilla was indicted for misdemeanor possession of marijuana, misdemeanor possession of drug paraphernalia, and felony trafficking in marijuana.

> He initially pleaded not guilty but was then offered a plea bargain that gave him five years in prison if he pleaded guilty to the misdemeanor possession and felony trafficking counts. During the plea discussions, Padilla's attorney advised him that he "did not have to worry about immigration status since he had been in this country so long." This advice was wrong. Like most drug offenses, other than most simple marijuana possession cases, Padilla's felony drug conviction was a deportable crime and an aggravated felony under immigration law. Shortly after Padilla entered a guilty plea, he was issued an immigration detainer.

Lillian Chu, Comment, *Crime and Banishment: Padilla v. Kentucky Debunks the Myth that Deportation Is Not Punishment*, 44 LOY. L.A. L. REV. 1073 (2011).

When the case reached the Supreme Court, the majority ruled that the lawyer's advice violated Mr. Padilla's Sixth Amendment right to counsel. Margaret Colgate Love and Gabriel Chin explain further:

> Even the two dissenters expressed sympathy with Mr. Padilla's situation, suggesting that he might have secured their vote if he had based his claim on the Due Process Clause rather than the Sixth Amendment.
>
> The *Padilla* decision clearly governs cases where a noncitizen is threatened with deportation on the basis of conviction. But if that were all, it would not "mark a major upheaval in Sixth Amendment law," as the concurring justices warned. While *Padilla*'s effects will be felt most immediately in the tens of thousands of criminal cases involving noncitizen defendants, defense lawyers must now concern themselves more generally with the broader legal effects of a criminal conviction on their clients. The systemic impact of this new obligation cannot be underestimated. *Padilla* may turn out to be the most important right to counsel case since *Gideon*, and the "Padilla advisory" may become as familiar a fixture of a criminal case as the Miranda warning.

Margaret Colgate Love and Gabriel J. Chin, *Padilla v. Kentucky: The Right to Counsel and the Collateral Consequences of Conviction*, 34–MAY CHAMPION 18, 18–19 (2010).

THE RIGHT TO COUNSEL IN CRIMINAL CASES, A NATIONAL CRISIS

Mary Sue Backus & Paul Marcus
57 Hastings L.J. 1031 (2006)

* * * In a case of mistaken identity, Henry Earl Clark of Dallas was charged with a drug offense in Tyler, Texas. After his arrest, it took six weeks in jail before he was assigned a lawyer, as he was too poor to afford one on his own. It took seven more weeks after the appointment of the

lawyer, until the case was dismissed, for it to become obvious that the police had arrested the wrong man. While in jail, Clark asked for quick action writing, "I [need to] get out of this godforsaken jail, get back to my job . . . I am not a drug user or dealer. I am a tax-paying American." During this time, he lost his job and his car, which was auctioned. After Clark was released, he spent several months in a homeless shelter. * * *

Sixteen-year-old Denise Lockett was retarded and pregnant. Her baby died when she delivered it in a toilet in her home in a South Georgia housing project. Although an autopsy found no indication that the baby's death had been caused by any intentional act, the prosecutor charged Lockett with first-degree murder. Her appointed lawyer had a contract to handle all the county's criminal cases, about 300 cases in a year, for a flat fee. He performed this work on top of that required by his private practice with paying clients. The lawyer conducted no investigation of the facts, introduced no evidence of his client's mental retardation or of the autopsy findings, and told her to plead guilty to manslaughter. She was sentenced to twenty years in prison. Tony Humphries was charged with jumping a subway turnstile in Atlanta to evade a $1.75 fare. He sat in jail for fifty-four days, far longer than the sentence he would have received if convicted, before a lawyer was appointed, at a cost to the taxpayers of $2330.

> A mother in Louisiana recently addressed a state legislative committee:
>
> My son Corey is a defendant in Calcasieu Parish, facing adult charges. He has been incarcerated for three months with no contact from court[-]appointed counsel. Corey and I have tried for three months to get a name and phone number of the appointed attorney. No one in the system can tell us exactly who the court[-]appointed attorney is. The court told us his public defender will be the same one he had for a juvenile adjudication. The court[-]appointed counsel told me he does not represent my son. The court clerk's office cannot help me or my son. We are navigating the system alone.
>
> Eight weeks ago we filed a motion for bond reduction. We have heard nothing—not even a letter of acknowledgement from the court that it received our motion. Without a lawyer to advocate on Corey's behalf, we are defenseless. How many more months will go by without contact from a lawyer? How many more months will go by without investigation into the case?

* * *

The Chief Public Defender of Fairfax County, Virginia (metropolitan Washington, D.C.) resigned in July 2005, after just ten months in the position. She said that even with legislative reforms in Virginia her office had so many clients and so few lawyers that the attorneys simply could not adequately represent the defendants at trials and on appeal. Last year, the twenty lawyers in the office defended more than 8000 clients.

The first rule of the American Bar Association's Model Rules of Professional Conduct indicates that "competent representation" requires "the legal knowledge, skill, thoroughness and preparation reasonably necessary for the representation." Yet in Broward County, Florida, the elected public defender felt compelled last year to forbid his attorneys from advising indigent criminal defendants to plead guilty unless they have had "meaningful contact" with their clients in advance. The head of the office said that public defenders are often ill-informed about their clients' cases and circumstances before advising them to take pleas offered by prosecutors at arraignment. "It's not fair to make life-altering decisions while handcuffed to a chair with fifty people standing around. . . . They meet with an attorney for sixty seconds, then they plead guilty and surrender their rights. . . . That's going to stop," the director stated. * * *

Poor people account for more than 80% of individuals prosecuted. These criminal defendants plead guilty approximately 90% of the time. In those cases, more than half the lawyers entered pleas for their clients without spending any significant time on the cases, without interviewing witnesses or filing motions. Sometimes they barely spoke with their clients.

An attorney was found to have entered pleas of guilty for more than 300 defendants without ever taking a matter to trial. In one case from Mississippi, a woman accused of a minor shoplifting offense spent a year in jail, before any trial, without even speaking to her appointed counsel. In some places, one lawyer may handle more than twenty criminal cases in a single day, with a flat rate of $50 per case. In others, some defense lawyers providing counsel to indigent defendants under a state contract system can be responsible for more than 1000 cases per year. In one major metropolitan area, San Jose, California, numerous defense attorneys failed to take simple steps to investigate and prepare their cases for trial. Some attorneys went to trial without ever meeting their clients outside the courtroom. Some neglected to interview obvious alibi witnesses. Some accepted without question reports from prosecutors' medical and forensic experts that were ripe for challenge. * * *

Is there a remedy for an outrageous state of affairs that leads to greater risks for the public and the deprivation of constitutional rights? Of course, such a remedy exists, and we have known this for decades. The remedy is the well-recognized approach of decent financial support from the government for indigent defense, and the presence of well-prepared, reasonably paid, resourceful lawyers. * * *

III. The Basis of the Right to Counsel

* * *

In 1932, the Court decided in *Powell v. Alabama* that the Due Process Clause of the Fourteenth Amendment required that an indigent defendant on trial for a capital offense be provided counsel. While the facts there were extreme, the Justices' language * * * was very broad. The Court expanded the right to representation when it later held in *Johnson v. Zerbst* that an individual accused of a felony in a federal court has a right to appointed counsel under the Sixth Amendment if he or she is unable to afford an attorney. In a major retreat, however, the Justices soon decided in the well-known case of *Betts v. Brady* that the right to counsel in the federal constitution could not be applied routinely to states through the Due Process Clause of the Fourteenth Amendment. The *Betts* decision lasted for two decades.

Finally, in 1963, the Supreme Court unanimously reversed *Betts* and ruled in *Gideon v. Wainwright* that the Sixth Amendment right to counsel applied to defendants charged with felonies in state court under the Due Process Clause. In oft-cited language, the Justices concluded that "any person haled into court, who is too poor to hire a lawyer, cannot be assured of a fair trial unless counsel is provided for him." Justice Black, writing for the Court, found that average citizens lack the necessary legal skills to be able to mount an effective defense. The result, he stated, is that indigent defendants cannot be ensured a fair trial without the guiding hand of counsel. The decision in *Gideon* was based on the principle that all individuals in the criminal justice system must be offered a fair opportunity to defend against charges brought against them. The Court reasoned that the lack of counsel for most indigent defendants presented a direct threat to the equality and fairness of the judicial process:

> From the very beginning, our state and national constitutions and laws have laid great emphasis on procedural and substantive safeguards designed to assure fair trials before impartial tribunals in which every defendant stands equal before the law. This noble ideal cannot be realized if the poor man charged with crime has to face his accusers without a lawyer to assist him.

A criminal defendant's right to counsel "may not be deemed fundamental and essential to fair trials in some countries, but it is in ours."

Gideon certainly did not answer all the key questions involved with the Sixth Amendment right to counsel. Still, it set the principal benchmark against which the American criminal justice systems today must be measured. * * *

V. The Crisis

A. Financial Support

By every measure in every report analyzing the U.S. criminal justice system, the defense function for poor people is drastically underfinanced. * * *

1. Funding

Methods of funding indigent defense differ among all fifty states and the District of Columbia. A nationwide study a few years ago revealed that in twenty-three states the state government is responsible for providing 100% of funding for indigent defense. In contrast, two states, Pennsylvania and Utah, provide no funding at the state level and leave the responsibility solely to individual counties. The District of Columbia, of course, receives all of its funding from the federal government.

The remaining states vary greatly in the amount of funds provided by the state and by county governments and the methods through which those funds are derived. In some states, the public defense system is financed mainly by the state with minimum contributions by counties. Other states leave it to the county to establish a system of public defense and then either reimburse a percentage of the costs or provide supplemental funding. A few states, on the other hand, require counties to pay all costs at the trial level; the state then bears the responsibility for any appeals. * * *

Many states, including California, Mississippi, and Arizona, starkly illustrate the funding problems of indigent defense programs. None, however, is more startling and sobering than the Massachusetts experience, and this in a state which provides excellent oversight and training for its defense counsel. In 2003, court-appointed attorneys representing indigent defendants in Suffolk County, Massachusetts refused to take on new cases. Their stand was the result of a dispute over back pay from the previous year. After two days, the Governor signed a spending measure that made up for the amount owed.

The concern of public defenders and appointed counsel in Massachusetts is not simply that they are not getting paid what they are owed, but that the rates at which they are paid are desperately inadequate. In 2003, the state paid its appointed counsel the third-lowest rate in the nation. For district court cases, court-appointed attorneys received $30 an hour, which was five dollars less than they had been paid seven years earlier. For superior court cases, the rate was $39, and in murder cases an attorney could earn $54 an hour. Believing these rates to be so low as to violate the defendants' right to effective assistance of counsel, attorneys sued the state to force an increase. The Massachusetts defenders sought raises in hourly rates to $60 for district court cases, $90 for superior court cases, and $120 for murder cases. Because of the low pay and high caseloads, the number of attorneys willing to act as appointed counsel declined by 9% from the late 1990s through 2003. In some places the number of available attorneys declined by 10%. The same problem surfaced with state-employed lawyers * * *.

The chief counsel for the governing state agency illustrated the problem with ensuring quality counsel in Massachusetts for indigent clients. His example focused on an attorney who had come to Massachusetts from the University of Michigan. However, after five years of service, the $39,000 annual salary she made in Massachusetts could not compete with the $74,000 salary she received when she accepted a position with the Washington, D.C. Public Defender Service. * * *

In 2004, the Massachusetts Supreme Judicial Court found that indigent defendants were in fact not receiving the constitutionally guaranteed right to counsel. The ruling said that, as a consequence, defendants could be jailed only for seven days without a lawyer and that after forty-five days without seeing a lawyer charges would be dropped. One county judge followed the ruling and, despite objections, released three defendants charged with drug offenses. What the court did not do, however, was order a pay raise for defenders, though the judges' language is strong:

> Public safety . . . comes with a cost. One of the components of that cost is the level of compensation at which counsel for indigent defendants will provide the representation required by our Constitution. . . . The inadequacy of compensation for private attorneys who represent indigent criminal defendants has persisted for many years. The continuation of what is now an unconstitutional state of affairs cannot be tolerated.

In 2004, the Massachusetts legislature did raise fees for appointed counsel, but not to the levels sought. Instead of hourly increases to $60, $90, and $120, legislators added an addition $7.50 per hour. A state commission had recommended much greater increases in hourly pay rates. Two years after the Suffolk County defenders refused to take on further cases, threats of a work stoppage arose again.

A major, and potentially very positive, legislative development then occurred in July 2005, when the state legislature passed even more significant changes for Massachusetts. This legislation raised compensation levels higher, with counsel in district court receiving $50 per hour, lawyers in superior court getting $60 ($100 per hour for homicide cases), and restrictions being imposed on the number of hours court-appointed attorneys could bill the state annually (1400).

2. Caseloads

Firmly enmeshed in the funding dilemma is the problem of overwhelming caseloads carried by public defenders and appointed counsel. As a result, defendants can often spend weeks or months without meeting their attorneys and defense lawyers sometimes have just minutes to prepare for court hearings or even trials. At a 1998 press conference, National Association of Criminal Defense Lawyers president Gerald B. Lefcourt commented:

> But no matter how dedicated or idealistic, a public defender carrying a caseload of as many as 700 cases a year, with no investigator, no secretary, no paralegal, no law library, no computer, none of the resources that police and prosecutors take for granted—that lawyer cannot effectively represent his clients.

In 1973, the National Advisory Commission on Criminal Justice Standards and Goals set forth recommendations for limits on public defender caseloads. The NAC stated that a single attorney in a year should not carry more than 150 felonies, or more than 400 misdemeanors, or more than 200 juvenile cases or more than twenty-five appeals. If an attorney handles the limit in one category then those are all the cases that person is to handle. Many lawyers throughout the nation do not come close to meeting that standard.

By 2001 the Clark County (Nevada) Public Defender Office had juvenile caseloads at about seven times the NAC recommended limit. Each of the two attorneys on the juvenile division staff had caseloads approaching 1500. A NLADA survey found that as the cases in the division increased from 1993 through 2001, the focus of the attorneys was not so much on representing their clients as it was "about processing cases." The evidence they present shows a more than 50% decrease in the amount of time available to the office to dispose of a case. In 1993, an average case took about sixty-three days to complete. By 2001, it was down to approximately twenty-six days. * * *

In Calcasieu Parish, Louisiana, nine defendants waited two years for their trials to begin. As a result, the state supreme court said that courts could stop capital prosecutions against indigent defendants until more funding became available. Because of lack of funding, public defenders in Calcasieu Parish carry caseloads at nearly four times the ABA recommended levels. Another account put the number in Calcasieu at almost six times the ABA limits. In Louisiana's Ninth Judicial District, public defenders have caseloads much closer to the ABA limit than in Calcasieu. But in the Ninth District it is estimated that nine more attorneys are nevertheless needed to meet the caseload burden.

3. Compensation

Of course, a great deal of funding for indigent defense goes into paying the attorneys representing the defendants. Depending on the type of indigent defense system used by a state or county, payment may be in the form of set salaries linked to full or part-time employment, or fees based on a contract rate, or on an hourly basis. And, as with the general funding issue, the question is whether the amount available is sufficient. The answer, generally, is no.

a. Fees

For court-appointed counsel, states or counties often set limits on the hourly rates and total compensation for the attorney. The most discussed, and criticized, system is Virginia's. Here there are "hard caps" on the amount a court-appointed attorney is to be paid, regardless of the length of the trial or the total hours she spent working on it. * * *

While court-appointed attorneys in Virginia may claim up to $90 per hour in fees, they are faced with the lowest payment cap in the nation, $1235. But, that total is only for attorneys representing defendants who face twenty years to life in prison; if the potential sentence is for fewer than twenty years in prison the cap is $395. And, for a misdemeanor punishable by jail time the cap is $112. These caps are not waivable. * * *

b. Salaries

In addition to fees and flat contract rate payments, there are thousands of public defenders who receive annual salaries. Salaried public defenders sometimes face paychecks that are less than their counterparts in prosecutor offices, despite an ABA-adopted standard that public defenders and prosecutors be paid at "comparable" rates. In many states the parity does exist. In others, however, the defense lawyers receive lower salaries.

In Baton Rouge, the twenty-seven attorneys earn between $18,000 and $35,000 annually, figures that are about 30% less than the salaries in the district attorney's office. Public defender salaries in Alameda County, California ranged much higher than in Baton Rouge, anywhere in excess of $50,000 to greater than $130,000, but the top prosecutor salaries there far exceeded those of the public defender office. In Georgia, entry-level district attorney and public defender positions both start out at the same annual salary, but the upper limit on the public defender salary scale is lower than that of the district attorney salary. The average salary for a Portland, Oregon public defender in 2000 was $45,426 compared to $61,638 for a prosecutor there.

The key problem may not necessarily be a disparity in salaries between prosecutors and defense lawyers, though such a disparity certainly exists in many parts of our country. Rather, the more serious dilemma may be that both sets of lawyers, at the state level, are paid too little. In many states, including Alaska, Maryland, Idaho, Mississippi, Ohio, Illinois, California, Massachusetts, and New Mexico, prosecuting and defending lawyers are paid less than $40,000 per year. * * *

B. The Special and Hidden Costs: Finding Lawyers to Represent Unpopular Clients

* * *

[N]ot all members of the public understand why an attorney should be willing to represent the accused. They may have little knowledge of a lawyer's professional obligations or the workings of an adversary system of justice. This creates the perception of lawyers as "hired guns," willing to represent anyone who can pay the fee (ironically, these difficult cases are often taken on appointment for little or no pay). This misperception leads to criticism, making it even harder to find attorneys willing to take on difficult cases. Large law firms may want to avoid being associated with unpopular causes because of the way it affects their professional image. Lawyers in smaller communities could risk losing a significant amount of business by defending someone unpopular in their community.

An attorney with political aspirations may have to worry about being labeled soft on crime and criticized for trying to help criminals exploit loopholes in the law. The 2005 Virginia gubernatorial race is a sad example of this. During the campaign, one of the candidates was criticized in print and in television ads for being an "ACLU lawyer" who defends death row inmates. The attorney, then state lieutenant governor, had handled two death-row appeals cases, though not with the ACLU. He was appointed counsel in both cases. The criticism was most unfortunate as it received wide coverage and it was so misguided. Death penalty appeals can be especially time consuming, difficult, and thankless. There is a great deal of pressure because a person's life is on the line. The pay, if any, is almost always well below what a lawyer could make in private practice. Taking on these cases shows the kind of character and professionalism that a lawyer should be able to cite with pride in an election campaign. * * *

D. Access to Counsel

Although constitutionally entitled to legal representation, a surprising number of indigent criminal defendants are denied counsel entirely. Referred to as "the dirty little secret of the criminal justice system," poor defendants are often pressured into pleading guilty, waiving their right to counsel or representing themselves without ever speaking to a lawyer about the merits of their case or the legal consequences of their actions. Stringent eligibility requirements, which can result in coerced self-representation, and the high incidence of defendants ill-advisedly waiving their right to counsel, systematically deprive poor defendants of their legal representation.

These routine practices, in addition to abuses of the plea bargaining process, dispose of cases quickly, but a crowded court docket moves along without regard for the rights of the accused. Shockingly, there are still areas of the country that simply fail to provide defense attorneys to certain classes of poor criminal defendants at all. * * *

1. Invalid Waiver as Denial

Despite the "obvious truth" that "lawyers in criminal courts are necessities, not luxuries," a defendant may choose to waive her right to counsel. To be valid however, a waiver must be voluntary, knowing and intelligent. Given the presumption against the waiver of fundamental constitutional rights, the judge has an obligation to make a thorough inquiry into the particular facts of the case, including the background, experience, and conduct of the accused before finding that a defendant has waived the right to an attorney. * * *

A city judge in Troy, New York was removed from the bench by the New York Commission on Judicial Conduct, in part for failing to advise defendants of their right to assigned counsel. He defended the practice of jailing defendants for several days without advising them of their right to counsel and then offering their freedom if they changed their plea to guilty. The judge explained at his disciplinary proceeding that he assumed the repeat offenders who came before him knew their rights, while others were not alert enough to understand what he would have said had he informed them of their rights. * * *

At times, the lack of a valid waiver goes beyond an individual judge's failure to make the appropriate inquiry and is systemic in nature. In the Rhode Island district courts, the arraignment process is so confusing defendants regularly waive counsel without an appreciation of what they are doing. During arraignment, a video tape explaining legal rights is played for a large group of defendants. The tape informs the defendants that they have a right to counsel and will be referred to the public defender if they cannot afford counsel. However, the video does not explain how or when the defendant can talk to the public defender. Some defendants may not even be aware that a public defender is a lawyer. After viewing the video, defendants are asked to enter a plea. The video does not explain that a not guilty plea must be entered before a defendant can be referred to the public defender. Many are under the impression that they must assert once and for all whether they are guilty or innocent. Most do not realize a not guilty plea can be changed after meeting with a lawyer. Throughout this process the defendants are not asked whether they want to waive their right to counsel. "The judge will generally make no inquiry whatsoever into the defendant's background, the defendant's educational history, the defendant's mental or physical condition, or the defendant's prior dealings with attorneys." * * *

2. Abuse of Plea Bargains

Invalid waivers of counsel are frequently linked to plea bargain abuse. Few defendants waive counsel with the intention of representing themselves at a trial. Rather, most waive counsel and immediately plead guilty to take advantage of a deal being offered by the prosecutor or judge. Observers of Georgia courts describe a process involving mass arraignments in which groups of defendants are informed of their rights by a judge. The judge then leaves the courtroom and the prosecutors take over. Each defendant lines up to meet privately with the prosecutor. Once each defendant has met with the prosecutor, the judge returns. At this point every defendant informs the judge that he would like to waive counsel and plead guilty.

Despite national standards that call for judges to refrain from participating in plea negotiations, judges sometimes play a more active role in the plea bargain process in order to resolve cases efficiently. The Troy, New York judge described above used a combination of exorbitant bail and a taste of jail to coerce defendants into pleading guilty. If a defendant indicated that she wanted to retain counsel or that she was too poor to do so, the judge set excessive bail and adjourned the case for a few days. Upon return to court, the judge asked whether the defendant would like to change the plea to guilty and be released. Most did, of course. This judge handled more than 3000 criminal cases a year, but in a three-year period, presided over only four trials. In upholding the judge's removal from the bench, the majority of a deeply divided New York Court of Appeals found that "coupled with a failure to advise these defendants of their right to assigned counsel, [the judge's] imposition of punitive bail all but guaranteed that defendants would be coerced into pleading guilty: it was the only way to get out of jail." * * *

Even when defendants manage to get court-appointed counsel it does not guarantee they will avoid being pressured into plea bargains. * * * "[M]eet 'em and plead 'em lawyers," in the interest of speed and efficiency, may encourage a plea bargain that is not be the best choice for a defendant. Heavy caseloads, per-case fees, and payment caps create incentives for appointed counsel to dispose of cases as quickly as possible. For example, an attorney in Georgia working on a fixed contract model only went to trial three times in a four-year span. Over this same span, his clients pleaded guilty 313 times. It seems unlikely that all 313 defendants were best served by pleading guilty. This is especially true in light of the fact that many guilty pleas were entered after only a few minutes of discussion between the attorney and client.

3. Eligibility Standards

Although states have an obligation to provide attorneys for poor criminal defendants, neither *Gideon* nor the right to counsel cases that followed have offered any guidelines for determining who qualifies for court-appointed counsel. * * * The myriad approaches to determining ency that states have employed, and the wide variations in how principles are enforced, result in unequal access to counsel across the nation. In short, a poor defendant denied appointed counsel in one state might be entitled to appointed counsel had she been charged in another jurisdiction.

In Wisconsin, a defendant must make $3000 or less to be appointed counsel. A person can qualify for food stamps and Medicaid but be ruled wealthy enough to retain his own attorney. It is estimated that each year 11,000 people who would be appointed counsel by standards used in other states are denied counsel by the state of Wisconsin. A judge in Kittitas County, Washington routinely denies counsel for college students because in his view an "able-bodied, employable young person with no dependents and virtually no debt [who] chooses to forgo available employment so that he can attain an college degree" is outside the definition of indigent. In one case, an unsuccessful defendant there had an annual income of $3600. In another instance, a judge denied appointed representation to a poor defendant when the contract lawyer questioned the defendant's eligibility because he had failed to list his wedding ring, a necklace and a wristwatch as assets on the application he submitted for representation.

Limiting eligibility to only the absolute destitute denies representation to a huge stratum of the population that is excluded from public counsel, but unable to afford private attorneys. As a result, these defendants have to go to extreme measures to secure counsel. James Daringer, a defendant accused of arson, found himself in this situation. He had a job earning $21,000 per year, so he did not qualify for court-appointed counsel, but because of debts and other liabilities he did not have enough money to hire a lawyer. He had to choose between representing himself in court and quitting his job so he could qualify for a public defender. Facing up to seven years in prison, Daringer chose to quit his job so he would meet the eligibility standards for the public defenders' office. * * *

E. Ethics and Professional Responsibility

The challenges facing defenders, including overwhelming caseloads, lack of supervision and training, inadequate compensation and resources, and political pressure, all raise significant ethical issues for defense attorneys, prosecutors, and judges. Although professional standards for defenders are clear, systemic deficiencies push defenders to compromise their efforts on behalf of clients. These questionable compromises undermine ethical standards and, in turn, contribute to the denigration of the legal profession and the criminal justice system. Judges, prosecutors, lawyer disciplinary bodies, and defenders themselves are loath to call attention to these ethical failings. As one notable commentator concluded, "there is a huge chasm between what ethics rules demand and how lawyers actually represent indigent defendants." * * *

Ethically a lawyer is required to serve her clients with competence and diligence. The lawyer must be thorough, adequately prepared, and a zealous advocate on behalf of the client's interests. Regular communication is expected in order to keep the client reasonably informed and to respond to the client's reasonable requests for information. In addition, a lawyer is required to consult with the client regarding how the lawyer will pursue important objectives and to explain matters to clients so that they may make informed decisions.

In practice, the average lawyer working in an overburdened public defender office, or as an appointed or contract attorney whose compensation is so anemic that the hourly wage barely covers overhead expenses, may do none of these things. The problem arises, for instance, with a lawyer carrying a misdemeanor caseload three times the size of the national recommended standards, who meets a client for the first time just before court is called into session. That attorney simply does not have the time or the resources to investigate, prepare, or communicate adequately with the client so that the client can make an informed decision and the attorney can advocate zealously for his client's best interests. Even where the matters are not complex, sheer volume can preclude anything other than an assembly line approach, which falls far short of professional standards. Such is the case for the two contract defenders in Allen County, Indiana, who were assigned 2668 misdemeanor cases last year. Each attorney makes less than $2000 a month and maintains a private practice on the side. Not surprisingly, the overwhelming majority of defendants plead guilty; only twelve went to trial in a year. * * *

The recent ABA report assessing the status of *Gideon*'s mandate across the nation * * * found that "defense lawyers throughout the country are violating these ethical rules by failing to provide competent, diligent, continuous, and conflict-free representation." As disturbing as it is to suggest that ethical violations are commonplace, it is even more alarming that courts and disciplinary authorities routinely overlook these breaches of professional ethics. The likelihood of any individual defender being subjected to discipline for violation of the minimum levels of competence or zealousness is small. Most disciplinary agencies seem reluctant to bring charges against defenders whose conduct breaches ethical rules, perhaps because it seems unfair to blame an individual attorney when the failings are more a function of systemic inadequacies. The reluctance to sanction defenders of the indigent may also reflect the concern that sanctions could discourage other lawyers from accepting cases of indigent defendants. Such a result would exacerbate the problem of an already short supply of attorneys willing to take on this type of work.

Another possible ethics enforcement mechanism, malpractice actions by defendants, is likely to be as unavailing as recourse to lawyer disciplinary bodies has been. Many states require that a plaintiff must first succeed in obtaining post-conviction relief for ineffective assistance of counsel before bringing a malpractice claim. Moreover, some courts, including some that require post-conviction relief, have held that the plaintiff must effectively demonstrate her actual innocence, not just that she would have been acquitted save for the attorney's negligence. * * *

The Supreme Court established a two-part test for determining when counsel is constitutionally ineffective in its 1984 decision in *Strickland v. Washington*. First, "a convicted defendant [who] complains of the ineffectiveness of counsel's assistance . . . must show that counsel's representation fell below an objective standard of reasonableness." There are no specific guidelines for determining whether counsel meets an objective standard of reasonableness. Instead, "[t]he proper measure of attorney performance remains simply reasonableness under prevailing professional norms . . . considering all the circumstances." The second element of an ineffective assistance of counsel claim is that "any deficiencies in counsel's performance must be prejudicial to the defense." To satisfy the prejudice prong, the "defendant must show that there is a reasonable probability that, but for counsel's unprofessional errors, the result of that proceeding would have been different. Reasonable probability is a probability sufficient to undermine confidence in the outcome."

Despite some strong rhetoric in support of competent representation, chilling examples abound of abysmal representation that was nevertheless upheld under this constitutional test. Unbelievably, courts have relied upon *Strickland* to refuse to find ineffective assistance of counsel even where the defense attorney was silent during the entire trial, shared delusions about his involvement in a murder conspiracy with the jury, or was arrested on the way to the courthouse for driving with a .27 blood-alcohol content.

Not surprisingly, the two-prong *Strickland* test has been widely criticized as betraying the promise of *Gideon*. In practice the test is nearly impossible to meet. Thus, as courts continue to apply the demands of the analysis to attorney performance, the definition of acceptable lawyer behavior departs further and further from ethical standards and substandard lawyering is routinely upheld. * * *

VII. Recommendations

State and local governments have had more than forty years to respond to *Gideon*'s trumpet call, yet the evidence is overwhelming and undeniable that many states have simply failed to meet their constitutional obligation to provide competent legal representation to criminal defendants who are unable to afford an attorney. The comprehensive national research by the National Committee on the Right to Counsel provides compelling support for the conclusion that that we have a true constitutional crisis. * * *

A. Independent Structure Recommendation 1: Establishing an independent, statewide nonpartisan authority responsible for the defense function should be the cornerstone of any reform of a state's indigent defense system. * * *

In addition to insulating the defense function from political and judicial pressures, a statewide oversight entity provides a mechanism for achieving many of the key components of an effective public defense delivery system and should:

- establish attorney qualification standards;
- coordinate eligibility standards to ensure consistency of access to public representation;
- facilitate appropriate appointments, matching attorney experience with the complexity of the cases;
- monitor and evaluate attorney performance and track caseloads;
- develop and provide training, both to entry-level defenders and advanced practitioners;
- provide access to technology and other resources; and
- serve as an advocate in the political process and provide a voice for the support of indigent defense. * * *

B. Competent Attorneys Recommendation 2: States must establish and enforce standards for attorneys who represent poor criminal defendants, including minimum qualifications, training, and performance requirements.

Without competent attorneys, no system of public representation of poor defendants will be successful. Regardless of the type of delivery system a state chooses to provide indigent defense services—contract, court-appointed, public defender or some hybrid—states should ensure that each defense attorney has at least minimum qualifications in criminal defense. * * *

C. Caseloads Recommendation 3: States must establish and enforce appropriate workload limits to prevent the overburdening of defenders and avoid undermining the quality of representation they are able to deliver. * * *

1. Caseload Standards

To ensure that defenders have sufficient time to devote to each client, states must control workloads. The most direct route is to establish caseload limits. * * *

2. Decriminalization to Reduce Crowded Dockets

States can take steps to reduce crowded dockets by decriminalizing certain non-serious misdemeanors, e.g., operating a vehicle with a suspended license, or with no license or insurance; shoplifting; disorderly conduct; disturbing the peace; or trespassing. States could reevaluate those misdemeanors that carry possible jail time, but for which incarceration is rarely sought or imposed, and treat them as civil infractions. This would serve several purposes. By reducing crowded court dockets, decriminalization can relieve some of the pressure on courts to move cases through the system quickly at any cost. In turn, this would provide judges with additional time to devote to more serious cases. In addition, removing these cases from the criminal docket would lighten the caseload of defenders and prosecutors, and also reduce the funds needed to provide state-funded defenders. The savings could then be used to fund other needs in a resource-starved defense system.

3. Alternative Justice Programs

States could expand the use of alternative justice programs such as diversion into drug courts, mental health courts, or alternative treatment programs. Problem-solving courts, such as community, domestic violence, drug, and mental health courts, may hold promise for reducing caseloads.* * *

D. Compensation Recommendation 4: Fair compensation, including adequate overhead and a fair fee, should be paid to all publicly funded defenders. * * *

In pursuing this goal of fair compensation, states should consider:

1. Salary Parity with Equivalent Prosecution Attorneys (Where Prosecutors are Fairly Compensated)

Salary parity is more than just a question of economic fairness. Parity also eliminates the appearance that the government values the defense function is valued less than the prosecution function. Equalizing compensation between defenders and prosecutors acknowledges the equivalent roles the two play in the criminal justice system.

2. Law Student-Loan Forgiveness Programs for Public Defenders and Prosecutors

Low pay and significant law school student-loan debt leave many defenders and prosecutors struggling financially and discourage many talented lawyers from careers in public service. Loan forgiveness programs, similar to those offered to doctors, nurses, and teachers, reduce a certain portion of student-loan debt for those who work in underserved areas. This would make it easier to attract and keep good, experienced lawyers as public defenders and prosecutors.

E. Proper Tools Recommendation 5: States must equip their indigent defense systems with the appropriate tools to enable a defender to deliver competent representation. This includes staff support, such as investigators, paralegals, and secretaries; technology and research capabilities; and access to independent experts and other professional services. * * *

2. Federal Resources

The federal government should establish an independent, federally funded defender resource center to assist and strengthen state and local indigent defense systems. Such a center could help states provide competent criminal representation for poor defendants by offering training, support, research assistance, brief and motion banks, advice on identifying and using experts and other services. * * *

VIII. Generating Reform

The essential recommendations outlined above * * * are neither new nor particularly visionary. We know how to structure, staff and fund an effective indigent system. Despite four decades of repeated calls for reform, many states have failed to take action. The challenge is not in knowing what to do to address the indigent defense crisis, but rather how to compel state legislatures and executives to establish, fund, and support a constitutionally adequate indigent defense system. Unfortunately, appealing to constitutional sensitivities has not worked in the face of strained state budgets, political pressures, a lack of a constituency to advocate for poor criminal defendants, and the popularity of "tough on crime" rhetoric. * * *

The task of protecting the rights of poor defendants, and thus ensuring the fairness of our courts, the legitimacy of criminal convictions and the integrity of criminal justice, requires the concerted effort of all. Federal, state and local governments, prosecutors, defenders, judges, bar and professional associations, law firms, law schools, and the media all have a role to play in upholding the promise of *Gideon*.

LAWYERING AND LEARNING IN PROBLEM-SOLVING COURTS

Paul Holland

34 Wash. U. J.L. & Pol'y 185 (2010)

* * *

In a problem-solving drug court, defendants are assessed to determine whether their alleged criminal conduct was linked to untreated substance abuse. In exchange for the opportunity to receive treatment as part of the process of resolving their criminal case, defendants are required to submit to an extended period of judicial supervision during which interim sanctions (including short jail stays) may be imposed or rewards could be granted. Those who succeed have their charges reduced or dismissed or their convictions vacated. Failure, if prolonged or severe enough to warrant termination from the program, results in traditional sanctions.

The introduction of the problem-solving drug court was more a matter of pragmatic improvisation than methodical theoretical design. In time, this innovation and the political movement behind it became enmeshed with the developing theory of therapeutic jurisprudence. The central premises of therapeutic jurisprudence are that interactions with the justice system necessarily have an impact on an individual's psychological or emotional well-being and that the system should be designed to minimize emotional or psychological harm and maximize benefit to the extent possible consistent with other system objectives. Viewed in this light, the traditional handling of drug-related cases amounted to a significant missed opportunity for personal transformation and community improvement.

The extent to which this therapeutic orientation has come to define the problem-solving approach is evident from this reflection from a defense attorney practicing in a mental health court (i.e., a court addressing crimes allegedly committed by the mentally ill):

> Recently, the judge, the social worker, the assistant district attorney, and I discussed with each other and with the client her need for hospitalization. She was so depressed that she did not have the strength to take her medication as the judge had ordered. The kindness and compassion that were expressed towards this woman stood in stark contrast to what would be more likely to occur in another courtroom—the shackling of a client and removal of that person to jail for failing to comply with the judge's directive.

A close look at this description reveals the extent to which problem-solving justice reorients the judicial process. The comment focuses on the client's "need" and the professionals' goodwill (i.e., their "kindness and compassion"). There is no discussion of the defendant's guilt or the lawyers' (or judge's) analysis. The verbs used—specifically, "discussed" and "expressed"—describe activities more closely associated with a therapist's office than a courtroom, such as the hypothetical courtroom that the defender invokes for contrast, in which the primary issue is the defendant's action (or failure to act) and in which the judge wields power bluntly, constrained to do little but order merciless (or at the very least, dispassionate) shackling.

B. Problem-Solving Judging: Performing Authority

The fusion of justice and therapy in problem-solving courts has altered the roles and relationships of all participants. As put in its strongest form by two drug court proponents, "[t]he drug offender becomes a client of the court, and judge, prosecutor, and defense counsel must shed their traditional roles and take on roles that will facilitate an offender's recovery from the disease of addiction." Seeing a defendant as "a client of the court" marks a radical change from the traditional notion of the judge as a "detached, neutral referee." The "client of the court" label also connotes a consumerist understanding of the defendant's experience which further situates problem-solving courts within the "dominant strain(s)" of modern American culture. The defendant, the person whose alleged unlawful actions have given rise to the proceedings, can assert a legitimate expectation of receiving services from the process.

Judges in these courts do not spend much time performing traditional judicial tasks, such as finding facts and interpreting law. Instead, they "verify that the exhaustive information on the progress of each defendant . . . comports with [their] own perception and . . . ritualize the imposition of graduated rewards or punishments. Instead of assessing contested stories from competing parties, the judge typically receives a consensus report from the court "team." The report offers a summary of the participant's performance since he or she was last before the court. It is this report, produced through the pre-hearing staffing process, described more within, that the judge must verify when he or she encounters the "client" herself. This verification is not merely a matter of establishing or checking facts. Indeed, the judge's task is more complex, not readily discernible by clear proof nor reducible to a conclusive articulation. The judge is essentially assessing the person's commitment to and capacity for transformation, something that neither legal education nor judicial experience necessarily prepares the judge to do. Assuming the judge determines that the team's report has accurately charted the participant's compliance, the judge's task is to communicate with the participant in a way that induces the desired future behavior (specifically, consistency for those who are succeeding, and change for those who are struggling). * * *

Problem-solving court judges can exercise artful directorial control over their calendars because of the work done in the pre-court meetings, events that have no analog in conventional courts. At these meetings, representatives of the court (judge, probation officers, and other court services personnel), lawyers for the state and the defendant/participant, and affiliated treatment providers share information about each participant and discuss what action the court should take. Options range from termination (with traditional punishment) to successful discharge or, as it is often termed, "graduation." Most of the time, of course, the team must address the broad array of options in between. Should the participant receive additional services? Is some intermediate sanction necessary? Should previously imposed restrictions be eased as a reward for progress toward treatment goals? * * *

Timothy Casey, defender and clinician, decries the loss of exclusivity and primary responsibility for the client's fate when "problem-solving courts . . . remove the attorney from the process." Defense attorneys are literally present, but they are no longer the distinctive protective and potentially disruptive force [that they are in conventional proceedings]. Problem-solving court defendants must interact directly with a range of others who share responsibility for their success. Tamar Meekins, another defender-turned-clinical teacher, laments the devaluing of the attorney-client relationship that results when "the non-legal team members may have greater interaction with, or develop a closer relationship to, the defendant than the defense attorney." Like Casey, Meekins sees defense counsel without "a functional representational role" in problem-solving courts. Meekins identifies an equally grave danger in the relationships that the defender, supplanted from primacy in the client's eyes, is likely to develop with other court actors: "[T]he defender's ability to represent her client might be materially limited because of the lawyer's personal interest in maintaining professional relationships with other members of the team."

Deprived of the galvanizing contests that mark the days of a trial lawyer, defenders in problem-solving courts nevertheless perform distinctive and vital tasks. Their work begins with the defendant's decision to enter a problem-solving court program. This threshold moment has its obvious therapeutic implications, but a lawyer's priorities at this point ought to be fairly conventional, i.e., ensuring that defendants receive full information, candid advice, and time to make a considered decision. [Bruce] Wexler suggests that defendants be allowed, even encouraged, to watch problem-solving court proceedings and even visit service providers before making their decision. Wexler imagines that "[a] lawyer, or paralegal, might play an important role in maximizing the vicarious learning by sitting through the session and explaining to the . . . client exactly what is happening." These tasks are not as dramatic as cross-examining a witness or delivering a closing argument, but they can be quite challenging, especially for defenders in transition to the new role. The defender must be capable of representing the process to the client without unduly promoting the court or cynically tearing it down. Counsel should likewise assume a traditional posture when a client is facing termination from a problem-solving court. At that moment, the court has ceased working to solve the client's underlying problem and is deciding merely the amount of sanctions to impose once and for all. At all points between entry and exit (successful or otherwise), the defender must continue the effort to maintain balance and clarity, as described by Jane Spinak, a clinician and defender with considerable experience with alternative courts:

> A more nuanced role is required of the defender, combining, at a minimum, her understanding of the individual client, the client's legal status, the effectiveness of the client's treatment, and the multiple messages the other participants are sending, so that each time the defender can determine, with the client, the appropriate response.

* * * The problem-solving court community is intended to work constructively rather than competitively. Relationships between any two members (e.g., those between judge and participant or defense counsel and probation officer) need not interfere with or detract from other relationships (e.g., that between defense counsel and client). Instead, the multiple ties reinforce each other. The defense lawyer is better able to communicate with and advocate for the client because of her rapport with other community members, and the client is better able to take advantage of the lawyer's advice because of reduced dependence upon it. Unlike representation in a trial paradigm, where everything hinges on a single contest, representation in a problem-solving court is a continuous campaign, requiring coordination—and far more sharing of responsibility—between lawyer and client. Even more important than their increased in-court speaking role, clients embody their case directly through interactions outside of counsel's presence, let alone control. Nevertheless, counsel has a vital role to play in helping the client prepare for these interactions. Just as lawyers traditionally prepare a client to testify, they can also role-play meetings with treatment court actors. These sessions are more difficult to simulate than virtually any cross-examination because they are not governed by a well-defined set of rules in the way that evidentiary hearings are. Defender offices, perhaps assisted by law clinics, might need to develop protocols with non-lawyer professionals from other disciplines in order to provide their clients with the greatest chance for success.

This preparatory role-playing is only superficially similar to preparing a client to testify or otherwise appear in court. Trial lawyers are taught that a first impression can be the difference between winning and losing. In problem-solving courts, however, where participants will have repeated and extended exposure to the judge and other influential actors, a good first impression is merely a nice start. It will be of little long-term benefit if the client is not able to achieve and maintain the substantial and long-term behavior change that is the court's objective. Defense counsel's ability to attain a distinctive "understanding of the individual client," to use Spinak's phrase, can prove highly valuable in keeping the client on track and keeping other court actors invested in the client's success. This is a less triumphal vision than that of a * * * champion, but it is neither less important nor less difficult.

RESTORATIVE JUSTICE IN THE TWENTY-FIRST CENTURY: A SOCIAL MOVEMENT FULL OF OPPORTUNITIES AND PITFALLS

Mark S. Umbreit, Betty Vos, Robert B. Coates, Elizabeth Lightfoot
89 Marq. L. Rev. 251 (2005)

Most contemporary criminal justice systems focus on law violation, the need to hold offenders accountable and punish them, and other state interests. Actual crime victims are quite subsidiary to the process and generally have no legal standing in the proceedings. Crime is viewed as having been committed against the state, which, therefore, essentially owns the conflict and determines how to respond to it. The resulting criminal justice system is almost entirely offender driven.

Restorative justice offers a very different way of understanding and responding to crime. Instead of viewing the state as the primary victim in criminal acts and placing victims, offenders, and the community in passive roles, restorative justice recognizes crime as being directed against individual people. It is grounded in the belief that those most affected by crime should have the opportunity to become actively involved in resolving the conflict. Repairing harm and restoring losses, allowing offenders to take direct responsibility for their actions, and assisting victims to move beyond vulnerability towards some degree of closure stand in sharp contrast to the values and practices of the conventional criminal justice system with its focus on past criminal behavior through ever-increasing levels of punishment. * * *

Restorative justice values, principles, and practices hearken back to * * * earlier paradigms, not only in British and American history, but also in numerous indigenous cultures throughout the world. Among these are many Native American tribes within the United States, the Aboriginal or First Nation people of Canada, the Maori in New Zealand, Native Hawaiians, African tribal councils, the Afghani practice of jirga, the Arab or Palestinian practice of Sulha, and many of the ancient Celtic practices found in the Brehon laws.

In addition, the values of restorative justice are deeply rooted in the ancient principles of Judeo-Christian culture that have always emphasized crime as being a violation against people and families, rather than "the state." * * *

The most succinct definition of restorative justice is offered by Howard Zehr, whom many consider the leading visionary and architect of the restorative justice movement. His seminal book, *Changing Lenses*, provided the conceptual framework for the movement and has influenced policy makers and practitioners throughout the world. According to Zehr, "Restorative justice is a process to involve, to the extent possible, those who have a stake in a specific offense and to collectively identify and address harms, needs, and obligations, in order to heal and put things as right as possible."

Instead of focusing upon the weaknesses or deficits of offenders and crime victims, restorative justice attempts to draw upon the strengths of these individuals and their capacity to openly address the need to repair the harm caused. Restorative justice denounces criminal behavior yet emphasizes the need to treat offenders with respect and to reintegrate them into the larger community in ways that can lead to lawful behavior.

From a restorative perspective, the primary stakeholders are understood to be individual victims and their families, victimized communities, and offenders and their families. The state and its legal justice system also clearly have an interest as a stakeholder but are seen as more removed from direct impact. Thus the needs of those most directly affected by the crime come first. Wherever possible, opportunities for direct engagement in the process of doing justice through various forms of dialogue are central to the practice of restorative justice.

Like many reform movements, in its early years the restorative justice movement focused on contrasting its values and principles with those of the status quo. The phrase "retributive justice" emerged to describe the conventional criminal justice system approach, particularly regarding its emphasis on offenders getting what they deserved.

Following more than twenty-five years of practice, research, and continuing analysis, Zehr has come to a different understanding, stating that such a sharp polarization between retributive and restorative justice is somewhat misleading. The philosopher of law, Conrad Brunk, argues that on a theoretical level, retribution and restoration are not the polar opposites that many assume. He notes that both actually have much in common: a desire to vindicate by some type of reciprocal action and some type of proportional relationship between the criminal act and the response to it. Retributive theory and restorative theory, however, differ significantly in how to "even the score"—how to make things right. Retributive theory holds that the imposition of some form of pain will vindicate, most frequently deprivation of liberty and even loss of life in some cases. Restorative theory argues that "what truly vindicates is acknowledgement of victims' harms and needs, combined with an active effort to encourage offenders to take responsibility, make right the wrongs, and address the causes of their behavior." * * *

The conventional criminal justice system focuses upon three questions: (1) What laws have been broken?; (2) Who did it?; and (3) What do they deserve? From a restorative justice perspective, an entirely different set of questions are asked: (1) Who has been hurt?; (2) What are their needs?; and (3) Whose obligations are these?

Restorative justice is not a list of specific programs or a clear blueprint for systemic change. It requires a radically different way of viewing, understanding, and responding to the presence of crime within our communities. Thus, an increased interest is emerging in addressing the broader, system-level implications of restorative justice principles. Among others, Braithwaite speaks of restorative justice with these larger dimensions in mind, emphasizing that restorative justice is far more than reforming the criminal justice system. It offers a way of transforming the entire legal system, while also impacting family life, workplace behavior, and even political conduct. Braithwaite's vision of restorative justice is nothing less than changing the way we do justice in the world. * * *

1. Program Examples

In Orange County, California, a victim-offender mediation and conferencing program receives nearly one thousand referrals of juvenile offenders and their victims each year. This program is supported by a large government grant and provides much needed support, assistance, and restoration for victims of crime, while also holding these young people accountable to their communities. By diverting these cases from further penetration into the justice system, if the victim's needs are met, the county also benefits from a significant cost reduction in the already overcrowded court system. The program in Orange County is part of a much larger network of more than 1500 victim-offender mediation and conferencing programs in seventeen countries, working with both juvenile and adult courts.

In several United States cities, prosecuting attorney offices routinely offer choices for victims of crime to actively participate in the justice system, to participate in restorative dialogue with the offender and others affected by the crime, and to meet whatever other needs these individuals are facing. A program in Indianapolis works closely with the police department in offering family group conferencing services in which young offenders and their families meet the individuals they have victimized and work toward repairing the harm, resulting in a significant reduction in recidivism among these offenders.

Another dialogue-based format was creatively used in Eugene, Oregon, following a hate crime against the local Muslim community that occurred within hours of the September 11 attacks. The prosecutor's office gave the victimized representatives of the Muslim community a choice of either following the conventional path of prosecution and severe punishment or the restorative justice path of participating in a neighborhood accountability board including face-to-face conversations with the offender and others in the community who were affected by this crime. The victims elected to meet in dialogue; together they were able to talk openly about the full impact of this hate crime and to develop a specific plan to repair the harm and promote a greater sense of tolerance and peace within the community.

In several jurisdictions, restorative justice procedures are being used to enable ethnic communities to access elements of their traditional means of handling infractions and breaches of trust among themselves. The Hmong peacemaking circles in St. Paul, Minnesota, receive referrals from local judges in cases involving Hmong participants so that the offense is handled in a more culturally appropriate way that fosters peacemaking and accountability. In Canada, aboriginal groups are utilizing the circle format of restorative justice dialogue to handle a wide range of offenses within the community.

Restorative justice dialogue responses are increasingly being offered to victims of severe and violent crime, driven by requests from victims for such opportunities. Departments of corrections in Texas, Ohio, Pennsylvania, and several other states have initiated statewide victim-offender mediation and dialogue programs through their victim services units. In such programs, victims of severe violence, including homicide, meet in facilitated dialogue with the offenders who have harmed them as part of their search for meaning and some measure of closure in the wake of trauma. A retired Wisconsin Supreme Court Justice facilitates dialogue groups in a state prison among prisoners and with several victims of severe violence in an effort to ingrain the full human impact of the prisoners' behavior upon victims and their communities.

Most recently, restorative practices are emerging as part of the healing process for victims of political violence. The Truth and Reconciliation Commission hearings in South Africa were established to foster national healing in the wake of severe violent political conflict as the apartheid system of racial segregation and oppression was dismantled. A victim-offender mediation was held in Israel between two Israeli-Palestinian youth and a young Israeli mother who had been assaulted and robbed; families of both the offenders and the victim were involved. Both the Jewish and the Palestinian communities actively participated and forged a path toward greater understanding, accountability, and mutual respect. And in the last few years, a former prisoner who was an icon of the Irish Republican Army ("IRA") movement in Northern Ireland met face-to-face with the daughter of one of the men he killed in their joint search for greater understanding, meaning, and peace in their lives.

2. Systemic Change Examples

As many advocates point out, restorative justice is a process, not a program. Therefore, some proponents are hopeful that a restorative justice framework can be used to foster systemic change, and such changes are beginning to occur. For example, within Minnesota, the State Department of Corrections established a policy to handle letters of apology by prisoners to their victims in a highly restorative and victim-centered manner. It encouraged and assisted prisoners who wanted to write such letters. The letters were then deposited in a victim apology letter bank in the central office for viewing by the prisoners' victims who were willing to read the letters.

Broad systemic change initiatives have been undertaken in a number of other countries. For example, in 1988 Austria adopted federal legislation that promoted the use of victim-offender mediation throughout the country. In 1989 legislation was adopted in New Zealand that totally restructured its youth justice system based on the traditional practices of its indigenous people, the Maori, and principles consistent with restorative justice. The largest volume of youth justice cases now go to family group conferences, rather than to court. This change has resulted in a significant reduction in both court cases and incarcerations, with no evidence of increased recidivism. And a nationwide systemic change effort has been undertaken in the United Kingdom through its policy commitment to adopt restorative justice principles and practices throughout the country. These changes are focused on increased participation by crime victims, youth accountability boards, and different forms of victim-offender mediation and dialogue. * * *

B. Opportunities for Expanding the Vision

* * * [M]any opportunities for new and widened impact * * * are listed below; many others continue to emerge.

Initiating a system-wide commitment to providing local citizens who are victimized by all but the most serious violent crime. Both parties would retain the legal right to go before the formal criminal or juvenile justice system if either felt that they were not treated fairly or were dissatisfied with the outcome of the restorative justice intervention. Such a policy would place restorative justice in the forefront of our collective response to crime, rather than consigning it to a marginal position as an option for only a select number of individuals. This policy would also result in huge cost savings.

Developing an increasing number of hybrids that integrate the strengths and limitations of each individual restorative justice intervention. For example, in more serious cases the use of victim-offender mediation on a small or intimate level could first be offered to the specific victim and offender. This could be followed by a session involving a number of family members and support people. Then, even this could be followed at a later time with a much larger community intervention involving a peacemaking circle of perhaps twenty to thirty individuals. Case examples of such combinations go all the way back to the experience of Genesee County, New York, in responding to a sniper shooting case in the early 1980s. Examples also include a more recent case in Dakota County, Minnesota in which the response to a pipe bomb incident by students in a high school resulted in combining elements of victim-offender mediation, family group conferencing, and a community peacemaking circle.

Increasing the use of surrogate victim-offender community dialogue. Encounters with surrogates can be a partial response to the large volume of crime victims whose offenders are never caught. Such victims are equally in need of gaining a greater understanding of why people commit such crimes and letting others in the community know about the impact on their lives. Often, they also find it beneficial to help hold other similar offenders accountable for their actions even though their own offender was never caught. Dialogue groups in prisons and other correctional facilities that include offenders, victims of similar crimes, and community members have been shown to benefit all who are involved at a relatively low cost. Examples of this exist in the states of Minnesota, Washington, and Wisconsin.

Applying restorative justice principles and practices in school settings from elementary level through college. Examples of this include the use of peacemaking circles to deal with student conflicts in an entire school district in Minnesota and other schools throughout the country that use various forms of victim-offender mediation, peer mediation, family group conferencing, circles, or other types of restorative dialogue. * * *

Offering more support for victims of severe violence. This would include greatly expanding the opportunities for victim-offender dialogue for those victims who seek to meet. It would also involve much wider use of victim intervention projects that respond to the needs of victims immediately, whether or not there ever is any direct engagement with the offender.

Developing strong legislative support for public resources being appropriated to support the restorative justice movement, based on evidence of its effectiveness in reducing recidivism, cutting costs, and increasing victim and citizen satisfaction with the justice process. Such initiatives would also involve building stronger alliances with the crime victim advocacy community through focusing on joint interests between restorative justice advocates and crime victim advocates.

Building ever-increasing bridges between the dominant culture and the many ethnic groups and communities of color within our society. One approach already being utilized is that of tapping into the ancient wisdom among many indigenous people, who have for centuries practiced elements of what today is called restorative justice.

Using the principles of restorative justice to engage in a new framework for research on the public policy and human impact of the death penalty.

Strengthening the very fabric of community and civic responsibility through increasing involvement of neighbors and citizens in restorative community-based justice initiatives that provide opportunities for more frequent and meaningful contact with each other in activities that benefit all of society.

V. Conclusion

The restorative justice movement is having an increasing impact upon criminal justice system policymakers and practitioners throughout the world. As a relatively young reform effort, the restorative justice movement holds a great deal of promise as we enter the twenty-first century. By drawing upon many traditional values of the past, from many different cultures, we have the opportunity to build a far more accountable, understandable, and healing system of justice and law that can lead to a greater sense of community through active victim and citizen involvement in restorative initiatives.

APPENDIX

MODEL PENAL CODE

■ ■ ■

PART I. GENERAL PROVISIONS

ARTICLE 1. PRELIMINARY

* * *

Section 1.02. Purposes; Principles of Construction.

(1) The general purposes of the provisions governing the definition of offenses are:

(a) to forbid and prevent conduct that unjustifiably and inexcusably inflicts or threatens substantial harm to individual or public interests;

(b) to subject to public control persons whose conduct indicates that they are disposed to commit crimes;

(c) to safeguard conduct that is without fault from condemnation as criminal;

(d) to give fair warning of the nature of the conduct declared to constitute an offense;

(e) to differentiate on reasonable grounds between serious and minor offenses.

(2) The general purposes of the provisions governing the sentencing and treatment of offenders are:

(a) to prevent the commission of offenses;

(b) to promote the correction and rehabilitation of offenders;

(c) to safeguard offenders against excessive, disproportionate or arbitrary punishment;

(d) to give fair warning of the nature of the sentences that may be imposed on conviction of an offense;

(e) to differentiate among offenders with a view to a just individualization in their treatment;

(f) to define, coordinate and harmonize the powers, duties and functions of the courts and of administrative officers and agencies responsible for dealing with offenders;

(g) to advance the use of generally accepted scientific methods and knowledge in the sentencing and treatment of offenders;

(h) to integrate responsibility for the administration of the correctional system in a State Department of Correction [or other single department or agency].

(3) The provisions of the Code shall be construed according to the fair import of their terms but when the language is susceptible of differing constructions it shall be interpreted to further the general purposes stated in this Section and the special purposes of the particular provision involved. The discretionary powers conferred by the Code shall be exercised in accordance with the criteria stated in the Code and, insofar as such criteria are not decisive, to further the general purposes stated in this Section. * * *

Section 1.04. Classes of Crimes; Violations.

(1) An offense defined by this Code or by any other statute of this State, for which a sentence of [death or of] imprisonment is authorized, constitutes a crime. Crimes are classified as felonies, misdemeanors or petty misdemeanors.

(2) A crime is a felony if it is so designated in this Code or if persons convicted thereof may be sentenced [to death or] to imprisonment for a term that, apart from an extended term, is in excess of one year.

(3) A crime is a misdemeanor if it is so designated in this Code or in a statute other than this Code enacted subsequent thereto.

(4) A crime is a petty misdemeanor if it is so designated in this Code or in a statute other than this Code enacted subsequent thereto or if it is defined by a statute other than this Code that now provides that persons convicted thereof may be sentenced to imprisonment for a term of which the maximum is less than one year.

(5) An offense defined by this Code or by any other statute of this State constitutes a violation if it is so designated in this Code or in the law defining the offense or if no other sentence than a fine, or fine and forfeiture or other civil penalty is authorized upon conviction or if it is defined by a statute other than this Code that now provides that the offense shall not constitute a crime. A violation does not constitute a

crime and conviction of a violation shall not give rise to any disability or legal disadvantage based on conviction of a criminal offense.

(6) Any offense declared by law to constitute a crime, without specification of the grade thereof or of the sentence authorized upon conviction, is a misdemeanor.

(7) An offense defined by any statute of this State other than this Code shall be classified as provided in this Section and the sentence that may be imposed upon conviction thereof shall hereafter be governed by this Code. * * *

Section 1.13. General Definitions.

In this Code, unless a different meaning plainly is required:

(1) "statute" includes the Constitution and a local law or ordinance of a political subdivision of the State;

(2) "act" or "action" means a bodily movement whether voluntary or involuntary;

(3) "voluntary" has the meaning specified in Section 2.01;

(4) "omission" means a failure to act;

(5) "conduct" means an action or omission and its accompanying state of mind, or, where relevant, a series of acts and omissions;

(6) "actor" includes, where relevant, a person guilty of an omission;

(7) "acted" includes, where relevant, "omitted to act";

(8) "person," "he" and "actor" include any natural person and, where relevant, a corporation or an unincorporated association;

(9) "element of an offense" means (i) such conduct or (ii) such attendant circumstances or (iii) such a result of conduct as

(a) is included in the description of the forbidden conduct in the definition of the offense; or

(b) establishes the required kind of culpability; or

(c) negatives an excuse or justification for such conduct; or

(d) negatives a defense under the statute of limitations; or

(e) establishes jurisdiction or venue;

(10) "material element of an offense" means an element that does not relate exclusively to the statute of limitations, jurisdiction, venue, or to any other matter similarly unconnected with (i) the harm or evil, incident to conduct, sought to be prevented by the law defining the offense, or (ii) the existence of a justification or excuse for such conduct;

(11) "purposely" has the meaning specified in Section 2.02 and equivalent terms such as "with purpose," "designed" or "with design" have the same meaning;

(12) "intentionally" or "with intent" means purposely;

(13) "knowingly" has the meaning specified in Section 2.02 and equivalent terms such as "knowing" or "with knowledge" have the same meaning;

(14) "recklessly" has the meaning specified in Section 2.02 and equivalent terms such as "recklessness" or "with recklessness" have the same meaning;

(15) "negligently" has the meaning specified in Section 2.02 and equivalent terms such as "negligence" or "with negligence" have the same meaning;

(16) "reasonably believes" or "reasonable belief" designates a belief that the actor is not reckless or negligent in holding.

ARTICLE 2. GENERAL PRINCIPLES OF LIABILITY

Section 2.01. Requirement of Voluntary Act; Omission as Basis of Liability; Possession as an Act.

(1) A person is not guilty of an offense unless his liability is based on conduct that includes a voluntary act or the omission to perform an act of which he is physically capable.

(2) The following are not voluntary acts within the meaning of this Section:

(a) a reflex or convulsion;

(b) a bodily movement during unconsciousness or sleep;

(c) conduct during hypnosis or resulting from hypnotic suggestion;

(d) a bodily movement that otherwise is not a product of the effort or determination of the actor, either conscious or habitual.

(3) Liability for the commission of an offense may not be based on an omission unaccompanied by action unless:

(a) the omission is expressly made sufficient by the law defining the offense; or

(b) a duty to perform the omitted act is otherwise imposed by law.

(4) Possession is an act, within the meaning of this Section, if the possessor knowingly procured or received the thing possessed or was aware of his control thereof for a sufficient period to have been able to terminate his possession.

Section 2.02. General Requirements of Culpability.

(1) *Minimum Requirements of Culpability.* Except as provided in Section 2.05, a person is not guilty of an offense unless he acted purposely, knowingly, recklessly or negligently, as the law may require, with respect to each material element of the offense.

(2) *Kinds of Culpability Defined.*

(a) *Purposely.*

A person acts purposely with respect to a material element of an offense when:

(i) if the element involves the nature of his conduct or a result thereof, it is his conscious object to engage in conduct of that nature or to cause such a result; and

(ii) if the element involves the attendant circumstances, he is aware of the existence of such circumstances or he believes or hopes that they exist.

(b) *Knowingly.*

A person acts knowingly with respect to a material element of an offense when:

(i) if the element involves the nature of his conduct or the attendant circumstances, he is aware that his conduct is of that nature or that such circumstances exist; and

(ii) if the element involves a result of his conduct, he is aware that it is practically certain that his conduct will cause such a result.

(c) *Recklessly.*

A person acts recklessly with respect to a material element of an offense when he consciously disregards a substantial and unjustifiable risk that the material element exists or will result from his conduct. The risk must be of such a nature and degree that, considering the nature and purpose of the actor's conduct and the circumstances known to him, its disregard involves a gross deviation from the standard of conduct that a law-abiding person would observe in the actor's situation.

(d) *Negligently.*

A person acts negligently with respect to a material element of an offense when he should be aware of a substantial and unjustifiable risk that the material element exists or will result from his conduct. The risk must be of such a nature and degree that the actor's failure to perceive it, considering the nature and purpose of his conduct and the circumstances known to him, involves a gross deviation from the standard of care that a reasonable person would observe in the actor's situation.

(3) *Culpability Required Unless Otherwise Provided.* When the culpability sufficient to establish a material element of an offense is not prescribed by law, such element is established if a person acts purposely, knowingly or recklessly with respect thereto.

(4) *Prescribed Culpability Requirement Applies to All Material Elements.* When the law defining an offense prescribes the kind of culpability that is sufficient for the commission of an offense, without distinguishing among the material elements thereof, such provision shall apply to all the material elements of the offense, unless a contrary purpose plainly appears.

(5) *Substitutes for Negligence, Recklessness and Knowledge.* When the law provides that negligence suffices to establish an element of an offense, such element also is established if a person acts purposely, knowingly or recklessly. When recklessness suffices to establish an element, such element also is established if a person acts purposely or knowingly. When acting knowingly suffices to establish an element, such element also is established if a person acts purposely.

(6) *Requirement of Purpose Satisfied if Purpose Is Conditional.* When a particular purpose is an element of an offense, the element is established although such purpose is conditional, unless the condition negatives the harm or evil sought to be prevented by the law defining the offense.

(7) *Requirement of Knowledge Satisfied by Knowledge of High Probability.* When knowledge of the existence of a particular fact is an element of an offense, such knowledge is established if a person is aware of a high probability of its existence, unless he actually believes that it does not exist.

(8) *Requirement of Wilfulness Satisfied by Acting Knowingly.* A requirement that an offense be committed wilfully is satisfied if a person acts knowingly with respect to the material elements of the offense, unless a purpose to impose further requirements appears.

(9) *Culpability as to Illegality of Conduct.* Neither knowledge nor recklessness or negligence as to whether conduct constitutes an offense or as to the existence, meaning or application of the law determining the elements of an offense is an element of such offense, unless the definition of the offense or the Code so provides.

(10) *Culpability as Determinant of Grade of Offense.* When the grade or degree of an offense depends on whether the offense is committed purposely, knowingly, recklessly or negligently, its grade or degree shall

be the lowest for which the determinative kind of culpability is established with respect to any material element of the offense.

Section 2.03. Causal Relationship Between Conduct and Result; Divergence Between Result Designed or Contemplated and Actual Result or Between Probable and Actual Result.

(1) Conduct is the cause of a result when:

(a) it is an antecedent but for which the result in question would not have occurred; and

(b) the relationship between the conduct and result satisfies any additional causal requirements imposed by the Code or by the law defining the offense.

(2) When purposely or knowingly causing a particular result is an element of an offense, the element is not established if the actual result is not within the purpose or the contemplation of the actor unless:

(a) the actual result differs from that designed or contemplated, as the case may be, only in the respect that a different person or different property is injured or affected or that the injury or harm designed or contemplated would have been more serious or more extensive than that caused; or

(b) the actual result involves the same kind of injury or harm as that designed or contemplated and is not too remote or accidental in its occurrence to have a [just] bearing on the actor's liability or on the gravity of his offense.

(3) When recklessly or negligently causing a particular result is an element of an offense, the element is not established if the actual result is not within the risk of which the actor is aware or, in the case of negligence, of which he should be aware unless:

(a) the actual result differs from the probable result only in the respect that a different person or different property is injured or affected or that the probable injury or harm would have been more serious or more extensive than that caused; or

(b) the actual result involves the same kind of injury or harm as the probable result and is not too remote or accidental in its occurrence to have a [just] bearing on the actor's liability or on the gravity of his offense.

(4) When causing a particular result is a material element of an offense for which absolute liability is imposed by law, the element is not established unless the actual result is a probable consequence of the actor's conduct.

Section 2.04. Ignorance or Mistake.

(1) Ignorance or mistake as to a matter of fact or law is a defense if:

(a) the ignorance or mistake negatives the purpose, knowledge, belief, recklessness or negligence required to establish a material element of the offense; or

(b) the law provides that the state of mind established by such ignorance or mistake constitutes a defense.

(2) Although ignorance or mistake would otherwise afford a defense to the offense charged, the defense is not available if the defendant would be guilty of another offense had the situation been as he supposed. In such case, however, the ignorance or mistake of the defendant shall reduce the grade and degree of the offense of which he may be convicted to those of the offense of which he would be guilty had the situation been as he supposed.

(3) A belief that conduct does not legally constitute an offense is a defense to a prosecution for that offense based upon such conduct when:

(a) the statute or other enactment defining the offense is not known to the actor and has not been published or otherwise reasonably made available prior to the conduct alleged; or

(b) he acts in reasonable reliance upon an official statement of the law, afterward determined to be invalid or erroneous, contained in (i) a statute or other enactment; (ii) a judicial decision, opinion or judgment; (iii) an administrative order or grant of permission; or (iv) an official interpretation of the public officer or body charged by law with responsibility for the interpretation, administration or enforcement of the law defining the offense.

(4) The defendant must prove a defense arising under Subsection (3) of this Section by a preponderance of evidence.

Section 2.05. When Culpability Requirements Are Inapplicable to Violations and to Offenses Defined by Other Statutes; Effect of Absolute Liability in Reducing Grade of Offense to Violation.

(1) The requirements of culpability prescribed by Sections 2.01 and 2.02 do not apply to:

(a) offenses that constitute violations, unless the requirement involved is included in the definition of the offense or the Court determines that its application is consistent with effective enforcement of the law defining the offense; or

(b) offenses defined by statutes other than the Code, insofar as a legislative purpose to impose absolute liability for such offenses or with respect to any material element thereof plainly appears.

(2) Notwithstanding any other provision of existing law and unless a subsequent statute otherwise provides:

(a) when absolute liability is imposed with respect to any material element of an offense defined by a statute other than the Code and a conviction is based upon such liability, the offense constitutes a violation; and

(b) although absolute liability is imposed by law with respect to one or more of the material elements of an offense defined by a statute other than the Code, the culpable commission of the offense may be charged and proved, in which event negligence with respect to such elements constitutes sufficient culpability and the classification of the offense and the sentence that may be imposed therefor upon conviction are determined by Section 1.04 and Article 6 of the Code.

Section 2.06. Liability for Conduct of Another; Complicity.

(1) A person is guilty of an offense if it is committed by his own conduct or by the conduct of another person for which he is legally accountable, or both.

(2) A person is legally accountable for the conduct of another person when:

(a) acting with the kind of culpability that is sufficient for the commission of the offense, he causes an innocent or irresponsible person to engage in such conduct; or

(b) he is made accountable for the conduct of such other person by the Code or by the law defining the offense; or

(c) he is an accomplice of such other person in the commission of the offense.

(3) A person is an accomplice of another person in the commission of an offense if:

(a) with the purpose of promoting or facilitating the commission of the offense, he

(i) solicits such other person to commit it, or

(ii) aids or agrees or attempts to aid such other person in planning or committing it, or

(iii) having a legal duty to prevent the commission of the offense, fails to make proper effort so to do; or

(b) his conduct is expressly declared by law to establish his complicity.

(4) When causing a particular result is an element of an offense, an accomplice in the conduct causing such result is an accomplice in the commission of that offense if he acts with the kind of culpability, if any, with respect to that result that is sufficient for the commission of the offense.

(5) A person who is legally incapable of committing a particular offense himself may be guilty thereof if it is committed by the conduct of another person for which he is legally accountable, unless such liability is inconsistent with the purpose of the provision establishing his incapacity.

(6) Unless otherwise provided by the Code or by the law defining the offense, a person is not an accomplice in an offense committed by another person if:

(a) he is a victim of that offense; or

(b) the offense is so defined that his conduct is inevitably incident to its commission; or

(c) he terminates his complicity prior to the commission of the offense and

(i) wholly deprives it of effectiveness in the commission of the offense; or

(ii) gives timely warning to the law enforcement authorities or otherwise makes proper effort to prevent the commission of the offense.

(7) An accomplice may be convicted on proof of the commission of the offense and of his complicity therein, though the person claimed to have committed the offense has not been prosecuted or convicted or has been convicted of a different offense or degree of offense or has an immunity to prosecution or conviction or has been acquitted.

Section 2.07. Liability of Corporations, Unincorporated Associations and Persons Acting, or Under a Duty to Act, in Their Behalf.

(1) A corporation may be convicted of the commission of an offense if:

(a) the offense is a violation or the offense is defined by a statute other than the Code in which a legislative purpose to impose liability on corporations plainly appears and the conduct is performed by an agent of the corporation acting in behalf of the corporation within the scope of his office or employment, except that if the law defining the offense designates the agents for whose conduct the corporation is accountable or the circumstances under which it is accountable, such provisions shall apply; or

(b) the offense consists of an omission to discharge a specific duty of affirmative performance imposed on corporations by law; or

(c) the commission of the offense was authorized, requested, commanded, performed or recklessly tolerated by the board of directors or by a high managerial agent acting in behalf of the corporation within the scope of his office or employment.

(2) When absolute liability is imposed for the commission of an offense, a legislative purpose to impose liability on a corporation shall be assumed, unless the contrary plainly appears.

(3) An unincorporated association may be convicted of the commission of an offense if:

(a) the offense is defined by a statute other than the Code that expressly provides for the liability of such an association and the conduct is performed by an agent of the association acting in behalf of the association within the scope of his office or employment, except that if the law defining the offense designates the agents for whose conduct the association is accountable or the circumstances under which it is accountable, such provisions shall apply; or

(b) the offense consists of an omission to discharge a specific duty of affirmative performance imposed on associations by law.

(4) As used in this Section:

(a) "corporation" does not include an entity organized as or by a governmental agency for the execution of a governmental program;

(b) "agent" means any director, officer, servant, employee or other person authorized to act in behalf of the corporation or association and, in the case of an unincorporated association, a member of such association;

(c) "high managerial agent" means an officer of a corporation or an unincorporated association, or, in the case of a partnership, a partner, or any other agent of a corporation or association having duties of such responsibility that his conduct may fairly be assumed to represent the policy of the corporation or association.

(5) In any prosecution of a corporation or an unincorporated association for the commission of an offense included within the terms of Subsection (1)(a) or Subsection (3)(a) of this Section, other than an offense for which absolute liability has been imposed, it shall be a defense if the defendant proves by a preponderance of evidence that the high managerial agent

having supervisory responsibility over the subject matter of the offense employed due diligence to prevent its commission. This paragraph shall not apply if it is plainly inconsistent with the legislative purpose in defining the particular offense.

(6)(a) A person is legally accountable for any conduct he performs or causes to be performed in the name of the corporation or an unincorporated association or in its behalf to the same extent as if it were performed in his own name or behalf.

(b) Whenever a duty to act is imposed by law upon a corporation or an unincorporated association, any agent of the corporation or association having primary responsibility for the discharge of the duty is legally accountable for a reckless omission to perform the required act to the same extent as if the duty were imposed by law directly upon himself.

(c) When a person is convicted of an offense by reason of his legal accountability for the conduct of a corporation or an unincorporated association, he is subject to the sentence authorized by law when a natural person is convicted of an offense of the grade and the degree involved.

Section 2.08. Intoxication.

(1) Except as provided in Subsection (4) of this Section, intoxication of the actor is not a defense unless it negatives an element of the offense.

(2) When recklessness establishes an element of the offense, if the actor, due to self-induced intoxication, is unaware of a risk of which he would have been aware had he been sober, such unawareness is immaterial.

(3) Intoxication does not, in itself, constitute mental disease within the meaning of Section 4.01.

(4) Intoxication that (a) is not self-induced or (b) is pathological is an affirmative defense if by reason of such intoxication the actor at the time of his conduct lacks substantial capacity either to appreciate its criminality [wrongfulness] or to conform his conduct to the requirements of law.

(5) *Definitions.* In this Section unless a different meaning plainly is required:

(a) "intoxication" means a disturbance of mental or physical capacities resulting from the introduction of substances into the body;

(b) "self-induced intoxication" means intoxication caused by substances that the actor knowingly introduces into his body, the tendency of which to cause intoxication he knows or ought to know, unless he introduces them pursuant to medical advice or under such circumstances as would afford a defense to a charge of crime;

(c) "pathological intoxication" means intoxication grossly excessive in degree, given the amount of the intoxicant, to which the actor does not know he is susceptible.

Section 2.09. Duress.

(1) It is an affirmative defense that the actor engaged in the conduct charged to constitute an offense because he was coerced to do so by the use of, or a threat to use, unlawful force against his person or the person of another, that a person of reasonable firmness in his situation would have been unable to resist.

(2) The defense provided by this Section is unavailable if the actor recklessly placed himself in a situation in which it was probable that he would be subjected to duress. The defense is also unavailable if he was negligent in placing himself in such a situation, whenever negligence suffices to establish culpability for the offense charged.

(3) It is not a defense that a woman acted on the command of her husband, unless she acted under such coercion as would establish a defense under this Section. [The presumption that a woman acting in the presence of her husband is coerced is abolished.]

(4) When the conduct of the actor would otherwise be justifiable under Section 3.02, this Section does not preclude such defense.

Section 2.10. Military Orders.

It is an affirmative defense that the actor, in engaging in the conduct charged to constitute an offense, does no more than execute an order of his superior in the armed services that he does not know to be unlawful.

Section 2.11. Consent.

(1) *In General.* The consent of the victim to conduct charged to constitute an offense or to the result thereof is a defense if such consent negatives an element of the offense or precludes the infliction of the harm or evil sought to be prevented by the law defining the offense.

(2) *Consent to Bodily Injury.* When conduct is charged to constitute an offense because it causes or threatens bodily injury, consent to such conduct or to the infliction of such injury is a defense if:

(a) the bodily injury consented to or threatened by the conduct consented to is not serious; or

(b) the conduct and the injury are reasonably foreseeable hazards of joint participation in a lawful athletic contest or competitive sport or other concerted activity not forbidden by law; or

(c) the consent establishes a justification for the conduct under Article 3 of the Code.

(3) *Ineffective Consent.* Unless otherwise provided by the Code or by the law defining the offense, assent does not constitute consent if:

(a) it is given by a person who is legally incompetent to authorize the conduct charged to constitute the offense; or

(b) it is given by a person who by reason of youth, mental disease or defect or intoxication is manifestly unable or known by the actor to be unable to make a reasonable judgment as to the nature or harmfulness of the conduct charged to constitute the offense; or

(c) it is given by a person whose improvident consent is sought to be prevented by the law defining the offense; or

(d) it is induced by force, duress or deception of a kind sought to be prevented by the law defining the offense.

Section 2.12. De Minimis Infractions.

The Court shall dismiss a prosecution if, having regard to the nature of the conduct charged to constitute an offense and the nature of the attendant circumstances, it finds that the defendant's conduct:

(1) was within a customary license or tolerance, neither expressly negatived by the person whose interest was infringed nor inconsistent with the purpose of the law defining the offense; or

(2) did not actually cause or threaten the harm or evil sought to be prevented by the law defining the offense or did so only to an extent too trivial to warrant the condemnation of conviction; or

(3) presents such other extenuations that it cannot reasonably be regarded as envisaged by the legislature in forbidding the offense.

The Court shall not dismiss a prosecution under Subsection (3) of this Section without filing a written statement of its reasons.

Section 2.13. Entrapment.

(1) A public law enforcement official or a person acting in cooperation with such an official perpetrates an entrapment if for the purpose of obtaining evidence of the commission of an offense, he induces or encourages another person to engage in conduct constituting such offense by either:

(a) making knowingly false representations designed to induce the belief that such conduct is not prohibited; or

(b) employing methods of persuasion or inducement that create a substantial risk that such an offense will be committed by persons other than those who are ready to commit it.

(2) Except as provided in Subsection (3) of this Section, a person prosecuted for an offense shall be acquitted if he proves by a preponderance of evidence that his conduct occurred in response to an entrapment. The issue of entrapment shall be tried by the Court in the absence of the jury.

(3) The defense afforded by this Section is unavailable when causing or threatening bodily injury is an element of the offense charged and the prosecution is based on conduct causing or threatening such injury to a person other than the person perpetrating the entrapment.

ARTICLE 3. GENERAL PRINCIPLES OF JUSTIFICATION

Section 3.01. Justification an Affirmative Defense; Civil Remedies Unaffected.

(1) In any prosecution based on conduct that is justifiable under this Article, justification is an affirmative defense.

(2) The fact that conduct is justifiable under this Article does not abolish or impair any remedy for such conduct that is available in any civil action.

Section 3.02. Justification Generally: Choice of Evils.

(1) Conduct that the actor believes to be necessary to avoid a harm or evil to himself or to another is justifiable, provided that:

(a) the harm or evil sought to be avoided by such conduct is greater than that sought to be prevented by the law defining the offense charged; and

(b) neither the Code nor other law defining the offense provides exceptions or defenses dealing with the specific situation involved; and

(c) a legislative purpose to exclude the justification claimed does not otherwise plainly appear.

(2) When the actor was reckless or negligent in bringing about the situation requiring a choice of harms or evils or in appraising the necessity for his conduct, the justification afforded by this Section is unavailable in a prosecution for any offense for which recklessness or negligence, as the case may be, suffices to establish culpability.

Section 3.03. Execution of Public Duty.

(1) Except as provided in Subsection (2) of this Section, conduct is justifiable when it is required or authorized by:

(a) the law defining the duties or functions of a public officer or the assistance to be rendered to such officer in the performance of his duties; or

(b) the law governing the execution of legal process; or

(c) the judgment or order of a competent court or tribunal; or

(d) the law governing the armed services or the lawful conduct of war; or

(e) any other provision of law imposing a public duty.

(2) The other sections of this Article apply to:

(a) the use of force upon or toward the person of another for any of the purposes dealt with in such sections; and

(b) the use of deadly force for any purpose, unless the use of such force is otherwise expressly authorized by law or occurs in the lawful conduct of war.

(3) The justification afforded by Subsection (1) of this Section applies:

(a) when the actor believes his conduct to be required or authorized by the judgment or direction of a competent court or tribunal or in the lawful execution of legal process, notwithstanding lack of jurisdiction of the court or defect in the legal process; and

(b) when the actor believes his conduct to be required or authorized to assist a public officer in the performance of his duties, notwithstanding that the officer exceeded his legal authority.

Section 3.04. Use of Force in Self-Protection.

(1) *Use of Force Justifiable for Protection of the Person.* Subject to the provisions of this Section and of Section 3.09, the use of force upon or toward another person is justifiable when the actor believes that such force is immediately necessary for the purpose of protecting himself against the use of unlawful force by such other person on the present occasion.

(2) *Limitations on Justifying Necessity for Use of Force.*

(a) The use of force is not justifiable under this Section:

(i) to resist an arrest that the actor knows is being made by a peace officer, although the arrest is unlawful; or

(ii) to resist force used by the occupier or possessor of property or by another person on his behalf, where the actor knows that the person using the force is doing so under a claim of right to protect the property, except that this limitation shall not apply if:

(A) the actor is a public officer acting in the performance of his duties or a person lawfully assisting him therein or a person making or assisting in a lawful arrest; or

(B) the actor has been unlawfully dispossessed of the property and is making a re-entry or recaption justified by Section 3.06; or

(C) the actor believes that such force is necessary to protect himself against death or serious bodily injury.

(b) The use of deadly force is not justifiable under this Section unless the actor believes that such force is necessary to protect himself against death, serious bodily injury, kidnapping or sexual intercourse compelled by force or threat; nor is it justifiable if:

(i) the actor, with the purpose of causing death or serious bodily injury, provoked the use of force against himself in the same encounter; or

(ii) the actor knows that he can avoid the necessity of using such force with complete safety by retreating or by surrendering possession of a thing to a person asserting a claim of right thereto or by complying with a demand that he abstain from any action that he has no duty to take, except that:

(A) the actor is not obliged to retreat from his dwelling or place of work, unless he was the initial aggressor or is assailed in his place of work by another person whose place of work the actor knows it to be; and

(B) a public officer justified in using force in the performance of his duties or a person justified in using force in his assistance or a person justified in using force in making an arrest or preventing an escape is not obliged to desist from efforts to perform such duty, effect such arrest or prevent such escape because of resistance or threatened resistance by or on behalf of the person against whom such action is directed.

(c) Except as required by paragraphs (a) and (b) of this Subsection, a person employing protective force may estimate the necessity thereof under the circumstances as he believes them to be when the force is used, without retreating, surrendering possession, doing any other act that he has no legal duty to do or abstaining from any lawful action.

(3) *Use of Confinement as Protective Force.* The justification afforded by this Section extends to the use of confinement as protective force only if the actor takes all reasonable measures to terminate the confinement as soon as he knows that he safely can, unless the person confined has been arrested on a charge of crime.

Section 3.05. Use of Force for the Protection of Other Persons.

(1) Subject to the provisions of this Section and of Section 3.09, the use of force upon or toward the person of another is justifiable to protect a third person when:

(a) the actor would be justified under Section 3.04 in using such force to protect himself against the injury he believes to be threatened to the person whom he seeks to protect; and

(b) under the circumstances as the actor believes them to be, the person whom he seeks to protect would be justified in using such protective force; and

(c) the actor believes that his intervention is necessary for the protection of such other person.

(2) Notwithstanding Subsection (1) of this Section:

(a) when the actor would be obliged under Section 3.04 to retreat, to surrender the possession of a thing or to comply with a demand before using force in self-protection, he is not obliged to do so before using force for the protection of another person, unless he knows that he can thereby secure the complete safety of such other person; and

(b) when the person whom the actor seeks to protect would be obliged under Section 3.04 to retreat, to surrender the possession of a thing or to comply with a demand if he knew that he could obtain complete safety by so doing, the actor is obliged to try to cause him to do so before using force in his protection if the actor knows that he can obtain complete safety in that way; and

(c) neither the actor nor the person whom he seeks to protect is obliged to retreat when in the other's dwelling or place of work to any greater extent than in his own.

Section 3.06. Use of Force for Protection of Property.

(1) *Use of Force Justifiable for Protection of Property.* Subject to the provisions of this Section and of Section 3.09, the use of force upon or toward the person of another is justifiable when the actor believes that such force is immediately necessary:

(a) to prevent or terminate an unlawful entry or other trespass upon land or a trespass against or the unlawful carrying away of tangible, movable property, provided that such land or movable property is, or is believed by the actor to be, in his possession or in the possession of another person for whose protection he acts; or

(b) to effect an entry or re-entry upon land or to retake tangible movable property, provided that the actor believes that he or the person by whose authority he acts or a person from whom he or such other person derives title was unlawfully dispossessed of such land or movable property and is entitled to possession, and provided, further, that:

(i) the force is used immediately or on fresh pursuit after such dispossession; or

(ii) the actor believes that the person against whom he uses force has no claim of right to the possession of the property and, in the case of land, the circumstances, as the actor believes them to be, are of such urgency that it would be an exceptional hardship to postpone the entry or re-entry until a court order is obtained.

(2) *Meaning of Possession.* For the purposes of Subsection (1) of this Section:

(a) a person who has parted with the custody of property to another who refuses to restore it to him is no longer in possession, unless the property is movable and was and still is located on land in his possession;

(b) a person who has been dispossessed of land does not regain possession thereof merely by setting foot thereon;

(c) a person who has a license to use or occupy real property is deemed to be in possession thereof except against the licensor acting under claim of right.

(3) *Limitations on Justifiable Use of Force.*

(a) *Request to Desist.* The use of force is justifiable under this Section only if the actor first requests the person against whom such force is used to desist from his interference with the property, unless the actor believes that:

(i) such request would be useless; or

(ii) it would be dangerous to himself or another person to make the request; or

(iii) substantial harm will be done to the physical condition of the property that is sought to be protected before the request can effectively be made.

(b) *Exclusion of Trespasser.* The use of force to prevent or terminate a trespass is not justifiable under this Section if the actor knows that the exclusion of the trespasser will expose him to substantial danger of serious bodily injury.

(c) *Resistance of Lawful Re-entry or Recaption.* The use of force to prevent an entry or re-entry upon land or the recaption of movable property is not justifiable under this Section, although the actor believes that such re-entry or recaption is unlawful, if:

(i) the re-entry or recaption is made by or on behalf of a person who was actually dispossessed of the property; and

(ii) it is otherwise justifiable under Subsection (1)(b) of this Section.

(d) *Use of Deadly Force.* The use of deadly force is not justifiable under this Section unless the actor believes that:

(i) the person against whom the force is used is attempting to dispossess him of his dwelling otherwise than under a claim of right to its possession; or

(ii) the person against whom the force is used is attempting to commit or consummate arson, burglary, robbery or other felonious theft or property destruction and either:

(A) has employed or threatened deadly force against or in the presence of the actor; or

(B) the use of force other than deadly force to prevent the commission or the consummation of the crime would expose the actor or another in his presence to substantial danger of serious bodily injury.

(4) *Use of Confinement as Protective Force.* The justification afforded by this Section extends to the use of confinement as protective force only if the actor takes all reasonable measures to terminate the confinement as soon as he knows that he can do so with safety to the property, unless the person confined has been arrested on a charge of crime.

(5) *Use of Device to Protect Property.* The justification afforded by this Section extends to the use of a device for the purpose of protecting property only if:

(a) the device is not designed to cause or known to create a substantial risk of causing death or serious bodily injury; and

(b) the use of the particular device to protect the property from entry or trespass is reasonable under the circumstances, as the actor believes them to be; and

(c) the device is one customarily used for such a purpose or reasonable care is taken to make known to probable intruders the fact that it is used.

(6) *Use of Force to Pass Wrongful Obstructor.* The use of force to pass a person whom the actor believes to be purposely or knowingly and unjustifiably obstructing the actor from going to a place to which he may lawfully go is justifiable, provided that:

(a) the actor believes that the person against whom he uses force has no claim of right to obstruct the actor; and

(b) the actor is not being obstructed from entry or movement on land that he knows to be in the possession or custody of the person obstructing him, or in the possession or custody of another person by whose authority the obstructor acts, unless the circumstances, as the actor believes them to be, are of such urgency that it would not be reasonable to postpone the entry or movement on such land until a court order is obtained; and

(c) the force used is not greater than would be justifiable if the person obstructing the actor were using force against him to prevent his passage.

Section 3.07. Use of Force in Law Enforcement.

(1) *Use of Force Justifiable to Effect an Arrest.* Subject to the provisions of this Section and of Section 3.09, the use of force upon or toward the person of another is justifiable when the actor is making or assisting in making an arrest and the actor believes that such force is immediately necessary to effect a lawful arrest.

(2) *Limitations on the Use of Force.*

(a) The use of force is not justifiable under this Section unless:

(i) the actor makes known the purpose of the arrest or believes that it is otherwise known by or cannot reasonably be made known to the person to be arrested; and

(ii) when the arrest is made under a warrant, the warrant is valid or believed by the actor to be valid.

(b) The use of deadly force is not justifiable under this Section unless:

(i) the arrest is for a felony; and

(ii) the person effecting the arrest is authorized to act as a peace officer or is assisting a person whom he believes to be authorized to act as a peace officer; and

(iii) the actor believes that the force employed creates no substantial risk of injury to innocent persons; and

(iv) the actor believes that:

(A) the crime for which the arrest is made involved conduct including the use or threatened use of deadly force; or

(B) there is a substantial risk that the person to be arrested will cause death or serious bodily injury if his apprehension is delayed.

(3) *Use of Force to Prevent Escape from Custody.* The use of force to prevent the escape of an arrested person from custody is justifiable when the force could justifiably have been employed to effect the arrest under which the person is in custody, except that a guard or other person authorized to act as a peace officer is justified in using any force, including deadly force, that he believes to be immediately necessary to prevent the escape of a person from a jail, prison, or other institution for the detention of persons charged with or convicted of a crime.

(4) *Use of Force by Private Person Assisting an Unlawful Arrest.*

(a) A private person who is summoned by a peace officer to assist in effecting an unlawful arrest, is justified in using any force that he would be justified in using if the arrest were lawful, provided that he does not believe the arrest is unlawful.

(b) A private person who assists another private person in effecting an unlawful arrest, or who, not being summoned, assists a peace officer in effecting an unlawful arrest, is justified in using any force that he would be justified in using if the arrest were lawful, provided that (i) he believes the arrest is lawful, and (ii) the arrest would be lawful if the facts were as he believes them to be.

(5) *Use of Force to Prevent Suicide or the Commission of a Crime.*

(a) The use of force upon or toward the person of another is justifiable when the actor believes that such force is immediately necessary to prevent such other person from committing suicide, inflicting serious bodily injury upon himself, committing or consummating the commission of a crime involving or threatening bodily injury, damage to or loss of property or a breach of the peace, except that:

(i) any limitations imposed by the other provisions of this Article on the justifiable use of force in self-protection, for the protection of others, the protection of property, the effectuation of an arrest or the prevention of an escape from custody shall apply notwithstanding the criminality of the conduct against which such force is used; and

(ii) the use of deadly force is not in any event justifiable under this Subsection unless:

(A) the actor believes that there is a substantial risk that the person whom he seeks to prevent from committing a crime will cause death or serious bodily injury to another unless the commission or the consummation of the crime is prevented and that the use of such force presents no substantial risk of injury to innocent persons; or

(B) the actor believes that the use of such force is necessary to suppress a riot or mutiny after the rioters or mutineers have been ordered to disperse and warned, in any particular manner that the law may require, that such force will be used if they do not obey.

(b) The justification afforded by this Subsection extends to the use of confinement as preventive force only if the actor takes all reasonable measures to terminate the confinement as soon as he knows that he safely can, unless the person confined has been arrested on a charge of crime.

Section 3.08. Use of Force by Persons with Special Responsibility for Care, Discipline or Safety of Others.

The use of force upon or toward the person of another is justifiable if:

(1) the actor is the parent or guardian or other person similarly responsible for the general care and supervision of a minor or a person acting at the request of such parent, guardian or other responsible person and:

(a) the force is used for the purpose of safeguarding or promoting the welfare of the minor, including the prevention or punishment of his misconduct; and

(b) the force used is not designed to cause or known to create a substantial risk of causing death, serious bodily injury, disfigurement, extreme pain or mental distress or gross degradation; or

(2) the actor is a teacher or a person otherwise entrusted with the care or supervision for a special purpose of a minor and:

(a) the actor believes that the force used is necessary to further such special purpose, including the maintenance of reasonable discipline in a school, class or other group, and that the use of such force is consistent with the welfare of the minor; and

(b) the degree of force, if it had been used by the parent or guardian of the minor, would not be unjustifiable under Subsection (1)(b) of this Section; or

(3) the actor is the guardian or other person similarly responsible for the general care and supervision of an incompetent person and:

(a) the force is used for the purpose of safeguarding or promoting the welfare of the incompetent person, including the prevention of his misconduct, or, when such incompetent person is in a hospital or other institution for his care and custody, for the maintenance of reasonable discipline in such institution; and

(b) the force used is not designed to cause or known to create a substantial risk of causing death, serious bodily injury, disfigurement, extreme or unnecessary pain, mental distress, or humiliation; or

(4) the actor is a doctor or other therapist or a person assisting him at his direction and:

(a) the force is used for the purpose of administering a recognized form of treatment that the actor believes to be adapted to promoting the physical or mental health of the patient; and

(b) the treatment is administered with the consent of the patient or, if the patient is a minor or an incompetent person, with the consent of his parent or guardian or other person legally competent to consent in his behalf, or the treatment is administered in an emergency when the actor believes that no one competent to consent can be consulted and that a reasonable person, wishing to safeguard the welfare of the patient, would consent; or

(5) the actor is a warden or other authorized official of a correctional institution and:

(a) he believes that the force used is necessary for the purpose of enforcing the lawful rules or procedures of the institution, unless his belief in the lawfulness of the rule or procedure sought to be enforced is erroneous and his error is due to ignorance or mistake as to the provisions of the Code, any other provision of the criminal law or the law governing the administration of the institution; and

(b) the nature or degree of force used is not forbidden by Article 303 or 304 of the Code; and

(c) if deadly force is used, its use is otherwise justifiable under this Article; or

(6) the actor is a person responsible for the safety of a vessel or an aircraft or a person acting at his direction and:

(a) he believes that the force used is necessary to prevent interference with the operation of the vessel or aircraft or obstruction of the execution of a lawful order, unless his belief in the lawfulness of the order is erroneous and his error is due to ignorance or mistake as to the law defining his authority; and

(b) if deadly force is used, its use is otherwise justifiable under this Article; or

(7) the actor is a person who is authorized or required by law to maintain order or decorum in a vehicle, train or other carrier or in a place where others are assembled, and:

(a) he believes that the force used is necessary for such purpose; and

(b) the force used is not designed to cause or known to create a substantial risk of causing death, bodily injury, or extreme mental distress.

Section 3.09. Mistake of Law as to Unlawfulness of Force or Legality of Arrest; Reckless or Negligent Use of Otherwise Justifiable Force; Reckless or Negligent Injury or Risk of Injury to Innocent Persons.

(1) The justification afforded by Sections 3.04 to 3.07, inclusive, is unavailable when:

(a) the actor's belief in the unlawfulness of the force or conduct against which he employs protective force or his belief in the lawfulness of an arrest that he endeavors to effect by force is erroneous; and

(b) his error is due to ignorance or mistake as to the provisions of the Code, any other provision of the criminal law or the law governing the legality of an arrest or search.

(2) When the actor believes that the use of force upon or toward the person of another is necessary for any of the purposes for which such belief would establish a justification under Sections 3.03 to 3.08 but the actor is reckless or negligent in having such belief or in acquiring or failing to acquire any knowledge or belief that is material to the justifiability of his use of force, the justification afforded by those Sections

is unavailable in a prosecution for an offense for which recklessness or negligence, as the case may be, suffices to establish culpability.

(3) When the actor is justified under Sections 3.03 to 3.08 in using force upon or toward the person of another but he recklessly or negligently injures or creates a risk of injury to innocent persons, the justification afforded by those Sections is unavailable in a prosecution for such recklessness or negligence towards innocent persons.

Section 3.10. Justification in Property Crimes.

Conduct involving the appropriation, seizure or destruction of, damage to, intrusion on or interference with property is justifiable under circumstances that would establish a defense of privilege in a civil action based thereon, unless:

(1) the Code or the law defining the offense deals with the specific situation involved; or

(2) a legislative purpose to exclude the justification claimed otherwise plainly appears.

Section 3.11. Definitions.

In this Article, unless a different meaning plainly is required:

(1) "unlawful force" means force, including confinement, that is employed without the consent of the person against whom it is directed and the employment of which constitutes an offense or actionable tort or would constitute such offense or tort except for a defense (such as the absence of intent, negligence, or mental capacity; duress; youth; or diplomatic status) not amounting to a privilege to use the force. Assent constitutes consent, within the meaning of this Section, whether or not it otherwise is legally effective, except assent to the infliction of death or serious bodily injury.

(2) "deadly force" means force that the actor uses with the purpose of causing or that he knows to create a substantial risk of causing death or serious bodily injury. Purposely firing a firearm in the direction of another person or at a vehicle in which another person is believed to be constitutes deadly force. A threat to cause death or serious bodily injury, by the production of a weapon or otherwise, so long as the actor's purpose is limited to creating an apprehension that he will use deadly force if necessary, does not constitute deadly force.

(3) "dwelling" means any building or structure, though movable or temporary, or a portion thereof, that is for the time being the actor's home or place of lodging.

ARTICLE 4.RESPONSIBILITY

Section 4.01. Mental Disease or Defect Excluding Responsibility.

(1) A person is not responsible for criminal conduct if at the time of such conduct as a result of mental disease or defect he lacks substantial capacity either to appreciate the criminality [wrongfulness] of his conduct or to conform his conduct to the requirements of law.

(2) As used in this Article, the terms "mental disease or defect" do not include an abnormality manifested only by repeated criminal or otherwise antisocial conduct.

Section 4.02. Evidence of Mental Disease or Defect Admissible When Relevant to Element of the Offense [; Mental Disease or Defect Impairing Capacity as Ground for Mitigation of Punishment in Capital Cases].

(1) Evidence that the defendant suffered from a mental disease or defect is admissible whenever it is relevant to prove that the defendant did or did not have a state of mind that is an element of the offense.

[(2) Whenever the jury or the Court is authorized to determine or to recommend whether or not the defendant shall be sentenced to death or imprisonment upon conviction, evidence that the capacity of the defendant to appreciate the criminality [wrongfulness] of his conduct or to conform his conduct to the requirements of law was impaired as a result of mental disease or defect is admissible in favor of sentence of imprisonment.]

Section 4.03. Mental Disease or Defect Excluding Responsibility Is Affirmative Defense; Requirement of Notice; Form of Verdict and Judgment When Finding of Irresponsibility Is Made.

(1) Mental disease or defect excluding responsibility is an affirmative defense.

(2) Evidence of mental disease or defect excluding responsibility is not admissible unless the defendant, at the time of entering his plea of not guilty or within ten days thereafter or at such later time as the Court may for good cause permit, files a written notice of his purpose to rely on such defense.

(3) When the defendant is acquitted on the ground of mental disease or defect excluding responsibility, the verdict and the judgment shall so state.

Section 4.04. Mental Disease or Defect Excluding Fitness to Proceed.

No person who as a result of mental disease or defect lacks capacity to understand the proceedings against him or to assist in his own defense shall be tried, convicted or sentenced for the commission of an offense so long as such incapacity endures. * * *

Section 4.10. Immaturity Excluding Criminal Conviction; Transfer of Proceedings to Juvenile Court.

(1) A person shall not be tried for or convicted of an offense if:

(a) at the time of the conduct charged to constitute the offense he was less than sixteen years of age [, in which case the Juvenile Court shall have exclusive jurisdiction*]; or

(b) at the time of the conduct charged to constitute the offense he was sixteen or seventeen years of age, unless:

(i) the Juvenile Court has no jurisdiction over him, or

(ii) the Juvenile Court has entered an order waiving jurisdiction and consenting to the institution of criminal proceedings against him.

(2) No court shall have jurisdiction to try or convict a person of an offense if criminal proceedings against him are barred by Subsection (1) of this Section. When it appears that a person charged with the commission of an offense may be of such an age that criminal proceedings may be barred under Subsection (1) of this Section, the Court shall hold a hearing thereon, and the burden shall be on the prosecution to establish to the satisfaction of the Court that the criminal proceeding is not barred upon such grounds. If the Court determines that the proceeding is barred, custody of the person charged shall be surrendered to the Juvenile Court, and the case, including all papers and processes relating thereto, shall be transferred.

ARTICLE 5. INCHOATE CRIMES

Section 5.01. Criminal Attempt.

(1) *Definition of Attempt.* A person is guilty of an attempt to commit a crime if, acting with the kind of culpability otherwise required for commission of the crime, he:

(a) purposely engages in conduct that would constitute the crime if the attendant circumstances were as he believes them to be; or

(b) when causing a particular result is an element of the crime, does or omits to do anything with the purpose of causing or with

* The bracketed words are unnecessary if the Juvenile Court Act so provides or is amended accordingly.

the belief that it will cause such result without further conduct on his part; or

(c) purposely does or omits to do anything that, under the circumstances as he believes them to be, is an act or omission constituting a substantial step in a course of conduct planned to culminate in his commission of the crime.

(2) *Conduct That May Be Held Substantial Step Under Subsection (1)(c).* Conduct shall not be held to constitute a substantial step under Subsection (1)(c) of this Section unless it is strongly corroborative of the actor's criminal purpose. Without negativing the sufficiency of other conduct, the following, if strongly corroborative of the actor's criminal purpose, shall not be held insufficient as a matter of law:

(a) lying in wait, searching for or following the contemplated victim of the crime;

(b) enticing or seeking to entice the contemplated victim of the crime to go to the place contemplated for its commission;

(c) reconnoitering the place contemplated for the commission of the crime;

(d) unlawful entry of a structure, vehicle or enclosure in which it is contemplated that the crime will be committed;

(e) possession of materials to be employed in the commission of the crime, that are specially designed for such unlawful use or that can serve no lawful purpose of the actor under the circumstances;

(f) possession, collection or fabrication of materials to be employed in the commission of the crime, at or near the place contemplated for its commission, if such possession, collection or fabrication serves no lawful purpose of the actor under the circumstances;

(g) soliciting an innocent agent to engage in conduct constituting an element of the crime.

(3) *Conduct Designed to Aid Another in Commission of a Crime.* A person who engages in conduct designed to aid another to commit a crime that would establish his complicity under Section 2.06 if the crime were committed by such other person, is guilty of an attempt to commit the crime, although the crime is not committed or attempted by such other person.

(4) *Renunciation of Criminal Purpose.* When the actor's conduct would otherwise constitute an attempt under Subsection (1)(b) or (1)(c) of this Section, it is an affirmative defense that he abandoned his effort to commit the crime or otherwise prevented its commission, under

circumstances manifesting a complete and voluntary renunciation of his criminal purpose. The establishment of such defense does not, however, affect the liability of an accomplice who did not join in such abandonment or prevention.

Within the meaning of this Article, renunciation of criminal purpose is not voluntary if it is motivated, in whole or in part, by circumstances, not present or apparent at the inception of the actor's course of conduct, that increase the probability of detection or apprehension or that make more difficult the accomplishment of the criminal purpose. Renunciation is not complete if it is motivated by a decision to postpone the criminal conduct until a more advantageous time or to transfer the criminal effort to another but similar objective or victim.

Section 5.02. Criminal Solicitation.

(1) *Definition of Solicitation.* A person is guilty of solicitation to commit a crime if with the purpose of promoting or facilitating its commission he commands, encourages or requests another person to engage in specific conduct that would constitute such crime or an attempt to commit such crime or would establish his complicity in its commission or attempted commission.

(2) *Uncommunicated Solicitation.* It is immaterial under Subsection (1) of this Section that the actor fails to communicate with the person he solicits to commit a crime if his conduct was designed to effect such communication.

(3) *Renunciation of Criminal Purpose.* It is an affirmative defense that the actor, after soliciting another person to commit a crime, persuaded him not to do so or otherwise prevented the commission of the crime, under circumstances manifesting a complete and voluntary renunciation of his criminal purpose.

Section 5.03. Criminal Conspiracy.

(1) *Definition of Conspiracy.* A person is guilty of conspiracy with another person or persons to commit a crime if with the purpose of promoting or facilitating its commission he:

(a) agrees with such other person or persons that they or one or more of them will engage in conduct that constitutes such crime or an attempt or solicitation to commit such crime; or

(b) agrees to aid such other person or persons in the planning or commission of such crime or of an attempt or solicitation to commit such crime.

(2) *Scope of Conspiratorial Relationship.* If a person guilty of conspiracy, as defined by Subsection (1) of this Section, knows that a person with whom he conspires to commit a crime has conspired with another person

or persons to commit the same crime, he is guilty of conspiring with such other person or persons, whether or not he knows their identity, to commit such crime.

(3) *Conspiracy with Multiple Criminal Objectives.* If a person conspires to commit a number of crimes, he is guilty of only one conspiracy so long as such multiple crimes are the object of the same agreement or continuous conspiratorial relationship.

(4) *Joinder and Venue in Conspiracy Prosecutions.*

(a) Subject to the provisions of paragraph (b) of this Subsection, two or more persons charged with criminal conspiracy may be prosecuted jointly if:

(i) they are charged with conspiring with one another; or

(ii) the conspiracies alleged, whether they have the same or different parties, are so related that they constitute different aspects of a scheme of organized criminal conduct.

(b) In any joint prosecution under paragraph (a) of this Subsection:

(i) no defendant shall be charged with a conspiracy in any county [parish or district] other than one in which he entered into such conspiracy or in which an overt act pursuant to such conspiracy was done by him or by a person with whom he conspired; and

(ii) neither the liability of any defendant nor the admissibility against him of evidence of acts or declarations of another shall be enlarged by such joinder; and

(iii) the Court shall order a severance or take a special verdict as to any defendant who so requests, if it deems it necessary or appropriate to promote the fair determination of his guilt or innocence, and shall take any other proper measures to protect the fairness of the trial.

(5) *Overt Act.* No person may be convicted of conspiracy to commit a crime, other than a felony of the first or second degree, unless an overt act in pursuance of such conspiracy is alleged and proved to have been done by him or by a person with whom he conspired.

(6) *Renunciation of Criminal Purpose.* It is an affirmative defense that the actor, after conspiring to commit a crime, thwarted the success of the conspiracy, under circumstances manifesting a complete and voluntary renunciation of his criminal purpose.

(7) *Duration of Conspiracy*. For purposes of Section 1.06(4):

(a) conspiracy is a continuing course of conduct that terminates when the crime or crimes that are its object are committed or the agreement that they be committed is abandoned by the defendant and by those with whom he conspired; and

(b) such abandonment is presumed if neither the defendant nor anyone with whom he conspired does any overt act in pursuance of the conspiracy during the applicable period of limitation; and

(c) if an individual abandons the agreement, the conspiracy is terminated as to him only if and when he advises those with whom he conspired of his abandonment or he informs the law enforcement authorities of the existence of the conspiracy and of his participation therein.

Section 5.04. Incapacity, Irresponsibility or Immunity of Party to Solicitation or Conspiracy.

(1) Except as provided in Subsection (2) of this Section, it is immaterial to the liability of a person who solicits or conspires with another to commit a crime that:

(a) he or the person whom he solicits or with whom he conspires does not occupy a particular position or have a particular characteristic that is an element of such crime, if he believes that one of them does; or

(b) the person whom he solicits or with whom he conspires is irresponsible or has an immunity to prosecution or conviction for the commission of the crime.

(2) It is a defense to a charge of solicitation or conspiracy to commit a crime that if the criminal object were achieved, the actor would not be guilty of a crime under the law defining the offense or as an accomplice under Section 2.06(5) or 2.06(6)(a) or (6)(b).

Section 5.05. Grading of Criminal Attempt, Solicitation and Conspiracy; Mitigation in Cases of Lesser Danger; Multiple Convictions Barred.

(1) Grading. Except as otherwise provided in this Section, attempt, solicitation and conspiracy are crimes of the same grade and degree as the most serious offense that is attempted or solicited or is an object of the conspiracy. An attempt, solicitation or conspiracy to commit a [capital crime or a] felony of the first degree is a felony of the second degree.

(2) Mitigation. If the particular conduct charged to constitute a criminal attempt, solicitation or conspiracy is so inherently unlikely to result or culminate in the commission of a crime that neither such conduct nor the actor presents a public danger warranting the grading of such offense

under this Section, the Court shall exercise its power under Section 6.12 to enter judgment and impose sentence for a crime of lower grade or degree or, in extreme cases, may dismiss the prosecution.

(3) Multiple Convictions. A person may not be convicted of more than one offense defined by this Article for conduct designed to commit or to culminate in the commission of the same crime.

Section 5.06. Possessing Instruments of Crime; Weapons.

(1) Criminal Instruments Generally. A person commits a misdemeanor if he possesses any instrument of crime with purpose to employ it criminally. "Instrument of crime" means:

(a) anything specially made or specially adapted for criminal use; or

(b) anything commonly used for criminal purposes and possessed by the actor under circumstances that do not negative unlawful purpose.

(2) Presumption of Criminal Purpose from Possession of Weapon. If a person possesses a firearm or other weapon on or about his person, in a vehicle occupied by him, or otherwise readily available for use, it is presumed that he had the purpose to employ it criminally, unless:

(a) the weapon is possessed in the actor's home or place of business;

(b) the actor is licensed or otherwise authorized by law to possess such weapon; or

(c) the weapon is of a type commonly used in lawful sport.

"Weapon" means anything readily capable of lethal use and possessed under circumstances not manifestly appropriate for lawful uses that it may have; the term includes a firearm that is not loaded or lacks a clip or other component to render it immediately operable, and components that can readily be assembled into a weapon.

(3) Presumptions as to Possession of Criminal Instruments in Automobiles. If a weapon or other instrument of crime is found in an automobile, it is presumed to be in the possession of the occupant if there is but one. If there is more than one occupant, it is presumed to be in the possession of all, except under the following circumstances:

(a) it is found upon the person of one of the occupants;

(b) the automobile is not a stolen one and the weapon or instrument is found out of view in a glove compartment, car trunk, or other enclosed customary depository, in which case it is presumed to be in the possession of the occupant or occupants who own or have authority to operate the automobile;

(c) in the case of a taxicab, a weapon or instrument found in the passengers' portion of the vehicle is presumed to be in the possession of all the passengers, if there are any, and, if not, in the possession of the driver. * * *

ARTICLE 6. AUTHORIZED DISPOSITION OF OFFENDERS.

Section 6.01. Degrees of Felonies.

(1) Felonies defined by this Code are classified, for the purpose of sentence, into three degrees, as follows:

(a) felonies of the first degree;

(b) felonies of the second degree;

(c) felonies of the third degree.

A felony is of the first or second degree when it is so designated by the Code. A crime declared to be a felony, without specification of degree, is of the third degree.

(2) Notwithstanding any other provision of law, a felony defined by any statute of this State other than this Code shall constitute, for the purpose of sentence, a felony of the third degree. * * *

Section 6.04. Penalties Against Corporations and Unincorporated Associations; Forfeiture of Corporate Charter or Revocation of Certificate Authorizing Foreign Corporation to Do Business in the State.

(1) The Court may suspend the sentence of a corporation or an unincorporated association that has been convicted of an offense or may sentence it to pay a fine authorized by Section 6.03.

(2)(a) The [prosecuting attorney] is authorized to institute civil proceedings in the appropriate court of general jurisdiction to forfeit the charter of a corporation organized under the laws of this State or to revoke the certificate authorizing a foreign corporation to conduct business in this State. The Court may order the charter forfeited or the certificate revoked upon finding

(i) that the board of directors or a high managerial agent acting in behalf of the corporation has, in conducting the corporation's affairs, purposely engaged in a persistent course of criminal conduct and

(ii) that for the prevention of future criminal conduct of the same character, the public interest requires the charter of the corporation to be forfeited and the corporation to be dissolved or the certificate to be revoked.

(b) When a corporation is convicted of a crime or a high managerial agent of a corporation, as defined in Section 2.07, is convicted of a crime committed in the conduct of the affairs of the corporation, the Court, in sentencing the corporation or the agent, may direct the [prosecuting attorney] to institute proceedings authorized by paragraph (a) of this Subsection.

(c) The proceedings authorized by paragraph (a) of this Subsection shall be conducted in accordance with the procedures authorized by law for the involuntary dissolution of a corporation or the revocation of the certificate authorizing a foreign corporation to conduct business in this State. Such proceedings shall be deemed additional to any other proceedings authorized by law for the purpose of forfeiting the charter of a corporation or revoking the certificate of a foreign corporation. * * *

Section 6.06. Sentence of Imprisonment for Felony; Ordinary Terms.

A person who has been convicted of a felony may be sentenced to imprisonment, as follows:

(1) in the case of a felony of the first degree, for a term the minimum of which shall be fixed by the Court at not less than one year nor more than ten years, and the maximum of which shall be life imprisonment;

(2) in the case of a felony of the second degree, for a term the minimum of which shall be fixed by the Court at not less than one year nor more than three years, and the maximum of which shall be ten years;

(3) in the case of a felony of the third degree, for a term the minimum of which shall be fixed by the Court at not less than one year nor more than two years, and the maximum of which shall be five years. * * *

Section 6.08. Sentence of Imprisonment for Misdemeanors and Petty Misdemeanors; Ordinary Terms.

A person who has been convicted of a misdemeanor or a petty misdemeanor may be sentenced to imprisonment for a definite term which shall be fixed by the Court and shall not exceed one year in the case of a misdemeanor or thirty days in the case of a petty misdemeanor. * * *

Section 6.12. Reduction of Conviction by Court to Lesser Degree of Felony or to Misdemeanor.

If, when a person has been convicted of a felony, the Court, having regard to the nature and circumstances of the crime and to the history and character of the defendant, is of the view that it would be unduly harsh to sentence the offender in accordance with the Code, the Court may enter judgment of conviction for a lesser degree of felony or for a misdemeanor and impose sentence accordingly. * * *

PART II. DEFINITION OF SPECIFIC CRIMES

OFFENSES INVOLVING DANGER TO THE PERSON

ARTICLE 210. CRIMINAL HOMICIDE

Section 210.0. Definitions.

In Articles 210–213, unless a different meaning plainly is required:

(1) "human being" means a person who has been born and is alive;

(2) "bodily injury" means physical pain, illness or any impairment of physical condition;

(3) "serious bodily injury" means bodily injury which creates a substantial risk of death or which causes serious, permanent disfigurement, or protracted loss or impairment of the function of any bodily member or organ;

(4) "deadly weapon" means any firearm or other weapon, device, instrument, material or substance, whether animate or inanimate, which in the manner it is used or is intended to be used is known to be capable of producing death or serious bodily injury.

Section 210.1. Criminal Homicide.

(1) A person is guilty of criminal homicide if he purposely, knowingly, recklessly or negligently causes the death of another human being.

(2) Criminal homicide is murder, manslaughter or negligent homicide.

Section 210.2. Murder.

(1) Except as provided in Section 210.3(1)(b), criminal homicide constitutes murder when:

(a) it is committed purposely or knowingly; or

(b) it is committed recklessly under circumstances manifesting extreme indifference to the value of human life. Such recklessness and indifference are presumed if the actor is engaged or is an accomplice in the commission of, or an attempt to commit, or flight after committing or attempting to commit robbery, rape or deviate sexual intercourse by force or threat of force, arson, burglary, kidnapping or felonious escape.

(2) Murder is a felony of the first degree [but a person convicted of murder may be sentenced to death, as provided in Section 210.6].

Section 210.3. Manslaughter.

(1) Criminal homicide constitutes manslaughter when:

(a) it is committed recklessly; or

(b) a homicide which would otherwise be murder is committed under the influence of extreme mental or emotional disturbance for which there is reasonable explanation or excuse. The reasonableness of such explanation or excuse shall be determined from the viewpoint of a person in the actor's situation under the circumstances as he believes them to be.

(2) Manslaughter is a felony of the second degree.

Section 210.4. Negligent Homicide.

(1) Criminal homicide constitutes negligent homicide when it is committed negligently.

(2) Negligent homicide is a felony of the third degree.

Section 210.5. Causing or Aiding Suicide.

(1) *Causing Suicide as Criminal Homicide.* A person may be convicted of criminal homicide for causing another to commit suicide only if he purposely causes such suicide by force, duress or deception.

(2) *Aiding or Soliciting Suicide as an Independent Offense.* A person who purposely aids or solicits another to commit suicide is guilty of a felony of the second degree if his conduct causes such suicide or an attempted suicide, and otherwise of a misdemeanor.

Section 210.6. Sentence of Death for Murder; Further Proceedings to Determine Sentence.

(1) *Death Sentence Excluded.* When a defendant is found guilty of murder, the Court shall impose sentence for a felony of the first degree if it is satisfied that:

(a) none of the aggravating circumstances enumerated in Subsection (3) of this Section was established by the evidence at the trial or will be established if further proceedings are initiated under Subsection (2) of this Section; or

(b) substantial mitigating circumstances, established by the evidence at the trial, call for leniency; or

(c) the defendant, with the consent of the prosecuting attorney and the approval of the Court, pleaded guilty to murder as a felony of the first degree; or

(d) the defendant was under 18 years of age at the time of the commission of the crime; or

(e) the defendant's physical or mental condition calls for leniency; or

(f) although the evidence suffices to sustain the verdict, it does not foreclose all doubt respecting the defendant's guilt.

(2) *Determination by Court or by Court and Jury.* Unless the Court imposes sentence under Subsection (1) of this Section, it shall conduct a separate proceeding to determine whether the defendant should be sentenced for a felony of the first degree or sentenced to death. The proceeding shall be conducted before the Court alone if the defendant was convicted by a Court sitting without a jury or upon his plea of guilty or if the prosecuting attorney and the defendant waive a jury with respect to sentence. In other cases it shall be conducted before the Court sitting with the jury which determined the defendant's guilt or, if the Court for good cause shown discharges that jury, with a new jury empanelled for the purpose.

In the proceeding, evidence may be presented as to any matter that the Court deems relevant to sentence, including but not limited to the nature and circumstances of the crime, the defendant's character, background, history, mental and physical condition and any of the aggravating or mitigating circumstances enumerated in Subsections (3) and (4) of this Section. Any such evidence, not legally privileged, which the Court deems to have probative force, may be received, regardless of its admissibility under the exclusionary rules of evidence, provided that the defendant's counsel is accorded a fair opportunity to rebut such evidence. The prosecuting attorney and the defendant or his counsel shall be permitted to present argument for or against sentence of death.

The determination whether sentence of death shall be imposed shall be in the discretion of the Court, except that when the proceeding is conducted before the Court sitting with a jury, the Court shall not impose sentence of death unless it submits to the jury the issue whether the defendant should be sentenced to death or to imprisonment and the jury returns a verdict that the sentence should be death. If the jury is unable to reach a unanimous verdict, the Court shall dismiss the jury and impose sentence for a felony of the first degree.

The Court, in exercising its discretion as to sentence, and the jury, in determining upon its verdict, shall take into account the aggravating and mitigating circumstances enumerated in Subsections (3) and (4) and any other facts that it deems relevant, but it shall not impose or recommend sentence of death unless it finds one of the aggravating circumstances enumerated in Subsection (3) and further finds that there are no mitigating circumstances sufficiently substantial to call for leniency. When the issue is submitted to the jury, the Court shall so instruct and also shall inform the jury of the nature of the sentence of imprisonment that may be imposed, including its implication with respect to possible release upon parole, if the jury verdict is against sentence of death.

Alternative formulation of Subsection (2):

(2) *Determination by Court.* Unless the Court imposes sentence under Subsection (1) of this Section, it shall conduct a separate proceeding to determine whether the defendant should be sentenced for a felony of the first degree or sentenced to death. In the proceeding, the Court, in accordance with Section 7.07, shall consider the report of the pre-sentence investigation and, if a psychiatric examination has been ordered, the report of such examination. In addition, evidence may be presented as to any matter that the Court deems relevant to sentence, including but not limited to the nature and circumstances of the crime, the defendant's character, background, history, mental and physical condition and any of the aggravating or mitigating circumstances enumerated in Subsections (3) and (4) of this Section. Any such evidence, not legally privileged, which the Court deems to have probative force, may be received, regardless of its admissibility under the exclusionary rules of evidence, provided that the defendant's counsel is accorded a fair opportunity to rebut such evidence. The prosecuting attorney and the defendant or his counsel shall be permitted to present argument for or against sentence of death.

The determination whether sentence of death shall be imposed shall be in the discretion of the Court. In exercising such discretion, the Court shall take into account the aggravating and mitigating circumstances enumerated in Subsections (3) and (4) and any other facts that it deems relevant but shall not impose sentence of death unless it finds one of the aggravating circumstances enumerated in Subsection (3) and further finds that there are no mitigating circumstances sufficiently substantial to call for leniency.

(3) *Aggravating Circumstances.*

(a) The murder was committed by a convict under sentence of imprisonment.

(b) The defendant was previously convicted of another murder or of a felony involving the use or threat of violence to the person.

(c) At the time the murder was committed the defendant also committed another murder.

(d) The defendant knowingly created a great risk of death to many persons.

(e) The murder was committed while the defendant was engaged or was an accomplice in the commission of, or an attempt to commit, or flight after committing or attempting to commit robbery, rape or deviate sexual intercourse by force or threat of force, arson, burglary or kidnapping.

(f) The murder was committed for the purpose of avoiding or preventing a lawful arrest or effecting an escape from lawful custody.

(g) The murder was committed for pecuniary gain.

(h) The murder was especially heinous, atrocious or cruel, manifesting exceptional depravity.

(4) *Mitigating Circumstances.*

(a) The defendant has no significant history of prior criminal activity.

(b) The murder was committed while the defendant was under the influence of extreme mental or emotional disturbance.

(c) The victim was a participant in the defendant's homicidal conduct or consented to the homicidal act.

(d) The murder was committed under circumstances which the defendant believed to provide a moral justification or extenuation for his conduct.

(e) The defendant was an accomplice in a murder committed by another person and his participation in the homicidal act was relatively minor.

(f) The defendant acted under duress or under the domination of another person.

(g) At the time of the murder, the capacity of the defendant to appreciate the criminality [wrongfulness] of his conduct or to conform his conduct to the requirements of law was impaired as a result of mental disease or defect or intoxication.

(h) The youth of the defendant at the time of the crime.]

ARTICLE 211. ASSAULT; RECKLESS ENDANGERING; THREATS

Section 211.0. Definitions.

In this Article, the definitions given in Section 210.0 apply unless a different meaning plainly is required.

Section 211.1. Assault.

(1) *Simple Assault.* A person is guilty of assault if he:

(a) attempts to cause or purposely, knowingly or recklessly causes bodily injury to another; or

(b) negligently causes bodily injury to another with a deadly weapon; or

(c) attempts by physical menace to put another in fear of imminent serious bodily injury.

Simple assault is a misdemeanor unless committed in a fight or scuffle entered into by mutual consent, in which case it is a petty misdemeanor.

(2) *Aggravated Assault.* A person is guilty of aggravated assault if he:

(a) attempts to cause serious bodily injury to another, or causes such injury purposely, knowingly or recklessly under circumstances manifesting extreme indifference to the value of human life; or

(b) attempts to cause or purposely or knowingly causes bodily injury to another with a deadly weapon.

Aggravated assault under paragraph (a) is a felony of the second degree; aggravated assault under paragraph (b) is a felony of the third degree.

Section 211.2. Recklessly Endangering Another Person.

A person commits a misdemeanor if he recklessly engages in conduct which places or may place another person in danger of death or serious bodily injury. Recklessness and danger shall be presumed where a person knowingly points a firearm at or in the direction of another, whether or not the actor believed the firearm to be loaded.

Section 211.3. Terroristic Threats.

A person is guilty of a felony of the third degree if he threatens to commit any crime of violence with purpose to terrorize another or to cause evacuation of a building, place of assembly, or facility of public transportation, or otherwise to cause serious public inconvenience, or in reckless disregard of the risk of causing such terror or inconvenience.

ARTICLE 212. KIDNAPPING AND RELATED OFFENSES; COERCION

Section 212.0. Definitions.

In this Article, the definitions given in Section 210.0 apply unless a different meaning plainly is required.

Section 212.1 Kidnapping.

A person is guilty of kidnapping if he unlawfully removes another from his place of residence or business, or a substantial distance from the vicinity where he is found, or if he unlawfully confines another for a substantial period in a place of isolation, with any of the following purposes:

(a) to hold for ransom or reward, or as a shield or hostage; or

(b) to facilitate commission of any felony or flight thereafter; or

(c) to inflict bodily injury on or to terrorize the victim or another; or

(d) to interfere with the performance of any governmental or political function.

Kidnapping is a felony of the first degree unless the actor voluntarily releases the victim alive and in a safe place prior to trial, in which case it is a felony of the second degree. A removal or confinement is unlawful within the meaning of this Section if it is accomplished by force, threat or deception, or, in the case of a person who is under the age of 14 or incompetent, if it is accomplished without the consent of a parent, guardian or other person responsible for general supervision of his welfare.

Section 212.2. Felonious Restraint.

A person commits a felony of the third degree if he knowingly:

(a) restrains another unlawfully in circumstances exposing him to risk of serious bodily injury; or

(b) holds another in a condition of involuntary servitude.

Section 212.3. False Imprisonment.

A person commits a misdemeanor if he knowingly restrains another unlawfully so as to interfere substantially with his liberty.

Section 212.4. Interference with Custody.

(1) *Custody of Children.* A person commits an offense if he knowingly or recklessly takes or entices any child under the age of 18 from the custody of its parent, guardian or other lawful custodian, when he has no privilege to do so. It is an affirmative defense that:

(a) the actor believed that his action was necessary to preserve the child from danger to its welfare; or

(b) the child, being at the time not less than 14 years old, was taken away at its own instigation without enticement and without purpose to commit a criminal offense with or against the child.

Proof that the child was below the critical age gives rise to a presumption that the actor knew the child's age or acted in reckless disregard thereof. The offense is a misdemeanor unless the actor, not being a parent or person in equivalent relation to the child, acted with knowledge that his conduct would cause serious alarm for the child's safety, or in reckless disregard of a likelihood of causing such alarm, in which case the offense is a felony of the third degree.

(2) *Custody of Committed Persons.* A person is guilty of a misdemeanor if he knowingly or recklessly takes or entices any committed person away from lawful custody when he is not privileged to do so. "Committed person" means, in addition to anyone committed under judicial warrant, any orphan, neglected or delinquent child, mentally defective or insane person, or other dependent or incompetent person entrusted to another's custody by or through a recognized social agency or otherwise by authority of law.

Section 212.5. Criminal Coercion.

(1) *Offense Defined.* A person is guilty of criminal coercion if, with purpose unlawfully to restrict another's freedom of action to his detriment, he threatens to:

(a) commit any criminal offense; or

(b) accuse anyone of a criminal offense; or

(c) expose any secret tending to subject any person to hatred, contempt or ridicule, or to impair his credit or business repute; or

(d) take or withhold action as an official, or cause an official to take or withhold action.

It is an affirmative defense to prosecution based on paragraphs (b), (c) or (d) that the actor believed the accusation or secret to be true or the proposed official action justified and that his purpose was limited to compelling the other to behave in a way reasonably related to the circumstances which were the subject of the accusation, exposure or proposed official action, as by desisting from further misbehavior, making good a wrong done, refraining from taking any action or responsibility for which the actor believes the other disqualified.

(2) *Grading.* Criminal coercion is a misdemeanor unless the threat is to commit a felony or the actor's purpose is felonious, in which cases the offense is a felony of the third degree.

ARTICLE 213. SEXUAL OFFENSES

Section 213.0. Definitions.

In this Article, unless a different meaning plainly is required:

(1) the definitions given in Section 210.0 apply;

(2) "Sexual intercourse" includes intercourse per os or per anum, with some penetration however slight; emission is not required;

(3) "Deviate sexual intercourse" means sexual intercourse per os or per anum between human beings who are not husband and wife, and any form of sexual intercourse with an animal.

Section 213.1. Rape and Related Offenses.

(1) *Rape.* A male who has sexual intercourse with a female not his wife is guilty of rape if:

(a) he compels her to submit by force or by threat of imminent death, serious bodily injury, extreme pain or kidnapping, to be inflicted on anyone; or

(b) he has substantially impaired her power to appraise or control her conduct by administering or employing without her knowledge drugs, intoxicants or other means for the purpose of preventing resistance; or

(c) the female is unconscious; or

(d) the female is less than 10 years old.

Rape is a felony of the second degree unless (i) in the course thereof the actor inflicts serious bodily injury upon anyone, or (ii) the victim was not a voluntary social companion of the actor upon the occasion of the crime and had not previously permitted him sexual liberties, in which cases the offense is a felony of the first degree.

(2) *Gross Sexual Imposition.* A male who has sexual intercourse with a female not his wife commits a felony of the third degree if:

(a) he compels her to submit by any threat that would prevent resistance by a woman of ordinary resolution; or

(b) he knows that she suffers from a mental disease or defect which renders her incapable of appraising the nature of her conduct; or

(c) he knows that she is unaware that a sexual act is being committed upon her or that she submits because she mistakenly supposes that he is her husband.

Section 213.2. Deviate Sexual Intercourse by Force or Imposition.

(1) *By Force or Its Equivalent.* A person who engages in deviate sexual intercourse with another person, or who causes another to engage in deviate sexual intercourse, commits a felony of the second degree if:

(a) he compels the other person to participate by force or by threat of imminent death, serious bodily injury, extreme pain or kidnapping, to be inflicted on anyone; or

(b) he has substantially impaired the other person's power to appraise or control his conduct, by administering or employing without the knowledge of the other person drugs, intoxicants or other means for the purpose of preventing resistance; or

(c) the other person is unconscious; or

(d) the other person is less than 10 years old.

(2) *By Other Imposition.* A person who engages in deviate sexual intercourse with another person, or who causes another to engage in deviate sexual intercourse, commits a felony of the third degree if:

(a) he compels the other person to participate by any threat that would prevent resistance by a person of ordinary resolution; or

(b) he knows that the other person suffers from a mental disease or defect which renders him incapable of appraising the nature of his conduct; or

(c) he knows that the other person submits because he is unaware that a sexual act is being committed upon him.

Section 213.3. Corruption of Minors and Seduction.

(1) *Offense Defined.* A male who has sexual intercourse with a female not his wife, or any person who engages in deviate sexual intercourse or causes another to engage in deviate sexual intercourse, is guilty of an offense if:

(a) the other person is less than [16] years old and the actor is at least [four] years older than the other person; or

(b) the other person is less than 21 years old and the actor is his guardian or otherwise responsible for general supervision of his welfare; or

(c) the other person is in custody of law or detained in a hospital or other institution and the actor has supervisory or disciplinary authority over him; or

(d) the other person is a female who is induced to participate by a promise of marriage which the actor does not mean to perform.

(2) *Grading.* An offense under paragraph (a) of Subsection (1) is a felony of the third degree. Otherwise an offense under this section is a misdemeanor.

Section 213.4. Sexual Assault.

A person who has sexual contact with another not his spouse, or causes such other to have sexual contact with him, is guilty of sexual assault, a misdemeanor, if:

(1) he knows that the contact is offensive to the other person; or

(2) he knows that the other person suffers from a mental disease or defect which renders him or her incapable of appraising the nature of his or her conduct; or

(3) he knows that the other person is unaware that a sexual act is being committed; or

(4) the other person is less than 10 years old; or

(5) he has substantially impaired the other person's power to appraise or control his or her conduct, by administering or employing without the other's knowledge drugs, intoxicants or other means for the purpose of preventing resistance; or

(6) the other person is less than [16] years old and the actor is at least [four] years older than the other person; or

(7) the other person is less than 21 years old and the actor is his guardian or otherwise responsible for general supervision of his welfare; or

(8) the other person is in custody of law or detained in a hospital or other institution and the actor has supervisory or disciplinary authority over him.

Sexual contact is any touching of the sexual or other intimate parts of the person for the purpose of arousing or gratifying sexual desire.

Section 213.5. Indecent Exposure.

A person commits a misdemeanor if, for the purpose of arousing or gratifying sexual desire of himself or of any person other than his spouse, he exposes his genitals under circumstances in which he knows his conduct is likely to cause affront or alarm.

Section 213.6. Provisions Generally Applicable to Article 213.

(1) *Mistake as to Age.* Whenever in this Article the criminality of conduct depends on a child's being below the age of 10, it is no defense that the actor did not know the child's age, or reasonably believed the child to be older than 10. When criminality depends on the child's being below a critical age other than 10, it is a defense for the actor to prove by a preponderance of the evidence that he reasonably believed the child to be above the critical age.

(2) *Spouse Relationships.* Whenever in this Article the definition of an offense excludes conduct with a spouse, the exclusion shall be deemed to extend to persons living as man and wife, regardless of the legal status of their relationship. The exclusion shall be inoperative as respects spouses ...ng apart under a decree of judicial separation. Where the definition of ... excludes conduct with a spouse or conduct by a woman, this ...de conviction of a spouse or woman as accomplice in a ... e or she causes another person, not within the ... .

...scuous Complainants. It is a defense to prosecution ...3.3 and paragraphs (6), (7) and (8) of Section 213.4 for the actor to prove by a preponderance of the evidence that the alleged victim had, prior to the time of the offense charged, engaged promiscuously in sexual relations with others.

(4) *Prompt Complaint.* No prosecution may be instituted or maintained under this Article unless the alleged offense was brought to the notice of public authority within [3] months of its occurrence or, where the alleged victim was less than [16] years old or otherwise incompetent to make complaint, within [3] months after a parent, guardian or other competent person specially interested in the victim learns of the offense.

(5) *Testimony of Complainants.* No person shall be convicted of any felony under this Article upon the uncorroborated testimony of the alleged victim. Corroboration may be circumstantial. In any prosecution before a jury for an offense under this Article, the jury shall be instructed to evaluate the testimony of a victim or complaining witness with special care in view of the emotional involvement of the witness and the difficulty of determining the truth with respect to alleged sexual activities carried out in private.

OFFENSES AGAINST PROPERTY

ARTICLE 220. ARSON, CRIMINAL MISCHIEF, AND OTHER PROPERTY DESTRUCTION

Section 220.1. Arson and Related Offenses.

(1) *Arson.* A person is guilty of arson, a felony of the second degree, if he starts a fire or causes an explosion with the purpose of:

(a) destroying a building or occupied structure of another; or

(b) destroying or damaging any property, whether his own or another's, to collect insurance for such loss. It shall be an affirmative defense to prosecution under this paragraph that the actor's conduct did not recklessly endanger any building or occupied structure of another or place any other person in danger of death or bodily injury.

(2) *Reckless Burning or Exploding.* A person commits a felony of the third degree if he purposely starts a fire or causes an explosion, whether on his own property or another's, and thereby recklessly:

(a) places another person in danger of death or bodily injury; or

(b) places a building or occupied structure of another in danger of damage or destruction.

(3) *Failure to Control or Report Dangerous Fire.* A person who knows that a fire is endangering life or a substantial amount of property of another and fails to take reasonable measures to put out or control the fire, when

he can do so without substantial risk to himself, or to give a prompt fire alarm, commits a misdemeanor if:

(a) he knows that he is under an official, contractual, or other legal duty to prevent or combat the fire; or

(b) the fire was started, albeit lawfully, by him or with his assent, or on property in his custody or control.

(4) *Definitions.* "Occupied structure" means any structure, vehicle or place adapted for overnight accommodation of persons, or for carrying on business therein, whether or not a person is actually present. Property is that of another, for the purposes of this section, if anyone other than the actor has a possessory or proprietary interest therein. If a building or structure is divided into separately occupied units, any unit not occupied by the actor is an occupied structure of another.

Section 220.2. Causing or Risking Catastrophe.

(1) *Causing Catastrophe.* A person who causes a catastrophe by explosion, fire, flood, avalanche, collapse of building, release of poison gas, radioactive material or other harmful or destructive force or substance, or by any other means of causing potentially widespread injury or damage, commits a felony of the second degree if he does so purposely or knowingly, or a felony of the third degree if he does so recklessly.

(2) *Risking Catastrophe.* A person is guilty of a misdemeanor if he recklessly creates a risk of catastrophe in the employment of fire, explosives or other dangerous means listed in Subsection (1).

(3) *Failure to Prevent Catastrophe.* A person who knowingly or recklessly fails to take reasonable measures to prevent or mitigate a catastrophe commits a misdemeanor if:

(a) he knows that he is under an official, contractual or other legal duty to take such measures; or

(b) he did or assented to the act causing or threatening the catastrophe.

Section 220.3. Criminal Mischief.

(1) *Offense Defined.* A person is guilty of criminal mischief if he:

(a) damages tangible property of another purposely, recklessly, or by negligence in the employment of fire, explosives, or other dangerous means listed in Section 220.2(1); or

(b) purposely or recklessly tampers with tangible property of another so as to endanger person or property; or

(c) purposely or recklessly causes another to suffer pecuniary loss by deception or threat.

(2) *Grading.* Criminal mischief is a felony of the third degree if the actor purposely causes pecuniary loss in excess of $5,000, or a substantial interruption or impairment of public communication, transportation, supply of water, gas or power, or other public service. It is a misdemeanor if the actor purposely causes pecuniary loss in excess of $100, or a petty misdemeanor if he purposely or recklessly causes pecuniary loss in excess of $25. Otherwise criminal mischief is a violation.

ARTICLE 221. BURGLARY AND OTHER CRIMINAL INTRUSION

Section 221.0. Definitions.

In this Article, unless a different meaning plainly is required:

(1) "occupied structure" means any structure, vehicle or place adapted for overnight accommodation of persons, or for carrying on business therein, whether or not a person is actually present.

(2) "night" means the period between thirty minutes past sunset and thirty minutes before sunrise.

Section 221.1. Burglary.

(1) *Burglary Defined.* A person is guilty of burglary if he enters a building or occupied structure, or separately secured or occupied portion thereof, with purpose to commit a crime therein, unless the premises are at the time open to the public or the actor is licensed or privileged to enter. It is an affirmative defense to prosecution for burglary that the building or structure was abandoned.

(2) *Grading.* Burglary is a felony of the second degree if it is perpetrated in the dwelling of another at night, or if, in the course of committing the offense, the actor:

(a) purposely, knowingly or recklessly inflicts or attempts to inflict bodily injury on anyone; or

(b) is armed with explosives or a deadly weapon.

Otherwise, burglary is a felony of the third degree. An act shall be deemed "in the course of committing" an offense if it occurs in an attempt to commit the offense or in flight after the attempt or commission.

(3) Multiple Convictions. A person may not be convicted both for burglary and for the offense which it was his purpose to commit after the burglarious entry or for an attempt to commit that offense, unless the additional offense constitutes a felony of the first or second degree.

Section 221.2. Criminal Trespass.

(1) *Buildings* and Occupied Structures. A person commits an offense if, knowing that he is not licensed or privileged to do so, he enters or

surreptitiously remains in any building or occupied structure, or separately secured or occupied portion thereof. An offense under this Subsection is a misdemeanor if it is committed in a dwelling at night. Otherwise it is a petty misdemeanor.

(2) *Defiant Trespasser.* A person commits an offense if, knowing that he is not licensed or privileged to do so, he enters or remains in any place as to which notice against trespass is given by:

(a) actual communication to the actor; or

(b) posting in a manner prescribed by law or reasonably likely to come to the attention of intruders; or

(c) fencing or other enclosure manifestly designed to exclude intruders.

An offense under this Subsection constitutes a petty misdemeanor if the offender defies an order to leave personally communicated to him by the owner of the premises or other authorized person. Otherwise it is a violation.

(3) *Defenses.* It is an affirmative defense to prosecution under this Section that:

(a) a building or occupied structure involved in an offense under Subsection (1) was abandoned; or

(b) the premises were at the time open to members of the public and the actor complied with all lawful conditions imposed on access to or remaining in the premises; or

(c) the actor reasonably believed that the owner of the premises, or other person empowered to license access thereto, would have licensed him to enter or remain.

ARTICLE 222. ROBBERY

Section 222.1. Robbery.

(1) *Robbery Defined.* A person is guilty of robbery if, in the course of committing a theft, he:

(a) inflicts serious bodily injury upon another; or

(b) threatens another with or purposely puts him in fear of immediate serious bodily injury; or

(c) commits or threatens immediately to commit any felony of the first or second degree.

An act shall be deemed "in the course of committing a theft" if it occurs in an attempt to commit theft or in flight after the attempt or commission.

(2) *Grading*. Robbery is a felony of the second degree, except that it is a felony of the first degree if in the course of committing the theft the actor attempts to kill anyone, or purposely inflicts or attempts to inflict serious bodily injury.

ARTICLE 223. THEFT AND RELATED OFFENSES

Section 223.0. Definitions.

In this Article, unless a different meaning plainly is required:

(1) "deprive" means: (a) to withhold property of another permanently or for so extended a period as to appropriate a major portion of its economic value, or with intent to restore only upon payment of reward or other compensation; or (b) to dispose of the property so as to make it unlikely that the owner will recover it.

(2) "financial institution" means a bank, insurance company, credit union, building and loan association, investment trust or other organization held out to the public as a place of deposit of funds or medium of savings or collective investment.

(3) "government" means the United States, any State, county, municipality, or other political unit, or any department, agency or subdivision of any of the foregoing, or any corporation or other association carrying out the functions of government.

(4) "movable property" means property the location of which can be changed, including things growing on, affixed to, or found in land, and documents although the rights represented thereby have no physical location; "immovable property" is all other property.

(5) "obtain" means: (a) in relation to property, to bring about a transfer or purported transfer of a legal interest in the property, whether to the obtainer or another; or (b) in relation to labor or service, to secure performance thereof.

(6) "property" means anything of value, including real estate, tangible and intangible personal property, contract rights, choses-in-action and other interests in or claims to wealth, admission or transportation tickets, captured or domestic animals, food and drink, electric or other power.

(7) "property of another" includes property in which any person other than the actor has an interest which the actor is not privileged to infringe, regardless of the fact that the actor also has an interest in the property and regardless of the fact that the other person might be precluded from civil recovery because the property was used in an unlawful transaction or was subject to forfeiture as contraband. Property in possession of the actor shall not be deemed property of another who has only a security interest therein, even if legal title is in the creditor pursuant to a conditional sales contract or other security agreement.

Section 223.1. Consolidation of Theft Offenses; Grading; Provisions Applicable to Theft Generally.

(1) *Consolidation of Theft Offenses.* Conduct denominated theft in this Article constitutes a single offense. An accusation of theft may be supported by evidence that it was committed in any manner that would be theft under this Article, notwithstanding the specification of a different manner in the indictment or information, subject only to the power of the Court to ensure fair trial by granting a continuance or other appropriate relief where the conduct of the defense would be prejudiced by lack of fair notice or by surprise.

(2) *Grading of Theft Offenses.*

(a) Theft constitutes a felony of the third degree if the amount involved exceeds $500, or if the property stolen is a firearm, automobile, airplane, motorcycle, motor boat, or other motor-propelled vehicle, or in the case of theft by receiving stolen property, if the receiver is in the business of buying or selling stolen property.

(b) Theft not within the preceding paragraph constitutes a misdemeanor, except that if the property was not taken from the person or by threat, or in breach of a fiduciary obligation, and the actor proves by a preponderance of the evidence that the amount involved was less than $50, the offense constitutes a petty misdemeanor.

(c) The amount involved in a theft shall be deemed to be the highest value, by any reasonable standard, of the property or services which the actor stole or attempted to steal. Amounts involved in thefts committed pursuant to one scheme or course of conduct, whether from the same person or several persons, may be aggregated in determining the grade of the offense.

(3) *Claim of Right.* It is an affirmative defense to prosecution for theft that the actor:

(a) was unaware that the property or service was that of another; or

(b) acted under an honest claim of right to the property or service involved or that he had a right to acquire or dispose of it as he did; or

(c) took property exposed for sale, intending to purchase and pay for it promptly, or reasonably believing that the owner, if present, would have consented.

(4) *Theft from Spouse.* It is no defense that theft was from the actor's spouse, except that misappropriation of household and personal effects, or

other property normally accessible to both spouses, is theft only if it occurs after the parties have ceased living together.

Section 223.2. Theft by Unlawful Taking or Disposition.

(1) *Movable Property.* A person is guilty of theft if he unlawfully takes, or exercises unlawful control over, movable property of another with purpose to deprive him thereof.

(2) *Immovable Property.* A person is guilty of theft if he unlawfully transfers immovable property of another or any interest therein with purpose to benefit himself or another not entitled thereto.

Section 223.3. Theft by Deception.

A person is guilty of theft if he purposely obtains property of another by deception. A person deceives if he purposely:

(1) creates or reinforces a false impression, including false impressions as to law, value, intention or other state of mind; but deception as to a person's intention to perform a promise shall not be inferred from the fact alone that he did not subsequently perform the promise; or

(2) prevents another from acquiring information which would affect his judgment of a transaction; or

(3) fails to correct a false impression which the deceiver previously created or reinforced, or which the deceiver knows to be influencing another to whom he stands in a fiduciary or confidential relationship; or

(4) fails to disclose a known lien, adverse claim or other legal impediment to the enjoyment of property which he transfers or encumbers in consideration for the property obtained, whether such impediment is or is not valid, or is or is not a matter of official record.

The term "deceive" does not, however, include falsity as to matters having no pecuniary significance, or puffing by statements unlikely to deceive ordinary persons in the group addressed.

Section 223.4. Theft by Extortion.

A person is guilty of theft if he purposely obtains property of another by threatening to:

(1) inflict bodily injury on anyone or commit any other criminal offense; or

(2) accuse anyone of a criminal offense; or

(3) expose any secret tending to subject any person to hatred, contempt or ridicule, or to impair his credit or business repute; or

(4) take or withhold action as an official, or cause an official to take or withhold action; or

(5) bring about or continue a strike, boycott or other collective unofficial action, if the property is not demanded or received for the benefit of the group in whose interest the actor purports to act; or

(6) testify or provide information or withhold testimony or information with respect to another's legal claim or defense; or

(7) inflict any other harm which would not benefit the actor.

It is an affirmative defense to prosecution based on paragraphs (2), (3) or (4) that the property obtained by threat of accusation, exposure, lawsuit or other invocation of official action was honestly claimed as restitution or indemnification for harm done in the circumstances to which such accusation, exposure, lawsuit or other official action relates, or as compensation for property or lawful services.

Section 223.5. Theft of Property Lost, Mislaid, or Delivered by Mistake.

A person who comes into control of property of another that he knows to have been lost, mislaid, or delivered under a mistake as to the nature or amount of the property or the identity of the recipient is guilty of theft if, with purpose to deprive the owner thereof, he fails to take reasonable measures to restore the property to a person entitled to have it.

Section 223.6. Receiving Stolen Property.

(1) *Receiving.* A person is guilty of theft if he purposely receives, retains, or disposes of movable property of another knowing that it has been stolen, or believing that it has probably been stolen, unless the property is received, retained, or disposed with purpose to restore it to the owner. "Receiving" means acquiring possession, control or title, or lending on the security of the property.

(2) *Presumption of Knowledge.* The requisite knowledge or belief is presumed in the case of a dealer who:

> (a) is found in possession or control of property stolen from two or more persons on separate occasions; or
>
> (b) has received stolen property in another transaction within the year preceding the transaction charged; or
>
> (c) being a dealer in property of the sort received, acquires it for a consideration which he knows is far below its reasonable value.

"Dealer" means a person in the business of buying or selling goods including a pawnbroker.

Section 223.7. Theft of Services.

(1) A person is guilty of theft is he purposely obtains services which he knows are available only for compensation, by deception or threat, or by

false token or other means to avoid payment for the service. "Services" includes labor, professional service, transportation, telephone or other public service, accommodation in hotels, restaurants or elsewhere, admission to exhibitions, use of vehicles or other movable property. Where compensation for service is ordinarily paid immediately upon the rendering of such service, as in the case of hotels and restaurants, refusal to pay or absconding without payment or offer to pay gives rise to a presumption that the service was obtained by deception as to intention to pay.

(2) A person commits theft if, having control over the disposition of services of others, to which he is not entitled, he knowingly diverts such services to his own benefit or to the benefit of another not entitled thereto.

Section 223.8. Theft by Failure to Make Required Disposition of Funds Received.

A person who purposely obtains property upon agreement, or subject to a known legal obligation, to make specified payment or other disposition, whether from such property or its proceeds or from his own property to be reserved in equivalent amount, is guilty of theft if he deals with the property obtained as his own and fails to make the required payment or disposition. The foregoing applies notwithstanding that it may be impossible to identify particular property as belonging to the victim at the time of the actor's failure to make the required payment or disposition. An officer or employee of the government or of a financial institution is presumed: (i) to know any legal obligation relevant to his criminal liability under this Section, and (ii) to have dealt with the property as his own if he fails to pay or account upon lawful demand, or if an audit reveals a shortage or falsification of accounts.

Section 223.9. Unauthorized Use of Automobiles and Other Vehicles.

A person commits a misdemeanor if he operates another's automobile, airplane, motorcycle, motorboat, or other motor-propelled vehicle without consent of the owner. It is an affirmative defense to prosecution under this Section that the actor reasonably believed that the owner would have consented to the operation had he known of it.

ARTICLE 224. FORGERY AND FRAUDULENT PRACTICES

Section 224.0. Definitions.

In this Article, the definitions given in Section 223.0 apply unless a different meaning plainly is required.

Section 224.1. Forgery.

(1) *Definition.* A person is guilty of forgery if, with purpose to defraud or injure anyone, or with knowledge that he is facilitating a fraud or injury to be perpetrated by anyone, the actor:

(a) alters any writing of another without his authority; or

(b) makes, completes, executes, authenticates, issues or transfers any writing so that it purports to be the act of another who did not authorize that act, or to have been executed at a time or place or in a numbered sequence other than was in fact the case, or to be a copy of an original when no such original existed; or

(c) utters any writing which he knows to be forged in a manner specified in paragraphs (a) or (b).

"Writing" includes printing or any other method of recording information, money, coins, tokens, stamps, seals, credit cards, badges, trade-marks, and other symbols of value, right, privilege, or identification.

(2) *Grading.* Forgery is a felony of the second degree if the writing is or purports to be part of an issue of money, securities, postage or revenue stamps, or other instruments issued by the government, or part of an issue of stock, bonds or other instruments representing interests in or claims against any property or enterprise. Forgery is a felony of the third degree if the writing is or purports to be a will, deed, contract, release, commercial instrument, or other document evidencing, creating, transferring, altering, terminating, or otherwise affecting legal relations. Otherwise forgery is a misdemeanor. * * *

Section 224.5. Bad Checks.

A person who issues or passes a check or similar sight order for the payment of money, knowing that it will not be honored by the drawee, commits a misdemeanor. For the purpose of this Section as well as in any prosecution for theft committed by means of a bad check, an issuer is presumed to know that the check or order (other than a post-dated check or order) would not be paid, if:

(1) the issuer had no account with the drawee at the time the check or order was issued; or

(2) payment was refused by the drawee for lack of funds, upon presentation within 30 days after issue, and the issuer failed to make good within 10 days after receiving notice of that refusal.

Section 224.6. Credit Cards.

A person commits an offense if he uses a credit card for the purpose of obtaining property or services with knowledge that:

(1) the card is stolen or forged; or

(2) the card has been revoked or cancelled; or

(3) for any other reason his use of the card is unauthorized by the issuer.

It is an affirmative defense to prosecution under paragraph (3) if the actor proves by a preponderance of the evidence that he had the purpose and ability to meet all obligations to the issuer arising out of his use of the card. "Credit card" means a writing or other evidence of an undertaking to pay for property or services delivered or rendered to or upon the order of a designated person or bearer. An offense under this Section is a felony of the third degree if the value of the property or services secured or sought to be secured by means of the credit card exceeds $500; otherwise it is a misdemeanor.

Section 224.7. Deceptive Business Practices.

A person commits a misdemeanor if in the course of business he:

(1) uses or possesses for use a false weight or measure, or any other device for falsely determining or recording any quality or quantity; or

(2) sells, offers or exposes for sale, or delivers less than the represented quantity of any commodity or service; or

(3) takes or attempts to take more than the represented quantity of any commodity or service when as buyer he furnishes the weight or measure; or

(4) sells, offers or exposes for sale adulterated or mislabeled commodities. "Adulterated" means varying from the standard of composition or quality prescribed by or pursuant to any statute providing criminal penalties for such variance, or set by established commercial usage. "Mislabeled" means varying from the standard of truth or disclosure in labeling prescribed by or pursuant to any statute providing criminal penalties for such variance, or set by established commercial usage; or

(5) makes a false or misleading statement in any advertisement addressed to the public or to a substantial segment thereof for the purpose of promoting the purchase or sale of property or services; or

(6) makes a false or misleading written statement for the purpose of obtaining property or credit; or

(7) makes a false or misleading written statement for the purpose of promoting the sale of securities, or omits information required by law to be disclosed in written documents relating to securities.

It is an affirmative defense to prosecution under this Section if the defendant proves by a preponderance of the evidence that his conduct was not knowingly or recklessly deceptive. * * *

OFFENSES AGAINST THE FAMILY

ARTICLE 230. OFFENSES AGAINST THE FAMILY

Section 230.1. Bigamy and Polygamy.

(1) Bigamy. A married person is guilty of bigamy, a misdemeanor, if he contracts or purports to contract another marriage, unless at the time of the subsequent marriage:

(a) the actor believes that the prior spouse is dead; or

(b) the actor and the prior spouse have been living apart for five consecutive years throughout which the prior spouse was not known by the actor to be alive; or

(c) a Court has entered a judgment purporting to terminate or annul any prior disqualifying marriage, and the actor does not know that judgment to be invalid; or

(d) the actor reasonably believes that he is legally eligible to remarry.

(2) Polygamy. A person is guilty of polygamy, a felony of the third degree, if he marries or cohabits with more than one spouse at a time in purported exercise of the right of plural marriage. The offense is a continuing one until all cohabitation and claim of marriage with more than one spouse terminates. This section does not apply to parties to a polygamous marriage, lawful in the country of which they are residents or nationals, while they are in transit through or temporarily visiting this State.

(3) Other Party to Bigamous or Polygamous Marriage. A person is guilty of bigamy or polygamy, as the case may be, if he contracts or purports to contract marriage with another knowing that the other is thereby committing bigamy or polygamy.

Section 230.2. Incest.

A person is guilty of incest, a felony of the third degree, if he knowingly marries or cohabits or has sexual intercourse with an ancestor or descendant, a brother or sister of the whole or half blood [or an uncle, aunt, nephew or niece of the whole blood]. "Cohabit" means to live together under the representation or appearance of being married. The relationships referred to herein include blood relationships without regard to legitimacy, and relationship of parent and child by adoption. * * *

Section 230.4. Endangering Welfare of Children.

A parent, guardian, or other person supervising the welfare of a child under 18 commits a misdemeanor if he knowingly endangers the child's welfare by violating a duty of care, protection or support.

Section 230.5. Persistent Nonsupport.

A person commits a misdemeanor if he persistently fails to provide support which he can provide and which he knows he is legally obliged to provide to a spouse, child or other dependent. * * *

OFFENSES AGAINST PUBLIC ORDER AND DECENCY

ARTICLE 250. RIOT, DISORDERLY CONDUCT, AND RELATED OFFENSES

Section 250.1. Riot; Failure to Disperse.

(1) *Riot.* A person is guilty of riot, a felony of the third degree, if he participates with [two] or more others in a course of disorderly conduct:

(a) with purpose to commit or facilitate the commission of a felony or misdemeanor;

(b) with purpose to prevent or coerce official action; or

(c) when the actor or any other participant to the knowledge of the actor uses or plans to use a firearm or other deadly weapon.

(2) *Failure of Disorderly Persons to Disperse upon Official Order.* Where [three] or more persons are participating in a course of disorderly conduct likely to cause substantial harm or serious inconvenience, annoyance or alarm, a peace officer or other public servant engaged in executing or enforcing the law may order the participants and others in the immediate vicinity to disperse. A person who refuses or knowingly fails to obey such an order commits a misdemeanor.

Section 250.2. Disorderly Conduct.

(1) *Offense Defined.* A person is guilty of disorderly conduct if, with purpose to cause public inconvenience, annoyance or alarm, or recklessly creating a risk thereof, he:

(a) engages in fighting or threatening, or in violent or tumultuous behavior; or

(b) makes unreasonable noise or offensively coarse utterance, gesture or display, or addresses abusive language to any person present; or

(c) creates a hazardous or physically offensive condition by any act which serves no legitimate purpose of the actor.

"Public" means affecting or likely to affect persons in a place to which the public or a substantial group has access; among the places included are highways, transport facilities, schools, prisons, apartment houses, places of business or amusement, or any neighborhood.

(2) *Grading.* An offense under this section is a petty misdemeanor if the actor's purpose is to cause substantial harm or serious inconvenience, or

if he persists in disorderly conduct after reasonable warning or request to desist. Otherwise disorderly conduct is a violation. * * *

Section 250.4. Harassment.

A person commits a petty misdemeanor if, with purpose to harass another, he:

(1) makes a telephone call without purpose of legitimate communication; or

(2) insults, taunts or challenges another in a manner likely to provoke violent or disorderly response; or

(3) makes repeated communications anonymously or at extremely inconvenient hours, or in offensively coarse language; or

(4) subjects another to an offensive touching; or

(5) engages in any other course of alarming conduct serving no legitimate purpose of the actor.

Section 250.5. Public Drunkenness; Drug Incapacitation.

A person is guilty of an offense if he appears in any public place manifestly under the influence of alcohol, narcotics or other drug, not therapeutically administered, to the degree that he may endanger himself or other persons or property, or annoy persons in his vicinity. An offense under this Section constitutes a petty misdemeanor if the actor has been convicted hereunder twice before within a period of one year. Otherwise the offense constitutes a violation.

Section 250.6. Loitering or Prowling.

A person commits a violation if he loiters or prowls in a place, at a time, or in a manner not usual for law-abiding individuals under circumstances that warrant alarm for the safety of persons or property in the vicinity. Among the circumstances which may be considered in determining whether such alarm is warranted is the fact that the actor takes flight upon appearance of a peace officer, refuses to identify himself, or manifestly endeavors to conceal himself or any object. Unless flight by the actor or other circumstance makes it impracticable, a peace officer shall prior to any arrest for an offense under this section afford the actor an opportunity to dispel any alarm which would otherwise be warranted, by requesting him to identify himself and explain his presence and conduct. No person shall be convicted of an offense under this Section if the peace officer did not comply with the preceding sentence, or if it appears at trial that the explanation given by the actor was true and, if believed by the peace officer at the time, would have dispelled the alarm. * * *

ARTICLE 251. PUBLIC INDECENCY

Section 251.1. Open Lewdness.

A person commits a petty misdemeanor if he does any lewd act which he knows is likely to be observed by others who would be affronted or alarmed.

Section 251.2. Prostitution and Related Offenses.

(1) *Prostitution.* A person is guilty of prostitution, a petty misdemeanor, if he or she:

(a) is an inmate of a house of prostitution or otherwise engages in sexual activity as a business; or

(b) loiters in or within view of any public place for the purpose of being hired to engage in sexual activity.

"Sexual activity" includes homosexual and other deviate sexual relations. A "house of prostitution" is any place where prostitution or promotion of prostitution is regularly carried on by one person under the control, management or supervision of another. An "inmate" is a person who engages in prostitution in or through the agency of a house of prostitution. "Public place" means any place to which the public or any substantial group thereof has access.

(2) *Promoting Prostitution.* A person who knowingly promotes prostitution of another commits a misdemeanor or felony as provided in Subsection (3). The following acts shall, without limitation of the foregoing, constitute promoting prostitution:

(a) owning, controlling, managing, supervising or otherwise keeping, alone or in association with others, a house of prostitution or a prostitution business; or

(b) procuring an inmate for a house of prostitution or a place in a house of prostitution for one who would be an inmate; or

(c) encouraging, inducing, or otherwise purposely causing another to become or remain a prostitute; or

(d) soliciting a person to patronize a prostitute; or

(e) procuring a prostitute for a patron; or

(f) transporting a person into or within this state with purpose to promote that person's engaging in prostitution, or procuring or paying for transportation with that purpose; or

(g) leasing or otherwise permitting a place controlled by the actor, alone or in association with others, to be regularly used for prostitution or the promotion of prostitution, or failure to make reasonable effort to abate such use by ejecting the tenant, notifying law enforcement authorities, or other legally available means; or

(h) soliciting, receiving, or agreeing to receive any benefit for doing or agreeing to do anything forbidden by this Subsection.

(3) *Grading of Offenses Under Subsection* (2). An offense under Subsection (2) constitutes a felony of the third degree if:

(a) the offense falls within paragraph (a), (b) or (c) of Subsection (2); or

(b) the actor compels another to engage in or promote prostitution; or

(c) the actor promotes prostitution of a child under 16, whether or not he is aware of the child's age; or

(d) the actor promotes prostitution of his wife, child, ward or any person for whose care, protection or support he is responsible.

Otherwise the offense is a misdemeanor.

(4) *Presumption from Living off Prostitutes.* A person, other than the prostitute or the prostitute's minor child or other legal dependent incapable of self-support, who is supported in whole or substantial part by the proceeds of prostitution is presumed to be knowingly promoting prostitution in violation of Subsection (2).

(5) *Patronizing Prostitutes.* A person commits a violation if he hires a prostitute to engage in sexual activity with him, or if he enters or remains in a house of prostitution for the purpose of engaging in sexual activity.

(6) *Evidence.* On the issue whether a place is a house of prostitution the following shall be admissible evidence: its general repute; the repute of the persons who reside in or frequent the place; the frequency, timing and duration of visits by non-residents. Testimony of a person against his spouse shall be admissible to prove offenses under this Section.

Section 251.3. Loitering to Solicit Deviate Sexual Relations.

A person is guilty of a petty misdemeanor if he loiters in or near any public place for the purpose of soliciting or being solicited to engage in deviate sexual relations.

INDEX

References are to Pages